THE
ESSENTIAL
MIDDLE
EAST

Also by Dilip Hiro

NON-FICTION

Iraq: In the Eye of the Storm (2002)

War Without End: The Rise of Islamist Terrorism and Global Response (2002)

India: The Rough Guide Chronicle (2002)

Neighbors, Not Friends: Iraq and Iran After the Gulf Wars (2001)

Sharing the Promised Land: A Tale of Israelis and Palestinians (1999)

Dictionary of the Middle East (1996)

The Middle East (1996)

Between Marx and Muhammad: The Changing Face of Central Asia (1995)

Lebanon, Fire and Embers: A History of the Lebanese Civil War (1993)

Desert Shield to Desert Storm: The Second Gulf War (1992)

Black British, White British: A History of Race Relations in Britain (1991)

The Longest War: The Iran-Iraq Military Conflict (1991)

Holy Wars: The Rise of Islamic Fundamentalism (1989)

Iran: The Revolution Within (1988)

Iran Under the Ayatollahs (1985)

Inside the Middle East (1982)

Inside India Today (1977)

The Untouchables of India (1975)

Black British, White British (1973)

The Indian Family in Britain (1969)

FICTION

Three Plays (1985)

Interior, Exchange, Exterior (Poems, 1980)

Apply, Apply, No Reply & A Clean Break (Two Plays, 1978)

To Anchor a Cloud (Play, 1972)

A Triangular View (Novel, 1969)

THE ESSENTIAL MIDDLE EAST

A COMPREHENSIVE GUIDE

Dilip Hiro

CARROLL & GRAF PUBLISHERS
NEW YORK

THE ESSENTIAL MIDDLE EAST
A Comprehensive Guide

Carroll & Graf Publishers
An Imprint of Avalon Publishing Group Inc.
161 William St., 16th Floor
New York, NY 10038

First Carroll & Graf edition 2003

First published in 1996 by Macmillan Press Ltd, UK

Library of Congress Cataloging-in-Publication Data is available.

ISBN: 0-7867-1269-4

Interior Design by Paul Paddock
Printed in the United States of America
Distributed by Publishers Group West

Contents

List of Maps vi

Using this Guide vi

Preface viii

Maps ix

The Guide 1

Subject Index 593

General Index 597

List of Maps

Map 1   The Ottoman Empire ca 1800   X

Map 2   The Middle East Today   XII

Map 3   Palestine 1947: UN Partition Plan   XIV

Map 4   Jerusalem 1947: UN Administration Plan   XIV

Map 5   Israel 1949: UN Armistice Lines   XIV

Map 6   Jerusalem 1949: Armistice Lines   XIV

Map 7   Israel and The Occupied Arab Territories 1967   XV

Map 8   Jerusalem 1967 Under Israel   XV

Map 9   Israel-PLO May 1994 Interim Agreement: Gaza Strip   XV

Map 10 Israel-PLO Sept. 1995 Interim Agreement: West Bank   XV

Using this Guide

Abbreviations Used

9/11	September 11, 2001	ft	feet
abbr.	abbreviation	Gen.	General
A.D.	Anno Domini (L. Year of the Lord); used for the first millennium only	GDP	Gross Domestic Product
		GMT	Greenwich Mean Time
		i.e.	*id est* (L. that is)
A.H.	After Hijra	km	kilometer
a.k.a.	Also known as	lit.	literally
b.	born	lt.	lieutenant
B.C.	Before Christ	m	meter
bn	billion	mn	million
brig.	brigadier	pl.	plural
ca	circa	pop.	population
col.	colonel	qv	*quod vide* (L. which see)
cu	cubic	r.	regina/rex
d.	died	sing.	singular
der.	derivative	sq	square
est.	estimated	St	Saint
EUR	Euro	U.K.	United Kingdom
fig.	figuratively	U.N.	United Nations
		U.S./U.S.A.	United States of America

Alphabetical Order

The alphabetic order does not take into account spaces or hyphens—or the Arabic definite article 'al'/'el'.

In the Arab Middle East (a) the current rulers of Jordan and Saudi Arabia, and the past rulers of Egypt and Iraq are called kings; (b) the ruler of Oman, sultan; (c) the ruler of North Yemen, imam; and (d) the rest emirs. For (a), (b) and (c), see the first name of the ruler; and for (d) the family name. For the king of Iran, see the family name.

Alternative Spellings

The spelling given in the headword is preferable to the alternative(s) mentioned later.

Cross-References

The cross-reference in the form of [*qv*] means that further information about the subject is available under the word(s) after which it appears. No cross-reference is used for the countries of the Middle East, except for Palestine and Transjordan.

Index

In the indexes the page reference in bold type indicates the principal entry.

Preface

The best way to use this reference work is to look up the term(s) first in the General Index or the Subject Index.

This general-purpose guide pertains to the Middle East, a region that includes Bahrain, Egypt, Iran, Iraq, Israel, Jordan, Kuwait, Lebanon, Oman, the Palestinian Territories, Qatar, Saudi Arabia, Syria, the United Arab Emirates, and Yemen. The reason for this selection is given under the entry: Middle East.

The guide covers the following subjects: Arab-Israeli wars, biographies, Christianity and Christian sects, civil wars, country profiles, ethnic groups, geography, government, Gulf wars, historical places, history, hostages, international agreements and treaties, Islam and Islamic sects, Judaism and Jewish sects, languages, literature and writers, personalities, military and military leaders, miscellaneous, nonconventional biological-chemical-nuclear weapons, oil and gas, the peace process, politics, political ideologies, religious ideologies and ideologues, regional conflicts, reginal organizations, terrorism, tourist places, and the United Nations.

I have included only those personalities who made an impact on the politics, military, religion, or literature of a country or the region, and who reached adulthood around the turn of the twentieth century or later. Likewise, I have included only those international agreements, protocols, or treaties that were signed, or initialed, in the twentieth century. In the case of political, religious, or politico-religious parties and personalities, I have paid as much attention to those in power, now or in the past, as to those out of power.

Since standard ways of transliterating Arabic and Hebrew words require acutes, graves, ogoneks, and so on, and these are not used by the English-language news agencies or newspapers, I have opted for the spellings current in the English-language print media. Within this context I have been consistent—using, for instance, Halacha, not Halakha; Muslim, not Moslem; and Quran, not Koran.

London
May 2003
Dilip Hiro

The Ottoman Empire c.1800

The Middle East Today

THE MIDDLE EAST TODAY

**PALESTINE 1947
UN Partition Plan**

LEBANON

SYRIA

Nazareth

Jenin

Mediterranean

Sea

Tel Aviv
Jaffa

Jerusalem

Amman

Gaza

Hebron

Beersheba

SINAI/
EGYPT

International
Border of
Palestine

Arab Area

International
Area

Jewish Area

0 kilometres 50

0 miles 50

Eilat

Aqaba

**ISRAEL 1949
UN Armistice Lines**

LEBANON

SYRIA

Nazareth

Jenin

Mediterranean

Sea

Tel Aviv
(1)

WEST
BANK

Jerusalem
(2)

Amman

Hebron

Dead Sea

GAZA STRIP

Gaza

Beersheba

JORDAN

SINAI/
EGYPT

Armistice
Lines

(1) Internationally
recognised capital
of Israel

(2) Self-declared
capital of Israel

0 kilometres 50

0 miles 50

Eilat

Aqaba

**JERUSALEM 1947
UN Administration
Plan**

To Nablus

0 kilometres 4

0 miles 3

Motsa

To the Coast

Ein Karim

Jerusalem

Abu Dis

Beit
Safafa

Beit
Jella

Zur Bahar

To Hebron

N

☐ 1947 Jerusalem Municipal Boundary,
under the British Mandate

■ Special International Régime Boundary,
as proposed by the United Nations

■ Principal Suburbs (selected)

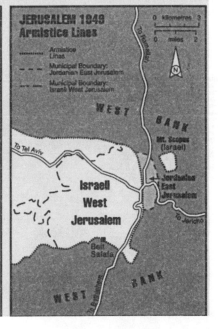

**JERUSALEM 1949
Armistice Lines**

To Ramallah

0 kilometres 3

0 miles 2

N

Armistice
Lines

Municipal Boundary:
Jordanian East Jerusalem

Municipal Boundary:
Israeli West Jerusalem

WEST

BANK

Mt. Scopus
(Israel)

To Tel Aviv

Jordanian
East
Jerusalem

Israeli

West

Jerusalem

To Jericho

Beit
Safafa

To Bethlehem

WEST

BANK

A

aal *(Arabic: of a family or clan):* The term *aal* is used in the case of Arab families or clans of distinction.

Aal Saud *(Arabic: House of Saud): see* House of Saud.

Abadan: *Iranian city* Pop. 257,000 (2003, est.). Situated on an island of the same name in the Shatt al Arab [*qv*], Abadan is called after its eighth-century founder, Abbad. It thrived as a port during the rule of the Abbasid dynasty (A.D. 751–1258). But with the silt from the Shatt al Arab expanding the delta gradually inward, its commercial importance declined. With the Shatt al Arab emerging as the boundary between the Persian and Ottoman Empires in the mid-seventeenth century, Abadan became a disputed territory. It was not until 1847 that Iran succeeded in acquiring it.

Soon after petroleum was discovered in the area in 1908, it became the site of an oil refinery owned by the Anglo-Persian Oil Company. In 1937, pressured by Iran and Britain, Iraq conceded to the thalweg principle that the median line of the deepest channel for the four miles of the Shatt al Arab opposite Abadan should delineate the international boundary. With the Iranian economy booming in the early mid-1970s due to high oil prices, Abadan prospered. The city participated in the revolutionary movement that overthrew the regime of Muhammad Reza Shah Pahlavi [*qv*] in 1979. It suffered heavily in the Iran-Iraq War (1980–88) [*qv*], when its oil facilities were destroyed. It has since been rebuilt.

Abbas, Mahmud (1935–): *Palestinian politician; prime minister of Palestinian Authority, 2003–* Born of middle-class parents in Safad, Palestine [*qv*], he and his family fled to Syria during the 1948–49 Arab-Israeli War [*qv*]. Abbas graduated in law at Damascus University and then earned a doctorate in history at the Oriental College, Moscow. In 1965 he was one of the founder members of Fatah [*qv*]. Three years later, he was elected a member of the Palestine National Council [*qv*]. As a moderate voice in the Palestinian leadership, he became a target for assassination by the Abu Nidal group [*qv*] in 1974 in Beirut [*qv*]. He was the chief initiator of clandestine contacts with leftist Jewish groups of Israel [*qv*].

Elected to the executive committee of the Palestine Liberation Organization [*qv*] in 1980, he was appointed as head of the PLO's department for national and international relations. In his book *The Road to Oslo,* published in 1994, he described the clandestine contacts in 1992 between the PLO, then a banned organization in Israel, and the leaders of the Labor [*qv*] and Likud [*qv*] parties. After Israel legalized the PLO in January 1993, PLO chairman Yasser Arafat [*qv*] put Abbas in charge of clandestine talks with Israel, which were held in Norway, where the Palestinian delegation was led by Ahmad Qrei.

On 13 September 1993, as the counterpart of Israeli foreign minister Shimon Peres [*qv*], Abbas signed the Declaration of Principles on Palestinian Self-Rule at the White House ceremony in Washington in the presence of U.S. President Bill Clinton (r. 1993–2001), Israeli Prime Minister Yitzhak Rabin [*qv*], and Arafat. In 1994 he moved to Gaza [*qv*]. Two years later Abbas was elected secretary-general of the PLO's executive committee, thus becoming Arafat's deputy in the PLO. He became the first prime minister of the Palestinian Authority [*qv*] in 2003.

Lacking in charisma, Abbas has little popular support and is widely considered as too accommodating toward Israel. His description of the two-year-old al Aqsa Intifada of 2000 [*qv*] as a disaster that had resulted in the Palestinian Authority losing all it had built up aptly summarized his viewpoint.

Abdul Aziz ibn Abdul Rahman al Saud (1879–1953): *founder and King of Saudi Arabia (r. 1932–53)* Born in Diraiya, central Arabia, Abdul grew up in Kuwait, where his ruling al Saud family was exiled following its defeat in 1891. In 1902 he regained Diraiya and neighboring Riyadh [*qv*] from the rival Rashid clan, which was allied with the Ottoman Empire. After consolidating his domain, he captured the Hasa region on the Gulf [*qv*] in 1913. Two years later, in the midst of the First World War, Britain, the most important European power in the region, recognized him as ruler of an independent Najd and Hasa. In 1920 he conquered the Asir region on the Red Sea. The next year he defeated his rival, Muhammad ibn Rashid, who was based in Shammar. After he had added more territories to his domain in 1922, he called himself the Sultan of Najd and its Dependencies.

He couched his campaigns in Islamic terms, as a struggle to punish either religious dissenters or those who had strayed from true Islam as encapsulated by Wahhabism [*qv*]. He also made it a point to marry into the family of the defeated tribal chief, thus consolidating his control of the captured territory. In the process he acquired 17 wives and sired 45 sons and 215 daughters. Among his spouses the most important were Hussah bint Ahmad al Sudairi, mother of seven sons, known as the Sudairi Seven, including Fahd [*qv*], Sultan, Nayif, and Salman; Jawhara bint Musaid al Jiluwi, mother of Khalid [*qv*]; Asi al Shuraim, mother of Abdullah [*qv*]; and Tarfa bint Abdullah al Shaikh, mother of Faisal [*qv*].

In 1924 Abdul defeated Sharif Hussein ibn Ali al Hashem in Hijaz [*qv*], and deposed him. Having declared himself King of Hijaz and Sultan of Najd and its Dependencies in January 1926 (later King of Hijaz and Najd and its Dependencies), Abdul sought international recognition. The following year Britain recognized him as King of Hijaz and Najd and its Dependencies. In 1929 he came into conflict with the militant section of the Ikhwan [*qv*], the armed wing of the Wahhabis, which had so far been his fighting force. Assisted by the British, then controlling Kuwait and Iraq, Abdul crushed the Ikhwan rebellion. In September 1932 he combined his two domains, comprising 77 percent of 1.12 million sq. miles/2.86 million sq. miles of the Arabian Peninsula [*qv*], into one—the Kingdom of Saudi Arabia—and called himself King of Saudi Arabia. He made his eldest son, Saud, crown prince, and Faisal the next in line.

Abdul faced an economic crisis caused by a severe drop in the tax paid by the pilgrims to Mecca [*qv*] following a decline in their numbers as a result of a global depression. It was against this background that he granted an oil concession to the Standard Oil Company of California in 1933 for £50,000 as an advance against future royalties on oil production. Modest commercial extraction, which started in 1938, was interrupted by the

Second World War, in which Abdul remained neutral. Despite growing links with U.S. petroleum corporations, Saudi Arabia failed to gain Washington's recognition until Abdul had a meeting in February 1945 with U.S. President Franklin Roosevelt aboard a U.S. warship in the Great Bitter Lake of the Suez Canal [qv]. Abdul was instrumental in getting the Arab League [qv] established in Cairo [qv] in March 1945. His Arab policy was conservative, committed to maintaining the status quo and shunning any dramatic moves toward the creation of larger Arab states through merger or confederation.

As a domineering and militarily successful tribal chief, Abdul behaved as an autocrat in his domestic policy. When he acquired the title King of Hijaz, he announced the establishment of a twenty-four-member Consultative Council, consisting of clergy, lay notables, and merchants in line with an injunction of the Quran [qv], which requires the governor to consult the governed. The Council played an insignificant role for a while and then became extinct. Following a dramatic increase in oil output after the Second World War, the economic boom overstretched the rudimentary institutions of the state, supervised by Abdul and some of his close aides, and undermined the traditional, spartan Wahhabi lifestyle of the House of Saud [qv]. Yet it was not until October 1953—a month before his death—that Abdul issued a decree appointing a council of ministers as an advisory body.

Abdul Ghani, Abdul Aziz (1939–): *Yemeni politician; North Yemeni prime minister, 1975–80, 1983–90, 1994–97* Born into a Shafii Sunni [qv] family in the Hujariya region of North Yemen, Abdul went to a teacher training college in Aden [qv], South Yemen. He then obtained an economics degree at a university in the United States. After his return to Aden he taught economics. When South Yemen became independent under a leftist regime in late 1967, he left for North Yemen, where he was appointed minister of economy and health. In 1971, after the formal end of an eight-year civil war in North Yemen [qv], he became governor of the Central Bank.

His absence from the country during the civil conflict; his Shafii origins, which set him apart from the fractious Zaidi Shia [qv] military officers and tribal leaders; and his technocratic background stood him in good stead. Following the coup by Col. Ibrahim Hamdi [qv] in June 1974, he was nominated to the ruling Military Command Council. In January 1975 Hamdi appointed him prime minister, a position he continued to hold, along with membership of the ruling Presidential Council—despite the assassination of Hamdi and his successor, Ahmad Hussein Ghashmi [qv]—until October 1980, when he was made vice president by President Ali Abdullah Salih [qv]. He took on the additional job of premier in November 1983 and stayed in that position until the unification of North and South Yemen in May 1990.

As a representative of the Shafiis, who were slightly more numerous than Zaidis in North Yemen, Abdul was assured of high office. In the five-strong Presidential Council for a united Yemen that followed, he was one of the three North Yemeni members. He retained his position when the first popularly elected parliament of united Yemen chose members of the new Presidential Council in October 1993. His main area of expertise remained finance, industry, and economic development. He supported Salih in the civil war [*qv*] that erupted in May 1994 and was appointed premier after it ended in July. Following the 1997 parliamentary poll, Abdul was replaced as the prime minister by Faraj Said Ghanim.

Abdul Ilah ibn Ali (1912–58): *Iraqi regent, 1939–53; crown prince, 1953–58* Son of Sharif Ali ibn Hussein, King of Hijaz (r. 1924–25) [*qv*], Abdul moved to Baghdad along with the family when Hijaz fell to Abdul Aziz ibn Abdul Rahman al Saud [*qv*] in 1925. Following the death in 1939 of his cousin and brother-in-law, King Ghazi of Iraq [*qv*], he became regent on behalf of four-year-old King Faisal II [*qv*]. After the seizure of power by anti-British officers, led by Rashid Ali Gailani [*qv*] in April 1941, the pro-British Abdul and the rest of the royal family fled. But two months later they returned to Baghdad [*qv*] following Gailani's defeat by the British. The poor performance of Iraqi troops in the Palestine War (1948–49) [*qv*] disappointed many Iraqis, who blamed the incompetence and corruption of Abdul for the national humiliation. When Faisal II came of age in 1953 and ascended the throne, he named Abdul crown prince. By then Abdul was widely regarded in Iraq as an agent of British imperialism. He was assassinated during the antimonarchist coup of 14 July 1958.

Abdul Maguid, Esmat (1923–): *Egyptian diplomat and politician; secretary-general of the Arab League, 1991–2001* Born into a middle-class family in Alexandria [*qv*], Abdul trained as a lawyer at universities in his native city and Paris. He joined the foreign service when he was twenty-seven. As a

career diplomat he rose steadily up the hierarchical ladder, becoming ambassador to France in 1970. When Anwar Sadat [*qv*] became president later that year, he named Abdul deputy foreign minister. From 1972 to 1983 he served as his country's chief representative to the United Nations. The following year he became foreign minister and deputy premier. In May 1991, following the expulsion of Iraq from occupied Kuwait, in which Egypt played an important role, Abdul was unanimously elected secretary-general of the Arab League [*qv*], the event signifying the restoration of Egypt as leader of the Arab world after twelve years of ostracization following its unilateral peace treaty with Israel in 1979 [*qv*]. In 2001, he was succeeded by Amr Moussa [*qv*].

Abdul Rahman, Omar (1938–): *Egyptian Islamist leader* Born into a poor peasant family in Gamaliya village, Daqaliya district, in the Nile [*qv*] delta, Abdul went blind in infancy as a result of diabetes. He was educated in local religious schools before joining al Azhar University [*qv*] in 1955. After securing a doctorate in literature in 1965 he became a lecturer in Islamic studies at the al Azhar's branch at Fahyum in the Nile delta.

As the prayer leader of the mosque in the nearby village of Fedmeen, he delivered sermons that were critical of the government, led by President Gamal Abdul Nasser [*qv*], and its ideology of Arab socialism [*qv*]. Following Egypt's defeat in the June 1967 Arab-Israeli War [*qv*], Abdul became more daring in his attacks on Nasser and Arab socialism. He was arrested in 1968 and expelled from al Azhar. On his release he criticized the official policies on religious trusts [*qv*] and Islam.

After the death of Nasser in September 1970, Abdul was arrested because of his call to the faithful not to pray for the soul of Nasser, whom he considered an atheist. He was released as part of the general amnesty President Anwar Sadat [qv] granted following his coup against Ali Sabri [qv] in May 1971.

Abdul became a lecturer on Islamic affairs at the University of Asyut in southern Egypt. Later that year he took a job as teacher of Islamic studies in Saudi Arabia [qv] (1971–78). He stayed in touch with Islamist activists in Egypt during his annual holidays there. On his return home he became a professor of Islamic studies at Asyut University.

He attacked Sadat for the Camp David Accords [qv] and economic liberalization, which according to him had led to moral and material corruption. After Sadat's assassination in October 1981 he was one of the twenty-four suspects who were arrested. He was accused of issuing a *fatwa* (a religious decree) for Sadat's assassination. But he was released, along with another suspect, due to lack of evidence.

Denied reinstatement as professor at Asyut University, Abdul settled at Fahyum and continued his attacks on the regime, now headed by President Hosni Mubarak [qv]. He was arrested in 1984 for delivering a subversive sermon, but was found not guilty. He urged his followers to join the Afghan Mujahedin, who, financed and trained by Saudi Arabia, America, and Pakistan, were conducting a jihad [qv] against the Soviet-backed regime in Afghanistan. Among those who followed his exhortation was his son Ahmad. Abdul continued his oppositional activities, including his demand that Egypt should be run exclusively according to the

Sharia [qv], and toured the country. His speeches inspired both al Gamaat al Islamiya [qv] and al Jihad al Islami [qv]. The government put him under house arrest in Fahyum and prevented him from speaking in public. In response he issued a fatwa allowing the faithful to capture weapons from the police and the military in order to carry out a jihad against the secular regime of President Mubarak.

In mid-1989, on the eve of the annual *hajj* [qv], he left Egypt. But instead of going to Mecca [qv], he arrived in Khartoum, the capital of Sudan, where a pro-Islamic military junta had seized power on 30 June 1989. Fearing retribution from Cairo, the Sudanese leaders refused him asylum. Abdul toured a few European capitals before visiting Pakistan and Afghanistan, where his two sons had reportedly joined the Ittihad-e Islami (Islamic Alliance), a pro-Saudi Afghan mujahedin group, which, along with other such factions, was funded and trained by the U.S. Central Intelligence Agency (CIA) working in conjunction with Pakistan's Inter-Service Intelligence.

In late 1989 Abdul received a tourist visa from the U.S. Embassy in Khartoum even though he was on the prohibited list. In America he ran a mosque in Brooklyn, popular with Egyptian, Sudanese, and Yemeni immigrants; obtained an immigrant visa; and moved to the adjoining state of New Jersey. From there his followers sent thousands of tapes of his sermons to Egypt. Following the bombing of the World Trade Center in New York in February 1993 and the aborting of a plan to bomb the United Nations and other targets some weeks later, Abdul was arrested as a suspect, found guilty in October 1995, and sentenced to life imprisonment for seditious conspiracy for a bombing plot. In early 1999, from his high security jail in the United States, he endorsed the unilateral cease-fire declared by al Gamaat al Islamiya.

Abdullah ibn Abdul Aziz al Saud (1923–): *Saudi Arabian crown prince, 1982–* Son of Abdul Aziz al Saud [*qv*] and Asi al Shuraim of the Rashid clan, which was defeated by Abdul Aziz in 1921, Abdullah was born and educated in Riyadh [*qv*]. He started his career as governor of Mecca [*qv*] and became deputy defense minister and commander of the National Guard [*qv*] in 1963. When Khalid ibn Abdul Aziz [*qv*] acceded the throne in 1975 he appointed Abdullah as second deputy premier. As commander of the National Guard, the most cohesive and reliable armed force in the kingdom, Abdullah was influential. He belonged to the innermost circle of senior Saudi princes. He headed the traditionalist-nationalist trend within the royal family, which was at odds with the modernist, pro-American faction led by Crown Prince Fahd ibn Abdul Aziz [*qv*], especially over the pace of economic development. He advocated a pan-Arabist policy and cultivated friendly relations with Syria, among others. He attempted to conciliate Syria and Iraq and bring the Lebanese Civil War (1975–90) [*qv*] to an end, but in vain. Once Fahd became king and prime minister in 1982, he named Abdullah crown prince and first deputy premier. During the Gulf crisis of 1990–91, unlike the defense minister, Prince Sultan ibn Abdul Aziz [*qv*], Abdullah was reluctant to invite U.S. forces to Saudi Arabia. He continued to command the

National Guard. He was distressed when a bomb at the National Guard training center in Riyadh in November 1995 killed seven people, including five American officers. Later that month, following a stroke, Fahd passed on his powers to Abdullah. Though, on recovery, Faisal nominally retrieved these powers three months later, there was less of Fahd's imprint on the administration during the subsequent years as Abdullah became the de facto ruler.

He tried to defuse internal tensions by conciliating political and religious dissidents at home and abroad. Yet he failed to address the long-running, contentious issue of the continued presence of the American troops on the Saudi soil, a subject that came to the fore in June 1996, when a huge explosion outside the Khobar Towers, a multistory residential block for U.S. military personnel, near Dhahran air base, killed nineteen American servicemen.

Abdullah continued the earlier policy of aiding the Taliban (lit., Religious Students), a faction of hardline Islamic fundamentalists [*qv*] in Afghanistan, created largely by Pakistan in late 1994, culminating in the recognition of the Taliban government in May 1997. In the region he mended fences with Iran [*qv*], especially after the election of Muhammad Khatami [*qv*] as president in August 1997. In early 1998 Abdullah refused to allow the United States to use Saudi bases to strike Iraq [*qv*] for the latter's failure to cooperate unconditionally with United Nations weapons inspectors. In July 2000 he advised Palestinian leader Yasser Arafat [*qv*] not to compromise on the future status of Jerusalem [*qv*] by conceding the sovereignty of the Dome of the Rock [*qv*] to Israel [*qv*] in his talks with Israeli prime minister Ehud Barak [*qv*] at Camp David.

Following the attacks on three American targets by hijacked aircraft on 11 September 2001, Abdullah violated the quota of the Organization of Petroleum Exporting Countries [*qv*] by increasing oil output by 500,000 barrels per day (bd), and shipped over 500,000 bd in Saudi tankers to America, thus lowering the oil price from $28 to $20 within weeks. Yet Washington's relations with Riyadh soured when it emerged that fifteen of the nineteen hijackers of 9/11 were Saudi nationals.

Abdullah I ibn Hussein al Hashem (1882–1951): *Emir of Transjordan, 1921– 46; King of Jordan, 1946–51* Son of Sharif Hussein ibn Ali al Hashem of Hijaz [*qv*], Abdullah was educated in Istanbul, where his father was kept under surveillance from 1891 until the coup by the Young Turks in 1908. From 1912 to 1914 Abdullah represented Mecca [*qv*] in the Ottoman parliament. He participated in the Arab revolt against the Ottomans that, led by his father, erupted in June 1916. When Sharif Hussein declared himself King of Hijaz in 1917, Abdullah became his foreign minister.

The disintegration of the Ottoman Empire in 1918 strengthened the hands of Sharif Hussein and his sons. However, the decision of a congress of Syrian notables in Damascus [*qv*] in March 1920 to crown Faisal ibn Hussein [*qv*], a younger brother of Abdullah, as king of Syria was rejected by Britain and France, the leading Allied members. In July French troops captured Damascus and put Faisal to flight. Abdullah assembled an army to expel the French from

Syria. He entered the British-mandated territory east of the Jordan River [*qv*], called Transjordan [*qv*], in January 1921 and set up a government in Amman [*qv*] two months later. In July London offered to recognize Abdullah's rule in Transjordan if he accepted the British mandate over it and Palestine [*qv*] (awarded to Britain by the League of Nations a year earlier) and renounced his plan to capture Syria. Abdullah consented, provided the clauses of the mandate about the founding of a National Home for the Jews [*qv*] were not applied to the Emirate of Transjordan. This was agreed and later endorsed by the League of Nations.

In April 1923 Britain announced that it would recognize Transjordan as an autonomous emirate under Emir Abdullah's rule if a constitutional regime were established there and a preferential treaty with London signed. Abdullah agreed and declared Transjordan "independent." But it was not until April 1928 that he proclaimed a constitution, which stipulated that legal and administrative authority should be exercised by the ruler through a legislative council. The resulting nominated body was powerless. It was only in 1939 that it was transformed into a cabinet and given some authority.

Tied to London and its subsidy, Abdullah remained loyal to Britain. In 1941 he dispatched Arab Legion troops, commanded by British officers, to Iraq to aid Britain in crushing the forces of Rashid Gailani [*qv*]. When London recognized the independence of Transjordan in May 1946, Abdullah changed its name to the Hashemite Kingdom of Jordan and called himself king. This necessitated revising the

1923 Anglo-Transjordan Treaty [*qv*], which was done in March 1948.

To extend his realm to Palestine, then being colonized by the Zionists [*qv*], Abdullah reached a clandestine, unwritten understanding with their leaders not to oppose the partitioning of Palestine, and the emergence of a Jewish state, if they let him take over the Arab part of Palestine. But the secret was leaked and the other constituents of the Arab League [*qv*] resolved to thwart the plan. In his clandestine meetings with Golda Meir [*qv*], a Zionist leader, in November 1947 and early May 1948, Abdullah reportedly explained his inability to stick to his agreement. The change also coincided with London's advice to him to seize control of the Arab segment of Palestine in league with other Arab countries rather than through a deal with the Zionist leaders.

After the Arab League's decision to dispatch troops to capture Palestine on the eve of the British departure on 14 May 1948, Abdullah became commander in chief of the forces from Egypt, Iraq, Jordan, Lebanon, and Syria. His Arab Legion captured substantial parts of Arab Palestine, while not attacking the zones allocated to the Jews in the United Nations partition plan of November 1947. In Jerusalem [*qv*], which was earmarked for international control, the Arab Legion seized the eastern part. In December, 2,000 Arab Palestinian delegates in Jericho [*qv*] acclaimed Abdullah as "King of all Palestine," which meant most of what could be saved from the Israelis.

He began to transform his military occupation of Arab Palestine into annexation, presenting his action as a response to orchestrated calls by local Palestinian notables to that effect. His move alarmed other Arab leaders. As before, Abdullah entered into a clandestine dialogue with the Zionist leaders in April 1949 to settle the sticky points about a truce between Jordan and Israel. The talks culminated in a draft nonaggression pact between the two countries in early 1950. Once again the secret leaked out. When pressured by fellow Arab leaders to scuttle his peace plans with Israel, he agreed, provided they let him annex Arab Palestine, which they did. Formal annexation followed in April and changed the character of Abdullah's realm. It now contained a large body of politicized Palestinians, who felt betrayed. Most of them considered Abdullah a traitor, a lackey of the British, who had made underhanded deals with the Zionists at the expense of Arab interests. In July 1951, Shukri Ashu, a young Palestinian, assassinated Abdullah as he entered al Aqsa Mosque in East Jerusalem [*qv*] for Friday prayers.

Abdullah II ibn Hussein al Hashem(1962–): *Jordanian king, 1999–* Born to King Hussein [*qv*] and Muna Gardiner, he was named the crown prince on birth. But fearing assassination, which would put an infant on the throne, King Hussein amended the constitution and named his younger brother Hassan as the crown prince. After attending prestigious private schools in Britain, Abdullah graduated from Sandhurst Military Academy before enrolling in Oxford University, where he graduated in international relations in 1984, and then spent an academic year at Georgetown University in Washington.

Pursuing a military career, he became a brigadier general in 1994. Four years later he was given command of the Jordanian Special Forces and promoted to major general. The King, suffering from terminal lymphatic cancer, and dissatisfied with the way Prince Hassan had conducted state affairs in his absence, revoked the amendment designating Hassan as crown prince barely a fortnight before his death on 7 February 1999, and named Abdullah the crown prince.

As a result, Abdullah acceded the throne with no experience in civil administration, politics, or diplomacy. Following the counsel of the senior advisers he inherited, Abdullah continued his father's friendly relations with Israel [*qv*] while reiterating that resolution of the Israeli-Palestinian conflict was a precondition for a lasting regional peace. Dependent on supply of Iraqi oil, he maintained cordial relations with Iraq [*qv*] and expressed distress at the continued suffering of Iraqis. After the installation of Bashar Assad [*qv*] as Syrian president in 2000, he improved ties with Syria [*qv*].

By presiding over the Arab League summit in Amman [*qv*] in March 2001, he became chairman of the Arab League [*qv*] for a year. It was in that role that he visited Washington in the aftermath of the terrorist attacks on the United States in September. The bill on free trade with Jordan, which had been languishing in U.S. Congress for three years, was passed in three weeks. The move helped Abdullah to advance much needed economic liberalization in Jordan.

abu (*Arabic: father*): A father in Arab society is traditionally referred to by the name of his first-born son. Sometimes, in clandestine or semi-clandestine groups, leaders adopt this honorific as a nom de plume, pseudonym, or nom de guerre. The best known examples pertain to the leadership of the Palestine Liberation Organization [*qv*]: Yasser Arafat (Abu Ammar) [*qv*], Khalid Wazir (Abu Jihad) [*qv*], and Salih Khalaf (Abu Iyad) [*qv*]. In some instances surnames begin with Abu: Abu(a)l-Fath, Abu(a)l-Kalam. Such surnames in North Africa as Bouteflika and Bourguiba are derivatives, respectively, of Abu Teflika and Abu Reguiba.

Abu Ammar: *see* Arafat, Yasser.

Abu Dhabi: *city and emirate in the United Arab Emirates* [*qv*].

Abu Dhabi city: *capital of United Arab Emirates and Abu Dhabi emirate* Pop. 520,000 (2002, est.). Located on the offshore island of the same name, Abu Dhabi was founded by members of the Aal bu Falah clan of the Bani Yas tribe in 1761. A quarter of a century later they transferred their base from the al Jiwa oasis to Abu Dhabi. In the early twentieth century its 6,000-odd inhabitants were dependent on pearl fishing and petty trading for their livelihood. It was not until the discovery and extraction of petroleum in the Abu Dhabi emirate in the early 1960s that its capital began to expand. Following the installation of Shaikh Zaid ibn Sultan al Nahyan [*qv*] as emir in 1966, ambitious plans to modernize Abu Dhabi were initiated. Within a decade it had been turned into a modern city with offices, hotels, light industry, and an international airport. With the formation of a confederation of seven emirates, called the United Arab Emirates [*qv*], in 1971, Abu Dhabi was selected as its interim capital, later confirmed as the capital city.

Abu Dhabi Emirate: Area 26,000 sq. miles/ 67,350 sq. km; pop. 1,186,000 (2001, est.); *see* United Arab Emirates.

Abu Iyad: *see* Khalaf, Salah.

Abu Jihad: *see* Wazir, Khalil.

Abu Mazen: *see* Abbas, Mahmud.

Abu Musa Island: *an offshore island in the Gulf* On the eve of the independence of the Trucial emirate of Sharjah [*qv*] in 1971, Muhammad Reza Shah Pahlavi [*qv*] of Iran pressed his claim to three islands at the mouth of the Gulf [*qv*], including Abu Musa. After Iranian troops had landed there, Britain, the erstwhile imperial power in the region, mediated. As a result, Sharjah and Iran agreed that both flags would fly on the island and that Iran would pay Sharjah an annual subsidy of £1.5 million until oil had been discovered in the principality. This arrangement survived the eight-year war between Iran and Iraq (1980–88) [*qv*], when Iraq, acting as self-appointed guardian of the Gulf's Arab states, demanded that Iran should quit the island. In September 1991 Sharjah protested that Iran had exceeded the privileges it had been allowed under the 1971 agreement. But its efforts to secure the involvement of the United Nations did not get far. In 1994 the Gulf Cooperation Council [*qv*] took up the matter and urged Iran to agree to refer the issue of its occupation of Abu Musa and Greater and Lesser Tumb Islands [*qv*] to the International Court of Justice, but to no avail. A decade later the matter remained unresolved.

Abu Nidal: *see* al Banna, Sabri.

Acre: *Israeli town* Pop. 48,600 (2003, est.). The commercial importance of Acre, a port on the Bay of Acre, dates back to the fifteenth century B.C., when it was renowned for its glass-making and purple-dyeing industries. King Ptolemy II of Egypt (r. 283–246 B.C.) changed its name from Accho to Ptolemais. When the Arabs captured it in A.D. 638 they called it Akka. Conquered by the crusaders (1104–87), it was renamed St. Jean d'Acre. When the Knights of St. John acquired it in 1191, they made it the capital of Palestine [*qv*]. Its surrender to the Saracens in 1291 heralded the decline of the Latin Kingdom of Jerusalem and the Crusades. It fell under the Ottomans (1517–1918), with a brief interregnum under Egypt (1832–40). It formed part of the Palestine that was formally placed under the British in 1922. The 1947 United Nations partition plan for Palestine assigned Acre, then an Arab settlement of 12,000, to the Arabs. But in the war that ensued the Zionist [*qv*] forces seized it and it was incorporated into Israel.

Its tourist offerings include the old town wall, an outstanding mosque built by Ahmad al Jazzar in the late eighteenth century, and a stunning view of the Bay of Haifa.

A.D.: *Abbr. of Anno Domini (Latin: Year of the Lord)* Since "the Lord" refers to Jesus Christ, Anno Domini supposedly begins with his birth. But by most estimations the actual starting point of the Years of the Lord was between 4 B.C. and 8 B.C.

Aden: *Yemeni city; capital of South Yemen* [*qv*], *1967–1990* Pop. 569,000 (2003, est.). Situated on the Gulf of Aden, the city has a commercial history stretching back to biblical times. It was conquered by Muslim Arabs in A.D. 636 and came under Ottoman Turkish rule in 1538. Britain arrived there by treaty in 1802 and took over the administration in 1839, incorporating it with India. This continued until 1937, when Aden was transformed into a crown colony. Following the opening of the Suez Canal [*qv*] in 1869, Aden became a coaling station on the sea route between Britain and India. In 1953 an oil refinery was erected there. Following the closure of the Suez Canal in June 1967, the refueling of ships declined sharply. Five months later Aden became the capital of independent South Yemen.

The new, leftist regime discontinued Aden's free-port status after three years. It also transformed the previous Royal Air Force base at Khaur Maskar, north of Aden, into an international airport. Its oil refinery began to receive crude oil from Iran after the revolution there in 1979.

Following the merger of North and South Yemen in 1990, Aden was maintained as a regional capital. But after the crushing of a rebellion by South Yemeni politicians by the central authorities in Sanaa [*qv*] in 1994, in which the city suffered damage, Aden's political importance declined.

Adonis: *see* Asbar, Ali Ahmad Said.

Aflaq, Michel (1910–89): *Syrian political thinker and politician* Born into a Greek Orthodox [*qv*] family in Damascus [*qv*], Aflaq received his higher education at the University of Sorbonne, Paris, where he came under leftist influence. Back in Damascus in 1934, he taught history at a prestigious secondary school. Together with Salah al Din Bitar [*qv*], a fellow teacher, in 1940, he established a study circle called the Movement of Arab Renaissance (*Baath*, in Arabic). They published pamphlets in which they expounded revolutionary, socialist Arab nationalism, committed to achieving Arab unity as the first step. In 1942 Aflaq devoted himself full-time to politics.

Once the mandate power, France, had left Syria in April 1946, Aflaq and Bitar secured a license for their group, now called the Party of Arab Renaissance. They decided to merge their faction with the one led by Zaki Arsuzi [*qv*]. Out of this, in April 1947, emerged the Arab Baath Party [*qv*] in Damascus. Aflaq was elected senior member of the executive committee of four. In August 1949, following a military coup by Col. Sami Hinnawi, Aflaq was appointed education minister. But when he failed to win a seat in the general election held three months later, he resigned.

In late 1952 he fled to Lebanon to escape arrest by the dictatorial regime of Col. Adib Shishkali [*qv*]. The next year he merged his group with Akram Hourani's Arab Socialist Party [*qv*] to form the Arab Baath Socialist Party [*qv*]. He remained the new party's secretary-general as well as its chief ideologue.

Following its seizure of power in March 1963, the ruling Baath party was riven into two factions: the moderate "civilian" wing and the radical "military" wing. When the military faction prevailed over its rival, Aflaq, who was associated with the latter, left for Lebanon. He retained his position as secretary-general of the National (i.e. All-Arab) Command of the Baath. The next year he left for Brazil. Following the successful coup in July 1968 by the Baath party in Iraq [*qv*], owing allegiance to his faction within the National Command, Aflaq was invited by Iraq to resume his leadership. He accepted, but in September 1970, when the Iraqi government failed to assist Palestinian commandos in their fight with Jordanian troops, Aflaq showed his displeasure by leaving Baghdad [*qv*] for Beirut [*qv*].

His estrangement lasted until 1974 when he returned to Baghdad to head the party's National Command. He enjoyed high status and much reverence in Baghdad. However, while the Iraqi regime regularly published his articles and tracts, it did not let him determine state policies and practices. During the Iran-Iraq War (1980–88) [qv], Aflaq was the butt of many attacks by Iran, anxious to depict Iraq, guided by a Christian, as a state that had deviated from Islam. Significantly, after his death in 1989 the Iraqi media disclosed that Aflaq had converted to Islam [qv] before his demise.

Agudat Israel *(Hebrew: Union of Israel): Israeli political party and international organization of ultra-Orthodox Jews* Agudat Israel was formed in Katowice, Poland, in 1912, largely by the ultra-Orthodox Jews [qv] of Germany, Poland, and Ukraine, to address Jewish problems from a religious perspective. A member had to accept the supremacy of the Torah [qv] in Jewish life. Its adherents in Palestine [qv] boycotted the quasi-governmental organs of the Yishuv [qv]. They did so primarily because the creation of Israel through human endeavor—such as the one by Zionist [qv] pioneers in Palestine—was against their belief that Israel, as a "peoplehood," would be redeemed by the Messiah [qv], and secondarily because they were against women's suffrage. They considered that Jews [qv] were a religious, not an ethnic, entity, and believed that Jewish problems could be solved only by the Torah.

When its members in Palestine accepted funds from the Jewish National Fund [qv] to set up kibbutzim [qv] and theological institutions, there was a split, with the dissenters forming the Neturei Karta [qv] in 1935. By the Second World War, Agudat claimed a world membership of 500,000 mainly ultra-Orthodox Jews. In 1947 its Central World Council set up international centers in New York, London, and Jerusalem [qv].

Once Israel was founded in 1948, Agudat decided to participate in the state's affairs. On the eve of the first general election in 1949 it combined with Poale Agudat Israel [qv] to form the Agudat bloc, which in turn allied with the Mizrahi bloc—Mizrahi [qv] and Poale HaMizrahi [qv]—to constitute the United Religious Front [qv]. It won sixteen seats and joined the government to run, inter alia, the religious affairs ministry. The Agudat bloc contested the 1951 election separately and won five seats. It joined the government, but quit in protest against the passing of a law prescribing conscription for women. While existing separately, the Agudat parties stayed in opposition during the era of Labor-dominated [qv] governments, which ended in 1977. Later they merged, winning four seats in 1981 and two seats in 1984. On the eve of the 1988 election they combined with two small religious groups to form the United Torah Judaism [qv].

A.H.: *Abbr. of After Hijra (Arabic: Migration)* The Islamic [qv] era began with the migration of the Prophet Muhammad from Mecca [qv] to Medina [qv] on A.D. 15 July 622 [qv].

Ahdut HaAvodah *(Hebrew: The Unity of Labor): Zionist political party in Palestine* Originating in the split in Poale Zion [qv], caused by increasing cooperation between socialist pioneers and the financial institutions of the World Zionist Organization [qv], the rightist, nationalist faction of Poale

Zion merged with the followers of Berle Katznelson, who were active in founding workers' institutions, to establish Ahdut HaAvodah in March 1919. It played an important role in the establishment of Haganah [*qv*] and Histadrut [*qv*]. It was instrumental in getting *Davar* (Word), the daily newspaper of Histadrut, started in 1925 under the editorship of Katznelson. In the spring of 1929 Ahdut HaAvodah and HaPoale HaTzair concluded a merger agreement and produced a common platform. A large majority of 2,500 Ahdut HaAvodah members ratified the amalgamation. In January 1930 a joint conference, representing 5,650 members, established Mapai [*qv*].

Ahdut HaAvodah-Poale Zion *(Hebrew: The Unity of Labor-Workers of Zion): Zionist political party in Palestine and Israel* Ahdut HaAvodah-Poale Zion was the result of the merger in April 1946 of the Tanua LeAhdut HaAvodah [*qv*] and the remnants of the Poale Zion (left) [*qv*]. It was popularly known as Ahdut HaAvodah. In early 1948 it combined with HaShomer HaTzair to establish Mapam [*qv*]. Protesting Mapam's tilt toward the Soviet bloc, which was seen as pursuing an anti-Zionist policy, Ahdut HaAvodah adherents decided in 1954 to acquire a separate identity. The party won ten parliamentary seats in 1955, seven in 1959, and eight in 1961. It became a junior partner in the Mapai-led [*qv*] coalition from 1955 onward. On the eve of the 1965 poll it signed an agreement for a *maarach* (alignment) with Mapai, the resulting bloc winning 45 seats out of 120. The maarach widened in 1968 to include Rafi [*qv*], and finally resulted in the merger of the three constituent parties into the Mifleget

HaAvodah HaYisraelit (the Israeli Labor Party) [*qv*].

Ahmad ibn Yahya (1895–1962): *ruler of North Yemen, 1948–62* Eldest son of Imam Yahya of the Hamid al Din branch of the Rassi dynasty, which for centuries had governed the northern and eastern highlands of Yemen, inhabited by Zaidi (Shia) [*qv*] tribes and later under the suzerainty of the Ottoman Turks, which ended in 1918. Bearing the title Saif al Islam (Sword of Islam), Ahmad assisted his father militarily as the latter tried to re-create the historical Greater Yemen by extending his realm to the Shafii (Sunni) [*qv*] region to the south. In the 1920s and 1930s he led campaigns to suppress tribal revolts. Following an abortive coup in February 1948, which resulted in the murder of his father, Ahmad assumed supreme power. Like his predecessors, he was elected *imam* [*qv*] (religious leader) by Zaidi chieftains and was called Imam Ahmad ibn Yahya.

On ascending the throne Ahmad pursued his father's ambition to re-create Greater Yemen by annexing the British protectorate of Aden. When London frustrated his plans, he turned militantly anti-British and befriended Egypt's pan-Arabist [*qv*] president, Gamal Abdul Nasser [*qv*]. In April 1956 he signed a mutual defense pact with Cairo that provided for a unified military command. He offered to join the United Arab Republic (UAR) [*qv*], the union of Egypt and Syria, soon after its formation in early 1958. The resulting loose federation of the UAR and North Yemen was named the Union of Arab States. By then Ahmad had concluded friendship treaties with Moscow, Peking, and other communist capitals.

At home Ahmad continued his father's despotic style of government, much facilitated by his program of modernizing the military. In August 1955 he crushed a coup attempt by a group of officers and two of his three brothers. After the breakup of the UAR in September 1961, Ahmad cut his ties with Nasser and began to attack him. Nasser retaliated by allowing the North Yemeni dissidents use of Cairo Radio for anti-Ahmad propaganda. Suffering from ill health, Ahmad passed on much of his authority to his eldest son, Muhammad al Badr [*qv*], before his death in September 1962, which triggered a military coup and ended the 1,064-year rule of the Rassi dynasty.

al Ahmar, Abdullah Hussein (1919–): *Yemeni politician* Son of Shaikh Hussein ibn Nasser al Ahmar, head of the Hashid tribal confederation, who was executed in 1959 for his part in a failed coup against Imam Ahmad ibn Yahya [*qv*], al Ahmar succeeded his father. When civil war erupted in September 1962, soon after Imam Ahmad's death, al Ahmar sided with the republicans. He was appointed governor of the Hajjah district northwest of the capital, Sanaa [*qv*]. In the republican camp he allied with conservative politicians and opposed radical military officers, especially President Abdullah Sallal [*qv*], a general who dominated the regime. His opposition to the participation of Egyptian forces in the conflict made him popular with Saudi Arabia, which backed the royalist camp. In September 1966, when President Sallal attempted to arrest al Ahmar in Sanaa, the latter fled to his tribal base and took up arms against the central authority. Once the Egyptian troops had withdrawn from

North Yemen after Egypt's defeat in the June 1967 Arab-Israel War [*qv*], al Ahmar returned to the capital with his forces. One of the plotters to depose Sallal in November 1967, he was a leading architect of the "Third Force" government led by President Abdul Rahman al Iryani [*qv*]. He won over most of the tribal leaders to the republican side and, assisted by Saudi Arabia, helped to conciliate the warring sides. The civil strife ended in 1970 with the formal abolition of the monarchy.

Following the promulgation of a new constitution in December 1970, stipulating a Consultative Assembly, partly elected and partly nominated, al Ahmar was elected its chairman. After Col. Ibrahim Hamdi [*qv*] carried out a bloodless coup in June 1974, he compelled al Ahmar to resign and disbanded the Assembly. The new constitution, promulgated by the Military Command Council, led by Hamdi, provided for a fully nominated Constituent People's Assembly (CPA) to act as a consultative body. Since Hamdi did not appoint al Ahmar as its member, relations between the two soured. In April 1977 al Ahmar led a rebellion against Sanaa in the north, which was crushed by Hamdi.

Following Hamdi's assassination in October, and the accession to power of Ahmad Hussein Ghashmi [*qv*], al Ahmar's relations with the center improved. He was appointed to the CPA. The succession to presidency of Ali Abdullah Salih [*qv*] after the assassination of Ghashmi in mid-1978 saw further improvement in al Ahmar's political fortunes. But his continued close links with Saudi Arabia, his opposition to improvement of ties between North Yemen and the Soviet Union, and his disapproval of unity between North and South Yemen inhibited any further rise in his influence.

With Salih proving more durable than anybody had foreseen, the situation in the tribal areas stabilized by the mid-1980s, and al Ahmar settled down to the role of an elder statesman. Following the unification of the two Yemens in May 1990, al Ahmar established the Yemeni Islah Group [*qv*], with an Islamist program. In the first multiparty general parliamentary election, held under universal suffrage in united Yemen in October 1993, the Islah won 62 of the 310 seats and al Ahmar was elected parliamentary speaker. In the 1994 Yemeni Civil War [*qv*], he actively sided with the government. Following the 1997 general election, in which the Islah secured fifty-three seats, he was reelected parliamentary speaker. With the tenure of the parliament extended to six years, al Ahmar's status remained unchanged until 2003.

Ahvaz: *Iranian city* Pop. 1,004,700 (2003, est.). The history of Ahvaz, situated on the banks of the Karun River, dates back to the Achaemenian Empire (539–330 B.C.). Ahvaz declined after that period but was revived by Sassanian King Ardeshir (r. A.D. 224–41), who dammed the river and called the settlement Hormuz Ardeshir. In ca. 275, near Ahvaz arose Gunde Shapur University, the greatest place of learning in its times. (Today, the city's university carries the historical name.) Following its capture in A.D. 637, the Arab conquerors changed its name to Suq al Ahvaz, the last word being the plural of Huzi/Khuzi, the local tribe.

Situated in the midst of fertile land that was particularly suitable for prized sugarcane, the city continued its prosperous existence throughout the Umayyad (A.D. 661–750) and Abbasid (A.D. 751–1258) Empires and after. But when the local dam broke in the mid-nineteenth century, the future of the city was doomed. It was saved later in the century by official plans to develop a new town across the river to complement the old settlement.

With the discovery of petroleum in the region in 1908, Ahvaz, now the capital of the oil-rich Khuzistan province, received a boost. Its prosperity continued for the next seven decades. As the center of the oil industry, it played a crucial role in the revolutionary movement that toppled the monarchy in Iran in 1979. In the Iran–Iraq War (1980–88) [*qv*] it became a frontline city and suffered some damage. It is now the seventh largest urban center in Iran [*qv*].

Aigptios: *see* Coptic Church and Copts.

al *(Arabic: the):* The Arabic definite article *al* is frequently used with proper nouns, especially places and people. For instance, Basra [*qv*] is written as al Basra in Arabic, and Nur al Din Attasi [*qv*] as Nur al Din al Attasi.

Al Jihad al Islami (Egypt): *Egyptian Islamic organization* The Egyptian authorities discovered the existence of Al Jihad al Islami, often called Al Jihad (AJ), in 1978 during Muslim-Copt [*qv*] riots. Its leadership council included Ismail Tantawi; Shaikh Omar Abdul Rahman [*qv*]; Muhammad Abdul Salam Faraj, an Islamist ideologue; Abbud Abdul Latif Zumur, a colonel in military intelligence who headed the group's operational wing; and Ayman Zawahiri [*qv*], a young surgeon. In his books, *Al Jihad: The Forgotten Pillar* and *The Absent Obligation,* Faraj argued that a true Muslim is obliged to struggle for the revival of the

Islamic *umma* [*qv*] and that Muslim groups or leaders who have turned away from the Sharia [*qv*] are apostates. Those who want to revive the Islamic umma are obliged to wage a jihad [*qv*] against the infidel state, the only acceptable form of jihad being armed struggle. A true Muslim must first confront the internal infidel (i.e., the Egyptian state) and then the external infidel (i.e., the non-Muslim world at large).

In early 1979 over 100 AJ members were charged with forming an antigovernment party. The next year Abdul Rahman issued a religious verdict that declared Egyptian President Anwar Sadat [*qv*] an infidel, thus making him a legitimate target for assassination. In early 1981 Faraj and Zumur devised a plan to assassinate Sadat and set up an Islamic state. On 6 October Lt. Khalid Ahmad Islambouli and three of his colleagues, armed with automatic weapons and hand grenades, attacked the review stand at the military parade in a Cairo [*qv*] suburb, killing Sadat and seven others.

Al Jihad leaders had visualized Sadat's assassination as a catalyst for a nationwide insurrection for the founding of an Islamic state. But there was an uprising only in Asyut, southern Egypt [*qv*], which left 188 dead. Most of the 3,000 Islamists jailed belonged to Al Jihad. It continued to have cells in the armed forces. Following his release after three years in jail for his participation in the plot to assassinate Sadat, in 1984, Zawahitri became the group's ideologue. He issued its first manifesto, *The Philosophy of Confrontation*. Its very title emphasized violence as a means of turning Egypt into an Islamic fundamentalist state. Thirty of its military members, including two majors, were tried in December 1986 for running training centers for subversives. After a series of Muslim-Copt clashes in the spring of 1987, the government arrested hundreds of Al Jihad members.

With Abdul Rahman emigrating in 1989, its activities declined. But with the return home of many veteran Islamist commandos after a successful jihad in Afghanistan against the leftist regime there in April 1992, Al Jihad, now calling itself the New Al Jihad, revived. It concentrated on assassinating high officials, such as ministers, but its two such attempts in 1993 failed. Government repression followed, including trials by military courts. By early 1997 these courts handed down eighty-seven death penalties to Islamic extremists. In 1999 Al Jihad's military leader, Adim Sigam, was killed, and 107 AJ members were tried for attempting to overthrow the government. Nine were given capital punishment. In early 2000 the leadership called on its followers to cease military activities and focus their attention on liberating Jerusalem [*qv*] from the Zionists [*qv*]. The government released a few hundred AJ detainees.

Al Qaida *(Arabic: The Base): Extremist Islamist organization* Al Qaida grew out of the Maktab al Khidmat (Bureau of Service [to the non-Afghan *mujahedin*]), established by Abdullah Azzam [*qv*] in Peshawar, Pakistan, in 1984. At the (Pakistan) Inter-Services Intelligence-U.S. CIA training camps established on both sides of the Afghan-Pakistan frontier, the non-Afghan Mujahedin [*qv*] underwent military training—based on the manuals used by the U.S. Defense Department and the CIA, and translated into Persian [*qv*], Arabic [*qv*], and Urdu—as well as political education, which emphasized nationalism and Islam [*qv*]. Their leader was Osama Bin Laden [*qv*]. He declared the departure of the Soviet troops from Afghanistan in February 1989 as a victory for the anti-Soviet jihad [*qv*].

Following the assassination of Azzam in November, bin Laden decided to run Maktab al Khidmat under the new title of Al Qaida, but with a more ambitious aim of creating an international network of jihadis, those who had participated in the anti-Soviet jihad [*qv*].

His scheme took concrete shape during his five-year stay (May 1991–May 1996) in Sudan, where he set up a string of companies. He ran Al Qaida along corporate lines—with the policy-making Shura Council of Twelve served by four executive committees: military (headed by Muhamamd Atef [*qv*]), business, Islamic studies, and media and public relations. In 1993 Al Qaida had an estimated 1,000 members, most of them Afghan veterans.

Bin Laden used his financial resources to fund the activities of Al Qaida, which focused on waging jihad against the U.S. by either financing directly Al Qaida's terrorist actions or sponsoring like-minded groups worldwide, with their activists coming to Sudan for weapons training. He turned Al Qaida into an umbrella organization specializing in conducting jihad through violent means. By then, besides supporting about 5,000 mainly Arab fighters in the Balkans, where a civil war raged in Bosnia during 1992–95, Al Qaida's members were established in Albania, Britain, Lebanon [*qv*], Malaysia, the Netherlands, Pakistan, Romania, Russia, Saudi Arabia [*qv*], Turkey, and the United Arab Emirates [*qv*]. Also Al

Qaida established associate relationships with like-minded groups in Algeria, Chechnya, Egypt [*qv*], Ethiopia, Horn of Africa, Lebanon, Libya, Philippines, South Asia, Southeast Asia, Syria [*qv*], Tunisia, and Yemen [*qv*].

After bin Laden had moved his entourage to Afghanistan in 1996, Al Qaida grew further, partly because Mullah Muhammad Omar, the ruler of the Taliban-controlled Afghanistan, gave it free rein, partly because of the return of the veterans of the anti-Soviet jihad after being harassed by their governments, and partly because of the decline in the jihads in the Balkans, Chechnya, and Kashmir. It opened military training camps. Four years later, Al Qaida's 3,000 fighters would become the Taliban's 55th Brigade. Outside Afghanistan the estimated size of Al Qaida activists and sympathizers was put at 4,500 in sixty countries.

The U.S. held Al Qaida responsible for the bombing of the American embassies in Nairobi and Dar as Salaam in August 1998, which killed 227 people. It saw the hand of Al Qaida in the bombing of USS *Cole* in Aden [*qv*] in October 2000. And following the terrorist attacks in New York and Washington in September 2001, U.S. President George W. Bush (r. 2001–) held Al Qaida and bin Laden responsible.

During Washington's Afghanistan campaign from October to December 2001, two-thirds of Al Qaida fighters either died or were taken prisoner. The rest, including bin Laden and his ideological mentor, Ayman Zawahiri [*qv*], escaped, mostly to Pakistan.

By the end of 2002, the arrest of some 3,000 Al Qaida activists and sympathizers in ninety-eight countries had cut the size of the organization by two-thirds. Al Qaida now lacked a headquarters and training camps. With raised security in the U.S. and other Western countries, it switched to Western targets in non-Western countries. In 2002 it or its associates hit German tourists in Tunisia, French naval technicians in Pakistan, and Australian and Western tourists in Bali, Indonesia (killing 202), using vehicles carrying liquid gas (in Tunisia) or chlorate (Bali). Also with the transfer of terrorist technology and expertise from the center to the periphery, Al Qaida's associate groups became more active.

However, by early 2003, the remnants of Al Qaida inside Afghanistan had established an underground network to carry out guerrilla actions and assassinations, and set up a radio station. Its strength was back to where it was before the Pentagon's Afghanistan war.

With Atef dead, and bin Laden and al Zawahiri rendered virtually inoperative in their secret hideouts, the task of planning future attacks fell on Khalid Shaikh Muhammad [qv], who had played an important role in the 9/11 terrorist strikes. His arrest in Pakistan in March 2003 was a great setback to the organization.

Alawis *(Arabic: followers of Ali): Islamic sect* Also known as Alawites. The term Alawi came into vogue in Syria during the French mandate (1920–46), replacing the earlier terms: (1) Nusairi, derived (according to some scholars) from the name of the first theologian of the sect, Muhammad ibn Nusair, who in 245 A.H./A.D. 857 proclaimed himself *bab* (gate) to the tenth Shia [qv] Imam Ali Naqi and of his son, Muhammad, who died before him; and (2)

Ansariya, the name of the mountain range where they lived.

Alawis are an offshoot of the Twelver Shias [qv], sharing their belief that Imam Ali, cousin and son-in-law of the Prophet Muhammad, was the legitimate heir but was deprived of his status by the first three caliphs. They portray Ali as a bearer of divine essence and hold him in higher esteem than any of the earlier prophets mentioned in the Quran [qv], including Adam, Noah, Moses, and Jesus. They follow certain rituals derived from Christianity [qv], including the celebration of Christmas [qv] and Epiphany [qv], and from Zoroastrianism [qv], including Nawruz [qv]. Taqi al Din ibn Taimiya (1263–1328), an orthodox Sunni [qv] Syrian theologian, described them as more dangerous than Christians and urged a jihad [qv] against them.

The seven pillars of the Alawi sect include not only the five pillars of the Sunni sect— *shahada* (Islamic credo), *salat* (five prayers), *zakat* [qv] (alms), *hajj* [qv] (pilgrimage to Mecca [qv]), and *sawm* (fasting during Ramadan [qv])—but also jihad (holy struggle) and *waliya* (devotion to the Imam Ali family and hatred of their adversaries). They share their annual festivals with Shias, including Eid al Fitr [qv], Eid al Adha [qv], and Ashura [qv]. Imam Musa al Sadr [qv], an eminent Twelver Shia theologian based in Lebanon, ruled in 1974 that Alawis were part of the Shia school of Islam. Most present-day Alawis are settled as peasants, mainly in the mountainous region around Latakia [qv], a port city in Syria, where they constitute 12 to 15 percent of the national population. The best known Alawi politician is Bashar Assad [qv], president of Syria.

Aleppo: *Syrian city* Pop. 1,934,000 (2003, est.). The importance of Aleppo, with a history stretching back to ca. 2000 B.C., stems from the strategic position it occupied on the caravan route connecting the eastern Mediterranean region with the lands farther east. It was part of the Achaemenian Empire (539–330 B.C.), and it continued to prosper during the later Roman and Byzantine periods. It fell to Muslim Arabs [*qv*] in A.D. 637, and retained its commercial importance during the subsequent Islamic empires, from the Umayyads, who built the Great Mosque in A.D. 715, to the Ottoman Turks (1517–1918).

Under the Ottomans it emerged as the principal trading center in their Arab empire. With the decline of caravan transport, local entrepreneurs took to industry, especially leather, textile printing, and silk manufacture. By the early twentieth century Aleppo had emerged as a rival to Damascus [*qv*]. Besides the Great Mosque, the citadel, constructed in the thirteenth century, is a chief tourist attraction. Aleppo is now the largest city of Syria [*qv*].

Alexandria: *Egyptian city* Pop. 3,891,000 (2003, est.). Founded by Alexander the Great in 332 B.C., Alexandria was the capital of Ptolemies (323–30 B.C.). In 306 B.C. it became the site of the Bibliotheca Alexandrina, a library with 700,000 items, which was destroyed by fire in 47 B.C. As a major port it rivaled and then outstripped ancient Carthage to become the largest city in the Mediterranean region. It emerged as the leading center of Hellenic and Jewish arts and sciences. Later, in 30 B.C., it formed part of the Roman empire and was its most populous provincial capital, with 300,000 free citizens. After Muslim Arabs [*qv*] captured it in A.D. 642, they transferred the capital to al Fustat near Cairo [*qv*]. It became the second largest city of Egypt, a position it has maintained.

It is the headquarters of the Greek Orthodox [*qv*] patriarchate. A highly developed port, it is an important industrial center. Its main tourist offerings include the Hadrianic catacombs and Pompey's Pillar. In 2001 it became the site of a newly constructed library, named after its ancient predecessor, capable of holding four million volumes. Though possessing only a quarter-million books, it became the largest and the most advanced library in the Arab world.

Algiers Accord (1975): *see* Iran-Iraq Treaty of International Boundaries and Neighborliness (1975)/Treaty of Frontier and Good Neighborly Relations (Iran-Iraq, 1975).

Ali, Salim Rubai (1935–78): *South Yemeni politician; president 1969–78* Born into a middle-class family in Zinjibar near Aden [*qv*], Ali trained as a teacher. Later he studied law and became involved in a militantly anti-imperialist movement, the National Liberation Front (NLF) [*qv*]. In October 1963 he led a guerrilla campaign against the British in the Rafdan Mountains. Four years later the British left, handing over power to the NLF. Accused of factionalism by the NLF leadership, Ali chose to go into self-exile. But he continued to conspire.

In June 1969 President Qahtan al Shaabi [*qv*], a moderate, was ousted by the leftists within the NLF and replaced by a presidential council of five (later reduced to three), headed by Ali, who was elected to the NLF central committee and politbureau. The new regime purged the party and government of moderate elements. It carried out rapid socioeconomic changes at home and followed radical foreign policies.

By the mid-1970s, however, Ali had begun to show signs of pragmatism, especially concerning Saudi Arabia, which had been deeply hostile to socialist South Yemen. This put him at odds with the radical, pro-Moscow faction led by Abdul Fattah Ismail [*qv*], secretary-general of the NLF. The rivalry between the two intensified and became entangled with relations between North and South Yemen. The assassination of North Yemeni President Ibrahim Hamdi [*qv*] on the eve of his visit to Aden [*qv*] in October 1977 made matters worse. The differences between Ali and Ismail hardened around the structure of the proposed Yemen Socialist Party [*qv*], developmental strategy, and foreign relations, particularly with Saudi Arabia.

The break between the two rivals came in June 1978. A special emissary of Ali, dispatched to his North Yemeni counterpart, Ahmad Hussein Ghashmi [*qv*], succeeded in killing both the president and himself with explosives hidden in his briefcase. One version had it that Ali had sent his envoy to secure Ghashmi's assistance in a planned coup, but his adversaries had got wind of it and had replaced his emissary with their own. Just as this drama was unfolding in Sanaa [*qv*], the two rivals clashed in Aden. While Ali used the army to overcome his opponents, Ismail engaged the party's People's Militia. Ali lost and was executed.

Alignment Bloc (Israel): *see* Labor Alignment (Israel).

aliya *(Hebrew: ascent): Jewish immigration* *into Palestine* Figuratively, the term *aliya* means Jewish immigration into Palestine; its other meaning being "to a call up" a member of the congregation to read the scroll of the Jewish Law during a synagogue [*qv*] service.

Organized Jewish immigration into Palestine, inspired by the Zionist movement [*qv*], began in 1882. Between then and 1948 there were six *aliyot* (pl. of *aliya*). The first aliya (1882–1903) involved 25,000 Jews—mainly from Tsarist Russia, which was then engaged in periodic pogroms of Jews [*qv*]—and doubled the size of the Jewish community in Palestine, which was divided evenly between Sephardic [*qv*] and Ashkenazi Jews [*qv*].

The second aliya (1904–14) also consisted mainly of Jews from Russia, where the collapse of the 1905 revolution caused an upheaval and socialist-minded Jews sought a better future in Palestine. An intake of 40,000 Jews raised the size of the local community to 90,000. Subsequent emigration reduced the total to 50,000 on the eve of the First World War.

The third aliya (1919–23), inspired by the 1917 Balfour Declaration [*qv*], involved 35,000 Jews, chiefly from Russia and Russian Poland. As believers in socialism and the dignity of labor, these colonizers set up agricultural settlements (*kibbutzim*) [*qv*], cooperative villages (*moshavim*), and a general federation of labor. They also created an educational system, with Hebrew [*qv*] as the medium of instruction, and a host of self-governing institutions.

The fourth aliya (1924–31) brought 60,000 Jewish immigrants—principally middle-class Jews from Poland—to the Palestinian shores, raising the size of the

Jewish community to 190,000 by 1931. With the United States ceasing to be an open country for immigrants from 1924 onward, Jewish emigrants from Europe became more interested in Palestine. This, and the formation of the Jewish Agency for Palestine [*qv*] to finance Jewish immigration and act as the political representative of the Jews in Palestine, prepared the ground for a larger wave of immigration.

The fifth aliya (1932–40), consisting of two phases—1932–35 and 1936–40—saw the influx of 233,000 Jews into Palestine, with about a third from Nazi Germany and another third from Eastern Europe. During the first phase, which coincided with Nazi persecution of the Jews in Germany, 144,000 Jews arrived in Palestine. The rate slowed somewhat during 1936–38, and in May 1939 the British government's White Paper fixed the annual quota at 15,000 for the next five years. Taking into account illegal immigration, the total for the second phase of the fifth *aliya* was 89,000. The new arrivals were chiefly middle-class professionals and capitalists, and gave the vastly enlarged Jewish community in Palestine a distinctly European veneer. Despite their high birth rate, Sephardic Jews decreased from 50 percent to 20 percent of the population.

The sixth aliya (1941–47), which involved 120,000 Jewish immigrants from Europe, including 28,000 illegals, tilted the balance further in favor of the Ashkenazim. At the founding of Israel in May 1948, it had 710,000 Jewish inhabitants.

Allon, Yigal (1918–80): *Israeli military officer and politician* Born Yigal Faikovitch in a farming family in the Galilee village of Kfar Tavor, Allon went to agricultural school and was involved in establishing a kibbutz [*qv*] on the northern coastline of the Sea of Galilee. One of the founder members of the Palmah [*qv*] in 1941, he became its commander four years later. During the 1948–49 Arab-Israeli War [*qv*] he performed brilliantly, rising in rank to brigadier general and commander of the southern front at the age of thirty. Politically he was allied with Mapam [*qv*], which was formed in early 1948. When in late 1949 the government began to purge Mapam members who were considered too pro-Soviet from the upper ranks of the military, Allon lost his command.

Enrolled as a part-time student in Israel, he won a scholarship to Cambridge University in Britain. On returning to Israel he joined the Ahdut HaAvodah-Poale Zion [*qv*]. He was elected on its ticket to the Knesset [*qv*] in 1955. Four years later he resigned to become a research fellow at Oxford University in Britain. He reentered the Knesset in 1961. For the next seven years he was labor minister in the coalition governments led first by David Ben-Gurion [*qv*] and then by Levi Eshkol [*qv*].

On the eve of the June 1967 Arab-Israeli War [*qv*], to Allon's disappointment, Eshkol handed over the defense ministry to his bitter rival, Moshe Dayan [*qv*]. In a cabinet reshuffle in 1968 Allon was appointed deputy premier. He retained this position in the government led by Golda Meir [*qv*] in 1969, with additional responsibility for education and culture. Opposing Dayan's annexationist plan for the Occupied Territories [*qv*], Allon proposed that the populated areas of the West Bank [*qv*] be returned to Jordan, with Israel retaining only a strip along the

Jordan valley as a security belt. Neither plan was adopted by the government.

Following the October 1973 Arab-Israeli War [qv], which discredited Dayan as defense minister, Allon retained his position as deputy premier in the cabinet headed by Yitzhak Rabin [qv] and also took charge of the foreign ministry. He became part of the powerful triumvirate of former military officers—Allon (leftist), Rabin (centrist), and Shimon Peres [qv] (rightist)—in the government. Following Rabin's resignation as head of the Labor Party [qv] in April 1977 and the electoral defeat of the party in May, Allon built up a base to challenge the new leader, Peres. But before he could test his popularity he died.

A.M.: *Abbr. of Anno Mundi (Latin: Year of the World)* This pertains to the Jewish era that began with the estimated date of creation, according to Genesis in the Old Testament [qv]: 3760 B.C. Jews [qv] use this dating system. *See also* Jewish calendar.

Amal *(Arabic: acronym of Afwaj al-Muqawama al Lubnaniya, The Lebanese Resistance Detachments): Lebanese militia* Amal was formed in July 1975, a few months after the outbreak of civil war in Lebanon, as the armed wing of the Movement of the Disinherited, which had been established in February 1973 by a radical Shia leader, Imam Musa al Sadr [qv]. It was popularly known as *Amal* (Hope). After the "disappearance" of al Sadr in August 1978 during his visit to Libya, Amal came under the leadership of Shaikh Muhammad Mahdi Shams al Din and Hussein Husseini, who forged strong links with Iran after an Islamic revolution there in early 1979. It gained many recruits from the 300,000 Shia emigrants from southern Lebanon who had abandoned their homes as a result of Israeli bombings.

By spring of 1982 the leadership of Amal had passed on to Shaikh Shams al Din and Nabih Berri [qv], a layman Shia leader. Since Berri was close to Syria, Amal increasingly became a fixture of the policies being pursued by Damascus, especially in the ongoing civil strife. The victory of the pro-Syrian camp in Lebanon's civil war [qv] in October 1990 improved the status of Amal. However, following a government decision to dissolve all irregular forces, 2,800 militiamen of Amal, which at its peak had 14,000 men under arms, were enrolled into the regular Lebanese army in September 1991.

It continued to function as a political party and contested parliamentary polls, with its leader Berri being elected parliamentary speaker. In the 2000 general election, it allied with Hizbollah [qv], and together they won all of the twenty-three seats in the governorate of South Lebanon.

American hostage crisis in Tehran (1979–81): *see* Hostage taking and hostages.

American University in Beirut: Continuing the tradition of Christian missionaries from the United States who had been establishing schools and colleges in Lebanon since the 1830s, Dr. Daniel Bliss of the American Protestant Mission, having secured a charter from the state of New York in 1863 and raised funds in the United States and Britain, opened the Syrian Protestant College in Beirut in 1866. Despite its name, the college was nonsectarian. It soon acquired a school of medicine. In 1882 English replaced Arabic as the language of instruction. Following the end of the Ottoman rule in 1918 and the arrival of the French as victors, in 1920 the trustees changed its name to the American University in Beirut (AUB).

Education in the arts and sciences, imparted by the AUB to a student body drawn from all over the Arab world, helped create a class of Arab intellectuals with a wide perspective. The AUB thus performed a significant role in producing political leaders and stimulating Arab political and intellectual activity. It continued to function throughout the 1975–90 civil war [qv] (during which—in 1984—its president, Dr. Malcolm Kerr, was killed), and its hospital provided much-needed services. After the conflict, its research program focused on the reconstruction of Lebanon. Between 1870 and 2002, it awarded 66,107 degrees and diplomas.

American University in Cairo: Established in 1919, the American University in Cairo (AUC) was financed by United States citizens interested in furthering education in the Middle East. Dr. Charles Watson, its founding president, was born of missionary parents and grew up in the Egyptian city of Asyut. It provides American liberal arts and professional education in English to predominantly Egyptian students. In 1928, female students were accepted and by 1994 their ratio had climbed to 50 percent. Incorporated in the United States, the AUC operates within the framework of the cultural relations agreement signed between Egypt and the United States in 1962, which was renewed in 1975. Despite the best intentions of its founders, the AUC has remained an exclusive institution because of its small student body and high tuition fees.

Its student body of a little over 11,000 students in courses and training programs in 2002 was less than one percent of the national total.

Amichai, Yehuda (1924–2000): *Israeli poet and novelist* Born Yehuda Pfeuffer to a businessman father in Wurzberg, Germany, Amichai moved to Palestine [qv] along with his parents in 1936. After graduating from a religious high school in Jerusalem [qv], he enrolled in the British army in 1942. After the Second World War, he joined the Palmah [qv] and fought in the 1948–49 Arab-Israeli War [qv]. He went to the Hebrew University in Jerusalem in 1949 and began to write poetry.

Much influenced by W. H. Auden (d. 1973), a left-wing British poet famed for his personal poetry written in a casual tone, Amichai combined everyday Hebrew [qv] with the language used in the Old Testament [qv] and the Jewish prayer books. An iconoclast, he derided the spartan way of life preached by the pioneering Zionist [qv] leaders, especially David Ben-Gurion [qv], during the first decades of Israel and aspired unashamedly for bourgeois comforts. In 1962 his *Poems (1948–62)* became a best-seller.

By continuing to harness the flat idiom of daily life with images from the Hebrew Bible [qv] and Jewish liturgy, he transformed the rhythm and vocabulary of Hebrew poetry. His work, distinguished by its depth and virtuosity, was read widely. By the time he was seventy, he had published eleven volumes of poetry in Hebrew; two novels, including *Not of This Time, Not of This Place* (1963); and several short stories. His later poetry is criticized as being thematically unadventurous and covering old ground. His works were translated into twenty-five languages. The titles translated into English include *Love Poems, More Love Poems, Poems of Jerusalem, Open-Eyed Landscape, Great Tranquillity: Questions and Answers,* and *The World Is a Poem, and Other Stories* and *Yehuda Amichai: A Life of Poetry 1948–1994.*

After the 1967 Arab-Israeli War [*qv*], he became an advocate of peace with the Palestinians and a supporter of the Peace Now [*qv*] movement. He won the Israel Prize for literature in 1982.

Amman: *capital of Jordan* Pop. 1,293,000 (2003, est.). A city of hills, Amman's origins lie in distant antiquity, around 4000 B.C. Both its present and biblical names are derived from Ammon, the capital of the Ammonites, its full description being Rabba' Ir Bene Ammon (*Hebrew: Great City of Ammon's Sons*). It is the site of the battle in which Uriah met his death (the battle having been ordered by his supreme commander, King David), enabling his wife, Bathsheba, to marry King David.

When Egyptian King Ptolemy II Philadelphius (r. 283–246 B.C.) captured the settlement, he called it Philadelphia. This name survived the arrival of the Greeks, Romans, and Byzantines, and the city thrived under the Romans. After capturing it in A.D. 635, the Muslim Arabs renamed it Amman. It began to decline and by the early thirteenth century was reduced to ruins.

When faced with the problem of resettling the Circassian [*qv*] refugees from the Caucasian region of Tsarist Russia, Ottoman Sultan Abdul Hamid II (r. 1876–1909) hit upon the idea of directing them to the virtually defunct Amman in 1878. The revived Amman was still a village when Abdullah ibn Hussein [*qv*] camped there with his troops in 1921 on his way to Syria. Two years later it became the capital of Transjordan [*qv*].

From then onward it began to expand— a process accelerated by the influx of Palestinian refugees after the 1948–49 Palestine War [*qv*] and again after the June 1967 Arab-Israeli War [*qv*]. In September 1970 the city became the center of an armed conflict between Palestinian guerillas and the Jordanian army.

On the whole Amman has benefited greatly by the enterprise of its Palestinian residents and has become the financial, commercial, communications, political, and educational center of Jordan. Among its tourist offerings are a Roman amphitheater and the old citadel.

Anaiza tribal federation: (Also spelled Anaza.) Anaiza is one of the twenty-five major tribal federations in the Arabian Peninsula [*qv*]. It is considered noble because of its claim to lineal descent from Yaarab, the eponymous father of all Arabs. Its origins can be traced back to the fifteenth century and the territory around the town of Diraiya in the Najd region [*qv*]. The House of Saud [*qv*] belongs to the Masalikh clan of the Ruwalla tribe of the Anaiza federation. The ruling al Sabah clan [*qv*] of Kuwait is part of the Amarat tribe of the Anaiza federation. *See also* Tribalism.

Anglo-American Commission on Palestine (1946): After the Second World War, in order to deflect the pressure of the U.S. Congress and president to concede to Zionist demands to scrap its 1939 White Paper—limiting annual Jewish immigration to Palestine to 15,000—and to admit 100,000 Jewish refugees (camped in

Cyprus) into Palestine, Britain agreed to the appointment of a joint Anglo-American commission to study the Palestine problem. In its report, published in April 1946, the Commission proposed that Britain should continue its mandate, that 100,000 Jewish refugees be let into Palestine and that all illegal militias—primarily the 65,000-strong Zionist irregulars, armed with weapons from wartime munitions factories—be disbanded. London agreed to continue the mandate only if the United States shared the responsibility, which the latter refused. While the United States urged immediate admission of the Jewish refugees into Palestine, Britain made this conditional on the disarming of the Zionist militias, whose violent activities were increasingly threatening British life and property.

Anglo-Bahraini Agreement (1914): To ensure supplies of oil—the fuel adopted by the British navy in 1913—Britain imposed an agreement on Bahrain whereby the latter was barred from giving petroleum concessions to non-British companies without London's prior permission.

Anglo-Egyptian Treaty (1936): The outbreak of the Italian-Ethiopian War in 1935 made Britain, the dominant foreign power in Egypt, amenable to redefining Anglo-Egyptian ties. The result was the signing of an Anglo-Egyptian treaty in 1936, valid for twenty years. It gave Britain the exclusive right to equip and train the Egyptian military. While it required Egypt to expand its transport and communications facilities and make them available to the British forces, it entitled Britain to build as many new air bases as it wished. It signified a formal end to the posting of British troops

outside the Suez Canal [*qv*] zone, subject to Egypt building up its defense capabilities to a sufficient level. British troops were to be stationed specifically to guard the Suez Canal until such time that the two signatories agreed that Egypt could do the job alone. Britain retained the right to take over all defense and communications facilities in the event of war.

The treaty disappointed Egyptian nationalists. In the 1950 general election, the nationalist Wafd [*qv*] won decisively. Reflecting the popular mood, which sought to avenge the humiliation suffered by the Arabs in the Palestine War (1948–49) [*qv*], the Wafd government pressed Britain to withdraw its troops from Egypt. When London stonewalled, Cairo unilaterally abrogated the 1936 Treaty in October 1951. The ensuing official noncooperation, reinforced by popular guerrilla actions, made the British base in the Suez Canal zone virtually inoperative. The tussle between London and Cairo paved the way for the overthrow of the Egyptian monarchy in less than a year. The republican regime was anxious to see the departure of the 70,000 British troops who were occupying 300 sq. miles/777 sq. km of Egyptian territory. It signed an agreement with London in October 1954 for a British withdrawal by the end of the year.

Anglo-Iraqi Treaty (1922): After Britain, the mandate power in Iraq, had installed Faisal I ibn Hussein [*qv*] as king in August 1921, it decided to formalize its relations with Baghdad. It incorporated the terms of its League of Nations mandate into a treaty. The Iraqi government deliberated for more than a year before endorsing it. The Anglo-Iraqi Treaty of October 1922, which vested economic and military control of Iraq in British hands, was then placed before a constituent assembly elected in March 1924. The reluctant members ratified it only after the British high commissioner threatened to suspend the constitution drafted by the assembly. The 1922 treaty was superseded by a fresh document in 1930.

Anglo-Iraqi Treaty (1930): When oil was discovered in Iraq in 1927, Britain, the mandate power, decided to redefine its relations with Iraq. In September 1929 it agreed to sponsor Iraq's membership in the League of Nations. A year later a twenty-five-year treaty was signed, to be implemented after Iraq had entered the League of Nations as an independent state. It required Iraq to formulate a common foreign policy with Britain and allow the stationing of British forces on its soil, in exchange for a British guarantee to protect it against foreign attack. London ended its mandate over Iraq in October 1932. A major upheaval in 1941 in Iraq, involving a coup by Rashid Ali Gailani [qv] and its suppression, confirmed the supremacy of Britain over Iraqi nationalist forces.

After the Second World War, Britain tried to meet the widespread Iraqi, desire for full independence by renegotiating the terms of the 1930 treaty, presenting the new treaty (initialed by both sides in the British port city of Portsmouth in January 1948—the Portsmouth Agreement, valid for twenty years) as signifying an alliance between two equals. However, because it did not include British troop withdrawal from Iraq, it went down badly with the Iraqis. Large-scale demonstrations in Baghdad [qv] against the Portsmouth Agreement brought down the

government and aborted the new draft treaty, thus implicitly confirming the annulment of the earlier treaty.

Anglo-Jordanian Treaty (1948): After Transjordan had acquired independence in May 1946, its ruler, Abdullah ibn Hussein [qv], assumed the title of king and changed the name of his realm from the Emirate of Transjordan to the Hashemite Kingdom of Jordan. This necessitated revision of the 1923 Anglo-Transjordan Treaty. A revised version, valid for twenty years, was signed in March 1948. It incorporated the principle of mutual assistance in the event of war, and allowed Britain to use military bases in Jordan for an annual subsidy of £12 million to the king. In December 1955 Amman [qv] witnessed massive demonstrations against the treaty. This was followed by a call by parliament, elected in October 1956, for abrogation of the treaty. In January 1957 Egypt, Syria, and Saudi Arabia together offered to replace the British subsidy for at least ten years. The Jordanian monarch, Hussein ibn Talal [qv], approached London to end the treaty. This was done in March 1957.

Anglo-Kuwaiti Agreement (1913): To ensure supplies of oil—the fuel adopted by the British navy in 1913—Britain imposed an agreement on Kuwait that barred the latter from giving oil concessions to non-British companies without London's prior permission.

Anglo-Omani Agreement (1925): To ensure supplies of petroleum—the fuel adopted by the British navy in 1913—Britain imposed an agreement on Oman whereby the latter was barred from giving oil concessions to non-British companies without London's prior permission.

Anglo-Ottoman Convention (1913): In July 1913 Britain signed an Anglo-Ottoman Convention with Ottoman Sultan Muhammad VI (r. 1909–23). Among other things it recognized Kuwait as "an autonomous *caza* [i.e., administrative unit] of the [Ottoman] Empire" under Shaikh Mubarak I al Sabah, who had the status of an Ottoman *qaimmaqam* (governor). Mubarak's complete autonomy was recognized within an inner (red) circle of 40 mi/ 64 km radius, centered on Kuwait port, which included not only the islands of Warba and Bubiyan, but also Mashian, Failakah, Auhah, and Kabbar. Beyond that, in a segment of land with a radius of 140 mi /224 km, centered on Kuwait port, marking the outer (green) boundary defined by the Convention, Mubarak was authorized to collect tributes from the tribes. However, the outbreak of the First World War in August 1914, when the Ottomans sided with the Germans, invalidated the Convention and allowed London to announce that Kuwait was an "independent shaikhdom under British protection."

Anglo-Persian Agreement (1919): By the end of the First World War, the government of Persia (now Iran) was in such dire financial straits that only British subsidies could keep it afloat. This encouraged Britain's foreign minister, Lord Curzon, to realize his dream of turning Persia into a British protectorate. He concluded a secret agreement with Tehran in 1919 that gave Britain enormous political, economic, and military control over Persia. When the terms of the agreement were disclosed on the eve of a debate in the Persian parliament, there was furor not only in Persia, but also in the United States and Bolshevik Russia. The parliament refused to ratify it.

Anglo-Qatari agreement (1916): According to this treaty, Britain guaranteed the territorial integrity of Qatar, while Qatar agreed not to cede any mineral rights to a third party without Britain's prior consent.

Anglo-Transjordanian Treaty (1923): In late 1921 the British offered Transjordan to Abdullah ibn Hussein [*qv*] to dissuade him from marching into Syria, then under French occupation, to avenge the defeat of his brother, Faisal ibn Hussein [*qv*]. Abdullah became Emir of Transjordan in April 1922. A year later Britain announced that it would recognize the "independence" of Transjordan under Abdullah's rule if a constitutional regime were established and a preferential treaty with London signed. In May 1923 such a treaty was concluded. It required Transjordan, "an autonomous emirate," to formulate a common foreign policy with Britain, and allowed the stationing of British forces on its soil, in exchange for a British guarantee to protect it against foreign attack.

Anglo-Yemeni Treaty (1934): Soon after the First World War, Imam Yahya Hamid al Din (r. 1918–48) dispatched his forces to capture several border areas that London considered part of its Western Aden protectorate. Periodic efforts to negotiate a deal failed until 1934, when a forty-year Anglo-Yemeni Treaty of Peace and Friendship was signed in Sanaa [*qv*]. It accepted North Yemen's southern frontier as the status quo until future negotiations produced a final settlement.

Ansar-e Islam (*Kurdish/Persian: Helpers of Islam*): *Iraqi Kurdish Islamist group* It was one of the three recently established Islamist [*qv*] groups in Iraqi Kurdistan [*qv*] opposed to the draft agreement between representatives of the Iraqi Kurdistan Front (IKF) [*qv*] and the Baghdad government in June 1991 that led to the formation of the Islamic Movement of Kurdistan (IMK) [*qv*], the others being the Kurdish Hizbollah and the Kurdish Mujahedin.

Ten years later, when the Patriotic Union of Kurdistan (PUK) [*qv*], controlling southeastern Kurdistan, attacked Halabja [*qv*], the IMK headquarters, and expelled the IMK leadership, the organization split, reviving Ansar-e Islam. Its 500-strong armed force set up a fortified network of villages and outposts in the valleys east of Halabja, covering about 100 sq. miles/260 sq. km. From there it mounted periodic attacks on PUK targets.

Unable to overpower Ansar-e Islam insurgents, the PUK put it about in the summer of 2002 that the Islamist organization, fortified by the arrival of about 100 Al Qaida [*qv*] fugitives from Afghanistan, was now led by Abu Mussab Zarqawi, a Jordanian operative of Al Qaida who was allegedly in touch with the government in Baghdad [*qv*].

Ansariyas: *see* Alawis.

anti-Semitism: *prejudice against Jews* As the Jews [*qv*] are blamed for killing Jesus Christ, who was born a Jew, Christians [*qv*] have harbored feelings against Jews since the inception of their faith. This has resulted in periodic persecution of Jews, often involving expulsion, in Christian countries, where Jews came to be confined to specific areas—ghettoes. The earliest ghettoes were in eleventh-century Italy. They existed until the late nineteenth century in Austria, Bavaria, Germany, Italy, and Russia.

Restrictions on the trades that Jews could pursue led more and more of them to resort to money lending and thus gave popular prejudice an economic dimension.

After the emancipation of Jews in the late nineteenth century, pseudoscientific theories were advanced to prove the racial inferiority of Jews. In order to divert popular disaffection, political demagogues and certain governments (Russia being a prime example) blamed Jews for the ills of society. A forged document, claiming to outline a Jewish plan to dominate the world and entitled *Protocols of the Wise Men of Zion,* appeared in the early twentieth century in Tsarist Russia. Hatred of Jews, a Semitic race, reached its peak in Nazi Germany (1933–45), based on the theory of the superiority of the Aryan race, and resulted in the extermination of an estimated six million Jews in Europe, a phenomenon commonly described as the Holocaust.

Antiochene rite: *see* West Syriac rite.

Antonius, George (1892–1942): *Lebanese writer and thinker* Born into a Greek Orthodox [*qv*] family in Lebanon and educated in Egypt, Antonius settled in Palestine [*qv*] in 1921 after taking up a job with the education department there. Nine years later he joined the New York-based Institute of Current World Affairs headed by Charles Crane, cochairman of a U.S. commission on the Middle East [*qv*] in 1919.

A lucid writer and an eloquent speaker, Antonius became a leading spokesman of Palestinian Arabs. He testified before the (British) Peel Commission (1937) on Palestine and acted as an adviser to the Arab delegates to the Round Table Conference on Palestine in London in 1939.

The Arab Awakening, his book on Arab nationalism [*qv*], published in 1938, established him as an original thinker. He traced the roots of Arab renaissance to a nascent movement in Beirut in the 1880s, composed largely of Arab Christians educated in the Protestant and Catholic mission schools and colleges of Lebanon. In Palestinian politics he allied himself with radical Haajj Muhammad Amin al Husseini [*qv*].

Aoun, Michel (1935–): *Lebanese military officer and politician* Born to Maronite [*qv*] parents, Aoun graduated from Lebanon's Military Academy as an artillery officer. He underwent further training in France from 1958–59. He rose steadily in the army, which became increasingly fractured along religious lines as the Lebanese Civil War [*qv*], beginning in 1975, dragged on for many years. His second period of training was in the United States from 1978–80. Four years later President Amin Gemayel [*qv*] promoted him to brigadier general and appointed him military chief of staff.

In the absence of a properly elected president to follow him, Gemayel called on Aoun to form a temporary military government. When Aoun appointed five military officers as cabinet ministers, the three Muslim officers refused to serve. By declaring a "war of liberation" against Syria in March 1989, Aoun further alienated the Muslim population and militias. The resulting blockade of the limited area controlled by Aoun made his position tenuous. He rejected the National Reconciliation Charter [*qv*], which had been adopted by an overwhelming majority of the Lebanese parliamentarians meeting in Taif, Saudi Arabia, in October 1989. He ignored the election in November of Rene Muawad

as president and later (following Muawad's assassination) of Elias Hrawi [*qv*], as well as President Hrawi's dismissal of him. He continued to occupy the presidential palace in Baabda, a suburb of Beirut.

His clashes with the Lebanese Forces [*qv*], a Maronite [*qv*] militia, undercut his standing among Christians and further reduced his area of control. In October 1990 his troops collapsed when attacked by the joint forces of his Lebanese opponents and Syria. He took refuge in the French Embassy. The following August he left for France, after the Lebanese government had granted him conditional amnesty. His attempts since then to return to Lebanon [*qv*] have failed.

Aql, Said (1912–): *Lebanese writer* Born into a Maronite [*qv*] family in Zahle, Aql soon established himself as an outstanding poet with extraordinary lyrical powers. His use of symbols set a new trend in Arabic poetry, as did his (later) practice of using colloquial language instead of classical Arabic, a traditional practice in the Arab world. An intellectual, Aql believed that Lebanese identity was rooted in its distant Phoenician past and had little to do with Islam [*qv*] or Arabism [*qv*]. He went on to develop a version of the Latin alphabet that he claimed was more suitable to the "Lebanese" language.

Aql's ideas appealed to Maronite intellectuals who, during the period between the two world wars, were intent on giving shape to a Lebanese identity distinct from Syria and the Muslim-dominated Arab hinterland. With the tide of Arab nationalism [*qv*] rising after the Second World War, Aql's particularist thesis lost ground. But the later arrival of a large number of Palestinians in Lebanon revived Aql's ideology among Maronites, especially the ultranationalist militia, the Guardians of the Cedars [*qv*].

al Aqsa Intifada: *see* Second Intifada.

Arab Baath Party (Syria): Michel Aflaq [*qv*] and Salah al-Din Bitar [*qv*] established a study circle in Damascus [*qv*] in 1940 called the Movement of Arab Baath (Renaissance). They published pamphlets in which they expounded revolutionary, socialist Arab nationalism [*qv*], and were committed to achieving Arab unity as the first step. Once the mandate power, France, had left Syria in April 1946, they secured a license for their group, now called the Party of Arab Baath. They decided to merge their faction with the one led by Zaki Arsuzi [*qv*]. Out of this, in April 1947, emerged the Arab Baath Party in Damascus. Aflaq was elected senior member in the executive committee of four.

The party's basic principles were described as the unity and freedom of the Arab nation within its homeland, and a belief in the special mission of the Arab nation, the mission being to end colonialism and promote humanitarianism. To achieve this the party had to be nationalist, populist, socialist, and revolutionary. While the party rejected the concept of class conflict, it favored land reform; public ownership of natural resources, transport, and large-scale industry and financial institutions; trade unions of workers and peasants; the co-option of workers into management; and acceptance of "nonexploitative" private ownership and inheritance. It stood for a representative and constitutional form of government, as well as freedom of speech and association within the bounds of Arab nationalism.

Arab Baath Socialist Party: *see* Baath Socialist Party.

Arab Cooperation Council (1989–90): *a regional Arab organization* Consisting of Egypt, Iraq, Jordan, and North Yemen, the Arab Cooperation Council (ACC) was formed in Baghdad in February 1989. It brought together those Arab countries outside the Gulf Cooperation Council [*qv*] that had aided Iraq during its war with Iran from 1980–88 [*qv*]. However, the ACC decided on cooperation only in economic and nonmilitary fields. The fourth ACC summit in Amman [*qv*], in February 1990, decided to work toward ending Jewish emigration from the Soviet bloc to the occupied Palestinian and Arab territories. In April the ACC urged the comprehensive removal of all weapons of mass destruction in the Middle East. Iraq's invasion of Kuwait in August 1990 resulted in the disintegration of the ACC, with Egypt allying with the United States to forge an anti-Iraq alliance.

Arab Democratic Party (Israel): *Israeli political party* Formed in 1988 in Nazareth [*qv*], the Arab Democratic Party (ADP) aimed to unify Israeli Arabs [*qv*] behind a three-point program: recognition of the Palestinian people's right to self-determination, recognition of the Palestine Liberation Organization (PLO) [*qv*] as their sole representative, and the withdrawal of Israel from all the Occupied Arab Territories [*qv*]. It won one seat in the 1988 election and two in 1992. On the eve of the 1996 poll, it merged with another group to form the United Arab List, which secured four seats.

Arab Deterrent Force: *Arab League peacekeeping force in Lebanon, October 1976 to July 1982* The Arab League summit of

October 1976 ordered the deployment, for an initial period of six months, of a peace-keeping force—called the Arab Deterrent Force (ADF)—to maintain the cease-fire in the Lebanese Civil War [*qv*], which had broken out in April 1975. Its 30,000 troops were drawn from Syria (25,000), Saudi Arabia (2,000), Sudan (1,000), South Yemen (1,000), Libya (600), and the United Arab Emirates (500). It was to function under the Lebanese president. Libya soon withdrew its contingent. The ADF's mandate was renewed every six months.

The ADF became embroiled in skirmishes with Maronite [*qv*] irregulars. By the middle of 1979, with the departure of the Sudanese, Saudi, South Yemeni, and UAE troops, the ADF had become a purely Syrian force. In April 1980 it clashed with the leading Maronite militia near Zahle, which induced Israeli intervention. The ADF won.

In late June 1982, during the Israeli invasion of Lebanon [*qv*], the Arab League foreign ministers failed to extend the ADF's tenure, which was due to expire shortly. But the Lebanese government did not formally ask Syria, the only country providing ADF troops, to withdraw its troops, partly because it did not wish to put the Syrian forces on a par with Israel's by demanding their pullback. The ADF's mandate ended in July 1982. (Later the presence of the Syrian troops in Lebanon was formalized by the Lebanese authorities.)

Arab East: Arab East is the term applied to the Arabic-speaking Middle East [*qv*], excluding Arab North Africa (Algeria, Libya, Mauritania, Morocco, and Tunisia), Djibouti, Somalia and Sudan. It includes Bahrain, Egypt, Iraq, Jordan, Kuwait, Lebanon, the Occupied Arab Territories [*qv*], Oman, Qatar, Saudi Arabia, Syria, the United Arab Emirates, and Yemen.

Arab/Arabian Gulf: *see* The Gulf.

Arab Higher Committee (Palestine): The killing of Shaikh Izz al Din Qassam [*qv*], a popular Arab leader, by the British in an encounter in November 1935, and the discovery of an arms cache in a cement consignment for a Jewish builder in Jaffa, led the different Arab factions to form the Arab Higher Committee (AHC) in early 1936 under the leadership of Haajj Muhammed Amin al Husseini [*qv*]. The AHC rejected the British proposal for a legislative council, with fourteen Arabs and eight Jewish members, because of the overrepresentation of the Jewish minority. It called on its followers to stage a general strike on 1 April 1936. The strike, which developed into a general Arab rebellion, lasted until 12 October.

A month later a British royal commission, headed by Lord Peel, visited Palestine [*qv*]. In July 1937 the Peel Commission recommended partition. When the AHC rejected this, the British banned the committee in October. Its leader, al Husseini, fled to Lebanon. From there he continued to guide the AHC, which revived the Arab rebellion in 1938. The rebellion lasted until the spring of 1939.

Following the British White Paper of May 1939, which restricted Jewish immigration, the AHC was legalized. During the summer of 1946 the British tried to find common ground between the AHC and the Jewish Agency for Palestine [*qv*], but failed. The AHC, led by al Husseini, continued as representative of the Arab Palestinians during the subsequent events. In 1958 al Husseini proposed that the AHC should join the recently formed United Arab Republic [*qv*]. Egyptian President Gamal Abdul Nasser [*qv*] accepted this in principle, but postponed action until after Palestine had been liberated. With the formation of the Palestine Liberation Organization [*qv*] in 1964, the AHC became redundant.

Arab-Israeli War I (1948–49): *14 May 1948 to 7 January 1949* Often called the Palestine War, and (by Israelis) the War of Independence (Israel) [*qv*].

Background: In November 1947 the Arabs in Palestine [qv] rejected the United Nations partition plan, contained in General Assembly Resolution 181, which gave the Jews, owning 6 percent of the land, 53.5 percent of Palestine. At that time the Arab population was about 1,200,000, the Jewish about 650,000. In early 1948 the British advanced their date of departure to 15 May from 1 October, specified by the U.N. On 14 May the Yishuv [qv] National Council's thirteen-member People's Administration declared the establishment of Israel [qv]. Following an Arab League [qv] decision, Egypt, Iraq, Jordan, Lebanon, and Syria, along with Arab Palestinian fighters, resolved to attack Israel. The overall commander of the Arab forces was King Abdullah ibn Hussein [qv].

Opposing forces: The 26,000 Arab troops comprised 7,000 Egyptians; 4,000 Iraqis; 5,000 Jordanians; 2,000 Lebanese; 4,000 Palestinian irregulars; and 4,000 Syrians. Of these, only Jordan's Arab Legion, commanded by British General John Glubb [*qv*], was professionally led. The Lebanese and Syrian troops were former territorial militiamen. The Egyptian and Iraqi forces were badly led and were equipped with poor British-supplied arms. By the end of the first phase of the war in mid-June, the total number of Arab troops had increased to 35,000.

The Israeli force consisted of 30,000 fully mobilized Haganah [*qv*] soldiers (about two-thirds of whom were Second World War veterans), supported by 32,000 reserves, 15,000 armed Jewish settlement police, and 32,000 home guards. By the end of the first phase of the war in mid-June 1948, the Israeli combat force had doubled to 60,000.

Events: The armed conflict, which started on 14 May 1948, went through four phases: 14 May to 11 June, 9 to 18 July, 15 October to 6 November, and 21 November 1948 to 7 January 1949. The total combat period was four months.

14 May to 11 June: In the north, the Syrian and Lebanese forces, assisted by Palestinian irregulars, captured much of north-central Galilee. In the central sector, Jordan's Arab Legion occupied most of southern and eastern Jerusalem [*qv*], including the Old City, and held on to the Jerusalem-Tel Aviv [*qv*] road. In the southern sector, the Egyptian army, helped by the Palestinian irregulars, overran Gaza [*qv*] and then captured Ashdod. The other Egyptian column seized Beersheba and Hebron [*qv*], and linked up with the Arab Legion in Bethlehem [*qv*]. A U.N. cease-fire came into effect on 11 June.

9 to 18 July: In the northern sector, the Israelis spread out from Haifa [*qv*]. In the center they captured Lydda (Lod), Ramle, and the neighboring airport. The second

U.N. cease-fire went into force on 18 July and lasted until 15 October, except in the south. At the end of this truce, the Israeli forces were 90,000 strong.

15 October to 6 November: In the north, the Israelis captured the Hula valley and occupied a strip of southern Lebanon. In the central sector they broadened the Tel Aviv-Jerusalem axis. By capturing Beersheba in the south, they separated the Egyptian troops in Hebron and Faluja. The Egyptians evacuated Ashdod and Majdal to consolidate their positions in the Asluj-Gaza region. A U.N. truce went into effect on the southern front on 6 November. In the north and center, cease-fires took place on 30 November.

21 November 1948 to 7 January 1949: In the south, the Egyptians initially enlarged their area around Gaza and Asluj, but later their overall position deteriorated. The final truce between them and the Israelis came on 7 January 1949. On 1 December, 2,000 Arab Palestinian delegates in Jericho [*qv*] proclaimed Abdullah ibn Hussein "King of all Palestine," which meant most of what could be saved from the Israelis.

Human losses: Arab Palestinians: 16,000 dead, including those killed during January to mid-May 1948, 14,000 injured. Other Arabs: 2,500 dead. Jews: 6,000 dead.

Armistice agreements: Following negotiations between the warring parties on the Greek island of Rhodes, Israel concluded armistice agreements with Egypt on 24 February 1949, Lebanon on 23 March 1949, Jordan on 3 April 1949, and Syria on 20 July 1949. Iraq, which lacked common borders with Israel, signed no such agreement with the Jewish state.

These agreements divided up the territory allocated by the U.N. to the Arabs in Palestine (area 10,435 sq. miles/27,026 sq. km) among Egypt, Israel, and Jordan. Egypt retained control of the Gaza Strip [*qv*], measuring 146 sq. miles/378 sq. km, as an Egyptian-administered territory. Having acquired 2,220 sq. miles/5,750 sq km above the 5,600 sq. miles/14,500 sq. km allocated to it by the U.N. partition plan, Israel annexed them. Thus, the Jews, who formed nearly a third of the population of Palestine on the eve of the war, seized 75 percent of the country instead of the 54 percent allocated to them by the U.N. Having acquired 2,297 sq. miles/5,949 sq. km, King Abdullah annexed them, subject to final settlement. Jerusalem, earmarked for international administration by the U.N., was divided between Israel and Jordan, with Jordanian East Jerusalem measuring 2.5 sq. miles/6.5 sq. km. As for Lebanon and Syria, the international borders of Palestine became the armistice lines between them and Israel.

Arab-Israeli War II (1956): *see* Suez War (1956).

Arab-Israeli War III (1967): *5 to 10 June 1967* Often called the June 1967 War or the Six-Day War.

Background: Taking seriously Israel's threat to overthrow it, the nine-month-old radical Baathist regime in Syria signed a defense treaty with Egypt in November 1966. Early in April 1967 Israel attempted to cultivate disputed Arab land in the Syrian-Israeli demilitarized zone, thus triggering a confrontation. A month later Syria informed Egypt's president, Gamal Abdul Nasser [*qv*], of Israeli troop concentration along its border. Promising to aid Syria on 16 May,

Nasser dispatched Egyptian troops to eastern Sinai [*qv*]. Two days later he demanded the withdrawal of the United Nations Emergency Force (UNEF) [*qv*], which had been patrolling the truce lines since the end of the 1956 Suez War [*qv*] on the Egyptian side. UNEF withdrew immediately.

Having stationed Egyptian troops at the tip of the Tiran Straits [*qv*] in Sharm al Shaikh on 22 May, Nasser blockaded the straits, thus closing off the Israeli port of Eilat. This raised the temperature in the region. Reflecting the popular mood, King Hussein of Jordan [*qv*], hitherto hostile to Nasser, rushed to Cairo [*qv*] on 30 May to conclude a mutual defense pact and place his forces under Egyptian command. Israel had earlier told its superpower ally, the United States, that it would go to war if one or more of the following events occurred: the departure of UNEF; the blockading of the Tiran Straits; the signing of a Jordanian-Egyptian defense pact; and the dispatch of Iraqi forces to Jordan. By the end of May all but one of these eventualities had come to pass.

Opposing forces (Weapons): Combat aircraft: Israel 260, Egypt 434, Iraq 110, Jordan 28, Syria 90. Tanks: Israel 1,100; Egypt 1,200, Iraq 200, Jordan 287, Syria 750.

Events: Early in the morning of 5 June Israel mounted preemptive air and ground assaults. It attacked all seventeen Egyptian airfields and destroyed three-fifths of Egypt's warplanes, consisting of 365 fighters and 69 bombers. Egypt also lost 550 tanks in Sinai [*qv*]. Later in the day Israel struck at the Jordanian and Syrian air forces on the ground, destroying more than two-thirds of their combat aircraft. It rejected the United Nations Security Council's call for an immediate cease-fire on 6 June.

On the Egyptian front, Israel captured the Gaza Strip [*qv*] on 6 June, the day Egypt decided to withdraw its 80,000 soldiers and 1,000 tanks from the the Sinai Peninsula. Having occupied most of the peninsula by 8 June, Israel reached the Suez Canal [*qv*] the following day. On the Jordanian front, the Israelis had captured East Jerusalem [*qv*], Bethlehem [*qv*], Hebron [*qv*], Jenin, and Nablus [*qv*] by 7 June. The Israelis then accepted a U.N.-sponsored cease-fire on this front. The Syrian front witnessed artillery duels on the first four days. The Israelis violated the U.N.-sponsored truce on the fifth day (9 June) by launching an offensive to capture the Golan Heights [*qv*]. It had achieved this aim by the evening of the sixth day (10 June) when the final cease-fire came into effect. In the naval battle, the Israelis captured Sharm al Shaikh on 7 June, thus ending the blockade of the Straits of Tiran.

Human losses: Egyptians: 11,500 dead, the majority dying of thirst in the Sinai desert, 15,000 injured. Jordanians: (military) 2,000 dead, 5,000 injured; (civilians—of Palestinian origin) 4,000 dead, 1,000 injured. Syrians: 700 dead, 3,500 wounded. Israelis: 778 dead, 2,558 injured.

Weapon losses: Egypt: 264 aircraft, 700 tanks. Jordan: 22 aircraft, 125 tanks. Syria: 58 aircraft, 105 tanks. Israel: 40 aircraft, 100 tanks.

Arab-Israeli War IV (1973): *6 to 25 October 1973* Often called the October 1973 War, the Ramadan War (by Arabs), or the Yom Kippur War (by Israelis).

Background: Unlike previous armed conflicts, when Israel had taken the initiative, this time Egypt and Syria mounted pre-planned attacks on Israeli forces, but only those in the Occupied Arab Territories [qv] with the aim of regaining the Egyptian or Syrian land. They did so after having tired of peaceful attempts to recover their lands for more than six years. The Arab move, which came on the eve of the Yom Kippur [qv] holiday in Israel, took the Israelis completely by surprise.

Events: *6–8 October:* The Egyptian Second Army crossed the Suez Canal [qv] at Kantara and Ismailia in the central sector, and the Third Army did likewise at Port Suez in the south. On the Golan Heights [qv] front, the Syrians captured Mount Hermon and made gains at Khushniya.

8 October: The United States began an arms airlift using the planes of the Israeli airline, El Al.

9 October: Israeli military fully mobilized. The Soviet Union began to airlift arms to Egypt and Syria, the latter receiving two-thirds of the shipments.

10–12 October: Israel counterattacked on the Golan Heights front and advanced east of the armistice line north of Qunaitra to Saasa.

11 October: Egypt mounted an offensive to relieve the Syrians.

13 October: Washington began to use U.S. aircraft to ship weapons to Israel.

15 October: An Israeli offensive along the Suez succeeded in creating a wedge between the two Egyptian armies north of the Great Bitter Lake of the Suez and established a bridgehead near Deversoir on the western bank.

15–19 October: Repeated Arab attempts to regain Syrian territory on the Golan Heights were frustrated by the Israelis.

16 October: An Arab oil embargo [qv] was imposed on the military backers of Israel.

19 October: Having expanded the bridgehead, the Israelis pushed southward on the Egyptian soil in order to surround the Egyptian Third Army along the eastern bank.

21 October: Henry Kissinger, U.S. secretary of state, arrived in Moscow to negotiate a deal with Soviet leaders. By then the United States had airlifted 20,000 tons of weapons to Israel, plus 40 Phantom bombers, 48 A4 Skyhawk ground attack jets, and 12 C-130 transporters. (By the end of the airlift on 15 November, 33,500 tons of U.S. arms had been shipped to Israel, while Soviet arms shipments to Egypt and Syria amounted to 15,000 tons.)

22 October: Following Kissinger's successful talks in Moscow, a truce, specified by U.N. Security Council Resolution 338 [qv], went into effect at 1852 GMT. But soon after, Israel broke the cease-fire on the Golan front and regained Mount Herman.

23–24 October: Violating the truce on the Suez front, the Israelis rushed to Adabiya in the Gulf of Suez to encircle the Egyptian Third Army. But their attempts to seize Port Suez failed.

24 October: Moscow put on alert seven airborne divisions for airlifting to Egypt if the Israelis went ahead with their attempt to surround the Egyptian Third Army.

25 October: Washington put its military on "precautionary alert" because of Moscow's possible intervention in the war. U.N. Security Council Resolution 340, renewing its cease-fire call, went into effect, marking a formal end to the hostilities.

During the twenty-day conflict, as signatories to the Joint Defense and Economic Cooperation Treaty of the Arab League [*qv*], nine Arab states (Algeria, Iraq, Jordan, Kuwait, Libya, Morocco, Saudi Arabia, Sudan, and Tunisia) dispatched 50,000 troops and air units to Egypt and Syria, including 30,000 Iraqi troops sent to Syria. **Human losses** Egyptians: 9,000 dead, 15,000 injured. Syrians: 3,500 dead, 9,000 injured. Israelis: 2,552 dead, 6,027 injured. **Weapon losses** Egypt: 300 aircraft. Syria: 160 aircraft. Egypt and Syria combined: 1,800 tanks. Israel: 114 aircraft, 800-plus tanks.

Arab Jews: *Jews originating in Arab countries. See also* Oriental Jews and Sephardim.

Arab League: *a collective of independent Arab states* (Official title: League of Arab States). In early 1942, faced with the prospect of Germany conquering North Africa, including Egypt, Britain tried to sway popular Arab opinion toward the Allies by publicly favoring the idea of unity of the Arab world, extending from the Atlantic to the Persian Gulf [*qv*]. Having countered the German threat, soon after London acted behind the scenes to bring about a preliminary Arab conference in the Egyptian city of Alexandria [*qv*] in September–October 1944. It was attended by official representatives of Egypt, Iraq, Lebanon, North Yemen, Saudi Arabia, Syria, and Transjordan, as well as a Palestinian observer on behalf of Arab Palestinians. Their decision to form the League of Arab States—a cooperative of independent Arab countries—was ratified on 22 March 1945 in Cairo [*qv*] with the signing of an appropriate pact.

The first secretary-general of the Arab League, headquartered in Cairo, was Abdul Rahman Azzam, an Egyptian diplomat. With more and more Arabic-speaking countries becoming independent, membership of the League expanded to include Libya (1953), Sudan (1956), Morocco (1958), Tunisia (1958), Kuwait (1961), Algeria (1962), South Yemen (1967), Bahrain (1971), Oman (1971), Qatar (1971), the United Arab Emirates (1971), Mauritania (1973), Somalia (1974), the Palestine Liberation Organization (1974), and Djibouti (1977). With the union of North and South Yemen in May 1990, membership declined to twenty-one. Then, with the admission of Comros Island in 1996, the total rose to twenty-two.

In 1950 the Arab League members signed a Joint Defense and Economic Cooperation Treaty (JDECT) [*qv*], primarily to provide protection to member states against Israel. Four years later the Egyptian president, Gamal Abdul Nasser [*qv*], opposed Iraq's plan to join a Western-sponsored defense organization, arguing that such an arrangement by a JDECT member would link all JDECT affiliates to the West. Under the provisions of this treaty, in the October 1973 Arab-Israeli War [*qv*] nine Arab League members dispatched troops and air units to Egypt and Syria and engaged in hostilities with Israel. However, in May 1982, when Iraqi President Saddam Hussein [*qv*] tried to invoke the treaty to secure military aid from Arab League members, he failed. The reasons were: Iraq was not engaged in war with Israel, Iraq had started the armed conflict by invading Iran in September 1980, and such leading members of the Arab League as Syria and Libya had lined up with Iran.

Since 1948 the Arab League has been

enforcing an economic boycott of Israel from its office based in Damascus [qv]. Following its recognition by the United Nations in 1958 as a regional body, the Arab League has been acting inter alia as the U.N.'s Arab region educational, scientific, and cultural organization. It has been instrumental in creating an Arab postal union, an Arab union of wireless communication and telecommunication, a nationality code, and an Arab cultural treaty. It is the headquarters of seventeen Arab trade unions, including the union of iron and steel workers, and physicians and veterinarians. It now has eleven specialized ministerial councils and seventeen permanent technical committees.

Following Egypt's unilateral peace treaty with Israel in March 1979, an Arab League summit suspended Egypt's membership and the headquarters were moved to Tunis. Egypt was readmitted to the League in May 1989, and the headquarters were returned to Cairo in October 1990. Seven months later Esmat Abdul Maguid [qv], the erstwhile foreign minister of Egypt, was unanimously elected secretary-general of the Arab League. In 2001, Maguid was succeeded by Amir Moussa [qv].

In 2000, the total population of the Arab League States was 280 million.

Arab League Summits: Arab League members are normally represented by their foreign ministers at the meetings of the Arab League Council of Ministers, but from 1964 the member states started meeting at the head-of-state level.

First Summit: January 1964 in Cairo [qv]. It resolved to "struggle against the robbery of the waters of Jordan by Israel."

Second Summit: September 1964 in Alexandria [qv]. It welcomed the establishment of the Palestine Liberation Organization (PLO) [qv] to "liberate Palestine from Zionist imperialism."

Third Summit: September 1965 in Casablanca. It renounced "intra-Arab hostile propaganda."

Fourth Summit: 29 August–1 September 1967 in Khartoum. Held in the wake of the June 1967 Arab-Israeli War [qv], it reaffirmed Palestinians' rights in their own country and declared: "No negotiations with Israel, no treaty, no recognition of Israel."

Fifth Summit: December 1969 in Rabat. It called for the mobilization of all Arab states against Israel.

Sixth Summit: November 1973 in Algiers. Held in the wake of the October 1973 Arab-Israeli War [qv], it set down strict conditions for talks with Israel.

Seventh Summit: 30 October–2 November 1974 in Rabat. It declared the PLO to be "the sole and legitimate representative of the Palestinian people," with "the right to establish the independent state of Palestine on any liberated territory."

Eighth Summit: October 1976 in Cairo. It approved the formation of the Arab Deterrent Force [qv] for peacekeeping in the Lebanese Civil War [qv].

Ninth Summit: November 1978 in Baghdad [qv]. It condemned the Camp David Accords [qv] of September 1978 between Egypt and Israel and decided that pan-Arab sanctions against Egypt, including suspension of its League membership and severance of diplomatic relations, would go into effect when it signed a peace treaty with Israel.

Tenth Summit: November 1979 in Tunis. It deliberated over continued Israeli occupation of southern Lebanon following Israel's invasion of Lebanon in March 1978 [*qv*].

Eleventh Summit: November 1980 in Amman [*qv*]. It adopted a strategy for joint Arab economic action, dealing with pan-Arab development until 2000.

Twelfth Summit: November 1981 in Fez. After sharp disagreement over a peace plan drafted by Saudi Crown Prince Fahd [*qv*], which implied de facto recognition of Israel, the meeting was suspended after a few hours. So the September 1982 meeting in Fez became the Twelfth Summit. It adopted a peace plan similar to the one submitted by Fahd, now Saudi king. It demanded the withdrawal of Israel from the Arab territories occupied in 1967; the dismantling of Jewish settlements in these areas; Palestinian self-determination under the PLO, resulting in a Palestinian state in the West Bank [*qv*] and Gaza Strip [*qv*], with East Jerusalem [*qv*] as its capital; interim U.N. supervision of the West Bank and Gaza; and the guaranteeing of peace for all the states in the region by the U.N. Security Council.

Thirteenth Summit: August 1985 in Casablanca; boycotted by Algeria, Lebanon, Libya, South Yemen, and Syria. It failed to back the agreement between the PLO and Jordan envisaging talks with Israel on Palestinian rights.

Fourteenth Summit (extraordinary): November 1987 in Amman. It endorsed U.N. Security Council Resolution 598 of July 1987 [*qv*] on a cease-fire in the Iran-Iraq War [*qv*] and criticized Iran for prevaricating over its acceptance of the resolution. It also

declared that the resumption of diplomatic links with Egypt was an issue to be decided by individual members.

Fifteenth Summit: June 1988 in Casablanca. It decided to fund the PLO to continue the six-month-old Palestinian uprising in the Israeli-occupied territories.

Sixteenth Summit: May 1989 in Casablanca. It decided to readmit Egypt to the Arab League. It also set up a Tripartite Committee of the heads of state of Algeria, Morocco, and Saudi Arabia to secure a cease-fire in the Lebanese Civil War and restore constitutional government in Lebanon.

Seventeenth Summit: May 1990 in Baghdad. It condemned the recent large increase in the migration of Soviet Jews to Israel.

Eighteenth Summit: August 1990 in Cairo. Twelve members out of the twenty present condemned Iraq [*qv*] for its invasion and annexation of Kuwait [*qv*], and accepted the request of Saudi Arabia and other Gulf states to dispatch troops to assist their armed forces.

Nineteenth Summit: June 1995 in Cairo. Held after an unprecedented gap of nearly five years, this summit was also notable for the absence of an invitation to Iraq.

Twentieth Summit: October 2000 in Cairo. This emergency summit was convened to debate the Second Intifada [*qv*] of the Palestinians against Israeli occupation. Iraq was invited, thus signaling the end of the Arab League's boycott of Iraq due to its invasion of Kuwait. It called on its members to freeze their ties with Israel. It set up two funds to help the Palestinians struggling against the Israeli occupation.

Twenty-first Summit: March 2001 in

Amman. It was held in the aftermath of the election of hawkish Ariel Sharon [*qv*] as the Israeli prime minister. It decided to appoint Amr Mousa [*qv*] the League's new secretary-general.

Twenty-second Summit: March 2002 in Beirut. It adopted a peace plan of Saudi Crown Prince Abdullah [*qv*], offering Israel total peace with all the League members in exchange for its total withdrawal from all of the Occupied Arab Territories [*qv*]. It rejected exploitation of war on terrorism to threaten any Arab country and use of force against Iraq.

Twenty-third Summit: March 2003 in Sharam al Shaikh, Egypt. Describing an invasion of Iraq as a threat to Arab security, it declared that its members will not participate in any such war. This, however, allowed them room to let the United States use their military bases to invade Iraq.

Arab nationalism: Nationalism in the Arab world was defined in opposition to foreign rule, first by Ottoman Turkey and then by Britain and France. In the nineteenth century, Egyptians were in the forefront in rebelling against their Ottoman masters. The Ottoman sultan's recognition of Muhammad Ali as viceroy of Egypt in 1805 signified the special place the Ottomans were prepared to assign Egypt. In time Cairo [*qv*] became a haven for non-Egyptian Arab intellectuals who clashed with their Ottoman rulers. The relative freedom that Cairo afforded helped to engender Arab nationalism as well as pan-Islamism [*qv*].

With the supplanting of Ottoman power by that of Britain in the wake of the opening of the Suez Canal [*qv*] in 1869, Arab nation-alism grew in opposition to British influence. It reached a peak in 1882, when Col. Ahmad Arabi Pasha attempted militarily to end British interference in Egyptian affairs. He failed. The result was British occupation of Egypt, which provided a powerful foil to nationalists.

Elsewhere, especially in the Levant [*qv*], the educational institutions established by American and French missionaries in the 1860s provided fertile soil for the growth of Arab political revival, resulting in such secret associations as Al Ahd (The Covenant) and Al Fatat (The Young Woman). When the Ottoman regime suppressed these groups, their members fled to (post-1882) Egypt. But little of importance occurred until the First World War. During that conflict, anti-Ottoman feelings, harnessed by the British, escalated into the Arab Revolt of 1916, which was led by Hussein ibn Ali al Hashem of Hijaz. After the war the Arabs felt let down by the victorious Britain and France, which carved up the Arab world in their spheres of influence according to the secret Sykes Picot Pact [*qv*].

Arab nationalism in Egypt revolved around the Wafd [*qv*]. Elsewhere it centered around the Hashemite dynasty [*qv*], whose members ruled Iraq and Transjordan. But the close relationship between London and King Faisal II [*qv*]—illustrated by the latter's restoration by the British after they had crushed the successful nationalist coup in 1941—disappointed Arab nationalists. The behavior of another Hashemite, King Abdullah of Transjordan [*qv*], before and during the 1948–49 Palestine War [*qv*], further disappointed Arab nationalists.

By then the establishment of the Arab

League [qv] in 1945 had provided a regional perspective to Arab nationalism. Its base in Cairo set the scene for the merging of Egyptian nationalism with a larger Arab nationalism. This happened after the over-throw of the decadent monarchy in Egypt in 1952 by nationalist, republican officers led by Gamal Abdul Nasser [qv].

As the decade progressed, and especially after 1956, when Egypt finally secured the withdrawal of British troops from its soil after seventy-four years, Nasser came to symbolize Arab nationalism in its widest sense. But Nasserism [qv], which was associated more with the leader than an ideology, faced com-petition from Baathism [qv], which had emerged as a well-defined ideology in Syria. In 1990 Arab nationalism received a severe blow when Iraq, a proponent of Baathism, invaded and annexed Kuwait—the first instance since the founding of the Arab League of a member state acting so aggres-sively toward another.

Arab Nationalist Movement: *pan-Arab political party* The Arab Nationalist Move-ment (ANM) came into being in 1952 as a result of the merger of two groups, com-posed chiefly of the students and staff of the American University in Beirut [qv]. George Habash [qv], Nayif Hawatmeh [qv], and Ahmad Khatib [qv] were among the founders of the ANM, whose main slogan was: "Unity [of Arabs], Liberation [of Pales-tine], Revenge [against the Zionist state]." While they increasingly saw the need to rev-olutionize the Arab world in order to con-front the modern Jewish state, they placed much hope in the Egyptian military coup of 1952, especially as a vehicle to effect Arab unity. The ANM applauded the formation

of the United Arab Republic [qv] in 1958 and was disappointed when it broke up three years later. The subsequent failure of any of the three leading republics—Egypt, Syria, and Iraq—to unify left the ANM dis-appointed with both Nasserites [qv] and Baathists [qv].

Since the liberation of Palestine was its top priority, in the mid-1960s the ANM set up a Palestinian section with its own armed wing and began guerrilla actions against Israel.

In the rest of the Arab world, it did well in those regions where Nasserism and Baathism were comparatively weak, the main example being the Arabian Peninsula [qv]. It was the ANM's South Yemeni branch that first issued a call for armed action, in 1959, to frustrate the British plan to set up a Fed-eration of South Arabia, composed of the Aden Colony, the Eastern Protectorate States, and the Western Protectorate States. Four years later the ANM played an impor-tant role in welding together the various nationalist groups active in South Yemen when they held a congress in the North Yemeni capital of Sanaa [qv] and fostered the emergence of the National Front for the Lib-eration of South Yemen [qv], which decided to achieve independence through an armed struggle. It succeeded in 1967.

In adjoining Oman, in early 1962 the ANM's Dhofari supporters cooperated with the members of the leftist Dhofari Liberation Front (DFL) to secure an independent Dhofar. The outbreak of an insurrection in South Yemen in 1963 encouraged the ANM's Dhofari section to merge with the leftist DFL and start a guerrilla campaign in Dhofar, which continued for a decade.

The Arab defeat in the June 1967 Arab-

Israeli War [*qv*] finally destroyed the ANM's confidence in the Egyptian and Syrian regimes, and led to the pan-Arab body being divided into individual sections in different countries.

Arab Nationalist Movement (Kuwait): *see* National Cultural Club (Kuwait).

Arab Nationalist Movement (North Yemen): In the early 1960s, in North Yemen the Arab Nationalist Movement (ANM) backed Gamal Abdul Nasser [*qv*]. But later, following the reconciliation between Nasser and the Saudi monarch in the wake of the June 1967 Arab-Israeli War [*qv*], when the local Nasserites tried to reach a compromise with the royalists, the ANM opposed the move. During the siege of Sanaa [*qv*] by royal tribalists in January 1968, it armed the city's workers, traders, and civil servants to defend the capital. The monarchists lifted the siege in February. But once the royalist threat was over, the centrists within the republican camp consolidated their authority and attacked the leftists, including the ANM, purging ANM elements from the army and driving party cadres underground.

Arab Nationalist Movement (Palestine): In December 1967 the Palestinian section of the Arab Nationalist Movement, along with its armed affiliates, combined with the Syria-based Palestine Liberation Front to form the Popular Front for the Liberation of Palestine [*qv*].

Arab Nationalist Movement (Saudi Arabia): Starting as a clandestine group in Dhahran in 1964, the Arab Nationalist Movement graduated into something bigger in early 1966. During the next three years, the party built up a base among military officers, oil workers, civil servants, and teachers. Its planned coup in June 1969 was foiled only hours before its scheduled implementation. The subsequent arrest of 200 conspirators, followed by scores of executions, destroyed the party.

Arab socialism: Originating as "Egyptian socialism," the term was transformed to "Arab socialism" when Egypt and Syria merged in 1958 to form the United Arab Republic (UAR) [*qv*]. Its leading proponent was Egyptian President Gamal Abdul Nasser [*qv*]. He first imbibed the virtues of socialism through his friendship with Josip Tito of Yugoslavia and Jawaharlal Nehru of India, whom he first met at the nonaligned nations conference in Bandung, Indonesia, in April 1955. The 1956 Egyptian constitution provided for a National Union that, though composed of all political tendencies, stood for abolition of feudalism and exploitation and for the reorientation of private property for the higher interests of society. It stipulated that workers must be taken into management.

Following the breakup of the UAR in September 1961, Nasser accelerated his campaign against the urban rich in Egypt. A series of decrees introduced progressive income tax and the nationalization of insurance, banking, and major industrial and commercial companies. During the winter of 1961–62, Nasser drafted a 30,000-word Charter of National Action. After debating the document in Cairo in May 1962, the National Congress of the Popular Forces—consisting of trade unions, professional syndicates, and other voluntary groups—adopted it. The charter combined its belief in "scientific socialism" and the "struggle against exploitation and in favor of equal opportunities" with the aim of achieving the unity of "all the working forces of the people," including national capitalists. It argued that political and social democracy were indivisible, and that to assure freedom of choice in politics, a citizen must be freed of exploitation of all kinds and given equal opportunity to enjoy a fair share of the national wealth. The body that was to implement the changes was to be called the Arab Socialist Union [qv], composed of an alliance of five segments of the workforce: peasants, workers, intellectuals, soldiers, and national capitalists.

Declaring that his regime had ended the exploitation that had existed in the monarchical era, Nasser stressed that relations between different socioeconomic classes must now be peaceful. This differentiated Arab socialism from Marxist socialism, with its belief in perpetual conflict in a society with classes. Also, objecting to attaching an ethnic or a nationality label to socialism, the Marxists in Egypt preferred to express their belief in an Egyptian path to socialism.

Arab Socialist Party (Syria): The Arab Socialist Party (ASP) was founded by Akram Hourani, a lawyer from Hama [qv], in January 1950. By participating in the anti-French armed struggle after the Second World War, he had gained popularity with the officer corps of independent Syria. Following his advice, the government decided to disregard the social background of the applicants to the country's only armed forces academy in Homs [qv]. Since a military career was the only way a son of a poor or middle-income peasant could raise his social status, the academy attracted many applicants from this social class. Given the party's

commitment to ending feudalism and distributing state land to the landless, and its leadership of peasant agitation, it soon enjoyed a considerable following among young cadets and officers. Sharing their opposition to the dictatorial regime of Col. Adib Shishkali [qv], the leaders of the ASP and the Baath party [qv] decided in September 1953 to form the Arab Baath Socialist Party [qv], and did so six months later.

Arab Socialist Party of Egypt: Following the decision of President Anwar Sadat [qv] to introduce a multiparty system in Egypt, a joint commission of the ruling Arab Socialist Union (ASU) [qv] and parliament decided in May 1976 to license three forums: right, left and center. The center forum was represented by the Arab Socialist Party of Egypt (ASPE), led by the then prime minister, Mamdouh Salim. In the parliamentary poll that followed in October–November, the ASPE won 280 of the 342 elected seats. Sadat then announced that the forums could evolve into fully fledged parties. Soon after, he dissolved the mass organizations affiliated to the ASU and transferred all its district and provincial offices and officials to the ASPE. This was formalized by the Law of the System of Political Parties passed in June 1977.

However, when Sadat's peace overtures to Israel, signaled by his visit to Jerusalem [qv] in November, met with opposition, he devised means of supplanting the ASPE with a party of his own and went on to outlaw opposition forces after winning 98.3 percent of the votes in a referendum on "correcting" Egyptian democracy in May 1978. Three months later, after threatening to birch anybody who tried to disrupt his course of action, he announced the formation of the National Democratic Party (NDP) [qv] under his supervision. With 275 ASPE parliamentarians rushing to join the NDP even before it had announced its program, the ASPE collapsed.

Arab Socialist Union (Egypt): In May 1962 a National Congress of the Popular Forces, attended by trade unions, professional syndicates, and other voluntary groups, adopted the Charter of National Action. Besides explaining Arab socialism [qv] it specified the political structure upon which it was to be built. The body that was to implement the National Charter was to be called the Arab Socialist Union (ASU). It was perceived as an alliance of five segments of the workforce: peasants, workers, intellectuals, soldiers, and national capitalists. The ASU was established in November 1962. It has a pyramidal structure, with units of twenty at village, workplace, or neighborhood level forming the base, the executive committee led by the republic's president at the apex, and district and provincial committees in between. The ASU's legislative branch was called the National Assembly. In it, as in all other elected bodies of the ASU, 50 percent of the seats were given to workers and peasants (meaning those owning less than 26 acres/10.6 hectares).

In practice, the original intent of ensuring greater participation in the government by the masses was not realized, and the ASU's exceptionally broad base and lack of cohesion inhibited it from becoming an active political agency to effect a socialist transformation of society. Within the ASU, elections were held only for the provincial committees.

Therefore, instead of emerging as a popular body to guide the state's executive arm, the ASU became subordinate to the state, assisting civil and military bureaucracies to implement official policies decided by President Gamal Abdul Nasser [qv], his advisers, and the cabinet (many of whose members sat on the ASU's executive committee). Many Egyptians found that the best way to secure the cooperation of the increasingly powerful civil servants was by achieving an important position in the ASU, whose membership soared to six million in four years. As a result, a mutually supportive triad of rich farmers, state bureaucrats, and urban professionals grew up and monopolized power.

Following the creation of the ASU's central committee in July 1965, Nasser appointed Ali Sabri [qv], the leftish prime minister, as the ASU's secretary-general with a mandate to transform the organization into a cadre-based party. Soon the ASU's district and provincial committees were manned by salaried functionaries drawn from civil servants, business managers, teachers, lawyers, landowners, and factory floor managers, and trained at one of the three institutes of socialist studies. Sabri established the Socialist Youth Organization (SYO) as an auxiliary to the ASU, but with its own cadre, and soon built up its strength to 20,000. But after Egypt's defeat in the June 1967 Arab-Israeli War [qv], Nasser moderated his socialist leanings. He decided to reestablish the consensus that had existed before the creation of the ASU and SYO cadres. In October he dissolved the SYO, and in June 1968 he changed the ASU's structure back to the one prevalent in the pre-Sabri days.

After Nasser's death in September 1970

there was a revival of the debate on the ASU's role. President Anwar Sadat [*qv*] made it subservient to the state executive. After the October 1973 Arab-Israeli War [*qv*], parliament made ASU membership voluntary for participants in a political or trade union election. After debating whether the ASU should be divided into five parts, each one representing a different social class within the "working forces," an official commission recommended the formation of three forums within the ASU. Following the parliamentary poll of October-November 1976, the ASU lost its political role, but it remained the sole owner of all major newspaper publishing companies and retained its authority to issue a license for a new publication. In August 1978 Sadat's invitation to Mustafa Khalil, the ASU secretary-general, to head his newly announced party, the NDP, formally ended the ASU.

Arab West: The Arab West includes all the countries of Arab North Africa: Algeria, Libya, Mauritania, Morocco, and Tunisia. It is separated from the Arab East [*qv*] by the Libyan Desert.

Arabia: *see* Arabian Peninsula.

Arabian Peninsula: Area: about 1.12 million sq. miles/2.91 million sq. km; pop. 56.4 million (2002, est.). Peninsula, southwest Asia, between the Red Sea and the Gulf of Aqaba to the west, the Persian/Arabian Gulf [*qv*] and the Gulf of Oman to the east, and the Arabian Sea and the Gulf of Aden to the south. It is divided into Bahrain [*qv*], Kuwait [*qv*], Oman [*qv*], Qatar [*qv*], Saudi Arabia [*qv*], the United Arab Emirates [*qv*], and Yemen [*qv*]. Surrounded on three sides by mountains, the treeless penin-

sular plateau slopes eastwards toward the Persian Gulf, the region that is rich in petroleum [*qv*].

Most of the inhabitants of the region are to be found on the coastal plains, and they have maintained contact with the rest of Asia, stretching as far as the Philippines, and with the eastern coast of Africa. The history of these inhabitants goes back to antiquity, when Arabia was divided between the realms of Sheba and Maain. Besides those settled on the coast or in the interior oases, there are nomads and others, who transport goods between the Indian subcontinent and the Mediterranean.

They were all affected by the rise of Islam [*qv*] in the second and third decades of the seventh century. United by this new monotheistic faith, the Arabian tribes soon conquered adjoining territories. But after the Caliphate was moved in A.D. 661 from Medina [*qv*], the burial place of the Prophet Muhammad, the founder of Islam, to Damascus [*qv*], Arabia lost its primacy in the Islamic Empire. Later, in 1517, it became part of the Ottoman Empire and remained so for four centuries. In the mid-eighteenth century its central Najd region [*qv*] came under the influence of Wahhabism [*qv*]. One of its followers, Abdul Aziz ibn Abdul Rahman al Saud [*qv*], built up his kingdom, Saudi Arabia, following the collapse of the Ottoman Empire in the First World War.

Arabic language: Arabic belongs to the Semitic language family [*qv*], its sisters being Hebrew [*qv*] and Aramaic, and is written from right to left. It has been a written language at least since the early fourth century A.D. It has a two-part word structure: the root, consisting mostly of three consonants and providing the basic meaning; and the pattern, consisting of vowels, giving grammatical meaning to the word. Prefixes and suffixes serve the functions of the definite article, pronouns, and prepositions. For example, jihad [*qv*] and *mujahid* (one who conducts jihad) have the common root *jhd.* As the language of the Quran [*qv*], Arabic is the religious language of Muslims [*qv*], but it is also the language of Arabs [*qv*], no matter what their religious affiliation. The language as written in the Quran is known as Classical Arabic and links all the countries of the Arab world, from the Persian Gulf to the Atlantic. But the spoken language varies from region to region, and there are five major groups of dialects: those found in Iraq, the Arabian Peninsula, Syria, Egypt, and North Africa.

Arabism: *see* pan-Arabism.

Arabs: Arabs, who claim descent from Ismail/Ishmael, Prophet Abraham's son by Hagar, appear frequently in the Bible [*qv*] as Ishmaelites. In the Old Testament [*qv*] the Second Book of Chronicles (17:11) alludes to "some Arabs" bringing 7,700 sheep and 7,700 goats as a present to King Jehosophat of Judah (r. ca. 870 B.C. to ca. 851 B.C.), the term describing nomadic people from the eastern bank of the Jordan River [*qv*]. An inscription of King Shalmaneser III of Assyria in the eighth century B.C. refers to "Gindibu the Aribi" as a member of the group of rebelling notables whom he had defeated. Later inscriptions in Assyria and Babylon are full of allusions to *Aribi* or *Arab*, a term used for nomads inhabiting the northern and central Arabian Peninsula [*qv*]. During the rise of the Greek and Roman civilizations, the term came to include the inhabitants of the whole peninsula.

The word *Arab* is a derivative either of a Semitic root linked to nomadism, or of "abhar," meaning to pass or move. Nomadic Arabs worshipped nature—rocks, water springs, trees—or idols, and this continued until the arrival of Islam [*qv*] in the mid-seventh century. The Arabs settled in the oases came under the influence of such pre-Islamic religions as Judaism [*qv*] and Zoroastrianism [*qv*]. Later Islam took hold in the world of Arabs, who became its leading proselytizers. In modern times an Arab means someone who speaks Arabic [*qv*]. In 2003 there were an estimated 291 million Arabs living in twenty-two member states of the Arab League [*qv*].

Arafat, Yasser (1929–): *Palestinian politician; chairman of Palestine Liberation Organization, 1969– ; president of Palestinian Authority, 1994–* Born Mahmud Abdul Rahman Abdul Rauf Arafat al Qudwa, nicknamed Yasser (lit. carefree), to a merchant father who was originally from Khan Yunis in the Gaza Strip [*qv*] but later ran a shop in Jerusalem [*qv*]. Arafat was born in Cairo [*qv*] during his father's temporary residence there. Both he and his parents were in the Gaza Strip at the time of the 1948–49 Palestine War [*qv*]. Arafat graduated as a civil engineer in 1955 from Cairo University, where he was chairman of the local Palestinian Students Union. The union was based in the Gaza Strip, then under Egyptian control. During the Suez War [*qv*] (October–November 1956) Arafat was an engineer with the Egyptian army. He then took up a civil engineering job in Kuwait.

Along with Salah Khalaf [*qv*] and Khalil

Wazir [*qv*], fellow Palestinians from Gaza, Arafat formed a clandestine group called Fatah [*qv*] in 1958. Five years later it was allowed to open an office in Algiers, capital of the revolutionary state of Algeria, to train commandos. This was in line with the Fatah strategy of employing popular revolutionary violence to liberate the Palestinian homeland. In 1964 in Baathist-run Damascus [*qv*], guided by its chairman, Arafat, Fatah decided to launch guerrilla actions against Israel [*qv*] from Syria [*qv*]. The first operation was mounted on 1 January 1965. After the June 1967 Arab-Israeli War [*qv*] Arafat met Egyptian President Gamal Abdul Nasser [*qv*], who pledged support but no funds.

In March 1968 Fatah commandos engaged Israelis in a battle in the Jordanian border town of Karameh, which increased the popularity of Fatah and Arafat, known as Abu Ammar. Four months later Fatah ended its boycott of the Palestine National Council (PNC) [*qv*] of the Palestine Liberation Organization [*qv*]. Fatah delegates attended the fifth session of the PNC in Cairo in July 1968. With an estimated guerrilla force of 15,000, Fatah emerged as the PLO's largest constituent. The PNC elected Arafat chairman of the PLO's executive committee at its sixth session in early 1969.

Arafat, who had emerged as an arbiter between the leftist and rightist factions within Fatah, now extended his mediation skills to hold together a motley assortment of Palestinian groups—some Marxist-Leninist, some pan-Arabist, some funded by leading Arab states, and all possessing militias. He stuck to two basic positions: no single Arab regime should be allowed to co-opt the PLO; and all sociopolitical ideologies committed

to the liberation of Palestine [*qv*] must be accommodated. After the expulsion of the PLO from Amman [*qv*] in the wake of Palestinian battles with Jordanian forces in 1970–71, the PLO headquarters moved to Beirut [*qv*]. Here the PLO, under Arafat's leadership and financed by private and governmental contributions, channeled through the Palestine National Fund [*qv*], began to set up "a state within a state."

Following the Arab summit's decision in late October 1974 to recognize the PLO as the sole, legitimate representative of the Palestinian people, Arafat's status rose. The next month he addressed the General Assembly of the United Nations (where the PLO had been accorded observer status) in the course of its debate on the Palestinian issue.

By now the PNC had adopted the idea of establishing a homeland on the West Bank [*qv*] and the Gaza Strip [*qv*] as a step toward the final goal of liberating all of Palestine. Pro-Soviet groups affiliated to the PLO played an important role in getting this line adopted by the PNC. Ever since Arafat's visit to Moscow in July 1968, as part of an Egyptian delegation led by Nasser, the Soviet Union had taken a keen interest in Arafat and the PLO and backed its guerrilla activities as a lawful expression of the Palestinian people's right to self-defense in the face of continued military occupation. In the Lebanese Civil War [*qv*], which erupted in April 1975, Arafat and other Palestinian leaders sided with the leftist Lebanese National Movement [*qv*] to fight the right-wing Lebanese Forces [*qv*]. Arafat's vehement opposition to Egypt's U.S.-inspired effort to reach unilateral peace with Israel in 1977–78 turned Arafat politically leftward.

At Fatah's fourth congress in May 1980 it was decided to intensify the armed struggle against the Jewish state. As a result, following the Israeli invasion of Lebanon in June 1982, which culminated in the siege of Beirut, Israel reciprocated by compelling Arafat to remove the PLO headquarters and troops from that city in August 1982. He moved the PLO administrative staff to Tunis and dispersed the Palestinian fighters to several Arab states.

Following a series of meetings with King Hussein of Jordan [qv], in February 1985 Arafat agreed to joint Palestinian-Jordanian moves toward a peace settlement with Israel and the formation of a Palestine-Jordan confederation after the founding of an independent Palestine. But Arafat failed to win the backing of the majority of PLO constituents. In April 1987 his agreement with King Hussein was annulled, and the unity of the PLO was restored. Arafat's flirtation with King Hussein and Egypt's President Hosni Mubarak [qv] soured his relations with President Hafiz Assad [qv] of Syria, who wanted the PLO to coordinate its policies with him.

In November 1988 the PNC, meeting in Algiers, proclaimed the State of Palestine, with Arafat as its president, a status that was formally recognized by 91 of the 110 states that had accorded recognition to the PLO. Arafat's disavowal of terrorism against Israel and his declaration that the State of Palestine, consisting of the Gaza Strip, the West Bank, and East Jerusalem [qv], would coexist peacefully with Israel were endorsed by the PNC. The following month, addressing a special session of the U.N. General Assembly in Geneva, he repeated his earlier declarations. This led to open contact between the PLO and the United States, albeit at a low level. But when Arafat failed to condemn an unsuccessful Palestinian raid on an Israeli military target (which according to a PNC statement was still a legitimate activity), the United States suspended its talks with the PLO in June 1990.

This, and the rapidly increasing migration of Soviet Jews into Israel, led Arafat to ally himself with the radical leader of Iraq, President Saddam Hussein [qv]. He sided with the Iraqi leader during the crisis that followed Iraq's invasion and occupation of Kuwait in August 1990. This alienated him from the rulers of the rich Gulf states and resulted in the stoppage of their subventions to the PLO. It also distanced him from the presidents of Egypt and Syria, who joined the anti-Iraq alliance to counter the Iraqi aggression. Following Iraq's defeat in February 1991 Arafat tried to regain his lost popularity, an uphill task. Deprived of the advice and friendship of his long-time comrades Khalil Wazir (assassinated in April 1988) and Salah Khalaf (assassinated in January 1991), Arafat felt increasingly isolated.

During the preliminary talks leading up to a Middle East peace conference under the joint auspices of the United States and the Soviet Union in October 1991, Arafat agreed to Israel's demand that the Jordanian delegation should consist of an equal number of Jordanians and Palestinians acceptable to Israel. When the bilateral negotiations that followed proved sterile, Arafat set up a clandestine channel to conduct secret talks with Israel in Norway through his well-trusted aides. The resulting accord was signed in the presence of Arafat and Israeli Prime Minister Yitzhak Rabin [qv] by Mahmud Abbas [qv] and Shimon Peres [*qv*] in Washington on 13 September 1993, which became known as Oslo Accord I [*qv*]. It required Israel to vacate the Gaza Strip and the West Bank town of Jericho as a first step toward granting Palestinian autonomy in the Occupied Territories [*qv*]. In July 1994 Arafat moved to Gaza to administer the Gaza Strip and Jericho as president of the Palestinian Authority [*qv*]. He shared the 1994 Nobel Prize for Peace with Rabin and Peres. In September 1995 Arafat signed an autonomy agreement on the West Bank with Israel, which became known as Oslo Accord II [*qv*]. It divided the West Bank into A/B/C zones: A (three percent of the territory, covering seven major cities, including Hebron), full PA civil control with external security under Israel; B, joint control (24 percent of the territory, covering 465 villages), where Israel had the power to intervene at its own discretion to maintain overall security; and the rest as C (73 percent of the territory), under full Israeli control. But with the assassination of Rabin two months later, followed by the defeat of Peres by hardliner Benjamin Netanyahu [*qv*] in the prime ministerial contest in May 1996, the Oslo Accords began to unravel, especially after Netanyahu refused initially to meet Arafat. The reluctant signing of the Wye River Memorandum [*qv*] in October 1998, with Israel agreeing to hand over one percent of the West Bank to the A area and another 12 percent to the B area (maintaining full control over 60 percent of the West Bank) did little to reverse the trend. The situation improved with the election of Ehud Barak [*qv*] as Israel's prime minister in May 1999. But Arafat's summit meeting with Barak, chaired by U.S. President Bill Clinton at the presidential retreat of Camp David in July 2000 to reach the final settlement between Israel and the Palestinians, failed primarily over the issue of the status of the Noble Sanctuary [*qv*] in Jerusalem's Old City, with Barak insisting on Israeli sovereignty over the third holiest shrine of Islam [*qv*]. Barak's defeat by the hawkish Ariel Sharon [*qv*] in February 2001 against the background of the Second Intifada [*qv*] of the Palestinians opened a grim chapter for Arafat, who would come to be shunned by newly elected U.S. President George Walker Bush. As violence between the two sides escalated, Sharon systematically destroyed the Palestinian Authority's administrative and economic infrastructure—an enterprise that got a further boost when in June 2002 President Bush publicly called on the Palestinians to change their leadership. His subsequent statement that he envisioned an independent State of Palestine exisiting side by side with Israel in mutual security did little to raise the status of Arafat.

Arbil: *see* Irbil.

Arif, Abdul Rahman (1916–): *Iraqi military leader; president, 1966–68* Born into a middle-class family in Baghdad, Arif enrolled at the local military academy and became an officer. A nationalist and opposed to the pro-Western stance of the monarchical regime, he joined the Free Officers group that overthrew the royalist regime in July 1958.

When his younger brother, Abdul Salam Arif [*qv*], clashed with Abdul Karim Qasim [*qv*], who headed the republican regime, Arif's career came under a shadow. Abdul Salam's fall ended Arif's future prospects in the military. However, the catapulting to power of Abdul Salam Arif in the wake of the Baathist coup and assassination of Qasim resulted in Arif's appointment as acting chief of staff. Following the accidental death of Abdul Salam Arif in April 1966, Arif emerged as the presidential choice of the ruling Revolutionary Command Council. By continuing the overall policies of his dead sibling, Arif provided continuity. Although friendly with Egypt under its radical president, Abdul Gamal Nasser [qv], he preserved Iraq's independent stance. He continued his brother's autocratic style of government, but lacked his charisma and astuteness. Though he kept Iraq out of direct confrontation with Israel during the June 1967 Arab-Israeli War [qv], the negative effect of the Arab debacle rubbed off on his government. The opposition felt emboldened to demonstrate in the streets, demanding free elections. This paved the way for disaffected Baathist [qv] officers, led by Ahmad Hassan Bakr [qv] and the military intelligence chief, Abdul Rahman Nayif, to overthrow Arif in July 1969, forcing him into exile in Turkey. After many years in Turkey, he was allowed to return home.

Arif, Abdul Salam (1920–66): *Iraqi military and political leader; president, 1963–66* Born into a middle-class family in Baghdad, Arif enrolled at the military academy and became an officer. His experience in the Palestine War (1948–49) [qv], in which the Iraqi troops performed poorly, turned him against the pro-Western regime of King Faisal II [qv]. He played a leading role in organizing the Free Officers group that ended the monarchy in July 1958. During the coup he led the force that seized the capital.

In the subsequent republican regime he emerged as second only to Abdul Karim

Qasim [qv], serving as deputy chief of staff, deputy premier, and interior minister. However, he soon clashed with Qasim, who disagreed with his plan to lead Iraq into a union with the United Arab Republic [qv], consisting of Egypt and Syria. He lost all his jobs in September and soon found himself behind bars. Accused of conspiracy to kill Qasim and mount a coup, he was found guilty and sentenced to death. But his sentence was commuted by Qasim, who ordered his release in 1961. This time his conspiring, conducted in alliance with Baathist [qv] officers, culminated in the termination of the Qasim regime in February 1963. He became president, but without much power. However, finding the Baathists at odds with one another, he got rid of them and assumed full authority in November.

An admirer of Egypt's President Gamal Abdul Nasser [qv], Arif emulated his policy of enlarging the public sector by pursuing a policy of progressive nationalization. Arif embarked on a plan to unite Iraq and Egypt, starting with economic and military coordination and a joint presidential council. He tackled the long-running Kurdish [qv] problem and was on the verge of signing an accord with Kurdish insurgents when he was killed in an air crash in April 1966.

Arlosoroff, Chaim (1899–1933): *Israeli politician* Born in Romny, Ukraine, Arlosoroff moved with his family to Germany in 1905. He obtained a doctorate in economics at Berlin University. At the age of nineteen he joined HaPoale HaTzair [qv] and two years later became editor of the party's newspaper. At twenty-four he became a member of the executive of the World Zionist Organization [qv]. In 1924 Arlosoroff emigrated to Palestine [*qv*] and within two years became secretary of HaPoale HaTzair. Following the merger of HaPoel HaTzair and Ahdut HaAvodah [*qv*] to form Mapai [*qv*], Arlosoroff emerged as one of its main spokesmen. At the 1931 congress of the World Zionist Organization, he won a seat on the Jewish Agency [*qv*] executive committee and became head of its political department, dealing with international affairs. He maintained good relations with the British mandate and sought accommodation with the Arabs in Palestine.

Following Adolf Hitler's ascent to power in Germany in January 1933, Arlosoroff helped German Jews to emigrate to Palestine by striking a deal with the German government, that allowed Jews to depart with most of their property. This was denounced strongly by the right-wing Zionist Revisionists [*qv*] and their extremist faction in Palestine, Brit Habriyonim. In June 1933 Arlosoroff was killed during a stroll along the Tel Aviv [*qv*] seashore. Three suspects, all members of Brit Habriyonim, were arrested and tried by a British mandate court. Two were released for lack of evidence, but the third, Abraham Stavsky, was given a death sentence. He appealed and was acquitted due to insufficient evidence. Arlosoroff's murder split the Yishuv [*qv*] into two hostile camps, with leftist Zionists blaming the Revisionists and the latter blaming the Arabs for the killing. The controversy simmered on. In 1982 the Likud-led [*qv*] government of Israel instituted an inquiry. The report of the commission, published in June 1985, was inconclusive.

Armenian: *an ancient Indo-European people, originating from the Lake Van region in eastern Turkey* Armenians claim to be the descendants of Haik, a descendant of Noah, and call themselves Hayq (pl. of Hay). In the sixth century B.C. they became part of the Persian Empire and were called Armina. Later, in 189 B.C., the Armenians established an independent kingdom, which fell to the Romans in 69 B.C. Around A.D. 300 they became the first nation to adopt Christianity [*qv*], thanks to the efforts of St. Gregory the Illuminator, and since then religion has played an important role in their lives.

After a period full of vicissitudes, at times enjoying independent kingdoms, they became subjects of the Ottoman Empire in the sixteenth century. As a result of a continual struggle between the Tsarist, Persian, and Ottoman Empires, the Armenian-majority areas fell under different rulers. Between 1894 and 1915, Armenians suffered persecution and massacre under the Ottomans. In the course of the First World War, the Ottoman Turks, who considered the Armenians to be pro-Russian "fifth-columnists," decided to expel some 1.75 million of them from Turkey into Greater Syria [*qv*] and Palestine [*qv*]. Roughly a third managed to escape expulsion. Of the rest, an estimated 50 percent perished because of starvation or Turkish violence en route. Most of those who survived settled in North America, Western Europe, or the Transcaucasian region of the former Soviet Union, which included the Armenian Soviet Socialist Republic.

In the Middle East today, substantial Armenian communities exist in Lebanon and Iran. They belong to either the Armenian Orthodox Church [*qv*] or the Armenian Catholic Church [*qv*].

Armenian Catholic Church: *part of the Roman Catholic Church* [qv], *but performing an Eastern rite* The Armenian Catholic Church was established in 1742 by Abraham Artzivian, the Armenian Catholic Bishop of Aleppo [qv], after he was elected patriarch of Sis, the capital of Cilicia (now in Turkey). Its liturgical language is Classical Armenian. Following the Ottoman persecution of Armenians during the First World War, the Church was reorganized. In 1932 the head of the Church, called the Patriarch of the Catholic Armenians and Katholikos of Cilicia, moved the Church's headquarters to Beirut [qv]. In 1991 there were about 12,000 adherents in the Beirut diocese.

Armenian language: *a member of the western branch of the Indo-European languages* Though Armenian had become the dominant language in the Lake Van region of eastern Turkey by the seventh century B.C., it did not acquire an alphabet until the fourth century A.D.

Armenian Orthodox Church: Also called the Armenian Apostolic Church or the Armenian Apostolic (Orthodox) Church. The Armenian Orthodox Church split from the Eastern Orthodox Church [qv] in the fourth century and in A.D. 506 adopted the Monophysite doctrine; that is, the belief that Christ had a human and a divine nature, united in one person. Its liturgical language is Classical Armenian. After transfering to different sites, the headquarters of the Church, called the Catholicos of all Armenians, was returned in 1441 to Echmiadzin in present-day Armenia. While Echmiadzin continued to be the site of the Catholicos of all Armenians, the Catholicos

of Sis was moved to Antelias, Lebanon, in 1930. The latter's estimated one million adherents are scattered not only throughout Lebanon, Syria, Kuwait, Iran, and Cyprus, but also North America.

Arsuzi, Zaki (1908–68): *Syrian political thinker* Born into a lower-middle-class household in Antioch (renamed Antakya in 1939), Arsuzi went to Sorbonne University in Paris and obtained a degree in philosophy in 1931. The next year he became a schoolteacher in Antakya. Interested in poetry and the arts, Arsuzi established a club to help raise the appreciation of art. But the French mandate authorities closed it down and inadvertently turned Arsuzi's considerable talents toward nationalist politics. When his home province of Alexandretta was annexed to Turkey in June 1939, Arsuzi became a refugee in Damascus [qv]. There he gathered a group of young acolytes, whom he urged to bring about a renaissance in the Arab world. Despite losing his job because of his politics, Arsuzi continued his nationalist activities.

Following the departure of the French in 1946, efforts were made to amalgamate the pan-Arab groups led by Arsuzi and Michel Aflaq [qv]. These came to fruition in April 1947 with the founding conference of the Arab Baath Party [qv] in Damascus. In the absence of Arsuzi, his deputy, Wahib Ghanim, was elected to the four-member executive committee of the party. Among the youths that Ghanim, based in Latakia [qv], recruited to the new party was Hafiz Assad [qv]. When, following the Baathist coup of March 1963, Assad was assigned the task of creating a military imbued with Baathist ideology, he turned to Arsuzi for guidance. Arsuzi became Assad's constant companion on the latter's tours of military barracks, where he delivered lectures on Baathist ideology. He also penned effective editorials in party and military publications, and filled the ideological vacuum created by the rival Baath faction's allegiance to Aflaq.

Arvand Rud *(Persian: Arvand River): see* Shatt al Arab.

Asbar, Ali Ahmad Said (1930–): *Syrian poet domiciled in Lebanon* Born of an Alawi [*qv*] family in Kassabin, a village near Latakia [*qv*], Asbar obtained a philosophy degree from Damascus University in 1954, with special interest in sufism [*qv*]. A staunch member of the Syrian Social Nationalist Party [*qv*], whose leader, Antun Saada [*qv*], named him Adonis, Asbar received a long jail sentence for his subversive politics. In 1956 he escaped to Beirut [*qv*], where he combined further studies with journalism and literary writing, mainly poetry and criticism. He coedited *Shiar* (Poetry), a literary magazine, from 1956–63.

Influenced by the classical Shia [*qv*] poets he had studied as part of his Alawi upbringing, he started out as a conventional poet, publishing two volumes of verses in the conventional Arabic ode (*qasida*) style. But by the late 1950s he had begun to experiment with the prose poem (*qasidat al nathr*), infusing it with density and tension, metaphoric representation, and rhythms. His volume *Songs of Mihyar, the Damascene* (1961), broke fresh ground in its diction, syntax, and imagery. Instead of using traditional images, he employed a complex set— including the Tammuzian symbols of Adonis and Bal, biblical figures and symbols, and

such myths as that of Phoenix—to portray revolutionary change in a mystical light. He broke with traditional diction and style and employed a totally new syntax that was authoritative yet original. Considering classical Arabic as too intellectual and cerebral to express modern, urban life, he grappled with the roots of the words and explored their untapped potential through various rhythms, producing a language as robust as its classical counterpart. The complexity and creative exoticism of Asbar's poetry, and its association with modernity, made it doubly attractive to a generation of young poets. He condemned the present servility and repression in the Arab world and lamented the past, scarred by foreign invasions and inertia. Alluding to the phoenix, he put his hopes in the future.

Asbar's challenge to the traditions of language and poetry ran in tandem with his propensity for protest and defiance and his sociopolitical vision of liberation from the status quo. The humiliation and pain caused by the Arab defeat in the June 1967 Arab-Israeli War [*qv*] created a social environment that made both his political views and his poetry attractive. The resurgent hope and pride epitomized by the rise of the Palestinian resistance movement in the late 1960s tied up with his thesis: like Tammuz, the god of revival in the Babylonian religion, who is associated with Greek Adonis, the legendary phoenix is reborn out of the ashes of the fire that consumes it. By the time he had published *Introduction to Arab Poetry* (1971), marking the birth of postmodernist poetry in Arabic, the movement for radicalizing linguistic structures, coining new words, and experimenting with fresh metaphors had taken root. He had also established his own literary journal, *Mawaqif* (Attitudes) (1968–78). In *The Shock of Modernity* (1978) and *Manifesto of Modernity* (1980) he summarized his literary views, stating that "there is no trace of memory in my poetry in the cultural sense, neither on the level of heritage nor on the personal level."

When Lebanon plunged into a long, bloody civil war in 1975 [*qv*], Asbar departed for Paris, where he has kept up his writing and supplemented it with teaching. His views on Arabic have mellowed. In 1984 he stated that a rediscovery of "language is a rediscovery of Arabic's modern potential connotative possibilities, forgotten meanings and latent metaphorical dimensions." The only language in which he realized he could write was the terse, elevated language of classical Arabic poetry—disassembled, modulated, and revolutionized by him, yet possessing the aura of the old poetry and its rhetorical hold on readers and listeners.

Ashkenazim *(Hebrew: pl. of Ashkenaz, derivative of Ashk'naz, meaning Germany):* Literally, the term applies to all those from Germany; but in practice, from the ninth century onward it increasingly meant German Jews [*qv*] and their descendants, including those who had left the German lands. They are different from the Jews originating in Spain and Portugal, called Sephardim [*qv*], in their pronunciation of Hebrew [*qv*], their prayer rituals, and their mother tongue, Yiddish [*qv*]. Until the late fifteenth century Ashkenazim and Sephardim were almost equal in number, but by the late 1920s about 90 percent of the 16.5 million Jews worldwide were Ashkenazim, a term now applied to Jews of

northern or central European origin. Following the Holocaust during the Second World War, which resulted in the death of some six million Jews, the remaining 9.5 million Ashkenazim constituted 82 percent of the global Jewish population of 11.5 million. At the founding of Israel in 1948, Ashkenazim made up 80 percent of its Jewish population. However, due to the large intake of Jews from Arab states and the higher birth rate among them and Sephardim, the proportion of Ashkenazim in the Israeli Jewish population had fallen below 50 percent by the mid-1960s. Nowadays, due to the large-scale emigration of Jews from the former Soviet Union from 1990–99, Ashkenazim have acquired a narrow majority in Israel.

Ashura *(Arabic: Tenth, meaning 10th of Muharram): a fasting day for Muslims* In Islam [*qv*] it is the day when Allah created Adam and Eve, paradise and hell, the pen, and life and death. Tradition has it that the Prophet Muhammad fasted on this day.

Ashura *(Arabic: Tenth, meaning 10th of Muharram): an annual ritual of Shias* Ashura is the final day of the dramatic events of 1–10 Muharram 61 A.H. [*qv*] (A.D. 8–17 May 681) in Islamic history. The narrative of this period is recited annually by professional readers in the mosques and meeting halls of Shias [*qv*] and is mounted as the second act of a passion play of Islam [*qv*], accompanied by frenzied grief and tears, wailing, and self-flagellation in public by the faithful.

The narrative runs as follows. After the death in April A.D. 680 of Muwaiya ibn Abu Sufian—the Umayyad governor of Syria, who had challenged Ali ibn Abu Talib, a cousin and son-in-law of the Prophet Muhammad, for the caliphate—his son, Yazid, became the caliph. Hussein, the oldest surviving son of Ali, then living in Medina [qv], staked his claim to the caliphate on the grounds that it belonged to the House of the Prophet, of which he was the most senior member, and that Yazid was a usurper. His stance won him swift and fervent messages of support from the Iraqi town of Kufa [qv], a stronghold of Ali's partisans. This news reached Yazid, who rushed a trusted aide, Ubaidullah ibn Ziyad, to Kufa, where he neutralized the anti-Yazid forces.

By then the unsuspecting Hussein, accompanied by his family and seventy-two retainers, was well on his way to Kufa. On 1 Muharram 61 A.H. (A.D. 8 May 681) Hussein's entourage was intercepted near Karbala [qv], some 30 miles/48 km from Kufa, by Yazid's soldiers. For the next eight days their commander tried to obtain Hussein's unconditional surrender. But Hussein, believing in his right to the caliphate, resolved to do battle and perish rather than surrender or retreat. He also reckoned that his martyrdom would revitalize the claim of the House of the Prophet to the caliphate. On the morning of 10 Muharram, Hussein led his small band of partisans to confront Yazid's 4,000 heavily armed troops. His warriors fell one by one, and he was the last to die.

This heroic tragedy of a man of charisma and piety tells the faithful that the true believer should not shirk from challenging the established order if it has become unjust and oppressive, despite slender chances of overthrowing it.

Assad, Bashar (1965–): *Syrian military and political leader; president, 2000–* Born in Damascus [qv], Assad received his baccalaureate in 1982. He graduated as a physician, specializing in ophthalmology, and began practicing as an ophthalmologist at a military hospital outside Damascus in 1988. Four years later he went to London to specialize in ophthalmology. In 1994 he returned home after the death of his elder brother, Basil, in a car accident. As the head of the Syrian Computer Society, he initiated a computerization program. After passing the General Staff course in 1997, he was promoted to lieutenant colonel. He was put in charge of Syria's relations with Lebanon [qv]. Following the death of his father, Hafiz [qv], on 10 June 2000, he was promoted to lieutenant general, and named commander in chief. Once the age requirement for president was lowered from forty to thiry-four, he was elected president on 10 July 2000.

In foreign affairs, he maintained his father's freshly initiated policy of mending fences with Iraq [qv], which culminated in the reopening of the oil pipeline between the two neighbors in late 2000, with 200,000 barrels of Iraqi oil flowing daily into Syria. Assad stuck to the earlier Syrian position that Israel [qv] had to withdraw from all of the Golan Heights [qv] in return for total peace and normalization of relations. At home, when ninety-nine leading intellectuals demanded an end to the thirty-seven-year-old martial law, his government announced that the emergency laws had been suspended. His freeing of 600 political prisoners still left 1,500 politicians incarcerated. However, after the initial surge of liberalization, Assad slowed down the pace of political reform to placate the old guard in the Baath Party and the military and intelligence services.

In the wake of the 11 September 2001 attacks on the U.S. by Al Qaida [*qv*], Assad's government promptly offered intelligence to Washington, thus thawing Syria's relations with the sole superpower. But since it continued to support Lebanon's Hizbollah [*qv*], America kept Syria on its list of the countries that sponsor international terrorism.

Assad, Hafiz (1930–): *Syrian military and political leader; president, 1971–2000* Born Hafiz Wahhash in the family of a notable in Qurdaha, an Alawi [*qv*] village near Latakia [*qv*], Assad enrolled at the Homs [*qv*] military academy in 1951 and graduated as an air force pilot four years later. He underwent additional training in Egypt. Soon after the formation of the United Arab Republic [*qv*] in early 1958, he took a further flying course in the Soviet Union.

The dissolution of all Syrian parties, including the Baath [*qv*], of which Assad had been a longtime member, left him disgruntled. In early 1960, while serving in Egypt, he became one of the five founders of the clandestine Military Committee. After the secession of Syria from the UAR in September 1961 the Military Committee became active. It was the main force behind the Baathist coup in March 1963. Six months later Assad was elected to the regional (i.e., Syrian) high command of the Baath party. His de facto status as commander of the air force was formalized in December 1964 when he was promoted to major general.

In May 1965 he was elected to the national (i.e., all-Arab) high command of the party. In the growing discord between the moderate civilian and the radical military factions of the ruling party, Assad was firmly with the latter. His faction mounted a successful coup in February 1966, and he became defense minister. He now developed an Arab nationalist perspective, concentrating on winning a military contest with Israel, whereas his rival, Salah Jadid [*qv*], pursuing a socialist path, urged a revolutionary transformation of Syrian society. The high command of the Baath failed to resolve the conflict. Assad used his status as defense minister to consolidate his position in the military to challenge Jadid. This came in February 1969 and ended with Assad in ascendancy in the party high command and the government.

Deferring to advice from Cairo and Moscow, Assad refrained from monopolizing power, and inter alia retained Nur al Din Attasi [*qv*], a Jadid ally, as president. But because Jadid continued to dominate the party machine, the tussle between him and Assad was not fully resolved. The final clash came in November 1970 during the national congress of the Baath in Damascus [*qv*]. Assad gained full control, purging and arresting his adversaries. He assumed the additional offices of prime minister and secretary-general of the Baath, leaving the presidency to his nominee, Ahmad Khatib. Under his guidance, the new party high command nominated a 173-strong People's Assembly to draft a constitution.

In February 1971 the People's Assembly ratified the party high command's nomination of Assad as president, and this decision was confirmed in a referendum in March, when 99.2 percent of those participating voted Yes. When in January 1973 the draft constitution described Syria as a "democratic, popular, socialist state," an influential group of Muslim clerics attacked the document as "secular and atheistic," and demanded insertion of an article proclaiming Islam [qv] as the state religion. Assad temporised by persuading the People's Assembly to amend the constitution to specify that the president must be Muslim. But the clergy did not think this sufficient. Assad declared that the October 1973 Arab-Israeli War [qv] was a jihad [qv] against the enemies of Islam. In early 1974 he went on an umra [qv] to Mecca [qv], and this established him as a true believer. He was reelected president in 1978, 1985, and 1992.

Assad put Syria on a firm institutional path, with elections to the People's Assembly being held every four years. The Assembly is dominated by the Baath-led National Progressive Front [qv], formed in 1972, which includes pan-Arabists [qv], socialists, and communists [qv]. The real power lies with the high command of the Baath, which is led by Assad. Complementing it is the intelligence network that permeates all important segments of society and government. The major opposition force, the Muslim Brotherhood [qv], remains outlawed.

Assad's intervention in the Lebanese Civil War [qv] in mid-1976 to bolster the Christian camp revived the Islamist forces, who started a campaign of assassination and terrorism. This graduated into near-insurrection in Aleppo [qv] and Hama [qv] in March 1980, and reached a peak with an assassination attempt on Assad in June. In response, Assad went all out to crush the Islamists, who retreated and consolidated their position. Their violent activities resumed and culminated in an insurrection in Hama in February

1982. Assad hit back with unprecedented force and assumed control. Signs of fission within the ruling elite surfaced when Assad suffered a heart attack in November 1983. His younger brother, Rifaat [qv], tried to seize power but failed.

Assad finally overcame this crisis, which threatened to turn into civil war, in March 1984, the month in which he successfully aborted the Lebanese-Israeli peace treaty [qv] that Lebanon, cajoled by the United States, had initialed in May 1983 in the wake of the Israeli invasion of Lebanon [qv] about a year earlier. Assad's involvement in the Lebanese civil strife was based on his doctrine that a special relationship existed between Lebanon and Syria, and that the defection of Lebanon to the U.S.-Israel camp would present extreme danger to Syrian security. Assad persevered with his Lebanese involvement until finally, in October 1990, the pro-Syrian side won.

His relations with Egypt have fluctuated. Initially he strengthened his ties with Egypt, coordinating the war against Israel in October 1973, but he became disillusioned with Egyptian President Anwar Sadat [qv] when the latter began to pursue the policies that were to culminate in the bilateral peace treaty with Israel in 1979. Assad made Syria the centerpiece of the Steadfastness Front [qv], which included the Palestine Liberation Organization [qv], and opposed readmission of Egypt into the Arab League [qv], from which it had been expelled in 1979. He signed a Friendship Treaty with the Soviet Union in 1980.

Reflecting the divisions within the national (i.e., pan-Arab) command of the Baath party, with Michel Aflaq [qv] operone of its units for an attack on Deir Yassin village in April 1948, which resulted in the massacre of 254 Arabs—men, women, and children. During the first months of the Palestine War, Palmah and Haganah troops carried out dozens of raids on Arab villages with the primary aim of razing them. Thus 472 of the 755 (or five out of eight) Arab villages disappeared without a trace. Following David Ben-Gurion's [qv] decision, after the founding of Israel in May 1948, to merge all such forces into a national military organization, the general staff of the Palmah was dissolved in 1949.

pan-Arabism: Pan-Arabism is a doctrine that maintains that no matter where Arabs live, they are part of a single community. It first manifested itself in the Arab territory of the Ottoman Empire from 1876–78 when a written constitution, promulgated by Sultan Abdul Hamid II, provided some element of free expression. It reemerged in 1908 after the Young Turks in Istanbul had mounted a successful coup against the sultan, only to go underground soon after the new rulers adopted the traditional stance of Turkish superiority.

The outbreak of the First World War provided the Ottoman's Arab subjects and notables an option to further their nationalist cause by siding with the anti-Ottoman forces. By declaring an Arab revolt in 1916, the Hashemite governor of Hijaz [qv], Hussein ibn Ali, became the leader of pan-Arabism, with a plan to see the Arab territories formed into a single, independent Arab state after the defeat of the Ottomans. But this was contrary to the aims of the clandestine 1916 Sykes-Picot Pact [qv], signed by Britain and France. In the interwar period the al Hashem clan [qv], which ruled Iraqand Transjordan [qv],

remained the repositories of pan-Arabism. This changed in 1948 when, in order to annex parts of Palestine [qv] to his realm, King Abdullah ibn Hussein [qv] of Jordan tried to make a secret deal with the Zionists [qv]. Pan-Arab nationalists now viewed him as a traitor to their cause.

Following the 1948–49 Palestine War [qv] and the establishment of Israel, pan-Arabism centered on the Arab struggle for the retrieval of Palestine from the Zionists [qv]. With the Free Officers' successful coup in Egypt in 1952, the mantle of pan-Arab leadership fell on Gamal Abdul Nasser [qv], president of the most populous and strategic Arab country, which since its inception in 1945 had contributed little to pan-Arabism, except to provide headquarters to the Arab League [qv], a pan-Arab institution conceived originally by the British to further their interests in the region. Nasser's first step toward creating a unified Arab state in 1958—the merger of Egypt and Syria into the United Arab Republic [qv]—failed three years later. Yet on the eve of the June 1967 Arab-Israeli War [qv], he was able to lead a joint military command of Egypt, Syria, and Jordan.

After this conflict, which ended with Arab defeat, pan-Arabism revolved around the objective of recovering all Arab territories lost to Israel in Egypt, Syria, and Jordan. The military alliance of Egypt and Syria in October 1973, backed by the military and oil muscle of the rest of the Arab world, was the next manifestation of pan-Arabism. It proved to be the pinnacle of the movement. By signing a peace treaty with Israel in 1979, Egypt, under President Anwar Sadat [qv], destroyed the Arab consensus that there should be no unilateral peace treaty with

Israel. With this Egypt lost its leadership of pan-Arabism, leaving Syrian President Hafiz Assad [qv] to carry the banner. Assad was committed to retrieving all Occupied Arab Territories [qv] from Israel.

The attempt by President Saddam Hussein [qv] of Iraq to portray his war with Iran as a struggle for "all of the Arab homeland" against Persian expansionism, masquerading as pan-Islamism [qv], was only partially successful. With such important Arab states as Syria, Algeria, and Libya siding with Iran, Saddam Hussein failed to project himself as a latterday Nasser. Indeed his invasion and annexation of Kuwait in August 1990 severely split the Arab League and mortally weakened pan-Arabism. This became clear a year later when the Arab neighbors of Israel and the Palestinians agreed to negotiate with the Jewish state, not collectively under United Nations auspices as they had hitherto unitedly insisted, but bilaterally, as Israel had demanded.

What remains of pan-Arabism is the Arab League, consisting of twenty-two Arabic-speaking member countries, but even that institution was somewhat undermined by the emergence of the Gulf Cooperation Council [qv] in 1981, and the Arab Maghreb Union, encompassing five North African Arab states of Algeria, Libya, Mauritania, Morocco, and Tunisia, in 1989.

pan-Islamism: Pan-Islamism is a traditional doctrine that maintains that no matter where Muslims live, they belong to a universal Islamic *umma* (community) [qv]. It transcends linguistic, cultural, and other ethnic differences among Muslims.

Pan-Islamism proved useful to the Ottoman rulers in the late nineteenth century. Sultan Abdul Hamid II (r. 1876–1909) tried to regenerate cohesion in Ottoman society by mobilizing the masses around the Islamic banner and engendering a pan-Islamic movement. By manifesting personal piety, appointing Arabs [qv] to important posts at the court, and constructing a railway from Damascus [qv] to Mecca [qv] to promote the *hajj* [qv], he showed his commitment to pan-Islamism. In this he had the active backing of, among others, Jamal al Din Afghani (1838–97), a religious personality of varied talents, whom he invited to Constantinople (now Istanbul) in the early 1890s. Since Afghani played an active role in the religious-political life of all the important Islamic regions—Ottoman Turkey, Egypt, Iran, India, and Central Asia—he acquired a truly pan-Islamic perspective and realized that the Islamic *umma* as a whole was threatened by European powers.

The dissolution of the Ottoman Empire—the last in the series of Islamic empires—in the wake of the First World War, followed by the abolition of the caliphate in 1924 by the Republic of Turkey, was a blow to pan-Islamism. But a few years later, the pan-Islamic concept was relaunched on a popular scale in Egypt by the Muslim Brotherhood [qv]. The Egyptian Brotherhood set up sister organizations in Syria, Transjordan (now Jordan), and Palestine [qv]. The pan-Islamic movement in Egypt reached a climax in 1949, the year when the Muslim Brotherhood leader Hassan al Banna [qv] was assassinated.

In the course of popularizing pan-Arabism [qv] and then Arab socialism [qv], Egyptian President Gamal Abdul Nasser [qv] suppressed the Brotherhood. The mantle of pan-Islamism was then taken up by the House of Saud [*qv*], specifically King Faisal ibn Abdul Aziz [*qv*], a devout Muslim, who promoted it in the mid-1960s as a competing ideology to Nasser's Arab socialism. He failed, but in 1969 an abortive attempt to set fire to Islam's third holiest shrine, the al Aqsa mosque in Jerusalem [*qv*], created an environment in which King Faisal was able to sponsor the Islamic Conference Organization (ICO) [*qv*], composed of Muslim states throughout the world, later based in Jiddah [*qv*].

As a multinational body representing governments, the ICO paralleled the Arab League [*qv*]. However, what caught popular attention in both the Muslim and non-Muslim world was the successful Islamic revolution [*qv*] in Iran in early 1979, which overthrew the secular pro-Western regime of Muhammad Reza Shah Pahlavi [*qv*]. Article 10 of Iran's constitution requires the government to formulate its general policies with a view to "the merging and union of all Muslim peoples"; and Article 152 requires Iranian foreign policy to be based on "the defense of the rights of all Muslims." However, as Iran is populated mainly by Shias [*qv*], a minority sect within Islam [*qv*], its impact has been limited to such pockets in the Muslim world as Bahrain and the Shia communities in Lebanon and Iraq.

In 1991 the military regime in Algeria struck a blow against pan-Islamism by aborting the imminent electoral victory of the Front for Islamic Salvation.

Pasha, Nahas: *see* Nahas (Pasha), Mustafa.

Passover *(Hebrew: Pesach, der. of the root meaning "pass over"):* One of the four major Jewish festivals, lasting seven (in Israel) to eight (in the Diaspora [*qv*]) days, the term Passover strictly applies to the first day. It celebrates the "passing over" by destructive forces (on the eve of the Exodus when the Lord "smote the Land of Egypt," *Exodus* 12:13) of the Israelites, who had poured the blood of a lamb on their door posts to show they were children of God. The festival begins on the fifteenth of Nisan, the first month of the Jewish calendar [*qv*]. At the ceremonial evening meals on the first and second day of the festival there is a recitation of certain passages of Exodus. During the festival only unleavened bread is eaten, as a reminder that the Jews fleeing Egypt had no time to leaven their bread.

Patriotic Union of Kurdistan: *Iraqi Kurdish party* The Patriotic Union of Kurdistan (PUK) was formed in mid-1976 by the merger of the Kurdish Workers League and the Social Democratic Movement under the leadership of Jalal Talabani [*qv*]. Both PUK constituents had emerged from the Kurdistan Democratic Party (KDP) [*qv*] after its leader, Mustafa Barzani [*qv*], fled to Iran in the wake of the March 1975 Algiers Accord [*qv*]. Under Talabani—who, during his tenure as the KDP's envoy to Syria, had been influenced by the leftist Palestinian leaders George Habash [*qv*] and Nayif Hawatmeh [*qv*]—the PUK described itself as Marxist-Leninist. It conducted its armed struggle against the Baghdad regime as well as the KDP, which had its bastion in the northwest of the Kurdistan Autonomous Region (KAR) [*qv*]. Based at Yakhsamar in Suleimaniya province, the PUK was strong in the southeast.

With the outbreak of the Iran-Iraq War [*qv*] in September 1980 the chances of Kurdish guerrilla activity improved sharply, with the PUK concentrating its operations in its stronghold area. A PUK agreement with the KDP in 1982 to open all of the KAR to both parties failed to endure. Overall the PUK expanded at the KDP's expense. In 1984, yielding to the pressure of its war with Iran, the Baghdad government began to negotiate with the PUK, but nothing came of it. This laid the groundwork for the PUK's subsequent ties with Iran, which began to arm PUK activists. Iran tried to effect a reconciliation between the PUK and the KDP. This attempt bore fruit in May 1987, when the two parties combined with six others to form the Iraqi Kurdistan Front (IKF) [*qv*].

Both the PUK and the KDP set up liberated areas along Iraq's borders with Iran and Turkey. But with Iraq prevailing over Iran in 1988, the situation changed. Following the Baghdad regime's onslaught on nationalist Kurds in 1988, the PUK and other IKF constituents fled across the border to Iran or Syria. Baghdad demanded public recantation from PUK leaders before they would be allowed to submit their demands to the government.

The crisis created by the Iraqi invasion of Kuwait [*qv*] in August 1990 revived the PUK and other IKF members. In March 1991, soon after the end of the Second Gulf War [*qv*], the PUK and the KDP revolted against the central government, and within a few weeks they had taken over three-quarters of the KAR. But they were unable to withstand Baghdad's counteroffensive. The crushing of the rebellion caused an exodus of some 1.5 million Kurdish refugees.

Pressured by the United Nations Security Council, Iraq declared a cease-fire in the KAR in mid-April. Talabani was deputy leader of the IKF delegation that negotiated with Baghdad on the basis of the 1970 pact

between the central government and Kurdish autonomists. These talks ended in mid June with an agreement on the extent of Kurdish autonomy, which was designated to encourage the return of Kurdish refugees in order to revive the 3,800 villages that had been razed by the Iraqi government over the past seventeen years. However, Talabani recommended to IKF leaders that the deal should be rejected. In October Baghdad withdrew its last troops from the KAR.

Following the general election in the KAR in May 1992, held under the protection of Western air forces, the PUK shared power equally with the KDP. This arrangement, carried to the extremes, was applied even to teachers and policemen on the beat. In the ministries two different command structures emerged. With each party allowed to set up offices in the other's bastion (the KDP in the Kermanji-speaking northwest, and the PUK in the Sourani-speaking southeast) and trying to raise its strength at the expense of the other, traditional tensions between them rose sharply. As a party directed by urban-based leaders, the PUK remained antipathetic to the KDP's continuing tribal ways. In May 1994 clashes between them left more than 1,000 fighters and civilians dead. Despite periodic cease-fires, relations soured further when the PUK participated in the military plan by the Washington-funded Iraqi National Congress [*qv*] to overthrow Saddam Hussein in March 1995, while the KDP did not. The intermittent intra-Kurdish violence raised the total death toll to 3,000 by September 1995. And the PUK's capture of the regional capital of Irbil [*qv*] in December left the two sides intensely embittered.

It was against this background that the PUK found itself under attack in Irbil in late August 1996 by the KDP, bolstered by Saddam Hussein's tanks and artillery. The retreating PUK lost not only Irbil, but also all of its territory in the southeast, and its leaders and fighters took shelter in Iran. From their haven they launched a counteroffensive and recaptured all the lost territory except Irbil at the cost of the death toll of 2,000 in both camps. Initialing a temporary accord in October, mediated by American and British diplomats, the two sides agreed to discuss sharing of the customs revenue currently monopolized by the KDP as well as conducting a new parliamentary poll. Nothing came of it.

Following the passage of the Iraq Liberation Act by U.S. Congress in October 1998, which authorized the White House to designate Iraqi opposition groups eligible for military aid by Washington, the PUK found itself included on the list of six such factions. On the ground very little changed, with Kurdistan divided administratively into two sectors, with the PUK's territory ruled from Suleimaniya [*qv*].

It was not until September 2002, when Washington's plans to invade Iraq went into a higher gear, that the PUK decided to bury its hatchet with the KDP. Both parties coordinated their millitary plans on the eve of Gulf War III [*qv*] in 2003, and agreed to work together. But after the fall of Baghdad [*qv*] on 19 April, Talabani breached the agreement, and ordered the PUK militia to enter Kirkuk, thus leaving the KDP no option but to follow. The PUK publicly welcomed the U.S. pro-consul (Retd.) Gen. Jay Raynar when he visited Kurditan.

Peace Now: *An extra-parliamentary Israeli group* (Official title: Hebrew: *Shalom Achshav*) It was founded by 348 reserve officers and soldiers of the Israel Defense Forces [*qv*] to support the Camp David Accords [*qv*] between Israel [*qv*] and Egypt [*qv*] in 1978. Its primary function is to pressure the Israeli government to seek peace with the Arab [*qv*] neighbors as well as the Palestinians, whose right to an independent state it recognizes. It also accepts the idea that the municipal borders of Jerusalem [*qv*], expanded by Israel after the 1967 Six-Day War [*qv*], may be readjusted, and that the two states may have their capitals in Jerusalem, the Palestinians in the Arab areas, the Israelis in the Jewish neighborhoods. It advocates a peace treaty with Syria [*qv*] on the basis of total Israeli withdrawal from the Golan Heights [*qv*] for total normalization of relations by Syria.

A nonpartisan, volunteer movement with branches throughout the country, Peace Now's national secretariat, based in Tel Aviv [*qv*], decides policy with its branches conducting activities on an almost autonomous basis. It has sister organizations in America, Britain, Belgium, and the Netherlands.

As part of the final settlement with the Palestinians, Peace Now visualizes some Jewish settlements being absorbed into Israel, some disbanded, and the rest allowed to exist under Palestinian sovereignty and law. In the late 1980s, its Settlement Watch section began monitoring and documenting the expropriation of the Palestinian land and houses, the building of new Jewish settlements, and the expansion of the existing ones in the West Bank [*qv*], Gaza Strip [*qv*], and East Jerusalem [*qv*]. It publishes periodic updates on the subject and uses this information to lobby politicians and appeal to the judiciary.

Before the Oslo Accord of 1993 [*qv*], Peace Now leaders held clandestine talks with the Palestinian leaders abroad. After it, they organized many joint activities, vigils, marches, and symposia with the Palestinians. However, with the rising conflict between Israel and the Palestinians after the al Aqsa Intifada [*qv*] in September 2000, Peace Now became marginalized.

Its most dramatic achievement was in the case of Lebanon [*qv*]. It led the mass movement against Israel's 1982 invasion of Lebanon, mobilizing 400,000 people in a protest rally in Tel Aviv in the aftermath of the conflict and finally succeeding in securing Israel's withdrawal from south Lebanon in 2000. Also, as a result of its persistent lobbying, the Israeli public opinion favoring a Palestinian state rose from 1 percent in 1977 to over 50 percent in 1997.

Peace Process, Middle East:

(1) After the Arab-Israeli War, 1948–49 [*qv*]: Following the truces signed between Israel and its Arab adversaries in 1949, behind-the-scene efforts were made by the United States to secure Israel's recognition by one or more of its Arab neighbors. Washington was behind the military coup in Syria in March 1949 that put Col. Hosni Zaim [*qv*] in power. But when, as promised, he opened secret talks with Israel, he was overthrown in August. Later, when King Abdullah I ibn Hussein [*qv*] of Jordan established clandestine contact with Israeli leaders, he was assassinated in 1951. Israel's aggression toward Egypt in collusion with Britain and France in 1956 hardened the stance of Arab states toward Israel. In the mid-1960s competition between radical Egyptian President Gamal Abdul Nasser [*qv*] and conservative Saudi King Faisal ibn Abdul Aziz [*qv*] for leadership of the Arab world intensified, and neither could afford to be less than militantly anti-Zionist.

(2) After the June 1967 Arab-Israeli War [*qv*]: The Arab summit in Khartoum from 29 August to 1 September 1967 combined its rejection of Israel—no peace, no recognition, and no negotiation—with its insistence on the rights of the Palestinians in their own country. To ensure that Israel did not consolidate the territorial gains it had made in the 1967 conflict, Egypt initiated a War of Attrition [*qv*] in March 1969, which continued until mid-1970. In December 1969 U.S. Secretary of State William Rogers offered a peace plan, later called the Rogers Plan [*qv*], which opposed Israeli expansionism and recommended that any boundary modifications to pre-June 1967 Israel be limited to "insubstantial alternatives required for mutual security." This was rejected by both Egypt and Israel. Egypt wanted unconditional Israeli withdrawal from the Occupied Arab Territories [*qv*] before negotiating a peace agreement with it. In contrast, Israel wanted direct unconditional talks with its Arab adversaries.

As the War of Attrition escalated in 1970, Rogers revived his initiative and focused on securing a cease-fire, enabling the U.N. mediator, Gunnar Jarring, to get the peace process going under U.N. Security Council Resolution 242 [*qv*]. He presented this proposal to Egypt, Israel, Jordan, and Syria on 19 June 1970. After consulting the Soviet Union, Nasser accepted the Rogers proposal on 22 July. Jordan did so on 25 July, and the Israeli parliament followed suit on 31 July after the government had received certain secret assurances from U.S. President Richard Nixon. The ninety-day truce went into effect on 7 August 1970. Following the death in September of President Nasser, his successor, Anwar Sadat [qv], renewed the cease-fire, but the U.N. mediator's peace efforts got nowhere. Having failed to secure Israel's withdrawal from Sinai [qv], Sadat planned a military campaign, in conjunction with Syria, to retrieve the Arab territories occupied by Israel in 1967.

(3) After the October 1973 Arab-Israeli War [qv]: The one-day United Nations peace conference in Geneva on 22 December 1973, under the cochairmanship of the United States and the Soviet Union and attended by Israel, Egypt and Jordan, did not reassemble as planned, because Sadat chose to pursue a unilateral path in his talks with Israel through U.S. Secretary of State Henry Kissinger. The result was the Sinai I Agreement [qv] between Egypt and Israel in January 1974. Then came a truce between Syria and Israel on the Golan Heights [qv] in June 1974. Next followed the Sinai II Agreement [qv] between Egypt, and Israel, valid for three years and signed on 4 September 1975. Israel agreed to this deal only after it had received written guarantees from the United States that it would not have talks with the Palestine Liberation Organization (PLO) [qv] unless it ceased its terrorist activity against Israel and recognized Israel's right to exist in tranquillity.

In 1976, a U.S. presidential election year, the peace process came to a halt. It was only in October 1977, when the new U.S. Presi-

dent Jimmy Carter (president from 1977–81) had settled into his job, that a joint U.S.-Soviet Union declaration stated the terms for reconvening the Geneva conference in December. But Israel disapproved of this, and no such meeting took place. In November the dramatic visit of Sadat to Jerusalem [qv] to address the Israeli parliament altered the course of the peace process. The accords between Israel and Egypt, signed at Camp David, Maryland, in September 1978, covered relations between the two countries, and between Israel and the Palestinians, even though their sole representative, the Palestine Liberation Organization (PLO), did not participate in the talks. On 26 March 1979 Egypt and Israel signed a peace treaty in Washington. By the time the two countries exchanged ambassadors in February 1980, Israel had returned two-thirds of Sinai to Egypt. But 26 May 1980—the target date for an agreement on Palestinian self-rule—passed unnoticed. On 26 April 1982 Israel returned the last part of Sinai to Egypt.

Following the expulsion of the PLO from Beirut [qv], on 1 September 1982, U.S. President Ronald Reagan presented a peace plan that reaffirmed U.N. Security Council Resolution 242 [qv]. While explicitly excluding Israeli annexation, sovereignty, or domination over the Occupied Territories [qv], it also ruled out an independent Palestinian state. Instead it favored Palestinian self-government "in association with Jordan," and called on Jordan and the Palestinians to widen the 1978 Camp David Accords [qv] so that a self-governing Palestinian authority could be elected to succeed the Israeli rule. Israeli Premier Menachem Begin [qv] summarily rejected this proposal because he had not been consulted, and the Reagan Plan died an instant death.

On 6 September 1982 the Arab summit in Fez adopted an eight-point peace plan, which included Israel's withdrawal to its pre-1967 borders, the dismantling of settlements in the Occupied Arab Territories [qv], the exercising of Palestinian self-determination under the PLO to create a State of Palestine, with its capital in East Jerusalem [qv], the right of Palestinian refugees to return home or receive compensation, and a U.N. Security Council guarantee of peace for all the states of the region, including Palestine. Syria backed this plan.

After falling out with Syrian President Hafiz Assad [qv] in 1983, PLO Chairman Yasser Arafat [qv] began talks with King Hussein [qv] of Jordan early the following year. In February 1985 they announced a peace plan that envisaged Palestinians exercising their right to self-determination within the framework of a confederation of Jordan and Palestine, and a joint Jordanian-Palestinian delegation participating in peace talks organized under U.N. auspices. When Israel failed to respond to the proposal, Jordan ended its diplomatic collaboration with the PLO. The Palestine National Council [qv] canceled the 1985 agreement in April 1987. Meanwhile Syria pursued a policy of achieving strategic parity with Israel.

In February 1988 George Shultz, the U.S. Secretary of State, offered a plan that specified a negotiating period of six months between Israel and a Jordanian-Palestinian delegation to work out details of a transitional autonomy arrangement for the West Bank [qv] and Gaza [qv]. The arrangement would remain in force for three years, during which a final settlement would be negotiated. The talks would run concurrently with an international peace conference, involving the five permanent members of the U.N. Security Council and all the interested parties, on the basis of Security Council Resolutions 242 and 338 [qv]. Israeli Premier Yitzhak Shamir [qv] rejected the plan, calling it impractical. Since the Shultz Plan lacked any provision for a Palestinian state, the PLO turned it down. So did other Palestinian leaders, who saw it as a ploy to stunt the growth of the fledgling intifada [qv].

With King Hussein finally cutting administrative and legal links with the West Bank in July 1988, Israel's strategy of persuading Jordan to join the enlarged Camp David Accords became redundant. On the other hand, it opened the way for the Palestine National Council to issue a declaration of independence for "our Palestinian land" and renounce violence and terrorism at its session in Algiers in November 1988. After this, the United States established low-level contact with the PLO headquarters in Tunis.

During 1989, with the tide of Soviet Jewish immigration building up due to Moscow's relaxed policies—raising the total number of immigrants from 13,300 in 1988 to 199,500 two years later—a new factor entered the process. In June 1990 the United States suspended talks with the PLO when the latter failed to condemn attack on Israel by the radical Palestine Liberation Front, affiliated to the PLO, because its target was military.

During the crisis preceding the Second Gulf War [qv], the PLO backed Saddam

Hussein because he tied Iraq's evacuation of Kuwait to Israel's withdrawal from the Occupied Arab Territories, a linkage summarily rejected by the United States. On the other hand, when during his meeting with U.S. President George Bush (r. 1989-93) in Geneva in November 1990, President Assad pointed out the double standards used by Washington regarding Iraq and Israel, Bush assured him that after the war he would act as a catalyst between Israel and the Arabs in bringing about a peace settlement.

(4) After the Second Gulf War, 1991 [*qv*]: The defeat of Iraq, the only independently radical Arab state, provided an incentive to U.S. Secretary of State James Baker to revive the peace process. The chances of this improved in mid-July 1991 when Syria's President Assad—when told that if he agreed then the blame for failure would fall on Israel—made concessions on his terms for attending an international conference on Middle East peace. The preconditions by Israel, now ruled by a right-wing coalition government headed by Yitzhak Shamir, were the exclusion of the PLO from the talks; the inclusion of the Palestinians resident in the Occupied Territories but unconnected with the PLO in a joint Jordanian-Palestinian delegation; any settlement with the Palestinians to include a transitional period of autonomy under the Israelis; and the negotiations to be bilateral, with no third country acting as a mediator or arbiter. In return, Israel conceded the principle of land for peace as contained in U.N. Security Council Resolution 242.

The Middle East Peace Conference was held in Madrid on 30 October under the cochairmanship of the United States and the Soviet Union (later Russia). When in his speech, Shamir described Syria as a "terrorist state," the Syrian foreign minister, Faruq al Shaara, responded by holding up a picture of a poster showing Shamir as a wanted fugitive concerning the assassination of Lord Moyne, the British resident minister in the Middle East.

After the preliminaries, bilateral talks began between Israel and Syria, and Lebanon and the Jordanians-Palestinians. A second stream of multilateral negotiations concerning regional matters was also initiated. These included issues such as refugees, water, the economy, ecology, and regional security and disarmament. Syria and Lebanon boycotted these talks. In the course of the bilateral negotiations the Jordanian-Palestinian delegation split into two, and the contact between the Palestinian delegates and the PLO gradually became public. Moreover, the four Arab delegations coordinated their strategies at joint sessions, often held in Damascus [*qv*], before attending new rounds of talks. The bilateral talks made little progress despite the installation of a Labor led [*qv*] government following the defeat in June 1992 of Likud [*qv*] led by Israeli Premier Shamir—who later revealed that he had planned to keep the negotiations going for ten years. Nor did the situation alter when Bill Clinton succeeded George Bush (r. 1989–93) as U.S. president in January 1993. The tenth round, held in Washington in June–July, was as sterile as the preceding nine.

Unknown to the Americans or anybody else, the Israeli government and the PLO had entered into Norwegian-organized secret talks in Norway in January 1993. These resulted in an agreement on principles in late

August, which was initialed by the Israeli foreign minister, Shimon Peres [*qv*], and the PLO official, Ahmad Krai, in Oslo. The formal signing of the Israeli-PLO Accord [*qv*] took place in Washington on 13 September in the presence of President Clinton.

(5) After the Israeli-PLO Accord, September 1993 [*qv*]: Having ended the state of war between Jordan and Israel at a meeting in Washington in July 1994, King Hussein and Israeli Premier Yitzhak Rabin [*qv*] signed the Jordanian-Israeli Peace Treaty [*qv*] in October 1994.

In May 1994 the PLO and Israel signed an agreement in Cairo [*qv*] on interim Palestinian self-rule in the Gaza Strip and the West Bank town of Jericho [*qv*] under the Palestinian Authority (PA) [*qv*]. The PA started functioning in July. In September 1995 the PLO and Israel signed an agreement in Washington on interim Palestinian self-rule in the West Bank under the PA, requiring withdrawal of Israeli troops from seven West Bank cities by December, joint PA-Israeli control of 450 Palestinian villages, and continued Israeli control of 128 Jewish settlements. This became known as the Washington Accord [*qv*] or Oslo II Accord [*qv*].

Following the assassination of Rabin in November 1995, his successor, Shimon Peres, carried out the Israeli withdrawal from the West Bank villages as well as six West Bank cities (Hebron [*qv*] being the exception) by late December 1995. In January there were elections to the eighty-eight-member Palestinian Council, followed by the election of the executive president of the Palestinian Authority, in which Yasser Arafat won seven-eighths of the vote. Peres's defeat in May 1996 by his right-wing rival Benjamin Netanyahu [*qv*], who described the Oslo Accords [*qv*] as "evil," was a heavy blow to the peace process.

(6) Netanyahu's premiership, May 1996–May 1999: After renegotiating the terms for a partial withdrawal from Hebron, Netanyahu authorized the construction of a large Jewish settlement southeast of Jerusalem at Jabal abu Ghunaim, called Har Homa. This brought the peace process to a virtual standstill, while Netanyahu stated that any progress was conditional on the PA curbing the Islamist opposition and ending its political activities in Jerusalem. The deadline of September 1998 for further Israeli withdrawal specified in the Oslo Accord II passed without any movement in the peace process. In October at the Arafat-Netanyahu summit, chaired by U.S. President Bill Clinton at the Wye Plantation, Maryland, Israel agreed to withdraw from a further 13 percent of the West Bank in three phases, each conditional on the PA meeting specific security arrangements to be verified by the U.S. Central Intelligence Agency. Talks on the final settlement, involving Palestinian refugees, Jewish settlements, and Jerusalem, were set to start in November and continue until the expiration of the Oslo Accords on 4 May 1999. In practice the Israelis carried out only the first of the three redeployments. To dissuade Arafat from declaring unilaterally the establishment of the sovereign State of Palestine on 4 May 1999, Clinton addressed a letter to him reasserting his backing for the right of Palestinians to determine their future as "a free people on their own land."

(7) Ehud Barak [*qv*] as Israeli Prime Minister, May 1999–February 2001: In

September 1999 Israel withdrew from 7 percent of the West Bank, and in October opened a safe passageway between the West Bank and Gaza through the Israeli territory as specified in the Oslo Accords. In May 2000 Israel withdrew unconditionally from southern Lebanon as demanded by the U.N. Security Council Resolution 425 [*qv*] of March 1978. In early July Clinton invited Arafat and Barak to an open-ended summit at Camp David to reach a framework agreement on the final settlement. On 26 July the summit ended in failure chiefly due to unbridgeable differences between the two sides on the fate of the Palestinian refugees and the future of Jerusalem. Clinton announced that the negotiations were being deferred.

On 25 September Arafat visited Barak at the latter's home, and they said they would meet again four days later. But on 28 September, Likud leader Ariel Sharon [*qv*], surrounded by 1,000 armed police, toured the Noble Sanctuary/Temple Mount [*qv*] in Jerusalem's Old City, normally out of bounds to the Jews. Regarding this as a provocative move by Sharon to underscore Israeli sovereignty over Islam's third holiest site, Palestinians protested by throwing stones. The Palestinian demonstration that followed after the Friday's midday prayers at the al Aqsa Mosque on 29 September was curbed by the Israeli security forces with live ammunition which left seven Palestinians dead. This marked the start of the al Aqsa Intifada [*qv*], also known as the Second Intifada [*qv*]. Against the background of rising violence and weakening coalition government, Barak called for the election of the prime minister in late November 2000.

A month later the regional newspapers published the Clinton Plan, which visualized a demilitarized Palestinian state in Gaza and 95 percent of the West Bank, with the Palestinians getting the remainder area in the Negev desert next to the Gaza Strip. Whereas the Israelis would exercise sovereignty over the Jewish settlements in East Jerusalem, the Palestinians would do so only over the Arab neighborhoods. In the Old City, Israel would annex the Jewish Quarter and the Western Wall [*qv*] as well as enjoy "shared functional sovereignty" both "behind" the Western Wall and "under" the Noble Sanctuary. The estimated 3.7 million Palestinian refugees would have the right to return to the future State of Palestine, but not to Israel. Those rejecting this choice would be entitled to compensation and resettlement. In his meeting with Clinton on 3 January 2001, when Arafat sought clarifications, he was told that this plan would expire when Clinton left the White House on 20 January. However, the Israeli and Palestinian delegations, meeting in the Egyptian sea resort of Taba on 21 January, began negotiating with the Clinton Plan as the starting point. After a week they postponed the talks until after the prime ministerial contest on 6 February. In this poll Barak lost to Ariel Sharon [*qv*].

(8) Ariel Sharon [*qv*] as Israeli Prime Minister, February 2001– : Sharon got elected on the platform of continued expansion of Jewish settlements, Israeli sovereignty over all of the expanded Jerusalem, and no talks with the Palestinians until there was complete cessation of terrorism.

Reporting in May, former U.S. senator George Mitchell described Sharon's walkabout at the Noble Sanctuary in September

2000 as "provocative" and Israel's use against the Palestinian demonstrators as excessive. Equally, he criticized the Palestinians for firing on Israeli soldiers and Jewish settlers from the PA-controlled areas and rejected their demand for an international protection force due to Israel's opposition. Stating that a cessation of violence would be hard to sustain unless Israel stopped its settlement construction activity, he recommended a freeze on all such activity. The PA accepted the Mitchell Report. While disputing any link between Jewish settlement policy and Palestinian terrorism, Sharon accepted the report "in principle." Later that month, for the first time Israel used F16 jet fighters to attack targets in Nablus, killing thirteen Palestinian policemen, thus escalating the conflict.

In his talks with officials of the new U.S. administration of President George W. Bush, Arafat offered a cease-fire if Israel froze settlements, removed the blockades of the Palestinian urban centers, implemented the third redeployment under the Wye River Memorandum [qv], and resumed talks on final settlement from the point where they were left off at Taba in January. But following a suicide bomb attack in Tel Aviv [qv] in June, which killed twenty young Israelis, Arafat dropped his conditions and promised a full cease-fire, while refusing to arrest Islamist leaders.

Following the terrorist attacks on the U.S., both Arafat and Sharon condemned them. Arafat ordered a total cease-fire, which did not hold. By reoccupying the territories under the PA's jurisdiction, and destroying the security and administrative infrastructure of the PA, from March 2001 onward, Sharon undermined systematically all the elements of the peace process painstakingly built up by Rabin and Peres in the 1990s in cooperation with the Palestinians.

Once Yasser Arafat had appointed Mahmud Abbas [qv] the PA's prime minister, the road map for peace—drafted by America, the European Union, Russia and the U.N.—was unveiled.

Phase I (ending 31 May): While the Palestinians pledge an immediate cessation of terrorism Israel commits itself to "the two-nation vision of an independent, viable Palestinian state living in peace and security alongside Israel." Phase II (June-December 2003): As the PA dismantles the terrorists' infrastructure, Israel dismantles Jewish outposts in the Palestinian Territories and stops expanding existing settlements. An international peace conference creates a Palestinian state with "temporary" borders. Phase III (2004–05): After an Israeli-Palestinian deal on final borders, Jerusalem, Palestinian refugees and Jewish settlements, a second peace conference confirms the agreement and declares a formal end to the conflict.

Pentecost (*Greek: derivative of* pentekostos, *fiftieth*): *Christian and Jewish Festival* Also known as Whitsunday [qv]. In the Jewish calendar [qv] Pentecost comes fifty days after Passover [qv] and marks the end of the biblical Palestinian grain harvest, a period of forty-nine days or seven weeks. In the Bible [qv] it is called the Feast of Weeks/Harvest/First Fruits (*Shabuot* [qv] in Hebrew). It is also known as the anniversary of receiving of the Jewish Law, an aspect stressed by Reform Jews [qv]. In the Christian calendar [qv] Pentecost is celebrated on the seventh Sunday after Easter [qv] in memory of when the Holy Spirit descended upon the followers of Jesus Christ on the fiftieth day after his resurrection. The Church celebrates Pentecost as the Feast of the Holy Spirit and as its own birthday. During early Christianity [*qv*], converts were baptized during the festival. Since they wore white garments, the festival acquired the title Whit(e)sunday in the English-speaking world.

People's Democratic Republic of Yemen, 1970–90: *see* South Yemen.

People's Republic of South Yemen, 1967–70: *see* South Yemen.

Peres, Shimon (1923–): *Israeli politician; prime minister, 1984–86, 1995–96* Born Shimon Persky into a middle-class household in Poland, Peres was eleven when his family migrated to Palestine [*qv*]. After studying at an agricultural school, he joined a kibbutz. From 1941 to 1944 he was secretary of a Zionist youth group. Active within Haganah [*qv*] since 1941, he was promoted to its command six years later and assigned the task of procuring weapons. By the end of the Arab-Israeli War (1948–49) [*qv*], he had become commander of the Israeli navy. Between 1953 and 1959 he served as the defense ministry's director general. Among other things he reinforced Israel's military links with the Western nations, especially in the nuclear weapons program, developed with the assistance of France.

He entered the Knesset [*qv*] in 1959 on a Mapai [*qv*] ticket and has retained a seat ever since. From 1960 to 1965 he served as deputy defense minister. He left Mapai and became secretary-general of Rafi [*qv*], led by David Ben-Gurion [*qv*], in 1965. When the Labor Party [*qv*] was formed in 1968 Peres joined it and became its deputy secretary-general. The next year he joined Golda Meir's [*qv*] cabinet as minister without portfolio. He served as transport minister from 1971–74, followed by a short stint as information minister. Prime Minister Yitzhak Rabin [*qv*] appointed him defense minister from 1974–77.

In contravention of party policy, Peres compromised with the ultranationalist Gush Emunim [*qv*] when they set up a settlement in Kadum, thus setting the stage for Jewish colonization in central West Bank [*qv*].

In a determined challenge to Rabin for party leadership in 1976, Peres lost by 1,404 votes to 1,445. But following Rabin's resignation in the wake of the disclosure that, as Israel's ambassador to the U.S., his wife had maintained an active bank account there, an illegal act, party delegates elected Peres their leader. In the May 1977 election he lost to Likud [*qv*], led by Menachem Begin [*qv*]. After the indecisive result of the 1984 election, Peres concluded a coalition and rotation deal with Likud, now led by Yitzhak Shamir [*qv*], and became prime minister of a national unity government from 1984–86. Peres oversaw Israel's withdrawal from Lebanon (except for a border security strip), and reduced the inherited runaway inflation to a manageable level. He served as deputy premier and foreign minister from 1986–88. With the 1988 poll mirroring the previous stalemate, Peres renewed his power-sharing agreement with Likud. In the Shamir-led cabinet he became deputy premier and finance minister. Peres's differences with Shamir on how to proceed with the Middle East peace process led to his resignation from the government in March 1990 and Labor's withdrawal from the ruling coalition.

In the 1992 leadership contest he lost to his longtime rival, Rabin. After Labor's victory in the June 1992 poll Peres was appointed foreign minister. But Premier Rabin allowed him to deal only with multilateral talks with the Arab countries, initiated by the Middle East Peace Conference in Madrid in October 1991. Once Israel had lifted its ban on contact with the Palestine Liberation Organization (PLO) [qv] in January 1993, Peres became involved in the secret talks with the PLO in Norway. The resulting Israeli-PLO Accord [qv], concluded in September 1993 in Washington, was a personal triumph for him. A year later he saw his peace efforts elsewhere culminate in a Jordanian-Israeli Peace Treaty [qv]. He shared the 1994 Nobel Peace Prize with Rabin and Yasser Arafat [qv]. Following the assassination of Rabin in November 1995, Peres became prime minister.

He lost to Benjamin Netanyahu [qv] in the prime ministerial poll of May 1996. In the subsequent cabinet of Ehud Barak [qv], formed after the May 1999 election, he was appointed minister without portfolio. In the national unity government of Ariel Sharon [qv], formed in March 2001, he became foreign minister. As the member of the inner cabinet, which included him and Labor Defense Minister Binyamin Ben-Eliezer, Peres claimed to have moderated the more extreme actions proposed by Sharon to quell the Second Intifada [qv] of the Palestinians and curb Islamist terrorists. He resigned his post when the Labor Party decided to quit the national unity administration in November 2002.

Persia and Persians: Persia is a derivative of Parsa, modern Fars, the southern region of Iran. The Indo-European nomads who migrated into the area from the Caucasus around 1000 B.C. were known as Parsa. By the seventh century B.C. they were established in southern Iran, then part of the Assyrian Empire. From early on Persian rulers were associated with the Medes.

Cyrus the Great (600–529 B.C.), first of the Achaemenians, declared himself ruler of Media in 559 BC and expanded his realm into the great Persian Empire. The Persians borrowed Assyrian political structures and Babylonian and Egyptian arts. Darius I (r. 521–486 B.C.) established a centralized government and extended his empire east into modern Afghanistan and northwest India and as far north as the Danube River.

The empire began to decline from the mid-fifth century B.C., with regional governors acquiring greater powers and Egypt breaking away. Its death knell came when Alexander the Great (r. 336–23) defeated the Achaemenians on the Granicus in 334 B.C., and in the Battle of Guagamela in 331 B.C. he destroyed the entire Achaemenian Empire. Following Alexander's death, most of the Persian Empire fell to his successors, the Seleucids, who were unable to maintain control.

Parthia, which seceded in 250 B.C., emerged as a successor to the old Persian Empire. Following its decline a new empire of Sassanians emerged in A.D. 226. It reestablished Zoroastrianism [qv] as the state religion. The Sassanian Empire reached its peak under Anushirvan (r.531–79) and then declined until its overthrow by invading Muslim Arabs [qv] in A.D. 640. Islam [qv] replaced Zoroastrianism as the official religion, and the caliphate made Persia part of an Islamic empire, from which modern Iran was later to emerge.

Persian Gulf: *see* The Gulf.

Persian language: Also known as Farsi. The principal language of the Iranian branch of the Indo-European family, Persian is divided into (1) Old Persian, the language of ancient Persia, written in cuneiform characters and in use until the third century B.C.; (2)

Middle Persian, including Pahlavi [*qv*] and Parsi, the chief language of Zoroastrian [*qv*] and Manichaean literature, both written in Aramaic script and dominant between the third century B.C. and the ninth century A.D.; and (3) Modern Persian, dating from the ninth century A.D., written in the Arabic script and the language used in the finest examples of Persian literature.

Pesach *(Hebrew: Passover): see* Passover.

petroleum *(Latin: from petra, a rock + oleum, oil): see* oil.

Phalange and Phalangists (Lebanon): *Lebanese political party and militia* Official title: Lebanese Kataeb Social Democratic Party. The Phalange is a derivative of *phalanx* (or battalion), the literal translation of the Arabic word *Kataeb*. It was established in November 1936 by Pierre Gemayel [*qv*], who had been inspired by the Nazi Youth Movement rallies he had seen during his visit to the Berlin Olympics in the summer.

The party attracted Christian [*qv*] youths from the mountainous Metn region, the heartland of the Maronites [*qv*], and Christian students in Beirut [*qv*]. It participated in the talks that led to the National Pact of 1943 [*qv*], which formalized Christian domination of the state. Its popularity was enhanced by the discovery in 1949 of a plot by the Syrian Social Nationalist Party [*qv*] to merge Lebanon with Syria and the nationalist reaction that this aroused among Christians.

Its pro-Western stance and opposition to pan-Arabism [*qv*] led it to back President Camille Chamoun [*qv*] in the 1958 Lebanese Civil War [*qv*]. Its initial support for President Fuad Chehab [*qv*] waned when he tried to strengthen state powers at the expense of the financial and commercial oligarchs who had led the Phalange. By aligning with the parties of Chamoun and Raymond Edde in the 1968 poll, it increased its parliamentary share from four to nine among the thirty Maronite seats.

Its leaders began to highlight the presence of Palestinians, whose numbers had been boosted by the June 1967 Arab-Israeli War [*qv*] and the 1970–71 Jordanian Civil War [*qv*]. On the eve of the Lebanese Civil War of 1975–90 [*qv*] the party, now 20,000 strong, had a militia under the command of Bashir Gemayel [*qv*], who later became commander of a coalition of Maronite militias, the Lebanese Forces (LF) [*qv*]. Politically it was part of an umbrella organization called the Lebanese Front [*qv*], led by Chamoun. Working in collaboration with the U.S. and Israeli intelligence agencies, it confronted its adversaries, the Lebanese National Movement [*qv*], which was allied with the Palestinians. In mid-June 1976, facing defeat, its leaders welcomed Syrian armed intervention on their side. But since they refused to sever their ties with Israel, their relations with Syria turned frosty.

Intent on eliminating any serious rivals to his dominance in the Christian camp, in the summer of 1980 Bashir Gemayel used the Phalange militia to wipe out the militia of Chamoun's National Liberal Party [*qv*], and largely succeeded. In early 1982 he began to liaise with Israel in its plans to attack Lebanon. The invasion occurred in June, and by September the Phalange had been catapulted into the leading position, with Bashir Gemayel elected to the presidency. But his assassination some days before taking office changed the situation. Though his elder brother, Amin [*qv*], a Phalange member, won the presidential election, the party had lost its most ambitious leader, and the death of Pierre

Gemayel in August 1984 deprived it of a much respected patriarch.

In early 1985 Samir Geagea, a leading member of the LF Command Council, declared the LF independent of the Phalange in security, policing, and finance, thus depriving it of much of its influence. This occurred just at the point when it had agreed to hand over to the Lebanese government various public departments it had usurped and run in the Christian enclave for several years. In the subsequent fighting Geagea won full control of the LF, further reducing the power of Amin Gemayel. After Gemayel had stepped down as president of Lebanon in September 1988 and left the country, the party's influence declined further. Guided by Geagea, it backed the Taif Accord [qv]. This caused a rift in the Lebanese Front, with the anti-Geagea faction siding with Gen. Michel Aoun [qv], who challenged the newly elected President Elias Hrawi [qv]. After the defeat of Aoun in October 1990, many Phalange offices were taken over by the pro-Syrian forces. Later the party cooperated with the government in its plans to disarm the militias. The national unity government formed in December 1990 included Geagea and another Phalange leader, Georges Saade. But in March 1991 Geagea resigned and went on to transform the LF into a political party. Due to its decision to boycott the 1992 general election, the Phalange's influence waned. Its headquarters was blown up in December.

Poale Agudat Israel (*Hebrew: Workers of the Union of Israel*): *Israeli political party* Formed in Katowice, Poland, in 1922 as the worker's section of Agudat Israel [qv] to safeguard the rights of religious Jewish workers, Poale Agudat Israel (PAI) set up a branch in Palestine [qv] a year later. In 1933 it founded its first kibbutz [qv]. It began cooperating with the World Zionist Organization (WZO) [qv] in the colonization of Palestine, including organizing illegal immigration. After the establishment of Israel in 1948, it expanded its educational and settlement activities.

On the eve of the general election in 1949, it allied with Agudat Israel as well as Mizrahi [qv] and Poale HaMizrahi [qv] to form the United Religious Front [qv]. In the 1951 poll it joined with Agudat Israel to form the Torah Religious Front [qv], which won five seats. The Front participated in the next Mapai-led [qv] government, but quit in 1952 in protest against the law prescribing conscription for women. While maintaining a separate existence the two Agudat groups, winning two to six seats, stayed in opposition throughout the Mapai/Labor-led [qv] governments until May 1977, when the PAI won one seat and merged with Agudat Israel.

Poale HaMizrahi (*Hebrew: Workers of the Spiritual Center*): *Israeli political party* Also known as HaPoale HaMizrahi. Since the branch of the Mizrahi [qv] in Palestine had many workers, its younger members formed Poale HaMizrahi in 1921. In turn, Poale HaMizrahi formed a confederation of trade unions, a group of *kibbutizim* [qv], and a network of religiously oriented schools. It acquired a separate identity from its parent body. Both organizations participated in the Zionist movement [qv] and in the quasi-governmental organs of Yishuv [qv]. After the Second World War, it was active in sponsoring illegal Jewish immigration.

In the run-up to the Israeli general election in 1949 it allied with three other religious parties to form the United Religious Front [qv], which won sixteen seats and joined the government. In the 1951 poll it allied with Mizrahi and won ten seats, improving the total by one in the next election in 1955 and rejoining the coalition government. The next year Poale HaMizrahi united with Mizrahi to form Mafdal, the National Religious Party [*qv*].

Poale Zion *(Hebrew: Workers of Zion): Zionist organization in Palestine* The first Zionist workers' party, Poale Zion was formed in the Russian city of Minsk (now in Belarus) in 1900 with a program of socialism, Zionism [*qv*], and migration to Palestine [*qv*]. It set up a branch in Palestine. Growing cooperation between socialist pioneers and the World Zionist Organization (WZO) [*qv*] caused a split in Poale Zion, its leftist section leaving in 1919 to form Mopsi (Socialist Workers Party), and its rightist, nationalist faction merging with the followers of Berle Katznelson to found Ahdut HaAvodah [*qv*].

poll tax: *an across-the-board tax on every member of a group* To keep the Arab conquerors separate from the conquered people, the early caliphs of the Umayyad period (A.D. 661–750) confined their soldiers to garrison towns. They provided protection to the non-Muslim population on payment of a poll tax, a practice initiated by the Prophet Muhammad after his victory at Khaibar, an oasis populated by Jewish tribes. The practice continued among Muslim rulers, who exempted non-Muslim subjects from military service and charged them a poll tax in exchange for the provision of security, the last such example being during the Ottoman Empire, which ended in 1918. *See also dhimmis.*

Popular Bloc (Bahrain): *Bahraini political party* After the Bahraini constitution had been promulgated in June 1973, the Bahrain National Liberation Front allied with the Bahrain Nationalist Movement to form the Popular Bloc, with a nationalist-leftist program, under the leadership of Hussein Musa. In the election for the forty-two-member National Assembly, held on a restricted franchise of 30,000 adult males, it secured twenty-one of the thirty elected seats. Led by Muhsin Mahrun, Popular Bloc members demanded the introduction of income tax, trade union rights, votes for women, and the nationalization of large Western-owned companies. The ruler, Shaikh Isa al Khalifa [*qv*], responded by issuing a draconian state security law in October 1974. The Popular Bloc protested. Alleging that parliament had debated "foreign" ideas and principles, the ruler dissolved it in August 1975, arresting most Popular Bloc leaders and destroying their party.

Popular Democratic Party (Saudi Arabia): *Saudi political party* In 1970, former members of the Arab Nationalist Movement [*qv*], remnants of the local Baath party, and the Marxists outside the National Liberation Front combined to form the Popular Democratic Party (PDP). Committed to liberating Saudi Arabia from Western imperialism by an armed struggle, it stressed the need to form a broad national front to oppose the royal dictatorship. Unusually for a Saudi group, it set up a special women's section. It drew most of its support from students and petty civil servants. Since belonging to it was a capital offense, its membership inside the country was minuscule. As a largely expatriate body, active among Saudi students studying abroad and long-term exiles, it had no impact on domestic events. With the decline of radical politics by the late 1980s, it lost support even among Saudi expatriates.

Popular Front for the Liberation of the Occupied Arab Gulf (1968–71): At its second congress in September 1968 in South Yemen, a Marxist state, the Dhofari Liberation Front (DFL) decided to extend its revolutionary activities to the rest of Oman and other Gulf states [*qv*] and changed its name to the Popular Front for the Liberation of the Occupied Arab Gulf (PFLOAG). Opposed to imperialism, neocolonialism, and local oligarchies, the PFLOAG committed itself to achieving a socialist revolution and stressed the importance of Dhofar as a link between South Yemen and the Gulf states. Besides South Yemen, the People's Republic of China backed it.

Nearly two years later, having brought two-thirds of Dhofar under its control, the PFLOAG extended its activities to the Oman region of the sultanate. This alarmed the British, the dominant political power in the country, and led to a London-engineered coup that replaced Sultan Said ibn Taimur [*qv*] with his son, Qaboos [*qv*]. The latter initiated political-social reform and modernization and expanded the military under the British aegis. In response, the third congress of the PFLOAG in 1971 lowered its sights from effecting a socialist revolution to effecting a national democratic revolution. It opened party membership to non-Marxist nationalists and renamed itself the Popular Front for the Liberation of Oman and the Arab Gulf [*qv*].

Popular Front for the Liberation of Oman (1974–82): Faced with a vigorous onslaught by its enemy, the congress of the Popular Front for the Liberation of Oman and the Arab Gulf (PFLOAG) [*qv*], meeting in July 1974, decided to narrow its field of action to Oman and renamed its organization the Popular Front for the Liberation of Oman (PFLO). Within a year the Soviet Union had begun supplying arms to the PFLO and training its cadres. But this was not enough to enable it to withstand the offensives that the Omani army, along with the Iranian troops—assisted by Britain, Egypt and Jordan—launched in 1975. With South Yemen ceasing its assistance in order to placate Saudi Arabia, the PFLO agreed to a cease-fire in 1976. But once Iran had withdrawn most of its troops in early 1977, PFLO fighters began to regroup. However, their activities from 1978–79 did not go beyond sporadic attacks and assassinations. Once Oman and South Yemen had formally recognized each other and signed a normalization agreement in 1982, the PFLO ceased to exist.

Popular Front for the Liberation of Oman and the Arab Gulf (1971–74): In 1971 the third congress of the Popular Front for the Liberation of the Occupied Arab Gulf [*qv*] lowered its sights from effecting a socialist revolution to effecting a national democratic revolution. It opened party membership to non-Marxist nationalists and renamed itself the Popular Front for the Liberation of Oman and the Arab Gulf (PFLOAG). The resulting increase in its strength enabled it to withstand three offensives by the British-led Omani forces, backed by British counterinsurgency units, between October 1971 and September 1972. The Omani sultan and his British backers redoubled their efforts, securing aid and assistance from Saudi Arabia and Jordan, and finally from Iran, which entered the fray in 1973. Faced with this opposition, the next PFLOAG congress in July 1974 decided to limit its activities to Oman, and the organization was renamed the Popular Front for the Liberation of Oman (PFLO) [*qv*]. However, a PFLOAG branch was set up in Bahrain.

Once the British had departed from Bahrain in mid-1971 and the ruler, Shaikh Isa al Khalifa [*qv*], had made desultory moves to share power with his ministers, the PFLOAG's Bahraini section began to flex its muscles. Along with the Bahrain National Liberation Front, it twice called a general strike. Shaikh Isa agreed to hold elections to a constituent assembly, but because of his refusal to release all political prisoners and grant votes to women, the PFLOAG boycotted the poll. It did the same when a general election was held in December 1973. In the crackdown that followed the dissolution of parliament in August 1975, many PFLOAG leaders were jailed.

Popular Front for the Liberation of Palestine: *Palestinian political party* The Popular Front for the Liberation of Palestine (PFLP) was formed in December 1967 by a merger between the Palestinian section of the Arab Nationalist Movement [*qv*] and the Syria-based Palestine Liberation Front, under the leadership of George Habash [*qv*]. The next year it affiliated to the Palestine Liberation Organization (PLO) [*qv*]. At its first (open) congress in February 1969, the PFLP described Israel, the World Zionist movement [*qv*], world imperialism, and Arab reaction in the region as the enemies of the Palestinian cause. The PFLP resolved to mobilize Palestinian workers and peasants, in alliance with the petty bourgeoisie, and to start a guerrilla struggle as a step toward a

national liberation war. It emulated the organizational structure of a communist party.

The congress, elected by members every four years and meeting every alternate year, was the PFLP's highest body. It elected the central committee, which in turn chose the political bureau (*politburo*). The congress also had the authority to elect the secretary-general, a position occupied by Habash since the party's inception until his formal retirement due to ill health in April 2000.

The PFLP's campaign inside the Occupied Territories [*qv*] involved 220 armed operations in 1970. Between 7 and 9 September 1970 its members hijacked three airliners, took them to an abandoned airfield near Amman [*qv*], emptied them of passengers, and blew them up. This triggered fighting between the Palestinian commandos and the Jordanian army, which the former lost. The PFLP then moved its main operational base to Lebanon. Its militia was the third largest among Palestinian after Fatah [*qv*] and Saiqa [*qv*].

Making no distinction between Zionist objects or persons inside Israel or outside, it attacked Israeli targets abroad—mainly by hijacking airliners and making political demands. Between July 1968 and December 1973, when the party congress suspended its activity against Israeli targets abroad, the PFLP conducted sixteen foreign operations.

When in 1974 the Palestine National Council (PNC) [*qv*] accepted the idea of a Palestinian state on the West Bank [*qv*] and Gaza [*qv*] as an intermediate step toward the liberation of all of mandate Palestine, the PFLP boycotted the PLO executive committee and the central council. In the late 1970s, when the Soviet Union began to offer military training to PLO activists, the PFLP was included in the program. It ended its boycott of the PLO institutions in 1981.

After the expulsion of the PLO from Beirut [*qv*] in September 1982 the PFLP moved its headquarters to Damascus [*qv*], but did not join the Syrian-instigated fight against Yasser Arafat [*qv*] and Fatah [*qv*]. However, after Arafat's agreement with King Hussein [*qv*] of Jordan to pursue a joint negotiating strategy in early 1985, the PFLP joined with the pro-Syrian Palestinian factions to form the Palestine National Salvation Front. After the PNC had disowned Arafat's deal with King Hussein in April 1987, the PFLP rejoined the PLO executive committee and other PLO institutions. In November 1988, while opposing the resolution before the PNC to accept a Palestinian state in part of Palestine and peaceful coexistence with Israel, the PFLP accepted the majority decision to adopt the resolution.

During the crisis created by Iraq's invasion of Kuwait in August 1990, the PFLP backed President Saddam Hussein [*qv*], especially when the latter tried to link Iraq's evacuation of Kuwait to Israel's withdrawal from the Occupied Arab Territories [*qv*]. The PFLP opposed the Israeli-PLO Accord [*qv*] of September 1993 and the Jordanian-Israeli Peace Treaty [*qv*] of October 1994.

In 1999, Abu Ali Mustafa, the moderate deputy of Habash, was allowed to return to the West Bank [*qv*], where he set up office in Ramallah. After the formal retirement of Habash as the party's secretary-general in 2000, he succeeded Habash. In July 2001, after Mustafa was assassinated by the Israeli military, Ahmad Saadat, a hardliner,

became the secretary-general. Following the assassination of Israeli tourism minister Gen. Zeevi Rechavam in retribution for Mustafa's killing, in October by PFLP activists, Saadat was arrested by the Palestinian Authority [*qv*] under pressure by Israel.

Popular Front for the Liberation of Palestine-General Command: *Palestinian political party* Having merged his Palestine Liberation Front with the Palestinian section of the Arab Nationalist Movement [*qv*] to form the Popular Front for the Liberation of Palestine (PFLP) [*qv*] in late 1967, Ahmad Jibril [*qv*] led his supporters out of the PFLP about a year later to form the Popular Front for the Liberation of Palestine-General Command (PFLP-GC). It then affiliated to the Palestine Liberation Organization (PLO) [*qv*].

The PFLP-GC carried out several operations against Israel and Israeli targets, including planting a bomb onboard a Swissair flight from Zurich to Tel Aviv [*qv*] in February 1970, which exploded and killed forty-seven passengers and crew. Four years later, in a failed attempt to exchange their Israeli hostages—taken at Kiryat Shimona—for 100 Palestinian prisoners, three members of the PFLP-GC and eighteen Israelis were killed.

After the 1982 Israeli invasion of Lebanon [*qv*], when the PLO's constituents were forced to vacate Beirut [*qv*], the PFLP-GC moved its headquarters to Damascus [*qv*]. In 1983 it joined an anti-Yasser Arafat [*qv*] rebellion masterminded by Syrian President Hafiz Assad [*qv*]. In May 1985 Israel granted the release of 1,150 Palestinian detainees and convicted prisoners in exchange for three Israeli soldiers captured by the PFLP-GC during the 1982 Israeli invasion of Lebanon. In late November 1987, three PFLP-GC activists mounted a hangglider raid from southern Lebanon on an Israeli military outpost, resulting in six Israeli deaths. This proved pivotal in sparking the intifada [qv] on 9 December.

Although the PFLP-GC was secular, socialist, and nationalist, in the late-1980s it began to form links with Iran, with Jibril visiting Tehran periodically. PFLP-GC propaganda began referring to the "Arab and Islamic people" and the "Arab and Islamic region."

After the blowing up of a Pan-Am airliner near the Scottish town of Lockerbie in December 1988 (causing the death of 278 people, in probable retaliation for the U.S. Navy shooting down an Iranian civilian airliner in July 1988, killing 290 people), U.S. intelligence sources alleged that the PFLP-GC was responsible for the act (later the blame was shifted to the agents of Libya).

In the Kuwait crisis and the Second Gulf War [qv], the PFLP-GC backed Iraqi President Saddam Hussein [qv]. But despite brave statements before and during the conflict, it did not carry out any terrorist acts.

It rejected the Israeli-PLO Accord [qv] of September 1993, because it failed to concede Palestinians' right to self-determination and the right of refugees to return home.

With Jibril moving closer to Iran, the PFLP-GC split in 1999.

Popular Islamic Conferences (Iraq): During the 1980–88 Iran-Iraq War [qv], in order to parallel Tehran in the religious arena, Iraqi President Saddam Hussein [qv] sponsored the First Popular Islamic Conference in Baghdad in April 1983. Attended by 280 clergy and pious laymen from fifty countries, it was presided by Shaikh Ali Kashif Ghita, a leading Shia [qv] cleric from Najaf [qv] who was noted for his religious branding of Ayatollah Ruhollah Khomeini [qv] as a heretic. Having backed Iraq's position on the war (withdrawal to the international borders) the conference tried to mediate between the belligerents, an enterprise that failed due to Iran's hostility.

The Second Popular Islamic Conference was held in Baghdad in April 1985 and was attended by 300 Iraqi and foreign clerics and pious laymen. As before, it sided with Iraq in the conflict and urged all Muslim countries to sever their links with Iran. For the next few months, Iraqi clergy addressed rallies in Iraq explaining the conference resolutions. Their overall aim was to convince Iraqis that their regime revered Islam [qv], and that the Muslim world was behind Iraq in its struggle against the heretical leaders of Iran.

The third conference, meeting on 11 January 1991 in Baghdad, called for a jihad [qv] if Iraq was attacked by the U.S.-led coalition that had been formed to expel Iraq from Kuwait, which it had occupied since August 1990.

Progressive List for Peace (Israel): *Israeli political party* The Progressive List for Peace was formed in 1984 under the leadership of Muhammad Miari and Matityahu Peled, a retired Israeli general, on the eve of the 1984 general election. Its goals were recognition of the Palestine Liberation Organization (PLO) [qv] and the founding of a Palestinian state in the West Bank [qv] and Gaza [qv]. It won two seats in 1984 election, followed by one in 1988 and none in 1992.

Progressive Party (Israel): *Israel political party* Shortly after the founding of Israel in May 1948, the liberal "A" faction of the General Zionists [*qv*] left its parent body to combine with the German-dominated *Aliyah Hadasha* (New Immigrants) Party, a moderate faction, and *HaOved HaTzioni* (The Zionist Worker) to form the Progressive Party. With four to six deputies in the first four Knessets [*qv*], from 1949 to 1959 it participated in most of the Mapai-dominated [*qv*] governments. In 1961 it merged with the General Zionists to form the Liberal Party [*qv*].

Progressive Socialist Party (Lebanon): The Progressive Socialist Party (PSP) was formed in 1949 by Kamal Jumblat [*qv*]. Predominantly Druze [*qv*], it had some Sunni [*qv*], Shia [*qv*], and Christian [*qv*] members. The party adopted a pan-Arabist [*qv*], left-of-center program that opposed the confessionalism [*qv*] built into the 1943 National Pact [*qv*]. In the 1958 Lebanese Civil War [*qv*], Jumblat assumed leadership of the camp opposed to the pro-Western President Camille Chamoun [*qv*].

As political consciousness among Muslims increased due to the events in the region and the growing presence of armed Palestinian commandos, the importance of the party and its leader rose. It was an important member of the National Progressive Front, forged by Jumblat in 1969 and three years later enlarged and renamed the Front of National and Progressive Parties and Forces. With the outbreak of the Lebanese Civil War in April 1975 [*qv*], the leadership of the nationalist-leftist camp once again rested with the PSP chief, Kamal Jumblat. After his assassination in March 1977 his son, Walid

[*qv*], became the PSP leader. He moderated the party line and repaired relations with Syria, which had been soured by his father.

After the Israeli invasion of Lebanon [*qv*] in June 1982, the PSP found itself on the defensive against the onslaught of the Israeli-backed Maronite [*qv*] militias. In September 1983 the PSP militia played an important role in frustrating the Western attempt to bolster the Lebanese army, which was commanded largely by Maronite officers. In February 1984 the party militia allied with the fighters of Amal [*qv*] and expelled the Maronite-controlled Lebanese army from West Beirut.

The PSP was a leading actor at the reconciliation conference held in Switzerland in March 1984. But in December 1985 Jumblat, along with the commanders of Amal and the Lebanese Forces (breakaway faction) [*qv*], failed in his attempt to end the conflict on the basis of a "National Agreement to Solve the Lebanese Crisis." To frustrate the designs of Gen. Michel Aoun [*qv*], the PSP joined thirteen other parties in August 1989 to form the Lebanese National Front, which was committed to defeating Aoun's political and military program. The PSP had reservations about the Taif Accord [*qv*] because it did not sufficiently curtail presidential powers and did not treat Muslim Lebanese equitably. But aware of Syria's strong backing of the Accord, it desisted from protesting.

Following the end of the civil war in October 1990, some 2,800 fighters from the PSP militia, which at its peak had 15,500 armed men, were taken into the regular Lebanese army. Jumblat was appointed as a minister in the national unity government that followed. The PSP participated in the

1992 general election, and after his election to parliament, Jumblat became minister for displaced persons. Following the 1996 parliamentary poll, in which the PSP won ten seats, including seven of the eight seats reserved for Druzes, Jumblat returned to his old ministerial post. When the newly elected president, Emile Lahoud [*qv*], in 1998 named Salim Hoss [*qv*] as the prime minister, he did not offer Jumblat, a close ally of the outgoing Rafiq Hariri [*qv*], a place in his cabinet. In the 2000 parliamentary poll, Jumblat demanded the withdrawal of the Syrian troops from Lebanon, thus appearing to make a common cause with Maronite Christian [*qv*] politicians. With the general election results indicating a rejection of the Hoss government, President Lahoud naming Hariri as the new prime minister, and the PSP winning sixteen seats, including seven allocated to Druzes, Jumblat's nominee, Marwan Hamadeh, became minister of displaced persons.

Protestant Christians/Church: *Christian sect* In general, a Christian not belonging to the Roman Catholic Church [*qv*] or the Orthodox Church [*qv*] is described as Protestant. Protestants consider the Bible [*qv*] to be the central source of Christian teaching. Protestant churches emerged as part of a religious revolution in Western Europe in the sixteenth century, starting as a reform movement in the Catholic Church. The major Protestant schools are Adventist, Anabaptist, Baptist, Calvanist, Congregationalist, Lutheran, Methodist, Modernist, Presbyterian, Puritan, and Unitarian.

Protocol of Constantinople (1913): Under the terms of the Protocol of Tehran (1911) [*qv*], representatives of the Ottoman

Empire, Persia (now Iran), Russia, and Britain met in Constantinople (now Istanbul) to delineate the boundary from Mount Ararat to the Persian Gulf [*qv*] and redefine navigational rights in the Shatt al Arab [*qv*], which formed the fluvial border between Iran and the easternmost province of the Ottoman Empire. Since Britain, keen to develop an oil industry in Iran, needed extensive port facilities along the waterway, the new protocol awarded to Iran five small islands and one largish one in the Shatt al Arab between Muhammara (later Khorramshahr) and the sea. It was confirmed in 1914, and followed by the appointment of a Delimitation Commission, in which Britain and Russia had powers of arbitration. By the time the First World War broke out in mid-1914 a definitive map of the frontier had been produced and 227 boundary pillars installed.

Protocol of Tehran (1911): The Protocol of Tehran, signed in 1911, outlined a basis for negotiations between Persia (now Iran) and the Ottoman Empire, and set up a Joint Delimitation Commission consisting of representatives of the Ottoman Empire, Persia, Russia, and Britain.

Protocol of Uqair (1922): The Protocol of Uqair was imposed by Sir Percy Cox, the British high commissioner in Baghdad [*qv*], on Kuwait and Najd [*qv*] (later Saudi Arabia) in December 1922. It carved out a neutral zone between Najd and Kuwait (the Saudi Arabia-Kuwait Neutral Zone [*qv*]). It confirmed the inner (red) line of the 1913 Anglo-Ottoman Convention [*qv*] regarding Kuwait's southern border with Najd, but did not define Kuwait's northern frontier with Iraq. In April 1923, when Shaikh Ahmad I al Sabah [*qv*] of Kuwait claimed the outer (green) line of the 1913 Anglo-Ottoman Convention as applying to the area north of Kuwait port, Sir Percy replied that his claim to the frontier and offshore islands was recognized as far as London was concerned. This limited Iraq's access to the Gulf [*qv*]to a mere 36 miles/58 km of coastline infested with swamps and marshland, thus denying it the possibility of a deepwater harbor and of becoming an important naval power in the region. King Faisal I of Iraq [*qv*] was disappointed, but with his country under British mandate he had no choice but to ratify Iraq's boundaries with its neighbors as decided by the British official.

Q

Qaboos ibn Said (1940–): *Sultan of Oman, 1970– ; prime minister, 1970–* Born in Salalah, Qaboos was educated privately at the royal palace and then at a private college in Bury St. Edmunds, Britain. After graduating from the Royal Military Academy at Sandhurst, he served briefly with the British forces stationed in West Germany, and then took courses in social studies at a British university. After being recalled home in 1965, he was put under surveillance at the Salalah royal palace. Among his visitors were British expatriates whom his father, Sultan Said ibn Taimur [*qv*], trusted. Some of them were used by London to plot the deposition of Sultan Said, which occurred on 23 July 1970.

After becoming sultan as well as prime minister and defense and foreign minister, Qaboos ended Oman's isolation by securing

it membership in the Arab League [*qv*] and the United Nations. Aided by rising oil output, which reached a peak of 400,000 barrels per day in the mid-1970s, he built or expanded the economic infrastructure and provided social services to Omani nationals. He intensified the campaign against the leftist insurgency in Dhofar that had been in progress since 1963. He expanded the army with a large intake of foreign mercenaries, especially Pakistanis. In 1973 he turned to Iran for extra troops. With British, Saudi, Egyptian, Jordanian, and Iranian backing, he crushed the Dhofari rebellion by late 1975.

Qaboos was alone in the Arab world in endorsing Egypt's Camp David Accords [*qv*] with Israel, and did not cut ties with it after the signing of a peace treaty between the two countries. He was the only Gulf leader to sign a military accord with Washington in mid-1980, allowing it to use Oman's harbors and airports and to stockpile arms and ammunition on its soil. He ended his regional isolation after the outbreak of the Iran-Iraq War [*qv*] in September 1980 by taking a pro-Iraqi position along with other Gulf rulers. He was a cofounder of the Gulf Cooperation Council (GCC) [*qv*] in 1981. However, belated awareness of Oman's proximity to Iran at the mouth of the Hormuz Straits [*qv*] made Qaboos adopt a neutral stand in the First Gulf War. Along with other GCC rulers, he backed Kuwait after it had been occupied by Iran in August 1990. He joined the United States-led coalition against Iraq. After the war he signed a ten-year military access agreement with Washington.

While refusing to provide Oman with a written constitution, he transferred the existing 45 member advisory body into a 60 member counsultative council.

Having endorsed the Oslo Accord I [*qv*] in September 1993, he hosted a multilateral conference, sponsored as part of the Middle East peace process [*qv*], in Muscat [*qv*].

In the face of growing indications of popular disaffection at the absence of a written constitution and his refusal to share his absolute power, Qaboos promulgated a constitution in late 1996, which incorporated the already existing fully nominated consultative council with scant legislative authority. He had to deploy troops to curb rioting in Hajar. Qaboos responded by ordering direct elections to the consultative council in 2000.

The next year he renewed Oman's ten-year military access agreement with America. In Washington's war against the Taliban-administered Afghanistan in October 2001, Qaboos allowed the Pentagon use of its military facilities after it agreed to sell Oman advanced weapons worth $1.2 billion.

al Qaida: *see* Al Qaida

Qasim, Abdul Karim (1914–63): *Iraqi military leader and politician; prime minister, 1958–63* Born of a Sunni [*qv*] father and a Shia [*qv*] mother in a lower-middle-class home in Baghdad [*qv*], Qasim graduated from the local military academy and became a commissioned officer in 1938. He fought in the 1948–49 Palestine War [*qv*] as a lieutenant-colonel. Along with Col. Abdul Salam Arif [*qv*], Qasim led the Free Officers group from its formation in 1956. It overthrew King Faisal II [*qv*] on 14 July 1958, assassinated the royal family, and declared a republic. Instead of forming a military Revolutionary Command Council as the coup

leaders in Egypt had done in 1952, Qasim headed a civilian-dominated cabinet of 14 as the prime minister, with additional responsibility for defense as both defense minister and military chief of staff. He became known as the Sole Leader.

In the debate that followed on Iraq's unification with the United Arab Republic (UAR) [*qv*], Qasim led the anti-unity camp and ousted the pan-Arabist Arif from office in September. A year later he curbed the Communist Party [*qv*], which had backed him in his opposition to union with the UAR. By playing the pro-unionist and anti-unionist camps against each other, he became isolated, inadvertently paving the way for his own downfall. He carried out agrarian reform.

Having made peace with Kurdish nationalists, Qasim invited their leader, Mustafa Barzani [*qv*], to return home from the Soviet Union. But, when Barzani demanded autonomy, Qasim mounted a campaign against the Kurds [*qv*].

Qasim withdrew Iraq from the Baghdad Pact [*qv*]. He hosted a conference of Iran, Iraq, Kuwait, Saudi Arabia, and Venezuela in September 1960 to form the Organization of Petroleum Exporting Countries (OPEC) [*qv*] to serve as a collective bargaining agency. His decree in 1961 deprived the Iraq Petroleum Company (IPC) of 99.5 percent of the 160,000 sq. miles/414,400 sq. km originally allocated to it for prospecting. In June 1961, when Kuwait became independent, Qasim claimed that it was part of Iraq. This created a crisis, and Qasim found himself being opposed by, among others, the Arab League [*qv*], which sent a Joint Emergency Force to Kuwait. This defused the situation, but only after Kuwait had made substantial secret subventions to Iraq.

An alliance of Baathist [*qv*] civilians and military officers, and Abdul Salam Arif, toppled Qasim's regime on 8 February 1963 and executed Qasim and his close aides.

Qassam, Izz al Din (1881–1935): *Palestinian leader* Born into a religious family in Jabla, northern Syria, Qassam received an Islamic education in Latakia [*qv*] and joined al Azhar University [*qv*] in Cairo [*qv*]. There he fell under the influence of Muhammad Abdu, an Islamic thinker. On his return to Syria he worked as a preacher. When the French mandated Syria in 1920, he preached against the foreign rule. Following his participation in the resistance to the French mandate in the mid-1920s, he was sentenced to death in absentia.

Qassam fled to the Palestinian city of Haifa [*qv*] and became a preacher there. Calling for a jihad [*qv*] against the British mandate and the Zionist [*qv*] colonizers, he coined the slogan: "God's book in one hand and a rifle in the other." Qassam thus became the first Arab leader in Palestine [*qv*] to advocate an armed struggle against foreign colonizers and rulers. Since he considered workers and peasants to be the most dedicated classes, ready to sacrifice everything to gain the independence of Palestine, he was seen as a guardian of the poor. This won him popularity among those Palestinians who were not particularly religious. In late 1935 Qassam gathered some 800 armed men in Haifa and began marching toward the hills of the West Bank [*qv*] in an effort to overthrow the British forces and make Palestine independent. British reconnaissance planes soon tracked down his militiamen, and the British army engaged them in an uneven battle at Yaabad near Jenin. They lost, and Qassam was killed.

However, this first armed confrontation between Palestinians and the British, coupled with Qassam's martyrdom [*qv*], boosted Arab morale. It paved the way for the Arab Revolt, which erupted in 1936 and lasted three years, the first Palestinian Intifada [*qv*]. It is widely recognized that Qassam's philosophy, leadership, and advocacy of an armed struggle left a lasting impression on Palestinian political culture. This became apparent when during the intifada in the Occupied Territories [*qv*] in the late 1980s both Hamas [*qv*] and Islamic Jihad [*qv*] named their respective military wings the Izz al Din Qassam Brigade.

Qatar:

Official name: State of Qatar

Capital: Doha [*qv*]

Area: 4.416 sq. miles/11,437 sq. km

Population: 793,000 (2003, est.)

Gross domestic product (1999): $17.9 billion

National currency: Qatari Rial (QR); QR 1 = US$0.275 = £0.192 = EUR 0.31 (2001)

Form of government: monarchy

Official language: Arabic [*qv*]

Official religion: Islam [*qv*]

Administrative system: Qatar consists of nine municipalities.

Constitution: An interim constitution, promulgated in April 1970 by Shaikh Ahmad ibn Ali al Thani [*qv*], named the al Thanis [*qv*] as hereditary ruling family and invested the *emir* (head of state) with supreme power. It specified a ten-member cabinet, appointed and led by the emir as chief executive. The cabinet ministers were to be additional members of the twenty-three-strong consultative council, with twenty of its members chosen from forty popularly elected representatives. Such a council has yet to materialize. In 1999 the ruler set up a twenty-nine-member Municipal Council, elected by universal adult suffrage, as a consultative body to the Ministry of Municipal Affairs and Agriculture.

Advisory council: After ascending the throne in February 1972, Shaikh Khalifa ibn Hamad al Thani [*qv*] appointed a fully nominated advisory council of twenty members, who were empowered to advise the cabinet only on matters referred to it by the emir. The council was expanded to thirty members in 1975 and thirty-five in 1988. Since its formation, its four-year tenure has been extended repeatedly, the last such extension being given in 1998.

Ethnic composition (2002): Arab, 42 percent; South Asian, 30 percent; Iranian, 12 percent; other, 6 percent.

High officials:

Head of state: Shaikh Hamad ibn Khalifa al Thani, [*qv*] 1995–

Crown Prince: Shaikh Jassim ibn Hamad al Khalifa, 1995–

Prime minister: Shaikh Abdullah ibn Khalifa al Thani, 1995–

Speaker of the advisory council: Muhammad ibn Mubarak al Khalifa, 1998

History: By intervening in the Qatari-Bahraini battles of 1867–68, Britain became the dominant foreign influence in the politics of Qatar, ruled by the al Thani family. During the Ottoman suzerainty (1872–1916) the al Thanis, adherents of Wahhabism [*qv*], remained preeminent. The end of Ottoman rule brought Abdullah ibn

Qasim al Thani (1876–1948) and the British closer, a relationship that was formalized in the 1916 Anglo-Qatari Treaty [*qv*]. Britain guaranteed Qatar's territorial integrity against external aggression, while Qatar promised not to cede any rights, including mineral rights, to a third party without British consent. A subsidiary of the Iraq Petroleum Company struck oil in 1939, but commercial extraction did not start until 1948. Output rose to 32,000 barrels per day toward the end of Shaikh Abdullah's reign.

Shaikh Abdullah's successor, Shaikh Ali ibn Abdullah al Thani (r. 1948–60) [*qv*], was deposed by the British in 1960 in favor of Shaikh Ahmad ibn Ali al Thani (r. 1960–72). He took Qatar into the Organization of Petroleum Exporting Countries (OPEC) [*qv*] in 1961, and into the Organization of Arab Petroleum Exporting Countries (OAPEC) [*qv*] in 1970. In 1964, yielding to pressure from the National Unity Front [*qv*] and Britain, he appointed an advisory council with the authority to issue laws and decrees for "the fundamental principles and basic rules of overall policy." He promulgated an interim constitution in April 1970, which, by specifying a largely elected consultative council, marked an important step toward a representative government. It was only in that year that the apparatus of a modern state was set up in Qatar. But that left untouched the "rule of four quarters:" the first quarter of revenues for administration, the second to the princes, the third to the reserves controled by the royal clan, consisting of some 1,000 adult male al Thanis, and the remainder for economic development.

Shaikh Ali al Thani negotiated the termination of the 1916 Anglo-Qatari Treaty and declared Qatar independent in September 1971. But in February 1972 he was overthrown in a bloodless coup by Khalifa ibn Hamad al Thani [*qv*], then prime minister. By then Qatari oil output had reached 600,000 barrels per day. Its oil revenue soared to $5.4 billion in 1980, when its population was less than 250,000. The next year it was a cofounder of the Gulf Cooperation Council [*qv*]. Qatar supported Iraq [*qv*] in the First Gulf War [*qv*]. It backed Kuwait after it had been occupied by Iraq in August 1990, and joined the U.S.-led coalition against Iraq in the Second Gulf War [*qv*].

In June 1995 Shaikh Khalifa was overthrown by his son Shaikh Hamad al Thani [*qv*]. Later that year he allowed Israel to open a trade mission in Doha. His decision in 1996 to partly fund the Al Jazeera (i.e., The Gulf) satellite television channel licensed to function without censorship—an unprecedented practice in Arab states—gave the tiny emirate a high profile in the region and the Arab world at large. Despite pressure from Arab and Muslim countries, Qatar presided over the U.S.-sponsored Fourth Middle East and North Africa Economic Conference—aiming to foster economic ties between Israel and the Arab world—in Doha in November 1997. The ruler held the first direct election to the nationwide Municipal Council on the basis of universal franchise in 1999. The following year Qatar became chair of the Islamic Conference Organization [*qv*], but only after it had closed down the Israeli trade office in Doha. In 2002, when the U.S. found public opinion in Saudi Arabia [*qv*] rising against its military presence in the kingdom, it shifted much of its military facilities to the al Udaid air base in Qatar.

This base became the headquarters of the U.S. Central Command for the launching of the Operation Iraqi Freedom [*qv*] in March 2003 to overthrow the regime of President Saddam Hussein [*qv*] in Iraq.

Religious composition (2002): Muslim, 94 percent, of which Sunnis [*qv*] 85 percent (mostly Wahhabi [*qv*]), Shias, [*qv*] 9 percent; Christian [*qv*], 4 percent; other, 2 percent.

qisas *(Arabic: derivative of qasas, tracking the enemy's footsteps)* The concept in Islam [*qv*] of equal retaliation for harm inflicted, with a provision for forgiveness, it is encapsulated in the Quran [*qv*] (5:49): "A life for a life, an eye for an eye / a nose for a nose, an ear for an ear / a tooth for a tooth, and for wounds / retaliation; but whosoever foregoes it / as a freewill offering, that shall be for him / an expiation."

qiyas *(Arabic: to compare):* Qiyas is the method by which statements in the Quran [*qv*] and the Hadith [*qv*] are applied to situations not explicitly covered by these sources of the Islamic law. *See also ijtihad.*

Qom: Pop. 914,000 (2003, est.). As the burial place of Fatima Maasuma *(Arabic: one who shuns sin)*, sister of Imam Ali al Rida/Reza, the eighth imam of Twelver Shias [*qv*], Qom is the holiest place for Shias [*qv*] after Mecca [*qv*], Medina [*qv*], Najaf [*qv*], Karbala [*qv*], and Mashhad [*qv*]. It became an important religious settlement in the early eighth century A.D., with its Shia inhabitants resisting Sunni [*qv*] governors and their tax demands. Fatima Maasuma was buried here in A.D. 816, but the first dome over her grave was not built until the thirteenth century. The founders of the Safavid dynasty (1501–1736), Shah Ismail and Shah Tahmasp, continued the tradition of using Qom as the winter capital. The city became a place of Shia pilgrimage in the seventeenth century. The Qajar dynasty (1790–1925) continued the tradition of placing royal and noble mausoleums at Fatima's shrine, now adorned by a gilded dome.

The uncertain conditions in Iraq that followed the collapse of the Ottoman Empire in 1918 encouraged the leading Shia clerics of Najaf and Karbala to resurrect Qom as a center of Shia learning. This led to the founding of Iran's largest theological college, Faiziyya, there in 1920. Five years later, in his drive to gain legitimacy for his rule, Reza Khan Pahlavi [qv] canvassed support among the clerical leaders of Qom.

During the reign of his son, Muhammad Reza Shah Pahlavi [qv], the importance of Qom continued. Among the clerics it spawned was Ayatollah Ruhollah Khomeini [qv], who came to prominence in the early 1960s. Qom was the site of Khomeini's challenge to the shah's rule in June 1963. Matters settled down after his deportation the following year. But when the anti-shah movement began nationally in late 1977, Qom soon became a leading center of protest and resistance. With the success of the Islamic revolution [qv] in February 1979, the city's preeminence grew. It was the Khomeini's base after his return from abroad. Later he left it for Tehran [qv], mainly to avail himself of better medical facilities after suffering a heart ailment. Qom then became the headquarters of his deputy, Ayatollah Hussein Ali Montazeri [qv], who set up the secretariat of the World Organization of the Islamic Liberation Movements there.

Qom is an important junction for the petroleum and gas pipelines that run between the oil fields of Khuzistan and Tehran. The discovery of an oil field near Qom in 1956 boosted its prosperity.

al Quds *(Arabic: The holy—short form of* Beit al Muqudus, *The House of Holiness): see* Jerusalem.

Quran *(Arabic: Recitation):* Muslims [qv] regard the Quran, which is composed of the divine revelations received by the Prophet Muhammad (A.D. 570–632) over the last twenty years of his life from the eternal, heavenly Book, *al kitab,* accessible only to the immaculate, as the Word of Allah. According to the Prophet Muhammad, the revelations of the earlier (monotheistic) prophets and the scriptures of Jews [qv] and Christians [qv] were also based on the same heavenly tablet, so that they coincided in part with what He revealed. The Quran confirmed that the law was given to Moses, the Gospel to Jesus Christ, and the Book of Psalms to David. Jews and Christians were called *ahl al kitab,* People of the Book.

The revelations, conveyed piecemeal to the Prophet Muhammad and delivered in rhythmic Arabic [qv] prose, were initially memorized by his followers and used in prayers. They were subsequently taken down on palm leaves, camel bones, or leather patches. The work of compilation, assigned by Caliph Abu Bakr (r. A.D. 632–34) to the Prophet's secretary, Muhammad Zaid ibn Thabit, involved collecting scattered discourses and transcribing memorized revelations. It was completed before Abu Bakr's death and produced a sheaf of separate inscribed leaves.

The authorized version of the Quran was not issued until A.D. 651 by Caliph Othman (r. A.D. 644–56), who destroyed all other versions. It consists of 114 *suras* (chapters) of varying length to form a book of some 6,616 verses. Until his migration in A.D. mid-622 to Medina [*qv*] from Mecca [*qv*], the Prophet Muhammad was under attack by his opponents. In contrast, in Medina he became a civil and military governor and judge. This is reflected in the suras, the earlier ones often being shorter, more imaginative, and in rhymed prose; the later ones being generally longer and down-to-earth, full of legal and moral guidelines. Except for the short introductory sura, the others are arranged approximately according to their length, starting with the longest. Therefore, the earlier, shorter suras of the Meccan period appear later in the Quran. These advocate obedience to Allah in view of the forthcoming Day of Judgement. The later, longer suras of the Medinese period offer guidelines for the creation of social environment that is conducive to the moral existence demanded by Allah.

All the suras are emphatic about monotheism, urging the audience to accept no divinity except Allah. He is the one who has created the universe and maintains it, and is the most powerful and wise. He has given guidelines to human beings as to how they should conduct themselves in His revelations conveyed through the prophets; and He will judge them on the basis on the Day of Judgement. His strictness is balanced by His mercy and compassion. Human beings, who are capable of doing good or evil, have a choice, and are responsible for their deeds as individuals and as a group. They are enjoined to heed the Quran. It demands total submission to the will of Allah, and to His message as conveyed by His messenger, the Prophet

Muhammad. This means living within the moral-ethical guidelines as an individual believer and as a member of the community. On the Day of Reckoning each person's actions will be examined and judgment delivered. He/she will either enjoy the gardens of heaven or suffer the horror of hell.

The Medinese section of the Quran is concerned with commenting on social affairs and providing a corpus of law.

It deals firstly with the external and internal security of the Islamic *umma* [*qv*] (community). The task of protecting it form external threats lies with all its members. The security of the individual and the property of individuals within the community is ensured through the old tribal custom of retribution, *qisas* [*qv*]. Secondly, family life is regulated. Thirdly, certain ethical and legal injunctions must be obeyed. Intoxicants, flesh of swine, games of chance, and hoarding are forbidden. Fraud, slander, perjury, hypocrisy, corruption, extravagance, and arrogance are condemned. Punishments for, inter alia, stealing, murder, and adultery are stated.

As the paramount authority for the Muslim community, the Quran is the ultimate source and continual inspiration of Islam [*qv*]. Pious Muslims memorize it. Often social and political gatherings begin with recitations from it. Together with the Hadith [*qv*], it constitutes the Sharia [*qv*].

Qutb, Sayyid Muhammad (1906–66): *Islamist ideologue* Born into a poor, but notable, family near Asyut, Sayyid Qutb trained as a teacher in Cairo [*qv*] and became a school inspector with the Ministry of Education. He was a prolific writer, as much at ease with essays and literary criticism as with fiction.

In 1948 the ministry sent him to a university in Colorado, USA, for further studies. His three years in America convinced him that society was racist and sexually depraved, and he concluded that the West was in a civilizational decline. He became interested in his Islamic roots and Islam [qv]. On his return to Egypt in 1951, the education ministry found his anti-American views so objectionable that it asked him to resign.

Later in his *Islam and the Problem of Civilization,* posing a rhetorical question—"What should be done about America and the West, given their overwhelming danger to humanity?"—he answered that a sentence of death should be passed on them. Decades later, such views would be expressed by Osama bin Laden [qv] and his intellectual mentor, Ayman Zawahiri [qv].

He joined the Muslim Brotherhood [qv] and soon became one of its eminent members. Following the ban on the Brotherhood in 1954, he was arrested and held in a concentration camp. Here he wrote his classic *Maalim fi al Tariq* (Signposts on the Road), which is the primer for radical Islamists [qv] worldwide. It was smuggled out and published in 1964, the year Qutb along with other Brotherhood detainees were released. In his book, Qutb divided social systems into two categories: the Order of Islam and the Order of Jahiliya (Ignorance), which was decadent and ignorant, the type that had existed in Arabia before Prophet Muhammad had received the Word of God, when men revered not God, but other men disguised as deities. He argued that the regime of President Abdul Gamal Nasser [qv] was a modern version of Jahiliya. This earned him the approval and respect of young Brothers and the opprobrium of the political and religious establishment.

The militant members of the (still clandestine) Muslim Brotherhood drafted Qutb into the leadership. They wanted him to avenge the persecution of the Brotherhood in the mid-1950s. By inclination a thinker, he wished to avoid violence. But when his radical followers pressed for a jihad [qv] to be waged against the social order he had himself labeled *jahiliya* because of its betrayal of Islamic precepts, Qutb could find no way out.

During his trial in 1966 he did not contest the charge of sedition, and instead tried to explain his position ideologically, arguing that the bonds of ideology and belief were sturdier than those of patriotism based upon region, and that the false distinction among Muslims on a regional basis was an expression of the Crusading and Zionist [qv] imperialism that had to be eradicated. In his view, *watan* (homeland) was not a land, but the community of believers, *umma* [qv]. He argued that once the Brothers had declared someone to be *jahil,* ignorant, they had the right to attack his person or property, a right granted in Islam, and that if in the course of performing this religious duty of waging a jihad against unbelievers, a Brother found himself on the path of sedition, so be it. The responsibility for creating such a situation lay with those who through their policies had created such circumstances. His subsequent execution turned him into a martyr in the eyes of his followers, gaining his thesis a wider acceptance in the Arab [qv] world and beyond.

Among his books, translated into English, are *Signposts on the Road; Islam: The Religion of the Future;* and *Social Justice in Islam.*

al Quwatli, Shukri (1891–1967): *Syrian politician; president 1943–49, 1955–58* Born into a rich land-owning family in Damascus [*qv*], Quwalti was active in Arab nationalist politics as a youth, joining the clandestine al Fatat society. The Ottoman government imprisoned him during the First World War. He was appointed governor of Damascus (1918–19) by Faisal I ibn Hussein [*qv*]. Following Faisal's defeat by the French, in 1920 Quwalti went into exile, operating mainly from Egypt or Europe. The French mandate in Syria condemned him to death in absentia. When his sentence was lifted in 1931, Quwalti returned home to head the National Bloc, which demanded independence. Following the Franco-Syrian Treaty of 1936 [*qv*], Quwalti became minister of defense and finance from 1936–39.

After a brief exile from 1941–43, when the pro-Nazi French government, based in Vichy, controlled Syria, he returned to Damascus to lead the National Bloc. It won overwhelmingly at the polls, and Quwalti became president from 1943. He led the final struggle for total independence. The National Bloc split into the National Party, led by Quwalti, and the People's Party. He was reelected president in 1948, but was overthrown by the army chief of staff, Col. Hosni Zaim [*qv*] in March 1949. He went into exile in Egypt and returned home after five years, following the downfall of Adib Shishkali [*qv*]. In the September 1954 elections his National Party did not do as well as the People's Party, but in the August 1955 presidential election, backed by the People's Party and Saudi funds, he beat his leftist rival, Khalid Azm.

Following an Israeli attack on the Syrian posts near Lake Tiberias in December, Quwalti strengthened Syria's ties with Moscow. Buffeted by U.S. and Iraqi plots to overthrow him, and pressured by his pan-Arabist military officers, he backed the idea of an Egyptian-Syrian federation. However, he was overruled by the officer corps, who advocated a merger. When this occurred in February 1958, Quwalti resigned, proposing Gamal Abdul Nasser [*qv*] as president of the United Arab Republic [*qv*].

R

Rabin, Yitzhak (1922–95): *Israeli military leader and politician; prime minister, 1974–77, 1992–95* Born into a middle-class Jewish family in Jerusalem [*qv*], Rabin graduated from an agricultural college in 1940. As a member of Palmah [*qv*] he participated in the Allied campaign in 1941 in Syria, then under a pro-Nazi French government. In the 1948–49 Arab-Israeli War [*qv*] he commanded a brigade that saw combat on the Jerusalem and Negev fronts. Rabin headed the Israeli military's tactical operations branch from 1950–52. Following his graduation from the British Staff College and promotion to general, he served as chief of the military's training department (1954–56), commander of the Northern Command (1956–59), chief of operations (1959–61), deputy chief of staff (1961–64), and chief of staff (1964–68). Under his command the Israeli armed forces performed brilliantly in the June 1967 Arab-Israeli War [*qv*]. Even while serving as ambassador to the United States

(1968–73) he advised the prime minister on important military matters.

After returning home, Rabin joined the Labor Party [qv] and was elected to the Knesset [qv] in December 1973. He was given the labor portfolio in the cabinet formed by Golda Meir [qv] in March 1974. Following her resignation, Rabin challenged Shimon Peres [qv] for the Labor leadership. He won by 298 votes to 254 and became prime minister in June 1974. His achievements included the Sinai II Agreement [qv] with Egypt in September 1975, and the rebuilding of the military and the economy after the October 1973 Arab-Israeli War [qv].

Factionalism within Labor on the issue of the Occupied Arab Territories [qv] intensified, and a series of financial scandals involving party leaders came to the surface. In addition, Rabin's inexperience in civil administration, poor communicating skills, and strained relations with Defense Minister Shimon Peres hurt the government's popular standing. Yet, in a fresh challenge by Peres to his leadership in early 1977, Rabin scraped through by forty-one votes in an electoral college of 3,000. In March it was revealed that during his ambassadorship in the United States, his wife, Leah, had maintained an active bank account in Washington, an illegal act according to the Israeli law. The next month he resigned as party leader.

Labor lost the general election in May, but Rabin remained politically active, becoming defense minister in the national unity government formed in 1984. Responding to the unpopularity of Israel's continued military involvement in Lebanon, he withdrew the Israeli troops from there, except for a small force posted in the border security strip. He retained the defense ministry in the next national unity government formed in 1988 and continued his hardline policy towards the Palestinian Intifada [qv] until Labor's withdrawal from the cabinet in 1990. He was elected Labor leader in 1992, and became prime minister of a Labor-led coalition after elections in June.

Rabin closely supervised the secret negotiations with the Palestine Liberation Organization (PLO) [qv] initiated by his foreign minister, Peres, and sanctified the Israeli-PLO Accord [qv]—signed in Washington in September 1993—by shaking the hand of his long-term enemy, Yasser Arafat [qv]. In October 1994 he signed the Jordanian-Israeli Peace Treaty [qv] with King Hussein [qv] at a common border site. He shared the 1994 Nobel Peace Prize with Peres and Arafat. In September 1995 he signed an agreement on self-rule for Palestinians in the West Bank, called the Oslo Accord II [qv]. He was assassinated in November in Tel Aviv [qv] by Yigal Amir, a fanatic Jewish Israeli.

Rafi (*Hebrew: acronym of* Reshima Poalei Israeli, *Israel Workers List): Israeli political party* Disagreeing with the decision of the Mapai [qv] convention in early 1965 to merge with the leftist Ahdut HaAvodah [qv], David Ben-Gurion [qv], supported by Shimon Peres [qv] and Moshe Dayan [qv], quit Mapai and offered their own list, Rafi, in the November 1965 general election. It won only ten seats in the Knesset [qv] versus Mapai's forty-five. Its membership of 25,000 was less than a tenth of Mapai's. In 1968 Rafi combined with Mapai and Ahdut HaAvodah to form the Israeli Labor Party [qv]. Refusing to accept the majority decision in Rafi, Ben-Gurion led a new group in the 1969 poll, which won only four seats.

Rafsanjani, Ali Akbar Hashemi (1933–): *Iranian religious and political leader; president 1989–* Born into a religious family in Behraman, Kerman province, Rafsanjani went to Qom [*qv*] for his theological studies. During the power struggle between Premier Muhammad Mussadiq [*qv*] and Muhammad Reza Shah Pahlavi [*qv*] from 1951–53, he sided with Mussadiq. Later he became a student of Ayatollah Ruhollah Khomeini [*qv*] in Qom. After Khomeini's deportation in 1964, Rafsanjani stayed in contact with him, handled Islamic charities on his behalf, and consulted him on political affairs. Rafsanjani was arrested and tortured in the mid-1970s.

One of the cofounders of the Tehran [*qv*] branch of the Association of Combatant Clergy Organization of Militant Clergy (OMC) [*qv*], Rafsanjani was actively involved in the 1977–78 revolutionary movement, particularly the formation of the Revolutionary Komitehs [*qv*]. He was one of the members of the Islamic Revolutionary Council and a cofounder of the Islamic Republican Party (IRP) [*qv*]. He was later appointed deputy minister of the interior. He was an active member of the 1979 Assembly of Experts [*qv*], charged with drafting the constitution. After his election as a Majlis [*qv*] deputy from Tehran [*qv*], he was voted speaker of the house in July 1980, a post to which he was reelected every year until the dissolution of the chamber in 1984. As the Majlis speaker he played a pivotal role in the impeachment of President Bani-Sadr [*qv*] in June 1981. In 1982, after the election of a new Assembly of Experts [*qv*],

Rafsanjani was chosen its vice president. He acted as Khomeini's personal representative on the Supreme Defense Council.

During the Iran-Iraq War [*qv*], when in mid-1982 Iran recovered the area lost earlier to its foe, Rafsanjani advocated advancing into Iraq if the latter did not meet Iran's demands, including a compensation payment of $100 billion for war damages. After his election to the Majlis in 1984, he was reelected speaker, a position confirmed annually for the next four years. On the sixth anniversary of the war (September 1986), Rafsanjani remarked that the regime had been able to use the war to awaken the people and fight the problems threatening the revolution. Following Iran's military setbacks in the spring of 1988, Khomeini put Rafsanjani in overall charge of the war effort. Having realistically assessed the deteriorating situation, in mid-July 1988 he persuaded the Assembly of Experts to recommend to Khomeini the truce called for earlier by the United Nations Security Council. Khomeini accepted the recommendation.

After Khomeini's death in June 1989, when President Ali Husseini Khamanei [*qv*] was promoted to succeed him, Rafsanjani resigned his speakership and ran for the presidency. He secured 95 percent of the votes on a turn-out of 70 percent. According to the amended constitution, Rafsanjani ruled without the premier, becoming the executive president, excluded radicals from his government and introduced economic liberalization. He pursued a pragmatic path in foreign policy, improving relations with Germany, France, Japan and the Soviet Union (later Russia). But due to a drop in oil prices, the economy suffered and inflation rose. As a result his popular vote in the 1993 presidential poll fell to 63 percent on a voter turnout of 56 percent. His performance during the second term was lackluster.

In 1997 Khamanei appointed him president of the Expediency Consultation Council System. In that capacity he acted as a mediator to resolve differences between the president, parliament, and the Guardians Council [qv]—as well as a consultant to the Leader on the formation of general policies. His efforts to return to the leadership of the parliament failed when he trailed embarrassingly poorly in the general election of 2001, which he contested from Tehran, once his stronghold. Now reform-oriented residents of the capital regarded him as a conservative surrounded by a coterie of corrupt men.

Rajai, Muhammad Ali (1933–81): *Iranian politician; prime minister, 1980–81, president, 1981* Born to a poor shopkeeper in Qasvin, Rajai quit school at sixteen and traveled to Tehran [qv], where he became a bricklayer. In 1951 he joined the air force as an orderly and then as a maintenance trainee. He was in contact with the Fedaiyan-e Islam [qv]. Five years later he enrolled at a teacher training college, graduating in 1959. He then taught in a provincial town. He was imprisoned briefly during the June 1963 uprising. After his release he became a high school teacher in Tehran.

Rajai joined the Liberation Movement [qv], and in 1967 he cofounded the Islamic Welfare and Mutual Assistance Foundation, a front organization for political activity. He joined the Mujahedin-e Khalq [qv] in 1970, but was unhappy with the leftward drift of the organization and left two years later. In November 1974 he was arrested on suspicion of planting a bomb outside the Tehran office of El Al, the Israeli airline. He was tortured, and scars were left on his feet. During his imprisonment he came into contact with Ayatollah Mahmud Taleqani [qv] and Ali Hussein Khamanei [qv]. He was released in November 1978.

After the revolution in February 1979, Rajai was appointed education minister. He accelerated the Islamisation of the education system. In August 1980, after he had been elected as a Majlis [qv] deputy, Rajai became the house's leading choice for premier. A reluctant President Abol Hassan Bani-Sadr [qv] appointed him prime minister.

Following the Iraqi invasion of Iran in September 1980, Rajai argued at the United Nations Security Council that the United States was the chief instigator.

Poles apart, socially and politically, Rajai and Bani-Sadr clashed often, and this was one of the factors that caused the downfall of the president in June 1981. In the presidential election that followed, Rajai, one of four candidates, won 88 percent of the votes. Under his presidency the government set up ad hoc committees in many places to deal with the violence of guerrillas led by the National Resistance Council [qv] and declared a state of emergency in the worst affected areas. An incendiary bomb killed Rajai and Premier Muhammad Javad Bahonar on 30 August during a National Security Council meeting.

Rajavi, Masud (1947–): *Iranian politician* Born into a middle-class family in Tabas, Khorasan province, Rajavi studied political science at Tehran University. In 1965 he joined the Mujahedin-e Khalq [qv] and five years later became a member of its central committee. He received guerrilla training at a Palestinian camp in Jordan. In 1971 he was one of the two Mujahedin-e Khalq leaders arrested for trying to abduct a top Western diplomat and was condemned to death. But under international pressure the government commuted his sentence. By the time he was released in December 1978, he was the only surviving central committee member of the Mujahedin-e Khalq, which participated actively in the revolutionary movement. After the victory of the Islamic revolution [qv], Rajavi supported autonomy for the Kurds [qv] and opposed secret revolutionary courts.

Since the Mujahedin-e Khalq had abstained in the referendum on the constitution, Ayatollah Ruhollah Khomeini [qv] disqualified Rajavi from contesting the presidential election in January 1980. Rajavi then backed Abol Hassan Bani-Sadr [qv], who was elected president. Later Rajavi cooperated with Bani-Sadr in the latter's struggle with the clerical leadership, which wanted to undermine his authority. Rajavi and his party were denounced by Khomeini as "hypocrites"—those claiming to be good Muslims, while following the secular ideology of Marxism and misguiding the faithful with their Marxist interpretations. Rajavi backed Bani-Sadr in June 1981 in the latter's confrontation with Khomeini.

After Bani-Sadr's dismissal from office, both he and Rajavi went underground. In July they flew to Paris together. There they jointly established the National Resistance Council [qv], which conducted sabotage and guerrilla attacks on suitable targets in Iran. The Islamic regime surmounted the challenge, which lasted from July 1981 to

September 1982, by using unrestrained force and propaganda. With the war against Iraq raging along the border, it convincingly labeled those creating disorder at home as unpatriotic agents of Baghdad. By holding a public meeting with Iraqi deputy premier Tariq Aziz [qv] in Paris in January 1983, Rajavi provided Iran with a propaganda tool and caused a split with Bani-Sadr. Under Iran's pressure, the French government expelled Rajavi from France. He then set up Mujahedin-e Khalq headquarters in Baghdad [qv].

Toward the end of the Iran-Iraq War [qv], in July 1988 Rajavi's forces, operating as the National Liberation Army, penetrated deep into Iran only to be surrounded by the Iranian troops and decimated. Despite Iraq's defeat in the Second Gulf War [qv] in 1991, followed by growing economic hardship in the country, Rajavi continued to receive aid from the Iraqi government, sharing his leadership of the Mujahedin-e Khalq with his wife, Miryam.

His organization mounted pinprick attacks along the Iraqi-Iranian border interspersed with rocket attacks on government offices in central Tehran [qv]. After many years of enjoying substantial support in U.S. Congress, the Mujahedin-e Khalq's standing in America suffered when the Bill Clinton administration listed it as a terrorist organization in 1997, thus making it illegal for those living in the United States to fund it. However, that left its support among the Iranian exiles living in Europe largely intact. With Washington mounting a global war on terrorism in the wake of attacks on it on 11 September 2001, there was no prospect of its rehabilitation there. And

Iraqi President Saddam Hussein, under increasing pressure by Washington, ensured that Rajavi kept a low profile. Following the attacks on the Mujahedin-e Khlaq bases during the Gulf War III [*qv*] in April 2003, Rajavi's whereabouts became a matter of speculation.

Rakah *(Hebrew: acronym of* Reshima Kommunistit Hadash, *New Communist List): Israeli political party* Rakah emerged as a result of a split in Maki [*qv*] in August 1965, when 2,000 Arab members and a section of the equally numerous Jewish members left the parent body. In the November 1965 election Rakah won three Knesset [*qv*] seats. Blaming Israel for aggression in the June 1967 Arab-Israeli War [*qv*], it opposed annexing any part of the Occupied Arab Territories [*qv*]. In the 1969 poll the party retained its three seats. In the 1973 election Rakah was the only group to demand Israeli withdrawal from all Occupied Arab Territories and recognition of Palestinian national rights. Its strength rose to four seats. In 1977 Rakah delegates to an international conference in Prague, Czechoslovakia, met the delegates of the Palestine Liberation Organization (PLO) [*qv*]. On the eve of the May 1977 election, Rakah merged with the Black Panther Party to form the Democratic Front for Peace and Equality, with the Hebrew acronym Hadash [*qv*], and secured five seats. *See also* Hadash.

Ramadan: *Islamic holy month of fasting* The Arabic root, *r-m-d,* refers to the heat of summer. The ninth month in the Islamic calendar [*qv*], Ramadan is regarded holy in Islam [*qv*] because it was on the night of 26–27 Ramadan, *Lailat al kadr* (Night of Power), that the first divine revelation was made to the Prophet Muhammad. During this month the faithful are required to undertake fasting, as stated in the Quran [*qv*] (2:179): "O believers, prescribed for you / is the Fast, even as it was prescribed for / those that were before you / the month of Ramadan, wherein the Quran / was sent down to be a guidance / to the people, and as clear signs / of the Guidance and the Salvation." During the month, between sunrise and sunset all adult Muslims are required to abstain from eating, drinking, smoking, and conjugal relations. Among other things this helps them to develop self-control.

Ramadan War (1973): Since Egypt and Syria started the war against Israel during Ramadan 1393 A.H. [*qv*], Arabs [*qv*] refer to the October 1973 Arab-Israeli War [*qv*] as the Ramadan War. *See* Arab-Israeli War IV.

Ras al Khaima Emirate: *a constituent of the United Arab Emirates* Area: 660 sq. miles/1,300 sq. km; pop. 171,000 (2001, est.). Ras al Khaima, ruled by Shaikh Saqr ibn Muhammad al Qasimi (r. 1948–), joined the United Arab Emirates (UAE) in February 1972. Commercial extraction of oil began on a modest scale in early 1984. By the late 1980s output had not exceeded 12,000 barrels a day.

Rastakhiz Party (Iran) *(Persian: Resurgence): Iranian political party* The Rastakhiz Party was established by Muhammad Reza Shah Pahlavi [*qv*] in March 1975 as the sole governing party after he had dissolved the ruling New Iran Party, founded by him in 1963, and the Mardom Party, the official opposition. By setting up a single governing party under Premier Amir Abbas Hoveida [*qv*], the shah co-opted the loyal opposition. In the Majlis elections of June 1975 Rastakhiz won 70 percent of the popular vote.

To tackle rising inflation the Rastakhiz government passed an antiprofiteering law and used Rastakhiz volunteers to monitor prices. They resorted to exacting levies from traders. When protest mounted in the autumn of 1977, the shah replaced Hoveida as premier with Jamshid Amuzgar, the leader of the liberal wing within Rastakhiz. To counter the rising protest movement, Rastakhiz officials set up Resistance Corps, consisting of policemen in civilian clothes, to break up opposition meetings. This led to attacks on Rastakhiz offices by anti-regime demonstrators. With the revolutionary movement gathering pace during the summer of 1978, the shah dissolved the party in September.

However, so hostile was the Islamic Republic of Iran to this party, that any Iranian who had ever belonged to it was automatically disqualified from contesting any public office, and this ban was applied strictly.

Ratz *(Hebrew: acronymn of Reshima Tzibori, Citizens List): Israeli political party* Ratz was formed by Shulamit Aloni in 1973 after her departure from the Labor Party [*qv*]. It was against Jewish settlements in the Occupied Territories [*qv*]. Its opposition to discrimination on the basis of religion, gender, or ethnicity made it attractive to secularists and women. It won three Knesset [*qv*] seats in the 1973 election, but only one in 1977. Having failed to secure a place in the subsequent parliamentary elections, it eventually won five seats in 1988. It then allied with Mapam [*qv*] and Shinui [*qv*] to form the Meretz [*qv*] alliance. Of the twelve seats won by Meretz in the 1992 election, six belonged to Ratz. It joined the Labor-led coalition. Its three ministers in the cabinet were notable for their strong support for the Oslo Accord I [*qv*] of September 1993.

Reform Judaism: The Jewish enlightenment, called *halaska*, during the latter half of the eighteenth century in eastern and central Europe led Jews away from the traditional belief in messianic redemption and toward a search for personal and communal fulfillment. In his book *Jerusalem* (1783), Moses Mendelssohn, a German Jew, argued that there was no contradiction between believing in a secular religion of reason and Judaism. The movement gathered pace after the 1789 French Revolution. It manifested itself among West European Jews in religious reform, with French Jews concentrating on reforming doctrine by emphasizing Judaism as a prophetic tradition and repudiating the binding nature of rabbinic law; and German Jews on worship—the latter institutionalizing reform in the mid-1840s. Thus, Reform Jews reject many of the restrictions of the Halacha [*qv*], use the vernacular in religious ceremonies, and curtail much of the ritual.

Religious endowment/trust: *Islamic institution. See* waqf.

Revisionist Zionists: *Zionist organization* Founded as the World Union of Revisionist Zionists in 1925 by Vladimir Jabotinsky [*qv*], it derived its name from its program of revising the Labor Zionist strategy of establishing a Jewish state in Palestine [*qv*] through colonization and returning to the original concept of Theodor Herzl (1860–1904) of Jewish statehood through international recognition of Jewish sovereignty over Palestine. Advocating a Jewish state on both sides of the Jordan River [*qv*], it opposed the 1922 decision of Britain, the mandate power in Palestine, to apply the idea of a Jewish homeland only to the west of the Jordan. Unlike Labor Zionists [*qv*], it gave priority to private capital to develop Palestine. At the seventeenth Zionist Congress [*qv*] in 1931, one-fifth of the delegates supported its stance. Efforts made later to conciliate its members with Labor Zionists in Palestine failed.

After the Zionist Congress in 1933 had resolved that "in all Zionist matters discipline in regard of the Zionist Organization [*qv*] must take precedence over the discipline of any other body," the Revisionists left and formed the New Zionist Organization (NZO) in 1935. In Palestine the party's youth movement, Betar, and the Revisionists within Haganah [*qv*] established Irgun Zvai Leumi [*qv*] in 1937. After David Ben-Gurion [*qv*], head of Israel's provisional government, had brought about the disbandment of Irgun in 1948, the Revisionists and former Irgun ranks combined to form the Herut [*qv*] Party under the leadership of Menachem Begin [*qv*].

Revolutionary Komitehs (Iran): Following Ayatollah Ruhollah Khomeini's [*qv*] taped messages in August 1978 from the Iraqi city of Najaf [*qv*], his senior clerical followers formed *Komitehs* (derivate of *Comite*, [*French, Committee*]) in mosques to guide those struggling against the regime of Muhammad Reza Pahlavi [*qv*]. Of all the spontaneous or preplanned bodies that sprouted during the final stage of the Islamic revolution [*qv*], the Revolutionary Komitehs proved to be the most broad-based and effective. As the anti-shah campaign escalated,

sympathetic soldiers secretly began to pass on arms to local Komitehs. They helped to distribute essential goods, including heating oil, during the last general strike. Once the shah had departed in January 1979, they took over administrative and police powers and reported to the Islamic Revolutionary Council, nominated by Khomeini before his return to Tehran [*qv*], and not to the government of Mahdi Bazargan [*qv*], appointed by him after his return. Following the outbreak of war with Iraq [*qv*] in September 1980, the government charged the Komitehs with rationing essential goods. They thus became part of the civilian administration.

Riyadh: *Capital of Saudi Arabia* Pop. 3,724,000 (2003, est.). Located in the middle of three valleys in the central Najd [*qv*] region, the oasis town of Riyadh became the center of the Wahhabi [*qv*] movement from the early nineteenth century. It became the capital of the House of Saud [*qv*] from 1824 to 1881, when it fell to the Rashid dynasty of Hail to the north. But the House of Saud returned when Abdul Aziz ibn Abdul Rahman al Saud [*qv*] recaptured Najd in 1902. Using Riyadh as his base, Abdul Aziz extended his realm from the eastern Hasa region to the western Hijaz [*qv*] and Asir. With the founding of the Kingdom of Saudi Arabia in 1932, Riyadh became its capital.

The discovery of oil in the east in 1933, followed by commercial production after the Second World War, had a dramatic impact on Riyadh, catapulting it from a medieval existence to modern life and turning it into a variant of a modern American city, but, due to Islamic strictures, without the leisure activities commonly available there. It is the country's leading educational and communications center, and is served by an airport, railway, and highways. It is the most populous city in the Arabian Peninsula.

Rogers Plan (1969): *a U.S. peace plan* In December 1969 U.S. Secretary of State William Rogers made public a peace plan he had earlier submitted to Israel, Egypt and Jordan—as well as to the Soviet Union, Britain, and France. It envisaged Israel's withdrawal to its 1967 borders, subject to minor modifications for mutual security, except for the Gaza Strip [*qv*], which was to be negotiated between Israel, Egypt, and Jordan. Palestinian refugees were to be either repatriated according to an agreed annual quota or given compensation. Other provisions included security arrangements, to be hammered out by the parties concerned. The final accords were to be negotiated under the chairmanship of Gunnar Jarring, the United Nations mediator. Israel rejected the plan, as did Egypt. This virtually killed the plan, but Rogers later mounted a more modest initiative aimed at bringing about a truce in the War of Attrition [*qv*], and this succeeded in August 1970.

Roman Catholic Christians/Church: *Christian sect* The term Roman Catholic Church came into vogue only in the nineteenth century. It applies to the Christian Church under the supreme authority of the pope, the historic Bishop of Rome. It took on a distinctive identity as a result of two major splits in the church—with the (Eastern) Orthodox Church [*qv*] in 1054, and within the Western church at the time of the Protestant [*qv*] Reformation in the mid-sixteenth century. The members of this church perform the Roman rites, the liturgy being said in Latin until the 1960s, and follow the practices of the church in Rome. They accept the teachings of the Bible [*qv*] and the interpretations offered by the Church, and subscribe to the doctrine that God conveys His grace to humans through sacraments. The Eucharist is therefore the center of Roman Catholic worship and is often performed with pomp and color. Particular emphasis is laid on the oneness and wholeness of the Christian body, which includes the dead as well as the living.

Different orders of priests, monks, and nuns are part of the body of the Roman Catholic Church. It has a hierarchical structure, extending from the parish priests to the pope at Vatican City in Rome, where the central administration is conducted by papal officials and commissions. The supremacy of the Bishop of Rome, the title first applied to the Apostle Peter, is derived from the New Testament [*qv*] (*Matthew* 16:18): "Peter: you are a rock and on this rock foundation I will build my church."

After the fall of the Western Roman Empire in A.D. 476, the pope also assumed the title of Pontifex Maximus, used earlier by Roman emperors in their high priestly functions. Rivalry between the pope and monarchs in Europe with regard to lay and religious power was a running theme in the Middle Ages (A.D. 476–1492). During the last two centuries of this era most churchmen were involved in politics and other worldly affairs. Before a belated attempt at reform within the church during this period and the first half of the sixteenth century could succeed in holding it together, the Protestant Reformation resulted in revolt and the Church's break-up.

The papacy was beset by "Catholic princes" until the late eighteenth century. In the nineteenth century, during the papacy of Pius IX (1846–78), came the declaration of papal infallibility in faith and doctrine, which hardened the rift between the Roman Catholic Church and its two major rivals.

Changes in the liturgy that have been introduced since the 1960s have led to greater use of the vernacular and increased participation by the congregation.

In the Middle East [qv], Roman Catholics have a patriarch in Jerusalem [qv] and apostolic delegates, called *nuncios*, in Baghdad [qv], Beirut [qv], and Cairo [qv].

Those churches that accept the supremacy of the pope but follow their own Eastern rites and customs are called Uniate [qv].

Rosh HaShana *(Hebrew: Head of the Year): Jewish festival* Rosh HaShana is the Jewish New Year festival and is held on the first two days of Tishri (September–October, according to the Christian Gregorian calendar [qv]; the seventh month of the Jewish calendar [qv] when arranged according to religious usage), which is believed to mark the creation of the world. It starts the Ten Days of Penitence, which end on the Day of Atonement—Yom Kippur [qv]. Rosh HaShana should be spent in prayer. The distinctive feature of the religious ritual of the day is the sounding of a ram's horn. Requesting a good year is the central theme of petitional prayers. Since Rosh HaShana is a major Jewish festival, work is prohibited.

Rumeila oil field (Iraq–Kuwait): An oil field in southern Iraq that extends into Kuwait, the exact division of Rumeila became entangled with the demarcation of the frontiers between the two neighbors on the eve of Iraq's invasion of Kuwait in August 1990. Baghdad claimed that since 1980 Kuwait had been extracting oil from it at the rate of 25,000 barrels a day, and that what it had taken was worth $2.4 billion. Kuwait denied the charge. Earlier, Iraq's agreement with the Soviet Union in 1969 to develop the Rumeila oil field in exchange for Iraqi oil strengthened its hand in its long dispute with Western-controlled Iraq Petroleum Company (IPC), which it nationalized in June 1972.

Russian Orthodox Church: *Christian sect* Of the six national churches in the Orthodox [qv] group, the Russian Orthodox Church, with its liturgy performed in Old Slavonic, is the most important. Originally based in Kiev (now capital of Ukraine) under Constantinople (now Istanbul), in 1589 the see was shifted to Moscow, where a patriarchate was established. This was replaced by a synod by Peter the Great (r. 1682–1725) in 1721. On the eve of the Bolshevik Revolution in 1917, the patriarchate was revived, only to be suppressed by the Bolsheviks, later Communists. It was again revived in 1943 during the Second World War in an attempt to foster Russian nationalism. Later the church and the state reached a modus vivendi, which survived until the collapse of the communist system in 1991. The Russian Cathedral is an important landmark in Jerusalem [qv] today.

S

Saada, Antun (1902–49): *Lebanese politician* Born to a Greek Orthodox [qv] doctor who migrated with his family to Brazil, Saada grew up there and worked on a magazine started by his father. In 1929 he traveled to Damascus [qv], where he became a journalist with al Ayyam (Arabic: The Days). Soon he moved to Beirut [qv], where he worked his way into the social and intellectual life of the American University of Beirut (AUB) [qv]. In late 1932 he established a secret society, which by 1935 had acquired several thousand members, with branches in Syria as well as Lebanon. Arguing that geography and history had given the inhabitants of Greater Syria [qv] a distinct identity, Saada expounded the concepts of a Greater Syrian nation (an ethnic fusion of Canaanites, Akkadians, Chaldeans, Assyrians, Aramaeans, and Hittites) and Syrian nationalism, which was at odds with both pan-Arabism [qv] and Lebanese nationalism, which was popular among the country's Christians [qv].

Saada demanded an end to the French mandate and independence for Syria-Lebanon. After he had brought the organization into the open as the Syrian Nationalist Party and held its first plenary conference in December 1935, he was jailed by the French. Following the electoral victory of the leftist Popular Front in France in 1936, he was freed. The next year his party was allowed to function legally after he had assured the authorities that it did not advocate destruction of the Lebanese entity.

In his book Nushu al-umam (Rise of Nations, 1938), he outlined the principles of his philosophy, the leading ones being that Syrians were a complete nation and that Syria's interests overrode all others. He allied these with a call for reform, including the separation of church and state, the removal of barriers between various sects and confessions, and the abolition of feudalism. His secular and antisectarian stance appealed to religious and racial minorities—Alawis [qv], Christians, Druzes [qv], and Kurds [qv]—who became a majority in the party leadership.

Saada visited Italy and Germany in late 1938 and was in the midst of his tour of South America when the Second World War broke out in September 1939. The French banned his party, charging its leaders with complicity with the Axis Powers, but they failed to prove their allegation. In 1941, after the party's leaders had altered the organization's name to the National Party, they were released.

When Saada returned to Lebanon in 1947, the country had regained its independence. He resumed his control over the organization, renaming it the Syrian Social Nationalist Party (SSNP) [qv]. Conflict between it and the Lebanese government revived, and Saada went underground. A compromise was reached, with Saada reaffirming his respect for Lebanon as an independent country. Following the Arab defeat in the 1948–49 Palestine War [qv], his argument against pan-Arabism and for Greater Syrian nationalism became attractive enough to instil traditional political leaders with a sense of insecurity. When Hosni Zaim [qv] seized power in Syria in March 1949, Saada hoped for his backing, but this did not materialize. In June 1949 armed clashes erupted between his party and the Phalangists [qv] in Beirut in what was officially described as a coup attempt by Saada He escaped to Syria to a warm welcome by Zaim. But under pressure from Lebanon and the anti-SSNP forces in Syria, Zaim agreed to Saada's extradition to Lebanon. After a secret, summary military trial, he was executed in July.

el Saadawi, Nawal (1931–): *Egyptian writer and feminist campaigner* Born into a middle-class family in the village of Kafr Tahla, el Saadawi trained as a doctor. She joined the Egyptian civil service and rose to become director general of health education at the ministry of health. After the publication of her first book, *Women and Sex* (1971), which showed a linkage between poverty and politics, and disease and politics, she was sacked from her job and the book was banned by the government of President Anwar Sadat [*qv*]. While working for the United Nations in Lebanon and Ethiopia as a doctor, she continued to publish novels, which were banned in Egypt. She campaigned for women's rights and expressed her left-wing views.

El Saadawi was among the several hundred dissident Egyptian intellectuals who were arrested in September 1981. Freed three months later by president Hosni Mubarak [*qv*], she resumed her writing and campaigning for women's rights in the Arab world. She founded the Arab Women's Solidarity Association to help repair the damage done to women by oppression and poverty. Her novel *The Fall of the Imam* (1987) drew a death threat from Islamic fundamentalists [*qv*], and for two years she lived under armed protection, ordered by the government.

Due to her opposition to the U.S.-led war against Iraq following that country's invasion of Kuwait, the authorities closed down the Arab Women's Solidarity Association in 1991. Though by then they had ceased to ban her books, she was barred from appearing on state-run television or radio. In the searing prose of her novels lies a passionate commitment to fighting injustice, but she remains conscious as a writer that a well-crafted story is one that can sustain itself without the politics. In 1991 she published an autobiographical work, *My Travels Around the World.* Then came *The Well of Life* (1993), containing two novellas focusing on the suffering of Arab women, and *The Innocence of the Devil* (1994), centered on two women in a mental hospital. She covered the subject of women's status in society in *Memoirs from the Women's Prison* (1994) and *Women at Point Zero* (1997). Her novels have been translated from Arabic into English by her husband, Sherif Hetata, a leftist writer who has spent thirteen years in jail for his political beliefs.

al Sabah, Abdullah III ibn Salim I (1895–1965): *ruler of Kuwait, 1950–65* Son of Shaikh Salim I, al Sabah, was ten years younger than his rival in the Jaber branch, Shaikh Ahmad I ibn Jaber II al Sabah, and at odds with the latter's pro-British leanings. Al Sabah's moment of glory came in July 1938, when he became president of the first elected parliament. But this lasted only until December, when the parliament was dissolved by Shaikh Ahmad I [*qv*].

During the Second World War, suspecting al Sabah of pro-Axis sympathies, the British excluded him from any position of authority.

Soon after al Sabah's accession to the throne in 1950, the Iranian oil crisis of 1951–53 boosted Kuwait's petroleum output. By 1955 Kuwait had become the leading oil exporter in the Gulf, a position it maintained until the end of al Sabah's rule.

As a result of London's complicity in the Suez War [*qv*] in 1956, anti-British feelings arose. Al Sabah demanded greater latitude in home affairs, and Britain met him halfway. But following the overthrow of the pro-Western monarchy in Iraq in July 1958, popular pressure grew on al Sabah to abrogate the 1899 Anglo-Kuwaiti Agreement [*qv*].

In September 1960 Kuwait became a founder member of the Organization of Petroleum Exporting Countries (OPEC) [*qv*].

Following the abrogation of the 1899 Anglo-Kuwaiti Agreement in June 1961, Britain officially recognized Kuwait as an independent country. When Baghdad claimed that Kuwait was Iraqi territory, al Sabah appealed for help from Britain and Saudi Arabia. London sent 6,000 troops and Riyadh a small contingent. Having acquired Arab League membership for Kuwait, al Sabah called on it for assistance, and the Arab League's Joint Emergency Force replaced the British troops.

In November 1962 al Sabah promulgated a constitution drafted by an assembly nominated by him. It specified a National Assembly elected on a franchise of one-tenth of adult male citizens. It lacked executive power, with the ruler having the exclusive right to appoint the government. Having conceded an elected parliament, al Sabah tried to determine its composition by manipulating the electoral system. Therefore, the parliament that emerged in January 1963 was a virtual rubber stamp. Al Sabah directed part of Kuwait's vast oil funds into foreign assistance. He also successfully effected Kuwait's transition from an obscure principality into a high profile, oil-rich state.

al Sabah, Ahmad I ibn Jabar II (1885–1950): *ruler of Kuwait, 1921–50* Son of Shaikh Jabar II al Sabah, al Sabah was the first in the Jabar line to reign over the principality. al Sabah's relations with Abdul Aziz ibn Saud [*qv*], the ruler of Najd [*qv*], deteriorated due to attacks by Ikhwan [*qv*], border disputes and the Najdi embargo on Kuwait's transit trade with the Arabian hinterland. The 1922 Protocol of Uqair [*qv*] resolved these problems, except for the Najdi embargo, which continued for the rest of the decade. In the early 1930s the domestic economy faltered due to the decline of the pearling industry, which had been damaged by cheap Japanese imports. However, there was an improvement in relations with Najd, which became part of Saudi Arabia in 1932.

Al Sabah granted the first oil concession in 1934 to the Western-owned Kuwait Oil Company (KOC). But it was not until 1938 that petroleum was found in commercial quantities. In the meantime al Sabah treated the fees and advance royalties paid by the KOC as his personal property. This angered the Kuwaiti notables, who demanded that the funds should be treated as government income and that al Sabah should restore the twelve-member advisory council he had disbanded on assuming power. Under popular pressure al Sabah accepted a constitution framed by a committee elected by the local Merchant Society. It passed on al Sabah's powers in domestic affairs to an elected parliament of fourteen. In July 1938 the parliament elected Shaikh Abdullah ibn Salim I al Sabah [*qv*] as its president. The diminution of al Sabah's authority was against the interests of Britain and the KOC. Encouraged by them, al Sabah dissolved parliament in

December and suppressed opposition. The sudden death in April 1939 of King Ghazi [*qv*] of Iraq, who had backed the opposition, further helped al Sabah.

During the Second World War, ignoring the pro-Axis sentiment prevalent among his subjects, al Sabah. sided with Britain as required by the 1899 Anglo-Kuwaiti Agreement. The sealing of the oil wells, combined with food shortages, led to much popular discontent. It was only in mid-1946 that petroleum exports could be resumed. The long rule of al Sabah was notable for the emergence of Kuwait as an oil state.

al Sabah, Jaber III ibn Ahmad I (1928–): *ruler of Kuwait, 1977–* Son of Shaikh Ahmad I ibn Jaber II al Sabah [*qv*], al Sabah continued the domestic policies of his predecessor, Shaikh Sabah III ibn Salim I al Sabah [*qv*], and showed no sign of reviving the National Assembly, which had been dissolved in 1976. With the Assembly's scrutinizing gaze removed, the ruling family had taken to lining its pockets at the expense of the state and leading merchants, thus creating distrust between the ruler and the ruled. Following Iran's Islamic revolution [*qv*] in early 1979 and the subsequent Shia [*qv*] protest in Kuwait, al Sabah further restricted the press and public assembly.

In early 1980 al Sabah appointed a constitutional committee to recommend amendments to the constitution. He approved the constitutional changes and called elections for the fifty-member National Assembly in February 1981. As no nationalist–leftist won a seat and the Islamic fundamentalists [*qv*] secured only six, al Sabah found the results deeply satisfying. But his regime was tarnished by the disastrous collapse of Kuwait's unofficial stock exchange in September 1982, leaving £97 billion in paper debt. The voters, restricted to only about a tenth of the adult population, showed their disapproval in the 1985 election by selecting five nationalist-leftists and eleven fundamentalists.

Al Sabah's policy of aiding Iraq [*qv*] in its war with Iran [*qv*], both financially and logistically, was unpopular with the Shias, who wanted Kuwait to stay neutral. On 25 May 1985 a suicide bomber driving a car packed with explosives made an unsuccessful attempt to assassinate al Sabah. Three weeks later a fire at the petroleum complex in Mina Ahmadi raged for a couple of days. The security lapse angered the National Assembly and the government resigned. On 3 July 1985 al Sabah dissolved the chamber and imposed censorship.

Kuwait's deepening alliance with Iraq in its war with Iran made its oil tankers vulnerable to attacks by Tehran. In the spring of 1987 al Sabah secured the assistance of the U.S. Navy, which protected Kuwaiti oil tankers by transferring them to a U.S.-based company.

Once the Iran-Iraq hostilities ended in August 1988, popular pressure built up for the restoration of parliament. Instead of reviving the National Assembly, al Sabah decided to introduce a National Council, an advisory body without legislative powers. When al Sabah held elections to it in June 1990 the opposition boycotted them.

He tried to use the $12–14 billion Kuwait had loaned to Iraq during the Iran-Iraq War as a lever to settle a border dispute with Iraq that dated back to 1961. He failed. He then flooded the oil market in order to lower the price and thus hurt Iraq economically. In retaliation Iraqi President Saddam Hussein [*qv*] invaded and occupied Kuwait on 3 August 1990. Al Sabah and most other members of the ruling family escaped first to Bahrain and then to Saudi Arabia. From his temporary headquarters in Taif, Saudi Arabia, al Sabah contributed $5 billion toward the cost the war against Iraq that was being planned by the United States. On his return home in March 1991, following the expulsion of Iraq from Kuwait by the U.S.-led coalition, al Sabah resisted opposition demands for the immediate revival of the National Assembly, with full legislative powers. In September he signed a ten-year defense cooperation agreement with the United States, allowing it to stockpile military supplies and conduct training exercises, as well as granting it access to Kuwait ports and airfields and stationing of American troops.

The election of thirty-one opposition candidates to the fifty-member parliament in the October 1992 poll indicated the degree of disaffection with his reign. Two years later, when the United States raised an alarm following the southward movement of Iraqi troops inside Iraq, al Sabah quickly mobilized his military. During the crises between Iraq and the United Nations over weapons inspection between 1995 and 1998, al Sabah was the only regional leader who publicly backed Washington's hawkish line against Baghdad.

In 1999, due to the recurring conflict between parliamentarians and the cabinet, he dissolved the National Assembly a year earlier. But in the general election the size of government supporters fell further from eighteen to twelve.

Al Sabah's policy of rapprochement with

Iran and Iraq stalled in the aftermath of the terrorist attacks on the United States in September 2001, followed by President George W. Bush's description of Iran and Iraq as members of the "Axis of evil." Al Sabah cooperated with the Bush administration in its preparations for invading Iraq in 2003 to the extent of letting U.S. forces take over nearly two-thirds of his country. He quietly welcomed the subsqent downfall of the Saddam Hussein regime in 2003.

al Sabah, Sabah III ibn Salim I (1913–77): *ruler of Kuwait, 1965–77* Son of Shaikh Salim I ibn Mubarak, al Sabah began his career as commander of the police force, a position he occupied from 1938 to 1959. He then headed the public health department. Following Kuwaiti independence in June 1961, al Sabah established the Ministry of Foreign Affairs and became its head as well as deputy premier. In October 1962 Shaikh Abdullah III ibn Salim I al Sabah [*qv*] appointed al Sabah, a member of the ruling family's Salim branch, crown prince even though, by precedence, the position should have gone to someone from the Jaber branch. Three months later Shaikh Abdullah III named him as prime minister, an office held until then by the ruler.

On becoming ruler in November 1965, al Sabah nominated a new cabinet. Several parliamentary deputies found his choice so unacceptable that they resigned in protest. To prevent this from happening again, al Sabah decided to rig the next general election. He directed Shaikh Jaber III ibn Ahmad I al Sabah [*qv*], prime minister since May 1966, and Shaikh Saad ibn Abdullah (later crown prince), minister of defense and the interior, to curb the opposition. They imposed censorship and disbanded journalists' and teachers' syndicates. The opposition demanded a rerun of the rigged 1967 general election, but to no avail.

In the June 1967 and October 1973 Arab-Israeli Wars [qv], al Sabah joined the Arab oil embargo [qv] against Israel's allies. The steep petroleum price rise in 1973–74 benefited al Sabah's regime. In 1975 Kuwait's annual oil income soared to $7.2 billion, but the state budget was able to absorb only $2.9 billion. Pressed by radical parliamentarians, al Sabah's government nationalized the Western-owned Kuwait Oil Company.

The Lebanese Civil War [qv], which started in April 1975 and involved the Palestinians living there, had an impact on Kuwait as it had a quarter of a million Palestinian residents. Disruption of the Lebanese press, which was considered the most free in the Arab world, encouraged the Kuwaiti papers (staffed largely by Palestinians) to provide uncensored news. Incensed, in August 1976 al Sabah suspended the National Assembly and imposed press censorship. He dissolved the chamber in September 1977.

al Sabah clan: *Kuwaiti ruling clan* The al Sabah clan is part of the Amarat tribe of the Anaiza tribal federation [qv]. After settling on the shores of Kuwait in 1710, the Anaizas developed trading facilities under the suzerainty of the Ottoman Turks. Of the three leading families who managed communal affairs, the al Sabahs were charged with administration and defense. Out of this arose, from 1752 onward, the al Sabahs' dynastic reign, the first ruler being Shaikh Sabah I al Sabah, and the second Abdullah I al Sabah (r.1756–1814).

In 1899 Shaikh Mubarak I al Sabah (r. 1896–1915) signed a secret treaty with the British whereby, for an annual subsidy of £1500, the Kuwaiti ruler accorded Britain the right of exclusive presence in Kuwait and control over its foreign policy. Shaikh Mubarak I was followed briefly by his older son, Shaikh Jaber II (b. 1865, r. 1915–17), who was deposed by the British for suspected pro-Ottoman sympathies during the First World War, and then by his younger son, Shaikh Salim I (b. 1875, r. 1917–21). Both sons established succession lines within the dynasty that were to share power, though not necessarily alternately. The Jaber branch ruled from 1921–50 (Shaikh Ahmad I ibn Jaber II al Sabah [qv]) and again from 1977 (Shaikh Jaber III ibn Ahmad I ibn al Sabah [qv]). The Salim branch reigned from 1950–65 (Shaikh Abdullah III ibn Salim I al Sabah [qv]) and again from 1965–77 (Shaikh Sabah III ibn Salim al Sabah [qv]). Shaikh Saad ibn Abdullah III, the crown prince since 1977, belongs to the Salim branch.

In 1965—four years after Kuwaiti independence—the title of the ruler was changed from *shaikh* to *emir* (Arabic: *ruler/commander*). In addition, the practice of having the head of the branch not currently occupying the throne to act as crown prince and prime minister was introduced. The leading members of the clan hold such vital ministerial portfolios as oil, defense, interior, and finance.

Sabastiya: *see* Samaria city.

Sabbath *(Hebrew: derivative of shabbat, repose):* Sabbath is the weekly day of rest prescribed for Jews [qv], Christians [qv], and Muslims [qv], although the precise day differs between the groups. Since, according to *Genesis,* God rested from the creation of the world on the seventh day (seven being the total number of spatial directions—forward, backward, above, below, right, left and center), Jews are required to abstain from constructive activity on the Sabbath, and praise the Creator (*Exodus* 20:11) or give thanks for their redemption (*Deuteronomy* 5:14). The Sabbath as a regular weekly fixture probably evolved during the Exile of the Israelites (586–400 B.C.) and replaced the earlier, irregular practice. The Jewish Sabbath, which falls on Saturday, is marked by three special meals and special prayers. An extract from the Torah [*qv*] is read in synagogues [*qv*] during morning service, followed by the chanting of the Haftara— a selection from *Prophets*. According to *Genesis* (1:5) "Evening passed and morning came—that was the first day," so a Jewish day begins in the evening. Hence, the Jewish Sabbath lasts from Friday sunset to Saturday sunset.

Likewise, the Muslim [*qv*] Sabbath lasts from Thursday nightfall to Friday nightfall. *Jumah*, the Arabic word for Friday, means "Assembling," when the believer is required to gather in the *jami masjid* (assembling mosque) for midday prayers. In the Hadith [*qv*] the Prophet Muhammad (A.D. 570–632) states: "Friday was ordered as a divine day of worship both for the Jew and the Christian, but they have acted contrary to the command. The Jew fixed Saturday and the Christian Sunday."

Since the early Christians observed the first day of the week, Monday, in commemoration of the Resurrection of Jesus Christ, Sunday became the Christian Sabbath.

sabra *(Arabic: cactus):* Sabra is the popular term for native-born Israeli Jews [*qv*] who,

like the local cactus plant, are thought to be prickly on the outside but soft and sweet on the inside. In 1996 only 21 percent of Israeli Jews were sabra.

Sabri, Ali (1920–91): *Egyptian military officer and politician; prime minister, 1962–65* Born in Cairo [*qv*], Sabri graduated from the Cairo Military Academy in 1939 and became a commissioned officer. A member of the Free Officers group, he liaised between its leadership and the U.S. Embassy before and during the July 1952 coup. Later he became close to President Gamal Abdul Nasser [*qv*], becoming director of his office. When Egypt and Syria merged to form the United Arab Republic (UAR) [*qv*] in 1958, Sabri was appointed minister for presidential affairs. Although the UAR split three years later, Sabri retained his position in the Egyptian administration. He was promoted to prime minister in September 1962 and kept that position for three years, after which he became one of the four vice presidents.

In July 1965 Nasser appointed him secretary-general of the Arab Socialist Union (ASU) [*qv*], with a mandate to transform it into a cadre-based popular organization. Sabri replaced the provincial and district ASU committees with executive bureaus, putting them under salaried functionaries who had been drawn from the civil service, business management, the factory floor, the teaching and legal professions, and the landowning class. He set up the Socialist Youth Organization (SYO) as an auxiliary to the ASU, but with its own cadre, and led the leftist faction within the ASU, advocating a larger public sector and closer ties with the Soviet Union. In 1966 the SYO carried out a campaign against feudalism. ASU and SYO activists played a crucial role in the demonstrations in Cairo on 9–10 June 1967 to persuade Nasser to reverse his decision to resign in the wake of Egypt's defeat in the Six Day War [qv]. Nasser stayed, but replaced his vice-presidents, including Sabri.

In a further rightward shift in his policies, Nasser reverted the ASU's structure back to that of the pre-1965 period. In September 1969 he demoted Sabri and his supporters in the ASU; and in December he appointed rightist Anwar Sadat [qv] as the only vice-president of the republic. After Nasser's death in September 1970, President Sadat named Sabri as one of his two vice-presidents. But the power struggle between Sadat and Sabri continued, with Sabri advocating maintaining the ASU as an independent body and Sadat favoring making it subservient to the state executive. Sadat's wishes prevailed, and Sabri and his close aides were arrested in May 1971. Sabri was charged with treason and abuse of power during Nasser's presidency. He was found guilty and condemned to death, but his sentence was commuted to life imprisonment. After his release in May 1981 he stayed away from public life.

Sadat, (Muhammad) Anwar (1918–81): *Egyptian military officer and politician; president, 1970–81; prime minister, 1973–74, 1980–81* Son of a petty civil servant in Mit Abul Kom village in the Nile [qv] delta, Sadat grew up in Cairo [qv]. He graduated from the Cairo Military Academy in 1938. Found guilty of spying for the Germans, Sadat, a captain in the signals corps, was jailed in the summer of 1942. He escaped in 1944 and went underground until the detention order was lifted. He spent two years in jail (1946–48) as a suspect in the assassination of Ahmad Osman, a cabinet minister, but was acquitted.

When his business venture failed, he rejoined the army in late 1949, regaining his rank of captain. He was posted to Rafah in the Sinai [qv], where he came into contact with Gamal Abdul Nasser [qv]. Sadat participated in the 22 July 1952 coup mounted by the Free Officers organization and secured a seat on the ruling eighteen-member Revolutionary Command Council (RCC). He liaised with the Muslim Brotherhood [qv], with which he had had friendly relations. Sadat edited *Al Gumhuriya* (The Republic), the regime's mouthpiece. From 1959 to 1969 he served as speaker of the parliament; and from 1964 to 1966 he was one of the four vice presidents.

When in 1965 Egypt established the Islamic Congress in Cairo to rally Muslim opinion abroad behind it, Sadat was chosen as its secretary-general. He was Egypt's representative at international Islamic gatherings, including a summit that led to the formation of the Islamic Conference Organization [qv] in September 1969. Three months later Nasser, performing a rightward shift, appointed Sadat as sole vice president. On Nasser's death in September 1970, Sadat became acting president. In mid-October he was elected president in a referendum, being the sole candidate.

Sadat's power struggle with Ali Sabri [qv] ended in May 1971 when he arrested Sabri and his close aides. In September Sadat promulgated a new constitution that played down the socialist guidelines of the earlier document. In mid-1973 he purged the leadership of the Arab Socialist Union (ASU) [qv] of leftists.

Sadat signed a fifteen-year Egyptian-Soviet Friendship Treaty [qv] in late May 1971. But in July 1972 he demanded that all Soviet military advisers in Egypt, who had arrived after the June 1967 Arab-Israeli War [qv], must leave the country within ten days. Some 15,000 Soviet personnel left, taking with them fighter aircraft, interceptors, and surface-to-air missiles. However, some of them gradually returned after October 1972 and again after February 1973. Following Sadat's rapprochement with Moscow in March 1973, Soviet arms shipments resumed.

Sadat became prime minister (stepping down in 1974) and began to plan an invasion of the Israeli-occupied Arab territories [qv]. During the October 1973 Arab-Israeli War [qv] the Egyptian troops performed unprecedentedly well, capturing land in the Sinai from the Israelis and retaining it. This enhanced Sadat's standing at home and in the region. But instead of pursuing peace under the auspices of the United Nations, he opted for U.S. mediation in his talks with Israel, thus breaking Arab ranks. After two interim disengagement agreements with Israel (Sinai I and Sinai II [qv], in 1974 and 1975) the peace process stalled.

Sadat's economic liberalization, involving the removal or reduction of subsidies on essentials, triggered countrywide bread riots in January 1977, the most serious upheaval since the anti-British rioting a quarter of a century earlier. It ceased only when Sadat canceled the price increases. He appealed for aid to the United States, which responded positively. After Moscow had refused to reschedule the Egyptian debts of US$10–12 billion, Sadat unilaterally abrogated the Soviet Friendship Treaty.

In November, in a dramatic move he addressed the Israeli Knesset [qv] in Jerusalem [qv], and this made him something of a hero in the Western world, a factor that paved the way for the commercial success of his autobiography, *In Search of Identity* (1978). Washington began to provide military aid to Egypt. Sadat signed the Camp David Accords [qv] with Israeli Premier Menachem Begin [qv] at the White House in Washington on 18 September 1978 in the presence of U.S. President Jimmy Carter.

At home, fearing a military coup, Sadat dismissed his chief of staff and defense minister, General Abdul Ghani Gamassy, and appointed National Democratic Party (NDP) [qv] leader Mustafa Khalil as prime minister to lead a "peace government" of technocrats and academics.

In March 1979 Sadat and Begin signed the bilateral Egyptian-Israeli Peace Treaty [qv] at the White House. This resulted in the immediate suspension of Egypt from the Arab League [qv] and the Islamic Conference Organization (ICO) [qv], and the severing of links by the Arab League members, except Oman. To overcome the increasing isolation of Egypt, Sadat assumed increased power at home. He dissolved parliament two years short of its normal tenure and rigged the first multiparty election in June 1979, his NDP securing 83 percent of the seats. He expelled the last of the remaining 200 Soviet civilian experts. Egypt became more dependent on the United States for economic survival.

After securing Khalil's resignation in May 1980, Sadat appointed himself prime minister. By immediately holding a stage-managed referendum, he abrogated the constitutional provision that limited the presidency to one six-year term. Sadat's peace treaty with Israel, and the rising corruption and ostentatiousness of the new rich, alienated the Islamic forces in Egypt, whom he had courted in the early years of his regime. The dismantling of the pricing mechanism introduced by the Nasser regime fueled inflation and brought much hardship to the working and lower-middle classes.

Contemptuous of opposition, both secular and religious, Sadat banned strikes and demonstrations and became increasingly intolerant and autocratic, indulging his fancy of imperial grandeur. His sweeping crackdown on dissidents in September 1981 resulted in some 2,000 arrests. The next month he was assassinated by four Islamic militants, led by Khlaid Ahmad Shawki Islambouli, during a military parade on the anniversary of the October 1973 Arab-Israeli War. In contrast to the mass grief demonstrated at the death of Nasser, most Egyptians were unmoved by Sadat's demise.

al Sadr, Musa (1928–78): *Lebanese/Iranian Islamic leader* Born into a religious family of Lebanese origin in Qom [*qv*], al Sadr was educated in secular and Islamic traditions before being sent to Tehran University, where he acquired a postgraduate degree in Islamic studies in 1956. Three years later the Shia [*qv*] establishment in Qom sent him to Lebanon as its representative to provide religious guidance to Lebanese Shias. Following al Sadr's condemnation of Muhammad Reza Shah Pahlavi [*qv*] for suppressing the countrywide protest in Iran led by Ayatollah Ruhollad Khomeini [*qv*] in June 1963, he was deprived of his Iranian nationality.

Al Sadr then acquired Lebanese citizenship. In 1967 he formed the Higher Shia Communal Council (HSCC), the first of its kind in the country, becoming a leading spokesman of Shias. Five years later the HSCC presented social, administrative, and economic demands to the government to ameliorate the living and working conditions of Shias. This charter became the manifesto of the multiconfessional Movement of the Disinherited that al Sadr founded in February 1973. It proved popular with Shias, who were dissatisfied with their traditional leaders.

Through rallies, demonstrations, and strikes al Sadr made Shias, the single largest sect, aware of their strength. When the Lebanese Civil War [*qv*] erupted in April 1975, al Sadr realized that unlike most other important religious sects, Shias did not have their own militia. He set up a militia adjunct to the Movement of the Disinherited in June 1975 and called it the Lebanese Resistance Detachments, which became popularly known by its Arabic acronym, Amal [*qv*]. It fought the Phalange militia [*qv*]. While opposed to the traditional Shia leadership, al Sadr remained friendly with the Sunni [*qv*] establishment, with whom he shared the demand for political parity between Muslims [*qv*] and Christians [*qv*].

During a trip to Libya in August 1978, al Sadr "disappeared." Libya insisted that al Sadr had left by plane for Italy, but his followers alleged that he had been detained or assassinated by his Libyan hosts. Lebanese Shias, routinely calling al Sadr "imam" [*qv*], regard him as a martyr, worthy of their veneration.

al Said, Nuri (1888–1958): *Iraqi military officer and politician; prime minister, 1930–32, 1939–40, 1941–44, 1946–47, 1949, 1950–52, 1954–57, 1958* Born in Baghdad [*qv*] to a Sunni [*qv*] family of mixed Arab-

Kurdish [*qv*] origin, al Said graduated from the Istanbul Military Academy and became a commissioned officer in the Ottoman army. In 1914 he joined the clandestine Arab nationalist group al Ahd (the Covenant). During the First World War, having defected from the Ottoman military in 1916, he joined the Arab revolt led by Sharif Hussein ibn Ali. He became chief of staff in the army of Faisal I ibn Hussein [*qv*]. After gaining the throne of Iraq in 1921, Faisal I appointed al Said as his chief of army staff. He became defense minister from 1922–24 and 1926–28 and was promoted to prime minister in 1930.

Al Said founded a political party named after the secret group he had joined earlier, al Ahd, even though he had abandoned his pan-Arabism [*qv*] and reached accommodation with the British mandate, an arrangement formalized in the Anglo-Iraqi Treaty of 1930 [*qv*], which provided the trappings but not the substance of independence. al Said was reappointed prime minister in 1939.

During the Second World War, the anti-British feeling in Iraq was so strong that, despite his pro-British learnings, al Said dared not join the Allies against the Axis Powers. In March 1940 he resigned as premier but agreed to join the next cabinet, led by Rashid Ali Gailani [*qv*], which lasted until January 1941. al Said stayed out of the next Gailani government, which took office in April. After al Said had been restored to the premiership by the British following their overthrow of Gailani in May 1941, he declared war against Germany in 1943. By the time he stepped down in June 1944, the groundwork for the founding of the Arab League [*qv*], inspired by the British, had been done.

After the war al Said served as prime minister in 1946–47, 1949, and 1950–52, before Faisal II [*qv*] came of age in 1953. Following a general election in June 1954, al Said was appointed as premier because the 1930 Anglo-Iraqi Treaty needed to be renegotiated before its expiration in 1955. Al Said's decision to join the Baghdad Pact [*qv*] in 1955, and his failure to condemn Egypt's aggressors in the Suez War [*qv*] of 1956, isolated Iraq from the rest of the Arab world. In 1957 he endorsed the Eisenhower Doctrine [*qv*], which offered help to Middle Eastern countries threatened by world communism or its regional allies.

Al Said's increasingly dictatorial ways, his manipulation of the electoral system, and his banning of political parties made the regime unpopular. When the Free Officers' group launched a successful coup in July 1958, it assassinated al Said along with the members of the royal family.

Said ibn Taimur ibn Faisal (1911–72): *Sultan of Oman, 1932–70* Son of Taimur ibn Faisal [*qv*], Said was enthroned by the British in 1932 after they had dethroned Sultan Taimur on the ground of fiscal irresponsibility. Reacting to his father's extravagance, Said took parsimony to extremes. He also monopolized power. Opposed to progress, he prevented his subjects from using, for instance, patent medicines, trousers, radio, books, and even spectacles.

In 1937 Said gave an oil concession to Petroleum Concessions (Oman). When, after the Second World War, it began explorations in the interior, which was controled by Imam [*qv*] Ghalib ibn Ali, problems ensued. Its exploration around the Buraimi oasis in 1951 upset Saudi Arabia, which claimed part of the oasis and occupied it. Said was also challenged by Imam Ghalib ibn Ali, who proclaimed the independent Imamate of Oman in 1954 and applied for membership of the Arab League [qv], which did not include the Sultanate of Oman. Said's forces, armed and led by the British, crushed the challenge by the end of 1955. Acting in collusion with the forces of Abu Dhabi, they also recovered the part of the Buraimi oasis that was occupied by the Saudis.

In 1957 the Imam's brother, Talib ibn Ali, encouraged by Saudi Arabia and Egypt, mounted a rebellion in the interior. Said called on the British to render him military assistance according to the Anglo-Omani Agreement of 1925 [qv]. The armed uprising dwindled into guerrilla actions. Egypt and the other states charged that the British had committed armed aggression against the Imamate of Oman and placed the matter before the United Nations. While the U.N. commission of enquiry failed to uphold the claim, several Arab countries succeeded in persuading the U.N. General Assembly to adopt a resolution demanding the end of British colonial presence in Oman. Nonetheless, after Said had withdrawn to his palace in Salalah, 600 miles/1,000 km southwest of Muscat [qv], in 1958, administrative control of the country passed almost totally into the hands of British civil servants, with London providing the funds for all development projects.

In 1962 Petroleum Development Oman, the successor to Petroleum Concessions (Oman), struck oil in commercial quantities. Petroleum income rose from $21 million in 1967 to $117 million three years later, but Said left the money untouched. By then Said faced a challenged to his authority from the inhabitants of Dhofar. The victory of the leftist forces in the adjoining South Yemen on the eve on the British withdrawal in November 1967 boosted the morale of Dhofari revolutionaries. This, and the total inflexibility of Said, made the British apprehensive. They engineered a coup in July 1970 and replaced Said with his son, Qaboos [qv].

Saiqa *(Arabic: Thunderbolt): Palestinian commando force* Saiqa is the military wing of the Vanguards of the Popular War of Liberation, sponsored by the Syrian Baath Party [qv] after the June 1967 Arab-Israeli War [qv]. It started commando actions against Israel from Jordan and joined the Palestine Liberation Organization (PLO) [qv]. It became the first Palestinian group to receive arms, secretly, from Moscow, and later training for its members in the Soviet Union. It was second in size only to the guerilla force of Fatah [qv]. When fighting broke out between Palestinian commandos and Jordanian troops in September 1970, it was Saiqa, then about 5,000 strong, that persuaded Syrian President Salah Jadid [qv] to give military aid to the Palestinians. They received arms, but when Jordan mounted a counteroffensive using tanks and planes, Syria's defense minister, Hafiz Assad [qv], refused to commit his air force.

Following Assad's seizure of power in November, he purged Saiqa of its leftist elements, appointed his protégé, Zuhair Mohsen, as secretary-general, and brought it under the control of the Syrian defense ministry. For most of the 1970s Mohsen headed the PLO's military department. At the Palestine National Council (PNC) [qv] session in June 1974, Saiqa backed the idea of setting up a "national authority" in the West Bank

[*qv*] and Gaza [*qv*] as an intermediate step toward liberating all of mandate Palestine. Mohsen's assassination in 1979 was a severe blow to Saiqa.

After it had been expelled from Beirut [*qv*] in 1982 and had based itself in Damascus [*qv*], Saiqa joined the pro-Syrian Palestine National Salvation Front against PLO Chairman Yasser Arafat [*qv*]. It opposed his attempts to make the PLO work in tandem with King Hussein [*qv*] of Jordan in the mid-1980s and continued to derive most of its strength from the Palestinian refugee camps in Syria. After the PNC had repudiated Arafat's deal with King Hussein in April 1987, it ended its boycott of the PLO institutions.

During the Kuwait crisis of 1990–91, taking its cue from Syria it opposed Arafat's backing of Iraqi President Saddam Hussein [*qv*]. In September 1993 it rejected Oslo Accord I [*qv*]. In 2000 its leader was Issam Qadi.

Salafiya movement and salafin *(Arabic: pl. of salafi, follower of ancestors): A Sunni Islamic reformist movement* A derivative of *salaf al salihin* (the pious ancestors), the Salafiya movement was influenced by Jamal al-Din Afghani (1838–97), an Islamic thinker who noted the militancy of the *salaf* (ancestors) of the early Islam. One of his disciples, Muhammad Abdu (1849–1905), stressed the impact that the salaf had had on the shaping of the Sharia [*qv*]. Muhammad Rashid Rida (1865–1935), a follower of Abdu, researched what the Prophet Muhammad and the *salaf al salihin* had done and said in order to apply that to contemporary conditions. He preferred to follow the concepts of the *salaf al salihin* rather than the four Sunni [*qv*] legal schools.

From the 1920s onward it became clear that the salafiya could be realized only if it won popular support. The movement's current adherents want conformity with the Islam of their salaf at the political level. They argued that since the Prophet Muhammad was succeeded by a caliph, chosen by the community, there can be no place for hereditary power in Islam. As such they are part of the religious opposition that exists, largely clandestinely, in the member states of the Gulf Cooperation Council [*qv*]. They have been especially active in Kuwait since the mid-1970s and want to establish a democratic republican regime there. Some Kuwaiti salafin participated in the armed uprising against the Saudi royal family at the Grand Mosque of Mecca [*qv*] in November 1979. As a quasi-political organization, the salafin won four seats in the Kuwaiti general election of 1992. They performed better in the subsequent polls, securing seven seats in 1999.

Salam, Saeb (1905–): *Lebanese politician; prime minister, 1952, 1953, 1960–61, 1970–73* Born into a notable Sunni [*qv*] family in Beirut [*qv*], Salem graduated from the American University of Beirut [*qv*] and finished his postgraduate studies at the London School of Economics and Political Science. He then managed the varied family agrarian and industrial interests. Elected to parliament in 1943, he retained a seat there until the 1972 election, except in 1957, when the election was rigged by President Camille Chamoun [*qv*]. In 1946 he became interior minister and served briefly as prime minister in 1952 and 1953. He was deputy prime minister in 1956, but resigned his post in protest at President Chamoun's refusal to condemn the Anglo-French-Israeli aggression against Egypt in the Suez War [*qv*]. In the 1958 civil strife he sided with the anti-Chamounist camp led by Kamal Jumblat [*qv*]. After serving as prime minister from 1960–61, he headed a group of Beirut-based Sunni parliamentarians that rivaled the one led by the Tripoli-based Rashid Karami [*qv*], who was the premier for most of the 1960s. When Suleiman Franjieh [*qv*] became president in 1970, he called on Salem to form the next government. Salem purged the army and civil service of the reformists inspired by ex-president Fuad Chehab [*qv*].

With the emergence of the Front of National and Progressive Parties and Forces under Kamal Jumblat in 1972, such traditional leaders as Salem lost ground. He resigned as prime minister in April 1973. Two years later, on the eve of the Lebanese Civil War [*qv*], he was one of the six former premiers who demanded that the army command council be reconstituted to give parity to Muslims [*qv*] and Christians [*qv*]. During the Israeli siege of Beirut in June–August 1982, Salem supervised the evacuation of Palestinian and Syrian forces from West Beirut.

After the assassination of Bashir Gemayel [*qv*] in September, Salem played a crucial role in the election of Amin Gemayel [*qv*] as president. Later, when Gemayel fell out with the nationalist-leftist constitutents of the Lebanese National Movement [*qv*], Salam failed to mobilize Muslims behind the president, highlighting the virtual collapse of Sunni power, mainly because the sect had failed to form a powerful militia of its own. As the civil conflict continued well into the 1980s, Salem's influence declined sharply.

Salih, Ali Abdullah (1942–): *Yemeni military officer and politician; president of North Yemen, 1978–90; president of Yemen, 1990–* A member of the Sanhan tribe of the Hashid tribal confederation, Salih was born in the northern region. After receiving a rudimentary education, he enrolled in the army as a soldier and rose rapidly through the ranks. After the assassination of President Ibrahim Hamid [*qv*] in October 1977, as commander of the Taiz region Salih assisted Ahmad Ghashmi [*qv*], chairman of the Military Council, to crush a rebellion by rival officers in April 1978. Ghashmi promoted Salih to deputy commander in chief of the army.

Following Ghashmi's assassination in June 1978, Salih became chief of staff and a member of the Presidential Council. A month later, seventy-six of the ninety-six People's Constituent Assembly members elected him president. To rally internal support he blamed South Yemen for Ghashmi's murder. In October he survived an attempted coup by a section of the army. But the following February, his troops failed to expel the National Democratic Front (NDF) [*qv*] forces from the areas they occupied along the border with South Yemen. Mediation by the Arab League [*qv*] led to an agreement by the two Yemens to unite within a year. When the concord proved stillborn, the NDF made a deal with Salih in mid-1980: formation of a national unity government to implement land reform and nonaligned foreign policy.

In October 1980 Salih replaced premier Abdul Aziz Abdul Ghani [*qv*] with Abdul Karim Iryani. However, having consolidated his power by purging the officer corps and placing his family and tribal kin in key positions, he did not invite the NDF to share power in a national unity government. In October 1981 Salih set up a 1,000-member General People's Congress [qv], partly by appointment and partly by indirect election.

When the need for arms rose sharply due to the introduction of conscription in 1979, Salih opted for Soviet weapons because of their cheapness. This upset Saudi Arabia, which suspended its budgetary aid of $300 million a year and all other economic aid. Following Salih's visit to Riyadh [qv] in August 1980, the Saudis partially resumed the aid. The next spring Salih arrested one of his close advisers, Abdullah Asnaj, for spying for Saudi Arabia and the United States. In October he visited Moscow. In 1984, when the Yemeni subsidiary of a U.S. oil company started to extract petroleum, he signed a Friendship and Cooperation Treaty with the Soviet Union [qv] during his second visit to Moscow.

At home he maintained a balance between the conservative tribal confederations in the north and the NDF in the south and managed to survive several assassination attempts. After being reelected president in 1983, Salih recalled Abdul Ghani to head the government. He maintained friendly relations with Saudi Arabia, the chief paymaster of North Yemen, while cultivating the leftist South Yemeni regime by periodically renewing the earlier agreement of eventual unity between the two Yemens. Following his reelection as president in 1988, he responded positively to the idea of an alliance of North Yemen with Egypt, Iraq, and Jordan, which materialized as the Arab Cooperation Council [qv] in early 1989. A steep decline in the economy of South Yemen resulted in the

uniting of the two Yemens in May 1990, with Salih becoming president of the united country.

In the Kuwait crisis of 1990–91 Salih refused to side with the Saudi-U.S. alliance against Iraq. Yemen, the only Arab member of the United Nations Security Council, voted against the U.S. stance and abstained on crucial resolutions on the Kuwait crisis and the Second Gulf War [qv]. The consequent Saudi retribution damaged the Yemeni economy. When the outcome of the April 1993 general election confirmed the existence of a political division along the old North-South divide, Salih's relations with his vice president, Ali Salim al Beidh [qv], soured. Salih won the subsequent Yemeni Civil War [qv] between the northern and southern forces in May–June 1994, when Saudi Arabia backed the southern camp. His prestige at home rose sharply.

In 1995 Salih was elevated to chairman of the GPC, a new post. Two years later the GPC improved its parliamentary strength from 123 to 187.

But his government encountered violent protest during 1997-98 when it tried to implement economic reform by cutting subsidies on basic necessities and fuel. Despite this, in the first direct presidential poll in 1999, he won 96.3 percent of the vote. In 2001 Salih replaced Abdul Karim Iryani as prime minister and appointed Abdul Qadir Bajammal as prime minister.

While Yemen's armed forces conducted their first joint military exercise with the U.S. forces in November 1998, Salih condemned Washington's Operation Desert Fox [qv] launched the next month. In October 2000 a suicide bomb attack on USS *Cole* while refueling in Aden [*qv*] killed seventeen sailors. The Islamic Army of Aden-Abyan claimed responsibility.

After the terrorist attacks on the United States in September 2001, Salih's government cooperated with Washington to capture Al Qaida [*qv*] activists based in Yemen.

Sallal, Abdullah (1917–2001): *Yemeni military officer and politician; president, 1962–67; prime minister, 1962–63, 1966–67* Born in a Zaidi [*qv*] blacksmith family in the north, Sallal was sent to Baghdad Military Academy, where he graduated in 1938. On his return home he was jailed briefly for suspected anti-regime activities. After his release he was permitted to resume his military career. He participated in the coup against Imam Yahya in early 1948, led by his personal adviser, Abdullah Wazir. But Wazir was overthrown the following month by Yahya's son, Crown Prince Ahmad ibn Yahya [*qv*], who succeeded his father. Sallal found himself condemned to death, but his sentence was commuted to a seven-year prison term. After his release he was appointed governor of Hodeida province.

Sallal became a protege of Crown Prince Muhammad al Badr [*qv*], who made him commander of his guard in 1956, and of the newly established military academy three years later. When al Badr acceeded the throne on 18 September 1962, he made Sallal, then a brigadier general, commander of the royal guard. Supported by a secret Nasserite [*qv*] group among military officers, Sallal carried out a successful coup against Imam al Badr on 26 September, but the ruler escaped unhurt. Sallal became president of the republic, promoting himself to field marshal, and led the republican camp in the Yemeni Civil War [*qv*], which continued until 1970. He concurrently assumed the prime ministry from 1962–63.

The republicans, deriving their main support from the Shafei (Sunni [*qv*]) tribes inhabiting the coastal plain and southern hills, were aided by Egypt, while the royalists, with a solid base among the Zaidi tribes in the north, were helped by the Saudis. Two and a half years of intense fighting were followed by a year of comparative lull. To placate the royalists, with a view to reaching an accommodation with them, Egyptian President Gamal Abdul Nasser [*qv*] placed Sallal under house arrest in Cairo [*qv*] and let the Presidential Council, of which Sallal was a member, run North Yemen.

With the failure of Nasser's peacemaking efforts, Sallal was allowed to return to Sanaa [*qv*] in September 1966. Besides resuming the presidency, Sallal took over the premiership and carried out a purge. He tried to regain the area lost to the monarchists in the war, but failed, partly because of the June 1967 Arab-Israeli War [*qv*], which diverted Egypt's resources. Cairo decided to withdraw its forces from North Yemen, and this weakened the position of Sallal, who was seen as an Egyptian protégé. He was overthrown in November 1967 during his visit to Moscow. He went into exile in Baghdad [*qv*], in October 1981. During the presidency of Ali Abdullah Salih [*qv*], he was allowed to return home, where he stayed away from public life.

Samaria: *Ancient kingdom* Called *Shomron* in Hebrew, Samaria covers the central zone of ancient Canaan/Palestine lying between the Jordan River [*qv*] and the Mediterranean Sea, and delineated by Galilee, the area to the west of Lake Galilee, to the north and Judea/Judah [qv] to the south. Its political and geographical center was Shechem, near present-day Nablus [qv].

It took the Israelites more than two centuries, from ca. 1250 B.C. to ca. 1030 B.C., to conquer and colonise Canaan. During the united Israelite Kingdom under King David (r. 1010–970 B.C)., northern Samaria was given to half of the tribe of Manasseh (the other halfwere settled to the east of the Jordan), and southern Samaria to the tribe of Ephraim.

Following the demise of King Solomon (r. 970–930 B.C.), the northern tribes, including Ephraim and Manasseh, split from their southern kinsmen, but retained the name Israelite Kingdom. Its capital at Tirzah (now Tall al Fariah) was shifted in 880 B.C. to Samaria City [qv]—these settlements and Shechem together forming an equilateral triangle, each side being 7 miles/10 km long. The kingdom fell to the Assyrians in 722 B.C. During the time of Jesus Christ (ca. 6 B.C.–A.D. 30) Samaria was ruled by the Romans.

Samaria city: Modern village of Sabastiya, also called Sebaste. Archaeological excavations during the early part of the twentieth century established that the history of Samaria city dates back to the late forth millennium B.C. During Old Testament [qv] times it became the capital of the (northern) Israelite Kingdom in 880 BC. It became the site of an acropolis, which contained a royal palace.

It was captured by the Assyrians, who enslaved most of its inhabitants and colonized it with Cutheans. The succeeding Persians retained it as an administrative center. After the capture of the region by Alexander the Great in 332 B.C., it became a Greek colony. It was destroyed by John Hyrcanus in 120 B.C., restored by Pompey (106–48 B.C.), a Roman general, and renamed Sebaste (Greek for Augusta) in honor of Roman Emperor Augustus (Sebastos in Greek) by Herod the Great (37–34 B.C.), and endowed with an Augustine temple, a forum and a basilica. After reaching a zenith in the late Roman Empire, it declined steadily during the Byzantine era (A.D. 476–1453), dwindling to a village during the Ottoman Empire (1517–1918), called Sabastiya.

Samaritans: *quasi-Jewish community.* This ancient Hebrew [qv]-speaking sect claims desent from the Kingdom of Israel when, following King Solomon's death in 920 B.C., the Samaritans formed the Kingdom of Israel and the Jews formed the Kingdom of Judah. They believe that Moses was the only prophet, and accept only the first five books of the Hebrew Bible [qv]. According to them, Abraham prepared to sacrifice his son Isaac not in Jerusalem [qv] but at Mount Gerizim that towers above Nablus [qv]. In 1917 there were only 146 Samaritans in the world. Sixty years later, they numbered 583, divided between settlement of Kiryat Luza on Mount Gerizim and Holon, south of Tel Aviv [qv]. They have preserved their language and culture. At Passover [qv], they all assemble at their synagogue on Mount Girizim to sacrifice sheep in a ritual similar to that of the ancient Jews. Those living in Kiryat Luza are entitled to elect one member to the Pale stinian Legislative Council. And those resident in Holon carry Israeli passports and serve in the military.

Samarra: *Iraqi town* Pop. 150,000 (1992, est.). According to the archaeological excavations of this century, the history of Samarra, located on the Tigris River [*qv*], dates back to the fifth millennium B.C. The present town, established during the third century A.D., reached its peak when Caliph al Mutasim (r. A.D. 833–41) abandoned Baghdad [*qv*] as the capital of the Abbasid Empire in A.D. 836 in its favor, endowing it with gardens and a palace. Though he renamed it Surra Manraa, the old name survived. By the time Caliph al Mutamid (r. A.D. 870–92) had returned the capital to Baghdad in A.D. 892, Samarra had spread many miles along the river. It was in Samarra that the last *imam* [*qv*] of the Twelvers Shias [*qv*], Muhammad al Qasim, the infant son of the eleventh Imam Hassan al Askari, went into spiritual occultation in A.D. 873.

Over the next four centuries the town declined dramatically. It has since revived. Its tourist offerings today include the minaret al Malwiya; the ziggurat, a temple tower of ancient Mesopotamia [*qv*] in the form of a stepped pyramid; and the Great Friday Mosque and the Abu Dulaf Mosque built during the ninth century. A pilgrimage place for Shias, it contains a copper-domed mosque that is sacred to them.

San Remo Agreement (1920): The San Remo Agreement is the title given to decisions regarding the Middle East [*qv*] made by the Supreme Council of the League of Nations (1920–1945), consisting of the major Allied powers—Belgium, Britain, France, Greece, Italy, and Japan (the United States did not join the League of Nations)—at its meeting in San Remo, Italy, in April 1920. The main decisions were as follows: Britain and France would decide the nature of the mandates for the region and submit their proposals to the League for debate and voting. France was awarded the mandates for Syria and Lebanon, and Britain for Palestine [*qv*] and Mesopotamia [*qv*] (later Iraq). The British mandate for Palestine included the Balfour Declaration [*qv*].

Sanaa: *capital of Yemen* Pop. 1,779,000 (2003, est.). Called Ghumdan in pre-Islamic times, Sanaa was a center of the Sabaeans, who arrived from the north in the tenth century B.C. They surrendered to the Arabs [*qv*] in the second century A.D. In A.D. 632 Ali, cousin and son-in-law of the Prophet Muhammad, converted its residents to Islam [*qv*].

Due to its central place in the Yemeni highlands, its fate has been shaped by the region's history, dominated by the Zaidi (Shia) [*qv*] tribes, whose rulers, called *imams* [*qv*], were in the habit of changing their capital. After losing its primacy for nearly four centuries, Sanaa found favor with Imam Abdul Wahhab ibn Tahir al Rassi (r. 1478–88). The Ottoman suzerainity over North Yemen from 1517 meant little to Sanaa, where the local imams held sway until 1872. Indigenous resistance to the Ottomans continued, culminating in a rebellion by Imam Yahya in 1911, which was suppressed. The treaty of 1913 limited him to the highlands, with Sanaa as his capital. After the Ottoman collapse, he reasserted his control of the coastal plain and the southern Shafii (Sunni) [*qv*] areas to the south, upgrading Sanaa into the national capital. But his son, Ahmad (r. 1948–62), moved the capital south to Taiz. After the 1962 revolution,

Sanaa once again became the premier city. During the 1962–70 civil war [*qv*], it suffered extensive damage. Sanaa is an important commercial and communications center. Its tourist attractions include the walled Old City, a Jewish quarter with gold and silver metalwork and embroidery workshops, and the Great Mosque.

Sarkis, Elias (1924–85): *Lebanese politician; president, 1976–82* Born into a middle-class Maronite [*qv*] family in Beirut [*qv*], Sarkis obtained a law degree from Saint Joseph University. From 1953 he worked in the legal section of the government's audit department. While investigating financial irregularities at the defense ministry, he drew the attention of President Fuad Chehab (president from 1958–64) [*qv*], who transferred him to his secretariat. Sarkis made the presidential bureau a leading center of power, and became its director general in 1962. After briefly serving President Charles Helou (president from 1964–70) [*qv*], Sarkis became governor of the Central Bank in 1966. Four years later he lost to Suleiman Franjieh [*qv*] in the presidential race by one vote. He came to represent moderate Maronite opinion, which was rare after the start of the Lebanese Civil War in April 1975 [*qv*].

Sarkis became a favorite of Syrian President Hafiz Assad [*qv*] following the latter's intervention in the war on the Maronite side in June 1976. The only candidate in the presidential election three months later, Sarkis won it. Working in conjunction with Assad, he replaced top officials with pro-Syrian nominees. When the Phalangists [*qv*] protested, he tried to limit Syrian power, but in vain.

His differences with Prime Minister Salim Hoss [*qv*] deepened. Sarkis saw national reconciliation as a prelude to curtailing Syria's influence in Lebanon, whereas Hoss regarded it as a preamble to implementing a security plan in coordination with the Syrian peacekeeping force. Efforts to bridge the gap between the two failed, and Hoss resigned in June 1980. Later in the year, the cabinet, led by Shafiq Wazzan, split in the face of a crisis created by a confrontation between the Phalangists and the Syrians in Zahle, a largely Greek Orthodox [*qv*] city.

In June 1982, within a week of invading Lebanon, the Israeli forces expelled Sarkis from his presidential palace in Baabda. By the time his term officially expired in September, Israel was very much in charge of Beirut [*qv*]. Sarkis retired from public life.

al Saud clan: *see* House of Saud.

al Saud, Abdul Aziz ibn Abdul Rahman: *see* Abdul Aziz ibn Abdul Rahman al Saud.

al Saud, Abdullah ibn Abdul Aziz: *see* Abdullah ibn Abdul Aziz al Saud.

al Saud, Fahd ibn Abdul Aziz: *see* Fahd ibn Abdul Aziz al Saud.

al Saud, Faisal ibn Abdul Aziz: *see* Faisal ibn Abdul Aziz al Saud.

al Saud, Khalid ibn Abdul Aziz: *see* Khalid ibn Abdul Aziz al Saud.

al Saud, Saud ibn Abdul Aziz (1902–69): *King of Saudi Arabia, 1953–64* After the death of his elder brother, Turki ibn Abdul Aziz (b. 1900), in 1919, Saud became the eldest son of King Abdul Aziz ibn Abdul Rahman al Saud [*qv*]. In 1926 King Abdul Aziz appointed Saud his viceroy in Najd [*qv*]. On the founding of the kingdom of Saudi Arabia in 1932, he named Saud crown prince. Two years later, along with his younger brother,

Faisal [*qv*], Saud carried out a victorious campaign against North Yemen [*qv*]. When, a month before his death in November 1953, King Abdul Aziz appointed a council of ministers, he named Saud its chairman. On succeeding his father, Saud retained the premiership and named Faisal crown prince.

With the sharp rise in oil revenues due to the growing demand for Saudi oil to fill the gap caused by the 1951–53 Iranian oil nationalization crisis, traditional, direct governance by the monarch proved inadequate when it came to handling the increasing fiscal and administrative complexities. The resulting chaos, compounded by Saud's extravagance and mismanagement, created a crisis. In 1958 he was compelled to appoint a new cabinet and hand over the premiership to Faisal. His deteriorating health led him to go abroad frequently for medical treatment. Yet he tried to regain full executive authority, and in 1960, after he had promised a constitutional monarchy, including a predominantly elected parliament, he succeeded. However, he reneged on his pledge for political reform.

After the republican coup in North Yemen in 1962, which implicitly threatened the future of the Saudi monarchy, Saud ceded his executive powers once again to Faisal, and Saudi Arabia became involved in the North Yemeni Civil War [*qv*]. In 1963, during Saud's long absences abroad for medical treatment, anti-Saud forces consolidated their position. As a result, in March 1964 Saud transferred all his powers to Faisal, who was named viceroy. In November the Supreme Religious Council and a group of seniormost princes deposed S. and named Faisal king.

Saud went into exile in Europe. In 1966, when rivalry between Egyptian president Gamal Abdul Nasser [*qv*] and King Faisal intensified, Nasser allowed Saud to settle in Cairo [*qv*] to strengthen his own anti-Faisal position. But when, following Egypt's defeat in the June 1967 Arab-Israeli War [*qv*], Nasser sought a rapprochement with Faisal, Saud lost his importance. He died in Athens, Greece, in February 1969, leaving behind fifty-two sons and fifty-five daughters.

Saudi Arabia:
Official name: Kingdom of Saudi Arabia
Capital: Riyadh [*qv*]
Area: 865,000 sq. miles/2,240,000 sq. km, including parts of the Saudi Arabia-Iraq and Saudi Arabia-Kuwait Neutral Zones [*qv*]
Population: 21,685 million (2003, est.)
Gross domestic product: $176.1 billion (2001)
National currency: Saudi Rial (SR); SR 1 = $0.267 = £0.187 =EUR 0.30 (2001)
Form of government: monarchy
Official language: Arabic [*qv*]
Official religion: Islam [*qv*]
Administrative regions: Saudi Arabia consists of four regions, divided into thirteen provinces, run by governors appointed by the monarch.
Constitution: In March 1992, sixty years after the founding of Saudi Arabia, King Fahd ibn Abdul Aziz al Saud [*qv*] issued the Basic Law of Government as a decree. It declared the Quran [*qv*] and the *Sunna* [*qv*] as the constitution of Saudi Arabia, which is described as a hereditary monarchy in the male descendants of Abdul Aziz ibn Abdul Rahman al Saud [*qv*]. The monarch is the head of state and the council of ministers, and the commander in chief of the military. He appoints the prime minister and other

ministers. The Basic Law provided for the appointment of a Consultative Council of sixty members and its chairman by the monarch for a four-year term. There was no provision for a legislature, political parties or trade unions.

Consultative Council: In August 1993 the first fully nominated sixty-member Consultative Council, with a four-year tenure, was named by the king. It was authorized to question the government, and any official action it disputed was to be referred to the monarch. Its strength was raised to ninety in 1997 and then to 120 four years later.

Ethnic composition (1990): Arab, 78 percent; Asian, 19 percent other, 3 percent.

Executive authority: Executive authority rests with the king, who rules through a council of ministers responsible to him.

High officials:

Head of state: King Fahd ibn Abdul Aziz [*qv*], 1982–

Prime minister: King Fahd ibn Abdul Aziz, 1982–

Crown prince and first deputy prime minister: Abdullah ibn Abdul Aziz al Saud [*qv*], 1982–

Head of the Supreme Religious Council: Shaikh Adul Aiz ibn Adulla al Saikh, 1999–

Chairman of the Consultative Council: Shaikh Muhammad ibn Ibrahim al Jubair, 2001

History (since ca. 1900): In 1902 Abdul Aziz ibn Abdul Rahman al Saud [*qv*] regained Diraiya and neighboring Riyadh [*qv*] from the rival Rashid clan, which was allied with the Ottoman Empire. After consolidating his domain, he captured the eastern Hasa region in 1913. Following the downfall of the Ottoman

Empire, he conquered the Asir region on the Red Sea in 1920. The next year he defeated his rival, Muhammad ibn Rashid, based in Shammar. After he had added more territories to his domain in 1922, he called himself the Sultan of Najd and its Dependencies. He couched his campaigns in Islamic terms, as a struggle to punish either religious dissenters or those who had strayed from true Islam as represented by Wahhabism [*qv*]. In 1924 he defeated Sharif Hussein ibn Ali al Hashem in Hijaz and deposed him.

Having declared himself King of Hijaz and Sultan of Najd and its Dependencies in January 1926, Abdul Aziz sought international recognition. The following year Britain recognized him as King of Hijaz and Najd and its Dependencies. In 1929 he fell out with the militant section of the Ikhwan [*qv*], the armed wing of the Wahhabis, which so far had been his fighting force. Assisted by the British, then controlling Kuwait and Iraq, he quelled the Ikhwan rebellion. In September 1932 he combined his domains, comprising about three-quarters of 1.12 million sq. miles/3.1 million sq. km of the Arabian Peninsula [*qv*], into one—the Kingdom of Saudi Arabia—and called himself King of Saudi Arabia.

Abdul Aziz granted an oil concession to the Standard Oil Company of California in 1933. Modest commercial extraction, which started in 1938, was interrupted by the Second World War, in which he remained neutral. As a domineering and militarily successful tribal chief, he behaved as an autocrat. Following a dramatic increase in oil output after the Second World War, the economic boom overstretched the rudimentary institutions of the state, supervised by him and some of his close aides, and undermined the traditional, spartan Wahhabi lifestyle of the House of Saud [*qv*]. Yet it was not until October 1953—a month before his death—that he appointed a council of ministers, chaired by his eldest son, Saud [*qv*], as an advisory body.

When Saud became king, he retained the premiership. However, he proved incapable of handling the fiscal and administrative complexities arising from the sharp growth in oil revenues caused by increased demand for Saudi oil due to the 1951–53 oil nationalization crisis in Iran. The resulting chaos, compounded by Saud's extravagance and mismanagement, created a crisis and led to a power struggle between him and his brother, Crown Prince Faisal [*qv*]. It was finally settled against Saud, who was forced to abdicate in 1964.

On ascending the throne, Faisal reneged on his promise of political reform that he had made as crown prince in 1962—especially the promulgation of a written constitution specifying a consultative council. Instead he harshly suppressed the opposition. He increased support to the royalist camp in the North Yemeni Civil War [*qv*], in which the republicans were being aided by Egyptian President Gamal Abdul Nasser [*qv*]. However, following the Arab defeat in the 1967 Six-Day War [*qv*], he buried his differences with Nasser. Faisal's efforts to establish a transnational organization of Muslim states succeeded in 1969, in the wake of an arson attempt on the al Aqsa Mosque in Jerusalem [*qv*], resulting in the formation of the Islamic Conference Organization [*qv*], based in Jiddah [*qv*].

During the 1973 Arab-Israeli War [*qv*], Faisal led the Arab oil embargo [*qv*] against the Western allies of Israel and backed the quadrupling of oil prices in 1973–74. Due to increased output and a sharp rise in price in 1973–74, Saudi oil income reached $22.57 billion in 1974, a 36-fold rise in a decade. Though he succeeded in having the oil embargo against Israel's Western allies lifted in March 1974, he was unwilling to go along fully with U.S. policy on the Middle East peace process [*qv*]. On 25 March 1975 he was assassinated by a young nephew, Prince Faisal ibn Musaid.

On becoming king, Khalid ibn Abdul Aziz [*qv*] freed political prisoners. He appointed a cabinet in which 15 of the 25 ministers were commoners, but he ensured that the crucial foreign, defense, interior, and National Guard [*qv*] ministries stayed with the House of Saud. He tried to end the Lebanese Civil War [*qv*], gave grants to the Palestine Liberation Organization (PLO) [*qv*], and opposed the Camp David Accords [*qv*]. He cut all links with Egypt after it had signed the Egyptian-Israeli Peace Treaty [*qv*] in March 1979.

In domestic affairs, Khalid represented the nationalist trend, committed to greater respect for tradition and slower economic development, which was in conflict with the pro-U.S. trend, stressing rapid economic development. When faced with an armed uprising at the Grand Mosque of Mecca [*qv*] in November 1979, he prevaricated and took a fortnight to quell it. Responding to the rise of a revolutionary Islamic regime in Iran, he, a pious Muslim, opted for stricter enforcement of Islamic injunctions in the kingdom. During 1981, the last full year of his reign, the kingdom earned a record oil revenue of $110 billion.

Of the two trends that had emerged among senior Saudi princes during Khalid's reign, King Fahd ibn Abdul Aziz belonged to the pro-U.S. school, favoring rapid economic progress. His Middle East peace plan (in exchange for the peaceful coexistence of all the states in the region, Israel would be required to evacuate all the Arab territories occupied in 1967, dismantle the Jewish settlements in these areas, and accept the founding of a Palestinian state) was adopted by the Arab League [*qv*] summit in September 1982. It remained the common Arab position on a comprehensive settlement until the Middle East Peace Conference [*qv*] in Madrid, Spain, nine years later.

In keeping with his vacillating manner, Fahd waited a whole week before making public his position on Iraq's invasion of Kuwait on 2 August 1990. He called on the United States and Arab countries to send troops to help protect Saudi Arabia and end the Iraqi occupation of Kuwait. The huge expenses incurred by Riyadh in the conduct of the Second Gulf War [*qv*], the rearming of the kingdom that followed the conflict, and the sharply reduced prices of oil, with annual petroleum income down to $43 billion, led his government to raise foreign loans to balance the budget. In May 1991 Shaikh Abdul Aziz al Baz handed Faisal a "Letter of Demands," signed by 400 leading ulama, judges, and academics, demanding a consultative council with powers to decided all domestic and foreign affaris, greater Islamization of state, social, economic, and educational institutions, punishment of those who had enriched themselves illegally; and

freedom of expression within the Sharia [*qv*]. Fahd ignored the petition.

Having made some concessions in the political and religious spheres, Fahd repressed further the dissident Islamic ulama at home and blocked financial assistance to Islamist militants abroad. He tightened ties with Washington still further, while the latter's dependence on Saudi petroleum grew. A quarter of America's oil imports now originated in Saudi Arabia, which had purchased $25 billion worth of U.S. arms between August 1990 and December 1992—by which time a formalized defense understanding between Riyadh and Washington was in place. The establishment of the fully nominated Consultative Council in 1993 did little to diminish disaffection. To silence opposition, the government detained 200 political dissidents in 1994. It was distressed when a bomb at the National Guard training center in Riyadh in November 1995 killed seven people, including five American officers. That month, following a stroke, Faisal passed on his powers to Crown Prince Abdullah. Though, on recovery, Faisal nominally retrieved these powers three months later, there was less of his imprint on the administration during the subsequent years as Abdullah became the de facto ruler.

Abdullah continued the policy of the kingdom aiding the Taliban (lit., Religious Students), a faction of hardline Islamic fundamentalists [*qv*] in Afghanistan, created largely by Pakistan in late 1994, which would later give refuge to Osama bin Laden [*qv*], a Saudi renegade. Saudi Arabia's financial and other assistance to the Taliban helped the latter to capture Kabul in September 1996. With this, the kingdom became part of the

Islamabad-Kabul-Riyadh triumvirate, which solidified when Saudi Arabia became the second country after Pakistan to recognize the Taliban regime in May 1997.

Relations with the United States began to fray after June 1996, when a huge explosion outside the Khobar Towers, a multistory residential block for U.S. military personnel, near Dhahran air base, left 19 American servicemen dead and injured another 400, including 107 Americans, and the Saudi authorities refused access to U.S. Federal Bureau of Investigation agents to interrogate the suspects.

In 1998, unemployment among Saudi citizens soared to 27 percent, twice the rate of five years earlier. But the House of Saud showed little sign of sharing its power with Saudi nationals.

As the custodian of Islam's two holiest shrines, the Saudi government advised Palestinian leader Yasser Arafat [qv] not to compromise on the sovereignty of the Noble Sanctuary [qv] in Jerusalem [qv] in his talks with Israeli Prime Minister Ehud Barak [qv] in July 2000. Following the outbreak of the Second Intifada [qv] in September, Crown Prince Abdullah backed the plan to set up two funds to aid the Palestinians at the Arab League [qv] summit.

A year later, following the attacks on three American targets by hijacked aircraft, Saudi-American relations soured further when 15 of the 19 hijackers turned out to be Saudi nationals.

Religious composition (1990:) Muslim 98 percent, of which Sunni [qv], 89 percent, mostly Shafii [qv] and Wahhabi [qv], and Shia, 8 percent; Christian, 1.5 percent; other, 0.5 percent.

Saudi Arabia-Iraq Neutral Zone: Area: 2,720 sq. miles/7,044 sq. km. Among other things, the Protocol of Uqair [qv] in December 1922 demarcated a neutral zone between Najd [qv] (later Saudi Arabia) and Iraq, adjacent to the western tip of the Saudi-Kuwaiti frontier. While being open to the nomad tribes of both countries for water and cattle grazing, it was a prohibited area for the construction of permanent (civilian or military) buildings. In 1938 Saudi Arabia and Iraq signed an agreement on administering the zone. In July 1975 the two neighbors divided the zone equally, with the new frontier running straight through it and each side assuming sovereignty over its part.

On the eve of Washington's war against the Taliban-controled Afghanistan in October 2001, Saudi Arabia refused to led the Pentagon use its state-of-art air operations command center built at Al Kharj base 150 miles/240 km southeast of Rigadh. It again denied the use of this facility when America launched its Operation Iraqi Freedom [qv] in March 2003.

Saudi Arabia-Kuwait Neutral Zone: Area: 2,230 sq. miles/5,770 sq. km. Among other things, the Protocol of Uqair [qv] in December 1922 demarcated, to the south of Kuwait, a neutral zone between Najd [qv] (later Saudi Arabia) and Kuwait. While remaining open to the nomad tribes of both countries for water and cattle grazing, it was a prohibited area for the construction of permanent (civilian or military) buildings. Two years after its independence in 1961, Kuwait concluded a further agreement with Saudi Arabia on the zone. In 1966 the two neighbors divided the area equally, each country integrating its respective territory into its central administration—except for natural resources, such as petroleum, which remain undivided, the offshore oil concessions being shared equally by the concessionaires of Saudi Arabia and Kuwait.

Sazman-e Cherikha-ye Fedai Khalq-e Iran *(Persian: Organization of People's Self-sacrificing Guerrillas): see* Fedai Khalq.

Sazman-e Mujahedin-e Khalq *(Persian: Organization of People's Holy Warriors): see* Mujahedin-e Khalq.

Sayyab, Badr Shakir (1926–64): *Iraqi poet* Born into a Shia [*qv*] family near Basra [*qv*], Sayyab secured a diploma from the Teachers' College, Baghdad [*qv*], where he specialized in Arabic and English literature. As a poet he came under the influence of T. S. Eliot (1888–1965), especially his poem *The Wasteland* (1922). Sayyab made his debut with a collection of poems, *The Wilted Flowers* (1947). Like Eliot, he discarded the idea of time as a linear progression and employed it flexibly as a permutation of the past, present, and future, merging and interlocking different eras and experiences. He made use of eternal images, historical archetypes, myths, proverbs, and folklore. Sayyab, who possessed impressive linguistic power, was outstandingly original in his imagery and exact in the choice of his words.

Overall, the impetus to discard the old and experiment with the new grew in the wake of the Arab defeat in the 1948–49 Palestine War [*qv*]. He and his fellow countrywoman, Nazik al Malaika (b. 1923), a highly talented poet—known later as part of "the generation of the catastrophe [of the Palestine War]"—became pioneers of the modernist movement in Arabic poetry. Their concepts dominated the poetry of the 1950s and most of the 1960s.

The volumes published by Sayyab in the mid 1950s (*In the Arab Maghreb, Song in the Month of August, Jaykur and the City*) were especially notable for the elevating rhythmical construction of the poems. Yet each collection had a different aura: *In the Arab Maghreb* had an enthusiastically heroic tone; *Song in the Month of August* was remarkable for its irony, a rare quality in Arabic literature; and *Jaykur and the City* made a tragic plea.

As a member of the underground Iraqi Communist Party [*qv*]—an act that cost him his teaching job in Baghdad—Sayyab's view was that society needed a redeemer, but redemption lay not with a heroic figure but with the masses, who, taking their destiny in their hands, would struggle and triumph. Since the defeat in Palestine [*qv*] was fresh and the feeling of redemption strong, and there was a popular yearning for Arab unity, Sayyab's perspectives were attractive. He aptly captured this view in the poem *The Song of Rain* (1954). In it he subtly incorporated the myth of Tammuz, the fertility god of Babylonia, to redeem life through rain and the arrival of spring.

He applauded the revolution of July 1958 in Iraq, which saw the end of the the pro-British monarchy. He celebrated the victory of the Algerian Front for National Liberation against French imperialism in 1962 by using the symbol of Sisyphus discarding his rock. During the regime of Abdul Karim Qasim (1958–63) Sayyab quit the Communist Party. After he was again sacked from his job, he left for Beirut, where he worked for *Shiar* (Poetry) magazine, coedited by Ali Ahmad Said Asbar [*qv*]. During his terminal illness he produced poetry of despair, often portraying himself as Job, an Old Testament [*qv*] prophet who suffered afflictions with fortitude and faith.

Second Gulf War: *see* Gulf War II (1991).

Second Intifada (2000–): Despite the failure of their talks in July 2000 at Camp David to reach a final settlement between Israel and the Palestinians, Israeli Prime Minister Ehud Barak [*qv*] and Palestine Liberation Organization [*qv*] Chairman Yasser Arafat [*qv*] had a cordial meeting at the former's home near Tel Aviv [*qv*] on 25 September, where they agreed to meet again four days later. But on 28 September, Likud leader Ariel Sharon [*qv*], surrounded by 1,000 armed police, toured the Noble Sanctuary/Temple Mount [*qv*] in Jerusalem's Old City, normally out of bounds to Jews [*qv*]—a move designed to underscore Israeli sovereignty over Islam's third holiest site. Regarding this as a provocative move by Sharon, the Palestinians [*qv*] protested by throwing stones.

The Palestinian demonstration that followed after the Friday's midday prayers at the al Aqsa Mosque on 29 September was curbed by the Israeli security forces with live ammunition, which left seven protesters dead. This marked the start of the al Aqsa Intifada [*qv*], also known as the Second Intifada [*qv*]. Barak sealed off the West Bank [*qv*] and Gaza Strip [*qv*] in October, as a result of which the Palestinian economy would lose $2.9 billion in the next six months, while Israel [*qv*] held back $430 million in tax revenue collected for the Palestinian Authority [*qv*].

Against the background of rising violence and weakening coalition government, Barak called for the election of the prime minister in February 2001. He lost to Ariel Sharon, who ran on a platform of continued expansion of Jewish settlements, Israeli sovereignty over all of Jerusalem, and no talks with the Palestinians until there was complete cessation of terrorism.

Consequently, the Second Intifada became more violent, with the Palestinians taking to the use of small arms, and the Islamist Palestinians groups like Hamas [*qv*] and the Islamic Jihad [*qv*] increasingly resorting to suicide bombings [*qv*] both in the Occupied Territories [*qv*] and Israel. It also led to the emergence of the Popular Resistance Committees (PRC) made up of all factions, including the secular Fatah [*qv*], which would go on to form its military wing, Tanzim, to specialize in suicide bombings.

Following the terrorist attacks on the U.S. in September 2001, Sharon made an unsuccessful attempt to get the U.S. administration of George Walker Bush (r. 2001–) to equate the Palestinian resistance to the Israeli military occupation with terrorism. He responded to periodic suicide bombings by Palestinians with escalating violence, pursuing his strategic aim of destroying the security and administrative infrastructure of the Palestinian Authority with armed helicopters, fighter aircraft, and gunboats, and ordering assassinations of suspected terrorists. Responding to a particularly lethal Palestinian suicide bombing in Israel on 27 March 2002, Sharon ordered the reoccupation of all the towns administered by Palestinian Authority (except Hebron [*qv*] and Jericho [*qv*]), thus effectively abrogating the Oslo Accords [*qv*], and placing Arafat under house arrest.

The first two years of the Second Intifada left 1,800 Palestinians dead and another 40,000 injured—directly affecting the life or limb of more than one out of 100 Palestinians—as well as 570 Israelis dead and another 3,000 wounded.

Semetic languages: A member of the Hamito-Semetic language family, the Semetic languages are divided into (1) northern peripheral, consisting of Akkadian (extinct); (2) northern central, including Canaanite, Amorite, Ugaritic, Phoenician and Punic, Aramaic, and ancient and modern Syriac and Hebrew [*qv*] (all extinct except modern Hebrew); (3) southern central, including Arabic [*qv*] and Maltese; and (4) southern peripheral, including southern Arabic and the languages of northern Ethiopia, such as Amharic and Tigre.

In the tenth century A.D., Judah ibn Quraish showed connections between Arabic, Aramaic, and Hebrew. But it was not until 1890 that William Wright came up with a systematic demonstration of this link. In 1781—referring to *Genesis* (10:1): "These are the descendants of Noah's sons: Shem, Ham and Japheth"—August Ludwig von Schlozer coined the title Shemitic/Semitic for these languages, which has since then stuck. Words in these languages are founded on a root made up of consonants, which provides the basic meaning of the word, and a vowel pattern that defines various shades of this meaning.

Semite: The term Semite/Shemite is based on *Genesis* (10:1): "These are the descendants of Noah's sons: Shem, Ham and Japheth." Initially those believed to be the descendants of Shem were called Semite. Nowadays the term applies to Arabs [*qv*], Akkadians of ancient Babylon, Assyrians,

Canaanites (including Phoenicians), Aramaean tribes (including Hebrews), and a large segment of northern Ethiopians because their languages are derived from the common Semitic root.

Sephardim *(Hebrew: pl. of* Sephardi, *derivative of* Sepharad/ *Spain):* In the Middle Ages (476–1492 AD), Sepharad meant Spain, and the term *Sephardi* was applied to the Jews [*qv*] of Spain. When expelled from Spain in 1492, and later from Portugal, most Sephardi Jews settled along the shores of the Mediterranean, establishing large, influential, and flourishing communities in Morocco, Italy, Greece, Turkey, Egypt, and the Levant [*qv*]. From the sixteenth century onward, differences between Sephardim and Ashkenazim [*qv*] became sharper. These pertained to synagogue architecture and rites (of Babylonian origin for Sephardim, and Palestinian origin for Ashkenazim), their pronunciation of Hebrew [*qv*], and their social customs. The mother tongue of Sephardim was Judeo-Spanish or Ladino [*qv*].

As inhabitants of Palestine [*qv*] since the late fifteenth century under the Ottomans, Sephardim claim the longest residency in Israel [*qv*], where they have had their own chief rabbi. After the founding of Israel in 1948, the immigrating Oriental Jews [*qv*]—originating in the Arab countries away from the Mediterranean, and in Iran and India, where their rites were neither Sephardic nor Ashkenazi—were classified Sephardic. With a large influx of Jewish immigrants from the Arab states, the percentage of Sephardim rose sharply. Due to this, and a higher birth rate among them, they became a majority in the mid-1960s. Three decades later they lost that position due to a large influx of Ashkenazim from the former Soviet Union. Sephardim are about one-fifth of the world Jewry.

Seveners: *see* Ismailis.

al Shaabi, Qahtan Muhammad (1920–81): *South Yemeni politician; president, 1967–69* Born into a notable family in the Lahej principality of the Aden Protectorate, al Shaabi received a secular education before joining the Lahej land department. He became its director in 1955. Three years later he joined the nationalist South Arabian League. He escaped to North Yemen in 1960 and, after the republican coup of September 1962, cofounded South Yemen's National Liberation Front (NLF) [*qv*] there. After the NLF had declared an armed struggle against the British in October 1963, al Shaabi became its leader. He also directed its fight against the moderate Front for the Liberation of South Yemen (FLOSY). Within three years the NLF had occupied all of the Protectorate and decimated FLOSY in the Aden Colony.

He negotiated South Yemen's independence with the British in Geneva in November 1967. Later that month, following independence, he became president as well as premier and chief of military staff of the People's Republic of South Yemen. When differences between NLF moderates, favoring Nasserite [*qv*] socialism, and NLF radicals, advocating Marxist-Leninist socialism, surfaced, al Shaabi sided with the former. Unwilling to split the party in view of the pressure on South Yemen from its conservative neighbors, he sought accommodation with the rival camp. But having tightened their control of the party machine and militia, the radical faction deposed al

Shaabi in June 1969. He was jailed in April 1970, and after his release he stayed away from public life.

Shabak *(Hebrew: acronym of* Sherut Betakhon Klali, *General Security Service): see* Shin Beth.

Shabuot *(Hebrew: Weeks): see* Pentecost. Also spelled Shavuot.

Shafii Code: *Sunni Islamic school* The Sunni [*qv*] Islamic school was named after Muhammad ibn Idris al Shafii (A.D. 767–820). A student of Islamic law in Medina [*qv*], along with Malik ibn Anas, the founder of the Maliki school [*qv*], Shafii familiarised himself with the Hanafi school [*qv*] by visiting Baghdad [*qv*]. Later settling in Cairo [*qv*], he greatly influenced the legal-administrative apparatus of the Abbasid Empire (A.D. 751–1258). He founded the science of religious jurisprudence *(fiqh* [*qv*]) on four pillars: the Quran [*qv*]; the Prophet's *sunna* [*qv*] (later to be recorded in the Hadith [*qv*]), analogical reasoning *(qiyas* [*qv*]), and the consensus *(ijma* [*qv*]) of the community. So far, *ijma* had been construed as consensus of *"ahl al hall wal aqd"* (those who loose and bind), a term embracing various types of representative of the community, including religious intellectuals, but Shafii enlarged it to include the whole community.

Analogical reasoning allowed the community to incorporate new situations into the Sharia [*qv*] (Islamic Law) without disturbing the primacy of the Quran and *sunna*. It also permitted individual opinions and differences, as sanctioned by the Prophet Muhammad's statement in the Hadith: "The differences of opinion among the learned within my community are [a sign of] God's grace." By pursuing this method the clergy could merge the Prophet Muhammad's teachings, Arab traditions, and non-Arab traditions into a single canonical system applicable to the life of all Muslims, Arab and non-Arab. Thus, Shafii's systemisation of the Sharia provided the foundation upon which a common identity of Muslims scattered around the world could be built. The Shafii school, founded by Shafii's disciples and originating in Egypt, reached southern Arabia and from there spread along the monsoon route to East Africa and Southeast Asia through Arab traders. Today it is particularly strong in Yemen.

Shah, Muhammad Reza: *see* Pahlavi, Muhammad Reza Shah.

Shah, Reza: *see* Pahlavi, Reza Shah.

Shamir, Yitzhak (1915–): *Israeli politician; prime minister, 1986–92.* Born Yitzhak Yazernitsky of a religious family in Poland, Shamir joined the Revisionist Zionist [*qv*] youth movement, Betar. He moved to Palestine [*qv*] in 1935 and two years later joined Irgun Zvai Leumi [*qv*]. When Irgun split in 1940, with Avraham Stern [*qv*] forming Lehi [*qv*], Shamir opted for the new group. After Stern's assassination in 1942, Shamir became one of the three commanders of Lehi in charge of organization and operations, which included the assassination in 1944 of Lord Moyne, the British resident minister in the Middle East. Arrested by the British in 1946, Shamir was dispatched to a detention camp in Eritrea. He escaped after four months and found his way to Paris, where he lived until the founding of Israel in May 1948.

After his arrival in Israel, Shamir became active with the political wing of Lehi, the Fighters Party. He joined Mossad [*qv*] in 1955 and served in various senior positions until 1965. After running a mattress factory for five years, he reentered politics by joining the Herut Party [*qv*]. Three years later he became chairman of the Herut executive, and in the December 1973 election he won a seat in the Knesset [*qv*]. He served as speaker from 1977–80 but opposed the Camp David Accords [*qv*], negotiated by the leader of his Likud [*qv*] Party, Menachem Begin [*qv*]. In the Knesset vote on the accords, he abstained. Shamir became foreign minister in 1980.

Following Begin's retirement in 1983, Shamir won the contest for party leadership and became premier, while retaining the foreign affairs portfolio. He inherited a military imbroglio in Lebanon, hyperinflation, and the collapse of several banks. After the stalemate result of the 1984 election, Shamir reached a rotation accord with Labor [*qv*] leader Shimon Peres [*qv*] in a national unity government. He served as deputy premier and foreign minister until 1986 and then became prime minister. After the 1988 poll Shamir continued as premier with his own coalition, first with Labor and then, from March 1990, with right-wing parties only.

In October 1991 he participated in the Middle East Peace Conference in Madrid [*qv*], while insisting on expanding Jewish settlements in the Occupied Arab Territories [*qv*]. The bilateral talks between Israel and its Arab neighbors made no progress, as Shamir, having lost the June 1992 election, revealed that he had planned to drag out the talks for ten years. In 1993 he stepped down as Likud leader. He was reelected to the Knesset in 1996 and 1999.

Sharett, Moshe (1894–1965): *Israeli politician; prime minister, 1953–55* Born Moshe Shertok in Russia to a religious Zionist [*qv*] militant, who moved his family to Palestine in 1906, Sharett graduated from a Jewish school in Tel Aviv [*qv*]. During the First World War he enrolled with the Ottoman Turkish military and rose to become an officer. After the war he joined the London School of Economics and Political Science.

On his return to Palestine [*qv*] in 1925, Sharett became a member of the editorial board of *Davar* (Word), the Histadrut [*qv*] newspaper. An activist of the Ahdut HaAvodah [*qv*], Sharett joined Mapai [*qv*] on its formation in 1930. Three years later he succeeded Chaim Arlosoroff [*qv*] as chief of the Jewish Agency's [*qv*] political department. In that capacity he led a campaign against the 1939 British White paper, which restricted Jewish immigration into Palestine. During the Second World War he encouraged Palestinian Jews to join the British army and helped to establish a Jewish brigade. After the war he led a Zionist political campaign that culminated in the United Nations resolving to partition Palestine in November 1947.

Following the founding of Israel six months later, Sharett was named foreign minister. He was elected to the Knesset [*qv*] in 1949 and retained a seat until his death. His pressure on Washington to sell arms to Israel led to the issuing of the Tripartite Declaration (by the United States, Britain, and France) [*qv*] in May 1950, which opposed any attempt to alter the truce boundaries by force. Sharett backed the United States when the Korean War erupted in June 1950.

While Sharett and Premier David Ben-Gurion [*qv*] agreed on the substance of foreign policies, Sharett's moderate, diplomatic style clashed with Ben-Gurion's hard, militarist style. Sharett succeeded Ben-Gurion when he resigned his office in 1953. From January 1954 Sharett was also foreign minister. His attempts to seek a peaceful settlement with Cairo foundered due to sabotage carried out by the Egyptian Jews [*qv*] acting as Israeli agents, masterminded by the defense ministry under Pinchas Lavon [*qv*], and the Israeli military's reprisals against Egyptian-administered Gaza [*qv*] after the execution of the Israeli agents' leaders.

After the July 1955 election he was appointed foreign minister by Ben-Gurion, who led the government. A year later, planning an attack on Egypt in Sinai [*qv*], Ben-Gurion compelled Sharett to resign from the cabinet. Sharett became the chief of Histadrut's publishing company. In 1960 he was elected chairman of the Jewish Agency's executive.

Sharia *(Arabic: way or road): Islamic Law* Consisting of divine revelation in the form of the Quran [*qv*] and the prophetic practice, *sunna* [*qv*] (as recorded in the Hadith [*qv*]), the Sharia completely governs the individual and the social life of the believer. The Quran provides the principles and the Hadith the details of their application. The Sharia is the basis for judging actions as good or evil.

By the time the Hadith had been compiled into six canonical collections in the mid-tenth century A.D., religious jurisprudents had studied all human actions and categorized them as obligatory (performance is rewarded, omission punished), recommended (performance is rewarded, omission is not punished), indifferent (neither punished nor rewarded), undesirable (disapproved but not punished), and prohibited (punished, with the degree of punishment depending on the severity of the sin—grave, venial, or tresspass). There were differences between Sunnis [*qv*] and Shias [*qv*] with regard to obligatory actions, the former prescribing five obligations and Shias enjoining more.

After categorizing human actions, jurisprudents graduated to prescribing exactly how the obligatory and recommended acts were to be performed. They also minutely pondered all bodily functions—eating, drinking, breathing, washing, urinating, defacating, farting, copulating, vomitting, bleeding, shaving—and prescribed how these were to be performed or dealt with, stressing the need to keep the body pure. Along with this went a code of social behavior that too was all-encompassing. The twin codes were so demanding that, even with the best will in the world, a believer was not able to abide by them all the time. On the other hand, it was the introduction of these codes into the lives of those who embraced Islam that has led to common behavioral patterns among all Muslims, whether they live in the Mauritanian desert or the Indonesian archipelago.

Shariati, Ali (1933–77): *Iranian Islamic thinker* Born into the family of an Islamic intellectual in Mazinan village near Mashhad [*qv*], Shariati grew up partly in Mazinan and partly in Mashhad. During the oil nationalization crisis of 1951–53, he backed Muhammad Mussadiq [*qv*] and was detained briefly. Trained as a teacher, he taught in elementary schools in rural areas.

In 1956, after Mashhad University had set up a faculty of letters, Shariati was able to pursue further studies in Arabic and French while working as a teacher.

Three years later he won a government scholarship to study sociology and Islamic studies at Paris University. He strived for a sociology that would interpret and analyze the realities of Third World life. In Paris Shariati met many intellectuals, philosophers, and scholars on Islam. He was influenced by the Algerian anti-imperialist struggle, which triumphed in 1962, and its ideologue Franz Fanon. However, while translating Fanon's *Wretched of the Earth* into Persian, Shariati challenged his views on religion and revolution.

After receiving his doctorate in sociology and theology in 1964, Shariati traveled home overland with his family and was arrested at the Turkish-Iranian frontier as a suspected subversive. Released six months later, he returned to his job as a teacher at a village school, then graduated to teaching at Mashhad University. After being dismissed from his post, Shariati moved to Tehran [*qv*] in 1967, where he lectured at the Husseinyeh Ershad, a socioreligious institution run by the Liberation Movement [*qv*]. His lectures, later published in fifty volumes, proved popular with college and senior high school students. In 1972 the government closed down the Husseinyeh Ershad, arrested Shariati, and banned most of his works. Three years later it placed him under house arrest. In May 1977 he was allowed to travel abroad. He went to Britain and died in Southampton in June—of a heart attack, according to the coroner's report.

Bitterly opposed to the regime of

Muhammad Reza Shah Pahlavi [*qv*], Shariati advocated participation in politics by the masses. He argued that Islam was not a conservative, fatalistic creed, but a revolutionary one, encompassing all aspects of life, particularly politics, which inspired the true believer to struggle against all forms of oppression, exploitation, and social injustice. Shariati found his inspiration in Shiism [*qv*], and his tools of analysis in Western social sciences. He did not want Shias to wait for the reappearance of the Hidden Iman, but to act forthwith to create a society based on equality. He was opposed to imperialism, political, economic, and cultural. In his *Intermediate School of Thought* (1973) he argued that Islam [*qv*] could be seen as an intermediate between socialism and capitalism, which adopted the advantages and positive aspects of other schools of thought while avoiding their negative aspects.

Shariatmadari, Muhammad Kazem (1903–86): *Iranian Islamic leader* Born into a religious, Azeri-speaking [*qv*] family in Tabriz [*qv*] in 1924, Shariatmadari went to Qom [*qv*] to undertake Islamic studies. After a decade in Qom he traveled to Najaf [*qv*] for further theological education. Returning to Tabriz in the late 1930s, he became a religious teacher. In 1950 Shariatmadari again moved to Qom, where he found himself in tune with the conservative Shia [*qv*] leader Ayatollah Muhammad Hussein Borujerdi and rose steadily in the clerical ranks. After Borujerdi's death in 1961, Shariatmadari was elevated to the rank of grand ayatollah, sharing this rare honor with two other clergymen: Muhammad Reza Golpaygani [*qv*] and Shehab al Din Marashi-Najafi.

During the June 1963 protest against the government-sponsored White Revolution [*qv*], he was arrested, but the experience did not radicalize him. In June 1970, when Muhammad Reza Shah Pahlavi [*qv*] sent his condolences on the death of Ayatollah Muhsin Hakim, the seniormost Shia cleric based in Najaf, Shariatmadari reaffirmed his loyalty to the monarch, thus widening the gap between himself and radical Ayatollah Ruhollah Khomeini [*qv*], who had been expelled from Iran five years earlier.

In January 1978, after the security forces had broken into his theological college in Qom and killed two of his students, he voiced opposition and demanded the return to the 1906–07 constitution. But it was not until the massacre of unarmed civilians by the security forces on 8 September 1978 in Tehran [*qv*] that Shariatmadari hardened his position. After the shah had installed a military government in November 1978, Shariatmadari joined his two fellow grand ayatollahs in Qom in their call for the dismantling of the political system. Nonetheless, when Shahpur Bakhtiar [*qv*] was appointed premier in early January 1979, Shariatmadari backed him.

After the revolution in February, Khomeini's leadership was balanced by Ayatollah Mahmud Taleqani [*qv*] on the left, and Shariatmadari on the right. With the death of Taleqani in September, the Islamic establishment became bipolar, with Shariatmadari leading the clerics who advocated nonintervention by the clergy in the day-to-day running of the government, in opposition to the interventionist school led by Khomeini. Shariatmadari abstained in the referendum on the Islamic constitution in December

1979, objecting to the excessive powers given to the Supreme Leader, Khomeini, and condemned the seizure of American diplomats as hostages [*qv*]. The differences between Shariatmadari and Khomeini became irreconcilable and were taken up by their respective followers in the streets of Tabriz and Qom in January 1980. Shariatmadari lost and was placed under house arrest.

Secret documents retrieved from the U.S. embassy showed that Shariatmadari had accepted funds for promoting nonalcoholic American drinks in Iran and that he had contacts in the U.S. Central Intelligence Agency. After the arrest of Shariatmadari's son-in-law, Ahmad Abbasi, in April 1982 for coplotting a coup—to be led by Sadiq Qutbzadeh, foreign minister from 1979–80—the government raided Shariatmadari's house and seminary and publicized his clandestine links with the CIA. Four years later Shariatmadari died of natural causes.

Sharjah Emirate: *a constituent of the United Arab Emirates* Area: 1,000 sq. miles/2,600 sq. km; pop. 520,000 (2001, est.). Sharjah, ruled by Shaikh Sultan ibn Muhammad al Qasimi (r. 1972–), is a founder member of the United Arab Emirates [*qv*]. Before the start of commercial extraction of oil in 1974, which had reached 60,000 barrels a day by the mid-1990s, a large part of Sharjah's income came from commemorative stamps, printed almost solely for philatelic purposes.

Sharon, Ariel (1928–): *Israeli military officer and politician; prime minister, 2001–* Born Ariel Shinerman of a Zionist [*qv*] family in Kafr Malal, Palestine [*qv*], Sharon joined Haganah [*qv*] as a youth. He fought in the Arab-Israeli War (1948–49) and continued his military career, working as an intelligence officer. He established Unit 101, composed exclusively of volunteers, to carry out swift cross-border reprisal attacks—one such operation against an Egyptian military camp in Gaza in February 1955 resulted in thirty-eight Egyptian deaths. When Unit 101 was incorporated into the paratroopers later in the years, Sharon became a paratroop commander.

During the Suez War in 1956 [*qv*], Sharon, leading a brigade, exceeded his orders and engaged in a battle that caused many victims. This slowed down his promotion. Only when Yitzhak Rabin [*qv*] became chief of staff in 1965 was Sharon promoted to head the training department of the general staff. Two years later he became a brigadier general. During the June 1967 Arab-Israeli War [*qv*] Sharon commanded a division on the southern front, capturing the Umm Katif range in the Sinai [*qv*]. In 1969 he was put in charge of the southern command. His iron-fist policy toward the Palestinian resistance to the Israeli occupation of the West Bank [*qv*] and Gaza [*qv*] proved controversial.

In mid-1973 he quit the army and entered politics by joining Gahal [*qv*]. Sharon was instrumental in the creation of Likud [*qv*] out of the merger of Gahal, the Free Center, the State Party (a remnant of Rafi [*qv*]), and the Eretz Yisrael [*qv*] movement. In the October 1973 Arab-Israeli War [*qv*] Sharon commanded a division that established a bridgehead over the Suez Canal [*qv*]. However, his later command of the division proved controversial. After being elected to the Knesset [*qv*] in December 1973, he resigned after some months to serve Labor Prime Minister Rabin as an adviser. In

1976 he formed his own group—*Shlomzion* (Peaceful Zion)—which won two seats in the 1977 election. He merged his group with the Herut [*qv*] faction of Likud and became minister of agriculture in the Likud-dominated government. He was also appointed chairman of the cabinet's (Jewish) settlement committee. Following the 1981 elections, he was named defense minister.

Once Israel had withdrawn its troops from the Sinai in April 1982, Sharon finalized his plans to attack Lebanon. Having launched the campaign with the ostensible aim of capturing a strip of Lebanese territory to rid it of Palestinian guerrillas, Sharon expanded it into a full-fledged war, advancing to Beirut [*qv*], besieging it for sixty-three days and bombarding it mercilessly from the land, air, and sea. Having secured the departure of Syrian and Palestine Liberation Organization (PLO) [*qv*] troops from Beirut, Sharon set out to become kingmaker in Lebanese politics by getting Bashir Gemayel [*qv*] elected president in September. He succeeded, only to see his protégé assassinated before he could take office.

Sharon allowed his Maronite [*qv*] allies a free hand to murder some 2,000 Palestinians [*qv*] in the refugee camps of Sabra and Shatila. A demonstration by about 400,000 Israelis compelled the government to appoint a commission of inquiry, headed by the chief supreme court judge, Yitzhak Kahan. Following a critical report by this commission, Sharon was forced to resign as defense minister in February 1983, although he retained a place in the cabinet as a minister without portfolio.

In the national unity government formed in September 1984, Prime Minister Shimon Peres [*qv*] appointed him minister of trade and industry and a member of the inner political cabinet. He held these jobs until January 1990. In the reconstituted cabinet led by Yitzhak Shamir [*qv*] in May 1990, Sharon became minister of housing and accelerated the building of Jewish settlements on the West Bank. After the Likud's defeat in the June 1992 election, Sharon lost his preeminence in Israeli politics. In 1996, Benjamin Netanyahu [*qv*] put Sharon in charge of a newly created Ministry of Infrastructure, elevating him to minister of foreign affairs in October 1998. Following Netanyahu's defeat in the prime ministerial contest in 1999 and his quitting of politics, Sharon was elected leader of the Likud.

Escorted by 1,000 armed police, Sharon toured the Noble Sanctuary [*qv*] in Jerusalem [*qv*] on 28 September 2000—a move designed to underscore Israeli sovereignty over Islam's third holiest site. The Palestinian demonstration that followed after the Friday's midday prayers at the al Aqsa Mosque the next day was curbed by the Israeli security forces with live ammunition, which left seven protesters dead. This marked the start of the al Aqsa Intifada [*qv*].

In the February 2001 prime ministerial contest, securing 62.4 percent of the vote, Sharon defeated the incumbent Ehud Barak [*qv*] by 25 percent on a platform of continued expansion of Jewish settlements, Israeli sovereignty over all of Jerusalem, and no talks with the Palestinians until there was complete cessation of terrorism. His national unity government included Labor [*qv*], now led by Binyamin Ben-Elizier. Israeli-Palestinian violence escalated while the newly installed U.S. administration of President

George W. Bush (r. 2001–) pursued a hands-off policy.

Following the terrorist attacks on the U.S in September, Sharon's attempt to equate the Palestinian resistance to Israeli military occupation to terrorism failed. He responded to periodic suicide bombings by Palestinians with escalating violence, pursuing his strategic aim of destroying the security and administrative infrastructure of the Palestinian Authority [qv] with armed helicopters, fighter aircraft, and gunboats, and ordering assassinations of suspected terrorists. Responding to a particularly lethal Palestinian suicide bombing in Israel on 27 March 2002, Sharon ordered the reoccupation of all the towns under Palestinian Authority (except Hebron [qv] and Jericho [qv]), thus effectively abrogating the Oslo Accords [qv]. His defiance of President Bush to vacate the occupied Palestinian towns was rewarded with an invitation to the White House and the sobriquet of "man of peace." He put PA President Yasser Arafat [qv] under house arrest in Ramallah.

In the Knesset poll of January 2003, his Likud [qv] party improved its strength from nineteen to thirty-eight. He formed a coalition government with strangly secularist shinui [qv] and far right secular parties.

Shas (Hebrew: abbreviation of Shomere Torah, Guardians of Torah): Israeli political party Shas was formed in 1984 by breakaway members of Agudat Israel [qv]. Its major backing came from Sephardic Jews [qv], many of them of Moroccan origin, who were critical of the Ashkenazi [qv] leadership of the existing religious political parties. Led by Moroccan-born Rabbi Arye Deri, it won four seats in the 1984 general election, six in 1988, and six in 1992. It joined the national unity governments formed in 1984 and 1988. After the 1992 election it participated in the Labor-led coalition government, and went along with the Oslo Accords [qv], with its spiritual leader, Rabbi Ovaida Yosef, declaring that peace was more important than territory. Despite the arrest of Deri on charges of corruption, Shas improved its size in the 1996 Knesset [qv] to ten seats. It coalesced with Likud [qv]. In the 1999 general election, its strength rose to seventeen, and it joined the government led by Labor's Ehud Barak [qv]. When Barak lost office two years later, Shas joined the national unity government led by Ariel Sharon [qv]. In the 2003 Knesset poll, its strength declined to eleven.

Shatt al Arab (Arabic: The Arab Stream): Beginning at Qurna, Iraq, with the confluence of the Euphrates [qv] and Tigris [qv] Rivers, the Shatt al Arab flows 120 miles/190 km southeast into the Gulf [qv], its width increasing from 150 ft/46 meters at Basra [qv] to 2,000 ft./610 meters at its mouth, and its discharge rising to 1,400 cu. meters/sec or 49,400 cu. ft./sec. For the last two-fifths of its length, it forms a fluvial border between Iran and Iraq. The demarcation of this frontier was a contentious issue between the two neighbors for a long time. The 1975 Algiers Accord [qv] settled the dispute for a while, but it was revived by Iraq five years later on the eve of its invasion of Iran, resulting in the Iran-Iraq War [qv]. In August 1990 Iraq stated its acceptance of the Algiers Accord, which divided the Shatt al Arab between the two sides along the deepest channel.

Shazar, Shneor Zalman (1889–1974):

Israeli politician; president 1963–73 Born Shneor Rubashov of a religious family in Saint Petersburg, Russia, Shazar joined the Poale Zion [*qv*] as a youth and assisted the group's leader, Don Ber Borochov [*qv*], in editing the party periodical. During the First World War he was a research student in Berlin, where he cofounded a branch of the Poale Zion.

In 1924 Shazar migrated to Palestine [*qv*], where he was active in politics and journalism. He became a leader of Ahdut HaAvodah [*qv*] and from 1930 of Mapai [*qv*], as well as being a member of the Histadrut [*qv*] executive and one of the editors of the Histadrut daily, *Davar* (Word). In 1944 he was appointed editor in chief of the newspaper.

Elected to the First Knesset [*qv*] in 1949, Shazar served as education minister from 1949–50. After he had left the government, he was elected to the Jewish Agency executive, becoming head of the department of education and culture in the Diaspora [*qv*], and then acting chairman of the Jewish Agency executive from 1957–61. Two years later he was elected president of Israel and was reelected in 1968.

Shehab, Fuad: *see* Chehab, Fuad.

Shia *(Arabic: Partisan): Islamic sect* Shia or Shiat means Shia/Shiat Ali, Partisans of Ali, cousin and son-in-law of the Prophet Muhammad (A.D. 570–632). By advocating strict adherence to the Quran [*qv*] and the *sunna* [*qv*], Ali came to represent idealism in Islam [*qv*]. His camp drew most of its support from pious Muslims and non-Arab Muslim clients, who felt discrimianted against by Arab [*qv*] Muslims. They were an important part of the coalition that engineered the Abbasid revolution in A.D. 751 against the Umayyad caliphs (A.D. 661–750), who they believed had deviated widely from the true Islamic path. But it was not too long before the Sunni [*qv*] Abbasid caliphs too began to slip away from the Quran and the *sunna*, thus allowing Shias to become the sole repositories of the vision of ideal Islam. The consequences were the subjugation of the Sunni caliph in Baghdad [*qv*] by a Shia king, Muizz al Dawla al Buyid, in A.D. 932, and the emergence of an Ismaili [*qv*] Shia caliphate, the Fatimids, in Cairo [*qv*] in A.D. 969. By then three branches of Shiism had crystallized: Zaidis [*qv*], Ismailis, and Imamis [*qv*].

During the Buyid hegemony in Baghdad (A.D. 932–1055) two collections of Shia Hadith [*qv*] were codified.

Shia domination lasted many generations, losing its grip first in Baghdad in 1055 and then in Cairo in 1171. Today Shias are a minority, being 12–15 percent of the total global Muslim population of about one billion. Of the forty-nine members of the Islamic Conference Organization (ICO) [*qv*] in 1994, only Bahrain, Iran, and Iraq were Shia-majority countries.

Shias differ from Sunnis [*qv*] in doctrine, ritual, law, theology, and religious organization. The Shia credo consists of five basic principles and ten duties. While sharing three principles with Sunnis—monotheism, i.e., there is only one God; prophethood, which is a means of communication between God and humankind; and resurrection, i.e., the souls of dead human beings will be raised by God on their Day of Judgement and their deeds on earth judged—Shias have two more: *imamat* [*qv*] and *aadl* (justice), the just nature of Allah. Their duties include daily prayers, fasting during Ramadan [*qv*], *khums* (an Islamic tithe) [*qv*], *zakat* (alms tax) [*qv*], *hajj* (pilgrimage to Mecca [*qv*]), encouraging virtue, discouraging evil, and loving Shia *imams* [*qv*] and their followers.

Shias believe that only those in the lineage of the Prophet Muhammad—and thus of his daughter, Fatima, and her husband, Ali—can govern Muslims on behalf of Allah, and that the imams, being divinely inspired, are infallible. Shias insist that the ruler must be just and that the Quran bears a pledge of sovereignty of the earth to the oppressed. Rooted in this pledge are the concepts of the return of the Hidden Imam—the arrival of the Mahdi [*qv*]—and the rehabilitation of society. That is, history is moving toward a predetermined goal and the forces of injustice will ultimately be defeated. This acts as a spur toward radical activism. (In contrast, Sunnis view Islamic history essentially as a drift away from the ideal community that existed under the rule of the first four Rightly Guided caliphs: Abu Bakr, Omar, Othman and Ali.)

The Shia ethos is different from the Sunni. Shia emotionalism finds outlets in mourning Imams Ali (assassinated), Hassan (poisoned), and Hussein (killed in battle), and in the heartrending entreaties offered at their shrines. Shias believe that through asceticism and suffering one can remove the ill-effects of the humiliation and persecution inflicted on them. During the Ashura [*qv*], the annual enactment of passion plays about the martyrdom of Imam Hussein, and self-flagellation by the faithful, provide outlets for expiating the guilt and pain originally felt by the inhabitants of Kufa [*qv*] for having abandoned Imam Hussein after having

invited him to their city to take charge. Sunnism offers no such outlets for its followers.

Finally, Shias and Sunnis organize religion and religious activities differently. Sunnis regard religious activities as the exclusive domain of the (Muslim) state. When the *ulama* [*qv*] act as judges or preachers or educators, they do so under the aegis of the state. There is scant opportunity for the ulama to organize religion on their own. In contrast, in Shia Iran, free of the Sunni Ottoman or Christian European influence, the leading *mujtahids* [*qv*], being recipients of the *khums* from their followers, maintained theological colleges and social welfare activities independent of the state. Also, by adopting the custom of naming the most revered colleague as the *marja-e taqlid* (source of emulation) [*qv*], whose independent opinion on the compatibility of major state decisions with Islam had to be sought, the religious hierarchy underlined its independence. Unlike in the Sunni religious establishment, Shia clerics are ranked from *thiqatalislam* (trust of Islam) to *hojatalislam* (proof of Islam) to *ayatollah* (sign of Allah) to *ayatollah-ozma* (grand ayatollah).

Shiat Ali *(Arabic: Partisan of Ali): see* Shia.

Shiite: *see* Shia.

Shin Beth *(Hebrew: acronym of* Sherut Betakhon, *Security Service): Israeli domestic security service* When Israel was founded in 1948, Shin Beth, headed by Isser Harel (1948–52), was the only civilian intelligence agency and covered domestic and foreign fields. After the formation of the foreign intelligence service, Mossad [*qv*], in 1951, Shin Beth's operations division was subdivided into the provision of security to high-ranking Israeli officials and the defense industry; monitoring the activities of Israeli Arabs [*qv*]; and counterintelligence, countering subversion by extremist groups; and surveillance of diplomats and foreign delegations. In the early 1950s one of the Israeli groups that drew Shin Beth's attention was Mapam [*qv*], then a partner in the Mapailed [*qv*] coalition.

After the June 1967 Arab-Israeli War [*qv*], Shin Beth began safeguarding Israel from its opponents within the Occupied Arab Territories [*qv*]. To do this it set up a network of Palestinian informers and made the local populace feel that they were everywhere. When, from later 1968, Palestinian groups started attacking Israeli aircraft on the ground or hijacking them, Shin Beth, then headed by Yosef Harmelin (1964–74), extended its operations abroad in pursuit of the terrorists. Following the assassination of Israeli athletes at the Olympics in Munich in September 1972 by the Black September Organization [*qv*], Shin Beth started running joint operations with Mossad in their hit-and-run campaign against Palestinian terrorists.

Under the directorship of Avraham Ahituv (1974–81), Shin Beth put under surveillance Kach [*qv*], founded by Rabbi Meir Kahane [*qv*]. It also found itself coping with terrorism by Jewish extremists in the Occupied Territories [*qv*] and Jerusalem [*qv*], which led among other things to the maiming by car bomb of two West Bank [*qv*] mayors in June 1980. The problem continued under Ahituv's successor, Avraham Shalom (1981–86), with Jewish terrorists killing four Arab students and injuring thirty-three in an attack on the Islamic College in Hebron [*qv*] in July 1983, and plotting to blow up the Dome of the Rock and al Aqsa mosque in the spring of 1984.

The unearthing of a cell of twenty Jewish fanatics followed Shin Beth's discovery of twelve bombs attached to Arab buses in East Jerusalem [*qv*].

In order to weaken the Palestine Liberation Organization (PLO) [*qv*], Shin Beth actively fostered Islamic groups among Palestinians in the late 1970s and early 1980s, a policy that culminated in the rise of Hamas [*qv*] in the wake of the intifada [*qv*]. The United National Leadership of the Uprising (UNLU) [*qv*] began targeting Israeli agents and informers, numbering about 20,000 in a population of 1.6 million. This proved so effective that Shin Beth chief Yosef Harmelin (1986–88) privately conceded the virtual demise of the informer network built up over a generation. Having failed to penetrate the UNLU, Shin Beth cooperated with the Israeli military to train special units of Arabic-speaking Israeli soldiers in civilian dress and dispatch them to the Occupied Territories to mix with the local population. They were also used to carry out executions of suspected Palestinian terrorists.

With the signing of the Israeli-PLO Accord [*qv*] in September 1993, Shin Beth began to protect PLO Chairman Yasser Arafat [*qv*]. Following the founding of the Palestinian Authority [*qv*] in July 1994, Shin Beth focused on penetrating its institutions. Now its main area of recruitment shifted to those Palestinians who were allowed to work in Israel. The shrinking size of this pool against the background of a revival of Israeli-Palestinian conflict after the assassination of Israeli Prime Minister Yitzhak Rabin [*qv*] in November 1995 proved no barrier to Shin Beth's success in recruiting Palestinian agents.

The launching of the al Aqsa Intifada [*qv*]

in September 2000 opened a new chapter in the history of Shin Beth. As the Israeli-Palestinian violence escalated, the number and frequency of Shin Beth's assassinations of suspected terrorists of all political hues, religious or secular, increased.

Shinui *(Hebrew: Change): Israeli political party* Official title: Shinui—*Mifleget HaMerkaz* (Change—Party of the Center). Shinui was formed in 1974 as a protest group in the aftermath of the October 1973 Arab-Israeli War [*qv*] by Amnon Rubinstein. It called for direct talks with Arab neighbors on the basis of territorial compromise and liberalization of the Israeli economy. In 1978 it combined with the remnants of the Democratic Movement for Change (DMC). It won three Knesset [*qv*] seats in the 1984 election and joined the national unity government. In 1986 it absorbed the Center Liberal Party and the Independent Liberal Party, and quit the government in May 1987. It won two seats in the 1988 election.

Later it allied with Mapam [*qv*] and Ratz [*qv*] to form the Meretz [*qv*] alliance on a platform that included separation of religion and state. Of the twelve seats secured by Meretz in the 1992 election, two belonged to Shinui, which joined the Labor-led [*qv*] coalition. In the 1996 poll it maintained its strength.

In the 1999 Knesset election, led by Yosef Lapid, Shinui entered the fray on its own on a strongly secular platform, severely attacking the privileges enjoyed by the Orthodox [qv] and ultra-Orthodox Jews [qv]. It won six seats and refused to join a coalition that included any religious group. Its principled stand paid dividends in the 2003 poll when, securing fifteen seats, it emerged as the third largest group in the Knesset. It joined the coalition government healed by Ariel Sharon [qv] when he agreed to its condition that religious parties be excluded from the government.

Shiraz: *Iranian city* Pop. 1,176,000 (2003, est.). The recorded history of Shiraz dates back to the period of the conquests by Alexander the Great (r. 336–23 B.C.). Part of the Fars region, it was a leading settlement during the reigns of the Seleucids (312–175 B.C.), Parthians (247 B.C.–A.D. 226) and Sassanians (A.D. 226–640). Following the defeat of the Sassanians by Muslim Arabs [*qv*], Shiraz entered the Islamic era. By the late fourteenth century, as the birthplace of Saadi (d. 1291) and Hafiz (d. 1389), outstanding Persian poets, and the site of the Congregational Mosque (A.D. 894), the New Mosque (1215), the Great Library (1218) and the Shah Chiragh Shrine (1349), it competed with Baghdad [*qv*] as a center of learning and piety.

Its fame attracted Tamerlane (1336–1405), the Mongol conqueror, who occupied it in 1387 and 1393. The city was sacked by Afghan invaders in 1724. It became the capital of the Zand dynasty (1750–94), whose founder, Karim Khan Zand, endowed it with outstanding buildings, including his mausoleum and the citadel. It was here that in 1844 Ali Muhammad Shirazi declared that he was the *bab* (gate) to the Hidden Imam, thus establishing the Babi movement [*qv*].

Besides the Islamic monuments and the garden tombs of Saadi and Hafiz, the city also offers as a tourist attraction the Church of Saint Simon the Zealot.

Shishkali, Adib (1901–64): *Syrian military leader and politician; president, 1953–54* Born into a middle-class Sunni [*qv*] family in Hama [*qv*], Shishkali pursued a military career by joining the Special Forces of the French mandate. A nationalist officer, he backed Rashid Ali Gailani [*qv*] in his fight with the British in 1941. He participated in the May 1945 uprising against the French. After Syria's independence in 1946, Shishkali fought the Zionists [*qv*] in the 1948–49 Palestine War [*qv*]. He played an important role in the coup by Col. Hosni Zaim [*qv*] in March 1949, but lost his military post on suspicion of disloyalty. After Col. Sami Hinnawi had seized power from Zaim in mid-August, he reinstated Shishkali, only to see himself overthrown by Shishkali four months later.

Shishkali allowed the parliamentary regime established by Hinnawi, with Nur al Din Attasi [*qv*] as president, to continue, naming himself deputy chief of staff. In late 1951, when the People's Party leader, Maruf Dwalibi, ignored Shishkali's demands while attempting to form the next government, he dissolved the parliament, dismissed President Attasi, and made his spokeman, General Fawzi Selu, president and premier. After banning all political parties in 1952, he founded the Arab Liberation Movement (ALM). But it failed to strike roots, and the parliament dominated by it remained unrepresentative. In June 1953 Shishkali became prime minister and was elected president with wide powers in a referendum.

A soldier at heart, Shishkali lacked a socioeconomic ideology with which to shape his policies, and his attempts at reform proved ill-conceived. His high-handedness toward the Alawi [*qv*] and Druze [*qv*] minorities created opposition to his rule in the Alawi and Druze regions. Hostile toward the Soviet Union but aware of the dangers of aligning with the United States or Britain, Shishkali sought the active cooperation of France. In the midst of strikes and demonstrations in Aleppo [*qv*] and elsewhere, caused by the government's mishandling of minor violence in the Druze Mountains, a mutiny by army officers in Aleppo in late February 1954 spread to all garrisons, except Damascus [*qv*], and ended only after he had left the country.

Shishkali subsequently lived in Lebanon, Saudi Arabia, and France. Charged with plotting a coup against the Syrian regime in 1957, Shishkali was tried in absentia and convicted. In 1960 he migrated to Brazil, where he was assassinated by a Druze in revenge for the bombing of the Druze Mountains, which had been ordered by him.

Shuqairi, Ahmad (1908–80): *Palestinian politician* Born into an eminent religious-political family in Acre [*qv*], Shuqairi trained as a lawyer at the Jerusalem Law School and the American University in Beirut [*qv*]. In 1945 he became director of a Palestinian office in New York, and later in Jerusalem [*qv*]. He served as a member of the Arab Higher Committee [*qv*] from March–June 1946. After the Palestine War (1948–49) [*qv*], Shuqairi moved to Damascus [*qv*]. He was a member of the Syrian delegation to the United Nations from 1949–50. From 1951–57 he was undersecretary for political affairs at the Arab League [*qv*]. He then served Saudi Arabia as minister of state of U.N. affairs and ambassador to the United Nations from 1957–62.

During his years at the United Nations he espoused the cause of Palestinians, often with vehement verbal attacks on Israel.

In 1963 Syria and Iraq proposed at the Arab League that a Palestine National Council [*qv*] be elected and that its chief delegate should occupy the Palestinian seat at the Arab League. The first Arab League summit [*qv*] in January 1964 directed Shuqairi to consult his countrymen and present a plan for the creation of an organization representing them. The result was the Palestinian National Charter [*qv*], adopted by a conference in East Jerusalem [*qv*] in May, which established the Palestine Liberation Organization (PLO) [*qv*]. Shuqairi was elected chairman of the PLO executive.

Under Shuqairi the PLO had the full backing of Egyptian President Gamal Abdul Nasser [*qv*], who allowed Shuqairi to run a radio station from Cairo [*qv*]. His extremist and contradictory statements, advocating the extermination of Israeli Jews, proved counterproductive since they played into the hands of Israel. On the eve of the June 1967 Arab-Israeli War [*qv*], Shuqairi, then heading a small Palestinian militia, indulged in hyperbolic rhetoric, creating a war psychosis that was out of proportion to the force he commanded. Following the Arab debacle in the war, Shuqairi was forced to resign his chairmanship of the PLO in December 1967. This ended his public life.

Sidon: *Lebanese city* Pop. 149,000 (2003, est.). The history of Sidon, an ancient Mediterranean port, goes back to the third millennium B.C. As a thriving commercial center it appears in the Old Testament [*qv*] and later in the epic poems of the Greek poet Homer, who lived before 700 B.C. It

was ruled by the Assyrians, Babylonians, Persians, Greeks, and Romans. King Herod (37–34 B.C.) and Jesus Christ (ca. 6 B.C.–A.D. 302) found it attractive. Its prosperity stemmed from glassware and purple dye industries.

In A.D. 637 Sidon fell to Muslim Arabs [*qv*]. During the Crusades (1095–1272) it was fiercely fought over by the two sides and underwent repeated destruction and reconstruction. It then came under the successive rule of the Mamelukes (1250–1517) and the Ottomans (1517–1918). It became part of the Vilayat of Lebanon under Fakhr al Din Maan (r. 1591–1633) and thrived as a port. It survived the disastrous earthquake of 1837. During the French mandate its port facilities were improved. After the 1948–49 Palestine War [*qv*], Palestinian refugees set up two camps near it.

Besides being the commercial center of the region, it is the terminus of the Trans-Arabian Pipeline for Saudi oil, which was shut off during the long Lebanese Civil War [*qv*]. Among its tourist offerings are the Temple of Ashmoon of the Phoenician era, and two Crusader forts.

Sinai Campaign (1956): This is the term used by Israelis for the Suez War (1956) [*qv*].

Sinai Peninsula: Area 23,500 sq. miles/61,000 sq. km. Sinai is a derivative of Sin, the ancient moon god, and has a recorded history dating back to the third millennium B.C. A triangular peninsula that connects Asia to Africa, the Sinai extends from its wide base on the Mediterranean to the Red Sea, whose two arms bound it on the west (Gulf of Suez) and the east (Gulf of Aqaba). In the south is Jebel Musa (*Arabic: Mount Moses*), known as

Mount Sinai in English, the site of the divine giving of the Law (tablets) to Moses. On its slope is the renowned Greek Orthodox [qv] monastery of Saint Catherine, founded in ca. A.D. 250, where the Codex Sinaiticus, one of the oldest manuscripts of the New Testament [qv], was discovered in the nineteenth century. The rest of the Sinai is a plateau sloping toward the Mediterranean Sea.

Oil, first struck in 1910, was not exploited until three years later. The site of fighting between Egypt and Israel during the Suez War [qv], the War of Attrition [qv], and the October 1973 Arab-Israeli War [qv], it was occupied by Israel between November 1956 and March 1957, and again from June 1967 to April 1982.

Sinai I Agreement (Egypt-Israel, 1974): Instead of using the United Nations to make peace with the Arabs after the October 1973 Arab-Israeli War [qv], Israel approached U.S. Secretary of State Henry Kissinger to bring about an agreement with Egypt. Egyptian President Anwar Sadat [qv] went along with this. The result was the Sinai I agreement on 18 January 1974 on the disengagement of the two armies in the Sinai [qv], Egypt making concessions, allowing Israel to control the Mitla and Gidi passes and limiting its own military presence east of the Suez [qv] to 7,000 troops and 30 tanks.

The agreement formally ended the wartime military alliance between Egypt and Syria and enabled Kissinger to persuade the Arab oil states to end the oil embargo [qv] against Israel's Western allies, imposed during the 1973 war.

Sinai II Agreement (Egypt-Israel, 1975): Consisting of three published and four secret documents, the Sinai II Agreement was signed by Israel and Egypt on 4 September 1975, with the United States playing a crucial mediating role. The disengagement in the Sinai [qv] required demilitarization of the Israeli-controled Mitla and Gidi passes, an Israeli withdrawal of 12–24 miles/20–40 km to create a wider United Nations buffer zone, and the posting of 200 American technicians to supervise the Egyptian and Israeli early warning systems. Israel returned the Abu Rudais oil field to Egypt. The signatories renounced the threat or use of force.

Of the four secret deals, three concerned Israel and one, Egypt. The United States promised to assist Egypt to erect an early warning system in Sinai and to consult it in the event of Israel violating the agreement. Washington reaffirmed its earlier commitment to help Israel maintain military superiority over its Arab neighbors, pledged $2.5 billion aid to Israel in 1975–76, and guaranteed oil deliveries from Iran or mainland USA. It also promised not to recognize or negotiate with the Palestine Liberation Organization (PLO) [qv] until it recognized Israel's right to exist and accepted U.N. Security Council Resolutions 242 and 338 [qv]. This cramped U.S. policymaking in the region until the late 1980s.

Sistani, Ali Husseini (1930–): *Iraqi religious leader* Born into a Shia [qv] religious family in Iran Mashhad [qv], Sistani pursued his theological studies in Qom [qv], where he became a student of Ayatollah Muhammad Hussein Borujerdi. In 1951, he traveled to Najaf [qv] where he studied under Grand Ayatollah Abol Qasim Khoei [qv]. After obtaining a degree in *ijtihad* [qv], interpretative reasoning of the Sharia [qv], Islamic law, in 1960—which entitled him to the honorific hojatalislam (lit. proof of Ilsam), he went back to Mashhad, only to stay there for a year.

On his return to Najaf, he spent three more years on theological research, and then began to teach *fiqh* [qv], Islamic jurisprudence. Like his mentor Khoei, he belonged to the quietist school among Shia clerics who wanted to focus exclusively on providing succor to the community in its spiritual life and social welfare—quite apart from those clergy who favored intervention in the affairs of the state. This distinction became all the more important after the coup by the secular Baath Party [qv] in 1968, and the repression of the Shia religious establishment that followed after Saddam Hussein [qv] became vice-president in 1975, and intensified in the aftermath of the Islamic revolution in Iran four years later. With this, the Iranian-born Shia clerics came under suspicion, which increased during the early period of the Iran-Iraq War [qv], but subsided when most Iraqi Shias proved loyal to their country and fought Iran. By the time the war ended in 1988, Sistani had acquired the status of an ayatollah, and gained popularity due partly to his spartan way of life.

Following the death in 1992 of Khoei whose funeral prayer was performed by him, the mantle of the *marja-e taqlid* (Arabic: source of emulation) [qv] passed not to him, as had been widely expected, but to the younger Ayatollah Muhammad Sadiq al Sadr due to the intervention by Saddam Hussein. But a breach occurred between Grand Ayatollah al Sadr and the Iraqi president in 1998 when he issued a religious decree calling on

Shias to attend Friday prayers in mosques, a step disapproved by Saddam. In February 1999, al Sadr and his two sons were shot dead as they left a mosque in Najaf. After blaming "foreign countries" for the assassinations, the government appointed Sistani as the marja-e taqlid, entitling him to the honorific of grand ayatollah.

After the deposition of Saddam Hussein in April 2003, the followers of al Sadr's grandson, Moqtada al Sadr, demanded that Sistani leave Najaf. This led his acolytes to take him to a safe house. In the political-administrative vacuum created by Saddam Hussein's ouster, the Najaf-based religious collective, dominated by Sistani, became the nerve center of the Shia network consisting of mosques nationwide to administer the neighborhoods in Iraq's urban centers, including providing armed vigilantes to maintain law and order.

Six-Day War (1967): *see* Arab-Israeli War III (1967).

Sneh, Moshe (1909–72): *Israeli politician* Born Moshe Kleinbaum in Radzin, Poland, Sneh obtained a medical degree at Warsaw University. Active in Zionist politics, he was elected chairman of the Zionist Student Union in Warsaw in 1930 and became a member of the central committee of the Zionist Organization in Poland two years later. In 1935 he was appointed as political editor of a Yiddish [qv] daily paper, *Haint* (Today), and elected chairman of the Zionist Organization in Poland. He served as an officer in the Polish army when the Second World War erupted.

He escaped to Palestine [qv] in 1940 and became head of Haganah's [qv] central command a year later. Elected to the Jewish

Agency [*qv*] executive in 1945, he became director of the political department of the Agency's European office. After his resignation from the Haganah central command in 1946, he was elected head of the illegal immigration department of the Jewish Agency. Impressed by the Soviet backing for the partitioning of Palestine in November 1947, Sneh advocated an alliance with Moscow. In January 1948 he joined the newly formed Mapam [*qv*], becoming a member of its executive committee and editor of its paper, *Al HaMishmar* (On the Guard).

He was elected to the Knesset [*qv*] in 1949 and retained a seat until 1965. Under his influence Mapam moved leftward, and this strained its relations with Mapai [*qv*]. But the trial and conviction of Mordechai Oran, an Israeli citizen and Mapam leader who was arrested as a Zionist spy in Prague in late 1952, created anti-Soviet feeling within Mapam ranks and led to Sneh's expulsion from the party. Sneh and his followers formed the Israeli Socialist Left Party, which merged into Maki [*qv*] in 1954. He became a leader of Maki and editor of its daily paper, *Kol Ha'Am* (Voice of the People). Within the party Sneh led the pro-Jewish faction, which criticised Moscow's ban on the emigration of Soviet Jews and its Middle East policies. By mid-1965 a split in the party became inevitable, and opponents of Sneh's faction left to form Rakah [*qv*]. supported the June 1967 Arab-Israeli War [*qv*] and opposed the unconditional withdrawal of Israel from the Occupied Arab Territories [*qv*]. A witty orator, Sneh was respected by even his toughest opponents.

Socialist Labor Party (Egypt): *Egyptian political party* After President Anwar Sadat

[*qv*] had drained the Arab Socialist Party of Egypt [*qv*] of almost all its parliamentary deputies by forming his own National Democratic Party [*qv*] in August 1978, he tried to create "honest" opposition by encouraging the formation of another rightist group, the Socialist Labor Party (SLP) [*qv*], under the leadership of Ibrahim Shukri. The SLP backed the Camp David Accords [*qv*] and the subsequent Egyptian-Israeli Peace Treaty [*qv*] in March 1979. In the June 1979 general election it won 26 seats in a house of 392 seats. When it retained only a fraction of these seats in the May 1984 poll, President Hosni Mubarak [*qv*] bolstered its strength by appointing four SLP members as parliamentary deputies. In the 1987 election it joined the alliance led by Muslim Brotherhood and won thirteen seats. Along with all other opposition groups, except the National Progressive Unionist Alliance [*qv*], the SLP boycotted the December 1990 election, demanding that the state of emergency be repealed and that the election be supervised by a nongovernmental body. In 1995 it won one parliamentary seat. In 2000 the state-controlled Political Parties Committee suspended it and its weekly paper *Al Shaab* (The People), which had been preeminent in exposing corruption in high places, for "exceeding its political mandate."

Socialist National Front (Lebanon): *Lebanese political party* Composed of opposition groups, the Socialist National Front (SNF) was formed in 1952. It was led by Camille Chamoun [*qv*], Kamal Jumblat [*qv*], and others concerned mainly with domestic reform. Following the resignation of President Bishara Khouri [*qv*] in

September 1952 in the wake of charges of corruption, the SNF's nominee, Chamoun, was elected president by parliament. By pursuing pro-Western foreign policies at odds with rising Arab nationalism [qv], Chamoun alienated himself from the predominantly Muslim SNF, now led by Jumblat.

Chamoun's rigging of the 1957 general election further widened the gap between him and the SNF. Matters came to a head in May 1958 when fighting erupted between Chamoun supporters and the SNF, marking the start of the first Lebanese Civil War [qv]. The induction of U.S. marines into the conflict by Chamoun enraged the SNF, which controled about a third of Lebanon. The conflict ended in a compromise, with Chamoun stepping down at the end of his term after dropping his plans for a constitutional amendment that would let him seek reelection. He was succeeded by General Fuad Chehab [qv]. During Chehab's presidency the SNF became dormant.

Society of Combatant Clerics (Iran): (Official title, *Persian: Majma-e Ruhaniyoun-e Mobraz)* Popularly known as Majma, it was formed on 21 March 1988 with the tacit backing of Ayatollah Ruhollah Khomeini [qv] after the dissolution of the ruling Islamic Republican Party [qv]. It was composed of socioeconomic radicals and headed by Hojatalislam Mahdi Karroubi. They broke away from the older Association of Combatant Clergy [qv]. Its members contested the 1988 parliamentary poll and gained a majority, with the leftist camp, including moderates, claiming the loyalty of two-thirds of the deputies. In the 1989 presidential election, the Majma backed Ali Akbar Hashemi

Rafsanjani [qv], then parliamentary speaker, who won. Karroubi was elected speaker for the rest of the tenure of the Third Parliament. When Majma members opposed Rafsanjani's economic liberalization program, he compromised by abandoning wholesale privatization and proceeding on a sector-by-sector basis. In the Fourth Parliament (1992–96), the Majma members became a minority. In the 1993 presidential contest it backed Rafsanjani. In the Fifth Parliament (1996–2000), too, the Majma remained a minority. In the 1997 presidential election, it backed Hojatalislam Muhammad Khatami [qv]. On the eve of the parliamentary poll in 2000, it formed an important part of the Second Khordad (23 May) Front, named after the date of Khatami's landslide victory. Karrubi was elected Speaker by 186 votes to none, with the parliament dominated by leftist and left-of-center deputies, with thirty of them belonging to the Majma.

Solh, Riyad (1894–1951): *Lebanese politician; prime minister, 1943–45, 1946–51* Also spelled Sulh. Born into a notable Sunni [qv] family in Beirut [qv], Solh joined the Arab nationalist movement as a youth. After studying law in Beirut, he went to Istanbul for further studies. During the First World War, Solh was condemned to death for his Arab nationalist activities, but was later pardoned and freed. After the war he became one of the assistants of Faisal ibn Hussein [qv] in Damascus [qv] and a cofounder of the nationalist Istiqlal Party. When Faisal was defeated, Solh fled from Syria. As a leader of the Syrian-Palestinian Congress, based first in Cairo [qv] and then in Geneva, Switzerland, he agitated for the independence of Greater Syria [qv] from the French mandate. Following the electoral victory of the leftist Popular Front in France in 1936, Solh returned home and became a leading Sunni leader of Lebanon.

During the Second World War Solh was one of the two main architects of the 1943 National Pact [qv], the other being Bishara Khouri [qv], a Maronite [qv] leader. He became prime minister (1943–45) and played a leading role in getting Lebanon chosen as a cofounder of the Arab League [qv]. After the war he again served as prime minister (1946–51). His government quelled an attempted coup by Syrian Social Nationalist Party (SSNP) [qv] activists, and executed the party chief, Antun Saada [qv], in mid-1949. In retaliation, SSNP militants assassinated Solh in July 1951 during his visit to Amman [qv].

South Lebanon Army: *Lebanese militia* Formed by Israel during its occupation of southern Lebanon from March to June 1978, the South Lebanon Army (SLA), consisting mainly of Christian militiamen, was put under the command of Saad Haddad, a former (Christian) Lebanese army major. About 2,000 strong, it was armed, trained, and financed by Israel. It patrolled the border zone inside Lebanon, an area 2.5–7 miles/4–12 km wide and 50 miles/80 km long, running from the Mediterranean to Kafr Shuba and populated by 40,000 Christians [qv], mostly Maronite [qv], and 60,000 Muslims [qv], mostly Shia [qv]. The SLA kept the Lebanese army and the Arab League's [qv] peacekeeping force out of its area. It acted as part of the Israel Defense Forces (IDF) when the latter invaded Lebanon [qv] in

June 1982. When Haddad died in January 1984, Israel appointed Antoine Lahad, a retired (Christian) Lebanese army major, to succeed him.

Upon its final withdrawal from Lebanon in June 1985, Israel handed over its positions in the self-declared security zone to the 3,000-strong SLA and left behind 1,000 Israeli troops as a back-up force. With this, the SLA became as much of a target of the Lebanese resistance against Israeli occupation as IDF troops. When the end of Amin Gemayel's [qv] presidency in September 1988 resulted in Gen. Michel Aoun [qv] claiming monopoly of power, Lahad pledged his loyalty to him. But this had no practical impact on the situation. Equally, the end of the civil war in October 1990 changed little as far as the SLA was concerned.

During the Second Gulf War [qv] (January–February 1991) there were armed exchanges between pro-Iraqi Palestinian commandos and the IDF-SLA alliance. Following the signing of the Lebanese-Syrian Treaty of Brotherhood, Cooperation, and Coordination [qv] in May 1991, which was condemned by Israel, the IDF-SLA alliance hardened its position. Israel responded to any attacks on SLA or IDF patrols, mainly by Hizbollah [qv] partisans, by launching air raids and aiming artillery fire at Hizbollah positions outside the strip. Since most Lebanese saw Hizbollah as a counterforce to the SLA, the government refrained from disarming Hizbollah.

On the eve of Israel's unconditional withdrawal from south Lebanon in May 2000, more than 6,000 present and past SLA troops escaped to Israel. The Lebanese government tried another 2,000 for serving in the SLA or for working inside Israel. It sentenced 800 former SLA soldiers to twenty-five years in jail.

South Yemen: Official title: People's Republic of South Yemen (1967–70); People's Democratic Republic of Yemen (1970–90). *See* Yemen: History.

South Yemeni-Soviet Friendship Treaty (1979): After several years of hesitation, often induced by the prospect of unity with North Yemen [*qv*], South Yemen signed a twenty-year friendship and cooperation treaty with the Soviet Union in October 1979 during a visit by its president, Abdul Fattah Ismail [*qv*], to Moscow. The treaty assured South Yemen of its survival, a top priority for a country beleaguered since its independence in 1967 by hostile neighbors: Saudi Arabia, Oman, and North Yemen.

Steadfastness Front: *Front of radical Arab states* Formed in Tripoli, Libya, in December 1977, in the wake of a visit to Jerusalem [*qv*] by Egyptian President Anwar Sadat [*qv*], the Steadfastness Front consisted of Algeria, Libya, the Palestine Liberation Organization (PLO) [*qv*], Syria, and South Yemen. An Iraqi representative attended the plenary session but walked out, considering the Front not radical enough. The Front upheld the official Arab League [*qv*] position of no negotiating with Israel until it had vacated all Occupied Arab Territories [*qv*]. Sadat reacted to its founding by severing diplomatic links with its constituents.

At its meeting in Damascus [*qv*] in September 1978, the Front opposed the July 1978 Arab League resolution against South Yemen and supported the Omani people's struggle for liberation. At its conference in April 1980, the Front formally recognized the Polisario's Saharan Arab Democratic Republic. In July 1980, South Yemen protested at the economic boycott decided, at Saudi Arabia's behest, by the Arab League by a majority vote, and in September the Front members met and opposed the League's action. The subsequent Arab summit canceled the resolution against South Yemen. This proved to be the Front's high point.

Under the leadership of President Chadli Ben-Jedid (president from 1979–91), Algeria began gradually to dissociate itself from the Front, a trend accelerated by its economic decline following the collapse of oil prices in the spring of 1986. At about the same time Libya became the target of air attacks by the United States, and this considerably chastened its leader, Muammar Qadhafi. Syrian president Hafiz Assad [*qv*] was too preoccupied with the developments in the Lebanese Civil War [*qv*] to nurture the Front. It ceased to exist by 1987.

Stern, Avraham ("Yair") (1907–42): *Israeli guerrilla leader* Born into a middle-class Jewish [*qv*] family in Poland, Stern migrated to Palestine [*qv*]. After graduating from a Jewish school in Jerusalem [*qv*], he studied philosophy at the Hebrew University.

A member of Haganah [*qv*], Stern played an active role during the 1929 interethnic riots. Two years later he quit Haganah and became one of the cofounders of the more militant Irgun B. When most of the Irgun B members returned to Haganah in 1937, Stern and his followers allied with Revisionist Zionists [*qv*] to set up Irgun Zvai Leumi [*qv*]. He became one of its top commanders. Opposed to its subordination to the Revisionist leadership, he clashed with Vladimir Jabotinsky [*qv*].

He went to Poland in 1938 to test the feasibility of an Irgun plan to transport 40,000 Jewish partisans to Palestine to stage an anti-British uprising there. Due to the gathering war clouds in Central Europe, Irgun had to rethink its agenda. After Stern's return to Palestine and the outbreak of the Second World War in September 1939, his differences with the Revisionist leadership sharpened. Disagreeing with their decision to stop attacking the British and start cooperating with Haganah, Stern argued that with Britain at war the time was right for the Zionists to pressure it to honor its promise to the Jewish people.

He left Irgun in June 1940. Three months later he founded Lehi [*qv*]. It argued that since the British were the number one enemy of Jews, and since fighting them was the top Jewish priority, there was no harm in negotiating with the German Nazis to achieve this aim. Lehi contacted the German embassy in Ankara. This, and the terrorist attacks against the British mandate, marginalized Lehi and Stern, who went underground. Discovered in a hideout during a British police raid in February 1942, Stern was shot dead. But Lehi, by now popularly known as the Stern Gang/Group [*qv*], survived.

Stern Gang/Group: *see* Lehi/Lehy.

Suez Canal: This Egyptian waterway—106 miles/170 km long, 197 ft./60 meters wide and 42.5 ft./13 meters deep—connects the Mediterranean Sea and the Gulf of Suez, and thus the Red Sea. Permission to construct the Suez Canal was granted by the Egyptian ruler Said ibn Abbas (r. 1854–63) to Ferdinand de Lesseps, a French engineer. The canal, started in 1859 by the Universal Suez Maritime Canal Company (USMCC),

was completed ten years later. Based in Paris, the USMCC, which was owned jointly by Britain and France, managed the Canal until its nationalization in July 1956, when Egypt set up the Egyptian Canal Authority (ECA) to run it. This also ended the British occupation of 3,000 sq. miles/7,790 sq. km in the Suez Canal Zone.

Egyptian President Gamal Abdul Nasser [*qv*] nationalized the Canal after the United States and Britain had humiliated him by withdrawing the World Bank loan for the construction of the Aswan High Dam [*qv*]. In 1958 compensation to the USMCC was agreed through the World Bank. Closed during the June 1967 Arab-Israeli War [*qv*] due to the presence of sunken ships and then due to the War of Attrition [*qv*], the Canal did not reopen until June 1975. In October, following the Sinai II Agreement [*qv*] between Israel and Egypt, Israeli cargo ships were permitted to use the canal. After the 1979 Egyptian-Israeli Peace Treaty [*qv*], Israeli warships were also allowed passage. With the Canal's enlargement completed in 1980, larger ships with 53 ft./16 meters draft were able to use it.

Suez War (1956):

Background: On 19 July 1956 the United States informed Egypt that it was withdrawing its offer of aid for the Aswan High Dam [*qv*], thus undermining the loan from the World Bank for Reconstruction and Development, which was predicated on the U.S. assistance. A week later Egyptian President Gamal Abdul Nasser [*qv*] nationalized the Suez Canal [*qv*], which was jointly owned by Britain and France. Following the debate on the matter by the United Nations Security Council, Egypt agreed on

11 October to the principles regarding running the Canal, including maintaining its status as an international waterway. On 24 October a secret Anglo-French-Israeli agreement on an invasion of Egypt was finalized.

Operations: On 29–30 October 1956 Israel invaded the Sinai [qv]. At 1800 hours on 30 October Britain and France gave a twenty-four-hour ultimatum to Egypt and Israel to cease hostilities and withdraw their troops 10 miles/16 km from the Suez Canal so as not to jeopardize freedom of shipping. As Israel's forces were some 30 miles/48 km from the canal, it accepted the ultimatum, but Egypt rejected it. Fighting between the two sides continued. When the deadline ended at 1800 hours on 31 October, Britain and France bombed Egypt's airfields, virtually destroying its air force, and continued attacking Egyptian military facilities for the next thirty-six hours. Cairo ordered its forces, sent earlier across the Canal into the Sinai, to retreat and thus avoid being encircled by the enemy. They had done so by 2 November. On that day the U.S. cooperated with the Soviet Union at the UN Security Council to sponsor the "Uniting for Peace" resolution, which condemned aggression against Egypt. The next day, while continuing to consolidate its position in the Sinai, Israel completed its occupation of the Gaza Strip [qv].

On 4 November the UN General Assembly voted to set up a U.N. Emergency Force (UNEF) [qv] to supervise the truce. On 5 November, British and French paratroopers landed at the northern (Port Said) and southern (Port Suez) ends of the Canal. Israel, advised by London and Paris, attached unrealistic conditions to its acceptance of the U.N. Security Council cease-fire resolution. The Soviet premier, Marshal Nikolai Bulganin, in a letter to his Israeli counterpart, David Ben-Gurion [qv], wrote: "It [the aggression] is sowing a hatred of the state of Israel among the peoples of the East such as cannot but make itself felt with regard to the future of Israel, and which puts in jeopardy the very existence of Israel as a state."

On the night of 5–6 November, British and French forces landed in the Port Said area and, after seizing the town, started to move south along the Canal, which had been blocked by the Egyptians with sunken ships. The recently reelected U.S. President Dwight Eisenhower applied economic pressure on Britian, with the U.S. Federal Reserve Board selling large amounts of British pounds, thus undermining the pound-dollar exchange rate. Yielding to the U.S.-Soviet pressure, the invading governments accepted a ceasefire from midnight on 6–7 November. By then Israel had occupied Gaza and most of the Sinai, including its southeastern tip, Sharm al Shaikh, at the mouth of the Gulf of Aqaba.

Losses: Egypt: 1,650 killed, 215 aircraft; Israel: 190 killed, 15 aircraft; Britain: 16 killed, 4 aircraft; France: 10 killed, 1 aircraft. **Aftermath:** The U.N. Emergency Force (UNEF) [qv], which was to supervise the truce, began arriving on 4 December. Britain and France completed their withdrawal by 23 December, handing over their positions to UNEF. Though Israel agreed to withdraw on 8 November it did not actually do so until 8 March 1957—and then only after the United States committed itself to standing by Israel's right of passage through the Gulf of Aqaba, ensuring that Gaza was not used again for launching guerrilla attacks against it, and assisting Israel, secretly, in its nuclear research program. On Israel's insistence UNEF troops were posted exclusively in Gaza and the Gulf of Aqaba region to safeguard Israeli shipping. Egypt was allowed to return to Gaza to administer it.

sufism *(Arabic: sufi, derivative of* suf, *wool; hence man of wool, ascetic): mystical philosophy in Islam* Subscribing to the general theory of mysticism [*qv*] that direct knowledge of God is attainable through intuition or insight, sufism is based on the doctrines and methods derived from the Quran [*qv*]. Some early Muslims undertook ascetic exercises, believing that this would bring them closer to God. They were inspired by the example of the Prophet Muhammad, who used to withdraw into a cave and undertake nightly vigils, and by the practices of Christian hermits. They stressed meditation and contemplation of God, and regarded involvement in worldly affairs, or pursuit of political power, as a distraction from the path of seeking Allah within. They came to be known as sufis—from the word *suf* (wool)—because of the woolen garments the pioneers among them wore as a sign of asceticism.

Hassan al Basri (d. A.D. 728) was the first known sufi personality. In time, two types of sufis emerged: ecstatic and sober. Among the latter, Abu Hamid Muhammad al Ghazali (1058–1111) was the most prominent. He tried to integrate the whole Islamic legal system with a spiritual infrastructure originating in the Prophet Muhammad's mystic consciousness. His work became the living document for the sufi orders/brotherhoods that sprang up soon after his death.

The first sufi order was Qadiriya. Founded by Baghdad-based Abdul Qadir al Gailani (1077–1166), it stressed piety and humanitarianism. A brotherhood consisted of aspirants (*murids*), who took an oath of allegiance to the guide, known as *shaikh, pir, or murshid.* Women were admitted as associate aspirants. The shaikh headed a hierarchy within the order that was linked by a chain of inherited sanctity (*baraka*) or kinship to the founding saint. This chain went back to early sufi founders, such as Hassan al Basri, and through them to the House of the Prophet or the Prophet Muhammad himself.

It was common for a sufi order to establish its own convents. An example of a mainstream brotherhood was Naqshbandi, established by Yusuf al Hamadani (d. 1140) but named after Baha al Din Naqshband (1318–89), a mystic born in Tajikistan. Naqshbandis believed that there was no *tariqa* (road) outside the Sharia [*qv*] and followed the maxim, "The exterior is for the world, the interior for Allah." Believing that piety was best expressed through social activity, they opposed withdrawal from the world. They are noted for their silent remembrance (*dhikr*) in mosques, undertaken to induce a state of collective ecstasy.

Whereas Islamic rituals were generally austere, sufi orders provided a framework within which rich and colorful liturgical practices were spawned in the form of devotional rituals by novices. Such ecstatic sufi orders as the Rifaiiya brotherhood, originating in Iraq, are an example. Rifaiiya followers went into frenzies, during which they would ride dangerous animals, walk into fires, ravage venomous reptiles, or mutilate themselves by placing iron rings in their ears, necks, and hands to demonstrate the supremacy of mind over matter.

Sufism grew rapidly between 1250 and 1500, when the caliphate was based in Cairo [*qv*] under Mamluk sultans (1250–1517), and when Islam penetrated central and western Africa and southern India and Southeast Asia along the land and sea routes used by Arab traders. Islam came into contact not only with paganism in Africa, but also with the advanced religions and civilizations of Hinduism and Buddhism in Asia. It was through the rise of sufism that Islam was often able to absorb the pre-Islamic beliefs and practices of the new converts. Today sufi brotherhoods exist, overtly or covertly, in most Muslim communities.

suicide bombing: *Suicide committed by detonating explosives either strapped to the body of a person or carried in a vehicle or a boat, or by ramming a building with flying aircraft* A suicide bomber either triggers the detonator while in the midst of his/her potential targets or drives a vehicle loaded with explosives into the target, killing himself/herself along with many others—the latter method often called truck bombing. The destruction of the Twin Towers of the World Trade Center in New York and part of the Pentagon in Washington on 11 September 2001 by ramming flying passenger aircraft into the buildings, resulting in the death of 3,052 people, opened a new chapter in suicide bombing. As a rule, the suicide bomber is supported by an operational cell that provides accommodation, transport, food, clothing, and security until he/she reaches the target, this cell often consisting of "sleepers," legal residents of a country with jobs and families.

It was on 18 April 1983 that truck bombing was first deployed, and the target was the U.S. embassy in Beirut [*qv*]. The driver rammed the embassy with his truck, loaded with high explosives, at high speed, and destroyed much of the building and killed sixty-three people, including seventeen Americans, of whom seven were Central Intelligence Agency officers. No group claimed responsibility, but the local Islamic Jihad [*qv*] was widely blamed.

Lebanon's Muslim [*qv*] terrorists did so in the course of the 1975–90 Civil War [*qv*], in which the U.S., France, Britain, and Italy had intervened on behalf of the Lebanese Christians [*qv*]. They followed up the bombing of the American Embassy with the truck bombing of the U.S. and French military headquarters in West Beirut, which left 300 dead. The person who killed him/herself in the process was regarded by radical Islamists [*qv*] as a martyr in the path of God, described in the Quran [*qv*] (Chapter 3, Verse 164) thus:

"Count not those who were slain in
  God's way as dead,
but rather living with their Lord,
  by Him provided,
rejoicing in the bounty that God
  has given them,
and joyful in those who remain
  behind and have not joined them,
because no fear shall be on them,
  neither shall they sorrow,
joyful in blessing and bounty from
  God,
and that God leaves not to waste
  the wage of the believers."

The method of being killed in "God's way" has varied. During the Iran-Iraq War (1980–88) [*qv*], Iranian leader Ayatollah Ruhollah Khomeini [*qv*] ruled that anybody who died in the war was a martyr. On the other side, Iraqi President Saddam Hussein [*qv*], though no scholar of Islam [*qv*], issued similar statements. Since suicide bombing was a recent phenomenon, it led to controversy among Muslim scholars. Those who opposed it argued that it was un-Islamic to kill innocent civilians. Those in favor reasoned that suicide bombing enabled Muslims to overcome their general weakness vis-à-vis their enemies.

However, suicide bombing ceased to be the monopoly of Islamic fundamentalists [*qv*]. By the beginning of the twenty-first century, it was adopted by ten organizations, both religious and secular, and used 160 times in thirteen countries, with Sri Lanka's Tamil rebels—Hindu by religion—fighting for an independent state, being the most frequent practitioners.

Whether sanctioned by religion or not, suicide bombing has proved effective. The conventional concept of security rests on deterrence, where the terrorist is killed or apprehended by the authorities. But the certain death of the suicide terrorist(s) precludes the captors extracting information, thereby enabling the terrorist group to undertake daring operations while protecting its cadres and organizational network.

In the case of the U.S. embassy bombings in Nairobi and Dar as Salam in August 1998, the authorities had quick success in apprehending the conspirators, because in each instance one of the terrorists chose not to commit suicide at the last moment.

Conversely, when both terrorists died in the ramming of USS *Cole* in October 2000, the Yemeni authorities took more than a year to arrest their coconspirators.

Similarly the black boxes saved from the crash of the third aircraft in rural Pennsylvania—instead of ramming Capitol Hill in Washington—provided useful clues to the U.S. authorities in identifying the nineteen suicide hijackers of the four planes.

During the first two years of the Second Intifada [*qv*] of the Palestinians [*qv*], seventy Palestinians, including three women, carried out suicide bombings. Those claiming these attacks were not only Hamas [*qv*] and the Islamic Jihad [*qv*], but also the Tanzim, affiliated to secular Fatah [*qv*].

sunna *(Arabic: custom, path):* In the pre-Islamic society of Arabia [*qv*] the term *sunna* applied to social practices based on ancestral precedents. After the rise of Islam [*qv*] under the Prophet Muhammad (A.D. 570–632), early converts took their cue either from the behavior of the Prophet's companions or the residents of Medina [*qv*], the capital of the Islamic realm. As for the later converts living away from Medina, codes based partly on local traditions and partly on the *sunna* evolved.

Though the Prophet Muhammad was an exemplar for Muslims, it was not until the eminent jurist Muhammad ibn Idris al Shafii (A.D. 767–820) had ruled that all legal decisions not stemming directly from the Quran [*qv*] must be based on a tradition going back to the Prophet Muhammad himself that a serious effort was made to compile the Prophet's sayings and doings—based on eyewitness accounts of his words, actions, and approbations.

Thus the *sunna* of the Prophet Muhammad was codified by Hadith [*qv*].

The authority of the *sunna* was reinforced when, reacting to the frequent fabrication of the Hadith by adherents of different doctrinal, legal, and political schools, leading jurists developed *ilm al hadith,* the method for testing the genuineness of individual tradition. The *sunna* was then employed in the exposition ofthe Quran and in *fiqh* [*qv*] (Islamic jurisprudence).

Sunnis *(Persian: derivative of* Ahl al sunna; *Arabic; People of the path [of the Prophet Muhammad]): Islamic sect* Sunnis are the leading sect within Islam. They regard the first four caliphs—Abu Bakr, Omar, Othman, and Ali (r. A.D. 656–61)—"Rightly Guided." They belong to one of the four schools of jurisprudence—Hanafi [*qv*], Maliki [*qv*], Shafii [*qv*], and Hanbali [*qv*]—and accept the six "authentic books" of al Hadith [*qv*], the first of which was compiled by Muhammad al Bukhari (d. A.D. 870).

They differ from the minorty Shia [*qv*] sect in doctrine, ritual, law, theology, and religious organization. They share only three of the five doctrines of Shiism: monotheism, i.e., there is only one God; prophethood, which is a means of communications between God and humankind; and resurrection, i.e. the souls of dead humans are raised by God on their Day of Judgement and their deeds on earth judged. Their five obligations—reciting the central Islamic precept ("There is no god but Allah, Muhammad is the Messenger of Allah"), daily prayers, fasting during Ramadan [*qv*], *zakat* (alms tax) [*qv*], and *hajj* (pilgrimage to Mecca) [*qv*]—are fewer than those required by Shias. Unlike Shias, Sunnis regard caliphs as fallible

interpreters of the Quran [*qv*] and the *sunna* [*qv*]. Sunnis do not share the concept of Mahdi [*qv*] with Shias, and view Islamic history essentially as a drift away from the ideal community that existed under the rule of the first four Rightly Guided caliphs.

Sunnis and Shias also differ on the organization of religion and religious activities. Sunnis regard religious activities as the exclusive domain of the (Muslim) state. When the ulama [*qv*] act as judges or preachers or educators, they do so under the aegis of the state. There is little scope for the *ulama* to organize religion outside the confines of the Muslim state.

The Sunni ethos, too, is different from the Shia. There is no emotional outlet for mourning the martyrdom of early Islamic leaders, as in the Ashura [*qv*] celebrations of Shias. The only exception lies with the Sufi orders [*qv*] within Sunnism, where believers are provided with something emotional or heartwarming—rituals that are performed collectively.

Finally, except for government-appointed religious officials such as *qadi* (judge), mufti (one who delivers fatwas, religious rulings), grand mufti and *shaikh-al-islam* (wise man of Islam), or professional theological teachers, called *maulawi* or *maulana* (learned man), Sunni clerics are not given the religious titles of their Shia counterparts.

Supreme Assembly of Islamic Revolution in Iraq: *Iraqi political organization (Arabic: Majlis al Aala lil Thawra al Islamiya fi al Iraq)* The Supreme Assembly of Islamic Revolution in Iraq (SAIRI) was formed in Tehran [*qv*] in November 1982 by three Iraqi Islamic organizations: al Daawa al Islamiya [*qv*], the Mujahedin Movement, and the Islamic Action Organization. Led by Ayatollah Muhammad Baqir al Hakim, a Shia [qv] cleric with a history of resistance to the Iraqi Baath [qv] regime, SAIRI aimed to found an Islamic state in Iraq [qv]. It raised an armed force (al Mujahedin) from among Iraqi exiles and prisoners of war, who then fought alongside the Iranians in the Iran-Iraq War [qv].

In late 1986 it participated in the Conference on Solidarity with the Iraqi People, held in Tehran and attended by the delegates of various Kurdish autonomist groups. But their decision to form a joint military committee remained unimplemented. After the Iran-Iraq War SAIRI's importance waned.

When Baghdad's control over the provinces weakened in the aftermath of the 1991 Gulf War [qv], SAIRI encouraged the Shias in southern Iraq to rebel against it. Its Iranian-based cadres crossed over into the rebel areas, unfurling its flag and the portraits of Ayatollahs al Hakim and Ruhollah Khomeini [qv]. The move proved counterproductive. Having fought Iran for eight years, most Iraqis, irrespective of their sectarian affiliation, were loath to see Iranian interference in their affairs. After the failure of the rebellion, SAIRI once again became quiescent. Later it tried to focus world attention on the plight of the (Shia) residents of the marshes in southern Iraqi, which were being drained by the central government in order to develop the area (economically and socially) and extract oil. But little came of it.

When Washington's Iraq Liberation Act, 1998, authorized the president to name Iraqi groups entitled to receiving military aid to topple the regime of Saddam Hussein [qv], President Bill Clinton named SAIRI as one such faction along with five others. But SAIRI, maintaining an army of 8,000 to 12,000 exiled Iraqis, rejected the entitlement, arguing that the American move made the Iraqi opposition appear as U.S. agents. By then the Iranian government had taken to using SAIRI to get even with the periodic pinprick attacks by the Baghdad [qv]-based Mujahedin-e Khalq [qv] along the Iranian-Iraqi border. In March 2000, when the Mujahedin activists inside Iran [qv] fired half a dozen mortars in central Tehran, SAIRI militants inside Iraq retaliated by firing mortars at a Baghdad neighborhood, killing four people.

In the spring of 2002, when the U.S. administration of President George W. Bush (r. 2001–) began preparing military plans to invade Iraq, it invited the six recognized Iraqi opposition factions to Washington, SAIRI representatives attended a meeting in August, thus reversing its pervious stance with the tacit approval of the Iranian government. Later it attended the Iraqi open conference in London where in the 65-member Advisory Committee it received a generous representation.

Following the overthrow of the Saddam Hussein regime by the Anglo-American forces in April 2003, the soldiers and activists of SAIRI returned to Iraq and took control of some Iraqi villages and towns along the Iranian border. SAIRI partisans also entered Najaj [qv] as Karbala [qv]. In conjuction with the followers of Gra Ayatollah Ahi Sistani [qv], they demanded that the occupying Anglo-American troops leave Iraq forthwith.

Supreme Council of Islamic Revolution in Iraq: *see* Supreme Assembly of Islamic Revolution in Iraq.

Sur: *see* Tyre.

Sykes-Picot Pact (Anglo-French, 1916): A secret pact between London and Paris was signed in May 1916 by Sir Mark Sykes, senior British diplomat, and Francois Geroges Picot, a former French consul in Beirut [*qv*], to carve up the Ottoman Empire among Britain, France, and Russia after their victory in the First World War. Its provisions contradicted various British statements and declarations (one of them in conjunction with France) during the war, as well as the contents of the correspondence between Sir Henry McMahon, the British high commissioner in Cairo [*qv*], and Hussein ibn Ali, the Arab governor of Hijaz [*qv*], which promised independence to the Arab territories of the Ottoman Empire after the victory of the Allies (Belgium, Britain, France, Greece, Italy, Japan, Montenegro, Russia, and Serbia) over the Central Powers (Austria–Hungary, Bulgaria, Germany, and the Ottoman Empire). An exchange of letters between Britain, France, and Russia in October 1916 finalized the pact. It was revealed in December 1917 by the Bolshevik regime in Russia, which published it in the official newspaper, Izvestia (Russian: News).

The Sykes-Picot Pact concerned the interests of Britain, France and Russia. After the victory Russia was to acquire Constantinople (now Istanbul), a strip on each side of the Bosphorus Straits, and large parts of of the four provinces of Turkey bordering Russia. As for the Ottoman Empire's Arab territory, in which Russia was uninterested, Britain and France made the following deal: British hegemony in the Baghdad and Basra provinces of Mesopotamia [*qv*]; French hegemony in Ottoman (Greater) Syria [*qv*] and Lesser Armenia (in Turkey); and an international zone in Palestine [*qv*], much smaller than the Palestine mandated to Britain in 1922. The rest was to be constituted into an independent Arab state or federation, divided into British and French spheres of influence.

synagogue *(Greek: assembly):* The terms for synagogue in Hebrew [*qv*] are: *beit ha-knesset* (house of the assembly), *beit ha-tefilla* (house of the prayer), and *beit ha-midrash* (house of the study). So a synagogue is a gathering place for prayer and religious study. Synagogues came into vogue after the razing of the First Temple (of Solomon) in 586 B.C., and rose in significance after the demolition of the Second Temple in A.D. 70. They became the site of three daily services as well as special ceremonies on the Sabbath [*qv*] and religious festivals.

Constructed with one end oriented toward Jerusalem [*qv*], synagogues tended to be basilical in design, with a gallery. In time they came to be embellished with mosaics, frescoes, and carvings. After Roman Emperor Constantine (r. A.D. 306–37) had adopted Christianity as the state religion in A.D. 313, old synagogues were demolished or converted to churches. Following the rise of Islam [*qv*] and an Islamic empire in the seventh century A.D., synagogues were allowed to be repaired in Muslim lands.

During the Middle Ages (A.D. 476–1492) synagogues emerged as the intellectual and social centers of Jewish life, the adjacent courtyards being used as law courts and for wedding ceremonies. Today a typical synagogue contains an ark (where the scrolls of the Torah [*qv*] are kept); an eternal light burning before the ark; two candelabra pews; and a raised platform, from which scriptural passages are read and, often, services conducted.

Segregation of the sexes, which is strictly observed by Orthodox Jews [qv], has been discontinued by Reform [qv] and Conservative [qv] Jewry. Among Diaspora [qv] Jews, synagogues are often independent, reflecting the local community's wishes in its construction, maintenance, choice of priest, called rabbi *(Hebrew: teacher)*, and officials.

Syria:

Official name: Arabic Republic of Syria

Capital: Damascus [qv]

Area: 71,500 sq. miles/185,180 sq. km

Population: 17,150,000 (2002, est.)

Gross domestic product: $17.6 billion (2001,est.)

National currency: Syrian Pound (SP); SP1 = US$0.089 = £0.062 = EUR 0.1 (2001)

Form of government: republic, president elected by voters

Official language: Arabic [qv]

Administrative system: Syria consists of thirteen governorates.

Constitution: The 1973 constitution, approved overwhelmingly in a referendum, describes Syria as a democratic, popular, socialist state, and requires that Islam [qv] should be the religion of the head of state. Executive power is vested with the president, who is elected directly by voters for a seven-year term. He has the authority to appoint or dismiss vice presidents, the prime minister, and individual ministers. He is also commander in chief of the military. Legislative power lies with the popularly elected 250-member People's Assembly, where eighty-four seats are reserved for independent members. Following the death of

President Hafiz Assad in 2000, the age requirement for president was lowered from forty to thirty-four.

Ethnic composition (2002): Arabs [qv], 90 percent; Kurds [qv], 6 percent; Armenians [qv] and others, 4 percent.

High officials:

Head of state: Bashar Assad [qv], 2000–

Vice presidents: (First) Abdul Halim Khaddam (political and foreign affairs), 2000– ; (Second) Muhammad Zuhair Masharka (internal and party affairs), 2000–

Prime minister: Muhammad Mustafa Mero, 2000–

Speaker of the People's Assembly: Abdul Qadir Qaddura, 1998–

History (since ca. 1900): Following a collapse of the four-century-long Ottoman rule in 1918, Greater Syria [qv] enjoyed a brief spell of self-rule under Faisal I ibn Hussein [qv] until his defeat by the French, the mandate power, in mid-1920. After enlarging the Vilayat of Lebanon at the expense of Syria, the French divided the area into Latakia, Jebel Druze, Aleppo, and Damascus, combining the last two in late 1924 to form the state of Syria.

It took France two years to quell the armed rebellion that erupted in Jebel Druze and spread elsewhere in 1925. The subsequent talks resulted in the convening of a national assembly in 1928. Dominated by the nationalist National Bloc, the assembly adopted a constitution that did not recognize the French mandate. Paris dissolved the parliament and imposed its own constitution in 1930. The parliament elected under this constitution reached an impasse with the French high commissioner on the terms of a treaty to replace the mandate and was suspended.

Popular protest reached a peak in early 1936 and shut down public services and markets for seven weeks. This compelled the French to negotiate with the National Bloc. Due to this installation of a leftist Popular Front government in Paris, these talks were successful. According to the Franco-Syrian Treaty [qv], initialed in September 1936, Paris agreed to grant independence to Syria in three years in exchange for long-term military, political, and economic privileges. A National Bloc government, elected in November 1936, was in power on the eve of the Second World War, when France suspended both the 1930 constitution and the government and imposed martial law.

After the occupation of northern France by Nazi Germany in 1940, and the subsequent establishment of a pro-German regime in Vichy in central France, control of the overseas French territories passed to the Vichy regime. It was defeated in Syria (and Lebanon) by British and Free French forces in June 1941, and Syria was granted (nominal) independence. When a general election was called in 1943, the National Bloc won handsomely. The next year Syria won the recognition of the United States and the Soviet Union. Because it declared war on Germany in February 1945, Syria was invited to the founding conference of the United Nations. At the end of the war France tried to reassert its authority in Syria, but failed. France finally left in April 1946.

Syria's unsuccessful participation in the 1948–49 Palestine War [qv] led to rioting and paved the way for the army coup that was launched in March 1949. Military rule lasted for five years under different rulers, the last of whom was Adib Shishkali [qv]. His overthrow was followed by the restoration of parliamentary democracy.

The first free election in the Middle East [qv] took place in Syria in September 1954, with women accorded universal suffrage. This led to the rise of radical groups, including the Baath party [qv]. When faced with a choice of aligning either with traditional parties, such as the National Bloc, or radical ones, such as the communists [qv], the Baath chose a way out by proposing Syria's union with Egypt. The resulting United Arab Republic (UAR) [qv] lasted from early 1958 to September 1961.

A secret Military Committee of Baathist officers was the main force behind a coup in March 1963. Factional infighting within the Baath was settled in favor of the radicals, led by Salah Jadid [qv], in early 1966. The new government, with Hafiz Assad [qv] as defense minister, pursued radical socioeconomic policies at home and actively opposed the conservative Arab government in the region. Though it successfully withstood the adverse effect its defeat in the June 1967 Arab-Israeli War [qv] had on its popular standing, the regime became divided on apportioning blame. The nationalist wing, led by Assad, blamed the socialist wing, headed by Jadid. A struggle ensued between the two factions, which Assad finally won in November 1970. Assad consolidated his presidency through a referendum in early 1971. By forming the Baathist-led National Progressive Front [qv] in 1972, he co-opted friendly parties.

The initial gains made by Syria on the Golan Heights [qv] front during the early phase of the October 1973 Arab-Israeli War [qv] were lost later. When, in the course of his intervention in the Lebanese Civil War [qv] in mid-1976, he sided with the Maronite Christian [qv] camp, there was an upsurge in support for the Muslim Brotherhood [qv]. It started a campaign of assassination and terrorism, which escalated into near-insurrection in Aleppo [qv] and Hama [qv] in March 1980, and reached a peak with an assassination attempt on Assad in June.

Assad went all out to crush the Islamists, and temporarily succeeded. The Brotherhood's violent activities resumed and culminated in an insurrection in Hama in February 1982. Assad hit back with unprecedented force, reimposing control at the cost of 5,000–10,000 lives. When he suffered a heart attack in November 1983, his power was challenged, unsuccessfully, by his younger brother, Rifat [qv].

Following the arrest and conviction in October 1986 of Nizar Hindawi (a Jordanian purportedly working in conjunction with the Syrian Embassy in London) for attempting to plant a bomb on an Israeli airliner in London, Britain broke off diplomatic relations with Syria. The United States recalled its ambassador from Damascus and placed Syria on the list of nations supporting international terrorism. The next year Syria closed down the training camps maintained on its territory by Abu Nidal [qv]. In September 1987 the U.S. ambassador returned to Damascus, but Washington retained Syria's name on its list of terrorist nations.

Meanwhile, Assad justified his continuing involvement in the Lebanese civil strife on the ground that defection of Lebanon to the U.S.-Israel camp would present great danger to Syrian security. He persevered, and in October 1990 the pro-Syrian side finally won in Lebanon. He was far less successful in dealing with the Palestine Liberation Organization (PLO) [qv], led by Yasser Arafat [qv]. Following Egypt's defection from the Arab camp in 1979, Assad embarked upon a plan to achieve strategic parity with Israel, an ambitious proposition to be implemented with active Soviet backing. Considering Palestinians an important part of an alliance to deal with Israel, he tried to bring Arafat under his wing. But Arafat, intent on maintaining the PLO's independence, resisted him. The subsequent Assad-inspired rebellion within Arafat's party, Fatah [qv], while weakening him made him, turn to moderate King Hussein [qv] of Jordan.

With the rapid decline of the Soviet Union as a superpower from 1989 onward, Syria had to soften its strategy toward Israel. It took a realistic view of the leadership that the United States, now the sole superpower, provided in reversing Iraq's occupation of Kuwait after August 1990. When Syria's attempt to persuade Iraqi President Saddam Hussein [qv] to evacuate Kuwait failed, it joined the U.S.-led anti-Iraq coalition and sent 30,000 troops to reinforce Saudi Arabia's defenses.

In October 1991 Syria agreed to participate in the Middle East Peace Conference [qv]—which was intended to lead to bilateral talks between Israel and its Arab enemies—having been assured that the conference would be held on the basis of U.N. Security Council Resolutions 242 and 338 [qv]. Syria disapproved of the Israeli-PLO Accord [qv] and the Jordanian-Israeli Peace Treaty [qv], but did nothing to undermine them. In its talks with Israel, it insisted on a clear Israeli commitment to vacate all of the Golan in return for total peace, and succeeded in getting the United States to play an active role in the negotiations.

Once Syria and Israel had agreed to a ten-point framework in late 1995, its representatives held talks at a venue in the United States in early 1996. But when suicide bombings by radical Islamist Palestinians killed fifty Israelis in late February–early March, Israeli Prime Minister Shimon Peres [qv] demanded that Syria condemn the attacks. Assad replied that these had nothing had nothing to do with his country. Peres unilaterally terminated the negotiations with Damascus. The situation remained unchanged during the three years when Benjamin Netanyahu [qv] was Israel's prime minister. Talks resumed after the election of Ehud Barak [qv] as Netanyahu's successor. In September 1999, U.S. Secretary of State Madeleine Albright backed the Syrian demand for total withdrawal from the Golan Heights. In December Barak met Syrian foreign minister Faruq al Shaara in Washington. Three months later U.S. President Bill Clinton presented Barak's proposals to Assad in Geneva. These included Israel retaining sovereignty over a narrow strip on the northeastern shore of Lake Tiberias to safeguard its water resources. Assad agreed to give Israel access to the strip but not sovereignty. The talks broke down. Assad died in June.

Three years earlier Assad had begun mending fences with Iraq by resuming economic links with Baghdad that had been broken in 1980 after Iraq's invasion of Iran. His successor, Bashar Assad, continued this policy—with the reopened pipeline between the two neighbors providing Syria with 200,000 barrels of oil per day for domestic consumption, thus making an equivalent amount available for export—as well as sticking to the Syrian position that Israel had to withdraw from all of the Golan Heights in return for total peace and normalisation of relations. Soon after Bashar assumed supreme power in Syria, ninety-nine leading intellectuals demanded an end to the martial law that had been in force since 1963. In response, the government announced that the emergency laws had been suspended. The release of 600 political prisoners, on top of another 225 freed by Hafiz Assad in the last days of his rule, still left 1,500 politicians in jail. After the initial surge of liberalization, Bashar Assad slowed down the pace of political reform to placate the old guard in the Baath party and the military and intelligence services. He maintained the Syrian force of 30,000 in Lebanon.

In the wake of the 11 September 2001 attacks on the U.S. by Al Qaida [qv], Syria, long opposed to Islamic fundamentalism [qv], offered intelligence assistance to Washington, thus thawing its relations with the sole superpower. But since Damascus continued to support Lebanon's Hizbollah [qv], America kept Syria on its list of the countries that sponsor international terrorism. On 1 January 2002, Syria became a nonpermanent member of the United Nations Security Council as a representative of the Arab member states. It voted for the Security Council Resolution 1441 [qv], thus making its adoption unanimous. It did so in order to avoid an invasion of Iraq by the United States. But as Washington prepared to invade Iraq despite satisfactory progress by U.N. inspectors in disarming Iraq of weapons of mass destruction, Syria warned against military action. When the U.S., backed by the U.K., invaded Iraq, Syria was the only Arab country to say publicly that the Anglo-American action was illegitimate. After Gulf War III [qv] it received public warnings from Washington not to harbor Iraqi fugitives.

Religious composition: (2002) Muslim [qv], 90 percent, of which Sunni [qv] 68 percent, Alawi [qv] 14 percent, Druze [qv] 6 percent, Ismailis [qv], 2 percent; Christian [qv], 9 percent; other 1 percent.

Syrian Catholic Church: *Christian sect* As a Uniate Church [qv], the Syrian Catholic Church accepts the primacy of the Pope but has retained its Eastern rites and customs. Attempts at reconciling the Syrian Orthodox Church [qv] with the Western church, based in Rome, in the mid-thirteenth century failed. But four centuries later some members began to convert to Catholicism [qv], while retaining their Liturgy of St. James in Syriac. The office of the Syrian Catholic Patriarch of Antioch was formalized in 1782. Since then the patriarch has been based in Deir Zafran, Sharfe, Aleppo [qv], Mardin (Turkey), and Beirut [qv].

Syrian Orthodox: *see* Orthodox Christians, Syrian.

Syrian Social Nationalist Party (Lebanon): *Lebanese political party* The Syrian Social Nationalist Party (SSNP) emerged in 1947 out of the Syrian Nationalist Party, founded in 1932 by Antun Saada [qv] with the aim of creating a Greater Syria [qv] that could accommodate all the people forming the Syrian nation, which Saada described as an ethnic fusion of Canaanites, Akkadians,

Chaldeans, Assyrians, Arameans, Hittites, and Metannis.

The SSNP combined opposition to the French mandate with secularism—including separation of church and state and removal of barriers between various sects and religions—and a state-directed program for modernizing society. The French banned the party in 1935, but it continued to function secretly. In 1938 Saada published *Nushu al-umam* (Rise of Nations), in which he argued the case for a unique Syrian identity.

The outbreak of the Second World War found Saade in Latin America on a mission to forge links with the Syrian settlers there. On his return to Lebanon in 1947 he reestablished control over the party, now renamed the Syrian Social Nationalist Party, which derived the majority of its support from the non-Maronite [qv] section of the Christian community. Due to his views on an all-embracing Syrian nationalism, he soon clashed with the Lebanese government. He went underground but was allowed to resurface after he had affirmed his acceptance of Lebanon as a sovereign state.

In June 1949 there was fighting in Beirut between the SSNP and the Phalange Party [qv], which, the SSNP alleged, had been provoked by the government of Riyadh Solh [qv]. The authorities described it as an attempted coup by the SSNP, arrested 2,000 SSNP members, and banned the party. Saada fled to Syria. Although received warmly by the Syrian leader, Hosni Zaim [qv], he was returned to Lebanon. Following a secret military trial he was executed; and in revenge SSNP militants assassinated Solh two years later. Though much weakened, the party continued to function semi-clandestinely until the lifting of the ban on transnational parties in 1970.

Led by Inaam Raad, the SSNP remained bitterly opposed to the Phalange. When the Lebanese Civil War [qv] broke out in April 1975, it allied with the Movement of the Disinherited, led by Musa al Sadr [qv], to form the pro-Syrian Nationalist Front. Habib Tanios Shartuni—who was responsible for blowing up the Phalange headquarters in Beirut in September 1982, killing president-elect Bashir Gemayel [qv]—was a member of the SSNP, which by then had emerged as a staunch ally of Syria in resisting Israel's ambitions in Lebanon. It emerged as an important element in the anti-Israeli front, conducting guerilla actions against the Israeli troops and their surrogate, the South Lebanese Army (SLA) [qv], in southern Lebanon. After the defeat of Gen. Michel Aoun [qv] in October 1990, SSNP militamen took over some of the offices of the Phalange, which had backed Aoun. In the national unity government formed two months later, Inaam Raad was appointed minister. The SSNP participated in the 1992 general election.

Later the party's leadership passed to Jibran Araiji.

Syrian-Soviet Friendship Treaty (1980): Following the 1979 Egyptian–Israeli Peace Treaty [qv], and because of mounting domestic and regional pressures on the Syrian regime and the outbreak of the Iran-Iraq War [qv] in September 1980, Syria's President Hafiz Assad [qv] signed a twenty-year Treaty of Friendship and Cooperation with the Soviet Union in Moscow in October 1980. It stipulated consultation "in the event of a situation jeopardizing the peace and security of either party." Later it was revealed that the treaty contained a secret clause dealing with the use of atomic weapons by a potential attacker, implying Israel. The treaty boosted Syria's confidence. Later there were unconfirmed reports that Moscow had stockpiled heavy weapons in Syria for use in the event of war between Syria and Israel. However, despite the treaty and Syria's involvement in Lebanon, the Soviet Union reacted passively to the Israeli invasion of Lebanon [qv] in June 1982, chiefly because of the rapidly deteriorating health of its leader, Leonid Brezhnev. With the collapse of the Soviet Union in 1991, the treaty lapsed.

T

Tabriz: *Iranian city* Pop. 1,213,000 (2003, est.). Capital of East Azerbaijan province, Tabriz is Iran's fourth largest city. Known as Tauris in ancient times, it was the capital of Atropaten, named after Atropates, a general of Alexander the Great (r. 336–23 B.C.). Its present name, a derivative of *tap riz,* meaning heat flow, refers to the hot springs surrounding it. Capital of the Ghazni dynasty, founded by Khan Mahmud Ghazan (r. 1295–1304), from the late thirteenth century, Tabriz fell to Tamerlane in 1392. Shah Ismail captured it from the Ottoman Turks in 1501 and founded the Safavid dynasty.

During the Second Russo-Iranian War (1827–28) it was occupied by the Russians. They reoccupied it during the First World War and stayed until the Bolshevik Revolution in October 1917. During the Second

World War the Soviets occupied the city in 1941, when it became an important link in the transportation of U.S. war materials from Iran's Gulf [*qv*] ports to the Soviet Union by rail.

Tabriz was the capital of the Autonomous Government of Azerbaijan, set up by the Democratic Party of Azerbaijan in December 1945, which lasted a year. It was at the forefront of the revolutionary movement in 1977–78, by which time it had emerged as an important commercial, industrial, and communications center, producing tractors, motorcycles, cement, textiles, and carpets.

Despite severe earthquakes, the last one to rock the city being in 1780, several of its historical monuments have survived. These include the early-fourteenth-century citadel and the mid-sixteenth-century Blue Mosque, so called because of its stunning blue tile decoration.

Taif Accord (Lebanese): *see* National Reconciliation Charter 1989 (Lebanon).

Taimur ibn Faisal (1885–1956): *Sultan of Oman, 1913–32* Born in Muscat [*qv*], Taimur succeeded his father, Faisal, in 1913. He inherited a country mired in a tribal revolt and heavy debts, and his attempt to buy peace failed. In 1915 the rebellious tribal leader Shaikh Isa ibn Salim al Harthi attacked the coastal region of Muscat-Batinah. Aided by the military of the British India government, Taimur repelled the insurgents and regained the coastal region, leaving the interior in the hands of Shaikh Isa al Harthi.

The subsequent uneasy peace allowed the British Political Agent in Muscat to initiate peace talks in 1918. The resulting Treaty of Sib [*qv*], signed in September 1920 between Taimur and "the people of Oman," recognized the authority of the sultan in external matters and guaranteed freedom of movement to the tribes and urban dwellers. Shaikh Isa, representing the tribal chiefs of the interior, promised not to break the peace or give refuge to wrongdoers from coastal towns. Taimur agreed not to raise taxes on coastal towns above 5 percent of the value of trade.

Since concluding a treaty with Shaikh Isa implied autonomy for the interior, Taimur was reluctant to do so. To overcome his reluctance, Britain gave him a loan to repay the debts he had incurred among the coastal traders. However, Taimur failed to show fiscal responsibility: he defaulted on his loan repayments and let the administrative machinery slacken. The efforts of British civil servants to salvage the situation failed, and in 1932 Britain forced Taimur to abdicate in favor of his son, Said [*qv*].

al Takfir wal Hijra (Egypt) *(Arabic: The Denunciation/Repentance and the Migration): Egyptian Islamic group* A clandestine group established in 1972, al Takfir wal Hijra came to light during the January 1977 rioting that followed the withdrawal of subsidies on daily necessities, when its members attacked nightclubs and bars in Cairo [*qv*]. It was led by Shukri Ahmad Mustafa, an agricultural engineer, who as a Muslim Brotherhood [*qv*] activist had spent six years in jail (1965–71). Though his followers called themselves al Gamaat al Muslimin (The Muslim Groups), the authorities pinned the title of al Takfir wal Hijra on them to sum up their ideology and tactics.

In his manuscript *Al Tawassumat* (The Searching Looks), Mustafa called on the faithful to avoid living among infidels, to spread their divine knowledge throughout the land, and to wage a jihad [*qv*] to establish an Islamic order. Arguing that atheists and their state, Egypt, would not be destroyed by Allah while the faithful lived among them, he advised Muslims to migrate and form a pure community along the lines of the Medinese polity of the Prophet Muhammad. Many of Mustafa's followers took to living in the caves and mountains of Minia in southern Egypt, where inter alia they underwent arms training. They were discovered by the security forces in September 1973, only to be pardoned by President Anwar Sadat [*qv*] after the Arab-Israeli War of October 1973 [*qv*].

Since Mustafa considered that religious functionaries were infidels, his followers boycotted prayers led by them, and instead prayed together in their homes. They married among themselves, withdrew their children from state schools, and refused to be drafted into the military. Organized into secret cells, they numbered 3,000–4,000 on the eve of the January 1977 riots. The government arrested sixty. When the demand of al Takfir wal Hijra activists to try them or free them was ignored, they forced the issue in July by kidnapping Shaikh Muhammad Hussein al Dhahabi, a former minister of religious trusts and al Azhar University [*qv*], for writing a newspaper article against their party. When their demand was refused, they killed Dhahabi. The subsequent repression led to the trial of 465 members by military courts. Of these, five, including Mustafa, were executed. Manyof its members then joined the al Gamaat al Islamiya [*qv*]. However, in the mid-1990s the party revived, and

245 of its members found themselves behind bars in 1996.

Talabani, Jalal (1934–): *Iraqi Kurdish leader* Born into a landowning family in Koy Sanjak, Irbil province, Talabani obtained a law degree at Baghdad University and practiced as a lawyer. A member of the Kurdistan Democratic Party (KDP) [*qv*] since his late teens, Talabani rose to become a member of its politbureau. Disagreeing with the accord that KDP leader Mustafa Barzani [*qv*] concluded with the Iraqi government in 1964, he quit the KDP and set up an "alternative" KDP in 1966. After being defeated by Barzani's followers, he fled to Iran and then to Baghdad [*qv*], where he sided with the government. When the KDP struck a deal with the Baathist [*qv*] regime in March 1970, Talabani returned to its headquarters in Hajj Omran. But he fell out with Barzani again, and left for Beirut [*qv*], where he came under the influence of leftist Palestinian leaders George Habash [*qv*] and Nayif Hawatmeh [*qv*]. He then moved to Damascus [*qv*] to become the KDP's envoy there.

Disagreeing with Barzani's decision to flee to Iran in the wake of the March 1975 Algiers Accord [*qv*], Talabani left the KDP to cofound the Kurdish Workers League. In mid-1976 it combined with the Social Democratic Movement to form the Patriotic Union of Kurdistan (PUK) [*qv*] under Talabani's leadership. The PUK, emerging strongly in the southeast Kurdistan Autonomous Region (KAR) [*qv*], came into armed conflict with the KDP in the late 1970s. The outbreak of the Iran-Iraq War [*qv*] in September 1980 lessened the hostility between the two parties as they concentrated on escalating their struggle against Baghdad. Talabani's agreement with the KDP in 1982 to open up all of the KAR to both parties helped the PUK to expand at the KDP's expense.

In 1984, pressured by the demands of its war with Iran, the Iraqi government began to negotiate with Talabani, but nothing came of it. This paved the way for Talabani's ties with Iran. In May 1985, along with Idris Barzani, Talabani met Iran's parliamentary speaker, Ali Akbar Hashemi Rafsanjani [qv], in Tehran. Prodded by Iran, Talabani made up with the KDP, and together they sponsored the formation, in May 1987, of the Iraqi Kurdistan Front (IKF) [qv]. The PUK set up liberated areas along Iraq's borders with Iran. But in the spring and summer of 1988 the Iraqi military recovered these areas, and Talabani and other PUK leaders fled to Syria.

Following Iraq's invasion of Kuwait in August 1990, Talabani was elected to a six-member coordination committee of the Iraqi opposition. After the Second Gulf War [qv], Talabani helped trigger a Kurdish uprising against Baghdad in early March 1991. It was successful but only briefly, and its crushing caused an exodus of some 1.5 million Kurdish refugees. Talabani was deputy leader of the IKF delegation that reached an accord with the central government in June on the basis of the 1970 pact between the central government and Kurdish autonomists. But he recommended its rejection to IKF leaders.

Following the general election for the KAR Legislative Council in May 1992, held under the protection provided by Western air forces, Talabani shared power equally with the KDP's Masud Barzani [qv]. Yet the traditional rivalry between the urban-based PUK and the rural-based KDP was far from over.

In May 1994 bloody clashes between the two left more than 1,000 people dead. Talabani's forces were also attacked by the Islamic Movement of Kurdistan [qv] (IMK), and his area of control shrank until late 1994, when a modus vivendi was worked out. The relations with the KDP deteriorated in the wake of the two factions taking opposite positions in the anti-Saddam coup plans in March 1995, with Kurdistan divided into two hostile zones. By September, Talabani controled the area containing two-thirds of the 3.2 million inhabitants of Kurdistan, including those in Irbil [qv]. But he lacked the resources to administer them. In order to obtain much needed arms and ammunition, he stopped aiding Iran's dissident Kurds and mended his fences with Tehran. This upset not only Barzani but also Saddam Hussein, and brought the two close together.

Emboldened by Iran's arms supplies, Talabani mounted an offensive against the KDP in August 1996. In return Barzani requested military aid from Saddam to retake Irbil from Talabani. Saddam obliged. Talabani lost to Barzani not only Irbil, but all of his territory. But, rearmed by Iran, Talabani's forces regained their part of Kurdistan minus Irbil.

The intra-Kurdish fighting undermined the American strategy of developing Kurdistan as the base for overthrowing Saddam, with the U.S. withdrawing its agents and funds from the area. Washington's efforts to conciliate Talabani with Barzani met with only partial success chiefly because his rival refused to share the hefty customs duties he collected on the illicit export of Iraqi oil to Turkey. After the passage of the Iraq Liberation Act by U.S. Congress in 1998, Talabani found the PUK certified as a faction that was entitled to Washington's military aid. But he did not seek it. Due to his boycott of the Kurdistan Legislative Council, that body lacked legitimacy.

When, after defeating the Taliban regime in Afghanistan in late 2001, the U.S. administration of President George W. Bush turned its attention to overthrowing Saddam's government by force, the importance of Talabani as well as Barzani rose. The high point came in August 2002 when Talabani and the leaders of five other recognized opposition groups were received in Washington by Vice President Dick Cheney.

On the eve of the Gulf War III [*qv*] in 2003, Talabani agreed to coordinate his party's millitary plans with those of the KDP. But after the fall of Baghdad [*qv*] on April 9 Talabani breached the agreement with the KDP and ordered his militia to enter Kirkuk. The KDP followed. Talabani publicly welcomed the U.S. pro-counsul (Retd.) Gen. Jay Rayner when he visited Kurdistan.

Talal ibn Abdullah al Hashem (1909–72): *King of Jordan, 1951–52* Born in Mecca [*qv*] to Abdullah ibn Hussein al Hashem [*qv*], Talal ascended the throne of Jordan in July 1951 following the assassination of his father. He issued a new constitution on 1 January 1952. It divided legislative power between the monarch and parliament, consisting of a fully nominated senate and an elected chamber of deputies. Talal's governing style deviated from the paternalism of his father. His rule was brief, as he was diagnosed as mentally ill. He was forced to abdicate in favor of his son Hussein, a minor, [*qv*], in August 1952 and was committed to a mental clinic in Istanbul, where he died twenty years later.

Taleqani, Mahmud (1910–79): *Iranian Islamic leader* Born into a religious Shia [*qv*] family in Taleqan village, Mazandaran province, Taleqani went to Qom [*qv*] for his Islamic studies. After graduating in 1938, he taught at a theological school in Tehran [*qv*]. In 1939 he was jailed for six months for delivering antigovernment lectures—the first of many imprisonments that kept him behind bars for more than fifteen years. During the 1951–53 oil nationalization movement, he backed Premier Muhammad Mussadiq [*qv*]. After the 1953 countercoup by Muhammad Reza Shah Pahlavi [*qv*], he was arrested for having once sheltered Navab Safavi, the Fedai Khalq [*qv*] leader. In the early 1960s, in association with Mahdi Bazargan [*qv*], Taleqani set up the Liberation Movement of Iran [*qv*]. He was sentenced to ten years of imprisonment in January 1964 for participating in the protest movement of June 1963.

Of his many books, *Labor and Property in Islam* was the best known. In it he argued that since God had created the world for all humankind and had no intention of dividing up society into exploiting and exploited segments, a classless society is enjoined by Islam [*qv*]. As such, Taleqani became popular with both Islamic and secular leftists. Known to be close to the Mujahedin-e Khalq [*qv*], he was arrested in June 1977 and charged with being linked to the party. He was tortured. Mounting public pressure during the revolutionary turmoil compelled the shah to release him in November 1978.

With one son active with the Mujahedine Khalq and another with the Fedaiyan-e Islam [*qv*], Taleqani was well-placed to weld a revolutionary coalition of Islamic and secular opposition forces, and he did so. He was a member of the Islamic Revolutionary Council (IRC), appointed by Ayatollah Ruhollah Khomeini [qv] from Paris. After the revolution in February 1979, he became its chairman. Following the arrest and torture of his two left-wing sons by the new regime in April, Taleqani left Tehran in protest at the return of despotism, but overcame his differences with Khomeini after a meeting with him a few days later. Khomeini appointed him as Friday prayer leader of Tehran, a great religious honor. He became Khomeini's chief troubleshooter. Due to his intervention, much bloodshed was avoided between the regime and the leftist forces, and also between the center and Kurdish [qv] autonomists. He was at ease with both Premier Bazargan and Khomeini, and he was also a bridge between the radical IRC and the moderate Bazargan government.

When it came to interpreting Islamic law, he took a position midway between Ayatollah Muhammad Kazem Shariatmadari [qv], who forbade intervention by clerics in daily administration, and Khomeini, who wanted an activist role for the clergy in all walks of life. In the framing of the Islamic constitution Taleqani insisted on a bill of rights for citizens and stressed the importance of individual freedom. In terms of popular support, which spanned a wide political spectrum, Taleqani was second only to Khomeini, upon whom he was a moderating influence.

Talmud *(Hebrew: learning):* The Talmud is a multivolume compilation of Jewish Oral Law, codified and compiled in Hebrew by Judah HaNassi around A.D. 200, with added commentaries, written in Aramaic,

during the next four centuries. Study in ancient academies was conducted orally, and it is not known when the Talmud was first written down. There are two versions of it: the Babylonian (completed in A.D. 500) and the Palestinian (completed in A.D. 400)—the former, with 2.5 million words, being three times the length of the latter.

The Babylonian Talmud is the authoritative version. It consists of the text of the Oral Law, the Mishna [qv], and other collections, including the Tosefta; and the Gemara [qv], the commentaries on the text. (Sometimes the term Talmud is used for the Gemara alone.) When Rabbi Shlomo Yitzhaki, known as Rashi, a leading interpreter of the Hebrew Bible [qv] in the eleventh century A.D., produced his commentary on the Talmud, the debates summarized in the Gemara became available to Jewish scholars at large. The comments of Rashi and his three grandsons were incorporated into later versions of the Talmud. The Babylonian Talmud was first published in Spain around 1482. The standard version, annotated in the sixteenth century, first appeared in Vilnius, Lithuania, in 1886, followed by thirty-six-volume translations of the Babylonian Talmud into German and English in the twentieth century.

The Mishna is divided into six orders *(sedarim)* and comprises sixty-three tractates, only 36.5 of which have commentaries. Though the main purpose of the Gemara was to summarize the debates among rabbis on the interpretation of the Mishna and judicial administration, it became a mass of information on a variety of subjects, with a nonlegal text called the Haggada. In a dialectical fashion, the Talmud presents a piece of legal text followed by various interpretations included in the Gemara and the works of Rashi and his three grandsons. Devout Jews [*qv*] regard the opinions given by the judges in the Talmud as having the force of law. The Talmud is of major significance to Orthodox Jews [*qv*], and their rabbis consult it when considering any matter of importance. This is particularly true in Israel.

Tanua LeAhdut HaAvodah *(Hebrew: Movement for Labor Unity): Zionist group in Palestine* When, in early 1944, David Ben-Gurion [*qv*] proposed to the Histadrut [*qv*] executive committee that the delegates chosen for an international trade union conference in London should seek its support for an independent Jewish state in Palestine [*qv*], many leftists disagreed. Those in Mapai [*qv*] left to found the Tanua LeAhdut HaAvoda. Rejecting Mapai's demand for the partitioning of Palestine, and the *HaShomer HaTzair's* (*Hebrew: The Young Guards*) call for a single binational state, the new group opted for a socialist Jewish state in all of Palestine. In 1946 it allied with the left-wing Poale Zion [*qv*].

taqlid *(Arabic: to hang around the neck):* Initially a practice of designating a sacrificial animal with a sign around its neck, but later extended to designating a public official with a badge or chain around his neck. Figuratively it meant public acceptance, or the traditional way of doing things. In religion it is the opposite of *ijtihad* [*qv*]. It imitates or rests on the opinions and interpretations of the past clerics of the Quran [*qv*] and the Hadith [*qv*]. *See* marja-e taqlid.

Tashnak Party (Lebanon) *(Armenian: Federation): Lebanese political party* The Tashnak, the leading party of Armenian Orthodox Christians [*qv*] in Lebanon, is center-right in its policies. During the 1975–90 Lebanese Civil War [*qv*], while being close to the Phalange Party [*qv*], it insisted on maintaining "positive neutrality." Claiming they wanted to eradicate gambling dens in the Armenian Orthodox districts in north-east Beirut [*qv*], the Phalangists attacked the area in 1979, but were repulsed by the Tashnak Party militia. The party stuck to its neutrality, and after the civil war maintained a low profile in Lebanese politics.

Tehran: *capital of Iran* Also spelled Teheran. Pop. 7,894,000 (2003, est.). Some 60 miles/100 km south of the Caspian Sea and situated at the foot of the Elbruz Mountains, Tehran is the most populous city in the Persian Gulf [*qv*] region. It is near the ancient settlement of Rages and the medieval Persian capital of Rey (now Reyshahar), which was razed by invading Mongols in 1220. It began to thrive during the Safavid rule (1501–1722), but it was not until three years after Aqa Muhammad Khan Qajar (r. 1779–90), the founder of the Qajar dynasty, had consolidated his rule and conquered Tehran in 1785 that it became the national capital. Modernized by Reza Shah Pahlavi (r. 1925–41) [*qv*], who overthrew the Qajars, the city has expanded and absorbed a large number of migrants from the provinces.

In late 1943 Tehran was the venue for the Allied summit conference between U.S. President Franklin Roosevelt, British Prime Minister Winston Churchill, and Soviet Premier Joseph Stalin, when they agreed on the scope and timing of military offensives against Germany and the creation of the

United Nations to handle the problems of peace. The participants also declared their respect for the sovereignty and territorial integrity of Iran.

During the last quarter-century of the reign of Muhammad Reza Shah Pahlavi (r. 1941–79) [*qv*], the growth of the city, fueled by rising oil revenue, was dramatic. The contrast between the affluent districts of the north at the foot of the mountain and the poor neighborhoods of the south became sharper.

Besides being the administrative center, Tehran is also the industrial hub of the country, producing nearly half of many of its manufactured goods. Its tourist attractions include the Gulistan, Saadabad and Maramar Palaces, which were turned into museums after the 1979 Islamic revolution [*qv*]; the Niavaran Palace, the former residence of the shah; the Baharstan Palace, housing the Majlis [*qv*]; and the Sepah-salar Mosque. The latest addition is the mausoleum of Ayatollah Ruhollah Khomeini [*qv*] on the southern outskirts of the city.

Tehiya (*Hebrew: renaissance*): *Israeli political party* Tehiya was formed in 1979 by Moshe Shamir after he had left Likud [*qv*] in protest at the Egyptian-Israeli Peace Treaty [*qv*], which involved returning all of Sinai [*qv*] to Egypt and uprooting the Jewish colonists there. Tehiya wanted Israel to assert its sovereignty over the Occupied Territories [*qv*] and accelerate the Jewish settlement program. In the 1984 election it won five seats, and in the 1988 election three. It joined the national unity administration that was formed in 1988, but withdrew in January 1992 in protest at the government's decision to continue to participate in the Middle East peace process [*qv*], initiated by the Middle East Peace Conference [*qv*] in Madrid three months earlier. In the June 1992 election it failed to win any seats.

Tel Aviv-Jaffa: *capital of Israel (internationally recognized)* Pop. 365,000 (2003, est.).

Jaffa: Claiming lineage from Japheth, son of Noah, Jaffa has over four millennia of history behind it. Ruled in turn by Canaanites, Egyptians, Philistines, Israelites, Persians, Greeks, Assyrians, Maccabaeans, and Romans, it was the see of a bishop in the Christian era. It fell to Muslim Arabs [qv] in A.D. 637 and remained under Muslim rule thereafter, except from 1126–87 and 1191–96, when it was held by the Crusaders. Fearing a fresh Crusade, the Cairo-based [qv] Mameluke ruler destroyed it. It was not until the late fifteenth century, under the Ottomans (r. 1517–1918), that Jaffa was revived to become a thriving port.

It was captured by the British army during the First World War in November 1917. After the Second World War there was sporadic fighting between the predominantly Arab Jaffa and its Jewish neighbor, Tel Aviv. Within a year of the founding of Israel in 1948, Jaffa was amalgamated with Tel Aviv and the enlarged entity called Tel Aviv-Jaffa. With the inauguration of a modern port at Ashdod in 1965, the port of Jaffa, hitherto the second largest in Israel, was closed.

Tel Aviv: Derivative of *Tel Havee* (Hill of Spring). Established as a Jewish suburb of Jaffa in 1909, Tel Aviv was named after the Hebrew translation of Theodor Herzl's novel *Altneuland (German: New Old Land)*. As the site of a Jewish secondary school, opened in honor of Herzl, it began to attract more and more Jewish inhabitants. It became a separate town in 1921. Following the Arab-Jewish riots of 1936, port facilities were installed there. On the eve of the establishment of Israel in May 1948 there was fighting between Jewish Tel Aviv and Arab Jaffa, which ended with the surrender of Jaffa and the flight of its Arab residents. The State of Israel was declared in Tel Aviv on 14 May 1948, and the countries that gave Israel diplomatic recognition opened their embassies there. These embassies stayed in Tel Aviv when the Israeli government and parliament moved to West Jerusalem [qv]. Tel Aviv is the headquarters of almost all Israeli political parties and newspapers. It is the leading commercial and industrial center, employing a larger number of people in industry than any other Israeli city.

Temple Mount: *Jewish holy site. See* Noble Sanctuary.

Terrorism: There is no universally accepted definition of terrorism. In the United States, three official definitions exist. According to the U.S. Defense Department: "Terrorism is the calculated use of violence or the threat of violence to inculcate fear, intended to coerce or intimidate governments or societies as to the pursuit of goals that are generally political, religious or ideological." According to the State Department: "Terrorism is premeditated, politically motivated violence perpetrated against non-combatant targets by sub-national groups or clandestine agents, usually intended to influence an audience." Finally, according to the Justice Department: "Terrorism is the unlawful use of force or violence against persons or property to intimidate or coerce a government, the

civilian population, or any segment thereof, in furtherance of political or social objectives." None of these matches the definition used by the British government in The Prevention of Terrorism Act, 2000: "The use or threat, for the purpose of advancing a political, religious or ideological cause of action which involves serious violence against any person or property, endangers the life of any person or creates a serious risk to the health or safety of the public or section of the public." The Uniting and Strengthening America by Providing Appropriate Tools Required to Intercept and Obstruct Terrorism (USA PATRIOT) Act, 2001, has two separate definitions of terrorism, both of them overlong and complicated.

Since terrorism is an international phenomenon, a globally accepted definition is essential. In the absence of it, the debate about the relationship, if any, between terrorism and resistance to military or colonial occupation remains unresolved. While the list of twenty-two terrorist groups published by Washington in November 2001 included Lebanon's Hizbollah [qv], thus resulting in its assets being frozen in the U.S., Lebanon [qv] refused to follow America's lead, arguing that it distinguished between those organizations that practiced terrorism and those that sought to liberate their occupied countries or territories by all means.

Another important factor in this case was whether a particular terrorist faction had a global reach—an essential prerequisite used by America to make its list of banned organizations. In the view of the Lebanese government, Hizbollah lacked a global reach.

Not an ideology like fascism, capitalism, socialism, or Islamic fundamentalism [qv], terrorism is a method that is open for deployment not only by individuals or groups, but also by governments. Indeed the term entered political vocabulary two centuries ago as part of the "Reign of Terror" or just "The Terror" (1793-94), unleashed by the government of the Republic of France, established a year earlier by the French revolutionaries, when some 12,000 people were executed as counterrevolutionaries.

In the Middle East [*qv*] the most dramatic example of state terrorism was in Syria [*qv*]. To crush the Islamist-inspired insurrection in Hama [*qv*], in February 1982 the government deployed thousands of troops to quell it. Before order was restored, between 5,000 and 10,000 people, including 1,000 soldiers, lay dead, and a quarter of the historic old city was razed. And the bombing of King David Hotel in Jerusalem [*qv*] by Irgun, [*qv*] led by Menachem Begin [*qv*], in April 1946, which killed ninety-six civilians, including fifteen Jews [*qv*], was the first massive terrorist political act of its kind in the Middle East of recent times.

al Thani, Ahmad ibn Ali (1911–78): *ruler of Qatar, 1960–72* Son of Shaikh Ali al Thani [*qv*], al Thani was born in Doha [*qv*]. Though installed on the throne by the British, he tried to show some independence. In 1961 he led Qatar into the newly formed Organization for Petroleum Exporting Countries (OPEC) [*qv*]. Three years later, yielding to pressure by the National Unity Front [*qv*] and Britain, he appointed an advisory council with the power to issue laws and decrees for "the fundamental principles and basic rules of overall policy." In April 1970 he promulgated an interim constitution, which, by specifying a largely elected consultative council, marked an important step toward a representative government. However that left untouched the "rule of four quarters": the first quarter of revenues for the administration, the second for the ruler, the third for the al Thani princes, and the fourth for economic development. Al Thani negotiated the ending of the 1916 Anglo-Qatari Treaty [*qv*] and declared Qatar independent in September 1971. Fueled by the proceeds of an oil output of 600,000 barrels a day, his extravagance reached unprecedented proportions. This, and his refusal to establish the advisory council specified by the 1970 constitution, paved the way for a bloodless coup by Premier Khalifa ibn Hamad al Thani [*qv*] in early 1972.

al Thani, Ali ibn Abdullah (1894–1976): *ruler of Qatar, 1948–60* Son of Shaikh Abdullah ibn Qasim, al Thani was born in Doha [*qv*]. With the death in 1947 of his elder brother, Hamad, the heir apparent and deputy ruler, al Thani was named to succeed him. Al Thani's accession to the throne coincided with the extraction of oil on a commercial scale. This allowed him to develop public services and build up an economic infrastructure. Being a Wahhabi [*qv*], al Thani moved cautiously in economic and political spheres, while basing the legitimacy of his rule on Islam [*qv*] and refusing to share power. This was unsatisfactory to the British, who made him abdicate in 1960 in favor of his son, Ahmad [*qv*].

al Thani, Hamad ibn Khalifa (1950–): *ruler of Qatar, 1995–* Born in Doha [*qv*], al Thani was educated there. After graduating from the Royal Military Academy in Sandhurst, Britain, in 1971, he joined the Qatari military as a major. Four years later he was promoted to major general and appointed commander in chief of the armed forces. After being named crown prince in May 1977, he was put in charge of the defense ministry. He continued his program of modernizing the military; and in his additional capacity as president of the Higher Planning Council, he began to modernize the state infrastructure. By the early 1990s he was involved in determining major domestic and foreign policies.

Under his leadership the Qatari military joined the U.S.-led coalition against Iraq in the Second Gulf War [*qv*]. But in 1994 he reconciled Qatar with Iraq while Saudi Arabia, the leader of the Gulf Cooperation Council [*qv*], was still hostile toward it. By reviving Qatar's border dispute with Saudi Arabia, he tried to reassert his country's independence. In June 1995, while his father, Shaikh Khalifa ibn Hamad al Thani [*qv*], was in Geneva, Switzerland, al Thani mounted a bloodless coup and ascended the throne.

At home he liberalized the government and in 2001 held the first ever local elections, based on a universal suffrage. He ended the censorship of the media and communicated with the press, explaining government policies. In 1996 he sponsored the establishment of the partially state-funded Al Jazeera television, giving it as much editorial freedom as was accorded to the British Broadcasting Corporation (BBC) by the British government. Aware of the domineering presence of Saudi Arabia in the Arabian Peninsula [*qv*], he often took stances in regional affairs—such as establishing trade ties with Israel and improving relatons with Iraq and Iran—that differed

from those of Riyadh in order to assert Qatar's independence.

As Chairman of the Islamic Conference Organization [*qv*], al Thani visited Washington to offer condolences to U.S. President George W. Bush after the September 11 2001 terrorist attacks on New York and Washington. The next year he allowed the Pentagon to shift most of its military facilities from Al Kharj air base in Saudi Arabia to al Ubaid air base in Qatar. This base became the operational headquarters of the U.S. Central Command for the launching of the Operation Iraqi Freedom [*qv*] in March 2003 to overthrow the regime of President Saddam Hussein [*qv*] of Iraq.

al Thani, Khalifa ibn Hamad (1930–): *ruler of Qatar, 1972–95* Son of Shaikh Hamad ibn Abdullah, the heir apparent who died before his father, al Thani was born in Doha. He started his administrative career as director of police and internal security, moved to education, and graduated to running the ministry of finance and petroleum affairs before being appointed prime minister and deputy ruler. He staged a palace coup in February 1972 to seize the throne, fearing that his uncle, Shaikh Ahmad [*qv*], would appoint his son, Abdul Aziz, to succeed him. Al Thani appointed a fully nominated advisory council of twenty members, with the power to advise the cabinet only on matters referred to it by him. He abolished the practice of allocating a quarter of the state's revenue to the personal account of the ruler. But by giving ten of the fifteen ministries to his brothers and sons, he consolidated his power. He tried to direct the process of modernization stimulated by the boom in oil production, which brought in a revenue of $5.4 billion in 1980, making the per capita income of Qatar one of the highest in the world. He financially backed Iraq in the 1980–88 Iran–Iraq War [*qv*] and was a cofounder of the Gulf Cooperation Council [*qv*] in 1981. While continuing to rule by decree, al Thani periodically expanded the advisory council. He joined the U.S.-led coalition against Iraq in the Second Gulf War [*qv*]. In June 1995, during his trip to Switzerland, al Thani was overthrown in a bloodless coup by his son, Hamad ibn Khalifa [*qv*], whom he had appointed crown prince in 1977. He went into exile in Abu Dhabi [*qv*].

al Thani dynasty: The progenitor of the al Thani dynasty was Shaikh Thani ibn Muhammad, who belonged to the Bani Tamim tribal confederation's Mudari tribe of Wahhabi [*qv*] persuasion, which had migrated to Qatar in the eighteenth century. After being under the authority of the al Khalifas [*qv*] of Bahrain, the al Thanis, led by Shaikh Qasim ibn Muhammad, found themselves installed as the ruling family by the British in the 1860s. They maintained their preeminence during the Ottoman suzerainty (1872–1916). The collapse of the Ottoman Empire brought Qasim's son, Shaikh Abdullah al Thani (1876–1948), closer to the British, who signed the 1916 Anglo-Qatari Agreement [*qv*] with him. He was succeeded by his son, Shaikh Ali al Thani (1894–1976) [*qv*], who in 1960 abdicated in favor of his son, Shaikh Ahmad (1911–78) [*qv*]. In a bloodless coup in 1972 Shaikh Ahmad was replaced by his first cousin, Shaikh Khalifa ibn Hamad al Thani [*qv*]. The al Thani clan was about 1,500 strong in the late 1990s.

Third Gulf War: *See* Gulf War III

Tigris River: Known in biblical times as Hiddekil, the Tigris River rises in the mountains of eastern Turkey and flows roughly 1,180 miles/1,900 km in a southeasterly direction through northern Syria and Iraq, where it joins the Euphrates River [*qv*] about 120 miles/190 km from the Persian Gulf [*qv*]. It provides irrigation for the fertile plain of Mesopotamia [*qv*].

Tiran Straits: Situated between Egypt's Sinai Peninsula [*qv*] and Saudi Arabia, the Straits of Tiran lie at the mouth of the Gulf of Aqaba, at the end of which is the Israeli port of Eilat, the country's only opening to the sea east of the Suez Canal [*qv*]. Following the 1956 Suez War [*qv*], a United Nations Emergency Force (UNEF) [*qv*] was stationed at Sharm al Shaikh at the mouth of the Straits to ensure its status as an international waterway. During the crisis preceding the June 1967 Arab-Israeli War [*qv*], Egypt asked the U.N. secretary-general to remove UNEF from Sharm al Shaikh. Once this was done, Egypt closed the straits to Israeli shipping. This escalated the crisis, which culminated in a war with devastating preemptive Israeli air attacks on Egypt, Syria, and Jordan.

Titles, Religious: (beginning with the highest rank)

(1) **Christianity** [*qv*]

Catholic [*qv*]

Pope

Cardinal

Patriarch

Archbishop/Primate

Bishop

Priest (often addressed as Father)

Deacon (often addressed as Father)

Orthodox [*qv*]

Armenian Orthodox [*qv*]:
Catholicos
Patriarch
Archbishop/Primate
Bishop
Priest
Deacon
Greek Orthodox [*qv*]:
Ecumenical Patriarch
Patriarch
Metropolitan
Archbishop
Bishop
Archimandrite
Priest
Other Orthodox denominations fall into one
of the above hierarchies.
Protestant [*qv*]
Archbishop/Primate
Bishop
Dean
Provost
Archdeacon
Canon
Priest (often addressed as Reverend)
Deacon (often addressed as Reverend)
(2) **Islam** [*qv*]
Shia [*qv*]
Hazrat (*Arabic: Threshold, a title accorded
to a prophet*)
Nabi (*Arabic: Apostle, a title accorded to
a prophet*)
Marja-e taqlid (*Arabic: Source of emulation*)
Ayatollah Ozma (*Arabic: Grand sign of
Allah*)
Ayatollah (*Arabic: Sign of Allah*)
Hojatalislam (*Arabic: Proof of Islam*)
Thiqatalislam (*Arabic: Trust of Islam*)
Mullah (der. of Mawla; *Arabic: Master or
learned man*)

Shaikh (*Arabic: Old Man; a title accorded
to a senior man of power*)
Sayyid (*Arabic: Lord or Prince; a heredi-
tary title accorded to a male descendant of the
Prophet Muhammad*)
haajj/haji: (*Arabic/Persian: one who has
performed the* hajj [*qv*])
These titles are not mutually exclusive.
Sufi [*qv*]
Hazrat (*Arabic: Threshold, a title accorded
to a prophet*)
Qutb (*Arabic: Pivot*)
Pir (*Persian: Guide*)
Ishan (*Persian: a title of respect, accorded to
a spiritual guide*)
Murshid (*Arabic: Guide*)
Shaikh (*Arabic: Old Man; a title accorded
to a senior man of power*)
These titles are not mutually exclusive.
Sunni [*qv*]
Hazrat (*Arabic: Threshold, a title accorded
to a prophet*)
Nabi (*Arabic: Apostle, a title accorded to a
prophet*)
Mahdi (*Arabic: One who is guided by Allah*)
Mujtahid (*Arabic: One who practices inter-
pretative reasoning/equivalent to Ayatollah*)
Shaikh-al-Islam (*Arabic: Wise man of Islam*)
Mufti al Azam (*Arabic: Grand deliverer of
fatwas, religious rulings*)
Mufti (*Arabic: One who delivers fatwas,
religious rulings*)
Qadi (*Arabic: Religious judge*)
Shaikh (*Arabic: Old Man; a title accorded
to a senior man of power*)
Maulana/Maulavi (der. of Mawla; *Arabic:
Master or learned man*)
Sayyid (*Arabic: Lord or Prince; a heredi-
tary title accorded to a male descendant of the
Prophet Muhammad*)

haajj/hajji: (*Arabic: One who has performed the* hajj [*qv*])
These titles are not mutually exclusive.
Titles, Secular: (in alphabetical order)
Emir (*Arabic: Commander or Prince*)
Emira (*Arabic: Princess*)
Fakhamah al Rais (*Arabic: His Excellency*)
Jalalah al Malik (*Arabic: His Majesty*)
Khan (*Turkish: Chieftain or Ruler*)
Malik (*Arabic: King*)
Malika (*Arabic: Queen*)
Mirza (*Persian: Son of Prince; a title accorded to a noble man*)
Pasha (*Turkish: Grandee or Governor*)
Shah (*Persian: King*)
Shaikh (*Arabic: Old Man; a title accorded to a senior man of power*)
Shaikha (*Arabic: Old Woman; a title accorded to a senior woman of power*)
Shahbanu (*Persian: Queen*)
Shah-en-Shah (*Persian: King of Kings*)
Sultan (*Arabic: Ruler*)

Torah (*Hebrew: law, precept*): Torah is the Hebrew name given to the first five books of the Old Testament [*qv*]: *Genesis, Exodus, Leviticus, Numbers,* and *Deuteronomy.* It is also know as the Written Law, the Law of Moses, and the Pentateuch (*Greek: Five Books*). Tradition has it that it was given by God to Moses on Mount Sinai during the wanderings of the Israelites in the Sinai Peninsula [*qv*] between ca. 1290 B.C. and ca. 1250 B.C. Strictly speaking, the Torah is the written text of the Pentateuch. Broadly speaking, though, it covers both the written text and detailed oral exposition conveyed to Moses, known in Judaism [*qv*] as the Oral Law.

Torah Religious Front: *Israeli political party* The Torah Religious Front is the name given to the alliance formed periodically by Agudat Israel [*qv*] and Poale Agudat Israel [*qv*] on the eve of a general election. These parties did so in 1955 and again in 1973, winning, respectively, six and five seats in the Knesset [*qv*].

Touma, Emile (1918–85): *Palestinian writer and politician* Born into a Greek Orthodox [*qv*] middle-class family in Haifa [*qv*], Touma moved to Jerusalem [*qv*] for his university education. He joined the Communist Party of Palestine (CPC) [*qv*] in 1939, then left it fours years later for the Arab-dominated League of National Liberation (LNL), which spawned the Federation of Arab Trade Unions and Labor Societies. Touma established the party journal *Al Ittihad* (*Arabic: The Unity*). Following the Soviet line of backing the partitioning of Palestine [*qv*] in late 1947, Touma remained in Israel after its establishment in May 1948. In October Maki [*qv*] was formed by a merger between the CPC and the remnants of the LNL, and Touma became one of its leaders, while maintaining his editorship of the *al Ittihad.* He received a doctorate in history at the Oriental Institute in Moscow.

When Maki split in 1965, Touma joined Rakah [*qv*], which was recognized by the international department of the Communist Party of the Soviet Union two years later. Touma was often the chief representative of Rakah at international assemblies. He was active, both as a journalist and author, in promoting the national rights of Palestinians in Israel and abroad. His views on the subject were summarized in his *Sixty Years of the National Movement in Palestine* (in Arabic), published in 1978. As secretary of the Arab People's Conference in Support of the

Palestine Revolution, he called a congress in December 1980, which was banned by the Israeli government. His death five years later was widely mourned by Israeli Arabs [*qv*] irrespective of their party affiliations.

Trablus: *see* Tripoli.

Transition Law 1949 (Israel): In February 1949 the Constituent Assembly, resulting from an election held on 25 January by the provisional government of Israel, passed the Transition Law. It declared Israel a republic, to be headed by a president, elected by a simple majority for a five-year term by the Knesset [*qv*], a single-chamber house of 120 deputies. The Knesset was to be elected by adult franchise under a system of proportional representation, the leader of the largest group being invited by the president to become the prime minister and form the government, which would exercise full executive powers. Having passed the Transition Law, and having decided to postpone indefinitely a written constitution, the Constituent Assembly transformed itself into the Knesset.

Transjordan: Transjordan was the name given in July 1922 to the region east of the Jordan River [*qv*] in what had previously been southern Syria, now occupied for more than a year by Abdullah ibn Hussein al Hashem [*qv*]. In May 1923, after Britain had recognized Emir Abdullah's rule and promised him an annual subsidy, it became the autonomous Emirate of Transjordan, which agreed to coordinate its foreign policy with London and allow the stationing of British troops on its soil.

In February 1928 Transjordan formally entered into a treaty with Britain. A British resident, by whose advice Abdullah agreed to

be guided, was then appointed. A basic law laying down the constitution was promulgated. When the Second World War erupted in 1939, Abdullah offered Britain his full support. After Transjordan acquired independence in May 1946, Abdullah assumed the title of king and renamed his realm the Hashemite Kingdom of Jordan. *See also* Jordan.

Treaty of Frontier and Good Neighborly Relations (Iran-Iraq, 1975): On 6 March 1975 Iraq's vice president, Saddam Hussein [*qv*], and Iran's king, Muhammad Reza Shah Pahlavi [*qv*], signed an accord in Algiers, Algeria. They agreed to delimit their fluvial boundaries along the Shatt al Arab [*qv*] according to the thalweg line (the median line of the deepest channel) and to end all infiltrations of a subversive nature. The latter provision applied chiefly to the Iranian-backed Kurdish insurgency against the Iraqi government. The Treaty of Frontier and Good Neighborly Relations, based on the Algiers Accord, was signed in Baghdad on 13 June and ratified by both parties on 17 September 1975.

A joint commission was appointed to demarcate the new land border in Iran's Qasr e Shirin area in the wake of (1) Iraq's claim that Iran retained territory in contravention of the 1913 Protocol of Constantinople [*qv*], and (2) the concession Iraq had made on the Shatt al Arab boundary, having so far claimed all of the waterway as its territory. Overall the treaty signified a victory for Iran as it incorporated the Iranian demand, made over sixty years earlier, that the thalweg principle be applied to the Shatt al Arab frontier. Harassed and exhausted by the Iranian-backed Kurdish insurgency, the Baghdad regime agreed to the Iranian demand.

However, on 17 September 1980, accusing Iran of violating the 1975 treaty by intervening in Iraq's domestic affairs by backing and financing the leaders of the revived Kurdish insurgency and by refusing to return to Iraq the border territories in the Qasr-e Shirin area it had retained in contravention of the 1913 Protocol of Constantinople, President Saddam Hussein abrogated the Treaty forthwith. Tearing up Iraq's copy of the document on television, he claimed that Iraq had thereby regained full sovereignty over the Shatt al Arab. He insisted that henceforth any Iranian ships using the waterway must engage Iraqi pilots and fly the Iraqi flag. Tehran refused. On 22 September 1980 Iraq invaded Iran, starting the Iran-Iraq War [*qv*], which lasted until August 1988.

During the talks that followed the truce, Iran blocked any United Nations moves to survey the Shatt al Arab to assess the work needed to clear it of sunken vessels and unexploded mines, arguing that according to the 1975 treaty, cleaning up the waterway was the joint responsibility of the signatories. Iraq said that the treaty contained four principles: noninterference in the internal affairs of the signatories; cessation of Iran's aid to the Iraqi Kurds; the return by Iran of the territory due to Iraq according to the 1913 Protocol; and delineation of the fluvial border along the mid-channel of the Shatt al Arab. Violation of any one of these principles—such as the gross interference by Iran in Iraq's domestic affairs that, Iraq claimed, started soon after the 1979 Islamic revolution [*qv*]—invalidated the whole treaty. Iran argued that the treaty dealt primarily with boundaries and could not be abrogated unilaterally. The matter remained unresolved until Iraq's occupation of Kuwait in early August 1990. In a letter to Iranian President Ali Akbar Hashemi Rafsanjani [*qv*] on 14 August, reversing his previous stand, President Saddam Hussein agreed to abide by the 1975 treaty.

Treaty of Iran-Iraq Frontier (1937): Signed on 4 July 1937, the Treaty of Iran-Iraq Frontier confirmed the land boundaries as set out in the 1913 Protocol of Constantinople [*qv*], confirmed in 1914, but amended slightly the fluvial frontier along the Shatt al Arab [*qv*]. Iraq conceded the thalweg (the median line of the deepest channel) principle for four miles opposite Abadan [*qv*], which housed an oil refinery of the Anglo-Persian Oil Company (APOC). The treaty stated that the Shatt al Arab was open for navigation to all the countries of the world. Even though the treaty was between the sovereign states of Iran and Iraq, independent since 1932, it took ample note of the diplomatic and commercial interests of Britain, the leading foreign power in both countries, and which dominated both APOC and the Iraq Petroleum Company, which had struck oil in northern Iraq in 1927.

Treaty of Good Neighborly Relations: (Iran-Iraq, 1949) Following the conclusion of the Treaty of Good Neighborly Relations in 1949, a supplement to the Treaty of Iran-Iraq Frontier (1937) [*qv*], mutual ties were raised to ambassadorial level.

Treaty of Jiddah (Anglo-Saudi, 1927): The May 1927 Treaty of Jiddah formalized relations between Britain and Abdul Aziz ibn Abdul Rahman al Saud [*qv*] after he had declared himself King of Hijaz [*qv*] and Sultan of Najd [*qv*] and its Dependencies in

1926. London recognized Abdul Aziz al Saud and his realm, and he in turn accepted Britain as protector of Oman and the principalities in the Gulf [qv].

Treaty of Lausanne (1923): After the Turks under Mustafa Kemal had rejected the Treaty of Sèvres [qv] and defeated the Greeks in their attempt to conquer western Turkey, there were negotiations between Turkey and the Allies of the First World War (Belgium, Britain, France, Greece, Italy, Japan, Romania, and the Kingdom of Serbs, Croats, and Slovenes [later Yugoslavia]), resulting in the Treaty of Lausanne, signed on 23 July 1923. Turkey renounced its claims to the non-Turkish provinces of the Ottoman Empire, and the Allies confirmed Turkish sovereignty over Anatolia. A convention dealing with the interests of the powers in the Bosphorus Straits, including the Soviet Union, was signed on the same day and added to the Treaty of Lausanne. It specified freedom of navigation for merchant ships of all nations in war and peace, and for warships of the powers in the straits in peace as well as the war, in which Turkey remained neutral.

Treaty of Muhammara (Najdi-Iraqi, 1922): The Treaty of Muhammara was signed in May 1922 to demarcate the border between Iraq and Najd [qv] (later Saudi Arabia). Later a neutral zone was created between the two countries according to the Protocol of Uqair [qv].

Treaty of Muslim Friendship and Arab Fraternity (Saudi-North Yemeni, 1934): The Treaty of Muslim Friendship and Arab Fraternity was signed between North Yemen and Saudi Arabia in May 1934 after a Saudi-initiated six-week war in March–April. The conflict had occurred in the wake of the failure of talks between the two sides in 1933 following attempts by North Yemen's Imam Yahya Hamid al Din in 1931–32 to reassert his authority among the tribes around the fringes of his mountain heartland in the reigns of Najran, Asir, and Tihama. Having overpowered the North Yemenis and captured Hodeida port, the Saudis accepted a cease-fire mainly because British, French, and Italian warships rushed to Hodeida, intent on curbing Saudi expansionism. The treaty, signed in Taif, Saudi Arabia, returned to Imam Yahya nearly half of the area he had lost in the war, including the southern part of the Tihama coastal plain, leaving the upland Najran and Asir in Saudi hands.

Treaty of Sèvres (1920): Signed on 10 August 1920 between Ottoman Sultan Muhammad VI's prime minister, Damad Ferid, and the victors of the First World War, the Treaty of Sèvres—based on the 30 October 1918 Mudros Armistice, which was tantamount to unconditional surrender on the part of the Ottomans— required the dismemberment not only of the Ottoman Empire, but also its nucleus, the Turkish heartland of Anatolia. The partitioning of Anatolia included turning the southeastern region, then containing the province of Mosul [qv], into an autonomous territory, with the prospect of full independence if recommended by the League of Nations, formed in January 1920. Rejected by the Turkish parliament, led by Mustafa Kemal, it was superseded by the Treaty of Lausanne [qv] on 23 July 1923.

Treaty of Sib (1920): The Treaty of Sib [qv] brokered by the British political agent in Muscat [qv] and signed in September 1920 between Sultan Taimur ibn Faisal [*qv*] and "the people of Oman," represented by Shaikh Isa ibn Salim al Harthi—recognized the authority of the sultan in external matters and guaranteed freedom of movement to the tribes and urban dwellers. As the leader of the tribal chiefs of the interior, Shaikh Isa promised not to break the peace or give refuge to wrongdoers from coastal towns, and Sultan Taimur agreed not to raise taxes on coastal towns above 5 percent of the value of trade. The treaty implied autonomy for the interior, though its extent was not specified, and became contentious in the 1950s.

tribalism: Based on common descent, a tribe (*Arabic: qabilah*) has a political organization above the levels of extended family (*Arabic: faghaz*) and clan (*Arabic: masheer*), and maintains its cohesiveness through blood solidarity. In the Arab world, tribes are often classified as noble or common. Tribes of the same category often combine to form federations or confederations. The average size of a tribal federation, containing two to five tribes, in Syria in the 1950s was 30,000. Nationally, only one-seventh of the Syrian population was then organized along tribal lines. In contrast, most of the people in the Arabian Peninsula [*qv*] were thus organized. There were about twenty-five major tribal federations in the peninsula, including Anaiza [*qv*], Awazim, Harb, Mutair, Qahtan, Rashid, and Utaiba. Due to the migrations of the past, tribal relationships exist across present-day national boundaries.

There are today about forty tribes or tribal federations in Saudi Arabia. The House of Saud [*qv*] belongs to the Ruwalla tribe (originally from Syria) of the Anaiza tribal federation of Najd [*qv*], Iraq, and Syria. The members of this federation are considered noble due to their claim to lineal descent from Yaarab, the eponymous father of all Arabs [*qv*]. Common (or non-noble) tribal federations, such as the Awazim, dating back to the fifteenth century in the Najd area, were only Arabized by intermarrying with noble lines. Tribal origins and loyalty are of great importance in recruitment to the National Guard [*qv*].

In Oman the struggle between the coast and the interior is rooted in tribalism. It basically revolves around two tribal confederations: one chiefly Ibadhi [*qv*], originally from Yemen and led by Bani Hina (also called Hinawi); the other largely Sunni [*qv*], originally from northern Arabia.

As monarchies, often with long-established ruling families, the six members of the Gulf Cooperation Council (GCC) [*qv*]—including the United Arab Emirates, composed of seven principalities—are strongly influenced by tribal considerations.

In North Yemen, the leading Hashid and Bakil confederations are the descendants of the Hamdan federation, an early convert to Islam. When the Hamid al Din family, a branch of the original al Rassi dynasty of the ninth century A.D., took over the reins of power in 1891, it largely succeeded in gaining the support of the Hashid and Bakil confederations. After Imam Ahmad ibn Yahya [*qv*] failed to provide safe conduct for the leader of the Hashid confederation in 1960, he lost the support of the key tribes. This weakened his position and paved the way for the overthrow of the monarchy. Following the establishment of the republic and the end of the civil war [*qv*] in 1970, the leaders of the Hashid and Bakil confederations, accounting for some 40 percent of the national population, continued to wield much power. Shaikh Abdullah Hussein al Ahmar [*qv*], leader of the Hashid confederation, used his 50,000 strong militia to secure a position of authority in the central government. President Ahmad Hussein Ghashmi [*qv*] belonged to the Hashid confederation; as does his successor, Ali Abdullah Salih (r. 1978–) [*qv*]. This enabled Salih to mobilize the hitherto pro-Saudi Hashid tribal leaders against Riyadh when skirmishes took place between North Yemeni and Saudi troops in October 1979.

In South Yemen the Marxist National Liberation Front [*qv*] and its successor, the Yemen Socialist Party [*qv*], mounted repeated campaigns against tribalism and succeeded to some extent. But in the periodic internecine fighting among government and party leaders, tribal affiliations counted as much as ideology.

The Iraqi Baathist Party [*qv*] took detribalizing steps after assuming power in 1968. It outlawed the use of surnames in order to mask the tribal or geographical origins of citizens. Hence Saddam Hussein [*qv*] stopped using his surname, al Tikriti, derived from the town of Tikrit. But under extreme pressure in the wake of Iraq's defeat in the 1991 Gulf War [*qv*], he successfully appealed to the loyalties of Sunni tribes and survived.

Tripartite Agreement (Anglo-Soviet-Iranian, 1942): This agreement was signed by Iran, Britain, and the Soviet Union in January 1942 following the occupation of Iran by British and Soviet troops in August 1941. It limited the Iranian army's role to one of maintaining internal security. It described the United States as an adjunct to Britain in the task of delivering supplies to the Soviet Union through Iran. It specified that the occupying troops would vacate Iran within seven months of the end of the war against the last member of the Axis Powers.

Tripartite Declaration (Anglo-American-French, 1950): The purpose of the Anglo-American-French declaration on the Middle East on 25 May 1950 was threefold: to help America coordinate its sale of weapons to Israel with Britain and France, the region's arms suppliers, according to the treaties they had signed with the Arab states; to outline the basic stance of the three leading Western powers concerning the principal problems of the region; and to pave the way for a regional defense pact. The document proclaimed the signatories' resolve to uphold the armistice boundaries agreed by Israel and its Arab neighbors in 1949, and pledged to sell Israel and the Arab states enough arms to help them meet their "legitimate needs for self-defense," and allow them to play their part in the defense of the region "as a whole." It set the scene for the creation of a regional defense treaty led by the Western powers. The three cosignatories and Turkey put forward to Egypt a proposal for a Middle East Defense Command, centered on the Suez Canal [*qv*] base. Egypt rejected the plan, but the Western powers persevered, and the concept finally emerged as the Baghdad Pact [*qv*] in February 1955.

Tripoli: *Lebanese city* Pop. 213,000 (2003, est.). Known in Arabic as Trabulus al Sham, Eastern Tripoli, in contradistinction to Trabulus al Gharb, Western Tripoli, in Libya,

Tripoli is Lebanon's second largest city, with a recorded history of over two and a half millennia.

Ruled in turn by the Persians, Greeks, and Romans, it fell to Muslim Arabs [qv] in A.D. 638. During the Crusades (1095–1272) it again changed hands and thrived as a seat of Christianity [qv] and learning, and as a trading center. It declined dramatically under the rule of the Cairo-based Mamelukes (1250–1517). Under the Ottomans (1517–1918) a new settlement, constructed a few miles inland, was linked to the old port area. After the collapse of the Ottoman Empire, France, the mandate power in the region, incorporated it into Greater Lebanon (later the Republic of Lebanon) in 1920. During the Second World War, it was liberated from the pro-German Vichy-based French government by British and Free French forces in 1941.

Part of the Sunni Muslim[qv]-majority region of northern Lebanon, it was a leading center of the forces opposed to President Camille Chamoun [qv] in the brief Lebanese Civil War [qv] of 1958. In the long Civil War of 1975–90 [qv], it joined the pro-Syrian, predominantly Muslim side. After the Palestine Liberation Organization (PLO) [qv] had been expelled from Beirut [qv] by the Israelis during their invasion of Lebanon in 1982 [qv], the PLO leader, Yasser Arafat [qv], tried to establish the PLO headquarters in Tripoli, but failed due to the opposition of the Syrian forces occupying most of northern Lebanon.

Despite these political upheavals, the importance of Tripoli as the terminus of an oil pipeline from Iraq and as a leading commercial and industrial center, has remained unimpaired. Its tourist attractions include the ruins of an old cathedral and castle; the Great Mosque, built to celebrate victory over the last of the Crusaders; the Teinal Mosque, completed in 1336; and the Tower of the Lions, erected in the late fifteenth century.

Trucial States: The Trucial States in the Lower Gulf [qv] included the principalities of Abu Dhabi [qv], Ajman, Dubai [qv], Fujaira, Ras al Khaima [qv], Sharjah [qv], and Umm al Qaiwan. By 1892, having signed exclusive agreements with London, the rulers of these emirates were conducting their foreign affairs through Britain, which appointed a political officer to the capital of each of the emirates. In 1952 Britain established the Trucial States Council (TSC), consisting of the rulers of the seven emirates, with its Development Office, funded by London, acting as its executive. The next year Britain replaced the local political officers with a political agent based in Sharjah and set up the Trucial Oman Scouts, a central military force charged with maintaining peace among the emirates. The TSC met regularly to discuss common problems.

With oil revenues beginning to rise in the 1960s, especially in Abu Dhabi, London's financial grants declined. In 1968 Britain initiated talks about the formation of an Arab Gulf Federation after its withdrawal in 1971. At a TSC meeting in July 1971 it was announced that all of the states except Ras al Khaima had agreed to form a federation prior to the departure of the British from the region by December 1971. This federation was named the United Arab Emirates.

Trumpeldor, Joseph/Yosef (1880–1920): *Zionist leader in Palestine* Born into a religious Jewish family in southern Russia, Trumpeldor was drafted into the Tsarist military and was severely injured at the Port Arthur front line in the 1904–05 Russo-Japanese War. When he had recuperated, he returned to the front and was captured. After his release in 1906 he returned to Russia, where he became the first Jewish commissioned officer in the army. During his law studies at St. Petersburg University, he organized a Zionist [*qv*] student body.

In 1912 he migrated to Palestine [*qv*] and joined the Degania kibbutz. At the start of the First World War in 1914, when he tried to leave for Russia, the Ottoman authorities deported him to Egypt. There Trumpeldor worked with Vladimir Jabotinsky [*qv*] to form Jewish battalions. In 1915 he served as second in command of the Zion Mule Corps, part of the British forces, on the Gallipoli front. After the dissolution of this corps, Trumpeldor traveled to London to form Jewish battalions within the British army.

After the February 1917 revolution in Russia, he returned to his homeland, where he set up the *HeHaltuz* (*Hebrew: The Pioneer*) organization to prepare Jewish youth for migration to Palestine. In late 1919 he returned to Palestine. In January 1920 the Jewish settlements in Upper Galilee, then part of Syria and under French control, became embroiled in the anti-French campaign by local Arabs. The Zionist leaders advised the Jewish settlers to evacuate the area until order had been restored. Disregarding this, Trumpeldor and his followers traveled to Tel Hai, near present-day Kfar Giladi, to assist its settlers. In the subsequent bloodshed, on 1 March Trumpeldor was one of the first to die. The Labor Battalions formed by fresh immigrants from southern Russia soon after his death were named after

him, as was the youth organization of the Revisionist Zionists [*qv*]—Berit (*Hebrew: Covenant*) Trumpeldor, Betar.

Tudeh Party of Iran *(Persian: masses):* Official name: Tudeh Party of Iran: Party of Iranian Working Class. The Tudeh Party, formed in January 1942, evolved out of the Communist Party of Iran (established in June 1920), which had helped to found the Soviet Republic of Gilan along the Caspian Sea. When the Tehran government crushed the republic in November 1921, the communist movement declined. However, its remnants managed to survive under the guise of local cultural and sports clubs. When the regime discovered this in 1931, it outlawed the formation of groups opposing constitutional monarchy or advocating communist ideology or conduct. In 1937, fifty-eight members of the Marxist Circle were convicted in Tehran [*qv*].

Following the occupation of Iran by Soviet and British troops in August 1941, and the deposition of Reza Shah Pahlavi [*qv*], all political prisoners were released. The communist movement revived. But to respect the law and make the new organization more attractive to peasants, workers, and artisans, former Marxist Circle members decided to form a democratic front, naming it the Tudeh Party, under the leadership of Taqi Arani. It grew dramatically. The demonstrations sponsored by it in the autumn of 1944 toppled the conservative government of Premier Muhammad Said. By staging a series of strikes in the oil industry, the pro-Tudeh trade union won concessions from the Anglo-Iranian Oil Company. In 1946 the party had 25,000 members and 75,000 sympathisers; and its trades union federation had 400,000 members. Its stress on modernism and progress in the sociocultural field especially appealed to women and young people.

In November 1946, Premier Ahmad Qavam Saltane arrested hundreds of Tudeh activists to forestall a threatened strike in Tehran. Claiming to restore normal conditions for parliamentary elections in Azerbaijan [qv], he sent troops to the province to overpower the year-old leftist National Government of Azerbaijan in Tabriz [qv], run by the Democratic Party of Azerbaijan.

The collapse of the government there as well as in Kurdistan [qv] was a setback to the Iranian communist movement as a whole. In protest, Tudeh leaders boycotted the 1947 election and concentrated on improving the party machine. In February 1949, claiming that his would-be assassin, an Islamist journalist, was a card-carrying member of a union affiliated to the pro-Tudeh labor federation, Muhammad Reza Shah Pahlavi [qv] suppressed the party. But with the oil nationalization movement rising in 1951, conditions for its revival improved. In mid-1952, changing its view of Premier Muhammad Mussadiq [qv] as an ally of the United States, it cooperated with his National Front [qv].

The Tudeh was active up to and soon after the shah's flight from Iran on 16 August 1953. When he returned three days later, his government repressed the party vengefully. It arrested 3,000 Tudeh activists, executing 54 and sentencing 200 to life imprisonment.

The party moved its headquarters to Eastern Europe, alternating between East Berlin and Prague. In 1960, having merged with the Democratic Party of Azerbaijan, the organization acquired a longer name—the Tudeh Party of Iran: Party of Iranian Working Class. Following a series of conferences in 1956–64, the party opted for peaceful means to effect the downfall of the shah and establish a democratic republic. This led to the exit of radicals, and the party membership fell to 3,000. However, assisted by the Communist parties of the Soviet Union, East Germany, France, and Italy, the Tudeh engaged fifty full-time cadres to run a radio station, based in Bulgaria, and brought out two publications.

In Iran it was no longer the favorite of leftist militants, who gravitated toward the newly established Fedai Khalq [qv] and Mujahedin-e Khalq [qv]. To counter this, starting in 1972 the party began to set up secret cells in Tehran University and in the oil and other major industries. Two years later it issued a call for the overthrow of the shah and the founding of a republic. Its membership in Europe and Iran rose to over 5,000. In the autumn of 1977 it revived its clandestine cells in major Iranian cities, and in September 1978 its leadership decided to establish contacts with Islamic revolutionaries. A month later it instructed its followers in the oil industry—a crucial area of its traditional strength—to support Ayatollah Ruhollah Khomeini's [qv] call for a strike. More than any other development, this determined the shah's fall. In December 1978, the Tudeh leaders instructed their followers to prepare for an armed uprising. They replaced Iraj Iskandri as first secretary with Nur al Din Kianouri. Tudeh activists participated in the final battles with the shah's forces from 9–13 February 1979 in Tehran and elsewhere.

Kianouri and his aides returned from

abroad to revive the party openly. In March the central committee met in Tehran, its first such meeting for a quarter of a century. In August the party described the political balance sheet of the regime of Ayatollah Khomeini as "positive": expelling the shah, declaring a republic, leaving the Western-dominated Central Treaty Organization [*qv*], breaking ties with Israel, and nationalizing banks and insurance companies. On the other handm it criticized the religious content of the draft constitution. In the elections to the 1979 Assembly of Experts [*qv*], its candidates secured only 50,000 votes.

Despite its backing for the government in its defense of Iranian territory when attacked by Iraq in September 1980, the authorities raided its office in Tehran and suspended its newspaper. This continued until the spring of 1981, when removing President Abol Hassan Bani-Sadr [*qv*] from office became an urgent official task. Given the Tudeh's anti-Bani-Sadr stance, the government tolerated its existence. But once the regime had overcome the crisis created by the Mujahedin-e Khalq and successfully held a presidential election in October 1981, it did not need the backing of nonviolent leftist parties.

When the Tudeh advised against marching into Iraq in June 1982 during the Iran-Iraq War [*qv*], it drew the ire of the authorities, who accelerated the purge of Tudeh members from official institutions. In February 1983 they arrested Kianouri and seventy other party leaders, charging them with spying for the Soviet bloc. In late April the Iranian television showed Kianouri admitting six major "misdeeds" by his party, including occasional espionage for the Soviet Union, not dissolving its secret sections, and

not surrendering all the arms it had secured during the rise of the revolutionary movement. On 4 May the government dissolved the Tudeh Party and arrested about 1,000 of its 2,500–3,000 members. Most of the remainder crossed into Afghanistan, where they assisted the ruling leftist party to organize industrial workers and improve the state propaganda apparatus.

In December 1983, eighty-seven members of the party's military section were found guilty of attempting to overthrow the regime and were sentenced to varying terms of imprisonment. In February 1984 there were further convictions, and ten Tudeh leaders were executed.

The party continued to exist abroad, with a large contingent in Kabul, Afghanistan. Its central committee met in East Berlin in January 1984, when it decided to establish fraternal relations with the Mujahedin-e Khalq [*qv*], then based in Paris. But this arrangement ended when the Mujahedin-e Khalq headquarters moved to Baghdad [*qv*] in 1986. The party split, with the breakaway section basing itself in Paris and the main body continuing its activities from East Berlin. With the merger of East and West Germany in 1990, and the reunification of East and West Berlin, the party lost its financial backing from East European communist parties. The downfall of the leftist regime in Kabul in April 1992 destroyed its last bastion in the region. Committed to the secularization and democratization of Iran, it continued to publish a journal, *Nameh Mardom (Persian: People's Journal)*, in Persian from Berlin.

Tumb/Tunb Islands: While implementing its plan to withdraw from the Gulf [*qv*] by December 1971, Britain, in consultation with the United States, chose Iran, under Muhammad Reza Shah Pahlavi [*qv*], to be the new guarantor of regional security and a bulwark against revolutionary change. Therefore, the shah decided to add the Lesser and Greater Tumbs, belonging to Ras al Khaima [*qv*], and Abu Musa [*qv*], belonging to Sharjah [*qv*], to Iran's Qeshm, Larak, and Hormuz Islands. Together these six islands form a crescent that guards the entrance to the strategic Hormuz Straits [*qv*]. On 30 November 1971, a day before the termination of the British treaty with Ras al Khaima, Iran occupied the uninhabited Lesser Tumb Island and captured Greater Tumb Island after some fighting.

After the 1979 Islamic revolution [*qv*] in Iran, the ownership of these islands became a contentious issue between Iran and Iraq, the latter claiming to be the guardian of the interests of the Gulf's Arab states. In April 1980 Baghdad called on Iran to vacate the Tumb Islands and Abu Musa. Tehran ignored the demand. During its eight-year war with Iraq [*qv*], the strategic importance of these islands became well established. In 1994 the Gulf Cooperation Council [*qv*] took up the matter on behalf of the United Arab Emirates [*qv*] and urged Iran to agree to refer the issue of its occupation of the Greater and Lesser Islands and Abu Musa Island to the International Court of Justice, but to no avail. The dispute continued to be a major barrier to cordial relations between Iran and the UAE.

Turkmen: Also spelled Turcoman or Turkoman. The term Turkmen applies to those who speak Turkmen, a member of the south Turkic language group. Those living east of the Caspian Sea—in Iran, Turkmenistan, Uzbekistan, and Afghanistan—are known as Trans-Caspian Turkmen. A much smaller number of Turkmen are scattered in pockets in northern Iraq and Syria. They are almost invariably Muslim [*qv*].

Twelvers: *see* Twelver Shias.

Twelver Shias: The predominant category among Shias [*qv*], Twelvers or Twelver Shias are so called because they believe in twelve *imams* [*qv*]: Ali, Hassan, Hussein, Zain al Abidin, Muhammad al Baqir, Jaafar al Sadiq, Musa al Kazem, Ali al Rida/Reza, Muhammad al Taqi Javad, Ali al Naqi, Hassan al Askari, and Muhammad al Qasim. They believe that Muhammad al Qasim, the infant son of the eleventh imam, went into occultation in Samarra [*qv*], Iraq, in A.D. 873, leaving behind four special assistants. As the last of them failed to name a successor, the line of divinely inspired imams became extinct in A.D. 940. Twelvers believe that the last imam will end his occultation at the end of time and will institute justice and order in the world, as well as punishing the enemies of Allah.

Tyre: *Lebanese town* Pop. 117,000 (2003, est.). A thriving city of ancient times, originally built on an island, Tyre has a history dating back to the third millennium B.C. Its ruler, Hiram, is mentioned as a supplier of building materials for the First Temple built by King Solomon (r. ca. 970–30 B.C.). By the ninth century B.C. Tyrians had set up colonies abroad, including Carthage (near modern Tunis). Tyre then came under the rule of the Assyrians and Achaemenians of Persia (550–330 B.C.). It withstood a siege by Alexander the Great (r. 336–23 B.C.) for several months, and fell to his forces only after he had constructed a causeway to the island—his legacy to the city. In retribution, he killed or enslaved some 40,000 Tyrians. Tyre recovered from the trauma to regain its importance as a commercial center for purple dye and silk-ware. After falling to the Egyptians, Greeks, and Romans it emerged as a Christian [qv] center, and is mentioned several times in the New Testament [qv]. It thrived under Muslim Arab [qv] rule from A.D. 638. Captured by the Crusaders in 1124, it became part of the Kingdom of Jerusalem and the burial place of Roman Emperor Frederick I Barbarossa (r. 1152–90). It was conquered by the Mamluks in 1291, who, fearing another Crusade, razed it. Its port silted up, and it declined to insignificance during the Ottoman times (1517–1918). The subsequent French mandate included it in Greater Lebanon (later the Republic of Lebanon). After the 1948–49 Palestine War [qv], Palestinian refugees set up a camp at nearby Rashidiya.

U

ulama/ulema *(Arabic: pl. of alim, possessor of* ilm, *knowledge):* Ulama is the term used collectively for religious-legal scholars of Islam [qv]. Since *ilm* in Islam means knowledge of the Quran [qv] and the *sunna* [qv], the ulama are theologians and canonists. They are the ultimate authority on the issues of law and theology, personifying the right of Muslims [qv] to govern themselves. In modern times, however, in Sunni [qv] countries they have by and large become government functionaries, with only a minority among them acting as independent thinkers on theology and canon law.

Ultra-Orthodox Jews *(Hebrew, Haredim):* The label ultra-Orthodox applies to those Jews who adhere to a strict interpretation of the Halakha [qv], Jewish Law. Full observance of the Halakha involves following all 613 religious prohibitions and obligations that regulate Jewish life—from trivial body functions to the organization of life in society—and separation between Jews and Gentiles. Ultra-Orthodox believe in divine intervention to reestablish the Jewish state of Israel [qv], and are opposed to the creation of Israel through human endeavour such as the one by the Zionists [qv] pioneers in Palestine [qv]. Later a majority cooperated with Zionists on the basis that Zionism [qv] could be put to the service of Judaism [qv] according to the Halakha. There are two major and one minor schools within ultra-Orthodoxy: Hassadim (*Hebrew, pious*); Mitnagdim (*Hebrew, opponents*), and Bratslavic, named after the Ukrainian town of Bratslav. Bearded adult males wear the garb of the East European ghetto—black trousers, thin long black coats and wide black hats, with their sidelocks, shaped into ringlets, dangling. Women wear long-sleeved dresses, their skirts falling well below the knees and covering the upper part of their heavy stockings, their hair shielded by a scarf or a wig. Television is off limits as one never knows when a semi-clad woman would appear on the screen. So too are newspapers and magazines. So the walls of the ultra-Orthodox neighborhoods are often plastered with news sheets. In Jerusalem ultra-Orthodox Jews live in Mea Shearim, Beit Israel, Geula, and Har Nof neighborhoods. They are exempted from conscription.

umm *(Arabic: mother):* It is customary among many Arabs to call a married woman the "umm" of her first-born son.

umma: A derivative of either the Arabic umm, meaning mother or source; or a loan-word from Hebrew [*qv*] *umma* or Aramaic *ummtha*; *umma* appears many times in the Quran [*qv*], always alluding to ethnic, linguistic, or religious groups who were part of Allah's plan of salvation. As the Prophet Muhammad progressed from his early days of struggle to become the ruler of a territory, his definition of *umma* changed, from the community of all Arabs, irrespective of their religious affiliation, to the community of all Muslims [*qv*]. Within a century of his death in A.D. 632 the *umma* spread far beyond Arabia and included different nations and races. In modern times the *umma,* now meaning the worldwide Islamic community as a whole, has carried more of a communal connotation than the more legalistic Dar al Islam (Domain of Islam). On the other hand, the annual hajj [*qv*] is a dramatic illustration of the existence of umma.

umra: *small pilgrimage to Mecca. Umra* involves the central ceremonies of the *hajj* [*qv*] for Muslims [*qv*]: circumambulating the Kaaba [*qv*] in Mecca [*qv*] and striding quickly between the Safa and Marwa hillocks. It can be performed at any time of the year with the exception of 8–10 Dhul Hijja, the days reserved for the hajj proper.

Uniate churches *(Russian: derivative of* uniyat, *union):* A group of Christian churches [*qv*] with Eastern rites that acknowledge the primacy of the pope of the Roman Catholic Church [*qv*] and accept the Roman Catholic Church in doctrine, but not in liturgy and customs.

It includes the Armenian Catholic Church [*qv*], the Chaldean Catholic Church [*qv*], the Greek Catholic Church [*qv*], the Maronite Catholic Church [*qv*], and the Syrian Catholic Church [*qv*].

Union of the Peoples of Arabian Peninsula (Saudi Arabia): An organization of Nasserite [*qv*] persuasion, established in the late 1950s and led by Nasser Said, the Union of the People of Arabian Peninsula (UPAP) aimed to rid Saudi Arabia [*qv*] of the monarchy. Banned in the Saudi kingdom, it maintained an office in Beirut [*qv*]. In 1966 it claimed responsibility for bomb explosions in such places as the defense ministry in Riyadh [*qv*] and the state security office in Dammam in the eastern oil region. After the death of President Gamal Abdul Nasser [*qv*] in 1970, its appeal waned. Following the takeover of the Grand Mosque in Mecca [*qv*] in November 1979 by Islamic militants, it briefly became active before going into hibernation again.

United Arab Emirates:

Official name: United Arab Emirates

Capital: Abu Dhabi [*qv*]

Area: 30,000 sq. miles/77,710 sq, km (Abu Dhabi, 26,000 sq. miles/67,350 sq. km; Ajman, 100 sq. miles/260 sq. km; Dubai [*qv*], 1,510 sq. miles/3,900 sq. km; Fujaira, 440 sq. miles/1,150 sq. km; Ras al Khaima, 660 sq. miles/1,700 sq. km; Sharjah [*qv*], 1,000 sq. miles/2,600 sq. km; and Umm al Qaiwain, 290 sq. miles/750 sq. km)

Population: 3,108,000 (2001, est.) (Abu Dhabi, 1,186,000; Ajman, 174,000; Dubai, 913,000; Fujaira, 98,000; Ras al Khaima, 171,000; Sharjah, 520,000; Umm al Qaiwain, 46,000)

Gross domestic product: $67.1 billion (2001)

National currency: UAE Dihram (Dh); Dh1 = U.S.$0.27 = £0.19 = EUR 0.31 (2001)

Form of government: monarchy; federation of seven emirates, each ruled by an emir, withthe seven emirs constituting the highestfederal authority: the Supreme Council of Emirs

Official language: Arabic [*qv*]

Official religion: Islam [*qv*]

Administrative system: The United Arab Emirates consists of seven constituent emirates, each ruled by a hereditary emir.

Constitution: The interim constitution, which came into effect in December 1971, specified a federal system for the constituent emirates. The seven-member Supreme Council of Emirs (SCE) is the highest federal body, which elects the president and vice president of the UAE from among its members. The president appoints the prime minister and the cabinet. The SCE's decisions must be approved by five emirs, including those of Abu Dhabi and Dubai. The legislative authority lies with the Federal National Council, a fully nominated consultative assembly of forty members, with a two-year tenure. The provisional constitution was extended every five years until 1996, when it was made permanent. Following this, Shaikh Zaid ibn Sultan al Nahyan [*qv*] was reelected president.

Federal National Council: This forty-member nominated legislative body is made up as follows: eight members each from Abu Dhabi and Dubai; six each from Ras al Khaima and Sharjah; and four each from Ajman, Fujaira, and Umm al Qaiwain. It debates legislation proposed by the cabinet and has the authority to amend or reject it.

Ethnic composition (2000): Arab, [*qv*] 40 percent; South Asian, 50 percent; Iranian, 5 percent; European, 1 percent; other 4 percent.

High officials:

President: Shaikh Zaid ibn Sultan al Nahyan, 1971–

Vice president: Shaikh Maktum ibn Rashid al Maktum [*qv*], 1990–

Prime Minister: Shaikh Maktum ibn Rashid al Maktum [*qv*], 1990–

Members of the Supreme Council of Emirs: Shaikh Zaid ibn Sultan al Nahyan (r. 1966–) of Abu Dhabi;

Shaikh Humaid ibn Rashid al Nuaimi (1981–) of Ajman;

Shaikh Maktum ibn Rashid al Maktum (r. 1990–) of Dubai;

Shaikh Hamad ibn Muhammad al Sharqi (r. 1974–) of Fujaira;

Shaikh Saqr ibn Muhammad al Qasimi (r. 1948–) of Ras al Khaima;

Shaikh Sultan ibn Muhammad al Qasimi (r. 1972–) of Sharjah;

Shaikh Rashid ibn Ahmad al Mualla (1981–) of Umm al Qaiwan.

Speaker of the Federal National Council: Muhammad ibn Khalifa Habtour

History (since ca. 1900): By 1892, having signed exclusive agreements with London, the rulers of the six emirates of the Lower Gulf [*qv*] (Abu Dhabi, Ajman, Dubai, Ras al Khaima, Sharjah, and Umm al Qaiwain) were conducting their foreign affairs through Britain, which appointed a political officer to the capital of each of the emirates. In 1952, after upgrading the province of Fujaira to an emirate, Britain established the Trucial States Council (TSC), consisting of the rulers of the seven emirates, with its Development Office, funded by London, acting as its executive. The next year Britain replaced the local political officers with a political agent based in Sharjah and set up the Trucial Oman Scouts, a central military force changed with maintaining peace among the emirates. The TSC met regularly to discuss common problems.

With oil revenues beginning to build up from the early 1960s, especially in Abu Dhabi, which accounted for seven-eighths of the area covered by the TSC, London's financial grants declined. This was especially true after 1966, when Shaikh Shakbut ibn Hamdan al Nahyan (r. 1928–66) was deposed by the British in favor of his younger brother, Shaikh Zaid, who was committed to economic development. When Dubai discovered offshore oil in 1966, the economic prospects of the TSC constituents improved.

In 1968 Britain initiated talks about the formation of an Arab Gulf Federation after its withdrawal in 1971. At the TSC meeting in July 1971 it was announced that all the states except Ras al Khaima had agreed to form a federation prior to the departure of the British from the region by December 1971. This federation was named the United Arab Emirates (UAE), with Shaikh Zaid al Nahyan as president and Shaikh Rashid al Maktum [qv] of Dubai as vice president.

When a single federal council of ministers came into being in December 1973, Shaikh Zaid al Nahyan abolished the Abu Dhabi cabinet and appointed a fifty-member Consultative Council in his emirate. To the detriment of the UAE, the personal rivalry between him and Vice President Rashid al Maktum persisted for many years. Following the Islamic revolution [qv] in Iran [qv] in early 1979, the Federal National Council and the federal cabinet demanded parliamentary democracy and unitary statehood. This alarmed the president and the vice president, who sank their differences. Shaikh Rashid became premier of the UAE, replacing his son, Shaikh Maktum al Maktum. In 1981 the UAE became a cofounder of the Gulf Cooperation Council [qv]

During the early phase of the Iran–Iraq War [qv] the UAE sided with Iraq [qv], providing it with financial aid. But as the conflict dragged on, with Iran gaining a stronger position than Iraq, the UAE took an increasingly neutral stance. During the spring of 1990 it allied with Kuwait in a strategy to harm the Iraqi economy by flooding the oil market and lowering the price of oil. Following the death of Shaikh Rashid in October 1990, Shaikh Maktum succeeded him as vice president and premier of the UAE and ruler of Dubai. In the 1991 Gulf War [qv] the UAE joined the anti-Iraq coalition led by the United States and contributed $5 billion to the war chest. In 1994, when the UAE extended its defense agreement signed in the aftermath of the Gulf War, it tried to persuade Iran to open talks on the status of Abu Musa [qv] and the Greater and Lesser Tumb Islands [qv], but failed. In 1995, Iran set up air defense systems on the islands; in the following year it inaugurated an electricity-generating plant on Greater Tunb. From 1995 onward, UAE President Shaikh Zayid appealed for the lifting of the U.N. sanctions on Iraq [qv]. The UAE sent food and medicine to Iraq in 1997 and 1998. It re-opened its embassy in Baghdad

[*qv*] in 2000. Following the terrorist attacks on the United States in September 2001, the UAE severed its diplomatic links with the Taliban regime in Afghanistan. While supporting Washington's campaign to punish the perpetrators of 9/11, the UAE urged the resumption of the Arab-Israeli peace process, and cautioned against any U.S. military action targeting an Arab regime. In the end it refrained from protesting publicly against the invasion of Iraq by the Anglo-American forces in March 2003.

Religious composition (2000): Muslim [*qv*], 78 percent; Christian, [*qv*] 10 percent; Hindu, 9 percent; other, 3 percent.

United Arab Republic (1958–61): In February 1958 Egypt and Syria merged to form the United Arab Republic (UAR). Part of the reason why the political and military leaders of Syria sought union with Egypt was to forestall the rise of leftists in their country. But once Syria had been incorporated into the UAR, its president, Gamal Abdul Nasser [*qv*], extended to the Syrian region his policy of nationalizing banking, insurance, and major industries. He thus alienated an important social class in Syria. Likewise, his ban on all political parties in Syria alienated almost all Syrian politicians; and the creation of a unified military command, in which Syrian officers were relegated to secondary positions, created discontent in the officer corps. These factors created widespread disaffection in Syria and prepared the ground for its secession from the UAR, which came in September 1961 amid much rancor.

United National Leadership of the Uprising (West Bank and Gaza): Following the spontaneous outbreak of the intifada [*qv*] in the Gaza Strip [*qv*], leaders of the groups affiliated to the outlawed Palestine Liberation Organization [*qv*] and based in the occupied West Bank [*qv*] and Gaza Strip [*qv*] combined to form the United National Leadership of the Uprising (UNLU). It functioned clandestinely and guided the intifada, often through leaflets. Despite the disparate nature of its constituents, it remained effective, mainly because repeated efforts by Israel's Shin Beth [*qv*] to infiltrate it failed.

United Nations Disengagement Observer Force (1974–): Following the disengagement agreement between the Syrian and Israeli forces on the Golan Heights [*qv*] on 31 May 1974, a United Nations Disengagement Observer Force (UNDOF) was posted to establish an area of separation and verify troop levels. UNDOF's 1,100 personnel were drawn from three European countries and Canada.

United Nations Emergency Force (1957–67): During the Suez War [*qv*], the United Nations General Assembly decided on 4 November 1956 to create a United Nations Emergency Force (UNEF)—composed of troops from countries not involved in the conflict—to supervise the cease-fire. With the truce taking effect on 7 November and UNEF units arriving in Egypt soon after, the British and French troops began to withdraw, completing the process by 23 December. On the insistence of Israel, which had completed its evacuation of Egypt by 8 March 1957, UNEF was stationed only on the Egyptian side of the Canal and in Egyptian-administered Gaza [*qv*]. It was required to safeguard Israeli shipping through the Gulf of Aqaba.

Nine years later tension in the region escalated when Israel warned Damascus—then militarily allied with Cairo—that it would retaliate vigorously if the guerrilla attacks on it from Syria continued. In mid-May 1967, Soviet, Syrian and Egyptian intelligence agencies warned Egyptian President Gamal Abdul Nasser [*qv*] that an Israeli attack on Syria was imminent. On 18 May Nasser asked the UN secretary-general to withdraw UNEF from Egypt, which he was entitled to do since U.N. forces are deployed in a country only so long as its government wishes. The secretary-general complied with Nasser's request. With the UNEF units gone from Sharm al Shaikh at the mouth of the Gulf of Aqaba, Nasser closed the waterway to Israeli shipping.

United Nations General Assembly Resolution 3236 (November 1974): At the end of a long debate on the "Question of Palestine," on 22 November 1974 the United Nations General Assembly reaffirmed the Palestinian people's right to self-determination, independence, and sovereignty and their right to return to their homes and properties.

United Nations Interim Force in Lebanon (1978–): Following the Israeli invasion of southern Lebanon [*qv*] on 14 March 1978, United Nations Security Council Resolution 425 [*qv*] of 19 March called on Israel to cease fire, and authorized the formation of the United Nations Interim Force in Lebanon (Unifil) to confirm the Israeli evacuation and assist the Lebanese government to assume effective control in the area. But when Israel carried out its major withdrawal in mid-June, it handed over its positions to a Christian militia, later called the South Lebanon Army (SLA) [*qv*], and did not allow the Beirut government to deploy its troops alongside the 5,300-strong Unifil force, drawn from ten countries and headquartered in Naqura.

With the second and larger Israeli invasion of Lebanon [*qv*] in June 1982, resulting in the occupation of southern Lebanon by Israel, Unifil's objective of assisting the Beirut government to assume effective control of southern Lebanon became more distant. Even though U.N. Security Council Resolution 425 pertained exclusively to Lebanon and had nothing to do with U.N. Security Council Resolution 242 of 1967 [*qv*], the basis of the Middle East peace process [*qv*] begun in October 1991, Israel insisted on interconnecting the two, linking Israel's evacuation of southern Lebanon to the conclusion of a Lebanese-Israeli peace treaty. Beirut refused. Following the unilateral Israeli withdrawal from southern Lebanon in May 2000, Unifil confirmed the evacuation. But, with Israel refusing the Shaaba Farms contiguous with Syria [*qv*], Hizbollah [*qv*] regarded the Israeli evacuation as incomplete and mounted periodic attacks on the Israeli positions on the Farms. So Israel insisted on Unifil continuing its mission.

United Nations Iran-Iraq Military Observer Group (1988–): Following acceptance of his implementation details for U.N. Security Council Resolution 598 [*qv*] on 8 August 1988, the U.N. secretary-general announced the formation of the United Nations Iran-Iraq Military Observer Group (UNIIMOG), consisting of 350 troops and officers drawn from twenty-five countries to supervise the cease-fire that was to come into effect on 20 August 1988.

United Nations Iraq-Kuwait Observer Mission (1991–): In line with U.N. Security

Council Resolution 687 [*qv*] of 3 April 1991, concerning the cease-fire in the Second Gulf War [*qv*] between Iraq and the U.S.-led coalition, the U.N. secretary-general selected a United Nations Iraq-Kuwait Military Observer Group (UNIKOM), composed of 320 military personnel from thirty-five countries, with the following mandate: to monitor the Khor Abdullah waterway and a demilitarized zone (DMZ) extending 10 kms into Iraq and 5 km into Kuwait from the agreed boundary between the two countries according to their agreement on 4 October 1963; and to deter violations of the boundary and observe hostile or potentially hostile actions. Following a fresh demarcation of the international frontier by a U.N. committee at the expense of Iraq in 1993, and its acceptance by Baghdad in November 1994, UNIKOM began to function within the new boundaries.

United Nations Monitoring, Verification and Inspection Commission (1999): According to the terms of paragraphs 1, 2, and 3 of U.N. Security Council Resolution 1284 (1999) [*qv*] on Iraq [*qv*], adopted on 17 December 1999, the secretary-general appointed the United Nations Monitoring, Verification, and Inspection Commission (Unmovic) to replace the United Nations Special Commission [*qv*] of 1991 and charged it to conduct on-site inspection of Iraq's biological, chemical, and missile facilities; to cooperate with the International Atomic Energy Commission (IAEA) regarding on-site inspection of Iraq's nuclear capabilities; and together establish and operate current and future ongoing monitoring and verification regimes to verify Iraq's continued compliance of its undertak-

ings in these areas. After UN Secretary-General Kofi Annan had appointed Hans Blix executive chairman of UNMOVIC in 2000, UNSCOM was dissolved. UNMOVIC recruited and trained about 100 inspectors from forty countries. It was not until late November 2002 that, following Iraq's acceptance of U.N. Security Council Resolution 1441 [*qv*], the UNMOVIC staff began performing their tasks.

United Nations Relief and Work Agency for Palestinian Refugees in the Near East (1949–): Following a resolution in December 1949 by the United Nations General Assembly to care for those Palestinians who had lost their homes and means of livelihood during the 1948–49 Palestine War [*qv*], the United Nations Relief and Work Agency for Palestinian Refugees in the Near East (UNRWA) was created at the U.N.'s offices in Vienna, Austria. This meant having to deal with 914,221 Palestinians, of whom some 500,000 qualified for UNRWA relief. Following Israel's seizure of the West Bank [*qv*] and the Gaza Strip [*qv*] during the June 1967 Arab-Israeli War [*qv*], there were a further 335,000 displaced Palestinians, of whom 193,600 were eligible for UNRWA support.

Financed by voluntary contributions of the member governments, UNRWA's mandate is renewed regularly to provide camps, food, clothing, schools, vocational training, and health clinics, often working in cooperation with the United Nations Educational, Scientific and Cultural Organization (UNESCO).

In 1980, of the 1,844,300 Palestinian refugees registered with UNRWA, about a third were in sixty-one camps scattered throughout the West Bank (20), the Gaza Strip (8), Jordan (10), Syria (10), and Lebanon (13). By 2000, the total had risen to 3,806,055, divided among the Gaza Strip (837,750), Jordan (1,609,566), Lebanon (380,072), Syria (387,526), and the West Bank (591,141). Following the escalation of Israeli-Palestinian violence due to the Second Intifada [*qv*], resulting in the blockade of the Palestinian Authority-controled zones by Israel, UNRWA became the prime agency to coordinate and supply emergency aid to the Palestinians. Its budget rose to $310 million in 2001. Due to Israel's long siege of the Palestinian towns and villages in 2001–02, the number of Palestinians whom UNRWA provided food aid rose tenfold to 1.1 million in 2003.

United Nations Security Council Resolution 242 (1967): Adopted unanimously on 22 November 1967.

The Security Council, Expressing its continuing concern with the grave situation in the Middle East,

Emphasizing the inadmissibility of the acquisition of territory by war and the need to work for a just and lasting peace in which every State in the area can live in security,

Emphasizing further that all Member States in their acceptance of the Charter of the United Nations have undertaken a commitment to act in accordance with Article 2 of the Charter,

1. *Affirms* that the fulfilment of Charter principles requires the establishment of a just and lasting peace in the Middle East which should includethe application of both the following principles:

(i) Withdrawal of Israel armed forces from territories occupied in the recent conflict;

(ii) Termination of all claims or states of belligerency and respect for and acknowledgement of the sovereignty, territorial integrity and political independence of every State in the area and their right to live in peace within secure and recognized borders from threats or acts of force;

2. *Affirms further* the necessity

(a) For guaranteeing freedom of navigation through international waterways in the area;

(b) For achieving a just settlement of the refugee problem;

(c) For guaranteeing the territorial inviolability and political independence of every State in the area, through measures including the establishment of demilitarized zones;

3. *Requests* the Secretary-General to designate a Special Representative to proceed to the Middle East to establish and maintain contacts with the States concerned in order to promote agreement and assist efforts to achieve a peaceful and accepted settlement in accordance with the provisions and principles of this resolution;

4. *Requests* the Secretary-General to report to the Security Council on the progress of the Special Representative as soon as possible.

United Nations Security Council Resolution 338 (October 1973): Adopted by fourteen votes to one, with one abstention (China) on 22 October 1973.

The Security Council (1.) *Calls upon* all parties to the present fighting to cease all firing and terminate all military activity immediately, no later than 12 hours after the moment of adoption of this decision, in the positions they now occupy; (2.) *Calls upon* the parties to start immediately afterthe cease-fire the implementation of SecurityCouncil resolution 242 (1967) in all of its parts; (3.) *Decides* that, immediately and concurrently with the cease-fire, negotiation shall start between the parties concerned under appropriate auspices at establishing a just and durable peace in the Middle East.

United Nations Security Council Resolution 425 (1978): Adopted on 19 March 1978 by twelve votes to one, with two abstentions (Czechoslovakia and the Soviet Union).

The Security Council, Taking note of the letters of the Permanent Representative of Lebanon [S/12600 and S/12606] and the Permanent Representative of Israel [S/12607], *Having heard* the statements of the Permanent Representatives of Lebanon and Israel, *Gravely concerned* at the deterioration of the situation in the Middle East and its consequences on the maintenance of international peace, *Convinced* that the present situation impedes the achievement of a just peace in the Middle East: (1) *Calls* for strict respect for the territorial integrity, sovereignty and political independence of Lebanon within its internationally recognized boundaries; (2) *Calls* upon Israel immediately to cease its military action against Lebanese territorial integrity and withdraw its forces from all Lebanese territory; (3) *Decides,* in the light of the request of the Government of Lebanon, to establish immediately under

its authority a United Nations interim force for Southern Lebanon for the purpose of confirming the withdrawal of the Israeli forces, restoring international peace and security and assisting the Government of Lebanon in ensuring the return of its effective authority in the area, the force to be composed of personnel drawn from Member States; (4) *Requests* the Secretary-General to report to the Council within twenty-four hours on the implementation of the present resolution.

It was not until May 2000, after it had lost nearly 1,000 soldiers, that Israel [*qv*] withdrew from southern Lebanon unconditionally.

United Nations Security Council Resolution 598 (1987): Adopted unanimously on 20 July 1987. The ten-clause resolution included the following operative clauses:

The Security Council . . .
Acting under Articles 39 and 40 of the Charter [of the United Nations],
1. *Demands* that, as a first step towards a negotiated settlement . . . Iran and Iraq observe an immediate cease-fire, discontinue all military actions on land, at sea and in the air, and withdraw all forces to the internationally recognized boundaries without delay;
2. *Requests* the Secretary-General to dispatch a team of United Nations observers to verify, confirm and supervise the cease-fire and withdrawal and further requests the Secretary-General to make necessary arrangements in consultation with the parties and to submit a report thereon to the Security Council;

3. *Urges* that prisoners-of-war be released and repatriated without delay after the cessation of active hostilities in accordance with the Third Geneva Convention of 12 August 1949;

4. *Calls* upon Iran and Iraq to cooperate with the Secretary-General in implementing this resolution and in mediation efforts to achieve a comprehensive, just and honorable settlement, acceptable to both sides, of all outstanding issues in accordance with the principles contained in the Charter of the United Nations . . .

6. *Requests* the Secretary-General to explore, in consultation with Iran and Iraq, the question of entrusting an impartial body with inquiring into responsibility for the conflict and to report to the Security Council as soon as possible;

7. *Recognizes* the magnitude of the damage inflicted . . . and the need for reconstruction efforts, with appropriate international assistance, once the conflict is ended and, in this regard requests the Secretary-General to assign a team of experts to study the question of reconstruction and to report to the Council.

United Nations Security Council Resolution 678 (1990): Adopted by the Security Council at its 2963rd meeting on 29 November 1990

The Security Council,

Recalling, and reaffirming its resolutions 660 (1990) of 2 August (1990), 661 (1990) of 6 August 1990, 662 (1990) of 9 August 1990, 664 (1990) of 18 August 1990, 665 (1990) of 25 August 1990, 666 (1990) of 13 September 1990, 667 (1990) of 16 September 1990, 669 (1990) of 24 September 1990, 670 (1990) of 25 September 1990, 674 (1990) of of 29 October 1990 and 677 (1990) of 28 November 1990.

Noting that, despite all efforts by the United Nations, Iraq refuses to comply with its obligation to implement resolution 660 (1990) and the above-mentioned subsequent relevant resolutions, in flagrant contempt of the Security Council,

Mindful of its duties and responsibilities under the Charter of the United Nations for the maintenance and preservation of internationalnd peace and security,

Determined to secure full compliance with its decisions,

Acting under Chapter VII of the Charter,

1. *Demands* that Iraq comply fully with resolution 660 (1990) and all subsequent relevant resolutions, and decides, while maintaining all its decisions, to allow Iraq one final opportunity, as a pause of goodwil, to do so;

2. *Authorizes* Member States co-operating with the Government of Kuwait, unless Iraq on or before 15 January 1991 fully implements, as set forth in paragraph 1 above, the foregoing resolutions, to use all necessary means to uphold and implement resolution 660 (1990) and all subsequent relevant resolutions and to restore international peace and security in the area;

3. *Requests* all States to provide appropriate support for the actions undertaken in pursuance of paragraph 2 of the present resolution;

4. *Requests* the States concerned to keep the Security Council regularly informed on the progress of actions undertaken

pursuant to paragraphs 2 and 3 of the present resolution;

5. *Decides* to remain seized of the matter.

United Nations Security Council Resolution 687 (1991): Adopted on 3 April 1991 by 12 votes to one (Cuba) with two abstentions (Ecuador and Yemen), the thirty-four-clause Security Council Resolution 687 contained the following operative paragraphs:

The Security Council. . .

Recalling its resolutions 660 [1990], 661 [1990], 662 [1990], 664 [1990], 665 [1990], 666 [1990], 667 [1990], 669 [1990], 670 [1990], 674 [1990], 677 [1990], 678 [1990], and 686 [1991],

Conscious of the need to take the following measures acting under Chapter VII of the Charter [of the United Nations],

1. Affirms all thirteen resolutions noted above, except as expressly changed below to achieve the goals of the resolution, including a formal cease-fire;

A

2–4. Concerning the international boundary between Iraq and Kuwait, calls on the Secretary-General to make arrangements to demarcate the boundary between Iraq and Kuwait;

B

5–6. Concerning immediate deployment of a United Nations observer unit to monitor the demilitarised zone along the international boundary;

C

7–13. Requires Iraq to accept the destruction, removal, or rendering harmless under international supervision of all chemical and biological weapons, and all research, development, support and manufacturing facilities; and all ballistic missiles with a range greater than 150 km; Requires the Secretary-General to appoint a Special Commission to carry out on-site inspection of Iraq's biological, chemical, and missile facilities and set up a monitoring system; Requests the Director-General of the International Atomic Energy Agency [IAEA] to carry out on-site inspection of Iraq's nuclear capabilities in cooperation with the Special Commission and set up a monitoring system;

14. Takes note that the actions under paragraphs 8–13 represent steps towards the goal of establishing in the Middle East a zone free from weapons of mass destruction and all missiles for their delivery.

D

15. Concerning the return of all Kuwaiti property seized by Iraq;

E

16–19. Concerning Iraq's liability for direct loss, damage, including depletion of natural resources, or injury to foreign Governments, nationals and corporations as a result of Iraq's invasion and occupation of Kuwait, with paragraph 19 directing the Secretary-General to recommend within thirty days to the Council the establishment of a Fund, financed by Iraq, to meet the requirements of the claimants, and a Commission to administer the Fund;

F

20–29. Concerning economic embargo against Iraq and its lifting;

20.The prohibitions against the sale or supply to Iraq of commodities or products, and prohibitions against financial transactions with Iraq, contained in resolution 661 [6 August 1990] shall not apply to foodstuffs and medicine;

21. The Security Council shall review the provisions of paragraph 20 every sixty days in the light of the policies and practices of the Government of Iraq, including the implementation of all relevant resolutions of the Security Council, for the purposes of determining whether to reduce or lift the prohibitions referred to therein;

22. Upon the approval of the Council of the program mentioned in paragraph 19 and upon Council agreement that Iraq has completed all actions contemplated in paragraphs 8 to 13, the prohibitions against the import [by other members of the United Nations] of commodities and products originating in Iraq, and the prohibitions against financial transactions related thereto contained in resolution 661 (1990) shall have no further force or effect. 24. *Decides* that in accordance with resolution 661 (1990) and subsequent related resolutions and until a further decision is taken by the Council, all States shall continue to prevent the sale or supply, or promotion or facilitation of such sale or supply, to Iraq by their nationals, or from their territories or using their flag or aircraft, of : (a) arms and related materials of all types . . . and spare parts and components and their means of production, for such equipment; (b) Items specified and defined in paragraphs 8 and 12 not otherwise covered above; (c) Technology under licensing or other transfer arrangements used in production, utilization or stockpiling of items specified in subparagraphs (a) and (b); (d) Personnel

or materials for training or technical support relating to the design, development, manufacture, use, maintenance or support of items in subparagraphs (a) and (b); 25. *Calls upon all States* and international organizations to act strictly in accordance with paragraph 24, notwithstanding the existence of any contracts, agreements, licenses and any other arrangements . . .

G

30–31. Concerning repatriation or return of all Kuwaiti and third-State nationals or their remains present in Iraq on or after 2 August 1990;

H

32. *Requires* Iraq to confirm that it will not commit or support any act of international terrorism;

I

33–34. On Iraq's official acceptance of the above provisions, a formal cease-fire becomes effective between Iraq and Kuwait and the Member States cooperating with Kuwait in accordance with resolution 678.

United Nations Security Council Resolution 1284 (1999): Adopted by eleven votes to none, with four abstentions (China, France, Malaysia, and Russia) on 17 December 1999.

The Security Council,

Recalling its previous relevant resolutions, including its resolutions 661 (1990) of 6 August 1990, 687 (1991) of 3 April 1991, 699 (1991) of 17 June 1991, 707 (1991) of 15 August 1991, 715 (1991) of 11 October 1991, 986 (1995) of 14 April 1995, 1051 (1996) of 27 March 1996,

1153 (1998) of 20 February 1998, 1175 (1998) of 19 June 1998, 1242 (1999) of 21 May 1999 and 1266 (1999) of 4 October 1999,

Recalling the approval by the Council in its resolution 715 (1991) of the plans for future ongoing monitoring and verification submitted by the Secretary-General and the Director General of the International Atomic Energy Agency (IAEA) in pursuance of paragraphs 10 and 13 of resolution 687 (1991),

Welcoming the reports of the three panels on Iraq (S/1999/356), and having held a comprehensive consideration of them and the recommendations contained in them,

Stressing the importance of a comprehensive approach to the full implementation of all relevant Security Council resolutions regarding Iraq and the need for Iraqi compliance with these resolutions,

Recalling the goal of establishing in the Middle East a zone free from weapons of mass destruction and all missiles for their delivery and the objective of a global ban on chemical weapons as referred to in paragraph 14 of resolution 687 (1991),

Concerned at the humanitarian situation in Iraq, and determined to improve that situation,

Recalling with concern that the repatriation and return of all Kuwaiti and third country nationals or their remains, present in Iraq on or after 2 August 1990, pursuant to paragraph 2 (c) of resolution 686 (1991) of 2 March 1991 and paragraph 30 of resolution 687 (1991), have not yet been fully carried out by Iraq,

Recalling that in its resolutions 686 (1991) and 687 (1991) the Council demanded that Iraq return in the shortest possible time all Kuwaiti property it had seized, and noting with regret that Iraq has still not complied fully with this demand,

Acknowledging the progress made by Iraq towards compliance with the provisions of resolution 687 (1991), but noting that, as a result of its failure to implement the relevant Council resolutions fully, the conditions do not exist which would enable the Council to take a decision pursuant to resolution 687 (1991) to lift the prohibitions referred to in that resolution,

Reiterating the commitment of all Member States to the sovereignty, territorial integrity and political independence of Kuwait, Iraq and the neighboring States,

Acting under Chapter VII of the Charter of the United Nations, and taking into account that operative provisions of this resolution relate to previous resolutions adopted under Chapter VII of the Charter,

A.

1. Decides to establish, as a subsidiary body of the Council, the United Nations Monitoring, Verification and Inspection Commission (UNMOVIC) which replaces the Special Commission established pursuant to paragraph 9 (b) of resolution 687 (1991);

2. Decides also that UNMOVIC will undertake the responsibilities mandated to the Special Commission by the Council with regard to the verification of compliance by Iraq with its obligations under paragraphs 8, 9 and 10 of resolution 687 (1991) and other related resolutions, that UNMOVIC will establish and operate, as was recommended by the

panel on disarmament and current and future ongoing monitoring and verification issues, a reinforced system of ongoing monitoring and verification, which will implement the plan approved by the Council in resolution 715 (1991) and address unresolved disarmament issues, and that UNMOVIC will identify, as necessary in accordance with its mandate, additional sites in Iraq to be covered by the reinforced system of ongoing monitoring and verification;

3. Reaffirms the provisions of the relevant resolutions with regard to the role of the IAEA in addressing compliance by Iraq with paragraphs 12 and 13 of resolution 687 (1991) and other related resolutions, and requests the Director General of the IAEA to maintain this role with the assistance and cooperation of UNMOVIC;

4. Reaffirms its resolutions 687 (1991), 699 (1991), 707 (1991), 715 (1991), 1051 (1996), 1154 (1998) and all other relevant resolutions and statements of its President, which establish the criteria for Iraqi compliance, affirms that the obligations of Iraq referred to in those resolutions and statements with regard to cooperation with the Special Commission, unrestricted access and provision of information will apply in respect of UNMOVIC, and decides in particular that Iraq shall allow UNMOVIC teams immediate, unconditional and unrestricted access to any and all areas, facilities, equipment, records and means of transport which they wish to inspect in accordance with the mandate of UNMOVIC, as well as to all officials and other persons under the authority of the Iraqi Government whom UNMOVIC wishes to interview so that UNMOVIC may fully discharge its mandate;

5. Requests the Secretary-General, within 30 days of the adoption of this resolution, to appoint, after consultation with and subject to the approval of the Council, an Executive Chairman of UNMOVIC who will take up his mandated tasks as soon as possible, and, in consultation with the Executive Chairman and the Council members, to appoint suitably qualified experts as a College of Commissioners for UNMOVIC which will meet regularly to review the implementation of this and other relevant resolutions and provide professional advice and guidance to the Executive Chairman, including on significant policy decisions and on written reports to be submitted to the Council through the Secretary-General;

6. Requests the Executive Chairman of UNMOVIC, within 45 days of his appointment, to submit to the Council, in consultation with and through the Secretary-General, for its approval an organizational plan for UNMOVIC, including its structure, staffing requirements, management guidelines, recruitment and training procedures, incorporating as appropriate the recommendations of the panel on disarmament and current and future ongoing monitoring and verification issues, and recognizing in particular the need for an effective, cooperative management structure for the new organization, for staffing with suitably qualified and experienced personnel, who would be regarded as international civil servants subject to Article 100 of the Charter of the United Nations, drawn from

the broadest possible geographical base, including as he deems necessary from international arms control organizations, and for the provision of high quality technical and cultural training;

7. Decides that UNMOVIC and the IAEA, not later than 60 days after they have both started work in Iraq, will each draw up, for approval by the Council, a work program for the discharge of their mandates, which will include both the implementation of the reinforced system of ongoing monitoring and verification, and the key remaining disarmament tasks to be completed by Iraq pursuant to its obligations to comply with the disarmament requirements of resolution 687 (1991) and other related resolutions, which constitute the governing standard of Iraqi compliance, and further decides that what is required of Iraq for the implementation of each task shall be clearly defined and precise;

8. Requests the Executive Chairman of UNMOVIC and the Director General of the IAEA, drawing on the expertise of other international organizations as appropriate, to establish a unit which will have the responsibilities of the joint unit constituted by the Special Commission and the Director General of the IAEA under paragraph 16 of the export/import mechanism approved by resolution 1051 (1996), and also requests the Executive Chairman of UNMOVIC, in consultation with the Director General of the IAEA, to resume the revision and updating of the lists of items and technology to which the mechanism applies;

9. Decides that the Government of Iraq shall be liable for the full costs of UNMOVIC and the IAEA in relation to their work under this and other related resolutions on Iraq;

10. Requests Member States to give full cooperation to UNMOVIC and the IAEA in the discharge of their mandates;

11. Decides that UNMOVIC shall take over all assets, liabilities and archives of the Special Commission, and that it shall assume the Special Commission's part in agreements existing between the Special Commission and Iraq and between the United Nations and Iraq, and affirms that the Executive Chairman, the Commissioners and the personnel serving with UNMOVIC shall have the rights, privileges, facilities and immunities of the Special Commission;

12. Requests the Executive Chairman of UNMOVIC to report, through the Secretary-General, to the Council, following consultation with the Commissioners, every three months on the work of UNMOVIC, pending submission of the first reports referred to in paragraph 33 below, and to report immediately when the reinforced system of ongoing monitoring and verification is fully operational in Iraq;

B.

13. Reiterates the obligation of Iraq, in furtherance of its commitment to facilitate the repatriation of all Kuwaiti and third country nationals referred to in paragraph 30 of resolution 687 (1991), to extend all necessary cooperation to the International Committee of the Red Cross, and calls upon the Government of Iraq to resume cooperation with the Tripartite Commission and

Technical Subcommittee established to facilitate work on this issue;

14. Requests the Secretary-General to report to the Council every four months on compliance by Iraq with its obligations regarding the repatriation or return of all Kuwaiti and third country nationals or their remains, to report every six months on the return of all Kuwaiti property, including archives, seized by Iraq, and to appoint a high-level coordinator for these issues;

C.

15. Authorizes States, notwithstanding the provisions of paragraphs 3 (a), 3 (b) and 4 of resolution 661 (1990) and subsequent relevant resolutions, to permit the import of any volume of petroleum and petroleum products originating in Iraq, including financial and other essential transactions directly relating thereto, as required for the purposes and on the conditions set out in paragraph 1 (a) and (b) and subsequent provisions of resolution 986 (1995) and related resolutions;

16. Underlines, in this context, its intention to take further action, including permitting the use of additional export routes for petroleum and petroleum products, under appropriate conditions otherwise consistent with the purpose and provisions of resolution 986 (1995) and related resolutions;

17. Directs the Committee established by resolution 661 (1990) to approve, on the basis of proposals from the Secretary-General, lists of humanitarian items, including foodstuffs, pharmaceutical and medical supplies, as well as basic or standard medical and agricultural equipment and basic or standard educational items, decides,

notwithstanding paragraph 3 of resolution 661 (1990) and paragraph 20 of resolution 687 (1991), that supplies of these items will not be submitted for approval of that Committee, except for items subject to the provisions of resolution 1051 (1996), and will be notified to the Secretary-General and financed in accordance with the provisions of paragraph 8 (a) and 8 (b) of resolution 986 (1995), and requests the Secretary-General to inform the Committee in a timely manner of all such notifications received and actions taken;

18. Requests the Committee established by resolution 661 (1990) to appoint, in accordance with resolutions 1175 (1998) and 1210 (1998), a group of experts, including independent inspection agents appointed by the Secretary-General in accordance with paragraph 6 of resolution 986 (1995), decides that this group will be mandated to approve speedily contracts for the parts and the equipments necessary to enable Iraq to increase its exports of petroleum and petroleum products, according to lists of parts and equipments approved by that Committee for each individual project, and requests the Secretary-General to continue to provide for the monitoring of these parts and equipments inside Iraq;

19. Encourages Member States and international organizations to provide supplementary humanitarian assistance to Iraq and published material of an educational character to Iraq;

20. Decides to suspend, for an initial period of six months from the date of the adoption of this resolution and subject to review, the implementation of paragraph 8 (g) of resolution 986 (1995);

21. Requests the Secretary-General to take steps to maximize, drawing as necessary on the advice of specialists, including representatives of international humanitarian organizations, the effectiveness of the arrangements set out in resolution 986 (1995) and related resolutions including the humanitarian benefit to the Iraqi population in all areas of the country, and further requests the Secretary-General to continue to enhance as necessary the United Nations observation process in Iraq, ensuring that all supplies under the humanitarian program are utilized as authorized, to bring to the attention of the Council any circumstances preventing or impeding effective and equitable distribution and to keep the Council informed of the steps taken towards the implementation of this paragraph;

22. Requests also the Secretary-General to minimize the cost of the United Nations activities associated with the implementation of resolution 986 (1995) as well as the cost of the independent inspection agents and the certified public accountants appointed by him, in accordance with paragraphs 6 and 7 of resolution 986 (1995);

23. Requests further the Secretary-General to provide Iraq and the Committee established by resolution 661 (1990) with a daily statement of the status of the escrow account established by paragraph 7 of resolution 986 (1995);

24. Requests the Secretary-General to make the necessary arrangements, subject to Security Council approval, to allow funds deposited in the escrow account established by resolution 986 (1995) to be used for the purchase of locally produced goods and to meet the local cost for essential civilian needs which have been funded in accordance with the provisions of resolution 986 (1995) and related resolutions, including, where appropriate, the cost of installation and training services;

25. Directs the Committee established by resolution 661 (1990) to take a decision on all applications in respect of humanitarian and essential civilian needs within a target of two working days of receipt of these applications from the Secretary-General, and to ensure that all approval and notification letters issued by the Committee stipulate delivery within a specified time, according to the nature of the items to be supplied, and requests the Secretary-General to notify the Committee of all applications for humanitarian items which are included in the list to which the export/import mechanism approved by resolution 1051 (1996) applies;

26. Decides that Hajj pilgrimage flights which do not transport cargo into or out of Iraq are exempt from the provisions of paragraph 3 of resolution 661 (1990) and resolution 670 (1990), provided timely notification of each flight is made to the Committee established by resolution 661 (1990), and requests the Secretary-General to make the necessary arrangements, for approval by the Security Council, to provide for reasonable expenses related to the Hajj pilgrimage to be met by funds in the escrow account established by resolution 986 (1995);

27. Calls upon the Government of Iraq:

(i) to take all steps to ensure the timely and equitable distribution of all humanitarian goods, in particular medical supplies, and to remove and avoid delays at its warehouses;

(ii) to address effectively the needs of vulnerable groups, including children, pregnant women, the disabled, the elderly and the mentally ill among others, and to allow freer access, without any discrimination, including on the basis of religion or nationality, by United Nations agencies and humanitarian organizations to all areas and sections of the population for evaluation of their nutritional and humanitarian condition;

(iii) to prioritize applications for humanitarian goods under the arrangements set out in resolution 986 (1995) and related resolutions;

(iv) to ensure that those involuntarily displaced receive humanitarian assistance without the need to demonstrate that they have resided for six months in their places of temporary residence;

(v) to extend full cooperation to the United Nations Office for Project Services mine-clearance program in the three northern Governorates of Iraq and to consider the initiation of the demining efforts in other Governorates;

28. Requests the Secretary-General to report on the progress made in meeting the humanitarian needs of the Iraqi people and on the revenues necessary to meet those needs, including recommendations on necessary additions to the current allocation for oil spare parts and equipment, on the basis of a comprehensive survey of the condition of the Iraqi oil production sector, not later than 60 days from the date of the adoption of this resolution and updated thereafter as necessary;

29. Expresses its readiness to authorize additions to the current allocation for oil spare parts and equipment, on the basis of the report and recommendations requested in paragraph 28 above, in order to meet the humanitarian purposes set out in resolution 986 (1995) and related resolutions;

30. Requests the Secretary-General to establish a group of experts, including oil industry experts, to report within 100 days of the date of adoption of this resolution on Iraq's existing petroleum production and export capacity and to make recommendations, to be updated as necessary, on alternatives for increasing Iraq's petroleum production and export capacity in a manner consistent with the purposes of relevant resolutions, and on the options for involving foreign oil companies in Iraq's oil sector, including investments, subject to appropriate monitoring and controls;

31. Notes that in the event of the Council acting as provided for in paragraph 33 of this resolution to suspend the prohibitions referred to in that paragraph, appropriate arrangements and procedures will need, subject to paragraph 35 below, to be agreed by the Council in good time beforehand, including suspension of provisions of resolution 986 (1995) and related resolutions;

32. Requests the Secretary-General to report to the Council on the implementation of paragraphs 15 to 30 of this resolution within 30 days of the adoption of this resolution;

D.

33. Expresses its intention, upon receipt of reports from the Executive Chairman of UNMOVIC and from the Director General of the IAEA that Iraq has cooperated

in all respects with UNMOVIC and the IAEA in particular in fulfilling the work programs in all the aspects referred to in paragraph 7 above, for a period of 120 days after the date on which the Council is in receipt of reports from both UNMOVIC and the IAEA that the reinforced system of ongoing monitoring and verification is fully operational, to suspend with the fundamental objective of improving the humanitarian situation in Iraq and securing the implementation of the Council's resolutions, for a period of 120 days renewable by the Council, and subject to the elaboration of effective financial and other operational measures to ensure that Iraq does not acquire prohibited items, prohibitions against the import of commodities and products originating in Iraq, and prohibitions against the sale, supply and delivery to Iraq of civilian commodities and products other than those referred to in paragraph 24 of resolution 687 (1991) or those to which the mechanism established by resolution 1051 (1996) applies;

34. Decides that in reporting to the Council for the purposes of paragraph 33 above, the Executive Chairman of UNMOVIC will include as a basis for his assessment the progress made in completing the tasks referred to in paragraph 7 above;

35. Decides that if at any time the Executive Chairman of UNMOVIC or the Director General of the IAEA reports that Iraq is not cooperating in all respects with UNMOVIC or the IAEA or if Iraq is in the process of acquiring any prohibited items, the suspension of the prohibitions referred to in paragraph 33 above shall terminate on the fifth working day following the report, unless the Council decides to the contrary;

36. Expresses its intention to approve arrangements for effective financial and other operational measures, including on the delivery of and payment for authorized civilian commodities and products to be sold or supplied to Iraq, in order to ensure that Iraq does not acquire prohibited items in the event of suspension of the prohibitions referred to in paragraph 33 above, to begin the elaboration of such measures not later than the date of the receipt of the initial reports referred to in paragraph 33 above, and to approve such arrangements before the Council decision in accordance with that paragraph;

37. Further expresses its intention to take steps, based on the report and recommendations requested in paragraph 30 above, and consistent with the purpose of resolution 986 (1995) and related resolutions, to enable Iraq to increase its petroleum production and export capacity, upon receipt of the reports relating to the cooperation in all respects with UNMOVIC and the IAEA referred to in paragraph 33 above;

38. Reaffirms its intention to act in accordance with the relevant provisions of resolution 687 (1991) on the termination of prohibitions referred to in that resolution;

39. Decides to remain actively seized of the matter and expresses its intention to consider action in accordance with paragraph 33 above no later than 12 months from the date of the adoption of this resolution provided the conditions set out in paragraph 33 above have been satisfied by Iraq.

United Nations Security Council Resolution 1441 (2002): Adopted unanimously on 8 November 2002.

The Security Council,

Recalling all its previous relevant resolutions, in particular its resolutions 661 (1990) of 6 August 1990, 678 (1990) of 29 November 1990, 686 (1991) of 2 March 1991, 687 (1991) of 3 April 1991, 688 (1991) of 5 April 1991, 707 (1991) of 15 August 1991, 715 (1991) of 11 October 1991, 986 (1995) of 14 April 1995, and 1284 (1999) of 17 December 1999, and all the relevant statements of its President,

Recalling also its resolution 1382 (2001) of 29 November 2001 and its intention to implement it fully,

Recognizing the threat Iraq's non-compliance with Council resolutions and proliferation of weapons of mass destruction and long-range missiles poses to international peace and security,

Recalling that its resolution 678 (1990) authorized Member States to use all necessary means to uphold and implement its resolution 660 (1990) of 2 August 1990 and all relevant resolutions subsequent to resolution 660 (1990) and to restore international peace and security in the area,

Further recalling that its resolution 687 (1991) imposed obligations on Iraq as a necessary step for achievement of its stated objective of restoring international peace and security in the area,

Deploring the fact that Iraq has not provided an accurate, full, final, and complete disclosure, as required by resolution 687 (1991), of all aspects of its programs to develop weapons of mass destruction and ballistic missiles with a range greater than one hundred and fifty kilometers, and of all holdings of such weapons, their components and production facilities and locations, as well as all other nuclear programs, including any which it claims are for purposes not related to nuclear-weapons-usable material,

Deploring further that Iraq repeatedly obstructed immediate, unconditional, and unrestricted access to sites designated by the United Nations Special Commission (UNSCOM) and the International Atomic Energy Agency (IAEA), failed to cooperate fully and unconditionally with UNSCOM and IAEA weapons. inspectors, as required by resolution 687 (1991), and ultimately ceased all cooperation with UNSCOM and the IAEA in 1998,

Deploring the absence, since December 1998, in Iraq of international monitoring, inspection, and verification, as required by relevant resolutions, of weapons of mass destruction and ballistic missiles, in spite of the Council's repeated demands that Iraq provide immediate, unconditional, and unrestricted access to the United Nations Monitoring, Verification and Inspection Commission (UNMOVIC), established in resolution 1284 (1999) as the successor organization to UNSCOM, and the IAEA, and regretting the consequent prolonging of the crisis in the region and the suffering of the Iraqi people,

Deploring also that the Government of Iraq has failed to comply with its commitments pursuant to resolution 687 (1991) with regard to terrorism, pursuant to resolution 688 (1991) to end repression of its civilian population and to provide access by international humanitarian organizations to all those in need of assistance in Iraq, and pursuant to resolutions 686 (1991), 687 (1991), and 1284 (1999) to return or cooperate in accounting for Kuwaiti and third country nationals wrongfully detained by Iraq, or to return Kuwaiti property wrongfully seized by Iraq,

Recalling that in its resolution 687 (1991) the Council declared that a cease-fire would be based on acceptance by Iraq of the provisions of that resolution, including the obligations on Iraq contained therein,

Determined to ensure full and immediate compliance by Iraq without conditions or restrictions with its obligations under resolution 687 (1991) and other relevant resolutions and recalling that the resolutions of the Council constitute the governing standard of Iraqi compliance,

Recalling that the effective operation of UNMOVIC, as the successor organization to the Special Commission, and the IAEA is essential for the implementation of resolution 687 (1991) and other relevant resolutions,

Noting that the letter dated 16 September 2002 from the Minister for Foreign Affairs of Iraq addressed to the Secretary-General is a necessary first step toward rectifying Iraq's continued failure to comply with relevant Council resolutions,

Noting further the letter dated 8 October 2002 from the Executive Chairman of UNMOVIC and the Director-General of the IAAEA to General Al-Saadi of th Government of Iraq laying out the practical arrangements, as a follow-up to their meeting in Vienna, that are prerequisites

for the resumption of inspections in Iraq by UNMOVIC and the IAEA, and expressing the gravest concern at the continued failure by the Government of Iraq to provide confirmation of the arrangements as laid out in that letter,

Reaffirming the commitment of all Member States to the sovereignty and territorial integrity of Iraq, Kuwait, and the neighboring States,

Commending the Secretary-General and members of the League of Arab States and its Secretary-General for their efforts in this regard,

Determined to secure full compliance with its decisions,

Acting under Chapter VII of the Charter of the United Nations,

1. *Decides* that Iraq has been and remains in material breach of its obligations under relevant resolutions, including resolution 687 (1991), in particular through Iraq's failure to cooperate with United Nations inspectors and the IAEA, and to complete the actions required under paragraphs 8 to 13 of resolution 687 (1991);

2. *Decides*, while acknowledging paragraph 1 above, to afford Iraq, by this resolution, a final opportunity to comply with its disarmament obligations under relevant resolutions of the Council; and accordingly decides to set up an enhanced inspection regime with the aim of bringing to full and verified completion the disarmament process established by resolution 687 (1991) and subsequent resolutions of the Council;

3. *Decides* that, in order to begin to comply with its disarmament obligations, in addition to submitting the required

biannual declarations, the Government of Iraq shall provide to UNMOVIC, the IAEA, and the Council, not later than 30 days from the date of this resolution, a currently accurate, full, and complete declaration of all aspects of its programs to develop chemical, biological, and nuclear weapons, ballistic missiles, and other delivery systems such as unmanned aerial vehicles and dispersal systems designed for use on aircraft, including any holdings and precise locations of such weapons, components, sub-components, stocks of agents, and related material and equipment, the locations and work of its research, development and production facilities, as well as all other chemical, biological, and nuclear programs, including any which it claims are for purposes not related to weapon production or material;

4. *Decides* that false statements or omissions in the declarations submitted by Iraq pursuant to this resolution and failure by Iraq at any time to comply with, and cooperate fully in the implementation of, this resolution shall constitute a further material breach of Iraq's obligations and will be reported to the Council for assessment in accordance with paragraphs 11 and[*] 12 below;

5. *Decides* that Iraq shall provide UNMOVIC and the IAEA immediate, unimpeded, unconditional, and unrestricted access to any and all, including underground, areas, facilities, buildings, equipment, records, and means of transport which they wish to inspect, as well as immediate, unimpeded, unrestricted, and private access to all officials and other persons whom UNMOVIC or the IAEA wish

to interview in the mode or location of UNMOVIC's or the IAEA's choice pursuant to any aspect of their mandates; further decides that UNMOVIC and the IAEA may at their discretion conduct interviews inside or outside of Iraq, may facilitate the travel of those interviewed and family members outside of Iraq, and that, at the sole discretion of UNMOVIC and the IAEA, such interviews may occur without the presence of observers from the Iraqi Government; and instructs UNMOVIC and requests the IAEA to resume inspections no later than 45 days following adoption of this resolution and to update the Council 60 days thereafter;

6. *Endorses* the 8 October 2002 letter from the Executive Chairman of UNMOVIC and the Director-General of the IAEA to General Al-Saadi of the Government of Iraq, which is annexed hereto, and decides that the contents of the letter shall be binding upon Iraq;

7. *Decides* further that, in view of the prolonged interruption by Iraq of the presence of UNMOVIC and the IAEA and in order for them to accomplish the tasks set forth in this resolution and all previous relevant resolutions and notwithstanding prior understandings, the Council hereby establishes the following revised or additional authorities, which shall be binding upon Iraq, to facilitate their work in Iraq:

– UNMOVIC and the IAEA shall determine the composition of their inspection teams and ensure that these teams are composed of the most qualified and experienced experts available;

– All UNMOVIC and IAEA personnel shall enjoy the privileges and immunities, corresponding to those of experts on mission, provided in the Convention on Privileges and Immunities of the United Nations and the Agreement on the Privileges and Immunities of the IAEA;

– UNMOVIC and the IAEA shall have unrestricted rights of entry into and out of Iraq, the right to free, unrestricted, and immediate movement to and from inspection sites, and the right to inspect any sites and buildings, including immediate, unimpeded, unconditional, and unrestricted access to Presidential Sites equal to that at other sites, notwithstanding the provisions of resolution 1154 (1998) of 2 March 1998;

– UNMOVIC and the IAEA shall have the right to be provided by Iraq the names of all personnel currently and formerly associated with Iraq's chemical, biological, nuclear, and ballistic missile programs and the associated research, development, and production facilities;

– Security of UNMOVIC and IAEA facilities shall be ensured by sufficient United Nations security guards;

– UNMOVIC and the IAEA shall have the right to declare, for the purposes of freezing a site to be inspected, exclusion zones, including surrounding areas and transit corridors, in which Iraq will suspend ground and aerial movement so that nothing is changed in or taken out of a site being inspected;

– UNMOVIC and the IAEA shall have the free and unrestricted use and landing of fixed- and rotary-winged aircraft, including manned and unmanned reconnaissance vehicles;

– UNMOVIC and the IAEA shall have

the right at their sole discretion verifiably to remove, destroy, or render harmless all prohibited weapons, subsystems, components, records, materials, and other related items, and the right to impound or close any facilities or equipment for the production thereof; and

– UNMOVIC and the IAEA shall have the right to free import and use of equipment or materials for inspections and to seize and export any equipment, materials, or documents taken during inspections, without search of UNMOVIC or IAEA personnel or official or personal baggage;

8. *Decides* further that Iraq shall not take or threaten hostile acts directed against any representative or personnel of the United Nations or the IAEA or of any Member State taking action to uphold any Council resolution;

9. *Requests* the Secretary-General immediately to notify Iraq of this resolution, which is binding on Iraq; demands that Iraq confirm within seven days of that notification its intention to comply fully with this resolution; and demands further that Iraq cooperate immediately, unconditionally, and actively with UNMOVIC and the IAEA;

10. *Requests* all Member States to give full support to UNMOVIC and the IAEA in the discharge of their mandates, including by providing any information related to prohibited programs or other aspects of their mandates, including on Iraqi attempts since 1998 to acquire prohibited items, and by recommending sites to be inspected, persons to be interviewed, conditions of such interviews, and data to be collected, the results of which shall be

reported to the Council by UNMOVIC and the IAEA;

11. *Directs* the Executive Chairman of UNMOVIC and the Director-General of the IAEA to report immediately to the Council any interference by Iraq with inspection activities, as well as any failure by Iraq to comply with its disarmament obligations, including its obligations regarding inspections under this resolution;

12. *Decides* to convene immediately upon receipt of a report in accordance with paragraphs 4 or 11 above, in order to consider the situation and the need for full compliance with all of the relevant Council resolutions in order to secure+ international peace and security;

13. *Recalls*, in that context, that the Council has repeatedly warned Iraq that it will face serious consequences as a result of its continued violations of its obligations;

14. *Decides* to remain seized of the matter.

---

* *As a result of two days of intense negotiations between France and Russia and the Anglo-American duo, the earlier word 'or' was changed to 'and'. + As a result of two days of intense negotiations between France and Russia and the Anglo-American duo, the earlier word 'restore' was changed to 'secure'. France and Russia wanted to ensure a meeting of the Security Council to discuss the inspectors' report before any military action was contemplated.*

United Nations Special Commission on Iraq (1991): According to the terms of paragraph 9 of UN Security Council Resolution 687 (1991) [*qv*], adopted on 3 April 1991, the secretary-general appointed a Special Commission to carry out on-site inspection of Iraq's biological, chemical, and missile facilities, and to cooperate with the International Atomic Energy Commission (IAEA) regarding on-site inspection of Iraq's nuclear capabilities and in setting up a monitoring system to verify Iraq's continued compliance of its undertakings in these areas. The United Nations Special Commission (UNSCOM) on Iraq [*qv*] was headed by Rolfe Ekeus, a Swedish diplomat.

In early 1995, with UNSCOM having virtually accomplished its disarming missions in chemical weapons and missiles, Ekeus turned increasingly to biological warfare agents. Following top-level defections from Iraq in August 1995, the Iraqi government conceded that it had produced anthrax and botulinum in 1989–90. Later it admitted producing larger quantities of these agents than initially declared. On his part, at the behest of Scott Ritter, an American chief inspector, Ekeus set up a Concealment Investigation Unit under Ritter to conduct Special Information Collection Missions (SICMs). For these Ritter requested and received assistance from the intelligence agencies of the United States and Israel.

For the SICMs to be successful, UNSCOM teams, headed by Ritter, initiated deliberately confrontational inspections exercises in order to make the Iraqi authorities activate its concealment mechanism for it to be detected by Ritter. The first such exercise in March 1996 failed to yield the expected result. In that month, while switching the monitoring system installed at 300 sites countrywide from collecting video images recorded by cameras on to a magnetic tape to transmitting video images using radio signals boosted by relays, the American signals-and-sensors technicians, working as UNSCOM staff, hid within the boosting stations antennas capable of intercepting microwave transmissions used by the Iraqi military. On the other hand, the second SICM in June, linked to an anti–Saddam Hussein [*qv*] coup—hatched by the U.S. Central Intelligence Agency, the British MI6, and Saudi and Jordanian intelligence agencies—also failed.

The covert cooperation between UNSCOM and America had deepened to the extent that Ritter gave regular briefings to the U.S. National Security Council before and after his inspection tours of Iraq. This relationship grew even stronger after Richard Butler, an Australian disarmament official, took over from Ekeus in July 1997. He pursued with greater vigor the strategy of using the SICMs to lay bare Baghdad's concealment mechanism.

In October Iraq's deputy prime minister, Tariq Aziz [*qv*], told the U.N. Security Council that it would not accept American personnel in UNSCOM teams, as they had shown more loyalty to the United States than to the United Nations. He provided a team of visiting U.N. diplomats sent by the secretary-general, Kofi Annan, with evidence to back up his espionage charges against the Americans on UNSCOM. When Iraq expelled six American inspectors, Butler pulled out all of them. U.S. President Bill Clinton (r. 1993–2001) ordered a military buildup in the region. But an American attack on Iraq was averted by the intervention of Russian President Boris Yeltsin (r. 1992–2000).

A crisis arose in early 1998 when Iraq refused inspections of eight presidential sites, being "sovereign." Following a visit to Baghdad [*qv*] by Annan, there was a seven-point agreement whereby Iraq undertook to accord UNSCOM "immediate, unconditional and unrestricted access," with inspection of the presidential sites to be conducted by a special group, and Annan pledged to bring the subject of lifting sanctions to the attention of the Security Council.

The inspection of presidential sites revealed nothing objectionable. Nor did intrusive, no-notice inspections of such other sensitive sites as the defense ministry yield anything incriminating. While Butler in his April 1998 report reported scant progress in disarmament due to a four-month long crisis, Aziz alleged that UNSCOM's intrusive inspections were meant to provide intelligence to Washington—a charge substantiated by the targets hit by the United States in its Operation Desert Fox [*qv*] in December, and the subsequent revelations made in the American press about the U.S. infiltration of UNSCOM.

In June Butler pointed out that Iraq had not accounted for 500 tons of missile rocket fuel and 1.7 tons of VX, a lethal nerve agent. Aziz claimed that Butler was deliberately focusing on minor issues in order to drag out the UNSCOM mission as wished by the United States. Saddam Hussein ordered that Iraq's cooperation with the inspection regimes of UNSCOM and the IAEA be suspended, while leaving their monitoring systems intact. Now the Clinton administration said that the crisis was between Iraq and the United Nations. Privately its officials stated that UNSCOM had outlived its usefulness, implying that it had achieved virtually all that it had set out to do. This view would later be echoed by Ritter, who would assert repeatedly that Iraq had been disarmed 90 to 95 percent.

Angered by the failure of the U.N. Security Council in October to mention anything about the lifting of sanctions following a debate on a comprehensive review of sanctions, Iraq stopped cooperating with UNSCOM and the IAEA in both inspecting and monitoring, demanding a quick review of its compliance in disarmament linked to a timetable to lift sanctions. Annan intervened, saying that if Iraq reversed its decision, the Council would settle the issue of a comprehensive review of Iraq's disarmament. Iraq agreed.

Butler worked closely with U.S. National Security Adviser Samuel Berger to carry out confrontational inspections during the second half of November. But given Iraq's cooperation, that ploy did not work. While France, Russia, and China considered Iraq's disarmament practically finished, expecting to complete the comprehensive review by Christmas and the embargo on oil lifted, U.S. officials wanted a credible basis for bombing Iraq against the background of imminent impeachment proceedings against Clinton. They therefore advised Butler to stiffen his special report to the Security Council on 15 December. In it Butler said that Iraq was not cooperating with UNSCOM. Advised by Peter Burleigh, the U.S. ambassador to the United Nations, Butler withdrew the UNSCOM staff from Baghdad without even informing the Council so that the U.S. could unleash its 100-hour blitzkrieg on Iraq—Operation Desert Fox—starting on 16 December afternoon Eastern Standard Time. By so doing,

Butler and Clinton brought about the vitual demise of UNSCOM, although it was officially disbanded in early 2000 after the adoption of U.N. Security Council Resolution 1284 [qv], which created the United Nations Monitoring, Verification, and Inspection Commission [qv].

During its existence, UNSCOM visited 700 sites and carried out 6,000 inspections. In biological warfare agents UNSCOM destroyed 8,400 liters (1,850 gallons) of anthrax; 19,000 liters (4180 gallons) of botulinum; 3,400 liters (750 gallons) of clostridium (gangerene gas); 2,200 liters (485 gallons) of aflatoxin; 10 liters (2 gallons) of ricin—as well as all the facilities for their research, development, and production. In the chemical weapons field UNSCOM destroyed 500–600 tons of mustard gas; 100–150 tons of nerve gasses—sarin and tabun; and 50–100 tons of VX nerve gas, and 480,000 liters (105,600 gallons) of chemical weapons agents; more than 450,000 gallons of precursor chemicals; and 30 chemical warheads—and 38,537 filled and empty chemical weapons munitions—and all the facilities for their research, development, and production. In the missiles and their delivery systems, UNSCOM destroyed eight types of delivery systems, 48 Scud missiles, six mobile launchers, eight fixed launch pads, and two fixed launch pads under construction.

United Nations Special Commission on Palestine (1947): On 15 May 1947 a special session of the United Nations General Assembly appointed an eleven-member Special Commission on Palestine, consisting of Australia, Canada, Czechoslovakia, Guatemala, India, Iran, the Netherlands, Peru, Sweden, Uruguay and Yugoslavia. While Arab Palestinians refused to cooperate with it, the Zionists [qv] took a contrary line. It submitted its report on 31 August 1947. Seven of its members proposed partitioning mandate Palestine into a Jewish state (53.5 percent of Palestine), an Arab state (45.4 percent), and Jerusalem [qv] and its suburbs (1.1 percent) under international trusteeship. India, Iran and Yugoslavia proposed an independent federal state composed of Arab and Jewish segments. On 29 November 1947 the U.N. General Assembly approved the majority proposal for partition by thirty-three votes to thirteen, with ten abstentions. With 72 percent of the voting members favoring partition, above the required two-thirds majority, partitioning Palestine became official U.N. policy. Challenging the U.N.'s authority to partition a country against the wishes of its majority, the Arab members proposed that the matter be referred to the International Court of Justice for its verdict, but their motion was defeated by twenty-one votes to twenty, with fifteen members abstaining.

United Nations Truce Supervision Organization (1948–): To assist the United Nations Mediator and the Truce Commission in supervising the cease-fire in the 1948-48 Arab-Israeli War [qv], the United Nations Truce Supervision Organization (UNTSO) was created in June 1948. After the formation of the United Nations Disengagement Observer Force in 1974 [qv] and the United Nations Interim Force in Lebanon in 1978 [qv], the UNTSO cooperated with them. In the mid-1990s, its 224 personnel, drawn from nineteen countries, were posted in Egypt, Israel, Jordan, Lebanon, and Syria.

United Religious Front: *Israeli political alliance* On the eve of the first general election in Israel, 1949, Agudat Israel [qv] and Poale Agudat Israel [qv] combined with Mizrahi [qv] and Poale HaMizrahi [qv] to form the United Religious Front. Winning sixteen seats (out of 120), the Front joined the government to run inter alia the Ministry of Religious Affairs. This enabled its constituents to determine the funding of religious councils and religious courts, as well as influence the composition and working of the Supreme Rabbinical Council, charged with supervising rabbis and synagogues [qv]. The Front's disagreement with Premier David Ben-Gurion [qv] on the degree of control over religious education in schools brought down the first Israeli government in mid-1951.

United States Middle East Force: The United States Middle East Force based itself in Bahrain according to a secret agreement signed by Washington and the emirate on the eve of Britain's withdrawal from there in 1971. It included the United States leasing naval facilities previously used by the British for an annual rental of £300,000. Bahrain thus became the official headquarters of the United States Middle East Force, even though as early as 1949 the U.S. Navy had established a presence there. Because of its proximity to the oil fields of Saudi Arabia, Qatar, and the United Arab Emirates, Bahrain was ideal for naval reconnaissance missions in the Gulf.

During the October 1973 Arab-Israeli War [qv], angered at the United States' support for Israel, the Bahraini ruler stated that he had abrogated the agreement with Washington. But what he had actually done was cancel the provision about providing fueling facilities to the U.S. Navy and raise the annual rental to £2 million. Later the Bahraini-U.S. military agreement, specifying naval and air facilities to the U.S. armed forces, was secretly renewed beyond its expiration date of June 1977. The Bahraini-U.S. link was confirmed in April 1980 when, following their unsuccessful attempt to free American hostages in Tehran [*qv*], U.S. military planes refueled in Bahrain before taking off for Turkey.

United Torah Judaism (Israel): *Israeli political party* Official title: *Yahadut HaTorah HaMeuhedet.* On the eve of the 1988 general election, Agudat Israel [*qv*] and Poale Agudat Israel [*qv*] merged with two smaller religious groups—Moria and Degel HaTorah—to form the United Torah Judaism. It won seven seats in that poll and four in the 1992 election. In 1990 it joined the Likud-led [*qv*] government after Labor [*qv*] quit the national unity cabinet. It maintained its strength in the 1996 Knesset [*qv*] poll, with a gain of one seat in the 1999 election, which it retained in the 2003 poll.

Universal Suez Maritime Canal Company: *see* Suez Canal.

al Utaiba, Juheiman ibn Saif (1939–80): *Saudi Arabian Islamic leader* Born in Sajir in Qasim province, al Utaiba was a grandson of an Ikhwan [*qv*] militant who died in 1929 in a battle against Abdul Aziz al Saud [*qv*]. At the age of eighteen he joined the National Guard [*qv*] and rose to become a corporal. Military discipline frustrated his fierce piety and vocal opposition to the

presence of non-Muslim Westerners in the Saudi kingdom's institutions, including the National Guard.

Al Utaiba left the National Guard in 1972 and enrolled at the Islamic University of Medina, where he became a student of Shaikh Abdul Aziz ibn Abdullah al Baz [*qv*], who advocated a return to the letter of the Quran [*qv*] and the *sunna* [*qv*]. Imbibing his teachings, al Utaiba applied them to the actions of the Saudi dynasty and concluded that it had deviated from the true path of Islam [*qv*]. This led to a clash with al Baz and expulsion from the university in 1974. On return to his native province, al Utaiba began to preach along the lines of the founder of Wahhabi [*qv*] doctrine, Shaikh Abdul Wahhab (1703–87).

A popular poet and writer on Islam, al Utaiba set up cells in numerous bedouin settlements in Qasim. In 1976 he and his followers moved to Riyadh [*qv*]. There he published a pamphlet in which he attacked the Saudi rulers for their deviation from the Sharia [*qv*], their greed and corruption, misuse of laws for their own benefit, and socializing with atheists and unbelievers. In the summer of 1978 the government arrested al Utaiba and ninety-eight of his followers in Riyadh. But once al Baz, now head of the Council of Ulama [*qv*], had ruled that their ideas were not treasonable, they were released after they promised not to undertake subversive actions or propaganda. They were kept under surveillance but managed to slip away.

Resorting to clandestine preaching, al Utaiba developed the idea of mahdi [*qv*] (messiah), which he allied to the traditional Wahhabi doctrine. In his brother-in-law, Muhammad ibn Abdullah al Qahtani, a former student of the Islamic University of Riyadh, he had found a mahdi with the name of the Prophet of Islam, and a surname that was a derivative of Qahtan, the legendary ancestor of Arabs [*qv*]. To this he tagged the notion widely held among Sunni Muslims [*qv*] that a *mujaddid* (renewer of faith), appears once every (Islamic) century. The new Islamic century was to begin on 1 Muharram 1400 A.H./20 November 1979.

On New Year's Eve, hundreds of al Utaiba's followers converged on the Grand Mosque in Mecca [*qv*], where they had concealed arms in the cellars and retreats of the vast complex. They planned to take hostage King Khalid al Saud [*qv*], who was expected to join the faithful for the first prayer of the century. Despite Khalid's absence, al Utaiba and his armed followers took over the mosque. After condemning the Saudi regime, al Utaiba introduced al Qahtani as the mahdi/mujaddid. It took the Saudi government a fortnight and the deployment of thousands of Saudi and Pakistani troops to regain the Grand Mosque. Qahtani was one of the 117 rebels killed in the operation, and al Utaiba was one of the 67 to be decapitated in January 1980.

V

Velayati, Ali Akbar (1945–): *Iranian politician* Born into a middle-class family, Velayati obtained a medical degree from Tehran University and engaged in postgraduate studies in the United States. On his return home he taught medicine at his old university in Tehran [*qv*]. A pious Muslim [*qv*], he was appointed deputy health minister in the first government after the 1979 Islamic revolution [*qv*]. He was elected to the Majlis [*qv*] in the early 1980 poll. In November he was appointed foreign minister. Following his election as president in October 1981, Ayatollah Ali Husseini Khamanei [*qv*] nominated Velayati as premier, but the Majlis rejected him by eighty votes to seventy-four.

As foreign minister, Velayati resolved the conflict between the regime's ideological commitment to export Islamic revolution and the norm of international diplomacy of noninterference in the internal affairs of a foreign country, by transferring the functions of his ministry's Islamic national liberation movements section to a nongovernmental body, the World Organization of the Islamic Liberation Movements, led by Ayatollah Hussein Ali Montazeri [*qv*] and based in Qom [*qv*].

During the 1980–88 Iran-Iraq War [*qv*], Velayati repeatedly tried to persuade the members of the Gulf Cooperation Council (GCC) [*qv*] to stay neutral in the conflict by stressing that peaceful coexistence with its neighbors was part of Iran's foreign policy. His efforts bore some fruit during the latter half of the long war. Soon after the U.N. Security Council adopted Resolution 598 [*qv*] in July 1987, Velayati succeeded in getting the influential West German foreign minister, Hans Dietrich Genscher, to publicly hold Iraq responsible for starting the Iran-Iraq War—an indication of the good relations Iran had established with West Germany.

Following Iran's acceptance of Resolution 598, Ayatollah Ruhollah Khomeini [*qv*] gave carte blanche to Velayati in his dealings with

Iraq [*qv*]. He proved a tough negotiator. In the end Iran succeeded in getting Iraq to reverse its decision of 1980 and reaccept the Algiers Accord [*qv*] in August 1990. During the crisis preceding the 1991 Gulf War [*qv*], Velayati managed to make a distinction between the Muslim people of Iraq and the Iraqi President Saddam Hussein [*qv*], and kept Iran out of the anti-Iraq alliance led by the United States, which had broken diplomatic and economic links with Tehran in 1979.

Under the presidency of Ali Akbar Hashemi Rafsanjani (1989–97) [*qv*], Velayati pursued the policy of reconciliation in the Gulf region not only with the Arab monarchies, but also with Iraq. Relations with the United States remained tense, with President Bill Clinton forming a new permanent Fifth Fleet to be stationed in Bahrain [*qv*] to patrol the Gulf [*qv*], chiefly to police Iran and enforce the naval blockade of Iraq. Following the election of Muhammad Khatami [*qv*] as president in 1997, Velayati was replaced by Kamal Kharrazi. Leader Ali Husseini Khamanei then appointed Velayati his adviser on foreign affairs.

Vilayet-e Faqih: *(Persian: Rule of the Religious Jurisprudent): Islamic doctrine* This doctrine, developed by Ayatollah Ruhollah Khomeini [*qv*] in his book *Hukumat-e Islam: Vilayet-e Faqih (Persian: Islamic government: Rule of the Faqih)* (1971), specified that an Islamic regime required an Islamic ruler who is thoroughly conversant with the Sharia [*qv*] and is just in its application: a Just Faqih. He should be assisted by jurisprudents at various levels of legislative, executive, and judicial bodies. The function of a popularly elected parliament, open to both lay believers and clerics, is to resolve the conflicts likely to arise in the implementation of Islamic doctrines. However, judicial functions are to be performed only by jurisprudents who are conversant with the Sharia. Such jurisprudents also oversee the actions of the legislative and executive branches. The overall supervision and guidance of parliament and judiciary rests with the Just Faqih, who must also ensure that the executive does not exceed its powers. After the establishment of the Islamic Republic of Iran in April 1979, the Vilayet-e Faqih doctrine became the backbone of the Islamic constitution adopted in December 1979.

W

Wafd *(Arabic: Delegation): Egyptian political party* The Wafd was formed in 1919 under the leadership of Saad Zaghloul (1860–1927), a lawyer. It was a coalition of different social classes seeking independence from the occupying power, Britain. Its name derived from the delegation Zaghloul led two days after the end of the First World War on 11 November 1918 to the British high commissioner in Cairo [*qv*], demanding that his delegation (*wafd*) be allowed to go to London to present its case for Egyptian independence. When this was refused, demonstrations and riots, tempered by talks, ensued over the next three years, with Wafdists demanding total independence for Egypt and Sudan. A unilateral British declaration in November 1922 granted (nominal) independence to Egypt, with British retaining responsibility for communications for the British Empire in the country, defending Egypt against direct or indirect aggression, safeguarding foreign interests and national minorities in Egypt, and protecting Sudan. This was underwritten by the Egyptian constitution, promulgated in 1923.

The Wafd won the subsequent general election, and Zaghloul became prime minister. After his death in 1927 the nationalist camp split between the Wafd, led by Mustafa Nahas Pasha [qv], and King Ahmad Fuad (r. 1922–36), with the monarch sacking Premier Nahas Pasha in 1931 and suspending the constitution. Just before his death in early 1936 the king reinstated the constitution.

The Wafd was returned to power with a large majority in the election of April 1936, when the Regency Council, headed by Nahas Pasha, reigned on behalf of sixteen-year-old King Faruq [qv]. In August 1936 the twenty-year Anglo-Egyptian Treaty [qv], retaining all four provisions of the 1922 Declaration except British protection for foreign interests and national minorities, was signed. When Faruq achieved adulthood in 1938, the tension between him and the Wafd revived. Faruq dismissed Nahas Pasha. When Italy entered the Second World War in May 1940, it had an impact on Egypt since Faruq was pro-Italian. The British demanded the dismissal of anti-British Premier Ali Mahir and his replacement by Nahas Pasha, who was ready to cooperate with London. Faruq refused. In February 1942, while German troops were advancing on Egypt from Libya and King Faruq was on the verge of appointing a new premier known to be anti-British, the British ambassador compelled the monarch, at the pain of

deposition, to choose Nahas Pasha for the job. Faruq complied. He remained in office until October 1944 and ensured Egypt's affiliation to the Arab League [qv].

After the Egyptian debacle in the 1948–49 Palestine War [qv], Faruq agreed to a reconciliation with Wafd leaders on the understanding that each side would overlook the incompetence and corruption of the other. Faruq ordered a general election in January 1950, which put the Wafd firmly in power. To maintain popular support. The Wafd government pressed London to withdraw its troops from Egypt. When Britain stonewalled, the Wafd unilaterally abrogated the 1936 Anglo-Egyptian Treaty (valid until 1956) in October 1951. It demanded immediate and unconditional British withdrawal from the Suez Canal [qv] zone. Guerrilla actions against British troops ensued, with leftist Wafdists taking part.

Following riots in Cairo in January 1952, the king dismissed the Wafd government. After a coup by the Free Officers in July 1952, the Wafd, along with other parties, was banned. A quarter of a century later, following the promulgation of the Law of the System of Political Parties in June 1977, Fuad Serag al Din, a veteran of the pre-1952 Wafd party, secured a license to establish the Neo-Wafd Party [qv].

Wahhabism and Wahhabis: *Islamic sect* Wahhabism is an Islamic doctrine developed by Muhammad ibn Abdul Wahhab (1703–87), a native of Najd [qv], a bastion of Hanbalis [qv]. The name was coined by the opponents of Abdul Wahhab: his followers called themselves Muwahidun (Unitarians), who accepted the Hanbali school as interpreted by Taqi al Din ibn Taimiya in the late fourteenth century. Abdul Wahhab condemned the medieval superstitions that had collected around the pristine teachings of Islam [qv]. Favoring *ijtihad* [qv] (reasoned interpretation of the Sharia [qv]), he opposed the codification of the Sharia into a comprehensive system of jurisprudence. He was especially against the cult of saints, who were often beseeched by believers to intercede on their behalf with Allah. He and his followers resorted to destroying the tombs of saints.

Unlike Hanbali practices, Abdul Wahhab made attendance at public prayer obligatory and forbade minarets in the building of mosques. Later, in alliance with the followers of Muhammad ibn Saud, who became the ruler of Najd in 1745 and founded the House of Saud [qv], Wahhabis mounted a campaign against idolatry, corruption, and adultery. Claiming authority from the Hadith [qv], they banned music, dancing and even poetry, an integral part of Arab life. They prohibited the use of silk, gold, ornaments, and jewelery.

Regarding themselves to be true believers, Wahhabis launched a jihad [qv] against all others—whom they described as apostates. In 1802 they attacked and looted Karbala [qv], a holy city of the Shias [qv]. Under Saud ibn Abdul Aziz (r. 1803–14), Wahhabi rule spread to the Iraqi and Syrian borders, and included the Hijaz [qv] region with the holy cities of Mecca [qv] and Medina [qv]. This led the Ottoman sultan to order the governor of Egypt, Muhammad Ali, to quell the movement. The result was the defeat and execution of Abdullah ibn Saud (r. 1814–18).

The power of the Wahhabi House of Saud waxed and waned until 1881, when it was expelled from the Riyadh region. But with Abdul Aziz ibn Abdul Rahman al Saud [qv], Wahhabism rose again in the Arabian Peninsula [qv]. He propagated the creed using military and state power and fostered the Ikhwan [qv] movement for the purpose. Considering themselves "the truly guided Islamic community," Wahhabis attacked polytheists, unbelievers, and hypocrites (i.e., those who claimed to be Muslim but whose behavior was un-Islamic). They labeled any deviation from the Sharia as innovation and therefore un-Islamic.

With oil riches flowing into the coffers of the Wahhabi state of Saudi Arabia since the late 1930s, the sect has lost some of its earlier militancy. The final authority lies with the head of the Supreme Religious Council in Saudi Arabia. It has adherents in Central Asia, Afghanistan, Pakistan, and India.

Wailing Wall: *The Western Wall of the Jewish temple in Jerusalem* Called *Kotel Ma'aravi* in Hebrew [qv], the Wailing Wall is part of the massive retaining wall, made up of stones, that the Roman king of Judaea/Judea, Herod the Great (37–34 B.C.), erected at the western, southern, and eastern borders of the Second Temple atop Mount Moriah in Jerusalem [qv] after extending the outer courtyard of the Temple. As the only remnant of the Second Temple, razed in A.D. 70, it is the most sacred site of Judaism [qv]. Since A.D. 70 Jews [qv] have visited it to grieve the destruction of the temple and pray. According to the Talmud [qv], divine presence has never departed from the Western Wall; and so the faithful say their prayers very close to the wall in the belief that the prayers will rise through the crevices to the Throne of Grace on Mount Moriah.

After the destruction of the Second Temple, Jews were permitted to enter Jerusalem only on the ninth of Av, the anniversary of the sacking of the temple. Since the pilgrims would ascend in silence and descend in tears, the wall acquired the epithet "Wailing." During the Muslim Arab [qv] rule from A.D. 638 onward, Jews were allowed to settle in Jerusalem and pray at the wall. The Ottoman Turks, who administered Jerusalem from 1516 for four centuries, formally recognized Jews' right to pray at the Wailing Wall.

In 1930, during the British mandate over Palestine, a League of Nations Commission examined the contending ownership claims by Jews and Muslims [qv] over the Wailing Wall and the adjoining area and declared Muslims the sole owners. The armistice agreement in April 1949 between Israel and Jordan, which controlled the Old City of Jerusalem containing the holy sites of Jews, Christians [qv], and Muslims [qv], provided for free access to sacred sites. But in practice Jordan denied access to the Wailing Wall to the Jews. The situation changed when the Israelis captured East Jerusalem [qv], including the Old City, in the June 1967 Arab-Israeli War [qv]. On Jewish holidays a large number of Jews pray at the Wailing Wall, divided by portable screens into separate prayer areas for women and men.

In the unsuccessful talks on final settlement of the Israel-Palestinian conflict between Israeli Prime Minister Ehud Barak [qv] and Palestine Liberation Organization [qv] Chairman Yasser Arafat [qv] in 2000, the latter agreed to Israel having sovereignty over the Wailing Wall.

waqf *(Arabic: prevent):* In Islamic law, *waqf,* the term popularly used for a religious trust, means "prevent a thing from becoming the property of a third person." Though in practice it meant the legal process by which an endowment was created, in common parlance the term was applied to the endowment *(mawquf)* itself. Anas ibn Malik (d. 796), founder of the Maliki school [qv], attributed the practice of religious trust to the *sunna* [qv]. The first major recorded example of waqf is that of Abu Bakr Muhammad ibn Ali al Madharai (d. A.D. 956) in Egypt. He turned his agricultural land into a waqf for the holy cities of Mecca [qv] and Medina [qv], and for other social purposes such as charities and religious education.

The waqfs, often administered by public officials, ameliorated poverty and advanced further education. On the other hand, the highconcentration of landed property and inefficient management had an adverse economic impact. During the latter period of the Ottoman Empire (1517–1918), waqfs accounted for nearly three-quarters of agricultural land. In the mid-1930s the waqf estates comprised one-seventh of the cultivated land in Egypt and one-sixth in Iran.

The central administration of waqfs in Egypt, begun in 1851, was formalized with a ministry in 1913. The League of Nations mandates over Syria, Palestine, Transjordan, and Iraq required that the mandatory powers should administer the waqfs in accordance with the Sharia [qv]. On independence the governments of these states—all with a Sunni [qv] majority except Iraq—took over the function. In a Shia [qv]-majority country such as Iran this role was traditionally played by senior clergy, who used the income to run educational, social, and charitable institutions and theological colleges. The Civil Code of 1928 authorized the Waqf Organization of the Ministry of Education to approve or disapprove budgets of waqfs, transform a waqf into private property or prohibit such a change, or take over a waqf with unknown administrators. Following the 1979 Islamic revolution [*qv*], this code was abrogated.

War of Attrition (Egypt-Israel) (1969–70): Following the Arab defeat in the June 1967 Arab-Israeli War [*qv*], Egyptian President Gamal Abdul Nasser [*qv*] went through the stages of "standing firm" by resisting Israel's diplomatic and military pressures, and "active deterrence"—i.e., keeping the conflict alive, thus preventing the status quo from congealing—to reach the final stage, the War of Attrition against Israeli positions along the Suez Canal [*qv*] on 8 March 1969. By then, helped by the Soviet Union, Nasser had reequipped the Egyptian military to its pre-June 1967 level. Israel responded by saturation bombing of Egyptian targets and deep penetration raids into Egypt. This drove Nasser deeper into the Soviets' embrace. With a sophisticated Soviet-built air defense umbrella in operation in the spring of 1970, Egypt managed to curtail Israel's capacity for massive reprisals.

Against this background Egypt and Israel accepted the initiative of U.S. Secretary of State William Rogers for a temporary, renewable cease-fire in August 1970. By then, the Israeli army had lost 2,659 soldiers, and the Egyptian military almost 10,000. Also, some 500,000 Egyptians from the Suez Canal zone had been turned into refugees.

War of the Establishment (Israel): *see* War of Independence (Israel).

War of Independence (Israel) (1948–49): Official title: Milhemet HaKomemiyut (*Hebrew: War of the Establishment*). Since the war between the Zionists [*qv*] in Palestine [*qv*] and their Arab neighbors erupted after the Declaration of the Establishment of the State of Israel by the Yishuv's [*qv*] People's Council on 14 May 1948, it was called the War of the Establishment. Later, politicians and historians took to calling it the War of Independence.

Washington Accord (1995): As required by Oslo I Accord [*qv*], the Israeli and Palestinian teams led respectively by Shimon Peres [*qv*] and Yasser Arafat [*qv*] negotiated a deal about the future of the West Bank [*qv*] and the advancement of Palestinian autonomy. Peres and Arafat initialed the final draft on 22 September 1995 in the Egyptian resort town of Taba. On 28 September they signed the agreement at the White House in Washington at a ceremony hosted by President Bill Clinton (r. 1993–2001). It became known as the Washington Accord or Oslo II Accord [*qv*].

With thirty-one Articles, seven Annexes and nine maps, the Accord was 314 pages long. It divided the West Bank into A, B and C Areas; and provided for elections and responsibilities for the Palestinian Legislative Council and the Palestinian Authority [*qv*] presidency; a phased release of the Palestinian prisoners; and a timetable for implementation.

Palestinian jurisdiction would begin after the elections. In Area A, the PA was to exercise full control over civil affairs and security; in Area B, the PA was to exercise control over civil affairs and public order, with Israelis taking charge of overall security; and in Area C, Israel [*qv*] was to exercise full control—including security, territorial jurisdiction and Jewish settlers.

Area A consisted of seven Palestinian cities —Bethlehem [*qv*], Hebron [*qv*], Jenin, Nablus [*qv*], Qalqilya, Ramallah and Tulkarm—and covered two per cent of the West Bank. Here the PA was required to guarantee freedom of movement to Israeli civilians and settlers through these urban centers and provide joint Palestinian-Israeli escorts for their vehicles. Area B included 465 villages, twenty-four percent of the territory and 63 per cent of the population. Here the Israel Defense Forces [*qv*] (IDF) had the power to intervene at its own discretion to maintain overall security. The rest of the West Bank, taking up seventy-three per cent of the land, was labeled Area C.

Finally, the Accord spelled out the powers of the PA presidency and the Legislative Council, both subject to review and final approval of Israel.

Full IDF evacuation of the Area A cities, except Hebron, was scheduled for the end of 1995, followed by a partial withdrawal from Hebron by 28 March 1996.

The IDF's evacuation, starting with Jenin on 13 November, reached a climax with its withdrawal from Bethlehem on 21 December, leading to a four-day party there, combining the celebration of Palestinian nationalism with Christmas [*qv*].

But due to the impending Israeli elections, Arafat allowed the partial evacuation of Hebron to be postponed in order to help Peres beat his Likud [*qv*] rival Benjamin Netanyahu [*qv*] in the prime ministerial contest in May 1996. But Peres lost. Netanyahu forestalled further implementation of the Accord. It was not until October 1998 that, under the Wye River Memorandum [*qv*] brokered personally by Clinton, he agreed to make some concessions to the Palestinians.

Wazir, Khalil (1935–88): *Palestinian political-military leader* Born into a middle-class household in Ramla, Palestine [*qv*], Wazir and his family fled during the 1948–49 Palestine War [*qv*]. He grew up in al Bureij refugee camp in the Gaza Strip [*qv*]. In 1954 he was selected by the Egyptian military, which administered Gaza, first for commando training, and then for further military instruction in Cairo [*qv*], where he met Yasser Arafat [*qv*]. Wazir was commissioned as a lieutenant in the Gazan brigade of the Egyptian army.

Before the capture of Gaza by Israel in the 1956 Suez War [*qv*], Wazir escaped to Cairo, where he became active in Palestinian student politics, dominated by Yasser Arafat. After spending a couple of years in Stuttgart, West Germany, along with Salah Khalaf [*qv*], Wazir traveled to Kuwait in early 1959 to join Arafat, who was running a construction business there. Together they established Fatah [*qv*], and Wazir returned to Stuttgart to organize the Palestinian students in West Germany.

Wazir was close to the National Liberation Front of Algeria, which won power in 1962. In December 1962 he and other leaders of Fatah went to Algiers, where the government authorized the opening of a Fatah office and training camps for Fatah activists. He visited Communist China in 1963. Arrested in January 1965 for sabotaging Israel's National Water Carrier from southern Lebanon, Wazir was put in jail, where he acquired the nom de guerre of Abu Jihad, Father of the Struggle. After his release in March he and Arafat moved to Syria. From there they traveled together to the Palestinian refugee camps on the West Bank [*qv*], then part of Jordan, to enroll recruits for Fatah. The military wing of Fatah, called Assifa *(Arabic: Storm)*, was headed by Wazir

With Fatah becoming the leading constituent of the Palestine Liberation Organization (PLO) [*qv*] in 1968, the importance of Assifa and Wazir rose. In the 1970s, as Fatah and Assifa, now based in Beirut [*qv*], became more active, carrying out numerous guerrilla operations, Wazir emerged as the right-hand man of Arafat, chairman of both Fatah and the PLO. Wazir backed Arafat in his continuing endeavor to impose PLO discipline and a centralized military command on the various PLO constituents without alienating any of them. After the expulsion of Fatah and the PLO from Beirut in 1982, Wazir moved with the party headquarters to Tunis, Tunisia. With the Palestinian fighters scattered in seven Arab countries, his task became onerous. On the other hand, his reputation as a conciliator remained unimpaired.

Following the outbreak of the intifada [*qv*] in December 1987, Wazir worked closely with the PLO's Occupied Homeland Directorate to give direction to the uprising. He ensured the success of the United National Leadership of the Uprising [*qv*]. He thus became a prime target for those in the Israeli government who felt that by eliminating him they would undermine the intifada, which Israel had failed to achieve so far. Hence, Wazir was assassinated by a Mossad [*qv*] hit team in April 1988 at his Tunis home. He was buried in Damascus [*qv*].

Weizman, Ezer (1924–): *Israeli military leader and politician; president, 1993–* Born into a prominent Jewish family in Caesarea, Palestine [*qv*], Weizman enrolled in the Royal Air Force during the Second World War and became a pilot. Following demobilization, he joined Irgun [*qv*]. During the

1948–49 Arab-Israeli War [*qv*] he was one of the first Israeli pilots. After the war he became an officer in the Israeli air force, rising to commander of the air force, 1958–66. Under his command, the air force prepared its plan to destroy the air power of its Arab neighbors, which it implemented efficiently during the June 1967 Arab-Israeli War [*qv*]. Weizman was appointed appointed chief of operations of the Israel Defense Forces.

When Weizman realized in 1969 that there was no chance of becoming chief of staff, he resigned and joined Gahal [*qv*]. Elected to the Knesset [*qv*], he became minister of transport in the national unity cabinet from 1969–70. When Gahal left the government in August 1970 in protest against the majority decision to accept a cease-fire in the War of Attrition [*qv*], Weizman followed suit. He was elected chairman of the executive committee of Gahal, a position he held until he fell out with the party leader, Menachem Begin [*qv*], in late 1972.

Weizman was persuaded to return to politics in early 1977, when he was appointed head of the Likud [*qv*] election headquarters. Likud won and Weizman became defense minister from 1977–80. He played an important role in the peace talks with Egypt. When the Palestinian autonomy provisions in the Camp David Accords [*qv*] were not implemented by the deadline of May 1980, he resigned, hoping the government would fall. It did not.

In the 1984 election his group, Yahad *(Hebrew: Together)*, won three seats. The stalemated election result gave him the chance to choose the next premier. Weizman opted for Shimon Peres [*qv*], who headed the subsequent national unity government, in which Weizman became minister without portfolio and a member of the inner political cabinet. Yahad joined Labor [*qv*].

Weizman headed the Labor election headquarters in 1988, but failed to repeat his 1977 success for Likud. In the next national unity cabinet, Weizman became minister of science and a member of the inner political cabinet. In early 1990, following a revelation by Premier Yitzhak Shamir [*qv*] that Weizman had violated official policy and law by meeting a Palestine Liberation Organization (PLO) [*qv*] official in Geneva, he resigned. Three years later, after the Labor-led government had lifted the ban on the PLO, Weizman was elected president of Israel. He resigned prematurely in 2000 after revelations that he had received $300,000 in undeclared cash gifts from two foreign businessmen during 1985-93.

West Bank (of the Jordan River): *Palestinian Territory* Area: 2,297 sq. miles/5,949 sq. km, including enlarged East Jerusalem (27 sq. miles/69 sq. km). Pop., excluding enlarged East Jerusalem [*qv*]: 2.3 million Palestinians (2003, est.), 220,000 Jewish settlers in 188 settlements. In the 1948–49 Arab-Israeli War [*qv*], Jordan's army managed to retain an enclave on the west bank of the River Jordan [*qv*], including the eastern part of Jerusalem [*qv*]. Egypt's army held the semidesert Gaza Strip [*qv*]. Together the two territories comprised about half of the area allocated to the Palestinian Arabs by the United Nations partition plan of November 1947. Jordan annexed the West Bank, including East Jerusalem, in April 1950. In the June 1967 Arab-Israeli War [*qv*], Israel captured the West Bank and Gaza. The population figures, according to a census taken in September 1967, were: West Bank,

589,000, Gaza 380,800. The military occupation of these territories was nominally changed in 1981 to "civil administration" working under military commanders. Jordan continued to pay its civil servants in the West Bank, and with Jordanian banks functioning in the territory, the Jordanian dinar was legal tender.

In 1968 militant Jews established their presence in the center of Hebron [*qv*]. They won the approval of the Labor [*qv*] government two years later, when they set a colony, called Kiryat Arba, near Hebron. In August 1973 the ruling Labor Party formally reversed its policy of merely holding on to the Arab Territories until the Arab states were ready to negotiate peace with it directly and adopted the Galili Document, which allowed Jewish individuals and public bodies to purchase land in the Occupied Arab Territories [*qv*] and the government to supplement the hitherto privately funded settlement program.

Once Jordan had accepted the decision of the Arab League [*qv*] summit in October–November 1974 that the Palestine Liberation Organization (PLO) [*qv*] was the sole and legitimate representative of the Palestinian people, its legal position in the West Bank became tenuous. The local elections held in April 1976 in the territory showed that almost all of the twenty-four mayors were supporters in varying degrees of the Palestine National Front, a front organization of the PLO, which was banned. By May 1977, when Labor was replaced by Likud [*qv*] as the leading governing coalition partner, there were thirty-two Jewish settlements in the West Bank, most of them authorized.

The Camp David Accords between Israel and Egypt [*qv*] in September 1978 included an agreement for autonomy for the Palestinians in the West Bank and Gaza to be implemented by 26 May 1980. Since the PLO was not party to these talks and wanted nothing less than a Palestinian state, this arrangement was stillborn.

Israel indefinitely postponed the local elections due in April 1980. The number of Jewish settlements continued to increase, and the existing ones grew more populous. The Palestinian Intifada [qv], which started in Gaza in December 1987, spread to the West Bank. In July 1988 Jordan cut its ties with the territory. The seizure and/or purchase of land by Israel and Jewish individuals and organizations continued so that by the time the Oslo Accord I [qv] was signed in September 1993, over half of the land had passed into Israeli or Jewish hands. Two years later the PLO and Israel signed the Oslo Accord II [qv], specifying Israeli troop withdrawal from seven cities, joint Palestinian-Israeli control of 450 Palestinian villages, and continued Israeli control of Jewish settlements. This happened in late 1995, except in Hebron [qv]. However, the existing 128 Jewish settlements were expanded and new ones established, the chief source of the Palestinian disaffection with the Oslo Accords. Following the eruption of the Second Intifada [qv] in September 2000, relations between Israel and the Palestinians soured. The situation worsened after the election of Ariel Sharon [qv] as Israeli prime minister in February 2001 on the platform of expanding Jewish settlement on the West Bank. As the number of protesting Palestinians killed by the Israeli military rose and Islamist Palestinians resorted increasingly to suicide bombings, Israel reoccupied the West Bank towns and cities in April 2002. Aside from brief and intermittent evacuation of the Palestinian urban centers, this reoccupation continued.

West Jerusalem: Area: 13 sq. miles/34 sq. km in 1948, 20 sq. miles /54 sq. km in 1993; pop. 651,000 (2002, est.). West Jerusalem, captured by Israeli forces in the 1948–49 Arab-Israeli War [qv] and retained by Israel, measured 13 sq. miles/34 sq. km.

In December 1949 Israel moved its capital to West Jerusalem, a move not recognized by the international community. Following its victory in the Six-Day War [qv], Israel added a vastly enlarged East Jerusalem [qv] to West Jerusalem on 28 June 1967 by extending its laws to the eastern sector. Additions in March 1985 and May 1993 expanded the area covered by West Jerusalem to 20 sq. miles/54 sq. km. Virtually all of its residents were Jewish.

West Syriac rite: *Christian rite* The West Syriac rite, initially called the Antiochene rite—the seminal system of liturgical practices and customs for almost all Eastern rites—originated in the patriarchate of Antioch, and is so called to distinguish it from the East Syriac rite [qv]. The liturgy of Saint James, a derivative of the Jerusalem-Antiochene rite, is the basis of the liturgy for the Syrian Orthodox [qv], Syrian Catholics [qv], and Maronite Catholics [qv].

Western hostages (in Lebanon): *see* Hostage taking and hostages.

Western Wall: *see* Wailing Wall.

White Guard (Saudi Arabia): *see* National Guard (Saudi Arabia).

White Revolution (Iran): In early January 1963 Muhammad Reza Shah Pahlavi [qv] launched a six-point socioeconomic reform package called the White Revolution. It consisted of agrarian reform, forest nationalization, the sale of public sector factories to pay compensation to landlords for land above the official ceiling, votes for women, profit-sharing in industry, and the eradication of illiteracy. According to official figures it was endorsed by 99.9 percent of those participating in a referendum on it on 25 January.

Opposition to the White Revolution, emanating primarily from hostility to the monarchical regime, came from both the secularist National Front [qv] and militant Muslim clerics. The latter were incensed by the shah's threat to amend the 1962 Land Reform Act to include lands belonging to the religious trusts [qv], which were managed by the clergy. Street protest was encouraged by Ayatollah Ruhollah Khomeini [qv], who described the White Revolution as phony. The unrest reached a peak in early June 1963 and culminated in a nationwide uprising in which many thousands of people were said to have been killed by the security forces. Khomeini was deported.

The Shah celebrated the tenth anniversary of the White Revolution in January 1973 by announcing that the National Iranian Oil Company would take over the ownership and all operation of the Western oil consortium that had been running the petroleum industry since 1954.

Whitsunday: *see* Pentecost.

World Islamic Front for Jihad against Crusaders and Jews: Official title: *Al Jabah al Islamiya al Alamiyah li Qital al Yahud wa al Salibiyin* At their base in Afghanistan, Osama bin Laden [qv] of Al Qaida [qv], Ayman al Zawahiri [qv] of Al Jihad al Islami [qv], Abu Yasser Rifia Ahmad Taha of al Gamaat al Islamiya [qv], Mir Hamza of Jamiat al Ulama (Pakistan), and Fazl ul Rahman of Harkat Al Jihad, (Bangladesh), announced the formation of the World Islamic Front for Jihad against Crusaders and Jews—or the World Islamic Front for Jihad (WIFFJ) for short—in February 1998.

In their communiqué they referred to America's continuing aggression against the Iraqi people—using the Arabian Peninsula [qv] as the staging post for the bombing of Iraq [qv]—as their evidence of the American occupation of the Peninsula since the 1991 Gulf War [qv]. Having caused the death of one million Iraqis through economic sanctions, Washington was intent on fragmenting and destroying Iraq. Its aims were to advance the interests of Israel [qv]; divert attention away from Israel's occupation of Jerusalem [qv] and its murder of the Palestinians [qv]; destroy Iraq; and fragment large Muslim countries like Saudi Arabia [qv], Egypt [qv], and Sudan into mini-states in order to ensure Israel's survival and the continued American occupation of the Arabian Peninsula. Committing of such crimes and sins by the Americans was tantamount to a declaration of war on Allah, Prophet Muhammad, and Muslims [qv].

Therefore, the communiqué added, "The ruling to kill the Americans and their allies—civilians and military—is an individual duty for every Muslim who can do it in any country in which it is possible to do it in, in order to liberate the al Aqsa Mosque [in Jerusalem] and the Holy Mosque [in Mecca (qv)] from their grip, and for their armies to leave all the lands of Islam [qv], defeated, and unable to threaten any Muslim." It called upon Muslim *ulama* [qv], leaders, young believers, and soldiers to attack the American troops and their allies and displace those Muslim regimes that were supporting them.

In March, the forty-member Council of Senior Ulama of Afghanistan met to debate the presence of the American troops in the Arabian Peninsula, and decided that the WIFFJ's call to jihad [qv] against America and Israel was in line with the Sharia [qv].

World Muslim League (Official title: *Arabic: Rabitat al Alam al Mussalmeen*): Propaganda issued by Egypt [qv] under President Gamal Abdul Nasser [qv] against the Saudi royal family led Crown Prince Faisal ibn Abdul Aziz [qv] to establish the World Muslim League (WML) in Geneva in 1962. Its function was to hold seminars and conferences on Islam [qv], and to generally act as a mouthpiece of Saudi Arabia in its interpretation of Islam. Its charter stated that the allegiance of the Muslim world should be to the Islamic doctrine and the overall interests of the Muslim *umma* [qv], above allegiance to nationalism or any other "ism." Faisal employed many exiled members of the Egyptian Muslim Brotherhood [qv] at the WML.

After the founding of the Islamic Conference Organization (ICO) [qv] in 1969, headquartered in Jiddah [qv], the WML was moved to Mecca [qv]. It remained tied to the House of Saud [qv] and reflected the official policies of Saudi Arabia.

During the 1990–91 Kuwait crisis, when Iraq alleged that infidel troops in Saudi Arabia had defiled the holiest shrines of Islam in Mecca and Medina [qv], the WML pointed out that the conflict along the Saudi–Kuwaiti border was 900 miles/1,500 km from the holy sanctuaries. The WML-sponsored conference of 350 Muslim *ulama* [qv] from eighty countries in Mecca stated that since the Saudi government had invited foreign troops for self-defense, its action was in line with the Sharia [qv]. But its proposal to form an Islamic force under ICO supervision, to which its members could appeal in the event of armed conflict among them, was not implemented.

World Union of Zionist Revisionists: *see* Revisionist Zionists.

World Zionist Organization: Following the adoption of a new constitution in 1960, the Zionist Organization (ZO) [qv], established in 1897, became the World Zionist Organization (WZO). At its founding by the First Zionist Congress [qv] in Basle, Switzerland, the Zionist Organization adopted a program summarized thus: "Zionism [qv] strives to create for the Jewish people a home in Palestine [qv] secured by public law." It elected Theodor Herzl (1860–1904), chief ideologue of political Zionism, as president. Herzl based the organization in Vienna, Austria, where he lived. The fifteen-strong executive committee ran such departments as political (meaning external affairs), information, land and development (in Palestine), immigration and absorption (in Palestine), and Torah [qv] education and culture (in the Diaspora [qv]).

The Fifth Zionist Congress in 1901 set up the Jewish National Fund (JNF) [qv] under the Zionist Organization's land and development section to finance the (communal) purchase of land in Palestine. Most of the Hovevei Zion *(Hebrew: Lovers of Zion)* societies, active in Russia, affiliated to the organization. When David Wolffsohn succeeded Herzl as president in 1905, he moved the headquarters to Cologne, Germany, his home base.

The Seventh Zionist Congress in 1905 rejected Britain's offer of land in Uganda for the Jewish homeland, and those who disagreed with the decision left the organization. The conflict between those wanted to focus on securing a Jewish homeland through diplomatic means and those who wanted to concentrate on colonizing Palestine was resolved by deciding to work on both fronts simultaneously, with the tenth Zionist Congress in 1911 electing Otto Warburg, an advocate of "synthetic Zionism." The headquarters moved to Warburg's home base, Berlin. The organization opened a Palestine Office in Jaffa [qv]. In 1915, during the First World War, the headquarters was moved to neutral Copenhagen in Denmark. In Palestine there was increasing cooperation between socialist pioneers and the Zionist Organization's financial institutions. Upon Chaim Weizmann's election as president in 1921, the headquarters moved to his base, London.

Following the 1922 British mandate, providing for a "Jewish agency" in Palestine to cooperate with the government of Palestine in establishing a Jewish national home there, Britain gave this role to the Zionist Organization, which appointed the Zionist executive in Palestine with its own chairman—Nahum Sokolow, based in Jerusalem [qv]—for the purpose. At Chaim Weizmann's initiative, the sixteenth Zionist Congress in 1929 established a proper Jewish Agency for Palestine [qv] with its own executive, consisting of an equal number of Zionists and non-Zionists—i.e., those who supported the idea of a Jewish national home in Palestine but did not subscribe to political Zionism.

After the Eighteenth Zionist Congress in 1933 had resolved that "in all Zionist matters discipline in regard of the Zionist Organization must take precedence over the discipline of any other body," the Revisionist Zionists [qv] left. They returned to the Zionist Organization at the Twenty-second Congress in December 1946, which—taking its cue from the resolution of the American Zionist Congress in May 1942 at the Biltmore Hotel, New York—demanded the formation of an independent Jewish state in all of Palestine. After the Congress had failed to reelect Weizmann president, the meetings of the Zionist Organization executive were cochaired by Nahum Goldmann and Berl Locker for the next ten years.

In Palestine, with the resignation of the last non-Zionist from the Jewish Agency executive in 1947, the distinction between the Zionist executive in Palestine and the executive of the Jewish Agency for Palestine disappeared, David Ben-Gurion [qv] being the chairman of both. His appointment as head of the London-based Zionist Organization's defense department enabled him to bring the various Jewish armed organizations in Palestine under a single command on the eve of the 1948–49 Arab-Israeli War [qv].

Following the Twenty-third Zionist Congress, held in Jerusalem in 1951, the headquarters was transferred from London to Jerusalem. The Zionist Organization continued to function as before, except that its departmental heads now worked in conjunction with their counterparts in the Israeli civil service. In between the congresses the Zionist General Council, reflecting the composition of the latest congress, functioned as a supervisory body. Its size increased from 25 in 1921 to 129 in 1968. It was the General Council that adopted a new constitution in 1960. Goldmann continued as president of the renamed Zionist Organization until 1968.

After that the highest office of the World Zionist Organization was held by the chairman of the Zionist Executive, Louis Pincus.

Wye River Memorandum (1998): Following the mediation by U.S. President Bill Clinton (r. 1993–2001), an agreement hammered out by the Israeli and Palestinian delegations at a series of meetings at the Wye Plantation, Maryland, Israeli Prime Minister Benjamin Netanyahu [qv] and Palestinian leader Yasser Arafat [qv] signed a document—called Wye Memorandum/Accord—on 15 October 1998 to facilitate the implementation of the Washington Accord [qv] of September 1995. This involved Israel transferring a further 13 percent of the West Bank to the Palestinian Authority (PA) [qv] in two stages, and entering into immediate final status talks with the Palestinians with the aim of achieving an agreement by 4 May 1999. In return, the PA agreed to combat terrorism and confiscate illegal weapons, and the Palestine Liberation Organization [qv] pledged to reaffirm the nullification of those provisions of the Palestine National Charter [qv] that were inconsistent with the provisions of the 1993 Oslo Accords [qv].

Y

Yamani, Ahmad Zaki (1930–): *Saudi oil expert and politician* Born into the family of a religious judge in Mecca [qv], Yamani studied law, first at Cairo University and then at New York and Harvard Universities in the United States.

In 1958 Crown Prince Faisal ibn Abdul Aziz [qv] appointed Yamani as adviser to the cabinet. Two years later he was promoted to minister of state, and in 1962 to minister of petroleum and mineral resources. In the mid-1960s he became chairman of the state-owned General Petroleum and Mineral Organization and a director of the Arabian American Oil Company (Aramco).

As a pragmatist, Yamani tried to persuade King Faisal, critical of the United States' staunchly pro-Israeli stance, to cooperate with the United States in formulating Saudi policies on oil output and pricing. His efforts were successful, and Yamani became a close adviser of the monarch.

Yamani served as secretary-general of the Organization of Petroleum Exporting Countries (OPEC) [qv] from 1968–69. He backed Faisal's strategy to use the oil weapon during the October 1973 Arab-Israeli War [qv], thus endorsing his newly formed perception that petroleum could no longer be divorced from Middle Eastern politics. Equally, Yamani supported Faisal's decision to lift the Arab oil embargo [qv] against the United States in March 1974, even though the conditions requiring Israel's evacuation of the Occupied Arab Territories [qv] and the granting of Palestinian rights had not been met.

On 21 December 1975, when OPEC oil ministers, meeting in Vienna, were taken hostage by the commandos led by Ilich Ramirez Sanchez—alias Carlos Martinez—Yamani was one of their chief targets. He was freed two days later in Algiers after a clandestine deal involving between $5 million and $50 million had been made between Saudi Arabia and Martinez.

Yamani lobbied hard, and successfully, to maintain OPEC's share of global output, even if that resulted in lower oil prices. He thus became leader of the pro-Western camp within OPEC. He implemented the policy of Saudi Arabia, acting in tandem with Kuwait, to produce above its OPEC quota and thus depress the price of oil in order to impair Iran's ability to continue the Iran-Iraq War [qv]. This cut the price by nearly two-thirds between December 1985 and July 1986, to $10 a barrel. In August, yielding to pressure from other OPEC members, Yamani agreed to fresh OPEC output figures, which raised the price to $14–16 a barrel. In early October 1986, after meeting the Iranian oil minister in Riyadh [qv], King Fahd ibn Abdul Aziz [qv] backed the idea of a fixed price of $18 a barrel. When Yamani refused to endorse this, Fahd dismissed him on 29 October.

Yamani retired from public life and devoted himself to private business, including the Center for Global Energy Studies, London. In the mid-1990s, with political and financial crisis brewing in Saudi Arabia, Yamani, based in Jiddah [qv], became a center of attraction for disaffected businessmen and religious leaders.

Yassin, Ahmad (1936–): *Palestinian leader* Born into a land-owning household in Jora in Palestine [qv], a village near the northern border of what later became the Gaza Strip [qv], Yassin and his family sought shelter in a refugee camp in the Gaza Strip during the First Arab-Israeli War (1848–49) [qv]. He joined the clandestine Muslim Brotherhood (Egypt) [qv] in the mid-1950s, a few years after suffering crippling injuries in a sporting accident, which left him wheelchair-bound. He worked as a schoolteacher in Gaza City [qv] from 1957 to 1964, when

he enrolled as a student of English at Ain Shams University, Cairo [qv]. Following repression of the Brotherhood in Egypt and Gaza in 1966, he was imprisoned.

After the Gaza Strip was occupied by Israel in 1967, he was released. He resumed teaching as well as leading the reorganized Muslim Brotherhood. He urged his followers to purge society of social-moral ills, arguing that Islamization of society was a precondition for the establishment of an Islamic state in a liberated Palestine, thus skirting the contentious issue of resistance to the Israeli occupation. In the autumn of 1973 the Israeli military authorities issued a license to Yassin to establish the Islamic Center to run social, religious, and welfare institutions, thus entitling it to receive *zakat* [qv], religious tax, from the believers. With the secular Palestine Liberation Organization [qv] emerging as a powerful force in the Occupied Territories [qv] from the mid-1970s, Israel decided to encourage the growth of the Islamic Center, with the military governor of the Gaza Strip, Brigadier General Yitzhak Segev, funding the mosques run by the Islamic Center.

In 1983 Israel began altering this policy partly because the Islamic Jihad [qv], a recently established Islamist organization, had resorted to pursing a militantly anti-Israeli stance. In 1984 Israel arrested Yassin for illegal possession of arms and sentenced him to a thirteen-year jail term. But in 1985, as part of a prisoner exchange deal between Israel and the Popular Front for the Liberation of Palestine-General Command [qv], Yassin was released.

He resumed social work in Gaza. But when the intifada [qv] erupted in late 1987, Yassin and his colleagues in the Islamic

Center could no longer resist pressure from their nationalist grass roots to engage in a political struggle against their Israeli occupiers. The result was the founding of Hamas [*qv*] as the activist arm of the Islamic Center/Muslim Brotherhood. Yassin was arrested in 1989 and sentenced to fifteen years imprisonment for conspiring to abduct two Israeli soldiers. As a result of another prisoner exchange in the wake of Mossad's failed attempt to assassinate, in Amman, Khalid Mashaal, a leader of Hamas in Jordan, in 1997, Yassin was freed in 1997.

He resumed his leadership of Hamas, reiterating that the organization would continue to resist Israeli occupation by all means. He was put under house arrest after he had criticized the Palestinian Authority (PA) [*qv*] for signing the Wye River Memorandum [*qv*] in October 1998. But as the Wye Memorandum unraveled, relations between Yassin and the PA thawed. With the outbreak of the Second Intifada [*qv*] in September 2000 and the subsequent pulverizing of the PA by Israel, the differences between Yassin and the PA narrowed.

Yazidis: *A religious group* The origin of the Yazidi doctrine—an amalgam of pagan, Sabaean, Shamanistic, Manichaean, Zoroastrian [*qv*], Jewish [*qv*], Christian [*qv*], and Islamic [*qv*] elements—is unknown. Totaling about 100,000, Yazidis are to be found in northeastern Syria, northern Iraq, and the Trans-Caucasian republics. Though they often speak a Kurdish [*qv*] dialect, their scriptures are written in Arabic [*qv*].

Their principal divine figure is the Peacock Angel, the supreme angel of the seven angels who ruled the universe after it had been created by God. Violation of divine laws can be expiated by the transmigration of souls. Yazidis believe that their chief saint, Shaikh Adi, a Muslim mystic in the twelfth century, acquired divine status through the transmigration of his soul. His tomb, situated north of Mosul [*qv*], is the site of an annual pilgrimage.

Though Yazidis do not believe in evil, sin, and the devil, they are often described as devil worshipers.

Yemen:

Official name: Republic of Yemen

Capital: Sanaa [*qv*]

Area: 182,280 sq. miles/472,100 sq. km, excluding 23,070 sq. miles/59,770 sq. km claimed by North Yemen along the undemarcated eastern frontier with Saudi Arabia

Population: 18,885,000 (2002, est.), with 79 percent in (old) North Yemen [*qv*] and 21 percent in (old) South Yemen [*qv*]

Gross domestic product: $6.7 billion (2001)

National currencies: Yemeni Rial (YR); YR1 = US$0.006 = £0.004 = EUR 0.0065 (2001)

Form of government: republic, president elected by popular vote

Official language: Arabic [*qv*]

Official religion: Islam [*qv*]

Administrative system: Yemen consists of seventeen provinces.

Constitution: The Yemeni constitution, based on a document endorsed by North Yemen [*qv*] and South Yemen [*qv*] in 1981, was approved by a referendum in May 1991, a year after the proclamation of the united Republic of Yemen. Describing the republic as "an independent, indivisible state," it specifies Islam and Arabic as the state religion and state language, respectively. The Sharia

[*qv*] is the primary source of legislation. Power rests with the people, who exercise it through elections and referendums. The state guarantees freedom of expression and assembly within the law. The republic's economy is founded on safeguarding private property and assuring Islamic social justice, while striving to develop the state sector as the main means of production.

In September 1994, twenty-nine articles were added to the constitution and fifty-two articles were amended. Further changes, adopted by the lower house of parliament in November 2000, were approved by a referendum three months later. According to the revised document, the president is to be elected for seven years by universal suffrage. He is empowered to nominate the vice president. He first appoints the prime minister and then, advised by him, the rest of the cabinet. The legislative power rests with the lower chamber of parliament, the House of Representatives, elected for six years by universal suffrage. By contrast, the upper chamber, the Consultative Council, is nominated by the president. The revised constitution reaffirms a multi party democracy.

Ethnic composition (2000): Arab, 99 percent; other, 1 percent.

High officials:

President: Ali Abdullah Salih [*qv*], 1999–

Vice president: Abd Rabbo Mansur al Hadi, 1999–

Prime minister: Abdul Qadir Bajammal, 2001–

Speaker of the House of Representatives: Shaikh Abdullah Hussein al Ahmar [*qv*], 1997–

History (since ca. 1900):

North Yemen: (Before the unification of North and South Yemen in 1990) Official name: Yemen Arab Republic; area: 77,220 sq. miles/200,000 sq. km; pop.: 9,274,000 (1986 census).

At the turn of the twentieth century North Yemen, under the nominal suzerainty of the Ottoman Turks, was ruled by Imam Yahya Hamid al Din (1869–1948). By rebelling against the Ottoman Empire in 1911, he obtained wider powers. During the First World War he was loyal to the Ottomans. With the collapse of the Ottoman Empire in 1918, North Yemen became fully independent, and Imam Yahya aspired to re-create the historic Greater Yemen. In 1925 he regained Hodeida port, which had been occupied in 1921 by the ruler of the neighboring Asir region with British connivance. The resulting dispute over Asir culminated in war in 1934 between North Yemen and Saudi Arabia, started by the latter. Having overpowered the North Yemenis and captured Hodeida port, the Saudis accepted a cease-fire mainly because British, French, and Italian warships rushed to Hodeida, intent on curbing Saudi expansionism. The Treaty of Muslim Friendship and Arab Fraternity [*qv*] returned to Imam Yahya nearly half of the area he had lost in war, including the southern part of the Tihama coastal plain—leaving the upland Najran and Asir in Saudi hands.

Following an abortive coup in February 1948, which resulted in the murder of his father, Ahmad ibn Yahya [*qv*] assumed supreme power. When his ambition to re-create Greater Yemen at the expense of the British Protectorate of Aden was frustrated by London, in 1956 he signed a mutual defense pact with Egypt, then ruled by President Gamal Abdul Nasser [*qv*]. In 1958 he formed a loose federation of North Yemen and the United Arab Republic (UAR) [*qv*], called the Union of Arab States. By then he had concluded friendship treaties with Moscow, Peking, and other communist capitals. After the breakup of the UAR in September 1961, he cut his ties with Egypt and began attacking Nasser, who reciprocated. Soon after Imam Ahmad's death in September 1962, a military coup led by Brigadier General Abdullah Sallal [*qv*] ended the 1,064-year rule of the al Rassi dynasty.

A North Yemeni Civil War [*qv*] broke out. The republicans, deriving their major support from the Shafei (Sunni [*qv*]) tribes inhabiting the coastal plain and the southern hills, were aided by Egypt, while the royalists, with a solid base among the Zaidi [*qv*] tribes in the north, were helped by the Saudis. In 1967 Sallal tried to regain the area lost in the war, but failed, partly because of the June 1967 Arab-Israeli War [*qv*], which diverted Egypt's resources. Cairo decided to withdraw its forces from North Yemen, and this weakened the position of Sallal. He was overthrown in November 1967 during his visit to Moscow by forces led by Abdul Rahman al Iryani [*qv*].

In March 1970, following complex negotiations, the civil war ended and a governmental system—based on a presidential council and a nominated consultative council—emerged. The first post-civil war president, al Iryani, was deposed in 1974; the second and third, Ibrahim Hamdi [*qv*] and Ahmad Hussein Ghashmi [*qv*], were assassinated in October 1977 and June 1978, respectively. Ali Abdullah Salih, deputy commander in chief, succeeded Ghashmi. He legitimized his power by gaining the backing of the People's Constituent Assembly (CPA). In October 1980 Salih replaced Premier Abdul Aziz Abdul Ghani with Abdul Karim Iryani to placate leftist opposition at home. In October 1981 he established a 1000-member General People's Congress [*qv*], partly by appointment and partly by indirect elections, and two months later he signed an agreement with South Yemen on unity.

Oil production, which began modestly in 1984, picked up rapidly. Salih maintained friendly relations with Saudi Arabia, the chief paymaster of North Yemen, while cultivating the leftist South Yemen by periodically renewing the 1981 agreement on eventual unity between the two Yemens. Following his reelection as president in 1988, he responded positively to the idea of an alliance of North Yemen with Egypt, Iraq, and Jordan, which materialized as the Arab Cooperation Council [*qv*] in early 1989.

South Yemen: (Before the unification of North and South Yemen in 1990) Official name: People's Democratic Republic of Yemen; area: 130,070 sq. miles/336,870 sq. km; pop.: 2,121,000 (1986, est.).

At the turn of the twentieth century, Britain ruled the Aden Colony through a governor attached to the India Office in London, and the Aden Protectorate, consisting of twenty-three provinces, through local rulers. After the First World War, Britain frustrated Imam Yahya's attempt to annex parts of the Aden Protectorate. It split the Protectorate from the India Office in 1927 and from the Aden Colony ten years later. In 1947 it introduced a fully nominated legislative assembly in the Aden Colony. In 1962 it offered a plan to knit together the Colony and the Protectorate into the Federation of South Arabia. This was opposed among others by the National Front for the Liberation of South Yemen

[*qv*], popularly called the NLF. It achieved power in late 1967 by launching a successful armed struggle against the British.

Following the founding of the People's Republic of South Yemen, differences between moderate and radical elements within the NLF came to the fore in June 1969, resulting in the victory of the hardliners. A new, radical constitution was promulgated in November 1970. By the time the sixth congress of the NLF was held in March 1975, the regime felt secure. In October the NLF decided to widen its base by forming the United Political Organization-National Front (UPO-NF) to be reconstituted in 1978. Following the assassination of North Yemeni President Ahmad Ghashmi in June 1978, there was fighting in Aden [*qv*], which President Salim Rubai Ali [*qv*] lost.

In October the UPO-NF was transformed into the Yemen Socialist Party (YSP) [*qv*]. The radical policies of Abdul Fattah Ismail [*qv*], chairman of the Presidential Council, did not go down well with his erstwhile ally Ali Nasser Muhammad [*qv*]. In April 1980 Ismail was forced to resign and go into exile in Moscow, leaving Muhammad as the sole leader. Five years later Ismail returned, following mediation by the Communist Party of the Soviet Union. He was appointed secretary-general of the YSP's central committee, a position without power. In January 1986 the rapprochement broke down. In the subsequent fighting Ismail lost his life, but his radical side won, and Ali Salim al Beidh [*qv*] emerged as leader of the YSP.

With the presidency going to a technocrat, Haidar al Attas, al Beidh emerged as the real power wielder. He began to moderate his radical stance and introduced economic and political reform—especially after Moscow cut its aid from $400 million in 1988 to $50 million in 1989. This accelerated the drive toward unification with North Yemen, which occurred the following year.

Republic of Yemen: (After unification of North and South Yemen in 1990) Upon unification on 22 May 1990, Salih became president and al Beidh vice president of the Republic of Yemen. The five-member Presidential Council consisted of three North Yemeni and two South Yemeni leaders. However, the two constituents maintained separate armed forces and broadcasting facilities. By September more than thirty new political groups had formed, the Islamic Yemeni Islah Group (YIG) [*qv*] being the most important.

Since Yemen—the only Arab country on the United Nations Security Council—refused to follow Saudi Arabia into the U.S.-led coalition against Iraq after its occupation of Kuwait in August 1990, Riyadh retaliated by withdrawing the special treatment accorded to Yemeni nationals. The resulting exodus of 850,000 Yemenis from Saudi Arabia depressed the already troubled Yemeni economy. Yemen voted against U.N. Security Council Resolution 678 (authorizing member states to use "all necessary means" to reverse Iraq's evacuation of Kuwait) in November 1990. In early January 1991, Yemen's peace plan to avert a war against Iraq failed to prevent the Second Gulf War [*qv*].

At home, voters endorsed the new constitution in May 1991. But the multiparty general election based on universal suffrage, the first of its kind in the Arabian Peninsula [*qv*] and promised within a year, did not take place until April 1993. Out of 301 parliamentary seats, the General People's Congress (GPC)—now turned into a political party—won over 40 percent, followed by the Yemeni Islah Group and the YSP. Ali Salim al Beidh, the leader of the YSP, which had so far shared power with the GPC, objected to President Salih co-opting the YIG into the new coalition government. Blaming Salih for the lack of progress on unification, al Beidh left Sanaa for Aden in August, setting the scene for a conflict that escalated into the Yemeni Civil War [qv] in April 1994, during which al Beidh declared South Yemen independent. South Yemen's independence was not recognized by any other country, and al Beidh's side lost in July. The victorious Salih and the GPC consolidated their power and Yemeni unity.

The next year, Salih was elevated to chairman of the GPC, a new post. In 1997 the GPC improved its parliamentary strength by sixty-four seats, partly due to the boycott of the polls by the Yemen Socialist Party, which had fifty-six deputies in the old legislature. But that did not lessen the problem the new government faced when trying to implement economic liberalization, prescribed by the International Monetary Fund, by phasing out subsidies on basic necessities and fuel. Also, the outlying mountainous regions under effective rule by the tribal chiefs remained out of governmental control. Nonetheless, in the first popular poll for the presidency in 1999, Salih secured more than 96 percent of the ballots. The next year, he called the first ever local elections. In April 2001 he promoted foreign minister Abdul Qadir Bajammal as the prime minister.

In foreign policy, Yemen strengthened its ties with the United States. It conducted its first joint military exercise with the U.S.

forces in November 1998. But that did not inhibit it from condemning Washington's Operation Desert Fox [qv] against Iraq in December. However, its earlier agreement to let the U.S. Navy use Aden for refueling went ahead in 1999. On 12 October 2000 a harbor skiff, laden with explosives, and piloted by two suicide bombers, struck the USS *Cole*, refueling in Aden port, and killed seventeen sailors. The attack, claimed by the Islamic Army of Aden-Abyan, was believed to be linked to the Al Qaida [qv] network. The Yemeni government cooperated fully with Washington to track down the culprits.

Following the terrorist attacks on the United States in September 2001, cooperation between the two governments increased, with the American policymakers being aware that the mountainous terrain of Yemen, the homeland of the bin Ladens, was ideal for setting up terrorist training camps.

Legislature: The House of Representatives—People's Constituent Assembly made up of the 159-member of North Yemen, the 111-member Supreme People's Council of South Yemen, and 31 new members appointed by President Salih—functioned from May 1990 to April 1993, when fresh elections, based on universal suffrage, were held to the 301-strong chamber. The result was as follows: General People's Congress, 123; Yemeni Islah Group, 62; Yemen Socialist Party, 56; other parties, 13; independents, 47. The outcome of the parliamentary poll in April 1997 was General People's Congress, 187; Yemeni Islah Group, 53; other parties (except Yemen Socialist Party), 7; independents, 54.

Religious composition (2000): Muslim, 99.8 percent, of which Sunnis, 53 percent and (Zaidi) Shias [*qv*], 46.8 percent; other, 0.2 percent.

Yemen Arab Republic: *see* North Yemen under Yemen—History.

Yemen Socialist Party: *Political party in South Yemen and Yemen* The National Liberation Front–sponsored (NLF) [*qv*] unification congress, held in October 1975, decided to weld the NLF, the Vanguard Party (a Baathist group), and the Popular Democratic Union (a Communist group) to form the United Political Organization-National Front as a transitional body to graduate into the Yemen Socialist Party (YSP) in October 1978. It was a Marxist-Leninist vanguard party, committed to building scientific socialism in South Yemen. Its first secretary-general was Abdul Fattah Ismail [*qv*]. After his exile to Moscow in April, the post went to Ali Nasser Muhammad [*qv*]. Muhammad lost the January 1986 internecine fighting, and the party's top position went to Ali Salim al Beidh [*qv*]. Under his leadership the YSP began to moderate its policies, a trend accelerated by the collapse of the Moscow-led socialist bloc that followed the demolition of the Berlin Wall in late 1989, resulting in the party distancing itself from Marxism-Leninism and adopting a social-democratic program.

Following the unification of the two Yemens in May 1990, the YSP was allowed to function in former North Yemen. But it failed to gain support there. All of the fifty-six parliamentary seats it won in the April 1993 election were from former South Yemen. During the civil war in the spring of 1994, the YSP was divided on the question of declaring former South Yemen independent. After the defeat of Vice President al

Beidh and his followers in the conflict, the party's standing suffered.

Objecting to the voter registration irregularities, the YSP, led by Ali Salih Obad, and several other opposition groups, boycotted the 1997 general election. The party leaders continued to be the target of assassination by Islamist militants. It was not until 1998 that it was able to hold a national conference—after a gap of ten years—in the southern city of Dali, when it elected a new political bureau. And it was only in 2000 that it managed to convene a conference in Sanaa [*qv*].

Yemeni Civil War (1962–70): *see* North Yemeni Civil War.

Yemeni Civil War (1994): The failure of the North-based General People's Congress [*qv*] and the South-based Yemen Socialist Party (YSP) [*qv*] to win parliamentary seats across the old border in the April 1993 election sowed the seeds of a conflict that within a year culminated in a civil war. The graduated process of unification had allowed President Ali Abdullah Salih [*qv*] and Vice President Ali Salim al Beidh [*qv*] to retain their authority over the respective armed forces of North and South Yemen. But as a gesture of unification, some units from each army were posted away from their native region.

The Northern forces' attack on the Southern units at Dhamar and Amran in former North Yemen on 27 April signaled the start of a civil war. It also established the offensive strategy of the North, with the South put on the defensive, both militarily and politically. Efforts by the Arab League [*qv*], Egypt, and the U.N. Security Council to bring about a cease-fire failed as President Salih stuck rigidly to his slogan: "Unity or death!"

On 22 May 1994, the fourth anniversary of unification, al Beidh declared South Yemen independent, calling it the Democratic Republic of Yemen (DRY). Al Beidh put his pro-Saudi vice president, Shaikh Abdul Rahman Jifri, in charge of defending Aden [*qv*], while himself retreating to Mukalla, 375 miles/600 km to the east. The Southern leaders lobbied hard to win international recognition for the DRY, but failed. Even Saudi Arabia, which had backed their moves, equivocated, concentrating on securing a cease-fire through the U.N. Security Council, thus providing the DRY with breathing space. Salih was adamant on keeping outsiders out of what he insisted was "an internal Yemeni affair."

On the ground the Southerners put up stiff resistance, but when the attacking Northerners cut off Aden's water and electricity supplies, its fall became inevitable. The North's forces also captured Mukalla, and al Beidh and his close aides fled to Saudi Arabia. The conflict ended on 4 July with more than 35,000 casualties, including some 10,000 fatalities, although the government put the figure at 1,000.

One version of the events maintains that al Beidh, acting in collusion with Riyadh, began to escalate the political crisis in August 1993 as a preamble to a military coup against Salih. The purported plan was to use the South's contingents posted in Dhamar and Amran, backed by the militia of the Bakil tribal confederation, to besiege Sanaa [*qv*] on 5 May and overthrow Salih. But intelligence sources loyal to Salih got wind of the South's plans, and the Northern forces attacked the Southern units of Dhamar and Amran on 27 April.

Yemeni Islah Group: *Yemeni political party* Official title: *Al Tajami al Yemeni lil Islah* (The Yemeni Group for Reform). Following the legislation of political parties after the Yemeni unification in May 1990, the Islamic and Zaidi [*qv*] tribal forces combined to form the Yemeni Islah Group (YIG), led by Shaikh Abdullah Hussein al Ahmar [*qv*] and Shaikh Abdul Wahhab al Anisi. Objecting to the provision in the 1991 draft constitution that the Sharia [*qv*] was to be the main source of legislation, it demanded that the Sharia should be the sole source and urged a boycott of the referendum on the constitution. However, it fought the general election held under that constitution in April 1993 and won sixty-two seats, more than the number gained by the Yemen Socialist Party [*qv*].

President Ali Abdullah Salih [*qv*] included the YIG in the new coalition government, and the position of parliamentary speaker went to its leader, al Ahmar. In October Salih gave up one of the three General People's Congress [*qv*] seats on the five-member Presidential Council to the YIG to maintain its support, which became crucial during the Yemeni Civil War [*qv*] the following spring.

During and after the conflict, Islah members were active in attacking those aspects of life in former South Yemen they considered un-Islamic, including bars, women in jeans, and the government-owned brewery in Aden [*qv*]. In the 1997 parliamentary poll, the YIG secured fifty-three seats and its leader al Ahmar was reelected speaker of the House of Representatives. In the first ever local elections in April 2001, the YIG presented a challenge to the ruling General People's Congress [*qv*], but won only 22 percent of the vote. Nonetheless, the government implemented a 1992 law requiring incorporation of religious educational centers, run by the YIG, into the state educational system. This further soured relations between the YIG and the governing party.

Yemeni War (1972): The emergence of a hardline leftist government in South Yemen in mid-1969 alarmed North Yemen and Saudi Arabia. In cooperation with South Yemeni emigrés in North Yemen and Saudi Arabia, Riyadh and Sanaa went on an offensive against Aden by leading a series of attacks along the South Yemen border in September 1972. The Arab League [*qv*] mediated. The warning by Aden that the Soviet Union would not stand idly by if there were a full-fledged invasion of South Yemen dissuaded Saudi Arabia from intervening directly. With the Arab League's assistance, a truce went into effect on 28 October 1972, with the warring sides announcing, astonishingly, that the two Yemens had agreed to work toward economic and political unification.

Yemeni War (1979): The victory of the leftist faction over its rival within the ruling National Liberation Front (NLF) in South Yemen [*qv*] in June 1978, and South Yemen's alleged complicity in the assassination of North Yemeni President Ahmad Hussein Ghashmi [*qv*], led Saudi Arabia to urge the Arab League [*qv*] to impose sanctions against South Yemen. It did so in July. Relations between Aden and Sanaa deteriorated. With North Yemeni National Democratic Front (NDF) [*qv*] forces, aided by Aden, occupying areas along the border

with South Yemen, the two Yemens went to war in February 1979. On 22 February NDF fighters captured border towns and penetrated 12 miles/19 km inside North Yemen with the intention of cutting off the strategic Taiz-Sanaa highway. Riyadh put its own forces on alert and paid $387 million to the United States to airlift heavy weapons to North Yemen. A cease-fire was arranged by Syria and Iraq on 2 March.

Yemeni-British Treaty (1934): *see* Anglo-Yemeni Treaty (1934).

Yiddish language *(German: derivative of Judisch, Jewish):* A medieval German of the Middle Rhine region, developed under the influences of Hebrew [*qv*] and Slavic, Yiddish was spoken by most Ashkenazi [*qv*] Jews from the Middle Ages. Modern Yiddish, written in Hebrew characters and dating from about 1700, can be divided into Western Yiddish, now extinct, and Eastern Yiddish. The latter is subdivided into a northern dialect (Lithuania) and a southern one (from Poland to Rumania). Yiddish spelling was standardized by the Yiddish Scientific Institute, based in Vilnius, Lithuania, in 1937, when there were 10–12 million Yiddish speakers. Following the Holocaust during the Second World War, this number halved. Once predominant among West European and North American Jews, Yiddish is now rarely spoken by them outside of the Hassadic [*qv*] communities.

Yishuv *(Hebrew: Settlement):* The term Yishuv means the Jewish community in Palestine [*qv*], starting with the first *aliya* [*qv*] in 1882 and ending with the founding of Israel in May 1948. Used in contrast to the term *Diaspora* [*qv*], the Yishuv was viewed as the vanguard of world Jewry, laying the groundwork for the Jewish state in Palestine.

Yom Kippur *(Hebrew: Day of Atonement):* Observed on the tenth day of Tishri, the first month in the Jewish calendar [*qv*] and falling between early September and early October, Yom Kippur is the Sabbath [*qv*] of Sabbaths, a day of fasting and prayer for forgiveness of sins. Rabbinical tradition describes Yom Kippur as the day on which Moses came down from Mount Sinai with the second set of tablets of the Law and declared divine pardon for the sins of the Golden Calf. In ancient times the high priest was allowed to enter the inner sanctum of the Temple on this day, dressed in white linen, signifying purity and humility. On Yom Kippur, Jews are required to confess their ethical lapses and other human failings. The evening service concludes with the declaration: "Next year in Jerusalem [*qv*]."

Yom Kippur War (1973): *see* Arab-Israeli War IV (1973).

Z

Zahal: *(Hebrew: acronym of Zvai Haganah Le Israel, Defense Force for Israel): see* Military in Israel.

Zahedi, Fazlullah (1880–1963): *Iranian politician; prime minister, 1953–55* Born into a landlord family in Hamadan, Zahedi graduated from the Military Academy in Tehran [*qv*] in 1916. He joined the Cossack brigade, which participated in the successful campaign against the Soviet Republic of Gilan in 1921, and rose to the rank of major general during the reign of Reza Shah Pahlavi [*qv*].

Following Reza Shah's deposition in 1941 by Britain and the Soviet Union, and their occupation of Iran, the British arrested Zahedi for suspected pro-German activities in 1943. Elected senator in 1946, Zahedi undermined the coalition government of Premier Ahmad Qawam al Saltane. He was so opposed to the pro-British Premier Ali Razmara that he flirted with the National Front [*qv*], briefly becoming interior minister under the first government of Muhammad Mussadiq [*qv*] in 1951, before concluding that the monarchy and military would stand or fall together. He then turned against Mussadiq.

Under the guise of the Retired Officers Club, Zahedi organized the secret Committee to Save the Fatherland, consisting of the military officers retired by Mussadiq in 1952. By late July 1953 the Committee had become one of the two clandestine forces planning the overthrow of the Mussadiq government, the other being the U.S. Central Intelligence Agency (CIA). Before fleeing Iran on 16 August, Muhammad Reza Shah Pahlavi [*qv*] dismissed Mussadiq and appointed Zahedi, then underground, as prime minister. Three days later, as Mussadiq ordered the army and the police to restore order in Tehran, pro-shah troops arrived from Hamadan, a stronghold of Zahedi. Zahedi led an assault on Mussadiq's residence and captured him after a nine-hour battle.

A third of Premier Zahedi's cabinet were generals. Together with the shah, Zahedi followed a three-pronged policy toward the opposition: annihilation of the Tudeh Party [*qv*], repression of the National Front [*qv*], and surveillance of independent-minded clerics. He resumed links with Britain and handed over the country's petroleum industry to a Western oil consortium. Zahedi was dismissed from his office in April 1955, a sign of the Shah's growing confidence.

Zaidis: *Shia Muslim sect* Zaidis share the first four Imams of Twelver Shias [*qv*]—Ali, Hussein, Hassan, and Zain al Abidin, a grandson of Imam Ali, a son-in-law of the Prophet Muhammad (A.D. 570–632)—but follow a different line with Zaid, son of Muhammad ibn al Hanafiya and half-brother of Imam Hussein ibn Ali. According to Zaidis, any descendent of Ali can be an imam [*qv*]; what he has to demonstrate is his ability to rule according to the Sharia [*qv*]. Since they do not claim infallibility for their imams [*qv*], who are elected by notables of the Zaidi community, they are in least conflict with the Sunni doctrine [*qv*]. Zaidi principalities existed in northern Iran and Yemen in the ninth century AD. The Zaidi state of Yemen, established by Imam Yahya ibn Hussein al Rassi in (North) Yemen in A.D. 898 continued, with some interruptions, until 1962.

Zaim, Hosni (1890–1949): *Syrian military leader and politician; president, 1949* Born into a Kurdish [*qv*] family in Aleppo [*qv*], Zaim was trained to become an officer in the Ottoman Turkish army. After the First World War he was drafted into the special forces formed by the French mandate authority. He stayed with the pro-German government of France, based in Vichy, during the Second World War. Following the defeat of the Vichy forces by the British and the Free French in 1941, Zaim was jailed. After his release, he was allowed to rejoin the Syrian army and rose rapidly in

rank. During the 1948–49 Palestine War [*qv*] he was promoted to brigadier and appointed chief of staff.

Working in conjunction with the U.S. Embassy in Damascus [*qv*], intent on securing recognition of Israel by its Arab neighbors, Zaim mounted the country's first military coup on 30 March 1949. He deposed the popularly elected president, Shukri al Quwatli [*qv*], dissolved parliament, and established military rule. As a result of a rigged referendum in late June, he was elected president with wide powers.

On 20 July he signed an armistice agreement with Israel whereby he gave up the small enclave Syria held in Palestine [*qv*]. Pro-American in foreign policy, Zaim backed Washington's proposal for a Middle East military pact. Through the United States he attempted to establish contact with Israeli leaders, indicating that he was interested in peace. This, and his partiality toward the Kurdish and Circassian [*qv*] units in the army, caused much disaffection. On 14 August a group of military officers, led by Col. Sami Hinnawi, staged a coup against Zaim. Following a summary trial by a military court, he was executed.

zakat (*Arabic: derivative of zakaa, to be pure*): The performing of *zakat,* mentioned in the Quran [*qv*] as the "freewill offerings for 'the poor and needy . . . the ransoming of slaves, debtors in God's way and the traveller," was later refined as obligatory charity by the believer and included in the five pillars of Islam [*qv*]. The underlying principle is that a Muslim should purify his/her wealth by paying his/her dues to the community, which spends the resources for social purposes. With the introduction of *fiqh* [*qv*] (Islamic jurisprudence), *zakat* was prescribed as a religious tax and regulated. The Shafii school [*qv*], for instance, prescribed *zakat* on cereal and fruit crops, livestock, gold and silver, and merchandise, the tax varying from 10 percent on crops to 2.5 percent on merchandise and gold and silver. In modern times *zakat* is either paid to the government of a Muslim country or to a Muslim religious-legal scholar, to be spent in ways prescribed by the Sharia [*qv*].

Zawahiri, Ayman (1950– ; a.k.a. Abu Muhammad; Muhammad Ibrahim): *Egyptian Islamist ideologue-politician* Son of a pharmacology professor at Cairo University, and grandson of Rabiaa Zawahiri, the Grand Shaikh of al Azhar University [*qv*], Zawahiri graduated as a surgeon from Cairo University's medical school in 1978. He was one of the founders of Al Jihad al Islami [*qv*], headed by Ismail Tantawi. Following Tantawi's departure for West Germany, Zawahiri became Al Jihad's leader. After the assassination of President Muhammad Anwar Sadat [*qv*] in 1981, Zawahiri was jailed for three years for participating in the assassination plot. Following his release, Al Jihad issued its first manifesto, *The Philosophy of Confrontation.*

In 1986 Zawahiri traveled to Pakistan and joined the medical corps in Peshawar to serve the Islamist Mujahedin fighting the Soviets and the Soviet-backed regime in Afghanistan. Here he met Osama bin Laden [*qv*]. He established a branch of Al Jihad in Peshawar as well as a monthly magazine, *Al Ghazu* (The Conquest). In 1994, soon after an exiled bin Laden made Khartoum, Sudan, his base, Zawahiri joined him. When in November 1995, the truck bombing of the Egyptian embassy in Islamabad left eighteen dead, the Egyptian government blamed Zawahiri. By now Zawahiri had become bin Laden's mentor.

In 1997, Zawahiri moved to Afghanistan to join bin Laden there. It was there that in February 1998, Al Jihad, led by Zawahiri, allied with the Al Qaida network of bin Laden to form the World Islamic Front for Jihad against Crusaders and Jews [*qv*], with Al Jihad members concentrating on forging documents, transferring money, and arranging communications, and Zawahiri emerging as the ideologue of the World Islamic Front.

On 4 November 1998 a U.S. federal grand jury returned a 238-count indictment—covering 227 murders caused by the bombings of the American embassies in Nairobi and Dar as Salam in August 1998 and eleven other charges—against bin Laden and sixteen others, including Zawahiri, and charging them with leading a terrorist conspiracy from 1989 to the present, working in concert with other terrorists to build weapons and attack American military installations. Following the terrorist attacks on the United States on 11 September 2001, Zawahiri was named as one of the leading conspirators. He was sitting next to bin Laden when the latter broadcast a twenty-minute statement on Al Jazeera TV on 7 October 2001 after the United States started bombing Afghanistan. Zawahiri is believed to have escaped into Pakistan's tribal areas adjacent to the Afghan border.

Zion: Zion is the Canaanite name of the hill upon which Jerusalem [*qv*] stood. In the Old Testament [*qv*] the name pertains to the easternmost hill of Jerusalem, which was the site of the royal palace—the center of Hebrew government and worship—built by King David (r. 1010–970 B.C.) of Israel. Following the destruction of Jerusalem by the Babylonians and the exile of the Jews in 586 B.C., Zion became embedded in the communal psyche. It was the site to which the Jews would be restored, where they would find Yahweh/Jehovah. Thus, over the centuries Zion acquired the connotation of the Jewish homeland and was adopted by those nineteenth-century Jews who wanted to set up a Jewish national center or state in Palestine [qv].

Zionism and Zionists: *A Jewish doctrine and movement* The term Zionism, named after Zion [qv], the hill in ancient Jerusalem [qv] upon which the royal palace of King David (r. 1010–970 B.C.) was built, was coined by Nathan Birnbaum in 1893. It was applied to the Jewish nationalist movement that aimed to create a Jewish state or national center in Ottoman Palestine [qv], the historic homeland of the ancestors of Jews. Until then the aspiration to return to Zion had been couched in religious terms and expressed in the liturgy. The movement gained ground among the Jews of Europe in the nineteenth century, when the political emancipation of the Jewish communities and their assimilation into the mainstream culture failed to secure them full acceptance.

In 1862 Moses Hess, a German Jew, published a book entitled *Rome and Jerusalem,* which advocated the return of Jews to Palestine and the creation of a spiritual center there for the Jewish Diaspora [qv]. This was religious Zionism, which called on Jews to return to Zion for religious reasons. The idea was adopted by the Hov-

evei Zion *(Hebrew: Lovers of Zion)* societies that sprang up in Russia soon after the pogroms of 1881–82 following the assassination of Tsar Alexander II. They organized the first immigration wave *(aliya* [qv]) into Palestine. This was seen as part of an effort to create a spiritual center for Jewish civilization by such Jewish thinkers as Ahad HaAam (1875–1927), who stressed the significance of maintaining a Jewish national culture, including developing Hebrew [qv] as a modern language.

It was left to Theodor Herzl (1860–1904), an Austro-Hungarian Jewish journalist, to give a political dimension to the concept of Zionism. In his pamphlet *Der Judenstaat (German: The Jewish State)* (1896) he argued for a Jewish homeland to be set up—preferably, but not necessarily, in Ottoman Palestine—and that it should be secured through an international agreement. The next year Herzl convened the first Zionist Congress [qv] in Basle, Switzerland. It established the Zionist Organization [qv]—later called the World Zionist Organization (WZO) [qv]—which stated: "Zionism strives to create for the Jewish people a home in Palestine secured by public law." Most of the Hovevei Zion societies affiliated to the WZO, based in Vienna, Austria. The Ottoman sultan turned down Herzl's proposal for autonomy for Palestine, which was not a single administrative unit of the empire. Britain offered 6,000 sq. miles/15,550 sq. km of virgin land in Uganda to WZO in 1903, but the seventh Zionist Congress in 1905 rejected the overture.

With the failure of the Russian revolution of 1905, and the subsequent repression and pogroms, the migration of Russian Jewish youths to Palestine increased, as did support for the Zionist movement among European Jews. Since many of the Russian settlers were socialists (Marxist and non-Marxist), there was rise of socialist Zionism in Palestine, which by 1914 had some 90,000 Jews.

When the First World War erupted political Zionism became dominant, with the Russian Jews settled in Britain taking over its leadership. Two such figures, Chaim Weizmann and Nahum Sokolow, played a crucial role in securing the Balfour Declaration [qv] from the British government in late 1917. It pledged official backing for the creation of a Jewish national home in Palestine and was incorporated into Britain's League of Nations mandate over Palestine in 1922. The mandate made a Jewish agency—the WZO until 1929 and then the Jewish Agency for Palestine [qv], working in conjunction with the government in Palestine—responsible for Jewish immigration and settlement. The 1920s and 1930s witnessed the development and consolidation of Jewish life in Palestine, funded by the WZO, which was financed mainly by American Jews. The Jewish community in Palestine was represented by an elected Vaad Leumi (National Council), a trade union federation, Histadrut [qv], and a militia, Haganah [qv].

The Jewish population increased from 108,000 in 1925 to 446,000 in 1939. Seeing their proportion in the national population rapidly decreasing, Arabs protested, rioting in 1921 and 1926 and staging a revolt from 1936 to 1939. In 1939 this led to the British imposing a limit of 75,000 Jewish immigrants over the next five years. But illegal immigration grew. In November 1947 the United Nations General Assembly, the successor to the League of Nations, recom-mended a swift end to the British mandate over Palestine and partitioning of the country, giving Jews, then 30 percent of the population, 53.5 percent of Palestine, and internationalizing Jerusalem and its suburbs, covering a little over 1 percent of Palestine. The WZO accepted the U.N. plan, the Arabs rejected it. Civil conflict erupted.

The founding of the State of Israel on 14 May 1948 triggered the Arab-Israeli War [qv]. During this war, besides occupying the Jewish sector allocated to it by the United Nations, Israel annexed half of the area allotted to the Arabs—reducing their share to 23.4 percent of Palestine, including part of Jerusalem—and expelled some 760,000 Arabs, who became refugees. The affiliates to the WZO in seventy countries continued to provide financial backing to Israel and to encourage Jews to settle there. In the June 1967 Arab–Israeli War [qv], Israel occupied the remainder of Palestine.

On 10 November 1975 the U.N. General Assembly passed Resolution 3379, which defined Zionism as "a form of racism and racial discrimination" by 72 votes to 35, with 32 abstentions. Sixteen years later, on 16 December 1991, the U.N. General Assembly revoked this resolution by 111 votes to 25, with 13 abstentions.

Unable to quell the intifada [qv] of the Palestinians [qv], which erupted in the Occupied Territories [qv] in 1987, Israel signed an accord on Palestinian autonomy with the Palestinian Liberation Organization (PLO) [qv], called the Oslo Accord I [qv], in 1993, thus recognizing the right of Palestinians to their own state within the boundaries of the Palestine of the British Mandate.

Zionist Congresses: The first Zionist Congress was convened by Theodor Herzl

(1860–1904) in Basle, Switzerland, in 1897. It established the Zionist Organization [qv]—later called the World Zionist Organization (WZO) [qv]—and stated: "Zionism [qv] strives to create for the Jewish people a home in Palestine [qv] secured by public law." It elected a fifteen-strong executive committee and a president, Theodor Herzl (1860–1904), and became the legislative body of the WZO.

The fifthth Zionist Congress in 1901 set up the Jewish National Fund (JNF) [qv] under the WZO's land and development section to finance the (communal) purchase of land in Palestine. The seventh Congress in 1905 rejected Britain's offer of land in Uganda for the Jewish homeland. The tenth Congress in 1911 elected Otto Warburg as president of the WZO: he wanted to work on both diplomatic and colonization fronts to achieve the Jewish homeland in Palestine. The twelfth Congress in 1921 thanked Britain for the Balfour Declaration [qv]. The increase in registered Zionists (who elected delegates based on territorial unions and affiliated party unions) from 164,333 in 1907 to 855,590 in 1921 indicated the popularity of the movement.

At President Chaim Weizmann's behest, the sixteenth Zionist Congress in 1929 established a proper Jewish Agency for Palestine [qv] with its own executive, consisting of an equal number of Zionists and non-Zionists, i.e., those who supported the idea of a Jewish national home in Palestine but did not subscribe to political Zionism.

After the eighteenth Zionist Congress in 1933 had resolved that "in all Zionist matters discipline in regard of the Zionist Organization must take precedence over the discipline of any other body," the Revisionist Zionists [qv] left. They returned to the WZO at the twenty-second Congress in December 1946 (elected by 2,159,840 Zionists), which—taking its cue from the resolution of the American Zionist Congress in May 1942 at the Biltmore Hotel, New York—demanded the formation of an independent Jewish state in all of Palestine.

The twenty-third Congress, held in Jerusalem [qv] in 1951, formulated its objectives in the light of the founding of Israel: consolidation of Israel and the ingathering of Jews in the Diaspora [qv]. It resolved to move the WZO headquarters from London to Jerusalem. The twenty-sixth Congress in 1964 endorsed the new constitution adopted in 1960 by the General Council, which inter alia formalized the practice of holding a congress every four years.

Zionist Organization: Founded in 1897, the Zionist Organization renamed itself the World Zionist Organization [qv] in 1960. See World Zionist Organization.

Zoroastrianism and Zoroastrians: Zoroastrianism is an ancient religion that is named after its founder, Zoroaster or Zarathustra (ca. 628–551 B.C.). It arose in ancient Persia [qv], where society was divided into three castes: priests, warriors, and herdsmen and agriculturists. This is mirrored in Zoroastrianism, where particular *daivas* (heavenly ones) or gods, are associated with each caste. Above all these gods is Ahura Mazda *(Old Persian: Wise Lord),* who, according to the *gathas* (verses) attributed to Zoroaster, is the creator of heaven and earth and the supreme lawmaker. At the beginning of creation his twin sons, Spenta Mainyu (Generous Spirit) and Angra Mainyu (Destructive Spirit), engaged in any ongoing struggle and threw the world into turmoil, which only the virtuous would survive to witness a new creation. A similar dualism runs through Zoroastrian cosmology, which divides the history of the universe into four ages of 3,000 years each, where the eternal struggle is between Ahura Mazda, who lives in the light, and Ahriman (derivative of Angra Mainyu, Evil Spirit), who lives in the dark.

Zoroaster's teaching is based on the *Avesta*, the scripture in the ancient Persian language [*qv*] of Avestan, which includes various texts such as the *Yasna* (Sacrifice), the *Yashts*, and the *Vendidad.* The *Yasna* includes verses attributed to Zoroaster, even though the text was not assembled in written form until about a millennium after Zoroaster's death. He stressed ethical and ritual purity and retained the ancient cult of fire. During the fire ceremony the *Yasna* is recited and *haoma* (an unfermented or intoxicating beverage) is consumed.

Since Ahura Mazda rules over all others and is the father of all spirits, both good and evil, Zoroastrianism is considered monotheistic. It had an impact on Christianity [*qv*] and Islam [*qv*]. Each of the three castes in Persia regarded Zoroaster as a model. His doctrine spread to present-day Afghanistan and Tajikistan as well as Iran and Kurdistan [*qv*]. It flourished in the Achaemenian period (550–330 B.C.), suffered neglect during the Greek period that followed Alexander the Great's conquest in 330 B.C., and began to revive at the end of the Parthian Empire (247 B.C.–A.D. 226). It became the state religion during the Sassanian period (A.D. 226–640). Under Sassanian rule the *Avesta* was compiled and translated into the vernac-

ular, Pahlavi [*qv*]. In addition the dualistic doctrine, which had begun to replace the monotheism of the gathas during the Achaemenian period, became the norm.

With the arrival of Islam [*qv*] in Persia and Afghanistan, the hold of Zoroastrianism began to wane. It survived until the tenth century, when diehard Zoroastrians migrated to the western coast of India, where they are now known as Parsis. A small minority survived in Iran. The constitution of the Islamic Republic of Iran recognizes Zoroastrians, along with Christians and Jews [*qv*], as a religious minority and allocates them one representative in a parliament of 270 members. In the late 1990s there were an estimated 50,000 Zoroastrians in Iran.

The Zoroastrian calendar, based on a solar cycle, consists of twelve months of thirty days each. The additional five or six days are kept for "remembering the dead."

Subject Index

Arab-Israeli wars, 32-36, 321-322, 372-373, 445, 490, 491, 497-499, 521, 538-539, 540-542, 567

biographies, 1-9, 11-12, 13-15, 19-20, 21-22, 23-24, 28-30, 45-50, 51-53, 54-59, 61-62, 64-65, 70-71, 74-77, 78-84, 85, 86, 86-89, 89-93, 95-98, 98-100, 100-101, 104-105, 105-107, 121-123, 125, 127-128, 132-133, 133-136, 140-141, 142, 144-146, 148-149, 151-152, 171-172, 173-174, 175-176, 179-181, 182-183, 184-185, 185-186, 190-191, 193-203, 204, 221, 230-231, 240-241, 241-242, 250-252, 259-261, 262-264, 264-265, 265-269, 269-271, 272-277, 294-295, 295-296, 296-297, 310-311, 312-314, 319-320, 330-331, 333-338, 343, 350, 352-354, 355-357, 367, 368, 369-370, 397-400, 421-422, 432-434, 438-441, 442-444, 449-455, 456-461, 462-465, 468-469, 474-475, 477, 478-479, 480-482, 482-484, 484-485, 489-490, 491-493, 494-495, 496-497, 511, 512-515, 519-521, 523-524, 529-530, 561-563, 568-570, 575-577, 585-586, 586, 587

Christianity and Christian sects, 10, 51, 86, 93-95, 105, 107-109, 117-118, 119-120, 127, 132, 133, 141, 151, 152, 190, 242-244, 256, 316-317, 321, 350-351, 367-368, 369, 395-396, 431, 448-449, 449, 509, 521, 521-523, 534, 571

civil wars, 30-31, 109-110, 256-257, 297-300, 342, 372, 389-390, 582-583

country profiles, 72-74, 128-130, 208-211, 231-234, 254-256, 288-291, 304-307, 362, 364-365, 371-372, 387-389, 434-436, 469-473, 482, 496, 505-509, 524, 534-538, 577-582

ethnic groups, 45, 50, 53, 63, 78, 82-83, 83-84, 109, 218, 235-236, 249-250, 280-281, 281-288, 329, 395, 411-414, 422, 456, 466, 476-477, 512-514, 533, 534

geography, 60-61, 62-63, 125, 126-127, 133, 139-140, 144, 149-150, 150-151, 154, 186, 190, 256, 281-282, 291-292, 308, 314, 320-321, 321, 355, 368, 370-371, 465-466, 484, 490-491, 497, 521, 529, 570-571, 587-588

government, 1, 2-4, 6-9, 13-15, 45-49, 54-58, 59-60, 70-71, 76-77, 78-79, 81-82, 86, 86-88, 89-92, 105-107, 132-133, 133-136, 136, 140-141, 142, 144-145, 148, 152-153, 173-174, 179, 180-181, 185, 185-186, 190-191, 193-201, 221, 230-231, 263-264, 265-266, 267-271, 272-273, 294-295, 312-314, 319-320, 331-333, 333-335, 339, 341-342, 350, 352-354, 355-357, 362, 364-365, 367, 368, 397-400, 407-408, 421-422, 432-434, 440-441, 442-443, 447, 451-455, 456-459, 459-461, 462-465, 468-469, 477, 478-479, 482-484, 484-485, 486-488, 489, 494-496, 511, 519-521, 523, 569-570, 585-586, 586

Gulf wars, 154-170, 176, 391, 539-540, 542-559

historical places, 1, 9, 9-10, 10-11, 15, 19, 24, 44, 66, 70, 71, 84-85, 89, 93 101-102, 121, 126-127, 143-144, 153, 174, 183-184, 190, 220, 222, 242-244, 252-253, 264, 281, 295, 317-319, 333, 343-344, 351-352, 354-355, 367-368, 371, 436-437, 447-448, 466, 467, 467-468, 488, 490, 490-491, 510-511, 516-517, 517-518, 528-529, 533-534, 571

history, 77-78, 118-119, 127, 132, 144, 149-150, 150-151, 177, 190, 259, 285, 320-321,

372-373, 374, 400-402, 422, 465-466, 496, 497, 504, 524, 529, 570-571, 571-572

hostages, 191-193, 212-213

international agreements and treaties, 25-27, 102-103, 130-131, 140, 211-212, 213-214, 219-220, 238-239, 253-254, 257, 302-303, 372, 396, 431-432, 473-474, 496, 510, 524-527, 528

Islam and Islamic sects, 12, 18, 53-54, 63-64, 85, 117-118, 124-125, 125-126, 131, 136, 140, 150, 172-173, 174-175, 176, 177-179, 179-180, 181, 186, 190, 203-204, 204-205, 206-207, 213, 222-223, 223-225, 231, 240, 242-244, 253, 261-262, 264, 271-272, 277-278, 310, 314, 316, 317, 318-319, 331, 338, 339, 341, 350-351, 371, 420-421, 425, 436, 437-438, 445, 446, 462, 477-478, 479-480, 485-486, 499-500, 501-502, 516, 521-523, 533, 534, 564-565, 566-567, 573, 586, 586-587

Judaism and Jewish sects, 20-21, 22, 28, 36, 53, 118, 125, 144, 147, 170, 176-177, 180, 182, 190, 242-248, 249-250, 257-259, 262, 317, 321, 322, 329, 350-351, 370, 371, 395, 396, 411, 446, 449, 455-456, 466, 476-477, 477, 504-505, 515-516, 523, 534, 565-566, 573-575, 584-585
languages, 44-45, 51, 63, 120, 183, 281, 294, 400, 422-423, 476, 584

literature and writers, 23-24, 28-29, 29-30, 52-53, 93-95, 121-122, 125, 151-152, 172, 175-176, 204, 250-251, 310-311, 313-314, 397, 437-438, 438-439, 451, 474-475, 523-524

military and military leaders, 29, 54-55, 55-58, 76-77, 81-82, 104, 106-107, 122-123, 148, 148-149, 174, 194-199, 205-206, 220-221, 294-295, 300-301, 307-308, 322, 322-329, 333-335, 339-341, 343, 355-357, 360-361,

365-366, 368, 408-409, 423-424, 433-434, 443-445, 457-459, 463-465, 482-484, 489, 495-496, 496-497, 500-501, 560-561, 569-570, 585, 586

miscellaneous, 1, 9, 15, 20-21, 22-23, 24, 28, 31, 44, 60-61, 69-70, 71-72, 85, 86, 89, 95, 98, 101, 103, 125, 126, 131, 139, 147-148, 171, 176, 186-188, 203, 261, 278, 367, 527-528, 534, 577, 590-591

nonconventional/biological-chemical-nuclear weapons, 323-327

oil and gas, 366, 373-387, 391-394, 449

peace process, 61-62, 396, 414-420, 448, 575

personalities, 1, 4, 295-296, 296-297, 333, 449-451, 459, 480-482, 489-490, 561-563, 563, 575-577

political ideologies, 39-40, 41-42, 43-44, 66-69, 293-294, 296, 309-310, 314-316, 357-358, 361-362, 366, 409-411, 425, 529-530, 573-575, 582, 584-585, 588-590

politics and politicians, 1-2, 3-4, 4-6, 11-12, 12-13, 15-18, 19-20, 21-22, 22, 27-28, 28-29, 30, 31-32, 40-41, 42-44, 45-48, 49-50, 51-52, 54-59, 60, 62, 64-65, 66-69, 74-76, 78-84, 86, 86-89, 89-91, 92-93, 95-98, 98-100, 104-105, 106-107, 110-117, 120-121, 121-124, 127-128, 132-133, 136-139, 140-141, 141-143, 144-147, 148, 153, 170, 171-172, 173-174, 177-179, 180, 180-181, 185, 188-190, 190-191, 193-194, 195-199, 201-203, 207-208, 218-219, 221, 223, 225-226, 226-229, 230-231, 234-235, 239-240, 248-249, 251-252, 259-261, 262-264, 265, 266-267, 269-271, 272-274, 279-281, 281, 282-285, 292-294, 302, 308-310, 311-312, 314-316, 319-320, 329-331, 333-335, 339-341, 343, 344-350, 352-353, 355-357, 358-360, 361-

362, 362-364, 365-366, 367, 368-369, 369-370, 390, 394-395, 402-407, 411-414, 421-422, 423-425, 425-429, 429-431, 440-445, 445-446, 446-447, 461-462, 462-465, 475-476, 477, 478-479, 482-484, 484-485, 488, 489, 492-495, 502-503, 509-510, 511-514, 514-515, 516, 517, 523-524, 529-532, 534, 538, 560, 561, 563-564, 568-570, 572-573, 582, 583-584, 584-585, 585-586, 586, 587

regional conflicts, 10, 24-25, 147-148, 207-208, 236-238, 248, 278-279, 321-322, 402-407, 467, 475-476, 484, 490, 521, 532-533, 539, 542, 559-560, 567, 584

regional organizations, 30, 36-39, 153-154, 224-225, 496, 538, 573

religious ideologies and ideologues, 4, 5, 6, 15-16, 16-18, 22, 27-28, 60, 65, 79-80, 95-98, 107-108, 110, 120-121, 139, 142-143, 170, 188-190, 205-206, 223, 225-226, 227-230, 246-248, 264-265, 269-271, 274-277, 296, 330-331, 336-338, 339, 344-350, 365, 370, 394-395, 410-411, 424-425, 434, 438-439, 446-447, 480-482, 491-492, 494, 500-501, 502-503, 511-512, 517, 523, 560, 561, 563, 572-573, 573-575, 576-577, 583-584, 587, 587-590

terrorism, 4, 5, 6, 15-16, 16-18, 61-62, 86-88, 95-98, 100, 142-143, 177-179, 220-221, 307-308, 335-338, 478, 496-497, 500-501, 518-519, 572-573, 587

tourist places, 10, 19, 24, 70, 71, 84-85, 89, 93, 101-102, 121, 127, 174, 177, 183-184, 190, 220, 222, 242-244, 264, 295, 317-318, 333, 343-344, 351-352, 354-355, 367-368, 436-437, 467, 467-468, 488, 490, 510-511, 516-517, 517-518, 528-529, 533-534, 571

United Nations, 538-560

General Index

Page references in bold type indicate principal entries.
For a name starting with "al," see its second part.

aal, **1**

Aal bu Falah clan, 9

Aal bu Said dynasty, 388

Aal Saud. *See* House of Saud

Abadan, Iran, **1**, 155, 211, 525

Abbad, 1

Abbas, Mahmud (Abu Mazen), **1-2**, 47, 80, 239, 332, 333, 420

Abbas I, Shah, 318

Abbasi, Ahmad, 482

Abbasid Empire, 15, 71, 84, 121, 172, 179, 203, 205, 231, 333, 400, 467, 477, 485

Abdu, Muhammad, 205, 434, 462

Abdul Aziz ibn Abdul Rahman al Saud (Ibn Saud), **2-3**, 4, 6, 44, 133, 134, 186, 193, 205, 252, 267, 317, 318, 319, 355, 447, 452, 468, 469, 470, 525-26, 561

Abdul Ghani, Abdul Aziz, **3-4**, 463, 464

Abdul Ilah ibn Ali, **4**, 136, 142

Abdul Maguid, Esmat, **4**, 37

Abdul Rahman, Omar, **4-6**, 15, 16, 143

Abdul-Alim, Abdullah, 148

Abdullah ibn Abdul Aziz al Saud, crown prince of Saudi Arabia 2, **6**-7, 39, 58, 134, 268, 360, 470, 472, 473

Abdullah I ibn Hussein al Hashem, king of Jordan, 7-**8**, 24, 26, 27, 32-33, 39, 181, 254, 255, 296, 319-20, 409, 414, 514, 524

Abdullah II ibn Hussein al Hashem, king of Jordan, **8-9**, 254, 255-56

Abdullah, Tayseer. *See* Atef, Muhammad

al Abidin, Zain, 231, 533, 586

Abraham, 45, 94, 108, 175, 183, 222, 242, 257, 262, 351

Absent Obligation, The (Faraj), 15-16

abu, 9

Abu Ammar. *See* Arafat, Yasser

Abu Dhabi city, United Arab Emirates, **9**, 153, 535

Abu Dhabi Emirate,**9**, 353-54, 383, 392, 393, 407, 461, 521, 529, 535, 536, 537

Abu Hafs. *See* Atef, Muhammad

Abu Iyad. *See* Khalaf, Salah

Abu Jihad. *See* Wazir, Khalil

Abu Khadija. *See* Atef, Muhammad

Abu Mazen. *See* Abbas, Mahmud

Abu Musa Island, **10**, 80, 154, 533, 537

Abu Nidal, 1, 267, 507

Achaemenian Empire, 15, 19, 422, 533, 591

Acre, Israel, **10**, 72, 172

A.D., **10**

Adam, 18, 53, 222

Aden, Gulf of, 10, 44

Aden, South Yemen, 3, **10-11**, 13, 17, 20, 27, 88, 98, 179, 337, 359, 361, 464, 578, 581, 583

Adhimiya, Iraq, 169

Admoni, Nahum, 331

Adonis. *See* Asbar, Ali Ahmad Said

Afghani, Jamal al-Din, 205, 410, 462

Afghanistan, 5, 6, 16-18, 28, 61, 65, 78, 95-96, 98, 103, 110, 113, 143, 179, 318, 335, 472, 488, 532, 538, 565, 572, 573, 587, 591

   U.S. war against (2001), 17, 18, 83, 162, 198, 211, 217, 271, 273, 284, 337, 389, 433, 473, 514

Aflaq, Michel, **11-12**, 30, 51, 52, 56, 69, 99, 100, 173

Afram, Fadi, 300

Afshar, Nadir Shah, 318

Agudat Israel, **12**, 182, 247, 370, 424, 484, 523, 560, 561

A.H., **12**

Al Ahali (journal), 338, 363

Ahdut HaAvodah, **12-13**, 90, 92, 152, 180, 186, 293, 425, 441, 479, 485

Ahdut HaAvodah-Poale Zion, **13**, 21, 91, 123, 292, 294, 310, 314, 315, 316

Ahituv, Avraham, 487

Ahmad ibn Yahya, **13-14**, 70, 221, 465, 467, 527, 578

al Ahmar, Abdullah Hussein, **14-15**, 148, 179, 372, 528, 578, 583

al Ahmar, Hussein ibn Nasser, 14

Al Ahram (newspaper), 122, 184, 311

Al Ahram Iqtisadi (magazine), 101

Al Ahrar (magazine), 308

Ahvaz, Iran, **15**

Aideed, Muhammad Farah, 61, 97

Aigptios. *See* Coptic Church and Copts

al Aini, Muhsin, 179

Al Akhbar (journal), 115, 338

Akka, 10

al, **15**

Al Jihad al Islami (al Jihad/AJ), 5, **15-16**, 61, 143, 335, 572, 587

Al Jihad: The Forgotten Pillar (Faraj), 15-16

Al Qaida, **16-18**, 28, 61, 65, 95, 96-98, 198, 217, 335, 337-38, 465, 508, 572, 581, 587 (*see also* Gulf War III)

Ala, Hussein, 139, 265

Alawi, Iyad, 218, 219

Alawis (Alawites), **18**, 52, 55, 58, 62, 118, 307, 348, 349, 450, 489, 509

Alawites. *See* Alawis

Albania, 17, 357

Albright, Madeleine, 57, 508

al-Din, Adnan Saad, 349

Aleppo, Syria, **19**, 51, 56, 151, 173, 250, 261, 288, 348, 349, 489, 507

Alexander the Great, 19, 62, 66, 70, 121, 144, 243, 258, 400, 422, 466, 488, 533, 591

Alexandretta, 51

Alexandria, Egypt, 4, **19**, 36, 37, 60, 143, 151, 175, 249, 353

Algeria, 17, 36, 38, 44, 46, 62, 97, 137, 192, 270, 300, 321, 327, 364, 391, 392, 393, 394, 402, 410, 411, 480, 496, 568

Algiers, 37, 46, 47, 211, 406, 416, 524, 568, 575

Algiers Accord (1975), 195, 211, 216, 275, 283, 284, 287, 390, 411, 484, 512, 524, 563

Ali, Hussein (Baha Ullah), 71

Ali, Imam (cousin and son-in-law of Prophet Muhammad). *See* Talib, Ali ibn Abu

Ali, Muhammad, 39, 118, 565

Ali, Salim Rubai, 19-20, 148, 230, 336, 580

Alignment Bloc. *See* Labor Alignment (Israel)

aliya, **20-21**, 278, 395, 401, 584, 588

Aliya Hadasha, 147

Allaf, Kazem, 192

Allah, 53, 70, 72, 175, 204, 206, 222, 349, 371, 438, 486, 499, 533, 535, 572

Allenby, Edmund, 240, 296

Allied Powers (First World War), 78, 135, 467, 504, 516, 526

Allies (Second World War), 36, 111, 112, 136, 220, 269, 277, 397, 399, 440

Allon, Yigal, 21-22, 200

al-Majid, Ali Hassan, 167

Aloni, Shulamit, 446

Altalena (ship), 221

A.M., **22**

Amal, **22**, 92-93, 115, 188, 189, 190, 223, 227, 299, 306, 343, 430, 459

Amarat tribe, 24

Amer, Abdul Hakim, 368

America. *See* United States of America

American hostage crisis in Tehran. *See* Hostage taking and hostages

American University in Beirut (AUB), **22-23**, 40, 89, 104, 171, 190, 192, 227, 260, 273, 450, 462, 489

American University in Cairo (AUC), 23, 102

Amichai, Yehuda, **23-24**

Amin, Abdul Munim, 142

Amin, Abdullah, 68

Amir, Yigal, 441

Amit, Meir, 331

Amman, Jordan, 7, 9, 26, 30, **24**, 38, 46, 80, 88, 109, 124, 137, 166, 171, 178, 254, 352, 405, 406, 407, 427

Amnesty International, 158

al Amri, Hassan, 179

Amuzgar, Jamshid, 193, 446

Anahita (journal), 125

Anaiza tribal federation, **24**, 193, 269, 291, 455, 527

Anglo-American Commission on Palestine, 24-25

Anglo-Bahraini Agreement, 25

Anglo-Egyptian Treaty, 25, 111, 129, 136, 344, 353, 564

Anglo-Iraqi Treaty (1922), 25-26, 112

Anglo-Iraqi Treaty (1930), 26, 142, 460

Anglo-Jordanian Treaty, 26, 199, 352

Anglo-Kuwaiti Agreement, 26, 452, 453

Anglo-Omani Agreement, 26, 461

Anglo-Ottoman Convention, 27, 289, 431-32

Anglo-Persian Agreement, 27, 209

Anglo-Persian Oil Company, 1, 211

Anglo-Qatari Agreement, 27, 435, 519

Anglo-Transjordanian Treaty, 8, 26, 27

Anglo-Yemeni Treaty, 27

Angola, 164, 249

al Anisi, Abdul Wahhab, 583

Annan, Kofi, 164, 198, 391, 540, 558, 559

Ansar-e Islam, 27-28, 163, 228

Ansariyas. See Alawis

Antakya, Syria, 51

Antar, Ali, 88, 337

anti-Semitism, 28, 94-95, 490 (see also Holocaust)

Antioch, Syria, 51

Antiochene rite. See West Syriac rite

Antiochus IV, 180, 243, 258

Antonius, George, 28-29

Aoun, Michel, 29, 68, 141, 145, 188, 191, 194, 223, 294, 299-300, 301, 302, 306, 361, 364, 424, 430, 495

Aqaba, Gulf of, 44, 201, 498-99, 521, 538-39

Aql, Said, 29-30, 153

al Aqsa Intifada. See Second Intifada

al Aqsa Mosque, 8, 97, 135, 170, 202, 224, 244, 371, 411, 419, 471, 475, 487, 572

Arab Awakening, The (Antonius), 29

Arab Baath Party, 11, 30, 51, 66, 67, 68, 99

Arab Baath Socialist Party, 11, 30, 42, 69, 99, 167, 195, 302

Arab Cooperation Council (ACC), 30, 147, 200, 334, 464, 579

Arab Democratic Party (ADP), 30

Arab Deterrent Force (ADF), 30-31, 37, 267

Arab East, 31, 44, 113, 114, 346, 356

Arab (Arabian) Gulf. See Gulf, the

Arab Higher Committee (AHC), 31-32, 202, 203, 352, 489

Arab-Israeli War I (1948-49; Palestine War; War of Independence), 4, 21, 23, 24, 25, 32-33, 39, 45, 49, 65, 79, 90, 111, 115, 121, 123, 127, 129, 132, 136, 144, 149, 171, 183, 184, 203, 216, 235, 242, 249, 250, 253, 254, 277, 305, 315, 344, 347, 348, 352, 355, 368, 370, 395, 408, 409, 414, 421, 433, 440, 450, 474, 482, 489, 490, 506, 534, 540, 560, 564, 568, 569, 570, 571, 576, 586, 589

Arab-Israeli War II (1956). See Suez War

Arab-Israeli War III (June 1967; Six-Day War), 4, 14, 21, 24, 33-34, 37, 40, 41, 43, 45, 49, 52, 57, 65, 66, 68, 69, 80, 81, 87, 91, 112, 114, 116, 122, 127, 128, 129, 133, 135, 137, 142, 144, 149, 152, 170, 171, 182, 183, 185, 186, 199, 240, 241, 242, 244, 247, 249, 251, 253, 255, 263, 296, 305, 309, 312, 316, 334, 338, 345, 346, 347, 348, 357, 365, 372-73, 374, 391, 397, 403, 406, 409, 413, 414, 423, 440, 445, 455, 456, 458, 461, 465, 469, 471, 482, 487, 490, 493, 497, 506, 521, 540, 566, 567, 569, 570, 571, 579

Arab-Israeli War IV (1973; Ramadan War), 22, 34-36, 37, 44, 56, 81, 123, 131, 142-43, 149, 182, 199-200, 232, 253, 255, 263, 265, 273, 305, 309, 320, 321, 326, 338, 349, 363, 374, 377, 379, 381, 386, 387, 391, 393, 403, 415, 441, 445, 455, 458, 471, 482, 488, 491, 512, 560, 575

Arab Jews, 36 (see also Oriental Jews; Sephardim)

Arab League, 3, 4, 32, 36-37, 39, 45, 56, 130, 133, 137, 157, 198, 200, 203, 253, 255, 256, 303, 305, 320, 321, 333, 334, 353, 364, 389, 391, 409, 410, 411, 432, 433, 452, 458, 460, 461, 463, 489, 495, 495, 496, 564, 582, 584

Arab League Summits, 9, 30-31, 37-39, 200, 217, 256, 295, 300, 306, 333, 335, 402, 472, 473, 490, 570

Arab Legion, 7, 8, 148-49, 352

Arab Maghreb Union, 410

Arab nationalism, 11, 29, 30, **39-40**, 55, 66, 106, 135, 140, 185, 203, 260, 352, 353, 494

Arab Nationalist Movement (ANM), **40-41**, 68, 114, 171, 182, 273, 358, 494

Arab Nationalist Movement (Kuwait). *See* National Cultural Club (Kuwait)

Arab Nationalist Movement (North Yemen), **41**

Arab Nationalist Movement (Palestine), **41**, 427, 428

Arab Nationalist Movement (Saudi Arabia), **41**, 116, 425

Arab Revolt of 1916, 39

Arab socialism, 4, 11, **41-42**, 43, 111, 345, 357, 410-11 (*see also* Nasser, Gamal Abdul)

Arab Socialist Party (Syria), 11, **42**, 66, 69, 241

Arab Socialist Party of Egypt (ASPE), **42-43**, 345, 359, 493

Arab Socialist Union (ASU), 42, **43-44**, 112, 142, 184, 308, 338, 345, 356, 357, 359, 363, 455-56

Arab West, **44**

Arabia. *See* Arabian Peninsula

Arabian Peninsula, 2, 24, 40, **44**, 45, 153, 222, 291, 321, 448, 470, 520, 527, 580

Arabian Sea, 44, 153, 159, 190

Arabic language, **44-45**, 52, 53, 64, 72, 121, 128, 175, 183, 214, 231, 254, 282, 289, 304, 311, 313, 362, 387, 434, 437, 469, 474, 505, 536, 577

Arabism. See pan-Arabism

Arabs, **45**, 209, 215, 232, 243, 254, 289, 295, 301, 304, 307, 318, 321, 352, 388, 400, 405, 406, 422, 435, 467, 470, 488, 490, 505, 517, 527, 534, 535, 536, 562, 566, 578 (*See also* Israeli Arabs)

Arafat, Yasser (Abu Ammar), 1-2, 6-7, **45-48**, 57, 80, 81, 92, 122, 124, 136-38, 154, 171, 178, 182, 200, 201, 233, 234, 235, 239, 252, 255, 266-67, 332, 334, 335, 370, 402-8, 416, 418, 420, 422, 428, 441, 462, 473, 475, 484, 487, 507, 529, 566, 567, 568-69, 575

Araiji, Jibran, 510

Arani, Taqi, 530

Aras River, 62, 63

Arbil. *See* Irbil

Ardeshire, King, 15

Arens, Moshe, 369

Argentina, 159, 173, 249

Argov, Shlomo, 298

Arif, Abdul Rahman, **48-49**, 67, 76, 216

Arif, Abdul Salam, 48-**49**, 67, 76, 195, 216, 433, 434

Arif-Yazdi, Muhammad Reza, 209

Arlosoroff, Chaim, **49-50**, 90, 314, 479

Armenia, 51, 281

Armenian Catholic Church, 50, **51**, 117, 307, 535

Armenian language, **51**

Armenian Orthodox Church, 50, **51**, 93, 118, 211, 516

Armenians, **50**, 63, 114, 116, 152, 209, 254, 304, 505

Arsuzi, Zaki, 11, 30, **51-52**, 99

Artaxerxes, King of Persia, 258

Artzivian, Abraham, 51

Arvand Rud. *See* Shatt al Arab

Asbar, Ali Ahmad Said, **52-53**, 474

Asfour, Hassan, 116

Ashdod, Israel, 32, 33

Ashkenazim, 20, 21, **53**, 170, 186, 233, 247, 259, 370, 395, 476, 484, 584

Ashu, Shukri, 8

Ashura (fasting day for Muslims), **53**

Ashura (annual ritual of Shias), 18, **53-54**, 230, 264, 317, 394, 486, 502

Asia Minor, 109

Asians, 470

al Askari, Hassan (imam), 231, 310, 467, 486, 533

Asluj, 33

Asnaj, Abdullah, 464

Assad, Bashar, 9, 18, **54-55**, 266, 350, 505, 508

Assad, Hafiz, 47, 51-52, 54, **55-58**, 59, 62, 69, 75, 77, 93, 100, 117, 140, 141, 145, 150, 173-74, 188, 196, 225, 226, 237, 241-42, 252, 257, 260, 266, 288, 298, 299, 302, 303, 322, 348, 349, 363, 402, 406, 410, 416, 417, 429, 461, 468, 496, 505, 506-8, 510

Assad, Rifaat, 56, **58-59**, 507

Assembly of Experts, Iran (1979), **59**, 78, 250, 270, 276, 330, 442

Assembly of Experts, Iran (1982-), **59-60**, 150, 208, 229, 270, 442

Association of Combatant Clergy, **60**, 272, 330, 442

Assyria, 45, 121, 139, 258, 400, 422, 466, 490, 517, 533

Assyrian Christians. *See* Nestorian Christians

Aswan High Dam, **60-61**, 356, 371, 497

Asyut, Egypt, 16

Asyut University, 5, 143

Ataturk, Mustafa Kemal, 288

Atef, Khadija, 62

Atef, Muhammed, 17, 18, **61-62**, 96, 337

Attar, Issam, 350

al Attas, Haidar, 88, 580

Attasi, Nur al Din, 55, **62**, 241, 489

Aurelian, Roman Emperor, 190

Australia, 72, 159, 165, 249

Austria, 28, 293

Austria-Hungary, 77, 78, 152

Axis Powers, 450, 453, 528

Ayash, Yahya, 178

Ayub, Tariq, 168

Ayubi, Salah al Din. *See* Saladin

Ayubid dynasty, 286, 400

Al Ayyam (periodical), 450

Azal, Sobh-e, 71

Azerbaijan, Iran, **62-63**, 209, 281, 373, 398, 531

Azeri language, **63**

Azeris, **63**, 209, 272

al Azhar University, 4, **63-64**, 65, 102, 202, 205, 331, 345, 348, 434, 512, 587

Aziz, Ali Abdullah, 228

Aziz, Muhammad ibn Abdul, 267, 268

Aziz, Osman Abdullah, 228

Aziz, Saud ibn Abdul, 193

Aziz, Tariq, **64-65**, 105, 120, 157, 159, 340, 366, 444, 558

Azm, Khalid, 440

Aznar, Jose Maria, 164-65

Azores, 164

Azzam, Abdul Rahman, 36

Azzam, Abdullah, 16, 17, **65**, 96

Baalbek, Lebanon, **66**, 188, 223

Baath party. *See* Baath Socialist Party

Baath Socialist Party, **66**, 425

Baath Socialist Party (Iraq), 64, **66-67,** 68, 76, 100, 113, 120, 191, 195, 214, 216, 217, 218, 264, 275, 282, 287, 288, 355, 362-63, 377, 434, 492, 503, 512, 528

Baath Socialist Party (Jordan), **67-68**, 80, 114, 352

Baath Socialist Party (Lebanon), **68**, 92, 260, 264, 358

Baath Socialist Party (North Yemen), **68**, 358

Baath Socialist Party (South Yemen), **68**

Baath Socialist Party (Syria), 33, 42, 55, 56, 58, 62, **68-69**, 75, 117, 137, 173, 177, 241, 266, 267, 288, 348, 349, 356, 363, 382, 461, 506

Baathism and Baathists, 40, 49, 51-52, 54 (*see also* Baath Socialist Party)

Babis and Babism, **69-70**, 71, 488

Babylon, 45, **70**, 94, 102, 125, 242, 258, 400, 422, 490

Babylonia, 70

al Badr, Muhammad, 14, **70-71**, 372, 465

Baghdad, Iraq, 4, 11-12, 26, 30, 37, 38, 48, 49, 56, 66, **71**, 77, 80, 81, 82, 104, 116, 121, 142, 148, 157, 161, 173, 214, 215, 226, 249, 286, 366, 413, 449, 485, 488, 504, 558 (*see also* Gulf War III)

Baghdad Pact, 114, 149, 199, 210, 216, 321, 352, 356, 398, 433, 460, 528 (*see also* Central Treaty Organization)

Bagheri, Amir Bahman, 192

Baha, Abdul, 72, 174

Baha Ullah. *See* Ali, Hussein

Bahais, 70, **71-72**, 118, 139, 174, 211, 249

Bahonar, Muhammad Javad, 340, 365, 443

Bahrain, 25, 31, 36, 44, **72-74**, 153, 154, 159, 268-69, 314, 322-23, 374-75, 385, 391, 411, 425, 427, 485

   Britain and, 25, 73, 269, 314, 385, 560

Bahrain National Liberation Front. *See* Popular Bloc

Bajakian, Adrenee, 294
Bajammal, Abdul Qadir, 464, 578, 581
Bakdash, Khalid, **74-75**, 115, 116, 117
Baker, James, 159, 201, 322, 417
Baker, Muhammad ibn Abu, 222
Bakhtiar, Shahpur, **75-76**, 230, 399, 481
Bakil tribal confederation, 70, 148, 527-28, 583
Bakr, Ahmad Hassan, 49, 57, 67, **76-77**, 195, 196
Balawi, Abdul Hakam, 332
Balfour, Arthur James, 77-78
Balfour Declaration, 20, **77-78**, 249, 279, 400, 401, 405, 589, 590
Bali, Indonesia, 18
Balkans, 17, 97
Baluchis, **78**, 209, 272, 337
Bandung, Indonesia, 41, 356
Bangladesh, 159, 572
Bani Yas tribe, 9, 313
Bani-Sadr, Abol Hassan, **78-79**, 139, 229, 276, 280, 285, 340, 360, 365, 366, 442, 443, 444, 532
al Banna, Hassan, **79-80**, 205, 344, 346, 347, 410
al Banna, Sabri, **80-81**
al Baqir, Muhammad, 231, 533
Baradaeus, Jacob, 396
El Baradei, Muhammad, 162-63, 325
Barak, Ehud, 7, 48, 57-58, **81-82**, 149, 189, 233, 235, 236, 239, 293, 320, 335, 365, 370, 390, 408, 419, 422, 473, 475, 483, 484, 508, 566
Barake, Muhammad, 172
Barcelona, Spain, 164
Barbarossa, Frederick I, 534
Barikiban, Ahmad, 59, 330
Barzani, Idris, 82, 283, 513
Barzani, Masud, **82-83**, 197, 283-84, 285, 287, 513
Barzani, Mustafa, 82, **83-84**, 281, 282-83, 285, 286, 411, 433, 512
Barzani, Ubaidullah, 82, 281
Basle, Switzerland, 245, 293, 573, 588, 590
Basra, Iraq, **84-85**, 142, 155, 156, 165, 166, 167, 168, 215, 286, 323, 504

al Basri, Hassan, 499
bat, **85**
Bayan (Shirazi), 70
Baybar, Sultan, 183
Bayununi, Muhammad, 225
al Baz, Abdul Aziz ibn Abdullah, **85**, 472, 561
bazaar, bazaaris, **85-86**, 230
Bazargan, Mahdi, 78, **86**, 230, 275, 308-9, 360, 447, 514, 515
B.C., **86**
B.C.E., 86
Beersheba, Israel, 32, 33
Begin, Menachem Wolfovitch, **86-88**, 102,123, 133, 141, 142, 146, 185, 220, 238, 247, 308, 309, 416, 421, 447, 458, 478, 519, 569
Behbehani, Muhammad Baqir, 316
Beheshti, Muhammad, 60, 270
al Beidh, Ali Salim, **88-89**, 337, 464, 580, 581, 582, 583
Beirut Arab University, 89
Beirut, Lebanon, 11, 29, 46, 47, 51, 52, 66, 68, 77, 81, 88, **89**, 92, 100, 102, 104, 106, 114, 115, 116, 117, 122, 124, 137-38, 144, 146, 151, 166, 181, 182, 192, 212, 227, 232, 295, 298, 302, 304, 306, 342, 400, 406, 415, 423, 428, 449, 462, 463, 483, 500, 510, 529, 535
Belkeziz, Abdel Ouahed, 225
ben, **89**
Ben-Eliezer, Binyamin, 422, 483
Ben-Gurion, David, 21, 23, 87, **89-91**, 123, 132, 133, 141, 187, 221, 240, 245, 295, 314, 315, 329, 367, 409, 421, 441, 447, 479, 498, 515, 560, 574
Ben-Jedid, Chadli, 496
Ben-Zvi, Yitzhak, **91-92**
Berger, Samuel, 559
Berlin, Germany, 132, 146, 152, 285, 423, 574
Bernadotte, Folke, 308
Berri, Nabih, 22, **92-93**, 141, 145, 304
Betar, 87, 240, 262, 447, 478
Bethlehem, West Bank, 32, 34, **93**, 407, 568
Bible, 45, **93-95**, 431, 448
Bikfaya, Lebanon, 146
Bilkman, Ukraine, 151

bin, **95**
bin Laden, Muhammad, 62
bin Laden, Muhammad Awad, 95
bin Laden, Osama, 17-18, 61, 62, 65, **95-98**,
    110, 162, 167, 198, 234, 336, 439, 472, 572,
    581, 587
Birnbaum, Nathan, 588
bint, **98**
Bishara, Abdullah, 153
Bishara, Azmi, **98-99**, 236, 358
Bitar, Salah al Din, 11, 30, **99-100**, 173
Black September Organization, **100**, 332
Blair, Tony, 198
Bliss, Daniel, 22
Blix, Hans, 162-64, 540
Bonaparte, Napoleon, 102
Book of Certitude, The (Baha Ullah), 72
Borochov, Don Ber, **100**, 293, 294, 485
Borujerdi, Muhammad Hussein, 150, 275, 481, 491
Boustani, Emile, 263
Boutros-Ghali, Boutros, **101**, 119
Brest-Litovsky, Poland, 86
Brezhnev, Leonid, 200, 214, 237, 510
Britain, 2, 10-11, 17, 36, 39, 104, 107, 117,
    128, 142, 148, 156, 278, 279, 322, 386, 529
    Bahrain and, 25, 73, 269, 314, 385, 560
    Egypt and, 25, 39, 40, 60, 79, 102, 111, 129,
        310, 321, 368, 392, 497, 528, 563-64 (*see
        also* Suez War)
    France and, 149, 391, 528 (*see also* Sykes-
        Picot Pact)
    Iran/Persia and, 10, 27, 139, 159, 190, 209-
        10, 213, 264, 397-98, 431, 525, 528, 530,
        532-33, 585, 586
    Iraq and, 2, 4, 7, 25-26, 82, 135, 148-49,
        159, 160, 202-3, 206, 215-16, 218, 249,
        286, 354-355, 377, 391, 399-400, 401,
        431-32, 467, 525 (*see also* Gulf War III;
        Operation Desert Fox)
    Israel and, 90, 232, 307, 315, 479, 528
        (*see also* Suez War)
    Jordan/Transjordan and, 7-8, 26, 27, 135,
        149, 181, 206, 249, 254, 255, 296, 401,
        524 (*see also* Sykes-Picot Pact)

    Kuwait and, 2, 26, 27, 162, 289, 385, 451-52,
        455 (*see also* Gulf War II)
    Lebanon and, 105-6, 149, 238, 299, 362
    North Yemen and, 13, 578
    Oman and, 26, 205-6, 385, 388, 390, 426,
        432, 461, 511, 526
    Palestine and, 7, 24-25, 31, 87, 90, 144, 174,
        183, 202-3, 240, 244, 245, 307, 373, 385,
        400-401, 434, 447, 467, 497, 566 (*see also*
        Balfour Declaration; Sykes-Picot Pact)
    Qatar and, 27, 125, 385, 435, 519, 521
    Saudi Arabia and, 2, 205-6, 252, 392, 470,
        525-26
    South Yemen and, 19, 40, 88, 361, 477, 579-
        80
    Soviet Union and, 528
    Syria and, 7, 123, 149, 489, 507, 509
    U.S. and, 24-25, 528 (*see also* Gulf War III;
        Operation Desert Fox)
    Yemen and, 27
Bu, **101**
Bubiyan Island, 27, 158, 289
Buckley, William, 192, 212, 227
Buddhism, 500
Bukhara, Uzbekistan, 125
al Bukhari, Muhammad, 173, 502
Bulganin, Marshal Nikolai, 498
Bulgaria, 77, 396
Burg, Avraham, 232
Burleigh, Peter, 391, 559
Bush, George H. W., 158, 159, 160, 196, 197,
    198, 216, 417
Bush, George Walker, 17, 48, 81, 98, 105, 108, 126,
    130, 211, 217, 198, 219, 256, 271, 273, 284,
    291, 335, 420, 454, 475, 484, 503, 514, 520
Butler, Richard, 161, 198, 216, 391, 558, 559
al Buyid, Muiz al Dawla, 485
Byblos, Lebanon, **101**
Byzantine Empire, 19, 89, 109, 243, 321, 400

Cairo, Egypt, 3, 36, 37, 38, 39, 40, 45, 46, 63,
    79, 80, 100, **101-2**, 119, 122, 126, 128, 128,
    131, 136, 137, 142, 151, 173, 176, 180, 249,
    305, 335, 405, 406, 407, 449, 485, 494

Cairo Agreement, **102**, 185, 263, 333, 357

Cameroon, 164

Camp David, 7, 48, 82, 178, 233, 239, 335, 371, 419

Camp David Accords, 5, 37, 88, 101, **102-3**, 130, 137, 200, 255, 267-68, 359, 413, 415-16, 432, 458, 471, 475, 478, 493, 569, 570

Canaan, 257, 400, 465-66, 517

Canada, 89, 92, 159, 160

Cape Town, South Africa, 127

Carter Doctrine, **103**

Carter, Jimmy, 102, 192, 268, 322, 399, 415, 458

Carthage, 19

Casablanca, Morocco, 37, 38, 224

Caspian Sea, 63, 119

Castro, Fidel, 138

Catholics, Armenian. *See* Armenian Catholic Church

Catholics, Assyrian. *See* Nestorian Christians

Catholics, Chaldean. *See* Chaldean Catholic Church

Catholics, Greek. *See* Greek Catholic Church

Catholics, Maronite. *See* Maronite Catholic Church

Catholics, Orthodox. *See* Orthodox Christians/Church

Catholics, Roman. *See* Roman Catholic Christians/Church

Catholics, Syrian. *See* Syrian Catholic Church

Catroux, Georges, 362

C.E., *104*

Central Asia, 395, 410, 565

Central Intelligence Agency (CIA), 5, 16, 96, 97, 104-5, 145, 166, 192, 210, 212, 216, 218-19, 227, 331, 335, 350, 398, 418, 482, 500, 558, 585

Central Powers (First World War), 77, 504

Central Treaty Organization (CENTO), **104**, 532

Cerularius, Michael, 109, 396

Chalabi, Ahmad, **104-5**, 219

Chaldean Catholic Church, 64, **105**, 117, 218, 369, 535

Chamoun, Camille Nimr, **105-6**, 107, 115, 140, 141, 145, 146, 185, 259, 263, 297, 298, 300, 305, 361, 423, 430, 462-63, 493-94, 529

Chamoun, Danny, 301, 361

Chamoun, Dory, 361

Chapman, Thomas, 296

Chavez, Hugo, 198, 217, 394

Chechnya, 17, 97

Chehab, Fuad, **106-7**, 146, 185, 297, 305, 423, 463, 468, 494

Cheney, Dick, 83, 219, 284, 514

Chernenko, Konstantin, 372

China, 60, 65, 158, 161, 164, 179, 391, 426, 559, 568

Chirac, Jacques, 169

Christian calendars, **107**

Christian fundamentalism, **107-8**

Christianity and Christians, 18, 22, 28, 29, 50, 56, 74, 93, 106, **108-9**, 114-15, 116, 118, 119, 120, 121, 124, 130, 137, 141, 145, 151, 152, 172, 190, 209, 211, 218, 222, 234, 235, 243, 256, 259, 272, 291, 300, 305, 306, 310, 321, 351, 362, 367, 371, 389, 400, 421, 430, 436, 437, 450, 455, 459, 463, 473, 504, 509, 521-22, 529, 535, 538, 566, 591

Christians, Catholic, 351, 509 (*see also* Armenian Catholic Church; Nestorian Christians; Chaldean Catholic Church; Greek Catholic Church; Maronite Catholic Church; Orthodox Christians; Roman Catholic Christians; Syrian Catholic Church)

Christians, Eastern. *See* Orthodox Christians/Church

Christians, Protestant. *See* Protestant Christians/Church

Christmas, 18, **109**, 568

church, **109**

Churchill, Winston, 296, 516

CIA. *See* Central Intelligence Agency

Cicilia, 51

Circassians, 24, **109**, 254, 586

Citizens Rights Party. *See* Ratz

Civil War in Jordan. *See* Jordanian Civil War

Civil War in Lebanon. *See* Lebanese Civil War

Civil War in North Yemen. *See* North Yemeni Civil War

Civil War in Oman. *See* Omani Civil War

Civil War in Yemen. *See* Yemeni Civil War

Clarification of Points of the Sharia (Khomeini), 275

Clinton, Bill, 1, 48, 82, 98, 126, 130, 161, 197, 201, 217, 233, 239, 257, 370, 405, 406, 407, 417, 418-19, 444, 503, 508, 558, 559, 563, 567, 568, 575

Cologne, Germany, 573

Comintern (Communist International), 111, 114, 115, 116

Committee for Advice and Reform (CAR), **110**

Committee for the Defense of Legitimate Rights, **110**

Communist Action Organization, 302

Communist Movement in Egypt, **110-12**

Communist Movement in Israel, 368 (*see also* Maki; Rakah)

Communist Party of Iran. *See* Tudeh Party of Iran

Communist Party of Iraq (CPI), 111, **112-13**, 191, 218, 338, 362-63, 433, 474

Communist Party of Jordan (CPJ), **114**

Communist Party of Lebanon, **114-15**, 260, 302, 358

Communist Party of Palestine (Palestine People's Party), **115-16**, 172, 312, 403, 404-5, 407, 523

Communist Party of Saudi Arabia, **116**

Communist Party of Syria, 56, 75, **116-17**, 363

Communist Party of Syria and Lebanon, 75, 114, 116

Comros Island, 36

confessionalism, **117-18**, 260, 298, 301, 304, 364, 430

Conservative Judaism, 118, 259, 504

Constantine I, Roman Emperor, 93, 108, 190, 243, 367, 504

Constantinople (later Istanbul), 400, 431, 504

Constitutional Revolution (Iran), **118-19**, 209, 312, 316, 341

Copenhagen, Denmark, 574

Coptic Church and Copts, 101, 102, 111, **119-20**, 130, 142, 368

Coptic language, 119, **120**

Council of Guardians, 59 (*see also* Guardians Council)

Cox, Percy, 431-42

Crane, Charles, 28, 279

crude oil. *See* oil

Crusades and Crusaders, 10, 89, 101, 102, 144, 174, 177, 183, 242, 244, 261, 295, 316, 352, 367, 371, 396, 397, 400, 490, 517, 529

Cuba, 138, 158

Curiel, Henri, 249

Curzon, Lord, 27

Cyril VI, patriarch of Antioch, 151

Cyprus, 51, 105, 122, 321, 396

Cyrus the Great, 70, 258, 422

Czech Republic, 165

Czechoslovakia, 159, 356

al Daawa, **120-21**, 196, 502

Dagan, Meir, 333

Dakar, Senegal, 224

Damascus, Syria, 7, 11, 19, 30, 37, 44, 46, 51, 54, 55, 58, 66, 69, 74, 84, 99, 100, 104, 117, **121**, 124, 135, 137, 151, 166, 173, 182, 250, 303, 319, 322, 348, 396, 406, 407, 417, 428, 462, 505

Damour, Lebanon, 237

Danzig, Abraham, 177

Daqiliya district, Egypt, 4

Dar as Salaam, Tanzania, 17, 61, 98, 337, 501, 587

Darabi, Kazem, 285

al Darazi, Muhammad, 125-26

d'Arcy, William Knox, 375, 385

Darius I, 249, 422

Darwish, Mahmud, **121-22**, 407

Dashnak Party, **122**

Davar (newspaper), 152, 479, 485

David, King of Israel, 24, 93, 132, 183, 242, 248, 258, 437, 466, 588

Day of Atonement. *See* Yom Kippur

Dayan, Moshe, 21, 122-23, 133, 320, 441

De Cuellar, Javier Perez, 227
De Gaulle, Charles, 362
De Lesseps, Ferdinand, 497
Debbas, Charles, 277
Declaration of Principles on Palestinian Self-Rule, 1
Deir al Assad, 121
Deir Yassin village, 87, 220, 307, 409
Deiral Qamar, Lebanon, 105
Democratic Front for the Liberation of Palestine,
   116, 137, 182, **123-24**, 240, 403, 404
Democratic Front for Peace and Equality.
   See Hadash
Der Judenstaat (Herzl), 588
Der Moement (newspaper), 152
Deri, Arye, 484
al Dhahabi, Muhammad Hussein, 512
Dhahran, Saudi Arabia, 6, 41
dhimmis, **124-25**, 253
Dhofar province, Oman, 40, 380, 388, 389, 432, 461
Dhofari Liberation Front, 40, 389, 426
Di Velt (newspaper), 152
Diaspora, **125**, 245, 248-49, 259, 293, 296, 312,
   370, 406, 407, 485, 504, 573, 584, 588, 590
Diego Garcia, 103
al Din, Adnan Saad, 225, 226
al Din, Muhammad Mahdi Shams, 22, 92
al Din, Yahya Hamid, 27, 191, 526, 578, 579
Diraiya, Arabia, 2, 24, 193, 470
Diwaniya, Iraq, 169
Djibouti, 36
Dodge, David, 192, 227
Doha, Qatar, **125**, 162, 225, 434, 436
Dome of the Rock, 7, 170, 202, 244, 335, 487
   (*see also* Noble Sanctuary)
Domitian, Emperor of Rome, 95
donum, **125**
Dowlatabadi, Mahmud, **125**
Druze, 92, 114, 116, 118, **125-26**, 149, 234,
   235, 256, 259, 260-61, 299, 307, 343, 430,
   431, 450, 489, 509
Dual Containment policy, **126**, 211, 285
Dubai, United Arab Emirates, **126**, 383, 529,
   535, 536
Dubai city, United Arab Emirates, **126-27**

Dubai Emirate, **127**, 312-13, 537
Dwalibi, Maruf, 489

East Africa, 291, 336, 343, 344
East Bank, 114, **127**, 254
East Jerusalem, 8, 33, 34, 37, 47, **127**, 177, 201,
   207, 231, 235, 239, 242, 244, 249, 257, 330,
   358, 371, 373, 403, 405, 406, 408, 414, 416,
   490, 566, 570, 571
East Syriac rite, 571 (*see also* Chaldean Catholic
   Church)
Easter, **127**, 132
Eastern Europe, 395
Eastern (Orthodox) Church, 51, 151, 351, 448
   (*see also* Orthodox Christian Church)
Eban, Abba/Aubrey, **127-28**, 200
Echmiadzin, Armenia, 51
Economics of Divine Unity, The (Bani-Sadr), 79
Ecuador, 392, 394
Edde, Raymond, 146, 263, 423
Eddi, Emile, 141
Egypt, 17, 30, 31, 36, 40, 41, 89, 92, 97, 101,
   105, **128-30**, 139, 142, 151, 154, 157, 249,
   311, 318, 319, 321, 375, 385, 391, 410, 476,
   517, 534
   Arab League and, 4, 37, 38, 56, 130, 200,
      334, 409, 458, 564
   Britain and, 25, 39, 40, 60, 79, 102, 111,
      129, 136, 310, 321, 344, 353, 368, 392,
      497, 528, 563-64 (*see also* Suez War)
   France and, 111, 528 (*see also* Suez War)
   Iran and, 399
   Iraq and, 4, 30, 36, 47, 49, 76, 159, 160, 327,
      332, 333, 346
   Israel and, 4, 32-36, 42, 46, 91, 94, 111, 142-
      43, 184, 203, 246, 247, 257-58, 295, 356-
      57, 411, 415, 441, 458, 479, 491 (*see also*
      Camp David Accords; Egyptian-Israeli
      Peace Treaty; Suez War; War of Attrition)
   Jordan and, 26, 34, 36, 103, 199, 200, 255,
      334, 356, 409
   Kuwait and, 4, 30, 36
   leaders, 10, 79, 126, 184, 333-35, 338, 353,
      355, 368, 456, 457, 587

Lebanon and. *See* Cairo Agreement
military, 323, 327
North Yemen and, 13, 41, 129, 221, 356,
372, 578-79
Oman and, 388, 389, 390, 426, 432, 458,
461
Palestine/PLO and, 333, 347, 400, 402 (*see
also* Cairo Agreement)
political parties, 42, 110, 292, 308, 344, 359,
363, 368, 493, 563
Saudi Arabia and, 36, 267, 334, 346, 357,
372, 392, 414, 469, 471, 573
Soviet Union and, 35, 60, 130, 131, 184, 334,
338, 356, 359, 415, 456, 458, 498, 567
Syria and, 13, 35-36, 55, 56, 75, 117, 255,
348, 356, 409, 440 (*see also* United Arab
Republic)
U.S. and, 23, 30, 60, 130, 334, 335, 338,
346, 356, 357, 368, 392, 458, 491, 497,
498, 528, 572 (*see also* Camp David
Accords)
Yemen and, 14, 465, 582-83
(*see also* Peace Process)
Egyptian-Israeli Peace Treaty (1979), 56, 119,
123, 129-30, **130-31**, 232, 267, 305, 334,
338, 342, 346, 364, 373, 375, 392, 406, 409-
10, 415, 458, 471, 493, 497, 510, 517
Egyptian-Soviet Friendship Treaty, **131**, 458
Eid al Adha, 18, **131**
Eid al Fitr, 18, **131**
Eilat, Israel, 34
Eisenhower Doctrine, 103, 106, **131**, 297, 305,
398, 460
Eisenhower, Dwight, 131, 498
Ekeus, Rolf, 198, 216, 391, 557, 559
el. *See* al
El Salvador, 244
Elam, 139
Elazer, David, 123
Eliezer, Binyamin Ben, 293
England. *See* Britain
Entebbe, Uganda, 332
Epiphany, 18, **132**
Erbil. *See* Irbil

Eretz Yisrael, **132**, 185, 309, 364, 482
Esfahan. *See* Isfahan
Eshkol, Levi, 21, 87, 91, 123, 128, **132-33**, 295,
315, 320
Ethiopia, 17, 25, 97
Euphrates River, 70, **133**, 150, 167, 271, 281,
320, 484
Eve, 53, 252

Fadlallah, Muhammad Hussein, 188
Fahd ibn Abdul Aziz al Saud, king of Saudi
Arabia, 2, 6, 38, 85, **133-34**, 158, 219, 267,
268, 360, 382, 469, 470, 472, 576
Fahyum, Egypt, 4, 5
Failakah, 27
Faisal ibn Abdul Aziz al Saud, king of Saudi
Arabia, 2, 133, **134-35**, 224, 253, 267, 357,
372, 374, 392, 411, 414, 469, 471, 573, 575
Faisal I ibn Hussein al Hashem, king of Iraq, 7,
25, 27, **135**, 148, 151, 181, 202, 215-16,
279, 296, 355, 360, 432, 440, 460, 494, 505
Faisal II ibn Ghazi al Hashem, king of Iraq, 4,
39, 49, **136**, 142, 297, 433, 460
Faisal, Yusuf, 75, 117
Falastinuna (magazine), 137
Fanon, Franz, 480
faqih, **136**, 152
Farah, Shahbanu, 274
Faraj, Muhammad Abdul Salam, 15-16
Farsi Island, 156
Farsi language. *See* Persian language
Faruq, king of Egypt, 129, **136**, 353, 355, 357, 564
Fatah, 1, 46, 57, 80, 92, **136-38**, 171, 178, 266-
67, 317, 403, 404, 407, 408, 428, 501, 507,
568-69
Fatah (Revolutionary Council). *See* Abu Nidal
Fatima (daughter of Muhammad), 181, 231,
319, 486
Fatimi, Hussein, 139
Fatimid dynasty, 102, 231, 244, 286, 400, 485
al Fawwaz, Khalid, 110
Fedai Khalq, **138-39**, 514, 531
Fedaiyan-e Islam, **139**, 265, 338, 443, 514
feddan, **139**

Fedmeen, Egypt, **4**
Ferid, Damad, 526
Fertile Crescent, **139-40**, 180, 321
Fez, Morocco, 38, 133, 416
fiqh, 65, 85, 136, **140**, 150, 203, 477, 492, 502, 587
First Gulf War. *See* Gulf War I
First Intifada. *See* Intifada
First World War, 2, 20, 27, 39, 44, 50, 51, 77, 89, 92, 121, 129, 135, 148, 149, 150, 152, 181, 186, 202, 209, 240, 252, 289, 296, 317, 319, 333, 386, 409, 410, 431, 440, 455, 460, 479, 494, 504, 510, 517, 530, 563, 578, 579, 586, 589
Fiver Shias. *See* Zaidis
Ford, Gerald, 403
France, 39, 79, 145, 156, 223, 259, 279
    Britain and, 149, 391, 528 (*see also* Sykes-Picot Pact)
    Egypt and, 111, 528 (*see also* Suez War)
    Iran and, 190, 340, 442, 444
    Iraq and, 64, 65, 82, 159, 160, 161, 162, 164, 169, 196, 559
    Israel and, 90, 326, 342, 479, 528 (*see also* Suez War)
    Lebanon and, 23, 89, 114, 115, 140, 146, 149, 238, 277, 299, 304-5, 317-18, 308, 342, 362, 450, 467, 490, 495, 509 (*see also*Sykes-Picot Pact)
    Syria and, 7, 11, 18, 27, 30, 42, 99, 116-17, 121, 123, 135, 140, 149, 177, 308, 317-18, 342, 348, 450, 467, 489, 505-6 (*see also* Sykes-Picot Pact)
    U.S. and, 391, 528
Franco-Lebanese Treaty, **140**, 305
Franco-Syrian Treaty, **140**, 440, 506
Franjieh clan, **141**
Franjieh, Hamid, 140, 141
Franjieh, Suleiman, **140-41**, 145, 146, 263, 298, 305, 463, 468
Franjieh, Tony, 140, 145, 298
Frankel, Zacharias, 118
Freedom Movement of Iran. *See* Liberation Movement of Iran

Freetown, Sierra Leone, 92
Freij, Elias, 407
Front for Steadfastness and Resistance. *See* Steadfastness Front
Fuad, Ahmad, 129, 136, 564
Fundamentals: The Testimony to Truth, 108

Gabon, 392, 394
Gahal, 87, 133, **141-42**, 185, 308, 309, 320, 482, 569
al Gailani, Abdul Qadir, 499
Gailani, Rashid Ali, 4, 7, 26, 136, **142**, 149, 202-3, 216, 377, 460, 489
Galilee, 32, 108, 121
al Gamaat al Islamiya, 5, 6, 130, **142-43**, 335, 572
al Gamaat al Muslimin. *See* al Takfir wal Hijra
Gamaliya village, Egypt, 4
Gamassy, Abdul Ghani, 458
Gardiner, Muna, 8
Garner, Jay, 169
gas. *See* natural gas
Gaza city, Gaza Strip, 32, 33, 48, 91, **143-44**, 178
Gaza Strip, 33, 34, 38, 45, 46, 47, 48, 80, 81, 103, 124, 137, 138, **144**, 154, 171, 172, 177, 178, 179, 182, 203, 207, 228, 231, 232, 236, 239, 242, 257, 262, 329, 333, 347, 373, 404, 406, 407, 408, 414, 416, 418, 419, 428, 429, 448, 462, 475, 479, 482, 498, 499, 538, 540, 541, 568, 570- 71, 576
Geagea, Samir, 301, 424
Gemara, **144**, 177, 322, 515
Gemayel, Amin, 29, 92, 141, **144-45**, 188, 260, 264, 299, 302-3, 305, 423, 424, 463, 495
Gemayel, Bashir, 140-41, 144, **145-46**, 260, 297, 298, 300, 301, 305, 332, 342, 361, 423, 463, 483, 510
Gemayel, Pierre, 140, 141, 145, **146**, 263, 298, 301, 423, 424
General People's Congress, **146-47**, 464, 582, 583, 584
General Zionists, **147**, 308, 430
Geneva Conventions on War, 58, **147-48**, 244, 542

Geneva, Switzerland, 47, 147, 159, 181, 299, 321, 392, 404, 415, 417, 477, 494, 508, 570

Genscher, Hans Dietrich, 562

Germany, 12, 21, 27, 28, 36, 49, 50, 53, 72, 75, 77, 78, 87, 118, 136, 146, 159, 164, 209, 259, 289, 353, 362, 397, 399, 442, 457, 497, 506, 516, 529, 532, 564, 585, 586

Gesher, 390

al Ghadr, Naji, 372

Ghani, Abdul Aziz Abdul, 579

Ghanim, Faraj Said, 4

Ghanim, Wahib, 51

Ghanoum, Alia Hamida, 95

Ghashmi, Ahmad Hussein, 3, 14, 20, **148**, 463, 528, 579, 580, 584

Ghazala, Abdul Halim Abu, 334

al Ghazali, Abu Hamid Muhammad, 223, 499

Ghazan, Khan Mahmud, 510

Ghazi ibn Faisal I al Hashem, king of Iraq, 4, 136, **148**, 289, 453

Al Ghazu (magazine), 587

Ghita, Ali Kashif, 429

Ghom. *See* Qom

Gilani, Ayatollah Muhammad Muhammadi, 209

Gilani, Fathullah, 209

Glubb (Pasha), Sir John Bagot, 32, **148-49**, 198, 352

Golan Heights, 34, 35, 54, 57, 69, 123, **149-50**, 231, 232, 241, 373, 413, 415, 507, 508, 538

Goldmann, Nahum, 574

Goldstein, Baruch, 170, 184

Golpaygani, Muhammad Reza Musavi, **150**, 481

Gordon, Aaron David, 293, 295

Goshe, Samir, 405

Great Bitter Lake, 3, 35

Great Britain. *See* Britain

Greater Lebanon, 151, 304

Greater Syria, 50, 66, 109, 135, **150-51**, 202, 362, 450, 504, 505, 509

Greater Tumb/Tunb Island. *See* Tumb/Tunb Islands

Greater Yemen, 13

Greece/Greek empire, 45, 140, 159, 258, 317, 400, 466, 476, 490, 517, 526, 529, 534, 591

Greek Catholic Church, 118, **151**, 182, 307, 535

Greek Orthodox Church, 11, 19, 28, 93, 118, **151**, 171, 307, 362, 468

Greenburg, Uri Zvi, **151-52**

Gregorian calendar, 127, **152** (*see also* Christian calendars)

Gregorian Orthodox Church, **152**

Gregory the Illuminator, Saint, 50, 152

Gregory XIII (pope), 107, 152, 316

Guardians Council, 59, 60, 86, **152-53**, 208, 271, 343, 443

Guardians of the Cedars, 30, **153**, 300, 301

Gulbenkian, C. S., 377, 380, 385

Gulf, the (Arab/Arabian/Persian Gulf), 2, 10, 44, 73, 103, 126, 133, **153**, 154, 162, 314, 321m 343, 344, 368, 385, 386, 393, 532

Gulf Cooperation Council (GCC), 10, 30, 73, 269, **153-54**, 389, 410, 432, 436, 462, 520, 521, 527, 533, 537, 562

Gulf states, **154**, 178, 196, 210, 216, 385, 385, 389, 404, 406, 426

Gulf War I (1980-88). *See* Iran-Iraq War

Gulf War II (1991), 38, 40, 47, 57, 64-65, 67, 69, 71, 74, 80, 82, 84, 85, 96, 104, 113, 121, 133, 138, 147, 149, 154, **157-61**, 171, 178, 194, 196-97, 200, 212, 216, 219, 220, 224, 249, 252, 255, 264, 269, 274, 281, 282, 283, 287-88, 290, 292, 300, 322, 326, 332, 334, 346, 347, 348, 355, 363, 378, 379, 382, 387, 392, 404, 410, 412, 417, 428, 429, 444, 449, 450, 454, 462, 464, 472, 495, 503, 507, 513, 520, 521, 525, 528, 537, 540, 543-57, 563, 572, 573, 580

Gulf War III (2003), 6, 65, 67, 71, 83, 85, 98, 105, 113, **161-70**, 195, 197-98, 271, 273, 284, 333, 341, 354, 366, 413, 436, 445, 473, 503, 508-9

Al Gumhuriya (periodical), 457

Gush Emunim, **170**, 247, 365, 421

ha, **171**

HaAm, Ahad, 588

HaAhdut (journal), 89, 92

Habash, George, 40, **171-72**, 182, 273, 411, 427, 512

Habib, Philip, 238
Habibi, Emile Shukri, **172**
Habtour, Muhammad ibn Khalifa, 536
Hadash, **172**, 236, 445
Haddad, Naim, 362
Haddad, Saad, 237, 303, 495
Haddad, Wadi, 100
al Hadi, Abd Rabbo Mansur, 578
Hadith, **172-73**, 204, 222, 224, 344, 436, 438,
    455, 477, 479, 485, 502, 516, 565
Hadrian, Roman emperor, 243
Hafiz, Amin, 99, **173-74**, 226
Haganah, 13, 32, 87, 122-23, 132, **174**, 187,
    220, 221, 240, 278, 308, 315, 367, 408, 409,
    421, 447, 482, 492, 496, 589
Hagar, 45, 175, 262
Haifa, 32, 72, 159, 172, **174**, 236, 434
Hairi-Yazdi, Abdul Karim, 150, 275
hajj, 98, 131, **174-75**, 222, 252, 262, 318, 319,
    394, 488, 535, 550
Hajj Umran, Iraq, 155
al Hakim, Fatimid Caliph, 125-26, 176
al Hakim, Muhammad Baqir, 503
Hakim, Muhsin, 120, 274, 481
al Hakim, Tawfiq, **175-76**
Hakimi, Ibrahim, 350
Hakimiya, **176**
Halabja, Iraq, 28, **176**, 228
Halacha, **176-77**, 247, 322, 396, 446, 534
Hama, Syria, 42, 56, 58, **177**, 225, 349, 519
Hamad, Sultan, 343
Hamadan, Iran, 78
al Hamadani, Yusuf, 499
Hamadeh, Marwan, 431
Hamadi, Saadoun, 161, 215
Hamas, **177-79**, 207, 257, 317, 333, 347, 407,
    434, 475, 487, 501, 577
Hamdi, Abdullah, 179
Hamdi, Ibrahim, 3, 14, 20, 68, 148, **179**, 221,
    358, 463, 579
Hamid II, Abdul, 24, 181, 263, 409, 410
Al HaMishmar (paper), 493
Hammurabi, 70
Hamuda, Yahya, 403

Hamza, Mir, 572
Hamzeh ibn Hussein al Hashem, crown prince of
    Jordan, 254
Hanafi Code, **179-80**, 205, 209, 281, 477, 502
HaNasi, Judah, 177, 259, 515
Hanbal, Ahmad ibn, 180
Hanbali Code, **180**, 205, 502, 564
Hanukkah, **180**
HaPoale HaTzair, 13, 49, 50, 90, 132, **180**, 186,
    293, 314
HaPoale HaTzair (journal), 180
Har Homa/Jabal Abu Ghneim, 178
Haram al Sharif. *See* Noble Sanctuary
Harbi, Khalid, 98
Harel, Isser, 331, 486
Hariri, Rafiq, **180-81**, 191, 294, 304, 431
al Haritihi, Hamoud Abdullah, 388
Harkat al Jihad, 572
Harmelin, Yosef, 487
al Harthi, Isa ibn Salim, 511, 527
Hasa region, 2
al Hashem clan, 39, 124, 135, **181**, 182, 318,
    409
Hashemi, Taha, 142
al Hashemi, Yassin, 148
Hashid tribal confederation, 14, 70, 148, 372,
    463, 527-28
Haskel, Mary, 250
HaShomer, 174
HaShomer HaTzair, 13, 278, 294, 315, 515
Hassadic Jews, 151, **182**, 351, 584
Hassan, Bilal, 124, 182
Hassan, Hussein Kamil, 197, 216
Hassan ibn Hussein al Hashem, Crown Prince of
    Jordan, 8, 9, 199, 201
Hassan, Khalid, 137
Hassan, King of Morocco, 58
Hawa, Said, 225
Hawatmeh, Nayif, 40, 123, **182-83**, 411, 512
Hazhir, Abdul Hussein, 139
Heath, Edward, 374, 392
Hebrew Bible. *See* Old Testament
Hebrew language, 23, 44, 53, 93, 118, 121, 152,
    183, 231, 235, 258, 476, 584, 588

Hebrew Resistance Movement, 307

Hebron, West Bank, 32, 33, 34, 48, 170, 178, **183-84**, 234, 243, 418, 475, 484, 487, 568, 570, 571

Heikal, Muhammad Hassanein, **184-85**

Hejailan, Jamil Ibrahim, 154

Helmi, Ali Mustafa Kamal, 129

Helou, Charles, 146, **185**, 263, 305, 468

Heraclitus, Emperor, 243

Hermon, Mount, 35, 256

Herod the Great, King, 183, 242, 243, 466, 490, 565

Heroes of Israel (Herzog), 186

Herut, 87, 141, 152, **185**, 308, 447, 478, 483

Herzl, Theodor, 446, 573, 588, 589-90

Herzog, Chaim, **185-86**

Herzog, Isaac, 185

Hess, Moses, 588

Hetata, Sherif, 451

hijab. *See* Islamic dress

Hijaz, Saudi Arabia, 2, 4, 7, 39, 134, 135, 148, 181, **186**, 318, 525, 565

Hillah, Iraq, 167, 169

al Hilli, Jamal al-Din ibn Yusuf, 205

Hina, Bani, 527

Hindawi, Nizar, 507

Hindus, 291, 389, 500, 538

Hinnawi, Sami, 11, 489, 586

Histadrut, 13, 90, 91, 92, 132, 152, 180, 185, **186-88**, 295, 307, 315, 319, 390, 479, 485, 516, 589

Hitler, Adolf, 50, 203, 399

Hittites, 183

Hizbollah, 22, 55, 93, 115, **188-90**, 223, 227, 228, 299, 306, 316, 347, 495, 508, 518, 539

Hobeika, Elie, 141, 145, 261

Hofi, Yitzhak, 331

Hogarth, D. G., 296

Holocaust, 28, 53, 397, 584

Holy City. *See* Jerusalem

Holy Land, **190**

Homs, Syria, 42, 55, 58, 62, 173, **190**, 201, 241

Hormuz Ardeshir, 15

Hormuz, Straits of, 153, **190**, 423, 533

Hormuzis, 343

Hoss, Salim, **190-91**, 261, 294, 430, 468

hostage taking and hostages, 100, 188, 189, **191-93**, 227, 251, 332, 482, 561 (*see also*Irangate Affair)

Hourani, Akram, 11, 42, 75

House of Saud, 2, 3, 24, 267, **193**, 411, 447, 527, 565, 573

Hoveida, Amir Abbas, 72, **193-94**, 445

Hrawi, Elias, 29, 93, 181, 191, **194**, 294, 300, 301, 306, 424

al Hudaibi, Hassan Islam, 344

Hujariya region, North Yemen, 3

Humaidan, Ibrahim, 73

Hussein ibn Ali al Hashem, 2, 7, 39, 135, 181, 186, 252, 318, 319, 409, 470

Hussein ibn Talal al Hashem, King of Jordan, 8, 9, 26, 34, 47, 57, 80, 124, 138, 149, 171, **199-201**, 255, 256, 257, 332, 346-47, 352, 357, 373, 406, 416, 418, 428, 441, 462, 507, 514

Hussein, Imam, 231, 317, 486, 586

Hussein, Qusay Saddam, 165, **194-95**, 199

Hussein, Saddam, 36, 47, 57, 64, 65, 66, 76, 77, 80, 81, 82, 83, 84, 105, 113, 120, 138, 154, 155, 171, 194, **195-99**, 200, 211, 215, 216, 218, 226, 264, 271, 274, 283-83, 287, 290, 332, 334, 335, 341, 346, 347, 354, 355, 391, 404, 410, 412-13, 428, 429, 436, 445, 454, 462, 501, 503, 507, 513, 520, 524, 525, 528, 558, 563 (*see also* Gulf War II; Gulf War III)

Hussein, Uday, 165, 195

al Husseini, Abdul Qadir, 203

al Husseini clan, **203**

al Husseini, Faisal, **201-2**, 203, 407

al Husseini, Haajj Muhammad Amin, 29, 31-32, **202-3**, 407

al Husseini, Hassan, 203

Husseini, Hussein, 22

al Husseini, Hussein, 203

al Husseini, Izz al-Din, 280, 284

al Husseini, Kamel, 202

al Husseini, Musa Kazim, 203

al Husseini, Mustafa, 203

al Husseini, Salim, 203
al Husseini, Taher, 203
Hyrcanus, John, 466

Ibadh, Abdullah ibn, 203
Ibadhis, **203-4**, 253, 272, 389, 527
ibn. *See* bin
Ibn Abbas, Said, 497
Ibn Affan, Othman, 203, 206, 222, 252, 281,
    438, 486, 502
Ibn Ali, Ghalib, 388, 460, 461
Ibn Ali, Hamza, 126
Ibn Ali, Hussein, 264, 339, 460, 504
Ibn Ali, Isa I, 269
Ibn Ali, Talib, 461
Ibn Anas, Malik, 314, 477
Ibn Baz, Abdul Aziz ibn Abdullah. *See* al Baz,
    Abdul Aziz ibn Abdullah
Ibn Hussein, Ali, 4
Ibn Jaafar, Abdullah, 231
Ibn Jaafar, Ismail, 231
Ibn Khattab, Omar (caliph), 84, 206, 222, 243,
    319, 486, 502
Ibn Malik, Anas, 566
Ibn Marwan, Abdul Malik, 243-44, 371
Ibn Muhammad, Abdul Aziz, 193
Ibn Muhammad, Thani, 521
Ibn Musaid, Faisal, 135, 471
Ibn Muwaiya, Yazid, 264
Ibn Rashid, Muhammad, 2, 470
Ibn Saud. *See* Abdul Aziz ibn Abdul Rahman al
    Saud
Ibn Saud, Abdullah, 193, 565
Ibn Saud, Muhammad, 180, 193, 565
Ibn Sultan, Khalid, 159
Ibn Sultan, Sayyid Turki ibn Said, 387
Ibn Sultan, Shakbut, 354
Ibn Taimiya, Taqi al Din, 18, 564
Ibn Thabit, Muhammad Zaid, 437
Ibn Thani, Muhammad, 125
Ibn Ziyad, Ubaidullah, 54
Ibrahim, Izzat, 215
Idris, Yusuf, **204**
Al Ihya al Arabi (journal), 100

ijma, **204-5**, 314
ijtihad, 85, 180, 204, **205**, 341, 492, 565
Ikhwan, 2, 134, **205-6**, 267, 317, 360, 452, 470,
    561, 565
Ikhwan al Muslimin. *See* Muslim Brotherhood
imam, **206**
imamat, **206-7**
Imamis. *See* Twelver Shias
In Search of Identity (Sadat), 458
Independent Nasserites, 302, 343
India, 10-11, 41, 72, 77, 291, 344, 395, 396,
    401, 410, 565
Indonesia, 18, 41, 356, 392, 394
Inqilab-e Islami (newspaper), 78
*Inquiry and Clarification of Many Hajj and Umra
    Issues* (al Baz), 85
Intermediate School of Thought (Shariati), 481
Inter-Service Intelligence, Pakistan, 5, 16, 96
intifada, 170, 177, **207-8**, 228, 232, 233, 252,
    347, 404, 416, 428, 434, 441, 538, 569, 571,
    576
Iran, 10, 50, 51, 74, 78, 104, 139, 152, 153,
    154, **208-11**, 231, 281, 286, 289, 312, 313,
    314, 318, 344, 367, 395, 410, 435, 485, 536,
    589, 591
    Britain and, 139, 190, 209-10, 213, 264, 397-
        98, 399-400, 431, 525, 528, 530, 533,
        585, 586
    Egypt and, 399
    France and, 190, 340, 442, 444
    Iraq and, 83-84, 113, 120, 154, 157, 211-12,
        228, 273, 283, 524-25, 539 (*see also* Iran-
        Iraq War)
    Israel and, 532
    Jordan and, 346
    Kuwait and, 291, 453, 454
    leaders, 59-60, 75, 78, 86, 150, 193, 264,
        269, 272, 274, 330, 343, 350, 397, 399,
        442-43, 459, 481, 514, 562, 585
    Lebanon and, 22, 188, 227, 277
    Libya and, 36, 254, 270, 410
    military, 323
    Oman and, 390, 426-27, 432
    Palestine/PLO and, 252

political parties, 138-39, 229, 284, 308, 339, 359, 365, 494

Russia and, 213-14, 510

Saudi Arabia and, 6, 394-95

Soviet Union and, 63, 83-84, 190, 209, 213-14, 280, 284, 285, 350, 397, 399-400, 442, 511, 528, 530, 585 (*see also* Iranian-Soviet Treaty)

Syria and, 36, 254, 270, 410

U.S. and, 75, 126, 190, 191-93, 209-11, 214, 270-71, 276, 291, 375, 398-99, 443, 444-45, 563, 585 (*see also* Iran-Iraq War; Iran-gate Affair)

(*see also*Constitutional Revolution; Islamic Revolution; oil and gas industry [Iran])

Iran-Contra Affair. *See* Irangate Affair

Irangate Affair, 188, 192, **212-13**, 227, 332

Iranian calendar, **213**

Iranian-Russian Treaty, **213-14**

Iranian-Soviet Treaty of Guarantee and Neutrality, **214**

Iran-Iraq Frontier Treaty, **211**, 525

Iran-Iraq Treaty of International Boundaries and Good Neighborliness, 154, 157, **211-12**, 524-25

Iran-Iraq War (Gulf War I), 1, 10, 12, 15, 30, 36, 38, 57, 64, 67, 71, 74, 76, 79, 80, 82, 84, 86, 120-21, 126, 153, **154-57**, 158, 176, 188, 190, 192, 194, 196, 200, 210, 224, 253, 255, 269, 270, 273-74, 276, 280, 285, 287, 290, 309, 317, 323, 324, 334, 340, 354, 366, 376, 377-78, 379, 381-82, 386, 389, 393, 410, 411-12, 429, 432, 442, 443, 444, 447, 453, 484, 492, 501, 503, 510, 512, 521, 525, 533, 537, 542, 562

Iraq, 1, 30, 31, 40, 74, 97, 105, 133, 139, 154, **214-18**, 279, 281, 286, 320, 321, 395, 396, 411, 485, 496, 566

Baath coup, 11, 49, 64, 66, 113, 120, 195, 214, 264, 275, 362

Britain and, 2, 4, 7, 25-26, 82, 112, 135, 142, 148-49, 159, 160, 202-3, 206, 215-16, 218, 249, 286, 354-55, 377, 391, 399-400, 401, 431-32, 460, 467, 525 (*see also* Gulf War III; Operation Desert Fox)

Egypt and, 4, 30, 36, 47, 49, 76, 159, 160, 327, 332, 334, 346

France and, 64, 65, 82, 159, 160, 164, 169, 196, 559

Iran and, 83-84, 113, 120, 154, 157, 211-12, 228, 273, 283, 524-25, 539 (*see also* Iran-Iraq War)

Israel and, 32-34, 249, 326-27, 332

Jordan/Transjordan and, 7, 9, 136, 149, 165, 200, 218, 224, 255, 256

Kuwait and, 4, 30, 47, 64, 120, 165, 218, 224, 289-90, 291, 295, 378, 433, 452, 453, 454, 539-40 (*see also* Gulf War II)

leaders, 4, 39, 48-49, 64, 76, 82, 104, 135-36, 142, 148, 194, 195, 274, 433, 459, 491, 512

military, 323-25, 327

North Yemen and, 68, 584

Oman and, 159, 390, 432

Palestine/PLO and, 11, 47, 80, 402, 404, 417, 462

political parties/groups, 66, 120, 358, 362, 411, 502

Russia and, 65, 161, 162, 164, 197, 559

Saudi Arabia and, 6, 158, 159, 160, 161, 214, 218, 295, 378, 469, 473, 526, 576

South Yemen and, 68

Soviet Union and, 64, 156, 196, 219-20, 283, 377

Syria and, 36, 47, 54, 57, 58, 77, 80, 159, 162, 164, 173, 196, 440, 507, 508-9

United Arab Republic and, 113

U.S. and, 6, 30, 64, 80, 81, 82-83, 104, 105, 121, 126, 196, 211, 218-19, 291, 377, 443, 572 (*see also* Gulf War II; Gulf War III; Iran-Iraq War; Operation Desert Fox)

Yemen and, 464, 580

(*see also* oil and gas industry [Iraq]; Persia and Persians; United Nations Special Commission on Iraq)

Iraqi invasion of Kuwait. *See* Gulf War II

Iraqi Kurdistan Front (IKF), 28, **218**, 228, 287, 412, 513

Iraqi National Accord, 104, **218-19**

Iraqi National Congress, 104, **219**, 412
Iraqi-Saudi Non-Aggression Pact, **219**
Iraqi-Soviet Friendship Treaty, **219-20**
Iraq-Najd Neutral Zone. *See* Saudi Arabia-Iraq Neutral Zone
Iraq-Saudi Arabia Neutral Zone. *See* Saudi Arabia-Iraq Neutral Zone
Irbil, Iraq, 83, 197, **220**, 413, 513
Irgun Zvai Leumi, 87, 174, 185, **220-21**, 241, 307, 308, 315, 408, 447, 478, 496-97, 519, 569
Iryani, Abdul Karim, 463, 464, 579
al Iryani, Abdul Rahman, 14, **221**, 372, 579
Isfahan, Iran, **222**
Iskandri, Iraj, 531
Ishmael. *See* Ismail
Islam and Muslims, 12, 17, 44, 45, 48, 53, 56, 61, 63, 64, 65, 70, 72, 74, 79, 93, 96, 97, 106, 109, 118, 119, 124, 125-26, 128, 130, 135, 137, 140, 142, 145, 146, 153, 172, 174, 179, 183, 186, 205, 206, 208, 211, 214, 215, 218, **222-23**, 226, 234, 253, 254, 256, 261, 268, 289, 297, 300, 305, 307, 318, 319, 331, 344, 348, 349, 362, 371, 387, 389, 422, 429, 434, 436, 445, 455, 459, 463, 467, 469, 501, 504, 505, 509, 514, 519, 522-23, 534, 535, 536, 538, 565, 566, 572, 573, 577, 581, 586, 591 (*see also* Alawis; Hanafi; Hanbali; Ibadhis; Islamism; Jaafari; Kharijis; Maliki; pan-Islamism; Quran; Shafii; Sharia; Shia; sufism; Sunni; Wahhabi; Zaidi)
Islam and the Problem of Civilization (Qutb), 439
Islamabad, Pakistan, 65, 225, 587
Islambouli, Khalid Ahmad, 16, 143
Islambouli, Muhammad Shawki, 143, 459
Islamic Action Front. *See* Muslim Brotherhood (Jordan)
Islamic Amal, 188, *223*
Islamic banking, **223-24**
Islamic calendar, **224**
Islamic Conference Organization, 135, 154, **224-25**, 226, 253, 273, 276, 371, 395, 411, 436, 457, 458, 471, 485, 520, 573
Islamic Consultative Assembly. *See* Majlis

Islamic dress, **225**
Islamic Front of Syria, **225-26**, 350
Islamic fundamentalism, 6, 16, 134, 143, 180, **226**, 273, 334, 345, 360, 451, 453, 472, 501, 508
Islamic Government: Rule of the Faqih (Khomeini), 275
Islamic Iranian Participation Front, **226-27**, 272
Islamic Jihad (Egypt). See al Jihad al Islami (Egypt)
Islamic Jihad (Lebanon), 192, 212, 223, **227**, 317
Islamic Jihad (Palestine), 178, 188, **227-28**, 317, 333, 407, 434, 475, 500, 501, 576
Islamic Law, 78, 204, 205, 205, 206, 223 (*see also* fiqh; Hanafi Code; Hanbali Code; Quran; Sharia; sunna)
Islamic Majlis (Iran). *See* Majlis
Islamic Movement of Kurdistan (IMK), 28, **228**, 283, 513
Islamic Republican Party, 59, 60, 79, **229**, 270, 277, 309, 343, 442, 494
Islamic Revolution (Iran), 60, 72, 73, 78, 82, 104, 120, 143, 150, 157, 196, 212, 214, 225, 226, **229-30**, 265, 268, 269, 270, 283, 309, 317, 330, 343, 346, 354, 381, 387, 411, 437, 444, 447, 453, 471, 492, 517, 525, 533, 537, 562, 567
Islamic Revolutionary Komitehs. *See* Revolutionary Komitehs
Islamism and Islamists, 15,16, 27-28, 56, 57, 61, 62, 65, 74, 95, 96, 130, 143, 177, 201, **230**, 407, 439, 500, 508, 571 (*see also* Islamic fundamentalism)
Ismail (Ishmael), 45, 175, 262
Ismail, Abdul Fattah, 20, 88, **230-31**, 336, 496, 580, 582
Ismail, Mahmud, 404
Ismail, Shah of Persia, 71, 318, 333, 436, 510
Ismailia, Egypt, 35, 79
Ismailis, 125-26, **231**, 485, 509
Israel, 12, 99, 113, 126, 127, 132, 135, 138, 139, 147, 183, 185, **231-34**, 259, 263, 278, 378, 466, 492, 517, 524

Britain and, 90, 232, 307, 315, 479, 528 (*see also* Suez War)

Egypt and, 4, 32-36, 42, 46, 91, 94, 111, 142-43, 184, 203, 246, 247, 257-58, 295, 356-57, 411, 415, 441, 458, 479, 491, 497 (*see also* Camp David Accords; Egyptian-Israeli Peace Treaty; Suez War)

founding in 1948, 12, 21, 32, 80, 90, 130, 183, 186, 232, 249, 278, 279-80, 307, 348, 370, 402, 405, 409, 476, 518, 567, 584, 589, 590

France and, 90, 326, 479, 528 (*see also* Suez War)

Iran and, 532

Iraq and, 32-34, 326-27, 332

Jordan/Transjordan and, 8, 9, 21-22, 32-34, 37, 68, 81, 103, 124, 199-201, 255, 257, 319-20, 566 (*see also* Jordanian-Israeli Peace Treaty)

leaders, 21, 49, 81, 86, 89, 91, 122, 127, 132, 185, 262, 265, 295, 319, 367, 369, 421, 440, 478-79, 482, 484-85, 569

Lebanon and, 31, 32-33, 37-38, 47, 81, 82, 92, 100, 141, 223, 236, 257, 298-99, 301, 305, 306, 421, 423, 441, 478, 510, 542 (*see also* Hizbollah; Israeli Invasion of Lebanon; Lebanese-Israeli Peace Treaty)

military, 325-27

Palestine/PLO and, 1, 6-7, 30, 32-33, 40, 81, 82, 100, 124, 236, 238, 248, 251, 257, 293, 314-15, 329, 332-33, 342, 347, 356-57, 371, 400, 404, 413, 427-29, 445, 462, 475, 483, 487, 529, 566, 570 (*see also* Arab-Israeli Wars I-IV; Fatah; Hamas; intifada; Irgun; Oslo Accords I & II; Wye River Memorandum)

political parties/groups, 12, 13, 30, 141, 234-35, 239, 262, 292-94, 308, 309, 310, 312, 314-15, 320, 329, 358, 365, 366, 390, 424, 429, 430, 441, 445, 446, 484, 488, 517, 523, 560, 561

Soviet Union and, 91, 316, 325, 493, 510

Syria and, 32-36, 54, 57-58, 81, 100, 137, 149, 237-38, 342, 356-57, 373, 413, 440, 507-8, 510, 538

U.S. and, 34, 35, 87, 90, 91, 302, 315, 342, 377, 391, 458, 479, 483-84, 491, 498-99, 528, 572, 575 (*see also* Camp David Accords)

(*see also* Judaism and Jews; Peace Process)

Israel BeAliya, **234-35**

Israel BeItainu, **235**, 330, 366

Israel Defense Forces (IDF), 81, 87, 90, 221, 237, 307, 413, 495, 568, 569 (*see also* Military in Israel)

Israeli Arabs, 30, 99, 172, **235-36**, 358, 487, 524

Israeli Invasion of Lebanon (1978), 38, 88, 153, 232, **236-237**, 298, 539

Israeli Invasion of Lebanon (1982), 47, 56, 88, 89, 102, 122, 131, 137, 145-46, 181, 188, 192, 225, 232, **237-38**, 252, 264, 267, 298, 309, 332, 334, 342, 402, 403-4, 414, 428, 430, 463, 483, 495, 510, 539

Israeli Labor Party. *See* Labor Party, Israeli

Israeli Socialist Organization, 124, **239-40**

Israeli-Palestine Liberation Organization Accord. *See* Oslo Accord I

Israel's Finest Hour (Herzog), 186

Istanbul, 7, 77, 89, 92, 135

Al Istiqlal (paper), 228

Italy, 25, 28, 136, 142, 159, 160, 164, 238, 279, 299, 342, 476, 564

Al Ittihad (journal), 121, 172, 523

Ittihad-e Islami (Islamic Alliance), 5

Jaafari Code, 209, **240**

Jabotinsky, Vladimir Zeev, 87, 132, **240-41**, 446, 496, 530

Jacobite Christians. *See* Orthodox Christians, Syrian

Jacobsen, David, 227

Al Jadid (journal), 121

Jadid, Salah, 55, 58, 62, 69, 173, **241-42**, 461, 506

Jaffa, 31, 80, **242**, 574

Jalalabad, Afghanistan, 97

al Jamahir, 64

Jame. *See* Association of Combatant Clergy

Jamiat al Ulama, 572

al Jamri, Abdul Amir, 74, 268
Japan, 153, 161, 442
Jarring, Gunnar, 414, 448
Javad, Muhammad al Taqi, 533
Al Jazeera TV, 166, 168, 436, 520, 587
al Jazzar, Ahmad, 10
Jbail. See Byblos
Jeddah. See Jiddah
Jenin, Palestine, 34, 65, 568
Jericho, West Bank, 8, 33, 48, 81, 233, 234, 239, 242, 333, 373, 404, 418, 475, 484
Jerusalem, 6, 8, 16, 32, 42, 48, 77, 87, 94, 97, 123, 128, 132, 135, 180, 220, 224, 228, 231, 242-44, 262, 307-8, 319, 335, 366, 370, 371, 397, 400, 401, 413, 414, 449, 458, 471, 483, 487, 496, 504, 519, 560, 565, 570, 572, 574, 588, 590
Jerusalem (Mendelssohn), 446
Jerusalem, Latin Kingdom of, 10, 89, 101, 244, 400, 534
Jesus Christ, 10, 18, 86, 93, 94-95, 107-8, 109, 127, 132, 151, 222, 243, 256, 321, 367, 371, 420, 437, 456, 490
Jewish Agency for Palestine, 21, 31, 50, 90, 128, 132, 244-46, 279, 319, 479, 485, 492-93, 574, 589, 590
Jewish Bible. See Bible
Jewish calendar, 246
Jewish festivals, 246
Jewish (Judaistic) fundamentalism, 246-48
Jewish migration. See under Judaism and Jews
Jewish National Fund, 12, 248, 573, 590
Jewish nationalism, 180, 183, 248-49
Jews. See Judaism and Jews
Jews in Arab Middle East, 249-50
Jews in Iran, 250
Jibran (Gibran), Khalil, 250-51
Jibril, Ahmad, 251-52, 428
Jiddah, Saudi Arabia, 65, 95, 96, 98, 135, 158, 224, 252-53, 296, 319, 372, 411, 471, 573, 576
Jifri, Abdul Rahman, 583
jihad, 16, 17, 65, 96, 97, 253, 348, 429, 434, 512, 565, 573

al Jiluwi, Jawrah bint Musaid, 2, 267
Joint Defense and Economic Cooperation Treaty (JDECT), 36, 253-54
Jordan, 30, 31, 65, 67, 104, 115, 124, 127, 135, 137, 151, 183, 254-56, 327, 345, 373, 378, 541
    Britain and, 7-8, 26, 149, 181, 199, 249, 254, 255, 352
    Egypt and, 26, 34, 36, 103, 199, 200, 255, 334, 346, 357, 409
    Iran and, 346
    Iraq and, 9, 136, 165, 200, 218, 224, 255, 256, 347
    Israel and, 8, 9, 21-22, 32-34, 37, 68, 81, 103, 124, 199-201, 255, 257, 566 (see also Jordanian-Israeli Peace Treaty)
    leaders, 7, 8, 181, 199, 352, 514
    Lebanon and, 201, 257
    Oman and, 390, 426-27, 432
    Palestine/PLO and, 8, 11, 24, 38, 46, 47, 80, 100, 137, 182, 199-201, 255, 256-57, 347, 352, 357, 402, 406, 409, 428, 461, 462, 570
    political parties, 67, 114, 346, 358
    Saudi Arabia and, 26, 200, 346
    Soviet Union and, 200, 352
    Syria and, 9, 26, 36, 80, 199, 200, 201, 255, 257, 346, 409, 507
    U.S. and, 9, 199-201, 256-57, 347
    (see also Peace Process; Transjordan)
Jordan River, 7, 45, 121, 127, 132, 137, 144, 254, 256, 447, 570
Jordanian Civil War, 256-57, 423
Jordanian-Israeli Peace Treaty, 233, 255, 257, 293, 322, 347, 371, 418, 422, 428, 441, 507
al Jubair, Muhammad ibn Ibrahim, 470
Judah, Kingdom of, 45, 94, 132, 242, 243, 258, 466
Judaism and Jews, 7, 32, 45, 78, 93, 108, 111, 118, 124, 125, 137, 149, 152, 176, 180, 183, 209, 211, 222, 232, 234, 243, 245, 257-59, 272, 310, 321, 329, 351, 365, 371, 400, 437, 455, 476, 523, 565, 566
    Jewish migration, 20-21, 24-25, 30, 38, 47, 50,

53, 90, 100, 132, 174, 187, 202, 233, 234-35, 244, 245, 249-50, 279, 293, 296, 312, 329, 352, 395, 404, 408, 424, 425, 476, 530, 573, 588-89 (*see also* aliya; White Paper) (*see also* anti-Semitism; Zionism)
Judaism, Conservative. *See* Conservative Judaism
Judaism, Orthodox. *See* Orthodox Judaism
Judaism, Reform. *See* Reform Judaism
Judaism, ultra-Orthodox. *See* Ultra-Orthodox Judaism
Judea, 170, 258, **259**, 400
Judeo-Spanish language. *See* Ladino language
Julian Christian Calendar, **259**
Julius Caesar, 107, 191, 259
Julius III (pope), 105
Jumaah, Numan, 369
Jumblat clan, **261**
Jumblat, Fuad, 261
Jumblat, Kamal, 107, 115, 141, 145, **259-60**, 261, 297, 302, 305, 358, 430, 463, 493-94
Jumblat, Nazira, 261
Jumblat, Walid, 141, **260-61**, 302, 305, 430
Jumhouri-ye Islami (newspaper), 343
al Jumhuriya, 64
June 1967 Arab-Israeli War. *See* Arab-Israeli War III
Juul, Mona, 239

Kaaba, 175, 186, **261**, 318, 319, 535
kabbala. *See* mysticism in Judaism
Kabul, Afghanistan, 62, 97, 210, 472, 532
Kach, **262**, 487
Kahan, Yitzhak, 483
Kahane, Meir, **262-63**, 487
Kandahar, Afghanistan, 97
Karachi, Pakistan, 80
Karameh, Jordan, 46, 137
Karami, Omar, 181, 261
Karami, Rashid, 141, 144, 146, 191, 260, **263-64**, 463
Karbala, Iraq, 54, 70, 166, 167, 168, **264**, 275, 281, 565
Al Karmel (journal), 122
Karo, Joseph, 177

Karrubi, Mahdi, 209, 494
Karun River, 15, 153
Kashani, Abol Qasim, **264-65**, 338
Kashmir, 17, 97
Kasravi, Ahmad, 139
Kassabin, Syria, 52
Kataeb Party. *See* Phalange Party
Katowice, Poland, 12
Katzav, Moshe, 232, **265**
Katzir, Ephraim, **265-66**
Katznelson, Berle, 13, 90, 425
al Kazem, Musa, 533
Kemal, Mustafa, 526
Kennedy, John F., 398
Kerensky, Alexander, 101
Kerr, Malcolm, 23
Khaddam, Abdul Halim, **266**, 505
Khalaf, Salah (Abu Iyad), 9, 45, 47, 81, 136, 137, **266-67**, 568
Khalid ibn Abdul Aziz al Saud, king of Saudi Arabia, 2, 6, 85, 133, **267-68**, 360, 471-72, 562
al Khalifa dynasty, 73, **269**, 314, 521
al Khalifa, Hamad ibn Isa II, 73, 74, **268**
al Khalifa, Isa II ibn Salman, 73, 74, **268-69**, 425, 427
al Khalifa, Jassim ibn Hamad, 435
al Khalifa, Khalifa ibn Salman, 73
al Khalifa, Muhammad ibn Mubarak, 435
al Khalifa, Salman II ibn Hamad, 73, **269**
Khalil, Mustafa, 44, 359, 458
Khalilzad, Zalmay, 169
Khamanei, Ali Husseini, 59, 60, 209, 210-11, 229, **269-71**, 272-73, 276, 330, 343, 442, 443, 562, 563
Khan, Hulagu, 205, 333
Khan, Reza. *See* Pahlavi, Reza Shah
al Kharafi, Jassim, 289
Kharg, Iran, 155, 190, 376
Kharijis, 203, 223, 253, **271-72**
Kharrazi, Kamal, 563
Khartoum, Sudan, 5, 37, 61, 96, 256, 414, 587
Khatami, Muhammad, 6, 209, 210-11, 227, 271, **272-73**, 494, 563

Khatami, Muhammad Reza, 227, 272, 343

Khatib, Ahmad, 40, 55, **273**, 358

al Khattar, Muhammad, 348

Khaur Maskar, South Yemen, 11

Khiyabani, Musa, 340

Khobar Towers, 6, 473

Khoei, Abol Qasim, **274**, 316, 491

Khomeini, Ayatollah Ruhollah Musavi, 59, 60, 75-76, 78, 79, 86, 138-39, 150, 157, 190, 192, 206, 208, 210, 229, 265, 269, 272, **274-77**, 280, 285, 309, 316, 323, 330, 340, 343, 355, 366, 393, 394, 398, 399, 429, 437, 442, 444, 447, 459, 481, 494, 501, 503, 515, 517, 531-32, 562, 563, 572

Khorranshahr, Iran, 155

Khouri, Bishara, 106, 141, 185, 259, **277**, 305, 362, 493, 495

Khouri, Ilya, 407

Khrushchev, Nikita, 62

khums, 150, **277-78**, 486

Khuzistan province, Iran, 15, 216, 376, 437

Kianouri, Nur al Din, 531-32

kibbutzim, 12, 20, 21, 122, 132, **278**, 296, 314, 319, 397, 408, 421, 424, 530

Kiev, Ukraine, 100, 101

King David Hotel, 87, 220, 519

King, Henri, 279

King-Crane Commission, **278-79**

Kirkuk, Iraq, 166, 169, 286, 377, 385, 413

Kiryat Arba, 170, 183, 184, 570

Kissinger, Henry, 35, 297, 322, 374, 392, 415, 491

Klinberg, Marcus, 325

Knesset, **279-80**, 458, 524

Kol Ha'Am (newspaper), 493

Komala-e Jian-e Kordestan, **280-81**, 285, 365

Kook, Abraham Yitzhak, 247

Kook, Zvi Yehuda, 247

Koran. *See* Quran

Kordestan. *See* Kurdistan, Iran

Kordestan Democratic Party of Iran. *See* Kurdistan Democratic Party of Iran

Krai, Ahmad, 407, 418

Kuala Lumpur, Malaysia, 225

Kufa, Iraq, 54, 179, **281**, 486

al Kulini, Abu Jaafar Muhammad, 173

al Kummi, Abu Jaafar Muhammad, 173

Kurdish Democratic Party. *See* Kurdistan Democratic Party

Kurdish Hizbollah, 28

Kurdish language, 84, 214, **281**, 282, 283, 285, 286

Kurdish Majahedin, 28

Kurdish Republic of Mahabad, 82, 282, 284 (*see also* Kurdistan Republic)

Kurdish Revolutionary Party, **281**

Kurdistan Autonomous Region (Iraq), 28, 67, 105, 113, 156, 214, 218, 220, 228, **282**, 286, 287, 324, 411, 512

Kurdistan Democratic Party, Iraq (KDP), 82, 120, 166, 197, 218, 219, 220, 228, 280, 281, **282-84**, 286, 411, 512, 513

Kurdistan Democratic Party of Iran, 84, **284-85**, 365

Kurdistan Front. *See* Iraqi Kurdistan Front

Kurdistan (Kordestan), Iran, 209, **282**, 398, 531, 591

Kurdistan region, **281**

Kurdistan Republic, 83, **285**

Kurds, **286**, 367, 450

Kurds in Iran, 63, 83, 138, 209, **286**, 444, 515

Kurds in Iraq, 49, 76, 82-84, 113, 156, 167, 169, 176, 195, 196, 215, 216, **286-88**, 362, 433, 503, 524, 525 (*see also* Iraqi Kurdistan Front; Kurdistan Autonomous Region)

Kurds in Syria, 74, 115, 116, **288**, 505, 586

Kut, Iraq, 167

Kuwait, 2, 31, 36, 44, 51, 74, 136-37, 153, 154, 202, **288-91**, 568

    Britain and, 2, 26, 27, 162, 289, 385, 451-52, 453, 455

    Egypt and, 4, 36

    Iran and, 291, 453, 454

    Iraq and, 4, 30, 47, 64, 120, 165, 218, 224, 289-90, 291, 295, 433, 452, 453, 454, 539-40 (*see also* Gulf War II)

    leaders, 273, 451-55

    military, 327

political parties/groups, 358
Saudi Arabia and, 288, 289, 431, 452, 469, 473-74, 576
Syria and, 36, 69
U.S. and, 30, 162, 291, 453, 454 (*see also* Gulf War II)
(*see also* oil and gas industry [Kuwait])
Kuwait City, Kuwait, 160, 288, **291-92**
Kuwait crisis (1990-91). *See* Gulf War II
Kuwaiti-Saudi Neutral Zone. *See* Saudi Arabia-Kuwait Neutral Zone

Labor Alignment. *See* Labor-Mapam Alignment
Labor and Property in Islam (Taleqani), 514
Labor Islamic Alliance, **292**, 308, 346
Labor Party (Israel), 1, 12, 13, 22, 82, 91, 123, 170, 185, 186-88, 233, 235, 236, 239, 265, **292-93**, 294, 310, 315, 320, 322, 365, 367, 390, 397, 404, 417, 421, 441, 441, 446, 478, 483, 484, 561, 570
Labor Zionism and Zionists, 147, 240, **293-94**, 446, 447
Labor-Mapam Alignment, 292, **294**, 310
Ladino language, **294**, 395, 476
Lahad, Antoine, 495
Lahoud, Emile, 181, 191, 261, **294-95**, 304, 306, 431
Lahoud, Jamil, 294
Lake, Tony, 218, 219
Land of Israel. *See* Eretz Yisrael
Lapid, Yosef, 488
Larsen, Terje, 239
Latakia, Syria, 18, 51, 59, 250, **295**
Lausanne, Switzerland, 145, 146, 181, 264, 299, 305
Lavon, Pinchas, 91, **295-96,** 315, 397, 479
Law of Return (1950), **296**, 365
Lawrence of Arabia. *See* Lawrence, Thomas Edward
Lawrence, Thomas Edward, **296-97**
League of Arab States. *See* Arab League
League of National Liberation, 312
League of Nations, 7, 25, 26, 78, 135, 140, 151, 216, 249, 279, 304, 389, 401, 467, 566, 589

Lebanese Civil War (1958), 68, 106, 115, 140, 146, 185, 263, **297**, 305, 423, 494
Lebanese Civil War (1975-90), 6, 22, 23, 29, 31, 37, 38, 46, 53, 56, 68, 69, 89, 92, 104, 106, 114, 115, 117, 122, 124, 137, 144, 145, 146, 153, 181, 185, 191, 192, 194, 212, 223, 259, 260, 261, 263, 266, 267, 294, **297-300**, 302, 305, 307, 332, 342, 349, 361, 364, 402, 423, 430, 455, 459, 463, 468, 471, 490, 496, 500, 507, 510, 516, 529
Lebanese Forces, 29, 46, 137, 144, 297, 299, **300-301**, 306, 423, 430
Lebanese Front, 106, 140, 145, 146, 260, 297, 298, 300, **301**, 302, 305, 423, 424
Lebanese National Movement, 46, 115, 124, 137, 146, 260, 297, **302**, 305, 402, 423, 463
Lebanese-Israeli (Putative) Peace Treaty, 56, 144-45, 260, 264, 300, **302-3**, 305
Lebanese-Palestine Liberation Organization Agreement. *See* Cairo Agreement
Lebanese-Syrian Treaty of Brotherhood, Cooperation, and Coordination, 194, 300, **303, 306**, 322, 495
Lebanon, 11, 17, 29, 31, 31, 36, 38, 50, 51, 97, 100, 104, 105, 117, 121, 126, 135, 137, 151, 178, 191, 249, **304-7**, 322, 345, 358, 411, 541
Britain and, 105-6, 149, 238, 298, 362
Egypt and. *See* Cairo Agreement
France and, 23, 89, 106, 114, 115, 140, 146, 149, 238, 277, 299, 304-5, 308, 317-18, 342, 362, 450, 467, 495, 509 (*see also* Sykes-Picot Pact)
Iran and, 22, 188, 227, 277 (*see also* Irangate Affair)
Israel and, 31, 32-33, 37-38, 47, 81, 82, 92, 100, 141, 223, 236, 257, 298-99, 301, 305, 306, 421, 423, 441, 478, 510, 542 (*see also* Hizbollah; Israeli Invasion of Lebanon; Lebanese-Israeli Peace Treaty)
Jordan and, 201, 257
leaders, 29, 92, 105-6, 140, 144-46, 180, 185, 190, 194, 277, 294, 449, 459, 462, 468, 494

military, 327, 343, 495
Palestine/PLO and, 92, 106, 146, 260, 297-
99, 342, 343, 406 (*see also* Cairo Agreement; Lebanese National Movement)
political parties/groups, 68, 114, 153, 188,
223, 300-302, 358, 423, 430, 493, 509,
516
Saudi Arabia and, 6, 31, 38, 299, 364, 471
South Yemen and, 31
Soviet Union and, 510
Sudan and, 31
Syria and, 22, 29, 31, 54, 55, 56, 57, 69, 92-
93, 141, 144-45, 149, 191, 194, 223, 237-
38, 260, 261, 266, 294-95, 298-300, 302,
304, 305-6, 308, 317-18, 327, 342, 361,
362, 423, 430, 450, 468, 507, 508, 510,
529 (*see also* Lebanese-Syrian Treaty)
U.S. and, 31, 106, 144, 227-38, 294, 297,
298, 299, 302, 305, 342, 423, 518
(*see also* Lebanese Civil War; Peace Process)
Lebanon, Mount, 89, 301, 316
Lehi/Lehy (Stern Gang/Group), 174, 220, **307-
8**, 315, 408, 478, 497
Leo IX, Pope, 109, 396
Lesser Tumb (Tunb) Island. *See* Tumb/Tunb
Islands
Leumi, Vaad, 589
Levant, 39, 121, **308**, 476
Levinger, Moshe, 170
Levy, David, 390
Liberal Party, 87, 141, 147, 185, **308**, 430
Liberal Socialist Party, 292, **308**, 346
Liberation Movement of Iran (LMI), 86, **308-9**,
339, 360, 443, 480, 514
Libya, 17, 22, 31, 36, 38, 44, 80, 97, 136, 254,
270, 271, 298, 321, 327, 353, 391, 392, 393,
402, 410, 428, 459, 496, 564
Lieberman, Avigdor, 235
Likud, 1, 50, 82, 87, 123, 142, 170, 233, 234,
235, 239, 247, 265, 292, 294, **309-10**, 316,
320, 364, 369, 370, 417, 421, 478, 482, 484,
517, 561, 567, 569, 570
Little Tumb (Tunb) Island. *See* Tumb/Tunb
Islands

Lloyd George, David, 77, 78
Locker, Berl, 574
Lockerbie, Scotland, 429
Lockwood, Al, 165
London, England, 105, 110, 128, 164, 503, 574
L'Orient le Jour, 185
Lydda (Lod), Israel, 32, 123, 171

Maalim fi al Tariq (Qutb), 439
Maan, Fakhr al Din, 261, 367, 490
Maarach, 91, 294, 310, 315
Maasuma, Fatima, 436
Mabovitch, Moshe, 319
Maccabeans, 400, 517
Maccabeus, Judas, 180, 243, 317
al Madharai, Abu Bakr Muhammad ibn Ali, 566
Madrid, Spain, 133, 178 (*see also* Middle East
Peace Conference, 1991)
Mafdal. *See* National Religious Party
mahdi, 310, 486, 502, 561
Mahdavi-Kani, Muhammad Reza, 60
Mahfouz, Naguib, **310-11**
Mahir, Ali, 564
Mahmud, Abid Hamid, 195
Mahoul, Issam, 326
Mahrun, Muhsin, 425
Maimon/Maimonides, Moses Ben, 177
al Majali, Abdul Hadi, 254
al Majid, Ali, 197
al Majid, Hussein Abd, 195
Majlis, **311-12**
Majlis al Shura, 73
Majnoon Islands, 155, 157
Maki, 121, 172, 236, 240, **312,** 316, 445, 493,
523
Maktab al Khidmat, 16, 17, 61, 65, 95
al Maktum, Maktum ibn Rashid, **312**, 313, 536,
537
al Maktum, Rashid ibn Said, **312-13**, 354, 537
Malaika, Nazik, **313-14**, 474
Maliki Code, 180, 209, **314**, 319, 477, 502, 566
Mamlukes, 101, 102, 179, 180, 181, 183, 400,
490, 500, 517, 529, 534
Manaf, Hashem ibn Abdul, 144, 181

Manama, Bahrain, **314**

Al Manar, 79

Manifesto of Modernity (Asbar), 53

Mansour district, Iraq, 168

Mansur, 71

Mapai, 13, 50, 90-91, 92, 123, 128, 132, 141, 151, 180, 265, 278, 292, 293-94, 295, 310, **314-15**, 319, 320, 364, 421, 424, 430, 441, 479, 485, 487, 493, 516

Mapam, 13, 21, 236, 292, 294, 310, 312, **315-16**, 320, 446, 487, 488, 493

Marashi-Najafi, Shehab al Din, 150, 481

marja-e taqlid, 150, 276, 278, **316**, 486

Maron, John, 316

Maron/Maro, Saint, 316

Maronite Catholic Church, 29, 31, 69, 93, 105, 106, 118, 140, 141, 144, 145, 146, 153, 185, 188, 194, 227, 251, 260-61, 263, 297, 298, 300, 301, 302, 304, 305, 306, 307, **316-17**, 342, 349, 361, 364, 402, 423, 430, 431, 468, 483, 495, 495, 507, 535, 571

martyrdom, 229, 258, 317, 362, 434, 500, 502 (*see also* suicide bombing)

Maruf, Taha Muhyi al Din, 215, 287

Masalikh clan, 24

al Masaari, Muhammad, 110

Mashaal, Khalid, 333, 577

Masharka, Muhammad Zuhair, 505

Mashhad, Iran, **317-18**, 341

Mashian, 27

Masirah Island, Oman, 389

Masjid-e Suleiman, Iran, 373, 375, 385

al Massallat, Subha Talfa, 195

Mauritania, 36, 44, 410

Mawaqif (journal), 53

McCarthy, John, 193, 227

McFarlane, Robert, 212-13

McMahon, Henry, 504

Mecca, Saudi Arabia, 2, 6, 7, 12, 56, 85, 95, 97, 126, 133, 135, 150, 153, 175, 181, 186, 213, 222, 224, 252, 261, 262, 268, **318-19**, 331, 349, 354, 360, 438, 471, 535, 562, 565, 566, 572, 573

Medes, 62, 422

Medina, Saudi Arabia, 12, 44, 54, 133, 186, 213, 222, 224, 262, **319**, 348, 354, 438, 501, 565, 566, 573

Mediterranean Sea, 159, 308, 321, 368

Meir (Meyerson), Golda, 8, 21, 123, 200, **319-20**, 421, 441

Melchior, Michael, 390

Melkite Christians. *See* Greek Catholic Church

Mendelssohn, Moses, 446

Menoufia, Egypt, 61

Meretz, 292, 316, 446, **320**, 488

Mero, Muhammad Mustafa, 505

al Meshad, Yahya, 327, 332

Meshkini, Ayatollah Ali, 209

Mesopotamia, 71, 105, 133, 139, 215, 257, 281, 286, 296, **320-21**, 504, 521

Messiah, 12, **321**, 370

Metni, Nasib, 297

Meyerson, Morris, 319

Mexico, 164, 387, 394

Miari, Muhammad, 429

Middle East, 101, 109, **321**, 394

Middle East Defense Organization, **322**

Middle East Peace Conference (Geneva, 1973), **321-22**

Middle East Peace Conference (Madrid, 1991), 47, 57, 133, 178, 194, 201, 255, 306, **322**, 329, 347, 404, 417, 422, 472, 478, 507, 517

Middle East Treaty Organization (METO), 104

Midrash, **322**

Mifleget HaAvodah HaYisraelit (Israeli Labor Party), 13

Mikunis, Shamuel, 312

Military in Bahrain, **322-23**

Military in Egypt, **323**

Military in Iran, **323**

Military in Iraq, **323-25**

Military in Israel, **325-27**

Military in Jordan, **327**

Military in Kuwait, **327**

Military in Lebanon, **327**

Military in Oman, **327**

Military in Qatar, **328**

Military in Saudi Arabia, **328**

Military in Syria, **328**
Military in United Arab Emirates, **328**
Military in Yemen, **329**
Minsk, Belarus, 100, 293, 425
Mishna, 144, 177, 183, 322, 515 (*see also* Talmud)
Mitchell, George, 420
Mizan (paper), 309
Mizrachi, 329 (*see also* Oriental Jews)
Mizrahi, 12, **329**, 364, 424-25, 560
Mohtashemi, Ali Akbar, 188, 223, 227
Mohieddin, Khalid, 111 (*see also* Muhyi al Din, Khalid)
Mohsen, Zuhair, 461-62
Moledet, 235, **329-30**, 366
Mongols, 71, 84, 121, 244, 318, 333, 488, 516
Montazeri, Hussein Ali, 59, 60, **330-31**, 437, 562
Morocco, 36, 38, 44, 58, 159, 225, 300, 321, 364, 410, 476
Moscow, 13, 35, 46, 59, 75, 82, 84, 88, 160, 372
Moses, 18, 93, 94, 177, 222, 242, 258, 351, 371, 437, 466, 491, 523
mosque, **331**
Mossad, 100, 228, 325, 326-27, **331-33**, 397, 398, 477, 486, 487, 569, 577
Mosul, Iraq, 64, 71, 105, 120, 166, 169, 216, 220, 286, **333**, 526
Most Holy Book, The (Baha Ullah), 72
Motahhari, Murtaza, 60
Motevaselian, Ahmad, 192
Mougneih, Imad, 227
Moussa, Amr, 4, 39, 333
Moyne, Lord, 307, 417, 478
al Mualla, Rashid ibn Ahmad, 536
Muawad, Rene, 29, 194, 300
Mubarak, (Muhammad) Hosni, 5, 47, 101, 119, 129, 130, 143, 185, **333-35**, 345, 359, 369, 451, 493
Muhammad, Ali, **335-36**
Muhammad, Ali Nasser, 88, 230, **336-37**, 580, 582
Muhammad, Aziz, 113

Muhammad, Khalid Shaikh, 18, **337-38**
Muhammad, Prophet (Muhammad ibn Abdullah al Quraish), 12, 18, 44, 53, 54, 70, 85, 86, 124, 126, 144, 172-73, 181, 183, 186, 204, 205, 206, 213, 222, 223, 224, 243, 262, 271, 314, 317, 318, 331, 354, 371, 425, 437, 438, 439, 445, 455, 462, 477, 486, 499, 501, 512, 535, 572, 586
Muhammad, Qazi, 284, 285
Muhammad IV, Sultan, 252, 526
Muhammad VI, Sultan, 27
Muhammad, Zahid, 337
Muhammadiya, Egypt, 79
Muhyi al Din, Khalid, 338, 363
al Muizz, 244
mujahed, **338**
Mujahedini, **339**, 502, 587
Mujahedin-e Islam, 264, **339**
Mujahedin-e Khalq, 79, 139, 229, 276, **339-41**, 365, 366, 443-44, 503, 514, 531, 532
mujtahid, 205, 276, 278, 316, **341**, 386
al Muktana, Baha al Din, 126
Mukhabarat, **341-42**
Multi-National Force (in Lebanon, 1982-84), 238, 299 **342**
Multinational Force and Observers, **342**
Munich, Germany, 100, 332, 487
Muqadam, Muhammad, 192
Murabitun, **343**, 358
Murad, Mustafa Kamel, 308
al Muradi, Abdul Rahman ibn Mujlam, 272
Musa, Hussein, 425
Musavi, Abbas, 189
Musavi, Hussein, 223
Musavi, Mir Hussein, 272, **343**
Musavi, Muhsin, 192
Muscat, Oman, **343-44**, 387, 433, 526
Muslim Brotherhood (Egypt), 79, 205, 292, 308, **344-46**, 355, 368, 369, 410, 439, 455, 493, 511, 573, 576
Muslim Brotherhood (Jordan), 256, **346-47**, 348, 410
Muslim Brotherhood (Palestine), 207, **347**, 410
Muslim Brotherhood (Saudi Arabia), **347-48**

Muslim Brotherhood (Syria), 56, 69, 117, 177, 225, 226, **348-50**, 410, 507

Muslims. *See* Islam and Muslims

Mussadiq, Muhammad, 75, 86, 265, **350**, 360, 375, 398, 442, 480, 514, 531, 585

Mustafa, Abu Ali, 428

Mustafa, Shukri Ahmad, 511

al Mutamid, Caliph, 467

al Mutasim, Caliph, 467

Muwahhidun. *See* Wahhabism and Wahhabis

My Turn to Speak (Bani-Sadr), 79

mysticism, **350-51**, 499

mysticism in Christianity, 351

mysticism in Islam. *See* sufism

mysticism in Judaism, 351

Nablus, West Bank, 34, 80, **351-52M**, 420, 568

Nabulsi, Suleiman, 67, 114, 199, 255, **352-53**

Nadr, Fuad Abu, 301

Nahas (Pasha), Mustafa, 136, **353**, 564

al Nahyan, Shakbut ibn Hamdan, 537

al Nahyan, Zaid ibn Sultan, 9, 313, **353-54**, 536, 537

Nairobi, Kenya, 17, 61, 98, 336, 337, 501, 587

Najab, Suleiman, 116, 405

Najaf, Iraq, 60, 70, 78, 120, 166, 167, 210, 229, 275, 281, **354-55**, 399, 447

Najd, Saudi Arabia, 2, 24, 44, 180, 186, 205, **355**, 452, 468, 525, 526, 527

Nameh Mardom (journal), 532

al Naqi, Ali, 18, 533

Naqi, Muhammad, 18

Naqshband, Baha al Din, 499

al Naqshbandi, Ahmad Abdul Qadir, 215

Nasiriya, Iraq, 166, 167, 169

Nassar, Fuad, 114

Nasser, Gamal Abdul, 4-5, 13, 14, 32, 33-34, 36, 39, 41-42, 43, 46, 49, 60, 64, 69, 99, 102, 111, 112, 115, 117, 119, 129, 131, 135, 136, 137, 140, 171, 176, 182, 221, 241, 263, 338, 345, 346, 348, **355-57**, 368, 369, 372, 409, 410-11, 414, 415, 439, 440, 455-56, 465, 469, 471, 490, 497, 535, 538, 539, 567, 573, 579

Nasserism and Nasserites, 40, 112, 113, 115, 173, 184, 302, 348, **357-58**, 359, 362, 363, 465, 477, 535

Nast, Muhammad Abu, 143

National and Progressive Front, 56, **358**

National Consultative Assembly. *See* Majlis

National Cultural Club (NCC), 273, **358**

National Democratic Assembly-Balad, **358**

National Democratic Front (NDF), 68, 179, **358-59**, 463, 584

National Democratic Party (NDP), 43, 101, 129, 130, 167, 292, 333, **359**, 458, 493

National Front (Iran), 75, 76, 78, 86, 308, 350, **359-60**, 530, 572, 585

National Front for the Liberation of South Yemen, 40, 579-80 (*see also* National Liberation Front)

National Guard (Saudi Arabia), 6, 206, 267, **360-61**, 372, 394, 471, 527, 561

National Liberal Party, 106, 298, 300, 301, **361**, 423

National Liberation Front (NLF), 19, 68, 88, 230, 336, **361-62**, 477, 528, 582, 584

National Pact, 118, 249, 277, 300, 301, 304, **362**, 423, 430, 495

National Progressive and Patriotic Front, 67, 76, 113, 281, **362-63**

National Progressive Front, 69, 75, 117, 260, **363**, 430, 506

National Progressive Unionist Alliance, 112, 338, 358, **363-64**, 493

National Reconciliation Charter (Taif Accord), 29, 93, 141,189, 193, 194, 261, 266, 300, 301, 306, 362, **364-65**, 424, 430, 526

National Religious Party (Mafdal), 170, 247, 329, **365**, 425

National Resistance Council (NRC), 79, 280, 285, **365-66**, 443, 444

National Union, 235, 330, **366**

National Unity Front, **366**, 435, 519

natural gas, **366**

Navon, Yitzhak, 265, **367**

Nawar, Ali Abu, 199, 352

Nawruz, 18, **367**

Nayif, Abdul Rahman, 49, 76

Nazareth, Israel, 30, 98, **367-68**

Nazis, 21, 28, 75, 87, 117, 145, 149, 152, 307, 397, 423, 440, 440, 497, 506

Near East, 321, **368**

Nebuchadnezzar, King, 70, 243

Neguib, Muhammad, 136, 338, 355-56, **368**

Nehru, Jawaharlal, 41, 356

Neo-Wafd Party, 292, 345, 359, **368-69**, 564

Nestorian (Assyrian) Christians, 105, 211, 218, **369**

Netanyahu, Benjamin, 48, 57, 82, 178, 201, 233, 235, 239, 265, 310, 330, 333, 365, **369-70**, 407, 408, 418, 422, 483, 508, 568, 575

Neturei Karta, 12, **370**

New Testament, 107, 108, 367, 534 (*see also* Bible)

New York City, N.Y., 17, 89, 98, 130, 337, 500

Nile River, 60, 61, 101, **370-71**

Nixon, Richard, 374, 391, 415

Nobel Prize for Literature, 310

Nobel Prize for Peace, 48, 88, 422, 441

Noble Sanctuary, 48, 82, 127, 233, **371**, 419, 420, 473, 475, 483

Nohra, Maurice, 115

Nokrashi (Pasha), Mahmud Fahmi, 344

NonConventional weapons. *See* military: *individual countries:* nonconventional weapons

North Africa, 36, 44, 109, 314, 321, 395, 400, 410

North America, 51

North Atlantic Treaty Organization (NATO), 104, 159

North Korea, 126, 211

North Yemen, 27, 30, 36, 191, 206, 250, 360, 371, 383, 395, 527 (*see also* Yemen: history)

@index2:Britain and, 13, 578

Egypt and, 13, 41, 129, 221, 356, 372, 578-79

Iraq and, 68, 584

leaders, 3, 13, 70, 179, 221, 463

PLO and, 402

political parties/groups, 68, 358

Saudi Arabia and, 71, 134, 179, 336, 358, 372, 464, 469, 526, 528, 578, 579, 584

South Yemen and, 3, 11, 15, 20, 88, 179, 221, 337, 358-59, 463-64, 496, 579, 580, 582, 584

Soviet Union and, 14, 70, 179, 372, 464

Syria and, 13, 584

U.S. and, 584

North Yemeni Civil War, 3, 71, 135, 356, **372**, 469, 471, 527

North Yemeni-Soviet Friendship Treaty, **372**, 464

Norway, 1, 47, 159, 386, 387, 394, 404, 407, 417-18, 422

Nouri, Adnan, 218, 219

Nouri, Ali Akbar Nateq, 210, 271, 272

al Nuami, Humaid ibn Rashid, 536

Nuarashi, Hahmud Fahmi, 79

Nuclear weapons. *See* military: *individual countries:* nonconventional weapons

al Numan, Abu Hanifa, 179, 281

Numan, Yassin, 88

Nusair, Muhammad ibn, 18

Nusairis. *See* Alawis

Nushu al-umam (Saada), 450, 509

OAPEC. *See* Organization of Arab Petroleum Exporting Countries

Obad, Ali Salih, 582

Obeid, Atif, 129

Obeid, Abdul Karim, 188

Occupied Arab Territories, 30, 31, 35, 39, 91, 123, 147, 158, 160, 170, 172, 296, 312, 320, 322, 357, 358, 365, **372-73**, 374, 392, 397, 404, 410, 414, 416, 417, 428, 441, 445, 478, 487, 493, 496, 570, 575

Occupied Territories, 21, 30, 48, 123, 177, 182, 201, 207, 228, 233, 239, 322, 347, 366, 370, 373, 370, 403, 406, 415, 427, 434, 446, 475, 487, 517, 576, 589

October 1973 Arab-Israeli War. *See* Arab-Israeli War IV

oil, 44, 103, 153, 273, 366, 373, 491, 496

oil and gas embargoes, 35, **374**, 381, 455, 471, 491, 575

oil and gas industry (Bahrain), 25, 73, 314, **374-75**, 385, 391 oil and gas industry (Egypt), **375**, 385, 391

oil and gas industry (Iran), 1, 15, 86, 139, 154, 156, 190, 209, 210, 230, 264-65, 290, 318, 350, 360, 373, **375-76**, 379, 381, 385, 392, 393, 394, 398, 399, 431, 442, 451, 469, 471, 517, 530, 531, 572, 576, 586

oil and gas industry (Iraq), 9, 26, 54, 83, 84, 155, 156, 157, 165, 167, 169, 195, 216, 217, 220, 255, 284, 286, 290, **376-78**, 383, 385, 391, 392, 392, 393, 394, 401, 433, 449, 503, 508, 513, 525, 551

oil and gas industry (Israel), **378**

oil and gas industry (Jordan), **378**

oil and gas industry (Kuwait), 26, 156, 157, 160, 290, 291, 354, 376, **378-79**, 382, 383, 385, 386, 391, 392, 393, 394, 449, 451, 452, 453, 455, 474, 537, 576

oil and gas industry (Oman), 26, **379-80**, 385, 387, 392, 394, 432, 460, 461

oil and gas industry (Qatar), 125, 366, **380**, 385, 391, 392, 393, 394, 435, 436, 520-21, 560

oil and gas industry (Saudi Arabia), 2-3, 7, 134, 156, 376, 379, **381-82**, 385, 386, 387, 391, 392, 393, 394, 447, 460-61, 469, 470, 471, 472, 474, 490, 560, 575-76

oil and gas industry (Syria), 162, 169, **382-83**, 385, 391, 508

oil and gas industry (United Arab Emirates), 9, 126, 157, 313, 354, 378, 382, **383**, 386, 391, 392, 445, 529, 537, 560

oil and gas industry (Yemen), 11, **383-84**, 385, 464, 579

oil and gas reserves, **386-87**

oil industry (Middle East), 196, 373, **384-85**, 391-94

oil measurements, **385**

oil prices, **385-86**

Old Testament, 23, 45, 107, 122, 321, 322, 351, 523 (*see also* Bible)

Oman, 31, 36, 40, 44, 88, 153, 154, 203, 272, 327-38, 343-44, **387-89**, 496, 526-27
   Britain and, 26, 205-6, 385, 388, 390, 426, 432, 461, 511, 526
   Egypt and, 388, 389, 390, 426, 432, 458, 461

Iran and, 390, 426-27, 432

Iraq and, 159, 390, 432

Jordan and, 390, 426-27, 432

leaders, 432, 460, 511

Saudi Arabia and, 388, 390, 426-27, 432, 460-61

South Yemen and, 388-39, 426, 496

Soviet Union and, 426

U.S. and, 103, 389, 432, 433

   (*see also* oil and gas industry [Oman])

Oman, Gulf of, 44, 153, 159

Omani Civil War, 389-90

Omar, Caliph. *See* Ibn Khattab, Omar

Omar, Mullah Muhammad, 17, 97, 98

Omar, Sultan Ahmad, 358

One Israel, 82, 293, **390**

One Nation, 188, **390**

OPEC. *See* Organization of Petroleum Exporting Countries

Operation Big Pines. *See* Israeli Invasion of Lebanon (1982)

Operation Desert Fox, 161, 198, 217, **391**, 464, 538, 559, 581

Operation Desert Sabre. *See* Gulf War II

Operation Desert Shield. *See* Gulf War II

Operation Desert Storm. *See* Gulf War II

Operation Iraqi Freedom. *See* Gulf War III

Operation Litani. *See* Israeli Invasion of Lebanon (1978)

Operation Peace in Galilee. *See* Israeli Invasion of Lebanon (1978)

Oran, Mordechai, 493

Organization of Arab Petroleum Exporting Countries (OAPEC), 374, 375, 377, *391-92*, 393, 435

Organization of Islamic Conference. See Islamic Conference Organization

Organization of Petroleum Exporting Countries (OPEC), 7, 157, 198, 217, 374, 376, 378, 380, 381-82, 385, 386, 387, **392-94**, 433, 435, 452, 519, 575

Organization of the Islamic Revolution in the Arabian Peninsula, **394-95**

Oriental Jews, 172, **395**

Orthodox Christians/Church, 95, 109, 127, 218, 369, **395-96**, 449

Orthodox Christians, Armenian. *See* Armenian Orthodox Church

Orthodox Christians, Greek. *See* Greek Orthodox Church

Orthodox Christians, Gregorian. *See* Armenian Orthodox Church

Orthodox Christians, Russian. *See* Russian Orthodox Church

Orthodox Christians, Syrian, 118, **396**, 571

Orthodox Eastern Church. *See* Orthodox Christians/Church

Orthodox Judaism, 118, 259, 262, **396**, 488, 505, 516

Oslo Accord I (1993; Israeli-Palestine Liberation Organization Accord), 47-48, 116, 122, 144, 170, 171, 178, 182, 201, 207, 228, 233, 236, **238-39**, 242, 252, 322, 332, 333, 334, 365, 370, 373, 402, 404, 405, 406, 407, 414, 418, 422, 428, 429, 433, 441, 446, 462, 487, 507, 567, 571, 575, 589

Oslo Accord II (1995; Washington Accord), 48, 81, 154, 184, 236, 407, 408, 418, 441, **567-68**, 571, 575

Oslo Accords, 233, 370, 396, 418-19, 475, 484

Osman, Ahmad, 457

Ottoman Empire, 1, 2, 7, 10, 13, 19, 27, 39, 44, 50, 66, 71, 77, 89, 101, 102, 109, 121, 135, 144, 148, 150, 174, 177, 179, 180, 181, 183, 186, 190, 193, 202, 215, 220, 223, 240, 244, 252, 254, 286, 289, 295, 296, 317-18, 319, 333, 354, 355, 367, 368, 385, 395, 400, 409, 410, 425, 431, 435, 437, 455, 460, 466, 467, 470, 476, 490, 504, 505, 510, 521, 526, 529, 565, 566, 566, 578, 588

Oz, Amos, **396**

Pahlavi, Farah, 399

Pahlavi, Muhammad Reza Shah, 1, 10, 63, 75, 84, 103, 139, 188, 191, 193, 195, 209, 211, 214, 229, 250, 264, 274, 275, 283, 284, 287, 317, 350, 360, 375, 386, **397-99**, 400, 411,

437, 442, 445, 447, 459, 481, 514, 517, 524, 531, 533, 571, 585

Pahlavi, Reza Cyrus, 76, 399

Pahlavi, Reza Shah (Reza Khan), 63, 72, 143, 209, 222, 339, 350, 397, **399-400**, 437, 516, 530, 585

Pahlavi dynasty, 63, 229-30, 267, 286, 376, **400**

Pahlavi language, **400**, 423, 591

Pakistan, 6, 16, 17, 18, 61, 65, 78, 98, 104, 159, 164, 211, 337, 390, 473, 565, 572

Palestine, 8, 10, 36, 46, 47, 49, 50, 87, 89, 92, 100, 123, 125, 126, 127, 132, 135, 137, 138, 139, 152, 177, 182, 183, 259, 278, 293, 296, 395, **400-402**, 504, 534, 566, 584, 588

   Britain and, 7, 24-25, 31, 87, 90, 144, 174, 183, 202-3, 240, 244, 245, 307, 373, 385, 400-401, 434, 447, 467, 497, 566 (*see also* Balfour Declaration; Sykes-Picot Pact)

   Egypt and, 333, 347, 400

   Iraq and, 11, 80, 202-3, 462

   Israel and, 1, 6-7, 40, 100, 236, 248, 257, 314-15, 329, 400, 413, 427, 462, 566 (*see also* Arab-Israeli Wars I-IV; Fatah; Hamas; intifada; Irgun; Oslo Accords I & II; Palestinian Liberation Organization; Wye River Memorandum)

   Jordan and, 8, 11, 24, 46, 80, 100, 137, 182, 199-201, 255, 347, 409, 428

   leaders, 1, 28, 45, 80, 171-72, 182, 201, 202, 251, 266, 434, 489, 523, 568, 576

   Lebanon and, 92, 106, 146

   partitioning, 8, 10, 32, 33, 111, 112, 115, 117, 172, 174, 202, 232, 244, 245, 307, 312, 315, 367, 401-2, 404, 405, 408, 493, 523, 560, 570, 589 (*see also* Peel Commission)

   political parties, 12, 13, 116, 147, 180, 329, 347, 427, 428

   Saudi Arabia and, 154, 473

   Soviet Union and, 90, 111, 112, 115, 117, 428, 461, 493, 523

   Syria and, 80, 149, 279, 428, 461, 494, 586

   U.S. and, 24-25, 90, 183, 279, 572

   (*see also* Peace Process)

Palestine Liberation Army (PLA), 201, 238, 257, **402**, 403

Palestine Liberation Front, 41, 405, 427, 428

Palestine Liberation Organization (PLO), 32, 36, 37, 38, 46-48, 56, 89,116, 122, 124, 137, 146, 154, 171, 178, 182, 200, 201, 203, 207, 224, 267, **402-5**, 406-7, 427, 490, 496, 538, 569, 570, 576

@index2:Egypt and, 402 (*see also* Cairo Agreement)

Iran and, 252

Iraq and, 47, 404, 417, 462

Israel and, 1, 30, 81, 82, 124, 251, 257, 293, 332-33, 342, 347, 356-57, 371, 404, 427-29, 445, 475, 483, 487, 529, 575 (*see also* Arab-Israeli Wars I-IV; Oslo Accords I & II)

Jordan and, 38, 46, 69, 80, 200-201, 255, 256-57, 353, 357, 402, 406, 462, 570

leaders, 1-2, 45, 65, 80

Lebanon and, 260, 297-99, 342, 343, 402, 406 (*see also* Cairo Agreement; Lebanese National Movement)

Saudi Arabia and, 267, 471

Soviet Union and, 46, 182, 312

Syria and, 57, 69, 342, 356-57, 402, 406, 507

U.S. and, 47, 238, 342, 416, 483-84, 491 (*see also* Peace Process)

Palestine National Charter, 403, **405-6**, 490, 575

Palestine National Council, 1, 46, 80, 124, 137, 171, 182, 199, 200, 255, 267, 322, 403, 405, **406-7**, 416, 428, 461, 490

Palestine National Fund, 46, 403, **407**

Palestine National Liberation Army, **407**

Palestine People's Party. *See* Communist Party of Palestine

Palestine War. *See* Arab-Israeli War I

Palestinian Authority (PA), 1, 2, 45, 48, 116, 124, 138, 144, 178, 184, 201, 217, 228, 233, 234, 239, 242, 333, 370, 402, 405, **407-8**, 418, 420, 428, 475, 484, 487, 541, 567, 575, 577

Palestinian National Authority, **408**

Palestinian Territories, 151, 178, 183, 198, 217, 233, **408** (*see also* Occupied Territories)

Palmah, 21, 23, 278, **408-9**, 440

pan-Arabism, 6, 13, 46, 56, 67, 69, 76, 104, 106, 129, 142, 146, 153, 263, 288, 357, 372, 423, **409**, 430, 450, 460

pan-Islamism, 39, 346, **410**

Paris, France, 53, 59, 60, 76, 100, 122, 135, 139, 146, 175

Parthian Empire, 321, 400, 422, 488, 591

Party of Arab Baath/Renaissance, 11, 30

Pasha, Ahmad Arabi, 39

Pasha, Ibrahim, 150

Pasha, Nahas. *See* Nahas (Pasha), Mustafa

Passover, 234, 246, **411**, 466

Patriotic Union of Kurdistan (PUK), 28, 83, 104, 166, 218, 219, 220, 228, 281, 282, 283, 285, 287, **411-14**, 512

peace conference. *See* Middle East Peace Conference

Peace Now, 24, 397, **413**

Peace Process, Middle East, 149, 178, 194, 268, 292, 297, 306, 310, 333, **414-20**, 421, 433, 471, 517, 539

Peel Commission, 28, 31, 90, 202, 401

Peking, China, 13

Peled, Matityahu, 429

Pentecost, 127, 132, 246, **420-21**

People's Democratic Republic of Yemen. See South Yemen

People's Republic of South Yemen. See South Yemen

Peres, Shimon, 1, 22, 47-48, 57, 82, 178, 233, 236, 239, 265, 370, 418, 420, **421-22**, 441, 478, 483, 508, 567, 568, 569

Peretz, Amir, 390

Persia and Persians, 1, 27, 50, 62, 63, 70, 84, 94, 121, 209-10, 243, 286, 400, **422**, 431, 466, 490, 517, 529, 591 (*see also* Iran)

Persian Gulf. *See* Gulf, the

Persian language, 208,**422-23**

Pesach. *See* Passover

Peshawar, Pakistan, 16, 65, 95, 96, 337, 587

Peta Tikvah, Palestine, 180

petroleum. *See* oil

Pfeuffer, Yehuda. *See* Amichai, Yehuda

Phalange Party and Phalangists, 122, 144, 145, 146, 185, 192, 238, 297, 298-99, 301, 342, 343, 361, **423-24**, 450, 459, 468, 509-10, 516

Philippines, 17, 97

Philistines, 400, 517

Philosophy of Confrontation, The (Zawahiri), 16, 587

Phoenicia, 101, 139, 153

Picot, Francois Georges, 504

Pincus, Louis, 575

Pius IX, Pope, 449

Plonsk, Poland, 89

Poale Agudat Israel, 12, **424**, 523, 560, 561

Poale HaMizrahi, 12, 329, 365, **424-25**, 560

Poale Zion, 12-13, 89, 92, 100, 293, **425**, 485, 516

Poland, 12, 20, 87, 165, 182, 293, 396, 497

poll tax, **425**

Poltava, Ukraine, 91

Pompey (Roman general), 243, 258, 466

Popular Bloc, **425**

Popular Democratic Party, **425-26**

Popular Front for the Liberation of the Occupied Arab Gulf, 389, **426**

Popular Front for the Liberation of Oman, 390, **426**

Popular Front for the Liberation of Oman and the Arab Gulf, 390, **426-27**

Popular Front for the Liberation of Palestine, 41,123, 138, 171, 182, 251, 257, 330, 403, 405, 407, **427-28**

Popular Front for the Liberation of Palestine-General Command, 347, 403, 405, **428-29**, 576

Popular Islamic Conferences, **429**

Portsmouth Agreement, 26, 112

Portugal, 314, 343, 344, 476

Powell, Colin, 163

Prague, Czechoslovakia, 75, 117, 445, 493

Program for Islamic Action, The, 143

Progressive List for Peace, **429**

Progressive Party, 147, 308, **430**

Progressive Socialist Party, 259, 260, 302, **430-31**

Prophet, The (Jibran), 251

Protestant Christians/Church, 95, 108, 109, 118, 127, 250, 307, **431**, 448

Protocol of Constantinople, 211, **431**, 524-25

Protocol of Tehran, **431**

Protocol of Uqair, 289, **431-32**, 452, 473

Protocols of the Wise Men of Zion, 28

Ptolemais, 10

Ptolemy dynasty, 66, 400

Ptolemy II, King of Egypt, 10, 24

Qaboos ibn Said, 380, 387, 388, 389, 390, 426, **432-33**, 461

Qaddura, Abdul Qadir, 505

Qadi, Issam, 462

Qadir, Abdul, 201

Qaddumi, Faruq, 137, 138

Qadhafi, Muammar, 81, 496

al Qahtani, Muhammad ibn Abdullah, 561

Qaim, Iraq, 169

Qajar, Ahmad, 119, 399

Qajar dynasty, 437, 516

Qajar, Muhammad Khan, 516

Qajar, Muzzafar al Din, 118-19, 209

Qana, Lebanon, 189, 236

Qasim, Abdul Karim, 48, 49, 66, 76, 84, 112-13, 142, 195, 216, 282, 377, **433**, 474

al Qasim, Muhammad, 310, 457, 533

Qasim, Talat Fuad, 143

al Qasimi, Saqr ibn Muhammad, 445, 536

al Qasimi, Sultan ibn Muhammad, 482, 536

Qasimlou, Abdul Rahman, 285

Qassam, Izz al Din, 31, 177, **434**

al Qatabi, Abdullah Ali, 388

Qatar, 27, 31, 36, 44, 125, 153, 154, 159, 162, 328, 337, 366, **434-36**, 519-21
    Britain and, 27, 125, 385, 435, 519, 521
    (*see also* oil and gas industry [Qatar])

qisas, **436**, 438

qiyas, 205, 314, **436**

Qom, 118, 139, 150, **436-37**, 442, 459, 481, 491, 514, 562

Qrei, Ahmad, 1, 332

al Quds. *See* Jerusalem

Quhafa, Abu Bakr ibn Abu, 206, 222, 437, 486, 502
Qulaylat, Ibrahim, 343
Qunaitra, Syria, 35, 149
Quran (Koran), 3, 18, 44, 70, 85, 122, 172-73, 174, 180, 203, 205, 222, 223-24, 225, 243, 253, 314, 317, 319, 344, 436, **437-38**, 445, 469, 477, 479, 485, 486, 499, 500, 501-2, 516, 534, 535, 561, 586
Qurdaha, Syria, 55, 58
Qutb, Sayid Muhammad, **438-39**
Qutbzadeh, Sadiq, 482
al Quwatli, Shukri, **440**, 586

Raad, Inaam, 510
Rabat, Morocco, 37, 224
Rabbo, Yasser Abdu, 404
Rabin, Leah, 441
Rabin, Yitzhak, 1, 22, 47-48, 81, 128, 201, 233, 239, 257, 262, 292, 332, 364, 405, 418, 420, 421-22, **440-41**, 482, 487
Rafi, 13, 91, 123, 132, 186, 292, 294, 309, 315, 367, 421, **441-42**, 482
Rafsanjani, Ali Akbar Hashemi, 60, 209, 210, 229, 270-71, 272, 309, 343, **442-43**, 494, 513, 525, 563
al Ragheb, Ali Abu, 254
Rahman, Fazl ul, 572
Rajai, Muhammad Ali, 79, 229, 270, 276, 340, 365, **443**
Rajavi, Masud, 79, 285, 339, 365, **443-45**
Rajavi, Miryam, 444
Rakah, 172, 236, 312, **445**, 493, 523
Ramadan, 126, 131, 222, **445**, 486
Ramadan, Taha Yassin, 215
Ramadan War, **445** (*see also* Arab-Israeli War IV)
Ramallah, West Bank, 234, 408, 428, 484, 568
Ramle, Israel, 32, 123
Rantisi, Abdul Aziz, 178
Ras al Khaima Emirate, 383, **445**, 529, 522, 535, 537
Rashid, Amr Muhammad, 169
Rashid clan, 2, 6, 193, 470, 527
al Rashid, Haroon, 71, 317, 354

Rashid, Mahir Abdul, 194
Rashid, Sahour, 194
al Rassi, Abdul Wahhab ibn Tahir, 467
al Rassi, Yahya ibn Hussein, 586
Rassi dynasty, 13, 14, 527, 579
Rastakhiz Party, 193, 275, 330, **445**
Ratz, 320, **446**, 488
Rauf, Abdul Munim Abdul, 345
Razmara, Ali, 139, 585
Reagan, Ronald, 103, 126, 190, 192, 212, 213, 237, 415
Rechavam, Zeev, 329, 428
Red Sea, 2, 44, 159
Reform Judaism, 118, 259, 420, **446**, 504
Religious endowment/trust, 4 (*see also* waqf)
Revisionist Zionists, 50, 87, 151, 185, 220, 240, 262, **446-47**, 478, 496, 530, 574, 590
Revolt in the Desert (Lawrence), 297
Revolutionary Komitehs, 230, 280, 284, 331, 442, **447**
Rezai, Ahmad, 339
Rhodes, 33, 90
al Rida/Riza, Ali, 317, 318, 436, 533
Rida, Muhammad Rashid, 79, 205, 462
al Rifai, Zaid, 254
Ritter, Scott, 557
Riyadh, Saudi Arabia, 2, 6, 80, 85, 133, 134, 153, 154, 193, **447-48**, 469, 470, 535
Road to Oslo, The (Abbas), 1
Rogers Plan, 142, 256, 320, 414, **448**, 567
Rogers, William, 414, 448, 567
Rohan, Michael, 224, 371
Roman Catholic Christians/Church, 93, 95, 109, 118, 127, 151, 316, 367, 369, **448-49**, 535
Roman Empire, 19, 45, 50, 66, 89, 101, 108, 109, 121, 140, 242, 243, 248, 258, 259, 321, 400, 466, 490, 517, 529, 534
Rome and Jerusalem (Hess), 588
Rome, Italy, 80, 164, 307
Roosevelt, Franklin D., 3, 103, 516
Rosh HaShana, 246, **449**
Rothschild, Lord (Lionel Walter), 77
Round Table Conference on Palestine, 28
Royner, Jay, 83, 284, 514

Rubenstein, Amnon, 488
Rumeila oil field, 165, 166, 377, **449**
Russia, 17, 20, 24, 28, 92, 98, 101, 107, 109,
    119, 182, 259, 293, 387, 394, 396, 431, 504
    Iran/Persia and, 27, 63, 213-14, 510
    Iraq and, 65, 161, 162, 164, 197, 391, 559
Russian Orthodox Church, **449**
Ruwalla tribe, 24, 193, 527

Saada, Antun, 52, **449-51**, 495, 509
Saadat, Ahmad, 428
al Saadawi, Nawal, 451
Saade, Georges, 301
Saasa, 35
al Sabah, Abdullah I, 455
al Sabah, Abdullah III ibn Salim I, 290, **451-52**,
    454, 455
al Sabah, Ahmad I ibn Jaber II, 431-32, 451,
    452-53, 455
al Sabah clan, 24, 290, **455**
al Sabah, Jaber II, 452, 455
al Sabah, Jaber III ibn Ahmad I, 158, 273, 289,
    290, **453-54**, 455
al Sabah, Mubarak I, 27, 289, 455
al Sabah, Saad ibn Abdullah III, 289, 454, 455
al Sabah, Sabah I, 455
al Sabah, Sabah III ibn Salim I, **454-55**
al Sabah, Salim I ibn Mubarak, 451, 454, 455
Sabastiya. See Samaria city
Sabbath, 118, 396, **455-56**, 504
sabra, **456**
Sabri, Ali, 5, 43, 142, **456-57**
Sadat, (Muhammad) Anwar, 4, 5, 16, 42, 44, 56,
    61, 76-77, 88, 101, 102, 119, 129-30, 131,
    142-43, 184, 266, 321, 333, 338, 344, 345,
    359, 368, 369, 374, 392, 397, 399, 410, 415,
    451, **457-59**, 491, 493, 496, 512, 587
al Sadiq, Jaafar, 206, 231, 240, 533
Sadiq, Yusuf, 111
al Sadr, Muhammad Sadiq, 492
al Sadr, Musa, 18, 22, 92, 316, 349, **459**, 510
Safad, Palestine, 1
Safavi, Nawab (Mujtaba Mirlohi), 139, 514
Safavid dynasty, 436, 510, 516

Saffran, Said, 394
Said ibn Taimur ibn Faisal, 380, 388, 390, 426,
    432, **460-61**, 511
Said, Muhammad, 530
Said, Nasser, 535
al Said, Nuri, 142, 216, **459-60**
al Saikh, Adul Aiz ibn Adulla, 470
Saiqa, 403, 405, **461-62**
Saladin (Salah al Din Ayubi), 102, 244, 261,
    286, 288, 367
Salafiya movement and salafin, 291, 344, **462**
Salahuddin, 105, 218, 219
Salam, Saeb, 263, **462-63**
Salih, Ali Abdullah, 3, 4, 14, 15, 88, 147, 359,
    372, **463-65**, 528, 578, 579, 580, 582, 583
Salim I (Ottoman sultan), 181
Salim, Mamdouh, 42
Sallal, Abdullah, 14, 71, 221, 372, **465**, 579
al Saltane, Ahmad Qavam, 531, 585
Sanchez, Linda, 335
Samaria, 170, **465-66**
Samaria city, **466**
Samaritans, **466**
Samarra, Iraq, 71, **467**, 533
Smarrai, Wafiq, 219
Samuel, Herbert, 77-78, 202
San Remo Agreement, 78, 401, **467**
Sanaa, Yemen, 11, 14, 20, 27, 40, 41, 71, 88,
    148, 179, 250, 361, 465, **467-68**, 577, 583
Sanchez, Ilich Ramirez (Carlos Martinez), 575
Sanjabi, Karim, 75, 360
Saqr, Eteinne, 153
Saracens, 10
Sarkis, Elias, 140, 191, 238, 260, 264, 298, 305,
    468
Sassanian Empire, 84, 222, 321, 400, 422, 591
Saud, 193
al Saud, Abdul Aziz ibn Abdul Rahman. See
    Abdul Aziz ibn Abdul Rahman al Saud
al Saud, Abdullah ibn Abdul Aziz. See Abdullah
    ibn Abdul Aziz al Saud
al Saud clan. See House of Saud
al Saud, Fahd ibn Abdul Aziz. See Fahd ibn
    Abdul Aziz al Saud

al Saud, Faisal ibn Abdul Aziz. *See* Faisal ibn Abdul Aziz al Saud

Saud, House of. *See* House of Saud

al Saud, Khalid. *See* Khalid ibn Abdul Aziz al Saud

al Saud, Nayif ibn Abdul, 2, 268

al Saud, Salman, 2

al Saud, Saud ibn Abdul Aziz, king of Saudi Arabia, 2, 133, 134-35, 267, **468-69**, 471, 565

al Saud, Sultan ibn Abdul Aziz. *See* Sultan ibn Abdul Aziz al Saud

Saudi Arabia, 2, 17, 31, 36, 44, 61, 65, 89, 95, 110, 142, 153, 154, 186, 211, 224, 225, 337, 345, 355, 447, 468, **469-73**

@index2:Britain and, 2, 205-6, 252, 392, 470, 525-26

Egypt and, 36, 267, 334, 346, 357, 372, 392, 414, 469, 471, 473

Iran and, 6, 394-95, 576

Iraq and, 6, 158, 159, 160, 161, 214, 218, 295, 378, 469, 473, 526, 576

Jordan and, 26, 200

Kuwait and, 288, 289, 431, 452, 469, 576

leaders, 2, 6, 85, 133, 193, 267, 468, 561, 575

Lebanon and, 6, 31, 38, 299, 364, 471, 473-74

military, 328 (*see also* National Guard)

Oman and, 388, 390, 426-27, 432, 460-61

Palestine/PLO and, 154, 267, 471, 472

political parties/groups, 116, 347-48, 358, 425, 535

North Yemen and, 71, 134, 179, 336, 358, 372, 464, 469, 526, 528, 578, 579, 584

South Yemen and, 20, 496

Soviet Union and, 134

Syria and, 6, 7, 36, 69, 507

U.S. and, 3, 6, 96, 103, 133, 134, 158, 267-68, 392, 436, 471, 472, 473, 572, 575

Yemen and, 14, 148, 464, 580, 583, 584

(*see also* oil and gas industry [Saudi Arabia])

Saudi Arabia-Iraq Neutral Zone, 214, 469, **473**

Saudi Arabia-Kuwait Neutral Zone, 288, 289, 431, 469, **473-74**

Saul, King of Israel, 258

Sawt al Shaab (periodical), 117

Al Sayliya, Qatar, 162

Sayyab, Badr Shakir, 313, **474-75**

Sazman-e Cherikha-ye Fedai Khalq-e Iran. *See* Fedai Khalq

Sazman-e Mujahedin-e Khalq. *See* Mujahedin-e Khalq

Scheib, Israel, 307

Schmulevitz, Matitiahu, 308

Schwartz, Hillel, 249

Schwarzkopf, Norman, 159, 160

Second Gulf War. *See* Gulf War II

Second Intifada (al Aqsa Intifada), 2, 38, 48, 82, 124, 131, 138, 198, 217, 228, 233, 236, 239, 242, 255, 408, 414, 419, 422, **475-76**, 483, 487, 501, 541, 571, 577

Second World War, 3, 12, 24, 26, 29, 32, 42, 53, 63, 79, 90, 112, 115, 117, 123, 128, 136, 142, 152, 173, 174, 184, 186, 202, 209, 213, 216, 220, 241, 244, 249, 264, 269, 278, 286, 290, 291, 304, 315, 321, 344, 368, 377, 379, 380, 385, 386, 395, 397, 401, 424, 450, 451, 453, 460, 470, 473, 479, 497, 506, 509, 511, 517, 524, 529, 564, 569, 584

Segev, Yitzhak, 576

Seleucids, 66, 89, 295, 400, 422, 488

Seljuk Turks, 63, 222

Selu, Fawzi, 489

Semitic languages, 44, 183, **476**

Semite, **476**

Sephardim, 20, 21, 53, 249, 259, 294, 395, **476-77**, 484

September 11, 2001 (9/11), 7, 9, 17, 18, 55, 62, 81, 98, 110, 130, 162, 164, 198, 210, 217, 234, 271, 273, 291, 335, 337, 366, 444, 454, 473, 475, 484, 500, 508, 520, 538, 581, 587

Serag al Din, Fuad, 368-69, 564

Seven Pillars of Wisdom (Lawrence), 296

Seveners. *See* Ismailis

Seychelles, 202, 353

Al Shaab (newspaper), 493

al Shaabi, Qahtan Muhammad, 19, 230, 336, **477**

al Shaara, Faruq, 57, 417, 508

Shabak. *See* Shin Beth
Shabuot (Shavuot). *See* Pentecost
Shafii Code, 3, 13, 179, 180, 209, 314, 467, 473, **477-78**, 502, 587
Shafii, Jaafar, 280
al Shafii, Muhammad ibn Idris, 173, 204, 205, 206, 477, 501
Shafiq, Mustafa, 139
Shah, Ahmad, 209
Shah, Fath Ali, 318
Shah, Muhammad Reza. *See* Pahlavi, Muhammad Reza Shah
Shah, Reza. *See* Pahlavi, Reza Shah
al Shaikh, Tarfa bint Abdullah, 2, 134
Shallah, Ramadan, 228
Shalmaneser III, King of Assyria, 45
Shalom, Avraham, 487
Shamir, Moshe, 517
Shamir, Yitzhak, 233, 265, 292, 307, 309, 326, 369, 416, 417, 421, **478**, 483, 570
Shammar, 2, 193
Shammi, Abdullah, 228
Sharaf-Kindi, Sadiq, 285
Sharansky, Natan, 234
Sharett, Moshe, 91, 319, 367, **479**
Sharia, 5, 16, 64, 65, 85, 128, 139, 179, 180, 222, 226, 264, 274, 275, 278, 292, 316, 339, 341, 345, 346, 438, 462, 472, 477, **479-80**, 492, 499, 561, 563, 565, 566, 573, 578, 583, 586
Shariati, Ali, **480-81**
Shariatmadari, Muhammad Kazem, 150, 316, **481-82**, 515
Sharjah Emirate, 10, 126, 383, **482**, 529, 533, 535
Sharm al Shaikh, Egypt, 34, 39, 521, 539
Sharon, Ariel, 39, 48, 82, 178, 232, 233, 235, 236, 238, 293, 298, 310, 320, 330, 332, 333, 365, 370, 408, 419-20, 422, 475, **482-84**, 488, 571
al Sharqi, Hamad ibn Muhammad, 536
Shartuni, Habib Tanios, 510
Shas, 247, 292, **484**, 488
Shatt al Arab, 1, 84, 133, 153, 154, 155, 196, 211, 212, 431, **484**, 524-25

Shazar, Shneor Zalman, **484-85**
Sheba, 44
Shehab, Fuad. *See* Chehab, Fuad
Shemali, Fuad, 115, 116
Shia, 13, 22, 52, 53, 63, 70, 71, 73, 74, 76, 92, 93, 102, 115, 118, 120, 121, 144, 150, 167, 169, 173, 179, 188, 196, 205, 206, 211, 212, 218, 223, 223, 227, 229, 231, 256, 259, 264, 269, 274, 275, 277, 281, 291, 304, 306, 307, 308, 316, 317, 318, 339, 341, 349, 354, 355, 360, 362, 394, 411, 429, 430, 436, 437, 453, 459, 467, 473, 481, **485-86**, 492, 495, 503, 565, 566 (*see also* Amal; Ismailis; Jaafari; Twelver Shias; Zaidis)
Shiar (magazine), 52, 474
Shiat Ali. *See* Shia
Shiite. *See* Shia
Shikaki, Fathi Abdul Aziz, 228, 333
Shiloah, Reuven, 331
Shin Beth, 207, 332, **486-88**, 538
Shinui, 234, 320, 446, **488**
Al Shira (magazine), 212
Shiraz, Iran, 70, 250, **488**
Shirazi, Ali Muhammad, 69-70, 71, 488
Shishkali, Adib, 11, 42, 117, 173, 440, **489**, 506
Shock of Modernity, The (Asbar), 53
Shuaibi, Azmi, 408
Shuaun Falastiniyya (periodical), 122
Shukri, Ibrahim, 493
Shultz, Geroge, 299, 416
Shuqairi, Ahmad, 137, 403, 406, **489-90**
al Shuraim, Asi, 2, 6
Shuster, William, 119
Sidon, Lebanon, 181, 237, **490**
Sidqi, Bakr, 148
Sigam, Adim, 16
Signposts on the Road (Qutb), 439
Sinai Campaign, 123, **490** (*see also* Suez War)
Sinai, Mount, 93, 94, 176, 246, 258, 523
Sinai Peninsula, 34, 77, 81, 87, 91, 102-3, 123, 129, 130, 170, 232, 258, 305, 316, 342, 356, 372-73, 375, 415, 457, 458, 479, 482, 483, **490-91**, 498, 517, 523
Sinai I Agreement, 184, 415, 458, **491**

Sinai II Agreement, 415, 441, 458, **491**, 497
Sistani, Ali Husseini, **491-92**
Sistani, Mirza Ahi, 503
Six-Day War. *see also* Arab-Israeli War III
Sixty Years of the National Movement in Palestine
    (Touma), 523
Sneh, Moshe, 312, 315, **492-93**
Socialist Labor Party, 292, 308, 346, **493**
Socialist National Front, 259, 297, **493-94**
Socialist Youth Organization (SYO), 43, 456-57
Society of Combatant Clerics (Majma), 60, **494**
Sokolow, Nahum, 574, 589
Solh, Riyad, 362, **494-95**, 509
Solomon, King of Israel, 243, 258, 466, 533
Somalia, 36, 61, 97
South Asia, 17, 289, 388, 435, 536
South Lebanon Army, 153, 188, 237, 305, **495**,
    510, 539
South Yemen, 36, 38, 250, 384, 426, 461, **496**,
    528
@index2:Britain and, 19, 40, 88, 361, 477, 579
Iraq and, 68
leaders, 19, 88, 230, 336, 477
Lebanon and, 31
North Yemen and, 3, 11, 15, 20, 88, 147, 179,
    221, 337, 358-59, 463-64, 496, 579, 580,
    582, 584
political parties/groups, 68, 358, 361, 582
Saudi Arabia and, 20, 496, 584
Soviet Union and, 231, 336, 496, 584
(*see also* Yemen: history)
South Yemeni-Soviet Friendship Treaty, **496**
Soviet Union, 13, 30, 47, 50, 57, 87, 88, 104,
    111, 112, 139, 262-63, 271, 321, 322, 327,
    337
Afghanistan and, 17, 61, 65, 95-96, 103, 110
Britain and, 528
Egypt and, 35, 60, 130, 131, 184, 334, 338,
    359, 415, 456, 458, 498, 567
emigration of Jews, 38, 47, 53, 234, 296, 312,
    395, 404, 588
Iran/Persia and, 63, 83-84, 190, 209, 213-14,
    280, 284, 285, 350, 397, 399-400, 442,
    511, 528, 530, 585

Iraq and, 64, 156, 160, 196, 219-20, 283,
    377
Israel and, 91, 316, 325, 493, 510
Jordan and, 200, 352
Lebanon and, 510
North Yemen and, 14, 70, 179, 372, 464
Oman and, 426
Palestine/PLO and, 46, 90, 111, 112, 115,
    117, 182, 312, 428, 461, 493, 523
Saudi Arabia and, 134
South Yemen and, 231, 336, 496, 584
Syria and, 35, 55, 58, 237, 430, 489, 506-7
U.S. and, 35, 237, 498
Spain, 159, 164, 183, 476, 515
Spears, Edward, 117, 362
Stalin, Joseph, 516
Stavsky, Abraham, 50
Steadfastness Front, 56, **496**
Stern, Avraham ("Yair"), 307, 478, **496-97**
Stern Gang/Group. *See* Lehi/Lehy
Stockholm, Sweden, 147
Sudan, 5, 17, 31, 36, 96, 97, 136, 314, 321,
    402, 563-64, 572
al Sudeiri, Hussah bint Ahmad, 2, 133
Sudeiri Seven, 2, 133, 268
Suez Canal, 3, 11, 25, 34, 35, 39, 60, 77, 79,
    111, 129, 232, 252, 318, 353, 356, 386, 401,
    482, **497**, 521, 564, 567
Suez War (Arab-Israeli War II; Sinai Campaign),
    34, 45, 73, 91, 106, 115, 123, 144, 216, 232,
    249, 250, 266, 269, 312, 316, 321, 338, 356,
    386, 397, 414, 452, 460, 462, 482, 491, **497-
    99**, 521, 538, 568
Sufian, Muwaiya ibn Abu, 53, 223, 271, 281
sufism, 52, 223, 253, 344, **499-500**, 502
suicide bombing, 57, 61, 138, 178, 228, 234,
    453, 464, 475, 484, **500-501**, 508, 571
Sulaka, John, 105
Suleiman the Magnificent, Sultan, 244
Suleimaniyah, Iraq, 83, 411, 413
Sultan ibn Abdul Aziz al Saud, 2, 6, 268
Sumerians, 71
sunna, 203, 205, 222, 253, 310, 314, 319, 469,
    477, 479, 485, **501-2**, 534, 561

Sunnis, 3, 13, 18, 62, 64, 73, 74, 78, 99, 118, 120, 121, 126, 130, 142, 173, 177, 179, 180, 181, 190, 205, 206, 207, 211, 218, 223, 234, 235, 256, 259, 260, 269, 277, 285, 286, 291, 304, 307, 310, 316, 317, 341, 343, 344, 348, 349, 354, 358, 362, 389, 430, 436, 459, 465, 473, 477, 485, 486, 495, 502, 509, 529, 534, 561, 566, 579, 582, 586

Supreme Assembly of Islamic Revolution in Iraq (SAIRI), 82, 120-21, 169, 211, 341, **502-3**

Supreme Council of Islamic Revolution in Iraq. *See* Supreme Assembly of Islamic Revolution in Iraq

Sur. *See* Tyre

Surur, Ahmad Fathi, 129

Switzerland, 106, 266, 430

Sykes, Mark, 504

Sykes-Picot Pact, 39, 150-51, 409, **504**

synagogue, **504-5**

Syria, 17, 31, 36, 38, 40, 41, 51, 97, 99, 104, 105, 126, 137, 139, 142, 151, 154, 231, 250, 281, 286, 288, 322, 345, 396, 496, **505-9**, 541, 566

Britain and, 7, 123, 149, 489, 507, 509

Egypt and, 13, 35-36, 56, 75, 117, 255, 348, 356-57, 409, 440 (*see also* United Arab Republic)

France and, 7, 11, 18, 27, 30, 42, 99, 116-17, 121, 123, 135, 140, 149, 177, 308, 317-18, 342, 348, 450, 467, 489, 505-6 (*see also* Sykes-Picot Pact)

Iran and, 36, 254, 270, 410

Iraq and, 36, 47, 54, 57, 58, 77, 80, 159, 162, 164, 173, 196, 440, 507, 508-9

Israel and, 32-36, 54, 57-58, 81, 100, 137, 149, 237-38, 342, 356-57, 373, 413, 440, 507-8, 510, 538

Jordan/Transjordan and, 9, 26, 27, 36, 149, 199, 200, 201, 255, 257, 346, 409, 507

Kuwait and, 36, 69

leaders, 11, 51, 54, 55, 58, 62, 74, 99, 173, 180, 223, 241, 266, 440, 489, 586

Lebanon and, 22, 29, 31, 54, 55, 56, 57, 69, 92-93, 141, 144-45, 149, 191, 194, 223, 237-38,

260, 261, 266, 294-95, 298-300, 302, 304, 305-6, 308, 317-18, 327, 342, 361, 362, 423, 430, 450, 468, 507, 508, 510, 529 (*see also* Lebanese-Syrian Treaty)

military, 327, 328

North Yemen and, 13, 584

Palestine/PLO and, 57, 69, 149, 279, 342, 356-57, 402, 406, 428, 461, 495, 507, 586

political parties/groups, 42, 68, 116, 225, 348, 358, 363

Saudi Arabia and, 6, 7, 36, 57, 69, 507

Soviet Union and, 35, 55, 58, 237, 440, 489, 506-7

U.S. and, 54, 57, 58, 69, 279, 342, 440, 506-9, 586

(*see also* oil and gas industry [Syria]; Peace Process)

Syrian Catholic Church, 118, 509, 535, 571

Syrian Orthodox. *See* Orthodox Christians, Syrian

Syrian Protestant College, 22

Syrian Socialist Nationalist Party (SSNP), 52, 241, 302, 423, 450, 495, **509-10**

Syrian-Palestinian Cognress, 494

Syrian-Soviet Friendship Treaty, 56, 149, 327, **510**

Tabriz, Iran, 63, 70, 510-11, 531

Taha, Rihad, 169

Taha, Abu Yasser Rifia Ahmad, 572

Tahmasp, Shah, 436

Taif Accord. *See* National Reconciliation Charter

Taif, Saudi Arabia, 29, 93, 135, 364, 454

Taimur ibn Faisal, 388, 460, **511**, 527

al Takfir wal Hijra, **511-12**

Tal, Wasfi, 100

Talabani, Jalal, 83, 197, 283-84, 285, 287, 411-13, **512-14**

Talal ibn Abdullah al Hashem, king of Jordan, 199, 254, 255, **514**

Taleqani, Mahmud, 86, 270, 308, 330, 443, 481, **514-15**

Talfa, Khairallah, 195

Talfa, Sajida, 194

Talib, Ali ibn Abu, 53, 173, 206, 222-23, 231, 271, 281, 314, 319, 348, 354, 355, 467, 485, 486, 502, 533, 586

Taliban, 6, 17, 62, 83, 97, 98, 162, 211, 271, 273, 284, 389, 433, 472, 473, 514, 538

Talmud, 177, 182, 259, 370, **515-16**, 565

Tamerlane, 63, 71, 222, 369, 488, 510

Taimiya, Ahmad ibn, 180

Tantawi, Ismail, 15, 587

Tanua LeAhdut HaAvodah, 13, 294, **516**

taqlid, 516

Tareeq al Shaab (journal), 113

Tarif, Salah, 236

Tashnak Party, 516

Tehran, Iran, 60, 71, 72, 78, 82, 92, 118, 120, 125, 139, 156, 191, 208, 225, 270, 271, 272, 360, 365, 376, 437, 444, 481, **516-17**, 561

Tehiya, 330, **517**

Tel Aviv-Jaffa, Israel, 50, 87, 90, 159, 178, 231, 244, 332, 413, 420, **517-18**

Temple Mount, 247 (*see also* Noble Sanctuary)

Terceira Island, 164

terrorism, 18, 47, 55, 62, 79, 80, 97, 99, 124, 130, 162, 178, 183, 192, 212, 220, 224, 273, 306, 335, 336, 405, 415, 416, 420, 429, 444, 475, 487, 488, 507, **518-19**, 538, 553, 575 (*see also* September 11, 2001; suicide bombing)

Terzi, Zehdi, 403

thalweg principle, 1, 211, 212, 524, 525

al Thani, Abdullah ibn Khalifa, 435

al Thani, Abdullah ibn Qasim, 435, 519, 521

al Thani, Ahmad ibn Ali, 366, 434, 435, **519**, 520, 521

al Thani, Ali ibn Abdullah, 435, **519**, 521

al Thani dynasty, 366, 434, **521**

al Thani, Hamad ibn Khalifa, 435, 436, **519-20**

al Thani, Khalifa ibn Hamad, 435, 436, 519, **520-21**

al Thani, Qasim ibn Muhammad, 521

al Thawra (newspaper), 64

Theodara, Empress, 396

Theodosius I, Roman Emperor, 121

Third Gulf War. See Gulf War III

Thousand and One Nights, The, 71

Tiberias, Lake, 58, 149, 150, 508

Tigris River, 71, 133, 320, 333, 484, **521**

Tikrit, Iraq, 76, 169, 528

al Tikriti, Omar Ali, 218

Tiran Straits, 34, 343, 356-57, **521**

titles, religious, **521-23**

titles, secular, **523**

Tito, Josip, 41, 356

Titus, Roman emperor, 243

Tora Bora, 96

Torah, 12, 93, 177, 246, 258, 329, 370, 396, 456, **523**, 573

Torah Religious Front, 424, **523**

Toubi, Tawfiq, 312

Touma, Emile, 172, **523-24**

Tov, Israel Baal Shem, 182

Trablus. *See* Tripoli

Transition Law, **524**

Transjordan, 7, 24, 27, 36, 39, 148, **524**, 566
Britain and, 7-8, 26, 27, 135, 206, 254, 296, 401, 524 (*see also* Sykes-Picot Pact)
(*see also* Jordan)

Treaty of Frontier and Good Neighborly Relations, **524-25** (*see also* Iran-Iraq Treaty)

Treaty of Iran-Iraq Frontier, 211, **525**

Treaty of Good Neighborly Relations, **525**

Treaty of Jiddah, **525-26**

Treaty of Lausanne, 286, **526**

Treaty of Muhammara, **526**

Treaty of Muslim Friendship and Arab Fraternity, **526**, 578

Treaty of Sèvres, 286, **526**

Treaty of Sib, 388, 511, **526-27**

tribalism, 24, **527-28**

Tripartite Agreement, **528**

Tripartite Declaration, 90, 479, **528**

Tripoli, Lebanon, 297, 302, 402, **528-29**

Tripoli, Libya, 496, 528

Trucial States, 126, **529**, 536

Trumpeldor, Joseph/Yosef, 240, **529-30**

Tudeh Party of Iran, 139, 280, 350, 398, **530-32**, 585

Tumb/Tunb Islands, 10, 154, **532-33**, 537

Tunis, 37, 47, 81, 102, 138, 231, 332, 403, 405, 416, 569
Tunisia, 17, 18, 36, 44, 321, 338, 402, 410
Turkey, 17, 49, 50, 51, 63, 82, 100, 104, 109, 133, 151, 157, 186, 223, 275, 279, 281, 286, 286, 288, 321, 410, 476, 504, 526, 528 (*see also* Ottoman Empire)
Turki aibn Abdul Aziz, 468
Turkmen, 63, 209, 215, **533**
al Tusi, Abu Jaafar Muhammad, 173
Twelver Shias, 18, 206, 209, 231, 240, 310, 316, 317, 341, 436, 467, **533**, 586
Tyre, Lebanon, 101, 227, 237, **533-34**

Uganda, 72, 573, 590
Ukraine, 12, 132
ulama/ulema, 118, 180, 486, 502, **534**, 561, 572, 573
Ultra-Orthodox Jews, 12, 182, 247, 370, 488, **534**
Umayyad Empire, 15, 19, 53, 84, 121, 172, 244, 371, 400, 425, 485
umm, **535**
Umm Qasr, Iraq, 166, 169
umma, 16, 65, 175, 438, 439, **535**, 573
umra, 349, **535**
Uniate churches, 105, 151, 316, 449, 509, **535**
Union of Arab States, 13
Union of the Peoples of Arabian Peninsula (UPAP), **535**
United Arab Emirates (UAE), 9, 17, 31, 36, 44, 153, 154, 159, 312-13, 328, 353, 354, 445, 482, 527, 533, **535-38** (*see also* oil and gas industry [UAE])
United Arab List, 30
United Arab Republic (UAR), 13, 14, 32, 40, 41, 49, 55, 58, 68, 69, 75, 99, 113, 129, 142, 173, 199, 241, 288, 297, 338, 348, 356, 409, 433, 440, 455, 506, **538,** 579
United Kingdom, 159 (*see also* Gulf War III)
United National Leadership of the Uprising (West Bank and Gaza), 207, 404, 487, **538**, 569
United Nations, 5, 6, 8, 10, 38, 46, 47, 61, 67,

72, 97, 101, 105-6, 111, 128, 134, 147, 186, 373, 388, 432, 461, 489-90, 506, 517, 525
partition plan for Palestine, 10, 32, 33, 90, 172, 174, 232, 244, 245, 307, 312, 315, 367, 401-2, 404, 408, 560, 570, 589
United Nations Disengagement Observer Force, **538**, 560
United Nations Emergency Force (UNEF), 34, 356, 498-99, 521, **538-39**
United Nations General Assembly Resolution 181, 32, 401, 404
United Nations General Assembly Resolution 3236, 403, **539**
United Nations General Assembly Resolution 3379, 589
United Nations Interim Force in Lebanon (UNIFIL), 237, **539**, 560
United Nations Iran-Iraq Military Observer Group, **539**
United Nations Iraq-Kuwait Observer Mission, **539-40**
United Nations Monitoring, Verification and Inspection Commission (UNMOVIC), **540**, 546-48, 551-52, 553-57, 559
United Nations Relief and Work Agency for Palestinian Refugees in the Near East, 193, **540-41**
United Nations Security Council, 34, 38, 98, 149, 176, 582
Resolution 242, 57, 128, 137, 322, 335, 357, 414, 415, 416, 417, 491, 507, 539, **541**
Resolution 252, 127, 244
Resolution 267, 244
Resolution 271, 244
Resolution 298, 244
Resolution 338, 35, 57, 322, 416, 491, 507, **541-42**
Resolution 340, 35
Resolution 425, 189, 236, 306, 419, 539, **542**
Resolution 465, 147, 244
Resolution 476, 127, 244
Resolution 478, 127
Resolution 487, 326
Resolution 479, 155

Resolution 509, 237
Resolution 598, 38, 154, 156, 157, 196, 270, 539, **542-43**, 562
Resolution 660, 160
Resolution 661, 158
Resolution 678, 158, 159, **543-44**, 580
Resolution 687, 65, 161, 194, 197, 324, 540, **544-45**
Resolution 715, 197
Resolution 1284, 161, 198, 391, 540, **545-52**, 559
Resolution 1441, 162, 164, 165, 198, 217, 508, 540, **553-57**
United Nations Special Commission on Iraq, 65, 161, 195, 198, 216, 218, 324, 391, 540, 553, **557-59**
United Nations Special Commission on Palestine, 401, **559-60**
United Nations Truce Supervision Organization, **560**
United Religious Front, 12, 91, 329, 424, **560**
United States Middle East Force, 269, **560-61**
United States of America (U.S.), 17, 21, 47, 72, 78, 84, 92, 97-98, 101, 103, 104, 108, 122, 125, 149, 279, 293, 321, 322, 389, 476, 496, 528
    Afghanistan and, 17, 18, 83, 162, 198, 211, 217, 271, 273, 284, 337, 389, 433, 473, 514
    Bahrain and, 74, 269, 560-61, 563
    Britain and, 24-25 (see also Gulf War III; Operation Desert Fox)
    Egypt and, 23, 30, 60, 130, 334, 338, 346, 356, 368, 458, 491, 497, 498, 528, 572 (see also Camp David Accords)
    Iran/Persia and, 27, 75, 126, 190, 191-93, 209-11, 214, 270-71, 276, 291, 375, 398-99, 443, 444-45, 563, 585 (see also Iran-Iraq War; Irangate Affair)
    Iraq and, 30, 39, 57, 64, 80, 81, 82-83, 104, 105, 121, 126, 196, 218-19, 291, 377, 572 (see also Gulf War II; Gulf War III; Iran-Iraq War; Operation Desert Fox)
    Israel and, 34, 35, 87, 91, 108, 257, 302, 315, 342, 377, 391, 458, 479, 491, 498-99, 572, 575 (see also Camp David Accords; Tripartite Declaration)
    Jordan and, 9, 199-201, 256-57, 347
    Kuwait and, 30, 162, 291, 453, 454 (see also Gulf War II)
    Lebanon and, 56, 106, 144, 237-38, 294, 297, 302, 305, 342, 423, 518 (see also Irangate Affair)
    Middle East policies/plans. See Carter Doctrine; Dual Containment; Eisenhower Doctrine; Peace Process; Rogers Plan
    North Yemen and, 584
    Palestine/PLO and, 25, 47, 90, 183, 238, 342, 416, 491, 572
    Saudi Arabia and, 3, 6, 96, 103, 133, 134, 158, 267-68, 436, 471, 472, 473, 572, 575
    Soviet Union and, 35, 214, 237, 498
    Syria and, 55, 57, 58, 69, 342, 440, 506-9, 586
    Yemen and,, 464-65, 581 (see also USS Cole) (see also September 11, 2001)
United Torah Judaism, 12, 247, **561**
Universal Suez Maritime Canal Company, 60-61, 497 (see also Suez Canal)
Uqla, Adnan, 226
U.S. See United States of America
U.S. Defense Department, 16
USS Cole, 17, 98, 337, 464, 501, 581
al Utaiba, Juheiman ibn Saif, 85, 319, **561-62**

Vance, Cyrus, 214
Vanunu, Mordecai, 325, 326, 332
Velayati, Ali Akbar, **562-63**
Venezuela, 198, 217, 392, 394
Vespasian, Roman Emperor, 352
Vichy, France, 117, 149, 277, 304, 440, 506, 529, 586
Vienna, Austria, 80, 104, 219, 285, 392, 540, 573, 575, 588
Vilayet-e Faqih, 150, **563**
Vilner, Meir, 172, 312
Vilnius, Lithuania, 87, 293, 329, 515, 584

Wafd, 25, 39, 111, 119, 129, 136, 353, 368, **563-64**

Wahhab, Muhammad ibn Abdul, 85, 180, 561, 564

Wahhabism and Wahhabis, 2, 3, 44, 180, 193, 205, 252, 264, 317, 318, 354, 355, 435, 436, 447, 470, 471, 473, 519, 521, 561, **564-65**

Wailing Wall (Western Wall), 127, 202, 228, 243, 419, **565-66**

Waite, Terry, 188, 192

al Walid, Caliph, 331

waqf, **566-67**

War of Attrition (Egypt-Israel), 357, 414, 448, 491, 497, **567**, 569

War of the Establishment (Israel). See War of Independence (Israel)

War of Independence (Israel), **567** (see also Arab-Israeli War I)

Warba Island, 27, 158, 289

Warburg, Otto, 574, 590

Warsaw, Poland, 152

Washington Accord. See Oslo I Accord

Washington, D.C., 17, 47, 57, 83, 98, 102, 103, 130, 145, 178, 186, 210, 239, 404, 418, 458, 500, 508, 567

Watson, Charles, 23

Wazir, Abdullah, 465

Wazir, Intisar, 407

Wazir, Khalil (Abu Jihad), 9, 45, 47, 136, 137, 266-67, 332, 407, **568-69**

Wazzan, Shafiq, 468

Weizman, Ezer, 265, **569-70**

Weizmann, Chaim, 92, 296, 574, 589, 590

West Africa, 314

West Bank, 21, 38, 46, 47, 48, 67, 68, 80, 102, 114, 115-16, 123, 124, 127, 137, 138, 144, 154, 170, 171, 172, 177, 182, 184, 199-200, 201, 207, 228, 231, 232, 234, 236, 242, 247, 254, 257, 262, 329, 347, 370, 373, 406, 407, 408, 414, 416, 418, 419, 421, 428, 429, 434, 461, 475, 482, 487, 538, 540, 541, **570-71**, 567, 575

West Jerusalem, 149, 242, 244, 518, **571**

West Syriac (Antiochene) rite, 316, 396, **571**

Western hostages. See hostage taking and hostages

Western Wall. See Wailing Wall

White Guard (Saudi Arabia). See National Guard (Saudi Arabia)

White Paper, 21, 24, 31, 90, 220, 401, 479

White Revolution, 86, 210, 275, 309, 360, 398, 481, **571-72**

Whitsunday. See Pentecost

Wilson, Woodrow, 78, 278-79

Wolffsohn, David, 573

World Islamic Front for Jihad against Crusaders and Jews (WIFFJ), 97, 337, **572-73**, 587

World Muslim League (WML), 253, **573**

World Trade Center, 5, 98, 337, 500

World Union of Zionist Revisionists. See Revisionist Zionists

World War I. See First World War

World War II. See Second World War

World Zionist Organization (WZO), 12, 49, 50, 187, 240, 245, 248, 329, 370, 424, 425, 427, **573-75**, 588, 590

Wretched of the Earth (Fanon), 480

Wye River Memorandum, 48, 178, 201, 255, 370, 418, 420, 568, **575**, 577

Yaarab, 24, 527

Yafi, Abdullah, 263

Yahya, Imam, 13, 465, 467

Yamani, Ahmad Zaki, 382, **575-76**

Yassin, Adnan, 332

Yassin, Ahmad, 177, 178, 333, 347, **576-77**

Yatom, Danny, 331

Yazidis, 218, **577**

Yellin-Mor, Nathan, 307, 308

Yelstin, Boris, 558

Yemen, 17, 31, 44, 97, 110, 158, 231, 250, 395, 501, **577-82**

  Britain and, 27

  Egypt and, 14, 465, 582-83

  Iraq and, 464, 580

  leaders, 14, 88, 148, 463, 465

  military, 329

  PLO and, 402

  political parties, 146, 358, 582, 583

Saudi Arabia and, 14, 148, 464, 580, 583
  U.S. and, 464-65, 581 (*see also* USS Cole)
  (*see also* oil and gas industry [Yemen]; North
    Yemen; South Yemen)
Yemen Arab Republic. *See* Yemen: history: North
    Yemen
Yemen Socialist Party, 20, 68, 88, 147, 231, 337,
    362, 528, 580, **582**, 583
Yemeni Civil War (1962-70), 14, 68, 148, 221,
    465, 468
Yemeni Civil War (1994), 15, 88, 89, 147, 464,
    581, **582-83**
Yemeni Islah Group, 15, 147, 580, **583-84**
Yemeni War (1972), **584**
Yemeni War (1979), **584**
Yemeni-British Treaty. *See* Anglo-Yemeni Treaty
Yiddish language, 53, 152, **584**
Yishuv, 12, 32, 50, 90, 92, 245, 314, 424, 567,
    584-85
Yitzhaki, Shlomo (Rashi), 515
Yom Kippur, 35, 246, 449, **585**
Yom Kippur War. *See* Arab-Israeli War IV
Yosef, Ovaida, 484
Young Turks, 7, 135, 181, 409
Yousef, Ramzi Ahmad, 337
Yugoslavia, 41, 396

Zaghlul, Saad, 353, 563
Zahal, 174, **585** (*see also* Military in Israel)
Zahedi, Fazlullah, **585-86**
Zahle, Lebanon, 29, 31
Zaidis, 3, 13, 179, 206, 209, 221, 231, 372, 467,
    579, 582, 583, **586**
Zaim, Hosni, 414, 440, 450-51, 489, 509, **586**
zakat, 131, 177, 222, 486, 576, **586-87**
Zamir, Zvi, 331
Zand, Karim Khan, 488
Zanzibar, 344
Zarqawi, Abu Mussab, 28, 163
Zawahiri, Ayman (Abu Muhammad; Muhammad
    Ibrahim), 15, 16, 17, 18, 439, **587**, 572
Ze'evi, Rechavam, 235, 330
Zghorta, Lebanon, 140, 141
Zifri, Mustafa (Abu Ali Mustafa), 172

Zinjibar, South Yemen, 19
Zion, **587-88**
Zionism and Zionists, 8, 10, 12, 16, 20, 23, 24,
    25, 37, 77-78, 90, 91, 100, 111, 112, 114,
    115, 118, 124, 137, 147, 171, 174, 180, 202,
    216, 220, 236, 240, 247, 248-49, 278, 279,
    309, 312, 329, 344, 352, 367, 370, 405, 409,
    421, 424, 434, 489, 493, 497, 516, 529-30,
    534, 560, 567, **588-89**
Zionist Congresses, 245, 248, 293, 447, 573,
    574, 588, **589-90**
Zionist Organization, 245, 401, 447, 492, 573,
    588, **590** (*see also* World Zionist Organiza-
    tion)
Zoroastrianism and Zoroastrians, 18, 45, 62,
    124, 209, 211, 213, 272, 367, 400, 422, 423,
    590-91
Zubair, Iraq, 166, 167
Zumur, Abbud Abdul Latif, 15, 16
Zwahar Kill, 96

About the Author

DILIP HIRO writes for the *Washington Post, The Nation,* the *Wall Street Journal,* the *Los Angeles Times,* and many other publications. He is a frequent commentator on CNN, BBC, and Sky TV, among others. His twenty four books include *Iraq: In the Eye of the Storm, Sharing the Promised Land, Between Marx and Muhammad, Neighbors,* and *War Without End.*

ating from Baghdad [*qv*], Assad remained cool toward the Baathist regime in Iraq [*qv*], led first by Ahmad Hassan Bakr [*qv*] and then Saddam Hussein [*qv*]. There was a rapprochement with Iraq in 1978, but this proved to be transient. With Assad siding with Iran in the Iran-Iraq War (1980–88) [*qv*], relations between Syria and Iraq soured. Following Saddam Hussein's invasion and occupation of Kuwait in August 1990, Assad tried to persuade the Iraqi leader to call off his action. When that failed, Assad joined the anti-Iraq coalition led by the United States and sent troops to assist Saudi Arabia's defenses.

Since assuming power Assad has committed himself to divesting Israel of the territorial gains it made in Arab countries during the June 1967 Arab-Israeli War [*qv*]. However, his forces failed to retake the Golan Heights [*qv*] during the October 1973 war. Following a disengagement agreement with Israel, he has ensured that no guerrilla attacks are launched on Israel from Syria. Following Egypt's defection from the Arab camp in 1979, Assad embarked upon a plan to achieve strategic parity with Israel, a costly proposition. At the same time he tried to maintain a unified camp among Israel's Arab neighbors by thwarting any attempts at additional bilateral deals involving Israel. His success in Lebanon encouraged him to frustrate any such plans by Jordan's King Hussein [*qv*].

Considering the Palestinians an important part of any alliance to deal with Israel, Assad wished to become a mentor of the PLO chairman, Yasser Arafat [*qv*]. But the latter's resolve to maintain the independence of the PLO led to soured relations between the two leaders. By inciting a revolt against

Arafat's leadership within his own party, Fatah [*qv*], in 1983, Assad weakened his position.

With the decline of the Soviet Union as a superpower from 1989 onward, Assad had to lower his sights when it came to tackling the issue of Israel. In October 1991 he agreed to participate in the Middle East peace conference, which was meant to lead to bilateral talks between Israel and its Arab enemies. He ensured that the conference was held on the basis of U.N. Security Council Resolutions 242 and 338 [*qv*], calling on Israel to withdraw from the territories it occupied during the 1967 war. In the Syrian-Israeli talks, Assad insisted that Israel must promise to vacate the Golan Heights in return for total peace with Syria before details of a peace treaty could be fleshed out. He succeeded in getting the U.S. to play an active role in the Syrian-Israeli negotiations.

Once Syria and Israel had agreed to a ten-point framework in late 1995, its representatives held talks at an American venue in early 1996. But, when suicide bombings by radical Islamist Palestinians killed fifty Israelis in late February–early March, Israeli Prime Minister Shimon Peres [*qv*] demanded that Syria condemn the attacks. Assad replied that these explosions had nothing to do with Syria. Peres unilaterally terminated the negotiations with Damascus. The talks remained suspended during the three years when Benjamin Netanyahu [*qv*] was Israel's prime minister. They resumed after the election of Ehud Barak [*qv*] as Netanyahu's successor. In September 1999, U.S. Secretary of State Madeleine Albright backed Assad's demand for total withdrawal from the Golan. Three months later Barak met Syrian foreign minister Faruq al Shaara in Washington. In March 2000 U.S. President Bill Clinton presented Barak's proposals to Assad in Geneva. These included Israel retaining sovereignty over a narrow strip on the northeastern shore of Lake Tiberias to safeguard its water resources. Assad offered to give Israel access to the strip but not sovereignty. The talks broke down. Elsewhere, in 1997 he began repairing his relations with Iraq.

In the 1999 presidential referendum, Assad secured 99.98 percent of the valid votes, a shade lower than the figure of 99.99 percent in the referendum of 1992. During the last days of his rule, marked by his failing health, he released 225 political prisoners. Overall, his long rule was marked by his consistency and tenacity. A distant and authoritarian personality, he combined realism with a cool, calculating disposition.

Assad, Rifaat (1937–): *Syrian politician* Born in the family of a rural notable in Qurdaha, an Alawi [*qv*] village near Latakia [*qv*], Assad joined the Baath party [*qv*] in 1952. He did his military service during the period when Syria was part of the United Arab Republic [*qv*] (1958–61). After the Baathist coup of March 1963, Assad was put through a crash course at the Homs [*qv*] military academy. In 1965, during internal party struggles between the military and the civilian wings, he became commander of a special security force loyal to the Military Committee. His unit participated in the February 1966 coup, which resulted in the victory of the radicals. It was also active in the struggle against Salah Jadid [*qv*], first in February 1969 and then in November 1970. Assad thus established himself as a powerful ally of his elder brother, Hafiz [*qv*].

His force, now called the Defense Companies and responsible for maintaining internal security, became the best endowed organ of the army. In 1975 he became a member of the national high command of the Baath party and took charge of youth affairs. When the Islamic opposition stepped up its terrorist attacks on the regime, Assad's Defense Companies struck at it. Among the massacres attributed to this force was one in Hama [*qv*] in 1982, when 5,000 to 10,000 people were killed, including 1,000 soldiers. Capitalizing on his status, Assad had taken to enriching himself through means that were not always above criticism.

When President Assad suffered a heart attack in November 1983, he appointed a six-member committee to run the country; it did not include Assad. His Defense Companies, now 55,000 strong and equipped with tanks, artillery, aircraft, and helicopters, became a source of envy among other officers. His close ties with the pro-Western King Hassan of Morocco and the Saudi crown prince, Abdullah ibn Abdul Aziz [*qv*], and his preference for the United States over the Soviet Union made him politically suspect.

Tension between the elite forces loyal to President Assad and Assad's Defense Companies rose sharply in late February 1984. A fortnight later the Syrian leader appointed Assad as one of the three vice presidents but failed to divest Assad of the command of the Defense Companies. On 30 March, when the two forces loyal to one or other of the brothers were poised in Damascus [*qv*] for a confrontation, President Assad reportedly defused the crisis by holding a meeting with his younger sibling in the presence of their aging mother.

In May Assad was sent on a working visit to Moscow along with other officers, including his two chief rivals. He stayed abroad until he was recalled to Damascus six months later to act as vice president in charge of security, but the post was a sham. He did not resume command of the Defense Companies, which had lost much of their strength and prestige. In frustration Assad left for Paris, which became his base.

In 1992 Assad returned to Syria to attend his mother's funeral, and remained in the country. It was not until 1998 that Hafiz Assad formally sacked him as a vice president of Syria. He then went into exile. In late 1999 the government closed down a port in Latakia that had been built illegally by Assad, and warned him that he faced prosecution if he returned home. Following Hafiz Assad's death in 2000, Assad described the accession of Bashar Assad [*qv*] as unconstitutional.

Assembly of Experts, Iran (1979): After the proclamation of the Islamic Republic of Iran in April 1979, its leader, Ayatollah Ruhollah Khomeini [*qv*], decreed the election of a seventy-three-member Assembly of Experts—each member representing about half a million people—to review the draft constitution prepared by the government. Elected in August on universal suffrage, the Assembly, consisting of religious and lay members, was dominated by the ruling Islamic Republican Party [*qv*]. It approved a constitution of 175 articles, which was ratified in a referendum in December 1979. Articles 107 and 108 empowered the clerical members of the Council of Guardians [*qv*] to decide the qualifications of the experts and the size of their assembly, which was authorized to choose the (supreme)

leader or leadership council of three or five members.

Assembly of Experts, Iran (1982–): Elections to the eighty-two-strong Assembly of Experts, each representing about half a million people, were held in December 1982. Only Muslim clerics were allowed to contest. Seen as a permanent constitutional body, the Assembly met once a year, often away from the glare of the media. In November 1985 one of its members, Ahmad Barikban, leaked its earlier decision to name Ayatollah Hussein Ali Montazeri [*qv*] as the future (supreme) leader. But in early 1989 irreconcilable differences emerged between Montazeri and the current (supreme) leader, Ayatollah Ruhollah Khomeini [*qv*]. Montazeri resigned as the successor-designate in March. The Constitutional Review Council, which Khomeini appointed in April, was hard at work when Khomeini fell seriously ill and died on 3 June 1989. During an eight-hour session, the Assembly of Experts rejected the alternative of a (supreme) leadership council and instead voted President Ali Khamanei [*qv*] as the (supreme) Leader. After Khamanei took office, he decreed elections for a fresh Assembly of Experts, which had been given a tenure of eight years by the revised constitution. The newly elected Assembly in October 1990 (with an increased membership of ninety) endorsed Khamanei as the Leader for eight years, and set up a subcommittee to monitor the performance of the Leader. This subcommittee submits its (confidential) report to the Assembly which meets only twice a year. On the eve of the poll for the Assembly, in October 1998, the Guardians Council [*qv*] ruled that a layperson could contest the election provided he was found to be an expert on Islam according to its test. However, no non-cleric passed the test.

Association of Combatant Clergy (Iran): (*Persian: Jame-e Ruhaniyat-e Mobarez-e*) Popularly known as Jame, its nucleus was formed in 1976 when the clerical followers of Ayatollah Ruhollah Khomeini [*qv*] began meeting clandestinely in Tehran [*qv*] to exchange sociopolitical information. It arranged the smuggling of Khomeini's speeches on cassettes from the Iraqi city of Najaf [*qv*] into Iran [*qv*]. Its founders included Ayatollahs Murtaza Motahhari (assassinated in 1979) and Muhammad Beheshti (assassinated in 1981), and Hojatalislams Ali Akbar Hashemi Rafsanjani [*qv*] and Ali Khamanei [*qv*]. As the Islamic revolutionary movement built up in 1977–78, it became more active and began gradually to surface. It played a vital role in establishing local Revolutionary Komitehs (Committees) [*qv*]. After the revolution it became the new order's main instrument to transform the traditional religious infrastructure into a religio-political apparatus of the state. As the political arm of the clergy, it actively backed the ruling Islamic Republican Party [*qv*] in elections and referendums. Since engaging in everyday politics had hitherto been seen by traditional clerics as an extremist activity, the Jame acquired an aura of radicalism. After Beheshti's assassination in 1981, Ayatollah Hussein Ali Montazeri [*qv*] became its leader. He took a radical stance on many issues. In 1982, when Montazeri stepped down due to pressure of work, its leadership went to Muhammad Reza Mahdavi-Kani. As a leading member of the Guardians Council

[*qv*], he declared land reform and foreign trade nationalization bills to be un-Islamic, thus denting the Jame's radical image. This changed totally when its radical members quit to form the Society of Combatant Clerics [*qv*] in 1988, leaving it as a distinctly conservative organization. In the subsequent parliamentary polls it formed an alliance with other conservative bodies.

Assyrian Christians: *see* Nestorian Christians.

Aswan High Dam (Egypt): Successor to the Aswan Dam, the Aswan High Dam on the Nile is 1.24 miles/2 km long and 90ft/30m deep. It was the centerpiece of the economic plan of Egyptian President Gamal Abdul Nasser [*qv*], and was designed to transform the country's cotton-based economy into something more robust and varied by irrigating two million acres of land and boosting electric supplies several-fold. In February 1956 the World Bank for Reconstruction and Development (WBRD) agreed to loan Egypt $20 million if the United States and Britain provided it with credits of $70 million to meet the hard-currency costs of constructing the dam.

Ignoring warnings from Washington, Nasser continued to direct his foreign policies along a nonaligned path. In April 1956 he recognized the seven-year-old People's Republic of China, thus angering the United States, which wanted the new communist republic to remain isolated. On 19 July the United States informed Egypt that it had decided against providing aid for the Aswan High Dam, because it considered the Egyptian economy too fragile to support such an ambitious project. Britain followed suit. A week later, addressing a rally in Alexandria [*qv*], Nasser declared that the

Universal Suez Maritime Canal Company [*qv*], headquartered in Paris, would be nationalized forthwith and the management of the waterway would be assigned to an Egyptian Canal Authority, adding that foreign currency revenues from the Suez Canal [*qv*] would be used to finance the High Dam's construction.

The Soviet Union declared that nationalization of the Suez Canal was within Egypt's legal rights. It stepped in to buy Egyptian cotton, which accounted for 85 percent of the country's exports. It also signed an agreement with Egypt to provide the latter with low-interest loans amounting to $130 million and the services of 5,000 Soviet technicians. Construction work on the project started in 1960. By the time the Soviet leader, Nikita Khrushchev, had inaugurated the first stage of the High Dam in May 1964, Egypt's electricity output had trebled. When its final phase was completed in January 1971, the Aswan High Dam had the capacity to hold back from the tail-end of the Nile's autumn flood some five billion cubic meters of water. Its hydroelectric plants, producing 10,000 million kilowatt-hours of electricity, increased the country's electric output fivefold from its pre-1960 level.

Atef, Muhammad (1944–2001) (a.k.a. Abu Hafs, Abu Khadija, Tayseer Abdullah): Born Muhammad Sobhi abu Sitta in a poor, religious family in Menoufia, Egypt [*qv*], Atef grew up to be a tall man of 6'6" (1.98 meters). A devout Muslim, he trained as a police officer and rose through the ranks during the 1970s. He joined the clandestine Al Jihad group [*qv*] soon after its founding in 1978. When the expected Islamist insurrection against the govern-

ment failed to materialize in the wake of the assassination of President Anwar Sadat [*qv*] in October 1981, Atef became restless.

In 1983 he went to Pakistan to participate in the jihad [*qv*] against the Soviets in Afghanistan. Here he came into close contact with Osama bin Laden [*qv*], who found his police background useful in training Arabic-speaking *mujahedin* [*qv*]. He was one of the founders of Al Qaida [*qv*], which emerged from Maktab al Khidmat (*Persian: Bureau of Service* [to non-Afghan Mujahedin]), established in 1984. When bin Laden returned to Saudi Arabia [*qv*] in 1990, Atef stayed behind in Afghanistan.

The next year he joined bin Laden in Khartoum, Sudan, where Al Qaida began to function as an umbrella organization to coordinate the activities of extremist Islamist groups worldwide. He was a member of the policy-making Shura Council of twelve and head of the military committee. He acquired the nom de guerre of Abu Hafs.

In 1992–93, he supervised the military training of the tribes in neighboring Somalia opposed to the United Nations intervention there. He aided and abetted the attacks on U.S. troops within the U.N. force, as a consequence of which eighteen American soldiers were killed while hunting for Somali warlord Muhammad Farah Aideed and which left nearly five hundred Somalis dead.

He accompanied bin Laden on his return to Afghanistan in 1996 and took charge of training fresh Al Qaida recruits in the camps run by the organization. After the suicide bombings of the U.S. Embassies in Nairobi and Dar as Salam in August 1998, which killed 227 people, a U.S. federal grand jury returned a 238-count indictment (covering

227 murders and eleven other charges) against Atef and sixteen others, charging them with leading a terrorist conspiracy from 1989 to present, working in concert with other terrorist groups to build weapons and attack American military installations. Washington announced a $5 million reward for information leading to Atef's arrest.

In January 2001 Atef caught media attention wtih the video of the wedding of his daughter, Khadija, to Muhammad, eighteen-year-old son of Osama bin Laden. Following the terrorist attacks on the U.S. in September, Washington froze his assets along with those of eleven others. Soon after the evacuation of Kabul by the Taliban on 12–13 November, Atef was killed in an air strike by U.S. warplanes.

Attasi, Nur al Din (1929–1992): *Syrian politician; president 1966–70* Born into a landlord family of the Attasi clan, based in the countryside around Homs [*qv*], Attasi acquired a medical degree from Damascus University in 1955. He joined the Baath party [*qv*] as a youth. After his graduation he worked as a medical volunteer with the Algerian National Liberation Front. Following the Baathist coup of March 1963, Attasi became a member of the ruling National Council for the Revolutionary Command. He was interior minister from 1963–64, then deputy prime minister from 1964–65.

In the internecine fighting within the Baath party, he sided with the radical Military Committee, which included Hafiz Assad [*qv*] and Salah Jadid [*qv*], both Alawis [*qv*]. Following the capture of power by the Military Committee in February 1966, Assad and Jadid emerged as the real leaders. Aware that their Alawi origin was a political liability in a predominantly Sunni [*qv*] society, they used Attasi, a Sunni, as a front man. Attasi became president of Syria as well as secretary-general of the regional (i.e., Syrian) and national (i.e., pan-Arab) high commands of the Baath party. In 1968 he also headed the government. But his real authority was limited.

As rivalry between Assad and Jadid sharpened, Attasi inclined toward Jadid. Following the first skirmish between the two contenders in February 1969, which showed Assad to be the stronger party, Attasi retained his positions as part of a compromise. But when Assad finally won in November 1970 he dismissed Attasi as president, premier, and secretary-general of the Baath party and jailed him. His trial release in late 1980, when the Assad regime faced a severe Islamist challenge, ended when he failed to cooperate. However, his subsequent house arrest soon ended when he agreed to refrain from politics.

Azerbaijan (Iran): The name Azerbaijan is derived from Atropates (*Greek: protected by fire*), a lieutenant of Alexander the Great who, following his commander's victory over the Persian Empire in 328 B.C., founded an independent kingdom in the region. In Iran today Azerbaijan embraces the provinces of East Azerbaijan (pop. 4.11 million in 1986) and West Azerbaijan (pop. 1.97 million in 1986). The Aras River separates Iranian Azerbaijan from the Trans-Caucasian Democratic Republic of Azerbaijan (DRA). It is a chiefly mountainous region with fertile lowlands.

Settled by the Medes before the eighth century B.C., it became a province of the Persian Empire. Its town of Orumiyeh was the reputed birthplace of Zoroaster, the founder of Zoroastrianism [*qv*]. After a long spell as an independent kingdom after 328 B.C., it again became part of the Persian Empire in the third century A.D. Following the victory of the Muslim Arabs [*qv*] over the Persians in A.D. 637, the region fell under the Islamic caliphate and its population was converted to Islam [*qv*]. During the eleventh and twelfth centuries it was ruled by the Seljuk Turks, and in the fourteenth century by Tamerlane. From the early seventeenth to the early nineteenth century it was governed by the Persian shahs. In 1828, following his defeat by the Russians, the shah ceded all territory west of the Caspian Sea and north of the Aras River to Tsarist Russia. He organized the remainder as a province named Azerbaijan. In 1938 Reza Shah Pahlavi [*qv*] divided it into East Azerbaijan (capital, Orumiyeh) and West Azerbaijan (capital, Tabriz [*qv*]).

Following the entry of the Soviet Union into the Second World War in June 1941, its troops occupied these provinces of Iran, which was neutral in the conflict. In December 1945 the Democratic Party of Azerbaijan proclaimed the National Government of Azerbaijan, with Azeri [*qv*] as the official language. A year later, after the Soviet troops had withdrawn, the national government surrendered to the Iranian troops sent by Tehran.

Both East and West Azerbaijan are populated primarily by Azeris, who are largely Shia [*qv*], and secondarily by Kurds [*qv*] and Armenians [*qv*]. Like the majority Persian-speakers in Iran, they participated in the revolutionary movement that toppled Muhammad Reza Shah Pahlavi [*qv*] and ushered in an Islamic republic. Following the breakup of the Soviet Union in 1991, and the emergence of the Democratic Republic of Azerbaijan, contact between these provinces and the DRA increased sharply. However, predictions that, inspired by nationalism, the Azeris in Iran would secede and combine with the DRA to form Greater Azerbaijan proved ill-founded.

Azeri language: Also called the Azerbaijani language, it belongs to the southwest Turkic group of languages and is akin to Turkmen [*qv*] and modern Turkish of Turkey. Written in the Arabic script, it developed as a literary language in the first quarter of the nineteenth century. In Iran, during the rule of the Pahlavi dynasty (1921–79) [*qv*] its use was suppressed. Azeri-speaking Iranians make up about 17 percent of the national population. In the Soviet Republic of Azerbaijan (1920–91), the Arabic script used for Azeri was changed to Latin in 1922, and then to Cyrillic in 1939. After the founding of the Democratic Republic of Azerbaijan in 1992, the government decided to revert to Latin.

Azeris: Also called Azeri-Turks, these Turkic people speak a language that is akin to modern Turkish. In Iran they are the predominant majority in the provinces of East and West Azerbaijan [*qv*], with a combined population of 6.3 million in 2003.

al Azhar University (*Arabic: Resplendent*): *Islamic University in Cairo* Established in A.D. 977 in the al Azhar mosque in Cairo [*qv*] by the Fatimid caliphate (A.D. 969–1171), al Azhar University is the oldest institution of its kind in the world and the leading center for higher Islamic learning. It later became a model for European universities, based on the principle of combining a place of prayer with that of higher learning, and having students live on the premises. The gown worn by the teachers of classical universities of Europe today is a variation of the dress used by the religious teachers at al Azhar, who sat on chairs by a column while students squatted on the floor in front of them.

The traditional teaching practice continues, as does the stress on teaching the Sharia [qv], theology, and Arabic [qv]. The university imparts instruction in the four schools of Sunni Islam [qv]. In the last quarter of the nineteenth century, philosophy was added to the curriculum.

But it was not until two years after President Gamal Abdul Nasser [qv] had nationalized the university that a major reform of the curriculum was carried out. As a result, several nontraditional disciplines such as social sciences were introduced and a hospital and medical faculty added. A supplementary campus was set up at Nasr City. But even the nonreligious faculties stress the study of Islam [qv].

Women were admitted in 1962, but they continue to be instructed separately from men. Al Azhar University attracts students from all over the world. In 2001, just under 189,000 students were enrolled at al Azhar and its affiliated institutions. Its rector is recognized as the highest Islamic authority in Egypt.

Aziz, Tariq (1936–): *Iraqi politician* Born Mikhail Yahunna of a Chaldean Catholic [qv] family in Mosul [qv], Aziz obtained a postgraduate degree from Baghdad University in the early 1950s. He joined the clandestine Baath party [qv] soon after it was established in Iraq in 1950. After the overthrow of the monarchy in July 1958, he joined *al Jumhuriya* (The Republic) as a journalist. Following the Baathist coup in March 1963 he became editor of the party's mouthpiece, *al Jamahir* (The Peoples). Despite the ups and downs experienced by the Baath party during the next five years, Aziz remained loyal to the party. When it seized power for the second time, in July 1968, it was better organized and led. It established a daily newspaper, *al Thawra* (The Revolution), in 1969, and Aziz was appointed editor.

Like many other young party members, Aziz was attracted to Saddam Hussein [qv], the youthful leader. With Saddam's star rising, Aziz moved closer to the center of power. In 1972 he was appointed to the highest ruling body, the Revolutionary Command Council. Two years later he was elected to the national (i.e., pan-Arab) high command of the Baath party and was made minister of information. In 1977 he was elected to the regional (i.e., Iraqi) high command of the Baath, a position of greater import than a cabinet post. Saddam Hussein became president in July 1979 and appointed Aziz deputy prime minister. In April 1980 he was the target of an unsuccessful assassination attempt by Islamic militants. In January 1981 Aziz took up the additional job of foreign minister.

During the Iran-Iraq War (1980–88) [qv] Tehran used Aziz's high office in Iraq as proof that the Iraqi regime was run by infidels. During the war Aziz was active in maintaining cordial relations not only with the Soviet Union, the traditional ally of Iraq, but also with France and, from 1984 onward, the United States. In the course of the Gulf crisis—triggered by the Iraqi invasion of Kuwait in August 1990 and culminating in a war between Iraq and the U.S.-led coalition in January 1991—he emerged as the chief spokesman and negotiator for Iraq in the media and around the negotiating table. His fluency in English and experience as foreign minister proved useful assets to President Saddam Hussein. In March 1991 he reverted to being deputy premier and was Iraq's top negotiator in its dealings with the United Nations, including the U.N. Special Commission (Unscom) on disarming Iraq [*qv*]. His repeated efforts to have the United Nations lift sanctions against Iraq failed in the absence of a clean bill of health from Unscom, a precondition for ending the sanctions, as stated in the U.N. Security Council Resolution 687 of April 1991 [*qv*]. However, as the roving ambassador of Saddam Hussein, he succeeded in improving Iraq's relations with the rest of the Arab world as well as China, France, and Russia.

After the Gulf War III [*qv*] in 2003, he surrendered to the occupying U.S. Forces.

Azzam, Abdullah (1941–89): *Palestinian Islamist ideologue* Born in Jenin, Palestine [*qv*], Azzam and his parents fled to Jordan [*qv*] during the 1948–49 Arab-Israeli War [*qv*]. After graduating in Islamic theology from Damascus University in 1966, he fought in the June 1967 Arab-Israeli War [*qv*]. He then pursued further religious education at al Azhar University [*qv*] and obtained a doctorate in *fiqh* [*qv*], Islamic jurisprudence, in 1973. After teaching the Sharia [*qv*] briefly at Jordan University, Amman [*qv*], he moved to Saudi Arabia [*qv*] to lecture at King Abdul Aziz University in Jiddah [*qv*]. His taped lectures became popular among young pious Saudis such as Osama bin Laden [*qv*]. Azzam held that jihad [*qv*] was compulsory for a true

Muslim, and that only by engaging in jihad would the faithful be able to revive the Islamic *umma* [*qv*] under a caliph as a prelude to restoring the glory of Islam [*qv*].

Attracted by the anti-Soviet jihad in Afghanistan that got going in 1980, Azzam traveled to Pakistan, where he became a lecturer in Islamic studies at Islamic University in Islamabad. Once the scheme of recruiting Arab [*qv*] volunteers for the jihad, called *Mujahedin* [*qv*], initiated by bin Laden, had become established in the early 1980s, Azzam moved to Peshawar, where bin Laden was based. Later bin Laden, who treated Azzam as his mentor, extended this program to non-Arab Muslims [*qv*] outside the region.

In 1984 Azzam set up the Maktab al Khidmat (*Persian: Bureau of Service* [to the Mujahedin]) primarily as a reception center for the newly arrived recruits. During his worldwide travels to raise funds for the Maktab, he visited the al Khifa Refugee Center, Brooklyn, implementing the official U.S. policy of encouraging American Muslims to join the anti-Soviet jihad in Afghanistan, in 1987. By then the Maktab had started providing social welfare to the widows and orphans of the non-Afghan Mujahedin.

Once the Soviets withdrew completely from Afghanistan in February 1989, Azzam claimed victory for the jihad. Seven months later a car bomb killed Azzam and his two sons as they were entering their mosque for the Friday prayer. This shattered bin Laden, who then resolved to continue running Maktab al Khidmat under the new title of Al Qaida [*qv*], but with a more ambitious aim of creating an international network of those who had participated in the anti-Soviet jihad.

B

Baalbek: *Lebanese town* Pop. 24,000 (2002, est.) Baalbek is the site of an ancient city dedicated to the worship of Baal or Bel, the sun god, its name in Greek being Heliopolis, Sun City. Its recorded history goes back to the time when Alexander the Great (r. 336–23 B.C.) conquered Greater Syria [*qv*] in 332 B.C. After Alexander's death, Baalbek came under the rule of the Ptolemies, Seleucids, and Romans, when it thrived. It became part of the Islamic caliphate in A.D. 637; and this continued under different dynasties until the dissolution of the Ottoman Empire in 1918. Major excavations around the turn of the twentieth century revealed two Roman temple complexes: one dedicated to Jupiter, Venus, and Mercury; the other to Bacchus.

Baath party: *see* Baath Socialist Party.

Baath Socialist Party: *pan-Arab political party* Officially called the Arab Baath Socialist Party, it emerged in March 1954 in Damascus [*qv*] from the amalgamation of the Arab Baath Party [*qv*] and the Arab Socialist Party [*qv*]. The party's basic principles were unity and freedom of the Arab nation within its homeland, and a belief in the special mission of the Arab nation, that mission being to end colonialism and promote humanitarianism. To achieve these ends, the party had to be nationalist, populist, socialist, and revolutionary. While the party rejected the concept of class conflict, it favored land reform; public ownership of natural resources, transport, large-scale industry, and financial institutions; trade unions of workers and peasants; the co-option of workers into management; and acceptance of nonexploitative private ownership and inheritance. It stood for a representative and constitutional form of government and for freedom of speech and association within the bounds of Arab nationalism [*qv*].

According to the Baath Socialist Party, Arabs [*qv*] form a single nation that is currently divided into various regions (countries). Therefore, the party is headed by a National Command that covers the whole Arab world and serves as the central executive authority. Under it are certain Regional Commands in those Arab states where the party is strong enough to justify the establishment of one. Below the Regional Commands are branches. These are composed of sections made up of divisions, each of which consists of a few three-member cells. Until 1966 the National Command was based in Damascus. A split in it that year led to a breakaway group establishing itself first in Beirut [*qv*] and then, following the Baathist coup in Iraq in July 1968, in Baghdad [*qv*].

Baath Socialist Party (Iraq): The Baath Socialist Party in Iraq, which started secretly as the Arab Baath Party [*qv*] in 1950, had 208 members in 1954. It held its first (clandestine) regional congress in late 1955, when it decided to cooperate with other nationalist groups. It played only a marginal role in the military coup that overthrew the monarchy in 1958. Despite being suppressed by the new ruler, Abdul Karim Qasim [*qv*], the party increased in size. By the time the Baathists, joined by non-Baathist sympathisers, overthrew Qasim in February 1963, the party had about 1,000 active members and 15,000 sympathizers. Once in power, the Baathists fell out among themselves, allowing the non-Baathist Abdul Salam Arif [*qv*] to usurp power in November 1963.

The failure of Iraqi President Abdul Rahman Arif [*qv*] to participate fully in the June 1967 Arab-Israeli War [*qv*] was used by the Baathists to build up their popular support. In mid-July 1968 an alliance of Baathist leaders and non-Baathist military officers overthrew Arif, and a fortnight later the Baathists elbowed out the non-Baathist conspirators and seized total power. By then the party had 5,000 active members.

The governing five-member Revolutionary Command Council (RCC), headed by President Ahmad Hassan Bakr [*qv*], institutionalized the interweaving of the party with state machinery and with secular society at large. The interim constitution of July 1970 formalized party supremacy by stating that the RCC, the highest state body, had the right to select its new members from the regional (i.e., national) leadership of the Baath. The party tightened its grip over the armed forces, police, and intelligence. Once Saddam Hussein [*qv*], who had earlier built up the party's militia, had acquired a seat on the RCC in November 1969, he busied himself with restructuring and strengthening the party. To broaden the popular base of the regime, the RCC sponsored the formation of the National Progressive and Patriotic Front [*qv*] in July 1973, with the Baath firmly in the lead.

Iraq's war with Iran (1980–88) [*qv*] brought about a marked change in the Baath. In the name of increasing production, the importance of Baathist socialism was minimized and the private sector was encouraged to grow at the expense of the public sector. The concept of pan-Arabism [*qv*] was made subservient to the idea of Iraqi nationalism, which was used as the prime force to motivate citizens to join the war effort. During the Kuwait crisis of 1990–91, the party machine was put to full use to shore up support for the regime. After Iraq's defeat in the Second Gulf War (1991) [*qv*] the regime came to rely heavily on the loyalty and tenacity of the party ranks and leaders. As United Nations economic sanctions against Iraq drastically lowered living standards, the government ensured the loyalty of party cadres by singling them out for economic perks. In the parliamentary elections of 1980, 1984, 1989, 1996, and 2000, the Baath won 183, 188, 138, 169, and 142 seats, respectively, out of 250—except in 1996 and 2000, when the thirty seats allocated to the Kurdish Autonomous Region [*qv*] were nominated by President Saddam Hussein [*qv*].

During the Third Gulf War [*qv*] in 2003, the invading Anglo-American forces made a point of destroying the party offices. With the fall of Saddam Hussein, the party collapsed.

Baath Socialist Party (Jordan): The Baath Socialist Party in Jordan evolved out of the Arab Baath Party [*qv*], which, founded secretly in 1948, received a boost from the incorporation of the West Bank [*qv*] into the Hashemite Kingdom of Jordan in 1950. It was part of the nationalist-leftist alliance, led by Suleiman Nabulsi [*qv*], which emerged as the leading parliamentary group in the 1956 election. Its leaders and a large majority of its members came from the urban educated class, with teachers and students forming its backbone. Later, despite a repressive ban on all political activity in 1957, the Baath continued to exist clandestinely. From 1958–1961 it was helped by the United Arab Republic (UAR) [*qv*], to mount antimonarchist agitation. After the collapse of the UAR, the Syrian Baathists [*qv*], following their seizure of power in 1963, lent their support. The loss of the West Bank to Israel in the June 1967 Arab-Israeli War [*qv*] resulted in a dramatic weakening of the party in Jordan, from which it failed to recover.

Baath Socialist Party (Lebanon): The Baath Socialist Party in Lebanon, which started as the Arab Baath Party [*qv*] in 1948, was hobbled by the enforcement of a law, passed in 1949, that banned parties linked to extraterritorial organizations. Yet in the tolerant climate created by the speedy end to the 1958 Lebanese Civil War [*qv*], the party was able to host the fourth national (i.e., pan-Arab) congress of the Baath Socialist Party in Beirut [*qv*] in 1959. It did so again in 1968 for the pro-Iraqi faction of the pan-Arab party. After the ban on groups with extraterritorial ties had been officially lifted in 1970, the Baath was able to function legally.

During the Lebanese Civil War [*qv*] from April 1975 onward Syria fostered its faction of the Lebanese Baath, which set up its own militia. In July 1987 it joined the Unification and Liberation Front of seven nationalist and progressive parties. Two years later the party, led by Abdullah Amin, joined the Lebanese National Front: fourteen Lebanese and four Lebanon-based Palestinian groups with a program to scrap the confessional system, end the Israeli presence, and defeat the forces of Gen. Michel Aoun [*qv*]. In the national

unity government, formed in December 1990, Amin was given a post. He continued to lead the pro-Syrian group.

Baath Socialist Party (North Yemen): The first Baath Socialist Party cells were set up in North Yemen in 1955–56. After the end of the Yemeni Civil War [*qv*] in 1970, North Yemen began to receive a substantial amount of aid from Iraq, and this enabled the Iraqi Baathists [*qv*] to foster the party in North Yemen. President Ibrahim Hamdi [*qv*] allowed centrist and leftist groups, such as the Baath, to function semi-clandestinely (due to the official ban on political parties) to help him counterbalance the pro-Saudi conservatives. In 1976 the Baath party merged with the Democratic Party of Popular Unity, a leftist group, and the Revolutionary Democratic Party, consisting of former members of the Arab Nationalist Movement [*qv*], to establish the National Democratic Front [*qv*].

Baath Socialist Party (South Yemen): The first Baath Socialist Party cells were set up in South Yemen in 1955–56. After independence in 1967 the party was free to function openly. With South Yemen becoming a recipient of aid from Iraq, the Baath's future seemed assured. But later, as the ruling National Liberation Front [*qv*] proceeded with its plans to bring all parties under the umbrella of the United Political Organization-National Front as a prelude to forming the Yemen Socialist Party [*qv*] in 1978, Baath leaders reluctantly dissolved the group.

Baath Socialist Party (Syria): In Syria the Arab Baath Party [*qv*], an urban-based group, turned militant by absorbing the predominantly peasant membership of the

Arab Socialist Party [*qv*] and becoming the Arab Baath Socialist Party. However, after the founding of the United Arab Republic (UAR) [*qv*] in 1958, UAR President Gamal Abdul Nasser [*qv*] suppressed the Baath in Syria. A coup by Syrian military officers against the Nasser regime in 1961 resulted in Syria seceding from the UAR. However desirable, Syria's secession ran counter to the Baath party's pan-Arabism [*qv*].

After the party had captured power in March 1963, it became divided into two factions: an anti-Marxist, chiefly civilian wing headed by Michel Aflaq [*qv*], and a radical, primarily military wing led by Gen. Salah Jadid [*qv*]. The conflict between them was not resolved until early 1966, when the radicals seized total power and drove Aflaq into exile. What contributed greatly to their victory was the military support given by Gen. Hafiz Assad [*qv*], the air force commander.

Following Syria's defeat in the June 1967 Arab-Israeli War [*qv*], once again two factions emerged within the party. The political wing, led by Jadid, stressed combining economic development with a people's war to liberate the occupied Golan Heights [*qv*]. The military faction, led by Assad, proposed sticking with conventional warfare and ending Syria's isolation by moderating its internal and external policies. Using his position as defense minister, Assad curbed the political wing's influence in the military, but he failed to wrest control of the party from the Jadid faction.

When in September 1970 Assad refused to provide air support to the Palestine Liberation Organization [*qv*] in its fight with the Jordanian army, a schism developed in the party and the government. A fortnight-long

congress of the party in Damascus in November failed to resolve the conflct. As the congress ended, Assad mounted a bloodless coup and arrested top party and military leaders. He then took measures to moderate the party's policies and leadership, and in March 1972 made it share power with the other groups in the National Progressive Front [*qv*].

Assad's intervention in the Lebanese Civil War [*qv*] in June 1976 on the side of the right-wing Maronites [*qv*] led to quiet rumblings in the party. Aware of this, he tried to explain his stance to the nation. Aware too of rising corruption within the party, Assad called a special congress in late 1979 to address the problem. The congress replaced two-thirds of the regional (i.e., national) command of the party and appointed a commission to ensure that no party member used his position for personal gain. During the armed struggle by the opposition Muslim Brotherhood [*qv*] in 1980–82, the party rallied around the regime. When Assad sided with Saudi Arabia and the U.S. during the Kuwait crisis of 1990–91, there were murmurs of disapproval among party ranks. But these died down as Assad consolidated Syria's position in Lebanon after the end of the civil war there in October 1990. In the 1994 general election, the Baath party, a member of the National Progressive Front, gained less than half of the 250 parliamentary seats. In the 1998 parliamentary pool, the party won 135 seats. In the election held in 2003 the party maintained its previous strength.

Baathism and Baathists: *see* Baath Socialist Party.

Babis: *religious sect* The origin of Babis goes back to 20 May 1844, the day when Ali

Muhammad Shirazi (1819–50)—a native of the Iranian city of Shiraz [*qv*] who studied theology at the Shia [*qv*] centers of Najaf and Karbala [*qv*]—declared himself to be the *bab* (gate) to the Hidden Imam. In his sermons he advanced a progressive concept of prophets, arguing that each prophet brought a new message superseding the previous one. Proclaiming himself a prophet, he published a new scripture, *Bayan* (Declaration), which contained laws superseding many in the Quran [*qv*]. This turned Muslim [*qv*] clergy against him. His followers, Babis, broke away from Islam [*qv*] in 1848. He was executed on 9 July 1850 in Tabriz [*qv*] for challenging a basic Islamic tenet that Muhammad was the last prophet of Allah. During the next few years, the Iranian government suppressed the Babi movement, which later evolved into the Bahai movement [*qv*].

Babylon: *Iraqi town* Pop. 15,000 (1991, est.). One of the oldest places in the world and a leading city in ancient times, Babylon—situated by the Euphrates River [*qv*], which has since changed course—was the capital of Babylonia nearly four millennia ago during the reign of Hammurabi (1792–50 B.C.) and retained that position for about a thousand years. Most of its ruins—situated near the Iraqi town of al Hilleh and first excavated by German archaeologists from 1899–1914—have been restored to an approximation of what existed at the height of the city's prosperity under King Nebuchadnezzar (r. 605–562 B.C.). At that time it was the world's largest settlement, covering 2,500 acres/1,000 hectares.

To immortalize himself Nebuchadnezzar ordered that each of the bricks laid to erect temples and other buildings (the Ishtar Gate; the Temple of Marduk; the ziggurat, popularly called the Tower of Babel, which was the city's name in Arabic [*qv*] and Hebrew [*qv*]) should carry the following words in cuneiform writing: "Nebuchadnezzar, King of Babylonia, son of Nabopolassar, King of Babylonia, am I." After it fell to the Persians under Cyrus the Great in 539 B.C., it continued to be the leading city of the world. It surrendered to Alexander the Great in 331 B.C.; and it was here, his planned capital, that he died eight years later in Nebuchadnezzar's palace.

al Badr, Muhammad (1926–96): *ruler of North Yemen, 1962* As the eldest son of Iman Ahmad ibn Yahya [*qv*], al Badr assisted his father in administering North Yemen and fulfilling specific assignments. In 1955, when Iman Ahmad faced an armed revolt by two of his brothers, al Badr mobilized the Bakil and Hashid tribal confederations and saved his father's throne. Al Badr was named crown prince. He encouraged his father to sign a friendship and trade treaty with the Soviet Union. In 1956 al Badr undertook a tour of Soviet bloc countries, and this led to a series of friendship and commercial agreements between North Yemen and several communist states. During his father's trip abroad for medical treatment in 1960, al Badr introduced some of the reforms promised by him, only to see them rescinded on his father's return.

After succeeding his father on 18 September 1962, al Badr tried to reduce growing opposition by granting an immediate amnesty to political detainees. But eight days later, the commander of the royal guard,

Brigadier General Abdullah Sallal [*qv*], staged a coup against him. Al Badr managed to flee to the north, where he rallied the tribes against the new regime in Sanaa [*qv*]. The resulting civil war [*qv*] lasted until 1970. As the rapprochement between the royalist and republican sides, brokered by Saudi Arabia, was based on acceptance of a republic in North Yemen, al Badr went into self-exile in Britain.

Baghdad: *capital of Iraq* Pop. 5,772,000 (2003, est.). Baghdad is a derivative of "*bagdad*," a Persian [*qv*] term, meaning "gift of God." Situated by the Tigris River [*qv*], Baghdad has attracted traders and travelers since the Sumerian age (ca. fifth millennium B.C.). Its recorded history, however, dates back to A.D. 763 when it was founded by the second Abbasid caliph, Mansur (r. A.D. 754–75), who made it his capital. It reached its pinnacle of prosperity as a commercial center under Caliph Haroon al Rashid (r. A.D. 786–809), a state well captured in many episodes of *The Thousand and One Nights*. The city suffered a setback in A.D. 836 when the Abbasid capital was moved to Samarra [*qv*]. This lasted until A.D. 892. Baghdad suffered severely from the invasion of the Mongols in 1258, which ended the Abbasid rule, and faced a similar fate twice more—in 1400 under Tamerlane and in 1524 under Shah Ismail of Persia. When it came under Ottoman suzerainty in 1638, its population was less than 15,000.

Following the collapse of the Ottoman Empire in 1918, and the subsequent creation of Iraq by the amalgamation of Mesopotamia [*qv*] and the province of Mosul [*qv*], Baghdad was made the Iraqi capital. Since then the oil wealth of the country has had an invigorating effect on the city. Besides commerce, it developed industry, transport, and financial services. Funded by a dramatic rise in oil revenues in the mid-1970s, modernization gathered pace. During the Iran-Iraq War (1980–88) [*qv*], Baghdad was an intermittent target of Iranian aerial bombing and ground-to-ground missile attacks. During the six-week Second Gulf War (1990–91) [*qv*], it suffered considerable damage. Most of it was repaired within a decade. During the Third Gulf War (2003) [*qv*], the invading Anglo-American forces destroyed scores of public buildings. And in the chaos and anarchy that followed the fall of the city, the looters and arsonists ransacked and torched all the museums and ministries—except the oil ministry guarded heavily by the occupying American forces.

Among its tourist offerings are the Mustansiriya Law College and the Abbasid Palace, built in the second quarter of the thirteenth century.

Baghdad Pact (1955): *see* Central Treaty Organization.

Bahais: *religious faith* The founder of the Bahai faith was Hussein Ali (1817–92), a Shia [*qv*] native of Tehran [*qv*] and half-brother of Sobh-e Azal, the chosen successor of Ali Muhammad Shirazi, the founder of Babism [*qv*]. A few years after Shirazi's execution in 1850, Hussein Ali became the leader of the exiled Babi community of Baghdad [*qv*]. In 1863 he declared himself *Baha Ullah/Bahaollah* (Glory of Allah), a manifestation of God, whose arrival had been predicted by his predecessor, Shirazi, the Bab. As almost all Babis followed Baha Ullah, they came to be called Bahais.

Baha Ullah authored major works, including *The Most Holy Book* and *The Book of Certitude,* setting out the laws and explaining the nature of God and religion, as well as numerous meditations, prayers, sermons, and letters. His eldest son, Abdul Baha (1844–1921), buried in Haifa [*qv*], is regarded by Bahais to be the infallible interpreter of Baha Ullah's teachings.

By the time of Baha Ullah's death in 1892 in Acre [*qv*], Bahaism had evolved as a universalist, pacifist faith without clergy, its beliefs including unity of all religions, equality of sexes, and spartan living. Its temples are open to people of all faiths, and Bahais are encouraged to open temples and build schools, hospitals, and orphanages around them. Bahaism requires its followers to be monogamous, fast for nineteen days in a year, and offer daily prayers. The Bahai community governs itself through elected bodies, starting at the local level and graduating to the global, with the Universal House of Justice, based in Haifa, at the top, administering the Bahai commonwealth. The Bahai calendar, which commences on the day of the spring equinox, consists of 19 months with nineteen days each, plus four intercalary days.

Among other things, Baha Ullah said that religion continuously evolves. Since this ran counter to the traditional view of Islam [*qv*] as the last, most perfect, revealed Word of Allah, the clergy in Iran declared Bahaism heretical. Nonetheless, the number of followers of Bahaism increased steadily. Responding to a campaign against them in the early 1930s, Reza Shah Pahlavi [*qv*] closed down Bahai schools. During the anti-Bahai campaign in 1955 Tehran's governor personally seized the local Bahai spiritual center. But the Shah resisted demands to outlaw Bahaism and purge the government of Bahais, estimated to be 10,000 to 1,000,000 strong. When the Universal House of Justice in Haifa complained to the United Nations on human rights grounds, the Iranian representative at the United Nations claimed there were no Bahais in Iran. Yielding to the pressure of the Islamic revolutionary movement (1977–78), the shah forced his court minister, Amir Abbas Hoveida [*qv*], to resign, and dismissed his own Bahai physician as well as four Bahai generals.

After the founding of the Islamic republic in Iran in 1979, Bahais faced persecution and closure of their temples. Most of them fled the country, and those who remained limited themselves to prayers at home. Outside the Middle East, Bahai centers exist in the United States, Germany, India, Uganda, Australia, and Panama. In 2000, there were more than 83,000 Bahai centers worldwide.

Bahrain:

Official name: State of Bahrain

Capital: Manama [*qv*]

Area: 273 sq. miles/707 sq. km

Population: 656,400 (2002, est.)

Gross domestic product: US$6.80 billion (1999, est.)

National currency: Bahraini Dinar (BD); BD 1 = US$2.66 = £1.69 = EUR 2.93 (2000)

Form of government: constitutional monarchy; cabinet nominated by the ruler

Official language: Arabic [*qv*]

Official religion: Islam [*qv*]

Administrative regions: Bahrain is divided into twelve administrative regions.

Constitution: The ruler of Bahrain became a sovereign in August 1971 with the abrogation of Bahrain's 1892 treaty with Britain, allowing the latter to conduct its external affairs and defense. The constitution, drafted by a partly elected constituent assembly, specified a National Assembly of forty-two, with thirty deputies to be elected on a limited franchise. The first Assembly, elected in December 1973, was dissolved in August 1975 and the constitution suspended. A quarter-century later, the Supreme National Committee, appointed by the ruler, recommended a transition to a two-chamber parliament, consisting of a popularly elected Assembly and a fully nominated Consultative Council. This was endorsed by a popular referendum in February 2001.

Consultative Council: Established in 1992, and called Majlis al Shura, this council—with a four-year tenure—and nominated by the ruler, is an advisory body and lacks legislative powers. Its initial size of thirty members was later raised to forty. In 2000, of the nineteen new appointees, four were women, including a Christian [*qv*], and one Jew [*qv*].

Ethnic composition: (2000) Arab, 73 percent; South Asian, 19 percent; Iranian, 7 percent; other, 1 percent.

Executive authority: Executive authority rests with the ruler. As head of a council of ministers appointed by the ruler, the prime minister is in charge of running the day-to-day administration.

High officials:

Head of state: Shaikh Hamad ibn Isa II al Khalifa, [*qv*] 1999–

Crown prince: Shaikh Salman ibn Hamad al Khalifa, [*qv*] 1999–

Prime minister: Shaikh Khalifa ibn Salman al Khalifa

Speaker of the Consultative Council: Ibrahim Humaidan

History (since ca. 1900): The Khalifa dynasty, which has ruled the thirty-three-island archipelago of Bahrain since 1783, signed a series of treaties with Britain in 1861, 1880, and 1892, turning Bahrain into a British protectorate and the base of British residency in the Persian Gulf [*qv*]. In 1932 Bahrain became the first Gulf territory to discover oil. The oil workers' efforts to gain trade union rights in the late 1930s failed.

Bahrainis showed their rising political consciousness by mounting anti-British demonstrations during the 1956 Suez War [*qv*], when Britain, France, and Israel together attacked Egypt. After the accession of Shaikh Isa II al Khalifa [*qv*] in 1961, there were demonstrations for political reform. But this protest and an oil workers' strike in 1965 were in vain. It was not until 1970 that the ruler temporized by appointing a twelve-member advisory Council of State. As the British prepared to leave in 1971, he transformed the council into a cabinet and charged it with framing a constitution. Severe rioting and strikes in March and September 1972 led Shaikh Isa to concede a forty-two-member constituent assembly, half elected and half nominated, to draft a constitution. These elections were held on a limited franchise in December 1972. The constituent assembly submitted a constitution to the emir in June 1973. He approved it. Elections to the National Assembly were held on a limited franchise in December, but the emir dissolved the parliament and suspended the constitution in August 1975.

With 60 percent of its nationals being Shia [qv], Bahrain was most affected by the Islamic revolution in Shia-majority Iran in 1979. When the Islamic opposition demanded that Bahrain be declared an Islamic republic, Shaikh Isa II, a Sunni [qv], reacted with a heavy hand. In 1981 Bahrain became a member of the Gulf Cooperation Council [qv]. Early the next year, the government arrested sixty people on the charge of plotting a coup. In the Iran-Iraq War [qv] Bahrain sided with Iraq. During the Kuwait crisis (1990–91) Bahrain took a firm pro-Kuwaiti line. To meet the rising demand for reform the emir appointed a thirty-member advisory council in late 1992, which held its inaugural session in January 1993. This proved insufficient, and in December 1994 widespread anti-regime demonstrations broke out, with protesters calling for the restoration of the dissolved parliament. Government repression followed, but violent protest, inspired partly by the Islamic Liberation Front of Bahrain, revived in March, leading to large-scale arrests and curfews. By April 1995 the disturbances and the state action had led to the deaths of sixteen people, injuries to scores, and 1,600 arrests. In July the ruler agreed to let Washington base its Fifth Fleet in Bahrain. His decision in September 1996 to enlarge the Consultative Council and let half of its forty members be elected indirectly through professional and cultural organizations did not satisfy the opposition demanding a return to the 1973 constitution. The number of people killed in arson attacks and bombings rose to thirty. In 1998

the State Security Court imposed heavy sentences on convicted political dissidents.

The situation changed in March 1999 when Crown Prince Shaikh Hamad became the ruler on the death of his father. He reshuffled the cabinet and released over 300 political detainees. When in July the State Security Court sentenced the leading oppositionist, Shaikh Abdul Amir al Jamri, to ten years imprisonment, the new ruler pardoned him. But in December, while promising to hold local elections on the basis of universal suffrage, he failed to mention the timetable. A year later, the Supreme National Committee, appointed by him, drafted a National Action Charter, which recommended a constitutional monarchy and a bicameral parliament. A referendum held in February 2001 endorsed the National Action Charter. Shaikh Hamad declared Bahrain to be a constitutional monarchy. In the election to the forty-member National Assembly, boycotted by the main opposition groups, twenty-one seats were won by secularists or moderate Islamists [qv].

Legislature: With the reintroduction of the popularly elected National Assembly in October 2002, the legislative powers reverted to it.

Religious composition (2000): Muslim, 85 percent; Christian; 7 percent; other, 8 percent. Among Muslims, Shias; 60 percent; Sunni, 40 percent. The Khalifa dynasty is Sunni.

Bahrain National Liberation Front: *see* Popular Bloc (Bahrain).

Bakdash, Khalid (1912–1995): *Syrian politician* Born into a Kurdish [qv] family in Damascus [qv], Bakdash obtained a law degree at Damascus University. Politically active while in his teens, Bakdash became the secretary-general of the Communist Party of Syria and Lebanon [qv] in 1936. He was jailed by the French mandate. On his release he traveled to Moscow and enrolled at the Communist International College. After Syrian independence in 1946, he returned to Damascus. By the early 1950s he and Akram Hourani were acknowledged to be among the country's most able politicians. In 1954 he was elected to parliament.

During the preliminary talks between Egypt and Syria on unity in 1957, Bakdash proposed a federal tie. When this was rejected, he and other communist leaders, anticipating the dissolution of all political parties in Syria, went into self-exile in Prague, Czechoslovakia. Bakdash called for Syria's secession from the United Arab Republic [qv]. But when this happened, in September 1961, the new Syrian rulers refused to allow him or any other communist leader to return home. The Baathists [qv], who seized power in March 1963, maintained a similar stance, although the radical Baathists' victory in February 1966 changed the situation somewhat. When Bakdash returned to Damascus in the autumn, the regime reluctantly accepted his presence on the condition that he would not hold meetings or make speeches.

In 1968 he was replaced as secretary-general of the Communist Party of Syria [qv]. Four years later President Hafiz Assad [qv] implemented Bakdash's proposal for the creation of a broad-based National Progressive Front [qv]. With his election as the party's secretary-general in 1974, he resumed his position as the Arab world's most senior

communist leader until he was replaced by Yusuf Faisal.

Bakhtiar, Shahpur (1914–91): *Iranian politician; prime minister, 1979* Born into a family belonging to the powerful Bakhtiar tribe, Bakhtiar finished his higher education at Paris University in 1940 with a doctorate in international law and political science. He enrolled in the French army to fight Nazi Germany. On returning to Iran in 1946, he took up a job with the labor ministry and served for two years. He joined the Iran Party, a secular nationalist group, which in 1949 combined with two other organizations to form the National Front [qv], led by Muhammad Mussadiq [qv]. Bakhtiar became deputy minister of labor in the Mussadiq government from 1951–52.

Following the downfall of Mussadiq in August 1953 and the suspension of normal political activity, Bakhtiar turned to practicing law. This brought him into conflict with the regime, especially after the establishment of the secret police, Savak, in 1957. He was detained briefly in 1961. As the antigovernment protest gathered pace in the autumn of 1977, Bakhtiar and Karim Sanjabi, another lawyer, revived the National Front. Rattled by the rising revolutionary movement, Muhammad Reza Shah Pahlavi [qv], anxious to co-opt a politician not associated with his regime but acceptable to the United States, turned to Bakhtiar On 29 December 1978 Bakhtiar agreed to form a government on the (unwritten) condition that the Shah would go abroad for holiday immediately, and that on his return he would act as a consitutional monarch. Bakhtiar tried to reach a compromise with Ayatollah

Ruhollah Khomeini [qv], then in Paris, but the latter declared his government illegal. To gain popular support, Bakhtiar released all political prisoners and promised to disband Savak. But he failed in his gamble, and the National Front expelled him. When on 11 February 1979 military leaders declared themselves neutral in the standoff between Bakhtiar and Khomeini, now heading a parallel government in Iran, Bakhtiar went underground before escaping to Paris.

He was the mastermind behind a failed coup attempt in July 1980 against the Islamic regime in Iran. He then cooperated with Iraqi President Saddam Hussein [qv] as the latter prepared for an invasion of Iran in September. He founded the monarchist National Resistance Movement in 1982 and remained a loyal supporter of the young pretender, Reza Cyrus Pahlavi. After an unsuccessful attempt on his life in 1980, Bakhtiar was given official protection by the French government. Despite this, he was assassinated in August 1991.

Bakr, Ahmad Hassan (1912–82): *Iraqi officer and politician; president, 1968–79* Born into the al Tikriti clan from Tikrit, Bakr enrolled in the army in 1938 and graduated from the Baghdad Military Academy four years later. He secretly joined the Baath party [qv] in 1956 when he was a colonel. He was a leader of the Free Officers Organization, which staged the republican coup in July 1958. A pan-Arabist [qv], he wanted a union between Iraq and Egypt and sided with Abdul Salam Arif [qv] against Abdul Karim Qasim [qv]. With Qasim emerging as the sole leader, Bakr lost his army post. He played an important part in the Baathist coup against Qasim in February 1963 and became prime minister, winning a promotion to major general. At the sixth national congress of the Baath party in October, he was elected to the national command. After the dismissal of his Baathist government by President Abdul Salam Arif in November, Bakr continued as deputy premier for a few months.

His elevation to secretary-general of the Baath regional command in 1965 ended the internecine party divisions. This allowed the party and its military adherents to concentrate on regaining power. In mid-July 1968 Bakr headed the group of Baathist and non-Baathist officers who overthrew President Abdul Rahman Arif [qv] and made him president. A fortnight later he ousted his erstwhile non-Baathist ally, Premier Colonel Abdul Razzaq Nayif. Besides being the new prime minister, Bakr was chairman of the ruling Revolutionary Command Council (RCC) and the military chief of staff. In 1969 he became field marshal.

In conjunction with Saddam Hussein [qv], a close relative, Bakr focused on widening his power base in the officer corps. In the internecine party divisions Bakr tried to play a mediating role, which, given his seniority, suited him. He reached an accord with rebellious Kurds [qv] in 1970, and three years later he inaugurated a broad-based National Progressive and Patriotic Front [qv]. But his strategy for countering the growing discontent among Shias [qv] by conciliating Shia dissidents and accommodating party ideology to the rising wave of Islamic revival did not prevail. Saddam Hussein, the rising star, overruled it.

The sudden move by Egyptian President Anwar Sadat [qv] in late 1977 to make unilateral peace with Israel led the regimes of Bakr and President Hafiz Assad [*qv*] of Syria to bury the hatchet. A visit by Assad to Baghdad [*qv*] in October 1978 set the scene for the unification of their republics. Sensing that Saddam Hussein was not genuinely interested in a union, Bakr sent a secret message to Assad during his visit to Baghdad in mid-June 1979 to expedite the unity negotiations. Informed of Bakr's move, Saddam Hussein acted against him swiftly. A month later, on the eve of the eleventh anniversary of the Baathist revolution, Saddam Hussein secured Bakr's resignation from all his governmental and party posts on "health grounds." Bakr spent his last years under house arrest in ignominy.

Balfour Declaration (1917): Balfour Declaration is the title given to an important policy statement on Palestine [*qv*] by Britain in November 1917 in the form of a letter from the British foreign secretary, Arthur James (later Lord) Balfour, in the coalition government of Prime Minister David Lloyd George, to a prominent British Zionist [*qv*] leader, Lord Rothschild (born Lionel Walter):

Foreign Office
2nd November 1917
Dear Lord Rothschild:

I have much pleasure in conveying to you on behalf of His Majesty's Government the following declaration of our sympathy with Jewish Zionist aspirations which has been submitted to, and approved by, the Cabinet. 'His Majesty's Government view with favor the establishment in Palestine of a National Home for the Jewish people, and will use their best endeavours to facilitate the achievement of this object, it being clearly understood that nothing shall be done which may prejudice the civil and religious rights of existing non-Jewish communities in Palestine, or the rights and political status enjoyed by Jews in any other country.' I should be grateful if you would bring this declaration to the knowledge of the Zionist Federation.

Yours sincerely,
(Arthur James Balfour)

The Balfour Declaration applied to Palestine, which then lacked geographical or political existence with defined borders. In the Ottoman Empire, Palestine was scattered over the *sanjak* (county or district) of Jerusalem and the *vilayat* (province) of Beirut, Jerusalem [*qv*] and its suburbs being ruled directly from Istanbul. The Balfour Declaration arose out of the convergence of Britain's imperial aims with Zionist aspirations, which came to the fore during the First World War (August 1914–November 1918), when Britain was pitted against the Central Powers, consisting of Germany, Austria-Hungary, Bulgaria, and Ottoman Turkey. The January 1915 Ottoman offensive against the Suez Canal [*qv*] across the Sinai Peninsula [*qv*] made London realize the strategic importance of Palestine in defending the Suez Canal, Britain's lifeline to India, and led it to resolve to control Palestine after winning the war.

In a memorandum to the cabinet in March 1915, Sir Herbert Samuel (later appointed British High Commissioner for

Palestine), a Zionist, proposed establishing a Jewish homeland in Palestine as a cornerstone of British policy in the Middle East. Until then the world Jewry, concentrated in Germany, Austria-Hungary, and the United States, had by and large remained neutral in the war. With the United States joining the conflict in April 1917 on the Allied side, the role of American Jewry became important. In order to gain its active cooperation in September, the pro-Zionists in the British government, led by Prime Minister Lloyd George and Foreign Minister Balfour, proposed backing the Zionist cause but failed to win cabinet approval. They then sought the advice of U.S. President Woodrow Wilson, known to be a pro-Zionist. Wilson replied that time was inopportune for anything more than a statement of general sympathy for the Zionists. The next month, responding to Zionist pleas and rumors of Germany wooing the Zionist movement, Lloyd George and Balfour again broached the subject with Wilson. After some hesitation he approved a draft statement, which, following minor editing, was issued by Balfour on 2 November 1917 in the form of a letter to Lord Rothschild. Endorsed by the chief Allied Powers, it was included in the San Remo Agreement of 1920 [*qv*] and incorporated into the British mandate over Palestine authorized by the League of Nations in July 1922.

Baluchis: *nomadic community with a tribal structure* Baluchis are to be found in present-day Iran, Pakistan, and Afghanistan. Their recorded history goes back to the tenth century A.D. Adherents of Sunnism [*qv*] in Islam [*qv*], they are now a settled community in Iran, concentrated in the Sistan and

Baluchistan province and forming 2.5 percent of the national population. After the Islamic revolution in 1979, their demand that the Sunni codes of the Islamic law [*qv*] be recognized on a par with the Shia code was accepted by the constitution makers.

Bani-Sadr, Abol Hassan (1933–): *Iranian politician; president, 1980–81* Born into a religious family in Hamadan, Bani-Sadr pursued his university education in Tehran [*qv*], specializing in economics, sociology, and Islamic law [*qv*]. He was sympathetic to the National Front [*qv*]. For participating in an antigovernment demonstration in June 1963, Bani-Sadr served a four-month jail sentence. He won a scholarship to Sorbonne University, Paris. After gaining a doctorate in sociology and economics, he stayed on in Paris.

During a visit to Najaf [*qv*], Iraq, in 1972 for his father's funeral, he met there with Ayatollah Ruhollah Khomeini [*qv*]. Bani-Sadr then strengthened his ties with the Islamic Student Society in Paris. When Khomeini arrived in Paris in early October 1978 from Iraq, Bani-Sadr became a member of the Ayatollah's inner circle of advisers. On his return home with Khomeini six months later, Bani-Sadr became Iran's chief architect of economic policies. Through his newspaper, *Inqilab-e Islami* (Islamic Revolution), he urged radical policies and was glad to see the government of Mahdi Bazargan [*qv*] fall in early November.

In the new cabinet Bani-Sadr became minister of economy and finance. As a member of the Assembly of Experts [*qv*], he succeeded in getting a bill of rights incorporated into the constitution. By winning 75 percent of the votes in the presidential poll in

January 1980, albeit with Khomeini's backing, Bani-Sadr enhanced his stature. Khomeini appointed him commander in chief of the military.

With the outbreak of hostilities with Iraq in September 1980, Bani-Sadr's handling of the war came under the critical scrutiny of leaders of the Islamic Republican Party [qv], the majority party in parliament, which was at odds with Bani-Sadr. He also clashed with Premier Muhammad Ali Rajai [qv], who had been foisted on him by parliament. Initially Khomeini tried to mediate between the two sides, but as Bani-Sadr began to court the Mujahedin-e Khalq [qv], a party detested by the Ayatollah, he turned against Bani-Sadr. On 20 June 1981 the Iranian parliament found Bani-Sadr incompetent, and Khomeini dismissed him as president. Bani-Sadr went underground and then, along with Masud Rajavi [qv], the Mujahedin-e Khalq chief, escaped to France.

The National Resistance Council (NRC) [qv], formed by Bani-Sadr and Rajavi, masterminded a successful campaign of assassination and terror. But when Rajavi began to collaborate with Iraq, which was still engaged in a bloody war with Iran, Bani-Sadr broke with Rajavi in April 1984 and quit the NRC. He continued his political activities, independently, from a Paris suburb.

In *The Economics of Divine Unity,* published before the revolution, Bani-Sadr expounded Islamic economics, rejected capitalism and Soviet socialism, and argued that Islamic teachings were a means to a just and equitable society. He encapsulated his later political experiences in *My Turn to Speak.*

al Banna, Hassan (1906–49): *Egyptian Islamic leader* Born into a religious family in the Nile delta town of Muhammadiya, al Banna graduated from Cairo Teachers College. He became a primary school teacher in Ismailiya, capital of the British-occupied Suez Canal [qv] zone. An avid reader of *Al Manar* (The Lighthouse), edited by Muhammad Rashid Rida, al Banna was much inflenced by the writings of this Islamic thinker. In 1928 he established the Muslim Brotherhood [qv] as a youth club, its main stress being on moral and social reform through communication, information, and propaganda. It then turned into a political-religious movement, which argued that Islam [qv] was a total ideology, offering an all-pervasive system to regulate every detail of the political, economic, social, and cultural life of believers. Based in Cairo [qv] since 1933, and led by the charismatic, spartan al Banna, the Brotherhood had spawned 500 branches by 1940, drawing its support from students, civil servants, artisans, petty traders, and middle-income peasants. After the Second World War, as the anti-British struggle escalated, the popularity of the Brotherhood, with its strong anti-imperialist credentials, soared, and al Banna claimed a Brotherhood membership of 500,000 in 1946.

He held the Egyptian political establishment solely responsible for the Arab debacle in the 1948 Palestine War [qv], and the Brotherhood's secret cells began to engage in terrorist and subversive activities. Prime Minister Mahmud Fahmi Nuqrashi retaliated by banning the Brotherhood in December 1948. Three weeks later Nuqrashi was assassinated by a Brotherhood activist. This led to further repression of the organization. On 12 February 1949 al Banna was killed by secret service agents in Cairo. He left behind his memoirs as well as numerous published speeches and articles.

al Banna, Sabri (1937–2002): *Palestinian leader* Born into a prosperous, plantation-owning family in Jaffa [*qv*], al Banna and his family fled to the al Bureij refugee camp in the Gaza Strip [*qv*] after the establishment of Israel in May 1948. They then moved to the West Bank [*qv*] city of Nablus [*qv*]. While working as an electrician's assistant, al Banna joined the Baath party of Jordan [*qv*] in 1955. Following the failed coup in 1957 against the regime of King Hussein [*qv*], the Baath party was suppressed. Al Banna moved to Riyadh [*qv*], where he established an electrical business and joined a secret Fatah [*qv*] cell. In 1967 he was expelled from Saudi Arabia after joining in a demonstration following the Arab defeat in the Six-Day War [*qv*].

His trading company in Amman [*qv*] became a useful conduit for Fatah. In 1969, when he was a member of the Fatah Revolutionary Council, al Banna was appointed Fatah's representative in Sudan. In July 1970 he was transferred to Baghdad [*qv*] as Fatah's envoy. There he began to echo the views of the Iraqi regime rather than represent Fatah's interests. Soon he started to work for the Iraqi secret service. Following his criticism of the decision of the Palestine National Council [*qv*] in mid-1974 to set up a "national authority" on any "liberated" territory in Palestine [*qv*], al Banna was expelled from Fatah. In November he was found guilty by a Fatah court, based in Beirut [*qv*], of plotting to kill a Fatah leader, Mahmud Abbas (nom de guerre: Abu Mazin) [*qv*], and was sentenced to death in absentia.

Encouraged by Iraq, he set up his own group—Fatah: The Revolutionary Council [*qv*]. The group was generously funded by Iraq, which used it to settle scores with Syria in 1976–77. Al Banna's activities from Baghdad ended in 1983, when in order to qualify for aid from Washington for the Iran-Iraq War [*qv*], Iraqi President Saddam Hussein [*qv*] expelled him and his men to show that Iraq was distancing itself from international terrorism.

Al Banna was then hired by Syria, which used his group as part of its coercive attempt to dissuade King Hussein of Jordan [*qv*] from making a unilateral deal with Israel. When King Hussein and Yasser Arafat [*qv*], chairman of the Palestine Liberation Organization (PLO) [*qv*], devised a joint plan in early 1985, al Banna joined with Abu Musa, another Syria-backed Fatah dissident, to destroy the accord and prevent any prospect of an agreements being reached between Hussein, Arafat, and Israel. In late 1985 al Banna's gunmen attacked counters of the Israeli El Al airline in Vienna and Rome and hijacked a Pan-American aircraft on the ground in Karachi. In mid-1986 Syria expelled al Banna and his group from Damascus [*qv*]. They reportedly took refuge in Libya, which became their main haven for almost eleven years.

Once the Iran-Iraq War [*qv*] was over in 1988, freeing Iraq from the need to placate the U.S., al Banna turned successfully to Baghdad for assistance. In 1990 he tried to wrest control of the Fatah-dominated Palestinian refugee camps in southern Lebanon, but failed. During the Gulf crisis (August 1990 to March 1991) al Banna was allegedly bribed by the Saudi authorities to refrain from carrying out assassinations and sabotage in the Saudi kingdom for Iraq. In January 1991 al Banna's agent, working as a bodyguard, assassinated Salah Khalaf [*qv*], the PLO's second-in-command in Tunis.

When, by 1996–97, the Libyan leader Muammar Qadhafi had found him to be a political liability, al Banna and his dwindled number of followers reportedly moved to Cairo [*qv*] to offer their mercenary services to Egypt in its drive against Islamist insurgents. This lasted a few years. In 1999, al Banna, an isolated figure, returned to Baghdad. There he became a liability to Saddam Hussein after 9/11 when the Iraqi leader reckoned that U.S. President George W. Bush could use al Banna's presence in Baghdad as a rationale to attack Iraq. In August 2002, the Iraqi government claimed that al Banna had entered the country illegally and that when confronted by a security unit in his Baghdad apartment, he committed suicide. Other reports suggested that al Banna had been killed by the Iraqi security unit in a shoot-out.

Barak, Ehud (1942–): *Israeli military and political leader; prime minister 1999–2001*
Born Ehud Brog in Kibbutz Mishmar HaSharon. He altered his family name to Barak *(Hebrew: lightning)* on joining the Israel Defense Forces (IDF) [*qv*] in 1959. During the 1967 Six-Day War [*qv*], Barak served as a reconnaissance group commander. In 1972, as the head of the *Seyeret (Hebrew: der. of reconnaissance) Makal (Hebrew: acronym for "General Staff")*, he led a successful assault on the Palestinians who had hijacked a Belgian airliner at Ben-Gurion Airport in Israel. In April 1973, Barak, dressed as a woman, led a commando unit into Beirut [*qv*] to assassinate three Pales-

tinian leaders. During the Arab-Israeli War that erupted six months later, Barak was a tank battalion commander on the southern front in Sinai. He then enrolled at Hebrew University, Jerusalem [*qv*], where he graduated in physics and mathematics, followed by a master's degree in engineering-economic systems from Stanford University, California, in 1978.

During the Israeli invasion of Lebanon in June 1982 [*qv*] Barak, now a major general, was the deputy commander of the IDF in Lebanon. In April 1983, he was appointed head of the IDF's intelligence branch. In January 1986, he was promoted to commander of the IDF Central Command, and then to deputy chief of staff in May 1987. In April 1991, he assumed the post of the fourteenth Chief of the General Staff and was promoted to the rank of lieutenant general, the highest in the Israeli military.

Following Israel's agreement with the Palestine Liberation Organization [*qv*] in May 1994, Barak supervised the IDF's redeployment in the Gaza Strip [*qv*] and Jericho [*qv*]. He played a central role in finalizing the peace treaty with Jordan [*qv*], signed in 1994, and met with his Syrian counterpart as part of the Syrian-Israeli negotiations. By the time he retired from the IDF in mid-1995, he had won the "Distinguished Service Medal" and four other citations for courage and operational excellence, the highest ever by an Israeli soldier.

Prime Minister Yitzhak Rabin [*qv*] then appointed him minister of the interior. In that capacity he did not vote for the Oslo Accord II [*qv*] that Rabin signed with Palestinian leader Yasser Arafat [*qv*]. After Rabin's assassination in November, Prime Minister

Shimon Peres [*qv*] appointed Barak minister of foreign affairs. In the 1996 general election Barak was elected to the Knesset. Later that year he was elected chairman of the Labor Party [*qv*]. In 1999 he formed the One Israel Party [*qv*], an alliance of Labor, Gesher, and Meimad.

In May 1999, Barak defeated his Likud [*qv*] rival Benjamin Netanyahu [*qv*] in the prime ministerial contest by a large margin. In the new cabinet Barak also took charge of the defense ministry. He kept his election promise by withdrawing unconditionally from south Lebanon. He became the first Israeli leader to state the terms for a final settlement with the PLO on the Palestinian refugees, Jewish settlements, Jerusalem, and final borders. But his talks with Arafat, chaired by U.S. President Bill Clinton, at Camp David in July 2000, failed—chiefly on the status of the Noble Sanctuary [*qv*] in the Old City when Barak insisted on having Israeli sovereignty over the revered Islamic site. The subsequent eruption of the Second Intifada [*qv*] by the Palestinians undermined his standing, and he called a special prime ministerial poll. He lost to Likud's Ariel Sharon [*qv*]. He resigned as leader of the Labor Party and as a Knesset member.

Barzani, Masud (1947–): *Iraqi Kurdish leader* Born during the tumultuous times that followed the collapse of the Kurdish Republic of Mahabad [*qv*], led militarily by his father, Mustafa [*qv*], Barzani grew up in Moscow. After a two-year stay in Baghdad [*qv*] following the republican coup of 1958, the family returned to Barzan in northern Iraq. With the defection in the early 1970s of one of his elder brothers, Ubaidullah, to the Baghdad government, the burden of

assisting their father in his political and military endeavors fell on Barzani and his remaining brother, Idris. After Mustafa's departure for the United States in 1976, the leadership of the Kurdistan Democratic Party (KDP) [*qv*] was exercised by Barzani and Idris. When they moved to Iran after the Islamic revolution in early 1979, Tehran began to lend them its support.

The outbreak of the Iran-Iraq War [*qv*] in September 1980 compelled Baghdad to reduce its troops in the Kurdish areas. This led to an expansion of the Iraqi border area under KDP control. In late 1986 Barzani attended a conference organized in Tehran [*qv*] by the Supreme Assembly of the Islamic Revolution in Iraq (SAIRI) [*qv*]. However, its attempt to coordinate the military activities of all anti-Saddam parties failed, because the secular leadership of the KDP felt uneasy about coalescing with the predominantly Islamic forces. With the death of Idris in 1987, Barzani became the sole leader of the KDP.

During the long Iran-Iraq war, Barzani's KDP had managed to set up liberated zones along the Iraqi border with Iran. However, when the conflict ended in 1988, Iraqi President Saddam Hussein [*qv*] launched a campaign of vengeance against the KDP stronghold. Later, when the Iraqi forces were defeated in the Second Gulf War [*qv*] in early 1991, Barzani led a Kurdish rebellion against the central government. Its suppression caused a massive exodus of Kurds into Turkey and intervention by the anti-Iraq Western coalition. Barzani's subsequent talks with the Baghdad government failed to lead to a successful conclusion. Protected by the air forces of the United States, Britain, and France,

Barzani's KDP, along with other Kurdish parties, held assembly elections in May 1992. Barzani shared power equally with Jalal Talabani [*qv*], the leader of the Patriotic Union of Kurdistan (PUK) [*qv*]. Yet the traditional rivalry between the two parties continued. In May 1994 intra-Kurdish clashes left over 1,000 people dead. It was not until six months later that, assisted by mediators, Barzani worked out a modus vivendi with Talabani. But Barzani's relations with his rival soured again when their two factions took opposite positions in the anti-Saddam coup plans in March 1995. With this, Kurdistan divided into two hostile zones. By September, Barzani's jurisdiction was reduced to a third of the region. But with the illicit Iraqi oil supplies passing through his territory, providing hefty customs duties, Barzani had much cash, part of which he used to buy arms and ammunition, some of them from Saddam. Talabani's rapprochement with Iran upset both Barzani and Saddam. When Talabani, freshly armed with Iranian-supplied weapons, attacked KDP's positions in August 1996, Barzani appealed to Saddam for military assistance to retake Irbil [*qv*] from Talabani. Saddam obliged. Barzani captured not only Irbil, but all of Talabani's territory, only to lose all except Irbil when Talabani, armed by Iran, counterattacked. The unprecedented intra-Kurdish violence undermined the American strategy of developing Kurdistan as the base for overthrowing Saddam. The U.S. withdrew its agents and funds from the area. Washington's efforts to conciliate the two rivals were successful only partially because Barzani refused to share the large customs duties he collected on the illicit export of Iraqi oil to Turkey. After the passage of the Iraq Liberation Act by U.S.

Congress in 1998, Barzani found the KDP certified as a faction that was entitled to Washington's military aid.

When, after defeating the Taliban regime in Afghanistan in December 2001, the U.S. administration of President George W. Bush turned its attention to ousting Saddam's government by force, the importance of Barzani as well as Talabani rose. However, when the leaders of the KDP and other five Iraqi groups were invited to Washington to meet Vice President Dick Cheney in August 2002, Barzani did not go. But he coordinated his military strategy with Talabani when America, backed by Britain, prepared to invade Iraq in March 2003. After the fall of the Saddam Hussein regime in April, Barzani publicly welcomed the U.S. pro-consul (Retd.) Gen. Jay Rayner when he visited Kurdistan.

Barzani, Mustafa (1904–79): *Iraqi Kurdish leader* Born into the family of a notable in Barzan, northern Iraq, Barzani grew up to be a leader of the Barzani tribe, which was traditionally opposed to the authority of the government, whether based in Mosul [*qv*] or Baghdad [*qv*]. Along with his elder brother, Ahmad, Barzani led the Kurdish struggle for independence in 1931–32. Following its suppression in 1935, the two brothers were exiled to Suleimaniyah. Escaping in 1942, Barzani led another unsuccessful rebellion.

Along with 1,000 armed followers, he crossed into the Kurdish region of Iran, which, along with the rest of country north of the latitude of Tehran [*qv*], had been under Soviet occupation since August 1941. When the State of Kurdistan Republic [*qv*] was founded there in December 1945,

Barzani was appointed its commander in chief. Following the Soviet departure in May 1946, the republic, run by the Kurdish Democratic Party (KDP) [*qv*], was crushed by the Tehran government in December 1946. Along with his followers, Barzani crossed the Iranian border into Soviet Trans-Caucasia in June 1947. In Moscow he enrolled at the Institute of Languages.

Following the 1958 coup against the Iraqi monarchy, Barzani returned to Iraq and backed the new regime under Abdul Karim Qasim [*qv*], who legalized the KDP. However, when Barzani advanced a plan for autonomy Qasim rejected it. The KDP revolted. In September 1961 Qasim mounted an offensive against the Kurdish insurgents. During the subsequent years, despite changes in the regime in Baghdad, relations between the central government and Barzani did not improve. It was not until March 1970 that the two sides reached a settlement, to be implemented over the next four years. This agreement conceded to several of the Kurdish demands, including recognition of Kurdish ethnicity on a par with Arab and the official use of the Kurdish language [*qv*] in Kurdish-majority areas. But there was mistrust on both sides and the pact failed to hold.

In March 1974 Barzani once again led his followers to fight the Iraqi government. This time he had the active backing of Muhammad Reza Shah Pahlavi [*qv*] of Iran, who wanted to weaken the pro-Moscow regime in Baghdad. By early 1975 the conflict was threatening to escalate into a full-scale war between Iraq and Iran. In an effort to avert this, Baghdad and Tehran reached an accord in March 1975, which resulted in

Iran cutting off military and logistical aid to Barzani's men. His rebellion failed. After escaping to Iran, Barzani fled to the United States and settled in northern Virginia, where he died in 1979.

Basra: *Iraqi city* Pop. 1,377,000 (2003, est.). Located beside the Shatt al Arab [*qv*], Basra is the site of an ancient settlement. Because of its strategic position, Caliph Omar (r. A.D. 634–44) set up a military camp there in A.D. 636. It was from Basra that Muslim Arabs conducted their campaigns against the Sassanian rulers of Persia. It evolved as a center of literary and scientific knowledge, commerce, and finance. In the early eighth century A.D. it fostered rebellions against the Umayyad caliphate based in Damascus [*qv*]. When the Abbasids succeeded the Umayyads in 750 they favored Baghdad [*qv*] over Basra. An attack by militant Qarmatian Muslims in A.D. 923 severely damaged the city. It suffered heavily under the Mongol invasions of the thirteenth century, which finally led to its destruction. In the early 1500s a new settlement, bearing the name of Basra, was founded a few kilometers further up the Shatt al Arab. The settlement prospered and grew.

In more recent times, a rail link with Baghdad and the discovery of oil in southern Iraq have boosted its fortunes. However, the outbreak of the Iran-Iraq War [*qv*] in 1980 turned it into a frontline city. In 1987, during the Iranian advance, the city center came within the range of artillery fire and suffered heavily, with two-thirds of its population fleeing. At the time of the Second Gulf War [*qv*], it was near the front line with Kuwait, but the damage this time was a result of air and missile attacks. Since then, the city has been reconstructed. It again suffered damage when the Anglo-American forces invaded Iraq in March 2003 and occupied it.

bat *(Hebrew: daughter):* The traditional Jewish custom of identifying a woman as a *bat* of his father is seldom manifested nowadays in secular Western societies. Nonetheless every female Jew has a Hebrew name given to her at birth, and used in synagogue [*qv*] and at marriage and burial.

al Baz, Abdul Aziz ibn Abdullah (1911–99): *Saudi Arabian religious leader* Born into a religious family in Riyadh [*qv*], al Baz studied the Quran [*qv*] and Sharia [*qv*]. After going blind at sixteen he became a student of Shaikh Muhammad ibn Abdul Wahhab, the grand mufti, to train as an Islamic judge. He was appointed a judge in the Kharj region, where he served from 1938–52. He then became professor of the Sharia and *fiqh* [*qv*] at the University of Riyadh from 1953–60. An orthodox cleric, he was made vice president of the Islamic University of Medina at its inception in 1961. In an article published in two Saudi newspapers in September 1965, he stated that the sun was moving in its orbit, as God has ordained, and that the earth was stationary and spread out by God for His creation. When this proved controversial, he denied it, saying that the earth was flat, but maintained that it was static.

In 1969 he was promoted to president of Medina Islamic University. Rejecting *ijtihad* [*qv*] of any kind, he urged a return to the letter of the scriptures. Among al Baz's students in 1972 in the Sharia faculty was Juheiman ibn Saif al Utaiba [*qv*]. In 1975 al Baz was appointed president of the twenty-one-member Higher Council of Ulema,

established four years earlier. In that capacity he concluded in the summer of 1978 that the ideas propagated by al Utaiba were not treasonable. However, when al Utaiba led an armed uprising at the Grand Mosque in Mecca [*qv*] in late 1979, he ruled that King Khalid ibn Abdul Aziz [*qv*] was entitled to use force to regain control of the holy mosque.

When Iraq invaded Kuwait in August 1990, al Baz initially argued against the Council's sanctioning of non-Muslim troops on Saudi soil, although he later changed his mind. In November 1990 he issued a religious verdict forbidding women to drive. On the eve of the U.S.-led Gulf War [*qv*] in January 1991, he issued a call for jihad [*qv*] by the forces under King Fahd ibn Abdul Aziz [*qv*] against the forces of President Saddam Hussein [*qv*], whom he described as a blasphemer for claiming to be a descendant of the Prophet Muhammad, something he had done several years earlier.

In May 1991 al Baz passed on to King Fahd a petition signed by more than 400 leading religious scholars, judges, and academics, demanding a consultative assembly; full Islamization of all social, economic, administrative, military and educational institutions; and disassociation from non-Islamic pacts and treaties. The next year he was appointed grand mufti of Saudi Arabia, a job that had been left vacant since 1969, and president of the Supreme Religious Council. Among his several books is *Inquiry and Clarification of Many Hajj and Umra Issues.*

bazaar, bazaaris *(Persian: marketplace, traders):* The word bazaar originated in Iran and spread to Arabia, Turkey, North Africa, and South Asia. *Bazaaris* are those who sell in bazaars—traders. Since the Prophet

Muhammad, the founder of Islam [*qv*], was a trader, there has been much affinity between bazaaris and the mosque. In modern times bazaaris played a particularly important role in bringing about the 1979 Islamic revolution in Iran [*qv*].

Bazargan, Mahdi (1905–95): *Iranian politician; prime minister, 1979* Born into a wealthy trading family in Tabriz [*qv*], Bazargan obtained an engineering degree from Paris University. After spending some years in Paris, he returned to Iran, where he began to teach engineering at Tehran University in 1941. He joined the Iran Party, which merged with two other groups in 1949 to form the National Front [*qv*], headed by Muhammad Mussadiq [*qv*]. During Mussadiq's premiership (1951–53), he became the managing director of the newly nationalized petroleum industry, managed by the National Iranian Oil Company.

In May 1955 Bazargan was arrested on the charges of treason and was detained until 1960. He teamed up with Ayatollah Mahmud Taleqani [*qv*] to form the Liberation Movement of Iran (LMI) [*qv*] in 1961. When he called for a boycott of a referendum on the government-inspired "white revolution" [*qv*] in 1963, he was given a ten-year sentence. After his release he stayed out of politics until the first stirrings of the anti-regime agitation in the autumn of 1977, when he became a cofounder of the Human Rights Association.

On 1 February 1979 Bazargan was nominated by Ayatollah Ruhollah Khomeini [*qv*] to head a provisional Islamic government. His appointment reassured the large, modern middle class. He served for nine months, resigning in protest at the militant students' seizure of the U.S. Embassy and diplomats. He had found that most of his authority was being usurped by such bodies as the Islamic Revolutionary Council (of which he was a member) and the Revolutionary Guards Corps. The following year he was elected leader of the LMI members of parliament.

By the spring of 1983 his party was the only prerevolutionary political group that was not banned, despite the fact that he opposed the official policy of continuing the war with Iraq after Iran had gained the upper hand in mid-1982. However, in protest against the lack of campaigning facilities, Bazargan's LMI boycotted the 1984 parliamentary elections. In 1985 his candidacy for president was rejected by the Guardians Council [*qv*]. Ignoring calls for action against Bazargan, Khomeini allowed him freedom of movement, including foreign travel, while denying him facilities for propagating his consistently critical views. This policy continued after Khomeini's death in 1989.

B.C.: *Before Christ* The era before the birth of Jesus Christ (derivative of the Greek word *Christos*, Anointed). The date originally assigned to Christ's birth is now believed to be about four to eight years too late; that is, he is believed to have been born between 4 and 8 B.C., and not A.D. 0 [*qv*].

B.C.E.: *Before Common Era* Some non-Christians use this term instead of the B.C. [*qv*] with its religious connotation.

Begin, Menachem Wolfovitch (1913–92): *Israeli politician; prime minister, 1977–83* Born in Brest-Litovsk (then in Poland, later in Russia), Begin obtained a law degree at the University of Warsaw. At sixteen he joined the youth organization of the Revisionist Zionists [*qv*], Betar. More extremist than Vladimir Zeev Jabotinsky [*qv*], the founder of the Revisionist movement, Begin challenged him in 1938 after being appointed commander of Betar in Poland. On the eve of the Nazi invasion of Poland in 1939, Begin fled to Vilnius, Lithuania, then under Soviet occupation. In 1940 he was sentenced to eight years' hard labor in a Siberian camp. But after the Soviet Union had joined the Second World War in mid-1941, Begin was released and drafted into the Free Polish army. He arrived in Palestine in 1942 as a soldier of that force.

After his demobilization in 1943, he was appointed commander of the underground Irgun Zvai Leumi [*qv*] (National Military Organization). Begin declared an armed struggle against the British mandate in January 1944, a call he repeated in October 1945 after the end of the war. The Irgun's terrorist activities led the British to offer a £10,000 reward for his arrest. In July 1946 the Irgun bombed the British mandate government offices in the King David Hotel, Jerusalem [*qv*], killing ninety-one British, Arab, and Jewish officials and staff. Following this, the Haganah [*qv*], the main military forces of the Jewish community in Palestine, stopped cooperating with the Irgun.

Begin was one of the chief planners of the attack on the Arab village of Deir Yassin near Jerusalem on 10 April 1948, resulting in the massacre of 254 men, women, and children—an event that caused the intended massive exodus of Arabs [*qv*] from Palestine. Led by Begin, the Irgun ranks refused to be absorbed into the Israel Defense Forces (IDF) formed by the provisional government

of David Ben-Gurion [*qv*] on 26 May 1948. They participated in the war against the Arab states as a separate entity. This continued until late June, when Ben-Gurion, clashing with Begin on the question of delivery of arms and volunteers to the Irgun aboard a freighter anchored off Tel Aviv [*qv*], ordered his forces to destroy the ship. In September Begin disbanded the Irgun, but soon former Irgun and Revisionist Zionist ranks reemerged as the Herut [*qv*] Party under Begin's leadership.

In 1949 Begin was elected to the Knesset [*qv*] and remained a member until 1984—his membership interrupted by a fifteen-month suspension in January 1952 for inciting a mob to attack the Knesset in protest against reparations to Israel from West Germany. In the first five general elections, his Herut Party won about 12 percent of the votes, emerging as the largest opposition faction in the parliament. He led his group in an authoritarian way and brooked no challenge. In 1965, at his behest, Herut joined with the Liberal Party [*qv*] to form the Gahal bloc [*qv*], which won 21 percent of the seats in that year's general election. On the eve of the June 1967 Arab-Israeli War [*qv*], Begin joined the national unity government headed by Levi Eshkol [*qv*]. He stayed in cabinet until July 1970 when—protesting against the majority decision to accept a U.S. peace plan that envisaged Israel's withdrawal from Sinai [*qv*]—he resigned and resumed his opposition role. In 1973 when the Likud bloc [*qv*], containing all the right-wing parties, was formed, Begin was elected its leader. Following Likud's electoral success in May 1977, Begin became prime minister, a position he held for more than six years. He signed the Camp David Accords [*qv*] with Egyptian President Anwar Sadat [*qv*] in September 1978, which in turn led to the conclusion of a peace treaty between Israel and Egypt. That year he and Sadat won the Nobel Peace Prize.

He twice ordered the invasion and occupation of Lebanon: in March 1978 and June 1982. The first occupation, limited to southern Lebanon, ended shortly. But the second invasion, when the Israelis advanced as far as Beirut [*qv*] and began to dictate the politics of Lebanon, proved controversial. Growing public criticism and the Israeli death toll in Lebanon, combined with an annual inflation rate of 400 percent, led to Begin's resignation in August 1983. He had also been depressed by the death of his wife, Aliza, nine months earlier.

al Beidh, Ali Salim (1938–): *South Yemeni and Yemeni politician* Born into a religious family in the Hadramaut region, al Beidh participated in the armed nationalist struggle of the South Yemen conducted by the National Liberation Front (NLF) [*qv*] against Britain. Soon after independence in 1967, al Beidh, a radical, fell foul of the moderate faction that dominated the NLF. But after the radicals had finally prevailed over their rivals in 1971, his star rose steadily. In 1973 al Beidh became planning minister, moving three years later to the Ministry of Municipal Affairs. In April 1980—after Premier Ali Nasser Muhammad [*qv*] had ousted his rival, President Abdul Fattah Ismail [*qv*]—al Beidh was promoted to deputy prime minister.

Al Beidh then allied himself with Vice President Ali Antar to oppose President Muhammad's increasingly moderate policies.

The return of Ismail from self-exile in Moscow in 1985 intensified the factional struggle. In the armed confrontation that ensued between the Muhammad and Ismail camps in January 1986, al Beidh sided with the latter. With Ismail, Antar, and others dead and Muhammad exiled, al Beidh emerged as the only top party leader to survive the conflict. He was elected secretary-general of the ruling Yemen Socialist Party [*qv*].

With the presidency and premiership going to technocrats, Haidar al Attas and Yassin Numan, al Beidh held the reins of real power. He began to moderate his radical stance and introduce economic and political reform—a tendency accelerated by the rapid decline of the Soviet bloc from 1989 onward. He expedited the plans for unification of South and North Yemen that had been agreed in principle earlier. When a united Yemen emerged in May 1990, albeit with two armies, he became its vice president.

The unification process proved more problematic than had been anticipated. In August 1993, blaming President Ali Abdullah Salih [*qv*] for lack of progress, al Beidh left Sanaa [*qv*] for Aden [*qv*]. Despite his reelection as vice president two months later by the newly elected parliament, he did not return to Sanaa. The subsequent signing by the two leaders of a Document of Agreement and Bond in Amman [*qv*] in February 1994 failed to dissipate the crisis. Following the eruption of a civil war [*qv*] between the two former states in April, al Beidh declared South Yemen independent in May. This was not formally recognized by any country of the world. Just before the defeat of the South Yemeni military in early July, he fled to neighboring Oman, and then to Saudi

Arabia. In 1996 as leader of the National Opposition Front, al Beidh demanded a referendum in the south to secure better terms for the region. Two years later he was sentenced to death in absentia for his role in the 1994 Civil War.

Beirut: *capital of Lebanon* Pop. 1,171,000 (2003, est.). The principal port of the country at the foot of Mount Lebanon, Beirut has a history stretching back to the Phoenician era (ca. 1250 B.C.), when it was known as Berytus. An important commercial center, it thrived under the rule of the Selucuids, Romans, and Byzantines. It fell to Muslim Arabs in A.D. 636. During the Crusades it was seized by the Crusaders in 1110, who retained it until 1291 as part of the Latin Kingdom of Jerusalem. During the Ottoman period it became capital of the Vilayat of Lebanon, an autonomous province of the empire from 1861 onward. In 1920 the French mandate authorities made it capital of Greater Lebanon, created by adding areas to the east, north, and south of the Vilayat of Lebanon. It expanded greatly after Lebanese independence in 1946 and became the leading financial center of the Middle East, losing that position after the Lebanese Civil War of 1975–90 [*qv*].

During the long conflict the city became divided into exclusively Christian East Beirut, situated on al Ashrafiya hill, and predominantly Muslim West Beirut, on al Musaitiba hill. From 1972 to 1982 Beirut was the headquarters of the Palestine Liberation Organization [*qv*]. The civil war and the Israeli invasion of Lebanon in June–August 1982 [*qv*] played havoc with the city. Despite the violence, its two leading educational institutions, the American University in Beirut [*qv*] and Beirut Arab University, continued to function. By the mid-1990s reconstruction plans had been finalized, and efforts to implement them were well advanced by 2003.

ben *(Hebrew: son):* The traditional Jewish custom of identifying a man as a *ben* (son) of his father is seldom manifested nowadays in secular Western societies. Nonetheless every male Jew has a Hebrew name given to him at circumcision (on the eighth day after birth), confirmed at bar mitzah *(Hebrew: lit., son of commandments; fig. coming of age)*, and used in synagogue [*qv*] service and at marriage and burial.

Ben-Gurion, David (1886–1973): *Israeli politician; prime minister, 1948–53, 1955–63* Born David Green in Plonsk, Poland, Ben-Gurion, the son of a lawyer, went to Warsaw University in 1904. There he joined the Poale Zion [*qv*] and two years later left for Palestine [*qv*], where he became a farmhand. He was a cofounder of the Poale Zion journal, *HaAhdut* (The Unity). In 1912 Ben-Gurion enrolled at the University of Istanbul to study Turkish law and government. The outbreak of the First World War took him back to Palestine. In 1915 he was deported as a troublemaker and sailed for New York. There he joined an American battalion of the Jewish Legion, which was being formed as part of the British army. Trained in Canada, Ben-Gurion arrived in Egypt as a member of the 40th Royal Fusiliers.

In postwar Palestine the Poale Zion split, its leftist section leaving in 1919 and forming Mopsi (*Mifleget Poalim Sozialistim*, Socialist Workers Party). Its rightist, nationalist section—led among others by Ben-Gurion—combined with the followers of Berle Katznelson to form Ahdut HaAvodah [qv]. Soon Ahdut HaAvodah and HaPoale HaTzair [qv] took the lead in constituting an umbrella organization to encompass all labor-pioneer parties of Zionist persuasion: Histadrut [qv]. With successive elections to Histadrut conferences showing Ahdut HaAvodah and HaPoale HaTzair to be the main parties, pressure grew on their leaders to seek a merger. This led to the founding of Mapai [qv] in January 1930 under the stewardship of Chaim Arlosoroff [qv]. Following the murder of Arlosoroff in 1933, Ben-Gurion was elected head of Mapai. Two years later he became leader of the executive committee of the Jewish Agency for Palestine [qv], soon to be recognized by the British mandate as the official representative of the Jews in Palestine.

Differing with his colleagues in the Mapai leadership, Ben-Gurion favored the 1937 Peel Commission's partition proposal. He opposed the British White Paper of 1939, which limited Jewish immigration into Palestine to an annual average of 15,000 for the next five years. But he could not remain anti-British once the Second World War had erupted in September 1939. He encouraged fellow Jews to join the British Africa Corps.

In 1942 he was the main instigator behind the resolution of the American Zionist Organization: that the founding of a Jewish state in Palestine should be the prime objective of Zionism [qv]. After the war, backed by Jewish Agency funds, Ben-Gurion, in his role of Histadrut chief, began to purchase arms in Europe. His appointment as head of the Zionist Organization's [qv] defense department in December 1946 enabled him to bring the various Jewish armed organizations in Palestine under a single command. Early in 1947, noticing the convergence of U.S. and Soviet positions on the partitioning of Palestine, the National Council (Vaad Leumi) of the Yishuv [qv], led by Ben-Gurion, began to formulate plans to consolidate the Jewish sector in Palestine, militarily and otherwise. By the time the United Nations adopted the partition plan in November 1947 the Yishuv had a large professional army, supported by 79,000 reserves, armed police, and home guards.

By spring 1948, at the behest of Ben-Gurion, the Jewish Agency had transferred all its executive powers to the people's administrative committee of the Yishuv assembly's National Council. It was this committee of thirteen, headed by Ben-Gurion and functioning as the provisional government, that declared the founding of the State of Israel on 14 May 1948 in Tel Aviv [qv]. Twelve days later it established the Israel Defense Forces (IDF) consisting of 60,000 troops, with Ben-Gurion as defense minister. It performed well in the Arab-Israeli War I [qv], also known as the War of Independence (of Israel) [qv], which lasted from mid-May 1948 to early January 1949, when armistice agreements were signed between Israel and its four Arab adversaries on the Greek island of Rhodes.

Mapai emerged as the largest party in the January 1949 election, winning 46 of the 120 seats in the Knesset [qv], and Ben-Gurion became prime minister. He welcomed the Tripartite (Anglo-American-French) Declaration of May 1950 [qv], which opposed any attempt to change the armistice boundaries of Israel set in January 1949, and promised to supply arms to Arabs and Israelis only to the extent that they did not create an "imbalance." The United Religious Front's [*qv*] disagreement with Ben-Gurion on the degree of governmental control over religious education in schools caused the downfall of his government in mid-1951. In the Second Knesset Mapai won forty-five seats. Having played a leading role in shaping the basic outline of Israel's internal and external policies, Ben-Gurion resigned as prime minister in December 1953 and retired to his kibbutz in the Negev.

Moshe Sharett [*qv*] became premier. His defense minister, Pinchas Lavon [*qv*], authorized a sabotage campaign in Egypt. The campaign backfired and Lavon resigned. Ben-Gurion was brought into the cabinet in early 1955 as defense minister. In response to the execution of two ringleaders of the Jewish espionage-sabotage cell in Egypt, Ben-Gurion ordered a massive attack on an Egyptian military camp in Gaza [*qv*], which resulted in thirty-nine Egyptian deaths. The escalating tension resulted in Ben-Gurion becoming prime minister in late 1955. Within a year he was involved in invading and occupying the Sinai Peninsula [*qv*] in collusion with Britain and France in the Suez War [*qv*]. Under pressure from the United States and the Soviet Union, he withdrew the Israeli troops from the Sinai in March 1957.

His next coalition government, formed after elections in November 1959, proved unstable, with the old controversy about Lavon's "security mishap" resurfacing in 1960. When a cabinet committee exonerated Lavon in early 1961 Ben-Gurion threatened to resign as prime minister and defense minister, insisting on a judicial inquiry. As a compromise, and in exchange for the shelving of further investigation into the affair, Lavon stepped down as secretary-general of Histadrut [*qv*]. Ben-Gurion headed the coalition government formed after the August 1961 poll, but found that he lacked the kind of authority he had exercised before. He resigned from the government in 1963 and began campaigning against his successor, Levi Eshkol [*qv*].

Aware of the declining popularity of Mapai, its leadership recommended an alignment (*maarach*) between it and Ahdut HaAvodah-Poale Zion [*qv*]. This was ratified by the Mapai convention in February 1965. Disagreeing with this, Ben-Gurion and his followers left Mapai and offered their own list, Rafi [*qv*], in the November 1965 election. Rafi won ten seats and the Mapai-Ahdut HaAvodah-Poale Zion Maarach [*qv*] forty-five. Ben-Gurion's personal popularity proved unequal to the institutional strength of his former party. After the June 1967 Arab-Israeli War [*qv*], Ben-Gurion opposed the annexation of the Occupied Arab Territories [*qv*]. In 1968 the maarach was widened to include Rafi, leading to the merger of the three constituents into the Israeli Labor Party [*qv*]. Ben-Gurion founded a new group, LaAam (To the People), which won four seats in the 1969 poll. The following year he quit politics. He died in 1973, leaving behind many diaries that have since been published.

Ben-Zvi, Yitzhak (1884–1963): *Israeli politician; president, 1952–63* Born Yitzhak Shimshilevitch in Poltava, Ukraine, Ben-Zvi became a Zionist [*qv*] in his youth. In

1906 Ben-Zvi cofounded Poale Zion [*qv*] in Russia before migrating to Palestine [*qv*] the next year. He was one of the founders of the HaShomer self-defense association and editor of *HaAhdut* (The Unity), the organ of the Poale Zion in Palestine. In 1912 Ben-Zvi enrolled at the University of Istanbul to study Turkish law and government. The outbreak of the First World War brought him back to Palestine. In 1915 he was deported as a troublemaker and journeyed to New York. There he joined an American battalion of the Jewish Legion that was being formed as part of the British army. Trained in Canada, Ben-Zvi arrived in Egypt as a member of the 40th Royal Fusiliers.

Following his return to Palestine after the First World War, he became a cofounder of Ahdut HaAvodah [*qv*] in 1919, Histadrut [*qv*] in 1920, and Mapai [*qv*] in 1930. From 1931 to 1948 he was president of the National Council of the representative assembly of the Yishuv [*qv*]. Ben-Zvi was a Mapai member of the Knesset [*qv*] from 1949 until his election as president in December 1952 following the death of President Chaim Weizmann. He was reelected president in 1957 and 1962, and like his predecessor, he died in office.

Berri, Nabih (1938–): *Lebanese politician* Born into a Lebanese Shia [*qv*] merchant family that settled in Freetown, Sierra Leone, Berri returned to Tibnin in southern Lebanon, the town of his ancestors. During his days as a law student at the Lebanese University of Beirut, he joined the semi-clandestine Baath party [*qv*]. After a brief enrollment at Sorbonne University, Paris, and a short stay in Freetown, he went to the United States. There he married a Lebanese American and raised a family before returning to Lebanon in early 1975. Berri allied with Imam Musa Sadr [*qv*], a radical Shia leader, and helped to establish a militia, Amal [*qv*]. Starting as a member of Amal's leadership council, Berri became its secretary-general in 1978 after the "disappearance" of Sadr. Under Berri's stewardship Amal became one of the most effective militias in the Lebanese civil conflict. In October 1981 he led an Amal delegation to Tehran [*qv*]. At the Amal conference in April 1982 he shared the leadership with Shaikh Muhammad Mahdi Shams al Din, a Shia cleric.

Following Israel's occupation of southern and central Lebanon in June 1982, Berri encouraged Shia resistance to the Israeli occupiers. He became one of the leading opponents of President Amin Gemayel [*qv*] when the latter initialed a peace treaty with Israel [*qv*] in May 1983. Responding to Gemayel's order to the Lebanese army to raze the Shia suburbs of Beirut [*qv*] in February 1984, Berri issued a successful call to fellow Muslims in the Lebanese army to defy the president. Aided by the Druze [*qv*] militia, Amal captured West Beirut and weakened the presidency of Gemayel, who then abrogated the draft peace treaty with Israel. In the national unity government that followed, Berri became minister of south Lebanon and reconstruction.

Berri had close ties with Syria. At its behest his militia attacked the Palestinian camps based in Beirut and southern Lebanon in order to weaken the control of Yasser Arafat's Fatah [*qv*] over them. Berri was one of the three leading militia commanders to sign the

"National Agreement to Solve the Lebanese Crisis" in December 1985, but the document proved stillborn. From 1988 onward Berri allowed Amal to be used by Syrian President Hafiz Assad [*qv*] to contain the growth of Hizbollah [*qv*], a radical Shia organization, whenever it suited him. Berri had reservations about the Syrian-brokered National Reconciliation Charter [*qv*]—agreed in Taif, Saudi Arabia, in October 1989—because of its inequity toward Shias, but dropped them under pressure from Assad.

The next month, following the election of Elias Hrawi [*qv*] as president, Berri was given a post in the new cabinet under Salim Hoss [*qv*]. In June 1990 Berri was one of the forty appointees to fill the vacant or newly created seats in parliament. Following the victory of the pro-Syrian, predominantly Muslim forces over their right-wing Maronite adversaries in October 1990, Amal and the other militias were disbanded, a proportion of Amal's members being absorbed into the regular army. Following a fresh parliamentary poll in 1992, Berri became speaker of parliament. He was reelected speaker after the 1996 and 2000 general elections.

Bethlehem: *West Bank town (Arabic: Beit lahm; Hebrew: Beth lehem: house of bread/Lahmu, a goddess)* Pop. 25,000 (2003, est.). Known in Old Testament [*qv*] times as Ephrat, Bethlehem was the scene of the Book of Ruth and the home of King David (r. ca. 1010–970 B.C.). It was the birthplace of Jesus Christ (ca. 6 B.C.—A.D. 30) and is a holy place for Christians [*qv*]. Roman Emperor Constantine I (r. A.D. 306–37) built a basilica at the site of Jesus's birth. When the settlement fell to Muslim Arabs [*qv*] in A.D. 637 it was left untouched. The church of Nativity standing there today is shared by the Armenian Orthodox Church [*qv*] (which has the Grotto of the Nativity, containing the manger that is believed to have warmed the newborn Jesus), the Roman Catholic Church [*qv*] (which owns the site of the birth, marked by a fourteen-point star on a marble stone), and the Greek Orthodox Church [*qv*] (which possesses the High Altar standing above the Grotto).

Bible: *Christian scripture* "Bible" is the diminutive of *byblos*, the Greek word for "papyrus" (an ancient writing material), meaning book. The Bible is regarded by Christians [*qv*] as the word of God delivered through divinely directed authors. It is composed of the Old Testament and the New Testament. The longer Old Testament, also called the Hebrew Bible [*qv*], is a record of the testament (solemn covenant) made by God with man and revealed to Moses (d. ca. 1250 B.C.) on Mount Sinai. It was written mostly in Hebrew [*qv*] between 1200 B.C. and 100 B.C. and is accepted as a holy scripture by both Jews [*qv*] and Christians [*qv*]. The shorter New Testament is a record of the fulfillment of the Old Testament and of the fresh covenant, encapsulated in the life and death of Jesus Christ, between God and Christians. It was written mainly in Greek within a century of Christ's death (ca. A.D. 30) and is accepted as a holy scripture by Christians only.

The modern Old Testament is based on the Hebrew Bible which, originally consisting of twenty-four books, is divided into: (1) The Law/Pentateuch/Torah [*qv*], containing five books; (2) The Prophets, containing eight books; and (3) The Holy

Writings/Hagiographia, containing eleven books.

(1) The Pentateuch spans the period between the creation of the universe (ca. 3760 B.C.) and the death of Moses (ca. 1250 B.C.). *Genesis,* the first book, begins with the creation of the universe and ends with Joseph, a great-grandson of Abraham (ca. 1800 B.C.), becoming an adviser to the Egyptian king. The four remaining works deal with the activities of Moses and the covenant between God and the Israelites. *Exodus* describes the deliverance of the Israelites from four centuries of bondage in Egypt, God's present of the Law to Moses on Mount Sinai, and His covenant with the Israelites. *Leviticus* deals chiefly with the rituals of worship. *Numbers* describes the wanderings of the Israelites in the Sinai desert for forty years. In *Deuteronomy* Moses summarizes the Law, and the book ends with a description of his death on the frontiers of the Promised Land.

(2) The Prophets is a record of the activities of the divinely inspired men (prophets), who lived during the ninth through fifth centuries B.C. Their books cover the history of the period between the death of Moses and the fall of the Kingdom of Judah in the sixth century B.C.

(3) The Holy Writings is a collection of books of poetry, songs, aphorisms, prophecy, and history. *Psalms* (ca. third century B.C.) contains the hymns and prayers used to worship JHVH (pronounced Yahweh), the sacred name of God. *Job* (ca. sixth century B.C.) is a narrative poem about a man named Job, who was beset by disasters. *Proverbs* (ca. fourth century B.C.) is a collection of aphorisms and epigrams about

human existence, offering a positive, pragmatic philosophy of life. *Song of Songs* (ca. tenth century B.C.) contains wedding songs. *Ruth* (ca. fourth century B.C.) is the story of the marriage of Ruth, a Moabite woman, to Boaz, a Hebrew landowner. *Lamentations* (ca. mid-sixth century B.C.) consists of poems lamenting the destruction of Jerusalem [qv] and the First Temple. *Ecclesiastes* (ca. third century B.C.), like *Proverbs,* contains maxims, but their general tone is skeptical. *Esther* (ca. second century B.C.) is the tale of Esther, the Hebrew wife of a Persian king, Ahasuerus, whose courageous actions save the Jewish community from an evil prime minister. The next three books—*Chronicles, Ezra,* and *Nehemiah,* which are attributed to a scribe at the Second Temple (537–350 B.C.) and written around 250 B.C.—are historical works that update the chronicle of the Jews, including the return of the exiled Jews to Jerusalem, the restoration of its walls by Nehemia (445 B.C.), and the legal reforms of Ezra (397 B.C.). *Daniel* (ca. 165 B.C.), the last book, begins with the capture of the Prophet Daniel in Babylon and the fall of the city to the Persians, and ends with a revelation of the end of history, proclaiming the arrival of the Kingdom of God.

Of the twenty-seven books of the New Testament, twenty-one are epistles. The New Testament begins with *The Gospels*—a book each by Matthew, Mark, Luke, and John, disciples of Jesus Christ, who describe his life and teachings. The first three works, called *Synoptic Gospels,* are somewhat similar and are nowadays judged to be anti-Semitic [qv]. *The Gospel According to John,* instead of focusing on Jesus's biography as the other disciples did, concentrates on the theme of Jesus as the word of God made flesh. It too is considered anti-Semitic. The fifth book, *The Acts of the Apostles,* ascribed to Luke, describes the history of early Christianity led by Peter (d. A.D. 67) as well as the missionary work of Paul (d. A.D. 65). Then follow *The Epistles*—attributed to Paul (fourteen epistles), and to James, Peter, John, and Jude, disciples of Jesus Christ. The epistles are addressed to the young churches and deal chiefly with Christian doctrine and worship. The New Testament ends with *Revelation,* a prophetic book written during the rule of Domitian (r. A.D. 81–96), most probably by more than one person, including John. In the traditional apocalyptic style of Hebrew literature, the book describes the catastrophes that will presage the Day of Judgement at the end of history.

Because Christians later split into three major churches—Roman Catholic [*qv*], Orthodox (Catholic) [*qv*] and Protestant [*qv*]—different versions of the Bible are in use today. Since the Roman Catholic Old Testament in Latin was translated from the Septuagint (the Greek translation of the Hebrew Bible rendered in the third century B.C.), and not from the later Hebrew Bible of Jamnia, it includes seven books not contained in the later version. This, and the division of single books into two or more, explains why there are as many as forty-six books in the Roman Catholic Old Testament. As a translation of the Septuagint they are arranged differently from the Hebrew Bible: The Pentateuch, The Historical Books, The Didactic Books, The Prophetical Books, and The Historical Books. The Protestant Old Testament has 39 books, arranged in the same way as those in the Roman Catholic Bible, but without the last collection of Historical Books. The Orthodox (Catholic) Church, consisting largely of Greek or Slavic churches, uses either the Septuagint for the Old Testament and the Greek New Testament (for Greek churches), or their translations into Old Church Slavonic (for the Slavic churches).

bin *(Arabic: son):* It is customary for an Arab male from the Arabian Peninsula [*qv*] to identify himself as the *bin* (son) of his father, followed by his surname, often prefixed with *al* (the). Those of high social rank tend to include more than one generation in the name.

bin Laden, Osama (1957–): *Saudi Islamist, leader of Al Qaida* Son of Muhammad Awad bin Laden—a bricklayer from South Yemen [*qv*], who, after settling in Saudi city of Jiddah [*qv*], became a leading construction magnate—and Alia Hamida Ghanoum, the youngest of his eleven wives, in Jiddah. After finishing his secondary education in 1974 at an elite high school, he graduated in civil engineering at King Abdul Aziz University in 1978. He regarded those who mounted the armed uprising in Mecca [*qv*] in November 1979 as "true Muslims [*qv*]."

After visiting the Pakistani city of Peshawar in the spring of 1980, he successfully lobbied his brothers, relatives, and friends to support the anti-Soviet struggle in Afghanistan. He returned to Pakistan with the hefty donations he had collected in Saudi Arabia [*qv*], and several Afghan and Pakistani employees of Saudi Binladin Group, owned by his family, to set up an office to support non-Afghan mujahedin [qv] in cooperation with Pakistan's Inter-Services Intelligence (ISI) and the U.S. Central Intelligence Agency (CIA), which oversaw the conduct of the anti-Soviet campaign. Bin Laden came under the influence of Abdullah Azzam [qv], who in 1984 established the Maktab al Khidmat (Bureau of Service [to the non-Afghan mujahedin]) in Peshawar—a seed out of which would grow Al Qaida (The Base) [qv] later. Besides vetting non-Afghan volunteers and sending them to one of the constituents of the seven-party Afghan Mujahedin Alliance, bin Laden supervised the construction of roads and the refurbishing of caves for storing weapons in the Mujahedin-controlled areas. He also participated in guerrilla actions and armed encounters.

At the ISI-CIA training camps established on both sides of the Afghan-Pakistan frontier, the volunteers underwent military training—based on the manuals used by the U.S. Defense Department and the CIA, and translated into Persian [qv], Arabic [qv], and Urdu—as well as political education, which emphasized nationalism and Islam [qv].

In 1986 bin Laden oversaw the construction of a tunnel complex at Zhwahar Killi in the vicinity of Khost near the Pakistani border, to house a training center, weapons store, and medical facility with electricity, piped water, as well as a jail for prisoners of war. The new base was to be an addition to the already existing nearby cave complex at Tora Bora, which had proved impervious to Soviet-Afghan assaults. When the Soviets left Afghanistan in February 1989, bin Laden declared it to be a victory for the jihad [qv]. Following the assassination of Azzam in

November, bin Laden resolved to continue running Maktab al Khidmat under the new title of Al Qaida, but with a more ambitious aim of creating an international network of jihadis, those who had participated in the anti-Soviet jihad.

Frustrated by the internecine violence among Afghan Mujahedin, centered on ethnicity among Afghan Mujahedin, that erupted after the Soviet withdrawal, bin Laden returned to Jiddah in the spring of 1990. Here he became a much sought-after speaker, and his taped speeches became bestsellers. During the crisis caused by Iraq's invasion of Kuwait [qv] in August, bin Laden offered the Saudi government a plan to defend the kingdom by mobilizing citizens as well as his veteran mujahdein. It was rejected. Along with many fellow-Saudis, bin Laden disapproved of the stationing of more than half a million Western troops, predominantly American, on the Saudi soil. When, after the successful end of the Second Gulf War [qv] in February 1991, many thousands of U.S. soldiers stayed on in the kingdom, bin Laden protested vehemently.

He left the kingdom for Sudan, ruled by an Islamist [qv] military government. In Khartoum he set up several different businesses. During his five years there, bin Laden ran Al Qaida along corporate lines—with the policy-making Shura Council of twelve served by four executive committees: military (headed by Muhamamd Atef [qv]), business, Islamic studies, and media and public relations. Bin Laden kept up his attacks on the continued presence of infidel soldiers on Arabia's holy soil and the regime that allowed it.

Bin Laden pursued his political-religious

agenda of waging jihad against the United States by either financing directly Al Qaida's terrorist actions or sponsoring like-minded groups abroad, while offering to train their activists at Al Qaida camps in Sudan, thus turning Al Qaida into an umbrella organization, specializing in conducting jihad violently. It established associate relationships with like-minded groups in Algeria, Chechnya, Egypt, Ethiopia, Lebanon, Libya, Philippines, Syria, and Yemen, and maintained guest houses in different countries. In 1992–93, bin Laden intervened in the civil war in Somalia, with Atef supervising the training of the Somali tribes opposed to the United Nations intervention in the conflict. Later bin Laden would be accused by America of aiding and abetting the attacks on U.S. troops within the U.N. force, as a result of which eighteen American soldiers died while hunting for Somali warlord Muhammad Farah Aideed—as did nearly 500 Somalis.

In early 1994 the Saudi government revoked bin Laden's citizenship and froze his assets—estimated to be $20–25 million. There was an unsuccessful attempt at his life. He responded by establishing the Committee for Advice and Reform [*qv*] (CAR), with the purported aim of promoting peaceful reform in Saudi Arabia, and opened an office in London.

To see its name removed from Washington's list of states that support international terrorism, Sudan's government agreed in early 1996 to put bin Laden under surveillance, thus following the lead of the CIA, which by then had set up a special Bin Laden Station, an unprecedented step taken regarding an individual. Sudan's gesture was not enough. But neither the United States wanted bin Laden for itself (as it lacked evidence to prove his guilt for killing Americans), nor Saudi Arabia. So in May 1996 bin Laden and his entourage left for Jalalabad in Afghanistan, then in the throes of a civil war between a ramshackle government in Kabul and the newly arisen, Pakistan-backed Taliban. The area where bin Laden took refuge was outside Taliban control. It was only after the Taliban had captured Kabul and the areas to its east in September that bin Laden sought its protection. He got it after the Taliban's spiritual leader, Mullah Muhammad Omar, based in Kandahar, had accepted bin Laden's oath of loyalty to him.

In return, bin Laden ordered several hundred of his experienced militia to fight alongside the Taliban in the civil war. His fighters consisted of those veterans of the anti-Soviet jihad who on returning home had been intolerably harassed by their governments, and the post-1989 Mujahedin, dispirited by the decline in the jihads in the Balkans, Chechnya, and Kashmir. Assisted by bin Laden's veterans, Mullah Omar's government extended its control over 85 percent of Afghanistan.

On the eve of the formation of the World Islamic Front for Jihad against Crusaders and Jews [*qv*] in February 1998, bin Laden and four other Islamist leaders deplored the suffering of the Palestinians and Iraqi people and declared it to be the religious duty of Muslims everywhere to kill the Americans and their allies—civilian and military—wherever possible in order to liberate the al Aqsa mosque (in Jerusalem [*qv*]) and the Holy Mosque (in Mecca [*qv*]) from their control.

Following the detonation of huge bombs at the U.S. embassies in Nairobi and Dar as Salaam on 7 August 1998, which killed 227 people, Washington held bin Laden responsible for the deadly blasts and called on the Taliban to hand him over. Mullah Omar refused. By now bin Laden was listed among the "Ten Most Wanted Fugitives" by the U.S. Federal Bureau of Investigation (FBI), with a $5 million reward for information leading to his arrest, a sum that would later be raised to $25 million.

America saw the hand of bin Laden's Al Qaida in the bombing of the USS *Cole* in Aden [*qv*] in October 2000. Two months later, working together with Russia, the U.S. administration of President Bill Clinton (r. 1993–2001) had the U.N. Security Council demand the extradition of bin Laden from the Taliban-controlled Afghanistan within a month, on pain of an imposition of an arms embargo on the Taliban regime. Mullah Omar defied the resolution. And the subsequent ban brought him and bin Laden closer, with bin Laden's well-trained non-Afghan fighters now forming the Taliban's 55th Brigade.

The public trial in February 2001 in New York of four Al Qaida operatives, charged with conspiracy for the bombings in Nairobi and Dar as Salam, gave him a higher profile in the Muslim world and increased his influence over Mullah Omar. When, following the terrorist attacks in New York and Washington on 11 September, the U.S. administration of President George W. Bush (r. 2001–) held bin Laden responsible and called on Mullah Omar to hand him over to America, the latter argued that bin Laden could not have been the culprit.

In the course of bin Laden's videotaped meeting with a visiting radical cleric from Jiddah, named Khalid Harbi, he named nine of the 9/11 hijackers, adding that they had been instructed to go to America but were told of the operation just before boarding the planes. Bin Laden also revealed that he and other plotters had discussed the extent of the damage that would be caused to the Twin Towers of the World Trade Center in New York City by the impact of the flying aircraft. The videotape, obtained by the United States in the third week of November (after the flight of the Taliban from Kabul on 12–13 November), was released to the media in mid-December 2001.

By then bin Laden had escaped to the tribal area along the Afghanistan-Pakistan border and found a sanctuary there. He took to sending audiotaped statements to Al Jazeera satellite television, timing them to coincide with the first anniversary of 9/11 or the high point of the *hajj* [*qv*] in February 2003 during the American military buildup to invade Iraq [*qv*].

bint *(Arabic: daughter):* It is customary for an Arab female to identify herself as the *bint* (daughter) of her father, followed by his surname, often prefixed with *al* (the).

Bishara, Azmi (1956–): *Israeli Arab academic and politician* Born into a middle-class family in Nazareth [*qv*], Bishara founded the National Committee of Arab High School Students in 1974. Later, while enrolled at Haifa University for a degree in political science, he established the Arab Students Union, which elected him as its chairman. After receiving a doctorate in philosophy from Humboldt University in Germany in 1986, Bishara taught cultural studies and philosophy at Bir Zeit University near Ramallah, West Bank [*qv*], and also worked as a senior researcher at the Van Leer Institute in Jerusalem [*qv*]. Along with his Israeli colleagues, he founded the Palestinian Institute for Research of Democracy.

In 1996 he was elected to the Knesset [*qv*] as a member of the United Arab List. On the eve of the 1999 poll he founded the National Democratic Assembly, Balad [*qv*], and got elected on its ticket. In early 2001 he became the first Israeli Arab [*qv*] to enter the race for prime minister. However, he withdrew at the last moment without endorsing any other candidate. In November, the Knesset lifted his immunity accorded to parliamentarians so that the attorney general could initiate criminal proceedings against him under the Prevention of Terrorism Ordinance (1948) regarding the speeches he delivered in Israel [*qv*] in June 2000 and at a memorial service in Syria [*qv*] a year later, in which he upheld the right to resist the Israeli occupation of the Palestinian territories. It was the first time that the Knesset stripped the immunity of one of its members because of his political statements made in the course of performing his duty as an elected representative.

On the eve of the 2003 parliamentary poll, the Israeli election commission barred him by twenty-two votes to nineteen from contesting the election, but the High Court overturned the ban. He retained his seat.

Bitar, Salah al Din (1912–80): *Syrian politician* Born into a prominent Sunni [*qv*] family in Damascus [*qv*], Bitar received his higher education at Damascus University, followed by Sorbonne University, Paris. Back in the Syrian capital in 1934, he taught mathematics and physics at a prestigious secondary school. In 1940, together with Michel Aflaq [*qv*], a fellow teacher, he established a study circle called the Movement of Arab Renaissance (*Baath*, in Arabic). They published pamphlets in which they expounded revolutionary socialist Arab nationalism, committed to achieving Arab unity as the first step. Once the mandate power, France, had left Syria in April 1946, Bitar and Aflaq secured a license for their group, now called the Party of Arab Renaissance. They decided to merge their faction with the one led by Zaki Arsuzi [*qv*]. Out of this in April 1947 emerged the Arab Baath Party [*qv*] in Damascus. Bitar was elected to its four-member executive committee.

In 1954 Bitar became a member of parliament. As foreign minister in 1956–57 he actively backed the idea of a union between Syria and Egypt. The next year, following the formation of the United Arab Republic (UAR) [*qv*], Bitar became its minister of national guidance. But when UAR President Gamal Abdul Nasser [*qv*] dissolved the Arab Baath Socialist Party [*qv*] in 1959, Bitar resigned. After the Baathist coup of March 1963, he became prime minister but lost his seat in the Baath party's national command.

As the Baathist Military Committee tightened its grip over the party and the government, Bitar identified with the civilian wing of the party. He found himself out of favor and intermittently ceded the premiership to General Hafiz Amin, until February 1966, when the civilian faction was ousted.

Bitar escaped to Lebanon. In 1969 he was sentenced to death in absentia in Damascus. Soon after Hafiz Assad [*qv*] seized power in November 1970, he pardoned Bitar.

During his exile in Beirut [*qv*] Bitar kept away from the Baathist national command led by Aflaq, which forged links with the Baathist regime of Iraq. From Beirut he moved to Paris. In January 1978 he was invited to Damascus for talks with President Assad, but the two leaders failed to reconcile their views. After his return to Paris, Bitar started publishing a journal, *Al Ihya al Arabi* (The Arab Revival), which became a mobilizing forum for various Syrian opposition groups in exile. He was assassinated in Paris in July 1980. Syrian complicity in the killing, though not proven, was widely suspected.

Black September Organization: *A Palestinian group* This Palestinian group, led by Wadi Haddad, was formed by militant members of Fatah [*qv*] soon after the defeat of the Palestinian commandos by the Jordanian army in Jordan in September 1970, and was named after that month. Following the assassination in November 1971 of Jordanian Premier Wasfi Tal in Cairo [*qv*], the four Palestinians claiming responsibility for it declared that they belonged to the Black September Organization (BSO).

Eight BSO members took hostage nine of the eleven Israeli athletes at the Olympic village near Munich, Germany, on 5 September 1972, the remaining two Israelis having died earlier in the struggle. Their demand that they and their hostages be put aboard an aircraft was met. But at the airport there was a shoot-out between them and the German security forces. All nine Israeli athletes were killed—eight of them by the German security personnel—as were five Palestinians. The remaining three hostage takers were captured.

The macabre drama was reported live by some 6,000 newspersons and the largest gathering of television equipment ever assembled, thus inadvertently highlighting the existence of Palestinians as a people nursing deeply felt grievances. In retribution, Israel's three-day-long air raids on Palestinian refugee camps in Syria and Lebanon killed 200 to 500 people, mostly civilians. Later, Mossad [*qv*] assassinated twelve Palestinians believed to have been involved in the Munich attack.

Borochov, Dov Ber (1881–1917): *Zionist thinker* Born in Kiev, Ukraine, Borochov became the leading ideologue of Zionist socialism. He started out as a member of the Russian Social Democratic Labor Party, but in 1900 left to become a cofounder of Poale Zion [*qv*] in Minsk, Belarus. He offered a program of socialism, Zionism, and migration to Palestine [*qv*] and argued that before Jews could launch a class struggle they first had to achieve nationhood, and for that they had to have a country of their own.

He chose Palestine partly because it was regarded as the historic homeland of Jews [*qv*], and partly because, being a "derelict country," it held interest only for minor and medium Jewish capitalists—not the big ones—and thus offered revolutionary promise for the Jewish proletariat, which was to be fostered there. He regarded local Arabs [*qv*] as Turkish subjects lacking national consciousness and visualized their assimilation, economic and cultural, into the Jewish nation as it developed economically under Jewish initiative and leadership. He left Russia in 1907 and returned ten years later to attend the Congress of Minorities called by the Alexander Kerensky regime. He died in Kiev.

Boutros-Ghali, Boutros (1922–): *Egyptian politician; United Nations secretary-general, (1992–96)* Born into a prominent Coptic [*qv*] family that was active in nationalist politics in Cairo [*qv*], Boutros-Ghali received higher education at Cairo University and then Paris University, where he obtained diplomas in political science and economics and a doctorate in international law in 1949. Boutros-Ghali then taught international law and international affairs at Cairo University. In 1960 he founded the magazine *Al Ahram Iqtisadi* (Economic Al Ahram) and edited it for the next fifteen years. He also authored several studies of international problems.

In 1977 President Anwar Sadat [*qv*] appointed him minister of state for foreign affairs. Boutros-Ghali played a role in the negotiations that led to the Camp David Accords [*qv*] between Egypt and Israel in September 1978. He retained his position under the presidency of Hosni Mubarak [*qv*]. Boutros-Ghali was elected to parliament in 1987 as a member of the ruling National Democratic Party [*qv*] and was promoted to deputy minister for foreign affairs four years later. On 1 January 1992 he assumed the office of United Nations secretary-general for a period of five years. When fourteen of the fifteen U.N. Security Council members backed his bid for a second term, the United States vetoed it.

Bu (*Arabic: father*): Derivative of *abu* [*qv*].

Byblos: *Lebanese town* Pop. 29,000 (2002, est.). Known in Arabic as *Jbail*, a derivative of biblical *Gebal*, Byblos is one of the oldest settlements in the world. Since papyrus, the ancient writing material later used for making paper, was exported from Lebanon to the Aegean region through Byblos, the place-name became the source word in Greek for "book" and in English for "bible" and "bibliography."

Archaeological work conducted during the 1920s established that Byblos has been inhabited since the eighth millenium B.C. In ancient times it was part of the Egyptian empire and an important trading place for cedar and other wood. After the end of Egyptian suzerainty in the eleventh century B.C., Byblos emerged as the leading city of Phoenicia. Later, during the Roman era, it lost its supremacy to Tyre [*qv*]. In the course of the Crusades it was captured in 1103 by the Crusaders, who retained it until 1291 as part of the Latin Kingdom of Jerusalem. It then came under the successive rule of the Mamelukes and the Ottomans.

Today its tourist offerings include a necropolis, an Obelisk Temple, Phoenician ramparts, a Roman theater, and Crusader ramparts.

C

Cairo: *capital of Egypt* Pop. 7,938,000 (2003, est.). Cairo's Arabic name, al Qairah, means "the Victorious." Located at the head of the River Nile [*qv*] delta, Cairo is the commercial, financial, industrial, educational and cultural center of Egypt and the most populous city of the Middle East [*qv*].

The ancient Roman settlement of Babylon was situated nearby, and Memphis, the capital of ancient Egypt, was across the Nile. Near Memphis are the Pyramids of Giza, a suburb of Cairo. The oldest pyramid, the tomb of Pharaoh Khufu (Cheops), dates back to 2640 B.C.

After Muslim Arabs had conquered Egypt in A.D. 641, they established the new capital, al Fustat (the Encampment), near the fortress of Babylon. In A.D. 969, following their conquest of Egypt, the Fatimids, a Shia [*qv*] dynasty from Tunis, founded Cairo (2 miles/3 km north of al Fustat), as their capital. Since then Cairo has thrived. In the early twelfth century the Crusader plan to capture it failed. It became the capital of the Islamic empire under the Mamelukes (1260–1517). It then came under the suzerainty of the Ottomans. They lost it to Napoleon Bonaparte in 1798, briefly, and then to the British in 1882. After Egyptian independence in 1922, the monarchical regime confirmed Cairo as the country's capital.

As a city rich in history since ancient times, it provides numerous tourist attractions. The most important of these, besides the Pyramids, are the Muallaqa Coptic Church [*qv*]; the Citadel (1179) built by Saladin; the mosques of Ibn Tulun (A.D. 878), al Hakim (1010) and Muhammad Ali (1857); the Antiques Museum, spanning the pre-Islamic era from 3000 B.C. to A.D. 641; the Coptic Museum; the Museum of Islamic Art; and the medieval Khan-e-Khalili bazaar. The city is also the site of al Azhar University [*qv*] and the American University in Cairo [*qv*].

Cairo Agreement (Lebanese-PLO, 1969): Relations between Lebanon and the Palestine Liberation Organization [*qv*] soured when their forces clashed on Lebanese soil in late October 1969. Responding to a mediation offer by Egyptian President Gamal Abdul Nasser [*qv*], the two sides signed an accord, popularly known as the Cairo Agreement. Unofficial leaks revealed that it allowed the PLO to administer the Palestinian refugee camps and establish armed units and posts inside them, and also to hold transit routes and certain positions in southern Lebanon (which had emerged as a major Palestinian-Israeli battleground), in return for the PLO's promise to respect Lebanese sovereignty. Both sides broke the terms of the accord as and when expedient. Following the Israeli invasion of Lebanon in June 1982 [*qv*]—resulting in the PLO's expulsion from Beirut and the creation of an Israeli-enforced security zone in southern Lebanon—the Cairo Agreement became virtually moribund.

Camp David Accords (Egypt-Israel, 1978): These accords were hammered out at the U.S. presidential retreat of Camp David, Maryland, in September 1978 between Egyptian President Anwar Sadat [*qv*] and Israeli Premier Menachem Begin [*qv*], with the assistance of U.S. President Jimmy Carter. They were signed in Washington on 18 September 1978. They laid out the framework for a peace treaty between Egypt and Israel, and a resolution of the Palestinian problem.

The highlights of the accord concerning Egypt and Israel were as follows: Egypt would regain Sinai [*qv*] in exchange for an agreement to conclude a peace treaty and establish normal relations with Israel. The negotiations would establish security zones in Sinai and limit the forces of both sides stationed there.

Once the peace treaty was signed within three months (in practice it took six months), a phased pull-back by Israeli troops would start, the first such withdrawal to be within three to six months after the treaty, and the last two to three years later.

The highlights of the regional peace, especially concerning the Palestinians, were the following: Over a five-year transition period, the West Bank [*qv*] and Gaza Strip [*qv*] would gain autonomy and see the end of Israeli military rule, while Israel would maintain military camps on the West Bank. Jordan was to be invited into the negotiations and could have a security role if it wanted. During the transition period there would be talks on the final status of the West Bank and Gaza Strip between Israel, Egypt, Jordan (if it wished), and the elected representatives of resident Palestinians. During these negotiations there would be a freeze on new Israeli settlements on the West Bank and the Gaza Strip.

The Egypt-Israel peace treaty was signed on 26 March 1979 in Washington and endorsed by the parliaments of the two countries. In the first phase of Israeli withdrawal from the Sinai Peninsula, Israel vacated two-thirds of the peninsula from El Arish on the Mediterranean coast to Ras Muhammad on the Red Sea on 23 January 1980. The two sides exchanged ambassadors on 26 February 1980. The final Israeli withdrawal occurred on 26 April 1982.

The total cost to the United States of military and economic aid to Israel and Egypt, promised in order to secure the Camp David Accords, was put at $10 billion, with two-thirds going to Israel.

Carter Doctrine (1980): *U.S. policy on the*

Gulf region Responding to Soviet military intervention in Afghanistan in late December 1979, U.S. President Jimmy Carter, in his State of the Union address to the U.S. Congress on 24 January 1980, stated: "An attempt by any outside force to gain control of the Persian Gulf region will be regarded as an assault on the vital interests of the United States. It will be repelled by use of any means necessary, including military force." Conceptually, the Carter Doctrine was a virtual repetition of what President Franklin Roosevelt had said in 1943—"The defense of Saudi Arabia is vital to the defense of the United States"—and a reiteration of the Eisenhower Doctrine [*qv*] proclaimed in 1957.

In its application, it advanced the steps taken by the Carter administration soon after the downfall of Muhammad Reza Shah Pahlavi of Iran [*qv*] in February 1979: to establish a joint task force of 50,000, to be called the Rapid Deployment Force (RDF), for safeguarding Gulf oil supplies; to build up the U.S. Fifth Fleet operating from Diego Garcia near Mauritius in the Indian Ocean; and to seek long-term access to air and naval bases in the Gulf. But of the six pro-Western Gulf states approached by Washington, only Oman agreed to let the United States use its military bases. The RDF was headquartered in the United States at MacDill Air Force Base near Tampa, Florida, in March 1980. The next U.S. president, Ronald Reagan, declared in October 1982: "An attack on Saudi Arabia would be considered an attack on the United States."

Catholics, Armenian: *see* Armenian Catholic Church.

Catholics, Assyrian: *see* Nestorian Christians.

Catholics, Chaldean: *see* Chaldean Catholic Church.

Catholics, Greek: *see* Greek Catholic Church.

Catholics, Maronite: *see* Maronite Catholic Church.

Catholics, Orthodox: *see* Orthodox Christians Church.

Catholics, Roman: *see* Roman Catholic Christians Church.

Catholics, Syrian: *see* Syrian Catholic Church.

C.E.: *Abbr. of Common Era* This term is used by some non-Christian writers to denote A.D. [*qv*].

Central Treaty Organization: *multilateral defense pact involving Middle Eastern countries* A Western-sponsored regional alliance, briefly known as the Baghdad Pact [*qv*], it started as the Middle East Treaty Organization (METO) in 1954. As part of its global strategy to create a worldwide chain of anti-Soviet alliances, in February 1954 the United States encouraged Turkey, a member of the North Atlantic Treaty Organization (NATO), to sign a Pact of Mutual Cooperation with Pakistan. In April Washington concluded a military assistance agreement with Iraq, followed by a Pact of Mutual Assistance with Pakistan in May. This set the scene for the signing of a military agreement in February 1955 between Turkey and Iraq, the nucleus of the Baghdad Pact. Later that year Iran, Pakistan, and Britain joined the Baghdad Pact, which pledged military aid in the event of communist aggression against a fellow member. Western pressure on Jordan, Lebanon, and Syria to join failed due to popular, nationalist, pan-Arab [*qv*] feelings expressed in huge demonstrations. After the republican coup in July 1958, Iraq pulled out of the Baghdad Pact in March 1959, which was then officially, and popularly, called the Central Treaty Organization (CENTO). Since it was meant to provide defense against communist aggression, Pakistan's attempts to invoke it in its wars with India in 1965 and 1971 failed. Following the Islamic revolution [*qv*] in early 1979, Iran quit CENTO, destroying its geographical continuity and military effectiveness and hastening its demise.

Chalabi, Ahmad (1945–): *Iraqi politician* Born into a rich banking family in Baghdad, Ahmad Chalabi and his parents fled Baghdad [*qv*] in the wake of the antiroyalist coup in 1958. After university education in Beirut [*qv*], Chalabi enrolled at the Massachusetts Institute of Technology and then obtained a doctorate in mathematics at University of Chicago. He became a mathematics professor at the American University in Beirut [*qv*]. He stayed there until 1977, when, due to the escalating Lebanese Civil War, he moved to Amman [*qv*]. He established Petra Bank there, and within a decade it became the third largest in Jordan [*qv*], only to be seized by the Central Bank of Jordan in mid-1989 due to shady foreign exchange transactions. His reported flight to Damascus in the trunk of a friend's car [*qv*] damaged his reputation. He moved to London, where he later became a British citizen. In 1992 the State Security Court in Amman convicted him in absentia in two cases and sentenced him to three and twenty-two year jail terms. He denied the charges. In the wake of Iraq's invasion of Kuwait [*qv*] in 1990, he carved out a niche for himself in the Iraqi opposition circles in London.

The U.S. Central Intelligence Agency

recruited him as an asset partly because he lacked any constituency inside Iraq, so he was the least threatening to other opposition groups, each of which had some sort of contacts at home. In June 1992, at the convention of 300 opposition delegates in Vienna, bankrolled by the CIA, Chalabi was elected leader of the Iraqi National Congress (INC) [*qv*], an umbrella body that gained the affiliation of nearly twenty groups.

Chalabi moved to Salahuddin in Iraqi Kurdistan [*qv*], the headquarters of the INC, with a plan to develop the region as the launching pad to overthrow the regime of President Saddam Hussein [*qv*]. But his plan in March 1995 to combine a military coup against Saddam with a popular uprising in the area adjacent to Kurdistan failed when the United States withdrew its support for it, preferring to back an alternative plan by the Iraqi National Accord (INA) [*qv*].

In September 1996, following the intra-Kurdish fighting in which the Kurdistan Democratic Party [*qv*] successfully secured Saddam Hussein's military assistance to defeat its rival, the Patriotic Union of Kurdistan [*qv*], the CIA decided to pull out all of its 5,500 Arab and Kurdish agents, including the INC from Kurdistan.

Following passage of the Iraq Liberation Act in October 1998, the INC was recognized as one of the six factions that qualified for official U.S. assistance. But, in April 1999, protesting against Chalabi's high-handedness, the members of the INC's executive committee demoted Chalabi from chairman to ordinary member of the committee.

The hawkish officials of the administration of President George Walker Bush (r. 2001–) warmly adopted Chalabi, who had by then developed close relations with influential pro-Israeli lawmakers. By contrast, Chalabi was now shunned by the U.S. State Department and the CIA. At the Iraqi Open Opposition Conference in London in December 2002, Chalabi's proposal for a transitional government for Iraq in post-Saddam Iraq was rejected. He returned to Iraq four months later in the wake of the Anglo-American invasion of the country.

Chaldean Catholic Church: Originally made up of members of the Nestorian Church [*qv*], who broke away from it to follow John Sulaka, who had been appointed Patriarch of Catholic Nestorians by Roman Catholic [*qv*] Pope Julius III in 1551. The term Chaldean was used partly to differentiate it from the Nestorian Church of Cyprus, which had reconciled with Rome earlier, and partly because the followers were originally from Chaldea and Mesopotamia [*qv*]. One of the Uniate Churches [*qv*], the Chaldean Church follows East Syriac liturgy. Its Patriarch Catholicos of Babylon of the Chaldeans is based in Mosul [*qv*]. Its adherents in the Middle East [*qv*] are mainly in Iraq, Syria, Lebanon, and Egypt. The community in Iraq is 500,000 strong, and its best-known member is Tariq Aziz [*qv*].

Chamoun, Camille Nimr (1900–87): *Lebanese politician; president, 1952–58* Born into a Maronite [*qv*] family in Deiral Qamar, Chamoun acquired a degree from the French Law College of Beirut in 1925. He entered parliament nine years later and became finance minister (1938) and interior minister (1943). In 1944 he was Lebanon's envoy to Britain, and two years later he was the chief Lebanese representative at the United

Nations. On his return to Beirut [*qv*] in 1947, he served as a minister for a year. He parted company with President Bishara Khouri [*qv*] when the latter had the constitution amended to pave the way for his reelection to the presidency. Chamoun joined the opposition and became its choice to replace Khouri when, facing charges of corruption, he resigned in September 1952.

Disregarding the program of his supporters to concentrate on domestic reform, Chamoun focused on foreign affairs. Despite pressure from Muslim politicians, he did not break his links with Britain and France during the latter's aggression against Egypt in October 1956 in the Suez War [*qv*]. His open alignment with the West, coupled with his rigging of the 1957 general election and repression of the opposition, angered the pan-Arab camp. A civil war [*qv*] erupted in May 1958. When the pro-Western monarchy in Iraq was overthrown by pan-Arabist military officers in mid-July, Chamoun called for U.S. troops to be sent under the Eisenhower Doctrine [*qv*]. The arrival of the U.S. forces intensified the civil conflict. To expedite the departure of foreign troops, opposition parliamentarians agreed to vote for General Fuad Chehab [*qv*]—the army commander who had remained neutral in the war—as president in September.

Chamoun founded the National Liberal Party [*qv*]. In the 1968 election it joined the Triple Alliance to oppose those Christian candidates who, as Chehabists, wanted to marry Christian identity with Arab nationalism [*qv*]. Chamoun took an increasingly anti-Palestinian stance, afraid that, encouraged by the support of armed Palestinians, the Lebanese Muslims would strive to strip the Christians of their traditional power. At the beginning of the 1975–90 Lebanese Civil War [*qv*] between the pan-Arab, leftist, predominantly Muslim camp and the right-wing Christian camp, Chamoun emerged as the leader of the status-quoist Lebanese Front [*qv*], a confederation of largely Maronite organizations.

His party set up its own militia, the Tigers, commanded by his son, Danny. But the Tigers were defeated in a series of clashes with the militia of the Phalange Party [*qv*], a Maronite faction. After the ascendancy of the Phalange and its leaders, the Gemayels [*qv*], in the wake of the Israeli invasion of Lebanon in June 1982 [*qv*], the importance of Chamoun waned. Following the Second National Reconciliation Conference in March 1984 in Switzerland, Chamoun joined the national unity government, which he served until his death three years later.

Chehab, Fuad (1902–73): *Lebanese military leader and politician; president, 1958–64* Born into Maronite [*qv*] family, Chehab joined the army during the French mandate and rose to the rank of colonel. After the independence of Lebanon in 1946, he was promoted to general and appointed commander of the army. He modernized the force and maintained its neutrality during political crises. When the opposition mounted street demonstrations against the corrupt government of President Bishara Khouri [*qv*] in September 1952, Chehab kept the army in the barracks. Unable to withstand rising popular pressure, Khouri resigned. Under the new president, Camille Chamoun [*qv*], Chehab served briefly as prime minister as well as defense and interior minister. In the May 1958 civil war [*qv*] between pro-Western forces, led by President Chamoun, and nationalist-leftist forces, headed by Kamal Jumblat [*qv*], Chehab, commanding an 8,000-strong army, remained neutral. His impartiality paved the way for his election to the presidency and an end to the civil strife.

Reflecting the bipartisan backing he had received, Chehab maintained stability by aligning his external policies with those of the Arab hinterland and by co-opting the leaders of urban Muslims in ruling the country. At home, supported by military officers and technocrats, he tried to modernize the Lebanese political-administrative machine, which was steeped in feudal values and sectarian cleavages. His public works program, including road building in the rural north and south, accelerated migration into cities from the countryside, thus setting in motion the radicalization of Lebanese politics. After stepping down in 1964, he continued to wield influence through the parliamentarians and military and intelligence officers who remained loyal to him. But he resisted their pressure to stand for the presidency again in 1970.

Christian calendars: *Gregorian and Julian* The Christian calendar is solar. The one introduced by Roman Emperor Julius Caesar (102–44 B.C.) in 46 B.C. was called the Julian calendar, in which the year consisted of 365 days, each fourth year having 366 days, and the months bearing the same names, order, and length as now. But when it was discovered that a solar year consisted of 365.2422, not 365.2500, days—a difference of about eleven minutes annually—corrections had to be made for the past inconsistency and an appropriate step taken

for the future. This was done by Pope Gregory XIII (1502–85) in 1582, and the new calendar was called Gregorian. By redating 5 October 1582 as 15 October 1582, ten days were lost. For the future it was specified that for the centesimal years—1600, 1700, and so on—only those exactly divisible by 400 should be leap years. It was not until September 1752 that Britain and British colonies in the Americas adopted the Gregorian calendar. Russia did so after the Bolshevik Revolution in October 1917. The difference between the Julian and Gregorian calendars at that time was eleven days, extending to 12 days from 1800 to 1900, and thirteen from 1900 to 2000. Thus, since 1900, Julian 13 October has been the same as Gregorian 26 October.

In 1681 the Pope moved the New Year from the spring equinox (on 21 March) to 1 January, being the circumcision day of Jesus, born a Jew, his birthday, according to tradition, being 25 December—as in Jewish reckoning, where a new day starts after the sunset. According to a sixth century A.D. reckoning, the Christian era is computed to start with Jesus Christ's circumcision, and it is now recognized that this date has been put four to eight years too late.

Christian fundamentalism: Christian fundamentalism rests primarily on the belief that both the Old Testament [*qv*] and the New Testament [*qv*] are literal expressions of the Divine Truth, particularly in their moral–ethical commandments and sociopolitical injunctions, and that they are absolutely infallible. It rests secondarily on the belief in the divinity of Christ and in the salvation of the believer's soul by the effective action of Christ's life, death, and resurrection. The term "fundamentalism" came into vogue in the United States in the 1920s following the publication of the twelve-volume *Fundamentals: The Testimony to Truth.* It was presented as antithetical to modernism and liberalism, which generally informed the Protestant church [*qv*] in the United States. Christian fundamentalism has been particularly strong among Pentecostal Protestants in the U.S. southern states. Growing support for Christian fundamentalism in the United States, organized through such bodies as the Moral Majority, led to the Republican Party gaining a majority in both Houses of Congress in 1994. Since then the Christian right has carved out a powerful niche within the Republican Party, whose candidate George W. Bush won the presidency in 2000. Its pro-Israeli stance has been an important influence on the Bush administration's policies in the Middle East.

Christianity and Christians: Christianity arose out of the birth, crucifixion, and teachings of Jesus of Nazareth [*qv*], a settlement in the Roman province of Galilee. Born a Jew [*qv*], Jesus (ca. 6 B.C.–A.D. 28) was acclaimed as the Christ *(Greek: Anointed)* by his principal followers, called apostles, most of whom were also Jewish. They regarded Jesus as the Christ who had been sent to earth as part of God's earlier covenants with the prophets Abraham, Isaac, and Jacob.

Initially Christianity was a sect within Judaism [*qv*], a monotheistic faith. But following the unsuccessful Jewish uprising in A.D. 66–70 the Jewish element within the Christian community withered. Those believing in the one eternal truth and salvation, as laid down by Christ, followed the rites prescribed by him—especially baptism and the Eucharist *(Greek: thanksgiving)*, which includes the liturgy of the sacrament, consisting of the consecration and distribution of bread and wine, symbolizing the body and blood of Christ offered in sacrifice.

After the death of Christ, his teachings were compiled into four books, called *The Gospels,* which form the early part of the New Testament [*qv*]. While the apostle Peter exercised religious authority, the apostle Paul spread Christ's teachings among non-Jews.

The well-organized nature of Christianity made the state hostile to it, and its monotheistic doctrine clashed with pagan practices. As a result, early Christians were persecuted. The situation changed in A.D. 313 when Roman Emperor Constantine I (r. A.D. 306–37) adopted Christianity and made it the state religion.

The breakup of the Roman Empire in A.D. 395 into the Western and Eastern sections began to undermine the unity of the Christian church. The church council, established in A.D. 325 to adjudicate controversies, produced the dogma of the Trinity—the Father (God), the Son (Christ), and the Holy Spirit—in the sixth century A.D. Increasingly, though, the church was racked with differences on such issues as the number of natures Christ possessed (divine, or divine and human) and the relationship of the Holy Spirit to the Father and the Son. Also, following the barbarian attacks on the Western Roman Empire in the fifth century A.D., there was a political vacuum that was filled largely by the church, led by the Pope based in Rome, with Latin as the official language.

In contrast, in the Eastern Roman Empire the Byzantine rulers exercised control over the church, led by the Patriarch based in Constantinople (now Istanbul), where Greek was the official language.

Guided by Rome and Constantinople, Christian monks spread the faith among pagans all over Europe. (In the Middle East, Asia Minor, and North Africa, Christianity gave way to Islam [*qv*] in the seventh century A.D.) The drift between Western (Roman Catholic [*qv*]) and Eastern (Orthodox [*qv*]) churches became a formal breach in 1054 after mutual excommunications of the Patriarch of Constantinople, Michael Cerularius, and the Rome-based Pope Leo IX. However, both churches experienced increasing conflict between secular and church authorities. When Reformation came in the early sixteenth century, it produced fresh diversity in the Christian faith, leading to the emergence of reformed churches—commonly called Protestant [*qv*], signifying their exclusion from both the Roman Catholic and Eastern (Orthodox) sects.

While the long-established sects still maintain an elaborate version of early doctrines and rites, the more recent Protestant churches have restored pristine doctrines and forms, removing later additions and developments. Modern Christianity is marked by continued conflict between various sects, periodic attempts at unification, and an ongoing attempt to find a stable, well-defined relationship between religion and state. With two billion followers among the planet's six billion inhabitants in 2000, Christianity is the world's most popular religion.

Christians, Catholic: *see* individual Catholic categories.

Christians, Eastern (Orthodox): *see* Orthodox Christians Church and individual Orthodox Christian categories.

Christians, Protestant: *see* Protestant Christians Church.

Christmas: *Christian festival* A derivative of the Old English term *Cristes maesse,* Christ's mass, Christmas is an annual Christian festival celebrated by special gifts, greetings, and food on 25 December, commemorating the birth of Jesus Christ in ca. 6 B.C. (*see* Christian calendars).

church: The term "church" is used for both a community of Christians and a building for Christian worship. Early churches, built like Roman basilicas (halls of justice), were later given a cruciform shape by the addition of wings laid perpendicular to the nave. In the Eastern Roman Empire under the Byzantines, churches acquired the form of the Greek cross.

Circassians: Circassians, also known as Cherkess or Adighe, based in North Caucasia and speaking Circassian, abandoned Christianity [*qv*] for Islam [*qv*] in the seventeenth century under the influence of the Ottoman Turks. In 1829 the Ottomans ceded the region to Tsarist Russia. But Circassians resisted Russian domination until 1864. After that, many Circassian clans fled to Turkey and Greater Syria [*qv*]. Because the Ottoman sultan encouraged them to settle around Amman [*qv*], they now form a minority group in Jordan, where they are to be found in the army and the king's bodyguard.

Citizens Rights Party (Israel): *see* Ratz.

Civil War in Jordan (1970–71): *see* Jordanian Civil War (1970–71).

Civil War in Lebanon (1958): *see* Lebanese Civil War (1958).

Civil War in Lebanon (1975–90): *see* Lebanese Civil War (1975–90).

Civil War in North Yemen (1962–70): *see* North Yemeni Civil War (1962–70).

Civil War in Oman (1963–76): *see* Omani Civil War (1963–76).

Civil War in Yemen (1994): *see* Yemeni Civil War (1994).

Committee for Advice and Reform (Saudi Arabia): In July 1994 Osama bin Laden [*qv*] signed a document describing the Committee for Advice and Reform (CAR) as "an all-encompassing organization that aims at applying the teachings of God to all aspects of life" in general and promoting "peaceful and constructive reform" in the governance of "Arabia"—deliberately omitting the qualifying "Saudi"—and establishing its office in London, with Khalid al Fawwaz (b. 1957) its director. CAR's specific objectives were to eliminate all forms of *jahiliya* (pre-Islamic) rule and all aspects of injustice, and to reform the political system of (Saudi) Arabia by ridding it of corruption and injustice, and to revive the Islamic tradition of *hesba* (lit. accountability), which entitles citizens to bring charges against government officials. Fawwaz was a civil engineering graduate of King Fahd University in Dhahran, who joined the anti-Soviet jihad in early 1980s in Afghanistan, where he met bin Laden. In early 1994 he came to Britain, and took up an English language course at a local college. Fawwaz collected all the pertinent media publications, videotapes, and newspaper cuttings available in Britain. He had a full office working on that and supplying bin Laden with this information. After 9/11, Fawwaz was detained in London.

Committee for the Defense of Legitimate Rights (Saudi Arabia): Encouraged by the holding of the first multiparty general election in Yemen in April 1993, six Saudi human rights activists—professors, lawyers, and civil servants—established the Committee for the Defense of Legitimate Rights (CDLR). Aiming to strive to eliminate injustice and defend the legitimate rights of citizens, the CDLR called on Saudi citizens to report official acts of injustice to it and demanded political reform, including elections based on universal suffrage. The government arrested the CDLR's head, Professor Muhammad al Masaari, and sacked the remaining founders from their jobs.

The CDLR then moved its base to London, from where it continued its activities, led by al Masaari, making extensive use of faxes to receive information from Saudi Arabia and communicate with its supporters there. In September 1994 it revealed that, following demonstrations against the detention of two militant clergymen, there had been large-scale arrests. Unprecedently, this was later confirmed by the Saudi government, which was believed to be holding up to 300 protesters in jail by early 1995.

The Saudi efforts to get Masaari deported from Britain failed. Later, there was a split in the CDLR, with al Masaari's erstwhile colleague Saad al Faqih forming the rival Islamic Reform Movement. This and lack of funds left the CDLR weak and ineffective.

Communist Movement in Egypt: In 1921 a breakaway faction of the Socialist Party of Egypt founded the Communist Party of Egypt (CPE). On the eve of the group's admission to the Moscow-based

Communist International (Comintern) in 1923, its program included demands for Egypt's independence from Britain, land reform, and the recognition of existing trade unions. Its policy of calling strikes brought it into conflict with the government, leading to a ban in 1924 on the Confederation of Trade Unions dominated by it.

Facing persecution, the CPE failed to make much headway among peasants. The situation changed in 1936 when a tide of anti-imperialism swept the country following the unpopular Anglo-Egyptian Treaty [qv]. After the Soviet entry into the Second World War in mid-1941 on the Allied side, the official policy toward communists turned benign. In 1942 trade unions were legalized. The dramatic increase in the size of the working class, caused by the war, enabled communists, now represented largely by the Mouvement Egyptien de Liberation Nationale, and the smaller Iskra, to enlarge their influence among workers.

The two communist groups brought their respective unions under the umbrella of the Congress of Workers' Unions (CWU), with a membership of 115,000. In May 1947 they merged to form the Mouvement Democratique de Liberation Nationale (MDLN). Since a large section of the MDLN's 1,500 members were either Copts [qv] or Jews [qv], the party's strength was not overly damaged by the Soviet support for the partition of Palestine, voiced at the United Nations in November. But the government used the Soviet action to dub communists pro-Zionist and jail their leaders. Following a poor showing by the Egyptian troops in the Palestine War (1948–49) [qv], the much

weakened administration released all political prisoners, including communists. Once the freshly elected Wafd [qv] government had abrogated the 1936 Anglo-Egyptian Treaty in October 1951, the communists forged a united front with other anti-imperialist groups and participated in the anti-British guerrilla campaign in the Suez Canal [qv] zone. On the eve of the July 1952 coup, the Communist Party had 5,000 active members.

Two of the eighteen-strong ruling Revolutionary Command Council (RCC) were communist: Major Khalid Mohieddin [qv] and Colonel Yusuf Sadiq. But this had no impact on the actions of the RCC, which claimed to be nonideological. Once Gamal Abdul Nasser [qv] had consolidated his hold over the RCC, he removed Mohieddin and Sadiq from it. But facing an Anglo-French-Israeli attack on Egypt in October 1956, Nasser released hundreds of communist and leftist Wafd prisoners to let them organize popular resistance against the invaders.

Following a reconciliation between the MDLN and the smaller CPE, a party congress was held in early 1958. But the party split into two factions when the leadership was unable to forge an agreed policy toward Iraqi communists [qv] after the antiroyalist coup of July 1958 in Iraq. Since Arab socialism [qv] was enshrined into the Charter of National Action in June 1962, which expressed belief in scientific socialism and commitment to the struggle against exploitation, the two factions reacted differently. The moderates saw it as heralding the beginning of a socialist revolution, while the radicals regarded it as signifying nothing more than the introduction of state capitalism, since it rejected the concepts of class conflict and the abolition of private property.

Hundreds of radical communists continued to suffer imprisonment. However, in August 1963 Nasser followed up his nationalization of private companies with a decision to release political prisoners (of both left and right) in order to enlarge the base of the fledgling Arab Socialist Union (ASU) [*qv*]. This resulted in the freeing of some 600 communist prisoners by the spring of 1964. A year later the communist leadership, declaring that Nasser's regime had been following the road of noncapitalist development toward socialism, dissolved the party and advised individual members to join the ASU.

While using the organizational skills of the former communists, the Egyptian regime treated them with circumspection. Loyal to the Egyptian president, they played a prominent role in organising pro-Nasser demonstrations after the June 1967 Arab-Israeli War [*qv*]. However, rejecting their advice to strengthen the revolutionary cadres of the ASU, Nasser changed the ASU structure to placate traditional elements. After his death in September 1970, former communists demanded greater representation in the ASU secretariat and trade unions, but to no avail. Since the National Unity Law of September 1972 specified a heavy penalty for political activity outside the ASU, they found themselves in a dilemma. When parliament decided to allow three forums within the ASU, the communists allied with leftist Nasserites [*qv*] to form the National Progressive Unionist Alliance [*qv*] in May 1976.

Communist Movement in Israel: *see* Maki *and* Rakah.

Communist Party of Iran: *see* Tudeh Party of Iran.

Communist Party of Iraq: The Communist Party of Iraq (CPI) was established in March 1934. Two years later it went underground when the government banned the propagation of Bolshevik socialism. It was only after the Soviets had joined the Allies in the Second World War in mid-1941 that the authorities allowed the communist front organizations to function openly. They held their first congress in 1945. Active among workers, the party, with a membership of 3,000, also built up a following among teachers, students, and ethnic minorities in towns as well as peasants in villages. When it organized a strike of oil workers in July 1946, it faced government repression. It suffered a setback in late 1947 when the Soviets backed the Palestine partition plan. Yet in January 1948 it succeeded in organising demonstrations against the renegotiated 1930 Anglo-Iraqi Treaty [*qv*], called the Portsmouth Agreement. Having rescinded the agreement, the government jailed hundreds of communist activists. Undeterred, they turned prisons into recruiting centers while their comrades outside dominated the largest student body.

In 1956 the CPI joined the United National Front (UNF), which advocated political reform at home and an anti-imperialist and anti-Zionist struggle abroad. The UNF was in touch with the Free Officers Organization, which overthrew the monarchy in mid-1958. The CPI, now with 8,000 members, expanded its base among peasants by forming Peasant Leagues to help implement the agrarian reform decreed by the regime of Abdul Karim Qasim [*qv*]. It backed Qasim in his conflict with Nasserists [qv], who wanted to unite Iraq with the United Arab Republic [qv]. Though Qasim curtailed communist influence during the latter part of his rule, the CPI was the only party to fight alongside his forces against the Baathists [qv] in February 1963. It therefore became the target of the ruling Baathists' witch-hunt, which claimed the lives of 3,000 to 5,000 communists—the worst fate suffered by any political party in the Arab East [qv].

With the fall of the Baathist government in November 1963, the CPI returned to a semi-clandestine existence. Its leadership scaled down the party's objective of establishing a socialist regime, led by workers and peasants, to participating in a popular front government based on the alliance of all patriotic forces. This led to splits in the party in 1965 and 1967, but allowed its main body, led by moderate Aziz Muhammad, to reach a rapprochement with the Baathists, who by then had been driven underground.

Following the successful Baathist coup of July 1968, the regime permitted the CPI to function. It held its second congress in September 1970. In May 1972 its seven-year old clandestine journal, *Tareeq al Shaab* (The People's Path), was allowed to appear daily. On the fifth anniversary of the July 1968 revolution, the CPI and the Baath Party signed the National Action Charter, heralding the formation of the National Progressive and Patriotic Front (NPPF) [qv]. This required the CPI to be loyal to the Baathist revolution and refrain from labor agitation as well as dissemination of its ideology among students and troops. In return it was given two cabinet seats out of twenty-eight.

The third CPI congress, held in May 1976, concluded that Iraq had entered the stage of noncapitalist development and recommended a series of anticapitalist measures. But the regime, enriched by booming oil revenues, increased its trade links with the West and relaxed controls over private capital at home. With the Kurdish problem settled for the time being through an accord with Iran in March 1975, the government decided to curb communist influence. On their part, in March 1978 CPI leaders coupled their criticism of the regime with calls for a general election and parity with the Baathists in the government until the poll.

The next month, following the Marxist military coup in Afghanistan, Baghdad's policy toward the CPI hardened. The result was large-scale arrests of communist activists and the execution of thirty-six leaders for trying to form party cells in the army. The CPI left the NPPF, but without publicizing the fact. The official anticommunist drive intensified to the point where reports circulating in early 1979 mentioned some 1,900 communists "disappearing." In April the party daily, with a circulation of 50,000, was shut down. In early 1980 President Saddam Hussein [qv] barred the CPI from contesting the parliamentary elections to be held in June. CPI leaders condemned Saddam Hussein's invasion of Iran in September, arguing that it diverted Arab energy away from confronting the main Arab enemy in the region: Israel. Following the Second Gulf War [qv], the remnants of the party got a toehold in the Kurdistan Autonomous Region [qv], controlled by the anti-Saddam Kurdish parties. They decided not to join the U.S.-sponsored Iraqi opposition on the eve of the Gulf War III [qv].

Communist Party of Jordan: The Communist Party of Jordan (CPJ) evolved under the leadership of Fuad Nassar in June 1951 out of the eight-year-old League of National Liberation (LNL). Two months later it allied with the Baathists [*qv*] and the Arab Nationalist Movement [*qv*] to form the National Bloc to contest a general election. It scored 11 percent of the vote, enough to upset the government, which arrested the communist leadership and stiffened the anticommunist law of 1948.

Following the promulgation of a new constitution in 1952, which allowed licensed political parties, the CPJ cooperated with the Baathists and the National Socialist Party to form the National Front in the spring of 1954. Despite vote-rigging in the autumn election, two communists won. In 1955 the CPJ participated in the National Front campaign to keep Jordan out of the recently formed Baghdad Pact [*qv*] and get the election results annulled. The struggle was successful. In the poll of October 1956 the alliance of the CPJ, Baathists, and National Socialists won 40 percent of the vote, with the CPJ securing 13 percent. The inclusion of a communist in the government, led by Nabulsi, was unprecedented in the Arab East [*qv*]. In April 1957 the monarch dismissed the Nabulsi government, dissolved parliament, declared martial law, and jailed 200 of the 2,000 CPJ members. They were incarcerated until late 1964. A chastened party leadership adopted a moderate program of socioeconomic reform at home.

The loss of the West Bank [*qv*] to Israel in the June 1967 Arab-Israeli War [*qv*] deprived the party of nearly half of its members. But the subsequent increase in the Palestinian refugee population in Jordan and the emergence of armed Palestinian commandos radicalized CPJ's ranks. The party formed its own militia, the Ansars. However, once the government had expelled all Palestinian commandos by mid-1971 after bloody fighting, CPJ leaders dissolved the militia and reverted to the moderate aim of forming a national unity government of all national and progressive forces.

In May 1974 the CPJ resolved to establish a national front of antiroyalist forces in order to set up a "national liberated authority" on the East Bank [*qv*]. But the outbreak of civil war in Lebanon a year later diverted the CPJ's attention and energies. It participated in the conference of ten Arab communist parties in June 1978 in Beirut [*qv*], which decided to sharpen the anti-Zionist struggle. Its semi-clandestine existence ended in 1992 when, following the legalization of political parties, the CPJ became one of the nine parties to secure a license. It participated in the general election of 1993 but failed to win a seat.

Communist Party of Lebanon: The Communist movement in Lebanon started with the People's Party of Lebanon in 1924, composed of intellectuals and trade unionists. After it had absorbed the Spartacus Party, a leftist group, in 1925, it renamed itself the Communist Party of Syria and Lebanon (CPSL). Because of its support for the Druze [*qv*] rebellion (1925–27), its leaders were arrested by the French mandate. It was not until 1928 that the CPSL, dominated by Armenian Christians [*qv*], was admitted to the Moscow-based Communist International (Comintern). Accepting Comintern's advice to "Arabize" itself, in 1936 the party hierarchy replaced Fuad Shemali, a Christian [*qv*], with Khalid Bakdash [*qv*], a Syrian Kurd [*qv*].

The CPSL's adoption of a radical program of combining the anti-imperialist struggle with revolutionizing workers and peasants in Lebanon alarmed the French mandate, which refused to recognize its trade union wing. The situation changed in 1936 when the leftist Popular Front, backed by communists, assumed power in France. Between then and the outbreak of the Second World War, the party membership rose from 200 to 2,000. It participated in Lebanon's parliamentary poll in 1943. After the Lebanese independence in 1946, the strength of the CPL soared to 16,000. It suffered a setback when the Soviets endorsed the Palestine partition plan in late 1947. When CPL leaders backed the Soviet decision, the government banned the party and dissolved its trade union wing.

President Camille Chamoun's [*qv*] refusal to condemn the Anglo-French-Israeli invasion of Egypt in 1956 created a climate where the CPL succeeded in reestablishing its Arab nationalist credentials by siding with local Nasserists [*qv*]. In the 1958 Lebanese Civil War [*qv*], it sided with the leftist-nationalist camp against Chamoun. In March 1965 it joined the Front of National and Progressive Parties and Forces, led by Kamal Jumblat [*qv*], a Marxist. The decision of the party congress in 1968 to enlarge its membership was aided by the formal lifting of the ban on it (along with other parties with extraterritorial links) two years later. In 1974 it formed the National Union of Workers and Employees under its aegis.

On the eve of the 1975 Lebanese Civil War [*qv*], the CPL, along with the Organization of the Communist Action in Lebanon (OCAL), formed the hard core of the Lebanese National Movement (LNM) [*qv*], which fought the rightist camp. Unlike other Lebanese parties, the CPL combined military action with political education and propaganda. By the end of 1975 the party had a membership of 15,000, half of whom were Shia [*qv*]. In 1978 it hosted a conference of ten Arab communist parties in Beirut [*qv*], which decided to intensify the anti-Zionist struggle. By the end of the civil war, the CPL had lost most of its Shia supporters to Amal [*qv*] and Hizbollah [*qv*]. It was denied any role in the national unity government formed after the end of the civil war in October 1990. The CPL participated in the general elections of 1992, 1996, and 2000, but without any success. Led by Maurice Nohra, it published a weekly journal, *Al Akhbar* (The News), with a circulation of about 20,000. Many of its readers were intellectuals.

Communist Party of Palestine: The Communist Party of Palestine (PCP), founded in 1922, won the recognition of the Moscow-based Communist International (Comintern) two years later. With the dissolution of Comintern in May 1943—and thus the loss of an external overseeing organization—the simmering differences between the Jewish and Arab members surfaced. Most of the Arab members left to form the League of National Liberation (LNL). Soon the LNL enlarged its influence by absorbing the existing Arab leftist groups and establishing the Federation of Arab Trade Unions and Labor Societies.

After the Palestine War (1948–49) [*qv*] and the absorption of the West Bank [*qv*] into Jordan, the LNL transformed itself into the Communist Party of Jordan [*qv*] in June 1951. Sixteen years later, following the loss of the West Bank to Israel in the Six-Day Arab-Israeli War [*qv*], the PCP was revived clandestinely in the West Bank area. It also began to function in the Palestinian refugee camps and was close to the Democratic Front for the Liberation of Palestine [*qv*], which backed the idea of establishing a "national" authority in any part of "liberated" Palestine. It affiliated to the Palestine Liberation Organization (PLO) [*qv*] and participated in the conference of Arab communist parties in Beirut [*qv*] in June 1978, which decided to intensify the anti-Zionist struggle. In 1987 the party, then led by Suleiman Najab, was given seats on the Palestine National Council. Five years later it changed its name to the Palestine People's Party [*qv*], but retained Najab as its head. Hassan Asfour, one of the party's leaders, participated in the PLO's secret negotiations with Israel, which led to the Oslo Accord [*qv*]. It backed the Accord and the resulting Palestinian Authority [*qv*]. It is led by Suleiman Najab.

Communist Party of Saudi Arabia: The Communist Party of Saudi Arabia (CPSA), officially established in Baghdad in 1975, evolved out of the National Liberation Front (NLF), a Marxist group formed in 1958, whose roots went back to the Workers' Committees formed in the wake of strikes at oil fields in 1953. These committees continued to function secretly until the next wave of strikes in 1956 when, following government persecution, they disintegrated. Some of their members allied with local communists to form the National Reform Front, a clandestine organization

that subsequently renamed itself the National Liberation Front. The NLF demanded a democratic constitution with rights to establish political parties and trade unions, and to demonstrate or strike, and called on the state to take total control of oil resources, from prospecting to marketing. It supported the coup attempt led by the Saudi section of the Arab Nationalist Movement [*qv*] in June 1969. Three years after its formation, the CPSA attended the conference of ten Arab Communist parties in Beirut, which decided to intensify the anti-Zionist struggle. With opposition in Saudi Arabia turning more toward militant Islam from the late 1970s onward, the appeal of the CPSA, operating from outside the country, waned. Within the next decade, the party became almost moribund.

Communist Party of Syria: The Communist movement in Syria started in 1925 with the formation of the Communist Party of Syria and Lebanon (CPSL). Because of its support for the Druze [*qv*] rebellion (1925–27), its leaders were arrested by the French mandate. It was not until 1928 that the CPSL, dominated by Christian Armenians [*qv*], was admitted to the Moscow-based Communist International (Comintern). Accepting Comintern's advice to "Arabize" itself, in 1936 the party hierarchy replaced Fuad Shemali, a Christian [*qv*], with Khalid Bakdash [*qv*], a Syrian Kurd [*qv*].

The CPSL's adoption of a radical program of combining the anti-imperialist struggle with revolutionizing workers and peasants made it unpopular with the French mandate, which refused to recognize its trade union wing. The situation changed in 1936 when the leftist Popular Front, backed by the communists, assumed power in France. It continued to function until it was banned, along with other political parties, on the eve of the Second World War.

Its clandestine existence ended in July 1941 when the British and Free French forces, having defeated the troops loyal to the pro-Nazi French government based in Vichy, legalized all political groups. It participated in the parliamentary elections in the summer of 1943. During the first four years of its legal existence (1941–45), the Communist Party of Syria (CPS) raised its membership from 1,000 to 10,000. Later it played a prominent role in frustrating France's plans to reestablish its authority in Syria. But the Soviet decision to back the partition of Palestine in late 1947 severely damaged the CPS's standing. It was not until early 1954, when President Adib Shishkali [qv] dissolved parliament and disbanded all political parties, that an environment was created whereby the CPS lost its pariah status.

In the 1954 general election, the party won as many votes as the Baathists [qv]. Following the discovery in late 1956 and mid-1957 of Western-inspired plots against the Syrian government, the CPS was allowed to join the Popular Resistance Force, a paramilitary organization. Its membership of 18,000 was record. This unnerved the Baathists, who began to advocate union with Egypt. Anticipating a ban on political parties after the Syrian-Egyptian union in early 1958 under President Gamal Abdul Nasser [qv], CPS leaders went into self-exile in Prague, Czechoslovakia. Nasser responded to Bakdash's criticism by repressing the CPS. After the breakup of the UAR in 1961, the new

rulers of Syria did not allow the CPS leaders to return home. When the Baathist regime, established in March 1963, moved leftward, the CPS backed it, especially after it had allowed the party leadership to return to Damascus [qv] in 1966.

Initially the CPS opposed General Hafiz Assad's [qv] "correctionist" coup in November 1970. But when two years later he agreed to form the National Progressive Front [qv], the CPS backed him. Of those elected on a common NPF list in the 1973 election, eight were members of the CPS, believed to have a membership of 3,000 to 6,000. Assad's dispatch of Syrian troops in June 1976 to aid the rightist camp in the Lebanese Civil War [qv] strained relations between him and the CPS. The reduced CPS representation in the parliament of 1977 reflected Assad's lukewarm attitude toward the party. But when, in the face of a serious challenge to Assad from the Muslim Brotherhood [qv] in 1980–82, the CPS backed the regime, relations between the two sides improved. The party held its sixth congress in January 1987. In the 1990 general election, the CPS, led by Yusuf Faisal, secured eight seats. In the 1994, 1998, and 2003 parliamentary polls, it retained its eight seats. In 2001 it was allowed to publish the *Sawt al Shaab* (The People's Voice) fortnightly.

confessionalism (in Lebanon): Confessionalism is the term used for a social system that recognizes the principle of religious communities being vested with political authority. It has been operational in Lebanon since March 1943, when the British representative in Beirut, General Edward Spears, mediating between the feuding Muslims [*qv*] and Christians [*qv*], recommended a ratio of six Christian parliamentary seats to five Muslim, based on the 1932 census, which had classified the population under sixteen religions or sects: Armenian Catholic [*qv*], Chaldean Catholic [*qv*], Greek Catholic [*qv*], Maronite Catholic [*qv*], Roman Catholic [*qv*], Syrian Catholic [*qv*]; Armenian Orthodox [*qv*], Greek Orthodox [*qv*], Syrian Orthodox [*qv*]; Protestant [*qv*]; Bahai [*qv*]; Jew [*qv*]; Alawi [*qv*], Druze [*qv*], Shia [*qv*], and Sunni [*qv*]. This was accepted as part of the National Pact [*qv*], an unwritten supplement to the Lebanese constitution of 1926, which was given the status of an official decree by the French delegate-general in July 1943.

Conservative Judaism: Conservative Judaism, founded in 1845 in Germany, lies somewhere between Orthodox Judaism [*qv*] and Reform Judaism [*qv*]. While remaining faithful to the basic features of traditional Judaism, it accepts a certain adjustment of religious practices to suit the modern age. It considers the Jewish religion, culture, and national identity as an integral whole. It regards the Sabbath [*qv*] as sacred, respects the dietary injunctions, encourages the learning of Hebrew [*qv*], and backs the secular Zionist movement [*qv*]. Its chief ideologue, Zacharias Frankel (1801–75), urged examination of the Jewish Written and Oral Law in order to separate its essence from the elements reflective of contemporary times and then reinterpreting the essence to suit the current era. An estimated 48 percent of the world's Jews [*qv*] are followers of Conservative Judaism or Reform Judaism [*qv*].

Constitutional Revolution (Iran) (1907–11): Yielding to demonstrations in Tehran [*qv*] and Qom [*qv*] for an elected parliament, the Shah of Iran, Muzzafar al Din Qajar (r. 1896–1907), issued a decree in August 1906 stating that an "Assembly of Delegates" be elected by the *ulama* [*qv*], the Qajar family and nobles, landowners, merchants, and guilds. The 106-strong assembly, called the Majlis [*qv*], met in October. During the next two months it unanimously passed a set of Fundamental Laws. The document, modeled along the Belgian constitution, was framed within an Islamic context. The mortally ill shah signed it on 30 December, died five days later, and was succeeded by his son, Muhammad Ali (r. 1907–08). Some months later the Majlis produced the longer Supplementary Fundamental Laws, outlining a parliamentary form of government, with power concentrated in the legislature at the expense of the executive. When the shah refused to ratify the new document, there were demonstrations, as well as the assassination of his prime minister. The shah signed it on 7 October 1907. The two sets of Laws together formed the Iranian constitution and ushered in the Constitutional Revolution.

However, the shah was reluctant to become a figurehead monarch. He used an attempt to assassinate him in mid-June 1908 as a pretext to mount a coup against the elected government. On 23 June he ordered his palace guard to bomb the Majlis building, which was being defended by 7,000 lightly armed constitutionalists. In the ensuing fight, over 250 people were killed. He dissolved the First Majlis, declared martial law and waged a campaign of terror against his opponents. A civil war ensued, and by mid-July he had lost. Having secured refuge in the Russian embassy, he abdicated in favor of his twelve-year-old son, Ahmad.

In November 1909, the Second Majlis approved the appointment of William Shushter, an American economist, as the treasurer general to increase the state's falling revenue. He organized a special tax-collecting force and deployed it everywhere, including the northern region, regarded as a Russian zone of influence. In November 1911, having ordered his troops to occupy Iran's Caspian Sea ports of Enzali and Rasht, the Russian tsar gave an ultimatum that failure to remove Shuster within two days would lead to the Russian occupation of Tehran. Only after the deadline, when Russian troops had begun to march toward Tehran, did the Majlis vote to dismiss Shuster. To placate the tsar the Iranian regent dismissed the Majlis for having defied the Russian ultimatum. Though the regent did not abrogate the 1906–07 constitution, his dismissal of the Majlis marked the end of the Constitutional Revolution.

Coptic Church and Copts: *main Christian church in Egypt* The term Copt—derivative of the Greek word *Aigyptios,* meaning Egyptian, and derived from the hieroglyphic "Het-Ka Ptah," Temple of Ptah's spirit—was applied to all Egyptians before the Muslim Arab [*qv*] conquest in A.D. 641. After the Muslim rule, Copts meant those Egyptians who did not embrace Islam [*qv*] and continued to practice Christianity [*qv*]. In A.D. 451 the Roman church declared the Coptic Church, one of the oldest in the Christian world, heretic because of the latter's adop-

tion of the monophysite doctrine, which states that Christ had only one nature, not two (divine and human). The service books of the Coptic Church continue to be in Coptic [*qv*]. The church's head, the Patriarch of Alexandria and all Egypt, is based in Cairo [*qv*]. Its best known member is Boutros Boutros-Ghali [*qv*]. The official 1986 census put Copts at 5.6 percent of the national population of 48.2 million, a proportion that remained about the same in the 1996 census, with Egypt's inhabitants numbering 59.3 million. Since Copts and Muslims share the same name and many Copts prefer to be listed as Muslim in official documents to avoid discrimination, the census figures are widely believed to be about half the real ones. Before the 1952 revolution, Copts were active in the Wafd [*qv*]. President Gamal Abdul Nasser [*qv*] reserved certain constituencies for Copts and nominated ten Copts to parliament. In the absence of proper political leadership, Copts turned to the religious hierarchy to advance political demands. The draft law on apostasy, making it a capital offense, was withdrawn by President Anwar Sadat [*qv*] in 1977 when Coptic religious leaders went on a fast. After the Egyptian-Israeli peace treaty [*qv*] in March 1979, anti-Sadat sentiment turned anti-Copt since the government had blocked all legitimate channels of expressing opposition to the treaty. In March 1980 several Copts were killed in clashes in southern Egyptian towns. The rise of militant Islamic movement in the early- and mid-1990s strained relations between Muslims and Copts. These improved with the decline of Islamic militancy in the late 1990s. In 1995 President Hosni Mubarak [*qv*] nominated six Copt members of parliament, and in 2000 only four. The parliament lacked any elected Copt member.

Coptic language: A Hamito-Semitic language, derived from ancient Egyptian, Coptic was a living language in Egypt between the second and seventh centuries A.D. Written in the Greek alphabet, Coptic supplanted the religious expressions of the earlier Egyptian language with words borrowed from the Greek. Nowadays it is used only in the liturgy of the Coptic Church [*qv*].

Council of Guardians (Iran): *see* Guardians Council (Iran).

crude oil: *see* oil.

D

al Daawa (Iraq) *(Arabic: The Call): Iraqi political party* Official title: *Hizb al Daawa al Islamiya*, The Islamic Call Party. Following the secular Baathists' [*qv*] seizure of power in Iraq in July 1968, the government censored religious publications, closed several Islamic institutions, and began to harass Shia [*qv*] clergy. When Shia clerics urged their supporters to protest, further repression followed. Against this backdrop al Daawa al Islamiya was formed in 1969, clandestinely, with the blessing of Najaf-based Ayatollah Muhsin Hakim, the seniormost Shia cleric. When the governing regime, dominated by Sunni [*qv*] leaders, tried to interfere with some Shia rituals and weaken the authority of the religious hierarchy, al Daawa gained ground. In December 1974 Shia religious processions turned into antigovernment demonstrations. The authorities executed five al

Daawa leaders. At the same time they tried to placate the Shia masses by increasing the public development funds going to the Shia-dominated south.

Following the Islamic revolution [*qv*] in Shia-majority Iran in early 1979, the leadership in Tehran decided to encourage an Islamic movement in Iraq and aided al Daawa. Iraq responded by making al Daawa membership a capital offense. In March 1980 it executed ninety-four al Daawa activists for killing a score of Iraqi officials in 1979. The next month al Daawa militants tried but failed to assassinate the Iraq deputy premier, Tariq Aziz [*qv*], a Christian [*qv*]. Following the outbreak of the Iran-Iraq War [*qv*] in September, which necessitated blackouts, al Daawa, now backed by Iranian arms and training, intensified its sabotage and assassination campaign. Iraq's task of suppressing al Daawa became easier once the Iranians had marched into Iraq in June 1982. It was convincingly able to label the allies of Iran as traitors to Iraq. This caused a sharp drop in al Daawa's support.

In November al Daawa members in Iran cooperated with other Islamic organizations to form the Supreme Assembly of Islamic Revolution in Iraq (SAIRA) [*qv*] in Tehran. In December 1983 they set off five bombs in Kuwait, which had been aiding Iraq in its conflict with Iran. In 1985 al Daawa allied with secular Iraqi opposition, especially the Kurdistan Democratic Party [*qv*], which provided it with refuge in the Kurdish region to carry out its attacks on economic and military targets of the Baathist regime. On 9 April 1987 al Daawa militants made an unsuccessful attempt to assassinate President Saddam Hussein [*qv*] on the outskirts of Mosul [*qv*].

With the end of the Iran-Iraq War in August 1988 al Daawa's activities subsided. They revived when, in the wake of the Second Gulf War [*qv*], there was a Shia rebellion in the south in March 1991. With its failure, al Daawa once again become marginalized within Iraq.

In 2002, al Daawa formally split from SAIRAI when the latter decided to cooperate with U.S.-sponsored Iraqi opposition groups.

al Daawa al Islamiya (Iraq): *see* al Daawa.

Damascus: *capital of Syria* Pop. 1,862,000 (2003, est.). The history of Damascus stretches back to the third millennium B.C., and the city's present name is at least 3,500 years old. In ancient times it was ruled by the Assyrians and the Persians. It fell to Alexander the Great (r. 336–23 B.C.) and then to other rulers. After it was conquered by the Romans in 65 B.C., it became an important city of the Decapolis province east of the Jordan River [*qv*]. It was on his way to Damascus that the apostle Paul was converted to Christianity.

Damascus was captured by Muslim Arabs [*qv*] in A.D. 635 and became the capital of the Islamic empire of the Umayyads in A.D. 661. Its prosperity continued even after the Abbasids, who succeeded the Umayyads, moved the imperial capital to Baghdad [*qv*] in A.D. 763. It was sacked twice by the Mongols, first in 1258 and then about a century later. Conquered by the Ottoman Turks in 1517, it remained part of their empire for the next four centuries. It came under French mandate after the First World War and became the capital of semi-independent Syria in 1943. It has expanded since then and has become the commercial, financial,

industrial, educational, and cultural center of Syria and the leading city of the Levant [*qv*].

Its prime tourist attraction is the Great Mosque, also called the Umayyad Mosque, one of the finest Islamic monuments. The original site was home to a temple to Jupiter, built by the Greeks. In the fourth century A.D. it was replaced by the renowned church of St. John the Baptist, constructed by Roman Emperor Theodosius I (r. A.D. 379–395). The Umayyads transformed this church, containing the shrine of St. John the Baptist, into a mosque in A.D. 715.

Darwish, Mahmud (1941–): *Palestinian writer and poet* Born into a landowning Sunni [*qv*] family in Barwa village near Acre [*qv*], Darwish and his family escaped to Lebanon during the 1948–49 Palestine War [*qv*]. They later returned and settled in Deir al Assad village in Galilee. After finishing high school at Kafr Yasid, Darwish found work with an Arabic printer in Acre. He began publishing his poems in the Arabic-language press, including the literary monthly *Al Jadid* (The New) and the fortnightly *Al Ittihad* (The Unity), the publications of Maki [*qv*], the Israeli Communist Party. Later, having been appointed to the editorial boards of these journals, he became a journalist.

With the publication of three volumes of poetry—*Birds without Wings* (1961), *Lover from Palestine* (1964) and *Olive Leaves* (1964)—he established himself as an outstandingly talented poet who was fluent in both Arabic [*qv*] and Hebrew [*qv*]. Profoundly original, rich in imagery, and imbued with intense feelings, his lyrical verses conveyed the suffering of Palestinians who had been expelled from their homeland

and compelled to live in refugee camps. Though deeply disappointed by the humiliating defeat suffered by the Arabs in the June 1967 Arab-Israeli War (*qv*), in which Israel occupied the rest of Palestine [*qv*], in his poetry he kept up the image of the resistant hero who, inspired by the ideas of valour and self-sacrifice, struggles to achieve freedom.

After spending a year at a university in Moscow (1970), he decided not to return to Israel. He based himself in Cairo [*qv*], where he published articles and poems in the leading daily, *Al Ahram* (The Pyramids). When the Palestine Liberation Organization (PLO) [*qv*] moved to Beirut [*qv*] in 1972, he became editor of its monthly publication, *Shuaun Falastiniyya* (Palestinian Affairs). In 1975 he was appointed director of the PLO Research Center. The involvement of the PLO in the Lebanese Civil War [*qv*], in which some 3,000 Palestinian refugees were massacred in Tal Zaatar camp in East Beirut by the Phalangist militia [*qv*] in 1976, darkened the tone of Darwish's poetry. The low point came during the long siege of West Beirut during the Israel invasion of Lebanon [*qv*] in 1982, when he was with the PLO chairman, Yasser Arafat [*qv*].

Following the PLO's expulsion from Beirut, he penned poems to recapture the debilitating experience in *Ode to Beirut* (1982) and *A Eulogy for The Tall Shadow* (1983), both narrative works of considerable length. His voice was now tingled with a realism that recognized that bravery, just cause, and readiness to die would not suffice to redeem the hero in the present-day world of global power politics and high technology. His protagonist is now a man stretching himself to his limits, striving in the face of

continued exile and defeat. Darwish's earlier triumphant tone has given to the concept of a heroic victim, someone caught in a heroic deadlock, like a man dying while climbing. Such maturity has added to the power of his verse. Darwish often calls on the Old Testament [*qv*] prophets, especially notably Isaiah and Jeremiah, to condemn the Israeli acts of injustice against the Palestinians. Equally Darwish is unrivaled in his usage of the language, style, and motifs of the Quran and the prophetic tradition in his poetry.

While in Cyprus Darwish, was elected chairman of the Palestinian Writers and Journalists Association and edited its magazine. He received the Ibn Sina Prize, sponsored by the Soviet Union, in 1982, followed by the Lenin Peace Prize a year later. When a selection of his poems was translated into English (*The Music of Human Flesh,* 1980) he became known in Britain and the United States, where he took up residence in the late 1980s before moving to Paris. He was elected to the PLO executive in 1987 as an independent and was reelected four years later. Opposed to the Oslo Accord [*qv*] of September 1993, he resigned in protest. In Paris he has continued to edit *Al Karmel,* the Palestinian literary review. His latest volumes of poetry in English include *Psalms* (1994) and *The Adam of Two Edens* (2001).

Dashnak Party (Lebanon): *see* Tashnak Party (Lebanon).

Day of Atonement (Jewish): *see* Yom Kippur.

Dayan, Moshe (1915–81): *Israel military and political leader* Born in a Degania kibbutz [*qv*] near the Sea of Galilee, Dayan joined the Haganah [*qv*] when in his teens. Due to a lack of fluency in English, he discontinued his studies at the London School of Economics in 1935–36 and returned to Palestine [*qv*], where he participated in Haganah operations to counter the Arab Revolt (1936–39). Following a change in the British mandate policy at the start of the Second World War, the authorities suppressed the Haganah and sentenced Dayan to five years' imprisonment. After his release in early 1941, he led a British reconnaissance unit into Syria, then under a pro-Nazi French regime. He was wounded and lost his left eye.

During the Arab-Israeli War I (1948–49) [*qv*], after his battalion had captured Ramle and Lod, Dayan was appointed commander of the Jerusalem [*qv*] area. He became a protégé of Prime Minister David Ben-Gurion [*qv*], who was also defense minister. After serving as head of the southern command (1950) and the northern command (1952), he was promoted to chief of army operations. In 1953 he became chief of staff. His military leadership reached its apogee during the Suez War (October–November 1956) [*qv*], when Israel mounted its lighting Sinai campaign.

After retiring from the military in 1958, Dayan became a Mapai [*qv*] politician. Elected to parliament in 1959, he served as agriculture minister. He resigned in 1964 because of differences with Prime Minister Levi Eshkol [*qv*]. The next year he joined Rafi [*qv*] and was elected to parliament on its list, becoming part of the opposition. On the eve of the 1967 Six-Day War [*qv*], however, Premier Eshkol formed a national unity government, which included Dayan as defense minister.

With most Rafi leaders joining the enlarged Mapai-Ahdut HaAvodah-Poale Zion Aligment [*qv*] to form the Labor Party [*qv*] in 1968, Dayan returned to the political mainstream. He took a hawkish line on the Occupied Arab Territories [*qv*] and used threats to establish a breakaway group of his own to impose his views on his Labor colleagues. In April 1973 he mounted a campaign to annex the West Bank [*qv*], the Golan Heights [*qv*], and parts of the Sinai [*qv*]. He used his office to create Jewish colonies in the Occupied Territories [*qv*].

The surprise Egyptian-Syrian attack on the Israeli-occupied Arab territories in October 1973 shattered the invincible image of Israel and Dayan. Though Dayan recovered from the initial shock, and the Israeli military performed well later, the label of failure stuck to him. In March 1974 the official inquiry on the October 1973 Arab-Israeli War [*qv*] cleared Dayan and blamed the chief of staff, General David Elazer. When Elazer resigned, the pressure on Dayan to do the same mounted. He refused, forcing Premier Golda Meir [*qv*] to submit the resignation of the full cabinet. When Labor lost the May 1977 poll to Likud [*qv*], Dayan crossed the lines and became foreign minister under Premier Menachem Begin [*qv*].

He played an important part in the peace talks with Egypt, which culminated in the Israeli-Egyptian peace treaty [*qv*] in March 1979. Later that year he left the government and established his own group. In the 1981 election it won only two parliamentary seats.

Democratic Front for the Liberation of Palestine: *Palestinian political organization* A breakaway group of the Popular Front for the Liberation of Palestine (PFLP) [*qv*], the Democratic Front for the Liberation of Palestine (DFLP) was formed in 1969 by

Nayif Hawatmeh [*qv*] and Bilal Hassan. By launching guerrilla actions against Israel, it secured an invitation to join the Palestine Armed Struggle Command (PASC) run by the Palestine Liberation Organization (PLO) [*qv*]. Within a year the DFLP's guerrilla force of 1,200 became the fourth largest.

The DFLP stressed that the Palestinian and Jordanian struggles were complementary. Its first open congress, in August 1970 in Amman [*qv*], advocated the overthrow of the Hashemite dynasty and the founding of a democratic regime. But the bitter experience of September 1970—when Palestinian civilians and commandos suffered heavy losses at the hands of the Jordanian army—had a salutary effect on the DFLP.

Following its expulsion from Jordan to Beirut [*qv*], it moderated its criticism of other parties and regional Arab regimes. At the Palestine National Council (PNC) session in June 1974 the DFLP was the prime mover behind the PNC's acceptance of resolution calling for the establishment of a "national authority" in the West Bank [*qv*] and Gaza Strip [*qv*] as the first step toward the liberation of the "whole of Palestine." In Lebanon the DFLP allied with the leftist Lebanese National Movement (LNM) [*qv*] during the Lebanese Civil War [*qv*]. In line with its policy of talking to those Israelis who were either anti-Zionist or simply ready to recognize the Palestinians' right to "an independent national authority" in the West Bank and Gaza Strip, it held talks with the Israeli Socialist Organization [*qv*].

After its expulsion from Beirut in 1982, the DFLP moved its base to Damascus [*qv*]. In the mid-1980s it cooperated with other radical Palestinian groups to frustrate the plan of the PLO chairman, Yasser Arafat [*qv*], and King Hussein [*qv*] of Jordan to enter into secret peace talks with Israel. It strongly opposed the Israeli–PLO accord [*qv*] signed in September 1993, refusing to moderate its stance. As a result, a year later the Palestinian Authority (PA) [*qv*], arrested forty DFLP activists in 1994. It was not until October 1999 that the DFLP made its peace with the PA. This resulted in its name being removed from Washington's list of terrorist organizations. It participated in the al Aqsa Intifada [*qv*] launched by the Palestinians in September 2000. About a year later two DFLP members became the first Palestinians to infiltrate an Israeli military outpost in the Gaza Strip and kill three soldiers.

Democratic Front for Peace and Equality (Israel): *see* Hadash.

dhimmis: *non-Muslims in an Islamic state.* *Dhimmis* are members of *ahl al dhimma* (people of *dhimma*), meaning equality pertaining to the rights or obligations of an individual. In a social context, *dhimma* is a contract between Muslims and members of other religions—Judaism [*qv*] and Christianity [*qv*]—provided the latter accept Islamic rule. *Dhimma* is based on a verse in the Quran [*qv*] (IX, 29): "Fight those who believe not in God and the Last Day . . . until they pay the jizya (*Arabic: tribute*) out of their hand, and have been humbled." The Prophet Muhammad concluded pacts of submission and protection with the Jews of Khaibar and the Christians of Najran. Initially, only Jews and Christians were involved. But when it became necessary to consider Zoroastrians [*qv*], it was decided that by writing down their previously orally transmitted scripture, Avesta, they had attained the status of *ahl al kitab,* people of the Book. The payment of the *jizya* (tribute), which developed into a precise poll tax, gave a definite fiscal status to *dhimmis.* Muslim rulers were prohibited to accept jizya from apostates or from idolators in Arabia. However, they could accept it from idolators in other regions of the world.

diaspora *(Greek: a scattering):* The term "diaspora," meaning dispersion, was originally applied to the scattered colonies of Jews [*qv*] following their exile from Palestine to Babylon in 586 B.C. Later it was applied collectively to all Jews living outside Palestine [*qv*] in the rest of the Old World. With the migration of Europeans to the New World, the Jewish Diaspora extended to that region as well. In that diaspora, the largest number of Jews (5.6 million) are in the United States.

Nowadays, however, the term has acquired a secular meaning and applies to all communities that have been dispersed in recent times: the Armenians [*qv*] after their persecution during the First World War, the Palestinians after the Palestine War (1948–49) [*qv*], etc.

Doha: *capital of Qatar* Pop. 319,000 (2003, est.). A hotbed of piracy, the village of Doha (*Arabic: Bay*) was razed in 1867. It was revived by Shaikh Muhammad ibn Thani the next year under British patronage. After Qatar [*qv*] formally became a British protectorate in 1916, London maintained its political agent in Doha. Its inhabitants made their living by fishing, pearling, and trading. After oil was found in the nearby Dukhan area in 1939, and exploited on a commercial scale after the Second World War, Doha prospered, undergoing dramatic change. Following Qatar's independence in 1971, Doha expanded to the point that in the mid-1980s it accounted for three-fifths of the national population. It is now a modern city with a deepwater harbor.

Dome of the Rock: *see* Noble Sanctuary.

donum: *area measurement used in the Arab Middle East* [*qv*]. 1 donum = 0.26 acre = 0.11 hectare.

Dowlatabadi, Mahmud (1940–): *Iranian writer.* Born in Dowlatabad in the eastern province of Khorasan, in a poor family, Dowlatabadi moved to Tehran [*qv*] in his mid-teens. After completing a course in acting in 1960, he became a stage actor. He published his first short story in the mid-1960s in *Anahita,* named after a preeminent pre-Islamic princess, and graduated to writing novels. In 1974 he began working for the Association for Intellectual Development of Children and Young People. After the Islamic revolution in 1979, he started publishing a series of novels under the title *Kelidar,* a town of Kurdish people, whose day-to-day struggle for survival Dowlatabadi chronicles factually but in such an emotionally charged language that he grips the reader. This ten-volume saga published over a decade established Dowlatabadi as a literary giant of modern Persian literature. His other works include *The Unoccupied Place of Solooch (Persian: Jay-e Khali-e Solooch),* the story of the survival of a village woman and her three children after her abandonment by her husband, and *Yusuf's Day and Night,* an equally riveting work of social realism.

Druze: *Islamic sect* Druzes are members of a movement called Daraziyya, derived from Muhammad al Darazi (d. 1019), an Ismaili [*qv*] missionary from Bukhara, Uzbekistan, who became an adviser to Fatimid Caliph al

Hakim (r. 996–1021) in Cairo in 1017. Accepting the Ismail doctrine, Darazi regarded the *taawil* (inner truth) and its representative, the *imam* [*qv*], superior to the *tanzil* (outer truth) and its representative, the Prophet Muhammad, and attributed the living imam (al Hakim) with supernatural powers, embodying *al aql al kulli* (the highest cosmic intellect). This proved controversial.

After al Darazi's death, this mission was taken over by Hamza ibn Ali, an Iranian. He gave the al Hakim cult a definitive Druze form and described al Hakim as the embodiment of the Ultimate One, the present locus of the Creator. He thus went beyond the Ismaili taawil and the Sunni [*qv*] tanzil.

Druzes do not feel bound by two of the five pillars of Islam [*qv*]: fasting during Ramadan [*qv*] and pilgrimage to Mecca [*qv*]. They accept the seven commandments prescribed by Hamza and his successor, Baha al Din al Muktana: speaking the truth among the faithful; helping and defending one another; renouncing all former faiths; dissociating themselves from unbelievers; recognizing the unity of the Lord in all ages; being content with whatever the Lord does; and submitting to His orders as conveyed by His cosmic ranks. They believe that when al Hakim and Hamza ibn Ali—both of whom disappeared—reappear to establish universal justice, the especially pious among them will rule the human race.

As a heterodox sect, Druzes suffered persecution by the majority Sunni Muslims. This drove them to the mountainous region of Syria-Lebanon-Palestine. They are now to be found in southern Syria's Druze Mountain area, Lebanon's Shouf region, and Israel.

Dual Containment policy (United States): In May 1993 the U.S. administration of President Bill Clinton (r. 1993–2001) declared that in the Gulf [*qv*] it would contain both Iran [*qv*] and Iraq [*qv*], thus reversing the policies of the earlier administrations of Presidents George Bush (r. 1989–93) and Ronald Reagan (r. 1981-89) based on the doctrine of "zero sum" regarding these two Gulf neighbors; that is, weakening Iraq is tantamount to strengthening Iran, and vice versa. Clinton's successor, President George Walker Bush (2001–), would adopt a modified version of the Dual Containment policy under the rubric of the "Axis of evil" by adding North Korea to the list.

Dubai: *city and emirate in the United Arab Emirates.*

Dubai city: *capital of the Dubai Emirate of the United Arab Emirates* Pop. 873,000 (2003, est.). Established in 1799, Dubai became an important pearling center in the early twentieth century. With traders from India and Iran settling there, it developed as a trading port. Its commercial and political significance grew to the extent that London transferred its political agent for the Trucial States [*qv*] from Sharjah [*qv*] to Dubai in 1954. With discovery of offshore oil in 1966, the city's fortunes improved sharply. Its reputation as a center for free trade in gold, much in demand in the Indian subcontinent, also helped its prosperity. Following the independence of the Dubai emirate in 1971, the city became its capital. It acquired a modern port and drydocks in the 1970s. During the Iran-Iraq War (1980–88) [*qv*], the importance of Dubai as a center for reexporting Western goods to

Iran rose dramatically. A cosmopolitan metropolis with excellent financial facilities, Dubai is the largest city of the United Arab Emirates. It is becoming a popular sea resort with European tourists.

Dubai Emirate: Area 1,510 sq. miles/3,900 sq. km; pop. 913,000 (2001, est.); *see* United Arab Emirates.

E

East Bank: The terms East Bank and West Bank [*qv*] apply to the Jordan River [*qv*]. The territory on the East Bank belongs to Jordan [*qv*].

East Jerusalem: Area 2.5 sq. miles/6.5 sq. km in 1948, 28.5 sq. miles/73.7 sq. km in 1967; pop. 242,000 Arabs (2002, est.); 193,000 Jewish settlers (2002 est.). East Jerusalem, captured by the Arab forces in the 1948–49 Arab-Israeli War [*qv*] and retained by Jordan, measured 2.5 sq. miles/6.5 sq. km. It included the Old City, measuring about 0.4 sq. miles/1 sq. km and containing the Noble Sanctuary [*qv*], the Wailing Wall [*qv*] and the Church of the Holy Sepulchre, the burial place of Jesus Christ. It was captured by Israel on 7 June 1967 during the Six-Day War [*qv*]. On 28 June 1967 Israel added 25 sq. miles/65 sq. km of the West Bank [*qv*] territory to (Jordanian) East Jerusalem and extended its laws to the vastly enlarged area, a step repudiated by U.N. Security Council Resolution 252 (1968).

Thirteen years later the Israeli parliament passed a "basic law," which declared unified Jerusalem to be the indivisible capital of Israel. This was repudiated in U.N. Security Council Revolutions 476 (March 1980) and 478 (June 1980) by fourteen votes to none. Though the Arab residents of East Jerusalem were given the right to vote in local elections, no more than 5 percent exercised this right, thus emphasizing their commitment to having East Jerusalem as the capital of a future State of Palestine. By 1997 Israel had established twelve Jewish settlements in East Jerusalem. Of its estimated population of 425,000 in 2002, some 242,000 were Arab and 193,000 Jews. *See also* Jerusalem and West Jerusalem.

East Syriac rite: *see* Chaldean Catholic Church.

Easter: Derivative of *Eastre,* an ancient Teutonic goddess. An annual church celebration commemorating Christ's resurrection on the third day after his crucifixion, for Roman Catholics [*qv*] and Protestants [*qv*] (Western). Easter is the first Sunday after the full moon that falls on, or follows, the spring equinox (21 March in the Gregorian Christian calendar [*qv*]). If the full moon happens on a Sunday, Easter is celebrated a week later. Thus Easter Sunday falls between 22 March and 25 April. Due to the somewhat different calculations of the Orthodox Church [*qv*], the Orthodox Easter often comes one, four, or five weeks later, but sometimes it coincides with the Western Easter. In both cases, Easter determines the dates of all other movable church festivals, such as Lent and Pentecost [*qv*].

Eastern (Orthodox) Church: *see* Orthodox Christian Church.

Eban, Abba/Aubrey (1915–2001): *Israeli politician* Born Aubrey Solomon of a merchant family in Cape Town, South Africa, Eban was a baby when the family moved to

London, where his father died soon after. Some years later his mother married Isaac Eban. After gaining a degree in classics and oriental languages from Cambridge University in Britain, he worked as a research fellow. During the Second World War, he served with British military intelligence in Cairo [*qv*] and Jerusalem [*qv*] and was promoted to major. After the war, he joined the political department of the Jewish Agency [*qv*] and advised the Jewish Agency delegates to the special United Nations General Assembly to discuss Palestine [*qv*]. Following Israel's admission to the world body in 1949, Eban became head of the Israeli delegation to the United Nations. The next year he was also appointed ambassador to the United States. A skilled diplomat, he served in both positions until 1959.

On his return to Israel, he was elected to parliament as a Mapai [*qv*] candidate and retained his seat until 1988. He joined the government as minister without portfolio, then became minister of education and culture in 1960. Three years later he was promoted to the post of deputy premier by Prime Minister Levi Eshkol [*qv*]. In 1966 he became foreign minister, a job he kept for eight years. After the June 1967 Arab-Israeli War [*qv*], he actively participated in the drafting of the crucial U.N. Security Council Resolution 242 [*qv*]. When Yitzhak Rabin [*qv*] became prime minister in 1974, Eban failed to secure a seat in the cabinet. After the 1984 general election, he served as chairman of the Knesset [*qv*] committee on foreign affairs and defense for four years.

Egypt:
Official name: Arab Republic of Egypt
Capital: Cairo [*qv*]

Area: 385,230 sq. miles/997,740 sq. km
Population: 63,984,000 (2000, est.)
Gross domestic product: $96.2 billion (2000, est.)
National currency: Egyptian Pound (LE); LE 1 = US$0.26 = £0.18 = EUR 0.29 (2001)
Form of government: Republic, president elected by parliament, confirmed by voters
Official language: Arabic [*qv*]
Official religion: Islam [*qv*]
Administrative regions: Egypt is divided into twenty-six governorates (provinces).
Constitution: The 1971 constitution, approved by a referendum, was amended in 1990. It describes Egypt as an Arab republic with a democratic, socialist system. It prescribes Islam as the state religion and the Sharia [*qv*] as the "principal source" of legislation. It labels the political system as multiparty. The state ensures equality of men and women in accordance with the Sharia. It also safeguards the public sector and protects the assets of cooperative societies and trade unions. The constitution bans the propagation of atheism and any attack on "divine religion." It guarantees the right to peaceful assembly, freedom of the press, and freedom to travel.

The sole presidential candidate, who must be endorsed by at least two-thirds of parliamentary deputies, is offered to the voters for approval. He has a six-year tenure and can be elected for other terms. He exercises executive authority and appoints or dismisses vice presidents and ministers, including the premier. He also nominates ten members to the parliament, called the National Assembly. The Assembly, with at least 350 elected members, is elected for five years. It has the power to force a minister to resign. In the case of the prime minister, the Assembly has the right to submit an adversarial report to the president. Should the latter reject the report, the matter is put to a referendum. If the voters accept the report, the full cabinet must resign. If the voters reject it, then the president must dissolve the Assembly.

Consultative Council: Following amendments to the 1971 constitution in May 1980, a 210-member Consultative Council with a three-year term was established to preserve the principles of the 1952 republican revolution and the 1971 "correctionist" revolution by President Anwar Sadat [qv]. One-third of its members are appointed by the president. Since the first three elections were boycotted by the opposition, the ruling National Democratic Party [qv] filled all the elected seats. The opposition participated in the 1989 poll, but failed to win a single seat. In the 1995 election, the NDP won eighty-eight of the ninety contested seats, and the mid-term 1998 election, eighty-seven seats out of ninety, followed by seventy-four of the eighty-eight contested seats in 2001, with most opposition factions continuing their boycott.

Ethnic composition (2002): Arabs, 99.0 percent; others, 1.0 percent

Executive authority: Executive authority rests with the president, who is elected by the National Assembly and endorsed by voters.

High officials:

President: Hosni Mubarak, 1999–
Prime minister: Atif Obeid, 2000–
Speaker of the National Assembly: Ahmad Fathi Surur, 2000–

Speaker of the Consultative Council: Ali Mustafa Kamal Helmi, 2001–

History: On the eve of the First World War, London declared Egypt (which had been under British occupation since 1882) a protectorate. In 1922, although it now recognized Egypt as a sovereign state under King Ahmad Fuad (r. 1922–36), Britain continued to maintain its military occupation. The anti-imperialist movement, spearheaded by the Wafd [qv], gained momentum and resulted in the Anglo-Egyptian Treaty of 1936 [qv]. The treaty preserved many British privileges, including its military presence in the Suez Canal [qv] zone.

The poor performance of the Egyptian troops in the Palestine War (1948–49) [qv] encouraged nationalist officers to plan a coup. In 1952, organized as Free Officers, they seized power after overthrowing King Faruq [qv]. The new Revolutionary Command Council (RCC) was dominated by Gamal Abdul Nasser [qv]. It started a program of land reform and industrialization at home and advancement of pan Arabism [qv] in the region. Egypt combined with Syria in early 1958 to form the United Arab Republic [qv], but the UAR split in September 1961 in bitterness. Egypt helped the republican officers in North Yemen to consolidate their regime after a coup there in 1962. But its humiliating defeat by Israel in the 1967 Six-Day War [qv], resulting in the loss of Sinai [qv], undermined the leadership of Nasser.

After Nasser's death in 1970, the presidency passed to Anwar Sadat. In conjunction with Syria, he launched a surprise attack on the Israeli-occupied Sinai in October 1973. The Egyptians gave their best military performance yet. Sadat cut the twenty-year-old ties with the Soviet Union and turned to the United States for a compromise with Israel. His efforts culminated in an Egyptian-Israeli peace treaty [*qv*] in March 1979. To curb domestic opposition to the treaty, Sadat took increasingly repressive measures, thus losing popularity. He was assassinated in October 1981.

Sadat's successor, Hosni Mubarak [*qv*], tried to heal the wounds, and succeeded. During his presidency Egypt was readmitted to the Arab League in 1989, after a decade of isolation. He continued the economic liberalization of Sadat. Equally, there was no change from his predecessor's practice of periodic, rigged elections. Mubarak was reelected to the presidency for the second time in October 1993. He faced increasing opposition from militant Muslim [*qv*] groups, especially al Gammat al Islamiya [*qv*]. By the time he was renominated by the National Assembly for the presidency in 1999, his government had suppressed Islamic militancy by using unprecedented methods that caused concern in the U.S. administration of President Bill Clinton (r. 1993–2001). Following the Islamist terrorist attacks on New York and Washington in September 2001, however, American perceptions at the official level changed. While offering full cooperation to the United States in its war against Islamist terrorism, Mubarak advised U.S. President George W. Bush (r. 2001–) to address the Israeli-Palestinian conflict impartially and help forge an international convention on terrorism, but to no avail.

Legislature: The parliament, called the National Assembly, deals with legislation, general policy matters, and the budget. Of its 454 members, 444 are elected, the rest are appointed by the president. The main opposition parties boycotted the poll in November–December 1990, demanding the lifting of the state of emergency and supervision of the election by an independent body, not the interior ministry. Five years later, the NDP won 316 seats; independents, 115 (of whom 72 joined the NDP); and four opposition groups, 13. In the 2000 elections—when the polling stations were supervised by judges, and not interior ministry officials—the NDP secured 170 seats; independents, 234 (of whom 194 joined the NDP); and six opposition parties together, 39.

Religious composition (2002): Muslim, 94 percent; Christian [*qv*], 6 percent. Almost all Muslims are Sunni [*qv*]. Four out of five Christians are Copts [*qv*].

Egyptian-Israeli Peace Treaty (1979): The Egyptian-Israeli Peace Treaty, signed in March 1979, ended the state of war that had existed between the two countries since the founding of Israel in May 1948. It was based on the principles and procedures outlined in the Camp David Accords [*qv*] of September 1978. Within a year of the treaty, the signatories had exchanged ambassadors and Israel had returned two-thirds of occupied Sinai [*qv*] to Egypt. By April 1982 Israel had withdrawn from the rest of the peninsula. Arab League [*qv*] members denounced Egypt's deviation from the common Arab policy of working toward a comprehensive peace settlement with Israel, suspended it from the League and broke all relations with Cairo. Egypt's suspension from the Arab League lasted until 1989. Despite periodic tension between Israel and Egypt—such as during the Israeli invasion and occupation of Lebanon in June 1982 [*qv*] and the al Aqsa Intifada [*qv*] of 2000—the treaty has held.

Egyptian-Soviet Friendship Treaty (1971): The Egyptian-Soviet Friendship Treaty, valid for fifteen years, was negotiated in Cairo [*qv*] by Egyptian President Anwar Sadat [*qv*] and signed on 27 May 1971. According to the operative Articles 7 and 8, the signatories agreed to enter into immediate consultation in the event of any threat to peace, and to continue cooperation in developing Egypt's military potential. However, the existence of the treaty did not inhibit Sadat from expelling Soviet military personnel in July 1972. Whatever tensions this act of Sadat created, they subsided quickly. Before, during, and after the October 1973 Arab-Israeli War [*qv*], the Soviets supplied Egypt with massive cargoes of arms and ammunition. In 1975 Sadat, burdened with heavy foreign debt and rising budget deficit, approached Soviet leaders for a ten-year moratorium on debt repayments. They rejected his request. In return, Sadat refused to renew the annual trade pact. On 14 March 1976 he unilaterally abrogated the friendship treaty ten years before its expiration date.

Eid al Adha (*Arabic: Festival of Sacrifice): Islamic festival* One of the two canonical festivals, Eid al Adha is also known as Eid al Qurban (*Persian: Sacrifice*) or Eid al Kabir (the Major Festival). It falls on 10 Dhul Hijja, the last month of the Islamic calendar [*qv*], when the *hajj* [*qv*] is undertaken by the faithful. Completion of the hajj is celebrated by sacrificing a sheep, a camel, or a bovine animal. Even those Muslims who are not on hajj are required to sacrifice an animal. They are also required to participate in communal prayers. The faithful wear their best clothes, visit friends and relatives, and exchange presents.

Eid al Fitr (*Arabic: the festival of breaking the fast): Islamic festival* One of the two canonical festivals, Eid al Fitr is also called Eid al Saghir, the Minor Festival. It falls on 1 Shawaal, which follows Ramadan [*qv*], the month of fasting. Muslims are required to participate in communal prayers and to pay their *zakat* [*qv*] before the prayers. The faithful wear their best clothes, visit friends and relatives, and exchange presents. Since Eid al Fitr comes at the end of a month of fasting, it is a joyous occasion.

Eisenhower Doctrine (1957): Following the strengthening of ties between Egypt and the Soviet Union in late 1956, U.S. President Dwight Eisenhower sent a message on 5 January 1957 to U.S. Congress outlining a countervailing strategy for the Middle East, later to be called the Eisenhower Doctrine. It proposed joint measures by the U.S. Congress and the president to accelerate economic development of the region to help it maintain political independence; to provide military aid and cooperation on request; and, most importantly, to safeguard the territorial integrity and political independence of individual countries requesting such aid against overt aggression from any nation "controlled by international Communism" (a phrase that included Egypt under President Gamal Abdul Nasser [*qv*], who was seen by Washington as being under Soviet control). In March 1957 the U.S. Congress adopted the Eisenhower Doctrine.

el *(Arabic: the): see* al.

Epiphany *(Greek: from epiphania, manifestation): Christian festival* Also called the Twelfth Day, Little Christmas, and the Manifestation of Jesus Christ to the Gentiles, Epiphany is celebrated on 6 January, twelve days after Christmas, to commemorate the baptism of Jesus in the River Jordan [*qv*], the showing of Jesus to the Three Wise Men, and the Miracle of Cana. It ranks after Easter [*qv*] and Pentecost [*qv*].

Erbil: *see* Irbil.

Eretz Yisrael *(Hebrew: Land of Israel):* The term Eretz Yisrael is used to denote the Hebrew kingdom under David (r. 1010–970 B.C.) and Solomon (r. 970–930 B.C.). It measured about 17,500 sq. mi/45,320 sq. km, half the area lying to the east of River Jordan [*qv*]. To the west it was bounded by the Mediterranean; to the east by the Syrian desert; and to the south by the line connecting the Valley of Arish with Kadesh Barnea and the Valley of Zor south of the Dead Sea, and then running from River Arnon to Mount Hermon to the Valley of Iyon. In ca. 930 B.C. the Hebrew kingdom was split into the northern territory, called Israel, and the southern, called Judah.

Esfahan: *see* Isfahan.

Eshkol, Levi (1895–1969): *Israeli politician; prime minister 1963–69* Born Levi Shkolnik in Ukraine, Eshkol migrated to Palestine [*qv*] in 1914 and worked as a farmhand. Active with HaPoale HaTzair [*qv*], he cofounded Degania Beth kibbutz in 1920. Later he participated [*qv*] in establishing the housing company of the Histadrut [*qv*]. From 1934–37 he worked in the Palestine Office in Berlin to supervise the transfer of goods bought with money donated by German-Jewish immigrants in Palestine. On his return home he directed the Histadrut's Mekorot Water Company. In 1940 he took charge of the finances of the Haganah [*qv*], including arms procurement. During the Arab-Israeli War (1948–49) [*qv*], he became director-general of the defense ministry under David Ben-Gurion [*qv*], focusing on the war's economic and financial aspects.

Elected to the Jewish Agency [*qv*] executive in 1948, Eshkol supervised the settlement of immigrants and encouraged the founding of cooperative villages, *moshavim.* In 1951 he was elected to parliament on the Mapai [*qv*] list, and kept his seat until his demise. After a year as minister of agriculture and development, he served as finance minister, a position he retained until he succeeded Ben-Gurion as prime minister and defense minister in 1963. He liberalized the economy, and detached the broadcasting department from the prime minister's secretariat, transforming it into an independent authority. He removed the travel limitations that had been imposed on Israel's Arab [*qv*] citizens since 1948.

By sponsoring a cabinet decision to bring the remains of Vladimir Jabotinsky [*qv*] from New York to Israel for reburial in Jerusalem [*qv*], Eshkol lowered tensions between the government and right-wing opposition. Eshkol reinforced arms purchase agreements with the United States, thus strengthening the Israeli military. He withstood the challenge posed by the defection of Ben-Gurion, who founded his own group, Rafi [*qv*], in 1965, and headed the government formed after the general election later that year.

On the eve of the 1967 Six-Day War [*qv*],

Eshkol came under increased public pressure to broaden his administration. He set up a government of national unity and gave up the defense ministry to Moshe Dayan [*qv*]. By co-opting the right-wing Gahal [*qv*] and its leader, Menachem Begin [*qv*], into the government, Eshkol gave that party the respectability denied to it by Ben-Gurion. Ignoring his critics' charges of vacillation, he governed by consensus until his death.

Euphrates River: Known in biblical times as Perath, the Euphrates River rises in eastern Turkey and flows roughly 1,680 miles/2,700 km to Iraq, there joining the Tigris River [*qv*], about 120 miles/260 km from the Persian Gulf [*qv*], to form the Shatt al Arab [*qv*]. It provides irrigation for the fertile plain of Mesopotamia [*qv*], a cradle of ancient civilization.

F

Fahd ibn Abdul Aziz al Saud (1921–): *King of Saudi Arabia, 1982–* Born in Riyadh [*qv*] to Ibn Saud [*qv*] and Hassa bint Ahmad al Sudairi, Fahd was the eleventh son of Ibn Saud. He received a traditional education. During the rule of Saud ibn Abdul Aziz [*qv*], Fahd served first as education minister (1953–60) and then, from 1962, as interior minister. He continued in that position when Faisal ibn Abdul Aziz [*qv*] ascended the throne in 1964. Fahd was promoted to second deputy prime minister in 1967, and to first deputy prime minister two years later. When Khalid ibn Abdul Aziz [*qv*] became king in 1975, Fahd was named crown prince. On Khalid's death in June 1982, Fahd succeeded him. Eldest of the seven sons of Hassa bint Ahmad al Sudairi, his accession implied the dominance of the Sudairi Seven in the kingdom.

Of the two trends that had emerged among senior Saudi princes during Khalid's reign, Fahd belonged to the pro-American school, favoring rapid economic progress funded by Saudi Arabia's vast oil revenues, and opposed the nationalist trend, which was committed to a greater respect for tradition and slower economic development. In August 1981 he presented to the Arab League [*qv*] a Middle East peace plan that, in exchange for peaceful coexistence of all the states in the region, required Israeli to evacuate all the Arab territories occupied in 1967, the dismantling of the Jewish settlements in these areas, and the founding of a Palestinian state. It was adopted at the next summit in Fez, Morocco, in September 1982 and remained the common Arab position on a Middle East settlement until the Middle East conference in Madrid, Spain, nine years later. In 1986 he changed his title from "His Majesty" to the "Custodian of the Holy Mosques (of Mecca [*qv*] and Medina [*qv*])."

In keeping with his vacillating manner, Fahd waited a whole week before making public his position on Iraq's invasion of Kuwait on 2 August 1990. He called on the United States and Arab countries to send troops to help protect Saudi Arabia and end the Iraqi occupation of Kuwait. The huge expenses incurred by Riyadh in the conduct of the Second Gulf War [*qv*], the rearming of the kingdom that followed the conflict, and the sharply reduced prices of oil led Fahd's government to raise foreign loans to balance the budget.

Rising corruption and repression led to the growth of the Islamic fundamentalist movement, which drew its inspiration from the early days of the Ikhwan movement [*qv*], which had laid the foundation of the kingdom in the mid-1920s.

In August 1993 he appointed a fully nominated sixty-member Consultative Council. Having made some concessions in the political and religious spheres, Fahd moved to repress further the dissident Islamic *ulama* at home and block financial assistance to Islamist militants abroad. Abroad, he tightened ties with Washington still further, while the latter's dependence on Saudi petroleum grew. A quarter of America's oil imports now originated in Saudi Arabia, which had purchased $25 billion worth of U.S. arms between August 1990 and December 1992—by which date a less formalized defense agreement between Riyadh and Washington was reportedly in place.

To silence opposition, Fahd detained 200 political dissidents in 1994. He was distressed when a bomb at the National Guard training center in Riyadh in November 1995 killed seven people, including five American officers. That month, following a stroke, Fahd passed on his powers to Crown Prince Abdullah. Though, on recovery, Faisal nominally retrieved these powers three months later, there was less of his imprint on the administration during the subsequent years as Abdullah became the de facto ruler.

One of the richest men in the world, in the mid-1990s Fahd's personal wealth was estimated to be around $20 billion.

Faisal ibn Abdul Aziz al Saud (1904–75): *King of Saudi Arabia, 1964–75* Born in Riyadh to Ibn Saud [*qv*] and Tarfa bint Abdullah al Shaikh, Faisal was the fourth son of Ibn Saud and the second among those who survived. After receiving a traditional education and military training, Faisal served his father as governor of Hijaz [*qv*] from 1926. He undertook several foreign missions, including an official visit to the Soviet Union in 1934. During that year he led a successful campaign against North Yemen. Over time, Faisal emerged as foreign minister—inter alia leading Saudi delegations to the United Nations—without bearing such a title: autocratic Ibn Saud did not rule with the assistance of a formally appointed cabinet.

When Saud ibn Abdul Aziz [*qv*] became king in 1953, he nominated a cabinet as an advisory body, with Faisal as deputy prime minister and foreign minister. Faisal was also named crown prince. When, hit by an economic crisis and lacking any budget, the kingdom's administration came to a halt in 1958, the king put Faisal in charge of all state affairs, promoting him to prime minister, a position Saud had held so far. Two years later King Saud reappointed himself prime minister but did not interfere with the fiscal policies of Faisal, who cut expenditure, introduced a budget, and paid off state debts. Following the republican coup in North Yemen in September 1962, King Saud once again promoted Faisal to prime minister. To offset the threat to the future of the Saudi monarchy, Faisal promised constitutional, religious, judicial, social, and economic reforms—including the promulgation of a written constitution, specifying a consultative council. But he was unable to deliver, because King Saud refused to give up any of his powers. The resulting crisis was resolved in November 1964 when, pressured by senior princes and clergy, King Saud abdicated. Faisal ascended the throne. A pious Muslim, and son of a mother who came from the religious House of Shaikh, Faisal had the respect of the Islamic establishment.

He suppressed the opposition harshly. He increased support to the royalist camp in the North Yemeni Civil War [qv], in which the republicans were being aided by Egyptian President Gamal Abdul Nasser [qv]. But following the Arab defeat in the 1967 Six-Day War [qv], Faisal buried his differences with Nasser. Faisal's efforts to establish a transnational organization of Muslim states succeeded in 1969, in the wake of an arson attempt on the al Aqsa mosque, Jerusalem [qv], resulting in the formation of the Islamic Conference Organization [qv], based in Jiddah [qv]. On 25 March 1975 Faisal was assassinated by a young nephew, Prince Faisal ibn Musaid.

Faisal I ibn Hussein al Hashem (1885–1933): *King of Iraq, 1921–33* Third son of Hussein ibn Ali al Hashem [qv], Faisal was born in Taif, Hijaz [qv], but was raised in Istanbul, where his father was kept under surveillance by the Ottoman sultan. In 1908 Faisal returned to Hijaz along with his father, who was appointed governor of Mecca [qv] by the Young Turks after they had succeeded the sultan. Faisal worked closely with his father, traveling to Damascus [qv] in 1915 (during the First World War) to secure support for him from secret Arab nationalist groups there. The next year Hussein led an Arab revolt in Hijaz against the Ottomans. As commander of the northern force, Faisal focused on harassing the Turkish troops and marched into Transjordan [qv] in 1917 along with the victorious British. Entering Damascus [qv] in October 1918, Faisal established an Arab government under the aegis of the Allied military administration.

At the Paris Peace Conference, he staked the claim of his al Hashem family as the ruler of either an independent Arab kingdom or a federation of several emirates (principalities). France, which in 1916 had entered into a secret agreement with Britain called the Sykes–Picot Pact [qv], opposed Faisal's demands and insisted on keeping Syria under its control. An Arab national congress in Damascus in March 1920 declared Faisal king of (Greater) Syria [qv], composed of present-day Syria, Lebanon, Israel, Palestine [qv], and Jordan. The next month, at the behest of the Allies, the League of Nations' Supreme Council handed France a mandate to administer Syria. In July there was a fight between the forces of France and Faisal, which the latter lost.

Forced into exile, Faisal accepted Britain's invitation to go to London. To overcome nationalist opposition to its mandate in Iraq, Britain offered to make Faisal king of Iraq in March 1921. He accepted and was crowned in August. Caught between rising Iraqi nationalism and British suzerainty, Faisal pursued a middle course. By ratifying a constitution drafted by an assembly and holding parliamentary elections, he legitimized his regime. In 1930 he signed a treaty with Britain: it required him to coordinate his foreign policy with London, and to allow the stationing of British troops in Iraq in exchange for a British guarantee to protect Iraq against foreign attack. Britain ended its mandate in October 1932 and sponsored Iraq's membership of the League of Nations.

Faisal II ibn Ghazi al Hashem (1935–58): *King of Iraq, 1939–58* The only son of King Ghazi ibn Faisal I al Hashem [*qv*], Faisal as an infant succeeded his father under the regency of his uncle Abdul Ilah ibn Ali [*qv*]. Following the 1941 coup by the nationalist Rashid Ali Gailani [*qv*], Faisal and his mother fled, along with Abdul Ilah and other members of the royal family. Gailani was defeated, and that ensured the future of Faisal as king. Following the Second World War, Faisal was sent to Britain to be educated. On achieving his majority in 1953 he began to exercise royal authority, but found himself hamstrung by the powerful presence of Abdul Ilah. After the formation of the Arab Federation of Iraq and Jordan in February 1958, Faisal became its head. Five months later he was gunned down in the royal courtyard during a coup mounted by republican officers.

faqih: *Islamic jurisprudent* One who practices *fiqh* [*qv*] (*Arabic: knowledge*), the term for jurisprudence, the science of religious law in Islam [*qv*].

Faruq (1920–65): *King of Egypt, 1936–52* The only son of King Ahmad Fuad, Faruq received his education in Egypt and Britain. He succeeded his father in April 1936, but did not exercise royal authority until he became eighteen in February 1938. He pursued his father's policy of undermining the nationalist Wafd [*qv*].

Following the outbreak of the Second World War, he attempted to remain neutral, even though British troops were stationed in Egypt under the Anglo-Egyptian Treaty of 1936 [*qv*]. Italy's entry into the conflict on the German side in May 1940 complicated matters since Faruq had many close Italian friends and advisers. In February 1942, while German troops were advancing on Egypt from Libya, and Faruq was considering appointing a prime minister known to share widely prevalent anti-British views, the British ambassador in Cairo [*qv*] ordered tanks to surround his palace and gave him the choice of abdicating or appointing Mustafa Nahas (Pasha) [*qv*], a pro-British Wafd leader, prime minister. Faruq chose the latter.

While this secured the Allied position in Egypt for the rest of the war, it destroyed Faruq's prestige among his subjects. He tried to retrieve it by dismissing Nahas Pasha in October 1944. His standing suffered a further setback when the Egyptian army did badly in the Palestine War (1948–49) [*qv*] due to the incompetence and corruption of its senior officers, the obsolescence of its British-supplied arms, and erratic supplies of food and medicine.

To restore the nation's wounded pride, Faruq made peace with Wafd leaders and held a general election in 1950, which returned the Wafd to power. The next year, after abrogating the Anglo-Egyptian Treaty of 1936, the Wafd government declared Faruq King of Egypt and Sudan. He was deposed in July 1952 by the Free Officers, led by Gen. Muhammad Neguib [*qv*] and Col. Gamal Abdul Nasser [*qv*]. He and his family were allowed to leave for Italy, where he continued to maintain a luxurious lifestyle until his death thirteen years later.

Farsi language: *see* Persian language.

Fatah (*Arabic: Victory; reverse acronymn of* Harkat al Tahrir al Falastini, *Movement for the Liberation of Palestine*): Fatah was founded in 1958 by Yasser Arafat [*qv*], Salah Khalaf [*qv*], and Khalil Wazir [*qv*] in Kuwait.

They set up secret party cells in Kuwait and the Palestinian refugee camps in Jordan, Syria, and Lebanon, a process accelerated by the publication of a monthly magazine, *Falastinuna* (Our Palestine [*qv*]), in Beirut [*qv*] in 1959. By then the basic theory of Fatah ideology and tactics was that revolutionary violence, practiced by the masses, was the only way to liberate Palestine [*qv*] and liquidate all forms of Zionism [*qv*].

Fatah remained underground until 1964, when the Arab League [*qv*] established the Palestine Liberation Organization [*qv*] under the leadership of Ahmad Shuqairi [*qv*]. Of the radical Arab states then, only Algeria volunteered in 1963 to provide military training facilities to Fatah. In 1964, in Baathist-run Damascus [*qv*], Fatah leaders decided on guerrilla actions against Israel from Syria. The first such act, on 1 January 1965, was aimed at blowing up the pipes of Israel's National Water Carrier at Ain Bone on the west bank of Jordan River [*qv*]. Fatah then had about 200 members.

The loss of the West Bank [*qv*] and Gaza Strip [*qv*] to Israel in the June 1967 Arab-Israeli War [*qv*] weakened Shuqairi's position in the PLO, whose Palestine National Council [*qv*] had been boycotted by Fatah and other armed groups. Egyptian President Gamal Abdul Nasser [*qv*] met Fatah's chairman, Arafat, and promised to aid Fatah. In March 1968 Fatah members engaged in a much-publicized battle with Israel near the Jordanian border settlement of Karameh. This raised Fatah membership to 15,000.

By now Fatah's overall objective had emerged as the establishment of a democratic, secular state in all of (British) mandate Palestine with equal rights to Jews [*qv*], Muslims [*qv*], and Christians [*qv*]. In July 1968 Fatah and other armed groups attended the PNC session in Cairo, which rejected U.N. Security Council Resolution 242 [*qv*] mainly because it made no mention of Palestinians. Fatah emerged as the PLO's largest constituent. In early 1969 the PNC elected Arafat chairman of the PLO's executive committee, which included three more Fatah leaders. In 1970 Fatah, based in Amman [*qv*], claimed membership of some 40,000, with half of them active in its militia, *al Assifa* (the Storm). The party leadership was evenly divided between right and left, with Arafat often acting as a mediator between Salah Khalaf and Faruq Qaddumi on the left, and Khalid Hassan and Khalil Wazir on the right. But Fatah's involvement, along with other mainly leftist forces, in the Palestinian conflict with the Jordanian army in September 1970 moved it leftward. This changed after Fatah's expulsion from Jordan and its new base in Beirut [*qv*] in 1972.

Prodded by the Democratic Front for the Liberation of Palestine [*qv*], in June 1974 Fatah accepted the idea of a transition stage for achieving the liberation of mandate Palestine with an independent entity in the West Bank and Gaza Strip [*qv*]. In the Lebanese Civil War [*qv*], which started in 1975, Fatah, along with other Palestinian commando groups, sided with the leftist Lebanese National Movement [*qv*] to fight the right-wing Lebanese Forces [*qv*]. Its opposition to the Camp David Accords [*qv*] in 1978 led Fatah to adopt a radical stance, with its fourth congress in Damascus [*qv*] in May 1980 resolving to "liberate Palestine completely."

Following the Israeli invasion of Lebanon [*qv*] in June 1982, Fatah was expelled from

Beirut. From its new headquarters in Tunis, Arafat tried to reestablish a base in Lebanon, but failed. In the mid-1980s Fatah's policy of coordinating with King Hussein of Jordan [qv] with regard to peace talks with Israel failed to take off. In 1988 the Fatah leadership decided to disavow violence against Israel and backed moves for the declaration of the State of Palestine, with Arafat as its president. Having failed to build on this moderated policy, the party leaders backed Iraqi President Saddam Hussein [qv] when, having occupied Kuwait in August 1990, he tried to link Israeli evacuation of the West Bank and Gaza Strip to his evacuation of Kuwait, but in vain. They were divided on the Oslo Accord [qv] of September 1993, with Qaddumi opposing it. In the end, Fatah accepted the Accord. It became the political backbone of the Palestinian Authority [qv]. In the elections to the Palestinian Legislative Council in 1996, Fatah won fifty-five of the eighty-six contested seats, with seven other members describing themselves as Fatah Independents. Following the eruption of the al Aqsa Intifada [qv] in September 2000, it set up an armed wing in the West Bank and Gaza Strip, called *Tanzim* (lit., Organization), which resorted to suicide bombings against Israelis.

Fatah: *The Revolutionary Council; see* Abu Nidal.

Fedai Khalq *(Persian: Popular Self-sacrificers):* *Iranian political party* Official name: *Sazman-e Cherakha-ye Fedai Khalq-e Iraq* (Organization of Iranian People's Self-Sacrificing Guerrillas). Fedai Khaliq was formed in 1970 by the amalgamation of two leftist groups established in 1963 by university students inspired by the victorious revolutionary movements led by Fidel Castro in Cuba and Vo Nguyen Giap in Vietnam. Believing in the "Propaganda by the Deed" doctrine of Ernesto "Che" Guevara, a Latin American revolutionary, the party hoped that repression by the pro-Western monarchical regime in the wake of guerrilla attacks on selected targets would lead to increased resistance by the masses, which would culminate in a people's revolution.

Its first attack on a gendarmerie post in the littoral fringes of the Caspian forest in early 1971 received much publicity. This won the party hundreds of young recruits, mostly from middle-class families. The party cadres, often trained by the Popular Front for the Liberation of Palestine [qv] in the Palestinian camps of Lebanon, attacked police stations and banks as well as police and Savak (secret police) informers. During the next five years some 10,000 Fedai Khaliq members, actual or suspected, were jailed, and about 180 activists were killed. But the anticipated people's revolution failed to materialize. The party split into two factions, with the moderates focusing on political activity among industrial workers. When Savak became overstretched in the autumn of 1977, the Fedai Khalq revived its guerrilla activity and its supporters participated in anti-regime demonstrations.

After the revolution in early 1979, the party's demand for a share of power was rejected by Ayatollah Ruhollah Khomeini [qv] and it went into opposition. As government pressure mounted, hundreds of party activists left for the Kurdish region to join the Kurdish guerrilla movement there. The party split in June 1980 into "majority" and "minority" factions. Fedai Khalq (majority) advocated cooperation with the Islamic regime and allied with the Tudeh Party [*qv*], which followed a similar policy. It was allowed to function openly while the government battled with the Mujahedin-e Khalq [*qv*]. But in May 1983, after the Mujahedin-e Khalq had been crushed, the authorities turned against Fedai Khalq (majority). The party, which continued to exist secretly, suffered a setback when one of its safe houses in Tehran [*qv*] was discovered by police in 1989. Following the collapse of the Soviet bloc in 1989–91, party members, many of them living abroad, began to drift toward the adoption of secular social democracy as their objective.

Fedai Khalq (minority) opposed the Islamic regime and sided with Abol Hassan Bani-Sadr [*qv*] in his confrontation with Khomeini in June 1981, but was repressed. It was formally dissolved in 1987.

Fedaiyan-e Islam (*Persian: Self-sacrificers of Islam): Iranian religious-political group* Formed in 1945 by a young theological student, Nawab Safavi (alias Mujtaba Mirlohi), Fedaiyan-e Islam went beyond the customary Islamic call for the application of the Sharia [*qv*], as provided by the Iranian constitution of 1906–07, and demanded a ban on tobacco, alcohol, cinema, opium, gambling, and the wearing of foreign attire. It advocated the veil for women. It also demanded comprehensive land reform, the nationalization of industry, and various social welfare measures. It drew its following chiefly from the lower sections of the trading community—porters, shop assistants, hawkers, peddlers.

The group used assassination as a political weapon. In 1948 it assassinated Ahmad Kasravi, a leading secularist lawyer and historian, and Abdul Hussein Hazhir, a court minister who was considered pro-British and pro-Bahai [*qv*]. This was followed in March 1951 by the assassination of General Ali Razmara, a pro-British prime minister. When two months later Muhammad Mussadiq [*qv*] refused to share power with the party, it turned against him, and its activists tried to assassinate one of his aides, Hussein Fatimi. Even after the August 1953 coup against Mussadiq, the party did not moderate its antigovernment stance. It also condemned the oil agreement that Muhammad Reza Shah Pahlavi [*qv*] signed with the Western consortium in August 1954.

In November 1955 a Fedaiyan member tried unsuccessfully to kill Premier Hussein Ala, and the authorities mounted an all-out assault on the party. Four top leaders, including Safavi, were executed. Following the release of party members during the shah's last days in 1978, Fedaiyan-e Islam was revived by Sadiq Khalkhali, a prominent cleric in Qom [*qv*], as a shadowy organization. The assassination of Mustafa Shafiq, a nephew of the shah, in Paris in December 1979 was widely attributed to Fedaiyan-e Islam.

feddan: *area measurement used in the Arab Middle East* 1 feddan = 4 donums [*qv*] = 1.038 acres.

Fertile Crescent: *Crescent-shaped area between the Anatolian Mountains and the Arabian Desert* The Fertile Crescent covers ancient Elam (southwestern Iran), Mesopotamia [*qv*] (Iraq), Assyria (Syria), Phoenicia (Lebanon), and Palestine [*qv*] (Israel and the Palestinian territories [*qv*]). Sometimes the Nile valley of Egypt is included to emphasize the crescent shape. The cradle of ancient civilization, with irrigated agriculture going back to ca. 8000 B.C., it is the region that provided the base for the Greek and Roman civilizations.

fiqh: *Islamic jurisprudence. Fiqh* includes all aspects of religious, social, and political life—covering not only ritual and religious observances, the law of inheritance, property, and contracts, and criminal law, but also constitutional law, laws concerning state administration and the conduct of war. Islamic jurisprudence became established within a century of the emergence of Islam [*qv*] in A.D. 622.

First Gulf War: *see* Gulf War I (1980–88).

Fiver Shias: *see* Zaidis.

First Intifada: *see* Intifada.

Franco-Lebanese Treaty (1936): This treaty—signed between France, then ruled by the leftist Popular Front government, and Lebanon in November 1936—gave Lebanon considerable autonomy. The treaty was designed to pave the way for the end of the French mandate.

Franco-Syrian Treaty (1936): Following negotiations between the leftist Popular Front government in France and the nationalists in Syria, the Franco-Syrian Treaty was intialed in September 1936. Paris agreed to end its mandate in three years and sponsor Syrian membership of the League of Nations in exchange for long-term military, political, and economic privileges for France. But the French parliament refused to ratify it in 1939.

Franjieh, Suleiman (1910–93): *Lebanese politician; president, 1970–76* Born into the Maronite [*qv*] Franjieh clan [*qv*] at the Ihden palace, 12 miles/20km from Zghorta, Franjieh grew up in the shadow of his elder brother, Hamid. While Hamid

provided overall leadership to the clan, Franjieh supervised its organization and armed guards. After Hamid's retirement from public life in 1957, Franjieh became head of the clan and entered politics.

In the 1958 Civil War [*qv*], he sided with the pro-Nasser [*qv*] camp against the Maronite president, Camille Chamoun [*qv*]. Two years later he was elected to parliament. He served as a minister from 1960–61 and again from 1968–70. In his bid for presidency in August 1970, Franjieh received the support of Chamoun and Pierre Gemayel [*qv*]. He defeated Elias Sarkis [*qv*], though only by one vote. Franjieh's adoption of an anti-Palestinian stand, advocated by right-wing Maronites, made him unpopular with the pro-Palestinian, Arab nationalist Muslims [*qv*].

When the Lebanese Civil War [*qv*] erupted in April 1975, Franjieh turned to Syria, aware that only it had the power to end the conflict and introduce political reform. At the behest of Syrian President Hafiz Assad [*qv*], in early 1976 Franjieh issued a Constitutional Reform Document, which specified changing the 6:5 Christian-Muslim ratio in parliament to parity between the two communities. The reform failed to eventuate.

As the civil conflict intensified, Franjieh grew closer to the right-wing Maronites. In September 1976, at the end of his presidential tenure, he joined the Lebanese Front [*qv*], led politically by Chamoun and militarily by Bashir Gemayel [*qv*]. But when, in Bashir Gemayel's bid to eliminate any serious rival to his presidential ambitions, his henchmen assassinated Franjieh's son and heir, Tony, and his family in June 1978,

Franjieh turned vehemently against the Gemayel family and allied with the leftist pro-Syrian camp, led by Walid Jumblat [*qv*] and Rashid Karami [*qv*].

Along with other anti-Lebanese Front leaders, Franjieh denounced the draft peace treaty between Lebanon and Israel [*qv*], initialed in May 1983. While remaining close to Assad, Franjieh rejected the "National Agreement to Solve the Lebanese Crisis," signed in December 1985 by the three pro-Syrian militia leaders, Walid Jumblat, Nabih Berri [*qv*] and Elie Hobeika. However, still hostile toward the Gemayels, Franjieh backed these commanders when their militias attacked forces loyal to President Amin Gemayel [*qv*].

When the end of Gemayel's presidency in September 1988 resulted in the emergence of two governments, Franjieh opposed the anti-Syrian administration led by General Michel Aoun [*qv*]. A year later Franjieh backed the Taif Accord [*qv*], which followed the general line of his own Constitutional Reform Document of 1976. Franjieh supported the military moves by the pro-Syrian Lebanese forces and Syria against Aoun in October 1990, which ended the civil war. The following spring, in line with other irregulars, Franjieh's militia surrendered its weapons to the Syrian army. Unlike right-wing Maronites, his party participated in the 1992 parliamentary elections and won half of the 34 seats reserved for Maronites in a house of 128. With the right-wing Maronites ending their boycott of the general election in 1996, the share of his party in the Maronite seats declined.

Franjieh clan: The Maronite [*qv*] Franjieh clan is based in the Zghorta region at the northern boundary of the Maronite heartland, which stretches to Jezzine at the southern tip of Mount Lebanon. The northern Maronites are more tribal than sectarian, and their preeminent clan, the Franjiehs, has been in rivalry with Maronite chiefs of central Mount Lebanon—Emile Eddi, Bishara Khouri [*qv*], Camille Chamoun [*qv*], and Pierre Gemayel [*qv*]—over the leadership of Lebanese Christians [*qv*]. The Franjieh clan was formerly headed by Hamid Frajieh (1907–81), who entered parliament in 1937 and served as a minister in different governments. A presidential candidate in 1952, he withdrew in favor of Camille Chamoun. When he retired five years later due to illness, the clan leadership passed to his younger brother, Suleiman.

Freedom Movement of Iran: *see* Liberation Movement of Iran.

Front for Steadfastness and Resistance: *see* Steadfastness Front.

G

Gahal (*Hebrew: acronym of Gush Herut Liberalim, Herut-Liberals bloc*): *Israeli political party* Gahal was formed in 1965 by the merger of Herut [*qv*] and Liberalim (Liberals) [*qv*], under the leadership of Menachem Begin [*qv*]. Tempted by the chance of winning power in the November 1965 general election following the defection of David Ben-Gurion [*qv*] from Mapai [*qv*], Herut and the Liberals papered over their differences over equal rights for women and relations between the state and religion. By winning twenty-six seats Gahal became the second largest bloc in the new Knesset [*qv*].

An invitation to join the national unity government on the eve of the June 1967 Arab-Israeli War [*qv*] made it and Begin politically respectable. In the October 1969 poll it retained its twenty-six seats and joined the national unity cabinet that followed. Rejecting the Rogers cease-fire plan [*qv*], which had been accepted by all other parties in the cabinet, Gahal left the government in July 1970. On the eve of the December 1973 election, Gahal allied with three small right-wing groups to form Likud [*qv*].

Gailani, Rashid Ali (1892–1965): *Iraqi politician; prime minister, 1933, 1940–41*
Born into an eminent Sunni [*qv*] family in Baghdad [*qv*], Gailani obtained a degree from the Baghdad Law School and set up legal practice. After a brief stint as a judge, he entered politics. He served as minister of justice in 1924, then as minister of interior from 1925–28. A nationalist, he opposed the Anglo-Iraqi Treaty of 1930 [*qv*]. He became prime minister briefly in 1933. Two years later he was appointed interior minister, and in late 1938 he became chief of the cabinet.

During the Second World War, when politicians and military officers split into pro- and anti-British factions, Gailani headed the anti-British, nationalist camp. He became prime minister in March 1940. Three months later, when Italy declared war against Britain and its allies, he refused to cut links with Italy. He also refused to abide by Article 4 of the Anglo-Iraqi Treaty, which gave landing and transit rights to Britain in the event of war. He withstood British pressure until January 1941, when he stepped down. But his pro-British successor, Taha Hashemi, faced counterpressure from military officers and public opinion. Hashemi's resignation from office in early April 1941 led to Gailani reassuming the premiership and to the flight of the pro-British regent Abdul Ilah [*qv*], Nuri al Said [*qv*], and the child-king Faisal II [*qv*]. Britain landed troops in Basra [*qv*]. In his military confrontation with the British in May, Gailani lost and fled to Germany.

After the war he spent many years in Saudi Arabia, Egypt, and Syria. He returned to Baghdad after the July 1958 coup against King Faisal II. A pan-Arab nationalist, he did not find favor with Abdul Karim Qasim [*qv*]. After his failed coup attempt in conjunction with the United Arab Republic [*qv*] in December 1958, Gailani was sentenced to capital punishment, but Qasim commuted his sentence and freed him in October 1961. Gailani then stayed away from politics.

al Gamaat al Islamiya (Egypt) (*Arabic: The Islamic Groups*): *Egyptian Islamic movement*
After carrying out a coup against the leftist Ali Sabri [*qv*] and his followers in the ruling Arab Socialist Union [*qv*] in May 1971, President Anwar Sadat [*qv*] instructed Abdul Munim Amin, an army general with pro-Muslim Brotherhood [*qv*] sympathies, to establish, train, and arm 1,000 Islamic Groups—al Gamaat al Islamiya—in universities and factories to fight "atheist Marxism." The program was so successful that the al Gamaat acquired an independent existence. Al Gamaat activities accentuated the historical animosity between Muslims [*qv*] and Copts [*qv*], and led to attacks on Copts and their churches. When the government tried to discourage this, al Gamaat members demonstrated, calling on Sadat to intensify the struggle against Israel.

The October 1973 Arab-Israeli War [*qv*],

described as a victory for Egypt by the authorities, produced a lull in al Gamaat's activities, but the economic crisis that followed the war, and Egypt's step-by-step rapprochement with Israel, created conditions conducive to the rise of Islamic fundamentalism [qv]. In the spring 1978 election of university student union officials, al Gamaat won 60 percent of the posts. The impending signing of an Egyptian-Israeli peace treaty [qv] in March 1979 so angered al Gamaat students that they mounted protest demonstrations at Alexandria and Asyut universities—a daring step, since it made them liable to life imprisonment. Their slogans were: "No peace with Israel," "No privilege for the rich" and "No separation between Islam and state." They cheered the victory of the Islamic revolution [qv] in Iran and condemned the hospitality that Sadat accorded to the deposed Muhammad Reza Shah [qv] in Egypt. Sadat set up new disciplinary councils for university students and arrested hundreds of Islamists in September 1981. His assassination the next month was applauded by al Gamaat.

There was lull in its activities during the early phase of the presidency of Hosni Mubarak [qv]. But as he upheld the substance of Sadat's policy of maintaining a secular state, the gap between al Gamaat and the regime widened. The group's first manifesto, *The Program for Islamic Action,* issued in 1984, had a much wider focus than the one specified in that of *Al Jihad al Islami* [qv], with its almost exclusive stress on violent action. Al Gamaat activists, operating at the grassroots level, continued their social welfare work—religious education and health clinics—through local mosques under the general guidance of Shaikh Muhammad Abu Nasr, an eighty-year-old cleric. In the early 1990s, as the authorities began to repress Islamists, al Gamaat, bolstered by the return of its militants from Afghanistan, where they had acquired experience as guerrillas, escalated its anti-regime campaign. To hurt the economy, starting in October 1992 they began attacking foreign tourists. Over the next two years they killed some 450 policemen and tourists. By then there were an estimated 29,000 Islamist political detainees, two-thirds of them al Gamaat members. In April 1996 al Gamaat activists killed seventeen Greek tourists in Cairo [qv], mistaking them to be Israelis. This led to an intensified government crackdown. Among those who guided al Gamaat from abroad were Muhammad Shawki Islambouli, brother of Khalid, who was one of the assassins of President Sadat, and Talat Fuad Qasim, both based in Afghanistan.

In early 1999 al Gamaat leaders declared a unilateral cease-fire that was endorsed by Shaikh Abdul Rahman Omar [qv], serving a life sentence in an American jail. The government released over 5,000 al Gamaat members out of an estimated 20,000. By tightening its control of the mosques and the preachers, it reduced the potential for recruits for al Gamaat. It also frustrated the organization's attempt to transform itself into a recognized political party.

al Gamaat al Muslimin (Egypt): *see* al Takfir wal Hijra (Egypt).

gas: *see* natural gas.

Gaza city: *capital of the Gaza Strip* Pop. 408,000 (2003, est.). The recorded history of Gaza stretches back to the fifteenth century B.C. A thriving trading post, it is the reputed site of the temple to Dagon, which was razed by Samson. To punish its residents for their spirited resistance, Alexander the Great (r. 336–23 B.C.) condemned them to slavery. Gaza fell to Muslim Arabs in A.D. 635; and as it is the burial site of Prophet Muhammad's great grandfather, Hashem ibn Abdul Manaf, it has acquired religious significance. It changed hands during the Crusades and in 1517 passed into the control of the Ottoman Turks, who held it until 1917. It was part of the Palestine that came under British mandate five years later. After the Palestine War (1948–49) [*qv*], it became the capital of the Gaza Strip [*qv*]. In 1994 the Palestinian Authority [*qv*] made Gaza its base.

Gaza Strip: *Palestinian territory* Also called Gaza. Area 146 sq. miles/378 sq. km; pop. 1,330,000 (2003, est); 380,800 (1967 census). In the 1948–49 Palestine War [*qv*] the Arab armies managed to retain only a semidesert strip along the Mediterranean coast, later called the Gaza Strip, and an enclave on the west bank of the Jordan River [*qv*], later named the West Bank [*qv*]. From January 1949 the Gaza Strip was administered by Egypt, but it passed into the hands of the invading Israelis during the Suez War (October–November 1956) [*qv*]. Israel vacated it in March 1957.

In the June 1967 Arab-Israel War [*qv*], the Gaza Strip was once again captured by Israel. On 1 December 1981 it was put under civilian administrators, albeit working under a military command. On the eve of the signing of the Oslo Accord [*qv*] in September 1993, one-third of the Strip was taken up by sixteen Jewish settlements (4,500 settlers) and the out-of-bounds military zones. As a result

of the Israel-PLO agreement of May 1994, this area was further expanded due to the creation of buffer zones. Hence, only about 60 percent of the Strip came under the administration of the Palestinian Authority [*qv*].

Gemara *(Aramaic: Completion):* Gemara is a commentary on and a supplement to Mishna [*qv*], the text of the Jewish Oral Law. *See also* Talmud.

Gemayel, Amin (1942–): *Lebanese politician; president, 1982–88* Born in Beirut [*qv*] of a notable Maronite [*qv*] family, Gemayel obtained a degree in law from St. Joseph University. He started his professional life as a lawyer but soon branched out into business. He entered parliament in 1970 in a by-election, and retained his seat two years later in a general election. Unlike his younger brother, Bashir [*qv*], Gemayel was not active in the Phalange Party's [*qv*] militia and was not directly involved in the Lebanese Civil War [*qv*], which broke out in 1975. Once the Syrians had intervened in the conflict in 1976 on the side of the Maronites [*qv*], Gemayel established contact with them. He was catapulted into the presidency when Bashir was assassinated soon after being elected president in September 1982. Backed by Syria, he received the votes of all but one of the seventy-eight parliamentarians in attendance.

He initially won much support abroad and at home. Under U.S. pressure, in May 1983 he initialed a peace treaty with Israel, then occupying much of Lebanon. But in order to make Israel vacate Lebanese soil, he refused to sign the document, even after parliament had passed it by sixty-four votes to two. In retaliation Israel withdrew its protection of his regime. When Israel carried out a partial withdrawal in September 1983, fighting between different communities erupted and engulfed Muslim West Beirut, further reducing the power of Gemayel's government. In February 1984 his attempt to cow the Shia [qv] residents of West Beirut by deploying the army against them backfired, resulting in the breakup of the Lebanese army along religious lines. Finding himself with no outside protection—Israeli or Western—Gemayel decided to bury the Lebanese-Israeli Treaty [qv] and seek Syrian aid.

Following a National Reconciliation Conference in Lausanne, Switzerland, in March 1984, Gemayel appointed a national reconciliation government under Rashid Karami [qv] to implement political and constitutional reform. But after the death of his influential father, Pierre [qv], in August, his position in the Phalange Party weakened. The internecine fighting within the party damaged the standing of Gemayel, who was also attacked by pro-Syrian militia leaders such as Nabih Berri [qv] and Walid Jumblat [qv]. In return, Gemayel opposed the "National Agreement to Solve the Lebanese Crisis," brokered by Syria and signed by Berri, Jumblat, and Eli Hobeika of the Lebanese Forces [qv].

Among other things, this pact specified parliamentary parity between Muslims [qv] and Christians [qv] instead of the current 6:5 division in favor of Christians. This alienated Gemayel from Syrian President Hafiz Assad [qv]. The latter tried to undermine Gemayel's authority by aiding the militias of Berri and Jumblat as well as Suleiman Franjieh [qv], a Maronite rival of Gemayel. By staying away from the parliamentary session to elect a new president, rightist Maronite

deputies deprived it of a quorum, thus defeating Assad's plan to have his nominee elected as president. In September 1988, on his last day of office, Gemayel appointed his chief of staff, General Michel Aoun [qv], as his successor. A month later Gemayel went into exile in France, where he reverted to being a businessman. He returned to Lebanon in 2000.

Gemayel, Bashir (1947–82): *Lebanese politician; president-elect, 1982* Born into a notable Maronite [qv] family in Beirut [qv], Gemayel started his law and political science studies at St. Joseph University but did not finish them. Active in the Phalange Party [qv], Gemayel opposed the presence of Palestinian guerrillas in Lebanon. In the early 1970s he worked for a law firm in Washington, where he was recruited by the U.S. Central Intelligence Agency (CIA).

At the start of the Lebanese Civil War [qv], beginning in April 1975, Gemayel became commander of the Lebanese Forces [qv], the military wing of the Lebanese Front [qv], a coalition of rightist Maronite parties. He formalized his long-existing secret ties with Israel. Intent on becoming the next Lebanese president, he began to eliminate serious rivals, culminating in the assassination by his henchmen of Tony Franjieh, the eldest son of Suleiman Franjieh [qv], in June 1978. He then overpowered the militia of Camille Chamoun's [qv] party.

In December 1980, at his initiative, Lebanese Front leaders issued a manifesto that favored a federal or confederal system within a unified Lebanon. Gemayel tightened his links with Israel, which provided arms and training to his militia. During the Israeli invasion of Lebanon in June 1982

[*qv*], Gemayel's forces linked up with the Israelis on the outskirts of Beirut. The expulsion of the PLO and the Syrians from Beirut by the Israelis strengthened the Phalange and improved Gemayel's chances of achieving the highest office. On 23 August 1982 Gemayel was elected president, fifty-seven of the sixty-five parliamentarians having voted for him. In his secret meeting with the Israeli prime minister, Menachem Begin [*qv*], on 1 September, he agreed to exchange representatives with Israel. On 14 September 1982, eight days before Gemayel was to be installed in office, a bomb explosion at the Phalange headquarters in Beirut killed him and twenty-six others.

Gemayel, Pierre (1905–84): *Lebanese politician* Born into a notable Maronite [*qv*] clan in Bikfaya, Gemayel received his university education in Beirut [*qv*] and Paris and trained as a pharmacist. Interested in sports clubs, he was deeply impressed by the Nazi Youth Movement in Germany and by the Berlin Olympics in the summer of 1936. Later that year he founded the Phalange Party [*qv*]. He played little or no role in the anti-French nationalist movement and the crisis of 1943. It was only after Camille Chamoun [*qv*] had become president, nearly a decade later, that Gemayel came to the fore. In the Lebanese Civil War of May–July 1958 [*qv*], he sided with Chamoun against the pan-Arabist [*qv*] forces.

Following the election of Fuad Chehab [*qv*] in September 1958, Gemayel was appointed to the four-member interim cabinet. After his election to parliament in 1960, he became an almost constant fixture in the governments formed during the presidency of Chehab and Charles Helou

(1964–70) [*qv*], serving variously as minister of finance, public works, and health. In the 1968 general election, he allied with Chamoun and Raymond Edde to form the Triple Alliance, which described the activities of the Palestinian commandos in Lebanon as a serious threat to national security. In the 1970 presidential poll, he backed Suleiman Franjieh [*qv*].

With the onset of civil war in 1975 [*qv*] the importance of the Phalange militia increased, and with it the weight carried by Gemayel's youngest son, Bashir [*qv*], the militia commander. Once the Maronite camp had overcome the immediate threat from its enemy, the Lebanese National Movement [*qv*], with Syrian assistance in 1976–77, it turned to its long-standing though clandestine ally, Israel. In May 1978 Gemayel visited Israel and signed an arms and training agreement.

Two years later, when Bashir Gemayel used his fighters to overpower the militia of Chamoun, the two patriarchs decided to resolve the crisis by merging their political parties. In December they endorsed the Lebanese Front [*qv*] manifesto, which favored a federal or confederal system within a unified Lebanon. At the March 1984 National Reconciliation Conference in Lausanne, Gemayel allied with Chamoun in proposing to create a federal system composed of several cantons, but failed to win the backing of the assembly. The next month he joined the National Reconciliation government headed by Rashid Karami [*qv*]. In July he stepped down as chairman of the Phalange Party, and the following month he died.

General People's Congress (Yemen): *Yemeni political party* Having survived a few coup attempts by military officers since assuming power in October 1977, President Ali Abdullah Salih [*qv*], a lieutenant general, decided to consolidate his authority through political means. In October 1981 he set up a 1,000-member General People's Congress (GPC), partly by appointment and partly by indirect elections. Its program included the unification of North Yemen and South Yemen. The GPC backed Salih's reelection as president in 1983 and 1988. It also endorsed his decision to take North Yemen into the Arab Cooperation Council [*qv*] in early 1989.

On the eve of unification of North and South Yemen in May 1990, the GPC was transformed into a licensed political party. Its program included multiparty democracy at home and friendly relations with neighbors and Islamic countries. It backed Yemen's official stance of neutrality in the 1990–91 Kuwait crisis and the Gulf War [*qv*]. In the multiparty general election in Yemen in April 1993, the GPC won 123 seats in a house of 301 members and led the coalition government formed with the Yemen Socialist Party [*qv*] and the Yemeni Islah Group [*qv*]. It backed President Salih during the Yemeni Civil War [*qv*], which erupted in the spring of 1994. In the 1997 general election, it secured 187 seats and twenty-five of the twenty-nine cabinet posts.

General Zionists: *Zionist political party in Palestine* The term General Zionists (*Zionim Klaliyim*) was first used at the Zionist Congress of 1907 to denote delegates attached to neither labor Zionism [*qv*] nor religious Zionism. In Palestine the General Zionist party came into being in 1930. Since by then it had come to represent the

capitalist strand within Zionism, it drew the support of businessmen, industrialists, planters, and traders.

Four years later the party split into a liberal "A" faction (sympathetic to labor) and a conservative "B" faction (sympathetic to capital). These factions came together in 1944, but the unity did not last. Shortly after the founding of Israel in 1948, the liberal "A" faction left to combine with the German-dominated Aliya Hadasha (New Immigrants) to form the Progressive Party [*qv*]. During the 1950s the General Zionists saw their parliamentary strength fall from twenty to eight. Fear of further decline persuaded its leaders to seek a merger with the Progressives on the eve of the 1961 election, which led to the rise of the Liberals [*qv*].

Geneva Conventions on War (1949): *International treaties signed in Geneva* The last of the four Conventions—developed by an International Red Cross conference in Stockholm in August 1948 and ratified by United Nations members in Geneva on 12 August 1949—entitled "Relative to the Protection of Civilian Persons in Time of War" applies to Israel and the Occupied Arab Territories [*qv*] including Jerusalem [*qv*], according to several United Nations Security Council resolutions, including 465 (March 1980). It forbids the Occupying Power doing the following to the Protected Civilians: collective punishment and reprisals; deportation of individuals or groups; hostage taking; torture; unjustified destruction of property; and discrimination in treatment on the grounds of race, religion, national origin, or political affiliation. Article 47 states: "Protected persons . . . shall not be deprived of . . . the benefits of this Convention by any changes introduced, as the result of the occupation of a territory, into the institutions or government of the said territory, nor by any agreement concluded between the authorities of the occupied territories and the Occupying Power, nor by the annexation of the whole or part of the occupied territory." Article 49 (6) states: "The Occupying Power shall not deport or transfer parts of its own civilian population into the territory it occupies."

Ghashmi, Ahmad Hussein (1938–78): *Yemeni military officer and politician; president, 1977–78* Born in Hamada into a clan of the Hashid tribal confederation, Ghashmi was trained as an officer at the Baghdad Military Academy. During the civil war (1962–70) [*qv*] he liaised between the republican regime in Sanaa [*qv*] and the northern tribal confederations of Hashid and Bakil. His relations with the Hashid chief, Abdullah al Ahmar [*qv*], were tense. Following a coup by Col. Ibrahim Hamdi [*qv*] in June 1974, Lt. Col. Ghashmi was appointed deputy chief of staff and a member of the ruling Military Command Council (MCC).

A conservative, Ghashmi was considered pro-Saudi. After the assassination of Hamdi in October 1977 he became commander in chief and chairman of a three-man MCC. He revived the Constituent People's Assembly (CPA), disbanded earlier by Hamdi, and tried to mend fences with al Ahmar. His government repressed the nationalist-leftist forces. Guided by Saudi Arabia, Ghashmi purged the military and civil services of pro-Hamdi personnel. In March 1978 he dissolved the MCC, thus neutralizing the power of the paratroop commander, Major Abdullah Abdul-Alim, an erstwhile MCC member and a Hamdi loyalist. In April the CPA replaced the MCC with a Presidential Council and elected Ghashmi president. He was assassinated in June by the blast of a bomb hidden in a briefcase by an emissary of South Yemeni President Salim Rubai Ali [*qv*].

Ghazi ibn Faisal I al Hashem (1912–39): *King of Iraq, 1932–39* The only son of Faisal I ibn Hussein al Hashem [*qv*], Ghazi was born in Hijaz [*qv*] under the Ottoman rule. Following the installation of his father as king of Iraq in 1921, he became heir apparent. Educated partly in Baghdad [*qv*] and partly in Britain, Ghazi succeeded his father in 1933. During his rule, factions emerged among military officers. In October 1936 Ghazi encouraged commander in chief Bakr Sidqi to overthrow the unpopular civilian government of Yassin al Hashemi. Ghazi's nationalist, anti-British views won him popularity. He died as a result of an alleged car crash.

Ghom: *see* Qom.

Glubb (Pasha), Sir John Bagot (1897–1986): *British military officer in the Middle East* Born in Preston, Britain, Glubb was educated at Cheltenham College and the Royal Military Academy in Woolwich, London. During the First World War he was wounded in combat and was awarded the Military Cross. After the war he was sent to Iraq. He left the British military in 1926 to serve the Iraqi government as an administrative inspector. In 1930 he joined Transjordan's Arab Legion, an internal security force. There he concentrated on ending intertribal conflict among nomads. He became the Legion's second-in-command, rising to commander in 1938 and attaining the rank of lieutenant general.

Led by Glubb, the Arab Legion assisted Britain and its allies in 1941 in their attacks on the government of Rashid Ali Gailani [*qv*] in Iraq and on the troops of the pro-Nazi, French Vichy regime in Syria-Lebanon.

After the Palestine War (1948–49) [*qv*]—when the Arab Legion failed to capture West Jerusalem [*qv*]—Glubb, a symbol of British hegemony in the region, became a hate figure among Arab nationalists. When London pressured King Hussein [*qv*] to join the Baghdad Pact [*qv*] (in order to regain the privilege of securing military bases in times of war), the tide of nationalism rose and Glubb became the target.

To offset the rising popular charge that he was a puppet of Britain, King Hussein dismissed Glubb in March 1956. Glubb retired to Britain, where he lectured and wrote books mainly about Arab countries and peoples.

Golan Heights: *Syrian region* Also called the Golan Plateau. Area 454 sq. miles/1,176 sq. km; pop. 33,000 (1994, est.), divided equally among Jewish settlers and Syrian Druze [*qv*]. Part of Syria since the First World War, the western border of the Golan Heights, overlooking the Hula Valley and Lake Tiberias/Sea of Galilee, was fortified after the founding of Israel in 1948. It became a source of sniper and artillery attacks on Israelis in the region. After defeating Jordan in the 1967 Arab-Israeli War [*qv*], Israel attacked the Golan Heights on 9 June and captured its capital, Qunaitra, the next day. A cease-fire went into effect later that day. The fighting and subsequent Israeli actions reduced the Syrian population of 250,000 to about

8,000, mainly Druze. Israel declared that it would keep the Golan Heights.

In 1969 Syria gave Palestinian commandos greater freedom of action in the area. Since the U.S. peace plan of June 1970 made no mention of Israel evacuating the Heights, Syria rejected it. In the October 1973 Arab-Israeli War [*qv*], the Syrian offensive, launched on 6 October, limited itself to recovering the Golan Heights. However, Syria was unable to build on its initial success and failed to alter the status quo. After it had signed the Syrian-Soviet Friendship Treaty [*qv*] in October 1980, its spokesman said that any attempt by Israel to annex the occupied Golan Heights would lead Syria to take "any step or measure to secure our rights." But when on 14 December 1981 the Israeli government extended its laws to the Golan Heights and received parliamentary backing in the form of the Golan Annexation Law, Syria did nothing more than denounce the Israeli action and put its case before the U.N. Security Council, which declared the law "null and void."

Israel continued its policy of establishing Jewish settlements, which numbered twenty-five in 1992. As for Syria, before joining the Middle East peace process, initiated by the United States after the Second Gulf War (1991) [*qv*], it ensured that Israeli evacuation of the Golan Heights would be the principal subject of discussion in the subsequent bilateral talks. In mid-1994 the two sides entered into substantive negotiations linking Israel's evacuation of the Golan Heights with normalization of relations between them. Israel unilaterally broke off these talks in the spring of 1996. They resumed in 1999 after the election of Ehud Barak [*qv*] as Israel's prime minister. But they failed in March 2000 when Barak insisted on keeping a strip of the Golan along Lake Tiberias, which Syrian President Hafiz Assad [*qv*] refused.

Golpaygani, Muhammad Reza Musavi (1899–1993): *Iranian leader* Born in Golpaygan of a religious Shia [*qv*] family, Golpaygani lost his parents when young and was raised by his sisters. When he was sixteen he went to Arak to be a pupil of Ayatollah Abdul Karim Hairi-Yazdi, and moved with him to Qom [*qv*] in 1922. Having finished his studies in Arabic and theology, he began teaching Islamic jurisprudence, *fiqh* [*qv*].

After Hairi-Yazdi's death in 1937, Golpaygani rose in stature in the religious hierarchy, now led by Ayatollah Muhammad Hussein Borujerdi. Golpaygani was a conservative. After the death of Borujerdi in 1961, the leadership of conservative clerics fell on the triumvirate of Ayatollahs Golpaygani, Shehab al Din Marashi-Najafi, and Muhammad Kazem Shariatmadari [*qv*]. They opposed the idea of state takeover of land above a certain ceiling, an important part of the agrarian reform law of the government. This brought Golpaygani close to Ayatollah Ruhollah Khomeini [*qv*], an opponent of the regime.

When Khomeini was exiled in 1964, Golpaygani took over the administration of the prestigious Faiyziyya seminary in Qom. He offered the concept of Vilayat-e-Faqih (Rule of Jurisprudents) [*qv*], which assigned spiritual and temporal leadership of an Islamic community to jurisprudents. This was to be incorporated into the constitution of the Islamic Republic of Iran, founded in 1979. As a senior *marja-e taqlid* (source of emulation) [*qv*], Golpaygani received *khums* [*qv*] (one-fifth of the income of his followers) as religious dues. With this money he founded and sustained charitable projects in Iran and abroad—building and maintaining clinics, hospitals, orphanages, and religious and educational centers.

After the Islamic revolution in Iran [*qv*], he backed the new regime at crucial moments. In the mid-1980s, when there was growing division between conservatives and radicals, especially on the issue of Khomeini's succession, the conservatives backed Golpaygani. When Khomeini died in 1989 without having named a successor, the Assembly of Experts [*qv*] reportedly offered the position of (supreme) leader to Golpaygani. Being in poor health, he turned it down. As a cleric who had been in close contact with all the leading Shia personages of the twentieth century, Golpaygani was unique.

Greater Syria: Area: 119,690 sq. miles/ 310,000 sq. km. Greater (or Natural) Syria occupies the piece of territory enclosed by the Taurus Mountains to the north, the Mediterranean Sea to the west, the Arabian desert to the south, and the Euphrates River [*qv*] to the east. It was known historically as *Bilad al Sham,* or Country on the Left/North (of Mecca [*qv*]).

From 1831 to 1840, during an interregnum in the Ottoman rule that started in 1517, Greater Syria was governed as a single entity under Egyptian viceroy Ibrahim Pasha. With the return of direct Ottoman rule, Greater Syria was divided into several provinces. Following the Ottoman defeat in the First World War, the victors—Britain and France—split Greater Syria according to the Sykes-Picot Pact [*qv*], with the northern region (later forming the republics of Syria and Lebanon) going to France and the southern section (constituting Palestine and Transjordan) to Britain. This was denounced at the Syrian National Congress meeting in Damascus in July 1919, which demanded sovereignty for a united Syria-Palestine, but in vain.

The League of Nations Supreme Council confirmed the British and French claims in 1920 by giving them mandates over the new entities created out of the old Ottoman provinces. While these mandates were visualized by the League of Nations as a guardianship of young nations that were to be led to independence, France toppled the government of Faisal I ibn Hussein al Hashemi [*qv*] in Damascus [*qv*], established a colonial regime, and rearranged the borders by allocating parts of Syria to the Vilayat of Mount Lebanon to create Greater Lebanon. By surrendering sections of the Syrian province of Aleppo to Turkey in October 1921, France further reduced the size of Syria. As a result, the independent Syria that emerged in 1946 occupied 71,500 sq. miles/185,180 sq. km.

Greater Tumb/Tunb Island: *see* Tumb/Tunb Islands.

Greek Catholic Church: Also known as Greek-Melkite Catholic Church, the Greek Catholic Church is a Uniate Church [*qv*]. Those early Christians [*qv*] of Egypt and Syria who accepted the church council's ruling in 451 that Jesus Christ possessed two natures, human and divine, were labeled "malka" (*Syriac: royalist*) by their opponents. Since they followed the Byzantine rite, they stayed with the Eastern Orthodox Church [*qv*] after the major church schism in 1054. Due to the predominance of Greek colonizers (in Egypt and Syria) in its congregation, the church came to be known as Greek Orthodox [*qv*].

Periodic attempts at unification with the Roman Catholic Church [*qv*] did not succeed until 1724, when a Roman Catholic, Cyril VI, was elected Patriarch of Antioch. But only a third of Greek Orthodox members followed his lead, and they came to be called Greek/Greek-Melkite Catholics. They conduct their Byzantine liturgy in Arabic. Their head, the Patriarch of Antioch and all the East, resides alternatively in Damascus [*qv*], Beirut [*qv*], and Cairo [*qv*]. Of the 1.5 million Greek Catholics in the Middle East and the Western Hemisphere, 350,000 live in Lebanon. They are also to be found in Egypt, Jordan, Syria, and the Palestinian Territories [*qv*].

Greek Orthodox Church: Those early Christians [*qv*] of Egypt and Syria who accepted the church council's ruling in 451 that Jesus Christ possessed two natures, human and divine, were labelled "malka" (*Syriac: royalist*) by their opponents. Since they followed the Byzantine rite, they stayed with the Eastern Orthodox Church [*qv*] after the major church schism in 1054. Due to the predominance of Greek colonizers (in Egypt and Syria) in its congregation, the church came to be known as Greek Orthodox [*qv*]. The Patriarch of Alexandria and all Africa, based in Alexandria [*qv*], is the head of a community of 350,000 in Egypt. The Patriarch of Antioch and all the East, based in Damascus [*qv*], is the head of a community of 370,000 in Lebanon, the second largest Christian sect.

Greenburg, Uri Zvi (1896–1981): *Israeli poet* Born in Bilkman, Ukraine, of a religious Hassadic [*qv*] family, Greenburg was educated in the nearby city of Lvov. At sixteen he began to publish poetry in Hebrew [qv] and Yiddish [qv]. He served as a soldier in the Austro-Hungarian army in the First World War, deserting it in 1918 and returning home. He moved to Warsaw, Poland, where he published nihilistic poetry in 1921–22, and then to Berlin.

In late 1923 he migrated to Palestine [qv] and worked as a farmhand. Here Greenburg adopted Hebrew as his sole language of expression. A member of the Ahdut HaAvodah [qv], he contributed articles and poems to its journal. Later he became a regular contributor to *Davar* (Word), the newspaper of the Histadrut [qv]. His poetry of the period was influenced by such varied people as Jewish prophets and Walt Whitman, a contemporary American poet.

Following the 1929 Arab riots, Greenburg joined the Revisionist Zionists [qv]. He moved to Warsaw, where he edited *Di Velt* (*Yiddish: The World*), the Revisionists' newspaper, from 1931 to 1935, and then *Der Moement* (*Yiddish: The Moment*), from 1938 to 1939. His poetry reflected his rising politicization, and many of his poems were overtly partisan. While the Revisionist youth praised his collection *The Book of Accusation and Faith* (1937), his opponents saw racist undertones in it. With the eruption of the Second World War, Greenburg returned to Palestine.

After the war, the massacre of Jews by the Nazis had a profound impact on his writing. His poetry allied intense lament with insistent declarations of the Jews' resolve to survive and resurrect Jewish sovereignty. A collection of these poems, *Streets of the River* (1946), became a classic of Jewish literature.

Following the founding of Israel in 1948, he joined Herut [qv] and became a member of parliament. The leading poet of the radical right, he was a bitter opponent of the labor movement. Yet the Mapai-led [qv] government recognized his literary achievement, and the ministry of education and culture awarded him the Israel Prize in Hebrew literature in 1957. After the June 1967 Arab-Israeli War [qv] he became a founder of the Movement for Eretz Israel. A decade later he received the Bailik Prize for the third time.

Gregorian calendar: Named after Pope Gregory III in 1582. *See* Christian calendars.

Gregorian Orthodox Church: Since Armenians [qv] were converted to Christianity [qv] by Gregory the Illuminator, the Armenian Orthodox Church is also known as the Gregorian Orthodox Church. *See* Armenian Orthodox Church.

Guardians Council (Iran): Established by the 1979 constitution of the Islamic Republic of Iran, the task of the twelve-member Council of Guardians is to ensure that all laws and regulations passed by parliament are compatible with the Iranian constitution and Islamic percepts. It consists of (1) six "*faqihs* (Islamic jurisprudents, [qv]) conscious of current needs and the issues of the day," to be appointed by the Leader (of the Revolution), and (2) six jurists, specializing in different branches of Islamic law, to be elected by parliament from a list of qualified candidates submitted by the head of the judiciary, who is appointed by the Leader. The tenure of the Council is six years. The parliament is required to submit its regulations and bills to it. All the guardians vote on their compatibility with the constitution, but only the six *faqihs* do so on their compatibility with Islamic precepts. A regulation or law becomes effective only if it is judged to be compatible with both the constitution and Islamic precepts. The Council also vets all candidates for public office at the national level for their loyalty to the constitution and Islam and the results of the elections.

Guardians of the Cedars: *Lebanese political group* Named after the cedar, the national symbol of Lebanon, the Guardians of the Cedars emerged soon after the outbreak of the Lebanese Civil War in April 1975 [*qv*]. Led by Eteinne Saqr, the Guardians were ultranationalist Maronites [*qv*]. They were inspired by the writings of Said Aql [*qv*], who believed that Lebanese identity was rooted in its distant Phoenician past and had little to do with pan-Arabism [*qv*] or Islam [*qv*]. In January 1976 they combined with other Maronite militias to create a unified military command. Open about their links with Israel, many of them joined the Israeli-sponsored South Lebanon Army [*qv*], formed after the Israeli invasion of southern Lebanon [*qv*] in March 1978. In the fractured Maronite community of the late 1980s, they were one of the eight political or military factions. When the civil war ended in favor of their adversaries in October 1990, their influence declined. Their backing of the electoral boycott by the Maronites of the parliamentary poll of 1992 further marginalized them.

Gulf, the: Surface area, 92,500 sq. miles/240,000 sq. km; length 610 miles/990 km; width, 35–210 miles/56–340 km; depth, 120–300 ft./40–100 meters. An extension of the Arabian Sea between Iran [*qv*] and the Arabian Peninsula [*qv*], the Gulf is connected to the Gulf of Oman by the Straits of Hormuz [*qv*]. As the flow of fresh water into it from the Shatt al Arab [*qv*] and the Karun River is limited, and water temperatures are generally high, its salinity is high. Since the eight countries around the Gulf possess two-thirds of global petroleum reserves [*qv*] and produce between a quarter and a third of the world's oil, the Gulf is an area of prime importance to the West and Japan.

Gulf Cooperation Council: *Regional body consisting of Bahrain, Kuwait, Oman, Qatar, Saudi Arabia, and the United Arab Emirates* Official title: Cooperation Council for the Arab Gulf States *(Arabic: Majlis al Taawun li Dual al Khaleej al Arabiyah).* The idea of a regional body in the Gulf grew out of Saudi Arabia's proposal for an internal security pact with fellow monarchies on the Arabian Peninsula [*qv*] following an armed uprising in Mecca [*qv*] in late 1979. The matter became urgent when the Iran-Iraq War [*qv*] erupted in September 1980. Meeting in Abu Dhabi [*qv*], rulers of the six Gulf monarchies founded the Gulf Cooperation Council (GCC) on 26 May 1981. Its objectives were to coordinate the internal security, procurement of arms and national economies of member states, and to settle border disputes under the leadership of the Supreme Council, consisting of the heads of the member states.

Abdullah Bishara, a Kuwaiti diplomat, was appointed secretary-general of the GCC, whose secretariat was in Riyadh [*qv*]. In June 1982 the GCC foreign ministers' attempt to end the First Gulf War failed. A GCC communiqué in November condemned Iran [*qv*] for occupying Iraqi territory. However, continuation of the war helped the GCC to become a cohesive body, particularly in defense, where collectively the GCC states had 190,000 troops and 300 warplanes. In October 1984 the GCC conducted a three-week joint military exercise in the desert of the United Arab Emirates.

At the GCC summit in November, it was decided to set up a Rapid Deployment Force (RDF) of two brigades under a Saudi officer based in Riyadh. A year later the GCC summit pledged to continue its efforts to end the war in a manner that safeguarded the legitimate rights and interests of "the two sides." The next summit, in late 1987, urged the U.N. Security Council to implement its ceasefire resolution 598 [qv], passed in July.

Following Iraq's [qv] invasion and occupation of Kuwait in August 1990, the GCC condemned the Iraq action. It dispatched its RDF to the Saudi-Kuwait border. The GCC summit in December 1990 demanded the unconditional withdrawal of Iraq from Kuwait. The troops and air forces of GCC members participated in the Second Gulf War [qv] against Iraq. In March 1991 GCC ministers agreed to give grants to Egypt and Syria for the deployment of the 35,000 Egyptian and 20,000 Syrian troops as part of the backbone of an expanded Gulf defense force. But these plans were later abandoned.

The GCC states decided to suspend their subsidies to the Palestine Liberation Organization [qv] so long as Yasser Arafat [qv], who had sided with Iraq during the Gulf crisis and war of 1990–91, was its chairman. Following the PLO-Israeli accord in Washington in September 1993 [qv], GCC members ended their ostracization of the PLO and the Palestinians. Saudi

Arabia promised to contribute up to US$100 million over a five-year period to a development fund for the West Bank [qv] and Gaza Strip [qv]. A year later the GCC decided to end the secondary and tertiary embargo on trade with Israel. In 1997 the Supreme Council decided to appoint a thirty-member Consultative Council as an advisory body. In March 1999 the GCC condemned Iran for conducting military exercises around the waters of the Abu Musa [qv] and Tunb Islands [qv], over which the United Arab Emirates [qv] claimed jurisdiction. Later that year it set up a committee to facilitate direct talks between Iran and the UAE to settle the dispute, but nothing came of it. In 2001 the GCC's secretary-general was Jamil Ibrahim Hejailan.

Gulf states: Though eight countries border the Gulf [qv], the six monarchies that are collectively known as the Gulf states are Bahrain [qv], Kuwait [qv], Oman [qv], Qatar [qv], Saudi Arabia [qv], and the United Arab Emirates [qv]. The remaining states with shorelines along the Gulf are Iran [qv] and Iraq [qv].

Gulf War I (1980–88): *war between Iran and Iraq* Following a week-ong clash between Iraq and Iran in the disputed border territory in the central sector, Baghdad claimed on 10 September 1980 to have captured the area. A week later Iraqi President Saddam Hussein [qv] abrogated the 1975 Iran-Iraq Treaty of International Boundaries and Neighborliness [qv] and claimed full sovereignty over the Shatt al Arab [qv]. On 22 September Iraq invaded Iran at eight points on their mutual border and bombed Iranian military installations and economic targets.

The armed conflict, the longest conventional war of the twentieth century, went through the following phases.

Phase one: September 1980 to March 1981. Iraq advanced into Iran. On 28 September U.N. Security Council Resolution 479 urged a truce. Iraq announced its readiness to cease fire if Iran accepted its complete rights over the Shatt al Arab. Tehran rejected the resolution. By mid-November Iraq had captured Khorramshahr and besieged Abadan [qv]. It occupied 10,000 sq. miles/25,900 sq. km of Iranian territory in the southern and central sectors. The wet winter helped cause a military standoff.

Phase two: April 1981 to March 1982. Stalemate. While the Iranian military, much enlarged by a surge of patriotism among Iranians, blocked further Iraqi advance, it failed to lift the siege of Abadan. Various efforts by the United Nations and the Islamic Conference Organization [qv] to end the conflict foundered: Iran refused to negotiate so long as Iraq occupied its land.

Phase three: March 1982 to June 1982. Iran recovered the lost land. On 24 May 1982 Iran retook Khorramshahr and drove the Iraqis back to the international frontier. Iraq announced its readiness for a truce on 9 June. Tehran refused to cease fire until Saddam Hussein had been removed from office. On 20 June he declared that Iraq's voluntary withdrawal from Iran would be completed within ten days. But on 30 June Iraq still held some pockets of Iranian territory.

Phase four: July 1982 to March 1984. Iranians marched into Iraq. Having rejected the U.N. Security Council's call for a truce and withdrawal of the belligerents to the international border, Iran tried to conquer Basra [qv] in mid-July. With nine divisions locked in the largest infantry combat since the Second World War, fierce battles raged for a fortnight. Finally Iran managed to hold only 32 sq. miles/83 sq. km of Iraqi land. In October Iran reclaimed some territory in the northern sector. Iraq's air strikes on Iran's Nowruz offshore oil field in March 1983 caused the largest oil spill in the history of the Gulf. In April Iran's offensive in the southern sector to reach the strategic Basra-Baghdad highway failed. But its offensive in the north in July yielded it the Iraqi garrison town of Hajj Umran. In mid-February 1984 Iran launched a second attempt to cut off the Baghdad-Basra highway, but again failed. Following an offensive in the Haur al Hawizeh marshes in late February, Iran seized Iraq's oil-rich Majnoon Islands.

Phase five: April 1984 to January 1986. Renewed stalemate. Iraq escalated its attacks on Iranian oil tankers, using French-made Exocet air-to-ship (surface-skimmer) missiles, and intensified its air raids on the Kharg oil terminal, which handled most of Iran's petroleum exports. Iran retaliated by hitting ships serving the ports of Kuwait and Saudi Arabia, which were aiding Iraq, in the Lower Gulf [qv]. In October 1983, Iraq started using chemical weapons—at first mustard gas and then nerve gases. In March 1985 an Iranian brigade reached the Baghdad-Basra highway, but was unable to withstand the Iraqi counterattacks. In May Iraq intensified its tanker war and strikes on Kharg, reaching a peak in mid-August. All told, Iraq hit thirty-three ships in the Gulf in 1985, and Iran fourteen.

Phase six: February 1986 to January 1988. The war of attrition escalated, and the United States began to intervene on the Iraqi side. The Iranian assault in February 1986 in the south, which resulted in the capture of 310 sq. miles/800 sq. km in the Fao Peninsula, broke the stalemate. A determined effort by Iraq, which mounted 18,648 air missions between 9 February and 25 March 1986 (compared with 20,011 missions in the whole of 1985), to regain Fao met with failure. In March, following a report by U.N. experts on Iraq's use of poison gas, the U.N. Security Council combined its condemnation of Iraq for deploying chemical weapons with its disapproval of the prolongation of the conflict by Iran. The next month, flooding of the oil market by Kuwait and Saudi Arabia caused the price of petroleum to fall below $10 a barrel, down from $27 the previous December. This sharply reduced the oil income of Iran and Iraq, but the latter was cushioned by the approximately $10 billion a year it received in aid from its Gulf allies, the West and the Soviet Union.

From July, using covert official U.S. expertise, Iraq began to use its air force more aggressively than before, hitting Iran's economic and infrastructural targets and extending its air strikes to the Iranian oil terminals in the Lower Gulf. During 1986 Iraq struck eighty-six ships in the Gulf, and Iran forty-one. In January 1987 Iran's offensives in the south brought its forces within seven miles of Basra, but failed to capture it. During the spring the Iranians and their Iraqi Kurdish allies captured territory in Iraqi Kurdistan [qv]. On 20 July the U.N. Security Council unanimously passed Resolution 598 [qv], calling for a cease-fire and the withdrawal of warring forces. The ten-article text included a clause for an impartial commission to determine war responsibility, one of the major demands of Iran. Iraq said it would accept the resolution on condition that Iran did the same. Four days later a Kuwaiti supertanker on the first Gulf convoy escorted by U.S. warships hit a mine, believed to have been planted by Iran. The subsequent naval buildup by the United States, Britain and France brought sixty Western warships in the region.

On the seventh anniversary of the war, on 22 September 1987, Iraq had nearly 400 combat aircraft, six times the number of Iran's airworthy warplanes. Baghdad possessed 4,500 tanks, 3,200 armored fighting vehicles, and 2,800 artillery pieces versus Tehran's respective totals of 1,570, 1,800 and 1,750. Iraq had 955,000 regular troops versus Iran's 655,000; and Iraq's Popular Army, at 650,000, was slightly larger than Iran's Revolutionary Guards Corps, at 625,000.

In October the U.S. Navy sank three Iranian patrol boats near Farsi Island, claiming that Iran had fired on a U.S. patrol helicopter; and U.S. warships destroyed two Iranian offshore oil platforms in the Lower Gulf in retaliation for an Iranian missile attack on a U.S.-flagged supertanker docked in Kuwaiti waters. Tehran's capacity to mount major offensives was much reduced due to its shortage of manpower and money and the damage done to its bridges, factories, and power plants by ceaseless Iraqi bombing. **Phase seven:** February to June 1988. Iraq retook its lost territories. By introducing long-range surface-to-surface missiles in February 1988, Iraq was able to hit Tehran [qv] and demoralize the population. Iran retaliated by hitting Baghdad [*qv*], which was much nearer the international border. Between 16 and 18 April, Iraq recaptured the Fao Peninsula, using chemical weapons, while U.S. warships blew up two Iranian oil rigs, destroyed one Iranian frigate and immobilized another, and sank an Iranian missile boat. From 23–25 May, Iraq, using chemical arms, staged offensives in the northern and central sectors, and then in the south, regaining Shalamche. Between 19 and 25 June, Iraq recaptured Mehran in the central zone, using poison gases, and then the Majnoon Islands in the south.

Phase eight: July to 20 August 1988. Iraq failed to seize Iranian land. On 3 July a U.S. cruiser shot down an Iran Air airbus carrying 290 people over the Lower Gulf, mistaking it for a combat aircraft. On 18 July, Iran unconditionally accepted U.N. Security Council Resolution 598. Two days later Iran's leader, Ayatollah Ruhollah Khomeini [*qv*], stated that acceptance of a truce was "in the interest of the revolution and the system at this juncture." From 22–29 July, Iraq mounted offensives in the northern, central, and southern sectors to capture Iranian land. It failed in the north, but succeeded elsewhere. However, within a week Iran had regained its lost territory. On 20 August a truce came into effect under U.N. supervision. By then, Iraq had used 110,000 chemical munitions against Iran.

Human losses: Iran (official), 194,931 dead, consisting of 183,931 combatants, including those missing in action, and 11,000 civilians; Iran (unofficial est.), 300,000 dead; Iraq (unofficial est.), 160,000–240,000 dead.

Cost: Iran (est. by the Stockholm International Peace Research Institute), $74–91 billion, plus military imports of $11.26 billion; Iraq (est. by the Stockholm International Peace Research Institute), $94–112 billion, plus military imports of $41.94 billion. In July 1990 Iraq's deputy premier, Tariq Aziz [*qv*], put the military imports at $102 billion.

Outcome: Neither country lost much territory, nor was there a change of regime in either nation. The war enabled Khomeini to consolidate the Islamic revolution [*qv*]. With a million men in its military, Iraq emerged as the most powerful country in the region, outstripping Turkey and Egypt.

After the truce: On 12 August 1990 Iraq unilaterally agreed to abide by the 1975 Iran-Iraq Treaty of International Boundaries and Neighborliness, withdraw its forces from the occupied Iranian territory, and exchange prisoners of war. By the spring of 2000, the two countries had repatriated 100,000 prisoners of war. Each side rejected the other's figures on the remainder, with Baghdad claiming that Iran was still holding 13,000 Iraqi prisoners of war and Tehran alleging that Iraq was holding 2,800 Iranian prisoners.

Gulf War II (1991): *war between Iraq and the United States-led coalition.*

Background (mid-July to 1 August 1990): In mid-July Iraq complained to the Arab League [*qv*] that the oil glut caused by Kuwait and the United Arab Emirates (UAE) had caused the price to fall to $11–13 a barrel—far below the reference price of $18 set by the Organization of Petroleum Exporting Countries [*qv*]—and that a drop of $1 a barrel reduced Iraq's annual revenue by $1 billion. On 31 July Iraqi and Kuwaiti officials met in Jiddah [*qv*] against the background of some 100,000 Iraqi troops massed along the Kuwaiti border. The next day the talks failed. According to the Kuwaitis, they had refused to comply with Iraq's demands to write off the $12–14 billion Iraq had received from Kuwait during the Iran-Iraq War [*qv*], relinquish some of the Kuwaiti territory along the Iraqi border, and lease its Bubiyan and Warba Islands to Baghdad. According to the Iraqis, they had been unable to see any sign of willingness on the part of Kuwait to repair the economic damage it had inflicted on Iraq by depressing oil prices.

Iraqi invasion of Kuwait and its aftermath. *2 August 1990:* At 2 A.M. local time Iraqi forces invaded Kuwait and occupied it. The ruler, Shaikh Jaber III al Sabah [*qv*], and other members of the royal family fled to Saudi Arabia. The U.N. Security Council passed Resolution 660 by fourteen votes to none, condemning Iraqi aggression against Kuwait and demanding immediate withdrawal. The United States, Britain, and France froze Iraqi and Kuwaiti assets. The Soviet Union halted arms deliveries to Iraq.

3 August: The Arab League foreign ministers condemned Iraq's action by fourteen votes to one, with five abstentions and one walkout.

6 August: The U.N. Security Council passed Resolution 661 by thirteen votes to none, imposing mandatory sanctions and an embargo on Iraq and occupied Kuwait. Following a request by Saudi King Fahd ibn Abdul Aziz [*qv*] for the United States to bolster his country's defenses, U.S. President George Bush ordered fighter aircraft and troops to leave for Saudi Arabia.

8 August: Baghdad annexed Kuwait.

9 August: King Fahd condemned Iraq's invasion of Kuwait.

12 August: Iraqi President Saddam Hussein [*qv*] offered a peace initiative that involved the withdrawal of Israel from the Occupied Arab Territories [*qv*] in "Palestine, Syria, and Lebanon," and the formulation of arrangements for the "situation in Kuwait" in line with the U.N. resolutions.

2 October: Amnesty International, a London-based human rights organization, published a report portraying widespread arrests, torture, and summary executions in Kuwait by the occupying Iraqi forces.

8 November: Bush ordered a doubling of U.S. troops in the Gulf to 400,000.

15 November: Saddam Hussein proposed talks between Iraq and Saudi Arabia on regional problems, and between Iraq and the United States on wider issues. There was no response from Riyadh or Washington.

19 November: Iraq mobilized an additional 250,000 troops, with 100,000 to be sent to Kuwait immediately.

27 November: Testimonies of experts before the U.S. Senate Armed Services Committee showed a large majority favoring the economic option over the military option in forcing Iraq out of Kuwait.

29 November: The U.N. Security Council adopted Resolution 678 by twelve votes to two (Cuba and Yemen), with one abstention (China), authorizing "all necessary means" to implement the earlier resolutions in order "to restore international peace and security in the area," unless Iraq fully implemented these resolutions before 15 January 1991.

9 January 1991: Talks in Geneva between Tariq Aziz [*qv*], Iraq's foreign minister, and James Baker, U.S. Secretary of State, to resolve the crisis failed.

12 January: The U.S. Senate authorized President Bush by 53 votes to 47 to use the U.S. military pursuant to U.N. Security Council Resolution 678; the House of Representatives did likewise by 250 votes to 183.

14 January: Iraqi parliament unanimously decided to go to war rather than withdraw from Kuwait, and empowered President Saddam Hussein to conduct it.

Opposing forces (at the start):

Iraq: Baghdad had 545,000 troops in Kuwait and southern Iraq, equipped with 4,200 tanks and 150 combat helicopters, supported by 550 combat-ready warplanes.

U.S.-led coalition: coalition of the United States and twenty-eight other U.N. members: Argentina (naval); Australia (naval); Bahrain (ground, air); Bangladesh (ground); Belgium (air—in Turkey, naval); Canada (air, naval); Czechoslovakia (ground); Denmark (naval); Kuwait; Egypt (ground); France (ground, air, naval); Germany (air—in Turkey); Greece (naval); Italy (air, naval); Morocco (ground); Kuwait (ground); Netherlands (naval); New Zealand (air); Niger (ground); Norway (naval); Oman (ground, air); Pakistan (ground, naval); Qatar (ground, air), Saudi Arabia (ground, air, naval); Senegal (ground); Spain (naval); Syria (ground); United Arab Emirates (ground, air); United Kingdom (ground, air, naval). Of the 425,000 U.S. troops, 250,000 were army soldiers, 75,000 marines, 60,000 naval personnel, and 45,000 air force personnel. They were equipped with 2,200 tanks, 500 combat helicopters, and 1,500 warplanes. By the end of the war the number of the troops of the United States reached 697,000, and those of the United Kingdom and France 52,000 and 25,000, respectively. The twelve North Atlantic Treaty Organization members involved had deployed 107 warships in the Gulf, the northern Arabian Sea and the Gulf of Oman, the Red Sea and the eastern Mediterranean, with most of them enforcing the U.N. embargo. The U.S. naval personnel were armed with 700-plus nuclear weapons on warships and submarines. The Arab and Muslim troops totalled 220,000. They were under the command of Prince Khalid ibn Sultan of Saudi Arabia and were equipped with 1,200 tanks, 150 combat helicopters, and 350 warplanes. The overall commander of the coalition was Gen. Norman Schwarzkopf of the U.S. Army. (The figures at the end of the war were: 700,000 troops equipped with 4,000 tanks and 2,900 warplanes and helicopters.)

Events:

Air campaign (Operation Desert Storm): 16 January to 24 February:

16–23 January: The air campaign of the U.S.-led coalition began at 2330 GMT on 16 January/0230 local time on 17 January, with aerial bombing and the firing of cruise missiles from U.S. warships. On 18 January Iraq fired twelve Scud ground-to-ground missiles at Tel Aviv [*qv*] and Haifa [*qv*] in Israel, and four days later three more Iraqi Scuds landed in Tel Aviv. Coalition air sorties in the first week totalled 12,000 (half of which were combat sorties), and cruise missile firings numbered 216.

24–30 January: The coalition increased the number of daily air sorties to 3,000.

31 January–6 February: On 3 February

the number of coalition air missions reached a total of 41,000, with the U.S. share at 87 percent. Iraq broke diplomatic ties with the United States, Britain, France, Canada, Italy, Egypt, and Saudi Arabia.

7–13 February: During the fourth week, the coalition concentrated on destroying Iraq's transport infrastructure of bridges and roads.

14–20 February: On 15 February Iraq agreed to deal with U.N. Security Council Resolution 660 if the coalition forces left the region, if Israel withdrew from the Occupied Arab Territories, and if the nationalist and Islamic forces of Kuwait were allowed to settle the country's future. Moscow saw this as opening up a new stage in the ongoing conflict, but Kuwait, Saudi Arabia, and Egypt rejected it. President Bush called on the Iraqi people and military to remove Saddam Hussein from office and then comply with the U.N. resolutions. The five-week total of coalition air sorties reached 86,000.

21–24 February: On 21 February Iraq welcomed the Soviet eight-point peace plan, including Iraq's statement of intent to withdraw from Kuwait; a cease-fire; the actual evacuation; the abrogation of the U.N. sanctions once two-thirds of the Iraqi force had left, and the rest of the U.N. resolutions once all Iraqi troops had departed; and the monitoring of the cease-fire by a U.N. force. Bush rejected the plan and offered a list of twelve conditions, including total Iraqi withdrawal within a week, to be accepted by 1730 GMT on 23 February. At 1200 GMT on 23 February, Iraq said that following its acceptance of the Soviet peace plan, it had decided to withdraw from Kuwait immediately and unconditionally. At 1630 GMT the U.N.

Security Council began a closed-door session, with the Western powers declaring that they were not interested in bridging the gap between the Soviet plan and the U.S. terms. At 1800 GMT Bush ordered Gen. Schwarzkopf to expel the Iraqis from Kuwait. By then retreating Iraqis had begun to set Kuwaiti oil wells ablaze.

Ground campaign (Operation Desert Sabre): 24–28 February: At 0100 on 24 February the coalition launched its ground offensive, with ground troops advancing on two axes. The next day at 2130 GMT the Soviet Union presented a new peace plan, and an hour later Iraq accepted it. Baghdad ordered a withdrawal from Kuwait as part of its compliance with Security Council Resolution 660. On 26 February at 1150 the Iraqi forces were out of Kuwait City. U.S. troops blocked all exits for the Iraqi forces in the Kuwaiti theater of war. The killing of retreating Iraqi soldiers continued until a cease-fire forty hours later. On 27 February at 0530 GMT Iraq said that it had completed its evacuation of Kuwait. By then some 640 Kuwaiti oil wells were ablaze. The next day at 0200 GMT Bush ordered a truce if Iraq put down its arms. At 0440 GMT Iraq complied and a temporary cease-fire went into effect at 0500 GMT, thus ending 167 days of prewar crisis and 42 days of warfare. The final total of the coalition's air sorties reached 106,000. They dropped 141,000 tons of explosives, the equivalent of seven nuclear bombs dropped on the Japanese city of Hiroshima in 1945, and hit 700 targets, many of them repeatedly. The number of cruise missiles fired was 325.

Human losses: The U.S. Defense Intelligence Agency issued an estimate of 100,000

Iraqi deaths with an error factor of 50 percent. According to Iraq's deputy premier, Sadoun Hamadi, in the first twenty-six days of the war, the coalition bombing (by 65,000 air sorties) had killed 20,000 Iraqis; the additional figure for the remaining 41,000 sorties was 12,600. During the ground campaign, involving attacks on twelve retreating Iraqi divisions (150,000 troops), the fatalities were estimated at 25,000 to 30,000. The total estimated dead were therefore 57,600–62,600. Other estimates put this figure higher—at 100,000. Iraq has not released its official statistics.

Of the 376 coalition deaths, the U.S. sustained 266 (including 125 due to accidents during the seven-month field training prior to the war), and Britain, 29. An estimated 2,000 to 5,000 Kuwaitis, mostly civilians, died.

Weapons losses: Iraq, 30 warplanes; coalition, 21 warplanes.

Cost: Coalition total, $82 billion—Japan, $13 billion; Kuwait, $22 billion; Saudi Arabia, $29 billion; and United States, $18 billion. Saudi Arabia put its indirect costs at $22 billion. No official figures were released for Iraq. According to Sadoun Hamadi, the damage to Iraq's infrastructure during the first twenty-six days of war was $200 billion. Other estimates put the total damage to Iraq at $200 billion.

After the truce: U.N. Security Council Resolution 687 [*qv*] required Iraq to implement a U.N.-monitored program of disarming itself of weapons of mass destruction and intermediate and long-range ground-to-ground missiles before U.N. sanctions against it could be lifted. *See also* Operation Desert Fox, United Nations Security Council Resolution 687, United Nations Security Council Resolution 1284, and United Nations Security Council Resolution 1441.

Gulf War III (2003): *war between Iraq and the U.S.-U.K. alliance.*

Background (May 1991–December 1998): During this period the United Nations Special Commission (UNSCOM) [*qv*] on disarming Iraq [*qv*] of weapons of mass destruction disarmed Iraq of 90 to 95 percent of its proscribed arms. By mid-June 1998, Baghdad claimed to have disarmed fully and demanded that the U.N. economic sanctions be lifted as specified in Paragraphs 20 and 21 of the United Nations Security Council Resolution 687 [*qv*]. Richard Butler, head of UNSCOM, disagreed. The tension mounted between the U.S. administration of President Bill Clinton and Iraq. To enable Washington, acting in conjunction with London, to mount its Operation Desert Fox [*qv*] against the regime of Iraqi President Saddam Hussein [*qv*] as a penalty for its failure to provide unhindered, unconditional access to U.N. inspectors to any sites they wished, Butler withdrew the inspectors from Iraq. At the Security Council, China, France and Russia condemned the U.S.-U.K. action.

(December 1998–November 2003): The breach among the Permanent Five members of the Security Council proved so severe that it took a year before the Council adopted a new resolution on the subject—1284 [*qv*]—with China, France and Russia abstaining. Iraq did not accept this resolution. Starting August 2000, when several regional countries resumed flights to Baghdad [*qv*], the

U.N. sanctions began to erode, with Syria [qv] re-opening its oil pipeline with Iraq. George W. Bush, who became U.S. president in January 2001, continued the hard-line policy of his predecessor. Following the terrorist attacks on America in September, he stiffened further his stance toward Iraq, even though no evidence turned up to support his administration's early speculation that Saddam Hussein was in cahoots with Al Qaida [qv] and Osama bin Laden [qv] in perpetrating 9/11.

But when, having overthrown the Taliban regime in Afghanistan and having put bin Laden on the run, Bush looked for the next target in his global war on terror, Iraq reappeared as a prime candidate in the spring of 2002. Washington ratcheted up its anti-Saddam rhetoric after the Labor Day holiday in September, claiming that he had restarted his program of making nuclear weapons, and asserting that the Iraqis had made an unsuccessful attempt to buy 500 tons of uranium oxide from Niger in 2000, and had obtained aluminum tubing for centrifuges to enrich uranium. (Later both these claims would be proved false, with the International Atomic Energy Agency [IAEA] declaring the Niger documents to be forgeries.) These statements proved highly effective in persuading the U.S. Congress to give Bush war powers by a comfortable majority in October, even though on 16 September Iraq had agreed to the return of the inspectors of the United Nations Monitoring, Verification and Inspection Commission (UNMOVIC) [qv], headed by Hans Blix, a former Swedish foreign minister and director-general of the IAEA, and Muhammad El Baradei, the Egyptian head of the IAEA. Both Bush and

British Prime Minister Tony Blair began building up military presence in the Gulf [qv], with Kuwait [qv] providing its territory for the posting of American and British troops, and Qatar [qv] allowing the U.S. Central Command (Centcom) to set up its regional headquarters at Al Sayliya near Doha [qv].

Against this background the U.N. Security Council adopted Resolution 1441 [qv] unanimously on 8 November, with France and Russia asserting, rightly, that it did not authorize automatic military action against Iraq if the Baghdad government failed to meet its requirements. The resolution specified the most intrusive inspection regime ever devised. After some equivocation, Saddam Hussein accepted the resolution.

U.N. inspections started on 27 November. As specified in Resolution 1441, Iraq submitted a 12,000-page document detailing its programs of weapons of mass destruction and missiles. In their reports to the Security Council on 19 December, Blix and Baradei said that Iraq had provided prompt access to the 150 sites their teams had visited. The aluminum tubing that America and Britain had alluded to were for permissible Iraqi rockets and not for the proscribed nuclear weapons. By 18 January, 2003 the U.N. teams had visited all eleven sites mentioned by Bush and Blair as the premises used by Iraq in its revived program of weapons of mass destruction, and found no evidence to that effect. On 19–20 January, Iraq signed a ten-point agreement with Blix and Baradei promising further cooperation. Yet Bush kept saying that Saddam must disarm, and in the case of his refusal, the U.S.-led coalition would force him to do so and free the

Iraqi people, well aware that 52 percent of Americans would believe the White House if it asserted that it had evidence of a proscribed weapons program by Baghdad even if U.N. inspectors found nothing. At the same, time the Special Forces of United States and Britain began infiltrating Iraq to facilitate the invasion of the country by the Anglo-American troops.

In their 27 January report covering 300 inspections in two months (of which about 100 concerned the nuclear program) of 230 sites (out of a total of 700) by a staff of 260 drawn from 60 countries, Blix and Baradaei informed the Security Council that on the whole Iraq had cooperated well, giving their teams prompt access to all sites. Baradei said that his inspectors had visited presidential compounds and private residences but had discovered no evidence that Iraq has revived its nuclear weapons program since its elimination in the 1990s.

By contrast, in his presentation to the Security Council on 5 February, U.S. Secretary of State Colin Powell claimed that (1) there were up to two dozen Al Qaida operatives in Iraq, the most important being Abu Mussab Zarqawi; (2) the Ansar-e Islam [qv] operated a chemical poison factory in an enclave of Iraqi Kurdistan [qv]; (3) a missile brigade operating from outside Baghdad was dispersing proscribed rockets throughout the country; (4) Iraq possessed about eighteen mobile biological weapons laboratories; (5) Baghdad had a model of an unmanned drone capable of spraying chemical or germ weapons within a radius of 550 miles; and (6) Iraq moved contraband, with soldiers relocating munitions just before inspectors arrived. Finally, Powell referred to Tony Blair's nine-teen page dossier "Iraq: Its Infrastructure of Concealment, Deception and Intimidation," posted on his official website on 3 February, as a fine piece of evidence.

Critics argued that the presence of Al Qaida operatives in Iraq did not prove the government's involvement: such operatives lived not only in other Arab and Muslim countries but also in many western states. The visiting western journalists found the Ansar-e Islam's poison factory nothing but a derelict dump. Following the overthrow of Saddam Hussein's regime, the Anglo-American troops failed to find the alleged Iraqi missile brigade or the proscribed missiles. Four days before the start of Gulf War III on 20, March 2003, Iraq handed over to UNMOVIC videos of mobile biological laboratories, arguing that the videos showed that Iraq did not violate U.N. resolutions. When checked out by the U.N. inspectors, Iraq's single unmanned drone turned out to be a machine rusting on an airfield north of Baghdad. Likewise, when verified on the ground, Powell's interpretation of the satellite images of trucks moving banned parts turned out to be false. Equally damaging was the discovery made by a British researcher at Cambridge University that large chunks of what Blair had tried to pass of as hot official U.K. intelligence were lifted verbatim from old academic journals and magazines posted on the Internet. Yet 70 percent in the United States agreed with Powell that Iraq was deceiving.

Powell's presentation marked the end of the Bush administration's support of continued U.N. inspections and prepared the ground for military action despite Blix's report on 14 February that the 300 biological and chemical samples examined by

UNMOVIC were consistent with Iraq's dec-larations, and that the inspections were bridging the gap created in the United Nation's knowledge during its absence from December 1998 to November 2002, and despite rising opposition to war both in America and Europe.

On February 15, 15 to 20 million people in 60 countries marched in anti-war protest in 600 towns and cities, a quarter of them in the United States. The marches in London (1.5 million strong), Rome (over 2 million) and Barcelona (over 1 million) were the largest ever. Overall, more than 70 percent in Britain, Italy and Spain opposed the war. Yet their governments continued to back Bush in his belligerent stance.

Indeed, Spain was one of the three spon-sors of the draft resolution—the others being the United States and Britain—presented to the Security Council on 24 February. It stated that Iraq had failed to comply with, and cooperate fully in the implementation of Resolution 1441 and must therefore face "serious consequences." Disagreeing with this document, France, Russia and Germany (as a non-permanent member of the Security Council) issued a memorandum saying that a verifiable disarmament could be reached through the implementation of a clear pro-gram of action by the inspection agencies, with each task clearly defined; reinforced inspections; and a timeline for inspections and assessment, with the chief inspectors reporting every three weeks. This was rejected by the U.S.-U.K.-Spain trio.

In the United States, opposition to war rose from 18 percent at the end of January to 37 percent a month later, almost equal to the support for it.

On 6 March, Blix declared that Iraq was involved in "real and very fine disarmament" and that its cooperation had been "proac-tive." It had begun taking inspectors to the sites where it said it had unilaterally destroyed biological weapons.

At the Security Council the U.S.-U.K.-Spanish draft attracted one more vote, while five members—China, France, Germany, Russia and Syria—opposed it. Of the remaining six, Pakistan and Guinea indi-cated they would abstain, and a top official of Cameroon said that his country and France were "old friends." Given this, there was no prospect of the Anglo-American alliance getting its draft resolution adopted by the Council. Yet so strongly opposed were France and Russia to a war on Iraq that they individually threatened to veto the resolution if passed.

When Angola, Cameroon, Chile, Guinea, Mexico and Pakistan proposed giving Iraq forty-five days to disarm (versus France's 120 days), the United States rejected the proposal summarily.

In the United States, the anti-Saddam rhetoric reached a point where 42 percent believed that he was "personally" responsible for 9/11, and 55 percent believed that he gave direct support to Al Qaida.

On 14 March, when Bush, Blair and Spanish President Jose Maria Aznar decided to meet on the Portuguese Island of Terceira in the Azores, Iraq gave UNMOVIC a twenty-page document detailing the destruc-tion of 3.9 tons of VX nerve agent. The next day U.N. Secretary-General Kofi Annan said he believed war without the second resolu-tion by the Security Council would break international law, meaning a violation of the

U.N. Charter. Following the Bush-Blair-Aznar meeting, on March 16, when they decided to abandon their draft resolution at the Security Council, Bush gave Saddam Hussein and his sons—Uday and Qusay [*qv*]—forty-eight hours to leave Iraq, failing which Washington would mount military operations. Saddam rejected the ultimatum. On March 18, the House of Commons in London passed a motion by 412 to 149 votes—with the opposition Tories voting with most of the governing Labor Party members—which stated that "the United Kingdom must uphold the United Nation's authority as set out in [Resolution] 1441 and many resolutions preceding it, and therefore supports the decision that the United Kingdom should use all means to disarm Iraq."

Opposing forces:

Iraq: Baghdad had 389,000 troops, including 82,000 in the Republican Guard and 20,000 in the Special Republican Guard, and was equipped with 2,600 tanks and 100 combat helicopters, backed by 300 combat aircraft, only half of which were serviceable. Its active paramilitary force included 5,000 armed personnel of the Special Security Organization, 20,000 members of Saddam's *Fedayeen* (*Arabic: Self-sacrificers*) and 6,000 non-Iraqi Arab volunteers.

US-led coalition: A nominal coalition of forty-eight countries, with only five contributing combat troops—United States (255,000), Australia (2000), Britain (45,000), Czech Republic (200); Poland (200); and Slovakia (200)—the rest either merely expressing support for Washington's position or allowing U.S. military aircraft passage through their air spaces. The Anglo-American forces were equipped with 920 tanks, 600 warplanes, 300 combat helicopters, and 50 unmanned aerial vehicles. The U.S. navy deployed five aircraft-carrier battle groups, and the U.K. navy one .

Events:

March 20–26 (Week 1):

The Pentagon started its Operation Iraqi Freedom [*qv*] on March 20 at 0233 GMT (0533 Iraqi time) with four guided bunker-busting bombs, released by Stealth bombers, to strike the Republican Presidential Palace Complex in Baghdad where Saddam Hussein and his two sons were suspected of holding a meeting. Cruise missiles hit surrounding targets while Tomahawk missiles struck targets around Baghdad. At 0530 GMT the Iraqi president appeared on television to declare that "Iraq will carry out jihad [*qv*] against the invaders with the heroic army in the vanguard of Iraq of civilization, history and belief . . . Iraq will be victorious." Four hours later, Group Captain Al Lockwood, spokesman for the British forces in the Gulf said, "If I was a betting man, hopefully, we'll be in Baghdad in the next three or four days." At the Rumeila oil field west of Basra [*qv*], Iraqis set oil wells ablaze. At night, when U.S. Navy Seals and Royal Marine commandos under British command tried to capture oil and gas platforms in the Fao Peninsula, they encountered resistance.

Next morning, the U.S. Central Command (Centcom) mounted a four-prong ground attack on Iraq from Kuwait, with the U.S. 3rd Infantry Division heading north toward Baghdad. American and British Special Forces, infiltrating Iraq from Jordan [*qv*], claimed the capture of Iraq's H2 and H3 airfields in the western desert. The Centcom's claim of the capture of Umm Qasr (pop. 45,000) port was disputed, rightly, by Al Jazeera TV. The Centcom's quick and surgical strikes on the government buildings and presidential compounds in Baghdad, combined with e-mails and mobile phone calls to Iraqi generals to defect, failed to bring about the expected collapse of the regime.

At 1720 GMT (2020 Iraqi time) the Centcom unleashed its "Shock and awe" strategy with a series of staggering explosions, most of them in the Republican Presidential Palace Complex, in an awesome, murderous fireworks display, unlike any witnessed before.

Later the Centcom hit targets in Mosul [*qv*] and Kirkuk [*qv*]. In Kurdistan, the Kurdistan Democratic Party [*qv*] and the Patriotic Union of Kurdistan [*qv*] agreed to put their 35,000 militia, called *peshmargas* (Kurdish: those prepared to die) under the Centcom command.

On 20–21 March, the Centcom undertook 1,000 combat missions and discharged 600 cruise missiles.

On 22 March, the Iraqi TV showed Saddam Hussein meeting senior advisers. The Iraqi military set fire to oil-filled trenches around Baghdad to create smoke to obscure targets and mislead the guidance systems of bombs and missles. The Centcom claim of the capture of Nasiriya (pop. 300,000) was disputed, rightly, by Al Jazeera TV. The Anglo-American forces approached Basra [*qv*]. The Pentagon sources said that the Central Intelligence Agency's (CIA) Special Activities Division "may be" involved in talks between the United States and the Republican Guard generals. The total of the cruise missiles to hit Iraq reached 1,000.

In America, Bush's approval rating rose from 51 percent ten days earlier to 70 percent, while the disapproval points fell from 42 to 27 percent. A poll in Britain showed 56 percent saying that America and Britain were "right" to go to war against 36 percent saying "wrong."

On 23 March, the Centcom's claim of the capture of Zubair naval base remained unverified. Iraq claimed that seventy-seven civilians had died in the fighting in Basra. As U.S. troops approached Najaf [*qv*] and Karbala [*qv*] they met stiff resistance. Nightly bombing of Baghdad continued.

On 24 March, there were reports of resistance to the invading forces in Zubair. The next day, the 25th, the Centcom claimed control of all of the Rumeila oil field. Its claim of a civilian uprising in Basra was contradicted by the images shown by Al Jazeera's reporter inside the city, which was now besieged. The Iraqi resistance in Nasiriya continued. A fierce sandstorm hit Baghdad.

There were large protest marches in Amman [*qv*], Beirut [*qv*]and Damascus [*qv*].

On 26 March, the sandstorm and Iraqi resistance slowed down the American advance. The Centcom's final capture of Umm Qasr was confirmed by Al Jazeera TV. In Baghdad, a U.S. missile hit a busy market in the northern suburb of Al Shaab, killing forty-eight. On the outskirts of the capital, the Anglo-American Special Forces painted targets with lasers to guide bombs. U.S. paratroopers arrived at Bashur air strip in Kurdistan to open a front in the north.

In the first week of its invasion of Iraq, the Centcom mounted 5,700 air sorties, dropped 2,000 guided bombs, and fired 500 Tomahawk missiles.

27 March –2 April (Week 2):

On March 27, British troops distributed food packages in Zubair. U.S. troops began consolidating their positions outside Karbala. Across the "Karbala Gap," however, they faced 6,000 Iraqi regular army and Republican Guard soldiers. Small bands of Iraqi irregulars harassed the U.S. supply lines. There were big explosions in central Baghdad. The following day a missile struck a market in the suburb of Al Shuale, killing at least fifty-five. Two bunker-busting bombs destroyed the communications tower.

On 29 March, a suicide bomber—a Shia [*qv*] Iraqi soldier in civilian dress—killed four American soldiers in Najaf. There was no evidence he was responding to the call given by Osama bin Laden seven weeks earlier to Muslims worldwide, especially to those in Iraq, to conduct a jihad against the infidels' invasion of Iraq even though its regime was run by the Baath Socialist Party [*qv*], which, in bin Laden's view, had adopted the apostasy of socialism.

There were worldwide protest demonstrations against the war, including one in Port Said, Egypt [*qv*], organized by the ruling National Democratic Party [*qv*].

On 30 March, there was fierce fighting between the two warring sides in Najaf. In Nasiriya the Americans started building an extra bridge over the Euphrates [*qv*] to help unclog the supply lines to the forces northward. U.S. troops captured the airfield near Karbala after intense combat. In its round-the-clock bombardment of Baghdad, the Centcom destroyed two phone exchanges and the international trade-fair site.

The next day the British Marines captured the Abu Qassib suburb of Basra after a fifteen-hour battle. In Nasiriya the U.S. Marines were engaged in street fighting. On April 1, the U.S Marines, on reaching Kut, fought the units of the Iraqi Republican Guard, regular army and Fedayeen Saddam. U.S. soldiers besieged Najaf. Fighting broke out in Hillah. There was heavy bombing of Baghdad with low-flying aircraft swooping over.

On April 2, American troops encircled Karbala.

At the end of two weeks, the Centcom had flown 18,000 air sorties, launched 725 Tomahawk missiles, discharged 12,000 precision-guided munitions, and dropped 50 cluster bombs, and fired an unspecified number of cluster munitions. It had seized 600 of the 1,000 Iraqi oil wells in the south and the center.

3–9 April (Week 3):

On April 3, the Kurdish peshmargas attacked the Iraqi front lines in a big way. The Centcom's blackout bombs, which showered power cables with graphite filament and short-circuited electric grids, plunged Baghdad into darkness. U.S. troops seized Furat near Saddam International Airport, located six miles from Baghdad's city boundary. The capital was (in theory) safeguarded by 20,000 soldiers of the Special Republican Guard, whose commanders were unable to communicate with the Central Command, and an unknown number of the Fedayeen Saddam and foreign volunteers.

The following day, a British Special Forces unit staged a lightning raid on a premise inside Basra and reportedly killed General Ali Hassan al-Majid (b. 1938), commander of the southern Iraqi forces, and his bodyguards. After a day's combat, the U.S. troops captured Saddam International Airport. Central Baghdad was quiet with little evidence of troops, road blocks or other defenses. Most of the capital was without power or water after another night of bombing.

On 5 April, an armored column of thirty U.S. tanks went around in an arc in the southwest of Baghdad, adjacent to Saddam Airport. Iraqi TV showed Saddam Hussein attending a meeting with his sons, top aides and military commanders. The black-uniformed Fedayeen Saddam appeared on the streets for the first time.

On 6 April, in a three-pronged attack, the British troops, who had so far fired inter alia 2,000-plus cluster munitions around Basra, entered the city center; and the U.S. forces seized Karbala's central district. The 7,000 American soldiers stationed at the Saddam Airport repulsed an Iraqi counterattack.

The next day there was looting in Basra, and a large statue of Saddam Hussein was pulled down in Karbala.

With an advance group of special mine-clearing tanks clearing a path through 400 yards (366 meters) of minefields, a column of seventy U.S. tanks and sixty fighting vehicles, with air cover, conducted an armored raid along Highway 8 running through Baghdad, and headed for the district housing government offices and the Parade Ground and Victory Arches. American soldiers raided the New Presidential Palace, which contained Saddam Hussein's official residence.

On 8 April at 1200 GMT (1500 Iraqi time), the Centcom directed two satellite-guided bombs and two bunker-busting bombs at a restaurant in Mansour district following an intelligence tip-off that Saddam Hussein and his two sons and senior aides were there. The bombs left a 60 ft (20 meters) crater and killed fourteen. In two separate attacks the U.S. killed Tariq Ayub, an Al Jazeera TV reporter on the roof of his office in Baghdad, and two news agency photographers based at the Palestine Hotel. Iraqi TV went off the air. That day, all Republican Guard and Special Republican Guard soldiers melted away, reportedly as a result of a secret deal negotiated by top CIA officials between the Centcom and the Republican Guard General Command (which had lost contact with the Iraqi Central Command due to the disruption by the Pentagon of the Iraqi communications system and had realized that without air cover it was impossible to defend Baghdad), whereby the Republican Guard generals agreed to order their ranks to throw away their uniforms and go home in return for the Centcom's assurance that the deserters would not be chased and that it would airlift the Republican Guard leadership out of Iraq. This deal left the Special Republican Guard commanders no option but to follow suit. As a result, the number of the Iraqi prisoners of war remained unchanged—at 8,302. The deal did not apply to the regular army and the Fedayeen Saddam. When they sniped at the American troops from building tops, they were targeted by A10 attack aircraft. U.S. Marines seized Rashid Airport in eastern Baghdad.

On 9 April, celebrating crowds in Baghdad danced, looted and defaced the ubiquitous images of Saddam Hussein. The 20 ft. (6 meter) bronze statue of Saddam at the Fardaws Square in downtown Baghdad was pulled down with the help of a U.S. Marine tank. The Centcom declared the end of the regime of Saddam Hussein, who was to be sighted later that day in the streets of a northern neighborhood of Baghdad. Heavy fighting broke out at the border town of Qaim (next to Syria), defended by units of the Special Republican Guard.

In the past three weeks the Centcom had staged 30,000 air sorties, dropped 30,000 bombs and discharged 750 cruise missiles.

10–16 April (Week 4):

On 10 April, Baghdad descended into anarchy as underprivileged Shia mobs resorted to arson and looting. With the exception of the ministries of oil and interior, heavily guarded by U.S. troops, all the ministries were ransacked and burnt. In the north, Kurdish peshmargas entered Kirkuk after the Iraqi troops abandoned the city following heavy U.S. air raids. Tikrit, the home-town of Saddam Hussein, was bombed severely, with the U.S Special Forces guiding the bombing. At Diwaniya there was an eight-hour firefight as the Iraqis attacked U.S. supply lines, and there was intense combat in Hillah between the American troops and the Fedayeen Saddam. Umm Qasr was named as the base of the U.S. Office for Reconstruction and Humanitarian Assistance (ORHA) to be headed by retired U.S. general Jay Garner. The Centcom issued playing-card pictures of the fifty-five most wanted Iraqis.

French President Jacques Chirac said, "France, like all democracies, welcomes the fall of Saddam Hussein's dictatorship."

On April 11, the Kurdish peshmaragas and U.S. Special Forces entered Mosul [*qv*] after signs of Iraqi withdrawal. There was

celebration as well as looting. The next day there was fighting between Kurds and Arabs in Mosul, which is two-thirds Arab. In central Baghdad, Iraq's largest archaeological museum was looted, and many ancient artifacts were destroyed or stolen.

On 13 April, U.S. soldiers entered Tikrit, which looked deserted. But once inside, they faced a fierce attack by Iraqi tanks. The Pentagon claimed that of the fifty-five to sixty zones into which the Centcom had divided Baghdad, only ten to fifteen were not under its control, and whatever resistance persisted was mainly from the non-Iraqi foreign volunteers.

On 14 April, the Bush administration put a $200,000 bounty on Saddam's head. The next day Centcom conceded that it controlled only the western part of Tikrit, with its eastern part on the other side of the Tigris being under pro-Saddam forces. Having captured Qaim, the American troops cut off the Iraqi-Syrian oil pipeline. A meeting of eighty Iraqi delegates held at Talil air base near Nasiriya, opened by Jay Garner, head of the Office for Reconstruction and Humanitarian Assistance, and chaired by Zalmay Khalilzad, a personal envoy of President Bush, was attended by the two main Kurdish parties but boycotted by the Supreme Assembly of Islamic Revolution in Iraq [*qv*]. In nearby Nasiriya, 20,000 Shias demonstrated against the U.S. and for an Islamic Iraq, shouting "No to America, No to Saddam."

On 16 April, forty U.S. Marines raided the house of British-trained Dr Rihad Taha, the biologist wife of General Amr Muhammad Rashid, former oil minister, but failed to find evidence of Iraq's alleged weapons of mass destruction.

In the past four weeks, the Centcom had mounted 37,000 air sorties, launched 23,000 precision-guided missiles, fired 750 cruise missiles, and dropped 1,566 cluster bombs (1,500 by the United States, and the rest by Britain).

For all practical purposes, Gulf War III ended on 16 April, although it was not until 1 May that President Bush announced a formal end to the hostilities against Iraq.

Human losses: Iraq: civilians 5,425 to 7,041 (est.), soldiers 13,000 (est.); U.K.: soldiers 31; U.S.: soldiers 119.

Cost: $30 billion for the first twenty-eight days, or approximately $1.1 billion a day, with the U.K. bearing about 8 percent of the total.

Gush Emunim *(Hebrew: Bloc of the Faithful): Israeli political–religious movement* Founded in early 1974, the Gush Emunim grew out of a highly active group within the National Religious Party (NRP) [qv], formed after the 1967 Six-Day War [qv] to advocate the Jewish settlement of the Occupied Arab Territories [qv]. In 1970 it captured popular attention by establishing an unauthorized settlement at Kiryat Arba near Hebron [qv]. The presence of the NRP inside the cabinet, and the fact that the Labor-dominated [qv] government itself had initiated a program of colonization within six months of the 1967 war, meant that no action was taken against the settlers. The installation in May 1977 of the Likud-led [qv] government boosted the morale of the Gush, whose views on historical Jewish claims on Judea [qv] and Samaria [qv] had been endorsed by the powerful Ashkenazim [qv] Rabbinical Council.

Within three years of the start of the Likud administration, the Gush had established twenty illegal colonies on the West Bank [qv]. The plans of Gush extremists—known as "The Jewish Underground"—to blow up the Dome of the Rock [qv] and al Aqsa mosque in order to trigger a fresh war between Israel and the Arabs were diverted by their involvement in attacks of two Palestinian mayors in June 1980 in retaliation for the death of six Jewish militants in Hebron in May. When the final Israeli evacuation of Sinai [qv], including Yamit settlement, in April 1982 aroused little public protest, Gush militants postponed their demolition plan.

In July 1983 the stabbing of a Jewish settler in Hebron led to retribution by the Jewish settlers of Kiryat Arba. This in turn led to attacks on Israeli buses in early 1984. Gush extremists responded by planting bombs on five Arab buses, which were defused. The arrest in April 1984 of Gush militants revealed their plans against Muslim shrines, which were condemned by secular and religious authorities.

It was only after the Palestinian intifada [qv] had gathered momentum in the late 1980s that the Gush's influence began to wane, after reaching a peak of 50,000 members. It opposed the Oslo Accord [qv] of September 1993, and its militants applauded the murder of twenty-nine Palestinians who were praying at Hebron's Ibrahimi Mosque (called Tomb of the Patriarchs by the Jews [qv]) in February 1994 by a Kiryat Arba resident, Baruch Goldstein, a follower of Kiryat Arba-based Moshe Levinger, the best known leader of the Gush Emunim. *See also* Jewish fundamentalism.

H

ha *(Hebrew: the):* Used as a prefix, the definite article in Hebrew is often joined (in European languages) to the noun by a hyphen, or is written with no intervening space, for instance Ha-Poale or HaPoale.

Habash, George (1925–): *Palestinian leader* Born into a Greek Orthodox [*qv*] family in Lydda (later Lod), Habash moved to Amman [*qv*] with his parents after the Palestine War (1948–49) [*qv*]. He graduated in medicine from the American University in Beirut (AUB) [*qv*]. While at the AUB, in 1952 he cofounded the Arab Nationalist Movement (ANM) [*qv*]. Under his leadership the ANM's Palestinian members formed a "Preparatory Committee for Unified Palestinian Action" in early 1966. Overall, though, Habash put his faith in Egyptian President Gamal Abdul Nasser [*qv*] as the leader who would liberate Palestine through a conventional war with Israel. But the Arab defeat in the 1967 Six-Day War [*qv*] destroyed this scenario.

Habash founded the Popular Front for the Liberation of Palestine (PFLP) [*qv*], which affiliated with the Palestine Liberation Organization (PLO) [*qv*]. Believing that hijacking an airliner was more effective in drawing world attention to the plight of Palestinians than killing Israelis, Habash began to organize hijacks—the first target being an Israeli aircraft at Athens airport in December 1968. As he turned into a Marxist-Leninist, wedded to bringing about global revolution, he added international Zionism [*qv*], world imperialism, and Arab reaction to Israel to his list of enemies. He used the hijacking of three Western airliners

on 9 September 1970 to trigger a clash between Palestinian commandos and King Hussein of Jordan [*qv*], which escalated into large-scale fighting in which the Palestinians were defeated.

After the PFLP's expulsion from Amman, Habash relocated it in Beirut [*qv*]. When in 1974 the Palestine National Council (PNC) accepted the idea of a Palestinian state on the West Bank [*qv*] and the Gaza Strip [*qv*] as an "intermediate step" toward the liberation of Palestine, Habash rejected it and began a boycott of the PLO Executive Committee, of which he was a member. He continued this until 1981. After the expulsion of the PLO from Beirut in September 1982, Habash refrained from joining the Syrian-instigated attack against Yasser Arafat [*qv*] and Fatah [*qv*]. But following Arafat's agreement with King Hussein in early 1985 to initiate talks with Israel, Habash joined the Syrian-inspired Palestine National Salvation front of radical Palestinian groups. Two years later, after the Arafat-Hussein agreement had been reversed, Habash rejoined the PLO Executive Committee. In November 1988, while opposing the resolution before the PNC to accept a Palestinian state in part of Palestine and peaceful coexistence with Israel, he declared that he would abide by the decision of the majority (which adopted the resolution).

During the crisis created by Iraq's invasion of Kuwait in August 1990, Habash backed President Saddam Hussein [*qv*], especially after the latter tried to link the Kuwaiti issue to Israel's occupation of the Arab territories. He backed Iraq in its war with the U.S.-led coalition in early 1991. He opposed the Oslo Accord [*qv*] of September 1993. Afflicted with cancer, he gave up his leadership of the PFLP to his deputy, Mustafa Zifri, also known as Abu Ali Mustafa, in 2000.

Habibi, Emile Shukri (1921–96): *Palestinian writer and politician* Born into a Christian [qv] family in Haifa [qv], Habibi received his secondary school education in Haifa and Acre [qv]. After working in sundry jobs, he became an announcer with the Palestinian Broadcasting Service in 1940, the year he joined the Palestine Communist Party [qv]. Following the party line, he backed the 1947 United Nations partition plan for Palestine. After the founding of Israel in 1948, he stayed in the Jewish state. The party he belonged to, Maki [qv] (the Israeli Communist Party), opposed military administration of Arab-inhabited areas and fought discrimination against Arab citizens. He was elected to parliament in 1951, 1955, and 1961. Four years later, together with Emile Touma [qv] and Meir Vilner, Habibi left Maki and established Rakah [qv] (New Communist List). He failed to get reelected to parliament in 1965 and 1969, but was successful in 1973.

A prolific journalist dealing with literary, cultural, and political subjects, Habibi served on the editorial boards of important communist publications, becoming chief editor of the party organ, *Al Ittihad* (The Unity), from 1985–89. His collection of short stories, *The Sextet of the Six-Day War* (1969), relates the meetings between Israeli Arabs [qv] and their relatives living elsewhere. His best known volume, *The Secret Life of Saeed, the Ill-fated Pessoptimist* (1974), is a sardonic novel about an Arab antihero who wants to cooperate with the Israelis. Then followed *Lukaa bin Lukaa* (Lukaa, son of Lukaa)

(1980), *Ikhtiyaa* (1985) and *Suraya bint al Ghoul* (Saraya, daughter of the Ghoul) (1991). He won the Israel prize for literature in 1992, the first Israeli Arab [qv] to do so.

Hadash *(Hebrew: acronymn of* Hazit Demokratit le Shalom ve Leshivyon, *Democratic Front for Peace and Equality): Israeli political party* Formed in 1977 by the merger of Rakah [qv] and the Black Panther Party, Hadash adopted the following program: Israeli withdrawal from all Occupied Arab Territories [qv], the establishment of a Palestinian state in the West Bank [qv] and Gaza [qv], and an end to discrimination against Israeli Arabs [qv] and Oriental Jews [qv]. The number of Knesset [qv] seats won by Hadash has varied between three (in 1999) and five (in 1977). Its secretary-general is Muhammad Barake.

Hadith *(Arabic: Narrative): sayings and doings of the Prophet Muhammad* The original term "Al Hadith," meaning "The Tradition"—an account of the words and deeds of the Prophet Muhammad—is now used without "Al." With the spread of Islam [qv] after the Prophet Muhammad's death in A.D. 632, many of his companions settled in the conquered territories, which were administered first by the Umayyads (A.D. 661–750) and then the Abbasids (751–1258). Of the 6,616 verses in the Quran [qv], only eighty concerned legal issues, mainly about women, marriage, family, and inheritance. But since the Prophet Muhammad had governed a realm, there was an oral record of what he had said and done as a judge and administrator. As most of his companions had made note of what he did or said for their own guidance, their diligence later paved the way for codification of the Prophet's *sunna* (practice) when the eminent jurist Muhammad ibn Idris al Shafii (A.D. 767–820) ruled that all legal decisions not stemming directly from the Quran must be based on a tradition going back to the Prophet Muhammad himself.

The result was the Hadith—books of traditions, each tradition described by text and the chain of authority, going back to the original source. Some 2,700 acts and sayings of the Prophet were collected and published in six canonical works, called *Al Hadith,* the first collection being by Muhammad al Bukhari (d. A.D. 870). These were accepted by Sunnis [*qv*] and became a secondary source of guidance, the primary source being the Quran. Shias [*qv*], who accepted only those traditions that were traced through Imam Ali ibn Abu Talib, came up with their collections, compiled by Abu Jaafar Muhammad al Kulini (d. 939), Abu Jaafar Muhammad al Kummi (d. 991) and Abu Jaafar Muhammad al Tusi (d. 1068). In the event of dispute, a tradition can be abrogated only by another tradition.

Hafiz, Amin (1921–): *Syrian politician; president, 1963–66* The son of a Sunni [*qv*] policeman in Aleppo [*qv*], Hafiz became a noncommissioned officer in the French-Syrian Special Forces during the Second World War. He graduated from the Homs Military Academy in 1947. Following his participation in the coup against Adib Shishakli [*qv*] in 1954, he was appointed commandant of the Homs Military Academy. After the merger of Syria and Egypt into the United Arab Republic [*qv*] in 1958, Hafiz was sent to the Cairo military staff college as an instructor. When Syria seceded from the UAR in September 1961, Hafiz was recalled to Damascus [*qv*], then dispatched to Argentina as a military attaché.

After the Baath party [*qv*] seized power in March 1963, the powerful Military Committee promoted Hafiz to lieutenant general and appointed him interior minister and deputy premier. He joined the Baath party. Having foiled the Syrian Nasserists' [*qv*] attempt to capture power, he became defense minister and acting chief of staff as well as chairman of the Presidential Council. When Salah al Din Bitar [*qv*] resigned as premier in October 1963, Hafiz succeeded him. But Hafiz's order in April 1964 to shell the al Sultan mosque in Damascus to counter the Islamic challenge to the regime backfired. He gave up his premiership.

Despite his high governmental and party positions, he lacked real power, which belonged to the Military Committee from which he was excluded. In protest he went over to the civilian faction of the Baath party, led by Michel Aflaq [*qv*] and Bitar, which lacked a military figure. In August 1965 he ousted Salah Jadid [*qv*], head of the Military Committee, as chief of staff. But in the final showdown between the Military Committee and its rival faction in February 1966, Hafiz's side lost and he was imprisoned.

After his release from jail in June 1967 he went into exile in Lebanon. When the Aflaq-led faction of the Baath party seized power in Iraq about a year later, he moved to Baghdad [*qv*]. Following the seizure of power by Hafiz Assad [*qv*] in November 1970, more than 100 Syrians, including Hafiz and Aflaq, were tried for conspiring with Iraq to overthrow the Syrian regime in 1970 (before Assad's takeover). Hafiz, Aflaq and three others were sentenced to capital punishment, which was commuted by Assad. Hafiz continued his anti-Assad activities, later heading the National Alliance of the Liberation of Syria, an umbrella body of various anti-Assad factions.

Haganah *(Hebrew: Defense): Zionist military organization* Aware of the deep Arab resentment against Jewish immigration into Palestine [*qv*], young Zionists [*qv*] secretly transformed a voluntary body, HaShomer (The Watchmen), into Haganah, a militia, in 1920. Following the Arab-Jewish clashes of 1929, they accelerated the process of training and equipping Haganah volunteers with smuggled weapons. It was the discovery of such arms in the autumn of 1935 that triggered the Arab revolt of 1936–39. Haganah then had more than 10,000 relatively well-equipped members. During the latter, post-1938 phase of the Arab revolt, when the Arabs [*qv*] attacked not only British targets but also Jewish settlements, Haganah was fostered and armed by the British mandate. It carried out operations against the Arabs and manufactured arms at a clandestine factory.

Following the outbreak of the Second World War, the British legalized Haganah, which instructed its members to join the Jewish units within the British army. More than 27,000 Palestinian Jews did so. However, when the war was over Haganah turned against the British and engaged in the smuggling of Jewish immigrants. The British mounted a major campaign against it in June 1947, but met with only partial success.

By the time the United Nations adopted the partition plan in November 1947, Haganah had emerged as a professional army, supported by 79,000 reserves, armed police, and home guards. As 15 May 1948—the British withdrawal date—approached, interethnic violence intensified. Conscious of the fact that the area about to constitute the Jewish state, according to the U.N. plan, held almost as many Arabs as Jews [*qv*], Haganah along with Irgun Zvai Leumi [*qv*] and Lehi [*qv*] focused on expelling as many Arabs from this area as possible. With the founding of Israel in 1948, Haganah members were transferred to the Zvai Haganah Le Israel (Military Defense of Israel), known as Zahal [*qv*].

Haifa: *Israeli city* Pop. 280,000 (2003, est.). An important port, the recorded history of Haifa goes back two millennia. It was captured by Muslim Arabs [*qv*] in A.D. 638 and changed hands during the Crusades. It formed part of the Ottoman Empire in the sixteenth century. At the turn of the twentieth century, Haifa began to overtake Acre [*qv*], situated at the northern end of the same bay, as a port. After the defeat of the Ottomans in 1918 it became part of the Palestine [*qv*] placed under British mandate. It was the site of bitter battles between the Arabs and the Zionists on the eve of the founding of Israel in 1948, which resulted in all but 3,000 of its 50,000 Arab residents fleeing.

The city, located on Mount Carmel, is picturesque and has a large deepwater harbor. It is an important commercial, industrial, and communications center. The burial place of Abdul Baha, son of the founder of Bahaism [*qv*], Haifa is the international headquarters of the Bahai faith [*qv*].

hajj *(Arabic: setting out):* The fifth pillar of Islam [*qv*], *hajj* is decreed by the Quran [*qv*]

(3:97): "And pilgrimage to the House [of Allah] is incumbent upon people for the sake of Allah, [upon] everyone who is able to undertake the journey to it." The House of Allah, containing the sacred Black Stone, the Kaaba [*qv*], in the Saudi city of Mecca [*qv*], is believed to have been rebuilt several times since its original construction by Adam. Before entering Mecca—during 8–10 Dhul Hijja, the last month of the Islamic calendar [*qv*]—the pilgrim performs a ritual ablution and puts on two seamless pieces of white cloth (men only—women wear ordinary dress).

After entering the city, the pilgrim circumambulates the Kaaba counterclockwise seven times. Then he strides fast between the Safa and Marwa hillocks, respective symbols of caution and hope, pertaining to the search for water by Hagar for her son Ishmael/Ismail by the Prophet Abraham. Along with fellow pilgrims he must then stand on Arafat Hill, situated 12 miles/19 km to the east of the Kaaba, from midday to sunset, seeking enlightenment and salvation. Next the pilgrim must reach Mina, a site in the desert, and throw seven stones at each of the three pillars, the first of which is called the Great Devil. This is a reenactment of Abraham's stoning of the devil, when an inner voice whispered to him not to sacrifice his son, Ishmael, as he had been commanded to do. Finally, in a further reenactment of Abraham (when, having resolved to sacrifice his son, Ishmael, in the way of God, the ram of his renunciation appeared), the pilgrim sacrifices an animal: a sheep, goat, camel or cow. The pilgrim then has his face and head shaved whereupon he is entitled to call himself hajji or haajj.

Hajj is the most dramatic manifestation of the Muslim [*qv*] *umma* [*qv*].

In the 1990s there were a series of accidents, caused either by a fire in the pilgrims' tents or a surge among pilgrims on their way to a prescribed site, resulting in hundreds of deaths. This happened despite the fact that in 1988 the Saudi government fixed a quota of one pilgrim per thousand foreign Muslims.

In 2001, of the two million pilgrims, 1,364,000 were foreign Muslims, the rest Saudi.

al Hakim, Tawfiq (1898–1987): *Egyptian writer* Born of a Turkish father and an Egyptian mother in Alexandria [*qv*], al Hakim secured a law degree from Cairo University. In 1925 he went to Paris to obtain a doctorate in law. Instead of concentrating on his studies, he soaked himself in the cultural, artistic, and theatrical life of the city. Having written two plays before arriving in Paris, he took a keen interest in the works of George Bernard Shaw, Henrik Ibsen, Maurice Maeterlinck, and Luigi Pirandello. After his return to Egypt in 1928, albeit without a doctorate in law, he was appointed deputy prosecutor in Alexandria and then transferred to several towns as the county district attorney. In 1934 he became director of the education ministry's research department, moving five years later to the Ministry of Social Affairs' information service.

By then his literary career was well established. Having attempted light entertainment in *Ali Baba* (1926), al Hakim opted for authoring intellectual plays full of ideas and philosophic reflections. He retained his outstanding ability to write lucid dialogue in colloquial Arabic and single-handedly raised prose drama, until then considered low art, to the exalted level of Arabic poetry. He dealt with the conflict between pragmatic and idealist behavior in *A Bullet in the Heart* (1931), a comedy, and with the search for knowledge in *Shahrazad* (1934). *The Men of the Cave* (1935) is another play of ideas offering a Quranic version of the Christian legend of the Seven Sleepers of Ephesus. Inspired by Aristophanes's *Lysistrata,* he wrote *Praxa: or How to Govern* (1939), in which the entertaining element was stronger than the intellectual. It was the same in *Pygmalion* (1942). During the next decade he wrote *Solomon the Wise* (1943), *King Oedipus* (1949), *Mr. Kanduz's Property* (1950), a contemporary social comedy, and *If Youth Only Knew* (1950), in which an old man regains his youth by taking an elixir.

At the time of the 1952 revolution, al Hakim was director of the National Library in Cairo [*qv*]. He supported the new regime. In 1956 he was made a member of the National Arts Council, and four years later received the state prize for literature. His *Soft Hands* (1954) is about dignity of labor, and *The Deal* (1956) is about a small village's attempt to purchase land from a foreign company. *The Sultan's Dilemma* (1960) is an entertaining fantasy with a political message: a ruler who uses force to uphold freedom is hardly free himself. This indicated al Hakim's disappointment with the rule of President Gamal Abdul Nasser [*qv*]. He expressed this feeling more strongly after publication of *The Tree Climber* (1962) (a variation of the story of Adam, Eve, and the Tree) and *Shams al Nahr* (1965) (a princess in the *Arabian Nights* who refuses to marry a rich prince), in such political plays as *Fate of a Cockroach*

(1966), *Not a Thing out of Place* (1966) and *The Bank of Worry* (1967). After Nasser's death in 1970, al Hakim criticized him in his booklet *The Return of Consciousness* (1975). By then his plays had been translated into foreign languages and performed abroad. His novels, *Return of the Soul* (1933) and *Diary of a County District Attorney* (1937), had also been translated abroad.

Hakimiya: *Islamic sect* Hakimiya is the term used for those who followed the Fatimid Caliph al Hakim. *See* Druzes.

Halabja: *Iraqi Kurdish town, site of poison gas attacks by Iraq* Pop. 75,000 (2002, est.). During the Iran–Iraq War [*qv*], Iran and its Iraqi Kurdish allies captured Halabja, fifteen miles from the international border, on 13 March 1988. Three days later the Iraqi air force attacked it with poison gas bombs, killing between 3,200 and 6,800 people, mainly civilians, and injuring another 10,000. The pictures of men, women, and children frozen in instant death, relayed by the Iranian media, shocked the world. In killing its own unarmed citizens with chemical weapons, Iraq did something unprecedentedly abhorrent. The U.S. Defense Department asserted that Iran was partly responsible for the event. It was seven weeks before the U.N. Security Council condemned the use of chemical weapons by "both sides (Iraq and Iran)" and called on them to refrain from using such weapons in the future.

Halacha *(Hebrew: The Way): Jewish law* Also spelled Halakha. Halacha is a set of laws and ordinances that govern religious observances and the daily life and conduct of Jews [*qv*]. It preserves the Oral Law, originating with the revelation on Mount Sinai to Moses. The task of compiling the oral traditions of the law, and their interpretations, begun at the turn of the second century A.D., was completed in the early third century A.D. by Judah HaNasi and was called Mishna [*qv*]. Then began commentaries on Mishna, known as Gemara [*qv*], which also supplemented it; the two together forming the Talmud [*qv*]. Halacha is the legal section of the Talmud and excludes nonlegal text—poetical digressions, fables etc.—known as Hagadda. To take into account the changes caused by the passage of time, the original version of Halacha was revised by Moses Ben Maimon/Maimonides (d. 1204), Joseph Karo (d. 1575), and Abraham Danzig (d. 1820). In more recent times Halacha has come to include Midrash Halacha [*qv*], which pertains to the Written Law as revealed in the written scripture, the Torah [*qv*].

Hama: *Syrian city* Pop. 380,000 (2003, est.). An important ancient settlement, the recorded history of Hama goes back more than three millenia, when it was called Hamath. It underwent changes of names as well as rulers until it fell to Muslim Arabs in A.D. 638. It changed hands again during the Crusades. It came under Ottoman suzerainty in the early sixteenth century. After the defeat of the Ottomans in 1918, it became part of the Syria placed under the French mandate.

As the leading center of the Sunni [*qv*] religious establishment, Hama witnessed major skirmishes between Islamists and the security forces of the secular Baath [*qv*] regime in 1964 and 1980. In February 1982 there was an Islamist-inspired insurrection there. Before it was crushed, between 5,000 and 10,000 people died, including about 1,000 soldiers, and a quarter of the old city was razed.

Its tourist attractions include the seventh-century al Sultan mosque, originally a church; the citadel; and the gardens along the Orontes River, irrigated by giant, six-century-old waterwheels.

Hamas *(Arabic: zeal; acronym of* Harakat al Muqawama al Islami, *Movement of Islamic Resistance): Islamic organization in the West Bank, Gaza, and East Jerusalem* Established on 27 December 1987 by Shaikh Ahmad Yassin [*qv*] and six other leaders of the Muslim Brotherhood [*qv*] in the Occupied Territories [*qv*] soon after the outbreak of the intifada [*qv*], its charter described its short-term aim as reversing Israel's occupation of the West Bank [*qv*], Gaza Strip [*qv*], and East Jerusalem [*qv*], and founding an Islamic state approved by a referendum; and its long-term objective as establishing an Islamic state in all of (mandate) Palestine. Strongly opposed to drugs and alcohol, it called for a struggle against corruption and bribery.

It was financed mainly by its supporters worldwide, who made contributions to it as part of the *zakat* [*qv*] (Islamic tax). Most of its funds were spent on charity and the construction and running of clinics and mosques. A popular movement, it participated in both trade unions and chambers of commerce.

Active in the intifada, it set up its armed wing and named it after Izz al Din Qassam [*qv*], leader of the Arab intifada of 1936–39. Due to its decentralized structure, it was unaffected by Yassin's imprisonment in 1989 when the leadership of Hamas passed to

Abdul Aziz Rantisi. It became a recipient of grants from the Gulf states after they had decided to stop funding the Palestine Liberation Organization (PLO) [qv] for siding with Iraq during the 1990–91 Kuwait crisis. It opposed the PLO's decision to participate in the Middle East peace process initiated in October 1991 in Madrid, and rejected the Oslo Accord [qv], signed in Washington nearly two years later. By then it had emerged as the foremost opponent of Israel, which in December 1992 deported 413 leaders of Hamas and Islamic Jihad [qv] to south Lebanon.

After the PLO had set up the Palestinian Authority (PA) [qv] in the Gaza Strip in May 1994, with several Jewish settlements in the Strip still intact, Hamas reiterated its earlier position that it considered Jewish settlers and Israeli troops in the Palestinian Territories [qv] as an occupying force to be resisted. Following the arrest of 350 Hamas supporters in the Gaza Strip by the PA police in October 1994, after an Israeli soldier had been kidnapped near Tel Aviv [qv] by members of the Izz al Din Qassim Brigade, Hamas intensified its opposition to the PA.

It did not participate in the elections for the presidency of the Palestinian Authority and the Palestinian Legislative Council in Janruary 1996, as these stemmed from the Oslo Accord. In retaliation for Israel's assassination of Yahya Ayash—the alleged mastermind behind the suicide bombings by the Hamas's armed wing to avenge the killing in February 1994 of twenty-nine Palestinians in Hebron [qv]—in January 1996 in Gaza city, the al Qassam Brigade mounted a series of suicide bombings in Jerusalem [qv] and elsewhere during the run-up to the elections for the Israeli prime minister and parliament in May. These damaged the prospects of the incumbent Shimon Peres [qv], who lost to Benjamin Netanyahu. [qv].

Following Netanyahu's decision to authorize a controversial Jewish settlement at Har Homa/Jabal Abu Ghneim on the southern outskirts of Jerusalem in early 1997, Hamas's military wing resumed suicide bombings. Pressured by Israel, the PA suppressed Hamas. But in October Israel freed Shaikh Yassin in order to secure the release of its two intelligence agents caught trying to assassinate a Hamas leader in Amman [qv]. A year later the PA arrested Hamas leaders for criticizing it for its latest agreement with Israel, called the Wye River Memorandum [qv]. Yet Hamas attended the "national dialogue" meeting along with other opposition groups convened by Yasser Arafat [qv] in October 1999. Later, its leaders criticized the PA for attending the final settlement talks with Israel chaired by the United States at the presidential retreat of Camp David in July 2000. However, once, the al Aqsa Intifada [qv] erupted two months later, and Arafat resisted Israeli pressure to arrest Hamas leaders, the differences between the two sides disappeared. Indeed, Hamas became an important member of the newly formed local Popular Resistance Committees, its other constituents being the Islamic Jihad [qv] and radical members of Fatah [qv]. The armed wing of Hamas stepped up its suicide bomb attacks on Israelis, mostly civilian, within Israel. While the reoccupation of the West Bank towns and cities by the Israeli government of Ariel Sharon from the spring of 2002 onward limited the terrorist activities of al Qassam Brigade, it failed to stop them.

Hamas remained the second most popular Palestinian organization after secular Fatah [qv], with most of its support coming from the Gaza Strip.

Hamdi, Ibrahim (1943–77): *North Yemeni politician; president, 1974–77* Born of a religious Zaidi Shia [qv] father and a Shafii Sunni [qv] mother in Dhamar, Hamdi trained as an Islamic judge. After the 1962 antiroyalist coup, he joined the army on the republican side. Rising through the ranks, Hamdi became a close aide of General Hassan al Amri, who served as chief of staff and premier from 1967–69. In 1971 Prime Minister Muhsin al Aini appointed Hamdi deputy premier and interior minister. A year later he was promoted to lieutenant-colonel and made deputy chief of staff.

On 13 June 1974 Hamdi carried out a bloodless coup by securing the resignation of the ruling Republican Council members and Abdullah Hussein al Ahmar [qv], speaker of the Constituent People's Assembly (CPA), and assumed power as head of the newly created Military Command Council. He replaced many of the 3,000 army officers, often illiterate tribal chiefs, with young officers freshly trained at socialist bloc military academies, and dissolved the CPA, which was dominated by tribal nominees, in October 1975.

Distancing himself from Saudi Arabia, he began to pursue independent domestic and foreign policies. While maintaining a ban on political parties, he tolerated the clandestine formation of the National Democratic Front [qv] in 1976. As a consequence, he fell foul of tribal leaders at home and the Saudi royal family abroad. The disgruntled tribal chiefs attempted two coups, but in vain. Negotiations between them and Hamdi, initiated in early 1977, collapsed when Shaikh al Ahmar and his supporters occupied Saada and Khamir, compelling Hamdi to use force in July to quell the rebellion.

He improved relations with South Yemen as well as the Soviet Union. During the South Yemeni president's visit to Sanaa [qv] in August 1977, he and Hamdi agreed to unify their countries in four years' time. But two days before Hamdi's departure for Aden [qv] in October 1977 to sign a mutual defense pact, he was assassinated along with his brother Lt. Col. Abdullah Hamdi, commander of an elite brigade. These killings were widely believed to have been inspired by Riyadh.

Hanafi Code: *Sunni Islamic legal school* The Hanafi Code is the school of the Sharia [qv] founded by Abu Hanifa al Numan (A.D. 699–767), an Iranian merchant-scholar based in Kufa [qv], Iraq. Instead of codifying established practices, Abu Hanifa applied logic and consistency in legal doctrines, thus establishing a method for tackling future problems and expanding the jurisdiction of law in Muslim society.

On the whole the Hanafi Code is liberal and oriented toward urban society. Adopted by the Abbaside caliphs (751–1258), it spread east to Afghanistan and then to the Indian subcontinent, central Asia, and western China. It became the favored school of the Ottoman Turks. Once they had usurped the Caliphate from the Mamelukes and established an Islamic empire (1517–1918), the Hanafi doctrine became the official code. It has continued to enjoy official status even in those former

Ottoman territories where the majority of local Muslims follow a different school.

Hanbali Code: *Sunni Islamic legal school* The Hanbali Code is the school of the Sharia [*qv*] founded by Ahmad ibn Hanbal (A.D. 780–855). Opposed to the legal superstructure built upon the Quran [*qv*] and the *sunna* [*qv*], Hanbal argued that a legal decision must be reached by referring directly to the Quran and the sunna. He maintained that they constituted the law itself and were not merely its source, thus standing apart from those schools—Hanafi [*qv*], Maliki [*qv*], and Shafii [*qv*]—that had codified the Quran and the sunna into a comprehensive jurisprudential system.

Over time Hanbal's fundamentalist approach lost support in the sophisticated societies of the Fertile Crescent [*qv*] but retained its hold among the nomadic tribes of the Najd [*qv*]. In the early fouteenth century Ahmad ibn Taimiya (d. 1328) emerged as an eminent Hanbali reformist, condemning the practices of saint worship and tomb cult, and opposing the contemporary *ulama's* [*qv*] assertion that there was no further need of *ijtihad* [*qv*]. Thus, Hanbali jurists continued to practice ijtihad in those areas where the Quran and the sunna are vague. Timaya's views were well received by the Mameluke caliphs (1250–1517) in Cairo [*qv*]. During the subsequent Ottoman Empire, Muhammad ibn Abdul Wahhab (1703–87), a Najdi cleric, was inspired by Hanbal and Taimiya. In 1745 he formed an alliance with the ruler of Najd, Muhammad ibn Saud, who adopted the Wahhabi doctrine [*qv*].

Hanukkah (*Hebrew: dedication*): *Jewish festival* Hanukkah is an eight-day celebration, from 25 Kislev to 3 Tevet, to mark the rededication of the Holy Temple and altar in Jerusalem following the successful revolt in 165 B.C. by Judah the Maccabee against Antiochus IV, the Greek ruler of Syria. After the razing of the Second Holy Temple in A.D. 70, the festival was associated with the miracle of the cup of oil that burned for eight days on one day's supply of oil, and thus with the concept of an eternal flame. The celebration consists of lighting candles placed in a special eight-branched *menorah* —a candelabrum—with a candle added on each of the eight days, and playing games of chance with a dreidel, a four-sided top inscribed with Hebrew [*qv*] letters on its sides.

HaPoale HaTzair (*Hebrew: The Young Worker*): *Zionist party in Palestine* Founded in 1905 at Petah Tikvah, Palestine [*qv*], with a program of Jewish settlement on the land and advancement of Jewish labor, HaPoale HaTzair rejected the class struggle and emphasized Jewish nationalism [*qv*]. As believers in the slogan "Conquest of Labor," its members lived as manual workers. In 1907 they set up the journal *HaPoale HaTzair*. They established the first cooperative farm at Degania in 1911 and the first village settlement at Nahalal. They participated in the Histadrut [*qv*], founded in 1920. With HaPoale HaTzair emerging as one of the two leading forces in the Histadrut, the other being Ahdut HaAvodah [*qv*], pressure mounted for the two to merge. This happened in 1930, resulting in Mapai [*qv*].

Haram al Sharif: *see* Noble Sanctuary.

Hariri, Rafiq (1944–): *Lebanese politician; prime minister, 1992–98, 2000–* Born into a Sunni [*qv*] family in Sidon [*qv*], Hariri enrolled as a student of business administration at Beirut Arab University in 1965. The next year he left to become a teacher in Jiddah [*qv*], Saudi Arabia. Soon he joined a construction company and worked there until 1970. Hariri then established his own construction company. It thrived and he took over a French firm in 1978. He set up a branch of the company in Lebanon in 1980 in the midst of the Lebanese Civil War [*qv*]. By 1983 his business empire included banking, insurance, construction, light engineering, computer, and advertising companies.

Following the Israeli invasion of Lebanon in 1982 [*qv*], he offered the services of his firms to counter the effects of the long Israeli siege of Beirut [*qv*]. He participated in the National Reconciliation Conferences in Geneva and Lausanne, Switzerland, in 1983 and 1984. Once the civil war was over in 1990, his multinational companies, possessing assets worth billions of dollars, became involved in reconstruction.

After the general election held in August–October 1992, followed by a government led by Omar Karami, public attention focused on reconstruction and rehabilitation. Aware of Hariri's business acumen and high standing in international financial centers, President Elias Hrawi [*qv*] named him prime minister in October 1992. His appointment began to attract foreign investment. In late 1994, stung by charges of corruption, he resigned, but was later persuaded to retract his resignation.

Frustrated by the parliament's resistance to his reconstruction plans, he resigned again in May 1995, but was recalled. He formed a new government and backed the extension of President Elias Hrawi's [*qv*] term of office. In October 1996 he was invited to become the prime minister for the third time. Two years later President Emile Lahoud [*qv*] did not repeat the invitation. But in the parliamentary poll of 2000, Hariri's supporters scored such an overwhelming victory that Lahoud had no option but to call on Hariri to form the next cabinet.

al Hashem clan: *Jordan's ruling dynasty* Named after Hashem ibn Abdul Manaf, the great grandfather of the Prophet Muhammad, the Banu Hashem clan was part of the Qureish tribe of Arabia. In the tenth century al Hashems became the ruling family of Mecca [*qv*] and the surrounding province of Hijaz [*qv*]. This continued until 1517 when—following the Ottoman Sultan Salim I's victory over the Mamlukes in Egypt—the head of al Hashem ruling family, known as the Sharif (Noble), sent an envoy to present the keys of Mecca to the Ottoman sultan and offer him the title of the Protector of the Holy Places. The sultan accepted both.

In 1893 Sultan Abdul Hamid II exiled Sharif Hussein ibn Ali al Hashem—the thirty-seventh in line of descent from the Prophet Muhammad through his daughter, Fatima, and her husband, Imam Ali, and their son, Hassan—by forcing him to live in Constantinople (now Istanbul). His exile ended when the sultan was deposed in 1909 by the Young Turks.

In 1916, during the First World War, Sharif Hussein, allying with Britain against the Ottoman Turks, led the Arab revolt with the help of his sons: Ali, Abdullah [*qv*], Faisal [*qv*], and Zaid.

Hassadic Jews *(Hebrew: from hasedim, pious): leading ultra-Orthodox sect* The Hassadic sect was established in Poland by Israel Baal Shem Tov (1698–1740), a pious Jew [*qv*], who, rebelling against the literalism of the Talmud [*qv*], attempted to help religious but illiterate Jews to relate to the Jewish law and doctrine through emotional means. He devised a method of total surrender by the believer to God through mystical elevation, involving singing and dancing. As the leader of his group of disciples, a Hassadic rabbi acts as an intercessor between them and God, offering inspired advice.

Despite being branded heretics by the Talmudists in 1781, the size of the Hassadic community grew, especially in Poland and Russia. Beginning in the early twentieth century, a small minority migrated to Palestine [*qv*], preferring to live either in Jerusalem's [*qv*] Mea Shearim district or in self-enclosed communities such the Bnei Brak agricultural settlement near Tel Aviv [*qv*]. Politically they supported Agudat Israel [*qv*].

Hawatmeh, Nayif (1934–): *Palestinian leader* Born into a Greek Catholic [*qv*] family in Salt, Jordan, Hawatmeh was a cofounder of the Arab Nationalist Movement [*qv*] in Beirut [*qv*]. With the Arab defeat in the 1967 Six-Day War [*qv*], he became disillusioned with Egyptian President Gamal Abdul Nasser [*qv*], who he had seen as the leader to liberate Palestine [*qv*] through a conventional war with Israel.

When the Popular Front for the Liberation of Palestine (PFLP) [*qv*] was formed in 1968, Hawatmeh was one of its founders. But the PFLP's failure to form a broad national front of Palestinian organizations led Hawatmeh and Bilal Hassan to quit and establish the Democratic Front for the Liberation of Palestine (DFLP) [*qv*] in 1969, and to affiliate it with the Palestine Liberation Organization [*qv*]. Within a year Hawatmeh had expanded the DFLP's commando force to make it the fourth largest among Palestinian militias.

Stressing the complementarity of the Palestinian and Jordanian struggles, he advocated the overthrow of the Hashemite dynasty. But the bitter experience of September 1970—when the Palestinians suffered heavy losses at the hands of Jordanian troops—had a salutary effect on him.

Hawatmeh maintained good relations with the Soviet Communist Party and was instrumental in persuading Moscow, after the October 1973 Arab-Israeli War [*qv*], to recognize the PLO as the sole legitimate, representative body of the Palestinian people. He was also the prime mover in persuading the Palestine National Council (PNC) [*qv*], in mid-1974, to accept the idea of establishing a "national authority" in the West Bank [*qv*] and Gaza [*qv*] as the first step toward the liberation of all of Palestine.

After his expulsion from Beirut [*qv*], Hawatmeh relocated the DFLP in Damascus [*qv*]. He began to cooperate with the PFLP leader, George Habash [*qv*], in their policies toward Yasser Arafat [*qv*] and the peace process. Hawatmeh accepted the PNC decision in late 1988 to reject terrorism and limit the use of violence to military targets inside Israel and the Occupied Territories. He opposed the Israeli-PLO accord [*qv*] of September 1993.

Six years later he met Yasser Arafat [*qv*] in Cairo when they agreed to coordinate their positions on the PLO's final status talks with Israel. His later request to be allowed to return to the Palestinian Territories [*qv*] was rejected by Israel even though the DFLP was removed from the list of the terrorist organizations by the United States in 1999.

Hebrew Bible: *see* Old Testament.

Hebrew language: A member of the Canaanite group of Semitic languages [*qv*], Hebrew was the language of ancient Hebrews. The biblical Hebrew of the period before the Jewish Exile in 586 B.C. evolved into a more precise language (as used in the Mishna [*qv*]) in the first century A.D. The subsequent forms have been mixtures of these two variants. Literary Hebrew had come into its own by the early sixth century. During the Middle Ages (476–1492), Hebrew was the only medium of writing for the Jews [*qv*] of northwest Europe. In contrast the Jews in the Arab [*qv*] world and Spain used it only for artistic expression.

The emergence of modern Hebrew— an amalgam of the language at different stages—coincided with the rise of Jewish nationalism [*qv*] around 1880. Once again Hebrew became a spoken language among Jews. The Jewish community in Palestine [*qv*] made it the medium of instruction in Jewish schools in 1913. Later the British mandate recognized it as one of the three languages in Palestine, on a par with Arabic [*qv*] and English. It became an official language of Israel upon its founding in May 1948.

Hebron: *West Bank city* Pop. 137,000 (2003, est.). Called Hevron by the Jews [*qv*] and Al Khalil al Rahman (the Friend of the Merciful), a reference to Abraham, by the Arabs [*qv*], Hebron is sacred to both Jews and Muslims [*qv*], the latter revering Abraham as a founder of monotheism and an antecedent of the Prophet Muhammad.

Hebron was established in the eighteenth century B.C. by the Hittites. Tradition has it that Abraham, the founder of Judaism [*qv*], lived there and bought the Machpelah cave, which became the burial place for him and his wife, Sarah; their son Isaac and his wife, Rebecca; and their son, Jacob, and his wife, Leah. In ca. 1010 B.C. King David was anointed in Hebron, his capital for eight years, and King Herod the Great (r. 37–4 B.C.) tried to protect the Machpelah cave—the site of Abraham's tomb—by enclosing it within a wall. In the Bible Hebron also appears as Kiryat Arba *(Hebrew: Four Towns)* and Marme.

Hebron fell to Arab Muslims [*qv*] in A.D. 635, and changed hands during the Crusades, with the Crusaders administering it from 1100 to 1260. In 1267 Mameluke Sultan Baybar banned worship by non-Muslims at the Machpelah cave. Hebron came under Ottoman suzerainty in 1516. After the fall of the Ottomans in 1918, it became part of Palestine [*qv*] under the British mandate. Modern Hebron is situated east of the old settlement.

Following the Arab-Jewish riots in 1929, in which sixty-seven of the town's seven hundred Jews were killed, the rest of the community fled. Two years later some thirty Jewish families returned, but they left after the Arab uprising of 1936–39. Following the Palestine War (1948–49) [*qv*] Hebron came under Jordanian authority. This lasted until the 1967 Six-Day War [*qv*], when the town, with a population of 38,310, fell to the Israelis. They soon opened the Machpelah cave, now enclosed within the Mosque of Abraham, the Friend, to worship by Jews.

An attempt by militant Jews in 1968 to establish a Jewish settlement in a rented Palestinian hotel in Hebron failed, and they were moved to an Israeli military base near the city. In 1971 they were allowed to build a settlement, called Kiryat Arba, east of Hebron. Eight years later Jewish families returned to the old Jewish neighborhood in the city center. By the early 1990s Kiryat Arba, with a population of nearly 5,000, had become the second largest Jewish colony on the West Bank [*qv*] and a hotbed of Jewish extremists. One of them, Baruch Goldstein, shot dead twenty-nine Palestinians at prayer in the Mosque of Abraham (called Ibrahimi Mosque by Arabs (and Tomb of Patriarchs by Jews), on 25 February 1994.

Though included in the list of the Palestinian cities to be evacuated according to the Oslo Accord II [*qv*] of September 1995, Israel did not withdraw from it. A later agreement between Israel and the Palestinian Authority (PA) [*qv*] left the city divided into two parts, with the one containing the Ibrahimi Mosque/Tomb of the Patriarchs and the Jewish settlers under exclusive Israeli control.

Heikal, Muhammad Hassanein (1923–): *Egyptian journalist and politician* Born into a middle-class family in Cairo [*qv*], Heikal secured a degree in law and economics from Cairo University. After a year at the *Egyptian Gazette* in 1943 as a reporter, he joined the weekly *Rose al Yussuf* and then the *Akhbar al Yom* (the Daily News), covering the Second World War, the Greek Civil War, and the Palestine War (1948–49) [*qv*]. In 1953 he became editor of *Akhar*

Saa (Last Hour), an illustrated weekly, and in 1956 of the daily *Al Akhbar* (The News).

After the July 1952 revolution, he had become a friend of President Gamal Abdul Nasser and his aides. This led to his appointment in 1957 as the chief editor of *Al Ahram* (The Pyramids), the semi-official newspaper of Egypt. Under his stewardship *Al Ahram* shed its sensational style and became a sober, objective newspaper of quality in the Arab world. Heikal became the country's most powerful journalist and a confidant of President Nasser. The circulation of *Al Ahram* rose to 500,000 daily and 750,000 on Fridays in the mid-1960s.

In 1968 Heikal was appointed to the central committee of the Arab Socialist Union [*qv*], where he advocated less reliance on the Soviet Union and political liberalization at home. He became minister of information and national guidance in April 1970. After Nasser's death five months later, Heikal lost his job as national guidance minister, but remained editor of *Al Ahram*.

While maintaining his personal friendship with the new president, Anwar Sadat [*qv*], Heikal took to criticizing his deviation from Nasserist principles. Following *Al Ahram*'s criticism of the U.S.-brokered Sinai I Agreement [*qv*] between Egypt and Israel in January 1974, Sadat removed Heikal from his job and prohibited him from publishing articles in the Egyptian press. He took to writing for the foreign press in the Arab world and elsewhere. Following Heikal's opposition to Sadat's dramatic peace moves with Israel in late 1978, he was harassed by the police and deprived of his passport. Heikal was one of the important opponents that Sadat imprisoned in September 1981, a month before his assassination. Released by President Hosni Mubarak [*qv*], Heikal resumed his journalistic career, but failed to reach a rapport with the new leader.

He has published several books in English, including *Nasser: The Cairo Documents* (1972), *The Road to Ramadan* (1975), *The Sphinx and the Commissar* (1978), *Return of the Ayatollah* (1981), *Autumn of Fury: The Assassination of Sadat* (1983), *Illusions of Triumph: An Arab View of the Gulf War* (1992), and *Secret Channels: The Inside Story of Arab-Israeli Peace Negotiations* (1997).

Helou, Charles (1912–): *Lebanese politician; president, 1964–70* Also spelled Hilou. Born into a middle-class Maronite [*qv*] family in Beirut, Helou studied law and practiced as a lawyer and journalist. From 1935 to 1946 he was the managing editor of the daily *L'Orient le Jour (French: The Oriental Morning).*

One of the founders of the Phalange Party [*qv*], he left it to join the Constitutional Bloc of Bishara Khouri [*qv*]. Helou was elected to parliament in 1951 and held his seat for a decade, becoming minister of justice from 1954–55. Though he opposed the attempt by Camille Chamoun [*qv*] to win the presidency for a second term, he stayed out of the 1958 Lebanese Civil War [*qv*]. This helped him to win the presidency in 1964 as a nonpartisan candidate who also had the backing of the incumbent, Fuad Chehab [*qv*].

A weak leader, Helou lacked a political or military base of his own. The reforming drive initiated by Chehab slowed under him. But Helou maintained stability in the country by aligning his foreign policy with that of the Arab hinterland and co-opting the urban Muslim [*qv*] leadership in the running of the state, thus blending Lebanon's Christian identity with Arab nationalism [*qv*]. He kept Lebanon out of the June 1967 Arab-Israeli war [*qv*].

Aware that the unity of the Lebanese army would be threatened if the clashes between the army and the Palestinian commandos became more bloody and frequent, Helou approved the Cairo Agreement of 1969 [*qv*], by which Lebanon allowed the Palestine Liberation Organization [*qv*] control of the Palestinian refugee camps. During the 1975–90 Lebanese Civil War [*qv*], Helou was consulted as someone whose mediation might help to end the conflict.

Herut *(Hebrew: Freedom): Israeli political party* Official title: *Gush Herut* (Freedom Bloc). After the disbandment of Irgun [*qv*] in July 1948, its former ranks and Revisionist Zionists [*qv*] reemerged jointly as Gush Herut, headed by Menachem Begin [*qv*]. The party advocated establishing biblical Eretz Yisrael [*qv*] and separating trade unions from the various social services and business activities of the Labor [*qv*]-dominated Histadrut [*qv*]. It attracted those Jewish immigrants, especially from the Arab states, who had experienced difficulty in becoming assimilated into the new social order. Herut secured fourteen seats in the first Knesset [*qv*], eight in the second, fifteen in the third, seventeen in the fourth, and seventeen in the fifth (1961). Encouraged by the rift in Labor's ranks in 1963, Herut merged with the Liberals [*qv*] to form Gahal [*qv*].

Herzog, Chaim (1918–97): *Israeli politician; president, 1983–93* Son of the chief rabbi of Ireland, Isaac Herzog, Herzog was born in

Belfast, United Kingdom. When his father was appointed the Ashkenazi [*qv*] chief rabbi of Palestine [*qv*] in 1936, the family migrated to Palestine. After attending Jewish schools, Herzog studied law at the Palestine Law School, Jerusalem [*qv*], and then in London and Cambridge.

During the Second World War he worked as an intelligence officer in the British military. After the founding of Israel in 1948 he was appointed director of military intelligence. He then served as military attaché in Washington (1950–54), commander of the Jerusalem district and head of the southern command (1954–59), and chief of military intelligence (1959–62).

After his retirement from the military he took up law practice. He joined Rafi [*qv*] in 1965. During the June 1967 Arab-Israeli War [*qv*], Herzog acted as a commentator on Israeli radio. After serving briefly as the military governor of the West Bank [*qv*], he returned to his law practice. During the October 1973 Arab-Israeli War [*qv*], he once again became a commentator on Israeli radio.

He served as Israel's ambassador to the United Nations from 1975 to 1978. On his return home he resumed his political career with the Labor [*qv*] movement. In 1983 he was elected to parliament, and two years later he narrowly won the contest for the country's presidency. He was reelected in 1988. His seven books include *Israel's Finest Hour* (1967), *The War of Atonement* (1975), and *Heroes of Israel* (1990).

hijab *(Arabic: cover or screen): see* Islamic dress.

Hijaz: *western region of Saudi Arabia* Area 150,000 sq. miles/388,500 sq. km; pop. 6,64,000 (2002, est.). As the birthplace and spiritual center of Islam [*qv*], Hijaz is the Holy Land of Muslims [*qv*]. It contains Islam's holiest shrines—in Mecca [*qv*], the site of the Kaaba [*qv*] and the birthplace of the Prophet Muhammad and in Medina [*qv*], the burial place of the Prophet Muhammad. It was the nucleus of the early Islamic Empire.

In more recent times, having been a province of the Ottoman Empire since 1517, after the First World War it became an independent kingdom under Sharif Hussein ibn Ali al Hashem, who had been appointed the Protector of the Holy Places (of Mecca and Medina) by the Ottoman regime in 1908.

Following the abolition of the caliphate by the secular republic of Turkey in 1924, Sharif Hussein declared himself caliph. This angered Abdul Aziz ibn Abdul Rahman ibn Saud [*qv*], then king of Najd [*qv*], who conquered Hijaz in 1926 and declared himself king of Hijaz as well as of Najd. In 1932 he combined his two realms into the Kingdom of Saudi Arabia. Hijaz is now called the Western Region.

Histadrut *(Hebrew: Federation; abbr. of HaHistadrut HaKelalit shel HaOvedim HaIvirim be Eretz Yisrael, The General Federation of Workers in the Land of Israel): Israeli trade union federation and social welfare agency* In 1920 Ahdut HaAvodah [*qv*] and HaPoale HaTzair [*qv*] agreed to form an umbrella organization to encompass all labor-pioneer parties of Zionist [*qv*] persuasion. The result was the General Federation of Hebrew Workers in the Land of Israel. Its membership was limited to Jewish workers, artisans, and tradesmen. About three-fifths of the 7,000 Jewish workers in Palestine [*qv*] participated in electing delegates to the founding convention of Histadrut in December 1920 with 4,400 members. (Jewish workers numbered about one-seventh of their Arab [qv] counterparts.) The next year Histadrut established Solel Boneh, a large construction and public works company, and, in association with the World Zionist Organization [qv], the Workers' Bank. It thus emerged as a general-purpose body rather than an exclusively trade-union organization.

Though formed as a nonpolitical trade union federation, Histadrut engaged in offering vocational training, building public works, encouraging Jewish immigration, settling newcomers, and organizing defense through Haganah [qv]. Under the leadership of David Ben-Gurion [qv], its general secretary from 1920 to 1935, Histadrut emerged as a central pillar of the Zionist enterprise in Palestine: it ran a social security system, an educational network, and its own production and service cooperatives.

In 1943 it set up a special department for Arab workers. With the size of Arab labor force rising due to Arab migration into urban areas following the loss of their agricultural land to Jewish immigrants, the Arab membership of the General Federation of Hebrew Workers in the Land of Israel—first allowed in 1960—grew sharply. This led the leadership of the Federation, popularly called Histadrut, to drop the term "Hebrew" from its name in 1966.

Following a growing challenge in the late 1960s to Histadrut from non-Histadrut "action committees," in 1971 the Labor Party-dominated [qv] government passed a law that formalized Histadrut's monopoly as the "legal representative of workers." The

Histadrut is open to all workers, including the self-employed and professionals, as well as students, housewives, pensioners, and the jobless. Nearly 85 percent of all those eligible belonged to the Histadrut. The Histadrut engages in: (1) trade union organization, involving unions, labor councils, and professional federations; (2) social services, including health insurance (until 1995), pension and welfare; (3) educational and cultural activities; and (4) economic development undertaken by Hevrat HaOvedim (The Workers' Company).

In trade unions the Histadrut's primary unit is the workers' committee at the workplace; its secondary unit, the trade union; and its tertiary unit, the labor council, which is elected by all local trade unions and oversees not only union but also economic and cultural affairs. Then there are nationwide professional bodies and other national organizations. The labor councils and nationwide federations report to the Histadrut executive.

Its educational and cultural activities include workers' colleges, vocational schools, sports clubs, and theater and dance groups. The activities undertaken by the Workers' Company include the running of factories, construction companies, agricultural and transport cooperatives, a bank, an insurance company, and a publishing house.

Until 1995, when the National Health Insurance Law separated Histadrut from health care, its social services included General Sick Fund (*Hebrew: Kupat Holim Kelalit*), covering half of the adult population, and pension funds.

A year earlier, in the Histadrut elections, held every four years, the Labor Party lost control of the executive committee, and the subsequent leadership renamed the organization as New Histadrut. At that time it had 1,573,000 members (of whom 100,000 were Arab), and it employed about a third of all employees in Israel.

Following the exclusion of Histadrut from health care, its membership dropped sharply, reaching 627,000 in 1998. Its leadership has since then reverted to the Labor Party. One Nation [*qv*], a faction furthering the cause of workers and retirees and affiliated to Histadrut, contested the parliamentary polls of 1999 and 2003 and gained representation in the Knesset [*qv*].

Hizbollah (*Arabic: Party of Allah): Lebanese political-religious movement* More a movement than a party, Hizbollah emerged under the leadership of Shaikh Muhammad Hussein Fadlallah, a Shia [*qv*] cleric, after the Israeli invasion of Lebanon [*qv*] in June 1982, primarily to offer resistance to the Israeli occupation. It was the brainchild of Ali Akbar Mohtashemi, the Iranian ambassador to Syria from 1982–83.

Also active in domestic politics, it opposed the regime of President Amin Gemayel [*qv*] in alliance with the Islamic Jihad [*qv*] and the Islamic Amal [*qv*]. The three organizations together confronted the Lebanese army in early 1984. Hizbollah was close to the contingent of 2,000 Iranian revolutionary guards, based in Baalbek [*qv*], who had been sent to Lebanon in mid-1982 to fight the Israeli invaders. As it escalated its guerrilla attacks on Israeli targets in southern Lebanon, its military aid from Iran increased. By the spring of 1987 its armory included cannons as well as antitank and antiaircraft missiles. It had emerged as the leading Lebanese recipient of financial assistance from Iran, which funded its health, education, and other public services through its (domestic) Martyrs' Foundation.

In turn, Hizbollah tried to assist Iran by taking Western, especially American, hostages in Lebanon (under such labels as the Revolutionary Justice Organization and the Organization of the Oppressed of the Earth, which seized Terry Waite, the envoy of the Archbishop of Canterbury, in early 1987), on the ground that their captivity would inhibit U.S. military involvement in the First Gulf War (1980–88) [*qv*] on the Iraqi side. It also used the hostages as bargaining chips to secure supplies of U.S.-made weapons to Iran, which had been equipped with such military hardware during the rule of Muhammad Reza Shah Pahlavi [*qv*]—the root of the Irangate-Contra Affair [*qv*].

Though unsympathetic to its religious militancy, Syrian President Hafiz Assad [*qv*] found the party a suitable instrument to pressure Israeli and South Lebanon Army (SLA) [*qv*] troops in Israel's self-declared security zone in southern Lebanon. In January–February 1988 the skirmishes between Hizbollah and the SLA claimed forty Hizbollah lives. Later, to ensure that Hizbollah did not acquire political monopoly among Shias, Assad encouraged members of Amal [*qv*], a Shia party, to attack Hizbollah fighters in the southern suburbs of Beirut. But Hizbollah performed well. Its activities also brought it into direct conflict with Israel, whose commandos abducted Shaikh Abdul Karim Obeid, the party leader in the south, in July 1989.

The next month Hizbollah joined the front formed to confront the government of Gen. Michel Aoun [*qv*], the Maronite army commander. It criticized the Taif Accord [*qv*] as perpetuating the old system, with its downgrading of Shias, now the largest single sect in Lebanon, and hindering the creation of an Islamic state in Lebanon, its ultimate goal. But it desisted from pressing its objections too far. Syria allowed Hizbollah to play an important, though subsidiary, role in the final, successful attack on Aoun's forces in October 1990. But protesting at the lack of any official plan to reverse Israel's occupation of the south, Hizbollah refused to join the national unity government formed in December.

Following the disarming of all militias in Greater Beirut, Hizbollah moved its men and weapons to the southern Beqaa Valley and the mountain caves near the Israeli-occupied region, and increased its attacks on Israeli and SLA patrols in the area. As before, Israel responded by pounding Hizbollah's positions with air raids and artillery fire. In May 1991 the party's newly elected secretary-general, Shaikh Abbas Musavi, stated that so long as Israel remained inside Lebanon his irregulars would not surrender their weapons to the Lebanese government. Unwilling to cause a split within its ranks by attacking Hizbollah—demanding an unconditional Israeli withdrawal from southern Lebanon as required by Security Council Resolution 425 of March 1978—the government settled for receiving a list of 3,500 Hizbollah militiamen active in the south.

In late 1991 a three-way swap—involving 450 Lebanese and Palestinian detainees under the Israelis, seven dead or captured Israeli servicemen, and the remaining Western hostages—ended Hizbollah's involvement in hostage taking.

It won eight of the twenty-seven seats reserved for Shias in the 1992 parliamentary elections. Its killings of two Israeli soldiers in July 1993 brought about a weeklong artillery bombardment by Israel under the codename "Operation Accountability," which left 139 dead and 250,000 homeless. During 1994–95 Hizbollah mounted sporadic attacks on Israeli targets in south Lebanon. In April 1996, to stop Hizbollah's rocket attacks on northern Israel, the Israeli government mounted "Operation Grapes of Wrath," which targeted a power station north of Beirut, and which killed 170 to 200 Lebanese, mostly civilians, including 100 refugees sheltering at the United Nations base at Qana, and displaced 400,000.

In the 1996 parliamentary poll Hizbollah retained its four seats in the South and Nabatiya governorate, and, allying with Amal [*qv*], won twenty-two of the twenty-three seats in the Beqaa Valley governorate.

Limiting itself to Israeli and SLA targets in the occupied southern Lebanon, Hizbollah mounted 715 attacks in 1997 and 1,200 in 1998. It intensified its activities in the run-up to the Israeli elections in May 1999, when Ehud Barak [*qv*], Labor's candidate for prime minister, promised to disengage Israel from southern Lebanon. In May 2000, Israel withdrew unconditionally from southern Lebanon as required by the United Nations Security Council Resolution 425 of March 1978 [*qv*]. But because Israel did not withdraw from the Shaaba Farm adjacent to the Syrian border, Hizbollah did not regard the Israel evacuation complete and attacked it periodically.

In the 2000 parliamentary poll, the

Hizbollah-Amal alliance won all twenty-three seats in the South and Nabatiya governorate and performed equally well in the Beqaa Valley.

Holy City: *see* Jerusalem.

Holy Land: The term was first used in the Old Testament [*qv*] in Zechariah 2:12. *See* Palestine.

Homs: *Syrian city* Pop. 752,000 (2003, est.). Known in ancient times as Emesa, it was the site of a renowned temple to the sun god. It was the capital of Roman Emperor Aurelian (r. A.D. 270–75). With Christianity [*qv*] becoming the state religion under Emperor Constantine I (r. A.D. 306–37), most of the local residents embraced the new faith. Homs fell to Muslim Arabs [*qv*] in A.D. 636 and was renamed Hims. A failed Christian uprising in A.D. 855 resulted in Christianity being rooted out. Since then its Muslim character has remained strong. It became part of the Ottoman Empire in 1517, a status that remained unaltered until the dissolution of the empire four centuries later, when it was included in the Syria placed under the French mandate. The French established a military academy there, the only one of its kind in the country.

It is an important commercial, industrial, and transport center. A stronghold of Sunni Islam [*qv*], in 1973 Homs witnessed violent skirmishes between the security forces and demonstrators protesting against the secular nature of the new constitution. Its tourist offerings include Roman ruins and a citadel built in the middle ages.

Hormuz, Straits of: Situated between Iran and the northern tip of Trucial Oman, at its narrowest point the Straits of Hormuz is only 23 miles/37 km wide. The territorial waters of Iran and Oman, each 12 miles/19 km wide, overlap in the Straits. In late 1979, when 40 percent of the world's oil passed through the Straits, rising tension between the United States and the Islamic regime in Iran made the Straits the focus of attention for both Washington and Moscow. Scores of warships from both sides assembled in the international waters of the north Arabian Sea at the mouth of the Straits.

During the 1980–88 Iran-Iraq War [*qv*] the importance of the Straits increased. In September 1983 the Iranian leader, Ayatollah Ruhollah Khomeini [*qv*], threatened to close it if Iran's Kharg oil terminal in the Gulf were destroyed by Iraq. U.S. President Ronald Reagan reiterated the earlier U.S. position that the United States would intervene militarily to keep the Straits open to international shipping. He increased the U.S. naval presence in the area to thirty warships. Britain and France followed suit. The Soviets increased their presence in the Arabian Sea to twenty-six war vessels. The crisis subsided, and the Straits remained open.

Hoss, Salim (1929–): *Lebanese politician; prime minister, 1976–78, 1979–80, 1987–90, 1998–2000* Born into a Sunni [*qv*] family in Beirut [*qv*], Hoss received his postgraduate degree in economics and business administration at the American University in Beirut (AUB) [*qv*] and capped it with a doctorate in economics at a university in the United States in 1961.

After teaching economics at the AUB, he joined the Kuwait Development Fund as a financial adviser in 1964. Two years later he was appointed chairman of the Lebanese Banking Control Commission, and in 1973 he was named chairman of the Industrial Development Bank. He worked in conjunction with Elias Sarkis [*qv*], the Central Bank governor who was elected president in September 1976 in the midst of a Civil War [*qv*]. Three months later Hoss was invited to lead the Lebanese government. He selected an eight-member cabinet consisting wholly of technocrats.

In the civil conflict he generally took a pro-Muslim and pro-Damascus line. His second government of twelve ministers, formed in July 1979, inclined toward Syria. Whereas Sarkis viewed national reconciliation as a prelude to reducing Syria's influence in Lebanon, Hoss considered it a prelude to implementing a security plan in cooperation with Syria and the institutionalization of Lebanon's relationship with Syria. Hoss stayed on as premier until October 1980.

He accepted a ministerial post (labor and education) when a national unity government was formed in April 1984 under Rashid Karami [*qv*]. Following Karami's assassination on 1 June 1987, Hoss was named acting prime minister. With General Michel Aoun [*qv*] appointing a military cabinet in September 1988, Hoss became the head of a parallel government. His relations with the Aoun administration soured, with Aoun dissolving parliament in early November 1989 and Hoss calling his action illegal.

Following the election of Elias Hrawi [*qv*] as president on 24 November 1989, Hoss was called to form the next government. He announced a cabinet of fourteen, divided equally between Christians [*qv*] and Muslims [*qv*]. In December 1990, after all heavy weapons had been removed from Greater Beirut and the fifteen-year division of the city had been ended, Hoss resigned. After the election of Emile Lahoud [*qv*] as president in November 1998, Hoss was invited to head the next cabinet. He resigned two years later when the supporters of his predecessor, Rafiq Hariri [*qv*], won overwhelmingly in the parliamentary poll.

Hostage taking and hostages: *American hostages in Iran; Western hostages in Lebanon* Hostage taking for political reasons in the West and elsewhere has a long history, dating back at least to Roman Emperor Julius Caesar (102–44 B.C.), who, referring to his crossing of the Rhine River in 55 B.C., mentioned the conquered Ubii tribe establishing ties of friendship and giving hostages as a guarantee of good behavior in the future. In more recent times in the Middle East [*qv*], the ruler of North Yemen, Imam Yahya Hamid al Din (1869–1948), held the sons of the tribal leaders from the north hostage, while maintaining that they were being given religious instruction at his court. Following the repression of the Iraqi Communist Party [*qv*] in 1978, the Baathist regime [*qv*] in Baghdad adopted an official policy of holding hostage a member of the family of an absconding communist to force him to surrender.

American hostages in Iran: On 4 November 1979 militant Islamist students in Tehran [*qv*] occupied the embassy and took hostage sixty-seven American diplomats. This was done to secure the extradition of Muhammad Reza Shah Pahlavi [*qv*], then receiving medical treatment in New York, to face charges of corruption and violation of Iran's 1906–07 constitution, and to stop the United States from courting dissident elements in Iran, especially military officers.

The U.S. administration, under President James Carter, immediately froze Iran's large reserves in the United States, severed diplomatic relations, and, together with the European Community, imposed economic sanctions against Iran. Its attempt to rescue the hostages in April 1980 failed, and its agents in Iran, including the commander of the Iranian air force, Amir Bahman Bagheri, were exposed. The hostages were then dispersed to different locations.

Various secret attempts to resolve the crisis proved futile. Carter made the release of the American hostages a central issue in his campaign for reelection. This made the Iranian leader, Ayatollah Ruhollah Khomeini, [qv] intransigent. Along with the sluggish U.S. economy, the hostage issue was instrumental in the defeat of Carter by Ronald Reagan in the November 1980 presidential poll. In line with a secret deal between Iran and the United States, brokered by Algeria, the American hostages (now reduced to fifty-two due to earlier, individual releases) were freed in Algiers after 444 days in captivity within minutes of President Carter handing over the office to Reagan on 21 January 1981.

Western hostages in Lebanon: During the first twelve years of the 1975–90 Lebanese Civil War [qv], some 14,000 people were kidnapped, of whom about 10,000 were killed. The practice of kidnapping foreigners for political purposes was initiated by the Phalange Party [qv] in mid-March 1982 with the abduction in Beirut [qv] of four Iranian diplomats: Kazem Allaf, Ahmad Motevaselian, Muhsin Musavi and Muhammad Muqadam (they were later killed). In retaliation, three months later the Islamic Jihad [qv] kidnapped David Dodge, acting president of the American University in Beirut [qv].

Two months after the United States had put Iran on the list of nations that support international terrorism in January 1984, and decided to harden its policy of blocking worldwide arms sales to Iran—then engaged in the Iran-Iraq War [qv]—came the abduction of William Buckley, the U.S. Central Intelligence Agency (CIA) station chief in Beirut. Securing his release became the chief motive for the United States to enter into clandestine talks with Iran on the basis of arms-for-hostages, which surfaced as the Irangate Affair [qv] in November 1986. By then the pro-Iranian groups in Lebanon held more than a dozen Western, mainly American and British, hostages. Buckley was believed to have died in captivity.

A further addition to the list came in January 1987: Terry Waite, an envoy of the British Archbishop of Canterbury, who had been engaged in an effort to secure the release of earlier captives. The reasons for taking Western hostages were (1) to make even the situation about arms supplies to Iran in its war with Iraq; (2) to prevent Western military involvement on the Christian side in the civil war, as had happened in early 1984; and (3) to secure the release of hundreds of Lebanese and Palestinian prisoners held without charge by Israel in the wake of the 1982 Israeli invasion of Lebanon [qv].

Once the Iran-Iraq War had ended in August 1988, the motives behind holding Western hostages narrowed to (2) and (3). After the Western powers had endorsed the Taif

Accord [*qv*] of October 1989, and the Lebanese Civil War had ended a year later, the kidnappers' motive remained just (3). With the release in early August 1991 of John McCarthy, a British journalist, the U.N. secretary-general was inducted into the process. The release of the last three American captives and 450 Lebanese and Palestinian prisoners occurred about four months later, thus bringing to an end a decade-long saga.

House of Saud: *The ruling dynasty of Saudi Arabia* The House of Saud is named after Saud, a member of the Musalikh clan of the Ruwalla tribe of the Anaiza tribal federation [*qv*] at the turn of the eighteenth century in the Diraiya-Riyadh region. His son, Muhammad, who ruled the Diraiya emirate between 1726–65, embraced Wahhabism [*qv*] in 1745. Armed with this doctrine he expanded his domain, an enterprise carried on by his successors: Abdul Aziz ibn Muhammad (r. 1766–1803) and Saud ibn Abdul Aziz (r. 1803–14), who reached the Syrian and Iraqi frontiers. But under Abdullah ibn Saud (r. 1814–18) the House of Saud's fortunes waned, with Abdullah suffering defeat and eventual execution by the Ottoman sultan.

Over the next three-quarters of a century the House of Saud rose again, only to be suppressed when the rival House of Rashid of the Shammar tribe, backed by the Ottomans, overpowered Abdul Rahman ibn Faisal al Saud in his bastion of Diraiya in 1891. The surviving members of the House of Saud, including Abdul Aziz ibn Abdul Rahman al Saud (1879–1953) [*qv*], took refuge in Kuwait. He regained Riyadh in 1902 and began to expand his realm, which he named Saudi Arabia in 1932. With this

the House of Saud, Aal [*qv*] Saud (consisting of Abdul Aziz and his five brothers), became the ruling dynasty of Saudi Arabia. In 2000, the male progeny of these six brothers by wives and concubines totaled about 6,400.

Hoveida, Amir Abbas (1919–79): *Iranian politician; prime minister, 1968–77* Son of a Bahai [*qv*] father, Hoveida was born in Tehran. He received his postgraduate degree in political science and economics from a university in Brussels and his doctorate in economics from a university in Paris. Starting out as a diplomat, Hoveida served the Iranian missions in France, Germany, and Turkey. From 1952 to 1956 he was with the U.N. Relief and Work Agency (UNRWA) [*qv*] at its Geneva headquarters. In 1958 he was named a director of the National Iranian Oil Company, and in 1964 he was appointed treasury secretary. When the New Iran Party was formed in 1963 at the behest of Muhammad Reza Shah Pahlavi [*qv*], Hoveida was made its assistant secretary.

By now Hoveida had firmly established his loyalty to the shah, who rewarded him with the premiership in 1968. Willing to accept a subservient role, he learned to interpret adroitly what the shah wanted. As a consequence he retained his high office until August 1977, the longest uninterrupted tenure since the promulgation of the 1906–07 constitution. When the shah decided to do away with the formula of ruling and opposition parties in 1975 and to establish a single party—Rastakhiz (Renaissance) [*qv*]—he chose Hoveida as its secretary-general. In October 1976 Hoveida relinquished this post to Jamshid Amuzgar.

Despite Hoveida's long, loyal service, the

shah dismissed him when he needed a scapegoat to stem the rising revolutionary tide in mid-1977 and named him court minister. But as popular pressure rose, the shah arrested Hoveida along with eleven other leading personalities. Hoveida was tried and executed by the Islamic regime in April 1979.

Hrawi, Elias (1930–): *Lebanese politician; president, 1990–98* Born into a landowning Maronite [*qv*] family in the Zahle region, Hrawi obtained a degree in business administration at a Beirut university. He then managed the family lands. He became a parliamentary deputy in 1972, representing Zahle. Appointed minister of public works in 1980, Hrawi served for two years. During most of the 1975–90 Lebanese Civil War [*qv*], Zahle was under Syrian control and Hrawi maintained amiable relations with Damascus. Following the assassination of President Rene Muawad in November 1989, Hrawi emerged as the favorite. He was elected president by forty-seven of the fifty-two parliamentary deputies meeting in Shtura. He called for special bonds between Lebanon and Syria.

His attempt to overthrow the rival government of Gen. Michel Aoun [*qv*] through economic and diplomatic pressure failed. But he succeeded in securing support for the Taif Accord [*qv*] from a section of the Maronite community, and in reducing the area under Aoun's control to about a third of the Christian sector. In August 1990 Hrawi steered through parliament the constitutional reform outlined in the Taif Accord. Two months later he actively cooperated with Syria in a joint military plan to topple Aoun, which succeeded.

He then created Greater Beirut, free of armed militias, and appointed a government of national unity. He cooperated with Syria on security matters. In May 1991 he signed the Lebanese-Syrian Treaty of Brotherhood, Cooperation, and Coordination [*qv*], thus formalizing links with Syria in all important matters, including security and foreign affairs. His government participated in the Middle East peace process, heralded by the Middle East Peace Conference in Madrid in October 1991, coordinating Lebanon's stance with Syria's. His supporters' success in the general election of 1992, which was boycotted by right-wing Maronites, strengthened Hrawi's hand. In 1995 the parliament extended his presidency by three years.

Hussein, Qusay Saddam (1966–): *Iraqi politician* Born to Saddam Hussein [*qv*] and Sajida Talfa in Baghdad [*qv*], Hussein attended Exemplary Kharkh School run by his mother until 1979 when his father became president. To mobilize the population during the Iran-Iraq War [*qv*] Hussein took to going to official meetings in a tank. He married Sahour, daughter of Gen. Mahir Abdul Rashid, commander of the 7th Army Corps and one of the heroes of the war.

Following the 1991 Gulf War [*qv*], Saddam Hussein put him in charge of the Concealment Operations Committee (COC) to oversee and safeguard crucial information and material concerning the military programs prohibited by the Security Council Resolution 687 [*qv*].

The next year he became the head of the Nation Security Bureau consisting of five intelligence agencies: (1) General Security (GS, *Amn al Aam*); (2) General Intelligence Department (GID, *Dairat al Mukhabarat al Ammaa*); (3) Military Intelligence (MI, *Istikhabarat al Askariya*); (4) Special Security

Directorate (*Muderiye al Amn al Khas*); and (5) Military Security (MS, *Amn al Askariya*). He also supervised the elite Republican Guard.

During the mid-1990s, in the internal debates that raged in the extended family of Saddam Hussein on how to deal with the U.N. Special Commission (Unscom) [*qv*] and the International Atomic Energy Agency (IAEA), Hussein, and his elder brother, Uday, opposed concessions to the United Nations. Against the background of intensified suffering that the Iraqi people suffered due to the punishing U.N. sanctions, security around Saddam Hussein tightened to the extent that only Hussein and the president's private secretary, Abid Hamid Mahmud, knew his whereabouts.

In 2001, when Hussein was elected to the Baath Party [*qv*] Regional Command, he held the rank of major general. Unlike Uday—notorious for his violence, short temper and public tantrums—Hussein is intelligent, calculating, and quietly ruthless.

During the Gulf War III [*qv*], Hussein directed the Republican Guard until its top commanders, unable to communicate with him, made a secret deal with U.S. intelligence officials, and deserted. Having reportedly collected $1,000 million from the Central Bank on his father's behalf, he and Saddam went underground on 9 April.

Hussein, Saddam (1937–): *Iraqi politician; president, 1979–* Born into the Begat clan of the al Bu Nasir tribe in Auja, a village near Tikrit, the son of Hussein Abd al Majid, a landless peasant, and Subha Talfa al Massallat, Hussein was raised by his maternal uncle, Khairallah Talfa, due to the death of his father before his birth. After his arrival in Baghdad [*qv*] in 1955 for further education, Hussein joined the Arab Baath Socialist Party [*qv*]. Following the 1958 coup he engaged in fights between the Baathists and the followers of Premier Abdul Karim Qasim [*qv*]. A member of the team that tried, unsuccessfully, to assassinate Qasim in October 1959, Hussein was injured in the leg. He escaped to Syria [*qv*] and then to Egypt [*qv*], where he studied law at Cairo University.

After the Baathist seizure of power in 1963, Hussein returned to Iraq. When Abdul Salam Arif [*qv*] usurped power from the Baathists, Hussein was involved in an abortive attempt to overthrow Arif. He was imprisoned but managed to escape in July 1966. Elected assistant general secretary of the Baath party, he spent the next two years reorganizing the party. He was thirty-one when the Baath recaptured power in 1968.

Though not a member of the ruling Revolutionary Command Council (RCC), Hussein was quite influential due to his blood ties with RCC Chairman Ahmad Hassan Bakr [*qv*], a cousin of Khairallah Talfa. In late 1969 Hussein secured a place on the RCC. Thereafter, the Bakr-Hussein duo came to dominate the Baath party, mainly because of their cunning decimation of their RCC colleagues. Hussein busied himself with strengthening the party as well as resolving the problem with the Kurds [*qv*]. His foreign travels in 1972, in the wake of Iraq's nationalization of Western-owned Iraq Petroleum Company, took him to Moscow and Paris.

By the mid-1970s, Hussein had outstripped Bakr in leadership, cunning, ruthlessness, and organizational ability. It was he who signed the Algiers Accord [*qv*] with Muhammad Reza Shah Pahlavi [*qv*] of Iran in 1975, thus ending a bitter feud with

Tehran. By the late 1970s he felt powerful enough to overrule Bakr's strategy of conciliating Shia [qv] dissidents, inspired by the Islamic revolution in Shia-majority Iran. When Hussein found out in mid-June 1979 that Bakr had sent a secret message to Syrian President Hafiz Assad [qv] to expedite negotiations on unity between Syria and Iraq, he compelled Bakr to resign. On the eleventh anniversary of the Baathist revolution in mid-July, Hussein assumed supreme power.

In late July Hussein discovered a major "anti-state conspiracy" involving sixty-eight top Baathist civilian and military leaders. All were tried summarily, and twenty-one were executed. Hussein purged trade unions, the militia, student unions, and local and provincial governments of the elements he considered halfhearted in their support of him. While generous in funding the improvement of Shia shrines and conciliatory toward senior Shia clergy, he severely repressed such militant Shia bodies as al Daawa [qv].

In September 1980 Hussein invaded Iran to recover the eastern half of the Shatt al Arab [qv], which he had conceded to Tehran in the 1975 Algiers Accord. But as his troops made inroads into Iran, he expanded his war aim to include the incorporation of captured areas into Iraq on the basis that the majority of its inhabitants were ethnic Arabs [qv]. By mid-1982, when the Iranians had expelled the Iraqis from their territory, two outcomes were possible: a draw or an Iranian triumph. Afraid that Tehran's victory would destabilize the region, including the oil-rich Gulf states [qv], the United States, the Soviet Union, and France enhanced their military, economic, and intelligence aid to Hussein's regime.

By extending the fight to include the Gulf [qv] and its shipping from 1984 onward, Hussein succeeded in involving the United States in the conflict in the name of protecting oil shipping lanes—against Iran. By mid-1987 Tehran found itself with a second front, in the Gulf, facing the U.S. Navy.

Against this background, in the spring of 1988, Iraq, making extensive use of chemical weapons, staged a series of successful offensives to regain territory that had been lost to Iran from 1984–86. This compelled Tehran to accept unconditionally U.N. Security Council Resolution 598 [qv] of July 1987. The truce came into effect on 20 August 1988.

In the course of the eight-year Iran-Iraq War [qv], Hussein enlarged his military from 250,000 to 1,250,000, vastly expanded the industrial-military complex, and made much progress in developing or producing chemical, biological, and nuclear arms. Soon Hussein was applying his vastly increased intelligence and military machines— including chemical weapons—to root out insurgent nationalist Kurds in the north, who had largely allied with Iran during the First Gulf War [qv].

In August 1990 Hussein invaded Kuwait, a neighbor that had aided Iraq materially and logistically during its war with Iran. U.S. President George Bush took a lead in rallying the support of the international community to reverse the Iraqi aggression, and cobbled together an alliance of twenty-nine Western and Arab nations. The United Nations imposed a military and economic embargo on Iraq. When Hussein refused to withdraw Iraqi troops from Kuwait by the U.N. deadline of 15 January 1991, the U.S.-led coalition began an air campaign against Iraq and

Iraqi-occupied Kuwait, thus initiating the Second Gulf War [*qv*].

The unprecedentedly intense bombing continued for thirty-nine days and was followed by a ground offensive that lasted four days. Defeated, Hussein withdrew his forces from Kuwait, and a temporary truce came into effect on 28 February. In April Hussein accepted a humiliating U.N. Security Council Resolution 687 [*qv*] that outlined the cease-fire, war reparations, and the main conditions for the lifting of sanctions against Iraq: destruction of its medium-range missiles as well as its nonconventional arms and manufacturing facilities.

Despite intense efforts by the leading Western powers, Israel, and Saudi Arabia to have Hussein assassinated, or his regime overthrown by a coup, he survived. His military and intelligence apparatus remained effective. However, the Western imposition of a "no fly" restriction in the area above the 36th parallel virtually ended his control over the Kurdish region in October 1991. His power was cut further in August 1992 when the allies declared the predominantly Shia area of Iraq below the 32nd parallel as a "no fly" zone for Baghdad.

While economic sanctions caused high inflation and a dramatic drop in living standards, there were no signs that popular discontent against Hussein's regime had reached such proportions as to destabilize it. But his elation at Bush's defeat in the U.S. presidential election in November 1992 proved premature when President Bill Clinton continued Bush's hardline policy toward Hussein. A denouement came in late June 1993, when the U.S. Navy hit the Iraqi intelligence complex in Baghdad with missiles on the basis that Hussein had planned Bush's assassination during his trip to Kuwait in April.

By October 1994, having complied with all the conditions of U.N. Security Resolution 687 (concerning the Gulf War cease-fire) and Resolution 715 (concerning long-term monitoring of Iraq's military industry), Hussein felt that it was time for the United Nations to lift the economic sanctions. To force the issue to the top of the agenda he moved Iraqi troops southward. The United States construed this as a plan by Hussein to invade Kuwait again and dispatched its forces to the region. Hussein withdrew his troops to their precrisis positions, and at the Security Council Russia called for the lifting of the sanctions by the spring of 1995. The defection to Jordan of Gen. Hussein Kamil Hassan, a son-in-law of Hussein and minister of industry, in August 1995 created a crisis for Hussein. He overcame it by winning 99.96 percent backing in a referendum on another seven-year presidential term in October.

In February 1996, after the return of Hussein Kamil Hassan and his family to Baghdad, the erstwhile defector was killed in a gun battle by his uncle, Gen. Ali al Majid. The next month, Hussein called parliamentary elections after seven years. In September, he was invited by Masud Barzani [*qv*] of the Kurdistan Democratic Party [*qv*] to assist him in expelling his rival Jalal Talabani [*qv*] from the regional capital of Irbil [*qv*]. He did. In the process the Iraqi troops and intelligence agents destroyed the base that the United States had established in the region to overthrow Hussein before withdrawing from the area.

Hussein's relations with the United

Nations Special Commission (Unscom) [*qv*] on disarming Iraq of weapons of mass destruction deteriorated when Richard Butler, an Australian disarmament specialist, replaced Rolf Ekeus, a Swedish diplomat, as head of Unscom in mid-1997. A crisis with the United Nations in February 1998 was defused by the last-minute intervention by U.N. General Secretary Kofi Annan, who met Hussein in Baghdad. But the agreement lasted only until December when the United States, assisted by Britain, mounted its Operation Desert Fox [*qv*]. The United States fired 415 Cruise and Tomahawk missiles and dropped 600 laser-guided bombs at 100 Iraqi targets. Hussein's efforts to have an Arab League [*qv*] summit condemn the Anglo-American action and demand the lifting of sanctions on Iraq failed. Equally, the American attempt to get the Gulf monarchies involved in overthrowing Hussein got nowhere.

He rejected the new, comprehensive U.N. Security Council Resolution 1284 [*qv*] passed in December 1999, which required Iraq to readmit U.N. inspectors who had been withdrawn by Butler to enable the United States to mount its Operation Desert Fox. Confident of his improved standing at home, Hussein called the parliamentary poll in March 2000 on time. Five months later he received President Hugo Chavez of Venezuela, the current chairman of the Organization of Oil Exporting Countries [*qv*], in Baghdad. Soon the air travel ban on Iraq collapsed. In October, Hussein was invited to an Arab League summit after ten years, but he did not attend. He backed the Palestinian al Aqsa Intifada [*qv*] by sending food and medical aid to the Palestinian Territories [*qv*] and paying generous compensation to the families of the Palestinians killed in the uprising. This made Hussein all the more unpopular with the newly elected U.S. President George W. Bush (r. 2001–), whose father, President George H. W. Bush (r. 1989–93), had inflicted a humiliating defeat on Hussein in 1991. Within weeks of taking office in January 2001, Bush Jr. ordered air strikes against Iraqi targets on the basis that Iraq was improving its air defenses.

Following the terrorist attacks on the United States in September, the Bush administration tried to show that Hussein had links with Al Qaida [*qv*], but failed to provide any convincing evidence. After its failure to capture or kill Osama bin Laden [*qv*] during its Afghanistan War, it attempted to divert popular opinion in the United States against Hussein on the ground that he had failed to disarm Iraq of its weapons of mass destruction. The propaganda war against Hussein built up after the first anniversary of 9/11. When Hussein agreed to the return of U.N. inspectors unconditionally on 16 September 2002, the United States, backed by Britain, successfully lobbied the U.N. Security Council to adopt a much more rigorous regime of inspections outlined in Resolution 1441 [*qv*] in November.

Hussein accepted the new resolution. Within weeks, U.N. inspectors started working in Iraq. They found no evidence of weapons of mass destruction by mid-March 2003. But that did not alter the earlier agenda of U.S. President George W. Bush to bring about "regime change" in Iraq. He gave Hussein two days to leave Iraq. When, as expected, he did not, Bush, backed by British Prime Minister Tony Blair, ordered an invasion of Iraq, thus starting Gulf War

III [*qv*]. During the war Hussein appeared on television or in person on the streets until and including 9 April, when Baghdad fell to the invading forces. He disappeared, reportedly carrying $1,000 million in cash collected from the Central Bank by his son Qusay. In May, in an audio-taped statement, he called on Iraqis to resist "the foreigners."

Hussein ibn Talal al Hashem (1935–99): *King of Jordan, 1952–99* Born in Amman [*qv*], Hussein was educated at Victoria College, Alexandria [*qv*], and then at a private college in Harrow and at Sandhurst Military Academy in Britain. Following the deposition in August 1952 of his father, Talal ibn Abdullah al Hashem [*qv*], due to mental illness, Hussein was named king. But power was exercised by a regency council until the following May, when Hussein turned eighteen.

The new constitution promulgated in 1952 nominally provided a multiparty, two-chamber parliament, with the king as the constitutional head of state. Following Hussein's rigging of the general election in the autumn of 1954, the opposition demonstrated against the electoral malpractices and the Baghdad Pact [*qv*], which he was poised to join in December 1955. Bowing to popular pressure, he dismissed Gen. John Glubb [*qv*] and ordered fresh elections. The nationalist-leftist alliance won the largest bloc of seats in the autumn 1956 poll.

When the government headed by Premier Suleiman Nabulsi [*qv*] abrogated the 1948 Anglo-Jordanian Treaty [*qv*], which entitled Britain to maintain military bases in Jordan, Hussein acquiesced. In April 1957 he crushed an incipient coup by the Free Officers, led by his recently appointed chief of staff, General Ali Abu Nawar, and received U.S. aid under the Eisenhower doctrine [*qv*]. Hussein dismissed the Nabulsi government, dissolved parliament and political parties, and imposed martial law.

He countered the emergence of the United Arab Republic [*qv*] in early 1958 by sponsoring a federation of Jordan and Iraq, becoming its deputy head. But the federation disintegrated as a result of the Free Officers' coup in Iraq in July.

Despite several attempts, inspired by Egypt or Syria, to overthrow him, Hussein survived, partly because in exchange for a financial subsidy, he allowed U.S. intelligence agencies to operate freely in his kingdom. To avoid friction on succession, Hussein named his youngest brother, Hassan, crown prince in 1965.

In the charged atmosphere in the buildup to the June 1967 Arab-Israeli War [*qv*], Hussein joined the Egyptian-Syrian defense pact. The subsequent loss of the West Bank [*qv*] had a traumatic effect on Hussein and his subjects. A rise in the number of refugees from these territories, and growing militancy among the Palestinians in Jordan, led to fighting between Palestinian commandos and the Jordanian army in September 1970, which the latter won. A major offensive by the Jordanian army in July 1971 pushed the last of the Palestinian commandos out of the kingdom. The Palestine National Council (PNC) [*qv*], meeting in April 1972, rejected Hussein's plan for a United Arab Kingdom, consisting of the federated provinces of Jordan and Palestine, with East Jerusalem [*qv*] as its capital after Israel's withdrawal from the West Bank.

During the October 1973 Arab-Israeli

War [*qv*] Hussein rejected calls by Egypt, Syria, and Saudi Arabia to open a third front against Israel, and accepted Washington's advice to stay out of the conflict. With enhanced U.S. military and diplomatic backing, Hussein felt confident enough to resume the face-to-face talks with Israeli leaders that dated back to the period before the 1967 war and included Yigal Allon [*qv*], Abba Eban [*qv*], and Golda Meir [*qv*].

He continued to press for Israel's evacuation of the West Bank. This ceased only when a summit conference of the Arab League in October–November 1974 recognized the Palestine Liberation Organization (PLO) [*qv*] as the sole and legitimate representative of the Palestinian people, and supported the right of the Palestinian people to establish an independent national authority on any liberated territory of Palestine. Hussein reluctantly accepted the Arab League resolution. Dismissing West Bank members of the parliament, elected in April 1967, he suspended the chamber. He advocated a comprehensive peace settlement through a U.N.-sponsored conference.

By receiving a PLO delegation to Amman in February 1977, Hussein enhanced his standing in the Arab world. He refused to join the peace process initiated by the Camp David Accords [*qv*] between Egypt and Israel in September 1978. He now strengthened Jordan's ties with the Soviet Union, which he had first visited in 1967. He concluded an arms deal with Moscow in 1981 and backed the Soviet leader Leonid Brezhnev's call for an international conference on the Middle East crisis.

In the Iran-Iraq War (1980–88) [*qv*], Hussein sided with Iraq. This accelerated

Jordan's economic integration with Iraq. Emulating Iraqi President Saddam Hussein's [*qv*] example of giving his regime a parliamentary veneer, Hussein revived the suspended Jordanian parliament in January 1984. Ignoring the Arab League's suspension of Egypt from its membership since 1979, Hussein began to improve relations with Cairo from 1984 onward. In early 1985 Hussein concluded an agreement with the PLO chairman, Yasser Arafat [*qv*], on a future confederation of a Palestinian state and Jordan, and a joint approach to a Middle East peace settlement. But this deal was rejected by the Palestine National Council (PNC) [*qv*] in April 1987. Hussein responded by severing all of Jordan's legal and administrative links with the West Bank in July 1988.

He actively backed a move to establish the Arab Cooperation Council (ACC) [*qv*], an alliance of Jordan, Egypt, Iraq, and North Yemen. Following Iraq's invasion of Kuwait in August 1990, Hussein worked hard to provide an Arab solution for the crisis, but failed. He blamed the United States, Egypt, and Saudi Arabia for his failure and the subsequent escalation of the crisis into a full-scale war. Reflecting public opinion at home—well captured by the eighty-strong parliament elected in a free and fair election in November 1989, returning thirty-two Islamist deputies—Hussein combined his critical stance toward Washington with a pro-Baghdad tilt. This cost him dearly in Western capitals.

After the end of the Second Gulf War [*qv*], he tried to repair the damage by distancing himself from Saddam Hussein. He participated in the negotiations that preceded the holding of the Middle East Peace Conference [*qv*] in Madrid in October 1991, and agreed to a joint Jordanian-Palestinian delegation, as proposed by Israel. In August 1993, when the secret Israeli-PLO Accord [*qv*] became public, Hussein denounced it because it contradicted the agreed policy of the four Arab parties to pursue a joint strategy in their bilateral talks with Israel. But after a meeting with Arafat, he moderated his stance.

He continued to coordinate Jordan's position with Syria and Lebanon in his peace talks with Israel. He also allowed a fresh parliamentary poll in November 1993 (as scheduled) and was satisfied to see the Islamist forces doing less well than before. With the implementation of the Israeli-PLO Accord progressing, Hussein felt the need to join the process by resuming bilateral talks with Israel without consulting Syria and Lebanon. On 25 July 1994 in Washington, Hussein signed an agreement with Israeli Premier Yitzhak Rabin [*qv*], ending the state of belligerency between their countries. On 26 October they signed a peace treaty at a site in the Araba Valley along the Jordanian-Israeli border about 30 miles/48 km north of the Gulf of Aqaba. Four years later, invited by U.S. President Bill Clinton, Hussein intervened, successfully, in the Israeli-Palestinian talks at the Wye River Plantation near Washington. Just before his death due to lymph cancer, to the dismay and shock of Crown Prince Hassan, who had been acting as the monarch during Hussein's extended medical treatment in the United States, Hussein named his eldest son, Abdullah, as his heir.

al Husseini, Faisal (1940–2001): Born in Baghdad [*qv*] to Abdul Qadir, the field commander during the 1936–39 Arab

Revolt in Palestine [*qv*] during the time his family took refuge there, al Husseini grew up in Cairo [*qv*], where he obtained a university degree. He returned to East Jerusalem [*qv*]. After the establishment of the Palestine Liberation Organization [*qv*] in 1964, al Husseini worked briefly in the PLO's Jerusalem office. He then graduated from the Homs [*qv*] Military Academy as an officer of the Palestine Liberation Army [*qv*]. After the June 1967 Arab-Israeli War [*qv*], he worked with Yasser Arafat [*qv*] to set up a guerrilla infrastructure in the West Bank [*qv*]. He was arrested by the Israeli government and sentenced to a year in jail.

In 1979 he opened the Arab Studies Center in East Jerusalem, which the Israeli authorities regarded as a front for coordinating PLO activities in the Occupied Territories [*qv*]. It closed down the Center, and put al Husseini under administrative detention. After his release he was placed under city arrest for the next five years. Yet he emerged as the chief spokesman of the PLO on the West Bank [*qv*] in the late 1980s.

In the preliminary talks that led to the Middle East Peace Conference [*qv*] in Madrid in October 1991, he acted as a bridge between U.S. Secretary of State James Baker and Arafat. Al Husseini led the Palestinian delegation that negotiated with the Israelis after the Madrid conference.

In the cabinet of the Palestinian Authority [*qv*] appointed in 1994, al Husseini was given the portfolio of Jerusalem. He reopened the Arab Studies Center. During the prime ministry of Benjamin Netanyahu (r. 1996–99) [*qv*], the Center was closed down. During his trip to Kuwait [*qv*] to repair the damaged relations between the

Emirate and the PLO, al Husseini died of a heart attack.

al Husseini, Haajj Muhammad Amin (1897–1974): *Palestinian religious and political leader* Born into a prominent religious family in Jerusalem [*qv*], al Husseini received his secondary education in the city, studied for a year at al Azhar University [*qv*] in Cairo [*qv*], and then enrolled at the Ottoman school of administration in Istanbul. He served briefly as an officer in the Ottoman army during the First World War. After the war he became a recruiting officer for the army of Faisal ibn Hussein [*qv*] in Syria.

As the leader of an Arab nationalist group in Jerusalem, the Arab Club, he considered Palestine [*qv*] to be part of Greater Syria [*qv*] and opposed Jewish immigration into Palestine. Holding al Husseini responsible for anti-Jewish violence in April 1920, a British military court sentenced al Husseini, in absentia, to fifteen years in jail. He escaped to Damascus [*qv*]. The British high commissioner, Sir Herbert Samuel, pardoned al Husseini in August. The following March, to conciliate Arab opinion, Sir Herbert recommended that al Husseini should be made the grand mufti (religious judge) of Jerusalem when the job fell vacant on the death of his step-brother, Kamel al Husseini. This happened in May.

In December Sir Herbert ordered the establishment of a five-member Supreme Muslim Council—charged with running religious endowments and courts, and mosques—to be elected indirectly. It chose twenty-five-year-old al Husseini as its chairman. Having achieved supreme office among Palestinian Muslims, al Husseini opted for persuasion rather than violence. But that did not deflect him from pursuing his aim of making Palestine an independent Arab state. He began restoring the Dome of the Rock [*qv*] and al Aqsa Mosque, a step that enhanced his popularity among Arabs. His attempt to restrict Jewish rights at the Wailing Wall [*qv*] triggered a severe riot in August 1929.

His insistent demand that restrictions on Jewish immigration should be coupled with the establishment of an Arab national government made him the most significant political leader of Arab Palestinians. In April 1936, at his behest, various Arab groups united to form the Arab Higher Committee (AHC) [*qv*] under his leadership. Reacting to the discovery that the Zionists [*qv*] were smuggling arms, the AHC called a general strike, which escalated into a general Arab revolt that was backed by Syrian and Iraqi volunteers. Following the recommendation in July 1937 of the British-appointed Peel Commission to partition Palestine, Arab violence escalated. Three months later the British government dismissed al Husseini as chairman of the Supreme Muslim Council, which was disbanded, and banned the AHC, banishing its members to Seychelles in the Indian Ocean. al Husseini took refuge in the Muslim shrines of Jerusalem, and then managed to flee, first to Lebanon and then Syria. From there he continued to direct the Arab revolt, which ended in March 1939 with a death toll of 3,232 Arabs, 329 Jews, and 135 Britons.

Soon after the outbreak of the Second World War in September 1939, al Husseini arrived in Baghdad [*qv*] as a political refugee and began rallying anti-Zionist and anti-British sentiments in Iraq. He aided Rashid

Ali Gailani [*qv*] in his revolt against the royal family and the British in 1941. After the failure of Gailani's venture, al Husseini fled to Iran, then to (neutral) Turkey and the Balkans under the Axis Powers, and finally Germany, where he met Adolf Hitler, who received him as a leader of anti-British Arab nationalism [*qv*]. He attended Nazi rallies in Berlin and blessed those Bosnian Muslims who had joined the German military.

At the end of the war al Husseini was arrested by the French forces, but soon managed to escape (aboard a U.S. military aircraft) to Cairo. The Arab League [*qv*] appointed him chairman of the revived Arab Higher Committee to represent Arab Palestinians. Through his cousin Abdul Qadir al Husseini, who led the Palestinian fighters in the civil conflict that preceded the Palestine War (1948–49) [*qv*], al Husseini exercised influence inside Palestine. He lobbied successfully to get Egypt to join the Arab struggle against Israel.

After the Palestine War his attempts to form a government of all Palestine in the Egyptian-occupied Gaza Strip [*qv*] were cold-shouldered by Cairo. He moved to Beirut [*qv*] in 1959. With the establishment of the Palestine Liberation Organization [*qv*] in 1964, al Husseini's influence declined sharply, and he led an uneventful existence.

al Husseini clan: *prominent Palestinian family* Based in Jerusalem [*qv*], since the nineteenth century, al Husseinis have been religious and political leaders of the Arab community in the city, holding the offices of grand mufti (Islamic judge) and mayor. Hassan al Husseini was succeeded as the grand mufti by Taher al Husseini (d. 1856), Mustafa al Husseini (d. 1868), Taher al

Husseini (d. 1908), Kamel al Husseini (d. 1921), and his step-brother, Haajj Muhammad Amin al Husseini (d. 1974) [*qv*]. In the 1880s and 1890s Salim al Husseini was the mayor of Jerusalem, followed by Said al Husseini (1902–06). Then came Hussein al Husseini (d. 1918) and his son, Musa Kazim (1918–20). Both Musa Kazim al Husseini and Haajj Muhammad Amin al Husseini rose to prominence as the twentieth century progressed. Musa Kazim's son, Abdul Qadir al Husseini (b. 1908), died as a fighter in the civil strife that erupted before the Palestine War (1948–49) [*qv*]. His son, Faisal al Husseini [*qv*], emerged as the chief spokesman of the Palestine Liberation Organization (PLO) [*qv*] on the West Bank [*qv*] in the late 1980s.

I

Ibadhis: *Islamic sect* Ibadhis are named after Abdullah ibn Ibadh, a member of the Azd tribe of Oman, who started his life as a Khariji [*qv*]. In A.D. 685 he split with Khariji extremists, who considered that non-Khariji Muslims [*qv*] were polytheists, whereas he regarded them as mere infidels. Thus Ibadhism emerged as a pragmatist school within the Khariji movement. It sought to restore the concept of Islam [*qv*] and the Islamic state before it was allegedly corrupted by Caliph Othman ibn Affan (r. 644–56 A.D.). Ibadhis were then to be found in Iraq, Hijaz [*qv*], Central Arabia, Oman, and Iran. In A.D. 850 the Omani tribes, professing Ibadhism, split from the Abbasid Caliphate, based in Baghdad [*qv*], and set up an independent domain in the plateau of Jebel Akhdar, Green Mountain. Today two-thirds of Omani Muslims are Ibadhi.

ibn: *see* bin.

Ibn Baz, Abdul Aziz ibn Abdullah: *see* al Baz, Abdul Aziz ibn Abdullah.

Ibn Saud: *see* Abdul Aziz ibn Abdul Rahman al Saud.

Idris, Yusuf (1927–91): *Egyptian writer* Born in a village near Zagazig in the Nile [*qv*] delta, Idris obtained a medical degree from Cairo University in 1951. He became a doctor and health inspector, but his real interest lay in literature and journalism. He adopted short stories as his chief literary form and published five collections before he was thirty. Politically aware, he backed the 1952 republican revolution.

Writing in a realistic style, he used short stories to give shape to the aspiration of the underprivileged and present a set of priorities to the revolutionary regime. While talented enough to portray characters of different social classes, Idris focused on the frustrated man who found himself surrounded by oppression and failure. The other main theme that ran through his work was conflict between the individual and the group. In his first collection, *The Cheapest of Nights* (1954), he dealt with overpopulation. This was also the subject of his play *Farhat Republic*, produced in 1957, the year he published his first novella, *City Dregs*. His *Akhir al Duniya* (1961) was well received.

Dissatisfied with the Western dramatic structure, Idris turned to the forms used by popular entertainers in the Arab world—shadow plays and puppet theatre. *The Stooges* (1964) was a significant work that used a folk entertainment form to portray a subject of contemporary concern—freedom of expression—which created a sensation among the audience and critics alike. *The Striped* (1969) was another critical play dressed up as popular entertainment.

Idris became progressively introverted both in his plays and short stories. He authored psychological plays and drama of the absurd, attempting to create an original indigenous style capable of conveying subtle nuances of spiritual change. After 1961 he published seven collections of short stories. His themes were the futility and absurdity of existence, and a constant feeling of loneliness. Now his main character, instead of being an heroic failure, was often enigmatic and miraculous, who operated in a world that hovered between illusion and reality. Some of his stories were translated into foreign languages.

ijma *(Arabic: consensus):* One of the four pillars of Islamic jurisprudence *ijma* means consensus of the community, *umma* [*qv*]—the remaining pillars being the Quran [*qv*]; Prophet Muhammad's *sunna* [*qv*], later codified as the Hadith [*qv*]; and *ijtihad* [*qv*], interpretative reasoning. The function of *ijma* is to settle the theory or practice concerning the believer's behavior in matters specified by Allah (through the Quran) and the Prophet Muhammad (through the Hadith). Until Muhammad ibn Idris al Shafii (d. A.D. 820) founded the discipline of religious jurisprudence *(fiqh* [*qv*]), based on these pillars, *ijma* had been construed as consensus of "ahl al hall wal aqd" (people of loosening and binding), a term that embraces various types of representatives of the community, including religious intellectuals. But Shafii enlarged it to include the whole community. In more modern times Muhammad Abdu (d. 1905), an Egyptian Islamic thinker, interpreted *ijma* as public opinion.

ijtihad *(Arabic: applying effort [to form an opinion]): interpretative reasoning* With time it became necessary for Muslims [*qv*] and their rulers to interpret the Quran [*qv*] and the Prophet Muhammad's *sunna* [*qv*] (together forming the Islamic law) to address unprecedented situations. During the early Islamic era, *ijtihad* was freely practiced by the learned to interpret the Quran and the *sunna*, the interpretation being either arbitrary or based on analogy, *qiyas* [*qv*]. Its practitioners were called *mujtahids* [*qv*]. Muhammad ibn Idris al Shafii (d. A.D. 820) restricted *ijtihad* to analogy from the Quran and the *sunna*.

By the mid-ninth century A.D. four major schools of Islamic law—ranging between the rigid Hanbali school [*qv*] and the liberal Hanafi school [*qv*]—had emerged within Sunni Islam [*qv*]. In order not to upset the consensus thus gained with some new radical innovation, the clergy from the tenth century onward declared that the gates of *ijtihad* had been shut. As late as the early nineteenth century, the Mufti of Cairo's al Azhar University [*qv*] declared: "He who believes himself to be a mujtahid must be under the influence of his hallucinations and of the devil." This view was challenged by Jamal al-Din Afghani (d. 1897), a leading Islamic reformer, who stated that each believer had the right and responsibility to interpret the Quran and the Hadith himself. His stance was adopted later by Muhammad Abdu (d. 1905), an Egyptian Islamic scholar, and his acolyte Muhammad Rashid Rida (d.

1935). Rida inspired Hassan al Banna [*qv*], the founder of the Muslim Brotherhood [*qv*] in Egypt, who favored *ijtihad* so that Islam could face the problems of the modern world.

Unlike in Sunnism, in Shia Islam [*qv*] *ijtihad* did not remain dormant for long. The destruction in 1258 of the (Sunni) Abbasid caliphate by the Mongol ruler Hulagu Khan (1217–65) created a political-ideological vacuum in which the Shia doctrine thrived. Jamal al-Din ibn Yusuf al Hilli (1250–1325), a Shia thinker, rehabilitated the concept and practice of *ijtihad*.

Ikhwan *(Arabic: Brethren or brotherhood): Islamic military movement in Arabia* Abdul Aziz ibn Abdul Rahman al Saud [*qv*], the ruler of Najd [*qv*], conceived the idea of settling the nomadic tribes in colonies in order to teach them the tenets of Islam [*qv*] as a step toward replacing their customary law with Islamic Law [*qv*] and their traditional tribal bonds with religious ones. Implementing this idea after 1913, he called the settlements *hijra (Arabic: migration—from a life of ignorance to one of enlightment)* and the settlers, al Ikhwan. They were fired with zeal to spread the Wahhabi [*qv*] version of Islam to the farthest corners of the Arabian Peninsula [*qv*] and beyond.

By 1920 their colonies had become the primary source of soldiery to Abdul Aziz al Saud. During the next several years the Ikhwan helped him to expand his realm to nearly four-fifths of the Arabian Peninsula. In 1927 Britain, the most powerful foreign power in the region, recognized Abdul Aziz al Saud as King of Hijaz and Sultan of Najd and its Dependencies on the condition that he respected Britain as the protector of

Oman and the Gulf principalities as well as the territorial integrity of Iraq and Transjordan, then under British mandate.

Ignoring al Saud's agreement with Britain, some of the Ikhwan commanders continued to raid territories outside his domain. This led to conflict between the Ikhwan and al Saud in March 1929, with 8,000 Ikhwan facing 30,000 well-armed soldiers of al Saud. The rebel Ikhwan were defeated. Further battles followed, and it was not until January 1930 that the last of the defiant Ikhwan chiefs surrendered. Those Ikhwan commanders who had stayed loyal to al Saud received regular stipends. Soon their units were transformed into the National Guard [*qv*].

Ikhwan al Muslimin: *see* Muslim Brotherhood.

imam *(Arabic: model, one whose leadership or example is to be followed): religious leader* "Imam" is used as a noun and as a title. Shias [*qv*] use it for the religious leader at the highest level instead of the honorific caliph (from Arabic *khilafa:* vice regent) used by Sunnis [*qv*]. Thus Shias refer to Ali ibn Abu Talib as Imam Ali, whereas Sunnis call him Caliph Ali. Sunnis refer to the founders of their four legal schools as imams—for example, Imam Muhammad ibn Idris al Shafii. As the religious leader of Zaidi [*qv*] Shias in his country, the ruler of North Yemen carried the honorific of Imam. In modern times Ayatollah Ruhollah Khomeini [*qv*] was given this title by Iranian Shias. Finally, the leader of prayers at any mosque is called an imam.

imamat: *supreme leadership of Muslims after the Prophet Muhammad* Sunnis [*qv*] distinguish between the early caliphate of the (four) Rightly Guided Caliphs—Abu Bakr ibn Abu Quhafa, Omar ibn Khattab, Othman ibn Affan, and Ali ibn Abu Talib—and the latter *imamat,* which was characterized by worldly monarchy. Only the caliphs met the conditions of the true *imamat.* The required qualifications were membership of the Quraish tribe, to which the Prophet Muhammad had belonged, thorough knowledge of Islamic law and probity in upholding it, and the physical fitness as well as an ability to discharge the political-military duties of the high office. The Imam could be appointed by his predecessor or elected. The size of the electorate—or "ahl al hall wal aqd" (people of loosening and binding)—necessary to make their choice binding on the Muslim community varied between one and the "generality" of the electors, the election amounting to a selection of the "most exemplary" Muslim. His duties were to protect the religion from heterodoxy; dispense Islamic punishment and justice between disputants; maintain peace within the Muslim domain and defend it against foreign enemies; collect Islamic alms and taxes, and spend the revenue according to the law; and appoint sincere Muslims to assist him in the discharge of his duties.

Shias [*qv*] do not accept the *imamat* of Abu Bakr, Omar, and Othman, arguing that the Prophet Muhammad had designated Ali as his successor. The Twelver Shia [*qv*] doctrine, formulated by Imam Jaafar al Sadiq (d. 765), maintains that the Imam must be designated by Allah through the Prophet Muhammad or another Imam, he must be free from sin and error, and he must be the "most exemplary" of all Muslims. In sum,

Imams, being divinely inspired, are infallible, a view not shared by Sunnis.

Imamis: *see* Twelve Shias.

intifada *(Arabic: shivering or shaking off): Palestinian uprising against the Israeli occupation, 1987–93* Intifada erupted spontaneously in the Palestinian refugee camp of Jabaliya in the Gaza Strip [*qv*] on 9 December 1987, when thousands marched in protest against the killing of four Palestinians by an Israeli truck near the settlement. During the next several days rioting spread throughout the Gaza Strip and the West Bank [*qv*], including East Jerusalem [*qv*], with predominantly young protestors attacking Israeli forces with stones and petrol bombs, and the latter responding with tear gas and live ammunition, killing twenty-four Palestinians by the end of December. By then both the Palestine Liberation Organization (PLO) [*qv*], headquartered in Tunis, and the Islamic Center, the front organization of the Muslim Brotherhood [*qv*], based in the Occupied Territories [*qv*], had lent the spontaneous movement their support.

The intifada stemmed from twenty years of collective and individual frustration and humiliation that the Palestinians had endured in their dealings with the Jews and the Israeli authorities, both military and civilian. By early January 1988 the secular PLO had set up the United National Leadership of the Uprising (UNLU) [*qv*] to direct the movement, while the Islamic Center formed Hamas [*qv*] for the same purpose. Many of those involved were young, educated Palestinians, fluent in Hebrew [*qv*] and familiar with Israeli norms, who took over the communal leadership from the older generation

of Arab notables who professed peaceful coexistence with the Israelis.

UNLU and Hamas urged the Palestinians to resign from all government posts, stop using public services, withdraw money from Israeli banks, boycott all Israeli products, cease paying taxes, and join the strikes it called. UNLU committees issued circulars containing instructions in these matters, and urged all Palestinians to share the sacrifices required by the intifada. The Palestinians used charity funds to support the large number of families whose husbands or brothers were jailed. Actions by the Israeli security forces—involving firings, curfews, harassment, arrests, and house searches and demolitions—severely disrupted Palestinian life. During the first four years of the intifada, 1,413 Palestinians were killed—most of them by the Israeli security forces and a minority by fellow-Palestinians for being Israeli agents—and 90,000 (about one sixth of all male Palestinians above fifteen) were arrested.

The campaign against the Israeli agents intensified in the early 1990s and destroyed Shin Beth's [*qv*] 20,000-strong intelligence network among the Palestinians, making it extremely hard for the occupying Israeli authorities to reimpose full control and restore law and order. This, and the refusal of the Palestinians to call off the intifada, convinced the Israeli government of the futility of continued suppression of them and denial of their national identity and the right to self-rule, and paved the way for the Israeli-Palestine Liberation Organization Accord [*qv*] in September 1993. By the end of the intifada, 1,636 Palestinians, including 316 minors, had been killed—1,346 by the

Israeli security forces and 290 by Jewish civilians. This figure excluded those who were murdered by fellow-Palestinians for collaborating with Israel. By contrast, the death toll of the Israelis was one a month.

Iran:

Official name: Islamic Republic of Iran

Capital: Tehran [*qv*]

Area: 636,296 sq. miles/1,648,000 sq. km

Population: 66,620,000 (2002, est.)

Gross domestic product: $82 billion (2001, est.)

National currency: Iranian Rial (RI); RIs 1000 = US$0.57= £0.40 = EUR 0.64 (2001)

Form of government: republic, under Leader (of the Revolution)

Official language: Persian [*qv*]

Official religion: Islam [*qv*]

Administrative regions: Iran is divided into twenty-seven provinces.

Assembly of Experts: The 1979 constitution provided for the Assembly of Experts [*qv*] to select the Leader or Leadership Council of three to five members. The First Assembly, elected in 1982, was followed by the Second in 1990 after the constitution was amended in 1989 and the provision of the Leadership Council removed. The Third Assembly was elected in 1998.

Constitution: A draft constitution, submitted to the Assembly of Experts (1979) by the government in August 1979, was modified and then approved by a referendum in December. Another referendum in July 1989 approved fifty amendments to the constitution, including abolishing the premiership, and creating the Expediency Consultation Council System (ECCS) to resolve differences between parliament, presidency, and the Guardians Council [*qv*].

Iran is an Islamic republic, where social, political, and economic affairs were conducted according to the tenets of Islam [*qv*]. The constitution provides for an outstanding Islamic jurisprudent to be the Leader (of the Revolution). Standing above the executive, legislative, and judicial branches of the state, he has extensive powers, including exercising the supreme command of the armed forces and declaring war or peace in consultation with the Supreme National Security Council, and outlining general policies after consultation with the ECCS. He has the authority to appoint half the members of the Guardians Council, the head of the judiciary, and the chief of the joint staff. He can dismiss the (elected) president if the supreme court finds him derelict in his duties or the parliament declares him politically incompetent. Ayatollah Ruhollah Khomeini [*qv*], named as the first Leader, was assigned these powers for life. His successor is required to be chosen by a popularly elected Assembly of Experts (on Islam), consisting of clerics, for the eight-year tenure of the Assembly.

The president is the chief executive and is elected directly for a four-year term. Legislative authority rests with the Majlis, which is elected for a four-year term. Bills passed by the Majlis were vetted by the Guardians Council to ensure that they are in line with the constitution and Islamic precepts. The articles dealing with the basic rights of the individual provide for equal human, political, economic, social, and cultural rights for men and women.

The press and other publications are give a free rein except in matters deemed detrimental to Islamic principles and public morality. The formation of political and professional parties and associations, as well as religious societies is allowed provided they do not violate the principles of independence, national unity of Islamic criteria.

The constitution specifies Islam of the Twelver Jaafari school [*qv*] as the official religion, with other Islamic schools, including the Hanafi [*qv*], Maliki [*qv*], Shafii [*qv*], and Zaidi [*qv*], being accorded full respect. It recognizes Christians [*qv*], Jews [*qv*], and Zoroastrians [*qv*] as religious minorities, and allocates them a certain number of parliamentarians.

Ethnic composition: (2000) Persians [*qv*] 65 percent, Azeris [*qv*] 20 percent, Kurds [*qv*] 7 percent, Baluchis [*qv*] 2.5 percent, Arabs [*qv*] 3 percent, Turkmen [*qv*] 2 percent, Armenian [*qv*] 0.5 percent.

Executive authority: Executive authority rests with the president, who is elected directly by voters.

High officials:
Leader: Ayatollah Ali Husseini Khamanei [*qv*], 1998–
President: Muhammad Khatami [*qv*], 2001–
First vice president: Muhammad Reza Arif-Yazdi 2001–
Speaker of Parliament: Mahdi Karrubi, 2000–
Speaker of the Assembly of Experts: Ayatollah Ali Meshkini, 1998–
Chairman of the Council of Guardians: Ayatollah Muhammad Muhammadi Gilani, 1989–
Expediency Consultation Council System: Ali Akbar Hashemi Rafsanjani [*qv*] 1997–

History: The Constitutional Revolution [*qv*] in 1907, during the reign of Muzzafar al Din Qajar (r. 1896–1907)—which introduced a written constitution and an elected Majlis—collapsed in 1911 with the dissolution of the Second Majlis. By the end of the First World War the financial position of Iran (then Persia) was so dire that only British subsidies could keep it afloat. London and Tehran concluded the secret Anglo-Persian Agreement [*qv*] 1919, which turned Iran into a virtual protectorate of Britain. The Majlis refused to ratify it. Britain decided to supplant the weak Qajar power with a strong authority represented by Col. Reza Khan, commander of the elite Cossak Brigade. Reza Khan carried out a coup against the government of Fathullah Gilani in February 1921. He persuaded the Majlis to depose the Qajar monarch, Ahmad Shah, and appoint him king in December 1925.

As Reza Shah Pahlavi [*qv*], the new ruler established a strong, centralized state in Iran, implemented social reform, and renegotiated the oil concessions given to the British-owned Anglo-Persian (later Anglo-Iranian) Oil Company. In foreign affairs he cultivated Germany in the 1930s in order to offset the traditional influence of Britain and Russia (then the Soviet Union). In 1933 he changed the name of the country from Persia to Iran. Disapproving Reza Shah's neutrality during the Second World War, Britain and the Soviet Union occupied Iran in August 1941 and forced Reza Shah to abdicate in favor of his son Muhammad [*qv*].

Following the departure of the British and the Soviets after the war, Muhammad Reza Shah Pahlavi faced leftist autonomous governments in Azerbaijan [*qv*] and Kurdistan [*qv*]. Having overpowered them with U.S. assistance, he consolidated his authority.

In May 1951 nationalist Premier

Muhammad Mussadiq [*qv*] nationalized the Anglo-Iranian Oil Company. Britain protested, and oil exports stopped. In August 1952 the parliament gave Mussadiq emergency powers for six months, and renewed them for a year in January 1953. Mussadiq came into conflict with the shah over the control of the defense ministry. On 16 August the shah left the country.

However, the jubilation of the pro-Mussadiq forces was short-lived. Royalist officers, working in conjunction with the U.S. Central Intelligence Agency, mounted a counter-coup that resulted in the arrest of Mussadiq and the return of the shah on 19 August. A year later he offered oil concessions to a Western consortium. He strengthened his links with the West by joining the Baghdad Pact [*qv*]. He repressed domestic opposition, secular and Islamic, and set up a police state. Through his "white revolution" [*qv*] he broke the hold of the landed aristocracy and prepared the ground for the rise of capitalism. The enormous jump in oil revenues in the mid-1970s fueled his ambition to make Iran the fifth most powerful nation in the world.

The discontent of the burgeoning modern middle class—which had emerged during a quarter-century of repression that had destroyed all avenues of opposition, except the mosque, whose extensive network remained intact—combined with the alienation experienced by a large underclass of recent rural migrants produced by an overheated economy, created a protest movement that began to stir in the autumn of 1977. Within a year the movement—guided by Ayatollah Ruhollah Khomeini [*qv*], exiled in Najaf [*qv*], Iraq [*qv*]—acquired revolutionary proportions. It succeeded in overthrowing the shah, heralding an Islamic order under Khomeini in early 1979.

Several attempts were made by the displaced Iranian leaders to overthrow the new regime through a military coup. When the last of these failed in July 1980, the scene was set for a frontal attack on Islamic Iran, which had alienated not only the United States but also the neighboring Gulf states [*qv*]. Iraq invaded Iran in September 1980. Despite the chaotic state of its military, Iran was able to stop the Iraqi advance. Overall, the eight-year conflict enabled Khomeini to consolidate the revolution. When in the early summer of 1988 he realized that further military reverses at Iraqi hands would threaten the future of his regime, he agreed to a ceasefire. He died within a year.

The succession to Khomeini's office by Ayatollah Ali Khamanei, the erstwhile president, was smooth. So too was the elevation of Ali Akbar Hashemi Rafsanjani, the erstwhile speaker of parliament, to the presidency by popular vote. His liberalization of the economy achieved mixed results. That is why his vote declined to 63 percent at the next poll in 1993. Continued low prices for oil, the predominant export of Iran, was another factor in the country's economic ills.

In the 1997 general election, the parliamentary speaker, Hojatalislam Ali Akbar Nateq Nouri, the favored candidate of the religious establishment, was defeated by Hojatalislam Muhammad Khatami by a landslide margin. He initiated much-needed political reform, which was resisted by the conservative-dominated Majlis and orthodox clerics. Under his leadership the regime held the first local elections in February 1999, an exercise that created tens of thousands of elected representatives. Facing the crisis caused by the student protest in July, Khatami and Khamanei worked together to defuse it. That Khatami's reformist agenda had popular backing became apparent when in the 2000 general election voters gave a thumping majority to reformers in the Majlis. In the presidential poll in 2001, Khatami improved his vote by 9 percent to 78. He continued the economic liberalization initiated by his predecessor.

Following the attacks on the United States in September 2001, both Khatami and Khamanei condemned the killing of innocent civilians. In the Afghanistan campaign of the United States that followed, Iran—hostile to the Taliban administration in Kabul since its inception in 1996—stayed neutral, while welcoming the overthrow of the Taliban, which it had regarded as the brain child of Pakistan and Saudi Arabia [qv]. But that did not stop U.S. President George Walker Bush (r. 2001–) from including Iran in his "Axis of Evil" along with Iraq and North Korea, thus continuing the Dual Containment policy [qv] of the previous administration. That did not deter Iran from letting the Tehran-based Supreme Assembly of Islamic Revolution in Iraq [qv] join the Washington-backed Iraqi opposition groups.

Legislature: The parliament, officially called Majlis, deals with legislation, general policy matters, and the budget. Its 290 members, elected for a four-year term, include two Christians, one Zoroastrian, and one Jew. It has the right to impeach the president, who is then dismissed by the Leader.

Religious composition: (2002) Muslims [qv] 98.7 percent, of which Shia [qv] 90 percent, Sunni [qv] 8.7 percent; Bahai [qv] 0.7 percent; Christian 0.5 percent, affiliated mainly to the Armenian Orthodox [qv] and the Assyrian Churches [qv]; Jewish 0.05 percent; Zoroastrian 0.05 percent. Bahais are considered heretics and their institutions were banned in 1983.

Iran-Contra Affair: *see* Irangate Affair.

Iran-Iraq Frontier Treaty (1937): Signed on 4 July 1937, the Iran-Iraq Frontier Treaty declared the Shatt al Arab [qv] open for navigation to all countries of the world. It confirmed the land boundaries as set out in the 1913 Protocol of Constantinople [qv], and the *proces-verbaux* of the Delimitation of the Frontier Commission of 1914; and amended the Shatt al Arab frontiers, with Iraq conceding the thalweg (that is, the median line of the main navigable channel) principle for four miles facing Abadan [qv], the site of the Anglo-Persian Oil Company's refinery. Later Iraq said it had signed the treaty under duress.

Iran-Iraq Treaty of International Boundaries and Good Neighborliness (1975): The Treaty of International Boundaries and Good Neighborliness between Iran and Iraq evolved out of the accord concluded on 6 March 1975 in Algiers between Muhammad Reza Shah Pahlavi [qv] and Saddam Hussein [qv], then vice president of Iraq. The signatories agreed to delimit the land boundaries of their countries according to the 1913 Protocol of Constantinople [qv] and the *proces-verbaux* of the Delimitation of the Frontier Commission of 1914, to demarcate the fluvial frontiers of their countries according to the thalweg line (that is, along the median line of the main navigable channel), and to end all infiltrations of a subversive nature.

Once the demarcation of the land and river boundaries had been accomplished according to the Accord, Iran and Iraq signed the Treaty of International Boundaries and Good Neighborliness in Baghdad on 13 June 1975. Article 4 of the treaty stated that the provisions about the land and river frontiers, and stopping subversive infiltration "shall be final and permanent." After the respective constitutional requirements about international treaties had been met in both states, the treaty went into effect on 17 September 1975.

Since the treaty incorporated Iran's demand, first made sixty years earlier, that the thalweg principle be applied to the frontier along the Shatt al Arab [qv], it signified a victory for Iran. Later Iraq said that it had signed the treaty under duress. It unilaterally abrogated the treaty on 17 September 1980 before invading Iran. Iran protested. In mid-August 1990, following its invasion of Kuwait, Iraq agreed to abide by the treaty.

Iran-Iraq War (1980–88): *see* Gulf War I.

Irangate Affair (1986): *Secret U.S. arms-for-hostages deal with Iran* On 3 November 1986, *Al Shira* (The Sail), a Beirut-based magazine, disclosed that the United States had secretly sold weapons to Iran. Aware of Iran's geostrategic importance, Washington wanted to end the hostility that Tehran had shown toward the United States since the 1979 Islamic revolution [qv]. It also wanted to gain the freedom of the American captives taken by pro-Iranian groups in Lebanon, then in the midst of the long Lebanese Civil War [qv]. This sale of arms was contrary to the declared policies of U.S. President Ronald Reagan (r. 1981–89), whereby an arms embargo had been imposed on Tehran, and the United States had vowed not to deal with terrorists and hostage takers. The American officials involved in the clandestine deals passed on the moneys obtained from Iran to the Contra guerrillas fighting the leftist government in Nicaragua, thus contravening the ban that the U.S. Congress had imposed on financially assisting the ultraright-wing Nicaraguan insurgents.

The Islamic Jihad [qv] had captured William Buckley, the U.S. Central Intelligence Agency station chief in Beirut [qv], in March 1984. It coupled its demand for the freeing of seventeen Shias convicted in Kuwait on charges of bombing the U.S. and French Embassies with a call on Washington and Paris to end their arms embargo against Iran, then engaged in war with Iraq. By the end of May the number of American captives taken by the pro-Iranian groups in Lebanon had risen to five.

In early July 1985 Reagan allowed his National Security Adviser, Robert McFarlane, to propose that Tehran might influence the pro-Iranian Lebanese groups to free their American hostages in exchange for the sale of U.S.-made weapons to Iran. The money thus obtained was to be channelled to the Contra guerrillas fighting the leftist regime in Nicaragua, thus subverting the ban that the U.S. Congress had imposed on aiding the Contras.

Two months later, in exchange for the sale of 508 U.S.-made antitank missiles, one American hostage was released. But the second swap of 120 antiaircraft missiles and 4,000 antitank missiles for the remaining captives (excluding Buckley, who had died) became entangled. A U.S. delegation, led by

McFarlane, arrived in Tehran on 25 May 1986, but made no progress in repairing U.S. relations with Iran. After further shipment of seven tons of U.S.-made arms and ammunition in early July, one American hostage was freed. The release of a further captive came after 500 antitank missiles had been delivered to Iran in late October. With three Americans still in captivity, the Iranians had managed to make the U.S. negotiators appear poor bargainers.

The disclosure of secret U.S. arms sales to Iran had a devastating impact on U.S. and world public opinion. Reagan's approval rating fell from 67 percent to 46 percent, and paralyzed his administration for several months. Washington's Arab allies were shocked and incensed. This was particularly true of Iraq, which had been assured clandestinely since November 1983 that the United States would ensure that it was not defeated in its war with Iran.

Iranian calendar: In 1925 the Iranian parliament adopted the solar calendar beginning with the *hijra*, the migration of the Prophet Muhammad from Mecca [*qv*] to Medina [*qv*] in A.D. 622, which is also the starting point of the Islamic (lunar) era. The Iranian (solar) year begins on the spring equinox, 21 or 22 March, and is divided into six consecutive months of 31 days, and the rest of 30 days, except the last, which is normally 29 days long. The months—named after Zoroastarian [*qv*] angels—are Farvardin (31 days), Urdibehesht (31), Khurdad (31), Tir (31), Murdad (31), Shahrivar (31), Mihr (30), Aban (30), Azar (30), Dey (30), Bahman (30), and Isfand (29 days normally, 30 days in a leap year). To change an Iranian calendar date to a Christian date, add 621 or 622 depending on the month of the year. The Islamic Republic of Iran, founded in 1979, uses the Iranian calendar along with the Islamic one.

Iranian-Russian Treaty (1921): A twenty-five-article treaty was signed between Iran (then Persia) and Soviet Russia on 26 February 1921. Article 5 required the two parties to prohibit the formation or presence of "any organization or groups of persons . . . whose object is to engage in acts of hostility against Persia or Russia." This applied equally to troops. Both signatories agreed to prevent the presence of forces of a third party in cases where the presence of such forces would be regarded as "menace to the frontiers, interests or safety" of the other party. "If a third party should carry out a policy of usurpation by means of armed intervention in Persia, or if such power should desire to use Persian territory as a base of operations against Russia, or if a foreign power should threaten the frontiers of Federal Russia or those of its allies, and if the Persian government should not be able to put a stop to such menace after having been once called upon to do so by Russia, Russia shall have the right to advance her troops into the Persian interior for the purpose of carrying out the military options necessary for its defense," stated Article 6. "Russia undertakes, however, to withdraw her troops from Persian territory as soon as possible as the danger has been removed." In August 1941 these articles formed the basis for the Soviet march into northern Iran (which took place in coordination with Britain, its ally in the Second World War after June 1941, which advanced from the south).

When the revolutionary movement in

Iran against the pro-U.S. Muhammad Reza Shah Pahlavi [*qv*] began to escalate sharply during the autumn of 1978, raising the possibility of intervention by Washington, the Soviet leader, Leonid Brezhnev, warned the United States against interfering in Iran's domestic affairs. Aware that Articles 5 and 6 of the 1921 Treaty entitled Moscow to move its troops into Iran if it felt threatened by an armed intervention by a third party in Iran, U.S. Secretary of State Cyrus Vance stated publicly that Washington had no intention of becoming involved in Iran's internal affairs, a statement that boosted the morale of the anti-shah forces.

Iranian-Soviet Treaty of Guarantee and Neutrality (1927): On 1 October 1927 the Soviet Union signed a Treaty of Guarantee and Neutrality with Iran. The signatories agreed to refrain from aggression against each other and to remain neutral in the event of aggression by a third country. "Each of the contracting parties agrees to take no part . . . in political alliances or agreements directed against the safety of the territory or territorial waters of the contracting party or against the integrity, independence or sovereignty," stated Article 3. The same applied to economic boycotts or blockades organized by third parties. One of the two protocols accompanying the document reiterated that Article 6 of the 1921 Iranian-Russian Treaty [*qv*] should remain in force. Following the 1979 revolution in Iran, when the United States and the European Economic Community imposed economic sanctions against Iran after militant Iranian students had taken U.S. diplomats hostage, the Soviet Union refused to join the embargo.

Iraq *der. of eragh (Persian; lowland):*
Official name: Republic of Iraq
Capital: Baghdad [*qv*]
Area: 169,235 sq. miles/438,317 sq. km, excluding the Iraqi share of the Saudi Arabia-Iraq Neutral Zone [*qv*] at 1,360 sq. miles/3,522 sq. km
Population: 23,474,000 (2002, est.)
Gross domestic product: $26.7 billion (2000, est.)
National currency: Iraqi Dinar (IQD); IQD 1000 = US$0.50 = £0.80 = EUR 0.49 (2002)
Form of government: republic, with president elected by the Revolutionary Command Council to be endorsed in a referendum
Official language(s): Arabic [*qv*] in all of Iraq; and Kurdish [*qv*] only in the Kurdistan Autonomous Region [*qv*]
Official religion: Islam [*qv*]
Administrative regions: Iraq is divided into eighteen governorates (provinces), including the three—Irbil, Dohak, and Suleimaniya—that form the Kurdistan Autonomous Region.
Constitution: Following a coup by the Baath Socialist Party [*qv*] in July 1968, an interim constitution was promulgated in September. Amended in November 1969, it was replaced by another provisional version in July 1970. The latter document was amended in 1973 and 1974. A draft of the permanent constitution was submitted in March 1989 to the National Assembly [*qv*], an institution established in 1980. Though the Assembly approved it in July 1990, it remains to be put to a referendum for approval before its implementation.

The September 1968 constitution

describes Iraq as "democratic and sovereign," and Islam as the state religion. The state undertakes to safeguard freedom of religion, speech, and opinion. It also guarantees freedom of the press and the right to establish associations and trade unions within the law.

The highest authority in Iraq is the Revolutionary Command Council (RCC), which rules by two-thirds majority, and which was authorized to issue laws until the establishment of a parliament. The 1969 amendments made Iraq's president the supreme commander of the armed forces and chairman of the RCC.

The fifteen-article peace agreement that the Iraqi government signed with the Kurdish insurgents in March 1970 included a promise by it to amend the present constitution to declare that the people of Iraq consisted of two principal nationalities—the Arab [qv] and the Kurdish—and to confirm the national rights of Kurds [qv] and all other minorities within the framework of Iraqi unity, and to appoint a Kurd as a vice president of Iraq.

The 1970 interim constitution required that the president and vice president(s) be elected by a two-thirds majority of the RCC and that cabinet ministers be responsible to the president. The National Charter promulgated by the president in July 1973 mentioned the creation of a National Assembly. The law for Autonomy in Kurdistan, issued in March 1974, provided for a Legislative Council there. Following an RCC decree in March 1980, elections to the National Assembly and the Legislative Council were held respectively in June and September.

An amendment to the interim constitution by the RCC in September 1995 stipulated that the elected chairman of the RCC would become the Republic's president for seven years, subject to the approval by the National Assembly followed by an endorsement in a referendum.

Ethnic composition: (2002) Arab 78 percent, Kurd 18 percent, Turkmen [qv] 1.5 percent, other 2.5 percent.

Executive authority: Executive power rests with the republic's president, who is elected by a two-thirds majority of the Revolutionary Command Council, established by the leaders of the coup carried out in July 1968, and then endorsed in a referendum. The size of the RCC has varied from five to seventeen members. In 2000, it had eight members.

High officials:

President: Saddam Hussein, 2002–03

Vice presidents: Taha Yassin Ramadan 2002–03 ; Taha Muhyi al Din Maruf (an ethnic Kurd) 2002-03

Chairman of the RCC: Saddam Hussein, 2002–03

Vice chairman of the RCC: Izzat Ibrahim, 2002-03

Speaker of the National Assembly: Saadoun Hamadi, 2000–03

Speaker of the Legislative Council of Kurdistan: Ahmad Abdul Qadir al Naqshbandi, 1989–03

History (ca. 1900): At the turn of the twentieth century, the provinces of Basra and Baghdad in the Mesopotamian plain had been part of the Ottoman Empire since 1638. After the dissolution of the Ottoman Empire in 1918 the mandate over these provinces was given to the British, who, constituting them as Iraq, put them under the authority of King Faisal I ibn Hussein al

Hashem [*qv*] in 1921. Four years later, a League of Nations arbitration committee awarded Mosul province to Iraq, thus enlarging the country.

In 1932 the British mandate ended, but most Iraqis considered their independence incomplete so long as British troops were stationed on their soil. In April 1941 Premier Rashid Ali Gailani [*qv*] led a successful coup against the British. However, he was unable to withstand a British counteroffensive in May.

After the Second World War, the national sentiment turned strongly anti-Western and anti-Zionist [*qv*] in the wake of the Arab defeat in the Palestine War (1948–49) [*qv*]. But the Iraqi strongman Premier Nuri al Said [*qv*] overrode popular feelings, led Iraq into the Western-led Baghdad Pact [*qv*], and refused to condemn the Anglo-French-Israeli aggression in the Suez War (1956) [*qv*]. The result was a military coup by Free Officers led by Brigadier Abdul Karim Qasim [*qv*] in July 1958. He carried out socioeconomic reform, but was overthrown in 1963 by a group of Baathist [*qv*] officers working in conjunction with the American Central Intelligence Agency.

Due to a division among the Baathists, power passed to the non-Baathist, pro-Egyptian Abdul Salam Arif [*qv*], and then to his brother Abdul Rahman Arif [*qv*], who was overthrown by a Baathist coup in July 1968. Better organized than before, the Baathists consolidated their hold over power, and began a program of economic development. They were helped by a dramatic jump in oil prices in the mid-1970s.

The rebellion by nationalist Kurds that flared up in 1974 was pacified by striking a deal with Iran, which had been arming the Iraqi Kurds, in March 1975, known as the Algiers Accord [*qv*]. But with the rise of an Islamic republic in Iran, a Shia [*qv*] majority country, the Iraqi government found Islamic militancy gaining ground among its Shias. Iraq's President Saddam Hussein tried to tackle the problem by suppressing militant Shias at home and invading the oil-rich Iranian province of Khuzistan in September 1980. He had expected the conflict to last a month. It continued for ninety-five months, ending in August 1988. Nonetheless, thanks to the aid Iraq received from the Gulf states [*qv*] and the West, Iraq emerged as the most powerful Arab country.

Determined to make his weight felt in the region, in August 1990 Saddam Hussein invaded and occupied Kuwait, an emirate to which Iraq had in the past laid claim. In response, the United States, under President George Bush, led a coalition of nations in a successful war in early 1991, which ended the Iraqi occupation of Kuwait. Due to the U.N. embargo imposed in August 1990 the living standards of Iraqis declined sharply. Though by late 1994 Iraq claimed to have met almost all the conditions required for the lifting of the U.N. embargo, such a prospect seemed distant. It receded further when some statements on Iraq's weapons of mass destruction program made to Rolf Ekeus, head of the U.N. Special Commission (UNSCOM), by Gen. Hussein Kamil Hassan, former minister of military industrialization, after his defection in August 1995, clashed with those of the Iraqi government. Following the succession of Ekeus, a career diplomat, by Richard Butler, a disarmament specialist, two years later, there was further pressure on Iraq to submit full information on its progam of unconventional weapons, particularly biological warfare agents. The heightened tension between the two sides led to a four-day bombing of Iraq by America, backed by Britain, in December 1998, called Operation Desert Fox [qv], after Butler had withdrawn U.N. inspectors from Iraq. The efforts of the U.N. Security Council to get weapons inspectors back into Iraq under a new resolution a year later were spurned by Baghdad. The U.N.'s agreement to let Iraq export oil to purchase food and medicine for its citizens, which came into operation from December 1996, reduced the suffering of ordinary Iraqis. However, the fact that Iraq could sell oil only under U.N. supervision and deposit its earnings in a U.N. escrow account meant that the U.N.'s economic mandate over the country's most prized resource remained in place.

For the first time since the Iran-Iraq War, Iraq held its parliamentary poll on time—in March 2000. Five months later, the arrival in Baghdad of President Hugo Chavez of Venezuela, then chair of the Organization of Petroleum Exporting Countries (OPEC) [qv], in August by air in the course of his visits to the capitals of the OPEC member states started an erosion of the strict U.N. sanctions. In the aftermath of the outbreak of the Second Intifada [qv] by the Palestinians in September, Iraq was invited to an Arab League summit [qv] after ten years, but Saddam did not attend. Iraq sent food and medical aid to the Palestinian Territories [qv] via Jordan [qv]. And following the lead of the Palestinian Authority [qv], Iraq paid compensation to the families of the Palestinians killed in the Intifada.

The succession of Democrat U.S. President Bill Clinton by Republican George Walker Bush (r. 2001–) made no difference to American-Iraqi relations. Bush ordered air strikes against Iraqi targets on the ground that Iraq was improving its air defenses. And in the aftermath of the attacks on the United States in September, Washington tried hard to link Iraq with Al Qaida [qv], but failed. However, after overthrowing the Taliban regime in Afghanistan, Bush targeted Iraq on the ground that it had failed to disarm itself of weapons of mass destruction as required by the United Nations. His administration succeeded in getting the U.N. Security Council to adopt Resolution 1441 [qv] in November 2002, stipulating a rigorous inspection and monitoring regime in Iraq. Baghdad accepted the resolution. *See further* Gulf War III, [qv].

Legislature: Nationally, legislative power rests with the National Assembly; and regionally, with the Legislative Council of Kurdistan. The government's promise, contained in the National Charter of 1973, to convene a popularly elected parliament was kept in June 1980 when elections to the 250-member National Assembly were held on the basis of universal suffrage. The Baath party won 188 seats. In the poll for the Second National Assembly in October 1984 the Baath party's share declined to 183. In the Third National Assembly, elected in April 1989, the Baath party won 138 seats. The elections to the Legislative Council of Kurdistan were conducted in September 1980, August 1986, and September 1989. The next poll for the National Assembly was held in March 1996, when the Baath party increased its size to 169 seats, which fell to 142 in the 2000 election. The thirty seats allocated to the Kurdistan Autonomous Region were nominated by President Saddam Hussein.

Religious composition: (2002) Muslim 96 percent, of which Shia 62 percent, Sunni [*qv*] 34 percent; Christian [*qv*] 3 percent, of which Chaldean Catholic [*qv*] 2 percent, Nestorian [*qv*] 0.8 percent, Orthodox [*qv*] 0.2 percent; Yazidi [*qv*] 1 percent.

Iraq-Najd Neutral Zone: *see* Saudi Arabia-Iraq Neutral Zone.

Iraq-Saudi Arabia Neutral Zone: *see* Saudi Arabia-Iraq Neutral Zone.

Iraqi Kurdistan Front: In May 1987 six Iraqi Kurdish groups formed the Iraqi Kurdistan Front (IKF) with the aim of intensifying resistance to the repressive policies of Baghdad with regard to Iraqi Kurdistan [*qv*]. The IKF demanded recognition of Kurdish national rights within Iraq. Its members were the Kurdistan Democratic Party (KDP) [*qv*], the Patriotic Union of Kurdistan (PUK) [*qv*], the Kurdistan Socialist Party, the Kurdistan People's Democratic Party, the Kurdish Socialist Party, and the Communist Party of Iraq [*qv*]. Later the Kurdistan Toilers' Party and the Assyrian Association joined the IKF. After the Second Gulf War [*qv*] the IKF negotiated, unsuccessfully, with Baghdad. Most IKF parties contested the election to the 105-member Kurdistan National Assembly held in the Kurdistan Autonomous Region [*qv*] in May 1992 by an anti-Baghdad authority; but only the KDP and the PUK were successful, and shared power equally for the next two years.

Iraqi National Accord: *Iraqi political faction* Funded by Saudi Arabia's intelligence agency, *Istikhabart,* the Iraqi National Accord (INA) was established in 1990 by Adnan Nouri; Iyad Alawi, a physician; and Omar Ali al Tikriti, a diplomat—all of them defectors. London-based Nouri, former general in Iraq's Republican Guard, maintained contacts with the U.S. Central Intelligence Agency. Their sole objective was the overthrow of Iraqi President Saddam Hussein [*qv*] through a military coup, and they focused on recruiting defectors from the Iraqi military and Baath Party [*qv*].

Though the INA formally affiliated to the newly formed Iraqi National Congress [*qv*] in June 1992, it opened its own office in Iraqi Kurdistan [*qv*] and maintained direct contacts with the CIA. When, in March 1995, Nouri learned of the INC's plan to mount a frontal attack on the Iraqi troops, he successfully convinced U.S. National Security Adviser Tony Lake to withdraw Washington's support for the plan. Nonetheless, the INC went ahead. Its resulting failure soured relations between it and the INA. In October the INA was accused of blowing up the INC office in Salahuddin.

The INA's plan for a coup conceived by its specially formed military council, based in Jordan [*qv*]—backed not only by the CIA, but also by the intelligence agencies of Britain, Saudi Arabia, Jordan, and Kuwait [*qv*] was scheduled for 26 June 1996, in which U.S. intelligence and communications operatives, working as inspectors and support staff for the U.N. Special Commission (Unscom) [*qv*]—on disarming Iraq, were assigned the job of conveying coded messages to some of the leading military conspirators. But starting in mid-June, the Iraqi authorities began arresting the plotters.

Following the bitter intra-Kurdish violence in September, when the CIA withdrew its agents and informers from Iraqi Kurdistan, the INA left the region. Nouri split with Alawi and moved to Turkey. After the passage of the Iraq Liberation Act in October 1998, Washington recognized the INA as a group eligible for U.S. assistance. During the administration of U.S. President George Walker Bush (r. 2001–), the INA became the favorite of the CIA and the State Department. It participated in the Iraqi Open Opposition conference in London in late 2002.

Iraqi National Congress: *Iraqi political grouping* The Iraqi National Congress was formed in Vienna at the meeting of 300 Iraqi delegates, funded by the U.S. Central Intelligence Agency which used Ahmad Chalabi [*qv*] as the front man. Among the twenty factions that affiliated to it were the Iraqi National Accord [*qv*], the Kurdistan Democratic Party (KDP) [*qv*], and the Patriotic Union of Kurdistan (PUK) [*qv*].

Led by Chalabi, it committed itself to waging a war of liberation against the regime of Iraqi President Saddam Hussein [*qv*], with the objective of establishing a democratic Iraq. Working with the KDP and the PUK, it set up its headquarters in Salahuddin to develop Iraqi Kurdistan [*qv*] as the staging area for the overthrow of Saddam. Encouraged by the defection in late 1994 of Gen. Wafiq Samarrai, who headed Iraq's military intelligence in 1991–92, Chalabi and Samarrai devised a plan that was in theory an amalgam of a popular revolt and a military coup to oust Saddam. But since it involved mounting frontal assaults on Iraqi troops, necessitating U.S. intervention with its air force

and even ground forces, National Security Adviser Tony Lake withdrew all American support. Nonetheless, the INC along with the PUK mounted their assaults on 5 March 1995, which the KDP and the INA refused to join. Nothing came of the INC-PUK offensives. Relations between the INC and the INA deteriorated to the extent that the INC headquarters was blown up in October, allegedly by the INA.

Following the bitter intra-Kurdish violence in September 1996, when the CIA withdrew its agents and informers from Iraqi Kurdistan, the INC left the region and moved its head office to London. After the passing of the Iraq Liberation Act in October 1998, the United States recognized the INC as a group eligible for its assistance. During the administration of President George Walker Bush (r. 2001–), the INC became the favorite of the U.S. Defense Department and Vice President Dick Cheney's office. At the Iraqi Open Opposition conference in London in December 2002, the INC failed to get its proposal for a transitional government for the post-Saddam Iraq [*qv*] accepted.

Iraqi-Saudi Non-Aggression Pact (1989): The Iraqi-Saudi Non-Aggression Pact was signed in Baghdad [*qv*] on 27 March 1979 during a visit by Saudi King Fahd ibn Abdul Aziz [*qv*]. It spelled out the principles of "non-interference in the internal affairs of the two sisterly countries" and "non-use of force and armies between the two states." Following the Iraqi invasion of Kuwait in August 1990 and Saudi Arabia's participation in the U.S.-led anti-Iraq coalition, the pact lost its purpose.

Iraqi-Soviet Friendship Treaty (1972): In 1972 Iraq and the Soviet Union cemented their friendship, based on their common opposition to Western imperialism and Zionism [*qv*], with a twenty-year Iraqi-Soviet Friendship Treaty. It was signed in Baghdad on 9 April 1972. The signatories agreed to contact each other in case of "danger to the peace of either party or . . . danger to peace," and to refrain from joining any alliance with another country or group of countries against the other. They also resolved to "develop cooperation in the strengthening of their defense capacity." Following its invasion of Kuwait in August 1990, Iraq fell foul of the U.N. Security Council, and the Soviet Union, a permanent Council member, condemned the Iraqi action. With the disintegration of the Soviet Union in December 1991, the treaty expired.

Irbil: *Iraqi city* Also spelled Arbil, Erbil. Pop. 865,000 (2003, est.). One of the oldest settlements in the world, Irbil has a history dating back to antiquity. In more modern times it was part of the Mosul province under the Ottomans (1517–1918). With the transfer in 1925 of Mosul to Iraq, it came under the jurisdiction of Baghdad. Discovery of oil [*qv*] in the region helped to improve the economy of Irbil, an important trading center.

When, following an agreement between Kurdish nationalists and the central government, the Kurdistan Autonomous Region [*qv*] was created in 1974, Irbil was chosen as its capital. Once the Iraqi territory above the 36th parallel was turned into a "no fly zone" for the Baghdad government by the Western powers in October 1991 and the Iraqi 5th Army, headquartered in Irbil, was forced to leave, the city became the capital of a semi-independent Iraqi Kurdistan. During the next five years, it changed hands between the competing Kurdistan Democratic Party [*qv*] and the Patriotic Union of Kurdistan [*qv*]. Its tourist attractions include a medieval citadel.

Irgun Zvai Leumi *(Hebrew: National Military Organization):* Irgun was formed by the Revisionist Zionists [*qv*] in Palestine [*qv*] in 1937, during the Arab revolt (1936–39), as a result of their disagreement with Haganah [*qv*], which limited itself to responding to Arab guerrilla activity. Irgun organized "preventive strikes" against Arab targets.

Following the publication of the British White Paper of 1939, which limited Jewish migration to Palestine, it turned against the British mandate. Except briefly during the Second World War, when it respected the official Zionist policy of cooperation with the Allies, Irgun conducted an anti-British campaign. After the war Irgun, with 3–5,000 members and led by Menachem Begin [*qv*], began sabotaging military installations, attacking barracks, and executing British soldiers. It cooperated with the Stern Group [*qv*] in raiding armories, blowing up bridges and warplanes, mining roads, derailing trains, and sinking patrol boats. On 22 July 1946 in Jerusalem [*qv*] it blew up the King David Hotel, the location of the British mandate's civilian and military offices, killing ninety-one people, including fifteen Jews, the first massive terrorist act in recent times.

During the months preceding the founding of Israel in mid-May 1948, it cooperated with the Stern Group in carrying out concerted attacks on Arabs. On 9/10 April 1948, in an eight-hour attack on Deir Yassin village near Jerusalem their joint forces killed

254 men, women, and children—two-thirds of all inhabitants. They dynamited houses, looted, and raped. The tactic was effective: in the five weeks leading up to the establishment of Israel, some 300,000 Arabs fled from the areas included in the United Nations plan for a Jewish state, and another 80,000 from the territory marked for the Arab state.

Though Irgun, while retaining its own military structure, agreed on 13 April 1948 to accept overall Haganah command, Begin refused to let Irgun members be transferred along with Haganah personnel to the Israel Defense Forces [qv], formed by the provisional government of David Ben-Gurion [qv] on 26 May 1948. Irgun continued its fight against the Arab armies as a separate entity. In late June Ben-Gurion forbade Irgun leaders to deliver arms to their troops, scattered along the beaches, from the ship *Altalena*. When the latter defied him, Ben-Gurion ordered his forces to attack the ship. This led to the death of forty Irgun soldiers and Irgun's disbandment.

al Iryani, Abdul Rahman (1908–98): *Yemeni politician; president of North Yemen, 1967–74* Born into a notable Zaidi [qv] family in Saada, Iryani received religious education and trained as an Islamic judge. An opponent of the ruler, Imam Ahmad ibn Yahya [qv], he participated in an abortive coup in 1948. After serving a six-year prison sentence, he left first for Aden [qv] and then Cairo [qv], where he cofounded the Free Yemen movement. Following the successful republican coup in September 1962, Iryani returned home and participated in the Yemeni Civil War [qv] on the republican side. He became minister of justice (1962–63) and then minister of local government (1964).

Iryani belonged to the conservative faction that had links with the Zaidi tribes in the north. When, in a move to placate the royalists, the pro-republican Egyptian President Gamal Abdul Nasser [qv] compelled North Yemeni President Abdullah Sallal [qv] in April 1965 to live in Cairo, Iryani was made a member of the powerful Republican Council of Yemen. He helped organize a pro-republican tribal conference to bolster the influence of the conservative faction within the government.

Having failed to strike a deal with the royalists, Nasser freed Sallal in September 1966. On his return home Sallal purged his rivals, including Iryani, who now found himself under house arrest in Cairo. Following Nasser's decision to withdraw the Egyptian troops from North Yemen by December 1967, Sallal's position became untenable. He was overthrown in November by a group of leaders, who later formed the five-member Republican Council, with Iryani as chairman and therefore president of North Yemen.

He helped to reconcile the warring sides and end the civil strife in March 1970. After the promulgation of a new constitution in December, he was confirmed as president in March 1971 by a Consultative Council. In 1972, following clashes between North Yemen and South Yemen, Iryani and his South Yemeni counterpart agreed to work toward uniting the two Yemens. He was overthrown in a bloodless coup by Col. Ibrahim Hamdi [qv] in June 1974. He went into exile to Lebanon, and then to Syria. He was allowed to return home in October 1981.

Isfahan: *Iranian city* Also spelled Esfahan. Pop. 1,379,000 (2003 est.). Isfahan's recorded history goes back to the Sassanian period (A.D. 226–640), when it was known as Aspadana. Captured by Muslim Arabs [*qv*] in A.D. 642, it became the capital of the Seljuk dynasty in the mid-eleventh century. After the fall of the Seljuks in 1200 it lost its prominence. It survived a sacking by Tamerlane in 1387 to become the capital of Persia in 1598 under Shah Abbas I (r. 1588–1629). Abbas built the royal palace as well as the magnificent Royal Mosque and the Lutfullah Mosque, and made Isfahan one of the largest cities of the times. It fell to the invading Ghalzai Afghans in 1723 and lost its capital status.

Some two centuries later a concerted effort was made by the ruler, Reza Shah Pahlavi [*qv*] to rebuild and enlarge the city. Its traditional textile and metalwork industries expanded, and it became the site of an oil refinery and steel plant. Its tourist attractions include the Royal Mosque and the Julfa quarters of the Armenians [*qv*], dating back to 1605.

Islam and Muslims *(Arabic: submission [to God's will]):* The last of the three important monotheistic religions, which draws upon Judaism [*qv*] and Christianity [*qv*], Islam was founded by the Prophet Muhammad (A.D. 570–632), who was born in Mecca [*qv*]. Those who follow Islam are called Muslims. Their scripture is the Quran [*qv*], the Word of Allah, which was revealed to Muhammad (lit. praiseworthy) ibn Abdullah al Hashem, the last of a series of messengers of Allah to humans, beginning with Adam and including Abraham, Moses, and Jesus. Next in importance to Muslims is the *sunna* [*qv*] (custom)—the words and deeds of the Prophet Muhammad. The Quran and the *sunna,* later codified as the Hadith [*qv*], together form the Sharia [*qv*] (Islamic Law), which covers all aspects of religious, social, and political life, including state administration and conduct of war.

The Islamic credo rests on belief in Allah, the revealed books, the prophets, and the day of judgement. Five duties (called Pillars of Islam) are prescribed for Muslims. Believers must say at least once in their life: "There is no god but God, and Muhammad is the prophet of God." They must pray five times daily facing Mecca, and must take part in collective noon prayers on Fridays. They must pay *zakat* [*qv*] *(Arabic: purification),* a religious tax, to support the poor and needy. They must fast from dawn to dusk during Ramadan [*qv*]. They must undertake a *hajj* [*qv*] to Mecca once in their lives, if they can afford it.

After the death of the Prophet Muhammad, who during the last decade of his life governed a domain (capital, Medina [*qv*]), fought wars and acted as a judge and administrator, his duties were taken over by his vice regent, Caliph *(from Arabic: khalif)* Abu Bakr ibn Abu Quhafa (r. A.D. 632–34). He was followed by Omar ibn Khattab (r. A.D. 634–44) and Othman ibn Affan (r. A.D. 644–56), who was assassinated by Muhammad ibn Abu Bakr and other conspirators for his maladministration.

During the reign of Omar and Othman, the Islamic state expanded far beyond the Arabian Peninsula [*qv*], with local governors administering its distant parts. The rule of Caliph Ali ibn Abu Talib (r. A.D. 656–61), a cousin and son-in-law of the Prophet

Muhammad, was challenged by Muwaiya ibn Abu Sufian, governor of Syria. A civil war ensued, creating Shiat Ali, or Shias [qv], and Kharijis [qv], thus fracturing the unity of the Islamic world. Over the next two centuries four different codes of the Islamic Law developed among Sunnis [qv], the orthodox sect. A mystical streak within Islam, known as sufism [qv], was developed among others by Abu Hamid Muhammad al Ghazali (1058–1111).

The spread of Islam was rapid during the two centuries after the Prophet Muhammad's death, reaching central France in 732 A.D. From the twelfth century onward sufis were at the forefront of the religious expansion that took Islam into Turkey, Central Asia, the Indian subcontinent, and sub-Saharan Africa. Pious Muslims, trading over land and sea, became the harbingers of Islam in East Africa, West Africa, and Indonesia. In 2002, there were over 1.3 billion adherents of Islam worldwide.

Islamicism and Islamicists: *see* Islamism and Islamists.

Islamic Action Front (Jordan): *see* Muslim Brotherhood (Jordan).

Islamic Amal (Lebanon): *Lebanese religious-political organization* The Islamic Amal was established in July 1982 by Hussein Musavi, a member of the command council of Amal [qv], after he had left Amal in protest at its leaders' passivity toward Israel's occupation of two-fifths of Lebanon. He allied with the Iranian revolutionary guards based in Baalbek [qv], and attacked and occupied the nearby Lebanese army's barracks. Islamic Amal activists conducted guerrilla actions against the Israeli troops in southern Lebanon. At the behest of Ali

Akbar Mohtashemi, Iran's ambassador to Syria, the Islamic Amal allied with the Islamic Jihad [qv] and the Hizbollah [qv] to conduct anti-Israeli and anti-U.S. activities. In early 1984 the three organizations together confronted the Lebanese army. When General Michel Aoun [qv] escalated his struggle against Syria and its Lebanese allies in 1989, the Islamic Amal joined an anti-Aoun front of eighteen groups. Following the end of the Lebanese Civil War [qv] in October 1990, the influence of the Islamic Amal declined as the Hizbollah emerged as the main party of radical Shias.

Islamic banking: The Quran [qv] forbids usury: "Oh believers, fear you God; and give up the usury that is outstanding, if you are believers" (2:279); and "Oh believers, devour not usury, doubled and redoubled, and fear you God" (3:25). Money must be used only as a means of exchange. But since money is also used as commodity this injunction has proved problematic. Since the early days of Islam, legalistic innovations have been employed to get around this prohibition. The extreme example is the Islamic doctrine that states: "Neccesity makes prohibited things permissible." In the Ottoman Empire (1517–1918) banks charged and paid interest, sometimes disguised as commission.

The circumventing devices are *muraabaha, mudaaraba,* and *mushaaraka. Muraabaha* involves selling a commodity with a contract that it would be bought back later at a premium equaling the agreed interest. *Mudaaraba,* meaning "sleeping partnership," involves a sleeping partner providing cash for an activity undertaken by an active partner, any profits being shared.

Mushaaraka entails a depositor being treated as a partner who shares in the profits or losses. Over the past few decades, many banks that use one or more of these methods have emerged in Muslim countries, especially where laws are derived exclusively from the Quran and the Hadith [*qv*].

Islamic calendar: In Islam, as in Judaism [*qv*], a day starts with sunset. The Islamic calendar is dated from the sunset on 15 July A.D. 622, the start of the *hijra* (migration) of the Prophet Muhammad from Mecca [*qv*] to Medina [*qv*]. The Islamic year is lunar and contains 354 days, 8 hours, and 4.8 minutes. The Islamic months, and their duration, are Muharram (30 days), Safar (29), Rabia Awal (30), Rabia Thani (29), Jumada Awal (30), Jumada Thani (29), Rajab (30), Shaaban (29), Ramadan (29), Shawal (30), Dhul Qaada (29), and Dhul Hijja (30).

Since a lunar year is shorter than a solar one by about eleven days, it takes roughly thirty-four lunar years to equal thirty-three solar years. There is thus an approximate difference of three years between a lunar century and a solar one. A person aged 100 years by a solar calendar is 103 according to a lunar calendar. To convert an Islamic date to a Christian date, divide it by 1.031 and then add 621 or 622, depending on the month of the year.

Islamic Conference Organization (1969): An arson attack on al Aqsa Mosque in Jerusalem [*qv*], the third holiest shrine of Islam [*qv*], by Michael Rohan, an Australian fundamentalist Christian [*qv*], in August 1969 shocked the Muslim world. At the initiative of Saudi King Faisal ibn Abdul Aziz [*qv*], an Islamic summit conference attended by twenty-four Muslim countries met in Rabat, Morocco, in September. Out of this emerged the Islamic Conference Organization (ICO), the first official pan-Islamic institution of intergovernmental cooperation. Open to all Muslim-majority states, the ICO based itself in Jiddah [*qv*] in May 1971. Its charter, adopted in 1972, aims to promote Islamic solidarity; to coordinate efforts to safeguard Islamic holy places and support the Palestinian struggle for national rights; and to increase social, cultural, and economic cooperation among members.

Funded primarily by Saudi Arabia, it provided the kingdom with an opportunity to project itself as the leader of the Islamic world. In 1975 it set up al Quds [*qv*] committee to implement ICO resolutions on the status of Jerusalem. The ICO's attempt to emerge as a mediator in the Islamic world suffered a setback when its efforts to bring about a cease-fire in the war between two Muslim countries, Iran [*qv*] and Iraq [*qv*], in 1981 failed. Tehran boycotted the fourth summit in Casablanca, Morocco, in January 1984 because the ICO failed to send a team to Iran to inspect the damage done by Iraqi bombing of Iranian civilian areas. When the ICO secretariat refused to change the venue of the fifth summit in January 1987 in Kuwait [*qv*], which was closely allied to Iraq in its conflict against Iran, Tehran again boycotted the meeting. The summit urged a cease-fire in the Iran-Iraq War [*qv*].

The sixth summit in Dakar, Senegal, in December 1991 was boycotted by twelve Arab heads of state in protest at the invitation extended to the Palestine Liberation Organization (PLO) [*qv*] and Jordan [*qv*], which had sided with Iraq in the Second Gulf War [*qv*]. At the next summit in

Morocco in 1994, the ICO adopted a code of conduct on terrorism that required member states not to aid terrorism and to ensure that extremist organizations did not use their territory for attacks on other states. At the extraordinary summit held in Islamabad, Pakistan, the ICO resolved to apply international pressure on Israel to honor its agreements with the PLO. The seventh summit in Tehran in December 1997 called on ICO members to consider the U.S. Iran-Libya Sanctions Act of 1996 as invalid. It condemned terrorism but upheld the right of those under military occupation to resist the occupiers by all means. The next summit was held in Doha [*qv*] in 2000 after Qatar [*qv*] had closed down the Israeli trade mission in its capital.

In April 2002, the ICO foreign ministers, meeting in Kuala Lumpur, Malaysia, failed to agree on the definition of terror or terrorism [*qv*]. While calling for an internationally agreed definition of terrorism, their final communiqué specifically differentiated it from the resistance of a people under colonial or foreign occupation.

In 2003 the ICO had fifty-seven members, including the PLO, which was not a state. Its secretary-general was Abdel Ouahed Belkeziz, a Moroccan.

Islamic Consultative Assembly (Iran): *see* Majlis.

Islamic dress: Islamic dress applies to women, who are required to behave as stated in the Quranic verse (24:30–31): "And say to the believing women that they cast their eyes and guard their private parts . . . and let them cast their veils over their bosoms, and not reveal their adornment save to their husbands, or their fathers, or their husbands'

fathers, or their sons, or their husbands' sons, or their brothers, or their brothers' sons, or their sisters' sons, or their women . . . or children who have not yet attained knowledge of women's private parts." The intention is to avoid arousing sexual passion between men and women who are not spouses or are not intending to be. The *hijab* (veil), traditionally worn by Muslim women in public, always covers the head but not necessarily the face.

Islamic dress has been compulsory for women in Saudi Arabia ever since its founding in 1932. Following the Islamic revolution in Iran in 1979, it was made compulsory by law. Iran's urban working class and rural women wear a *chador*, an all-encompassing shroud.

Islamic Front of Syria: *Syrian political alliance* In 1980 the moderate faction of the Muslim Brotherhood [*qv*] combined with the Islamic Liberation Party (ILP), the Society of Abu Dharr (SAD), and the Northern Circle (NC) to form the Islamic Front of Syria (IFS). It was led by Shaikh Muhammad Bayununi (SAD), Adnan Saad al Din (Muslim Brotherhood), and Said Hawa (NC). To reassure the leftist and secular opposition, the IFS offered a program that was an amalgam of Islamic concepts and liberal democracy.

Once IFS leaders had reorganized their cadres, they resumed the armed struggle against the regime of President Hafiz Assad [*qv*]. In February 1981 they initiated an insurrection in Hama [*qv*] and, operating from Iraq, they appealed to Syrians to declare a "civil mutiny" against the regime. Assad repressed the uprising in Hama. In June Israel invaded Lebanon [*qv*], an event in which the

Syrian troops stationed in Lebanon became partially involved. This turned public attention away from Islamic resistance toward the government's anti-Israeli fight and weakened the Islamic movement.

The Muslim Brotherhood, the IFS's leading constituent, wanted the IFS to adopt its pro-Iraq policy. This split the IFS into "compromisers," led by Saad al Din, and "purists," headed by Adnan Uqla. The latter held that since Iraqi President Saddam Hussein [*qv*] had invaded the Islamic Republic of Iran he was anti-Islamic, and therefore cooperation with him could not be contemplated. The compromisers were prepared to work with anybody who was willing to help them overthrow the Assad regime.

In March 1982 Saad al-Din led the IFS into an alliance with seventeen other opposition groups to form the National Alliance for the Liberation of Syria under Amin Hafiz [*qv*] in Baghdad [*qv*]. It demanded a constitutional parliamentary regime, Islam as the state religion, and the Sharia [*qv*] as the main source of legislation. When the purists condemned Saad al-Din's move, their leader, Uqla, was expelled from the IFS. The infighting caused a dramatic drop in the fundamentalists' activities and popular support.

Islamic fundamentalism: Fundamentalism is the term used for the effort to define the fundamentals of a religion and adhere to them. One of the cardinal tenets of Islamic fundamentalism is to protect the purity of Islamic precepts from the adulteration of speculative exercises. Related to fundamentalism is Islamic revival or resurgence, a renewed interest in Islam. Behind all this is a drive to purify Islam in order to release all its vital force. In medieval times the drive for purification meant ridding Islam of superstition and/or scholastic legalism. That is, the fundamentalist response was purely internal. Today the response is both internal and external: to release Islam from its scholastic cobwebs as well as to rid it of ideas imbibed from the West.

Whether a Muslim-majority state today is fundamentalist or not can be judged by a single criterion: Is its legislation derived *solely* from the Sharia [*qv*] (Islamic Law)? By this standard Saudi Arabia is the oldest Islamic fundamentalist state in the world: since its inception in 1932 it has known nothing but the Sharia. However, what the Islamic revolution did in Iran in 1979 was to transform a secular state and society into a religious one, thus pioneering a model for Muslim countries with a secular background, the majority in the forty-nine-member Islamic Conference Organization [*qv*]. In the mid-1990s about a dozen of ICO member states were being run solely according to the Sharia.

See also Abdul Rahman, Omar; al Banna, Hassan; Osama bin Laden; al Gamaat al Islamiya (Egypt); Hamas; Hizbollah; Islamic Action Front (Jordan); Islamic Amal (Lebanon); Islamic Front of Syria; Islamic Jihad (Lebanon); Islamic Jihad (Palestine); Islamic Movement of Kurdistan; Islamic Revolution (Iran); Al Jihad al Islami (Egypt); Muslim Brotherhood (Egypt); Muslim Brotherhood (Jordan); Muslim Brotherhood (Palestine); Muslim Brotherhood (Saudi Arabia); Muslim Brotherhood (Syria); Al Qaida; and al Takfir wal Hijra.

Islamic Iranian Participation Front (Iran): Popularly known as *Moshakerat (Persian, participation)*. Formed on the eve of the first local elections in Iran in early 1999, the left-of-center Islamic Iranian Participation Front was led by Muhammad Reza Khatami, a younger brother of President Muhammad Khatami (r. 1997–) [qv]. It was the leading constituent of the 2nd Khrdad/23rd May Front, named after the date on which Khatami had scored his landslide victory in 1997, formed to contest the 2000 Majlis [qv] elections. Its program included greater media freedom, including private radio and television channels, and reform of government bureaucracy. While favoring attractive conditions for private capital in industry, it opposed privatizing state-owned oil, power, telecommunications, and tobacco industries. Of the 268 seats settled, the IIPF won 95. Muhammad Reza Khatami was elected deputy speaker of the Majlis. It remained the main bulwark of political reform in the country, which was resisted by the conservative parliamentarians and judiciary.

Islamic Jihad (Egypt): *see* Al Jihad al Islami (Egypt).

Islamic Jihad (Lebanon): The Islamic Jihad (IJ), a pro-Iranian Shia [qv] group, was formed in Lebanon in the spring of 1982. In retaliation for the kidnapping of four Iranian diplomats in Beirut [qv] in mid-March 1982 by Maronite [qv] militiamen, the group abducted David Dodge, the acting president of the American University of Beirut (AUB) [qv], in July. It was close to Ali Akbar Mohtashemi, Iran's ambassador to Syria (1982–83).

In April 1983 it truck-bombed the U.S. Embassy in West Beirut. Seventeen of the sixty-three people killed were American, most of them senior Central Intelligence Agency (CIA) operative. On 23 October 1983 IJ militants truck-bombed the U.S. Marines headquarters at Beirut International Airport, killing 241 troops, and the French paratroops in Bir Hassan district, killing fifty-nine soldiers. A similar explosion caused by another IJ activist destroyed the Israeli military headquarters in Tyre [qv], leaving sixty people dead, half of them Israelis. The IJ allied with the Islamic Amal [qv] and Hizbollah [qv] in early 1984 to confront the Lebanese army.

In March the IJ kidnapped William Buckley, the CIA station chief in Beirut. It promised to free him in exchange for the release of seventeen Shias [qv] who had been convicted in Kuwait on charges of bombing the U.S. and French embassies. In September the IJ exploded a car bomb inside the U.S. Embassy compound in East Beirut, killing eight people. The next month it released David Jacobsen, an American, as part of the hostages-for-arms deal between the United States and Iran, known as the Irangate Affair [qv].

Following the IJ's freeing of John McCarthy, a British journalist, in August 1991, U.N. Secretary-General Javier Perez de Cuellar became involved in securing the release of the remaining Western hostages and 450 Lebanese and Palestinians held without charge by Israel. In late 1991 a three-way swap—involving 450 Lebanese and Palestinian detainees under the Israelis, seven dead or captured Israeli servicemen, and the remaining Western hostages—ended the IJ's involvement in hostage taking. With Hizbollah dominating radical Shia life, the IJ, led most of the time by shadowy Imad Mougneih, faded away.

Islamic Jihad (Palestine): Dissatisfied with

the policies of the Muslim Brotherhood in the Occupied Territories [*qv*], its militant members split to form the Islamic Jihad (Palestine) in 1981. It captured media headlines when its activists threw hand grenades at a military graduation ceremony at the Western Wall [*qv*] in Jerusalem [*qv*] in October 1986. It claimed to be the main force behind the eruption of the Palestinian intifada [*qv*] a little over a year later. It cooperated with other groups in continuing the intifada. Opposed to the Israeli-Palestine Liberation Organization Accord of September 1993 [*qv*], it maintained its policy of violent attacks on Israeli targets in the West Bank [*qv*] and Gaza Strip [*qv*] and came into open conflict with the Palestinian Authority [*qv*] in late 1994. Its collective leadership kept a low profile, except for Shaikh Abdullah Shammi in Gaza [*qv*], where the group published a weekly paper, *Al Istiqlal* (The Independence). Its leader, Fathi Abdul Aziz Shikaki, was assassinated by Mossad [*qv*] agents in Malta in October 1995. He was succeeded by Ramadan Shallah. It participated actively in the al Aqsa Intifada [*qv*] that erupted in September 2000, and was responsible for a few suicide bombings. Some of its activists became victims of Israel's policy of "targeted killings."

Islamic Law: *see* Sharia.

Islamic Majlis (Iran): *see* Majlis.

Islamic Movement of Kurdistan: *Iraqi political organization* Their opposition to the draft agreement between representatives of the Iraqi Kurdistan Front (IKF) [*qv*] and the Baghdad government in June 1991 led the Kurdish Hizbollah, the Kurdish Mujahedin, and the Kurdish Ansar-e Islam [*qv*] to form the Islamic Movement of Kur-

distan (IMK) under the leadership of Shaikh Osman Abdullah Aziz and Shaikh Ali Abdullah Aziz. Later, when IKF constituents failed to ratify the draft agreement, the IMK cooperated with the IKF in setting up a freely elected administration in the Kurdistan Autonomous Region (KAR) [*qv*] after the Iraqi forces had left the region in October 1991. It acquired the mayoralty of Halabja [*qv*], its headquarters. It participated in the May 1992 general election, but failed to cross the required 7 percent threshold to qualify for seats in the Legislative Council.

In late 1993 it began to expand its base, through force, in southeast Kurdistan at the expense of the Patriotic Union of Kurdistan (PUK) [*qv*], which shared power with the Kurdistan Democratic Party (KDP) [*qv*] in the KAR. The bloody fighting between them in May–June 1994 enabled the IMK, with the assistance of the KDP and Iran [*qv*], to enlarge its area of control along the Iranian border.

As a result of a rapprochement between the PUK and the KDP in late 1994, the KAR government was expanded from ten to fifteen ministers, with one post going to the IMK. But this arrangement broke down when the PUK and the KDP fought each other in September 1996.

As Iran began to forge strong links with the PUK, it turned cool toward the IMK, and this led its constituents to squabble. The resulting weakness of the IMK encouraged the PUK to attack Halabja in September 2001, capture the town hall, and expel the IMK leadership. The formal demise of the IMK signaled the revival of its earlier constituents, including Ansar-e Islam.

Islamic Republican Party (Iran): The Islamic Republican Party (IRP) was established within a month of the February 1979 revolution by Iran's leading clerics, including Ali Akbar Hashemi Rafsanjani [*qv*] and Ali Hussein Khamanei [*qv*]. Its main aim was to guard the revolution and infuse Islamic principles into political, economic, cultural, and military spheres of society. As well as encouraging individuals to join it, the founders of the IRP urged the Islamic Associations [*qv*] to affiliate to it.

In the elections to the Assembly of Experts [*qv*], which was charged with drafting the constitution, forty-seven of the seventy-three members either belonged to the IRP or were sympathetic to it. IRP leaders were at the forefront of opposition to President Abol Hassan Bani-Sadr [*qv*] and his policies. Due to their endeavors, Bani-Sadr was impeached by 177 deputies, with one vote opposing, on 20 June 1981. Eight days later a bomb explosion triggered by Mujahedin-e Khalq [*qv*] activists killed seventy-four IRP leaders.

Following President Muhammad Ali Rajai's [*qv*] assassination in August, the IRP's secretary-general, Ali Khamanei, successfully contested the office in October 1981. Within two years the IRP and its allied groups occupied all political space. Yet by late 1984 its importance within the regime had declined: the factions of the party had become so deeply divided on socioeconomic issues, between conservatives and radicals, that their infighting was impeding the workings of the executive and the legislature. The differences between the two party wings became acute by mid-1986, and Ayatollah Ruhollah Khomeini [*qv*], the Supreme Leader, appointed a mediation council to conciliate them. After it failed, he had the party dissolved in July 1987.

Islamic Revolution (Iran): What started in early 1977 as a demand by Iranian intellectuals to abolish censorship ended up as a revolutionary overthrow of the most powerful pro-Western monarchy in the Middle East [*qv*], the Pahlavi shahs, two years later. The protest movement went through several stages, beginning with the revival of opposition parties at home and leading to the assuming of its stewardship by Ayatollah Ruhollah Khomeini [*qv*], then in exile in Najaf [*qv*], Iraq.

Khomeini made adroit use of Shia [*qv*] history and Iranian nationalism to attract ever-increasing support, and he united disparate anti-shah forces, both secular and religious, by his most radical demand: the deposition of Muhammad Reza Shah Pahlavi [*qv*]. Khomeini also devised an original set of strategies and tactics to neutralize the shah's 413,000-strong military. He advised his followers to confront the soldiers through martyrdom [*qv*], to let them kill as many as they wanted until they felt disgusted at their brutal behavior. At the same time he warned troops that firing at their brothers and sisters amounted to firing at the Quran [*qv*]. These words, coming as they did from an eminent religious authority, had a strong impact on the soldiers, who were often conscripts and overwhelmingly Shia.

Though the revolutionary movement included secular elements, only the religious segment could provide a national network down to the village level in the form of the mosque. Both as an institution and as a place of congregation, the mosque proved crucial.

Since the state could not regularly suppress the mosque, it offered opportunities to revolutionaries that no other place could. Therefore, Khomeini instructed the clergy to base the Revolutionary Komitehs [*qv*] in mosques.

What finally sealed the fate of the Pahlavi state was an indefinite strike by oil workers, ordered by Khomeini on 31 October 1978. This was a body blow to the state treasury, already reeling from the effects of strikes by *bazaaris* [*qv*], bank employees, customs officers, postal workers, and miners. Forced by the military government, appointed by the shah in early November, to return to work, the oil workers did so on condition that they would produce only enough to satisfy domestic demand.

The ten-day Shia ritual of Ashura [*qv*] in December enhanced religious feeling in the nation, now paralyzed by a strike of civil servants. The first signs of cracks in the army appeared, with soldiers deserting with their weapons. In desperation the shah appointed Shahpur Bakhtiar [*qv*], a secular opposition leader, prime minister and agreed to go abroad on holiday immediately. He did so on 16 January 1979, but it was not until 11 February—after Khomeini had returned home and appointed Mahdi Bazargan [*qv*] prime minister, and after pro-Khomeini forces had crushed an attempted coup by the Imperial Guard—that the Pahlavi rule finally ended. The human cost in terms of antiroyalist deaths was 10,000 to 40,000 and the Iranian military was down to 110,000 armed personnel. The members of the monarchical elite either fled or found themselves imprisoned.

Though nonreligious opposition had contributed substantially to the success of the revolution, it was denied its share of power. Since Khomeini, the movement's leader, was a religious authority, and the mosque provided the base for the movement, the end result was an Islamic revolution. Though other Middle Eastern countries had experienced dramatic change, often accompanied by the overthrow of the monarchy, the prime mover had been the military, and the means a coup. This was the first time that millions of ordinary, unarmed citizens had actively participated in a political process lasting many months and ended up not only toppling the ruler, but also decimating such institutions as the military. Since then no other Muslim-majority country has undergone such a revolutionary experience.

Islamic Revolutionary Komitehs (Iran): *see* Revolutionary Komitehs (Iran).

Islamism and Islamists: When Islam [*qv*] is used as a political ideology, it is described as Islamism, and its adherents are called Islamists. *See* also Islamic fundamentalism.

Ismail, Abdul Fattah (1936–86): *South Yemeni politician; president, 1978–80* Born into a peasant family in the Hujairiah region of North Yemen, Ismail traveled to Aden [*qv*] for further education. Here, employed by the British Petroleum Company, he took a keen interest in trade unionism. Active in the National Liberation Front (NLF) [*qv*], he became one of its leaders in 1964 and specialized in political and military affairs. After South Yemeni independence in late 1967 he was named minister of national guidance. In June 1969 Ismail's leftist faction overthrew President Qahtan al Shaabi [*qv*], and he became secretary-general of the NLF and a member of the Presidential Council under Salim Rubai Ali [*qv*].

Together with Ali Nasser Muhammad [*qv*], Ismail continued to lead the leftist wing and built up a strong party militia and intelligence network. Following a coup in August 1971, he and Muhammad consolidated their position. In June 1978 they clashed with President Ali, who lost his life. Muhammad became chairman of the Presidential Council, but six months later ceded that position to Ismail.

The radical policies of Ismail alienated Muhammad, who espoused a more pragmatic approach. In April 1980 Ismail was forced to resign his position and go into exile in Moscow. He spent five years there. Following the Soviet Communist Party's successful mediation between the South Yemeni factions, Ismail returned home. He was made secretary general of the ruling Yemen Socialist Party's [*qv*] central committee, a position that lacked power. The rapprochement between the factions broke down in January 1986. In the subsequent violence Muhammad was defeated, but Ismail lost his life.

Ismailis: *Islamic group* Part of Shia [*qv*] Islam, Ismailis are distinguished from the other sub-sects—Zaidis [*qv*] and Imamis or Twelvers [*qv*]—by the number of revered figures they regard as Imams [*qv*]. They share the first six Imams with Twelvers (Ali, Hassan, Hussein, Zain al Abidin, Muhammad al Baqir, and Jaafar al Sadiq). The seventh is Ismail, the older, militant son of al Sadiq, who died in A.D. 762 before his father. This created a rift among Shias since not all of them accepted as their Imam Ismail's younger brother, Abdullah ibn Jaafar, who died without a son.

Ismailis are also known as Seveners since they subscribe to the concept that the number seven, being the total of spatial directions—forward, backward, above, below, right, left, and center—is symbolic, and that in the case of Imams signifies the end of a cycle.

An Ismaili group set up the Fatimid (named after a daughter of the Prophet Muhammad and the wife of Imam Ali) caliphate in Tunis, which, after conquering Egypt in A.D. 969, rivaled the Abbasids, based in Baghdad [*qv*]. Their rule lasted until 1171. Today in the Middle East Ismailis are to be found in Iran, Syria, and Yemen.

Israel:

Official name: State of Israel

Capital: Tel Aviv [*qv*] (internationally recognized); Jerusalem [*qv*] (self-declared)

Area (pre-1967 borders): 7,820 sq. miles/ 20,255 sq. km

Population: 6,029,000 (2000, official est.), including Jewish settlers—176,000 (East Jerusalem [*qv*]), 182,000 (West Bank [*qv*]), 7,000 (Gaza Strip [*qv*]), and 20,000 (Golan Heights [*qv*])

Gross domestic product: $108.2 billion (2000 est.)

National currency: New Israeli Shekel (NIS); NIS 1 = US$0.24 = £0.17 = EUR 0.27 (2001)

Form of government: republic, parliamentary

Official languages: Hebrew and Arabic

Official religion: none

Administrative regions: Israel is divided into six districts.

Constitution: The Constituent Assembly, elected in January 1949, adopted a Transition Law in February. It declared Israel a republic, to be headed by a president who would be elected for a five-year term by the Knesset [qv] (parliament; a single chamber of 120 members) by a simple majority. The Knesset was to be elected by adult franchise under a system of proportional representation with the election threshold at 1 percent. The leader of the largest group would be invited by the president to become the prime minister and form the government, which would exercise executive authority. The Constituent Assembly then transformed itself into the First Knesset.

Following a debate on a report on the question of a written constitution by the Knesset's Committee on Constitution, Law, and Justice, the house decided in June 1950 to assign the task of preparing a draft constitution to the Committee "chapter by chapter . . . [with] each chapter submitted to the Knesset" and "all the chapters [after the Committee had finished its work] shall be incorporated into the Constitution." Between then and 1968, four such "chapters" were adopted by the Knesset: Basic Law: The Knesset (1958), fixing its term to four years; Basic Law: Lands in Israel (1959), creating the National Land Authority; Basic Law: The State President (1964), requiring him/her to be an Israeli citizen, resident in the country; and Basic Law: The Government (1968).

Ethnic composition (1999): Jews, 79 percent; Arabs, 21 percent.

Executive authority: Executive authority rests with the cabinet, headed by the prime minister, who is the leader of the largest group in parliament.

High officials:

President: Moshe Katzav, 2000–

Prime minister: Ariel Sharon, 2003–

Speaker of the Knesset: Reuven Rivlin, 2003–

History: Israel was established on 14 May 1948 at the end of the British mandate over Palestine [qv], which dated back to 1922. An immediate war with its Arab neighbors ended in January 1949, with Israel acquiring 21 percent more land than the about 54 percent allocated to it by the United Nations partition plan of 1947. Following Egyptian nationalization of the Suez Canal [qv] in July 1956, Israel colluded with Britain and France, invading Egypt in October and occupying Sinai [qv] and Gaza [qv]. Under U.N. and U.S. pressure it vacated these territories in March 1957.

During heightened tension in early June 1967 Israel staged preemptive strikes on the air forces of Egypt, Syria, and Jordan, and occupied the West Bank [qv], Gaza [qv], and the Golan Heights [qv]. This firmly established Israel's military superiority over its Arab neighbors and made it somewhat complacent. The attacks in October 1973 by Egypt and Syria on Israel to regain their lost territories of Sinai and the Golan came as a surprise to the Israelis. They rallied quickly but failed to reestablish the status quo ante. Mediation by the United States led to a peace treaty between Israel and Egypt in March 1979 on the principle of "land for peace."

Within six weeks of returning the last segment of Sinai and Egypt on 25 April 1982, Israel invaded Lebanon, occupying two-fifths of the country, including its capital, Beirut [qv]—a far more serious venture than the one in March 1978, when Israel had restricted itself to occupying about half of southern Lebanon, which was being used by Palestinian guerrillas for attacks on Israel.

After phased withdrawals from Lebanon ending in June 1985, Israel maintained a military presence in its self-declared security zone in southern Lebanon.

The situation in the occupied West Bank and Gaza deteriorated to the extent that in 1987 the Palestinian population mounted an uprising, or intifada [qv]. The intifada continued year after year, compelling Israel first to recognize and then to negotiate with the Palestine Liberation Organization (PLO) [qv]. The resulting Israeli-PLO Accord [qv] of September 1993 led to the formation of the Palestinian Authority [qv] in Gaza and the West Bank town of Jericho [qv] as a first step toward autonomy for the areas of mandate Palestine occupied by Israel since 1967.

The dominance of the Ashkenazi Jews [qv], a feature of Israel at its inception, lessened as large numbers of Jews arrived from the Arab states. This affected the political balance in the country, with the left-of-center Labor Party [qv], which had dominated governments since 1948, being relegated to opposition in 1977 by the right-wing Likud [qv]. But Likud's dominance did not last long. After the 1984 poll the two leading parties formed a national unity government, with premiership divided into a two-year term for each of the leaders: Labor's Shimon Peres [qv] and Likud's Yitzhak Shamir [qv].

This arrangement was repeated after the 1988 general election. But in 1990, disagreeing with Shamir's policy on pursuing peace, Labor withdrew from the national unity administration, hoping Likud would lose power. It did not. It co-opted ultranationalist groups into the government and finished its term in 1992. At the next poll Labor emerged as the leading party and became the dominant partner in the new coalition. Having achieved positive results in the peace process—an accord with the PLO and a peace treaty with Jordan—Labor planned to keep on this path with a view to gaining the directly elected premiership, to be introduced in 1996. It failed because its popular leader, Yitzhak Rabin [qv], was assassinated by a Jewish extremist in November 1995, and his successor Shimon Peres [qv] lost to his Likud rival Benjamin Netanyahu [qv] in the May 1996 poll. Without formally renouncing the Oslo Accord, he tried to wriggle out of it, in the process weakening it. But when, under American pressure, he signed a fresh deal under it, his ultrarightwing supporters abandoned him, depriving him of majority in the parliament. He lost to the Labor rival Ehud Barak [qv] in the elections—for the prime minister and the parliament—in May 1999. Barak withdrew Israeli troops from southern Lebanon a year later. But his final status talks with PLO leader Yasser Arafat, [qv] chaired by U.S. President Bill Clinton, at Camp David in July 2000 failed when Arafat found his terms unacceptable. A visit by Ariel Sharon [qv], the Likud leader, to the Noble Sanctuary/Temple Mount [qv] in September triggered the Palestinian al Aqsa Intifada [qv]. With his coalition government disintegrating, Barak resigned in December. He lost to Sharon in the prime ministerial contest in February 2001. Sharon demanded total cessation of violence by the Palestinians before peace talks could resume. Following that, he held out the prospect of freezing the present arrangement—whereby the Palestinian Authority (PA) [qv] controlled about 20 percent of the Palestinian Territories [qv]—and signing an extended truce with Israel. Soon the Palestinian intifada escalated from stones thrown at the Israeli troops to armed assaults on Israeli soldiers and settlers. The Sharon government escalated its response from army firings to besieging Palestinian enclaves to making military incursions into the areas under PA jurisdiction and assassinating suspected terrorists.

After the attacks on the United States in September 2001, Sharon tried, unsuccessfully, to bracket Arafat with Osama bin Laden [qv]. By ordering tanks and helicopter gunships into refugee camps in the West Bank in February 2002 to arrest wanted terrorists, Israel crossed a red line. Responding to the killing of seven Israeli soldiers in early March, Israel sent 20,000 troops and scores of tanks in the West Bank. For the first time the PA publicly called on the Palestinians to confront the invaders. A more severe reprisal followed the murder of twenty-seven Israeli Jews on Passover [qv], 27 March, by a Palestinian suicide bomber, when Israel mounted its Operation Defensive Wall, reoccupying all Palestinian towns and cities except Hebron [qv] and Jericho [qv], destroying Arafat's headquarters in Ramallah, and placing him under house arrest. By the time the Israeli offensive had ended a month later, 250 Palestinians were dead. In April the European Union parliament called on member states to impose political and trade sanctions against Israel for violating international and humanitarian law in its offensive against the Palestinians. With no end to periodic suicide bombings by the Palestinians, Israel reoccupied the West Bank towns and cities. Following the January 2003 parliamentary poll, in which in Likud doubled its

size to 38, Sharon formed a coalition government with strongly secularist Shinui [qv] and far right secular parties.

Legislature: The Knesset deals with legislation, general policy matters, the budget, and international treaties. It has the right to elect the state president by a simple majority, or dismiss him/her for misdemeanor. But a two-thirds majority is needed to declare the president too ill to perform his or her duties. In order to reduce the number of political parties, the Knesset passed a law requiring direct election for the prime minister, who then set out to form a coalition government. The first such poll took place in 1996 along with the one for the Knesset, with the second such set of elections conducted in 1999. But in 2001, there was only the prime ministerial contest, the last such exercise. In 2003 the electoral system reverted to the old arrangement since the new system failed to reduce the number of political factions.

Religious composition (2002): Jews, 80 percent, of which those of Asian origin, 12.5 percent; European-North American origin, 32 percent; Israel-born, 21 percent; and North African origin, 14.5 percent; Muslims [qv], 14.7 percent, of which Sunni [qv], 13 percent and Druze [qv], 1.7 percent; Christian [qv], 2.1 percent; unclassified, 3.2 percent.

Israel BeAliya *(Hebrew: Ascent into Israel): Israeli political party* Israel BeAliya was formed by Natan Sharansky in 1995. Born in Moscow in 1948, Sharansky migrated to Israel [qv] in 1986. As the number of Jews from the Soviet Union arriving in Israel rose sharply from the late 1980s, he saw a potential for a political party that catered to the needs of such migrants. In the 1996 Knesset [*qv*] poll, Israel BeAliya won seven seats. In the coalition government headed by Benjamin Netanyahu [*qv*] (r. 1996–99), Sharansky served as minister of industry and trade. He took a hard-line position on the peace process with the Palestinians [*qv*]. In the 1999 parliamentary election, his faction secured six seats. It joined the coalition government led by Ehud Barak [*qv*] (r. 1999–2001), with Sharanksy becoming minister of internal affairs. When Ariel Sharon [*qv*] succeeded Barak as the prime minister, Sharansky retained his ministry. In the 2003 general election, Israel BeAliya secured only two seats. Sharanksy resigned the party leadership. The two parliamentary deputies joined Likud [*qv*], raising its size to 40, and signalling the end of Israel BeAliya.

Israel Beltainu *(Hebrew: Israel our home): Israeli political party* Israel Beitainu was formed on the eve of the 1999 Knesset [*qv*] poll by Avigdor Lieberman, until then a close aide to Prime Minister Benjamin Netanyahu [*qv*] (r. 1996–99), leader of Likud [*qv*]. Born in the Soviet Republic of Moldavia, Lieberman was active in Likud politics, where he backed ultraright-wing policies. He founded the party as a rival to the older Israel BeAliyah [*qv*], which was popular with the Jewish immigrants from the former Soviet Union, who numbered almost one million by 1999. It won four seats on a secular, ultranationalist platform, opposing statehood for the Palestinians [*qv*] and proposing exile for their leader, Yasser Arafat [*qv*]. It did not join the national unity government formed by Ariel Sharon [*qv*] in March 2001. Following the assassination of the Moledet [*qv*] leader and

tourism minister Rechavam Zeevi in October, it formed an alliance with Moledet, called the National Union [*qv*]. When Sharon's government faced defeat in the Knesset after the exit of the Labor Party [*qv*] from the coalition in November 2002, the National Union backed Sharon, and Lieberman became a minister. In the 2003 general election it retained its share of four seats within the National Union's score of seven.

Israel Defense Forces: *see* Military in Israel.

Israeli Arabs: The term "Israeli Arabs" applies to those Arabs [*qv*] who did not leave Palestine before or during the 1948 Arab-Israeli War [*qv*] and acquired Israeli nationality. According to the Israeli census taken in November 1948, the 156,000 Israeli Arabs represented 18 percent of the total population. Due to natural growth this figure had risen to 1.32 million by 2000, including 232,000 living in East Jerusalem [*qv*], amounting to 20 percent of the Israeli population, including enlarged East Jerusalem.

Three-quarters of Israeli Arabs were Sunni Muslim [*qv*], about one-tenth Druze Muslim [*qv*] and the rest Christian [*qv*], and unclassified. More than 70 percent lived in the Northern District of Israel. Until 1966 they were severely restricted; for instance, they could not travel without the permission of the local military governor. They have been barred from joining the military, the exception being Druze males, who have their own units within the armed forces.

The education system for Israeli Arabs is separate from the Jewish, except at university level, where the medium of instruction is Hebrew [*qv*].

Politically, until 1958 Israeli Arabs were allowed to join only auxiliary bodies attached to the mainstream secular political parties. The lead of Mapam [qv] to open its doors to direct membership in 1958 was not followed by Labor [qv] until 1971. Because of this the separate Arab lists offered by Labor (the Progress and Development and the Arab Bedouin List) and Mapam lost their popularity. The 1973 election was the last one in which Labor won a parliamentary seat for its Arab list. The overall strength of Israeli Arab members of the 120-member Knesset [qv] has been five or six, with the left-wing Maki [qv]/Rakah [qv]/Hadash [qv] gaining the majority of the seats. In the 1992 election, eight Israeli Arabs were elected to parliament and two were appointed deputy minister. Angered by the Operation Grapes of Wrath [qv] in Lebanon ordered by Prime Minister Shimon Peres [qv], which killed 170 to 200 (Lebanese, mostly) civilians, including 102 refugees sheltering at a hill top in Qana, in April 1996, enough Israeli Arabs abstained to cause his defeat.

In the 1999 Knesset poll, the number of Israeli Arab members rose to twelve. Of these, nine belonged to the groups that were either exclusively or predominantly Arab and rejected Zionism [qv]. The 2003 general election saw the number of Israeli Arab parliamentarians decline to ten.

Israeli Arabs largely back the idea of a Palestinian state on the West Bank [qv] and Gaza [qv], and have been keen supporters of the Oslo Accords [qv] of 1993 and 1995. Soon after the eruption of the Second Intifada [qv] in September 2000, Israeli Arabs mounted a demonstration in support of the Palestinians. Firing by the Israeli security forces left thirteen protesters dead. This alienated Israeli Arabs from Prime Minister Ehud Barak [qv] (r. 1999–2001). By abstaining in the prime ministerial contest in February 2001, they contributed to his defeat by an unprecedented 25 percent. In this election, Azmi Bishara [qv] became the first Israeli Arab to enter the race for the high office, but he withdrew just before the pollling day.

In the national unity government of Ariel Sharon [qv], formed in March 2001, Salah Tarif, a Druze member of the Labor Party, became the first Israeli Arab to become a cabinet minister, albeit without portfolio.

Israeli Invasion of Lebanon (1978): Eleven Lebanon-based Palestinians reached northern Israel [qv] near Haifa [qv] secretly by boat on 11 March 1978. In their attacks on the beach and on a bus on the Haifa-Tel Aviv road they killed thirty-five Israelis. Nine of them died when overpowered by the Israeli forces.

Given the severity of the Palestinian action on the highway in central Israel, the government decided to solve the south Lebanese problem by removing about 5000 Palestinian guerrillas and their infrastructure from the area. On 14 March Israel invaded Lebanon with the aim of creating a 6 mile/10 km wide buffer zone along the 62 mile/100-km border. It dispatched 20,000–25,000 troops and used U.S.-made F-1 fighter planes and cluster bombs. Finding the Palestinians on the run, the Israelis captured half of southern Lebanon, about 10 percent of the country. By the time the Israelis had accepted U.N. Security Council Resolution 425 [qv] (calling for a cease-fire) on 21 March they had destroyed eighty-two villages, killed 2,000 people, mostly civilian, and displaced 160,000.

The Israeli withdrawal, which started on 11 April, took two months to complete and resulted in the Lebanese border zone (2–6 miles/4–12 km wide and 50 miles/80 km long) being put under the jurisdiction of an Israeli-funded Christian militia, called South Lebanon Army [*qv*], commanded by Saad Haddad, a former Lebanese army major. In the rest of the territory evacuated by the Israelis, the U.N. Interim Force in Lebanon (UNIFIL) [*qv*] took over from the departing troops.

The final and unconditional withdrawal of the Israeli forces from the Lebanese border zone took place in May 2000.

Israeli Invasion of Lebanon (1982): The second Israeli invasion of Lebanon, lasting from 6 June to 3 September 1982, went through the following phases.

Phase one: On the morning of 6 June 1982 Israel mounted Operation Peace in Galilee with the dual aim of securing the evacuation of all foreign forces from Lebanon and installing a regime in Beirut [*qv*] that would conclude a peace treaty with it. About 40,000 Israel Defense Forces (IDF) [*qv*] soldiers marched under heavy air cover into Lebanon across the land frontier, divided into eastern, central, and western sectors. This was supplemented by amphibious landings near Sidon [*qv*] and Tyre [*qv*].

Ignoring the U.N. Security Council Resolution 509 of 6 June, which called on Israel to withdraw immediately to its border with Lebanon, the IDF advanced along the coastal highway to Tyre and captured it the next day. Backed by more amphibious landings near Sidon, the IDF seized the city on 8 June. That night Israel's amphibious landings near Damour prepared the ground for the fall of the town the following day.

In the central sector the IDF column captured Litani River bridges and encircled Nabatiye, then pushed northwest to Sidon to link up with the other columns to besiege Sidon. By nightfall on 8 June the central IDF column had outflanked the Syrian forces in the southern Beqaa Valley, while its western column pressed eastward from Sidon into the Shouf Mountains to envelop Syria's forward positions at Jezzine before heading north. The IDF's eastern column concentrated on getting a foothold in southern Beqaa in order to advance to the strategic Beirut-Damascus highway.

Phase two: On the afternoon of 9 June, after Israeli electronic countermeasures had crippled Syria's radar, the IDF destroyed seventeen of the nineteen Syrian antiaircraft batteries. The ensuing air battle, involving 70 Syrian and 100 IDF supersonic jets, resulted in the loss of twenty-nine Syrian planes. Despite these losses, Syrian President Hafiz Assad [*qv*] deployed his air force on a large scale to slow down the Israeli advance. Damascus lost thirty-five more warplanes but gained valuable time.

On 10 June a Syrian armored division engaged an IDF armored brigade in the Rashaya area near the Lebanese–Syrian border, forcing the Israelis back several kilometers. The western IDF column reached the outskirts of Khalde, 3 miles/5 km from Beirut's international airport.

Assad dashed to Moscow, which led to activation of the hotline between the Soviet leader, Leonid Brezhnev, and U.S. President Ronald Reagan. Washington pressed its special envoy, Philip Habib, to intensify his peacemaking efforts.

Phase three: On 11 June a cease-fire between Israel and Syria went into effect, ending the fight in the eastern and central sectors. The next day Habib brokered a truce between Israel and the Palestine Liberation Organization (PLO) [*qv*].

Phase four: Ignoring the cease-fire with the PLO, on 13 June the IDF expelled Lebanese President Elias Sarkis [*qv*] from his palace in Baabda, an easterly suburb of Beirut [*qv*], and linked up with the militia of the Phalange Party [*qv*], thus besieging half a million Lebanese and Palestinians in the 3 sq. miles/8 sq. km of West Beirut. From 13 June to 12 July Israeli defense minister Gen. Ariel Sharon [*qv*], who was directing the invasion, tried to secure unconditional PLO surrender, first by heavy artillery salvos and then by staging air raids. This was coupled with the severing of water and electricity supplies as well as fuel and food.

Breaking the truce with the Syrians, the IDF attacked them on 22 June along the Beirut-Damascus highway east of Baabda and removed them from the road for 9 miles/15 km, up to Sofar. By the time the next cease-fire came into effect on 26 June the Israelis had seized the Dahr al Baidar pass, east of Sofar, along the Beirut-Damascus road.

Phase five: A truce between the PLO and the IDF lasted from 12 July to 21 July, when the Palestinians attacked the IDF behind its lines. From 22 July to 29 July the IDF staged a more intense bombing of West Beirut, combining it with a bombardment of the entire Syrian front in the Beqaa Valley. After a brief cease-fire, lasting until 31 July, from 1 August to 12 August the IDF subjected West Beirut to a more intense bombardment from the air, land, and sea, with Sharon resorting to saturation bombing for 11½ hours, using phosphorus shells and concussion bombs. Water supplies were cut off to let the city burn. Sharon's action angered Washington, which pressured Israeli Prime Minister Menachem Begin [*qv*] to intervene. As a result, the sixty-three-day siege of West Beirut ended, and peace returned on 13 August.

Phase six: On 19 August Israel accepted the evacuation plans of the PLO and Syria that had been brokered by Habib. Two days later, contingents of about 1,000 men each from the United States, Britain, France, and Italy—constituting the Multi-National Force (MNF) [*qv*] for peacekeeping—were deployed to ensure the safe withdrawal of PLO and Syrian troops. The last of the 8,144 PLO commandos, 3,500 Syrian-controlled Palestine Liberation Army (PLA) [*qv*] troops, and 2,700 Syrian soldiers left West Beirut on 1 September 1982.

At their peak the IDF deployed 76,000 troops, PLO fighters and their Lebanese allies amounted to 18,000, and the Syrian units to 25,000.

Human losses: Lebanese and Palestinians: 15,700 dead, including 1,110 PLO fighters and 1,350 Syrian troops; Israel: 350 dead. By the time of the final Israeli withdrawal in May 2000, the number had risen to over 1,000.

Weapon losses: Syria: 92 aircraft, 42 tanks; PLO: 20 tanks; Israel: 2 aircraft, 2 tanks.

Israeli Labor Party: *see* Labor Party, Israeli.

Israeli-Palestine Liberation Organization Accord (1993): Popularly known as the

Oslo I Accord. Following secret talks in Norway between Israeli and Palestine Liberation Organization (PLO) officials (called at the behest of Terje Larsen, a Norwegian sociologist, and his wife, Mona Juul, a diplomat, and lasting nearly a year), the two sides initialed a deal in Oslo in late August 1993. On 10 September Israel formally recognized the PLO after its chairman, Yasser Arafat [qv], had addressed a letter to Israeli Premier Yitzhak Rabin [qv] recognizing Israel's right to exist in peace and security. He also renounced violence and promised to ensure compliance of this by all PLO elements. The accord, called the Declaration of Principles (DOP), was signed on 13 September in Washington at the White House by Mahmud Abbas, the second-in-command of the PLO, and Shimon Peres [qv], the Israeli foreign minister, in the presence of Rabin, Arafat, and U.S. President Bill Clinton.

The accord provided for Palestinian self-rule for the Gaza Strip [qv] and the West Bank town of Jericho [qv]—with Israeli sovereignty over Jewish settlements in the Occupied Territories [qv]—as an interim stage, with talks on permanent agreement to begin after two years. The timetable was as follows.
13 October: The accord to come into force. Joint Israel-PLO Liaison Committee formed to implement it.
By 13 December: The two sides to agree on a protocol on the withdrawal of Israeli forces from the Gaza Strip and Jericho.
By 13 April 1994: Israel to complete military withdrawal from the Gaza Strip and Jericho. Israel to transfer powers to the Palestinian Authority [qv] nominated by the PLO.
By 13 July 1994: Elections to the Palestinian Council to be held, followed by the dissolution of Israel's military-run civil administration in the Occupied Territories, with its powers transferred to the Palestinian Authority.
By 13 December 1995: Israel and the Palestinians to start talks on permanent settlement, including the status of East Jerusalem [qv].
By 13 December 1999: permanent settlement to take effect.

In practice the implementation agreement was signed on 4 May 1994, and as head of the Palestinian Authority, Arafat set up his headquarters in Gaza City on 1 July. The implementation agreement on extending the jurisdiction of the Palestinian Authority to the West Bank [qv] and the holding of elections to the Palestinian Council was signed in September 1995, with the implementation to be completed by early 1996, a few months before the extended deadline (May 1996) for negotiation on the final status of the Occupied Territories and the Jewish settlements built there.

These plans went awry when Rabin was assassinated in November 1995, and his successor, Peres, was defeated by Likud leader Benjamin Netanyahu [qv] six months later. Netanyahu's defeat by his Labor rival Ehud Barak [qv] in May 1999 raised hopes. But the terms for the final settlement that he offered at the summit with Arafat and Clinton at Camp David in July 2000 did not satisfy Arafat. The eruption of the Palestinian al Aqsa Intifada [qv] in September and the refusal of Arafat to curb it undermined the basis on which the Oslo I Accord was founded.

Israeli Socialist Organization: *Israeli political party* Formed by a group of former

Jewish members of Maki [*qv*] in 1962, the Israeli Socialist Organization was better known by the name of its journal, *Mastzpen* (Compass). It opposed the June 1967 Arab-Israeli War [*qv*] and conducted dialogues with such Palestinian groups as the Democratic Front for the Liberation of Palestine [*qv*]. It was portrayed as a "traitor" party by the Zionist [*qv*] establishment. Sustained harassment and persecution of its members by official agencies led to its disintegration in the early 1970s.

J

Jaafari Code: *Shia Islamic legal school* This Islamic legal code is named after Imam Jaafar al Sadiq (A.D. 699–765), the sixth Imam of Twelver Shias [*qv*]. *See also* Hadith [*qv*].

Jabotinsky, Vladimir Zeev (1880–1940): *Revisionist Zionist leader* Born into a middle-class family in Odessa, Russia, Jabotinsky studied law in Berne, Switzerland, and Rome. On his return home he worked as a journalist with an Odessa newspaper. During the 1903 pogroms, he helped to organize local Jewish self-defense. Shocked by the pogroms, Jabotinsky joined the Zionist movement and attended the Sixth Zionist Congress in 1904. Two years later, as a delegate to the Congress of Russian Zionists, he helped to draft its program.

The outbreak of the First World War found Jabotinsky working as a journalist for a Moscow newspaper in Cairo [*qv*]. He met Joseph Trumpeldor [*qv*] in Alexandria [*qv*], and together they formed the Zion Mule Corps of young Jews who had been deported from Palestine [*qv*] by the Ottomans. They promoted the idea of establishing Jewish battalions to fight alongside the British to conquer Palestine [*qv*]. In 1917 London authorized the formation of the First Judean Regiment, popularly known as the Jewish Legion, and attached it to the British forces of General Edmund Allenby. As a lieutenant in the Legion, Jabotinsky saw combat in the Middle East and was decorated.

After the war Jabotinsky settled in Jerusalem [*qv*]. For his role in the Arab-Jewish riots in 1920 he was sentenced to fifteen years imprisonment, but was freed the next year as part of a general amnesty. He moved to London and was elected to the executive committee of the World Zionist Organization (WZO) [*qv*]. He resigned this post in 1923 when the committee refused to endorse his policy to pressure the British mandate to build a Jewish homeland in Palestine with its resources.

He formed the World Union of Revisionist Zionists in 1925, which affiliated to the WZO. He also founded Betar (acronym of *Berit Trumpeldor.* Covenant with Trumpeldor), a youth organization. At the 1931 Zionist Congress the fifty-two Revisionist Zionist [*qv*] delegates were the third largest group. Efforts to conciliate them with the Labor Zionists failed.

In Palestine, the Revisionists' attempt to seize the leadership of the Zionist movement was frustrated by the Labor Zionists, headed by David Ben-Gurion [*qv*]. Seceding from the WZO in 1935, the Revisionists established the New Zionist Organization (NZO), led by Jabotinsky. He advocated giving primacy to private capital to develop Palestine and was opposed to the Marxist concept of class struggle. He went to live in

Palestine, where he became editor of the NZO newspaper.

When he went abroad in 1936, the British refused to let him return to Palestine. By then the Irgun Zvai Leumi [qv], which had splintered from Haganah [qv] five years earlier, had come to take orders from Jabotinsky, who later became its supreme commander, even though, barred from Palestine, he spent his time in Eastern Europe, Paris, London, and New York.

When the Second World War erupted in 1939, Jabotinsky declared that the NZO would support the war effort. Determined to form a Jewish army, he visited the United States for this purpose in mid-1940. He died there and was buried in New York. His remains were exhumed and reburied in Israel in 1964.

Fluent in several languages, Jabotinsky was an essayist, poet, novelist, playwright, and translator.

Jacobite Christians: *see* Orthodox Christians, Syrian.

Jadid, Salah (1926–1993): *Syrian military leader and politician* Born into a notable Alawi [qv] family in Duwair Baabda, a village near Jablah port, Jadid trained as an officer at the Homs Military Academy. He began his army career as a lieutenant. Politically active, he was first a member of the Syrian Social Nationalist Party [qv], then the Arab Socialist Party [qv], and finally the Baath Socialist Party [qv]. Following the merger of Syria and Egypt into the United Arab Republic (UAR) [qv] in early 1958, Jadid was transferred to Egypt.

Angered at President Gamal Abdul Nasser's [qv] decision to dissolve the Baath party in Syria, he joined Hafiz Assad [qv] and two other Baathist officers to form, secretly, the Military Committee in 1959. It succeeded in taking Syria out of the UAR in September 1961. It also carried out a Baathist coup in Damascus [qv] on 8 March 1963. As a Military Committee leader, Jadid began to purge non-Baathist officers from the armed forces.

In October, promoted to major general, Jadid was named chief of staff. But a year later he lost his high office as a result of party infighting and was relegated to deputy secretary-general of the Baath regional command. But he fought back. The climax came in February 1966 when the military faction, led among others by Jadid, won an armed confrontation with its rival. Having gained a monopoly of authority, Jadid packed the government and the party regional command with his supporters, while himself remaining simply deputy secretary-general of the party. He promoted Nur al Din Attasi [qv] to secretary-general of the party and Assad to defense minister. He continued to lead a spartan existence and espouse leftist policies. Following an abortive military coup in September, Jadid and Assad purged the officer corps.

The Syrian defeat in the June 1967 Arab-Israeli War [qv], involving the loss of the Golan Heights [qv], was a strong blow to Jadid's regime. Among other things it created a rift between Jadid and Assad, who advocated pragmatic policies. With Jadid maintaining a tight grip over the party machine, Assad increased his control over the armed forces. In February 1969 Assad tried to usurp Jadid's power, but compromised in order to avoid bloodshed. But matters came to a head in September 1970, when, contrary to Jadid's promise, Assad failed to provide military aid to the Palestinian commandos battling the Jordanian army.

When Jadid convened an emergency National (i.e., pan-Arab) Congress of the Baath party on 30 October 1970 in Damascus, the meeting place was surrounded by pro-Assad soldiers. Once the congress had ended in acrimony on 12 November, the opponents of Assad, including Jadid, were arrested. He was held in the Mezze fortress prison until 1983. After his release he was kept under surveillance and barred from public life until, after a brief period of freedom, he was again detained at the Mezze prison where he died of illness.

Jaffa: Incorporated into Tel Aviv [*qv*] in 1949. *See* Tel Aviv-Jaffa.

Jbail: *see* Byblos.

Jeddah: *see* Jiddah.

Jericho: *West Bank town* Pop. 20,000 (1993, est.). One of the oldest settlements in the world, Jericho's history dates back to ca. 9000 B.C. A millennium or so later its few thousand inhabitants built a stone wall around the village. There were intermittent breaks in Jericho's history until 2300 B.C., when it was settled by Amorites, who were followed by Canaanites in ca. 1900 B.C. Its capture by Joshua, successor to Moses, around 1220 B.C., heralded the entry of Hebrews into Canaan, the Promised Land, and its fall to Babylon in 586 B.C. marked the end of the Kingdom of Judah.

During the reign of King Herod the Great (37–34 B.C.) the town was moved about a mile southward. The king built a palace, and he died there. In A.D. 68 the Romans destroyed the town. The Crusaders rebuilt it on a site about a mile east of the Old Testament [*qv*] settlement. A center of balsam groves, it became known as the City of Palms.

Jericho was part of the Palestine [*qv*] under the British mandate. After the Palestine War (1948–49) [*qv*], it was incorporated into Jordan, and when two camps for Arab refugees from Palestine were opened nearby, it became a center of activity. In the June 1967 Arab-Israeli War [*qv*] it fell to the Israelis and the town became depopulated. It was the only West Bank [*qv*] town to be included in the Oslo Accord [*qv*] of September 1993 for transfer to the Palestinian Authority [*qv*] along with the Gaza Strip in the first round. In 1998 it became the site of a casino, which proved popular with Israelis who were not allowed to gamble inside Israel. It closed down during the Second Intifada [*qv*].

Jerusalem: *Israeli/Palestinian city; self-declared capital of Israel* Area: East Jerusalem [*qv*] 2.5 sq. miles/6.5 sq. km in 1948, 28.5 sq. miles/73.7 sq. km in 1967; West Jerusalem [*qv*] 13 sq. miles/34 sq. km in 1948, 20 sq. miles/54 sq. km in 1993; pop. (2002, est.) East Jerusalem, 425,000; West Jerusalem, 651,000. Jerusalem is derivative of *Yerushalayim (Hebrew: Founded by [god] Shalem)*. Mentioned as Salem in the Old Testament [*qv*] (Genesis 14:18), Jerusalem is a settlement with a recorded history dating back to ca. 1900 B.C., when it was the capital of a Canaanite city-state and the site where Abraham was greeted by King Melchizedek. Though its ruler was defeated by the Hebrews under Joshua, the successor to Moses, around. 1220 B.C., it maintained its independence until its capture by David (r. 1010–970 B.C.) in ca. 1010 B.C. He made it the capital of united Israel and also—by transferring the Ark of the Covenant from Hebron [qv]—the religious center of his kingdom. He built the fortress of Zion, and his successor, King Solomon (r. 970–30 B.C.) built the First Temple in 952 B.C.

After the division of Israel, which followed Solomon, Jerusalem became the capital of the southern Kingdom of Judah until it was overrun by the Babylonian ruler Nebuchadnezzar (r. 605–562 B.C.) in 586 B.C., when most of the population was expelled and the First Temple razed. Under the succeeding Persian rule, Jewish sectarianism hardened. Allowed to return to Jerusalem in 538 B.C., the Jews [qv] began to construct the Second Temple, finishing it in 515 B.C. The Persians in Palestine [qv] were overpowered by Alexander the Great (r. 336–23 B.C.) in 333 B.C., and the succeeding Greek rulers tried to found a parallel city on Jerusalem's western edge.

The banning of Judaism [qv] in 168 B.C. by Antiochus IV (r. 175–63 B.C.) led to a Jewish revolt, headed by Judas Maccabeus. It was successful and resulted in the restoration of the Second Temple in 163 B.C. and the revival of the Jewish rule in Jerusalem under Jonathan in 152 B.C. The city became the capital of Judaea.

In 63 B.C. the Roman general Pompey captured Jerusalem, which fell in 40 B.C. to the Parthians, who were in turn overpowered by Roman King Herod the Great (r. 37–34 B.C.) three years later. In 20 B.C. Herod began to reconstruct the Second Temple on a large scale, building a surrounding esplanade, part of whose outer wall, built partly with stones from Solomon's First Temple, came to be known as the Western Wall [qv]. After Herod the city was governed by Roman procurators, called Pontius. Under one of them, Pilate, Jesus of Nazareth [qv], born a Jew, was crucified at nearby Calvary in ca. 30 A.D.

The repressive Roman administration led to another revolt by the Jews in A.D. 66 and its siege by Roman Emperor Titus (r. A.D. 40–81). It fell in A.D. 70 and the Second Temple was razed. Roman Emperor Hadrian (r. A.D. 117–38) seized and destroyed Jerusalem in A.D. 132. He then reconstructed it as a Roman colony, named *Aelia Capitalina* (Capital of Memory), and banned Jews.

With the conversion of Roman Emperor Constantine I (r. A.D. 306–37) to Christianity [qv] in A.D. 313, Jerusalem underwent a revival. The Church of the Holy Sepulchre, begun in A.D. 325 on the site of Jesus Christ's crucifixion at Calvary, was completed ten years later, and Jerusalem became a holy Christian city. In A.D. 614 it was seized by the Persians, who were overpowered by Byzantine Emperor Heraclitus (r. A.D. 610–41) in A.D. 628. The Byzantines were defeated by Muslim Arabs [qv] led by Caliph Omar (r. A.D. 634–44) in A.D. 637.

Jerusalem had been mentioned in the Quran [qv] (17:1): "Celebrated be the praises of Him who by night took His servant from the Masjid al Haram [the Sacred Mosque in Mecca" [qv] to the Masjid al Aqsa [the Remote Mosque in Jerusalem] the precinct of which we have blessed." At the site of the Sacred Rock, where the Prophet Muhammad had purportedly been carried on a winged animal on the night of his ascent to heaven, a mosque was built by Abdul Malik ibn

Marwan (r. A.D. 684–705), an Umayyad ruler, in A.D. 691 and called the Dome of the Rock [*qv*]. Under the Muslim rulers, Jews were allowed to return and Christians were given freedom of worship.

In A.D. 969 the city fell into the hands of the Fatimid ruler al Muizz (r. A.D. 955–78), and the church of the Holy Sepulchre was burnt down. The persecution of Christians continued and resulted in the First Crusade (1095–99). The Crusaders, led by Godfrey of Bouillon, captured Jerusalem and massacred Muslims and Jews. The city became the capital of the Latin Kingdom until its fall to the Muslim general Salah al Din (Saladin) Ayubi in 1187.

With brief interruptions, Jerusalem remained under Muslim control until 1917. Sacked by the Mongols in 1244, it came under Ottoman rule in 1517. Sultan Suleiman the Magnificent (r. 1520–66) rebuilt the city walls in 1541. By the late eighteenth to early nineteenth century, Jerusalem, confined to the Old City and measuring 0.4 sq. miles/1 sq. km, had fewer than 10,000 residents, a quarter of them Jewish. The Old City contained the Western Wall (sacred to Jews), the Church of the Holy Sepulchre (sacred to Christians), and the Dome of the Rock and al Aqsa mosque (sacred to Muslims). Once new buildings had been constructed outside the walled Old City, from 1855 onward, Jerusalem's population increased, reaching 68,000 in 1910. It was captured by the British forces in December 1917.

During the British mandate (1922–48), Jerusalem was the capital of Palestine. Tension between local Arabs and new Jewish immigrants led to riots in 1920, 1929, and 1936. After the Second World War, the city's population was 165,000, three-fifths of whom were Jewish. The United Nations partition plan of November 1947 specified an independent Jerusalem under U.N. administration.

After the Palestine War (1948–49) [*qv*], the city was divided into two parts: the Israeli sector included the west and south of the New City and was known as West Jerusalem [*qv*]; the Jordanian sector comprised the east and north of the New City and all of the Old City, and was known as East Jerusalem [*qv*]. In January 1950 Israel declared (West) Jerusalem its capital, but this was not recognized by foreign governments, which continued to maintain their embassies in Tel Aviv [*qv*].

During the June 1967 Arab-Israeli War [*qv*], the Israelis seized East Jerusalem from Jordan. They then attached 25 sq. miles/65 sq. km of the West Bank territory to it and extended Israeli laws to Greater East Jerusalem. The Jerusalem Law of 1980 extended Israeli sovereignty over the entire city. U.N. Security Council Resolution 476 of 30 June 1980 reaffirmed its earlier resolutions on the Holy City of Jerusalem—252 (1968), 267 (1969), 271 (1969), 298 (1971), and 465 (1980)—and reconfirmed that all measures taken by Israel (as the occupying power) that altered the character and status of the Holy City were legally invalid and violated the last of the four Geneva Conventions on War [*qv*]. Except Costa Rica and El Salvador, all the countries with diplomatic relations with Israel still maintain their embassies in Tel Aviv [*qv*].

Jewish Agency: *a Jewish organization for the ingathering of Jews in Israel* Full title: The

Jewish Agency for Palestine [*qv*]/Land of Israel. The 1922 British mandate for Palestine provided for the recognition of "an appropriate Jewish agency" for "advising and cooperating with the administration of Palestine in such economic, social and other matters as may affect the establishment of the Jewish national home and the interests of the Jewish population in Palestine," and that "the Zionist Organization [*qv*] . . . shall be recognized as such agency."

The Zionist Organization appointed a Zionist Executive in Palestine, with its own chairman and based in Jerusalem [*qv*]. Its functions were to act as the political representative of the Jews [*qv*] in Palestine, and to encourage and finance the ingathering of Diaspora [*qv*] Jews in Palestine. The Sixteenth Zionist Congress [*qv*] in 1929 formally created the Jewish Agency in Palestine "for discharging the functions of the Jewish agency as set forth in the Mandate" on the basis of parity between Zionists [*qv*] and non-Zionists (i.e., those who backed the idea of a Jewish national home without subscribing to political Zionism). Both the Zionist Executive and the Jewish Agency Executive shared the same chairman. The Jewish Agency negotiated with Britain and represented Jewish interests at the League of Nations.

In May 1942 David Ben-Gurion [*qv*]—chairman of both the Jewish Agency Executive and the Zionist Organization Executive in Palestine—convened an American Zionist Congress at the Biltmore Hotel, New York. It coupled its call for unrestricted Jewish immigration to Palestine with a demand that "Palestine be established as a Jewish Commonwealth integrated into the structure of the new democratic world."

This led to the steady departure of non-Zionists from the Agency Executive, accelerated in December 1946 by the endorsing of the Biltmore Hotel Resolution by the Twenty-second Zionist Congress in Basle, Switzerland, turning the agency into a purely Zionist organization by early 1947. It lobbied strongly at the newly formed United Nations, which finally offered a partition plan for Palestine in November 1947.

By May 1948, when Israel was established, the Agency had transferred all its executive powers to the people's administrative committee of the National Council of the Yishuv [*qv*] assembly, while retaining the functions of Jewish immigration and settlement in Israel. Its functions as an international nongovernmental body, coordinating all Jewish overseas endeavors in Israel, were formalized by Israel's Law of Status (1951), which codified statutory and conventional links between the Jewish Agency and Israel. The law states: "The [World] Zionist Organization, which is also the Jewish Agency for Palestine, deals as hitherto with immigration and directs the projects of absorption and settlement in the state."

A major reorganization in 1971 put the Jewish Agency in Israel in charge of practical work in Israel, leaving the World Zionist Organization [*qv*] to concentrate on the Diaspora [*qv*]. Its Assembly decides the basic policy, with the board of governors doing so between the Assembly sessions and the executive committee conducting day-to-day affairs.

The Jewish Agency is the overall collector of contributions to the Zionist cause throughout the world. Bearing different names—the United Jewish Appeal in America, the Joint Israel Appeal in Britain etc.—its *Keren Kayesod (Hebrew: Perpetual Fund)* operated in seventy countries. In 2000 its budget was $381 million.

Jewish Bible: *see* Old Testament.

Jewish calendar: The Jewish dating system is a compendium of lunar and solar cycles. The Jewish calendar consists of a lunar cycle of nineteen years. There is also a solar cycle of twenty-eight years, at the beginning of which the *tekufah* of Nisan (month)—the spring equinox—returns to the same day and the same hour. In the Jewish calendar, a day is counted from sunset to sunrise; a week consists of seven days; a month contains twenty-nine days, twelve hours, and 793 portions (1,080 portions equaling one hour); and a year has twelve lunar months (totaling 353 to 355 days) and about 11 days. In order to bring the calendar into line with the annual solar cycle, a thirteenth month of thirty days is intercalated in the 3rd, 6th, 8th, 11th, 14th, 17th, and 19th years of a nineteen-year cycle. A leap year may therefore have 383, 384, or 385 days, and is called defective, regular, or abundant. The same terms apply to a regular year with 353, 354, and 355 days.

The names of the months, arranged according to religious usage, are: Nisan (30 days, March–April of the Christian Gregorian calendar [*qv*]), Iyar (29, April–May), Sivan (30, May–June), Tammuz (29, June–July), Av (30, July–August), Elul (29, August–September), Tishri (30, September–October), Heshvan/Marheshvan (29/30, October–November), Kislev (29/30, November–December), Tevet (29, December–January), Shevat (30, January–February), and Adar (29/30, February–March). The thirteenth month of the leap year, Adar Sheni/Ve-Adar (29), is intercalated before Adar and so contains the religious observances normally occurring in Adar. The calendar begins with Tishri, its first day heralding Rosh HaShana (The New Year) [*qv*], which falls between 6 September and 4 October. Formalized by Hillel II in A.D. 358, it originates in 3761 B.C., the date traditionally given for the Creation in the Old Testament [*qv*]. The Jewish year is denoted by A.M. [*qv*]. The 301st lunar cycle started in 5701 A.M. (A.D. 1940–41).

To convert a Jewish year into Christian, deduct 3,760 from it.

Jewish festivals: Jewish festivals are divided into major and minor. The four major festivals—when work is prohibited and all males are required to attend religious observances at a synagogue [*qv*]—are: Pesah/Passover [*qv*] (15–22 Nisan), commemorating the Israelites' servitude in Egypt and the subsequent Exodus; Shabout (Feast of Weeks, or Pentecost [*qv*]), the anniversary of the revelation of the Torah [*qv*] at Mount Sinai, celebrated on 6–7 Sivan; the Days of Penitence/Judgement, beginning with Rosh HaShana [*qv*] on 1–2 Tishri and ending with Yom Kippur [*qv*] on 10 Tishri; and Sukkot/Tabernacles/Booths from 15–21 Tishri, commemorating the Israelites' wanderings after the Exodus. Minor holidays, when work is not prohibited, are: Simhath Torah (Rejoicing over the Law) on 23 Tishri; Hannukah [*qv*] from 25 Kislev to 2/3 Tebet; and Purim (Feast of Lots) on 14 Adar.

Jewish/Judaistic fundamentalism: Fundamentalism is the term used for the effort to define the fundamentals of a religion and adhere to them. In the case of Judaism, these fundamentals are contained in the *Halacha* [*qv*] (Jewish Law). The expunging of current Jewish precepts and practices of secular influences is a primary goal of Jewish fundamentalists. Related to fundamentalism is Judaistic revival or resurgence, renewed interest in Judaism [*qv*], or the *teshuva* (return) movement—a return to full observance of the Halacha, i.e., all 613 religious prohibitions and obligations that regulate Jewish life, from trivial daily bodily functions to the organization of life in society—and the separation of Jews and gentiles. Whether the Jewish state of Israel is fundamentalist or not can be judged by a single criterion: Is its legislation derived solely from the Halacha? At present the answer is No.

There is also the belief held by ultra-Orthodox Jews that Israel as a "peoplehood" would be redeemed only by a Messiah, from which stemmed their opposition to Zionism [*qv*], which was seen as a Jewish version of secular nationalism. Later a synthesis of "the divine concept" and "national sentiment"— offered by Abraham Yitzhak Kook (d. 1935), the first Ashkenazi [*qv*] chief rabbi of Palestine [*qv*]—gave rise to religious Zionism. After the founding of Israel in 1948, his son, Zvi Yehuda Kook (d. 1982), argued that the Zionists, despite their irreligiosity, were the inadvertent bearers of a messianic redemption and that the State of Israel was an unconscious instrument of the divine will. He attributed Israel's spectacular victory in June 1967 to divine intervention, and his followers called 1967 Year One of the Era of Redemption.

In early 1974 they established the Gush Emunim [*qv*]. It was one of the several manifestations of a rising *teshuva* (return) movement in Israel in the mid-1970s, the others being the opening of the great Talmudic colleges in Jerusalem [*qv*] for penitents and the coming to power of a religious-conservative coalition led by Likud [*qv*] in 1977. With Prime Minister Menachem Begin [*qv*] officially backing Jewish settlements in the West Bank [*qv*], the Gush made an advance in its program of re-Judaization from above. However, it was opposed to Begin's peace talks with Egypt and looked for ways of sabotaging the peace process. The foiling of a conspiracy involving Gush extremists in a plan to blow up the Muslim holy shrines on the Temple Mount [*qv*] in 1984 was a setback to the fundamentalist cause. The stress then returned to fundamentalism from below, which has been the program of several religious parties.

In the eleven general elections between 1949 and 1984, the fundamentalists won 12–15 percent of the votes—with two-thirds going to religious Zionists organized as the National Religious Party (NRP) [*qv*], and only one-third to the non-Zionists of Agudat Israel [*qv*]. But in the 1988 election, out of the total of 15 percent religious votes, the NRP secured only a quarter, with the ultra-Orthodox votes—consisting of Shas [*qv*] and United Torah Judaism [*qv*]—rising to three-quarters. In 1999, with Shas alone gaining 13 percent of the vote, the total for the religious parties rose to 21 percent.

Without specifically recognizing the legitimacy of the Zionist state of Israel, the non-Zionist religious parties have often delivered their supporters' votes in exchange for substantial government commitments, including enlarged subsidies for religious educational institutions. They have pursued a strategy of forcing the secular Israeli government to institute creeping Judaization, affecting all Jews in Israel. For instance, they made it accept their definition of Jewish identity "in accordance with the Halacha" when determining the credentials of Jewish converts coming from abroad.

Jewish National Fund: *fund for the purchase and development of land in Palestine/Israel* Official title: *Keren Kayemet LeIsrael (Hebrew: Perpetual Fund for Israel).* The Fifth Zionist Congress in 1901 set up a land and development section, which established the *Keren Kayemet LeIsrael,* popularly known as the Jewish National Fund (JNF), to buy land in Palestine [*qv*] for the settlement of Jews there. The JNF, an organ of the World Zionist Organization [*qv*], adopted the following principles: the purchase of land with communal contributions for communal ownership; plots to be available only for lease to Jews; land use to be supervised; and speculation to be prevented.

Starting modestly in 1905, the JNF resorted to large-scale land purchases from 1921 onward. It leased land for forty-nine years on the condition that lessees would forfeit their right to the land if they failed to work it, or did so with the help of hired labor. By the time Israel was established in May 1948 the JNF, now operating from Jerusalem [*qv*], had acquired nearly a quarter of a million acres. In 1949–50 the Israeli government handed over to it 600,000 additional acres belonging to the Arabs [*qv*] who had fled.

The JNF was turned into an Israeli-registered company in 1953. It collects funds in about seventy countries. In 1960 the JNF and the Israeli government, together owning 92 percent of Israeli territory, set up the National Land Authority to administer all the lands.

Jewish nationalism: Jewish nationalism is the concept that Jews form a nation that is entitled to develop its own distinctive identity. The Jewish commonwealth, established in ancient Israel under King David (r. 1010–970 B.C.), underwent divisions, decimation, and revival before its final destruction by the Romans in A.D. 70. Spread throughout the rest of the Roman Empire, Jews continued to believe in their nationhood.

Over the centuries anti-Jewish persecution pushed European Jews toward the less hospitable northeastern and central-northern parts of the continent. Here the idea of nationhood acquired a spiritual dimension at the expense of the political and gave rise to a belief that a messiah would restore sovereignty to Jews in their historical land.

Barred from agriculture, most Jews took to commerce and finance. The feeling of being stifled in ghettoes became stronger as Jews became increasingly familiar with liberal ideas following the 1789 French Revolution. Gradually they began to abandon the religious traditions of their antecedents. But their assimilationist tendency, encouraged by their emancipation in the late nineteenth century, was checked by the emergence and popularity of pseudoscientific theories proving the racial inferiority of Jews. The result was the rise of Jewish nationalism, which, on the eve of the First World War, fell into three categories: Diaspora [*qv*] nationalism, Zionism [*qv*], and Territorialism.

Arguing that Jews could develop their own special identity and culture as a minority regardless of where they lived,

Diaspora nationalists advocated that they should strive for cultural autonomy within their countries of domicile. Zionists emphasized the need for a Jewish homeland for Jews who were unwilling or unable to live elsewhere, which would also be a cultural-spiritual center for international Jewry. For historical reasons they focused on Palestine [qv] as the Jewish homeland. The Territorialists, while subscribing to the concept of the Jewish homeland, were prepared to explore such alternatives to Palestine as Argentina, Angola, Australia, and Iraq. They were overtaken by the Zionists due to the Balfour Declaration of 1917 [qv].

Jews: *see* Judaism and Jews.

Jews in Arab Middle East: In 1945 there were 870,000 Jews in the Arab Middle East [qv]. Following the founding of Israel [qv] and the First Arab-Israeli War [qv], their number fell to 70,000, with 600,000 migrating to Israel and the rest elsewhere.

Egypt: The recorded history of the Jewish community in Egypt dates back to 494 B.C. and the reign of Darius I (r. 521–486 B.C.). At the turn of the twentieth century there were about 40,000 Jews, mostly Sephardic [qv] and concentrated in Cairo [qv]. After the Second World War their number rose to 70,000, based mainly in Cairo and Alexandria [qv].

Jewish intellectuals were active in the leftist Mouvement Egyptien de Liberation National and the Iskra group, led respectively by Henri Curiel and Hillel Schwartz, both Jews [qv].

After the Palestine War (1948–49) [qv] most of the Jews left, with only 5,000 remaining. Still more departed after a group of Jews, acting as an Israeli espionage-sabotage cell, was caught in 1954. The 1956 census included just 450 Jews. The total rose to 1,631 in the 1976 census.

Iraq: Iraq under the British mandate had a substantial community of Jews, many of whom could trace their ancestry to ancient times. Following the passage of a law in 1931 that gave the community autonomy in its internal affairs, a network of Jewish schools, hospitals, and charitable institutions grew, mostly in Baghdad [qv]. On the eve of the Palestine War in 1948, there were an estimated 150,000 Jews in Iraq. After this conflict, most of them departed, mainly for Israel. A second exodus occurred after the Suez War [qv] of 1956. Unofficial estimates on the eve of the Second Gulf War [qv] in 1991 put the number of Jews in Iraq at 2,500, chiefly in Baghdad. By 2003 the figure had fallen to 50.

Jordan: Article 25 of the League of Nations Mandate for Britain, which went into force in September 1922, exempted Jordan (then Transjordan) from application of the Balfour Declaration [qv]. Jews were barred from acquiring land or settling in the country. During the 1948–49 Arab-Israeli War [qv], some 2,000 Jews living in the Old City of East Jerusalem [qv] surrendered to the Jordanian army and were later transferred to Israel.

Lebanon: A region under the Ottomans that proved popular with minority Islamic sects, Lebanon also attracted Jews. In the late nineteenth century they formed a small, thriving community in Beirut [qv]. The 1932 census showed Jews to be some 15,000 strong. The National Pact [qv] of 1943 included Jews in a grouping of non-Muslim minorities, along with Bahais [qv] and Protestant Christians [*qv*], and allotted the group one parliamentary seat.

After the Palestine War (1948–49) many Jews left, and more did so after the Suez War [*qv*]. In 1968 there were some 7,000 Jews in the country. The onset of a long civil war in 1975, and the prevailing chaotic conditions, involving abductions and hostage taking, made life for Jews difficult. By the early 1990s unofficial estimates put their number at 500–700. Their number dwindled to 20 in 1998.

Syria: The small, long-established Jewish communities in Damascus [*qv*], Aleppo [*qv*], and Latakia [*qv*] together totaled 25,000 on the eve of the Palestine War (1948–49 [*qv*]). A majority of them departed after this conflict, and more did so after the Suez War [*qv*]. In the mid-1960s the Jewish total declined to some 5,000. By 1994 it had fallen to 1,250, and to 100 by the late 1990s.

Yemen: North Yemen [*qv*] had a substantial community of Jews, mostly settled in Sanaa [*qv*] and the northern town of Saada, and many could trace their ancestry to ancient times. Following the Palestine War (1948–49), 42,000 Jews migrated to Israel. Less than 6,000 remained, and many of these departed after the Suez War [*qv*]. In the early 1990s unofficial estimates put their number at 2,000–2,500. In South Yemen some 7,000 Jews departed from the Aden Protectorate during and after the 1948–49 Palestine War. In the united Yemen of 2000, there were about 400 Jews.

Jews in Iran: Jews in Iran have a history dating back to antiquity. During the reign of Muhammad Reza Shah Pahlavi (r. 1941–79) [*qv*], Jews—along with other non-Muslim-recognized minorities—voted as a distinct group in parliamentary elections. This practice continued after the 1979 revolution. The number of Jews, estimated at 70,000 on the eve of the revolution, fell by 20,000 after it. The community elected one member to the Assembly of Experts (1979) [*qv*]—convened to draft an Islamic constitution, which recognized Jews as the People of the (Holy) Book—and entitled them to elect one deputy to the Majlis [*qv*]. In 1999, there were an estimated 35,000 Jews with fifty-six synagogues. The trial of thirteen Jews and nine Muslims [*qv*] in Shiraz [*qv*] on spying charges drew international attention. All but three Jews and two Muslims were found guilty, with the Jews sentenced to four to thirteen years in jail. On appeal their sentence was reduced by two to four years. However, all those still in prison in 2002 were released.

Jibran, Khalil (1883–1931): also spelled Gibran Khalil. *Lebanese writer* Born into a Maronite [*qv*] family in the village of Bishari, Jibran received his schooling in Beirut [*qv*] until 1895, when he left with his parents for Boston, USA. Three years later he traveled to Beirut [*qv*] to study Arabic [*qv*] and French at the Maronite al Hikma Institute. After his return to Boston, he took to writing and painting. He published his literary essays in 1903 in *al Muhajir (Arabic: The Migrant)*, a newspaper of expatriate Arabs. The next year, at an exhibition of his drawings, he met Mary Haskel, who became his life-long benefactor. She sent him to Paris in 1908 to study art.

Soon after his return to Boston in 1910, Jibran formed the Golden Chain, a political group committed to bringing about socio-political reform in Lebanon. In 1912 he settled in New York, where he continued to produce essays, poems, short stories, and paintings.

His collections of short stories—*Nymphs of the Valley* (1906) and *Rebellious Spirits* (1908)—all set in Lebanon, showed his romantic bent, belief in the inherent good-ness of humans, admiration for pastoral sur-roundings, and distrust of the institutions and bonds of civilized society. He expressed these ideas forcefully in his collection of essays, *A Tear and a Smile* (1914). He was influenced by the Bible [*qv*], Jean Rousseau, William Blake, and Friedrich Nietzsche. Though religious, he was anticlerical and opposed to the Maronite church hierarchy. He continued writing in Arabic prose until 1918, when he began to use English as well.

His lyrical style, supported by analogies and biblical metaphors, suited his romantic thoughts, the end result being musically poetic Arabic prose that was unique. His first book in English was *The Madman* (1918), which expressed optimistic pantheism, fol-lowed by *Twenty Drawings* (1919) and *The Forerunner* (1920). In his novel *Broken Wings* (1922) he attacked feudal lords and clerics in Lebanon who stood between the young hero and his rich beloved, a reflection of his per-sonal experience.

In 1920 he became a cofounder of the Pen Association, a literary club, and provided its members, many of them talented poets, with encouragement, inspiration, and intel-lectual leadership. He published his volume of Arabic poems *The Processions* in 1923. But far more important was his volume in Eng-lish, *The Prophet* (1923), in which he dis-cussed relations between man and man in a mystical fashion, an approach that won him critical acclaim and riches. The book became a classic and kept selling long after Jibran was dead. His next two volumes in English, *Sand and Foam* (1926) and *Jesus, the Son of Man* (1928), were also well received. He published *The Earth Gods* just before he died, and *The Wanderer* and *The Garden of the Prophet* appeared posthumously.

Jibril, Ahmad (1937–): *Palestinian leader*
Born of a Palestinian father and a Syrian mother in Yazour, a village near Jaffa [*qv*], Jibril and his family fled to Syria during the Palestine War (1948–49) [*qv*]. After fin-ishing his education, he joined the Syrian army and rose to be captain.

In the early 1960s he quit the army to participate in Palestinian politics, founding the Palestine Liberation Front. It was one of the constituents of the Popular Front for the Liberation of Palestine (PFLP) [*qv*], formed some months after the Arab defeat in the June 1967 Arab-Israeli War [*qv*]. Soon after the first clandestine PFLP congress in August 1968, Jibril and his supporters split to form the PFLP-General Command (PFLP-GC) [*qv*], which joined the Palestine Liberation Organization (PLO) [*qv*].

His small, tightly controlled faction car-ried out several operations against Israel and Israeli targets, including planting a bomb aboard a Swissair flight from Zurich to Tel Aviv [*qv*] in February 1970, which exploded and killed forty-seven passengers and crew. Four years later, in a failed attempt to exchange their Israeli hostages, taken in northern Israel, for 100 Palestinian prisoners, three members of Jibril's party and eighteen Israelis were killed.

Following the expulsion of the PLO from

Beirut in 1982, Jibril made Damascus [qv] the base of his group. He joined an anti-Yasser Arafat [qv] rebellion masterminded by Syrian President Hafiz Assad [qv]. In May 1985 Israel released 1,150 Palestinian prisoners in exchange for three Israeli soldiers whom Jibril's group had captured during the 1982 Israeli invasion of Lebanon [qv]. In late November 1987 a hang glider raid from southern Lebanon by three PFLP-GC activists on an Israeli military outpost, which resulted in six Israeli deaths, proved pivotal in sparking the Palestinian intifada [qv] on 9 December.

Though Jibril's party was secular, socialist, and nationalist, in the late 1980s he started to form links with Iran and visited Tehran [qv] periodically. His party propaganda began referring to the "Arab and Islamic people" and the "Arab and Islamic region." Despite threatening statements before and during the 1990–91 Kuwait crisis following Iraq's invasion of Kuwait, Jibril's group did not carry out any terrorist acts. He rejected the Israeli-PLO Accord [qv] of September 1993, primarily because the PLO failed to obtain Israeli agreement on the Palestinians' right to self-determination and the Palestinian refugees' right to return home. His continued opposition to the peace process led to a split in his party in 1999.

Jiddah: *Administrative capital of Saudi Arabia* Pop. 2,746,000 (2003, est.). The reputed site of the tomb of Eve, Jiddah/Jedda means "female ancestor." Situated on a narrow coastal plain, it has been an important port on the Red Sea since the pre-Islamic era. After the rise of Islam [qv], Caliph Othman (r. 644–56) designated it as the port for Muslims undertaking a *hajj* [qv] to Mecca [qv] by sea. This contributed to its prosperity. It also developed as a transit point for maritime trade between India and the Mediterranean region via Egypt. However, this settlement was to the south of present-day Jiddah.

When the Ottoman Turks conquered Egypt in 1517, Jiddah came under their authority. Sultan Muhammad IV (r. 1648–87) made it the official port of Mecca, a position until then held by the older port to the south. The opening of the Suez Canal [qv] in 1869 ended the transshipping role of Jiddah, but boosted the hajj travel, which became the lifeline of the city, now part of Hijaz [qv] province.

During the First World War, after the provincial governor, Sharif Hussein ibn Ali al Hashem, had led the Arab revolt against the Ottomans in 1916, Jiddah's Ottoman garrison surrendered to the British. Following the defeat of Sharif Hussein by Abdul Aziz al Saud [qv] in 1924, Jiddah passed to the victor. It was here in 1927 that Britain signed a treaty with Abdul Aziz al Saud, recognizing him as King of Hijaz and Najd [qv] and its Dependencies. Since then it has been the headquarters of the kingdom's foreign ministry and the site of foreign diplomatic missions.

As a Wahhabi [qv], King Abdul Aziz regarded the tomb of Eve as an idolatrous shrine and destroyed it in 1928.

For the next two decades Jiddah remained a walled settlement. Then, rid of its walls in 1947, and funded by the fast-rising oil revenue of Saudi Arabia, it expanded rapidly. It acquired new apartment blocks, hotels, banks, private and public offices, a university, and such industries as cement, food processing, oil refining, pottery, and steel rolling.

A new dock complex, named after King Faisal [*qv*], opened in 1973 to serve the growing commercial and pilgrimage traffic. In 1980 came the King Abdul Aziz International Airport, occupying an area of 40 sq. miles/104 sq. km. Both of these facilities are needed to serve the more than one million foreign Muslims who undertake the hajj annually. From 1932 to 1982, Jiddah was the kingdom's diplomatic capital.

It is the most cosmopolitan Saudi city, its residents coming not only from other parts of the Arab world, but also Asia, Africa, and Europe, and it is the headquarters of the Islamic Conference Organization [*qv*] as well as the World Muslim League [*qv*].

jihad *(Arabic: effort):* Full title in Arabic: jihad *fi sabil Allah* (Striving in the way of God). Literally, jihad means effort or struggle, which is waged in various forms—internal and external—and degrees, war being the most extreme. In its internal form, jihad is the inner struggle of moral discipline and commitment to Islam [*qv*] by a Muslim [*qv*]. However, it is jihad's external form that has interested most chroniclers.

Historically the term "jihad" has been used to describe an armed struggle by Muslims against unbelievers in their mission to advance Islam or counter danger to it. Among the several verses in the Quran [*qv*] that enjoin religious war on believers is (9:5): "Then, when the sacred months are away, / slay the idolaters wherever you find them, / and take them, and confine them, and lie in wait/for them at every place of ambush. But if they / repent, and perform the prayer, and pay the alms, then / let them go their way."

According to the *sunna* [*qv*], jihad is to be launched only after unbelievers have rejected the offer to Muslims or *dhimmis* [*qv*]. When a Muslim community is ruled by non-Muslims, a jihad can be justified only if Islam is suppressed. Kharijis [*qv*], and therefore Ibadhis [*qv*], regard jihad as the sixth pillar of Islam [*qv*]. Later, sufi [*qv*] thinkers distinguished between the "greater jihad," a struggle against one's base instincts, and the "lesser jihad," a struggle against unbelievers.

al Jihad al Islami: *See* Al Jihad al Islami.

Joint Defense and Economic Cooperation Treaty (Arab League, 1950): Following the failure of their military action against the newly founded Israel in the Palestine War (1948–49) [*qv*], the seven members of the Arab League [*qv*] signed a Joint Defense and Economic Cooperation Treaty (JDECT), aimed primarily at Israel, and ratified it in 1950. An early decision taken under this treaty was the League's resolution in November 1950 to continue the wartime blockade of Israel on the premise that the truce of January 1949 did not amount to a state of peace. When a new member was admitted to the League, it was required to join the JDECT.

In the Arab-Israeli Wars of 1967 [*qv*] (when the League had thirteen members) and 1973 [*qv*] (when the League had nineteen members), the combatant Arab states called for and received military aid from fellow members under the JDECT. But when in May 1982, during the Iran-Iraq War [*qv*], Iraq invoked the pact to secure military aid from members, it failed. This happened partly because the enemy was not Israel [*qv*], partly because Iraq [*qv*] had started the war, and partly because such leading Arab League members as Syria [*qv*] and Libya had sided with Iran.

Jordan:

Official name: Hashemite Kingdom of Jordan

Capital: Amman [*qv*]

Area: 34,442 sq. miles/89,206 sq. km

Population: 5,300,000 (2002, est.)

Gross domestic product: $7.8 billion (2000, est.)

National currency: Jordanian Dinar (JD); JD 1 = US$1.41 = £0.99 = EUR 1.59 (2001)

Form of government: monarchy

Official language: Arabic [*qv*]

Official religion: Islam [*qv*]

Administrative regions: Jordan is divided into eight governorates (provinces).

Constitution: The Hashemite Kingdom of Jordan is an independent sovereign state. Its governmental form is monarchical, with a parliament. The present constitution, approved by King Talal ibn Abdullah al Hashem [*qv*], has been in force since 1952. Executive power rests with the king, who exercises it through ministers. He appoints, dismisses, or accepts the resignation of the prime minister; and on his recommendation other ministers are appointed or dismissed, or their resignation accepted. He also appoints the members and president of the Senate, the upper house of parliament. The cabinet manages all state affairs. If the parliament's lower chamber, the House of Representatives, withdraws its confidence from the cabinet or any minister, the latter must resign. The king is the supreme commander of the armed forces.

Ethnic composition (2002): Arab, 98 percent, of which more than half are of Palestinian origin; Armenian, [*qv*] 1 percent; Circassians [*qv*], 1 percent.

Executive authority: Executive authority resides with the king, who exercises it through ministers appointed by him.

High officials:

Head of state: King Abdullah II ibn Hussein al Hashem [*qv*], 1999–

Crown Prince: Prince Hamzeh ibn Hussein al Hashem, 1999–

Prime minister: Ali Abu al Ragheb, 1999–

Speaker of the Senate: Zaid al Rifai, 1997–

Speaker of the House of Representatives: Abdul Hadi al Majali 1997–

History: Following the disintegration of the Ottoman Empire in 1918, Abdullah ibn Hussein al Hashem [*qv*] and his army entered the British-mandated area east of the Jordan River [*qv*] called Transjordan [*qv*], and set up a government in Amman in 1921. Britain agreed to recognize Abdullah's rule if he accepted Britain's mandate over it and Palestine [*qv*]. This he did. In 1923 Transjordan became an autonomous emirate, which agreed to formulate a common foreign policy with London and allowed Britain to station troops on its soil.

When Transjordan acquired independence in May 1946 Abdullah assumed the title of king and renamed the Emirate of Transjordan the Hashemite Kingdom of Jordan. The 1923 treaty was replaced by a new one in 1948. As a result of the Palestine War (1948–49) [*qv*], Jordan occupied 22 percent of Palestine, called the West Bank [*qv*]. West Bankers were given full Jordanian citizenship and equal parliamentary representation with East Bankers. After a general election in 1950, the new parliament declared the East Bank [*qv*] and West Bank united in the Hashemite Kingdom of Jordan.

Following the assassination of King Abdullah in 1951, his son Talal [qv] ascended the throne. Due to mental illness Talal abdicated the next year in favor of his son Hussein ibn Talal. His poll rigging in the 1954 general election was met by massive protest. Following a fair and free election in 1956, a national-leftist government under Suleiman Nabulsi [qv] came to power. It abrogated the 1948 treaty with Britain, and King Hussein acquiesced. But after he had crushed an incipient coup by his newly appointed chief of staff in 1957, he dismissed the Nabulsi government and dissolved parliament and all political parties. Though parliament was revived in 1963, political parties remained banned.

In the charged atmosphere during the buildup to the June 1967 Arab-Israeli War [qv], Jordan joined the Egyptian-Syrian defense treaty. After losing the West Bank to Israel, Jordan ended up with 250,000 refugees from the territory. Growing militancy among them and the Palestinians who had settled earlier in Jordan led to fighting between the Palestinian commandos and the Jordanian army in September 1970, which the latter won. Jordan stayed out of the October 1973 Arab-Israeli War [qv].

When the Arab League summit in October–November 1974 recognized the Palestine Liberation Organization (PLO) [qv] as the sole and legitimate representative of the Palestinian people, Jordan reluctantly accepted the resolution. Dismissing the West Bank half of the House of Representatives (HoR), King Hussein suspended it. Jordan refused to join the peace process begun by

the Camp David Accords [qv] in 1978. It sided with Iraq [qv] in the Iran-Iraq War (1980–88) [qv], thus accelerating its economic integration with Iraq. In 1984 King Hussein revived the HoR. His agreement with PLO Chairman Yasser Arafat [qv] in 1985 on a joint approach to a Middle East peace settlement was rejected by the Palestine National Council [qv] two years later. A free and fair election in 1989 resulted in an HoR with 40 percent Islamist membership.

During the Kuwait crisis following Iraq's invasion of Kuwait in August 1990, Jordan tried to find an Arab solution, but failed. Its stance during the Second Gulf War [qv] was pro-Iraq. Later it tried to repair the damage done to its standing in the West by distancing itself from Iraq. Before the Middle East Peace Conference in Madrid in October 1991, Jordan agreed to a joint Jordanian-Palestinian delegation. Three years later it became the second Arab country to sign a peace treaty with Israel. At the same time, Jordan's economic links with Iraq remained strong, with Baghdad supplying 75,000 barrels of oil per day, half of it free and the rest at a discount. These ties became stronger when Iraq was allowed to purchase food and medicine by selling oil, and it gave large contracts to Jordanian businessmen to supply food and medicine.

Whenever the Israeli-Palestinian talks ran into trouble, King Hussein intervened, successfully. The last time he did so was in October 1998 at the Wye River Plantation near Washington. His successor, King Abdullah II, lacked the seniority and experience of his father to play a mediating role in the Israeli-Palestinian peace process. Indeed the outbreak of the Second Intifada [qv] of the Palestinians in September 2000 created a crisis atmosphere in Jordan. As the host of the Arab summit in March 2001, Abdullah II tried to conciliate Iraq and Kuwait, but failed. At home, he dissolved the HoR in June 2001 and then postponed the parliamentary poll due in November.

Two months earlier, following the attacks on the United States, the George W. Bush administration increased Washington's economic assistance to Jordan with a view to securing the young monarch's active cooperation in its war on terrorism and to wean him away from Iraq. It also gave Jordan free access to the American market.

Legislature: The parliament, called the National Assembly, consists of a fully nominated Senate of thirty, and a popularly elected House of Representatives of eighty, which has a tenure of four years. In case either chamber turns down a bill acceptable to the other, or the monarch withholds his consent, then only a joint session of the two houses can pass it. Following the dissolution of the HoR and political parties in 1957, fresh elections were held in July 1963 and then in April 1967. After dismissing all thirty West Bank deputies, the king suspended the sixty-member House in February 1975. He revived it in January 1984. In July 1988 he dissolved it and formally cut Jordan's legal and administrative links with the West Bank. In November 1989 a fresh poll was held to the HoR, confined to the East Bank. After the legalization of political parties in September 1992, nine parties were licensed. In November 1993, in the first multiparty election since October 1956, the majority of seats went to independents, with the Islamic Action Front

[qv] securing sixteen seats, being the only party to win more than one seat. In the 1997 poll, its share dropped to eight seats, with the progovernment independents winning sixty.

Religious composition (2002): Muslim [qv], 94 percent, of whom Sunni [qv], 90 percent; Shia [qv], 2 percent; Druze 1 percent [qv]; Christian [qv], 5 percent.

Jordan River: Rising primarily at the foot of Mount Hermon in Syria and secondarily in Mount Anti-Lebanon, the Jordan is fed by the Hasbani, Banias, and Dan Rivers, and flows 220 miles/355 km into the Dead Sea. Its northern half delineates parts of the Jordanian-Israeli border and the Syrian–Israeli border. Its southern half lies in Jordan. Often mentioned in the Bible [qv], it was the scene of the baptism of Jesus Christ.

Jordanian Civil War (1970–71): Involving the Jordanian military and an alliance of Palestinian guerrillas and radical Jordanians, the civil conflict lasted from 15 to 25 September 1970. It resulted in a Jordanian victory and came to be known among Palestinians as Black September. With the increased presence of armed Palestinians in Jordan, there were periodic clashes between them and the 55,000-strong Jordanian military in the spring of 1970.

The truce between them, brokered by the Arab League [qv] in June, became tenuous when King Hussein ibn Talal [qv] accepted the (U.S.) Rogers Peace Plan [qv] in early August. Since his action contradicted the stance adopted by the fourth Arab League summit [qv] in Khartoum on peace with Israel, relations between him and the Palestine Liberation Organization (PLO) [qv] soured. Tension heightened following the blowing up of three Western airliners at an airfield near Amman [qv] by the Popular Front for the Liberation of Palestine (PFLP) [qv] on 12 September, after Israel had refused to release its Palestinian prisoners.

As the United States moved its warships and warplanes to the region, Hussein formed a military cabinet on 15 September. Fighting immediately erupted between the two sides in Amman and northern Jordan. On 19 September the tank units of the Syrian-based Palestine Liberation Army (PLA) [qv] crossed into the north of Jordan and captured Irbid. Hussein requested U.S. intervention, but Washington opted for a joint U.S.-Israel operation. However, the Jordanian army checked the Palestinian tank advance.

Assured of U.S. and Israeli backing, Hussein deployed his air force against the Palestinians in the Irbid area. With the Syrian air force under Gen. Hafiz Assad [qv] refusing to intervene on their behalf, the Palestinian armored units withdrew to Syria. A truce, mediated by the Arab League, went into force on 25 September.

Since Palestinian militia units were often posted inside refugee camps and used them as their bases, there was much fighting in the camps, and high casualties. About 4,000 Palestinians died. The United States airlifted arms to Jordan and increased its financial aid. Thus fortified, Hussein kept up pressure on the Palestinian commandos and finally expelled them in July 1971 after destroying the last centers of resistance in the hills near Ajloun.

Jordanian-Israeli Peace Treaty (1994): King Hussein ibn Talal [qv] of Jordan and Israeli Premier Yitzhak Rabin [qv] signed a peace treaty between the two countries on 26 October 1994 at a site in the Araba Valley along the Jordanian-Israeli border about 30 miles/48 km north of the Gulf of Aqaba. It was witnessed by U.S. President Bill Clinton. The treaty fixed the Israeli-Jordanian border along the lines demarcated at the time of the British mandate in 1922. Israel conceded Jordanian sovereignty over the 147 sq. miles/381 sq. km occupied by it, while Jordan leased 116 sq. miles/300 sq. km of it to Israel.

Jordan agreed that the Palestinian refugees would be settled where they were in Jordan in return for aid from the United States, i.e., the right of the Palestinian refugees to return home was forfeited. The treaty recognized Jordan's custodianship of the Muslim [qv] holy places in East Jerusalem [qv], thus undermining the Palestinian position. The treaty was condemned by Syria, Lebanon, the Palestine Liberation Organization (PLO) [qv], and Hamas [qv]— and ordinary Palestinians in Gaza [qv], the West Bank [qv], and East Jerusalem, who staged a protest strike.

Judaism and Jews: The oldest of major monotheistic creeds, Judaism is a compendium of law, tradition, and doctrine dating back to the Prophet Abraham in ca. 1900/1800 B.C. He was directed by God to leave his native Harran in northern Mesopotamia for Canaan (present-day Israel, Palestine, and southern Lebanon) with a solemn promise, the Covenant, that he would become the father of great nations there. His grandson Jacob received the name Israel and had twelve sons, from whom arose the twelve tribes of Israel. They migrated to Egypt, where they were enslaved in 1700 B.C., a condition they endured until God renewed his Covenant to Abraham by calling on Moses in the mid-thirteenth century B.C. to lead the descendants of Israel (the Israelites) out of Egypt, and giving them the Law through Moses on Mount Sinai during their forty years of wandering in the Sinai Peninsula [qv]. This provided a strong ethical foundation to the creed, with its stress on virtuous action.

The Israelites began to conquer and settle Canaan, but they were not yet a nation, only a confederation of tribes led by personages called Judges, such as Gideon and Samson. They set up altars and sanctuaries in Canaan, with the Ark of the Covenant deposited at Shiloh. These tribes were brought together under Saul (r. ca. 1030–10 B.C.), who established the Kingdom of Israel. His successor, David, son of Jesse (r. ca. 1010–970 B.C.) led the Israelite nation in obedience to God and brought the Ark of the Covenant to Jerusalem [qv] as a shrine for the God of Israel. His son Solomon (r. ca. 970–30 B.C.) built the First Temple.

The opposition to the evolution of a dynastic rule led to the northern tribes—who called their domain Israel—to break with the southern part, ruled by David's descendants and called Judah, with Jerusalem as its capital.

During the eighth century B.C., Prophet Amos declared that violations of the moral-ethical code of the Covenant would bring the wrath of God upon the Israelites.

In 722 B.C. Israel fell to Assyria, and many Israelites were expelled. Judah continued to exist, but from 605 B.C. the people of Judah, called Jews [qv], were taken into exile by the Babylonians. In 586 B.C. Jerusalem was destroyed and the First Temple razed, and the Israelites/Jews were exiled. They were allowed to return to Jerusalem in 538 B.C. by Persian King Cyrus the Great (600–529 B.C.). The Second Temple was completed by 515 B.C.

Though the new Covenant of God, promising a kingdom under a descendant of King David, was not fulfilled, Persian King Artaxerxes (r. 464–24 B.C.) declared the Torah [qv] (Written Law) to be the law for the Jews. This in turn led to the Oral Law. The conquest of the region by Alexander the Great (r. 336–23 B.C.) in 333 B.C. marked the emergence of Hellenistic Judaism. The banning of Judaism by the Greek ruler Antiochus IV (r. 175–63 B.C.) in 168 B.C. resulted in a Jewish revolt in 166 B.C., led by Judas Maccabaeus of the Hasmonaean family. He succeeded in gaining religious freedom for Jews three years later, but not political freedom. In his attempt to secure the latter he was killed in 160 B.C., giving rise to the concept of martyrdom [qv] in monotheistic religions.

The Jewish commonwealth was revived under Jonathan in 152 B.C. However, the Hellenization of Judaism continued, and the Torah, written originally in Hebrew [qv], was translated into Greek. Later the Jewish community split into Sadducees—often rich, conservative and ecclesiastical—who believed in the divinity of the Written Law, and Pharisees, often poor, progressive and lay, who espoused the Oral Law.

In 63 B.C. the Roman general Pompey captured the region, named it Judea (derivative of Judah) and incorporated it into the Roman Empire. Various attempts by Jews to set up an independent Jewish state failed.

Christianity [*qv*] emerged intially as a sect within Judaism. Restrictive decrees from Rome led to a Jewish revolt in A.D. 66–70, during which the Second Temple was destroyed.

With Jews now turning inward, their leadership increasingly came under eminent rabbis *(Hebrew: my teachers)*, beginning with Judah HaNasi (A.D. 175–220), who concentrated on developing the Talmud [*qv*]. During the Middle Ages (476–1492) two branches of Jewish culture evolved: Sephardim [*qv*] and Ashkenazim [*qv*]. Attempts to conciliate them, initiated in France, were thwarted when Jews were expelled from the country in 1306. German Jews underwent enlightenment, *haskala*, in the eighteenth century. From this emerged a religious reform of doctrine and worship, especially among the Jews of Germany and France. The reform among German Jews became institutionalized as Reform Judaism [*qv*] in the 1840s. This in turn spawned Conservative Judaism [*qv*], also in Germany. Most Jews, unaffected by either movement, remained Orthodox [*qv*] in their religious beliefs and practices. Modern secular Jewish thinkers tend to reinterpret Judaism as a historical process, centered on ethics and morals, or as religious nationalism. In 1998 there were 13.5 million Jews worldwide, with a little over a third living in Israel. Of the 8.6 million Jews in the Diaspora [*qv*], two-thirds lived in America. Elsewhere, France, with 600,000, had the largest number, followed by Russia, with 400,000.

Judaism, Conservative: *see* Conservative Judaism.

Judaism, Orthodox: *see* Orthodox Judaism.

Judaism, Reform: *see* Reform Judaism.

Judea: Judea was the name given by the Romans to the vassal kingdom in Palestine [*qv*], which came under their rule in 63 B.C. This lasted until A.D. 135, when it was renamed Palestina (Prima and Secunda). The term Judea was revived by Israel's right-wing government in 1977.

Judeo-Spanish language: *see* Ladino language.

Julian calendar: Introduced by Roman Emperor Julius Caesar (r. 59–44 B.C.) in 46 B.C. *see* Christian calendars.

Jumblat, Kamal (1917–77): *Lebanese politician* Born into a notable Druze [*qv*] family in Mukhtara village, Jumblat studied law and sociology at universities in Beirut [*qv*] and Paris. He was elected to parliament in 1947. The next year he became head of his clan, and in 1949 he established the Progressive Socialist Party [*qv*]. Though predominantly Druze, the party had Sunni [*qv*], Shia [*qv*], and Christian [*qv*] members, and it advocated abolition of the country's confessionalist system. Earlier, by marrying a woman from the competing Arsalan clan, he had softened the traditional rivalry between the Jumblats and the Arsalans.

Starting out as a supporter of Bishara Khouri [*qv*], Jumblat turned against him when he was accused of corruption in the summer of 1952. In alliance with Camille Chamoun [*qv*], Jumblat established the Socialist National Front [*qv*], and Chamoun succeeded Khouri after his resignation in September 1952. When Chamoun abandoned the Arab nationalist program upon which he had been elected president, Jumblat led an opposition alliance against him in May 1958. The resulting Lebanese Civil War [*qv*] lasted until the end of July. Jumblat was named education minister (1960–61) and interior minister (1961–63).

Jumblat's feudal background enabled him to exercise a strong influence over Druzes, whereas his leftist, Arab nationalist [qv] views made him popular with urban, mainstream Sunnis. A consistent opponent of confessionalism [qv], he provided a common framework to the leftist Lebanese groups and the Palestinian factions in the form of the National and Progressive Front in 1969. His legalization (when interior minister) of such transnational parties as the Communists [qv] and Baathists [qv] in 1970 enabled the Front to enlarge first in 1972 and then again in 1975 and emerge as the Lebanese National Movement (LNM) [qv], with Jumblat as its leader.

In the Lebanese Civil War [qv], which erupted in April 1975, Jumblat led the LNM against its opponent—the rightist Maronite coalition called the Lebanese Front [qv]. Jumblat formed an alliance with the Palestine Liberation Organization (PLO) [qv]. It was friendly with Syria. But when the LNM-PLO alliance captured two-thirds of Lebanon by April 1976, Syrian President Hafiz Assad [qv] revised his stance, fearing that total victory by the radical LNM-PLO alliance would result in Israeli military intervention and destabilization of the whole region, including Syria. In June Syria attacked LNM-PLO positions and spared the Lebanese Front a humiliating defeat.

Following the election of Elias Sarkis [qv], a Syrian nominee, as president in September, and a cease-fire in the civil war two months later, Jumblat accepted Sarkis as president. But as a Lebanese patriot, committed to maintaining a multiparty system in Lebanon, Jumblat resented the role of Assad, the authoritarian ruler of Syria, as the sole power broker in Beirut. In early 1977, when Jumblat attacked Assad's rule in Syria itself, he became the Syrian leader's number one enemy. Jumblat was assassinated in March 1977.

An intellectual of high caliber, Jumblat taught history of economic thought at Beirut University for several years and authored a few books on Lebanese politics.

Jumblat, Walid (1949–): *Lebanese politician* Born into a notable Druze [qv] family in Mukhtara village, Jumblat went to the American University in Beirut [qv] and then to a university in Paris. He was active with the militia of the Progressive Socialist Party (PSP) [qv]. Following the assassination of his father, Kamal [qv], in March 1977, Jumblat succeeded him as head of his clan, of the PSP, and of the Lebanese National Movement (LNM) [qv]. He moderated the LNM's stress on ending confessionalism and tried to work in cooperation with Syria. He condemned the election of Bashir Gemayel [qv] as president in August 1982.

After the initialing of a peace treaty between Israel and Lebanon [qv] in May 1983, Jumblat joined an alliance that had formed to overturn it. Following the withdrawal of the Israelis from the Shouf region in September 1983, his Druze militia expelled the Maronite [qv] forces who had arrived there on the coattails of the Israeli occupiers. In March the Lebanese-Israeli draft treaty was annulled.

Jumblat joined the national government formed under Rashid Karami [qv] as minister of public works. In October he helped form an alliance of six parties opposed to President Amin Gemayel [qv]. He extended

Druze control to the Mediterranean coast and the hills overlooking Beirut [*qv*] and its southeastern suburbs.

In late 1985 Jumblat was one of the three militia leaders who signed the "National Agreement to Solve the Lebanese Crisis," a detailed document outlining political reform and Lebanese-Syrian relations. But the accord was stillborn because the Maronite militia leader, Elie Hobeika, failed to persuade his camp to endorse it. Jumblat had reservations about the Taif Accord [*qv*], signed in September 1989, which he saw as giving too many concessions to the Maronites, but he suppressed his misgivings at Syria's behest. Two months later Jumblat was named minister of public works in the government of Salim Hoss [*qv*].

Following the end of the Lebanese Civil War [*qv*] in October 1990, when a national reconciliation government was formed under Omar Karami, Jumblat was made a minister without portfolio, and the following June he was nominated to the expanded parliament. His party contested the parliamentary elections in September 1992. Elected to parliament, he was appointed minister of displaced persons. In the 1996 poll his party won ten seats. In 1998 he and his party deputies abstained from voting for Emile Lahoud [*qv*], the choice of Syria, for president. Once Israel had withdrawn its troops unconditionally from south Lebanon in May 2000, Jumblat saw no rationale for Syria to deploy its troops in Lebanon. In the run-up to the general election three months later, he joined the Maronite leaders in demanding the withdrawal of the Syrian troops from Lebanon.

Jumblat clan: Also spelled Junblat. Of Kurdish [*qv*] origin, the Jumblats claim lineage from Salah al Din Ayubi (Saladin), who defeated the Crusaders in 1187. At first settled in the Aleppo [*qv*] region, they migrated to Lebanon on the invitation of the Druze [*qv*] ruler Fakhr al Din Maan (d. 1633), who was based in the Shouf region. They assimilated themselves into the local Druze community and became an important clan, based in Mukhtara village.

When power passed from the Maans to the Shehabis at the turn of the eighteenth century, the Jumblats struggled against the Shehabis. With the ousting of the Shehabis in 1840, the Jumblats emerged as one of the leading clans, competing with the Arsalan and Yazbaki clans for primacy among the Druzes.

Following the end of the Ottoman Empire in Lebanon in 1918, the successor French mandate tried to woo ethnic and religious minorities such as the Druzes, thus underwriting the continued importance of the Jumblats. After the assassination of Fuad Jumblat in 1922, power passed to his widow, Nazira. Their son, Kamal [*qv*], became an eminent Lebanese politician.

June 1967 Arab-Israeli War: *see* Arab-Israeli War III (1967).

K

Kaaba: (lit., cube) *Islamic shrine* The holiest shrine of Islam, the Kaaba, containing the sacred Black Stone, stands at the center of the Grand Mosque of Mecca [*qv*]. Built of gray stone, it is a 50 ft./15 meter high box-like structure, 40 ft./12 meters by 35 ft./10.5 meters, which rests on a marble base 1 ft./30 centimeters thick. Apart from its entrance door and a gilt water spout, it is always covered with a black cloth, which is changed annually after the *hajj* [*qv*].

Entry to the marble-floored interior is by a door in the northeastern wall. In the eastern corner near the door, the holy Black Stone is built into the wall 5 ft./1.5 meters above the ground. It consists of three large pieces of stone and several small ones, which are surrounded by a ring of stone held together by a silver band. Either solidified basaltic lava or basalt, the Black Stone has been worn smooth by touching and kissing over the centuries.

Opposite the northwest wall of the Kaaba is a semicircular white marble wall 3 ft./1 meter high, about 6 ft./2 meters from the north and west corners of the Kaaba. The space between the Kaaba and this wall is believed to contain the graves of Ismail/Ishmael and his mother, Hagar, the slave wife of Abraham. Nearby is a trough where legend has it that Ibrahim/Abraham and Ismail/Ishamael mixed the mortar to build the Kaaba.

Within two years of his migration from Mecca to Medina [*qv*] in A.D. 622, after failing to conciliate the local Jewish tribes, the Prophet Muhammad instructed that during prayer, instead of turning to Jerusalem [*qv*], believers should turn to the Kaaba in Mecca.

kabbala *(Hebrew: receiving or accepting [tradition]): see* mysticism in Judaism.

Kach *(Hebrew: Thus): Israeli political party*
The Kach was established in 1976 by Rabbi Meir Kahane [*qv*], an American Jew who settled in Israel [*qv*] in 1971. The group, known widely by its symbol of a clenched fist, was a Jewish fundamentalist [*qv*] party.

That is, it regarded Jews to be an exclusivist community, opposed to social or sexual intercourse with non-Jews, and insisted that only Jews had the right to live in the biblical Land of Israel. It therefore advocated expulsion of Arabs [*qv*] from the West Bank [*qv*] and the Gaza Strip [*qv*] as well as from Israel. Its members harassed Arabs, assaulted them in their homes, and smashed cars and shop windows in Arab districts.

In the 1984 Knesset [*qv*] elections, the Kach won 25,000 votes and Kahane became a deputy. The parliament then passed a law barring parties with a racist policy from contesting elections. When in 1988 the high court upheld the legislation and declared the Kach racist, it was prevented from participating in the general election that year. The opinion polls had showed its popular support to be 5 percent, or six deputies. After Kahane's assassination in 1990, his son, Baruch, set up the Kahane Hai *(Hebrew: Kahane Lives)* group. After Yitzhak Rabin's [*qv*] assassination in late 1995, both Kach and Kahane Hai were banned in Israel.

Kahane, Meir (1932–90): *Israeli politician*
Born Martin David Kahane, the son of a rabbi in Brooklyn, New York, Kahane joined the Betar, the youth movement of the Revisionist Zionists [*qv*], as a teenager. He obtained a law degree from New York University and was ordained as an Orthodox [*qv*] rabbi. He combined his religious work with editing the Brooklyn-based *Jewish Press*.

His increasingly militant views led him to establish in the mid-1960s the Jewish Defense League, which resorted to such violent acts as bombing in the cause of defending Jews. He coupled this with harassing the Soviet missions in New York to highlight Moscow's ill-treatment of Jews [*qv*]. During this period, Kahane claimed later, he had worked under cover for the Federal Bureau of Investigation as Michael King, the pseudonym he used to coauthor the book *The Jewish Stake in Vietnam.*

Declaring that the only way a Jew could escape from imbibing gentile values was to live in Israel [*qv*], he migrated there in 1971. After the October 1973 Arab-Israeli War [*qv*] Kahane became vehemently anti-Arab. In 1976 he set up Kach [*qv*]. He advocated the creation of a Jewish state exclusively for Jews so that they would be free from non-Jewish influences.

He became a Knesset [*qv*] deputy when his party, Kach, won 25,000 votes in the 1984 general election. His often controversial behavior in the Knesset led to a number of suspensions. But his popular standing rose, so that on the eve of the 1988 poll his party was poised to win six parliamentary seats. However, it was disqualified from contesting the general election. He was assassinated in New York in 1990.

Karami, Rashid (1921–87): *Lebanese politician; prime minister, 1955–60, 1961–64, 1965–66, 1966–68, 1969–70, 1975–76, and 1984–87* Born into a religious Sunni [*qv*] family in Tripoli [*qv*], Karami secured a law degree from Cairo University. He set up legal practice in Tripoli.

Following the death in 1950 of his father, Abdul Hamid, the chief Islamic judge of the city, Karami became the leader of local Muslims and their representative in parliament. He was named justice minister in 1951, then economy and social affairs minister (1953), and finally prime minister (1955).

Unlike traditional, conservative Sunni

leaders such as Saeb Salam [*qv*], Karami was a radical who supported the pan-Arabism [*qv*] of Egyptian President Gamal Abdul Nasser [*qv*]. In the 1958 Lebanese Civil War [*qv*] he sided with the pan-Arabists who fought the pro-Western President Camille Chamoun [*qv*]. After the conflict he led a national unity government from September 1958 to May 1960. For most of the 1960s he was the premier. During the June 1967 Arab-Israeli War [*qv*], he wanted Lebanon to enter the conflict but was opposed by the Maronite [*qv*] commander of the military, Gen. Emile Boustani.

In the May 1968 election Karami led the Democratic Parliamentary Forum, which emerged slightly behind its rival, the Triple Alliance of Camille Chamoun, Pierre Gemayel [*qv*], and Raymond Edde. However, the subsequent government, led by Abdullah Yafi, fell in December. The new cabinet, headed by Karami, excluded Triple Alliance leaders. In April he resigned when clashes between the Palestinian commandos and the Lebanese army got out of hand. But since no other premier was appointed by President Charles Helou [*qv*], Karami resumed his office after a satisfactory accord had been signed between the Palestine Liberation Organization (PLO) [*qv*] and Lebanon in November in Cairo [*qv*].

After the election of Suleiman Franjieh [*qv*] as president in 1970, Karami failed to win a further mandate for his premiership. Soon after the start of the Lebanese Civil War in April 1975 [*qv*], Franjieh appointed Karami prime minister in the hope that his stature would enable him to end the war. He failed, but continued as premier until December 1976, when the newly elected president, Elias Sarkis [*qv*], turned to Salim Hoss to lead the government. Tripoli, Karami's bastion, became the battleground between Islamists and secular Baathists [*qv*].

Following the Israeli invasion of Lebanon [*qv*] in June 1982, Karami joined the anti-Israeli camp and called for deferment of the presidential poll until after Israel's evacuation. When Amin Gemayel [*qv*] became president in September 1982, Karami joined the anti-Gemayel camp. He opposed the draft Lebanese-Israeli Peace Treaty [*qv*]. Following a reconciliation conference in Lausanne, Switzerland, Karami headed a national reconciliation government in April 1984. He fell out with President Gemayel in early 1986 after the latter refused to endorse the "National Agreement to Solve the Lebanese Crisis," signed by three leading militia leaders. Karami was assassinated in June 1987.

Karbala: *Iraqi city* Also called *Mashhad al Hussein (Arabic: Witness to Hussein)*. Pop. 572,000 (2003, est.). It is the site of the martyrdom [*qv*] of Imam Hussein ibn Ali at the hands of Yazid ibn Muwaiya in A.D. 681, which forms the climax of the Shia [*qv*] festival of Ashura [*qv*]. Over the centuries Karbala emerged as a center of Shia learning, and after the construction of the shrine of Imam Hussein, called the Great Martyr, it became one of the holiest cities of the Shias. It was attacked by Wahhabis [*qv*] in 1802, and Imam Hussein's shrine was stripped of all its embellishments.

Following the seizure of power in Iraq by secular Baathists [*qv*] in 1968, Karbala and its religious establishment came under a shadow. In the aftermath of the Second Gulf War [*qv*], Karbala became an important center of Shia uprising against President

Saddam Hussein [*qv*]. But the government troops quickly crushed the rebellion. After the downfall of the Saddam Hussein regime in 2003, Karbala emerged as a bastion of the Shia religious movement for the establishment of an Islamic State in Iraq.

The city's tourist attractions include the Mosque of Imam Hussein, which is capped with a golden dome.

Kashani, Abol Qasim (1884–1962): *Iranian religious-political leader* Born into a religious Shia [*qv*] family in Tehran [*qv*], Kashani grew up in Najaf [*qv*], Iraq, where he studied Islam [*qv*]. He returned to Iran in 1921 after Iraq had been placed under British mandate. During the interwar years, he emerged as a radical who opposed senior clerics' advice to juniors to stay away from politics. He became popular with second-rank clerics and itinerant mullahs. Kashani was arrested for his anti-British activities after the British had occupied Iran in August 1941 during the Second World War.

On his release after the war, he founded a political party, Mujahedin-e Islam [*qv*]. It demanded abrogation of all secular laws passed by the regime, the application of the Sharia [*qv*], as stated in the 1906–07 constitution, and the reintroduction of the veil for women.

Kashani was sent into forced exile in the northern city of Qazvin until late 1947. His third arrest, followed by banishment to Lebanon, came in the wake of a failed attempt on the life of Muhammad Reza Shah Pahlavi (r. 1941–79) [*qv*] on 4 February 1949. He was permitted to return home after a year.

The issue of the nationalization of the Anglo-Iranian Oil Company dominated the general election held from July 1949 to February 1950, in which Kashani participated. Elected to parliament, he advocated oil nationalization. In March parliament voted for it, and then for the appointment of Muhammad Mussadiq [*qv*] as premier. Kashani was moved as much by anti-imperialism as by a symbiotic relationship between religion and politics in Islam: the two main themes that were later to drive Ayatollah Ruhollah Khomeini [*qv*] and fuel the forces of Islamic revolution [*qv*]. In August Kashani was elected speaker of parliament for a year.

At Kashani's intercession, Mussadiq released twenty-eight members of the Fedaiyian-e Islam [*qv*], including the assassin of a prime minister. But the Kashani-Mussadiq alliance broke down when, in order to survive politically, Mussadiq began to rely increasingly on secular leftists. In January 1953 Kashani opposed Mussadiq's request for an extension of his emergency powers by a year. Following his failure to be reelected speaker of parliament in July, Kashani joined the anti-Mussadiq camp and, whether by design or chance, contributed to his overthrow in August 1953.

He opposed the oil agreement that the shah made with a Western oil consortium a year later. Following a failed Fedaiyin attempt to assassinate Prime Minister Hussein Ala, the government arrested Kashani, releasing him only after he had dissociated himself from the group. After his death his mantle of radical religious opposition to the shah was taken over by Kheomini.

Kataeb Party: *see* Phalange Party.

Katzav, Moshe (1945–): *Israeli president, 2000–* Born in Yazd, Iran [*qv*], Katzav's parents migrated to Israel [*qv*] in 1951, where he grew up in Kiryat Malachi. At twenty-four, while still a student at Hebrew University, Jerusalem [*qv*], he was elected the mayor of his town. In 1977 he was elected to the Knesset [*qv*] as a member of Likud [*qv*] and retained his seat until 2000. He served as the minister of labor and welfare in the National Unity Government of 1984–1988, then as the transportation minister under Yitzhak Shamir [*qv*] 1988–92. In the administration of Benjamin Netanyahu [*qv*] (1996–1999), he was appointed deputy prime minister and minister of tourism. Following Netanyahu's defeat, Katzav became the Knesset Opposition Likud chairman. When President Ezer Weizman [*qv*] resigned in 2000, Katzav faced Shimon Peres [*qv*] as his rival. Katzav won by a 63–57 vote majority and became Israel's eighth president.

Katzir, Ephraim (1916–): *Israeli scientist; president, 1973–78* Born Katchalsky in Kiev, Russia, Katzir arrived in Palestine [*qv*] as a child in 1925. He pursued his under- and postgraduate studies in biochemistry at the Hebrew University in Jerusalem [*qv*] and then taught there. In 1951 he became head of the biophysics department at the Weizmann Institute of Science. Katzir was awarded the Israel Prize for Life Sciences in 1959 and the Rothschild Prize in 1961. He served as chief scientist to the ministry of defense from 1966–68.

Interested in public affairs, he was a member of Mapai [*qv*]. In 1973, as the Labor Party [*qv*] candidate for the presidency, he defeated his rival, Yitzhak Navon [*qv*], by a narrow margin. During his term of office, Israel witnessed the October 1973 Arab-Israeli War [*qv*], the Likud [*qv*] victory in the 1977 election, and President Anwar Sadat's [*qv*] trip to Jerusalem [*qv*].

In 1980 Katzir established the Center for Biotechnology at Tel Aviv University and concentrated on scientific matters.

Khaddam, Abdul Halim (1932–): *Syrian politician; first vice-president, 1984–* Born into a poor Sunni [*qv*] family in Banias, Khaddam obtained a law degree at Damascus University, where he joined the Baath party [*qv*]. He worked as a lawyer and schoolteacher in the capital before entering civil service as a provincial governor under the Baathist regime from 1963—first in Hama [*qv*], then Qunaitra, and finally Damascus [*qv*].

A friend of Hafiz Assad [*qv*] since their senior school days (1949–51), Khaddam's career advanced in line with Assad's. In May 1969, after Assad had made his first, partly successful move to acquire supreme power, Khaddam was promoted to minister of economics and foreign trade. Once Assad had assumed full authority in late 1970, Khaddam became foreign minister and deputy premier.

Over time he established himself as a brilliant executor of Assad's foreign policies. Assad put him in charge of implementing Syria's policy in Lebanon, especially after the outbreak of the Lebanese Civil War [*qv*] there in April 1975. Khaddam helped to assemble a Committee for National Dialogue in September, which secured a month-long truce. Later he was the moving spirit behind the first and second Lebanese National Reconciliation Conferences in Switzerland (November 1983 and March 1984). In May 1984 Assad appointed Khaddam as one of the three vice presidents,

with special responsibility for Lebanese and foreign affairs.

Two months later Khaddam narrowly escaped death from a car bomb. He was the main force behind the forging of the Taif Accord [*qv*] in October 1989. His moment of glory came a year later when the Lebanese Civil War ended on Syria's terms.

He was confirmed in his post in 2000 by President Bashar Assad [*qv*].

Khalaf, Salah (1932–91): *Palestinian leader* Born into a middle-class household in Jaffa [*qv*], Khalaf and his family became refugees in al Bureij camp in the Gaza Strip [*qv*] in 1948. After graduating from a teacher training college in Cairo [*qv*], he worked as a teacher in the Gaza Strip, then under Egyptian administration. Spotted in 1954 by the Egyptian army as someone with leadership potential, he was given advanced military training. During a visit to Cairo he met Yasser Arafat [*qv*], then leader of the local Palestinian Student Federation. During the 1956 Suez War [*qv*], when Gaza fell to the Israelis, Khalaf left the territory. Later he enrolled as a student in Stuttgart, Germany.

In March 1959 Arafat, then working in Kuwait [*qv*], secured him an entry permit for Kuwait. That summer, together with Arafat and Khalil Wazir [*qv*], he became a cofounder of Fatah [*qv*]. Following his involvement in an attack on the Israeli National Water Carrier at Beit Netopha on 1 January 1965, launched from the Ein Hilwa Palestinian camp in southern Lebanon, Khalaf was arrested along with Arafat and jailed for two months. In prison they decided to adopt noms de guerre, Khalaf choosing Abu Iyad.

Helped by the Baathist [*qv*] government in Syria, Khalaf began to recruit for Fatah in Gaza and Jordan. In 1969 Khalaf and other Fatah leaders assumed control of the Palestine Liberation Organization (PLO). During the 1970s Khalaf emerged as a member of a triumvirate that dominated both Fatah and the PLO, his colleagues being Arafat and Wazir. With Arafat somewhere in the middle, Khalaf balanced the rightist tendencies of Wazir. During the June 1982 Israeli invasion of Lebanon [*qv*], as head of Fatah's security apparatus the defense of West Beirut fell mainly upon Khalaf.

Following the banishment of the PLO from Beirut [*qv*] to Tunis, and other setbacks that followed in the mid-1980s, Khalaf mellowed. In November 1988 he endorsed the resolution of the Palestine National Council (PNC) [*qv*] to abandon violence and accept peaceful coexistence with Israel, along with a Palestinian state to be established on the West Bank and Gaza. This, and the victory of the Fatah forces over the Abu Nidal [*qv*] group in the southern Lebanese Palestinian camps in mid-1990, turned Khalaf into a hate figure among militant Palestinian circles. He was assassinated in January 1991 at the PLO headquarters in Tunis by his bodyguard, described by PLO sources as Abu Nidal's agent.

Khalid ibn Abdul Aziz al Saud (1912–82): *King of Saudi Arabia, 1975–82* Born in Riyadh to Ibn Saud [*qv*] and Jawhara bint Musaid al Jiluwi, Khalid learned the Quran [*qv*] as a boy—as well as riding, tracking, and marksmanship. He then had his apprenticeship in politics, attending the daily assembly of his father. Khalid helped his father to suppress the Ikhwan [*qv*] rebellion

in 1929. After the establishment of Saudi Arabia three years later, he carried out royal missions in Germany and Britain. In 1943 Khalid and his elder brother, Faisal ibn Abdul Aziz [*qv*], traveled to the United States on an official assignment.

When Faisal was promoted to prime minister in September 1962, he appointed Khalid deputy prime minister. In 1963 Khalid was named commander of the newly formed National Guard [*qv*]. Once King Saud ibn Abdul Aziz [*qv*] had abdicated in late 1964, and Khalid's elder brother, Muhammad ibn Abdul Aziz, being ill, had given up his claim to the throne a few months later, Khalid was named crown prince in March 1965. A decade later he ascended the throne after the assassination of Faisal. He freed 150 political prisoners held by his predecessor.

His cabinet of twenty-five contained fifteen commoners, but retained the crucial foreign, defense, interior, and National Guard ministries with the House of Saud [*qv*]. He delegated authority to Crown Prince Fahd ibn Abdul Aziz [*qv*], partly because Khalid was susceptible to heart attacks. Khalid supported plans to end the civil war in Lebanon [*qv*], and funded the Arab Deterrent Force [*qv*] which was stationed there.

He gave grants to the Palestine Liberation Organization (PLO) and opposed the Camp David Accords [*qv*] of September 1978. He cut off all links with Egypt after it had signed a peace treaty with Israel in March 1979. Convinced that the United States, which was not able to save the Pahlavi dynasty [*qv*] in Iran in early 1979, would be unable to save the House of Saud, Khalid rebuffed U.S.

President James Carter's efforts to persuade him to join the Middle East peace process, inaugurated by the Camp David Accords.

In domestic affairs, along with Muhammad ibn Abdul Aziz and Abdullah ibn Abdul Aziz [qv], Khalid represented the nationalist trend (committed to greater respect for tradition and slower economic development), which was in conflict with the pro-U.S. trend (stressing rapid economic development funded by vast oil revenues) espoused by three Sudairi brothers: Fahd, Sultan ibn Abdul Aziz (defense minister), and Nayif ibn Abdul Aziz (interior minister).

When faced with an armed uprising at the Grand Mosque of Mecca [qv] in November 1979, Khalid prevaricated while Sultan urged rapid, massive action. It was a fortnight before the uprising was crushed, with 117 insurgents dead, followed by the execution of sixty-seven more. Responding to the rise of a revolutionary Islamic regime in Iran, Khalid, a pious Muslim, moved toward stricter enforcement of orthodox Islam and Islamic practices in the kingdom.

Despite open heart surgery in 1978, he suffered a minor coronary attack in early February 1980. A major one in June 1982 killed him.

al Khalifa, Hamad ibn Isa (1950–): *ruler of Bahrain, 1999–* Born in Riffa, al Khalifa was educated in Bahrain [qv]. On completing his junior secondary schooling in 1964, he was named crown prince. He finished his secondary education in Cambridge, United Kingdom, and then joined Mons Officer Cadet School in Aldershot. After graduating as a cadet in 1968, he returned home to command the newly established Bahrain Defense Force. In 1970, as head of the Defense Directorate, he became a member of the twelve-member advisory Council of State. On the eve of Bahraini independence in 1971, al Khalifa became the country's defense minister, a position he held until his elevation to ruler. In 1972 he enrolled at the U.S. Army Command and Staff College at Fort Leavenworth, Kansas, and graduated in the following year.

Though as deputy head of the al Khalifa Family Council he had much say in the running of the emirate, it was only after he ascended the throne in 1999 that he could implement the long overdue political reform. Al Khalifa immediately reshuffled the cabinet and freed more than 300 political detainees. When the State Security Court sentenced the leading opposition figure, Shaikh Abdul Amir al Jamri, to ten years in jail, al Khalifa pardoned him.

In 2000 when the Supreme National Committee, appointed by al Khalifa, drafted a National Action Charter, recommending a constitutional monarchy and a bicameral parliament, he held a referendum in early 2001. Once the electorate voted for the charter, al Khalifa declared Bahrain to be a constitutional monarchy. He held elections to the forty-member National Assembly in 2002.

al Khalifa, Isa II ibn Salman (1933–99): *ruler of Bahrain, 1961–99* Born in Manama [qv], al Khalifa was named heir apparent at twenty-four. He succeeded his father three years later. He faced increasing agitation by his subjects—including a strike by oil workers in 1965—for political reform. But it was not until January 1970 that he appointed an advisory twelve-member Council of State. As the British prepared to leave in 1971, he transformed it into a cabinet and charged it with framing a constitution. Severe rioting and strikes in March and September 1972 led al Khalifa to concede a forty-two-member constituent assembly, half elected and half nominated, to draft a constitution. It did so in mid-1973 and al Khalifa approved the document, which provided for a National Assembly with a four-year tenure. The elections to the Assembly were held on a limited franchise in December 1973. Al Khalifa dissolved parliament and suspended the constitution in August 1975.

Bahrain, with a Shia [qv] majority, was affected by the Islamic revolution [qv] in Shia-majority Iran. When the Islamic opposition demanded that Bahrain be declared an Islamic republic, al Khalifa, a Sunni [qv], reacted with a heavy hand. In May 1981 al Khalifa took Bahrain into the Gulf Cooperation Council [qv]. In January 1982 his government arrested sixty residents for plotting an Iranian-instigated coup. Al Khalifa sided with Iraq in the Iran–Iraq War (1980–88) [qv]. During the Kuwait crisis (1990–91), he took a firm pro-Kuwaiti line and contributed troops and warplanes to the war against Iraq.

To meet the rising demand for reform, he appointed a thirty-member advisory council in 1993, but kept the 1973 constitution suspended.

al Khalifa, Salman II ibn Hamad (1895–1961): *ruler of Bahrain, 1942–61* Born in Manama [qv], al Khalifa began to acquire administrative experience in his early twenties. He became the head of a department dealing with the properties of minors, and then graduated to the departments overseeing courts. During the Second World War al Khalifa sided with the Allies, and after the conflict he allowed the British navy to use Bahrain's docks and other facilities, later extending this privilege to the United States Middle East Force [qv]. Al Khalifa's close ties with Britain became a point of contention during the 1956 Suez War [qv], when the Anglo-French-Israeli alliance invaded Egypt, and his subjects mounted massive pro-Egyptian demonstrations.

al Khalifa dynasty: *Bahraini ruling dynasty* Following the migration of the al Khalifa clan of the Utaiba tribe of the Anaiza tribal federation [qv] from the Arabian Peninsula [qv] to the offshore islands of Bahrain, in 1783 the clan succeeded in wresting control of the islands from Iran (then Persia). The al Khalifas consolidated their hold by signing a series of treaties with Britain (in 1861, 1880, and 1892), turning Bahrain into a British protectorate.

After Shaikh Isa I ibn Ali was deposed by the British in 1923, his son Hamad (1873–1942) became the ruler. During his rule, oil was discovered in 1932, with output reaching 19,000 barrels a day in 1940. Oil revenue funded expanding public services while the ruler maintained tight control over his subjects, refusing trade union rights to workers despite a strike in the oil industry in 1938.

Khamanei, Ali Husseini (1939–): *Iranian religious-political leader; Leader, 1989* Born into a religious family in Mashhad [qv], Khamanei pursued his theological studies in Najaf [qv], Iraq, and then Qom [qv], where he became a student of Ayatollah Ruhollah Khomeini [qv]. He participated in the June 1963 antigovernment protest. After Khomeini's deportation to Turkey in late 1964, Khamanei returned to Mashhad, where he taught at the local theological college. During the next decade he was arrested six times for his antigovernment activities. His release from jail in 1975 was followed by internal exile in Iranshahr in the distant Baluchistan-Sistan province. This ended during the revolutionary upsurge of 1977–78, and enabled him to return to Mashhad and participate in the movement.

Khamanei was one of Khomeini's first appointees to the Islamic Revolutionary Council (IRC), which assumed supreme power after the Islamic revolution [*qv*]. He was a cofounder of the Islamic Republican Party [*qv*], which became the ruling party. Later the IRC appointed him its representative at the defense ministry, where he headed the political-ideological bureau, which was charged with inculcating service personnel with Islamic ideology and keeping a watchful eye on the officer corps. In 1979 he was elected to the Assembly of Experts [*qv*], which drafted the constitution. Following the death in September of Ayatollah Mahmud Taleqani [*qv*], Khomeini appointed Khamanei, then a *hojatalislam* (a grade lower than ayatollah), as the Friday prayer leader of Tehran [*qv*], a highly prestigious position.

Elected to the Majlis [*qv*] in early 1980, he was active in the IRP's parliamentary wing. In May he became Khomeini's personal representative on the Supreme Defense Council. During his sermon at a Tehran mosque on 27 June 1981, a bomb, hidden in a tape recorder placed near him, exploded, injuring his arm, lungs, and vocal cords. Following the assassination of the IRP's secretary-general, Muhammad Beheshti, the next

day, Khamanei was elected to this office; and following the assassination of President Muhammad Ali Rajai [*qv*] on 30 August, he was chosen as the IRP candidate for the presidency. He gained 95 percent of the votes. He was elected to the Assembly of Experts [*qv*] in 1982. In the summer of 1984 Khamanei toured the Arab countries that were backing Iran [*qv*] in its war with Iraq [*qv*]: Syria [*qv*], Libya, and Algeria.

He won 88.5 percent of the votes in the August 1985 presidential poll. But when he tried to replace his radical prime minister, Hussein Musavi [*qv*], he found his hands tied. He and Musavi belonged to the opposing factions within the IRP and could not reconcile their differences. As a result, Khomeini ordered the dissolution of the IRP in July 1987. A year later, instructed by Khomeini, Khamanei accepted U.N. Security Council Resolution 598 for a cease-fire in the Iran-Iraq War [*qv*].

Khamanei, promoted to ayatollah by Khomeini on his deathbed, became a *mujtahid* [*qv*], a constitutional requirement for the Leader. Following Khomeini's death on 3 June 1989, the hastily assembled Assembly of Experts implemented his deathbed wish by electing Khamanei the Leader by sixty votes to twelve.

While maintaining Khomeini's pattern of periodically issuing radical statements, he encouraged pragmatic President Ali Akbar Hashemi Rafsanjani [*qv*] to liberalize the economy, which had become highly centralized due to the Iran-Iraq War. The newly elected Second Assembly of Experts in 1990 confirmed Khamanei as the Leader for the duration of its tenure. He maintained a hardline stance toward America, which, in his view, became the sole hegemonistic power in the world after the collapse of the Soviet Union in 1991. At home he worked closely with Rafsanjani after his reelection in 1993 to further economic reform.

Khamanei endorsed the result of the 1997 presidential poll unhesitatingly even though it resulted in the defeat of Ali Akbar Nateq Nouri, the favorite of the religious establishment. The crisis caused by student rioting in Tehran in July 1999 brought Khamanei and the reformist President Muhammad Khatami [*qv*] together. They defused it by a combination of firmness, mobilization of popular support for the regime, and placating of the student leaders.

Alarmed by the overconfident euphoria displayed by the reformist camp following its overwhelming success in the first run of the parliamentary poll in March 2000, Khamanei ordered a clamp down of the reformist press through the judiciary on the ground that, if unchecked, the forces unleashed by reformers would replace the Islamic order with a secular one. His nomination of conservatives to the Guardians Council [*qv*] ensured an effective control over the reformist-dominated parliament.

He endorsed the repeat landslide victory of Khatami in the presidential election in 2001. With the United States extending its 1996 Iran-Libya Sanctions Act for another five years in 2001, the chances of Washington-Tehran rapprochement receded, and this suited Khamanei well.

On the other hand, Khamanei's strong condemnation of the Al Qaida in the terrorist attacks on the United States in September 2001 thawed relations between the two countries, which continued as Washington attacked

the Taliban regime in Afghanistan, much detested by Khamanei's government. But when U.S. President George W. Bush included Iran in his so-called Axis of Evil in early 2002, Khamanei and his aides lambasted Washington. Khamanei maintained silence as America ratcheted up pressure on Iraqi President Saddam Hussein [*qv*], whose aggression against Iran in 1980 had not been forgotten totally. But on the eve of the Gulf War III [*qv*] in March 2003 Khamanei warned the U.S. against invading Iraq. After the war he described the American occupation of Iraq as "worse than Saddam's dictatorship."

Khamanei is the author of several books on Islam and history.

Khan, Reza: *see* Pahlavi, Reza Shah.

Kharijis *(Arabic: Seceder; sing. of Khawarij): Islamic sect* During the battle of Siffin on the banks of the Euphrates [*qv*] in July A.D. 657 between Ali ibn Abu Talib and Muawiya ibn Abu Suffan about the succession to the caliphate, Muawiya proposed that he and Ali should settle their differences by referring them to two arbitrators, who would judge the matter according to the Quran [*qv*]. While a majority of Ali's forces accepted the proposal, several hundred protested against establishing a human tribunal above the divine word. They withdrew to a nearby village. Over the months their ranks swelled as more of Ali's soldiers deserted, especially after the arbitrators had ruled against Ali in March A.D. 658. They came to be called Khawarij (pl. of Khariji).

They denounced Ali's claim to the caliphate, declaring that that any pious Muslim was worthy of becoming caliph and did not have to belong either to the household of the Prophet Muhammad or his Quarish tribe. They branded infidel anyone who disagreed with their stance. In July A.D. 658 Ali attacked the Khawarij in their camp at Nahrawan and defeated them. But enough of them survived to continue the Kharaji movement and avenge the deaths of their comrades by Ali's forces. One of them, Abdul Rahman ibn Mujlam al Muradi, fatally stabbed Ali in January A.D. 661. A moderate school of Khawarij, known as Ibadhis [*qv*], is predominant in Oman today.

Khatami, Muhammad (1943–): Born in a religious family in Yazd, his father being a sayyid, a descendant of Prophet Muhammad, he pursued religious education in Qom [*qv*] where he obtained a degree in advanced theology. He then secured degrees in philosophy at Isfahan University and educational sciences at Tehran University. In Tehran [*qv*] he became an active member of the Association of Combatant Clergy [*qv*]. In 1978 he was sent to Hamburg, Germany, to head the Islamic Center that ran a Shia [*qv*] mosque. There he learned English and German. After the revolution he was elected a parliamentary deputy to the First Majlis [*qv*]. Ayatollah Ruhollah Khomeini [*qv*] appointed him head of the state-owned Kayhan Newspapers. In 1982 he became minister of culture and Islamic guidance in the cabinet of Prime Minister Mir Hussein Musavi [*qv*], a position that was confirmed by the two subsequent parliaments. When the conservative-dominated 1992 Majlis objected to his liberal views, he resigned. President Ali Akbar Hashemi Rafsanjani [*qv*] then appointed him an adviser to the presidential office. He also became head of the National Library.

On the polling day, 23 May (2 Khordad in Iranian calendar [*qv*]), 1997, an unprecedented 88 per cent of the 33 million electors participated. Of these, 20 million, or 69 percent of the total, favored Khatami, and only 25 percent Ali Akbar Nateq Nouri, the favorite of the religious establishment. With this the 54-year-old Khatami emerged as the second most powerful man in Iran. Electors preferred him because they wanted the government to tone down its ideological rhetoric and focus more on tackling such problems as inflation, joblessness, drug addiction and pollution in cities. Women and youth voted overwhelmingly for him. He advocated freedom and equality for women within an Islamic context. Khatami's emphasis on the rule of law appealed especially to the modern middle class. Finally, by having the courage to discuss publicly the role of ethnic and religious minorities—Christians [*qv*], Jews [*qv*], Zoroastrians [*qv*], Azeris [*qv*] and Baluchis [*qv*]—he won their vote.

At home, his government accorded greater freedoms to citizens. The crisis caused by the student rioting in Tehran in July 1999 brought Khatami and leader Ali Khamanei [*qv*] together. They defused it by a combination of firmness, mobilization of popular support for their regime and placating of the student leaders. Hopes rose when the reformist camp, headed by the left-of-center Islamic Iranian Participation Front [*qv*], led by Khatami's younger brother, Muhammad Reza, achieved overwhelming success in the first run of the parliamentary poll in March 2000. When Khamanei clamped down on the exuberant reformist press through the judiciary, Khatami did not protest, knowing well that the final authority lay with

Khamanei. Abroad Khatami's government mended its fences with the Gulf monarchies as well as Iraq [*qv*]. Khatami's hosting of the Islamic Conference Organization [*qv*] in December 1997 added to Iran's prestige abroad. His government also normalized relations with leading European nations.

In the June 2001 presidential election, Khatami won 78 percent of the vote on a lower turnout of 67 percent, with his nearest rival getting a mere 16 per cent of the ballots. Khatami was quick to condemn the terrorist attacks on the U.S., and his government was glad to see the downfall of the Taliban regime in Afghanistan with which it nearly went to war in September 1998. Since his administration cooperated actively with Washington to stabilize post-Taliban Afghanistan after America's Afghan Campaign that ended successfully in December 2001, Khatami was surprised and disappointed when President George W. Bush included Iran in his "Axis of Evil" in January 2002.

Given the continued resistance by the conservative judiciary, the pace of political reform at home slowed. At the same time firm oil prices helped Iran's economy. As the U.S. began its military build-up in the Gulf [*qv*] region, Khatami warned against attacking Iraq. And after the Anglo-American forces had occupied Iraq in April 2003, Khatami demanded that they leave the country.

Khatib, Ahmad (1940–): *Kuwaiti politician*
Born into a middle-class family in Kuwait, Khatib studied medicine at the American University of Beirut [*qv*], where he came under the influence of George Habash [*qv*]. Khatib was a cofounder of the Arab Nationalist Movement (ANM) [*qv*], based in Beirut [*qv*].

On his return in 1953 to Kuwait, then a British protectorate, Khatib established the National Cultural Club (NCC) [*qv*] as a front for the ANM to skirt the ban on political parties. The next year, the NCC contested elections to local councils and did well. In the first election to the fifty-member National Assembly in independent Kuwait in 1963, conducted on a limited franchise, four NCC members, including Khatib, and eight sympathizers won. The NCC protested against poll rigging in the 1967 general election, but to no avail.

In the next parliament, elected in 1971, Khatib, leading the nationalist-leftist bloc of six, concentrated as much on foreign affairs as on domestic ones. The October 1973 Arab-Israeli War [*qv*], and especially the use of oil as a diplomatic weapon, boosted the standing of Khatib's group. Though the fourth parliament, elected in 1975, continued to be dominated by the conservative tribal-merchant bloc, the tone of its proceedings became increasingly strident due largely to Khatib's leadership of the radical minority. He condemned the ruler's decision to suspend parliament in September 1976.

After Shaikh Jaber III al Sabah [*qv*] restored parliament, albeit with depleted powers under an amended constitution, in February 1981, he ensured the defeat of opposition candidates. Even Khatib failed to win. Four years later, though, Khatib managed a victory—one among five nationalist-leftists. To the government's chagrin he began to cooperate with the Islamic fundamentalists [*qv*] in parliament. Khatib criticized Shaikh Jaber III when he dissolved the house in July 1986.

Once the Iran-Iraq War [*qv*], in which

Kuwait sided with Iraq, had ended in August 1988, Khatib joined the movement for the restoration of the National Assembly. When the ruler conceded a seventy-five-member National Council (with one-third nominated members) with powers only to make recommendations, protest continued. On the eve of the poll in June 1990, Khatib and many others were arrested for advocating an election boycott.

Following the Iraqi occupation of Kuwait in August 1990, Baghdad tried to co-opt Khatib, but he refused. He went into exile. He returned to Kuwait after the Second Gulf War [*qv*]. In the poll to the restored National Assembly in October 1992, Khatib was elected a deputy.

Khoei, Abol Qasim (1899–1992): *Iraqi Islamic leader* Born into a religious Shia [*qv*] family in Khoy, Iranian Azerbaijan [*qv*], Khoei emigrated with his parents to Najaf [*qv*], Iraq, in 1912. There he pursued his Islamic studies and became an outstanding theological teacher. Settled in Najaf, he rose steadily in the Shia hierarchy, reaching the rank of ayatollah in the mid-1930s. Being of Iranian origin, Khoei built up a substantial following in Iran, where he was represented by his nominees in Qom [*qv*] and Mashhad [*qv*]. Following the death in 1961 of Ayatollah Muhammad Hussein Borujerdi, the seniormost Shia cleric in Iran, Khoei's status rose.

He kept up his teaching and a steady output of books on the Sharia [*qv*], religious biography, and Quranic commentary. He belonged to the quietist school among Shia clergy, who wanted to concentrate on providing succor to the community in its spiritual life and social welfare. Thus he stood apart from Ayatollah Ruhollah Khomeini [*qv*], an Iranian Shia leader who went to live in Najaf in 1965 and wanted clerics to be involved in politics.

On the death in 1970 of Ayatollah Muhsin Hakim, the status of *marja-e taqlid (Arabic: source of emulation)* [*qv*] passed to Khoei, who also acquired the title of grand ayatollah. His followers now spanned all of the Shia world, as did the activities of the al Kheoi Foundation. In the late 1970s he stayed out of the revolutionary movement in Iran. Equally, when Shahbanu Farah, wife of Muhammad Reza Shah Pahlavi (r. 1941–79) [*qv*], during her visit to Najaf in November 1978, called on him to make a conciliatory statement, Khoei refused.

Following his invasion of Iran, President Saddam Hussein [*qv*] sought Khoei's approval for his action, but Khoei maintained a studied silence. He did not break it when the Iraqi media claimed in May 1981 that Khoei had prayed for Saddam Hussein's health. The government curtailed sharply the size of his seminary in Najaf and imprisoned many of his students. When in April 1983 it organized the First Popular Islamic Conference in Baghdad [*qv*], Khoei and his family spurned the invitation to attend.

After the collapse of the Shia uprising in southern Iraq in the wake of the Second Gulf War [*qv*], Khoei, then seriously ill, was put under house arrest and coerced into appearing on television with Saddam Hussein. He was then moved to Kufa [*qv*], where he died in August 1992. He left behind some ninety books and pamphlets.

Khomeini, Ruhollah Musavi (1902–89): *Iranian religious–political leader: Leader, 1979–89* Born into a religious Shia [*qv*] family in Khomein, Khomeini was educated in theology at a religious school run by Ayatollah Abdul Karim Hairi-Yazdi in Arak. When Hairi-Yazdi moved to Qom [*qv*] in 1922, Khomeini went with him. Three years later Khomeini graduated in the Sharia [*qv*], ethics, and spiritual philosophy. Over the years he related ethical and spiritual problems to contemporary issues and taught his students to regard the addressing of current social problems as part of their religious duty.

In 1941 Khomeini published a book in which he attacked secularism. Four years later he graduated to the clerical rank of *hojatalislam (Arabic: proof of Islam)*, which allowed him to collect his own circle of disciples, who would accept his interpretations of the Sharia. After the death of Ayatollah Muhammad Hussein Borujerdi in 1961, urged by his students, Khomeini published a book entitled *Clarification of Points of the Sharia*. It secured him promotion to *ayatollah (Arabic: sign of Allah)*. This enabled Khomeini to assume the leadership of the radical clergy.

In 1963 he combined his criticism of the White Revolution [*qv*] with a personal attack on Muhammad Reza Shah Pahlavi (r. 1941–79) [*qv*]. His arrest on 5 June 1963 in Qom triggered a countrywide uprising. The shah used the army to crush it, reportedly causing the death of thousands. Pressured by clerics, the shah released Khomeini two months later and put him under house arrest in a Tehran [*qv*] suburb.

After his release in April 1964, Khomeini resumed his oppositional activities. In November he was expelled to Turkey. After living in the Turkish city of Bursa for a year, he

moved to Najaf [*qv*], Iraq. From there he kept up his campaign against the shah—an enterprise that the leftist Baathists [*qv*], who seized power in Iraq in 1968, found convenient, since they too were opposed to the pro-Western shah. In 1971 Khomeini condemned the celebrations of 2,500 years of unbroken monarchy in Iran, a claim that lacked historical evidence.

That year his book *Islamic Government: Rule of the Faqih*, based on a series of lectures, was published. In it Khomeini argued that instead of prescribing do's and don'ts for believers and waiting passively for the return of the Hidden Imam, the (Shia) clergy must attempt to oust corrupt officials and repressive regimes and replace them with ones led by just Islamic jurists. Unhappy at the mistreatment of Shia clerics by the Baathist regime, Khomeini sought permission in 1972 to leave for Lebanon, but was denied.

In 1975 Khomeini attacked the inauguration of a single party, the Rastakhiz [*qv*], in Iran. His call was taken up by many clergy and theological students. As a result of a rapprochement between Iraq and Iran in the wake of the Algiers Accord [*qv*], the number of Iranian pilgrims to Najaf and Karbala [*qv*] rose sharply, and this made it easier for Khomeini to guide his followers in their anti-shah campaign through smuggled tape recordings. These audiotapes became all the more important as the revolutionary process, consisting of massive and repeated demonstrations and strikes, gathered momentum through successive stages, from February 1977 to October 1978, when he was exiled to France.

The turning point in the movement had come in January 1978, when a scurrilous attack on him in a Tehran-based progovernment newspaper inflamed popular feelings and placed the initiative in the ongoing struggle firmly with Khomeini He made astute use of Shia history and Iranian nationalism to engender and intensify antiroyalist militancy among a rapidly growing circle of Iranians. He showed considerable shrewdness in uniting various disparate forces along the most radical demand—the deposition of the shah—and in causing the disintegration of the 413,000-strong military of the regime. By November 1978, operating from Neuphle-le-Chateau, a Paris suburb, Khomeini had put the shah on the defensive, and the economy, crippled by the stoppage of vital oil exports, was in a tailspin. On 13 January 1979, three days before the shah's final departure from Iran, Khomeini appointed the Islamic Revolutionary Council (IRC) to facilitate the formation of a provisional government to produce a constitution for an Islamic republic in Iran.

On his return to Tehran on 1 February 1979, Khomeini appointed Mahdi Bazargan [qv], a member of the IRC, as prime minister. Following a referendum based on universal suffrage, Khomeini announced the establishment of the Islamic Republic of Iran on 1 April. In August an elected Assembly of Experts (1979) [qv] debated the draft constitution, which incorporated the principle that Islamic jurisprudents would provide the leadership of the republic. Khomeini was named *marja-e taqlid (Arabic: source of emulation)* [qv], leading *mujtahid* [qv], and (Supreme) Leader.

He first isolated and then repressed all non-Islamic forces that had backed the revolutionary movement. He was equally hostile to the Mujahedin-e Khalq [qv], which combined Islam [qv] with Marxism. Khomeini turned against President Abol Hassan Bani-Sadr [qv] when the latter tried to foster a constituency outside Khomeinist circles. Having brought about Bani-Sadr's dismissal, constitutionally, Khomeini endorsed only those candidates for the presidency (Muhammad Ali Rajai [qv] and Ali Khamanei [qv]) who were his proven acolytes.

In the early crisis-ridden years of the Islamic Republic, Khomeini provided strong leadership and showed ruthlessness in crushing opposition, bent on either staging a military coup against the regime (monarchist strategy) or triggering a civil war (Mujahedin-e Khalq strategy).

Convinced that Iran could never be truly independent until it had excised U.S. influence from all walks of Iranian life, Khomeini kept up his campaign against the United States, the prime source to him of moral corruption and imperialist domination, describing it routinely as the "Great Satan." He was pleased when, following the storming of the U.S. Embassy in Tehran in November 1979, Washington cut off its diplomatic links with Iran.

Khomeini was incensed when, following Iraq's invasion of Iran in September 1980, neither the United Nations nor the Islamic Conference Organization (ICO) [qv] condemned the Iraqi action. However, Iraq's aggression helped Khomeini to rally Iranians on a patriotic platform and make his fractious supporters sink their differences on how to run the country, especially the economy. Conscious of the cementing effect of the Iran-Iraq War [qv], Khomeini repeatedly rejected offers of mediation and a cease-fire.

His attempts to export Islamic revolution to the neighboring countries failed. The Gulf monarchs, all Sunni [qv], managed to sideline Khomeini by successfully portraying him as a Shia leader of a non-Arab country. The only success Khomeini had in this regard was among the Shias of Lebanon. At home Khomeini managed to keep together the moderates and radicals within the ruling establishment by intermittently favoring one side and then the other. When he realized that the governing Islamic Republican Party (IRP) [qv] had become incurably faction-ridden, he ordered its disbandment in 1987.

Khomeini's radicalism did not blind him to reality. The military setbacks suffered by Iran in its war with Iraq in the spring of 1988 made him realize that if he did not stop fighting, the Islamic Republic would disintegrate, and that led him to accept the U.N.-brokered cease-fire in July 1988. Nonetheless, this was a bitter blow, described by him as "taking poison." He died within a year of making that decision—on 3 June 1989. He left behind an Iran with its territorial integrity intact, its Islamic regime well-entrenched, but its economy shattered.

Khouri, Bishara (1890–1964): *Lebanese politician; president, 1943–52* Born into a Maronite [qv] family in Beirut [qv], Khouri went to Paris to pursue his law studies. Returning home in 1911, he set up a legal practice. It was interrupted by the First World War, when Khouri left for Egypt. After returning to Beirut in 1919, he briefly practiced as a lawyer and then joined the judicial system, becoming a judge in 1923.

When the republican constitution went into effect under the French mandate in 1927, Khouri was named interior minister and then

promoted to prime minister, 1927–29. Three years later he was about to succeed Charles Debbas as president when the French suspended the constitution. This turned him into a nationalist, demanding a return to the constitution. When this happened, in 1936, Khouri contested the presidency but lost to Emile Edde by a thin margin. The constitution was suspended again by the pro-German government of France, based in Vichy, which assumed power in 1940. It was only after the Vichy forces were defeated by the Allies in Lebanon that the Free French reinstated the constitution.

Khouri led the Christian [qv] camp in its dispute with the Muslim [qv] side about sharing parliamentary seats. After the matter had been settled with the National Pact [qv] in March 1943 and approved by the Free French government, Khouri was elected president, unopposed, in September for a six-year term. Before the end of his office he instigated an amendment to the constitution to allow a second presidential term. This proved controversial, especially when it followed widespread charges of poll rigging in the 1947 parliamentary election. It inspired a concerted campaign by the opposition, which accused Khouri of corruption. Unable to withstand rising popular pressure, Khouri resigned in September 1952, midway through his second term.

At home Khouri co-opted urban Muslim leaders in administering the state; and he aligned his foreign policies with those of the Arab hinterland and participated in the Palestine War (1948–49) [qv].

khums *(Arabic: one-fifth): religious tithe applicable to Shia Muslims* One of the several duties incumbent upon Shias [qv], *khums,* amounting to one-fifth of a believer's trading profits, should be used for charitable purposes. Often a Shia hands over this sum to his *marja-e taqlid (Arabic: source of emulation)* [*qv*], a leading *mujtahid* [*qv*] whose interpretations of the Sharia [*qv*] he has agreed to accept and who uses it for social welfare.

kibbutzim *(Hebrew: communes; sing. kibbutz): rural communes in Palestine/Israel* Kibbutz is the term used for a settlement centered on a village and based on communal ownership of the means of production, with each member supplied with his/her personal needs. Sometimes the term *kvutzah* (pl. *kvutzot*) is used. Early Zionists [*qv*] thought collective or cooperative settlements to be the best way to reclaim Palestine [*qv*], and they established the first kibbutz in 1909. The second *aliya* (1904–14) [*qv*] inaugurated various types of communal living, including the establishment of the first kibbutz in 1909; and during the third *aliya* (1919–23) [*qv*] collectivism became popular within the labor movement. During the fourth *aliya* (1924–31) [*qv*] there was a split in the kibbutz movement, with the moderates being prepared to coexist with an expanding private sector and the radicals resolving to establish a countrywide commune.

Initially most of these settlements were affiliated to a federation called the Kibbutz Muhad (United Kibbutz), which was controlled by Mapai [*qv*]. But in 1927, with the formation of *HaShomer Hatzair* (The Young Guard), a revolutionary socialist group, nearly half of the kibbutzim affiliated to the left-wing federation called *Kibbutz Artzi* (Countrywide Kibbutz). At the end of the fifth *aliya* (1932–40) [*qv*] some 25,000 Jews, forming about 5 percent of the Jewish population, lived in kibbutzim or kvutzot.

During the Second World War many of their members joined the Jewish units of the British army. When Haganah [*qv*] decided to form the elite Palmah [*qv*] units, the Kibbutz Muhad helped with the project.

Following the founding of Israel [*qv*] in May 1948, the importance of kibbutzim in absorbing new arrivals declined sharply. In 1949 the concept of combining collectivism with military defense was realized in Nahal (acronym of *Noar Halutzi Lohem*: Fighting Pioneer Youth) settlements. The first Nahal settlement in Upper Galilee in 1951 was followed by many others in the border areas. In 1967 the Kibbutz Artzi, with 28,800 members on seventy-six settlements, became the largest kibbutz federation, followed by *Ihud HaKvutzot HaKibbutzim* (The Union of kvutzot and kibbutzim), with 25,300 members in seventy-six settlements, and the Kibbutz Muhad, with 22,800 members in fifty-eight settlements.

After the economic boom of 1968, labor shortages in Israel led many kibbutzim to break with the past and employ Arab labor. The number of kibbutzim fell from 300 in 1976 to about 250 in 1993 when, housing only 2.5 percent of Israel's population, they produced 40 percent of its agricultural and 8 percent of its industrial output. These figures declined further during the 1990s. In 2001, only 120,000 Israelis, forming a tiny 2 percent of the population, lived in kibbutzim.

King-Crane Commission (1919): *U.S. commission on the Middle East* Pursuing the self-determination doctrine he had been advocating, U.S. President Woodrow

Wilson, at the Paris Peace Conference of the Council of Four in March 1919, proposed that an Allied Commission on Mandates in (Ottoman) Turkey, consisting of U.S., British, French, and Italian members, be sent to the Middle East [qv] to consult the inhabitants on their political future. The Peace Conference endorsed the idea. But since the French were really against it and the British were at best lukewarm, three of the four Allied members soon withdrew from the Commission. As a result only the U.S. appointees (Dr. Henri King, president of Oberlin College, Ohio, and Charles Crane, a businessman interested in Christian missions in the Middle East) left for the region in May.

King and Crane received numerous petitions from varied quarters and interviewed all political leaders in Syria [qv] and Palestine [qv]. In their report, submitted in August, they concluded that an overwhelming majority, while opposed to the concept of mandate, agreed that there was a need for foreign assistance, provided it came from the United States, or, as a second alternative, Britain. They recommended a single mandate for a United Syria consisting of Syria and Palestine [qv], provided the mandate was for a limited period and its holder did not act as a colonial power. They further recommended that Faisal ibn Hussein [qv] should become king of United Syria and that Iraq should have an Arab monarch.

While sympathizing with Zionist aspirations and plans, they concluded that the "extreme Zionist program must be greatly modified if the civil and religious rights of the non-Jewish inhabitants of Palestine are to be protected in accordance with the terms of the Balfour Declaration [qv]." After discussions with Zionist leaders in Jerusalem [qv] they had concluded that "the Zionists looked forward to a practically complete dispossession of the present non-Jewish inhabitants of Palestine, by various forms of purchase." They therefore recommended that "Jewish immigration should be definitely limited and the project of making Palestine a distinctly Jewish commonwealth should be given up. There would then be no reason why Palestine could not be included in a united Syrian state." Britain and France ignored the report.

Since the United States withdrew from the Peace Conference in December 1919—a preamble to its refusal to join the League of Nations, which was formed the following month—the report lost its importance. It was not until December 1922 that it was published unofficially.

Knesset *(Hebrew: Assembly): Parliament of Israel* The Knesset and government of Israel evolved out of the People's Council, which was formed according to a joint decision by the National Council of the Jewish Community in Palestine and the Executive of the Jewish Agency [qv] on 1 March 1948. The thirty-seven members of the People's Council, appointed on 15 April 1948, came from the National Council of the Jewish Community, the Jewish Agency Executive, and other groups not represented in either of these bodies. Of these, thirteen were chosen to form the People's Administration.

On 15 May 1948, the end of British mandate in Palestine, the People's Council became the Provisional State Council; and the People's Administration, the provisional government of the State of

Israel. The Provisional State Council passed a law for the election of 120 members to the Constituent Assembly. Following this poll in January 1949, the Constituent Assembly adopted a Transition Law, which specified a unicameral parliament, to be called the Knesset, of 120 deputies, elected by universal suffrage using a proportional representation system, with the whole country forming a single constituency and the election threshold at 1 percent. The Constituent Assembly then transformed itself into the First Knesset.

It was not until 1958 that the "Basic Law: the Knesset" was passed. The law gave the Knesset the same powers as exercised by the British parliament; i.e., the Knesset is sovereign and its authority in legislative and other affairs is unlimited. Its tenure is four years, but it can dissolve itself before that. No quorum is needed. It elects the state president (a constitutional head) by a simple majority of those present and voting, for a maximum of two terms of five years each. The president invites the leader of the largest group in the Knesset to form a government. Once he or she has succeeded in doing so, with himself/herself as prime minister, and secured a vote of confidence in the Knesset, the cabinet is sworn in within a week. Starting with the 1992 Knesset poll, the election threshold was raised to 1.5 percent with a view to reducing political parties. When this did not happen, the Knesset passed a law mandating direct election for the prime minister, who then cobbled together a coalition government. The first such poll took place in 1996 along with the one for the Knesset, with the second such set of elections conducted in 1999. There was no decrease in the number of groups winning parliamentary seats. In 2001, however, there was only the prime ministerial contest, the last such exercise. In 2003 the electoral system reverted to the old arrangement.

Komala-e Jian-e Kordestan *(Kurdish: Association of Revival of Kurdistan): Kurdish organization in Iran* During the Soviet occupation of northern Iran (1941–46), nationalist Kurds secretly established the Komala-e Jian-e Kordestan, often called Komala, in 1943 in Mahabad. It had the support of the Soviet forces. After the founding of the Kurdish Democratic Party (KDP) [*qv*] in 1945, Komala members joined it and dissolved their group. It was revived as the Kurdish wing of the Communist Party of Iran (Marxist-Leninist) in 1969.

Under the leadership of Jaafar Shafii it participated in the 1977–78 revolutionary movement. In its strongholds in the northern Kurdish area it seized power through Revolutionary Komitehs [*qv*]. After the 1979 revolution it allied with the KDP and the followers of Shaikh Izz al-Din Husseini, a Mahabad-based Sunni [*qv*] religious leader, and demanded autonomy for the Kurds. When this was rejected by the Islamic regime in Tehran [*qv*], it took up arms against it and faced government persecution.

In the confrontation between Ayatollah Ruhollah Khomeini [*qv*] and President Abol Hassan Bani-Sadr [*qv*] in 1981, it sided with the latter, who lost. It then joined the National Resistance Council [*qv*]. As the Iran-Iraq War (1980–88) [*qv*] dragged on, Komala began to cooperate with Iraq. Therefore, Iran often combined its offensives against Iraq in the northern sector with attacks on Komala strongholds. After the war

Komala merged into the Communist Party of Iran and became the Kordestan Organization of the Communist Party of Iran (KOCPI). Following the Second Gulf War [*qv*], it moved its base to Iraqi Kurdistan near Suleimaniya administered by the Patriotic Union of Kurdistan (PUK) [*qv*]. But once the PUK had decided on repairing its strained relations with Iran in September 1996 after suffering a humiliating defeat by the rival Kurdistan Democratic Party [*qv*], the KOPCI lost its base in Iraq—and with it any importance it had.

Koran: *see* Quran.

Kordestan (Iran): *see* Kurdistan (Iran).

Kordestan Democratic Party of Iran: *see* Kurdistan Democratic Party of Iran.

Kufa: *Iraqi town* Pop. 47,000 (2000, est.). Situated north of Najaf [*qv*], Kufa lies along the banks of the Euphrates [*qv*] and has a history dating back to antiquity. A military base of Muslim Arabs [*qv*] in Mesopotamia [*qv*], Kufa grew in importance during early Islam [*qv*]. It was a center of rebellion against Caliph Othman (r. A.D. 644–56) and a bastion of support for Ali ibn Abu Talib in his struggle for the caliphate against Muwaiya ibn Abu Sufian, which led to the battle of Siffin.

After being a leading political-military center until A.D. 750, it turned into a cultural center for the next century, fostering such scholars as Abu Hanifa al Numan (d. A.D. 767), the founder of the Hanafi Code [*qv*]. It then turned into the cradle of Shiism [*qv*] for the next century. With the emergence of Najaf and Karbala [*qv*] as leading Shia holy shrines, the significance of Kufa declined.

Kurdish Democratic Party (Iraq): *see* Kurdistan Democratic Party (Iraq).

Kurdish language: The language of Kurds [*qv*], Kurdish is part of the Iranian branch of Indo-Iranian subfamily of the Eastern/Satem division of the Indo-European languages. Spoken in Kurdistan [*qv*], its northern dialect is called Kermanji and the southern, Surani, the latter being the literary form of the language. It is written in Arabic script using the Persian alphabet. In the Soviet Republic of Armenia, a modified version of the Cyrillic script was used for Kurdish.

Kurdish Republic of Mahabad (1945–46): *see* Kurdistan Republic (1945–46).

Kurdish Revolutionary Party (Iraq): *a breakaway group of the Kurdistan Democratic Party* The Kurdish Revolutionary Party (KRP) was formed in 1964 in protest against the authoritarian leadership of Mustafa Barzani [*qv*]. Following the agreement of the Kurdistan Democratic Party (KDP) with Baghdad in 1970, many KRP members returned to the parent body. But when the KDP failed to join the institutions inaugurated by the 1970 accord, there was a reverse flow, which involved inter alia Obeidallah Barzani, a son of Mustafa. The KRP had by then joined the National Progressive and Patriotic Front [*qv*].

Kurdistan *(Kurdish/Persian: Place of Kurds):* As a geographical expression, the term Kurdistan applies to the Kurdish-majority region in southwest Asia. It covers about 193,000 sq. miles/500,000 sq. km spread over northwestern Iran, northern Iraq, the northeastern corner of Syria, southeastern Turkey, the Nakhichevan enclave of Azerbaijan, and southern Armenia. The estimated number of Kurds living in these countries in 2000 was about 24 million

(Turkey, 13 million; Iran, 5.2 million; Iraq, 4.4 million; Syria, 1.0 million; and Azerbaijan and Armenia, 0.3 million), and it was reckoned that between 15 and 16 million of them lived in the "geographical" region of Kurdistan.

Kurdistan (Iran): *Iranian province* Also spelled Kordestan. Area: 9,652 sq. miles/ 24,998 sq. km; pop. 1,346,000 (1996 census). Established in 1961, Kurdistan is bordered by West Azerbaijan to its north, Gilan and Hamdan to its east, Kerman to its south, and Iraq to its west. Its population is predominantly Kurdish.

Kurdistan Autonomous Region (Iraq): Area: 14,923 sq. miles/38,650 sq. km; pop. 2,362,000 (1991, est.). An agreement between the Kurdistan Democratic Party (KDP) [*qv*] and the Iraqi government in March 1970 led to a Kurdistan Autonomous Region (KAR) being inaugurated four years later. Consisting of three Kurdish-majority governorates of Dohak, Irbil, and Suleimaniya in the north-northwest, it has an eighty-member Legislative Council and an Executive Council. The legislative deputies are elected, but the Executive Council members and chairman are appointed by the central government in Baghdad [*qv*]. Elections to the Legislative Council were held in September 1980, August 1986, and September 1989.

Kurdish [*qv*] is the official language for administration and education, and Arabic [*qv*] is a compulsory language in schools.

After the Second Gulf War (1991) [*qv*] the Baghdad government was deprived by the actions of the United States, Britain, and France (including the imposition of "no fly" restrictions) of its control of the KAR, which

began to function as a semi-independent entity. Fresh elections in May 1992 led to the sharing of power by the Kurdistan Democratic Party [*qv*] and the Patriotic Union of Kurdistan [*qv*], with the new government adopting its own flag. The power-sharing arrangement broke down after two years, and the American plan to develop the region as the springboard for overthrowing Saddam Hussein [*qv*] was scuttled in 1996. *See also* Kurds (Iraq), Kurdistan Democratic Party, and Patriotic Union of Kurdistan.

Kurdistan Democratic Party (Iraq): Official Kurdish title: *Partiya Demokrata Kurdistan.* Between the end of the Kurdish Republic of Mahabad [*qv*] in December 1946 and his crossing into the Soviet Union from Iran in June 1947, Mustafa Barzani [*qv*] set the guidelines for an Iraq-based Kurdish Democratic Party (KDP) [*qv*]. Inspired by Marxism-Leninism, it would dedicate itself to liberating Iraq from foreign imperialism and domestic reaction and would fight for Kurdish autonomy within Iraq.

Following the July 1958 revolution, Barzani was allowed to return home. He backed the new regime under Abdul Karim Qasim [*qv*], who legalized the KDP. The KDP renamed itself the Kurdistan Democratic Party (KDP) in 1959. But when Barzani advanced a plan for Kurdish autonomy, Qasim rejected it, and in September 1961 mounted an offensive against the strongholds of the KDP. During the subsequent years, despite changes in the regimes in Baghdad [*qv*], relations between the central government and the KDP remained poor.

In March 1969 the KDP resumed its armed struggle against the central government, now run by the Baath party [*qv*]. The fighting ended a year later with an accord that was to be implemented over a four-year period. It conceded to several of the KDP's demands, including recognition of Kurdish ethnicity on a par with Arab, and the official use of Kurdish [qv] in Kurdish-majority areas. But due to mistrust on both sides, the pact failed to hold.

After March 1974, when the government created the promised Kurdistan Autonomous Region (KAR) [qv], the KDP went on the warpath. Fighting ensued between the two sides. This time the KDP had the backing of Iran's Muhammad Reza Shah Pahlavi [qv], who wanted to weaken the pro-Moscow regime in Iraq. By early 1975 four-fifths of Iraq's 100,000 troops and nearly half of its 1,390 tanks were pinned down by 45,000 Kurdish guerrillas. The conflict threatened to escalate into a full-scale war between Iran and Iraq. To avert this, the two countries signed the Algiers Accord [qv], which resulted in Iran stopping military and logistical aid to the KDP. Barzani escaped to Iran.

The KDP leadership passed on to Barzani's sons, Idris and Masud [qv]. When they moved into Iran after the 1979 Islamic revolution [qv], Tehran began to provide them with aid. The outbreak of the Iran-Iraq War [qv] in 1980 compelled Baghdad to reduce its troops in the Kurdish areas. This led to an expansion in the Iraqi border area under KDP control. The KDP began to increase its cooperation with Iran. With the death of Idris Barzani in 1987, Masud became the KDP's sole leader. During the Iran-Iraq War it set up liberated zones, totaling 4,000 sq. miles/10,360 sq. km, along the Iraqi border with Iran. But starting in February 1988, Iraqi President Saddam

Hussein [qv] unleashed a seven-month campaign of vengeance against KDP strongholds that affected 3,800 villages and reclaimed the lost area.

KDP leaders escaped to Iran or Syria, but during the crisis created by Iraq's occupation of Kuwait in August 1990, which drew most of the Iraqi troops away from the KAR, they returned to the KAR. When Iraq was defeated in the Second Gulf War [qv] in early 1991, Masud Barzani led a Kurdish rebellion against Baghdad. Its suppression caused a massive exodus of Kurds into Turkey and Iran and the intervention of the U.S.-led anti-Iraq coalition.

Barzani's subsequent talks with Baghdad failed. Protected by the air forces of the United States, Britain, and France, the KDP, along with other Kurdish parties, held Legislative Council elections in May 1992. The KDP, commanding 25,000 troops and backed by 30,000 militiamen, shared power equally with the Patriotic Union of Kurdistan (PUK) [qv]. Two years later the arrangement broke down, with KDP and PUK partisans clashing violently. To reduce the PUK's area of control, the KDP began to ally itself with the Islamic Movement of Kurdistan [qv].

Yet the traditional rivalry between the two parties continued. In May 1994 intra-Kurdish clashes left over 1,000 people dead. It was not until six months later that, assisted by mediators, Barzani worked out a modus vivendi with Talabani. But Barzani's relations with his rival soured again when their two factions took opposite positions in the anti-Saddam coup plans in March 1995. With this, Kurdistan divided into two hostile zones. By September, Barzani's jurisdiction was reduced to a third of the region. But with the illicit Iraqi oil supplies passing through his territory, providing hefty customs duties, Barzani had much cash, part of which he used to buy arms and ammunition, some of them from Saddam Hussein. Talabani's rapprochement with Iran upset both Barzani and Saddam. When Talabani, freshly armed with Iranian-supplied weapons, attacked KDP's positions in August 1996, Barzani appealed to Saddam for military assistance to retake Irbil [*qv*] from Talabani. Saddam obliged. Barzani captured not only Irbil, but all of Talabani's territory, only to lose all except Irbil when Talabani, armed by Iran, counterattacked. The unprecedented intra-Kurdish violence undermined the American strategy of developing Kurdistan as the base for overthrowing Saddam. The United States withdrew its agents and funds from the area. Washington's efforts to conciliate the two rivals were successful only partially because Barzani refused to share the large customs duties he collected on the illicit export of Iraqi oil to Turkey. After the passage of the Iraq Liberation Act by the U.S. Congress in 1998, Barzani found the KDP certified as a faction that was entitled to Washington's military aid.

When, after defeating the Taliban regime in Afghanistan in December 2001, the U.S. administration of President George W. Bush turned its attention to ousting Saddam's government by force, the importance of Barzani as well as Talabani rose. However, when the leaders of the KDP and five other Iraqi groups were invited to Washington to meet Vice President Dick Cheney in August 2002, Barzani did not go.

Following the collapse of the Saddam Hussein regime in the face of an invasion by the Anglo-American forces in April 2003, Barzani publicly welcomed the U.S. proconsul (Retd.) Gen. Jay Rayner.

Kurdistan Democratic Party of Iran: *Iranian political party* In September 1945, when Iran's Kurdish region was under Soviet occupation, the Kurdish Democratic Party (KDP) *(Kurdish: Hizb-e Dimokrat-e Kurd)* was established in Mahabad by Qazi Muhammad, who had led an autonomous local council since 1941. The KDP demanded autonomy for the Kurds within Iran. Three months later it founded the State of Republic of Kurdistan/Kordestan *(Kurdish: Dawlat-e Jumhouri-ye Kurdistan),* popularly known as the National Government of Kordestan *(Kurdish: Hukumat-e Milli Kurdistan)* and often labeled by outsiders as the Kurdish Republic of Mahabad. Qazi Muhammad was appointed president. The republic lasted a year before being overthrown by the forces of Muhammad Reza Shah Pahlavi [*qv*] after the Soviet withdrawal in May 1946. The KDP went underground.

With a mild revival of armed resistance against the shah in the early 1970s, the party, now renamed the Kordestan Democratic Party of Iran (KDPI), began to flex its muscles. A complicating factor entered the equation when the shah began to arm Kurdish autonomists in Iraq in 1973–74, a policy that ended with the Algiers Accord [*qv*]. The KDPI participated in the revolutionary movement of 1977–78, when local power was seized in northern Kurdish areas by the Revolutionary Komitehs [*qv*], composed of the followers of Shaikh Izz al-Din Husseini, a Mahabad-based Sunni [*qv*] religious leader, and KDPI members.

After the revolution, when the central government, led by Ayatollah Ruhollah Khomeini [qv], tried to establish control in the Kurdish areas, the KDPI came into conflict with it. At its congress in April 1980 the KDPI demanded the use of the Kurdish language [qv] in schools, offices, and courts, and the redrawing of provincial borders to include all Kurds in one province. Efforts to reach a compromise with Tehran failed, and fighting broke out between the two sides.

The Iraqi invasion of Iran in September 1980 helped Khomeini in that it created a surge of nationalism in which ethnic differences were forgotten, for the time being. The KDPI backed President Abol Hassan Bani-Sadr [qv] in his confrontation with Khomeini in June 1981 and lost. Later both the KDPI and Komala [qv] joined the National Resistance Council [qv], headed by Bani-Sadr and Masud Rajavi [qv].

As the Iran-Iraq War (1980–88) [qv] dragged on, the KDPI began to side with Iraq. Its leader, Abdul Rahman Qasimlou, tried to reconcile Baghdad with its Kurdish nationalists and managed to get the central government and Jalal Talabani [qv] of the Patriotic Union of Kurdistan [qv] to negotiate in 1984–85. The talks failed. After the war, Talabani brokered a meeting between Qasimlou and Iranian officials in Vienna, Austria, in the autumn of 1989. Qasimlou was assassinated in Vienna, allegedly by Iranian agents. But the KDPI, having a 10,000-strong militia, withstood the shock.

Following the establishment of the no-fly zones in northern Iraq by America and Britain in late 1991, the Iraqi PUK began providing refuge to the KDPI forces, with their headquarters in the Iraqi border town of Qala Diza. They made a point of killing the personnel of Iran's Revolutionary Guard Corps, which in turn hit back. It was against this background that KDPI chief Sadiq Sharaf-Kindi and his three colleagues were murdered at a restaurant in Berlin in September 1992 by Kazem Darabi, an Iranian intelligence agent and his four Lebanese cohorts.

Tension between the KDPI and Iran rose sharply after Washington's adoption of the Dual Containment policy [qv] in May 1993. This continued until the summer of 1996 when Talabani reached a rapprochement with Tehran in order to get even with the rival Kurdistan Democratic Party [qv] of Masud Barzani [qv]. The Iranian forces then captured the KDPI stronghold inside Iraqi Kurdistan at Koy Sanjak, delivering an almost fatal blow to the group, reducing its fighting force to about 1,500.

It remained a member of the National Resistance Council.

Kurdistan Front: *see* Iraqi Kurdistan Front.

Kurdistan Republic (1945–46): Official title: State of Republic of Kurdistan *(Kurdish: Dawlat-e Jumhouri-ye Kurdistan)*, popularly known as the National Government of Kurdistan *(Kurdish: Hukumat-e Milli Kurdistan)*. It was formed in December 1945 by the Kurdish Democratic Party [qv], with Qazi Muhammad as its president and Mustafa Barzani [qv] as its commander in chief. Its capital was Mahabad. Kurdish [qv] became the official language in the government and schools, and the Iranian imperial army was replaced by a national army. The republic was overthrown by the forces of Tehran in December 1946, seven months after Soviet troops, stationed in the area since August 1941, had withdrawn.

Kurds: Kurds are members of an ethnic group that inhabit the Zagros and Taurus Mountains of southeastern Turkey, northwestern Iran, northern Iraq, and the adjacent areas in Syria and Nakhichevan. Descendants of Indo-European tribes, they appear in the history of the early empires of Mesopotamia [*qv*], where they are described as "Kardouchoi." They trace their distinct history as mountain people to the seventh century B.C., and this has been substantiated by recent excavations at Saaqez in Iran. These show Saaqez as the capital of a Kurdish region that was part of the Scythian empire, from the ninth to the third century B.C. It was not until the seventh century A.D. that they embraced Islam [*qv*]. Like Persians, who also embraced Islam, they retained their language, but unlike them, they remained predominantly Sunni [*qv*].

The Kurdish general, Salah al Din (Saladin) Ayubi, overpowered the Shia Fatimid dynasty in Egypt and established the Ayubid dynasty (1169–1250). During the Ottoman and Persian Empires there were periodic uprisings by Kurds against the central power. Kurdish nationalism manifested itself in the late ninteenth century inter alia in the publication of the first periodical in Kurdish (1897). Since the Treaty of Sèvres (1920) [*qv*], which specified an autonomous Kurdistan, was not ratified, and since the subsequent Treaty of Lausanne (1923) [*qv*] made no mention of it, the aspirations of Kurdish nationalists remained unfulfilled. *See also* Kurds in Iran, Kurds in Iraq, and Kurds in Syria.

Kurds in Iran: Nationally Kurds make up about 8 percent of the Iranian population. They are predominant in Kurdistan [*qv*] and are a substantial community in the provinces of East Azerbaijan (pop. 3.3 million), West Azerbaijan (pop. 2.5 million), Kerman (pop. 2.0 million), and Ilam (pop. 0.5 million). During the rule of the Pahlavi dynasty [*qv*], the teaching of Kurdish in schools was banned. *See also* Kurdistan Democratic Party of Iran.

Kurds in Iraq: Nationally Kurds [*qv*] accounted for about 19 percent of the Iraqi population. Of the 3.6 million Kurds in the country in 1991, nearly two-thirds were in the Kurdistan Autonomous Region [*qv*]. By amalgamating (in December 1925) the predominantly Kurdish province of Mosul, which was part of Turkey before the First World War, with Baghdad and Basra (former provinces of Mesopotamia [*qv*]) to create modern Iraq, the British unwittingly engendered a Kurdish problem for the enlarged country. In 1927 the importance of Mosul province rose sharply when a British-dominated company struck oil near Kirkuk.

During the Second World War, Mustafa Barzani [*qv*] led a failed rebellion. He fled to Iran, and later to the Soviet Union. Following the 1958 coup in Iraq, he returned home and backed the new republican regime. In exchange, Baghdad legalized the Kurdistan Democratic Party (KDP) [*qv*] and promulgated a constitution that stated: "Arabs and Kurds are associated in this nation." However, when Barzani advanced an autonomy plan, Baghdad rejected it. Fighting broke out between the two sides in September 1961 and continued until June 1966, when an agreement granted official recognition of the Kurdish language [*qv*] and proportional representation of Kurds in the civil service.

However, the accord failed to dissipate

mutual mistrust. In March 1969 the KDP resumed its armed struggle against the central government, now run by the Baath party [*qv*]. The fighting ended a year later with an accord that was to be implemented over a four-year period. The constitution of July 1970 recognized Kurds as one of the two nationalities of Iraq, and Kurdish as one of the two languages in the Kurdish region. But once again the agreement failed to hold.

Ignoring the noncooperation of the KDP, the Baghdad government enforced the Kurdish autonomy law in March 1974, including the appointment of a Kurd, Taha Muhyi al Din Maruf, a diplomat, as a vice president of the republic, the formation of the Kurdistan Autonomous Region (KAR) [*qv*], comprising the provinces of Dohak, Irbil, and Suleimaniya, and establishment of the (largely nominated) Kurdistan Legislative Council.

Fighting erupted again. This time the KDP had the active backing of Iran's Muhammad Reza Shah Pahlavi [*qv*], who wanted to weaken the pro-Moscow regime in Baghdad. At one point the KDP controlled a third of the KAR, and its 45,000 guerrillas pinned down four-fifths of Iraq's 100,000 troops and nearly half of its 1,390 tanks. The conflict resulted in 60,000 civilian and military casualties, the destruction of 40,000 homes in 700 villages, and 300,000 refugees. To avert the danger of the conflict escalating into a full-scale war between Iran and Iraq, the two countries signed the Algiers Accord [*qv*] in March 1975, which resulted in Iran cutting off military and logistical aid to the KDP. Barzani escaped to Iran.

During the 1980–88 Iran-Iraq War [*qv*] the activities of the Kurdish insurgents, allied with Tehran, compelled Iraq to deploy divisions in the north to the detriment of its war effort elsewhere. Taking advantage of the pressure of war on Baghdad, the KDP (now led by Masud Barzani [*qv*]) and the Patriotic Union of Kurdistan (PUK) [*qv*], headed by Jalal Talabani [*qv*], set up liberated zones along the borders with Iran and Turkey. Starting in February 1988 Iraqi President Saddam Hussein [*qv*] unleashed a seven-month campaign of vengeance against KDP strongholds, involving the use of chemical weapons and affecting 3,800 villages. Saddam reclaimed the area that had been lost to the insurgents, and the Kurdish leaders escaped to Iran or Syria.

During the crisis created by Iraq's occupation of Kuwait in August 1990, which drew most of the troops away from the KAR, the KDP leaders returned to Kurdistan. Following Iraq's defeat in the Second Gulf War [*qv*] the Kurdish nationalists persuaded the 100,000-strong local Iraqi army auxiliary force, made up of Kurds, to change sides. Within a week the rebels controlled the KAR and large parts of the oil-rich province of Tamim, including its capital, Kirkuk. In late March a government counterattack reversed the situation, causing an exodus of 1.5 million Kurds into Iran and Turkey.

Having fully regained the region, Baghdad signed a truce with the insurgents in mid-April. In the subsequent talks with the central government, Barzani, acting as leader of the Iraqi Kurdistan Front (IKF) [*qv*], reached a draft agreement in June whereby the Kurds would have predominant military and political authority over the KAR, with joint control of the army and police by the Kurdish authorities and Baghdad. In return, the Kurds had to surrender their heavy weapons and cut all links with outside powers. But despite further clarification of the agreement from Baghdad, Barzani failed to win the approval of the majority of IKF leaders.

With 16,000 Western troops deployed in the 3,600 sq. mile/9,325 sq. km security zone created by the U.S.-led anti-Iraq coalition in the Iraqi-Turkish border region, Baghdad was forced to withdraw its forces from the KAR by late October. Even after the U.S., Britain, and France, the three permanent Western members of the U.N. Security Council, had pulled out their troops from the area by the end of 1991, they continued their air surveillance of Iraq north of 36 degrees latitude from the Turkish air base of Incirlik. Thus protected, the Kurds conducted their own elections for parliament in May 1992 and chose their own government, which among other things had its own army and adopted its own flag. Kurds thus acquired a semi-independent administrative-political entity. *See further* Kurdistan Democratic Party and Patriotic Union of Kurdistan.

Kurds in Syria: Nationally Kurds [*qv*] make up about 6 percent of the Syrian population. Apart from a small community in Damascus [*qv*] dating back to the times of Salah al Din (Saladin) Ayubi (r. 1169–93), himself a Kurd, they are concentrated in the Jazira region in the northeast corner of the country and in the mountainous area north of Aleppo [*qv*] among the border with Turkey. Most of them arrived from Turkey during the interwar years, when a Kurdish revolt against the regime of Mustafa Kemal Ataturk failed in 1925.

Mirroring the situation in adjoining Iraq, the Kurds in Syria established the Kurdish Democratic Party (KDP) in 1957, demanding that Kurds be recognized as an ethnic group entitled to develop its own culture.

Following the merger of Syria with Egypt to form the United Arab Republic (UAR) [*qv*] in 1958, the new pan-Arabist regime repressed the KDP. This policy continued after Syria seceded from the UAR in 1961. A special census conducted in Jazira in late 1962 deprived 120,000 Kurds of Syrian nationality. After the pan-Arabist [*qv*] Baath party [*qv*] seized power in 1963, the government expelled many of the Kurds along the Turkish frontier and stripped many thousands of others of their Syrian nationality. It joined the Iraqi Baath [*qv*] government's war against the Kurds and adopted a policy of settling Arabs in the Jazira region while scattering the local Kurds into the interior, especially after oil had been found in the area. Applied haphazardly, this policy resulted in some 30,000 Jazira Kurds leaving the area by early 1971.

Later that year the government adopted a conciliatory position similar to the one taken by the Iraqi regime in its March 1970 declaration. The Baath congress recognized that the Kurdish and Arab peoples had equal rights and that the Kurds had a right to their own nationality, though not to separation. In late 1971 the government for the first time distributed land-reform land to Kurdish peasants in Jazira. In 1976 President Hafiz Assad [*qv*] officially renounced the population transfer plans for Jazira.

Kuwait:
Official name: State of Kuwait
Capital: Kuwait city
Area: 6,880 sq. miles/17,820 sq. km— including the Kuwaiti share of the Kuwait-Saudi Arabia Neutral Zone [*qv*] and the

Bubiyan and Warba offshore islands, with a combined area of 348 sq. miles/900 sq. km

Population: 2,117,000, including 815,000 Kuwaiti nationals (2003, est.)

Gross domestic product: $42.3 billion (2001)

National currency: Kuwaiti Dinar (KD); KD1 = US$3.26 = £2.27 (2001) = EUR 3.66 (2001)

Form of government: monarchy

Official language: Arabic [*qv*]

Official religion: Islam [*qv*]

Administrative regions: Kuwait is divided into five governorates (provinces).

Constitution: Following Kuwait's independence on 19 June 1961, the ruler appointed a constituent assembly in December. The constitution drafted by it was promulgated in November 1962. Kuwait is a hereditary emirate (principality) under the rulership of the descendants of Shaikh Mubarak I al Sabah (d. 1915). The constitution guarantees freedom of opinion, freedom of the press, and the freedom to perform religious rites, and allows the formation of trade unions and peaceful societies that stay within the law. A unicameral National Assembly of fifty members is elected for a four-year term by literate male Kuwaiti citizens who can prove that their family has been domiciled in Kuwait since 1921. The ruler can dissolve the Assembly, provided fresh elections are held within two months.

Ethnic composition (2002): Arab [*qv*], 80 percent; South Asian, 9 percent; Iranian, 4 percent; other, 7 percent.

Executive authority: Executive authority rests with the emir, who exercises it through a council of ministers. He appoints or dis-

misses the prime minister, or accepts his resignation. After consultation with the prime minister, the emir appoints or dismisses ministers, or accepts their resignation. Nonparliamentary ministers become ex-officio members of the National Assembly. A minister is responsible to the National Assembly, and following a vote of no confidence must resign. The emir is the supreme commander of the military and is authorized to declare defensive war, conclude peace agreements, and sign treaties.

High officials:

Head of state: Shaikh Jaber III ibn Ahmad I al Sabah [*qv*], 1977–

Crown prince and prime minister: Shaikh Saad ibn Abdullah III al Sabah, 1977–

Speaker of the National Assembly: Jassim al Kharafi, 1999–

History (since ca. 1900): At the turn of the twentieth century Kuwait was a British protectorate following a secret treaty between Shaikh Mubarak I al Sabah (r. 1896–1915) and London in 1899. The Anglo-Ottoman Convention of 1913 [*qv*], which recognized Kuwait as an autonomous principality of the Ottoman Empire under Shaikh Mubarak I, was invalidated by the Ottomans joining the Germans in the First World War. London now publicly declared Kuwait to be "an independent shaikhdom under British protectorate." After the war, the 1922 Protocol of Uqair [*qv*] defined Kuwait's borders and created the Kuwait-Najd [*qv*] (later Saudi Arabia) Neutral Zone. In 1937 the fourteen-member (elected) Kuwait Legislative Council voted ten to four for a union with Iraq [*qv*], then ruled by King Ghazi ibn Faisal [*qv*].

Following the development of the oil industry in Iraq and Iran [qv], the trading economy of Kuwait improved. Kuwait's oil exploration bore fruit in 1938 at Burgan, but the wells were plugged during the Second World War. In the postwar years, oil extraction and exports reached commercial proportions. The stoppage of oil exports from Iran from 1951–53 led to a rapid increase in the Kuwaiti output and a rise in local living standards.

Popular demand for political reform, including parliament, was not conceded by the ruler, Shaikh Abdullah III al Sabah [qv], until after political independence in June 1961. He appointed a constituent assembly in December and promulgated the constitution drafted by it in November 1962. Elections to the National Assembly on a limited franchise were held in 1963, 1967, 1971, and 1975.

Over the years the Assembly evolved into an institutional means of expression and access to the main sociopolitical elements—nomadic and sedentary tribes, urban merchants and businessmen, and political intellectuals and professionals. In August 1976 the ruler suspended four articles concerning the National Assembly as well as the Assembly, accusing it of "malicious behavior" and wasting time on legislation, and dissolved the Assembly a year later.

Kuwait prospered from the steep rise in the price of oil in the mid-1970s, and the state set up a national fund for future generations.

Yielding to popular pressure, Shaikh Jabar III al Sabah [qv] reinstated the National Assembly with depleted powers in early 1981. The new parliament proved to be a handmaiden of the ruler. However, in the Sixth National Assembly, elected in early 1985, there were five nationalist-leftists and eleven Islamists in a house of fifty. By offering a combined opposition and demanding an official inquiry into the disastrous collapse of the unofficial stock exchange in 1982, involving $97 billion in paper debts, they caused the al Sabah dynasty [qv] some unease. In July 1986 Shaikh Jabar III dissolved the Assembly again.

Once the Iran-Iraq War (1980–88) [qv], in which Kuwait had sided with Iraq, ended in August 1988, there was agitation for the restoration of the Assembly. When the ruler conceded a seventy-five-member National Council (one-third of whom were nominated), but with the power only to make recommendations, protest continued. The June 1990 poll was boycotted by the opposition. This, and Kuwait's attempt to weaken Iraq's economy by depressing oil prices by flooding the market, were major factors behind Iraqi President Saddam Hussein's [qv] decision to invade Kuwait in August 1990.

During the seven months of Iraqi occupation, Kuwait suffered wanton damage and Kuwaitis suffered exile and unprecedented brutality, including rape, summary execution, and the arbitrary confiscation of property. The Second Gulf War [qv] ended with the U.S.-led coalition expelling Iraq from Kuwait in February 1991. The country's funding of the 1991 Gulf War and its aftermath reduced the Kuwait Investment Authority's assets from $88.5 billion to $31.5 billion. Kuwait was restored to Shaikh Jabar III, who held elections to the Seventh National Assembly in October 1992. Of the fifty members, thity-one belonged to the opposition despite the government's success in quickly rebuilding the country's shattered oil economy.

Following Kuwait's signing of a ten-year defense pact with America, 5,000 U.S. troops were based in the country. In the recurring crises between Iraq and the United Nations during the 1990s, Kuwait stood out as the only Gulf monarchy that publicly backed Washington's plans to bomb Iraq. At home, due to the frequent conflict between parliamentarians and the cabinet, the ruler dissolved the parliament a year earlier. In the 1999 general election, the size of the government supporters fell from eighteen to twelve. In regional affairs, Kuwait's growing rapprochement with Iran and Iraq was halted by the terrorist attacks on the United States in September 2001, followed by President George W. Bush's description of Iran and Iraq as members of the "Axis of Evil."

Legislature: A single-chamber National Assembly of fifty members with a four-year tenure is elected by literate male Kuwaiti citizens belonging to families domiciled in Kuwait since 1921. The emir can dissolve the Assembly provided fresh elections are held within two months. But in August 1976 he suspended the four constitutional articles concerning the Assembly and dissolved it in 1977. After its restoration in early 1981, it was suspended again by the emir in July 1986.

Ministers are responsible, individually and collectively, to the Assembly, which must approve bills before the emir promulgates them as laws. If dissatisfied with the prime minister, the National Assembly can convey its lack of confidence in him to the emir, who must then dismiss him or dissolve the Assembly. Though political groups are not permitted, several semipolitical organizations are known to exist. In the October 1992 general election, among the factions that secured Assembly seats were the Islamic Constitutional Movement, a moderate Sunni [qv] group; the Kuwait Democratic Forum, a secular body; and Salafin [qv], a Sunni fundamentalist group.

In the 1999 general election, when only 113,000 Kuwait males (out of 793,000 Kuwait nationals) were entitled to vote, twenty seats were secured by Islamists—both Sunni and Shia (represented by the National Islamic Coalition)—fourteen by secular liberals, represented by the National Democratic Rally, founded in 1997, and the older Kuwait Democratic Front; twelve by government supporters; and the rest by independents.

Religious composition: (2002) Muslims [qv], 85 percent, of which Sunni [qv], 60 percent, Shia [qv] 25 percent; Christian [qv], 8 percent; Hindu, 7 percent.

Kuwait city: *capital of Kuwait* Pop. 343,500 (2003, est.). Kuwait *(Arabic: Little Fort)* was founded in 1710 by members of the Anaiza tribal confederation [qv] who migrated from the interior of the Arabian Peninsula [qv]. In 1776 the (British) East India Company established a base here, and it became an important link in the communication system between India and Britain.

Until 1921 the settlement was surrounded by a mud wall, and its residents lived by fishing, pearling, and trading with India and East Africa. Following the development of the emirate's petroleum industry after the Second World War, Kuwait city and its environs grew dramatically, a process accelerated by the razing of the mud wall in

1957. It emerged as a prosperous administrative, commercial, and financial center, with tree-lined roads and dotted with parks and gardens.

Its historical museum contains prehistoric artifacts from Failakah Island. The damage done to the city during its seven-month occupation by the Iraqis was repaired after the defeat of Iraq [*qv*] in the Second Gulf War [*qv*] in February 1991.

Kuwaiti-Saudi Neutral Zone: *see* Saudi Arabia-Kuwait Neutral Zone.

L

Labor Alignment (Israel): *Israeli political bloc See* Labor-Mapam Alignment.

Labor Islamic Alliance (Egypt): *Egyptian political party* On the eve of the April 1987 parliamentary poll, the semi-clandestine Muslim Brotherhood [*qv*] allied with the opposition Socialist Labor Party [*qv*] and Liberal Socialist Party [*qv*] to form the Labor Islamic Alliance (LSA). The secular groups joined the alliance in order to meet the electoral threshold of 8 percent of the total vote. Adopting the slogan "Islam is the solution," the LSA demanded that the Sharia [*qv*] should be the sole source of legislation.

Despite political harassment and the stuffing of ballot boxes with the votes of the dead, absent, and under-aged for the ruling National Democratic Party [*qv*], the LSA won 17 percent of the vote and sixty seats, displacing the Neo-Wafd Party [*qv*] as the main opposition group. LSA constituents boycotted the next general election when their demands that the emergency be repealed and that the poll be supervised by an independent, nongovernmental body were rejected.

Labor Party (Israeli): (Official title: *Hebrew: Mifleget HaAvodah HaYisraelit*) The alignment formed in 1965 between Mapai [*qv*] and Ahdut HaAvodah-Poale Zion [*qv*] was widened in January 1968 to include Rafi [*qv*], leading finally to the merger of the three into *Mifleget HaAvodah HaYisraelit* (The Israeli Labor Party). Contesting the 1969 and 1973 elections in alliance with Mapam [*qv*] as the Labor-Mapam Alignment [*qv*], its total score in the 1969 and 1973 elections was fifty-six and fifty-one seats, respectively. The Alignment became the leader of the coalition government. Continuing the same Alignment in 1977 and 1981, but securing only thirty-two and forty-seven seats, respectively, Labor lost power to Likud [*qv*]. In the 1984 election the Alignment won forty-four seats, three more than Likud, but the Labor leadership decided to form a national unity government with Likud. Disagreeing with this, Mapam (six seats) discontinued the Alignment. In January 1987 the three-member Yahad group merged with the Labor Party.

In the 1988 and 1992 elections Labor contested independently and won thirty-nine and forty-four seats, respectively. The national unity government that Labor formed with Likud in 1988 fell in March 1990 when its differences with Likud Premier Yitzhak Shamir [*qv*] on the Middle East peace process became irreconcilable. It acted as opposition until the June 1992 poll, when, led by Yitzhak Rabin [*qv*], it secured forty-four seats, twelve more than Likud. It formed a coalition government with Meretz [*qv*] and Shas [*qv*].

It signed a limited self-rule accord with the Palestine Liberation Organization [*qv*] in September 1993 and the Jordanian-Israel Peace Treaty [*qv*] in October 1994. It won thirty-four seats in the May 1996 general election. The One Israel (*Israel Ahat*, in Hebrew) [*qv*] alliance, led by it in the May 1999 poll, secured twenty-six seats. Following the defeat of its leader, Ehud Barak [*qv*], in the 2001 prime ministerial contest, Labor, led by Binyamin Ben Eliezer, joined the national unity government formed by Ariel Sharon [*qv*]. In the January 2003 parliamentary election Labor's share declined to 19.

Labor Zionism and Zionists: *political movement among Jews* The term Labor Zionist applies to those Zionists who wanted to blend Zionism [*qv*] with socialism. A month after the first Zionist Congress met in Basle, Switzerland, in August 1897, the Bund (i.e., League) was established in Vilna, Lithuania, as the general union for Jewish workers in Lithuania, Poland, and Russia. Three years later Poale Zion [*qv*] was established in Minsk, Russia, with a program of socialism, Zionism, and migration to Palestine [*qv*]. From Russia it spread to Austria and then to the United States. A survey of European Jews [*qv*] showed that less than a third of them worked in manufacturing or the construction industry, while nearly a half were engaged in distributive trades, with none in agriculture.

A leading Poale Zion ideologue, Dov Ber Borochov [*qv*], argued that Jews in the Diaspora [*qv*] were excluded from the larger class struggle because of their rootlessness. The solution lay in concentrating Jews in a country of their own, where they could develop the base of their own socioeconomic pyramid. What was needed, he concluded, was a land with a small population but a large potential for agricultural development. Borochov chose Palestine, partly because it was regarded as the historic homeland of Jews, and partly because, being a "derelict country," it was of interest only to small and medium Jewish capitalists—not the big ones—and thus offered revolutionary promise for the Jewish proletariat that was to be fostered there. He considered local Arabs as Turkish subjects, lacking national consciousness, and visualized their assimilation, economic and cultural, into the Jewish nation as it developed economically under Jewish initiative and leadership.

This emphasis on creating a Jewish working class in Palestine dovetailed with the views and actions of Aaron David Gordon (a Ukrainian Jew who arrived in Palestine in 1904) and his followers, who formed the HaPoale HaTzair [*qv*]. Gordon believed that the Jewish nation would recapture its lost spiritual values through manual labor and that the crux of the Jewish problem was not capital against labor but production versus parasitism. By draining marshes and setting up agricultural outposts, HaPoale HaTzair members helped to create Jewish wage labor in agriculture.

In 1919 the leftists within Poale Zion left to form Mopsi (the Socialist Workers Party). The Poale Zion's rightist, nationalist members merged with another group to form Ahdut HaAvodah [*qv*]. In January 1930 Ahdut HaAvodah and HaPoale HaTzair merged to form Mapai [*qv*]. Fifteen years later, having failed to persuade Mapai to adopt the ideas of class struggle and binational (Arab-Jewish) socialist revolution,

Hashomer HaTzair members left Mapai, merged with the leftist Tanua LeAhdut HaAvodah [*qv*] a year later, and emerged as Mapam [*qv*] in early 1948.

In Israel Borochov's influence was most marked in Mapam and Ahdut HaAvodah-Poale Zion [*qv*], and Gordon's in Mapai. As the dominant element in the coalition governments for the next three decades, the Labor Zionist parties were at the forefront of building the nation and the state. In January 1968 a merger of Mapai [*qv*] with Ahdut HaAvodah-Poale Zion and Rafi [*qv*] created the Israeli Labor Party [*qv*]. The Labor Zionist groups in the diaspora supported their counterparts in Israel, and each of them had its own world confederation.

Labor-Mapam Alignment: *Israeli political bloc* The Israeli Labor Party, which arose in January 1968 out of the merger of Mapai [*qv*], Ahdut HaAvodah-Poale Zion [*qv*], and Rafi [*qv*], forged an alliance with Mapam [*qv*]. Popularly called *Maarach* (Alignment), it won 46.2 percent of the vote and fifty-six parliamentary seats. The Alignment continued in the elections in 1973 (42.5 percent, fifty-one seats), 1977 (26.7 percent, thirty-two seats), 1981 (39.2 percent, forty-seven seats), and 1984 (36.7 percent, forty-four seats). When Labor decided to form a national unity government with Likud [*qv*] in 1984, Mapam ended the alignment and became an opposition group with six deputies.

Ladino language: Ladino, also known as Judeo-Spanish, the mother tongue of Sephardic Jews [*qv*], is a language of medieval Spanish origin. Written in Hebrew script, its vocabulary consists of Hebrew [*qv*] words as well as Portuguese, Greek, and Turkish. The first book in Ladino, published in Istanbul, appeared in 1510.

Lahoud, Emile (1936–): *Lebanese military and political leader; president, 1998–* Son of General Jamil Lahoud and Adrenee Bajakian in Baabdate, Lahoud was educated locally. After joining the Beirut Military Academy as a cadet in 1956, he graduated with the rank of lieutenant four years later after passing a naval engineering course in Britain.

He became commander of the second Fleet in 1966. By the time he acquired the rank of rear admiral in 1985, he had been through naval staff courses at the Naval Command College in Rhode Island, United States, twice. Two years earlier he had been appointed president of the military office in the defense ministry where Gen. Michel Aoun [*qv*] was chief of staff. In September 1989, toward the end of the 1975–1990 Lebanese Civil War [*qv*], Lahoud fell out with Aoun. Two months later, President Elias Hrawi [*qv*] promoted Lahoud to general and appointed him military chief of staff after dismissing Aoun. Lahoud led the campaign against Aoun in October 1990, which ended the civil war.

He rebuilt the shattered Lebanese armed forces and introduced conscription for male adults. He managed to maintain friendly relations with both Syria [*qv*] and America. In October 1998 he was elected president by 118 out of 128 parliamentarians. He invited Salim Hoss [*qv*] to form the next government and exercised greater presidential powers than his predecessor.

When the pro-Rafiq Hariri [*qv*] groups did well in the 2000 parliamentary poll, Lahoud called on Hariri to head the next cabinet. While Hariri agreed to focus on the economy, Lahoud took charge of defense and security. In that role Lahoud tied to curb the rising protest against the continued presence of Syrian troops in Lebanon [*qv*], which showed little sign of abating even after Syria had withdrawn 6,000 to 10,000 soldiers from Beirut [*qv*] and suburbs in the summer of 2001. He chaired the Twenty-second Arab League summit [*qv*] in March 2002, the first to be held in Beirut, where there was public reconciliation between Iraq [*qv*] and Kuwait [*qv*], and between Iraq and Saudi Arabia [*qv*].

Land of Israel: *see* Eretz Yisrael.

Latakia: *Syrian city* Pop. 417,000 (2003). Latakia's Arabic name, *Ladhikiya,* is derived from *Laodicea,* mother of Selecus II (d. 226 B.C.), a Greek ruler. A leading port during the Seleucid period in the third and second centuries B.C., it was destroyed by earthquakes twice before falling into the hands of invading Muslim Arabs [*qv*] in A.D. 638. From then until the French mandate in 1920, it came under the intermittent authority of Crusaders, Arabs, and Ottoman Turks.

Endowed with an excellent harbor, today it is the main port of Syria. Its local industry includes fishing, vegetable-oil extraction, tanning, and cotton ginning. Among its surviving monuments are Corinthian columns, called the Colonnade of Bacchus, and a Roman victory arch.

Lavon, Pinchas (1904–76): *Israeli politician* Born Lubianker in Lwow, Poland, Lavon was a cofounder of the Jewish youth movement built around the ideas of Aaron David Gordon. He migrated to Palestine [*qv*] in 1929. He became a joint secretary of Mapai [*qv*] in 1938–39. After serving as a member of the Histadrut [*qv*] executive for several years, he became its secretary-general in 1949–50. Elected to the First Knesset [*qv*] in 1949, he was a member until 1961. He was minister of agriculture from 1950–51 and then minister of defense from 1954–55.

In his second post he became the focus of the longest and most controversial political dispute in Israeli history. In 1954 an attempt by an Israeli spy network in Egypt, consisting of local Jews [*qv*], to destabilize the Egyptian regime and ruin its relations with the West—by planting bombs in cinemas, post offices, and railway stations as well as U.S. consulates and information centers—backfired. All thirteen Israeli agents were arrested. In February 1955, despite Lavon's protestations that the operation had been undertaken by a senior army officer without his knowledge, he was forced to resign as defense minister. The next year he was elected secretary-general of the Histadrut and stayed on until 1961.

In the summer of 1960, when new evidence backing Lavon's version of the "security mishap" surfaced, he demanded that his name be cleared. Prime Minister David Ben-Gurion [*qv*] refused to accept a ministerial inquiry into the affair, as proposed by a majority in the cabinet, and insisted on a judicial inquiry. Ben-Gurion resigned as premier in January 1961, but that was not the end of the Lavon affair. Indeed it continued until the mid-1960s, dragging the ruling party, Mapai, into a whirlpool, and weakening both it and its leader, Ben-Gurion. The Levi Eshkol government, formed in June 1963, fell in December 1964 amid continuing controversy about the Lavon affair.

He led a political group named *Min HaYesod* (From the Foundation), consisting chiefly of intellectuals and members of the kibbutzim [*qv*] who had split from Mapai in November 1964. Following the June 1967 Arab-Israeli War [*qv*], Lavon favored Israel's withdrawal from the Occupied Territories [*qv*].

Law of Return, 1950 (Israel): Adopted in July 1950, the Law of Return confirmed a provision in the 1948 Declaration of Independence of Israel [*qv*] by guaranteeing that "every Jew has the right to this country as an immigrant." Any Jew in the Diaspora [*qv*] wishing to settle in Israel is guaranteed an immigration visa, except those engaged in an activity "against the Jewish people" or likely to "endanger public health or security of the state." In August 1954 another exception was added: Jews "with a criminal past, likely to endanger public welfare." During the first twenty years of Israel, 1,290,771 Jews entered the country under the Law of Return. Of the nearly million Jews from the former Soviet Union who migrated to Israel between the decade of 1989–98 under this law, about a third were not Jews. They were allowed to settle in Israel because they were married to Jews.

Lawrence, Thomas Edward (1888–1935): *Lawrence of Arabia* Son of an Anglo-Irish baronet, Sir Thomas Chapman, Lawrence grew up in Oxford, Britain, and graduated from the city's Jesus College, specializing in medieval military architecture. Between 1911 and 1913 he worked under D. G. Hogarth, an Oxford archaeologist, in Mesopotomia [*qv*]. The next year he joined an exploratory project that took him from Gaza [*qv*] to Aqaba.

Following the outbreak of the First World War, Lawrence was sent to Cairo [*qv*], where he was assigned to military intelligence, and then in January 1916 to the Arab Bureau of Intelligence and diplomatic officers, established to define and implement Britain's role in the Arab revolt against Ottoman Turkey. In October Lawrence joined the British mission in Jiddah [*qv*]. Leading a small force behind the Ottoman lines, Lawrence carried out sabotage and guerilla operations. After mid-1917 he coordinated the Arab revolt with the British campaign, led by General Edmund Allenby. In December he was captured by the enemy, but managed to escape. In September 1918 Lawrence, now promoted to lieutenant colonel, entered Damascus [*qv*] with the Arab forces.

As a member of the British delegation to the Paris Peace Conference of the Council of Four in March 1919, he liaised with the Arabs and acted as adviser to Faisal ibn Hussein [*qv*]. His lobbying for Arab independence failed. This meant the end of the agreement that Lawrence had managed to broker between Faisal ibn Hussein and Chaim Weizmann, the Zionist [*qv*] leader, in London in January 1919, involving acceptance of Jewish immigration into Palestine [*qv*], since it was conditional on the Arabs obtaining their independence "as demanded."

When Colonial Secretary Winston Churchill set up the Middle East department in March 1921, he appointed Lawrence as his Arab affairs adviser. Lawrence was involved in Churchill's negotiations with Abdullah ibn Hussein [*qv*], which resulted in Transjordan [*qv*] being handed over to Abdullah under British protection.

Having finished his long memoirs, recounting his wartime experiences (*Seven Pillars of Wisdom*, 1922), he spent a few years pruning it and finding a publisher. It was published privately in 1926 and was followed by a summary, *Revolt in the Desert,* a year later. He was then at a Royal Air Force (RAF) base in India. He retired from the RAF in 1935 and died in a motorcycle accident soon after.

Lawrence of Arabia: *see* Lawrence, Thomas Edward.

League of Arab States: *see* Arab League.

Lebanese Civil War (1958): The 1958 Lebanese Civil War lasted from May to July. The gap between President Camille Chamoun [*qv*] and the oppositionist, mainly Muslim [*qv*] Socialist National Front (SNF) [*qv*], led by Kamal Jumblat [*qv*], widened after the formation of the United Arab Republic [*qv*] in February 1958, with Chamoun becoming increasingly intolerant of opposition. On 8 May, Nasib Metni, a Christian [*qv*] newspaper publisher, who had just served a jail sentence for criticizing the president, was killed. This led to antigovernment rioting in Tripoli [*qv*] that left thirty-five dead. The SNF organized countrywide strikes and Chamoun declared a state of emergency.

On 12 May civil war started between Chamoun partisans—the gendarmarie and the Maronite [*qv*] militia—and Jumblat supporters, with the army staying neutral. But when the fighting between the two sides intensified, the army intervened to end it. In mid-July, when the Jumblat camp controlled about a third of Lebanon, the pro-Western Iraqi monarch, Faisal II ibn Ghazi [*qv*], was overthrown by republican army officers.

Deprived of his only strong ally in the region, Chamoun requested military aid from the United States under the Eisenhower Doctrine [*qv*]. Soon 14,300 U.S. marines and airborne ground troops arrived and were backed up by the seventy-six-ship U.S. Sixth Fleet. The civil strife intensified briefly before coming to an end on 31 July, with both sides accepting the army commander, General Fuad Chehab [*qv*] as the sole presidential candidate. The war took a toll of about 1,400 to 4,000 Lebanese. The U.S. troop withdrawal was completed by 25 October.

Lebanese Civil War (1975–90): Traditional rivalry between left-leaning Muslim [*qv*] and rightist, mainly Maronite Christians [*qv*] was accentuated with the arrival in Lebanon in the early 1970s of the Palestinian commandos and the Palestine Liberation Organization (PLO) [*qv*]. Also by March 1975 the shuttle diplomacy of U.S. Secretary of State Henry Kissinger to further the Middle East peace process had run out of steam. It suited the United States to see the Arabs mired in a civil conflict that would distract their attention from the failure of U.S. diplomacy. An attack on the Palestinians by the Phalange [*qv*] militia in East Beirut on 13 April 1975 heralded the start of a civil war. That lasted until 13 October 1990 and went through the following phases:

Phase one: April 1975 to May 1976—ascendancy of the reformist alliance. Violence spread throughout the country. The main opposing camps were the Lebanese National Movement (LNM) [*qv*], led by Kamal Jumblat [*qv*], and the Lebanese Front [*qv*], headed by Camille Chamoun [*qv*], with its militia, the Lebanese Forces [*qv*], commanded by Bashir Gemayel [*qv*]. The PLO allied with the LNM and set up a joint command. The LNM demanded an end to confessionalism [qv] and reform of the political system to make it equitable to Muslims, who were now known to constitute a majority.

The Lebanese Front insisted on the expulsion of the armed Palestinians from Lebanon before discussing political and constitutional reform. During this phase both sides decided to eliminate hostile pockets within their enclaves. Intense countrywide fighting in January 1976 destroyed vital state institutions and public buildings, and caused the breakup of the Lebanese army. By early April the LNM-PLO alliance controlled two-thirds of the country. In desperation the Lebanese Front turned to Syria through President Suleiman Franjieh [qv]. Afraid that radical Lebanon, by giving the PLO wide latitude in its struggle with Israel, would provoke Israel, Syrian President Hafiz Assad [qv] decided to aid the Maronite-dominated Lebanese Front.

Phase two: June 1976 to February 1978— Syrian intervention and hegemony. The Syrian military intervention saved the Lebanese Front from total defeat. A subsequent cease-fire, brokered by Libya, prepared the ground for the election of a president. Elias Sarkis [qv], a Syrian nominee, won and took office in September 1976. Within two months a truce had taken hold in the country, except in southern Lebanon where the PLO's activities against Israel were being hampered by an Israeli-backed Christian militia.

Phase three: March to October 1978—first Israeli invasion [qv]. Following a Palestinian guerrilla attack in the Jewish state on 11 March 1978, Israel invaded southern Lebanon [qv]. In May Maronite leaders Pierre Gemayel [qv] and Camille Chamoun

visited Israeli for arms supplies. On 13 June a Phalange squad assassinated Tony Franjieh, son of Suleiman Franjieh, to eliminate any serious rival to Bashir Gemayel in his bid for the presidency.

Phase four: November 1978 to May 1982—consolidation of the Christian ministate. In May–June 1979 the Phalange began to clash with the National Liberal Party (NLP) [qv] militia. The conflict reached a climax in July 1980, with the Phalange defeating the NLP fighters. In the fighting between the Phalange and its Syrian opponents for the control of Mount Sanin, northwest of Zahle, in late April 1981, Israel intervened and shot down two Syrian helicopters. Three months later, following a three-way understanding between Israel, Syria, and the PLO, brokered by the United States, a cease-fire went into effect in southern Lebanon. After the Israeli defense minister, Ariel Sharon [qv], had conferred with LF commanders in January 1982 to plan an Israeli invasion of Lebanon, Israel resumed its arms shipments to the Maronite militias.

Phase five: June 1982 to February 1984— second Israeli invasion and its aftermath. Following a failed assassination attempt on the Israeli ambassador to Britain, Shlomo Argov, on 3 June, Israel invaded Lebanon. (For 6 June to 1 September 1982, see Israeli Invasion of Lebanon, 1982.) On 13 September president-elect Bashir Gemayel [qv] was killed in an explosion that destroyed the headquarters of his Phalange Party [qv]. Israeli units occupied Beirut [qv] with the aim of maintaining order and preventing retaliatory violence. Between 16 and 18 September some 2,000 Palestinian refugees were massacred by the Phalange militia in Beirut's Sabra and Shatila camps. On 20 September deployment of the Western Multi-National Force (MNF) [*qv*]—consisting of U.S., British, French, and Italian units—began. The next day Amin Gemayel [*qv*] was elected president by the parliament. On 29 September the Israelis left Beirut.

On 17 May 1983 Israel signed the Lebanese-Israeli Peace Treaty [*qv*] after the Lebanese parliament had adopted it by an overwhelming majority, but President Amin Gemayel withheld his signature. Following the Israelis' withdrawal from the Shouf region on 3 September, their positions were taken up by the Phalange militia and the Lebanese army. This led to fighting between them and the Druze-PLO alliance. The United States and France intervened with warplanes and warships on the side of the Lebanese army. A cease-fire was mediated by Saudi Arabia on 25 September. But the United States continued its reconnaissance missions over west-central Lebanon from its aircraft carriers. On 23 October truck bombing of U.S. and French military headquarters killed 241 U.S. and 59 French troops. The First National Reconciliation Conference was held in Geneva in early November.

After an attack on West Beirut's Shia [*qv*] suburbs by the Lebanese army and the Lebanese Forces (LF) on 3 February 1984, fighting erupted between the army and the LF on the one side and the Amal-Druze [*qv*] alliance on the other. U.S. warships intervened against the Muslims forces. Following the defection of Muslims from the Lebanese army, the Amal-Druze alliance expelled the (Christian) army from West Beirut. On 7 February 1984 the United States withdrew its troops from Beirut. The other members of the Western MNF followed suit.

Phase six: March 1984 to January 1986—return of Syrian hegemony. Encouraged by Assad, President Gemayel decided to abrogate the draft Lebanese-Israeli peace treaty: the Lebanese parliament did so on 5 March. Following the Second National Reconciliation Conference in Lausanne, Switzerland, in mid-March a national reconciliation government was formed. On 6 June 1985 Israel completed the last phase of its withdrawal from Lebanon by handing over its positions in southern Lebanon to the Christian militia run by it, but leaving behind 1,000 Israeli troops. In late December the commanders of Amal, the Druze militia, and the LF signed the National Agreement to Solve the Lebanese Crisis, outlining political reform and Lebanese-Syrian relations; but the agreement was stillborn as the LF commander was unable to secure the endorsement of his executive committee.

Phase seven: February 1986 to September 1988—limits of Syrian power. Following fighting between Amal and the Druze militia in West Beirut in February 1987, Syria sent its troops, withdrawn in September 1982, to restore order. In early April 1988 there were clashes between Amal and Hizbollah [*qv*] in southern Lebanon, and these continued until late May. Meanwhile, in mid-April Assad and U.S. Secretary of State George Shultz agreed to coordinate policy on political reform in Lebanon. When parliament failed to elect a new president, on 22 September 1988 outgoing President Gemayel instructed his chief of staff, General Michel Aoun [*qv*], to form a temporary military government. Of the five other officers he appointed to his cabinet, three Muslim officers refused to join.

Phase eight: October 1988 to September 1989—war of liberation, Aoun-style. Following his attack and suppression of the LF in the Christian enclave in February 1989, Aoun declared a war of liberation against Syria in mid-March. Syria imposed land and sea blockades on the Christian enclave. On 25 May the Sixteenth Arab League [*qv*] summit appointed a committee of the heads of Algeria, Morocco, and Saudi Arabia to settle the Lebanese crisis within six months. In mid-August fourteen Lebanese groups formed an anti-Aoun front.

Phase nine: October 1989 to October 1990—the Taif Accord [*qv*]. Between 30 September and 22 October, fifty-eight of the sixty-two (surviving) Lebanese parliamentarians debated the National Reconciliation Charter [*qv*] in Taif, Saudi Arabia, and adopted it. Aoun rejected it, but the Maronite Lebanese Front accepted it. After endorsing the Taif Accord on Lebanese soil at Qulayaat on 5 November, the Lebanese parliament elected Rene Muawad as president. He was assassinated on 22 November. Two days later parliament elected Elias Hrawi [*qv*] to the presidency.

From January to March 1990 there was intense fighting between Aoun loyalists and the LF. As a result, Aoun ended up with only a third of the Christian enclave. The LF declared allegiance to Hrawi. On 21 August parliament decided to overhaul the constitution as outlined in the Taif Accord. A month later Hrawi's decision to impose a land blockade on Aoun's enclave was backed by the LF. By now, in the midst of the crisis created by Iraq's invasion and occupation of Kuwait, Syria had joined the U.S.-led coalition against Iraq. On 13 October, in a joint air and ground campaign, the Lebanese and Syrian troops defeated Aoun's soldiers and brought the civil war to an end.

Human losses: The number of fatalities during the fifteen and a half years of war, including the 15,700 killed in the Second Israeli invasion, mainly civilians, was put at 150,000.

Economic damage: During the first seven years of conflict (before the Second Israeli invasion), the direct annual cost of the war was put at $900 million.

After the war: On 9 May 1991 parliament passed a law giving Muslims and Christians parity in the chamber, thus changing the 6:5 Christians-Muslim ratio of the 1943 National Pact [*qv*] and raising the size of the chamber from 99 to 108. On 22 May, Presidents Hrawi and Assad signed the Lebanese-Syrian Treaty of Brotherhood, Cooperation, and Coordination [*qv*], which required the two neighbors to coordinate their policies in foreign affairs, defense and economy.

Lebanese Forces: *Lebanese militia and political party* Formed in January 1976, the Lebanese Forces (LF) consisted of the Maronite [*qv*] militias of the Phalange [*qv*], the National Liberal Party [*qv*], the Guardians of the Cedars [*qv*], and al Tanzim. Its unified military command was headed by Bashir Gemayel [*qv*]. After his assassination in 1982 the new commander, Fadi Afram, adopted an openly pro-Israeli line, calling for talks between Lebanon and Israel. Following the abrogation of the draft Lebanese-Israeli Peace Treaty [*qv*] in March

1984, LF leadership passed to Fuad Abu Nadr. After a bloodless coup in March 1985, Samir Geagea assumed command of the LF.

In December 1989 Geagea's backing for the Taif Accord [qv] led to fighting between the LF and Gen. Michel Aoun [qv] commanding the (Christian) Lebanese army based in the Christian enclave. It intensified after Geagea had declared his allegiance in April 1990 to President Elias Hrawi [qv], who rivaled Aoun as head of state. Five months later the LF backed Hrawi's blockading of Aoun's enclave, now reduced to about a third of the Christian sector. At the time of Aoun's fall in October 1990, marking the end of the civil war, the LF was 10,000 strong, down from its peak of 20,000 under Bashir Gemayel, with 25,000 reserves.

Geagea was included in the national unity cabinet formed in December. The next year, in line with the official policy of integrating the members of all militias under the age of twenty-five into the regular armed forces, the government absorbed 6,500 LF men into the military. The LF then transformed itself into a political party. It boycotted the 1992 general election. In May 1994, following the bombing of a Maronite church in Jonieh earlier that year, the LF was banned and Geagea was arrested on charges of complicity in the explosion and the murder in October 1990 of Danny Chamoun, a son of Camille Chamoun [qv]. In 1995 he was sentenced to death, which was later commuted to life imprisonment.

Lebanese Front: *Lebanese political alliance* The Lebanese Front was formed in September 1976 as a confederation of the following Maronite [qv] Christian political parties: the Phalange Party [qv], National Liberal Party [qv], the Guardians of the Cedars [qv], and the Maronite League. It was headed by Camille Chamoun [qv]. The Front's constituents stressed their distinctness from the Arab world by emphasizing that Maronite history, centering on the church and Mount Lebanon, stood apart from mainstream Muslim Arabs [qv] and even non-Maronite Christians. In December 1980 the Front issued a manifesto calling for the replacement of the 1943 National Pact [qv] by some sort of federation or confederation within a unified Lebanon.

Though Chamoun was the nominal leader, Bashir Gemayel [qv] and his father, Pierre [qv], mattered more. Since Christians played a special role in Lebanon, they argued, they were entitled to a special position, irrespective of them being a minority. The Front tightened its links with Israel, which found it convenient to deal with a single Maronite political entity than with several. However, with Bashir Gemayel's murder in September 1982 and Israel's withdrawal from Lebanon in June 1985, the Front moderated its stance.

With the rise of Gen. Michel Aoun [qv] as a pretender to the presidency in September 1988, the Front became one of the three power centers in the Christian enclave, the remaining one being the Lebanese Forces [qv]. A year later the Front's parliamentary leader, Georges Saade, successfully opposed a proposal by the Lebanese parliament, meeting in Taif, Saudi Arabia, to discard confessionalism [qv] by a certain deadline. The internecine Christian fighting in early 1990 weakened the Front. With the end of the civil war [qv] in October, the Front, a creature of the conflict, lost its relevance.

Lebanese National Movement: *Lebanese-Palestinian political alliance* Formed on the eve of the April 1975–October 1990 Lebanese Civil War [*qv*], the Lebanese National Movement (LNM) was a confederation of various nationalist and progressive Muslim-dominated parties—including the Arab Baath Socialist Party [*qv*], the Progressive Socialist Party (PSP) [*qv*], the Syrian Social Nationalist Party [*qv*], the Communist Party [*qv*], the Communist Action Organization, the Popular Nasserist Organization and the Independent Nasserites. Led by Kamal Jumblat [*qv*], it demanded the abolition of the confessional system, amendment of the constitution to redefine the prerogatives of the various branches of the executive, and reorganization of the army.

It formed an alliance with the Palestine Liberation Organization (PLO) [*qv*] in its fight with the Maronite [*qv*] Lebanese Front [*qv*] and the Lebanese Forces [*qv*]. When the LNM-PLO alliance gained the upper hand in the fighting, Syria intervened in June 1976 on the side of the Christians [*qv*]. Its troops expelled LNM-PLO forces from the Christian areas they had captured. This, and the subsequent Syrian plan to legitimize its occupation of eastern and northern Lebanon, turned Jumblat into a vocal adversary of Syrian President Hafiz Assad [*qv*].

Kamal Jumblat's assassination in March 1977 deprived the LNM of a charismatic figure. The mantle passed on to his son, Walid [*qv*], who lacked experience and leadership qualities. He made his peace with Syria. Indeed, as the leader of both the PSP and the LNM, he coordinated his policies and actions with Damascus. While the Lebanese Front insisted on resolving the problem of the Syrian and Palestinian military presence before tackling the issue of political reform, the LNM wanted immediate reform while its Syrian and Palestinian allies were still able to lend it their support.

Israel's siege of Beirut [*qv*] in August 1982 resulted in the departure of both PLO and LNM fighters from West Beirut. This enfeebled the LNM. A year later, in July 1983, the constituents of the LNM gathered again (in Tripoli [*qv*]) to consult all other groups opposing the draft Lebanese-Israeli Peace Treaty [*qv*] that had been initialed two months earlier. Following its success in destroying the treaty, the LNM ceased to function as a coherent body. Its erstwhile constituents participated in the civil strife through their respective militias. They came together again briefly as the Lebanese National Front in August 1989 to overthrow Gen. Michel Aoun [*qv*].

Lebanese-Israeli (Putative) Peace Treaty (1983–84): Under U.S. pressure, President Amin Gemayel [*qv*], soon after assuming office in September 1982, agreed to enter into talks with Israel provided the United States acted as the mediator. This led to an agreed draft of a peace treaty between Lebanon and Israel in early May 1983. It formally ended the state of war between the two countries, and banned Lebanon from allowing the use of its territory or airspace for the passage of troops or military equipment from any state that did not have diplomatic relations with Israel. It also required Lebanon to abrogate any regulations, laws, or treaties that were in conflict with the Lebanese-Israeli accord, including all the commitments that Lebanon had made as a founder member of the Arab League [*qv*] since 1945. It curtailed the Lebanese government's power to station troops between the Zahrani and Awali rivers, and required it to recognize the Israeli-backed Christian militia, commanded by Saad Haddad, as the sole force authorized to patrol the area up to Zahrani, and allow the stationing of Lebanese-Israeli supervisory teams charged with detecting and destroying any armed guerrillas in the area.

The document was denounced by left-of-center forces in Lebanon and Syrian President Hafiz Assad [*qv*]. Its passing by sixty-four Lebanese members of parliament (to two opposing), followed by the signing of it by Israel, made little difference to their stance. They continued to express their opposition publicly. Protesting at Israel's continued occupation of a large part of Lebanon in the aftermath of the June 1982 Israeli invasion [*qv*], President Gemayel withheld his signature on the treaty. When, following a truck bombing of their military barracks that resulted in 300 U.S. and French deaths in October 1983, the four leading Western nations withdrew their peacekeeping contingents from Beirut [*qv*] in February 1984, Gemayel found himself without his Western guardians. He therefore decided to abrogate the treaty, and at his behest parliament did so almost unanimously on 5 March 1984.

Lebanese-Palestine Liberation Organization Agreement (1969): *see* Cairo Agreement (Lebanese-PLO, 1969).

Lebanese-Syrian Treaty of Brotherhood, Cooperation, and Coordination (1991): The six-article Lebanese-Syrian Treaty of Brotherhood, Cooperation, and Coordina-tion was signed by the presidents of the two countries in Damascus [*qv*] in May 1991. Article One enjoins the parties to "realize the highest degree of cooperation and coordination between them in all political, security, cultural, scientific, and other concerns . . . within the framework of the sovereignty and independence of each of them." Article Two requires the signatories to achieve cooperation and coordination in economics, agriculture, industry, commerce, transportation, communications, customs, and development. "The interrelationship of the two countries' security requires that Lebanon not be made the source of a threat to Syria's security or Syria to Lebanon's in any circumstances whatsoever," states Article Three. "Lebanon shall therefore not allow itself to become a passage or a base for any power or state or organization the purpose of which is the violation of Lebanon's security or Syria's security." Equally, Syria "shall not allow any action that threatens Lebanon's security, independence or sovereignty."

The next article specifies the formation of a Lebanese-Syrian military committee to determine the size and duration of the Syrian troops' presence in Lebanon. Article Five focuses on the contracting parties' foreign policy and requires them to coordinate their Arab and international policies. The last article specifies the formation of joint agencies at different levels to implement the treaty—from the Higher Council, consisting of the presidents, prime ministers, deputy prime ministers, and parliamentary speakers, to the committees on defense and security, foreign affairs, and economic and social affairs. In 2001, Lebanon and Syria created a customs union.

Lebanon:
Official name: Republic of Lebanon
Capital: Beirut [*qv*]
Area: 4,036 sq. miles/10,452 sq. km
Population: 3,620,000 (2003, est.), excluding 406,000 Palestinian refugees in camps
Gross domestic product: $16.6 billion (2001, est.)
National currency: Lebanese Pound (LP); LP 1000 = US$0.66 = £0.46 = EUR 0.75 (2001)
Form of government: republic, president elected by parliament
Official language: Arabic [*qv*]
Official religion: None
Administrative regions: Lebanon is divided into five governorates (provinces).
Constitution: Promulgated by the French mandate in May 1926, the constitution was amended in 1927, 1929, and 1943 by France, and in 1947 and 1990 by the Lebanese parliament, the last exercise resulting in changes to thirty-one articles. Lebanon is a multiparty, multireligious republic, where since 1943 confessionalism [*qv*] has been built into the political-administrative system. It specifies that the president of the republic is to be a Maronite Christian [*qv*], the prime minister a Sunni Muslim [*qv*], and the parliamentary speaker a Shia Muslim [*qv*].
Ethnic composition (2002): Arab, 95 percent; Armenian [*qv*], 4 percent; other, 1 percent.
Executive: The 1990 amendments to the constitution curtailed the power of the president, elected for a six-year term by parliament, and increased the authority of the cabinet, making it more autonomous. The president has the power to approve and implement laws passed by the National Assembly. However, his decisions must be cosigned by the prime minister, except when it is a question of appointing a prime minister—something he must do in consultation with the speaker of the Assembly and senior deputies. Cabinet ministers need not be Assembly members, but are responsible to it.
High officials:
President: Emile Lahoud [*qv*], 1998–
Prime minister: Rafiq Hariri [*qv*], 2000–
Speaker of the parliament: Nabih Berri [*qv*], 2000–
History: After receiving a mandate for (Greater) Syria from the League of Nations in 1920, France enlarged the ex-Ottoman Vilayat of Lebanon by adding areas to its north, west, and south, hitherto belonging to Syria, and calling the new entity Greater Lebanon. In 1926 it promulgated a republican constitution, with a parliament and an executive president elected by parliament, and the country was renamed the Republic of Lebanon. France suspended the constitution in 1932, and a census held in that year produced figures for sixteen recognized religious sects. In 1936 Paris reinstated the constitution, and the Franco-Lebanese Treaty [*qv*] signed in November gave considerable autonomy to Lebanon.

During the Second World War the pro-German government—formed in Vichy, central France—took over overseas French territories, including Lebanon, in 1940. The Vichy government's occupation of Lebanon was overthrown by British and Free French forces in June 1941, and Lebanon was given (nominal) independence. The National Pact [*qv*] of March 1943 provided a formula of six

Christian to five Muslim parliamentarians. In September Bishara Khouri [*qv*] was elected president. In 1945 Lebanon was one of the founder members of the Arab League [*qv*].

With the departure of the French in December 1946 Lebanon became fully independent. It participated in the Palestine War (1948–49) [*qv*] and signed a truce with Israel in March 1949. Khouri was reelected later that year, but was forced to resign in 1952 and was followed by Camille Chamoun [*qv*]. Chamoun subscribed to the Eisenhower Doctrine [*qv*] and solicited the help of U.S. troops in the midst of the May–July 1958 Lebanese Civil War [*qv*] between his forces and those of Kamal Jumblat [*qv*]. The succeeding president, Fuad Chehab [*qv*], tried to modernize Lebanon's political-administrative machinery, which was steeped in feudal values and sectarian cleavage. The reforming pace slowed down during the presidency of Charles Helou [*qv*].

Lebanon stayed out of the June 1967 Arab-Israeli War [*qv*]. The increasing presence of armed Palestinians led to clashes between them and the Lebanese army, but a modus vivendi was worked out through the 1969 Cairo Agreement [*qv*]. During the presidency of Suleiman Franjieh [*qv*], the Palestine Liberation Organization (PLO) [*qv*] set up its headquarters in Beirut [*qv*] in 1972. Lebanon stayed out of the 1973 Arab-Israeli War [*qv*].

In April 1975 the long Lebanese Civil War [*qv*] erupted. By the spring of 1976 the Lebanese National Movement (LNM)-PLO alliance controlled two-thirds of the country and Syria intervened on the side of the Christian Lebanese Front [*qv*]. In September Elias Sarkis [*qv*], a Syrian nominee, was elected

president. After the assassination of the LNM leader, Kamal Jumblat [*qv*], in March 1977, his son, Walid [*qv*], succeeded him.

Israel invaded southern Lebanon in March 1978 to destroy the PLO bases there. In June Israel withdrew, but handed over its posts in southern Lebanon to a Christian militia. The Maronite militias forged strong ties with Israel, but their attempts to extend their sway to Zahle in the Beqaa Valley in mid-1981 were frustrated by Syria, now maintaining 30,000 peacekeeping troops under the aegis of the Arab League and backing the Muslim camp.

In early June 1982, six weeks after completing its withdrawal from the Sinai Peninsula [*qv*] in late April 1982, under the terms of the Egyptian-Israeli Peace Treaty [*qv*], Israel again invaded Lebanon. It occupied two-fifths of the country, including Beirut [*qv*], and was instrumental in getting Bashir Gemayel [*qv*] elected president. But before he could take office, Gemayel was assassinated. The Israeli invasion ended on 1 September, after 11,644 PLO fighters and 2,700 Syrian troops had left West Beirut.

Amin Gemayel [*qv*] was elected president. Under U.S. pressure he initialed a draft peace treaty with Israel in May 1983. But strong domestic hostility to it, combined with Syrian opposition, resulted in the treaty being annulled in March 1984. Following a reconciliation conference in Lausanne, Switzerland, a national unity government was formed. In June 1985 Israel completed the last phase of its withdrawal, handing over its positions in southern Lebanon to its surrogate force, the South Lebanon Army (SLA) [*qv*]. In early 1987 Syria dispatched its troops into West Beirut to restore order following fighting between Amal [*qv*], a Shia [*qv*] militia, and an alliance of left-of-center non-Shia Muslim forces.

Following parliament's failure to elect a new president to succeed Gemayel, on 22 September 1988 he called on his chief of staff, Gen. Michel Aoun [*qv*], to form a temporary military government. Of the five officers appointed to the cabinet, all three Muslim officers refused to join. In May 1989 Aoun launched a "war of liberation" from Syria. Five months later Lebanese parliamentarians, meeting in Taif, Saudi Arabia, adopted the National Reconciliation Charter [*qv*], containing political reform, and later approved it at a meeting held inside Lebanon. They also elected Elias Hrawi [*qv*], a Syrian nominee, as president.

Aoun rejected the Taif Accord [*qv*], whereas the Maronite Lebanese Forces [*qv*] accepted it. This led to intra-Christian violence, in which Aoun did badly. After parliament had translated the Taif Accord into law, giving parity to Muslims and Christians in legislature and curtailing the powers of the Maronite president in August, the Lebanese and Syrian forces defeated Aoun's troops on 13 October 1990, thus ending the civil war. A national unity government disarmed the various militias, ended the division of the capital into East and West Beirut, and signed a Treaty of Brotherhood, Cooperation, and Coordination with Syria [*qv*] in May 1991.

Elections to an enlarged parliament were held between August and October 1992. Due to the election boycott by the Maronite-dominated parties, the new chamber and the consequent government were strongly pro-Syrian. Lebanon participated in the Middle East peace process that had been inaugurated by the Middle East Peace Conference in Madrid in October 1991 [*qv*], but, mirroring the impasse between Syria and Israel, its bilateral talks with Israel made little progress. The government called on Israel to vacate southern Lebanon unconditionally, as demanded by the 1978 U.N. Security Council Resolution 425 [*qv*], and allowed Hizbollah [*qv*] to function in the region as a counterforce to the SLA. Bound by the 1991 Lebanese-Syrian Treaty of Brotherhood, Cooperation, and Coordination [*qv*], it consulted Syria in its peace talks with Israel. Since Syria's negotiations with Israel made little progress, the Lebanese-Israeli talks proved inconclusive. Pressured by Hizbollah's attacks, Israel quit southern Lebanon in May 2000 unconditionally.

After the terrorist attacks on the U.S. in September 2001, Washington pressured Lebanon to ban Hizbollah. But the Lebanese government refused, arguing that it was a legitimate political group with a substantial presence in the parliament as well as a social welfare organization. President Emile Lahoud chaired the Twenty-second Arab League summit [*qv*] in March 2002 in Beirut, which called for devising a universally accepted definition of terrorism [*qv*].

Legislature: Called the National Assembly, parliament is a unicameral house with 128 members, divided equally among Christians and Muslims, who are elected on universal suffrage for a four-year term. It has legislative and constitutional powers. It is also an electoral college for the election of president. If it fails to choose a president by a two-thirds majority in the first secret ballot, it makes its choice by a simple majority. On constitutional matters a quorum of two-thirds is required, but other decisions are taken by a simple majority.

Following the eruption of the Lebanese Civil War in April 1975 [*qv*], the Assembly, elected in 1972, periodically extended its life until September 1992, when a fresh election was held under the amended constitution. The new share of Islamic sects, with the old share in parenthesis, was: Sunni, 27 (20); Shia, 27 (19); Druze [*qv*] 8 (6); and Alawi [*qv*], 2 (none). The new share of Christian sects was: Maronites, 34 (30); Greek Orthodox [*qv*], 14 (11); Greek Catholics [*qv*], 6 (6); Armenian Catholic and Armenian Orthodox [*qv*], 6 (5); Protestants [*qv*] and non-Muslim minorities, 4 (2).

Religious composition: (1986, unofficial estimate) Muslim, 60–73 percent, of which Shia, 31–39 percent, Sunni, 21–26 percent; Druze, 7 percent, Alawi, 1 percent; Christian, 26–39 percent, of which Maronite, 16–25 percent, Greek Orthodox; 5–6 percent; Greek Catholic, 3–4 percent, Armenian Catholic and Orthodox, 2–3 percent; Other, 1 percent.

Lehi/Lehy (*Hebrew: acronym of* Lohemei Herut Israel/Yisrael, *Fighters for Free Israel): Zionist militia* In June 1940 Avraham Stern [*qv*] and his followers, disagreeing with Irgun's [*qv*] decision to suspend its armed campaign against the British mandate, left Irgun, and established Lehi in September. Commonly known as the Stern Gang or Stern Group, Lehi argued that since the British were the number one enemy of Jews [*qv*], and since fighting them was the top Jewish priority, there was no harm in negotiating with the German Nazis to achieve this aim. As a consequence it contacted the German Embassy in Ankara.

This, and terrorist attacks against the British mandate, marginalized Lehi and Stern, who went underground.

Stern's death in February 1942 did not destroy Lehi. The leadership formally passed to the triumvirate of Yitzhak Shamir [*qv*], Nathan Yellin-Mor, and Israel Schieb in November. Its assassination policy resulted in the murder of Lord Moyne, British minister of state in Cairo, in November 1944. After the war, in order to coordinate underground activities, it joined with Irgun and Histadrut [*qv*] to form the Hebrew Resistance Movement (HRM) in November 1945. Among the joint operations it carried out with Irgun were the blowing up of the British embassy in Rome and the posting of letter bombs to British ministers, as well as killing British soldiers in Palestine [*qv*] and hanging their officers. Lehi attacked a military airfield as well as several railway depots and workshops.

After the disbanding of the HRM in October 1946, Lehi felt free to intensify its guerrilla activities: it attacked oil installations, military trains and vehicles, and British troops and policemen. Between November 1947 (the United Nations partition plan) and May 1948 (the founding of Israel), the 1,000-strong Lehi allied with the larger Irgun in concerted attacks on Arabs [*qv*], including a full-fledged offensive against the Arabs of Jaffa [*qv*] and an attack on Deir Yassin village near Jerusalem [*qv*] on 9–10 April 1948, killing 254 men, women, and children.

Following the establishment of Israel, the decision to dissolve Lehi and absorb its members into the Israel Defense Forces (IDF) did not apply to Jerusalem, which was given a separate status. Therefore, Lehi units continued to function in that city. In September the assassination of Count Folke Bernadotte, a Swedish diplomat acting as the U.N. mediator between Arabs and Jews, was claimed by *Hazit HaMoledet* (The Homeland Front), a subgroup of Lehi. Two Lehi leaders, Nathan Yellin-Mor and Matitiahu Schmulevitz, were found guilty and given eight and five years imprisonment, respectively, by a military court. But they were soon released as part of the general amnesty, and Yellin-Mor was elected to the Knesset [*qv*] in January 1949 on a Lehi ticket. The Israeli government treated Lehi members on a par with Haganah [*qv*] and Irgun when calculating pensions or redundancy payments for its civil servants.

Lesser Tumb Island: also spelled Lesser Tunb Island; *see* Tumb/Tunb Islands.

Levant *(French: derivative of lever, to rise, as applied to, say, sunrise):* Historically, the term was applied to the lands along the eastern shores of the Mediterranean. Subsequent to the French mandate of Syria and Lebanon in 1920, these countries were called the Levant States. Today the term Levant applies to the independent states of Syria and Lebanon.

Liberal Party (Israel): *Israeli political party* Official title: *Liberalim (Hebrew: Liberals).* The fear of a further fall in their electoral popularity drove the General Zionists [*qv*] to merge with the Progressive Party [*qv*] to form the Liberal Party on the eve of the 1961 general election. While endorsing the concept of a welfare state, it demanded encouragement for private enterprise. It won seventeen seats in the Knesset [*qv*]. In the 1965 poll it allied with Herut [*qv*] to form a bloc called Gahal [*qv*], under the leadership of Menachem Begin [*qv*].

Liberal Socialist Party (Egypt): *Egyptian political party* The Liberal Socialist Party (LSP) was formed in May 1976 by Mustafa Kamel Murad to represent the rightist forum within the Arab Socialist Union [*qv*]. It advocated liberal economic policies and greater freedom for private enterprise. It was allowed to publish a weekly magazine, *Al Ahrar* (The Free). In the general election in November it won twelve seats. This declined to three in the 1979 poll when Murad failed to be reelected.

The LSP's poor performance in the next two elections led its leadership to form an alliance with the Socialist Labor Party [*qv*] and the Muslim Brotherhood [*qv*] on the eve of the 1987 poll, especially as it had no chance of crossing the newly required threshold of 8 percent of the total vote to qualify for seats in parliament. The resulting Labor Islamic Alliance (LSA) [*qv*] won sixty seats, with the LSP's share at ten. Like its allies in the LSA, it boycotted the 1990 election when the government rejected their call to lift the state of emergency and conduct the poll under the supervision of a nongovernmental organization. In the 1995 poll it secured one seat, retaining it in the 2000 election.

Liberation Movement of Iran: *Iranian political party* After his release from jail (as a leader of the National Front [*qv*]) in 1961, Mahdi Bazargan [*qv*] teamed up with Ayatollah Mahmud Taleqani [*qv*] to form the Liberation Movement of Iran (LMI). They saw it as a link between Shiism [*qv*] and modern political ideas and movements. It was open to both lay and clerical Iranians. Bazargan urged the clergy to participate in politics.

Following his call for a boycott of the referendum on the White Revolution [qv] in January 1963, Bazargan was given a ten-year prison sentence, but this did not affect the spread of the LMI among Iranian students in Europe and North America. In late 1977, with the revolutionary movement gathering pace in Iran, the LMI revived at home. Its status was raised with the appointment of Bazargan as prime minister by Ayatollah Ruhollah Khomeini [qv] after the 1979 Islamic revolution [qv]. In the first parliamentary election it won 20 seats in a house of 270. Since it functioned as opposition it came under official pressure. The government shut down its paper, *Mizan (Persian: Scales),* on the ground that it had divulged military secrets. However, by the spring of 1983, when the political scene was occupied by the governing Islamic Republican Party [qv] and its smaller allies, the LMI was the only opposition group allowed to function.

In a parliamentary speech in August, Bazargan, who had opposed the Iranian invasion of Iraq two months earlier, criticized the government for labeling dissidents as heretics. In April 1985 Khomeini dismissed his appeals for a truce with Iraq as demoralizing to the armed forces. Undaunted, Bazargan and the LMI continued to describe war as lethal to Islam [qv] and revolution. In August 1985 Bazargan was disqualified as a candidate for the presidency.

Once the Iran-Iraq War [qv] had ended in 1988, the party lost its strongest card against the government. While a sharp decline in the majority for President Ali Akbar Hashemi Rafsanjani [qv] in 1993 showed that opposition to the government was rising, there was

little evidence to show that the LMI was the main beneficiary.

The death of Bazargan in 1995 caused a decline in the LMI's following. Though the party lacked an official license, the authorities allowed it to function. During the student protest in mid-1999, it emerged that some students favored the LMI. In 2001 the conservative-dominated judiciary arrested many party leaders, and in the following year the group was formally banned.

Likud *(Hebrew: Unity): Israeli political bloc* In the wake of the October 1973 Arab-Israeli War [qv], Gahal [qv] combined with the Free Center, the State Party (a remnant of Rafi [qv]), and the Eretz Yisrael movement to form Likud. What brought them together was their commitment to incorporating into Israel the Palestinian Arab territories occupied since the June 1967 Arab-Israeli War [qv].

Ideologically, Likud was an alliance of the conservative, capitalist, and ultranationalist trends within secular Zionism [qv]. It won 30.2 percent of the votes (thirty-nine seats) in the December 1973 poll and secured 33.4 percent of the votes (forty-three seats) in the May 1977 election, becoming the senior partner in the coalition government (including religious parties) headed by its leader, Menachem Begin [qv]. It repeated its winning performance in the July 1981 election and secured forty-seven seats.

Due to Israel's invasion of Lebanon [qv] in 1982 and its aftermath, resulting in the death of more than 500 soldiers, Likud's popularity declined. Begin resigned in August 1983 and was succeeded by Yitzhak Shamir [qv]. Likud's share of forty-one seats in the 1984 general election was a little more than Labor's [*qv*] thirty-eight. It formed a national unity government with Labor, with its leader becoming prime minister for a two-year term. The same happened after the 1988 election when, faced with the loss of a further two seats (to thirty-nine), Likud agreed to share power with Labor in a national unity government. When this arrangement broke down in March 1990 on the issue of the terms of a Middle East peace process, Likud managed to put together a coalition cabinet with the help of religious and ultraright parties. In the June 1992 poll, with its share of seats down to thirty-two, it lost power. Its leadership passed to Benjamin Netanyahu [*qv*]. In the May 1996 general election, it won twenty-two seats. After Netanyahu had stepped down as the party leader in the wake of his defeat in the prime ministerial contest in May 1999, and Likud's parliamentary strength had fallen to nineteen, its leadership went to Ariel Sharon [*qv*].

Little Tumb Island: also spelled Little Tunb Island; *see* Tumb-Tunb Islands.

M

Maarach *(Hebrew: Alignment): Israeli political alliance* Maarach is the popular term that was applied to the alliance between Mapai [*qv*] and Ahdut HaAvodah-Poale Zion [*qv*] in 1965—and then from 1969 to 1984 to the alliance between the Labor Party [*qv*] and Mapam [*qv*].

Mafdal *(Hebrew: acronymn of* Mifleget Datit Leumit, *National Religious Party): see* National Religious Party (Israel).

mahdi *(Arabic: The guided one, leader):* The concept of *mahdi,* the Rightly Guided One, who will end injustice and restore faith while claiming divine sanction, is well defined in Judaism [*qv*], Christianity [*qv*], and Twelver Shiism [*qv*]. Twelver Shias believe that the twelfth Imam Muhammad al Qasim, the infant son of the eleventh Imam Hassan al Askari, is their mahdi, who has been in spiritual occultation since A.D. 874 but will reappear to institute the rule of justice on earth before the Day of Judgement. Among Sunnis [*qv*] the prevalent concept is that of a *mujaddid* (renewer), who appears at the turn of every Islamic century to defend the *sunna* [*qv*] from innovation.

Mahfouz, Naguib (1911–): *Egyptian writer; winner of the Nobel Prize for Literature, 1988* Born into a merchant family in Cairo [*qv*], Mahfouz graduated in philosophy from Cairo University in 1934. After a brief period of teaching philosophy, he joined the civil service in 1939 and stayed on for thirty-three years. After serving in the ministry of religious endowments from 1939–54, he moved to the ministry of culture and national guidance as director of technical supervision, and later as director of the State Cinema Organization.

He discovered European fiction at university and avidly read in French such writers as Honore de Balzac, Albert Camus, Fyodor Dostoevsky, Gustave Flaubert, Walter Scott, Leo Tolstoy, and Emile Zola. *A Game of Fates* (1939), his first novel, was influenced by Walter Scott. Set in the era of the pharaohs, it dealt with an oppressive regime and the overthrow of foreign rule. As monarchical Egypt was then under British tutelage, the subject was contemporary.

After two more historical novels Mahfouz

turned to social realism with *A New Cairo* (1946). The book centerd on three university students—one a socialist, another a pious Muslim, and the third an opportunist. The next three novels—*Khan al Khalili* (1945), *Midaqq Alley* (1947), and *The Beginning and the End* (1949)—revolved around the lower middle classes in Cairo. The books had a large cast and examined prevailing social tensions. Balzac was his inspiration. Mahfouz stretched the bounds of literary Arabic [*qv*], understood from the Persian Gulf [*qv*] to the Atlantic, to compose realistic dialogue, a unique achievement—thus fashioning a device that allowed him and other Arabic writers to infuse social realism into their creative works and broaden their readership.

Next followed his most mature work, *The Trilogy* (1956–57): *Bayn al Qasryn* (The Palace Walk), *Qasr al Shawq* (The Palace of Desire), and *Al Sukkariyya* (The Sugar Street), named after Cairo streets. In it he offered an eyewitness account of Egypt between the First and Second World Wars through a thirty-year history of one Cairene family using a vernacular that had not been encountered before, with religious and political themes entertainingly intertwined. It made him a literary star in Egypt and elsewhere in the Arab world. In its length and scale *The Trilogy* remains unrivaled in Arabic literature. After seven years of silence came a serialization in *Al Ahram* (The Pyramids), the country's leading daily newspaper, of his *Children of Gebelaawi* (1964), an iconoclastic allegory of human life from Genesis to the present day, which concluded with a vision of man searching in a rubbish dump for clues about his salvation. So unsettling was this

work that the authorities did not allow it to be issued as a book in Egypt.

At the film broadcasting division of the ministry of culture and national guidance, he adapted several of his novels as films. He became a full-time writer in 1973 and continued his steady output of novels and short stories. By the time he won the Nobel Prize for Literature at the age of seventy-seven, he had authored thirty-two novels, thirteen volumes of short stories, and thirty screenplays. He had also emerged as the most widely translated Egyptian writer. After the Nobel Prize his novels were immediately translated into several languages.

Adrift in the Nile was published in 1993, followed by *The Harafish* in 1994, a story of an Egyptian family living in an alley over several centuries. While Mahfouz's works are not partisan, they are certainly political. A modest man of regular habits, he has always been a writer with a highly developed social conscience committed to social justice. He has also been robustly independent-minded, and was stabbed in Cairo in 1994 after being denounced as an "infidel" by Islamic extremists.

Nevertheless, he has continued to be as productive as before. Among his later publications are *Arabian Nights and Days* (1995); *The Honeymoon* (1995); *The Beggar. the Thief and the Dogs* (2000); *The Day the Leader Was Killed* (2001); *Naguib Mahfouz at Sidi Gaber: Reflections of a Nobel Laureate, 1994–2001* (2001); and *Voices from the Arab World: Ancient Egyptian Tales* (2003)—capped by *The Complete Mahfouz Library* (2002).

Majlis *(Arabic/Persian: Assembly): parliament in Iran* Majlis is the popular term that has been used for the Iranian parliament since its inception during the 1906–07 Constitutional Revolution [*qv*]. It is the longest-standing elected legislative body in the Middle East [*qv*]. *See also* Iran: Constitution, and Legislature.

Maki *(Hebrew: acronym of* Miflaga Kommunistit Israelit, *Israeli Communist Party): Israeli political party* Maki emerged in October 1948 out of the merger of the Communist Party of Palestine (CPP) [*qv*] and the remnants of the League of National Liberation (LNL). It recognized the State of Israel without accepting the Zionist doctrine of a link between the Jews [*qv*] in Israel and the Diaspora [*qv*]. It backed the right of Arab refugees to return to their homes, as well as the founding of a Palestinian state in the territory allotted to the Arabs in the United Nations partition plan of November 1947.

In the First Knesset (1949–51) [*qv*] it won four seats. It had 8,000 members in 1951. Benefiting from a split in Mapam [*qv*] in 1953, it increased its Knesset seats to six in the 1955 poll. Opposed to military administration of the Arab-inhabited areas, it fought discrimination against Arab citizens, then 4 percent of the population. It was the only party to oppose Israeli aggression in the 1956 Suez War [*qv*].

In the early 1960s, when the Soviet Union began to pursue pro-Arab policies, a cleavage developed in Maki. The pro-Arab faction proposed cooperation with the Arab Communist parties, whereas the pro-Jewish faction advocated alliance with certain Zionist workers' groups to form a popular front. Moscow's sympathy for the Palestine Liberation Organization [*qv*], and its continued refusal to allow Soviet Jews to emigrate, accentuated the division within Maki. In mid-1965 the pro-Arab wing, led by Meir Vilner and Tawfiq Toubi, left Maki to form Rakah [*qv*]. In the 1965 poll, led by Moshe Sneh [*qv*] and Shamuel Mikunis, Maki gained one seat.

Maki supported the June 1967 Arab-Israeli War [*qv*] and opposed unconditional Israeli withdrawal from the Occupied Arab Territories [*qv*]. In the 1969 election Maki retained its single seat, but failed to do so in the poll four years later. The party disintegrated in mid-1975.

al Maktum, Maktum ibn Rashid (1941–): *ruler of Dubai emirate in the United Arab Emirates, 1990–; vice president of the UAE, 1990–; prime minister of the UAE, 1971–79, 1990–* Born in Dubai *[qv]*, al Maktum was educated there and in Britain. He then began to acquire administrative experience in the Emirate of Dubai [*qv*]. After the formation of the United Arab Emirates (UAE) in December 1971, he was elected prime minister by the Supreme Council of Emirs. As a Western-educated royal, he got on well with the substantial community of Western oil and financial experts. Al Maktum continued as the UAE premier until July 1979 when he stepped down in favor of his father, Shaikh Rashid ibn Said Al Maktum [*qv*], becoming his deputy. After the death of Shaikh Rashid in October 1990, al Maktum took over his father's positions: vice president and premier of the UAE, and the ruler of the Dubai emirate. Under his leadership, Dubai has been developed successfully as a tourist resort for Europeans.

al Maktum, Rashid ibn Said (1914–90): *ruler of the Dubai emirate in the United Arab Emirates, 1958–90; vice-president of the*

UAE, 1971–90; prime minister of the UAE, 1979–90 Born in Dubai [qv], al Maktum belonged to the Aal bu Falasa section of the Bani Yas tribe. Despite his lack of formal schooling, he proved to be a good administrator and economist when he became ruler of the Dubai emirate in 1958. He turned Dubai into a leading entrepôt of eastern Arabia, basing its commercial prosperity initially on the importation and exportation of gold, the source of supply being banks in Switzerland and the destination India and Pakistan. Commercial oil production, which began in 1969, boosted the local economy.

Following the founding of the United Arab Emirates in July 1971, a Supreme Council of seven rulers was established, with Shaikh Zaid al Nahyan [qv] of Abu Dhabi [qv] as its president and al Maktum its vice president. Though both leaders realized the importance of cooperation to make a success of the fledgling UAE federation, personal rivalry between them persisted: al Maktum was a sophisticated entrepreneur, whereas Shaikh Zaid was a bedouin chief. But when the UAE faced the stormy winds of republicanism from Islamic Iran, both leaders realized the danger.

At the behest of Shaikh Zaid, the Supreme Council called on al Maktum to become the UAE's prime minister in July 1979. He agreed, taking over from his eldest son, Maktum ibn Rashid al Maktum [qv], and applying his considerable administrative and financial skills to the running of all of the UAE for the next decade.

Malaika, Nazik (1923–2001): *Iraqi poet* Born in Baghdad [qv] into a literary family—with both her parents being poets—Malaika composed her first poem in classical Arabic [qv] at ten. While a student at the Higher Teachers' Training College, she published her poetry—characterized by extraordinary terseness, eloquence, original use of imagery, and a sensitive ear for music—in newspapers and magazines.

Her first collection of poems, *Aashiqat Al-Layl* (Lover of Night), appeared in 1947. Two years later, her next collection, *Shazaya wa ramad* (Ashes and Shrapnel), helped launch free verse in Arabic as a new form for avant-garde poets—as part of the literary movement also pioneered by Badr Shakir Sayyab [qv]. At the same time Malaika became a strong advocate of women's rights. Her lectures on women's status in patriarchal societies appeared as books—*Woman between Passivity and Positive Morality* (1953) and *Fragmentation in Arab Society* (1954). By then she had obtained a master's degree in English literature from the University of Wisconsin, Madison, U.S.A.

On her return home, she became a lecturer at the Arabic department of the Education College in Baghdad. In 1962 she published a collection of essays on the merits and demerits of free verse and metrical poetry, *Qadaya 'l-shiar al-muaasir* (The Contemporary Poetry Issues).

In the late 1960s, however, Malaika began to distance herself from experimentalism while advocating socially conservative views, and reverted to traditional metrical poetry. These collections of her poems appeared between 1970 and 1978. She moved to Kuwait [qv] to teach at the University of Kuwait. A festschrift containing many essays on her work was published in 1985.

Following the invasion of Kuwait by Iraq [qv] in August 1990, she returned to

Baghdad. Then she moved to Cairo [*qv*]. There, a collection of her poems, *Youghiyar Alouanah Al-Bahr* (Leaving the Sea of Sorrow), most of them written a quarter-century ago, appeared in 1999.

Maliki Code: *Sunni Islamic school* The Maliki Code is the canonical school of Sunni Islam [*qv*], founded by Malik ibn Anas (A.D. 714–96), a jurist resident in Medina [*qv*]. Like other schools it is based on the Quran [*qv*], the *sunna* [*qv*], and *ijma* [*qv*]. But in the *sunna* (Tradition of the Prophet Muhammad and his Companions) Malik ibn Anas excludes Caliph Ali ibn Abu Talib, a cousin and son-in-law of the Prophet Muhammad, who is regarded by Sunnis as the last of the four Rightly Guided Caliphs. With regard to *ijma* (Consensus of the Community), Malik ibn Anas stated that if it fails to produce a solution to a problem, then *qiyas* [*qv*] (reasoning by analogy) should be practiced by a jurist to find one.

The Maliki Code's initial dominance of the Arab heartland of Islam gave way to the Shafii Code [*qv*]. An essentially conservative doctrine, it has persisted more in pastoral communities than elsewhere and is today the leading code in North Africa, West Africa, and Sudan.

Manama: *capital of Bahrain* Pop. 154,000 (2003, est.). Situated on Bahrain Island, Manama's recorded history dates back to 1345. It fell to the Portuguese in 1521, and then the Iranians in 1602. Iran's authority was overthrown by the local al Khalifa family [*qv*] in 1783. Following the treaties the al Khalifas signed with Britain between 1861 and 1892, turning Bahrain into a British protectorate, Manama became a seat of a British political agent under the regional political resident based in Bushehr, Iran. In 1946 the British political resident set up his office in Manama. This continued until 1971 when Manama became the capital of independent Bahrain.

Before the discovery of oil in 1932 the local economy centered on fishing, pearling, and trade. After the Second World War, the city rapidly developed as a commercial and financial center. It became a free port in 1958 and acquired deepwater shipping facilities four years later. With its modern harbor and ship-repair facilities, it has emerged as one of the leading ports in the Gulf [*qv*], containing two-fifths of the national population. It has also acquired a worldwide reputation as an offshore banking center.

Mapai *(Hebrew: acronym of* Mifleget Poalei Israel, *Israel Workers Party): Israeli political party* Mapai resulted from the merger of Ahdut HaAvodah-Poale Zion [*qv*] and HaPoale HaTzair [*qv*] in 1930. Of its 5,650 members, three-fifths were agriculturists. After the murder of its head, Chaim Arlosoroff [*qv*], in 1933 its leadership passed to David Ben-Gurion [*qv*]. Mapai dominated most of the institutions of the Yishuv [*qv*]: kibbutzim [*qv*], trade unions, militia, schools, and parliament. In the twenty-three-member National Council (i.e., cabinet) of the Yishuv Assembly, it often held eleven seats.

As its leaders began to focus on national problems, they diluted their socialist commitment. Despite strong opposition from leftists, the Mapai conference of 1941, representing some 20,000 members, adopted a program that focused on the founding of a Jewish state in Palestine [*qv*]. The party split on this issue in February 1944, with the leftists leaving. After the Second World War, Mapai led an anti-British campaign, which was joined by Haganah [qv], Irgun [qv], and Lehi [qv]. It favored partitioning Palestine into Jewish and Arab states and participated in the Arab-Israeli War (1948–49) [qv].

In the 1949 general election it emerged as the leading party, gaining 46 seats out of 120, a performance it repeated in the 1951 poll. It became the dominant partner in the coalition governments that followed. The crucial decisions taken between 1948 and 1952, which shaped the future of Israel, reflected its leaders' views. They chose a secular, not a theocratic, system; a capitalist economy managed by social democratic bureaucracy, and not socialism; and pro-Western foreign policy. After a dip in the 1955 election to forty seats, Mapai's share rose to forty-seven in the 1959 poll but fell to forty-two in 1961.

During the first-quarter-century of the state of Israel, when the population increased dramatically, the state and society changed considerably. Mapai's decision to open its membership to all socioeconomic groups further diluted its pioneering socialist ideals. The sharp growth in its size, reaching 200,000 members in 1964, created an unwieldy party bureaucracy.

The rivalry between Ben-Gurion and Pinchas Lavon [qv], centering on the latter's "security mishap" in 1954, which dragged on for a decade, damaged the party, reducing its vote in the 1960 Histadrut [qv] poll to 55 percent, down from the 80 percent it used to win in the 1930s. Having rid Lavon of his office in Histadrut and the government, Ben-Gurion did not rest content. He left the government in 1963 and began to campaign against Prime Minister Levi Eshkol [qv]. To meet the challenge, party leaders recommended an alliance with Ahdut HaAvodah-Poale Zion [qv]. The Mapai conference in 1964 accepted the recommendation. On the eve of the 1965 poll Mapai signed an agreement for a *maarach* (alignment) with Ahdut HaAvodah-Poale Zion, the resulting bloc winning forty-five seats. The Maarach, widened in 1968 to include Rafi [qv], finally resulted in the merger of the three constituent parties into the Israeli Labor Party [qv].

Mapam *(Hebrew: acronym of* Mifleget Poalei Meuhedet, *United Workers Party): Israeli political party* Once the November 1947 United Nations partition plan for Palestine [qv] had destroyed the idea of a binational (Arab-Jewish) state in Palestine, the barrier between the two major leftist organizations—Ahdut HaAvodah-Poale Zion [qv] and HaShomer HaTzair (The Young Guards)—was lifted, paving the way for their merger. This happened in January 1948, and the result was Mapam under the leadership of Moshe Sneh [qv]. It became the leading leftist force inside and outside parliament in Israel. Its nineteen-member bloc in the First Knesset [qv] (1949–51) attacked the Mapai-led government for accepting a large amount of financial aid from the United States. Mapam advocated organizing new immigrants into collective agrarian and industrial units, and nationalizing natural resources and large capitalist enterprises. In the elections to the Second Knesset in 1951 it won fifteen seats. But during the term of this parliament it lost two deputies to Mapai [qv]; two, including Sneh, to

Maki [*qv*]; and four to the revived Ahdut HaAvodah–Poale Zion. The smaller contingent of nine in the Third Knesset (1955–59) was less leftist and less pro-Soviet. Indeed it became a partner in the coalition government led by Mapai [*qv*].

Following the Suez War [*qv*], Mapam held demonstrations against Israel's withdrawal from the Sinai Peninsula [*qv*]. In the elections of 1959, 1961, and 1965, Mapam won eight or nine seats and coalesced with Mapai to form the government. When it supported the June 1967 Arab-Israeli War [*qv*], it lost some leftist members.

In January 1969 Mapam allied with the newly formed Labor Party [*qv*] to form the Labor-Mapam Alignment [*qv*], which performed erratically—down from fifty-six seats in 1969 to thirty-two in 1977, then rising to forty-seven in 1981. The Alignment held until September 1984 when, protesting against Labor's decision to form a national unity government with Likud [*qv*], Mapam ended it, taking its six deputies into opposition. In the 1988 election Mapam won three seats on its own. As part of the Meretz [*qv*] alliance, in the 1992 poll it secured four seats. Its share fell to two seats in the 1996 general election and rose to three in 1999.

marja-e taqlid *(Persian: source of emulation):* In Twelver Shiism [*qv*] the idea of a living *mujtahid* [*qv*] interpreting the Sharia [*qv*] took hold in the late eighteenth century. Muhammad Baqir Behbehani (d. 1793), a mujtahid based in Karbala [*qv*], ruled that every believer must choose a mujtahid to emulate, who was given the honorific of *marja-e taqlid.* In the religious establishment his standing was above that of *ayatollah ozma,* grand ayatollah, a title

that came into vogue in Iran during the 1907–11 Constitutional Revolution [*qv*]. He exercised far greater power than a leading Sunni [*qv*] cleric. He issued judgments on political matters impinging on Islamic principles independently of the temporal ruler, a development that had a profound impact on the subsequent history of Iran, a predominantly Shia country. Among the best known Shia *marja-e taqlids* of recent times have been Abol Qasim Khoei [*qv*], Ruhollah Khomeini [*qv*], Musa al Sadr [*qv*], and Muhammad Kazem Shari-atmadari [*qv*]. They carried the title of Grand Ayatollah. *See also* mujtahid and Titles, Religious (Shia Islam).

Maronite Catholic Church: *Christian sect* One of the Uniate churches [*qv*]—i.e., affiliated to the Roman Catholic Church [*qv*] but allowed to practice its own Eastern rites and customs—its adherents are called Maronites. They are followers of Saint Maron/Maro, a Christian hermit who lived in northeast Syria in the late fourth–early fifth century. Their migration to Mount Lebanon occurred in the late seventh century, and was led by St. John Maron, patriarch of Antioch. With the persecuted Christians from the plains taking refuge in these mountains over the next few centuries, the Maronite ranks grew steadily. During the Crusades (1095–1272), they sided with the Crusaders.

In 1182 their church acquired semiautonomous affiliation with the Vatican, which allowed them to retain their own West Syriac liturgy [*qv*] and have their own resident patriarch in Lebanon. Pope Gregory XIII established the Maronite College in Rome in 1585. In 1648 France proclaimed itself protector of

Catholics in the Ottoman Empire (1517–1918) and was so accepted. This was the beginning of a special relationship between France and the Maronites, which bloomed when Syria-Lebanon was placed under the French mandate after the First World War. Maronite and other Christian leaders cooperated actively with Paris in the creation of a Christian-dominated Greater Lebanon, later to be called the Republic of Lebanon.

Centuries of isolation in the mountains, combined with successful resistance to direct control by Muslim overlords, turned the Maronites into a community where religion and politics were inextricably mixed. Its immediate spiritual head is the Patriarch of Antioch and All The East, who resides in Bkirki near Jounieh port. Today Maronites are the largest Christian community in Lebanon, whose constitution requires that the republic's president should be a Maronite.

martyrdom *(Greek: derivative of* martus, *witness): the concept of dying in the cause of religion* In the course of securing political independence for the Jews [*qv*] from their Greek rulers, their leader, Judas Maccabaeus of the Hasmonaean family, lost his life in 160 B.C., thus giving rise to the concept of martyrdom in monotheistic religions. A martyr is one who dies for his or her faith. The concept of martyrdom was formalized and elevated by the Prophet Muhammad (A.D. 570–632). The appropriate verse in the Quran [*qv*] (3:163) reads: "Count not those who are slain in God's way as dead, / but rather living with their Lord, by Him provided, / rejoicing in the bounty that God has given them, / and joyful in those who remain behind and have not joined them."

In modern times martyrdom motivated the Ikhwan [*qv*], operating under Abdul Aziz al Saud [*qv*] from 1913 to 1928, to expand the realm of Wahhabi Islam [*qv*]. During the 1977–78 revolutionary movement in Iran, the deeply rooted martyr complex of Shias [*qv*]—which led thousands of Iranians, wearing white shrouds, used to cover corpses, to face the bullets of the army—was an important factor in demoralizing the government soldiers, who began to desert. In December 1978 the onset of the Ashura festival [*qv*], which centers on the martyrdom of Imam Hussein, called the Great Martyr, irrevocably turned the tide against the secular regime of Muhammad Reza Shah Pahlavi [*qv*].

The newly formed Islamic Republic of Iran established the Martyrs Foundation to look after the families of those who had died as martyrs before, during, and after the Islamic Revolution [*qv*]—a category that also included those who were killed in the 1980–88 Iran-Iraq War [*qv*], since they had perished while defending an Islamic republic. The concept of martyrdom was also instrumental in actions such as truck-bombing, involving the instant death of the driver, carried out by such Shia organizations in Lebanon as the Islamic Jihad [*qv*] and Hizbollah [*qv*]. Later it inspired similar actions by Hamas [*qv*] and Islamic Jihad [*qv*], Sunni [*qv*] groups, in the Occupied Territories [*qv*], as well as secular Fatah [*qv*]. *See also* suicide bombing.

Mashhad *(Arabic: a place of witness/sepulchral shrine): Iranian city* Pop. 2,061,000 (2003, est.). The settlement of Nukan, where Caliph Haroon al Rashid (r. A.D. 786–809) and Imam Ali al Rida/Reza (d. 818), the eighth imam of the Twelver Shias

[*qv*], were buried, acquired the name Mashhad or Mashhad-e Rida. In 1220 the Mongol invaders damaged it considerably. When the founder of the Safavid dynasty, Shah Ismail (r. 1501–24), adopted Shiism [*qv*] as the state religion, the importance of Mashhad rose.

It fell into the hands of Uzbek invaders and was not recovered until 1598 by Shah Abbas 1 (r. 1587–1629). He made the city attractive and a leading place of pilgrimage for Shias. Nadir Shah Afshar (r. 1736–47) turned Mashhad into the capital of Iran and built several monuments, including a mausoleum for himself. Following his assassination and a civil war, Mashhad became the capital of Khurasan province, a buffer zone between Iran and Afghanistan. Mashhad was finally brought under Iranian control in the early nineteenth century by Fath Ali Shah of the Qajar dynasty. The palace started by Crown Prince Mirza in 1833 was completed in 1876.

The leading city of eastern Iran, Mashhad serves the prosperous agricultural region of the country. It is the center of the wool trade and carpet making. In recent times the quadrupling of the oil price in 1973–74, which boosted the income of Iran, had a beneficial effect on Mashhad. In 1974 the city received 3,200,000 pilgrims, a fifteenfold increase over the previous decade, who came to visit the shrine of Imam Ali al Rida/Reza.

Mecca: *Saudi Arabian city* Pop. 1,615,000 (2003, est.). Known as Macoraba during the (Greco-Egyptian) Ptolemaic period (323–30 B.C.), Mecca was an ancient center of commerce. It was situated on the incense route from India to the Mediterranean region and had developed around the well of Zamzam and the sanctuary of Kaaba [*qv*], which were holy to Arab [*qv*] tribes before the rise of Islam [*qv*].

The birthplace of Prophet Muhammad ibn Abdullah al Quraish (A.D. 570–632), it was in Mecca that he passed on his first revelations to the early body of believers. The Prophet Muhammad's migration from Mecca in A.D. 622 marked the beginning of the Islamic era. Eight years later he conquered Mecca. As the site of the annual *hajj* [*qv*], Mecca became the most sacred city of Islam.

It was looted in A.D. 930 by Karmathians, a cyrpto-Muslim sect, who were responsible for the removal of the Black Stone from the Kaaba and its absence for twenty years. By the late eleventh century Mecca was administered by the al Hashem [*qv*] family, the governor bearing the title of *sharif* (noble). Together with the surrounding region of Hijaz [*qv*] it was dependent for its food on Egypt, being under the suzerainty of whoever controlled Cairo [*qv*]. When the Ottomans conquered Egypt in 1517, the control of Mecca fell to them. It came under Wahhabi [*qv*] rule from 1804–13. After the opening of the Suez Canal [*qv*] in 1869, there was improved communication between Istanbul and Mecca, now the capital of Hijaz. Hussein ibn Ali al Hashem became the sharif in 1908. In June 1916 he declared himself king of Hijaz, with Mecca as its capital. He was overthrown by Abdul Aziz al Saud [*qv*] in 1924. Mecca became part of Saudi Arabia and was closed to non-Muslims.

The economic and religious life of the city revolves around the hajj, which lasts about a week. The heart of Mecca is the Haram *(Arabic: Sanctuary),* the Grand Mosque. Situated at the center of the Old

City and containing the Kaaba, it was extensively renovated after a two-week siege by security forces to quell an armed uprising by over 300 Islamic militants, led by Juheiman al Utaiba [*qv*] on 1 Muharram 1400 A.H./20 November 1979.

Served by the seaport and airport facilities of Jiddah [*qv*] and transformed into a modern metropolis, Mecca is well equipped to serve the two million pilgrims who arrive during the hajj. During the hajj of 1987 it became the site of rioting, in which 402 pilgrims, mainly Iranians, died as a result of police gunfire and stampedes.

Medina *(Arabic: town): Saudi Arabian city* Pop. 843,000 (2003, est.). Also known in Arabic as *Madinat al Rasul Allah* (Town of the Messenger of Allah), Medina is the second holiest city of Islam [*qv*]. Called Yathrib in pre-Islamic times, this oasis town was possibly settled by some of the Jews [*qv*] expelled from Palestine [*qv*] in A.D. 135. After his migration from Mecca [*qv*] in A.D. 622, the Prophet Muhammad established a base here. Following his death ten years later Medina became the capital of the Islamic caliphate. This continued until A.D. 661, when the capital was moved to Damascus [*qv*].

It remained a center of Islamic learning, especially with regard to the Quran [*qv*] and the *sunna* [*qv*], and was the base, among others, of the founder of the Maliki Code [*qv*] in the eighth century. Later it came under the intermittent control of the *sharifs* (nobles) of Mecca and of Egypt. Following their seizure of Egypt in 1517, the Ottomans gained control of Medina. As the site of the Great Mosque, which contains the tombs of the Prophet Muhammad, his daughter

Fatima, wife of Caliph/Imam Ali, and Caliphs Abu Bakr and Omar, Medina had emerged as the second holiest place of Islam. The Ottoman suzerainty ended during the First World War. The subsequent rule by Sharif Hussein ibn Ali al Hashem gave way in 1924 to that of Abdul Aziz al Saud [*qv*]. It became part of Saudi Arabia and was closed to non-Muslims.

The economic and religious life of the city revolves around the *hajj* [*qv*], when most pilgrims combine their visit to Mecca with one to Medina. The nearby area is the site of the first mosque in Islam and the mosque commemorating the change of prayer direction from toward Jerusalem [*qv*] to toward Mecca.

Meir (Meyerson), Golda (1898–1978): *Israeli politician; prime minister, 1969–74* The daughter of Moshe Mabovitch, a carpenter in Kiev, Ukraine, Meir migrated with her family to Milwaukee in the United States when she was eight. She trained as a teacher and married Morris Meyerson, a bookkeeper, in 1917. Four years later they migrated to Palestine [*qv*] and joined a kibbutz [*qv*]. From 1926 she became active in the Histadrut [*qv*] and later Mapai [*qv*]. After separating from her husband in 1932, she spent two years in the United States with the Pioneer Women's Organization.

In 1936 she became head of the Histadrut's political department. She opposed the partition plan proposed by Britain's Peel Commission in 1937. Following the arrest in 1946 of Moshe Sharett [*qv*], head of the Jewish Agency's [*qv*] political department, dealing with foreign affairs, she replaced him. In that capacity she had secret meetings with Transjordan's ruler, Abdullah ibn Hussein [*qv*], in late November 1947 and again on 10 May 1948, to dissuade him from joining other members of the Arab League [*qv*] in attacking the imminent State of Israel [*qv*]. She failed.

She served briefly as head of the Israeli legation in Moscow until her election in early 1949 to the Knesset [*qv*], where she was to retain a seat for the next quarter of a century. Meir became labor minister from 1949–56, then foreign minister from 1956–66. After resigning from the cabinet, she was drafted as secretary-general of Mapai to heal internecine wounds. When Mapai transformed itself into the Labor Party [*qv*] in 1968, Meir retired from public life. But following the sudden death of Prime Minister Levi Eshkol [*qv*] in February 1969, she was elected to head the national unity government in order to stave off a power struggle within Labor. Her acceptance of the Rogers Peace Plan [*qv*] in July 1970 led to the exit of Gahal [*qv*] from the cabinet.

The attention of all political parties was focused on the impending general election in late October 1973, when Israel was attacked by Egypt and Syria on 6 October. During the conflict she provided strong leadership, including purportedly ordering the mounting of Israel's entire stock of twenty-five atomic bombs on specially adapted bombers. Though praised for her leadership during the October 1973 Arab-Israeli War [*qv*] by the official inquiry commission in March 1974, Meir decided to resign as premier (thus causing the entire cabinet to fall), partly to bring about the resignation of Moshe Dayan [*qv*]. In 1975 she received the Israel Prize for her contribution to Israeli society.

Melkite Christians: *see* Greek Catholic Church.

Meretz (*Hebrew: Energy): Israeli political alliance* Official title: *Meretz-Israel HaDemokratit* (Energy—The Democratic Israel). Having ended its alignment with the Labor Party [*qv*] in the aftermath of Labor's decision to form a national unity government with Likud [*qv*] in September 1984, Mapam [*qv*] formed the Meretz alliance with Shinui [*qv*] and Ratz [*qv*] after the 1988 general election, giving it a total strength of ten deputies. Its program included separation of religion and state, electoral reform, discontinuation of the construction of Jewish settlements in the Occupied Arab Territories [*qv*], and self-determination for Palestinians. It functioned as an opposition. In the 1992 election it secured twelve seats and joined the Labor-led coalition government. In 1996 it won nine seats and went into opposition. It secured ten seats in 1999 and joined the Labor-led coalition government headed by Ehud Barak [*qv*]. It stayed out of the national unity cabinet headed by Ariel Sharon [*qv*] in 2001. In the January 2003 parliamentary election, its strength declined to six seats.

Mesopotomia (*Greek: Land between the Rivers [Tigris and Euphrates]*): Covering the territory between the Tigris [*qv*] and Euphrates [*qv*] rivers and extending from the mountains of southern Turkey to the Persian Gulf [*qv*], Mesopotomia constitutes the greater part of modern Iraq [*qv*]. Archaelogical excavations, conducted over the past one and a half centuries, have provided evidence of civilization dating back to ca. 10 millennia B.C. Mesopotomia is the region where the earliest settled agrarian society evolved, with its irrigation systems, crafts, and buildings made of clay bricks. It was there that one of the first cities was built around 4000 B.C., and writing was invented in ca. 300 B.C. Incorporated into the Parthian Empire (250 B.C.–A.D. 226) in the second century B.C., it declined steadily. After 38 B.C. it became a buffer zone—first between the Parthian, and later Sassanian (A.D. 226–640), Empires; and then the Roman (27 B.C.–A.D. 395), and later Byzantine (395–1453), Empires. It was conquered by Muslim Arabs [qv] in A.D. 637. Since then its history has been that of Iraq.

messiah (*Hebrew: derivative of* mashiach, *meaning anointed):* Though the concept of a messiah is common to Judaism [qv] and Christianity [qv], it is viewed differently by Jews and Christians. Following their exile in 586 B.C., Jews [qv] aspired for restoration by a leader, who, like David (r. 1010–970 B.C.), would be a monarch as well as an epitome of piety. After their final dispersion in A.D. 135, Jews began to think of the messiah as someone who would end injustice, lead them to a restored Israel, and initiate the resurrection of the dead. Christians regard Jesus Christ as the Messiah promised in the Old Testament [qv]. The fact that, far from ending injustice, he suffered as its victim, makes no difference to his messianic status, according to Christians. *See also* mahdi.

Middle East: Early Western geographers divided the East into the Near East [qv] (the area extending from the Mediterranean Sea to the Persian Gulf [qv]; the Middle East (the region extending from the Persian Gulf to Southeast Asia); and the Far East (covering the regions facing the Pacific Ocean). But during the Second World War, when the term Middle East was applied to the

British military command in Egypt, the traditional definitions underwent a change and the Middle East encompassed the region previously called the Near East. Later, when the independent states of Libya, Tunisia, Algeria, and Morocco joined the Arab League [qv], the term Middle East was considered to include these countries as well. The best way out of this confusion is to think of the Middle East as consisting of a core and peripheries. The core includes Iran, the Fertile Crescent [qv], the Arabian Peninsula [qv], and Egypt. To its south lies Sudan, to its west Arab North Africa, and to its north Turkey and Cyprus. The narrowest definition of the Middle East includes only the core, and the widest, the core and its three peripheries.

Middle East Defense Organization: In an effort to link various Middle Eastern countries in a military alliance against the Soviet Union, London, backed by Washington, conceived the Middle East Defense Organization (MEDO) as a multilateral defense pact. Since it was centered on Britain's Middle East Defense Command, based in the Suez Canal [qv] zone, the nationalist government of Egypt rejected it in late October 1951. This led to efforts by Britain and the United States to encourage bilateral agreements with a view to creating a multilateral defense pact, which materialized in 1955 as the Baghdad Pact [qv].

Middle East Peace Conference (Geneva, 1973): Following the October 1973 Arab-Israeli War [qv], a Middle East Peace Conference was convened in Geneva on 21 December under the cochairmanship of the United States and the Soviet Union. It was attended by Egypt, Israel, and Jordan, but boycotted by Syria. Having instructed Israel and Egypt to negotiate the disengagement of their forces, the conference adjourned the next day in view of the imminent general election in Israel. But having won the election on 31 December, Israel's Labor [qv]-dominated government did not return to Geneva on 7 January as agreed. Instead it approached U.S. Secretary of State Henry Kissinger to use his personal diplomacy to bring about an agreement with Egypt. The Egyptian president, Anwar Sadat [qv], went along with this. Efforts by Washington and Moscow to reconvene the conference during the tenure of U.S. President Jimmy Carter (r. 1977–80) failed.

Middle East Peace Conference (Madrid, 1991): After the Second Gulf War [qv] the United States began to lobby actively for a Middle East Peace Conference. On 18 July 1991, following Syrian President Hafiz Assad's [qv] dramatic concessions on his terms for attending a peace conference, U.S. Secretary of State James Baker met him in Damascus [qv]. On 30 September the Palestine National Council [qv] agreed to attend such a gathering. It was held in Madrid, Spain, on 30 October 1991 under the cochairmanship of the United States and the Soviet Union (later Russia), and was attended by Israel, Syria, Lebanon, and Jordan (whose delegation included Palestinians from the Occupied Territories [qv]). All the parties agreed to honor U.N. Security Council Resolution 242 of November 1967 [qv], which called for the withdrawal of Israel from the Occupied Arab Territories [qv] in exchange for the peaceful coexistence of all the states in the region, and Resolution 338 of October

1973 [qv], which called on the concerned parties to implement Security Council Resolution 242.

The Madrid conference was followed by bilateral talks between Israel and the three Arab parties, held outside the Middle East. The bilateral negotiations between Israel and Jordan evolved into separate talks between the Israeli delegation and the Jordanian, and the Israeli delegation and the Palestinian, with the latter taking its orders from the Palestine Liberation Organization (PLO) [qv]. Secret negotiations between the PLO and Israel led to the Israeli-PLO Accord [qv] in September 1993. Thirteen months later a Jordanian-Israeli Peace Treaty [qv] was signed. Starting in 1994, talks between Israel and Syria were mediated by the United States, but those between Israel and Lebanon were put on hold, waiting for tangible progress on the Israeli-Syrian front in line with the 1991 Lebanese-Syrian Treaty of Brotherhood, Cooperation, and Coordination [qv].

Midrash *(Hebrew: investigation or study)*: Homiletical interpretations and embellishments of the Hebrew Bible [qv] by rabbis since ca. A.D. 200, Midrash is incorporated in the Mishna [qv]. Like the Gemara [qv], it contains material that pertains to Jewish Law, called Midrash Halacha [qv], and digressions in the form of rabbinic folklore, called Midrash Hagaada.

Military in Bahrain (2003): Total armed forces, 10,700; active, 10,700

Military expenditure as percent of GDP: 4.8 (2001)

Ground forces: regular army, active, 8,500

In-service equipment: tanks, 140; armored personnel carriers, 235; major artillery, 84

Air forces: regular air force, 1,200

In-service equipment: combat aircraft, 34; combat helicopters, 40

Naval forces: regular navy, 1,000

In-service equipment: surface combatants, 1 (frigate, 1); patrol and coastal combatants, 10

Military in Egypt (2003): Total armed forces: active, 443,000; reserves, 254,000

Military expenditure as percent of GDP: 4.7 (2001)

Ground forces: regular army, active, 320,000; reserves, 150,000

In-service equipment: tanks, 4,265; armored personnel carriers, 4,267; major artillery, 1,438

Air forces: (a) regular air force, active, 29,000; reserves, 20,000; (b) Regular air defense, active, 75,000; reserves, 70,000

In-service equipment: combat aircraft, 608; combat helicopters, 128

Naval forces: regular navy, active, 19,000; reserves, 14,000

In-service equipment: surface combatants, 11 (destroyers, 1; frigates, 10); patrol and coastal combatants, 39; mine warfare vessels, 12

Paramilitary: active, 332,000 (Central Security Forces, 250,000; National Guard, 60,000; Border Guard, 20,000; Coast Guard, 2000)

Military in Iran (2003): Total armed forces: active, 520,000; reserves, 350,000

Military expenditure as percent of GDP: 5.9 (2001)

Ground forces: (a) regular army, active, 325,000; reserves, 350,000; (b) Revolutionary Guard Corps, active, 100,000

In-service equipment: tanks, 1,565; armored personnel carriers, 590; major

artillery, 2,395; combat helicopters, 195; aircraft, 17

Air forces: regular air force, 37,000; air defense, 15,000

In-service equipment: combat aircraft, 360

Naval forces: (a) regular navy, 18,000; (b) Revolutionary Guard Corps, 20,000

In-service equipment: submarines, 6; surface combatants, 3 (frigates, 3); patrol and coastal combatants, 56; mine warfare vessels, 7

Paramilitary: active, Law Enforcement Forces, 40,000; reserves, Resistance Mobilization Force *(Persian: Niruyeh Moqawemat Basij)*, 300,000

Nonconventional weapons *Chemical:* There were unconfirmed reports of Iran deploying chemical weapons during its offensive against Basra in early 1987 during the Iran-Iraq War [*qv*]. Further use of such arms was discontinued when it was judged un-Islamic by Ayatollah Ruhollah Khomeini [*qv*].

Nuclear: After examining the nuclear power project in Bushahr in January 1995, the inspectors of the International Atomic Energy Agency (IAEA) said that they saw no evidence of military use of the power plant. Similar statements were issued by the IAEA after their six monthly visits to the site. When in early 2003 the Iranian government announced that it had discovered uranium mines and that it proposed to process the mineral for peaceful purposes, the IAEA said that it had known about these plans before.

Military in Iraq (2003): Total armed forces: active, 389,000; reserves, 650,000

Military expenditure as percent of GDP: 9.3 (2001)

Ground forces: regular army, active, 350,000; reserves, 630,000

In-service equipment: tanks, 2,600; armored personnel carriers, 1,800; major artillery, 2,100; combat helicopters, 100

Air forces: (a) regular air force, 20,000; (b) regular air defense, 17,000

In-service equipment: combat aircraft, 300

Naval forces: regular navy, active, 2,000

In-service equipment: patrol and coastal combatants, 6; mine warfare vessels, 3

Paramilitary: active, 44,000 (border guards, 9,000; Saddam's *fedayeen,* 20,000; security troops, 5,000)

Nonconventional weapons: *Biological:* Research in biological weapons began in 1985. Production of the biological warfare agents anthrax (*bacillus anthracis*) and botulinum (*clostridium botulinum*) started in 1989 and continued for a year. Implementing U.N. Security Council Resolution 687 [*qv*] of April 1991, the inspectors of the United Nations Special Commission (UNSCOM) [*qv*] for disarming Iraq demolished research facilities. By 1995 Iraq's claim to have destroyed all its stored agents was yet to be fully verified by UNSCOM. Later Iraq declared that it had 8,400 liters (1,850 gallons) of anthrax; 19,000 liters (4,180 gallons) of botulinum; 3,400 liters (750 gallons) of clostridium (gangerene gas); 2,200 liters (485 gallons) of aflatoxin; 10 liters (2gallons) of ricin. These were destroyed by UNSCOM. That left 15,300 kilograms (34,000 pounds) of bio-weapons growth media unaccounted for.

Chemical: Iraq began to use chemical weapons (mustard and nerve gases) in the 1980–88 Iran-Iraq War [*qv*] from October 1983 onward, culminating in large-scale deployment during the last months of the war, which ended in August 1988. During that year the government also used chemical weapons against Kurdish insurgents and civilians in the Kurdistan Autonomous Region [*qv*], resulting in an estimated 100,000 deaths. Following the implementation of U.N. Security Council Resolution 687 [*qv*] of April 1991, the four facilities for developing, producing, and storing were destroyed by UNSCOM.

The chemical warfare agents and quantities destroyed were 500–600 tons of mustard gas; 100–150 tons of nerve gases—sarin and tabun; and 50–100 tons of VX nerve gas. Also destroyed were 480,000 liters (105,600 gallons) of chemical weapons agents; over 450,000 gallons of precursor chemicals; and 30 chemical warheads—as well as 38,537 filled and empty chemical weapons munitions. That left 590,000 gallons of precursor chemicals unaccounted for.

Nuclear: Research and development in the nuclear weapons program was well advanced at the time of the 1991 Gulf War. In the course of implementing U.N. Security Council Resolution 687, the UNSCOM and the International Atomic Energy Agency examined 25,000 pages of documents, 700 rolls of film, and nineteen hours of videotape to assess the Iraqi Atomic Energy Commission's personnel and procurement of materials. They concluded that Iraq had not produced a detonator for an atom bomb, and had not accumulated sufficient enriched uranium to produce a nuclear weapon. If Iraq had been able to overcome these barriers, it would have acquired the ability to produce two or three atom bombs annually by 1995 or 1996 at the earliest. All military nuclear research and development facilities had been destroyed by U.N. inspectors by 1993. In its April 1998 report, the IAEA said, "Based on all credible information to date, the IAEA has found no indication of Iraq having achieved its program goal of producing nuclear weapons or of Iraq having retained a physical capability for the production of weapon-usable nuclear material or having clandestinely obtained such material." In February 2003, after carrying out 177 inspections at 125 sites since the previous November, IAEA chief Muhammad El Baradei basically repeated the earlier summary.

Military in Israel (2003): Total armed forces: active, 161,500; reserves, 437,000

Military expenditure as percent of GDP: 9.6 (2001)

Ground forces: regular army, active, 120,000; reserves, 410,000

In-service equipment: tanks, 3,750; armored personnel carriers, 10,400; major artillery, 1,455

Air forces: regular air force, active, 35,000; reserves, 22,000

In-service equipment: combat aircraft, 704; combat helicopters, 135

Naval forces: regular navy, active, 6,500; reserves, 5,000

In-service equipment: submarines, 3; patrol and coastal combatants, 48

Paramilitary: active, 8,050 (border police, 8,000; coast guard, 50)

Non-conventional weapons: *Biological and chemical:* The Israeli Institute for Biological Research (IIRB) at Nes Ziona, south of Tel Aviv [*qv*], established in 1952, is the Israeli military and intelligence community's front organization for developing, testing, and producing biological and chemical weapons. Access to Nes Ziona is denied even to the members of the Knesset's foreign affairs and defense committees concerned about the health risks to the residents of the area. The crash of an Israeli El Al aircraft southeast of Amsterdam on its way from New York to Tel Aviv in October 1992—which killed forty-seven and infected more than 1,000 people with respiratory and neurological ailments—was carrying 10 tons of chemicals, including hydrofluoric acid, isopropanol, and dimethyl methylphosphonate (DMMP)—three of the four ingredients needed to produce sarin nerve gas. The U.S. Office of Technology Assessment for Congress reported in 1993 that Israel had "undeclared offensive chemical warfare capabilities" and was "generally reported as having an undeclared offensive biological weapons program." In that year the Israeli government acknowledged that Marcus Klinberg, deputy head of the IIRB, was given a twenty year sentence in solitary confinement in 1983 for leaking information on Israel's biological weapons program to the Soviet Union—a stiffer sentence than the eighteen years of solitary confinement imposed in 1986 on Mordecai Vanunu (after he had been smuggled from Britain to Israel by Mossad [*qv*] agents) for leaking nuclear arms secrets. In September 1998, despite the protest by Nes Ziona's residents, the government decided to extend the IIRB site by a further forty-one acres.

Though Israel signed the Chemical Weapons Convention in 1993, its parliament has not yet ratified it. And Israel has not signed the Biological and Toxin Weapons Convention yet.

Nuclear: The Israel military nuclear program began in Dimona, near Beersheba in the Negev desert, in September 1957 following a secret agreement with France for the construction of a building and supply of a nuclear reactor capable of producing two low-yield weapons annually. A reprocessing plant to transform uranium into weapons-grade plutonium was completed in 1962. The French presence in Dimona continued until 1966. In early 1968 the plant began to produce four to five nuclear arms annually, and there were more than twenty-five such weapons by the time of the October 1973 Arab-Israeli War [*qv*].

According to the account by Mordecai Vanunu, a technician at the reprocessing plant (called Machon 2, which was capable of producing ten weapons a year) from August 1977 to July 1985, who took fifty-seven color photographs of the facility (published in the *Sunday Times* in London on 5 October 1986), Israel possessed about 200 nuclear weapons. In addition to the nuclear reactor and the reprocessing plant, there were six other Machons (facilities). Vanunu also claimed that since 1984 Israel had been manufacturing neutron bombs (two-stage thermonuclear devices that kill all living things within a given range). An analysis of his photographs led experts to conclude that Israel had the capacity to produce a low-yield neutron bomb.

During the 1991 Gulf War [*qv*], following Iraqi missile attacks on Israel, Premier Yitzhak Shamir [*qv*] put Israel on full nuclear alert and (according to U.S. satellite pictures) ordered mobile missile launchers armed with nuclear warheads to be deployed in the open, facing Iraq.

An article based on a study of Russian and French satellite pictures, and published in late 1994 in *Jane's Intelligence Review* (November 1994, Coulsdon, United Kingdom), gave the following locations for Israel's various military nuclear facilities: Soreq, south of Tel Aviv, on the Mediterranean (design and testing of nuclear weapons); Dimona in the Negev Desert (nuclear reactor and plutonium processing plant); Yodefat in northern Israel (assembly of weapons); and Kfar Zecharya in the Judean hills southwest of Jerusalem [*qv*] (storage of nuclear weapons in bunkers). As for delivery systems, there is a missile base at Kfar Zecharya that is equipped with Jericho I and Jericho II missiles (range 800 miles/1,300 km). Taking into account 60 Jericho II missiles (range/940 miles 1,500 km), older Jericho I missiles (range/310 miles 500 km), and an equal number of gravity atomic bombs (to be dropped by nuclear-capable F4 and F16 warplanes), as well as dozens of nuclear artillery shells, land mines, and special demolition devices, Israel has at least 200 nuclear weapons.

In 1997 *Jane's Intelligence Review* stated that Israel had over 400 thermonuclear and nuclear weapons. Three years later, Issam Mahoul, an Israeli Arab [*qv*] member of the Knesset [*qv*], put the number of Israeli nuclear warheads at 200 to 300.

Despite U.N. Security Council Resolution 487 of June 1981, Israel has not placed its nuclear facilities under IAEA safeguards.

Israel's efforts to sabotage the Iraqi nuclear program included the blowing up of two cores destined for the Tammuz nuclear reactor by Mossad operatives in April 1979 at the French port of La Seyne-sur-Mer; the assassination in Paris in June 1980 by Mossad agents of Yahya al Meshad, an Egyptian nuclear physicist overseeing the Iraqi-Egyptian cooperation on nuclear development; and the bombing on 4 June 1981 of the nuclear facility being constructed by the French near Baghdad [*qv*].

In the early 1970s, aware of Israel's nuclear weapons program, Egypt, Syria, Iraq, Libya, and Algeria set up special sections in their armed forces to deal with nuclear warfare. Given their military ties with the Soviet Union, the latter trained the members of these units in arming Soviet-made surface-to-surface Scud missiles with nuclear weapons. The secret clauses in the 1980 Syrian-Soviet Friendship Treaty [*qv*] provided for the supply of Soviet nuclear arms to Syria under certain conditions.

Military in Jordan (2003): Total armed forces: active, 100,240; reserves, 35,000

Military expenditure as percent of GDP: 8.5 (2001)

Ground forces: regular army, active, 84,700; reserves, 30,000

In-service equipment: tanks, 1,179; armored personnel carriers, 1,500; major artillery, 531

Air forces: regular air force, active, 15,000; reserves, 4,500

In-service equipment: combat aircraft, 101; combat helicopters, 22

Naval forces: regular navy, active, 540; reserves, 500

In-service equipment: patrol craft, 3

Paramilitary: active, 10,000 (of which, public security police, 10,000); reserves (civil militia), 35,000

Military in Kuwait (2003): Total armed forces: active, 15,000; reserves, 23,500

Military expenditure as percent of GDP: 12.1 (2001)

Ground forces: regular army, active, 10,000; reserves, 18,000

In-service equipment: tanks, 150; armored personnel carriers, 85; major artillery, 20

Air forces: regular air force, active, 2,500; reserves, 3,000

In-service equipment: combat aircraft, 105; combat helicopters, 15

Naval forces: regular navy, active, 2,500; reserves, 2,500

In-service equipment: patrol and coastal combatants, 4

Paramilitary: active (National Guard), 5,000

Military in Lebanon (2003): Total armed forces: active, 71,830

Military expenditure as percent of GDP: 3.5 (2001)

Ground forces: regular army, 70,000

In-service equipment: tanks, 327; armored personnel carriers, 1,338; major artillery, 160

Air forces: regular air force, 1,000

In-service equipment: combat aircraft, none in service

Naval forces: regular navy, 830

In-service equipment: patrol and coastal combatants, 7

Paramilitary: active, 13,000 (of which, internal security force, 13,000)

Syrian forces stationed in Lebanon: ground forces, 18,000

Military in Oman (2003): Total armed forces: active, 41,700

Military expenditure as percent of GDP: 14.5 (2001)

Ground forces: regular army, 25,000

In-service equipment: tanks, 117;

armored personnel carriers, 189; major artillery, 120

Air forces: regular air force, 4,100

In-service equipment: combat aircraft, 40

Naval forces: regular navy, 4,200

In-service equipment: patrol and coastal combatants, 13

Royal household: ground force, 6,000; air force, 250; naval force, 150

Paramilitary: active, 4,400 (tribal home guard, 4,000; coast guard, 400)

Military in Qatar (2003): Total armed forces: active, 12,400

Military expenditure as percent of GDP: 7.3 (2001)

Ground forces: regular army, 8,500

In-service equipment: tanks, 35; armored personnel carriers, 190; major artillery, 40

Air forces: regular air force, 2,100

In-service equipment: combat aircraft, 18; combat helicopters, 19

Naval forces: regular navy, 1,800

In-service equipment: patrol and coastal combatants, 7

Military in Saudi Arabia (2003): Total armed forces: active, 199,500; reserves, 25,000

Military expenditure as percent of GDP: 14.1 (2001)

Ground forces: (a) regular army, active, 75,000; (b) National Guard [*qv*], active, 75,000; reserves, 25,000

In-service equipment: tanks, 1,055; armored personnel carriers, 2,670; major artillery, 518; combat helicopters, 67

Air forces: (a) regular air force, 18,000; (b) air defense forces, 16,000

In-service equipment: combat aircraft, 294

Naval forces: regular navy, 12,500; regular marines, 3,000

In-service equipment: surface combatants 8 (frigates, 4; corvettes, 4); patrol and coastal combatants, 26; mine warfare vessels, 7

Paramilitary: active, 15,500 (frontier force, 10,500; coast guard, 5,000)

Military in Syria (2003): Total armed forces: active, 319,000; reserves, 354,000

Military expenditure as percent of GDP: 10.8 (2001)

Ground forces: regular army, active, 215,000; reserves, 280,000

In-service equipment: tanks, 9,400; armored personnel carriers, 1,600; major artillery, 2,080

Air forces: (a) regular air force, active, 40,000; reserves, 30,000; (b) Regular air defense, active, 60,000; reserves, 40,000

In-service equipment: combat aircraft, 611; combat helicopters, 90

Naval forces: regular navy, active, 4,000; reserves, 4,000

In-service equipment: surface combatants, 2 (frigates, 2); patrol and coastal combatants, 18; mine warfare vessels, 5

Paramilitary: active, 108,000 (gendarmerie, 8,000; people's militia, 100,000)

Military in United Arab Emirates (2003): Total armed forces: active, 41,500

Military expenditure as percent of GDP: 4.6. (2001)

Ground forces: regular army, 35,000

In-service equipment: tanks, 381; armored personnel carriers, 650; major artillery, 271

Air forces: regular air force, 4,000

In-service equipment: combat aircraft, 101; combat helicopters, 49

Naval forces: regular navy, 2,500

In-service equipment: surface combatants, 2 (frigates, 2); patrol and coastal combatants, 16

Military in Yemen (2003): Total armed forces: active, 66,500; reserves, 40,000

Military expenditure as percent of GDP: 8.9 (2001)

Ground forces: regular army, active, 60,000; reserves, 40,000

In-service equipment: tanks, 790; armored personnel carriers, 710; major artillery, 335

Air forces: (a) regular air force, 3,500; (b) air defense force, 1,500

In-service equipment: combat aircraft, 116; combat helicopters, 8

Naval forces: regular navy, 1,500

In-service equipment: patrol and coastal combatants, 11; mine warfare vessels, 6

Paramilitary: active, 50,000 (interior ministry force, 50,000); reserves, 20,000 (tribal levies, 20,000)

Mishna: *Text of the Jewish Oral Law. See* Talmud.

Mizrachi *(Hebrew: Oriental): the term commonly used for* Edot Mizrachi *(Hebrew: Oriental Peoples). See* Oriental Jews.

Mizrahi *(Hebrew: acronym of* Merkaz Rouhani, *Spiritual Center): political party in Palestine/Israel* Mizrahi was formed in 1902 by a group of rabbis in Vilnius, Lithuania, to counter growing secularization in the education of Jews [*qv*] in Europe. It marked the rise of religious Zionism as a distinct faction within the Zionist movement [*qv*], represented by the World Zionist Organization [*qv*]. The party advocated establishing a Jewish national home in Palestine [*qv*], based on the written Jewish law, the Torah [*qv*]. In Palestine Mizrahi ensured that the chief rabbinate was organized within the framework of the elected assembly.

In 1922 its younger members formed

Poale HaMizrahi [*qv*]. Mizrahi had one minister in the provisional government of Israel in 1948. It and the Poale HaMizrahi allied with other religious groups to form the United Religious Front (URF) to contest the first general election in 1949. The URF won sixteen seats and joined the government to run inter alia the ministry of religious affairs. The ministry decided how to finance religious councils and religious courts, and influenced the composition and working of the powerful rabbinical council.

In mid-1951 it brought down the government led by David Ben-Gurion [*qv*] on the issue of educating immigrant families and the URF's degree of control over religious education in schools. In the following election, Mizrahi and the Poale HaMizrahi together won ten seats and joined the coalition government. In 1956 the two groups combined to form the National Religious Party [*qv*].

Mohieddin, Khalid: *see* Muhyi al Din, Khalid.

Moledet *(Hebrew: Homeland): Israeli political party* The Moledet was established in 1988 by Gen. Rechavam Zeev with a program of expelling the Palestinians from the West Bank [*qv*] and Gaza [*qv*]. It won two seats in the 1988 poll and backed the national unity government that followed. Protesting against Israel's participation in the Middle East Peace Conference in Madrid [*qv*] in October 1991, it withdrew its backing from the administration three months later. In the June 1992 election it won three parliamentary seats. In 1994 it combined with the Tehiya [*qv*] to form the Moledet-Eretz Israel Faithful and the Tehiya. Four years later this bloc joined the coalition government led by Benjamin Netanyahu [*qv*]. In the 1999 general election, it won three seats. In March it joined the national unity government under Ariel Sharon [*qv*], and its leader Rechavam Ze'evi became minister of tourism. He was assassinated in October by the militants of the Popular Front for Liberation of Palestine [*qv*] at an East Jerusalem [*qv*] hotel where he had taken up residence. The Moledet then combined with Israel BeItainu [*qv*] to form the National Union [*qv*].

Montazeri, Hussein Ali (1921–): *Iranian religious-political leader* Born into a poor peasant family in Najafabad, Montazeri had his early theological education in Isfahan [*qv*]. He then went to Qom [*qv*] where he became a student of Ayatollah Ruhollah Khomeini [*qv*]. In the early 1960s he taught at the Faiziyya seminary in Qom, and participated in the antigovernment protest in June 1963.

An active member of the anti-shah clerical circles, he was close to Ayatollah Mahmud Taleqani [*qv*]. During the latter part of his exile, from 1964 to 1978, Khomeini appointed Montazeri as his personal representative in Iran. Montazeri was arrested during the anti-Rastakhiz Party [*qv*] protest in March 1975. Tortured in jail, he was released in November 1978 in the midst of a rising revolutionary movement. On his return to Iran in February 1979, Khomeini appointed Montazeri as Friday prayer leader of Qom, a highly prestigious position, and gave him a seat on the governing Islamic Revolutionary Council. Montazeri was elected as leader of the Association of Combatant Clergy [*qv*] and chairman of the Assembly of

Experts (1979) [*qv*], which was convened to draft a constitution. In 1980 Khomeini put him in charge of the secretariat of the Friday prayer leaders, based in Qom.

Montazeri took a radical stance on many issues. The official campaign to bolster Montazeri's standing gathered pace in the spring of 1983, when in all government offices Khomeini's portraits were accompanied by smaller pictures of Montazeri. But the radicals' attempt to have him named as successor to Khomeini by the Assembly of Experts (1982) [*qv*] failed. However, after a brief session of the Assembly in November 1985, one of its members, Ahmad Barikiban, revealed that the Assembly had in fact chosen Montazeri as Khomeini's successor. Montazeri continued in this position until March 1989 when Khomeini changed his mind about him.

Instead of following Khomeini's example of intermittently backing one or other faction within the ruling establishment, Montazeri consistently advocated moderate policies, such as allowing a fair degree of opposition and liberalizing the economy, thus alienating centrists and radicals. He also repeatedly stressed the failure of the Islamic revolution to deliver its promises while ignoring its achievements. Montazeri was offered the choice of sharing power with two others to constitute a Leadership Council of three, but rejected it, preferring to resign. He then immersed himself in religious teaching. When Khomeini died in June 1989, Montazeri was not on the list of candidates considered by the Assembly of Experts. Later, when he publicly questioned the religious learning and standing of Khomeini's successor, Ayatollah Ali Khamanei [*qv*], he was put under house arrest. In the late 1990s he set up his own Web site to express his views and communicate with others. In early 2003 the authorities lifted the restrictions on his movements.

mosque: *an Islamic place of public worship* In Arabic, *masjid* (place of prostration). The first mosque, built by the Prophet Muhammad (A.D. 570–632) at Quba near Medina [*qv*], was a simple courtyard. During the rule of Caliph al Walid (A.D. 705–15) the following elements were added to mosques: the *mihrab,* a semicircular niche in the center of the wall pointing to the *qiblah* (the direction of Mecca [*qv*]); and the *minbar,* a seat at the top of steps to the right of the niche used as a pulpit by the preacher *(khatib)* to deliver a sermon *(khutba)*. Since then mosques have often been fully or partially covered and provided with one or more minarets. Large mosques sometimes have cloisters for students of religion.

The head of a mosque is called *imam* [*qv*] and acts as the prayer leader. Sometimes he also acts as a religious instructor *(maulawi)*. There is also a *muezzin* (the caller to prayer), who uses the minaret to call believers to worship five times a day. Ritual prayers, called *salat* (Arabic) or *namaz* (Persian), are offered by barefoot men, gathered in rows on the floor, who bow and prostrate themselves under the guidance of the imam.

Ritual objects, pictures, and statues are not allowed inside mosques. Since believers are required to cleanse themselves before praying, a place for ablution, containing running water, is often either attached to the mosque or enclosed by it.

Muslims are required to pray collectively on Fridays, the Islamic holy day, and the Friday prayer sermon is especially important.

This led to the evolution of collective mosques *(jami masjid)* in cities with a large Muslim population. Over time such mosques became multipurpose public buildings, serving military, political, judicial, social, and educational purposes. A prime example of this was the al Azhar mosque in Cairo, which evolved into al Azhar University [*qv*] in A.D. 969. In modern times the nonreligious functions of mosques have been taken over by secular institutions, but they continue to impart elementary Islamic education to Muslim children in many countries.

After the establishment of an Islamic republic in Iran, mosques were put to traditional use, with neighborhood Revolutionary Komitehs [*qv*] basing themselves in mosques and conducting such state administration as issuing ration cards and recruiting volunteers to the Basij militia.

Mossad *(Hebrew: Institute): Israeli foreign intelligence service* Official title: *HaMossad LeModein Ve Tafkidim Meyuhadim* (Institute for Intelligence and Special Tasks). In April 1951 the Israeli government replaced the foreign ministry's political department (charged with gathering intelligence outside Israel) with Mossad and transferred it to the prime minister's office. Within two months of taking office its first director, Reuven Shiloah, signed a clandestine cooperation agreement with the U.S. Central Intelligence Agency (CIA). After Shiloah's resignation in September 1952, Isser Harel became director (1952–63). His successors were Gen. Meir Amit (1963–68); Maj. Gen. Zvi Zamir (1968–74); Maj. Gen. Yitzhak Hofi (1974–82); Nahum Admoni (1982–89); and Danny Yatom (1989-97). The name of the current director remains a state secret. In 1997 Mossad had 1,700 full-time employees. Together with Shin Beth [qv], it spent $1.1 billion annually, about 10 percent of the defense budget.

Some of the better known operations of Mossad since the early 1970s are as follows. Within a year of the killing of eleven Israeli athletes by Black September Organization [qv] commandos at the Munich Olympics in September 1972, Mossad operatives assassinated twelve Palestinians involved directly or indirectly with the event. Mossad arranged secret meetings between Prime Minister Yitzhak Rabin [qv] and King Hussein of Jordan [qv] in 1975 and 1977, one of which was in Tel Aviv [qv]. In July 1976 it organized the storming of the airport in Entebbe, Uganda, where 100 hostages who had been on an Air France flight from Tel Aviv were being held by two Palestinian guerrillas and two members of the German Baader-Meinhoff group to secure the release of forty Palestinian prisoners. In April 1979 Mossad operatives blew up two cores for the Tammuz nuclear reactor that were awaiting shipment to Iraq from the French port of La Seyne-sur-Mer. Fourteen months later in Paris, Mossad agents assassinated Yahya al Meshad, an Egyptian nuclear physicist overseeing an Iraq-Egyptian cooperation on nuclear development. On 4 June 1981 Mossad and Aman (Hebrew: *Amn, acronym of Agaf [Branch] Modein [Intelligence]*), the military intelligence arm, organized an Israeli air raid on Iraq and destroyed the nuclear facility being constructed near Baghdad [qv].

Based since 1975–76 in Jounieh, capital of the Christian enclave during the Lebanese Civil War [qv], and working in tandem with Bashir Gemayel [qv], the Mossad participated in the plan of Defense Minister Ariel Sharon [qv] for an Israeli invasion of Lebanon [qv], which was implemented in June 1982. Mossad and Aman organized an air raid on the headquarters of the Palestine Liberation Organization (PLO) [qv] in Tunis on 1 October 1985, killing fifty-six Palestinians. Mossad was deeply involved in the Irangate affair [qv], which came to light in November 1986. Earlier, in late September 1986, a Mossad agent, "Cindy," had lured Mordechai Vanunu—a shift manager at Israeli's Dimona nuclear plant from August 1977 to November 1985—to Rome from London, where he had passed on details of Israel's nuclear weapons production to the *Sunday Times,* which published them on 5 October. In Rome Vanunu was drugged by Mossad agents and taken to Israel, where he was sentenced to a long prison term. On 16 April 1988 a Mossad hit team assassinated a top Palestinian leader, Khalil Wazir [qv], in Tunis. But Mossad's repeated efforts to kill President Saddam Hussein [qv] before, during, and after the 1991 Second Gulf War [qv] failed.

In 1990 Mossad recruited Adnan Yassin, deputy to Abdul Hakam Balawi, head of the PLO's internal security in Tunis, as an agent. During the ultrasecret talks among the top PLO leaders in 1992–93, Mossad had Yassin plant bugs in the offices of Mahmoud Abbas [qv] and Ahmad Qrei, and convey the information by a radio transmitter to the Israeli embassies in Paris and Rome, from where it was passed on to top Israeli leadership engaged in sensitive negotiations with the PLO, which culminated in the Oslo Accord I [qv] in 1993. Thus Mossad enabled its political superiors to strike the most important accord with the PLO in the full knowledge of the strategy and tactics of Yasser Arafat [*qv*] and his second in command, Abbas.

In October 1995 its agents assassinated Fathi Abdul Aziz Shikaki, leader of the Islamic Jihad of Palestine [*qv*] in Malta. But Mossad's attempt to kill Khalid Mashaal, a Hamas [*qv*] leader, by pumping a chemical agent into his ear, in Amman [*qv*] in September 1997, failed, resulting in the arrest of two of its agents, carrying Canadian passports, and leading to Israel's release of Shaikh Ahmad Yassin [*qv*] and seventy-two other Palestinian prisoners in return for the agents' release.

In November 2002, Meir Dagan was appointed director-general of Mossad.

Mosul: *Iraqi city* Pop. 1,790,000 (2003, est.). A settlement with a long history and situated by the Tigris River [*qv*] opposite the ancient ruins of Nineveh, Mosul was the leading city of northern Mesopotamia [*qv*] by the time of the Abbasid caliphate (751–1258). It was sacked by the Mongol invader Hulagu in 1258 and subsequently lacked proper administration until its capture by the Iranian Shah Ismail (r. 1501–24) in 1508. It fell to the Ottoman Turks in 1538. As an important commercial center, it thrived during the Turkish rule. Following the Ottoman defeat in the First World War it lost its preeminence, but the discovery of oil in the region in 1927 changed its fortunes. It is the site of several mosques, including one with a leaning minaret, and churches. The capital of Nineveh province, Mosul is Iraq's second largest city. During the Gulf War III [*qv*] in March–April 2003, the city fell to the Kurdish Militias operating in alliance with the invading U.S. forces.

Moussa, Amr (1936–): *Egyptian diplomat and politician; secretary-general of the Arab League, 2001–* Born into a middle-class family in Cairo [*qv*], Moussa graduated in law from Cairo University in 1957. He then joined the Egyptian foreign service. He served as director of the international organizations department of the foreign ministry from 1977 to 1981. For the next four years he was Egypt's alternative representative at the United Nations. After his posting as his country's ambassador to India during 1987–90, he served as Egypt's permanent representative to the United Nations for a year. He was then promoted to foreign minister, a job he held for ten years.

He and President Hosni Mubarak [*qv*] were active in advising the Palestinian leadership during its secret talks with Israel [*qv*] that led to the Oslo I Accord [*qv*] in September 1993. They were equally involved in getting the two sides to sign the Cairo Agreement on the Gaza Strip [*qv*] and Jericho [*qv*], which led inter alia to the establishment of the Palestinian Authority [*qv*] in 1994. But their efforts to put the Middle East peace process back on track during the rule of Israeli Prime Minister Benjamin Netanyahu (1996–99) were largely unsuccessful. Against the backdrop of worsening Israeli-Palestinian relations in the wake of the Second Intifada [*qv*], Moussa and Mubarak came under pressure by radical Arab states to sever diplomatic relations with Israel, especially after the election of Ariel Sharon [*qv*] as Israel's prime minister. Which they managed to withstand it at the Twenty-second Arab League summit [*qv*], which appointed Moussa as its new secretary-general.

Mubarak, (Muhammad) Hosni (1928–):

Egyptian military leader and politician; president, 1981– Son of a court functionary and born in the Nile [*qv*] delta village of Kafr al Musaliha, Mubarak graduated from the air force academy in 1950. After serving as a fighter pilot from 1950–54, he taught at the air force academy, where he later became director general. Appointed commander of the West Cairo air base in 1961, Mubarak underwent courses at the Soviet General Staff Academy. In 1964 he was sent to the Frunze Military Academy in the Soviet Union, where he stayed for more than a year.

After Egypt's debacle in the June 1967 Arab-Israeli War [*qv*], Mubarak was returned to his earlier job of director general of the air force academy. Two years later he was appointed chief of staff of the air force and promoted to air vice marshal. In the October 1973 Arab-Israeli War [*qv*], under his command the air force performed well during the crucial initial hours, and he was promoted the next year to air marshal. In April 1975 President Anwar Sadat [*qv*] appointed Mubarak vice president since he lacked the potential of developing into a competing center of power. Mubarak became vice chairman of the ruling National Democratic Party (NDP) [*qv*] in 1976. As vice president, Mubarak followed Sadat's line in domestic and foreign affairs.

Following Sadat's assassination in October 1981, Mubarak took over as president. He also became leader of the NDP. After briefly moderating his stance toward Islamic fundamentalists [*qv*], Mubarak resumed Sadat's hardline policy. While continuing a close alliance with the United States he thawed Egypt's relations with the Soviet Union. He withdrew the Egyptian ambassador from Tel Aviv [*qv*] in protest against Israel's invasion of Lebanon in 1982, but rejected Arab demands to break diplomatic ties with Israel. He continued Sadat's policy of militarily aiding Iraq [*qv*] in the Iran-Iraq War [*qv*], hoping thus to erode the Arab League's [*qv*] policy of boycotting Egypt since the signing of the Egyptian-Israeli Peace Treaty [*qv*]. His success came in September 1984 when Jordan, Iraq's ally, resumed diplomatic ties with Cairo. After the final expulsion of Yasser Arafat [*qv*] from Lebanon in 1983, Mubarak helped him to reassemble his scattered forces.

In February 1986 a riotous mutiny by 17,000 conscripts of the Central Security Forces in Cairo threatened Mubarak's regime. Its suppression by Defense Minister Field Marshal Abdul Halim Abu Ghazala so enhanced Ghazala's prestige that Mubarak sacked him in April to get rid of a serious potential rival to his own authority. As the sole candidate, Mubarak was reelected president in 1987.

Mubarak led Egypt into the Arab Cooperation Council (ACC) [*qv*] in February 1989, and three months later Egypt was allowed to return to the Arab League. When Iraqi President Saddam Hussein [*qv*] occupied Kuwait in August 1990, Mubarak condemned his action. In the Arab League he led the majority that demanded Iraq's immediate and unconditional withdrawal. This ended the ACC. Mubarak sent Egyptian troops to Saudi Arabia to bolster Saudi defenses. As part of the U.S.-led coalition, the Egyptians participated in the Second Gulf War [*qv*], taking care not to enter Iraq.

Mubarak's policies proved unpopular with a growing segment of Egyptian society.

Almost all opposition groups boycotted the general election of 1990. Militant Islamist groups such as Gamaat al Islamiya [qv] and Jihad al Islami [qv] intensified their campaign against his regime in 1992. Nonetheless he was reelected president in 1993. He played an important role in bringing about an accord between Israel and the Palestine Liberation Organization [qv] in September 1993 and its subsequent implementation.

An attempt by al Gamaat al Islamiya to assassinate Mubarak during his visit to Addis Ababa to attend the Organization of African Union summit in June 1995 failed. By the late 1990s his campaign against Islamic militants had succeeded and the economy had improved. In the referendum, following his nomination for the presidency by the parliament in 1999, he secured a 94 percent vote on an official turnout of 79 percent. In July 2000 he advised Yasser Arafat [qv] not to compromise on the future status of Jerusalem [qv] by conceding the sovereignty of the Dome of the Rock [qv] to Israel in his talks with Israeli Prime Minister Ehud Barak [qv] at Camp David, and called for a united Arab stance in support of the Palestinians according to United Nations Security Council Resolution 242 [qv]. Later at his behest, Saddam Hussein was invited to the Arab League summit in Cairo [qv] after a decade.

Following the terrorist attacks on the United States in September 2001, Mubarak's calls for an international convention to define terrorism as a preamble to a worldwide campaign [qv] against it went unheeded by the administration of President George W. Bush. Nor were his repeated warnings against invading Iraq heeded.

Muhammad, Ali (1952–): *Egyptian military officer; Al Qaida leader* Born into a well-to-do family in Alexandria [qv], Muhammad enrolled at the military academy in Heliopolis, a suburb of Cairo [qv]. A tall, powerfully built man, he underwent paratrooper training and rose to the rank of major before leaving the army in 1984. During his military service he secretly joined the Al Jihad Al Islami [qv]. In 1980 he tried to ingratiate himself with the U.S. Central Intelligence Agency (CIA) in Egypt. Though rebuffed, he did not give up. Nor did the CIA.

In early 1986 he arrived in the United States with a visa waiver, a privilege that could be conferred on a visitor only with the blessing of the CIA or the State Department. He found a job as a security officer in Sunnyvale, California, and married Linda Sanchez, an American medical technician. In November he enlisted in the U.S. Army on a three-year contract and served as an army sergeant at the Special Forces headquarters at Fort Bragg, North Carolina. As an assistant instructor at the John F. Kennedy Special Warfare Center, Muhammad assisted the seminar director prepare classes on the history, politics, culture, and armed forces of the Middle East [qv]. A multilinguist, he was fluent in Hebrew [qv]. He was a frequent visitor at Al Khifa Refugee Center in Brooklyn, a recruiting center for American Muslim [qv] volunteers to join the anti-Soviet jihad [qv] in Afghanistan. During his annual army leave Muhammad traveled to Afghanistan to fight there. He returned with a belt of a Spetsnaz (Soviet Special Forces) soldier whom he claimed to have killed.

After an honorable discharge from the U.S. defense department, Muhammad started a leather import-export business. During his visits to New York, he imparted weapons training to the American Muslim militants attending Al Khifa Refugee Center. He found time and inclination to pursue a doctorate in Islamic studies.

In 1993 he applied unsuccessfully for a translator's job at the Federal Bureau of Investigation (FBI). After the failed attempt on Osama bin Laden's [qv] life in Sudan in 1994, Muhammad retrained his bodyguards, a fact he reportedly conceded in an FBI interview in 1997, when he and his wife moved from Santa Clara to Sacramento, where he was employed as a computer specialist at a music and video wholesaler. A search of their home revealed documents on surveillance of government targets, assassination techniques, planning of terrorist acts, and use of explosives.

After his arrest in 1998, he chose a plea bargain and turned a state witness in the U.S. case against bin Laden. His own trial was so sensitive that it was held in camera when it opened in late October 1998 in Manhattan—two and a half months after the bombing of the two U.S. embassies in East Africa. Muhammad told the court that he had "scouted out" the American Embassy in Nairobi at bin Laden's request.

Still in jail in early 2003, Muhammad expected to receive a light sentence.

Muhammad, Ali Nasser (1939–): *South Yemeni politician; president, 1978, 1980–86* Born in the Dathina tribal region of South Yemen, Muhammad trained as a teacher in Aden [qv]. While working as the headmaster of a school in his native area, he played an active role in the founding of the National Liberation Front (NLF) [qv] in 1963. During the armed campaign Muhammad led NLF guerrillas in the Beihan region. When South Yemen became independent in November 1967, Muhammad was appointed governor of Lahej province. Following the ousting of President Qahtan al Shaabi [qv] in June 1969, Muhammad was named local government minister, and, soon after, defense minister. In August 1971, along with Salim Rubai Ali [qv] and Abdul Fattah Ismail [qv], Muhammad became a member of the Presidential Council and premier.

The next year, when Saudi Arabia was poised to intervene in the conflict between South Yemen and North Yemen on the latter's side, his warning that the Soviet Union would not stand idly by if South Yemen were invaded by its neighbors proved effective.

After the NLF had devised a three-year political-economic plan for the transition from national democracy to socialism, differences developed between President Ali on the one hand and Muhammad and Ismail on the other. The NLF central committee decided in September 1977, and again in January 1978, to divest Ali of some of his many functions. In June he agreed to resign, but then reneged, leading to a one-day fight in which he lost his life. Muhammad took over the presidency, but ceded it to Ismail in December, while retaining the premiership and membership of the Presidential Council. Gradually Muhammad came into conflict with Ismail, as the latter insisted on maintaining a hard line at home and abroad, while Muhammad began to espouse a pragmatic approach. Ismail lost in April 1980 and went into exile in Moscow. As head of the state, the government, and the ruling Yemen Socialist Party [*qv*], Muhammad monopolized power and used it to moderate official policies. This earned him the disapproval of the deputy premier, Ali Salim al Beidh [*qv*], and the defense minister, Ali Antar, among others. The return of Ismail from Moscow in 1985 intensified factionalism. Muhammad's attempted coup to eliminate his radical rivals in January 1986 set off bitter fighting. Though Ismail and Antar were killed, Muhammad lost the battle. He fled to Ethiopia. The partial amnesty and introduction of a multiparty system on the eve of the unification of North and South Yemen in May 1990 did not apply to Muhammad. He was appointed to the five-member Presidential Council nominated by Ali Salim al Beidh [*qv*] after the latter's declaration of independence for South Yemen in 1994. The Council did not last long. In 1996, Muhammad was allowed to return to Yemen.

Muhammad, Khalid Shaikh (1965–): *Al Qaida leader* Born to Pakistani Baluchi [*qv*] parents, settled in Kuwait [*qv*] since 1961, Muhammad grew up in a suburb of Kuwait city [*qv*]. After finishing his secondary education in Kuwait, he went to the United States on a government grant. There he obtained a diploma in mechanical engineering from North Carolina Agricultural and Technical University, Greensboro, a largely African American college, in 1986. Instead of returning home, Muhammad went to Peshawar, Pakistan, to join his elder brother, Zahid, and his Kuwait-born nephew, Ramzi Ahmad Yousef—an electrical engineering graduate from a British university—both of whom had earlier joined the anti-Soviet jihad [*qv*], orchestrated and funded by America, Pakistan, and Saudi Arabia [*qv*].

When Yousef was arrested in Pakistan in February 1995 in connection with the bombing of the World Trade Center in New York two years earlier, which killed six people and injured 1,200, his chief coconspirator turned out to be Muhammad. It was Yousef who originally came up with the idea of deploying a hijacked passenger plane as a missile to hit a target. In January 1995, when Yousef and Muhammad were living in the Filipino capital of Manila, their apartment caught fire and the police ended up discovering a laptop computer with a plan to blow up ten America-bound passenger jets over the Pacific. They fled, with Muhammad moving to Qatar [*qv*], where he worked as a civil servant. But by the time the Qatari government, tipped off by the U.S. Federal Bureau of Investigation (FBI), got around to issuing an arrest warrant in 1996, Muhammad had absconded.

He formally joined Al Qaida [*qv*]. After the formation of the World Islamic Front for Jihad against Crusaders and Jews [*qv*] in February 1998, he was appointed to the military committee headed by Muhammad Atef [*qv*]. Impressed by his record, Atef reportedly made him his deputy. In that capacity, Muhammad is believed to have coordinated the bombings of the U.S. embassies in Nairobi and Dar as Salam in August 1998, the bombing of the USS *Cole* in Aden [*qv*] in October 2000, and the attacks in New York and Washington on 11 September 2001. With the death of Atef during the Afghan campaign by the United States in November, Muhammad became the head of the military committee of Al Qaida. The FBI put a reward of $25 million on his head. He was believed to be the mastermind behind the bombing of a synagogue in the Djerba Island of Tunisia in 2002, which killed twenty-one people, mainly German tourists. He was arrested in the Pakistani city of Rawalpindi in February 2003 and handed over to U.S. authorities.

Muhyi al Din, Khalid (1922–): *Egyptian politician* Born into a landowning family in the Nile [*qv*] delta, Muhyi graduated from the Royal Military Academy in Cairo [*qv*] and became a cavalry officer, reaching the rank of major. He also obtained an economics degree from the University of Cairo.

Active with the Free Officers organization, which staged a coup in July 1952, Muhyi was one of the two leftist members of the ruling eighteen-member Revolutionary Command Council (RCC). In the power struggle between President Muhammad Neguib [*qv*] and his deputy, Gamal Abdul Nasser [*qv*], the communists, including Muhyi, backed Neguib because he favored returning to a parliamentary system. When Nasser won he dismissed Muhyi from the RCC and put him under house arrest. But during the 1956 Suez War [*qv*] Nasser released hundreds of leftists, including Muhyi, so that they could organize resistance against the invaders of the Suez Canal zone.

Muhyi was named editor of a new pro-government daily, *Al Massaa (Arabic: The Evening)*, but he lost this job in 1959 when, reacting to the Iraqi Communists' [*qv*] opposition to the unification of Iraq with the United Arab Republic [*qv*], Nasser turned against local communists. It was not until 1964 that Nasser, responding to the changed situation in the region, began to co-opt communists. Muhyi was appointed chairman of the board of *Al Akhbar (Arabic: The News)*. He also became a member of the secretariat of the Arab Socialist Union (ASU) [*qv*], the new ruling party, and headed the ASU branch responsible for the press.

After Egypt's debacle in the June 1967 Arab-Israeli War [*qv*], Nasser began to cold-shoulder leftists and rejected Muhyi's proposal that the armed services be controlled by the ASU, with its cadre penetrating their institution, thus ending their isolation from society.

Muhyi received the Lenin Peace Prize from the Soviet Union in 1970. After Nasser's death that year, Muhyi's ties with the new government became tenuous. Muhyi attacked President Anwar Sadat's [*qv*] growing alliance with the United States, especially after the October 1973 Arab-Israeli War [*qv*], and economic liberalization, which hurt the poor. After the forums within the ASU were allowed to graduate to parties in 1977, Muhyi was elected leader of the National Progressive Unionist Alliance (NPUA) [*qv*]. The next year he became editor of its weekly paper, *Al Ahali* (The People). He opposed the Egyptian-Israeli Peace Treaty [*qv*].

He was one of the 240 secular dissidents arrested in September 1981, a month before Sadat's assassination. Though charged with security offenses, he was not tried. He was released soon after. Having failed to win a parliamentary seat in 1984 and 1987, he succeeded in 1990. The number of seats for his party rose to five and six respectively in the polls of 1995 and 2000.

mujahed: (pl. mujahedin) One who engages in *jihad* [*qv*].

Mujahedini: plural of Mujahed [*qv*].

Mujahedin-e Islam *(Persian: Combatants of Islam): Iranian political party* The Mujahedin-e Islam was formed in 1945 by Ayatollah Abol Qasim Kashani [*qv*], a nationalist cleric. It drew its strength from small traders, theological students, and older leaders of bazaari [*qv*] merchant families. It demanded cancellation of all the secular laws passed by Reza Shah Pahlavi [*qv*], the application of the Sharia [*qv*] as stated in the constitution of 1906–07, the veil for women, and protection for Iranian industries. It suffered a near-fatal blow in early 1949 when the banishment of Kashani to Lebanon was coupled with governmental repression. His return home in mid-1950 failed to revive the party, especially as another semi-clandestine group, Fedaiyan-e Islam [*qv*], had by then struck roots and won Kashani's patronage.

Mujahedin-e Khalq *(Persian: The People's Combatants): Iranian political party* Official title: *Sazman-e Mujahedin-e Khalq-e Iran* (Iranian People's Combatants' Organization). The Mujahedin-e Khalq was founded secretly in 1965 by young former members of the Liberation Movement [*qv*] who felt that their leaders were too moderate. It stressed the importance of religion, believing that Shia Islam [*qv*] would play a major role in inspiring the masses to join the revolution. Its chief ideologue, Ahmad Rezai, argued that the rebellions led by Shia Imams [*qv*], especially Hussein ibn Ali, were as much against the usurping Caliphs, who had abandoned the objective of establishing the Order of the Divine Unity (worship of One God and the founding of a classless society for universal good) as they

were against feudalists and rich merchants. In modern times true Muslims must strive to create a classless society by struggling against imperialism, capitalism, dictatorship, and conservative clericalism.

The party activists started their guerrilla actions in August 1971 with a view to disrupting the celebrations of 2,500 years of monarchy in October. The resulting government repression led to the killing or detention of virtually all founder members. But the party's action-oriented program attracted a steady stream of young recruits. Severe repression and an inflow of pro-Marxist recruits led to an attempt by party leaders to combine Islam [*qv*] and Marxism. While continuing to be inspired by Islam as an ideology and culture, they increasingly used Marxism as an analytical tool. This alienated many anti-Marxists who, finding themselves in a minority, left, thus strengthening the position of the Marxists at the expense of the centrists.

In mid-1975 the cental committee, dominated by Tehran-based leftists, adopted a manifesto that described Islam as "the ideology of the middle classes" and Marxism as "the ideology of the working class," concluding that Marxism was the truly revolutionary creed. The centrists, opposed to the philosophy of Marxism, split the party. Both wings carried out guerrilla actions and lost many cadres. In 1976 they decided to focus on propaganda, with the centrists targeting students, and on the Marxist workers.

Yielding to popular pressure in 1977–78, the government freed most Mujahedin prisoners. This strengthened both factions, who participated in many demonstrations. The release in December 1978 of Masud Rajavi

[*qv*], the only surviving member of the original central committee, boosted the Mujahedin's morale. Both factions were active during the events that culminated in the victory of the revolution in February 1979. The Marxist Mujahedin-e Khalq changed its name to the *Sazman-e Paykar dar Rah-e Azadi-e Tabaqah-e Kargar* (Combat Organization on the Road to Liberation of the Working Class), popularly called Paykar, with the centrist group retaining the original name under Rajavi's leadership.

When Mujahedin-e Khalq members refused to surrender their arms to the Islamic government, as ordered by Ayatollah Ruhollah Khomeini [*qv*], they came into conflict with the new regime. This culminated in open warfare on the eve of the implement of President Abol Hassan Bani-Sadr [*qv*] on 21 June 1981. Both Rajavi and Bani-Sadr went underground. On 28 June a bomb planted by Mujahedin-e Khalq members killed seventy-four leaders of the Islamic republic. A month later Rajavi and Bani-Sadr clandestinely flew from Tehran [*qv*] to France.

The party's armed struggle against the Khomeini regime continued, with its guerrillas, led by Musa Khiyabani, targeting revolutionary guards and parliamentarians. On 30 August its members detonated an incendiary device that killed President Muhammad Ali Rajai [*qv*] and Premier Muhammad Javad Bahonar. The government responded by imposing summary justice on those found guilty of violence. In February 1982, in a single attack, the security forces killed ten Mujahedin-e Khalq central committee members, including Khiyabani. By then the party claimed to have killed over 1,200 religious and political

leaders of the regime. The government put the number of executed Mujahedin at 4,000, with the party claiming twice that number.

With war against Iraq [*qv*] raging along the international border, the Tehran government successfully labeled those creating disorder at home as unpatriotic agents of Baghdad. Its efforts received a boost when the Mujahedin leader, Rajavi, publicly met the Iraqi deputy premier, Tariq Aziz [*qv*], in Paris in January 1983, a move that also caused a split between Rajavi and Bani-Sadr.

After the replacement of a socialist adminstration, sympathetic to the Mujahedin-e Khalq, with a center-right government in France, the authorities expelled Rajavi in June 1986 at the behest of Iran. He set up the party's headquarters in Baghdad [*qv*] and continued his activities from there. A year later, assisted by Iraq, Rajavi formed an armed wing of the party: the National Liberation Army (NLA). Toward the end of the Iran-Iraq War [*qv*], in late July 1988, the 7,000-strong NLA, operating under heavy Iraqi air cover, seized towns 60 miles/100 km into Iran along the Baghdad-Tehran highway. The Iranians cut off their supply lines and counterattacked. Up to 4,500 NLA and Iraqi troops were killed. As further punishment to the Mujahedin-e Khalq, the Iranian government also executed hundreds of jailed party members.

After Khomeini's death in June 1989, Iraqi President Saddam Hussein [*qv*] halted all anti-Iranian activities, including hostile broadcasts of the Mujahedin-e Khalq radio, in order to improve relations with post-Khomeini Iran. But the thaw did not last long. The Mujahedin-e Khalq continued to exist in Baghdad (maintaining 4,500 troops) in the same way that the Iranian-backed Supreme Assembly of the Islamic Revolution in Iraq [qv] did in Tehran—as an embarrassing irritant to the other side. Iran blamed the Mujahedin for the bomb explosions that occurred from time to time—such as the one in Mashhad [qv] on 21 June 1994—and in retribution fired missiles at its bases near the Iran-Iraq border. The Mujahedin continued their periodic pinprick attacks on Iran.

In October 1997 Washington declared the Mujahedin-e Khalq a terrorist organization, thus barring it from collecting funds in America, its chief source of income. However, as long as Iraq and Iran continued their old policy of backing each other's rebel groups, there was no prospect of the group being expelled from Iraq. Due to the student rioting in mid-1999 in Tehran, and the reformist victory in the Iranian parliamentary poll in the following year, the Mujahedin leadership visualized an intensified struggle between reformists and conservatives. In March 2000 its activists fired thirteen mortars at a residential area near the headquarters of the Islamic Revolutionary Guard Corps, their obvious target. Iran hit the group's military camps in Iraq, and the members of the Tehran-based Supreme Assembly of Islamic Revolution in Iraq [qv] fired mortars at a neighborhood in Baghdad.

During the Gulf War III [qv] the Mujahedin military bases were hit, but not destroyed, by as yet unidentified forces. The U.S. signed a cease-fire agreement with it, which required it to disarm. With this, its future became uncertain.

mujtahid *(Arabic: one who strives):* A mujtahid is one who practices *ijtihad* [qv], and the term applies to both Sunni [qv] and Shia [qv] clerics. In Twelver Shiism [qv] the idea of a living mujtahid interpreting the Sharia [qv] took hold in the late eighteenth century. This gave the mujtahid a far greater degree of power than that of a leading Sunni [qv] cleric. Shia mujtahids reached their judgments on political matters impinging on Islamic principles independently of the temporal ruler, a development that had a profound impact on the subsequent history of Iran [qv], a predominantly Shia country. In the Shia world the honorific "mujtahid" was replaced by "ayatollah" around the time of the 1907–11 Constitutional Revolution [qv] in Iran. In 2000 there were twenty-seven ayatollahs in that country.

Mukhabarat *(Arabic: lit., intelligence; fig., organization collecting information):* Mukhabarat is the popular term used in Arab countries for the intelligence apparatus both at home and abroad. More specifically, *Amn al Aam (Arabic: General Security)* focuses on general public and governmental property, with some of its employees monitoring the daily life of the populace, looking for any sign of dissent, and others operating at major police stations, specializing in interrogating and, if need be, torturing suspects. It maintains a large network of informers. By contrast, *Amn al Khas (Arabic: Special Security)* concentrates on protecting the head of state and his palaces and guesthouses. The largest organ of intelligence, *Dairat al Mukhabarat al Ammaa (Arabic: General Intelligence Department),* the official title of Mukhabarat, functions both internally and externally, with its agents attached to the country's embassies abroad. Its functions include keeping tabs on the governing and other political parties (if they are allowed); curbing local opposition; monitoring subversive activities and engaging in counterespionage; maintaining surveillance of all embassies and other foreign missions in the country and monitoring the state's embassies abroad; collecting intelligence overseas; and conducting sabotage and subversion against hostile countries and aiding the groups opposed to their regimes. Its armed forces counterpart is *Istikhabarat al Askariya (Arabic: Military Intelligence)*. Its functions include assessing chief military threats to the country; overseeing security and counterintelligence in the armed forces; ensuring the officers' loyalty to the regime; maintaining a network of informers in the countries of the region; and cooperating with foreign intelligence agencies. In addition, there is *Amn al Askariya (Arabic: Military Security)*. It is charged with maintaining internal security within the armed forces, a task it often performs by posting at least one unquestionably loyal officer in every military unit. So the generic term Mukhabarat covers up to five intelligence agencies.

Multi-National Force (in Lebanon, 1982–84): Following a seventy-day siege of Beirut [*qv*] during the 1982 Israeli invasion of Lebanon [*qv*], an agreement was brokered in August by the United States between Israel, Syria, and Lebanon that a Multi-National Force (MNF) composed of about 1,200 troops each from the United States, France, and Italy would be deployed to ensure the safe withdrawal of Palestine Liberation Organization (PLO) [*qv*] and Syrian forces from West Beirut. The evacuation was completed by 3 September, and the MNF left within a week.

On 13 September president-elect Bashir Gemayel [*qv*] was assassinated. Between sixteen and eighteen Christian Phalangist [*qv*] militiamen killed some 2,000 men, women, and children in the Palestinian camps of Sabra and Shatila in Beirut. The MNF was recalled and took up positions between the airport and the outskirts of the city. A British contingent of 150 men was added to the MNF.

About a year later the United States and France intervened with warplanes and warships in the Lebanese Civil War [*qv*] on the side of the Maronite-dominated [*qv*] Lebanese army. This angered the opposing, predominantly Muslim camp. On 23 October 1983 the truck-bombing of U.S. and military headquarters in West Beirut left 241 U.S. and 59 French troops dead. This shook the resolve of the United States and France to back the Lebanese army. In February 1984, despite the intervention of U.S. warplanes against them, the Muslim forces succeeded in expelling the Lebanese army from West Beirut. Washington ordered the withdrawal of its troops from Beirut, and London, Rome, and Paris followed suit. The MNF withdrawal was completed by 31 March 1984.

Multinational Force and Observers (1979): To ensure compliance with the provisions of the 1979 Egyptian-Israeli Peace Treaty [*qv*] concerning the level of forces of the two neighbors in and near the Sinai Peninsula [*qv*], a Multinational Force and Observers (MFO) of 2,600 troops from eleven countries was posted in the peninsula in August 1981. The MFO is also required to ensure freedom of navigation through the Straits of Tiran [*qv*].

Murabitun *(Arabic: Faithful of the Sermon): Lebanese militia* Formed in the early 1970s by Ibrahim Qulaylat, the Murabitun was the armed wing of the Independent Nasserite Movement (INM). Opposed to the traditional Sunni [*qv*] leadership, the Beirut-based INM had its following among poor Sunnis. It backed the Palestine Liberation Organization (PLO) [*qv*]. Part of the Lebanese National Movement (LNM) [*qv*] in the civil war of 1975–90 [*qv*], it was bitterly opposed to the Phalangists [*qv*]. With its peak strength not exceeding 3,000, it was the smallest militia. Due to its closeness to the PLO, it was expelled from Beirut [*qv*] along with the PLO by the Israelis in August 1982. Its attempt to return to West Beirut in February 1984 was frustrated by Amal [*qv*] and the Druze [*qv*] militia. Later, as PLO constituents began to rebuild their military strength in West Beirut, it did the same. Following the end of the civil war in October 1990, it was dissolved along with other militias.

Musavi, Mir Hussein (1941–): *Iranian politician; prime minister, 1981–89* Born in Khamane near Tabriz [*qv*], Musavi obtained a degree in architecture at a university in Tehran [*qv*] in 1969. An activist in Islamic circles, he was jailed briefly in 1973 for antigovernment activities. On his release he went to London to study interior design. Following the Islamic revolution [*qv*] in February 1979, he became a cofounder of the Islamic Republican Party [*qv*]. He was appointed chief editor of the party's daily paper, *Jumhouri-ye Islami* (Islamic Republic).

An economic radical, he favored nationalization of foreign and domestic trading. After a brief tenure as foreign minister, Musavi was appointed prime minister in October 1981. His government accelerated the pace of Islamization and the purging of official institutions of those with insufficient Islamic convictions. But its effort to implement radical land reform, involving the purchase of excess land by the state, was thwarted by the Guardians Council [*qv*] on the ground of inviolability of private property. His policies favoring the public sector were unpopular with traders and businessmen.

When, after his reelection as president in 1985, Ali Hussein Khamanei [*qv*] considered dropping Musavi as premier, Ayatollah Ruhollah Khomeini [*qv*], intent on maintaining a balance between radicals and moderates, publicly praised Musavi. An amendment to the constitution in 1989 abolished the office of premier. Upon his election as president in July 1989, Ali Akbar Hashemi Rafsanjani [*qv*] appointed Musavi as his adviser on political matters, a position that lacked the kind of power Musavi had exercised earlier. He continued in that position when Muhammad Khatami [*qv*] was elected president in 1997. Later, Leader Ayatollah Ali Khamanei [*qv*] nominated him to the Expediency Consultation Council System.

Muscat: *Capital of Oman* Pop. 797,000 (2003, est.). A port with a long history, Muscat was an important center for trading with the Gulf [*qv*] and East Africa by the thirteenth century. The Hormuzis, who then administered it, held supreme for three centuries before being overthrown by the Portuguese in 1508. After a century and a half the Portuguese gave way to the forces of the local imam [*qv*]. After Sultan Hamad had captured the port in the late eighteenth century the country was called Muscat and Oman, a name it retained until 1970.

Encircled by mountains, Muscat is a striking city with two sixteenth-century forts. It is an architectural museum, showing influences of the regions it has traded with over the centuries: India, Portugal, East Africa, and Zanzibar, Iran, and the Persian Gulf. Its population is equally cosmopolitan.

Muslim Brotherhood (Egypt): *Egyptian political-religious party* Official title: *Ikhwan al Muslimin (Arabic: Brotherhood of Muslims)*. In 1928 Hassan al Banna [*qv*] established the Muslim Brotherhood as a youth club committed to effecting moral and social reform through information and propaganda. But in 1939, responding to the popular movement against the 1936 Anglo-Egyptian Treaty [*qv*] and the 1936 Palestinian Arab uprising against the British mandate and Zionist colonization, it transformed itself into a political entity. It declared that Islam, based on the Quran [*qv*] and the Hadith [*qv*], is a comprehensive, self-evolving system, applicable to all times and places. According to al Banna, the Brotherhood was "a salafiya [*qv*] message, a Sunni [*qv*] way, a sufi [*qv*] truth, a political organization, an athletic group, a scientific and cultural union, an economic enterprise and a social idea." By 1940 it had established 500 branches, each with its own center, mosque, school, and club.

During the Second World War the Brotherhood's ranks swelled with students, civil servants, artisans, petty traders, and middle-income peasants. After the war the Brotherhood participated in an escalating anti-British struggle. In 1946 the party claimed 500,000 members with as many sympathizers, organized among 5,000 branches. Its volunteers fought in the 1948–49 Palestine War [*qv*]. Many Egyptian officers picked up the Brotherhood ideology, and the Brethren acquired military training from them.

Blaming Egypt's political establishment for the debacle in the 1948–49 conflict, the Brotherhood resorted to terrorist and subversive activities. The government declared martial law and banned the party in December 1948. Three weeks later Premier Mahmud Fahmi Nokrashi (Pasha) was assassinated by a Brotherhood member. This led to further repression of the party. Hassan al Banna argued that since the Brotherhood had been disbanded, the assassin could not be described as a member of it. In February 1949 al Banna was assassinated by secret service agents in Cairo [*qv*].

When martial law was lifted in 1950, the ban on the Brotherhood was removed and it was allowed to function as a religious body. However, the next year, following the election of moderate Hassan Islam al Hudaibi as leader, it was permitted to participate in politics. Supporting the government's abrogation of the Anglo-Egyptian Treaty, it declared a campaign against the British occupiers and participated in the January 1952 riots in Cairo.

The ban on political parties by the ruling Revolutionary Command Council (RCC) after the July 1952 coup did not apply to the Brotherhood, which was described as a religious body. Of the eighteen RCC members, four, including Anwar Sadat [*qv*], had been close to Brotherhood leaders. When the latter realized that as modernizers RCC members were more interested in spreading secular education, giving equal rights to women and implementing land reform than in applying the Sharia [*qv*] to all spheres of life, they began to oppose the new regime. The RCC banned the Brotherhood in February 1954.

On 23 October a Brotherhood activist, Abdul Munim Abdul Rauf, tried unsuccessfully to assassinate President Gamal Abdul Nasser [*qv*]. He and five other Brethren were executed, and more than 4,000 party activists were arrested. Several thousand Brethren fled to Syria, Saudi Arabia, Jordan, and Lebanon. In 1964, as part of a general amnesty, Nasser released the Brethren in order to co-opt them into the newly formed Arab Socialist Union [*qv*] as a counterforce to the communists [*qv*], who were also freed. But reconciliation between the two sides proved temporary. During the next two years there were three attempts by the Brethren to assassinate Nasser. This resulted in a trial of 365 Brethren followed by the execution of their top leaders in August 1966.

The humiliating defeat the Israelis inflicted on Egypt in June 1967 created a popular feeling that God had punished Arabs for turning away from their faith and tinkering with alien concepts such as Arab socialism [*qv*]. Sensing a change in the popular mood, Nasser released 1,000 Brethren in April 1968.

Reversing Nasser's policies, President Anwar Sadat promised that the Sharia would be the chief source of legislation and released all Brotherhood prisoners. Exiled Brethren began to return from Saudi Arabia and elsewhere, and this strengthened the Islamists at home. The changed conditions enabled the Brethren to reintegrate themselves into al Azhar University [*qv*], the official center of Islam, which had been purged of them by Nasser.

Fearful of the popular appeal of the Brotherhood, Sadat denied it a license to contest the 1976 general election as a distinct forum. Therefore, the Brethren ran either as independents or as members of the ruling Arab Socialist Party (ASP) [*qv*]. Nine were elected as independents, and another six as ASP members. When independent Brethren offered to cooperate with the government on certain conditions, the radicals within the party left to form militant groups. But because Sadat's economic policies increased disparity between rich and poor, and because he agreed to make peace with Israel without addressing the crucial Palestinian problem, Brotherhood leaders turned against him. Most of the nearly 2,000 dissidents arrested in September 1981 were Brethren or other Islamic fundamentalists [*qv*]. On 6 October Sadat was assassinated by four Islamist soldiers.

After an intense drive to crush Islamic militants, President Hosni Mubarak [*qv*] engaged al Azhar clerics to reeducate the imprisoned Brethren and other Islamists, two-fifths of whom were college or university students. Because the 1983 Election Law, like its predecessor, banned parties based on religion or atheism, the Brotherhood was barred from contesting the 1984 elections. It therefore allied with the Neo-Wafd Party [*qv*] and won eight seats, despite the fact that the poll was flagrantly rigged. Outside parliament, the Brotherhood, working in alliance with the Neo-Wafd [*qv*], succeeded in dominating the ruling bodies of influential syndicates of journalists, lawyers, doctors, and engineers.

In the 1987 elections the Brotherhood allied with the opposition Socialist Labor Party [*qv*] and the Liberal Socialist Party [*qv*] to form the Labor Islamic Alliance (LSA) [*qv*]. Despite the customary vote rigging and harassment of the opposition, the Brotherhood-led Alliance won 17 percent of the vote and sixty seats, of which thirty-seven were won by Brethren. They demanded the immediate application of the Sharia, the ending of Egypt's strategic and economic links with the United States, and the abrogation of the Egyptian-Israeli Peace Treaty [*qv*]. Like its allies in the LSA, the Brotherhood boycotted the 1990 election when the government rejected their joint call to lift the state of emergency and conduct the poll under the supervision of a nongovernmental body.

During the Kuwait crisis and the Gulf War [*qv*], the Brotherhood, a traditional ally of Saudi Arabia, largely supported Iraqi President Saddam Hussein [*qv*]. It fueled pan-Islamic [*qv*] feelings at the expense of the West. Due to its absence from parliament, it could no longer act as an intermediary between the government and the militant Islamic groups as they escalated their anti-regime campaign.

Allowed to contest the general election in 1995, the Brotherhood fielded 150 candidates, all of whom lost. In 1996 it was divested of its domination of the Bar Association, leaving only the Doctors Association under its control. Three years later twenty Brotherhood leaders were arrested on charges of plotting to overthrow the government and infiltrating professional syndicates. However, the Brotherhood was allowed to contest the 2000 general election, and won seventeen seats.

Muslim Brotherhood (Jordan): *Jordanian religious body with a political wing, called the Islamic Action Front* During his visits to Jordan (then Transjordan) between 1942 and 1945, Hassan al Banna [*qv*] set up Muslim Brotherhood branches in many towns. When the Brotherhood was first banned in Egypt in 1948, hundreds of its activists went into exile in other Arab states, including Jordan. The same thing happened in 1954, when the Brotherhood in Egypt was dissolved by President Gamal Abdul Nasser [*qv*].

Since King Hussein of Jordan [*qv*] was one of the Arab leaders Nasser tried to overthrow, the Jordanian Brotherhood turned increasingly pro-Hussein. When his throne was threatened by opposition demonstrations in 1956, it actively sided with him. In return, Hussein's ban on political parties in 1957 exempted the Brotherhood on the ground that it had been registered as a religious charity. His growing stress on the religious eminence of his antecedants as governors of Hijaz [*qv*], and thus guardians of Mecca [*qv*], endeared him to the Brotherhood.

During the decade after the June 1967 Arab-Israeli War [*qv*], with the star of Saudi Arabia rising in the Arab East [*qv*], King Hussein grew closer to Riyadh for financial and ideological reasons and began co-opting Brotherhood leaders into his regime. In the 1970s he allowed them to impart military training to members of Syria's Muslim Brotherhood [*qv*]. This enabled him to overcome their disapproval of his opposition to the 1979 Islamic revolution [*qv*] in Iran.

The Brotherhood participated in the November 1989 parliamentary election through its political wing, the Islamic Action

Front (IAF). The IAF emerged as the single largest group, with twenty-three deputies in a house of eighty; another nine, while describing themselves as independent Islamists, worked in tow with it. In October 1990 the IAF joined the government and ran five ministries. During the Kuwait crisis and the Gulf War [qv], the Brotherhood, deviating from its traditional pro-Saudi stance, supported Iraqi President Saddam Hussein [qv]. It was partly in deference to the IAF policy that King Hussein refused to join the U.S.-led alliance against Iraq. On the eve of the Middle East Peace Conference in Madrid [qv], the IAF ministers resigned in protest at Jordan's participation in the conference.

To thwart the possibility of the IAF emerging as a majority party in the November 1993 elections, conducted officially on a multiparty basis, the monarch modified the election law by decree. Unwilling to confront the king, the IAF decided to contest only thirty-six seats. It won sixteen and again emerged as the largest group in parliament. It opposed the Jordanian-Israeli Peace Treaty [qv] signed in October 1994. In the 1997 general election it won eight seats.

Muslim Brotherhood (Palestine): *religious-political organization in Palestine/the West Bank and Gaza* During his visits to Palestine [qv] between 1942 and 1945, Hassan al Banna [qv] set up Muslim Brotherhood branches in many towns. After the 1948–49 Palestine War [qv], the Gaza Strip [qv] came under Egyptian authority and the West Bank [qv] was annexed by Jordan. With this the fate of the Brotherhood in Gaza became intertwined with its Egyptian counterpart, and that of the

Brotherhood in the West Bank with its Jordanian counterpart.

After the June 1967 Arab-Israeli War [qv], Israel occupied the West Bank and Gaza. In order to weaken the Palestine Liberation Organization [qv] in the Occupied Territories [qv], in 1973 Israel issued a license to Shaikh Ahmad Yassin [qv], the Brotherhood leader in the Occupied Territories, to set up the Islamic Center as a charity to run social, religious, and welfare institutions. It encouraged the growth of Islamic Center/Muslim Brotherhood—funded chiefly by contributions from private and official sources in the Gulf states [qv]—as a counterpoint to the secular PLO to the extent of providing funds covertly to the mosques in the Occupied Territories, especially the Gaza Strip, considered sympathetic to it. But following the dramatic rise of Hizbollah [qv] in Lebanon, the Israeli government had second thoughts. It arrested Yassin in 1983 for illegal possession of arms and sentenced him to a long prison term. However, he was released two years later as part of a prison exchange deal between Israel and the Popular Front for the Liberation of Palestine-General Command [qv].

Yassin built on the popularity he had gained as a political convict of Israel and rapidly increased the membership of the Islamic Center/Muslim Brotherhood. With eruption of the intifada [qv] in December 1987, Yassin and six other leaders of the Brotherhood decided to join the mass movement against the Israeli occupiers. The result was the founding of Hamas [qv] as the activist arm of the Brotherhood.

Muslim Brotherhood (Saudi Arabia): Following the dissolution of the Muslim Brotherhood in Egypt in 1954, hundreds of Brethren took refuge in Saudi Arabia. After their leaders had convinced the Saudi monarch that Egyptian President Abdul Gamal Nasser [*qv*] was misusing al Azhar University [*qv*], they were given funds to set up the Islamic University of Medina {*qv*] in 1961. The university emerged as a bastion of the Brotherhood, which is allowed to function as a religious charity under the leadership of eminent theologians such as Shaikh Muhammad al Khattar. In their struggle against Nasser and Nasserism [*qv*], the Saudi monarchs began to fund the Brotherhood in different Arab countries, a practice that continued after Nasser's death in 1970 until the Second Gulf War [*qv*] in 1991.

Muslim Brotherhood (Syria): The Muslim Brotherhood in Syria emerged in the mid-1930s when Syrian students of theology returning from Egypt began to form branches in different cities under the title *Shabab Muhammad* (Youths of Muhammad). The most important of these, established in 1935 in Aleppo [*qv*], became the organization's headquarters. It stood for an end to the French mandate and for sociopolitical reform along Islamic lines. In 1944 the headquarters was moved to Damascus [*qv*]. Once the French had departed in 1946, it focused on socioeconomic issues. Most of its support came from urban petty traders and craftsmen. The founding of Israel and the Arab defeat in the Palestine War [*qv*] gave a boost to the Brotherhood and politicized it.

Following the dissolution of Egypt's Muslim Brotherhood in 1954, many Egyptian activists took refugee in Syria and strengthened and radicalized the local variant. Its program now demanded the founding of "a virtuous polity" that would implement the rules and teachings of Islam.

When Syria joined Egypt in 1958 to form the United Arab Republic (UAR) [*qv*], and the ban on political parties in Egypt was extended to Syria, the Brotherhood was formally dissolved. However, it continued to function underground. Growing disaffection with Gamal Abdul Nasser's [*qv*] presidency helped it to expand its base. In the election held in December 1961, a few months after Syria's secession from the UAR, it won ten seats, nearly half as many as the mainstream National Bloc. Following the Baathist [*qv*] coup in March 1963, the Brotherhood and other political parties were banned and parliament dissolved. It did badly in its confrontation with the government in 1964.

The Arab defeat in the June 1967 Arab-Israeli War [*qv*] split the party into moderates, advising caution, and radicals, advocating a jihad [*qv*] against the Baathists. With young Brethren receiving commando training from the Muslim Brotherhood [*qv*] in Jordan in the 1970s, the party's militarization gathered pace.

When Hafiz Assad [*qv*] became president in late 1971, the Brotherhood attacked the regime strongly because Assad was an Alawi [*qv*]. The party, composed of Sunnis [*qv*], who formed over two-thirds of the population, argued that since Alawis were neither Muslim nor People of the Book (Christian [*qv*] or Jew [*qv*]), they were infidels and idolators, who worshipped Imam Ali. Assad countered this by participating in prayers in various mosques throughout Syria. The Brotherhood condemned the 1973 constitution, which sanctified the leading position of the Baath party in Syria, described as a "democratic, popular, socialist state."

Pro-Brotherhood clerics demanded that Islam [qv] be declared the state religion. Antigovernment rioting followed. Assad compromised by directing parliament to specify that the head of state must be Muslim, and it complied. Unsatisfied, the clergy called for demonstrations, which turned violent. Heeding their call, many Sunnis boycotted the referendum on the constitution. Assad combined repression with co-option and offered state honors and higher salaries to the clergy. He described the October 1973 Arab-Israeli War [qv] as a jihad against the enemies of Islam and referred to the Syrian troops as the soldiers of Allah. In early 1974 he undertook an *umra* [qv] to Mecca [qv]. Later, Imam Musa al Sadr [qv], an eminent Shia [qv] theologian, issued a religious verdict that Alawis were part of Shia [qv] Islam.

These developments reduced tension between the two sides, but not for long. In mid-1976 Assad intervened militarily in the year-old Lebanese Civil War [qv] on the side of Maronite Christians [qv] against the alliance of Lebanese Muslims and Palestinians. This angered the Brotherhood, now led by Adnan Saad al-Din. The jihad it launched against the regime in July 1976 lasted four years. Its activists assassinated Baathist officials, Alawi leaders, and security personnel and informers in order to goad the government into increasing its repressive activities, thereby alienating large sections of society.

The increased activity swelled the party ranks. Between 1975 and 1978 the number of Brethren in Aleppo [qv] rose from 800 to 5,000 to 7,000. The national total of 30,000 members compared favorably with the ruling Baath's 200,000. A study of 1,384 fundamentalist prisoners (in 1982) showed 27.7 percent to be college or university students and 13.3 percent professionals.

In a calculated escalation in mid-1979, the party combined attacks on police stations, Baath party offices, and army units with large-scale demonstrations and strikes. In a daring assault on the Aleppo artillery school, it killed eighty-three Alawi cadets. Assad convened a special congress of the Baathists in January 1980 to examine the party and its policies. Two-thirds of the national command of the party was replaced, often by Sunnis, and the proportion of Sunnis in the cabinet was raised too.

Unimpressed, the Brotherhood called strikes in Aleppo and Hama [qv], which paralyzed those cities. Soon the national syndicates of lawyers, engineers, doctors, and academics joined in, demanding free elections and the freeing of political prisoners. Assad duly released 200 political prisoners, sacked several unpopular provincial governors, and increased imports of consumer goods. But the Aleppo and Hama merchants continued their shutdown. Assad dispatched elite troops to these cities. They arrested some 5,000 people and summarily executed several hundreds. The protest petered out.

Another wave of official retribution followed an unsuccessful assassination attempt on Assad on 25 June 1980. Parliament made membership of, or even association with, the Muslim Brotherhood a capital offense. Armed with this, the security forces went on a rampage, meting out summary justice, especially in Aleppo. With this the Islamic rebellion virtually collapsed. The Brotherhood split, with the moderate faction led by Issam Attar allying with smaller Islamic organizations to form the Islamic Front of Syria [*qv*] in October 1980.

In 1998 Hafiz Assad freed some Brotherhood leaders. And soon after succeeding his father, Bashar Assad [*qv*] ordered more releases. *See also* Islamic Front of Syria.

Muslims: *see* Islam and Muslims.

Mussadiq, Muhammad (1881–1967): *Iranian politician; prime minister, 1951–53* Son of a wealthy public official in Ahmadabad, Mussadiq pursued his university education in Paris and then obtained his doctorate in law at Lausanne University, Switzerland. On his return to Iran in 1914 he was named governor general of Fars province. Following the coup by Reza Khan [*qv*] in 1921, Mussadiq joined the government as minister of finance. He was elected to the Majlis [*qv*] in 1923, but when he opposed the coronation of Reza Khan as Shah of Iran in 1925, he was forced to retire from public life.

With the deposition of Reza Shah in 1941, Mussadiq's fortunes rose. He was elected to parliament in 1944. A nationalist, he led a successful campaign to deny granting of an oil concession to the Soviet Union in 1945. Three years later he challenged Muhammad Reza Shah Pahlavi's [*qv*] nominee for premier, Ibrahim Hakimi, and lost by a single vote. In 1949 he cofounded the National Front [*qv*]. His call to nationalize the oil concession given to the British-owned Anglo-Iranian Oil Company proved popular. In late April 1951 the Majlis decided by a large majority to go ahead with the nationalization and to appoint Mussadiq

as premier. This happened on 1 May 1951. Britain and other Western powers boycotted Iran's nationalized oil industry, and the economy suffered as a result.

With the middle classes forsaking him, Mussadiq depended increasingly on the support that the Tudeh Party [*qv*] could muster on the street and among oil workers and civil servants. This alienated Mussadiq from clerical circles. In mid-January 1953 he won a yearlong extension of his emergency powers from parliament. He clashed with the shah over the command of the armed forces. In July 1953, by asking his supporters in parliament to resign, he caused its de facto dissolution due to the lack of a quorum. Following endorsement of his decision in a referendum, Mussadiq declared on 12 August 1953 that he would order fresh parliamentary elections.

When the shah's attempt to dismiss Mussadiq failed, the shah fled. Following three days of demonstrations and counterdemonstrations, Mussadiq's civilian and military opponents, actively aided by the U.S. Central Intelligence Agency, mounted a successful coup against Mussadiq. By 19 August the shah was back in power. Tried for treason, Mussadiq was jailed for three years and barred from public life. After his release, he was kept under house arrest in Ahmadabad.

Muwahhidun (*Arabic: Unitarianism*): *see* Wahhabism and Wahhabis.

mysticism (*Greek: derivative of mystikos, belonging to secret rites*): Mysticism is the doctrine that direct knowledge of God, or some ultimate reality or spiritual truth, can be attained through intuition or insight, and in a way that is distinct from ordinary sense perception or the application of logical reasoning. The experience of the presence of God, or some ultimate reality or spiritual truth, often results in heightened consciousness and a sense of transcending the mundane world. During this experience new knowledge and awareness are often believed to be passed on to the mystic in unfamiliar ways. Forms of mysticism are to be found in all major religions as well as in secular experience.

mysticism in Christianty: An early example of Christian mysticism is Gnosticism, a religiophilosophical movement of the pre-Christian era, with the central doctrine that spiritual emancipation is attained through *gnosis* (knowledge), which saves the initiate from the intrinsic evil of matter. According to St. John of the Cross, union with God is the highest mystical experience and is attained by pursuing the path of purgatory, intended to excise sin, and then the path of illumination, which illuminates whatever is spiritual. Later the Desert Fathers developed the hermetic method of attaining mystical enlightenment. St. Augustine elaborated the concept of the Divine Light of Being, drawing heavily on neoplatonic ideas, which continued to interest later Christian mystics, including Meister Eckhart (d. 1329).

Mysticism has continued to thrive in the church and outside, and the long list of great Christian mystics includes St. Gregory I, St. Hildegard of Bingen, Hugh of St. Victor, St. Thomas Aquinas, St. Theresa of Avila, and St. Catherine of Siena. Its influence in Eastern Orthodox [*qv*] and Catholic Churches continues.

mysticism in Islam: *see* sufism.

mysticism in Judaism: The desire for immediate awareness of and communion with God is basic to Judaism. The visions of the Old Testament [*qv*] prophets and the apocalyptic images of later Judaism provided the foundations for Jewish mysticism. In the twelfth century, Jewish mystics adopted the term *kabbala (Hebrew: received [tradition])* —originally used to denote the (received) oral tradition, along with the Written Law—to stress the continuity of their mystical tradition since antiquity.

Kabbala reached its apogee at the beginning of the fourteenth century in the *Sepher HaZohar* (The Book of Splendor), attributed to Moses de Leon (d. 1305). It narrated the power and inner life of God and laid out the principles and commandments by which the true believer could regain the adherence to God that had been lost by the fall of humans from their original purity. Subsequent Jewish mysticism continued to be built upon this base. Rabbi Isaac Luria (d. 1572) and his followers, and the Hassadic [*qv*] masters of the eighteenth and nineteenth centuries represent important developments of Kabbala.

N

Nablus: *West Bank city* Also spelled Nabulus. Pop. 115,000 (2003, est.). The site of an ancient settlement with the Greek name of Neapolis (New City), Nablus sits between two mountains: Jerizim, a place where, legend has it, God issued his commandments to Moses, and Ebal, from where curses were hurled at those who defied Moses's Law. It is a twin of Shechem, a biblical settlement associated with Abraham (Genesis: 12:6) and Jacob (Genesis: 34:2).

Established by Roman Emperor Vespasian (r. A.D. 69–79) in A.D. 72, it thrived as an east–west gate between Mount Jerizim and Mount Ebal because it was endowed with an abundant water supply from springs. Captured by Muslim Arabs [*qv*] in A.D. 636, it remained under Muslim rule until 1917, except between 1099 and 1187, when it was ruled by the Crusaders. A severe earthquake destroyed much of it in 1927.

In the 1930s it was a leading center of Arab resistance to Jewish immigration into Palestine, and the birthplace of the Arab Higher Committee [*qv*] in 1936. Following the 1948–49 Palestine War [*qv*] it became part of Jordan, and later a center of Palestinian guerrilla activities against Israel. Following the Israeli occupation in 1967, it once again became the forefront of resistance. In 1976 Jewish militants set up a colony at Elon Moreh near the city. In 2002, its kasbah, the historic old city center, was destroyed by the reoccupying Israeli forces.

Its industry continues to be dominated by olive oil and soap production and handicrafts. Its tourist attractions include Jacob's Well and Joseph's grave as well as the al Kabir and al Nur mosques, both constructed on the ruins of Byzantine churches.

Nabulsi, Suleiman (1908–76): *Jordanian politician; prime minister, 1956–57* Born into a notable family in Salt, Jordan, Nabulsi graduated in law and social studies from the American University in Beirut [*qv*]. He joined the civil service and rose to be director of the state-owned Agricultural Bank, a post he held until 1946. He served as minister of finance and economy from 1947–49 and again from 1950–51.

He was Jordan's ambassador to Britain from 1953–54. This experience turned him into a staunch Arab nationalist and anti-Zionist and alienated him from the regime of King Hussein ibn Talal [*qv*]. He was exiled from the capital, Amman [*qv*], to a provincial town. Undaunted, he cofounded the National Socialist Party (NSP) and was elected its leader. Nabulsi entered into an electoral alliance with the Baathists [*qv*] and the Communist Front [*qv*], and formed the National Front (NF). Its attempt to win a majority in the forty-member parliament in the autumn of 1954 was frustrated by official poll rigging. It won twelve seats. However, as leader of the NF, the largest bloc in parliament, Nabulsi succeeded in preventing King Hussein from joining the Baghdad Pact [*qv*] in December 1955. He also succeeded in getting him to dissolve parliament.

In the free election of October 1956 the NF won sixteen seats, and Nabulsi was asked to form a government. It merged the Arab Legion with the (Palestinian-dominated) National Guard to create a 35,000-strong army. When parliament abrogated the 1948 Anglo-Jordanian Treaty [*qv*], the monarch did not overrule it. But when the cabinet decided to establish diplomatic relations with the Soviet Union and allow the Communist Front to publish a weekly newspaper, King Hussein warned it of the dangers of communist infiltration. Heeding this, Nabulsi banned the communist publication.

In April 1957 the king resisted a challenge from the Free Officers, led by Ali Abu Nawar, who had succeeded Sir John Bagot Glubb [*qv*] as chief of staff. He then dismissed Nabulsi's government, declared martial law, dissolved parliament as well as political parties and trade unions, and put Nabulsi under house arrest. Once freed,

Nabulsi resumed his leadership of the NSP. But with martial law in force, his area of operation was limited. When the Jordanian army and the Palestine Liberation Organization (PLO) [qv] clashed in 1970, he backed the latter. But by the mid-1970s he had changed sufficiently to merit royal appointment to the fully nominated senate in 1976.

Nahas (Pasha), Mustafa (1879–1965): *Egyptian politician; prime minister, 1928, 1930, 1935–37, 1942–44, 1950–52* Born into a wealthy Cairene family, Nahas obtained a law degree from the University of Cairo. After practicing as a lawyer, he joined the judicial system and served as a judge from 1904–19. He then participated in the nationalist movement and was exiled along with its leader, Saad Zaghlul, to the British-controlled Seychelles Islands. After their release they won parliamentary seats as Wafd Party [qv] candidates in the first general election under the 1923 constitution.

Nahas served in the Wafd government under Zaghlul. When Zaghlul died in 1927, Nahas succeeded him as leader of the party. In 1928 and 1930 he served as prime minister, but was forced by the monarch to resign. His efforts to see the parliamentary constitution reinstated succeeded in 1935, and his stewardship of the party's election campaign in May 1936 resulted in a Wafd victory. He formed the next government and three months later signed the new Anglo-Egyptian Treaty [qv], which granted Egypt independence but fell short of total sovereignty.

Nahas was dismissed from office in December 1937 by King Faruq [qv]. In February 1942, when German troops were advancing on Egypt from Libya, the British intervened militarily by surrounding the royal palace with tanks and gave Faruq the choice of abdicating or appointing the pro-British Nahas as prime minister. Faruq chose to invite Nahas to form a government. Nahas played a key role in the establishment of the Arab League [qv], a British-inspired enterprise. Following Nahas's inauguration of the League's preparatory conference in Alexandria [qv] in October 1944, he was dismissed again by the king. His party boycotted the election of January 1945, but participated in the poll of January 1950. Having won it on an Arab nationalist platform, Nahas headed the next government.

When his talks on the future of the 1936 Treaty and the British military presence in the Suez Canal [qv] zone failed, Nahas unilaterally abrogated the Treaty in 1951. He started a popular struggle to eject the British troops. This led to mounting violence, culminating in battles between Egyptian and British troops, the eruption of mob violence in January 1952, and the fall of his government.

Following the July 1952 coup, all political parties, including Wafd, were outlawed. Unlike many other politicians, who were tried for corruption, Nahas was left alone. He retired from public life.

al Nahyan, Zaid ibn Sultan (1915–): *President, United Arab Emirates, 1971–; ruler, the Abu Dhabi Emirate, 1966–* Born in al Ain to the ruling Aal [qv] Nahyan family of the Aal Bu Falah tribe, Nahyan learned the Quran [qv] as a boy, as well as falconry, riding, and marksmanship. He was appointed governor of the eastern province of the Abu Dhabi emirate (capital, al Ain) in 1946. He ruled it as a bedouin chief, consulting tribal notables and making himself accessible to ordinary people. When his elder brother, Shakbut ibn Sultan, ruler of the emirate since 1928, refused to use the revenue accruing from oil production (which began in 1960) to promote economic development, he was overthrown with the aid of Britain, the imperial power, in 1966, and replaced by Nahyan He appointed highly trained advisers and administrators to handle the emirate's burgeoning government revenues and activities.

It was primarily Abu Dhabi's rapidly growing oil revenues that encouraged the small neighboring emirates to agree to form the United Arab Emirates (UAE) in July 1971, five months before the scheduled British departure in December. Nahyan was elected president of the UAE for a five-year term and reelected four times.

As ruler of the Abu Dhabi emirate he appointed a cabinet led by a premier, responsible to him, in July 1971. When a single federal council of ministers came into being in December 1973, he abolished the Abu Dhabi cabinet and appointed a fifty-member consultative council.

To the detriment of the UAE, personal rivalry between Nahyan and Shaikh Rashid ibn Said al Maktum [qv], vice president of the UAE, persisted for many years. Following the Islamic republican revolution in Iran [qv] in early 1979, the nominated Federal National Council and the federal cabinet demanded parliamentary democracy and a unitary state. This alarmed Nahyan and Shaikh Rashid, who buried their differences. Rashid became prime minister of the UAE.

During the early phase of the 1980–88 Iran–Iraq War [qv], Nahyan sided with Baghdad. But as the conflict dragged on and Iran's position grew stronger, Nahyan took an increasingly neutral stance. Later, during the spring of 1990, he allied with Kuwait in its strategy to hurt the Iraqi economy by flooding the oil market and hence lowering prices. Later, troubled by the impoverishment and suffering of the Iraqi people caused by the U.N. sanctions, he called for their lifting, but to no avail. Equally his plan for President Saddam Hussein {qv] to step down to avoid an invasion of the Anglo-American forces in early 2003 got nowhere.

During Nahyan's rule the UAE emerged from being a collective of medieval emirates to an efficiently run modern state with one of the highest per capita incomes in the world.

Najaf: *Iraqi city* Pop. 550,000 (1991, est.). Also called *Mashhad Ali (Arabic: Witness to Ali),* Najaf is the burial place of Imam Ali ibn Abu Talib, a caliph (r. A.D. 656–61) and a cousin and son-in-law of the Prophet Muhammad (d. A.D. 632). Since Shias [qv] consider Ali to be the only legitimate caliph after the Prophet Muhammad, they regard his tomb in Najaf as the most sacred shrine after Mecca [qv] and Medina [qv].

The town is believed to have been established by Caliph Haroon al Rashid (r. 786–809). It has undergone dramatic vicissitudes since then. It was burned down by zealot Sunnis from Baghdad in 1051, but was soon rebuilt. When under Ottoman rule (from 1638–1918), the city was sacked twice by Wahhabi [qv] raiders (in 1806 and 1810) and Ali's mausoleum was stripped of all its furnishings. Led by resident *mujtahids* [qv], its Shia population rebelled against the Sunni [qv] Ottomans in 1842, 1852, and 1854, but were repressed. In 1920 the local populace offered stiff resistance to the British mandate in Iraq and opposed King Faisal I ibn Hussein [*qv*], considering him a British stooge.

During the republican era, beginning in 1958, Najaf became a seat of opposition to the secular regime of the Baath Party [*qv*], which seized power in 1968. From 1965–78 it was the base of exiled Ayatollah Ruhollah Khomeini [*qv*]. After the 1991 Gulf War [*qv*] it participated in the Shia uprising in southern Iraq against the regime of President Saddam Hussein [*qv*], which was quickly quelled. Following the collapse of the Saddam Hussein regime in 2003, Najaf emerged as the power center of the majority Shia community in Iraq, with clerical establishment in the city sending out instructions to mosques nation-wide as to how to fill the power vacuum caused by the sudden disappearance of the ubiquitous Baath Party state apparatus.

Najaf remains a leading center of Shah pilgrimage and burial. With its encircling wall mostly intact, it has retained the aura of a medieval settlement. Unlike Mecca and Medina, the city is open to non-Muslims, but they are not allowed to enter the shrine of Imam Ali.

Najd: *central region of Saudi Arabia* Pop. 4,838,000 (2000, est.). Also spelled Nejd. A chiefly rocky plateau with mountains to the west and desert to the east, north, and south, Najd has a string of oases. It was politically fragmented until 1745, when it became the center of the Wahhabi movement [*qv*]. More recently, Abdul Aziz ibn Abdul Rahman ibn Saud [*qv*] conquered the region from the Ottoman Turks in 1902. Since then it has been the geographical and ideological nucleus of the Saudi realm that Abdul Aziz created, which was finally named the Kingdom of Saudi Arabia in 1932, with the Najdi capital of Riyadh [*qv*] as its national capital. Now officially called the central region, it consists of Hail, Buraidah, and Riyadh provinces.

Nasser, Gamal Abdul (1918–70): *Egyptian military leader and politician; president, 1956–70; prime minister, 1954–56* Born in Bani Mor village, Asyut province, Nasser, son of a postal clerk, was a graduate of the Royal Military Academy in Cairo [*qv*]. After serving in Sudan for two years, Nasser returned to the military academy as an instructor in 1941. He underwent further training at the staff college and participated in the Palestine War (1948–49) [*qv*] as a major in the Egyptian army. Promoted to colonel in 1950, he was appointed lecturer at the Royal Military Academy.

Nasser was a charismatic leader of the clandestine Free Officers organization, which ousted King Faruq [*qv*] on 22 July 1952 and set up the ruling Revolutionary Command Council, with Brig. Gen. Muhammad Neguib [*qv*] as its head. Neguib favored reinstating the parliamentary system, but Nasser opposed him. Nasser won. Having banned political groups in January 1953, the regime sponsored a single party, the Liberation Rally. The power struggle between Nasser and Neguib intensified after the RCC declared a republic in June 1953 and appointed Premier Neguib as the republic's president. The differences between Nasser and Neguib came to the fore in February 1954 when the RCC banned the Muslim Brotherhood [*qv*] without consulting Neguib. His resignation as president and premier created a crisis, involving the mobilization of different military units by the two rivals. A compromise in April allowed Neguib to retain presidency but give up premiership. This lasted until November when the RCC dismissed Neguib as president and put him under house arrest. It chose Nasser as its chairman. After a new constitution was proclaimed in 1956, Nasser was elected president for a six-year term and reelected twice.

Starting out as a nonideological officer, committed only to ridding public life of corruption, Nasser turned increasingly ideological and radical as conservatives at home and the Western powers abroad tried to smother his Arab nationalist regime. At the first Non-Aligned Nations conference in Bandung, Indonesia, in April 1955, Nasser came under the influence of Premier Jawharlal Nehru of India and President Josip Tito of Yugoslavia, both committed to nonalignment. Nasser succeeded in stopping the expansion of the Western-sponsored Baghdad Pact [qv].

After America had refused to sell him arms, he accepted an arms sales offer from Czechoslovakia. When the United States reacted by withdrawing its offer of aid for the Aswan High Dam [qv] project, and getting the World Bank to do the same, Nasser nationalized the Suez Canal [qv] and accepted aid from Moscow. The resulting aggressive anti-Egyptian alliance of Britain, France, and Israel, which culminated in the Suez War [qv] in October–November 1956, further radicalized Nasser. He became the top political demon in the West and Israel. America, Britain, France, and Israel fielded teams to assassinate him. They failed. The withdrawal of the aggressors from Egypt by March 1957 raised Nasser's prestige at home and in the region.

Following the merger of Egypt and Syria into the United Arab Republic (UAR) [qv] in early 1958, Nasser was elected president of the UAR. He visited the Soviet Union for the first time as a leader of the Non-Aligned Movement. At home he suffered a major setback when Syria seceded from the UAR in September 1961, ending his hopes of gradually uniting the Arab East [qv] under his leadership. As Syria turned increasingly radical in its policies, Nasser quickened the pace of socioeconomic reform in Egypt so as not to be seen less militant than the Syrians. The land reform, launched a decade ago, was consolidated along with further nationalization of industries and services.

In 1962, at a convention of the delegates of peasants, workers, and intellectuals, Nasser inaugurated the Arab Socialist Union (ASU) [qv]. Later that year Nasser sided with the republicans in the civil war [qv] that erupted in the wake of a coup in North Yemen. In 1964 he hosted a summit of the Organization of African Unity in Cairo.

Following the ascendancy in Damascus [qv] in early 1966 of radical Baathists, who escalated the Palestinian guerrilla attacks against Israel, Nasser once again found himself upstaged by Syria. To overcome the problem, in November 1966, he signed a defense pact with Syria, which specified a joint command for the Egyptian and Syrian forces in the event of war. As tension rose in the spring of 1967, Israel warned Syria against allowing Palestinian operations from its soil. In mid-May, stung by taunts that he was hiding behind the protection of the United Nations Emergency Force (UNEF) [qv], posted in Sinai [qv] on the Egyptian side, Nasser called on the U.N. secretary-general to withdraw it. When this occurred, Nasser closed the Straits of Tiran [qv] to Israeli shipping, thus raising the stakes. King Hussein of Jordan [*qv*], who hitherto had been hostile to Nasser, rushed to sign a mutual defense pact with Egypt on 30 May. This was the zenith of Nasser's power and prestige.

Once Israel had realized that the international community would not force Nasser to reopen the Straits of Tiran to Israeli ships, on 5 June it mounted devastating preemptive attacks on the air forces of Egypt, Syria, and Jordan. The debacle of the June 1967 Arab-Israeli War [*qv*] virtually destroyed Nasser and Nasserism [*qv*]. For the time being, though, he contrived to turn defeat into victory. Taking responsibility for the defeat, he resigned. Popular demonstrations made him retract, but his retraction went beyond resignation and covered the whole gamut of his domestic and foreign policies. He moderated the stance of the ASU at home. In November 1967, he accepted U.N. Security Council Resolution 242 [*qv*], which called for the peaceful coexistence of Israel and the Arab states in return for Israel's evacuation of the Occupied Arab Territories [*qv*]. However, to prevent Israel from consolidating its occupation of Egyptian territory, Nasser initiated the War of Attrition [*qv*] in 1968 after reequipping his military with Soviet weaponry.

In the Arab world he reached a compromise with his arch enemy, the conservative Saudi King Faisal ibn Abdul Aziz [*qv*]. He withdrew Egyptian troops from the North Yemeni Civil War in December 1967. Yet he remained the elder statesman of the progressive Arab world. When conflict between the Palestine Liberation Organization (PLO) [*qv*] and Lebanon became explosive, both parties turned to Nasser for mediation. The result was the November 1969 Cairo Agreement [*qv*]. Equally, after the fight between the PLO

and the Jordanian army in mid-September 1970, the two sides approached Nasser for a rapprochement. It was the strain of these negotiations that caused Nasser to have a fatal heart attack. A charismatic figure, Nasser was the first Egyptian to rule Egypt for a very long time, since King Faruq's family was originally from Albania.

Nasserism and Nasserites: Nasserism is a sociopolitical doctrine based on the thoughts and actions of Gamal Abdul Nasser, president of Egypt [*qv*] (1954–70). Beginning as pan-Arab nationalism [*qv*], it evolved into Arab socialism [*qv*]. Unlike Baathism [*qv*], Nasserism was not a well-conceived thesis by one or more ideologues, but emerged as an ideology out of a series of practical responses to the problems, domestic and foreign, that Egypt, ruled by military officers from 1952 onward, faced as it tried to consolidate its newly won political and economic independence. Egyptian military officers led by Nasser developed an ideology and created, as a state fiat, a political organization to implement it after they had seized power, whereas the Baathists were a party with an ideology and cadre long before they acquired power.

Nasser's drift toward socialism reflected an emerging trend among Egyptian intellectuals and workers. But instead of implementing egalitarian socioeconomic reform with the assistance of a political party committed to the doctrine, he relied basically on state bureaucracy, with the Arab Socialist Union (ASU) [*qv*] acting more as an organizational façade than a real cadre-based party. During Nasser's rule, Nasserite parties sprouted in several Arab countries, including Syria, Iraq, Jordan, Lebanon, Saudi Arabia,

North Yemen, and South Yemen. But within a few years of his death these disappeared or became insignificant, except in Lebanon—where the Independent Nasserite Movement and its militia Murabitun [*qv*] continued to draw their support from Sunni Muslims [*qv*]—and Yemen [*qv*]. In Egypt, denied a license to constitute a party of their own, most of the Nasserites joined the National Progressive Unionist Alliance [*qv*]. In the early 1990s, they were allowed to form a party, which secured one seat in the 1995 general election and three in the 2000 poll.

National and Progressive Front (Lebanon): In 1969 Kamal Jumblat [*qv*] established the National and Progressive Front (NSF), consisting of leftist Lebanese parties and major Palestinian groups based in Lebanon. As interior minister he legalized such transnational parties as the Communist Party [*qv*] and the Baathist party [*qv*] in the summer of 1970, and they joined the NSF. In 1972 it was renamed the Front of National and Progressive Parties and Forces. *See also* the Lebanese National Movement.

National Consultative Assembly (Iran): *see* Majlis.

National Cultural Club (Kuwait): In 1953 Ahmad Khatib [*qv*] formed the National Cultural Club (NCC) as a front for the Arab Nationalist Movement (ANM) [*qv*]. It did well in the local elections held in 1954. The following year it revived demand for a legislative assembly that had first been made before the Second World War. By periodically mounting popular demonstrations in the capital, the NCC showed itself to be the chief political force in the country. In the first general election of 1963, four NCC/ANM members and eight sympa-

thizers won twelve of the fifty seats. Over the next decade, as the existence of quasi-political organizations became accepted, the need to use the NCC as a shield ended.

National Democratic Assembly-Balad: *Israeli Arab political party.* Established in 1999 by Azmi Bishara [*qv*], the National Democratic Assembly-Balad aims to change Israel [*qv*] from a Jewish state into a democratic state according equal treatment to all its citizens, Jews [*qv*] and Arabs [*qv*] alike, and demands autonomy over the Arab educational system and affirmative action for the Arab minority. It advocates Israel's withdrawal from all the Occupied Arab Territories [*qv*], and the establishment of an independent Palestinian state in the Occupied Territories [*qv*] with East Jerusalem [*qv*] as its capital. It won two seats in the 1999 Knesset [*qv*] poll and retained them in the 2003 election.

National Democratic Front (North Yemen): *North Yemeni political party* In 1976 the Revolutionary Democratic party, the (Marxist) Democratic Party of Popular Unity, and the Baathists [*qv*] secretly merged to form the National Democratic Front under the leadership of Sultan Ahmad Omar. Its aims were to consolidate national independence, which was threatened by reactionary Saudi Arabia, and to end feudalism.

Ignoring the ban on political parties, President Ibrahim Hamdi [*qv*] allowed the NDF to exist semi-clandestinely. It held its first secret congress in July 1978, when it called for unity between North and South Yemen. Its ranks were swelled by the defection in late 1978 of the paratroop commander, Major Abdullah Abdul-Alim, and his troops from the government of President Ali Abdullah Salih [qv]. Aided by South Yemen, the NDF captured the southern town of Harib in February 1979 and tried to extend its area of control. The fighting continued until early March, when South Yemen yielded to regional pressures and accepted a cease-fire.

The agreement of the presidents of the two Yemens to unite within a year was welcomed by the NDF. But when nothing came of it the NDF reached a compromise with Salih: he would allow the NDF to publish a newspaper in North Yemen if it stopped its radio broadcasts from South Yemen. As Salih consolidated his power in the 1980s, he squeezed out the NDF from North Yemen, leaving it with a base in Aden [qv], the South Yemeni capital. The NDF welcomed the unity of the two Yemens in 1990. In the general election of 1993 it won four seats in a house of 301.

National Democratic Party (Egypt): The National Democratic Party (NDP) was founded by President Anwar Sadat [qv] in August 1978 after the parliament, at his behest, had outlawed wide-ranging political activities such as preaching Marxism and class struggle, advocating laissez faire capitalism, demanding a religion-based state, etc. He called on Mustafa Khalil, then heading the weakened Arab Socialist Union [qv], to be its (nominal) president. Even before it had published its program, 275 of the 300 Arab Socialist Party [qv] parliamentarians joined it, thus assuring it of power.

Describing itself as "national, democratic, socialist, scientific, faithful, popular, revolutionary, humanist and nationalist," the NDP listed its enemies: the "followers of foreign ideologies" (i.e., Marxists), "those trying to take Egypt back to the pre-1952 era" (i.e., neo-Wafdists [qv]), and "the remnants of the totalitarian regime" (i.e., Nasserites [qv]). It stated that the effort to rebuild Egyptian society after the 1952 revolution had failed because the regime had tried to imitate "the system and culture of foreign occupation," the word "foreign" implying the Soviet Union. Describing its socioeconomic philosophy as "socialist democracy, Arab Islamic and Christian values, and the principles of the 1952 revolution after being corrected [in 1971 by Sadat]," its program states that the public sector must be limited to projects that "the people" felt necessary and that the economic policy of providing an open door to foreign capital must remain.

Following the Camp David Accords [qv] in September 1978, Sadat appointed Khalil as premier and became the NDP's president. In the 1979 parliamentary poll the NDP won 302 of the 362 elected seats. After Sadat's assassination in 1981, Hosni Mubarak [qv] became the NDP's president. In the general elections of 1984, 1987, and 1990—which, as in Sadat's period, were widely rigged—the NDP won 379, 380, and 354 seats, respectively, in a house of 438 to 444 seats, the last poll having been boycotted by all the major opposition parties. In the 1995 general election it secured 316 seats and then gained the loyalty of another 99 independents. In the 2000 poll it won 176 places, with a further 212 deputies, having been elected as independents, joining the party later.

National Front (Iran): *Iranian political party* In 1949 the Iran Party and the Democrat Party combined to form the National Front (NF) [qv] under the leadership of Muhammad Mussadiq [qv]. A secular, nationalist group, the NF demanded nationalization of the oil industry, which at the time was controlled by the British-owned Anglo-Iranian Oil Company (AIOC). This proved a popular move. In May 1951, with the support of Majlis [*qv*] members, it succeeded in having Mussadiq named as prime minister by Muhammad Reza Shah Pahlavi [*qv*]. It backed Mussadiq during the 1951–53 crisis caused by the nationalization of the AIOC.

When the shah fled in mid-August 1953 the party split, with one section calling for a republic and the other for a constitutional monarchy. Following the return of the shah, the NF was repressed. It made a comeback in the early 1960s and urged a boycott of the referendum on the state-sponsored White Revolution [*qv*] in 1963. As a result, it was again repressed and its leaders jailed.

The NF continued to attract support among Iranian students studying in the West. It revived at home in the early stages of the 1977–78 revolutionary movement, participating actively as one of the three major strands of the movement, the others being Islamic fundamentalism [*qv*] and Marxism. After the revolution the liberal, secular forces represented by the NF aspired to create social democracy in Iran.

In February 1979 Premier Mahdi Bazargan [*qv*] appointed Karim Sanjabi, the NF leader, as foreign minister. He resigned after the occupation of the U.S. Embassy in Tehran [*qv*] by militant students in November. The NF failed to win any seats in the 1980 general election. Later it was wooed by President Abol Hassan Bani-Sadr [*qv*]. It was considered an opposition group. But with most of the moderate democrats siding with the Liberation Movement [*qv*], the NF lost support sharply.

National Front for the Liberation of South Yemen: *see* National Liberation Front (South Yemen).

National Guard (Saudi Arabia): An armed force drawn from the most loyal of the tribes in Saudi Arabia, the National Guard was the new name given to the White Guard (formed in 1932) after the dissolution of the Ikhwan [*qv*]. The need to rename, rearm, and retrain this force arose in the aftermath of the overthow of the monarchy in North Yemen [*qv*] in September 1962. The National Guard was put under the command of Prince Khalid ibn Abdul Aziz [*qv*]. Its personnel were billeted outside the main urban centers, and its officers were the most pampered outside the royal family. King Faisal ibn Abdul Aziz [*qv*] rejected a proposal to merge the military and the National Guard, mainly because having two separate armed services enabled him to maintain a balance between the competing clans inside the kingdom.

As the kingdom's most reliable armed force, the National Guard deals with anything that remotely threatens the regime—be it a strike, a demonstration, a tribal revolt, or disaffection in the military. It was at the forefront of quelling the uprising by Islamic militants in Mecca [*qv*] and the demonstrations by Shias [*qv*] in the eastern province of Hasa in late 1979. With the ascendancy of Fahd ibn Abdul Aziz [*qv*] to the throne in 1982, Crown Prince Abdullah ibn Abdul Aziz [*qv*] became its commander. In 2003 it had 75,000 active troops and 25,000 reserves. Its arms included 730 armored personnel carriers and 70 major artillery pieces.

National Liberal Party (Lebanon): Camille Chamoun [*qv*] established the National Liberal Party (NLP) soon after stepping down as president in September 1958. It stressed Lebanese (as opposed to Arab) nationalism and economic liberalism based on private enterprise. It succeeded in attracting Lebanese outside the Maronite [*qv*] community. In the 1972 general election, campaigning in alliance with the Phalange [*qv*], it secured thirteen seats, the largest number won by any party.

During the initial phase of the 1975–90 Lebanese Civil War [*qv*], the NLP cooperated with the Phalange in building up the infrastructure of a state in the Christian area, with its capital in Jounieh, working for a "decentralized unity" of Lebanon [*qv*] and strengthening links with Israel. But once they had jointly thwarted the plans of the Lebanese government and the Syrian peacekeeping force to patrol Christian areas, the simmering tension between them over such matters as control over the illegal ports in the Christian enclave, often used for drug trafficking, boiled over. The NLP militia suffered heavily in the bloody clashes with the Phalangists in July 1980, and it suffered further setbacks in October. But following the assassination of Bashir Gemayel [*qv*] in September 1982, the party's chances of survival improved. With the bloody split in the Phalange militia in early 1986, the NLP's relative standing in the Christian enclave, which harbored eight Maronite centers of power, rose considerably.

After Chamoun's death in August 1987 the mantle of NLP leadership passed to his son Danny. In August 1990 he backed Gen. Michel Aoun [*qv*] when the latter challenged parliament's power to alter the constitution and pass reform laws. Danny Chaman and his family were murdered in the aftermath of Aoun's defeat in mid-October 1990. His younger brother, Dory Chamoun, became party president. He joined other Maronite parties in boycotting the 1992 general election. He boycotted the 1996 parliamentary poll, but not the 1998 municipal elections when the NLP captured several local councils. Once again he boycotted the parliamentary election in 2000 in protest at the presence of Syrian troops in Lebanon.

National Liberation Front (South Yemen): *South Yemeni political party* Official title: National Front for the Liberation of South Yemen. The National Liberation Front (NLF) was set up in Sanaa [*qv*], North Yemen, in early 1963 to achieve independence from Britain through an armed struggle. It launched its first armed attack in the Radfan mountains in October. During the course of two years it opened four fronts against the British and took the fight to Aden [*qv*].

The NLF also came into conflict with the moderate Front for the Liberation for the Occupied South Yemen (FLOSY). London's declaration in early 1966 that it would leave by December 1968 intensified the fight between the NLF and FLOSY. By August 1967 the NLF had emerged as the stronger party and had won the loyalty of the federal army. On the departure of the British three months later, it founded the People's Republic of South Yemen. The republic's constitution described the NLF as an alliance of the people's democratic forces, and its central committee, elected by the party congress, as the leading political organ.

Following a split in the regime in June

1969, the victorious leftists replaced the republic's presidency with a presidential council of five NLF leaders, later reduced to three. In March 1975 the party's sixth congress laid down a three-year political-economic plan for the transition from national democracy to socialism. In October a unification congress decided to weld the NLF, the (Baathist [*qv*]) Vanguard Party and the (Marxist) Popular Democratic Union into the United Political Organization-National Front, to be reconstituted as the Yemen Socialist Party [*qv*] in 1978.

National Pact, 1943 (Lebanon): *constitutional agreement* In March 1943, prodded by the British, the Free French, led by Charles de Gaulle—who had retaken Lebanon from the pro-German French government in June 1941 with British assistance—restored Lebanon's 1926 constitution. Gen. Edward Spears, the British representative in Beirut, mediated between feuding Muslims [*qv*] and Christians [*qv*] about the apportioning of parliamentary seats. Using the 1932 census, showing Christians to be 54 percent of the population, Spears recommended a ratio of six Christian seats to five Muslim. (Later the 6:5 ratio was also applied to posts in the civil service, judiciary, and military.) This was agreed by Riad Solh [*qv*], the Muslim leader, and Bishara Khouri [*qv*], the Christian leader, as part of the National Pact, an unwritten supplement to the constitution. It stipulated that the republic's president should be a Maronite Christian [*qv*], its prime minister a Sunni Muslim [*qv*], its parliamentary speaker a Shia Muslim [*qv*], and his deputy a Greek Orthodox [*qv*].

Accepting the existing frontiers of Lebanon, the Muslim leadership gave up its demand for union with Syria to re-create Greater Syria [*qv*]. In return its Christian counterpart agreed that Arabic should be the only official language of the republic, and that Lebanon should be free of any foreign (i.e., European) ties and should present an "Arab face" to the world. Some months later the National Pact was given the status of an official decree by the Free French government's General Georges Catroux.

In 1960 the number of parliamentary seats was increased from seventy-seven to ninety-nine, with fifty-four going to Christians and forty-five to Muslims. This lasted for thirty years, and then, as a result of the National Reconciliation Charter of 1989 [*qv*], the number of seats was raised to 128 and the proportion altered to parity between Christians and Muslims. *See also* Lebanon: Legislature.

National Progressive and Patriotic Front (Iraq): *Iraqi political alliance* In July 1973, on the fifth anniversary of the Baathist coup, the parties that had signed the National Action Charter formed the National Progressive and Patriotic Front (NPPF). The NPPF included the Baath Party [*qv*] as well as the Communist Party [*qv*] and the smaller Nasserist [*qv*] and Kurdish groups. Its secretary-general was Naim Haddad, a Baath Party leader.

The non-Baathist signatories to the charter were required to be loyal to the Baathist revolution and to refrain from spreading their ideologies among students and the military, as well as abstaining from labor agitation and helping to avert strikes. In return, some of the non-Baathist constituents of the NPPF were given seats in the cabinet, the Communists receiving a maximum of two, and the others one or none. But cabinet ministers were more heads of departments than makers of policy, which was formulated by the ruling (Baathist) Revolutionary Command Council. Due to increasing differences with the Baathist leadership, the Communist Party quit the NPPF in 1978.

When parliamentary elections were introduced in 1980, only NPPF constituents were allowed to contest. The Baathist candidates won 183 of the 250 seats, the rest going to the non-Baathist groups or independents. In the 1984 poll the Baathist share rose marginally to 188, but in the general election of 1989 it fell to 138, with non-Baathist NPPF groups and independents making gains. During the crisis leading to the 1991 Gulf War [*qv*], the NPPF was prominent in organizing pro-regime demonstrations. Its importance declined after the war. With the collapse of the Baath Party in 2003, it became moribund.

National Progressive Front (Syria): *Syrian political alliance* The National Progressive Front (NPF), formed in March 1972 on the ninth anniversary of the Baathist revolution, comprised the Baath Party [*qv*], the Communist Party [*qv*], the Arab Socialist Union (ASU), the Arab Socialist Movement (ASM), and the Organization of Socialist Unionists (OSU). Its eighteen-member leadership, headed by President Hafiz Assad [*qv*], included nine other Baathists and two members each from the four non-Baathist groups. The latter were given seats in the cabinet, but they were barred from enrolling members among students or military personnel. PNF policies were to be modeled along Baath congress resolutions. On such weighty matters as

going to war with Israel in October 1973, Assad consulted leaders of the PNF as well as the Baath Regional Command.

PNF constituents were allowed to contest elections. In the 1986 general election the Baath party won 129 of the 250 seats, the Communist Party 9, the three remaining parties of the NPF 57, the rest going to independents. The figures for the 1990 poll were Baathists, 134 seats; Communists, 8; the ASU, 8; the ASM, 5; the OSU, 7; and independents 84. In 1994 the Organization of Socialist Unionists split, with the breakaway faction calling itself Organization of Democratic Socialist Unionists (ODSU). It was allowed to join the PNF. In the 1994 election the Baath Party won less than half of the seats, with the PNF gaining a total of 167. In the 1998 parliamentary poll, the results were Baath, 135; Communists, 8; the ASU, 7; the ASM, 6; OSU, 7; and ODSU, 4. In the 2003 election the total was the same—167, divided among the constituents almost as before.

National Progressive Unionist Alliance (Egypt): *Egyptian political party* When, in May 1976, the government allowed the political role of the Arab Socialist Union [*qv*] to be taken over by three tribunes, the leftist forum was represented by the National Progressive Unionist Alliance (NPUA). Known by its Arabic acronym of Tagammu and consisting largely of Marxists and the leftist Nasserists [*qv*], the NPUA was led by Khalid Muhyi al Din [*qv*]. In the parliamentary poll of 1976 the NPUA won only two seats. This was in contrast to the large circulation of the party's weekly journal, *Al Ahali (Arabic: The Masses)*. To silence the journal, which vehemently opposed the Egyptian-Israeli Peace Treaty of

March 1979 [*qv*], the government amended the law so that only a party with ten parliamentary seats could publish a newspaper. In the subsequent polls the party failed to win a single seat because of the high threshold of 8 percent imposed by successive electoral laws. In the 1990 general election, held under changed electoral rules and boycotted by all the major opposition parties, the NPUA won 1.4 percent of the vote and two seats. At the next election in 1995 its strength rose to five, and then to six in 2000, when the party leadership claimed 160,000 members.

National Reconciliation Charter, 1989 (Lebanon): The National Reconciliation Charter is the document adopted by the Lebanese parliamentarians at their session in Taif, Saudi Arabia, in October 1989 to resolve the issues at the core of the Lebanese Civil War [*qv*]. The draft, prepared by the Arab League's [*qv*] troika (Algeria, Morocco, and Saudi Arabia) was debated by sixty-two deputies (accounting for all but nine of the surviving members), divided equally among Christians [*qv*] and Muslims [*qv*]. The final version was a compromise. Despite the Muslim majority in the national population (estimated at 60–75 percent), Muslim deputies agreed that Christians and Muslims should have an equal number of parliamentary seats, which would be increased from 99 to 128. They also consented to limit abolition of confessionalism [*qv*] only to the administrative apparatus over a long period of time, and allowed Christians to keep the presidency, albeit with reduced powers.

By accepting Syria's continued presence for at least two years after the national unity government had agreed on constitutional reform, Christian deputies provided Syria with legitimacy—something it had lost with the expiration of the 1976 Arab League mandate in mid-1982—and conceded Syria's strategic concerns in Lebanon.

All but four (Muslim) deputies voted for the charter. Fifty-eight deputies, forming four-fifths of the surviving members, and the speaker met on 4 November at the Qulayaat airstrip in northern Lebanon to ratify the charter. A national unity government was then formed to implement the charter, popularly known as the Taif Accord [*qv*]. By the end of 1989 most of the important foreign powers had declared their backing for it. Within the Christian camp Gen. Michel Aoun [*qv*] rejected it, whereas most other Maronite [*qv*] leaders accepted it.

Implementation began in August 1990. Of the forty-nine deputies participating in the voting, all but one opted to overhaul the 1926 constitution by altering three articles, specifically Articles 17, 52, and 53. Article 17, which stated that executive power should be vested in the president of the republic, was amended to read: "Executive power is assigned to the Council of Ministers." This council was to consist of an equal number of Muslim and Christian ministers. Article 53 formerly empowered the president to designate a prime minister for approval by parliament and to appoint or dismiss ministers. Now the president was required to consult the speaker and senior deputies before designating the prime minister, and the right to dismiss ministers became the prerogative of the cabinet. Likewise, Article 52, which authorized the president to negotiate and ratify international treaties, was modified to require the president to secure the consent of the prime minister and the approval of the cabinet before an international treaty could become operative. Overall, the agreed reform favored the cabinet, which emerged with greater power than the president, but a two-thirds majority was required for cabinet decisions.

The civil war ended in October, and to implement the next stage of the charter a second national unity government was formed in late December 1990. Its main task was to effect the administrative decentralization stipulated by the charter.

National Religious Party (Israel): *Israeli political party* Popularly known by its Hebrew acronym, Mafdal [*qv*], the National Religious Party (NRP) was formed in 1956 by the merger of Mizrahi [*qv*] and Poale HaMizrahi [*qv*]. In the general elections of 1959, 1961, 1965, and 1969 the NRP won 11 to 12 seats and joined Mapai [*qv*] or Labor [*qv*] to form a coalition government, and to run the education, religious affairs, and interior ministries.

Following the June 1967 Arab-Israeli War [*qv*], the NRP's commitment to creating the Eretz Yisrael [*qv*] of biblical times strengthened the hand of Labor hardliners and stiffened official policies toward the Occupied Arab Territories. The NRP spawned Gush Emunim [*qv*] with a program to colonize the Occupied Arab Territories [*qv*] and ensured that no action was taken against Gush settlers.

After the December 1973 poll, when it obtained ten seats, as a precondition for joining a Labor-led coalition government the NRP demanded that the Law of Return [*qv*]

be amended to exclude non-Orthodox [*qv*] converts to Judaism [*qv*]. When this was rejected the NRP refused to join the administration. It finally joined the cabinet led by Yitzhak Rabin [*qv*] in October 1974.

Following the May 1977 poll, when the NRP secured twelve seats, it became part of the Likud-led [*qv*] coalition government. A split in the party halved its Knesset [*qv*] strength to six in the 1981 election. Since then its presence in the Knesset has fluctuated between four and six. It opposed the 1993 Oslo Accord [*qv*].

In the 1996 poll it secured nine seats and joined the coalition government led by Benjamin Netanyahu [*qv*]. Its strength declined to five in the 1999 election. It joined the administration of Ehud Barak [*qv*]. And it was also part of the national unity government formed by Ariel Sharon [*qv*] in 2001. Its size rose to six in the 2003 poll, and joined the coalition government led by Sharon.

National Resistance Council (Iran): *Iranian political alliance* Following their escape from Iran to Paris in July 1981, Abol Hassan Bani-Sadr [*qv*] and Masud Rajavi [*qv*], head of the Mujahedin-e Khalq [*qv*], formed the National Resistance Council (NRC) to oppose violently the Islamic regime of Iran. It claimed responsibility for the bomb explosion in Tehran [*qv*] on 30 August that killed President Muhammad Ali Rajai [*qv*] and Premier Muhammad Javad Bahonar. In November it won the affiliation of the Kurdistan Democratic Party of Iran [*qv*] and the Komala-e Jian-e Kordestan [*qv*].

Of the NRC's constituent parts, the Mujahedin-e Khalq [*qv*] was the most active in the Persian-speaking heartland of Iran. In

August 1983 it claimed that during its two years of existence it had killed 2,800 Islamic officials and revolutionary guards in hundreds of offensive and defensive operations.

With the Iran-Iraq War [*qv*] dragging on, the NRC concentrated on this issue, advocating an immediate cease-fire and blaming Ayatollah Ruhollah Khomeini [*qv*] for continuing the conflict in order to divert public attention away from the worsening domestic problems. Rajavi's public meeting with the Iraqi vice premier, Tariq Aziz [*qv*], in Paris in January 1983 upset Bani-Sadr, who considered Iraq an enemy country. When efforts to patch up their differences failed, Bani-Sadr quit the NRC in early 1984.

With the shifting of the Mujahedin-e Khalq headquarters to Baghdad [*qv*] in 1986, the Iraqi capital became the center of NRC activities as well. The American ban on the Mujahedin in 1997 did not extend to the NRC. And even when it was imposed in the wake of the terrorists attacks on the United States in September 2001, it was not applied in practice. Indeed, the NRC, maintaining an office in Washington, periodically called for the lifting of ban on the Mujahedin with advertisements in American newspapers, endorsed by many members of the House of Representatives. Following the weakening of the Baghdad-based Mujahedin-e Khalq due to the Gulf War III [*qv*], the NRC's future became more uncertain.

National Union: *Israeli political bloc* Official title: (*Hebrew: Halchund HaLeumi*) Israel BeItainu [*qv*] and Moledet [*qv*] combined in late 2001 to form the National Union on the common platform of their opposition to the establishment of a Palestinian state, and their advocacy of "transfer" of the Palestinians [*qv*] from the Occupied Palestinian Territories [*qv*] and total Israeli jurisdiction over all of Jerusalem [*qv*]. In the 2003 Knesset [*qv*] poll, it won seven seats, with four for Israel BeItainu and the rest for Moledet.

National Unity Front (Qatar): *Qatari political party* The National Unity Front (NUF) was formed in 1963 to channel the discontent Qatari citizens felt at the squandering of oil wealth by the ruling al Thani clan [*qv*], coupled with its tight grip over political and economic power. The NUF organized a series of antigovernment demonstrations to demand a proper state budget, a representative council, and curbs on the unlimited prerogatives of the al Thanis. The ruler, Shaikh Ahmad ibn Ali al Thani [*qv*], combined his repression of the NUF with the appointment in 1964 of an advisory council with authority to issue laws and decrees concerning basic state policy.

natural gas: Natural gas is a mixture of several hydrocarbons and such inert gases as nitrogen and carbon dioxide. Among the hydrocarbons, methane (CH^4), a colorless, odorless gas, accounts for at least three-quarters of natural gas by volume, the other hydrocarbons being ethane, butane, and propane. Natural gas is found either on its own (unassociated) or along with petroleum [*qv*] (associated). The latter exists partly as a cap above an oil reservoir and partly dissolved in it. In newly exploited oil fields the presence of gas under pressure pushes the oil to the surface. The associated gas produced with petroleum is either used as a fuel or is reinjected or burned. Piped natural gas, used industrially and domestically, is methane.

Navon, Yitzhak (1921–): *Israeli politician; president, 1978–83* Born into a long-settled

Sephardic Jewish [*qv*] family in Jerusalem [*qv*], Navon became active in the Zionist movement [*qv*] in his youth. He enrolled with Haganah [*qv*] in the early 1940s and worked for its intelligence section. Upon the founding of Israel he joined its foreign service. After serving briefly as a diplomat in Argentina, Navon became political secretary to Foreign Minister Moshe Sharett [*qv*]. From 1952 to 1963 he worked as secretary to Premier David Ben-Gurion [*qv*] and became quite influential.

He joined Rafi [*qv*] in 1965 and was elected to the Knesset [*qv*] in that year. During his thirteen years in parliament, he became deputy speaker (1966–73) and chairman of the foreign affairs and defense committee (1974–77). In 1978 he was elected president by a parliament in which the right wing had the majority. He returned to the Knesset on the Labor [*qv*] list in 1984 and became deputy premier and minister of culture and education. Reelected in 1988, he resumed his earlier posts and held them until 1990.

Nawruz *(Kurdish/Persian: New Day):* The first day of the Iranian solar calendar and falling on the spring equinox, Nawruz is celebrated by Iranians, Kurds [*qv*], and Zoroastrians [*qv*].

Nazareth: *Israeli town* Pop. 64,000, of which Christian [*qv*], 53,000; Muslim [*qv*], 11,000 (2003, est.). The New Testament [*qv*] makes several mentions of Nazareth, a Jewish settlement, as the home town of Joseph and a place associated with the childhood of Jesus. It became a center of Christian pilgrimage after Roman Emperor Constantine (A.D. 306–37) had adopted Christianity [*qv*] as the state religion in A.D. 313 and built a church there.

Nazareth was one of the most prized towns during the Crusades, and having captured it in 1099, the Crusaders turned it into a leading ecclesiastical center. But once Salah al Din (Saladin) Ayubi (r. 1169–93) had defeated the Crusaders in 1187, Christian influence declined rapidly.

Following their conquest of Palestine [*qv*] in 1517, the Ottomans expelled the Christians from the town. This policy was reversed when Emir Fakhr al Din Maan (r. 1591–1633) extended his Vilayat of Lebanon to Lower Galilee. Following his permission to Christians to return to Nazareth, Franciscan monks resettled the old Crusader foundation in 1620 and constructed a church in 1730, which in 1909 was replaced by a basilica, the Roman Catholic Church [*qv*] of the Annunciation. It contains the Grotto of the Annunciation, where, according to the New Testament [*qv*], Archangel Gabriel appeared to the Virgin Mary to announce that she was to be the mother of Jesus.

Other religious sites in Nazareth are St. Mary's Well, the Church of Joseph on the site of Joseph's carpentry shop, the Synagogue-Church on the site of the synagogue [*qv*] where Jesus preached, and the Mensa Christi (Table of Christ) Church where Jesus reputedly dined with the Apostles after his resurrection.

Included in the Arab [*qv*] sector by the United Nations partition plan of 1947, Nazareth fell to Zionist [*qv*] forces in 1948. It is now the largest Arab town in Israel and an important market and trading center. For a long time it was a bastion of the Israeli communists [*qv*], who repeatedly have been elected to run the local government.

Near East: The term Near East was coined by Western geographers to distinguish it from the Middle East (running from the Persian Gulf [*qv*] to Southeast Asia) and the Far East (the region facing the Pacific Ocean). Extending from the Mediterranean Sea to the Persian Gulf, the Near East virtually coincided with the Ottoman Empire. But when the British government prefaced its military command in Egypt with the Middle East during the Second World War (1939–45), the nomenclature became confused. Since then the term Near East has disappeared in common parlance, although the foreign ministries of some important Western governments, chiefly the United States, continue to use it in the pre-Second World War context.

Neguib, Muhammad (1901–84): *Egyptian military leader and politician; prime minister, 1952–53, president, 1953–54* Born to an Egyptian military officer and his wife in Khartoum, Sudan, Neguib graduated from the Royal Military Academy in Cairo [*qv*]. As an army officer, he rose steadily in rank and was a brigadier in 1948 when Egypt participated in the Palestine War [*qv*]. Promoted to brigadier general in 1950, he became commander of the ground forces the following year.

Through Abdul Hakim Amer, his operations officer, Neguib was in touch with the Free Officers organization. He accepted its offer to head the Revolutionary Command Council (RCC) after the July 1952 coup. He also became commander in chief of the armed forces. After the resignation of the civilian government in September, the RCC appointed him premier and defense minister. Following the declaration of the republic in June 1953, the RCC confirmed him as prime minister and appointed him to the presidency, but relieved him of his top military position.

His differences with Gamal Abdul Nasser [*qv*], the real leader of the RCC and the republic, came to the fore in February 1954 when the RCC banned the Muslim Brotherhood [*qv*] without consulting him. His resignation as president and premier created a crisis involving the mobilization of different military units by the two leaders. A compromise in April allowed Neguib to retain the presidency, albeit with diminished powers, and lose the premiership. This lasted until November when the RCC dismissed him as president and put him under house arrest. He was freed in 1971 after the death of Nasser. He backed Anwar Sadat [*qv*], but did not reenter public life.

Neo-Wafd Party: *Egyptian political party* The Neo-Wafd Party was established by Fuad Serag al Din, a veteran of the Wafd Party [*qv*], in early 1978 when he won the loyalty of twenty-two parliamentarians, thus meeting the legal requirement for new political groups. The party, which was committed to secularism, private enterprise, and close ties with the United States, proved particularly attractive to Copts [*qv*]. But when parliament, guided by President Anwar Sadat [*qv*], passed a law specifying various penalties for those who inter alia had a record of belonging to "the corruptive elements before or after the 1952 revolution," the Neo-Wafd leadership disbanded the party in September 1978.

Serag al Din was one of the opposition leaders to be rounded up by Sadat three years later. President Hosni Mubarak [*qv*] reversed Sadat's policy, and the Neo-Wafd reemerged in August 1983. In the 1984 general election it allied with the (unlicensed) Muslim Brotherhood [*qv*], arguing that both parties had been suppressed by President Gamal Abdul Nasser [*qv*]. However, it adopted only eighteen of the candidates the Brotherhood offered. Of the fifty-eight Neo-Wafd deputies, only eight belonged to the Brotherhood.

In the 1987 poll the Neo-Wafd, contesting on its own, managed to cross the 8 percent threshold fixed by the electoral law and won thirty-six seats. Along with other major opposition groups, it boycotted the 1990 election, protesting against the continuing state of emergency and demanding supervision of the poll by a nongovernmental body. In the 1995 poll, it won six seats, followed by seven in 2000. On the death of Serag al Din during that year, Numan Jumaah became the party leader.

Nestorian Christians: *Christian sect* The Nestorian Church is based on the theology of Nestorius (d. ca A.D. 451), patriarch of Constantinople, who asserted that there were two separate persons in Christ—human and divine—morally united through the cooperation of their two wills. This contradicted the orthodox doctrine that the human and divine natures of Christ were inseparably joined in one person and partook of one divine substance—a doctrine reaffirmed by the Councils of Ephesus in A.D. 431, Chalcedon in A.D. 451 and Constantinople in A.D. 553. Only the Persian Church remained faithful to Nestorianism and emerged as the Nestorian Church. The invasion of the region by Tamerlane (d. 1405) virtually destroyed the church, leaving a few pockets of followers in Iran and Iraq. When a section of Nestorians reunited with the Roman Catholic Church [*qv*] in 1551, their church was called Chaldean/Chaldean Catholic [*qv*]/East Syriac [*qv*]. The rest of the community then became known as Assyrian Christians.

Netanyahu, Benjamin (1950–): *Israeli politician; prime minister, 1996–99* Born into the household of Bentzion Netanyahu, a right-wing academic, Netanyahu left for the United States when his father got a teaching job there in 1964. He returned to Israel three years later to do his military service and became a commander in an elite commando force. He returned to America to resume his university education at the Massachusetts Institute of Technology in Cambridge and obtained a master's degree in business administration in 1976. Netanyahu worked in America for three years and then became a furniture sales executive in Israel (1980–82). In 1982 Moshe Arens, Israel's ambassador to the United States, hired him as political counselor. Later he served as Israel's ambassador to the United Nations until 1984. On his return to Israel, he became a full-time director of the Jonathan Institute, which specialized in studying terrorism.

Elected to the Knesset [*qv*] on the Likud [*qv*] list in 1988, he became deputy foreign minister from 1988–91. He then served as deputy minister in Prime Minster Yitzhak Shamir's [*qv*] office from 1991–92. Reelected to parliament in 1992, Netanyahu, assisted by expertise and funds from his American Jewish friends, won the contest for the Likud leadership in 1993. He opposed the Oslo Accords [*qv*].

In the 1996 prime ministerial contest, Netanyahu defeated his rival Shimon Peres [*qv*] by one percent of the vote. His coalition government had the backing of 62 of the 120 members of the Knesset [*qv*]. By refusing to implement the previous government's agreement on troops withdrawal from the Occupied Territories [*qv*], and by pursuing such hardline policies as authorizing the construction of a highly controversial Jewish settlement at Har Homa/Jabal abu Ghnaim on the outskirts of Jerusalem [*qv*], Netanyahu devalued the Oslo Accords, much to the disapproval and frustration of the U.S. administration of President Bill Clinton (1993–2001). Following his signing of the Wye River Memorandum [*qv*], which required Israel to withdraw from 13 percent of the West Bank [*qv*], Netanyahu lost the support of the ultraright-wing factions in the Knesset. This resulted in the downfall of his government. In the May 1999 prime ministerial contest he lost to Ehud Barak [*qv*] by a plurality of 56 to 44 percent. He resigned from Likud leadership and the Knesset, and gave a series of lectures in the United States. In 2002 Israeli Prime Minister Ariel Sharon [*qv*] appointed him foreign minister. In the subsequent government in 2003, he became finance minister.

Neturei Karta *(Aramaic: Guardians of the [Holy] City): An ultra-Orthodox Jewish sect in Israel* The name Neturei Karta is derived from an allusion in the Talmud [*qv*] to students of the Torah [*qv*] as "guardians of the [holy] city." The group emerged in Palestine [*qv*] in 1935 following a split in Agudat Israel [*qv*] when it compromised its Poland-based parent body's policy of non-cooperation with the (World) Zionist Organization [*qv*]. Ten years later Neturei Karta and its sympathizers won a majority on the committee representing the Ashkenazi [*qv*] community of Jerusalem [*qv*].

During the run-up to the founding of Israel in 1948, Neturei Karta opposed the creation of a Jewish state in Palestine on the ground that such a state would not be founded exclusively on Jewish law and tradition, and that the return to Zion of the Diaspora [*qv*] Jews could not be taken in isolation from their redemption by the awaited Messiah [*qv*], who was charged with establishing a Jewish state and whose time had not yet come. During the 1948–49 Arab-Israeli War [*qv*], it called for internationalization of Jerusalem. Later it became the most known Jewish organization in Israel to refuse to recognize the Zionist [*qv*] state.

In 1980 the sect had about 6,000 members, living mainly in the Mea Shearim district of Jerusalem and the Bene Brak suburb of Tel Aviv [*qv*]. Periodically its adherents resort to stoning cars that pass near their neighborhoods on the Sabbath [*qv*]. Its leader, Rabbi Moshe Hirsch, who had public meetings with the Palestine Liberation Organization [*qv*] leader, Yasser Arafat [*qv*], in 1993 before the Israeli-PLO Accord [*qv*], was appointed to the Palestinian Authority [*qv*] in July 1994 to deal with the Jewish affairs of the Occupied Territories [*qv*].

New Testament: *see* Bible.

Nile River: Length 4,150 miles/6,680 km from its remotest headstream to the Mediterranean, including 1,875 miles/3,020 km of the Nile proper, formed by the junction of the Blue Nile and the White Nile at Khartoum, Sudan. The world's longest river, the Nile rises in the highlands south of the equator, flows through northeast Africa into the Mediterranean Sea, and drains 1,294,000 sq. miles/3,351,000 sq. km. Between Khartoum and Aswan the Nile falls 935 ft./285 meters in a series of six rapids. Flooding is caused by the Blue Nile being fed by heavy monsoon rains in Ethiopia. Efforts to tame the Nile go back six millennia. The building of several barrages and waterworks by the late nineteenth century made perennial irrigation possible. The Aswan Dam was completed in 1902, and the Aswan High Dam [qv] in 1971. After Cairo [qv], the Nile waters enter the delta, dividing chiefly between the Damietta and Rosetta channels. The river is an important means of transportation.

Noble Sanctuary: *Islamic site in Jerusalem* Built on Mount Moriah in the Old City of Jerusalem [qv], the Noble Sanctuary—which houses the Dome of the Rock and al Aqsa Mosque (The Distant Mosque) and measures 35 acres/0.14 sq. km—takes up about a third of the Muslim Quarter, which occupies nearly two-fifths of the historic Old City. It was from this spot that, having arrived there in the course of his night journey by a winged animal, and having prayed at the Rock of Foundation, the Prophet Muhammad, guided by Archangel Gabriel, ascended into the heavens by a ladder of light, where he received, it is believed, Allah's injunction on the prayers his followers were to perform.

The rock that the Dome of the Rock protects is the Rock of Foundation (of the world) of the Jewish legend, the Jewish temple's inner sanctum. The octagonal shape of the building surmounted by a dome—that is, a circle within an octagon—modeled on the then existing Church of Resurrection (later renamed the Church of the Holy Sepulchre), was symbolic in ancient times of the center of the world. Thus the Dome of the Rock is a synthesis in form and content of Judaism [qv], Christianity [qv], and Islam [qv]. It was built in A.D. 691 by Abdul Malik ibn Marwan (r. A.D. 684–705), an Umayyad ruler based in Damascus [qv]. During the Crusaders' rule (1099–1187), it was reconverted into a church and renamed the Temple of the Lord.

Al Aqsa is a plainer, traditionally built mosque. It has prayer niches dedicated to Moses and Jesus. An arson attack on it by Michael Rohan, an Australian fundamentalist Christian [qv], in August 1969, shocked the Muslim world and led inter alia to the founding of the Islamic Conference Organization [qv].

Following the annexation of East Jerusalem [qv] by Jordan, the Jordanian monarch acquired the custody of the Noble Sanctuary in 1950. When Israel occupied East Jerusalem in June 1967, it accepted the Jordanian custodianship. This was confirmed by the Jordanian-Israeli Peace Treaty [qv], which was signed in October 1994 and hotly disputed by the Palestine Liberation Organization [qv]. The future of the Noble Sanctuary proved to be main stumbling block in the Israeli-PLO final settlement talks in July 2000 at Camp David in Maryland.

Nonconventional weapons (Arab Middle East, Iran, and Israel): *see* each individual country's military: nonconventional weapons.

North Yemen: Official title: Yemen Arab Republic. *See* Yemen: history.

North Yemeni Civil War (1962–70): Following the overthrow of Imam Muhammad al Badr [*qv*] by pan-Arabist [*qv*] military officers in September 1962, Egyptian President Gamal Abdul Nasser [*qv*] agreed to help the republican side, which commanded only 6,000 troops. In January 1963 the Saudi White Guard, later renamed the National Guard [*qv*], moved to the North Yemen border at Jizan and Najran to help al Badr. This led to fighting between Saudi and Egyptian forces.

Initially the Zaidi [*qv*] tribesmen, inhabiting the northern region bordering Saudi Arabia, supported al Badr. But in the absence of a strong central authority, tribal leaders such as Shaikh Naji al Ghadr of the Bakil tribal confederation, commanding a private army of 12,000, and Shaikh Abdullah al Ahmar [*qv*], head of the Hashid tribal confederation, found it more profitable to distance themselves from the conflict or offer their services to the highest bidder. By August 1965 the royalists had regained about half of North Yemen.

Having placed the republican president, Abdullah Sallal [*qv*], under house arrest in Cairo [*qv*], Nasser met King Faisal in Jiddah [*qv*]. Talks between them went on for about a year, but ended in failure. Meanwhile, Abdul Rahman al Iryani [*qv*], a conservative member of the Republican Council, had managed to neutralize the tribal leaders. Though Sallal returned to Sanaa [*qv*] and resumed his office, his position was weakened when, following the Egyptian debacle in the June 1967 Arab-Israeli War [*qv*], Nasser agreed with the Saudi king to pull out his troops from North Yemen by December 1967.

With al Iryani replacing Sallal in November 1967, the political hue of the republican regime changed. The royalists made a bid to capture Saana, but the republicans, assisted by tribes and leftists, ended the siege in February 1968. The tribal forces then began to attack the leftists, and subsequent ascendancy of conservatives in the republican regime made it acceptable to more and more tribals.

By early 1969 Riyadh had ceased to back al Badr militarily. In March 1970 President al Iryani reached an agreement with Riyadh whereby Saudi subsidies to the royalists were stopped. Once the Saudis were reassured that a republican regime in Saana, dependent for its financial survival on them, would be no threat, they formally recognized it. A coalition government, including royalist ministers, was formed, and the Consultative Council of forty-five was expanded by eighteen nominees, all of whom were royalists.

The eight-year conflict caused some 200,000 deaths.

North Yemeni-Soviet Friendship Treaty (1984): It was signed by President Ali Abdullah Salih [*qv*] and Kostantin Chernenko in Moscow.

Nuclear weapons (Arab Middle East, Iran, and Israel): *see* each individual country's military: nonconventional weapons.

Nusairis: *see* Alawis.

O

Occupied Arab Territories (1967): During the June 1967 Arab-Israeli War [*qv*], Israel occupied Egypt's Sinai Peninsula [*qv*]; the Gaza Strip [*qv*], which had been administered by Egypt since 1949; the

West Bank [*qv*], including East Jerusalem [*qv*], which had been annexed by Jordan in 1950; and Syria's Golan Heights [*qv*]. The annexation by Israel of East Jerusalem in late June 1967 and of the Golan Heights in December 1981 was not formally recognized by any foreign government or the United Nations.

After its peace treaty with Egypt in March 1979, Israel returned the Sinai Peninsula to Egypt in three stages, ending in April 1982. Having accepted the Palestine Liberation Organization (PLO) [*qv*] as the sole representatives of the Palestinians in November 1974, King Hussein [*qv*] of Jordan severed all legal and administrative ties with the West Bank, including East Jerusalem, in July 1988. The Israeli-PLO Accord of September 1993 [*qv*] involved interim Palestinian self-rule in Gaza and the West Bank town of Jericho [*qv*], followed by an extension of autonomy to other parts of the West Bank and negotiations on the future of East Jerusalem and the final settlement. In 1994 the Israeli-Syrian talks centered on Syria's insistence on Israel's acceptance of full withdrawal from the Golan Heights on the model of the 1979 Egyptian-Israeli Peace Treaty [*qv*].

Occupied Territories (1967): The term Occupied Territories refers to those areas of Palestine [*qv*] under British mandate that were occupied by Israel in the June 1967 Arab-Israeli War [*qv*]; i.e., the West Bank [*qv*], including East Jerusalem [*qv*], and the Gaza Strip [*qv*].

October 1973 Arab-Israeli War: *see* Arab-Israeli War IV (1973).

oil: In its geological context "oil" is a shortened version of crude oil or, more appropriately,

petroleum [*qv*]. A mixture of hydrocarbons found underground in a gaseous or liquid state, the term oil is applied to the liquid form. It is often greenish or dark brown and sometimes black. Archaelogical excavations in Iraq and Iran indicate that oil in the form of bitumen was used for building roads and for coating the hulls of ships and walls. In more modern times petroleum replaced whale oil in lamps as an illuminating fuel. Its mining involves prospecting, drilling, and extraction. The first petroleum well was drilled in 1848 near Baku, the capital of Azerbaijan. It was not until 1859 that oil was struck first in the U.S. town of Titusville, Pennsylvania. In the Middle East [*qv*] the first commercial drilling for oil occurred in 1908 at Masjid-e Suleiman, Iran [*qv*].

After extraction, often called recovery, oil is refined by distillation, which separates it into fractions of varying volatility. These are put through chemical conversion processes, known as cracking and reforming, to produce a variety of end products: asphalt, cleaning agents, explosives, fertilizers, fibers, gasoline/petrol, jellies, jet fuel, paraffin/kerosene, medicines, naptha, paints, plastics, synthetic rubber, and waxes. Carbon accounts for 82–87 percent of the weight of crude oil, and hydrogen 12–15 percent. Of the three series of compounds contained in an oil, the paraffin series is the most extensive, ranging from methane gas to petrol/gasoline to waxes; followed by the naphthene series, yielding volatile liquids to tarry bitumens; and the aromatic series, yielding mainly benzene.

The arrival of the motor car, run on gasoline, at the turn of the twentieth century provided the single most important incentive to develop the oil industry.

Oil and gas embargoes, 1967 and 1973–74:
Oil embargoes were imposed by the Arab petroleum exporting countries in 1967 and 1973–74 against Western states that directly aided Israel in its war with Arab adversaries. The scale and speed of Israeli attacks on the Egyptian, Syrian, and Jordanian air bases in early June 1967 led Cairo and Amman to accuse Washington and London of direct participation in the Arab-Israeli conflict. An emergency meeting of the Arab petroleum-exporting countries in Baghdad [*qv*] decided to cut off oil supplies to the United States, Britain, and West Germany, but not France, which had condemned the Israeli action. The boycott lasted until the end of August 1967 and led to the formation in January 1968 of the Organization of Arab Petroleum Exporting Countries (OAPEC) [*qv*].

During the October 1973 Arab-Israeli War [*qv*], OAPEC oil ministers met in Kuwait [*qv*] on 16 October. The next day, reacting to U.S. President Richard Nixon's decision to airlift weapons to Israel on a massive scale, OAPEC members decided that "all Arab oil-exporting countries shall forthwith cut production by no less than 5 percent of the September production, and maintain the same rate of reduction each month until the Israeli forces are fully withdrawn from all Arab territories occupied during the [June] 1967 [Arab-Israeli] War [*qv*], and the legitimate rights of the Palestinian people are restored." They categorized the consumer countries as friendly, neutral, or hostile to the Arab cause, with friendly nations to be supplied at the September level, neutrals at a reduced level, and hostile ones not at all. They also confirmed the steep price rise decided earlier by

the Organization of Petroleum Exporting Countries (OPEC) [*qv*]. Saudi Arabia ordered a 25 percent cut in its output, then running at 8 million barrels a day, but Iraq ignored the OAPEC decision.

Unlike the June 1967 embargo, this one hurt the United States—partly because it was applied during autumn and winter when demand for heating oil was high, and partly because the United States had become more dependent on Arab oil. The OAPEC move reduced the annual U.S. gross domestic product by $10–20 billion.

The resolve of OAPEC members, especially of Saudi Arabia, began to falter. Aware of the staunchly anticommunist views of the Saudi monarch, Faisal ibn Abdul Aziz [*qv*], Edward Heath, prime minister of Britain (which was not on the Arab oil boycott list), argued publicly in late December that any prolonged oil squeeze would, by weakening the West, strengthen communism. It did not take long for President Anwar Sadat [*qv*], working in conjunction with U.S. Secretary of State Henry Kissinger, to convince Faisal to end the boycott. Faisal and Sadat then prevailed upon other members of OAPEC to end the five-month embargo on 18 March 1974 "as a token of Arab goodwill" to the West—even though the Israelis had not withdrawn from anywhere in the Occupied Arab Territories [*qv*] and the legitimate rights of the Palestinian people had not been restored.

Oil and gas industry (Bahrain): Oil reserves: 100 million barrels (2000), 0.1 percent of the world total; gas reserves: 90 billion cu. meters (2001), 0.1 percent of the world total.

In 1929 the Standard Oil Company of California combined with the Texas Company to form the Bahrain Petroleum Company (BAPCO) and registered it in Canada, a British dominion. BAPCO commenced commercial production in 1932. Output rose from 19,000 barrels per day in 1940 to 77,000 in 1970. It then declined, stabilizing at around 42,000 barrels per day in the early 1990s, and falling to 37,000 barrels per day in 2000. At that rate the reserves were expected to last until 2007. Gas output, at 24 million cu. meters per day in 2000, was expected to last until 2013. Bahrain [qv] was a founder member of the Organization of Arab Petroleum Exporting Countries [qv].

Oil and gas industry (Egypt): Oil reserves: 2.9 billion barrels (2001), 0.3 percent of the world total; gas reserves: 1,000 billion cu. meters (2000), 0.6 percent of the world total.

Though oil was first struck in 1886, it was not extracted commercially until 1913. It was only after the 1952 revolution that the government tried seriously to develop the industry. The loss of oil fields in the Sinai [qv] to Israel in 1967 was compensated by fresh discoveries in the Gulf of Suez and the Western Desert.

Following the establishment of the oil ministry in 1973, exploration and extraction gained pace, with output reaching 420,000 barrels per day in 1977 and then stabilizing at around 800,000 million barrels per day in 2000. At this production rate, Egypt's reserves will last until 2009. Egypt [qv], a founder member of the Organization of Arab Petroleum Exporting Countries (OAPEC) [qv], was suspended from OAPEC in 1979 as a result of the Egyptian–Israeli Peace Treaty [qv] but was readmitted a decade later. Gas production, which began in 1974, reached 49 million cu. meters per day

in 2000. At this rate, Egypt's reserves will last until 2055.

Oil and gas industry (Iran): Oil reserves: 98.7 billion barrels (2001), 8.5 percent of the world total; gas reserves: 23,000 billion cu. meters (2001), 14.8 percent of the world total.

Oil was found at Masjid-e Suleiman, southwest Iran [qv], in 1908 by a British prospector, William Knox d'Arcy, and commercially mined four years later. His firm expanded to become the Anglo-Persian Oil Company (APOC). With the British admirality's decision in 1913 to switch from coal to oil, the importance of petroleum increased. To ensure supplies Britain acquired a controlling share in APOC, whose name was changed to the Anglo-Iranian Oil Company (AIOC) following the renaming of Persia as Iran in 1933, and then British Petroleum.

Following the nationalization of the AIOC in 1951 and the founding of the National Iranian Oil Company (NIOC) in that year, the West boycotted Iran's oil, thus creating a crisis that culminated in a clash between nationalist Premier Muhammad Mussadiq [qv] and pro-Western Muhammad Reza Shah Pahlavi [qv] in August 1953, in which Mussadiq lost. On the advice of the United States the shah kept the oil nationalization law on the statute books, but downgraded the role of the NIOC. It leased the rights to, and management of, Iranian oil in 1954 for the next twenty-five years to a Western consortium, with the following share-out: AIOC, 40 percent; Royal Dutch Shell, 14 percent; five major U.S. oil companies (Exxon, Gulf, Mobil, Socal, and Texaco), 8 percent each; and Compagnie Francaise des Petroles, 6 percent. It was only in 1967 that

NIOC was able to market 100,000 barrels per day (b/d) on its own.

Encouraged by the self-reliant policies advocated by the Organization of Petroleum Exporting Countries (OPEC) [qv], of which Iran was a founder member, the shah pressed the consortium to renegotiate the leasing agreement. In July 1973 the NIOC took over all the operations and ownership of the Western oil consortium. Buoyed by the rise in production at 6 million b/d in 1974, and the quadrupling of oil prices in 1973–74, the shah visualized Iran becoming the fifth most powerful nation in the world. In 1977 the oil revenue of $19.5 billion provided three-quarters of the government's annual income. The strike of oil workers in October 1978 (when oil production was at 5.3 million b/d and domestic consumption at about 800,000 b/d), played a crucial role in the overthrow of the Pahlavi dynasty [qv]. The loss of Iran's supplies to the international oil market pushed the price from $13 to $20 a barrel. Therefore, with the resumption of exports at 3.2 million b/d in the spring of 1979, Iran earned more than it did with larger exports before the revolution of February 1979.

With the Western economic boycott of Iran following the takeover of the U.S. embassy in Tehran in November 1979, there was disruption of the Iranian oil supplies into the market, resulting in another price rise. The eruption of the Iran-Iraq War [qv] in September 1980, primarily in the Iranian oil province of Khuzistan, destabilized the market further, pushing the dollar price into the upper thirties in the spring of 1981. In the mid-1980s Iran's output fell to 1.4 million barrels per day, and then stagnated at 2.5 million barrels per day during the war.

Iran's chief oil terminal at Kharg Island became vulnerable to Iraqi air attacks. Iran survived by pumping oil at Kharg into its own tankers, which delivered the commodity to its customers at its offshore islands in the Lower Gulf [qv] outside the range of the Iraqi bombers.

The steep decline in the oil price from $28 to below $10 a barrel, caused by the flooding of the market by Saudi Arabia and Kuwait during the spring of 1986, reduced Tehran's oil income from $13.1 billion in 1985 to $7.2 billion, with average exports at 1.6 million b/d. This severely damaged its ability to conduct the war, which ended in August 1988.

After the war Iran increased its output steadily from 2.87 million b/d in 1989 to 3.62 million b/d in 1993, with exports around 2.5 million b/d and oil revenue at $14.5 billion. At the 2001 production rate of 3.55 million b/d, yielding an annual income of about $20 billion, Iran's reserves will last until 2070.

With the world's second largest gas reserves (after Russia), being consumed at the rate of 165 million cu. meters a day in 2000, it will take Iran 450 years to exhaust them.

Oil and gas industry (Iraq): Oil reserves: 112.5 billion barrels (2001), 10.7 percent of the world total; gas reserves: 3,110 billion cu. meters (2001), 2.0 percent of the world total.

The efforts of the Turkish Petroleum Company (TPC), owned largely by the Anglo-Persian Oil Company (APOC) after the First World War, bore fruit in 1927 when it struck oil in commercial quantities in the Kirkuk area. This increased the strategic and economic value of Palestine [qv] since it provided a gateway to the Iraqi oil fields through the British protectorate of Transjordan [*qv*] (now Jordan). Under Washington's pressure the TPC was reconstituted in 1931 as the Iraq Petroleum Company (IPC)—a 23.5 percent share each was held by government-owned British, French, and Dutch companies and two U.S. corporations, the remaining 6 percent by Partex, owned by C. S. Gulbenkian, a Portuguese businessman.

The oil output had reached such proportions by the Second World War that Britain intervened militarily to overthrow the nationalist government of Rashid Ali Gailani [*qv*] in 1941. In the late 1940s the Iraqi government required IPC to pay half of its profit as tax. After the 1958 revolution, Abdul Karim Qasim [*qv*] issued a decree in 1961 that deprived IPC of 99.5 percent of the 160,000 sq. miles/ 414,400 sq. km originally allocated to it for prospecting, covering almost the whole country, including oil-rich Rumeila [*qv*] in the south. The government set up its own Iraq National Oil Company (INOC). IPC challenged the law, and a partial compromise was reached in 1969. Meanwhile, government decrees of August and October 1967 gave the INOC wider powers and the exclusive right to develop the Rumeila oil field. To pressure Baghdad to reverse its hard-line policy, IPC halved the output of the Kirkuk oil fields in March 1972. In mid-May 1972 Iraq [*qv*] warned IPC that it would end the negotiations if its demands were not met within a fortnight. They were not, and IPC was nationalized in June. This marked the end of an era that had begun in 1912 under the rule of the Ottoman sultan.

The Soviet Union played an important role in giving confidence to Iraq to go ahead with nationalizing IPC. It also helped to develop Iraq's petroleum industry in exploration and extraction—as in the Rumeila oil fields—and in refining. The general message of the Soviets was that Iraq need not be totally dependent on Western capital and/or expertise in this industry.

Once it had consolidated its position, Iraq nationalized the American and Dutch interests in the Basrah Petroleum Company, operating in the south. It did so during the October 1973 Arab-Israeli War [*qv*], when feelings in the Arab world were running high against the United States and Holland, which openly and materially sided with Israel. On the other hand, Baghdad did not join the Organization of Arab Petroleum Exporting Countries (OAPEC) [*qv*] oil embargo against the states that aided Israel in the war.

The fivefold increase in revenue from petroleum exports in the mid-1970s provided an unprecedented boost to the morale of the ruling Baath Socialist Party [*qv*], which had seized power in 1968. The government raised the salaries of its civil servants and military personnel substantially. Its ambitious Five-Year Plan, 1976–80, promised a prosperous future for all. In 1979 and 1980, when the national population was less than 13million, the oil output exceeded 3.5 million b/d, with exports at 3.3 million b/d and oil income at $21.3 billion and $26.3 billion respectively.

The war with Iran started in September 1980, and oil output fell to 800,000 b/d in 1982. It rose to 1.75 million b/d in 1986, but the price fell to below $10 a barrel and Iraq's oil income plummeted to $7 billion. Baghdad was able to withstand the price crash because of the large grants it received from Saudi

Arabia and Kuwait. Later, Iraq built a pipeline that connected with a Saudi pipeline leading to the Red Sea port of Yanbu, thus supplementing its earlier pipeline running to the Turkish port of Dortyol.

Demanding parity with Iran in its export quota, from October 1986 to May 1988 Iraq ignored the output quotas agreed by the Organization of Petroleum Exporting Countries (OPEC) [*qv*]. Following the end of the Iran–Iraq War [*qv*] in August 1988, Iraq returned to the OPEC system when OPEC equalized the Iraqi and Iranian output quotas at 2.64 million b/d each. The following year Iraqi production reached 2.83 million b/d, with exports at 2.4 million b/d and export earnings at $12 billion. In the first half of 1990, production was 3.1 million b/d, but flooding of the market by Kuwait and the United Arab Emirates depressed the price from $18 to $12 a barrel, causing Iraq to lose nearly $20 million a day.

With Iraq's invasion of Kuwait in early August 1990, followed by immediate economic sanctions by the United Nations, Baghdad's oil exports ceased. From then on Iraqi oil output fell to 400,000 b/d, enough for domestic needs, lowering the annual average for 1990 to 2 million b/d. Three years later the figure was 455,000 b/d, including the 65,000 b/d that Jordan was allowed to import from Iraq as a special case. Starting December 1996, when Iraq was allowed by the United Nations Security Council to export enough petroleum to earn $2 billion in six months, the output rose. With the Security Council raising the six-monthly limit to $5.2 billion in the spring of 1998, the production for that year reached 2.2 million b/d. Further improvement occurred when the Security Council sanctioned sufficient funds for Iraq to repair its dilapidated oil industry. As a consequence of the Security Council removing the ceiling on the oil output of Iraq in December 1999, which had been exempted from OPEC quota since the end of the Second Gulf War [*qv*] in March 1991 due to its special circumstances, the figure for 2000 topped 2.63 million b/d, with Baghdad's oil exports earnings reaching $7.1 billion in the first six months of the year. At its 2000 rate of extraction, 3 million b/d, the Iraqi reserves will last until 2116.

Gas production rose from 16.2 million cu. meters per day in 1966 to 55.2 million cu. meters per day in 1979, but then declined sharply due to the conflict with Iran, recovering to 29.2 million cu. meters per day in 1989, with about a third being exported. At this rate Iraq's reserves will last until 2096.

Oil and gas industry (Israel): Oil was first found in Israel in 1955. The output peaked at 6,000 barrels per day and was down to 500 b/d from proven reserves of 4 million barrels. The production of natural gas, found in the Dead Sea region, remained steady at around 20 million cu. meters per day. It was expected to rise due to the reserves of 40,000 million cu. meters found in the Ashkelon area.

Oil and gas industry (Jordan): There is no oil extraction industry in Jordan. The production of natural gas, found in the northeast, was less than 1 million cu. meters per day in 2000, with the country's total deposits estimated at 6,440 million cu. meters.

Oil and gas industry (Kuwait): Oil reserves: 96.5 billion barrels (2001), 9.2 percent of the world total; gas reserves: 1,500 billion cu. meters (2001), 1.0 percent of the world total.

The Kuwait Oil Company (KOC), owned equally by the Anglo-Iranian Oil Company (now British Petroleum) and the (U.S.) Gulf Oil Company, obtained petroleum concessions in Kuwait [qv] in 1934 for seventy-four years. Commercial extraction began in 1938, the Burgan field proving to be a gigantic reserve of oil. Interrupted by the Second World War, production recommenced in 1946. Due to the Western boycott of the nationalized oil company in Iran in 1951, the output of Kuwaiti petroleum rose sharply. In 1956 Kuwait became the leading oil exporter in the region, with a total output of 1.1 million barrels per day (b/d), a position it maintained for a decade.

Pursuing the self-reliance policy of the Organization of Petroleum Exporting Countries (OPEC) [qv], Kuwait, one of OPEC's founder members, acquired 25 percent of the shares of KOC in October 1972, with provision for a further 2.5 percent annual increase in shareholding over the next decade. But after the October 1973 Arab-Israeli War [qv] and a dramatic jump in oil prices, the government acquired a majority holding in KOC immediately, buying the rest of the shares in March 1975. It also responded positively to parliament's demand that oil output be limited to a maximum of 2 million b/d.

Following the disruption of Iraqi oil supplies due to the outbreak of the Iran–Iraq War [qv] in September 1980, Kuwait volunteered to meet Iraq's obligations. Later it used oil as a weapon when, in alliance with Saudi Arabia, it flooded the market in early 1986, depressing the price from $28 to $10 a barrel, thus severely damaging Iran's ability to finance its war. The negative impact on Iraq was compensated by subventions to it from Kuwait and Saudi Arabia. After the war's end in August 1988, Kuwait insisted that Iraq should repay the $10–12 billion loaned to it by way of the oil supplied to Iraq's customers during the conflict. When Baghdad refused, Kuwait began to flood the petroleum market by exceeding its OPEC quota of 1.5 million b/d by 40 percent, thus depressing the price and hurting Iraq. This was the background to the Iraqi invasion and occupation of Kuwait in early August 1990. Just before retreating at the end of the 1991 Gulf War [qv], Iraqi troops set ablaze 640 of Kuwait's 800 oil wells. After the cease-fire the Kuwaiti government successfully concentrated on extinguishing the fires and repairing the damage to the industry.

In 1992 OPEC gave a special dispensation to Kuwait to produce without a fixed quota. In early 1993 OPEC fixed Kuwait's share at 1.6 million b/d, one-fifth less than its current output. Though its quota was increased to 1.7 million b/d later in the year, Kuwait insisted on 2 million b/d and produced nearly that much. In 2001 its output was 2.14 million b/d. At this rate Kuwait's reserves will last until 2124.

Kuwait's gas reserves, being consumed at the rate of 26 million cu. meters a day in 2001, will last until 2159.

Oil and gas industry (Oman): Oil reserves: 5.5 billion barrels (2000), 0.5 percent of the world total; gas reserves: 830 billion cu. meters (2000), 0.5 percent of the world total.

Exploration by the Anglo-Iranian Oil Company (AIOC), which obtained concessions in 1925, yielded nothing. In 1937 a subsidiary of the Iraq Petroleum Company (IPC), Petroleum Concessions (Oman), received a seventy-five-year concession for the whole country except Dhofar province, where a separate concession was granted to Dhofar Cities Service Petroleum Corporation in 1953. In that year Petroleum Development Oman (PDO), the successor to Petroleum Concessions (Oman), began serious exploration. Due to the continued failure to strike oil, all corporations except Royal Dutch Shell and Partex, owned by C. S. Gulbenkian, withdrew, leaving them respectively with 85 percent and 15 percent of the shares. The reconstituted company found oil in commercial quantities in 1962 in the central region. In 1967, when exports began, Partex sold part of its shares to Compagnie Francaise des Petroles.

Oil revenue rose from $21 million in 1964 to $117 million in 1970, when Sultan Said ibn Taimur [qv] was succeeded by his son Qaboos [qv]. Rising income from oil, though modest by Gulf standards, enabled Qaboos to build up Oman's infrastructure and provide public services to his subjects. In 1975 his government acquired a 60 percent share of the PDO, leaving the rest with Royal Dutch Shell (34 percent) and Compagnie Francaise des Petroles. During the 1970s oil output averaged 300,000 b/d. Production in Dhofar, which began in 1980, boosted the total. In 2001 the output was 959,000 b/d. At this rate Oman's reserves will last until 2017.

Oman's gas reserves, being consumed at the rate of 36.7 million cu. meters a day in 2001, will last until 2063.

Oil and gas industry (Qatar): Oil reserves: 15.2 billion barrels (2001), 1.5 percent of the world total; gas reserves: 14,400 billion cu. meters (2001), 9.3 percent of the world total.

The concession given in 1925 to the Anglo-Persian Oil Company, which yielded nothing, was transferred in 1935 to an Iraq Petroleum Company subsidiary, Petroleum Development (Qatar)—later renamed Qatar National Petroleum Company (QNPC). It struck oil in 1939, but work was interrupted by the Second World War and did not resume until 1948. Output rose from 32,000 barrels per day (b/d) in 1950 to 600,000 b/d in 1973.

Following its independence in 1971, Qatar [qv], a member of the Organization of Petroleum Exporting Countries (OPEC) [qv] since 1961, pursued self-reliant policies. A dramatic increase in its oil revenue due to a sharp price rise in 1973–74 enabled the Qatari government to buy the QNPC in two stages, in 1974 and 1976. In 1977 the state-owned Qatar General Petroleum Company (QGPC) became solely responsible for oil and gas production. After reaching a peak of 510,000 b/d in 1979, output averaged 350,000 b/d during the 1980s. Rising steadily from 420,000 b/d in 1991, it reached 783,000 b/d in 2001. At this rate Qatari oil will last until 2057.

The offshore North Field is the world's largest single deposit of unassociated gas, making Qatar the third largest possessor of natural gas in the world. In the 1980s the average output was 27.4 million cu. meters a day. The commissioning of the first phase of the North Field in 1991 doubled production, and the trend continued during the 1990s, with the output reaching 89 million cu. meters a day in 2001. At this rate Qatar's reserves will last until about 2355.

Oil and gas industry (Saudi Arabia): Oil reserves: 261.8 billion barrels (2001), 24.9 percent of the world total; gas reserves:

6,220 billion cu meters (2001), 4.0 percent of the world total.

In 1933 the Standard Oil Company of California (SOCAL) secured exploration rights in the eastern Hasa province with preferential rights elsewhere in the kingdom. In 1936 SOCAL invited Texaco to form a joint company, Caltex. It struck oil in 1938. Interrupted by the Second World War, exports resumed in 1946. Two years later Caltex expanded into a consortium of four U.S. companies—SOCAL (later Chevron), 30 percent; Texaco, 30 percent; Standard Oil Company of New Jersey (later Esso, then Exxon), 30percent; and Mobil Oil, 10 percent—called Arabian American Oil Company (Aramco). Output rose so sharply that Aramco's earnings jumped from $2.8 million in 1944 to $115 million five years later. The Saudi monarch required Aramco to pay half of its profits as tax.

In the course of administrative and fiscal reform, in 1962 the government set up the General Petroleum and Mineral Organization, known as Petromin, to increase state participation in the oil and gas industry. Petroleum output shot up from 1.3 million barrels per day (b/d) in 1940 to 8 million b/d in 1973 before the Arab-Israeli War [qv] in October. Saudi Arabia [qv] led the Arab oil embargo [qv] during the conflict and ensured that the embargo continued. Equally, when it decided to see it end in March 1974, its will prevailed.

Due to increased output and a sharp rise in price in 1973–74, Saudi oil income reached $22.57 billion in 1974, a 36-fold increase in a decade. Among other things this allowed Riyadh to pursue the self-reliance policy advocated by the Organization of Petroleum Exporting Countries (OPEC) [qv], of which it was a founder member. Saudi Arabia acquired a 25 percent share of Aramco, with provision for a further 2.5 percent annual increase in shareholding until the total reached 51 percent.

To fill the gap created in late 1978 by the stoppage of oil exports from Iran, which was in the midst of revolutionary turmoil, Saudi Arabia increased its output to 9.5 million b/d in 1979 and 10 million b/d a year later. Political turbulence in Iran after the Islamic revolution [qv] raised the price from $13 a barrel in early 1979 to $28 in May 1980, increasing Saudi Arabia's oil income to $106 billion in 1980 and enabling it to buy up the remaining Aramco shares, thus completing the nationlization of Aramco announced in 1978, with the new company renamed Saudi Aramco.

The outbreak of the Iran-Iraq War [qv] in September, resulting in extensive damage to both countries' oil industries and a drop in their exports, led to higher prices during 1981, reaching a spot price peak of $41 a barrel. With Saudi production steady at 10 million b/d, oil income reached a record $110 billion in 1981. To aid Iraq in its war against Iran, Saudi Arabia volunteered to honor its oil contracts.

When, due to high prices, worldwide demand for oil began to decline, Saudi Arabia cut its output sharply, first to 6.6 million b/d (1982) and then 4.8 million b/d (1984), to stabilize the price at $29 a barrel. It thus underlined its role as the swing producer within OPEC, who by adjusting its production could stabilize the price and keep the overall OPEC output within the agreed limits. However, in the process its oil income fell to $27 billion in 1985 at 3.6 million b/d.

Partly to increase OPEC's overall share of the world market in the face of price cutting by non-OPEC producers, and partly to depress the oil income of Iran, thus weakening its capacity to prolong its war with Iraq, Saudi Arabia, in alliance with Kuwait, began to flood the market with their sharply increased output—an average 50 percent more than in the previous year. This depressed the price from $28 a barrel in December 1985 to below $10 a barrel in July, and began to hurt the kingdom's economy. King Fahd ibn Abdul Aziz [qv] acted in October by sacking Ahmad Zaki Yamani [qv], the oil minister since 1962, and decided to limit output to raise prices. This policy prevailed at OPEC, which cut its total by 7.5 percent to 15.8 million b/d for the first half of 1987, the Saudi share being 4.1 million b/d. The price stabilized at little over the OPEC reference level of $18 a barrel.

This more or less held until the spring of 1990, when market flooding by Kuwait and the United Arab Emirates depressed the price to $12 a barrel. However, the Iraqi invasion and occupation of Kuwait in early August caused the spot price of oil to shoot up to $28 a barrel. An emergency meeting of OPEC allowed members to increase their output beyond the allocated quota due to the loss of 4 million b/d of oil previously exported by Iraq and Kuwait. With an average output of 6.84 million b/d, Saudi Arabia ended 1990 with oil income of $40.7 billion, more than twice the average figure for the past four years. With output running at 8.6 to 8.9 million b/d during the early 1990s, and the price fluctuating between $12 and $22 a barrel, Saudi Arabia's oil income in 1993 was nearly $43 billion. Oil prices fell sharply in 1998 due to the reduced demand in the Asian market caused by economic downturn. Saudi Arabia played a leading role in securing output cuts by OPEC and leading non-OPEC producers in 1999, and succeeded in getting the prices in the $22–28 per barrel range. By and large this range held for the next few years.

Possessor of the largest oil reserves in the world, and accounting for nearly one-eighth of world and one-third of OPEC output in 2001, Saudi Arabia will exhaust its reserves by 2087 at the current rate of production.

Saudi Arabia has the world's fourth largest gas reserves. These were being consumed at the rate of 177 million cu. meters a day in 1991 and should last until 2073.

Oil and gas industry (Syria): Oil reserves: 2.5 billion barrels (2001), 0.2 percent of the world total; gas reserves: 290 billion cu. meters (2001), 0.2 percent of the world total.

The Iraq Petroleum Company (IPC), which acquired oil concessions in Syria [qv] during the French mandate (1920–41), surrendered these to the government in 1951 after having failed to find petroleum. The concessions given in the mid-1950s to a West German-led consortium and U.S. company, which led to the discovery of petroleum, were canceled when the Baathist [qv] regime nationalized the oil industry in 1964 and set up the Syrian Petroleum Company (SPC) under the aegis of the General Petroleum Authority. Modest production began in 1968. In the mid-1970s Syria granted concessions to foreign companies. Their discoveries in the mid-1980s, especially in the country's northeast corner, nearly doubled the national output to 400,000 barrels per day in 1990. Continued steady increase took the figure to

600,000 barrels per day in 1995, when a decline set in, taking the total to 540,000 b/d in 2000. At this rate, Syrian reserves will last until 2013.

Natural gas production started in 1994 and reached 18 million cu. meters in 2000. At this rate the reserves will last until 2016.

Oil and gas industry (United Arab Emirates [UAE]): Oil reserves: 97.8 billion barrels (2001), 9.3 percent of the world total; gas reserves: 6,000 billion cu. meters (2001), 3.9 percent of the world total.

In 1939 the Trucial Coast Development Oil Company, later Abu Dhabi Petroleum company (ADPC), a subsidiary of the Iraq Petroleum Company (IPC), obtained exploration rights in Abu Dhabi [qv]. Another company to secure concessions was Abu Dhabi Marines Area (ADMA), formed in 1954 by British Petroleum and Compagnie Francaise des Petroles. Oil production started in 1962 on a modest scale. By 1978 the ADPC and ADMA had been restructured into the Abu Dhabi Company for Onshore Oil (ADCO) and ADMA-OPCO for offshore work. These companies accounted for 93 percent of Abu Dhabi's oil output, which amounted to 1.8 million barrels per day (b/d) on the eve of Iraq's invasion of Kuwait in August 1990.

Oil was discovered in Dubai [qv] in 1966 by the Dubai Petroleum Company (DPC), which in 1961 had taken over IPC's concession, held since 1937. Commercial production, which began in 1969, rose to 420,000 b/d at the time of Iraq's attack on Kuwait in August 1990. Petroleum was struck in Sharjah [qv]in 1974, and production reached 60,000 b/d in mid-1990. Oil was found in Ras al Khaima [qv] in 1984,

but by the late 1980s output had not exceeded 12,000 b/d.

The two sharp rises in the price of oil in the mid- and the late 1970s made the UAE, with less than a million people, one of the top five richest countries in the world. In July 1990 the UAE was producing 2.3 million b/d, more than twice the quota fixed by the Organization of Petroleum Exporting Countries (OPEC) [qv], of which it had been a member since 1974, thus causing the price to fall to $12 a barrel, a third below the $18 OPEC reference price.

With the temporary loss of Iraqi and Kuwaiti oil to the world market the UAE raised its output, which reached 2.6 million b/d in 1991, stabilized at around 2.4 million b/d (marginally above the OPEC limit of 2.24 million b/d), and brought the country an annual income of some $14 billion. At the 2001 production rate of 2.24 million b/d, the UAE's reserves will last until 2120.

With the fifth largest gas reserves in the world, being consumed at a rate of 113 million cu. meters a day in 2001, it will take the UAE until 2146 to exhaust them.

Oil and gas industry (Yemen): Oil reserves: 4 billion barrels (2001), 0.4 percent of the world total; gas reserves: 480 billion cu. meters (2001), 0.3 percent of the world total.

In North Yemen [qv], from the 1970s the state-owned oil company tried but failed to discover petroleum. However, in 1984 the Yemeni subsidiary of the U.S.-based Hunt Oil Company discovered oil in commercial quantities. Production increased rapidly and reached 200,000 barrels per day (b/d) on the eve of the unification of North and South Yemen [qv] in May 1990.

In South Yemen oil was struck in commercial quantities in 1987, and output remained at 10,000 b/d until the unification of the two Yemens. In the 1990s, Yemeni output rose steadily, reaching 396,000 b/d in 1999. At the 2001 production rate of 458,000 b/d, Yemen's reserves will last until 2025.

With its gas deposits being consumed at the rate of 174 million cu. meters a day in 2001, Yemen's reserves will last until 2076.

Oil and gas reserves (2001):

Oil reserves (2001):

World:	1,050 billion barrels
Middle East:	685.6 billion barrels, 65.3 percent of world total

The Gulf region:	64.7 percent
Bahrain	0.1 percent
Iran	8.5 percent
Iraq	10.7 percent
Kuwait	9.2 percent
Oman	0.5 percent
Qatar	1.5 percent
Saudi Arabia	24.9 percent
United Arab Emirates	9.3 percent

Outside the Gulf region: 1.0 percent of world total

Egypt	0.3 percent
Syria	0.3 percent
Yemen	0.4 percent

North America: 6.1 percent of world total. At the 2001 output of 14 million barrels a day for the United States, Canada, and Mexico, the North American reserves will last until 2015.

Former Soviet Union: 6.2 percent of world total. At the 2001 production rate of 8.7 million barrels a day, reserves will last until 2022.

Europe: 1.8 percent of world total. At the 2001 production of 6.8 million barrels a day, Europe's reserves will last until 2009. For Norway, at its 2001 output of 3.4 million barrels a day, its reserves will last until 2009; and for Britain, at its 2001 output of 2.5 million barrels a day its reserves will last until 2007.

Gas reserves (2001):

World:	155 trillion cu. meters, trillion being one million million
Middle East:	56.58 trillion cu. meters, 36.8 percent of world total

The Gulf region:	35.6 percent
Bahrain	0.1 percent
Iran	14.8 percent
Iraq	2.0 percent
Kuwait	1.0 percent
Oman	0.5 percent
Qatar	9.3 percent
Saudi Arabia	4.0 percent
United Arab Emirates	3.9 percent

Outside the Gulf region: 1.2 percent of world total

Egypt	0.6 percent
Syria	0.2 percent
Yemen	0.4 percent

North America: 4.9 percent of world total. At the 2001 output of 762 billion cu. meters per day, the reserves of North America (Canada, Mexico, and the United States) will last ten years.

Former Soviet Union: 36.2 percent of world total. At the 2001 production rate of 677 billion cu. meters per day, these reserves will last seventy-nine years.

Europe: 3.1 percent of world total. At the 2001 production of 293 billion cu. meters per day, these reserves will last sixteen years.

Oil industry (Middle East): Of the world's

proven oil reserves of 1,050 billion barrels in 2001, the Middle East [*qv*] had 686 billion barrels, or 65.3 percent of the total, with 64.2 percent in the Gulf states [*qv*], Iran, and Iraq, and the rest in Egypt, Syria, and Yemen.

Oil was first extracted commercially in 1908 by a British prospector, William Knox D'Arcy, at Masjid-e Suleiman in southwest Iran. His firm expanded to become the Anglo–Persian Oil Company (APOC). With the British admirality's decision in 1913 to switch from coal to oil, the importance of petroleum increased. To ensure supplies Britain acquired a controlling share in APOC. It also imposed a series of agreements on the rulers of Kuwait (1913), Bahrain (1914), Qatar (1916), the Lower Gulf emirates (mid-1920s), and Oman (mid-1920s), whereby they were barred from giving oil concessions to non-British companies without London's prior permission. The terms of oil concessions to British interests included long duration (60 to 95 years), vast areas (160,000 sq. miles/414,000 sq. km in Iraq, more than 500,000 sq. miles/1,295,000 sq. km in Saudi Arabia), exemption from local taxes, and paltry royalties to the host country, with the royalty treated as a rental proportional to the size of the yield, irrespective of the price of the extracted commodity. It varied between 3–8 British pennies/8–20 American cents per barrel of 35 imperial gallons.

After the First World War, APOC acquired three-quarters of the shares of the Turkish Petroleum Company (TPC), which had originally consisted of British, French, and German interests. TPC had begun to operate in Iraq in 1912 after winning an oil concession from the Ottoman sultan. APOC

found oil in commercial quantities in the northern region of Kirkuk in 1927. Petroleum on a commercial scale was next discovered in Bahrain in 1932, followed by Kuwait and Saudi Arabia in 1938.

By then the Anglo-Persian Oil Company had changed its name to the Anglo-Iranian Oil Company (now British Petroleum) following the renaming of Persia [*qv*] as Iran in 1933; and the Iraq Petroleum Company (IPC) had been created in 1931. Government-owned British, French, and Dutch companies, and two privately owned U.S. companies each held 23.5 percent of the shares of IPC; the remaining 6 percent being held by Partex, owned by C. S. Gulbenkian, a Portuguese businessman who had acted as a middleman during the Ottoman times.

After a halt in production during the Second World War, output rose sharply as more oil fields were discovered and tapped. By the late 1960s production in the Gulf [*qv*] amounted to 30 percent of the global total. In 2001 the Gulf region's output was 28.5 percent of the world total and 70 percent of the Organization of Petroleum Exporting Countries' (OPEC) [*qv*] total.

The recent histories of the following countries have been shaped largely or exclusively by oil: all six Gulf states [*qv*], Iran, Iraq, and Palestine [*qv*] under the British mandate.

Oil measurements (Based on world average crude oil gravity):

    1 barrel = 5 Imperial gallons/42 U.S. gallons

    1 long ton (2,240 lbs) = 7.42 barrels (used in Britain)

    1 metric ton (2,205 lbs) = 7.30 barrels (also called tonne)

    1 short ton (2,000 lbs) = 7.00 barrels

(used in North America)

1 tonne (2,205 lbs) = 7.30 barrels

Conversion table:

Long tons per year to barrels per day, divide by 49.2

Metric tons per year to barrels per day, divide by 50.0

Short tons per year to barrels per day, divide by 52.14

Tonnes per year to barrels per day, divide by 50.0

Oil prices: During 1861–80 the average worldwide price of a barrel of oil fluctuated between US$1 and $9 in money of the day, equivalent to $10 to $90 in 2001 U.S. dollars. It then settled down to $1 a barrel, rising to $3.50 during the First World War ($28 in today's money), and not returning to its $1 level until the early 1930s. During the Second World War the price rose modestly, but picked up during the postwar reconstruction. It moved up to $2 a barrel in the wake of the loss of Iranian supplies from 1951 to 1953 and the Suez War [*qv*] of 1956, which closed the Suez Canal [*qv*]. On the eve of the October 1973 Arab-Israeli War [*qv*] the average price of a barrel of oil from the Gulf [*qv*] region was $2.55. Between mid-October 1973 and 1 January 1974, the price of oil was increased from $2.55 to $11.65 a barrel ($43 in today's cash) by the Organization of Petroleum Exporting Countries (OPEC) [*qv*], with the host government's average takings rising fivefold, from $1.38 to $7 a barrel. For the next four years, increases kept pace with inflation, and in late 1978 oil was selling for $14 a barrel.

The overthrow of Muhammad Reza Shah Pahlavi [*qv*] of Iran in early 1979, partly caused by a strike in the Iranian oil industry, raised the price from $14 to $28 a barrel within a few months. The outbreak of the Iran-Iraq War [*qv*] in September 1980, resulting in extensive damage to both countries' oil industries and a drop in their oil exports, led to higher prices during 1981, reaching a spot price peak of $47 a barrel (equivalent to today's $78) but stabilizing at around $34 a barrel in the early 1980s. When, in response to the high price, worldwide demand for oil began to decline, Saudi Arabia, the largest OPEC producer, curtailed its output sharply to stabilize the price at $29 a barrel in 1984.

To meet the price-cutting challenge by non-OPEC Western producers such as Britain and Norway, and to enlarge OPEC's share of the market and damage Iran's war effort, Saudi Arabia and Kuwait began to flood the oil market from December 1985, depressing the price from $28 to less than $10 in July 1986. Hurt by the steep fall in its oil revenue, Saudi Arabia reversed the strategy and, in alliance with Iran, encouraged OPEC to aim for $18 a barrel by cutting overall production. By and large this aim was achieved, the dollar price rising to the low twenties in the spring of 1989. However, in early 1990, once again for political reasons (this time to put pressure on Iraq), Kuwait and the United Arab Emirates [*qv*] overproduced and reduced the price to $11 a barrel. The Iraqi invasion and occupation of Kuwait in early August caused the spot price of oil to reach $28 a barrel within a few weeks, the dollar price briefly rising to the high thirties. An emergency meeting of OPEC allowed members to increase their output beyond their allocated quotas due to the loss of the 4 million barrels a day that had previously been exported by Iraq and Kuwait.

After the Second Gulf War [*qv*] in early 1991, the price fluctuated around $20 until mid-1992, when Kuwait returned to its prewar production levels and resumed its exports. During the next two years the price hovered around $16 a barrel (equivalent to today's $20), only $2 above the prevalent figure in 1978. The reentry of Iraq, albeit on a limited scale, into the oil export market in December 1996 had a depressing effect on prices. They fell sharply in 1998 due to the reduced demand in the Asian market caused by economic down-turn combined with OPEC's decision to increase output. Saudi Arabia played a leading role in securing output cuts by OPEC and such leading non-OPEC producers as Mexico, Norway, Oman, and Russia in 1999, and succeeded in getting the prices in the $22–28 per barrel range. By and large this range held for the next few years, with the price shooting the $30 mark in 2000, and again in late 2002–early 2003.

In terms of the 2001 U.S. dollar, a barrel of oil cost between $10 and $90 during 1861–80. A century later, in 1960, the price was still $11 a barrel. The 1973 Arab-Israeli War and the 1979 Iranian Islamic revolution [*qv*] pushed the price to a peak of $78 in 1980. It then declined to $13 in 1998 (registering a decline of 70 percent in real terms since 1981)—reaching its mid-1950s level—before rising above $30 in 2000 and then falling to $27.

Old Testament: *see* Bible.

Oman:

Official name: Sultanate of Oman

Capital: Muscat [*qv*]

Area: 119,500 sq. miles/309,500 sq. km

Population: 2,714,000 (2002, est.)

Gross domestic product: $20.0 billion (2001, est.)

National currency: Omani Rial (OR); OR 1 = US$2.60 = £1.82 = EUR 2.93 (2001)

Form of government: monarchy

Official language: Arabic [*qv*]

Official religion: Islam [*qv*]

Administrative system: Oman consists of eight governorates, each divided into *vilayats/vilayas* (regions).

Constitution: In 1996 Sultan Qaboos issued the Basic Statute of State, the first such document. It describes Oman as Arab, Islamic, and independent, with its system of government being Sultani (Royal), hereditary in the male descendants of Sayyid Turki ibn Said ibn Sultan. It describes the Sultan as head of State as well as prime minister and supreme commander of the military. He heads a nominated council of ministers. While the constitution provides for the Consultative Council and the Council of State, it has no provision for political parties or trade unions.

Consultative Council: In 1981 the Sultan established a forty-five-member Consultative Council as an advisory body. Ten years later he added fifteen more members and restructured it. The Council was incorporated into the 1996 Basic Statute of State. Initially the Sultan appointed its members from among the nominees selected at the national polls. In 2000 this system was replaced by direct election based on limited franchise. The elected Consultative Council had eighty-three members. Its Speaker is appointed by the Sultan. The chamber, an advisory body, drafts legislation only on social and economic affairs for submission to the appropriate ministry. The Sultan appointed a new Council in 2000.

Council of State: This forty-one-member body, nominated by the Sultan, serves as a liaison between the government and its citizens.

Ethnic composition (2002): Arab 75 percent; South Asian, 22 percent; other, 3 percent.

High officials:

Head of state: Sultan Qaboos ibn Said [*qv*], 1970–

Prime minister: Sultan Qaboos ibn Said

Speaker of the Consultative Council: Abdullah Ali al Qatabi, 2000–

Speaker of the Council of State: Hamoud Abdullah al Harithi, 2000–

History since ca. 1850: The ruling Aal Bu Said dynasty reached its peak in the 1850s, when its empire extended to the eastern shores of Africa. Its collapse in the following decade so weakened the ruling family that it was overpowered by tribes from the interior. In 1871 the British attacked Muscat and restored the Aal Bu Saids to power. Oman thus became a de facto colony of Britain.

In 1915 the traditional rivalry between the coast and the hinterland resurfaced, and the tribes of the interior, led by the *imam* [*qv*], attacked Muscat. Britain intervened on behalf of the sultan. The subsequent uneasy peace was formalized in 1920 in the Treaty of Sib [*qv*] between Sultan Taimur ibn Faisal [*qv*] and the tribal leaders, who recognized the sultan's authority in external affairs. The treaty guaranteed freedom of movement to the tribes and urban dwellers, with the sultan agreeing not to raise taxes above 5 percent of the value of trade in coastal towns. The signing of a treaty with the imam implied

autonomy for the interior. But its extent became contentious, with the sultan maintaining that the treaty recognized the imamate as autonomous only in local and socioreligious affairs.

The reasonable modus vivendi between the sultan and the tribal chiefs of the interior broke down again in the mid-1950s. Encouraged by Saudi Arabia, which was feuding with Oman over the Buraimi oasis straddling their borders, Imam Ghalib ibn Ali proclaimed the independent Imamate of Oman in 1954. The forces of Sultan Said ibn Taimur [*qv*], armed and led by the British, quelled the uprising. Acting in collusion with the forces of Abu Dhabi [*qv*], they also recovered the area of Buraimi oasis occupied by the Saudis.

In 1957 the imam's brother, Talib ibn Ali, urged on by Saudi Arabia and Egypt, mounted a rebellion in the interior. With the assistance of the British, the sultan reduced the uprising to sporadic guerrilla actions. Claiming that Britain had committed an act of aggression against the Imamate of Oman, Egypt and other Arab states placed the matter before the United Nations. While the U.N. Commission of Inquiry failed to uphold the claim of popular opposition to the sultan, several Arab countries succeeded in persuading the U.N. General Assembly to adopt a resolution demanding the end of British colonial presence in Oman.

During the 1960s, though oil revenues began to rise, Sultan Said showed no sign of spending these funds on building the infrastructure of a modern state. He also faced armed rebellion in the southwestern region of Dhofar, which received an impetus from the victory of the leftist forces in adjoining South Yemen in 1967. The British engineered a coup in July 1970 to replace Said with his only son, Qaboos. Under Qaboos, Oman joined the Arab League [qv] and the United Nations. With the funds provided by oil revenues and subventions by Kuwait and the United Arab Emirates, the new ruler expanded the economic infrastructure and public services. In 1975 the government succeeded in ending the insurgency in Dhofar.

Alone among the Arab Gulf states [qv], Oman showed a willingness for U.S. forces to use its military facilities, especially the ones on its offshore Masirah Island after Britain had withdrawn its forces from it in 1977. Alone among the Arab League members, it refused to cut relations with Egypt after the latter's peace treaty with Israel in 1979. In June 1980 it signed a military cooperation agreement with the United States whereby, in exchange for U.S. military and economic aid, the United States could use Oman's air and naval facilities and conduct military exercises.

Oman joined the Gulf Cooperation Council [qv] in May 1981. Later that year Sultan Qaboos nominated a forty-five-member Consultative Council as an advisory body. Having sided with Iraq in the early phases of the 1980–88 Iran-Iraq War [qv], Oman later adopted a neutral stand. Along with other GCC members it backed Kuwait after the latter's occupation by Iraq in August 1990. It joined the U.S.-led coalition against Iraq in the 1991 Gulf War [qv]. Later that year Sultan Qaboos expanded and restructured the Consultative Council. The arrest of 200 Omanis in 1994 was attributed to the authorities' efforts to curb Islamist militancy. There were increasing signs of popular disaffection at the absence of a written constitu-

tion and the refusal of the Sultan to share his absolute power. In response, Sultan Qaboos promulgated a constitution in late 1996. But it failed to give legislative powers to the Consultative Council. There were riots in Hajar, which were curbed by the military, and student protest erupted at Sultan Qaboos University when the authorities banned meetings. In the first directly elected Consultative Council in 2000, two women won seats. In 2001, Oman renewed its ten-year military access agreement with America. In Washington's war against the Taliban-administered Afghanistan in October 2001, Oman allowed the Pentagon use of its military facilities.

Religious composition (1994 census): Muslim, 54 percent, of which three-quarters Ibadhi [qv], the rest Sunni [qv]; Hindu (mostly expatriates), 28 percent; Christian, 15 percent; other, 3 percent.

Omani Civil War (1963–76): In 1963 the Dhofar region, annexed by the Sultan of Oman in 1876 and covering two-fifths of the sultanate, erupted into a secessionist rebellion. Within two years the uprising had turned into a sustained armed struggle led by the Dhofari Liberation Front (DLF). The leftists' capture of power in adjoining South Yemen in November 1967 gave a boost to the DLF. In September 1968 it decided to extend its revolutionary activities to the rest of Oman and other Gulf states and changed its name to the Popular Front for the Liberation of the Occupied Arab Gulf (PFLOAG) [qv]. Having secured large parts of Dhofar, the PFLOAG launched campaigns against slavery, illiteracy, tribalism, and the oppression of women.

With two-thirds of Dhofar under its control, the PFLOAG extended its guerrilla activity to the Oman region of the sultanate in June 1970. This alarmed the British, the dominant political and commercial power in the country, who engineered a coup in July and replaced the old, inflexible Sultan Said ibn Taimur [qv] with his young son, Qaboos [qv]. Qaboos initiated sociopolitical reform and modernization, and rapid expansion of the military under British aegis. In response, the PFLOAG decided in July 1971 to lower the party's objective of achieving a socialist revolution to that of a national democratic revolution and opened its membership to non-Marxist nationalists. The party was renamed the Popular Front for the Liberation of Oman and the Arab Gulf [qv], but the acronym remained the same (PFLOAG).

The resulting increase in the strength of the PFLOAG enabled it to withstand the repeated offensives that the British-led Omani troops, in conjunction with Britain's counterinsurgency force, the Special Air Service (SAS), mounted between October 1971 and December 1972. By recruiting a large number of Pakistani mercenaries, Sultan Qaboos also increased the size of his military—fivefold to 12,500. He also received generous funding from Saudi Arabia to purchase arms, and Iran loaned him helicopters. When these measures failed to defeat PFLOAG insurgents, Tehran dispatched troops to Dhofar in 1973, and the guerrillas began to suffer as a result of the increased size of their enemy.

In July 1974 the PFLOAG leaders decided to concentrate on Oman and therefore renamed their organization the Popular Front for the Liberation of Oman (PFLO) [qv]. In 1975, while foreign assistance for Oman increased sharply, with Iran injecting more combat troops, Jordan and Egypt sending military advisers, and Saudi Arabia donating money, outside aid for the PFLO dried up. Following the Algiers Accord in March 1975 [qv], Iraq withdrew its backing of the PFLO. With Saudi Arabia offering a rapprochement to South Yemen, the latter ceased to assist the PFLO.

In October 1975 the Omani military, working in conjunction with some 25,000 Iranian troops and the British SAS, launched a major offensive against the PFLO guerrillas, estimated to be 5,000–10,000 strong. By December the Omani government claimed to have crushed the revolutionary movement at the cost of some 400 Omani, British, Iranian, and Jordanian troops. Saudi Arabia helped to negotiate a truce in 1976, whereby an amnesty was offered to those who had fought on the PFLO side.

One Israel: *Israeli political grouping.* Official title: *(Hebrew: Israel Ahat)* Formed on the eve of the 1999 Israeli elections at the behest of Ehud Barak [qv], it consisted of Labor [qv]; Gesher, a small faction formed by David Levy in 1996; and Maimad, a moderate religious faction led by Rabbi Michael Melchior. Barak won the prime ministerial contest, and One Israel won twenty-six Knesset [qv] seats, improving on Labor's nineteen.

One Nation: *Israeli political group.* Official title: *(Hebrew: Am Ahatm)* A party of workers and retirees affiliated to Histadrut [qv], founded by Amir Peretz on the eve of the 1999 parliamentary poll, in which it secured two seats. In the 2003 general election, which it fought on economic issues, its strength rose to three.

Operation Big Pines: *see* Israeli Invasion of Lebanon, 1982.

Operation Desert Fox: Relations of Iraqi President Saddam Hussein [*qv*] with the United Nations Special Commission (UNSCOM) [*qv*] on disarming Iraq of weapons of mass destruction deteriorated when Richard Butler, an Australian disarmament specialist, replaced Rolf Ekeus, a Swedish diplomat, as head of UNSCOM in mid-1997. A crisis with the United Nations in February 1998 was defused by the last-minute intervention by U.N. secretary-general Kofi Annan, who met Saddam in Baghdad [*qv*]. But the agreement lasted only until mid-December when the United States, assisted by the United Kingdom, mounted its four-day Operation Desert Fox after Butler had withdrawn U.N. inspectors from Iraq on the private advice of Peter Burleigh, the U.S. ambassador to the United Nations, without even informing the other Security Council members. The United States fired 415 Cruise and Tomahawk missiles (ninety more than during the Second Gulf War [*qv*]) and dropped 600 laser-guided bombs at 100 Iraqi targets.

China, France, and Russia condemned the U.S.-U.K. action. The breach among the Permanent Five members of the Security Council was so severe that it took a year before the Council adopted a new resolution on the subject—1284 [*qv*]—with China, France, and Russia abstaining. Saddam Hussein's efforts to have the Arab League [*qv*] foreign ministers' meeting in January 1999 condemn the Anglo-American action and demand the lifting of sanctions on Iraq failed. Equally, Washington's attempt to get the Gulf monarchies involved in overthrowing Saddam Hussein got nowhere.

Operation Desert Sabre: *see* Gulf War II.

Operation Desert Shield: *see* Gulf War II.

Operation Desert Storm: *see* Gulf War II.

Operation Iraqi Freedom: *see* Gulf War III or Third Gulf War.

Operation Litani: *see* Israeli Invasion of Lebanon, 1978.

Operation Peace in Galilee: *see* Israeli Invasion of Lebanon, 1978.

Organization of Arab Petroleum Exporting Countries: The Organization of Arab Petroleum Exporting Countries (OAPEC) was formed in Kuwait [*qv*] in January 1968 in the aftermath of the Arab defeat in the June 1967 Arab-Israeli War [*qv*], and consisted of Algeria, Iraq, Kuwait, Libya, and Saudi Arabia. Membership of OAPEC required oil to be the main source of national income, and its objective was to safeguard the interests of its members. In 1970 Qatar joined the organization. In 1971, when the condition about oil being the chief source of income was dropped, OAPEC's size rose by four—Bahrain, Egypt, Syria and the United Arab Emirates—bringing its total membership to ten.

During the October 1973 Arab-Israeli War [*qv*], OAPEC members, reacting to U.S. President Richard Nixon's order to airlift weapons to Israel on a massive scale, decided on 17 October to cut output by 5 percent of the September figure and to maintain the same rate of reduction each month until the Israeli forces had withdrawn from all Arab territories occupied during the 1967 war and the Palestinians' legitimate rights had been restored. Consumer countries were categorized as friendly, neutral or hostile to the Arab cause. Friendly nations would be supplied at the September level, neutrals at a reduced level, and hostile ones not at all. OAPEC also confirmed the steep price rise decided earlier by the Organization of Petroleum Exporting Countries (OPEC) [*qv*]. Saudi Arabia ordered a 25 percent cut in its output, then running at 8 million barrels a day, but Iraq ignored the OAPEC decision.

The embargo hurt the United States, reducing its annual gross domestic product by $10–20 billion. Aware of the anticommunist views of the Saudi monarch, Faisal ibn Abdul Aziz [*qv*], Edward Heath, prime minister of Britain (which was not on the Arab oil boycott list), warned him that any prolonged oil squeeze would, by weakening the West, strengthen communism. Egyptian President Anwar Sadat [*qv*], working in conjunction with U.S. Secretary of State Henry Kissinger, convinced Faisal to end the boycott. Faisal and Sadat then prevailed upon the other members of OAPEC to end the five-month embargo on 18 March 1974 as a token of Arab goodwill to the West—even though the Israelis had not withdrawn from anywhere in the Occupied Arab Territories [*qv*] and the legitimate rights of the Palestinian people had not been restored.

Following the Egyptian-Israeli Peace Treaty [*qv*] in 1979, Egypt was suspended from OAPEC's membership. It was readmitted ten years later.

Even though its output was more than 700,000 barrels a day in the early 1990s, Oman did not apply to join OAPEC.

During the Iraqi occupation of Kuwait in 1990–91, the OAPEC headquarters was moved to Cairo [*qv*]. After the Second Gulf War [*qv*] the headquarters returned to Kuwait.

Total OAPEC output in 2001 was 28 percent of the global aggregate.

Organization of Islamic Conference: *see* Islamic Conference Organization.

Organization of Petroleum Exporting Countries: The Organization of Petroleum Exporting Countries (OPEC) [*qv*] is an international body to coordinate the hydrocarbon policies of its constituents. Following a meeting in Baghdad [*qv*] in September 1960 of the representatives of Iran [*qv*], Iraq [*qv*], Kuwait [*qv*], Saudi Arabia, and Venezuela, it was formally inaugurated in January 1961 in Geneva (the headquarters being moved to Vienna in 1965). Its subsequent members included Qatar [*qv*] (1961), Indonesia and Libya (1962), Abu Dhabi [*qv*] (1967), which transferred to the United Arab Emirates [*qv*] (UAE) in 1974, Algeria (1969), Nigeria (1971), Ecuador (1973), and Gabon (1975).

The major oil companies were opposed to OPEC's aims and policies, outlined in June 1962. The OPEC document stated that until the final goal of nationalization of hydrocarbon resources had been achieved, the government of a member state should ensure that the contracted arrangements with the concessionaires specify maximum governmental participation and control over all aspects of their operations. It called on the member states to set a tax reference price and gradually reduce the area of existing concessions. The oil majors were particularly opposed to OPEC's demand that they must maintain accounts as stipulated by the local government and make them available at all times for official inspection.

During the period 1948–60 the average rate of return on the capital of oil corporations operating in the Gulf [*qv*], producing nearly a third of the global output in 1960, was 111 percent. In 1968 British Petroleum, Royal Dutch-Shell and five U.S. oil majors—Exxon, Gulf, Mobil, SOCAL, and Texaco—together controled 77.9 percent of world's oil production, 60.9 percent of refining and 55.6 percent of the marketing facilities. But with many independent U.S. petroleum corporations, as well as Japanese and Italian companies, offering favorable terms to the producing countries and acquiring an increasingly important role in the industry, the situation changed.

In 1970 Libya's year-old republican regime imposed production cuts on oil companies as a pressure tactic to secure higher taxes and royalties. To offset the ripple effect, the oil majors negotiated with Iran, Iraq, and Saudi Arabia as the representatives of all Gulf [*qv*] producer territories, reaching a satisfactory arrangement in February 1971. In October 1972 the national oil companies of Abu Dhabi, Kuwait, Qatar, and Saudi Arabia acquired 25 percent of the shares of the foreign concessionaires, with an agreement for a further 2.5 percent annual increase in shareholding for the next decade.

In September 1973, aware of the energy crisis facing their main Western consumer countries, and intent on securing compensation for the latest devaluation of the U.S. dollar (the currency used in oil transactions), OPEC members decided to double the price from $2.55 to $5.09 a barrel. The talks with the oil majors on the subject scheduled for October were postponed due to the outbreak of the Arab-Israeli War [*qv*]. The hawkish stand taken by the Organization of Arab Petroleum Exporting Countries (OAPEC)

[*qv*] during the conflict led to the earlier OPEC price rise remaining in force without the consent of the oil majors. In late November Algeria raised the price of its crude from $4.80 to $9.25 a barrel; and three weeks later the oil ministers of the eight Gulf states pushed the figure to $11.65, effective from 1 January 1974. This became the price of OPEC, producing 55 percent of the world's oil. Thus within three months the price jumped from $2.55 to $11.65, with the host government's average takings per barrel rising from $1.38 to $7.

To offset inflation in the West and the concomitant diminution in the value of the U.S. dollar, OPEC raised the oil price thrice in five years, taking it to about $14 a barrel in mid-1977. The comparative stability of price and supplies was shaken in late 1978 by the political turmoil in Iran. Responding to a call by Ayatollah Ruhollah Khomeini [*qv*], the oil workers of Iran went on strike, halting Iranian oil exports, then running at 4.5 million barrels a day. The disruption of supplies in the winter of 1978–79 pushed up the price to $28 a barrel. After the price rise in 1980, when OPEC produced 45 percent of the global total, its unity became frayed mainly because of the outbreak of war between its two important members, Iran and Iraq. Falling demand in the West led OPEC to reduce output and lower prices from 1983 onward. The flooding of the market by Kuwait and Saudi Arabia in 1986, aimed at weakening Iran in its war with Iraq, lowered the price to below $10 a barrel in April and severely damaged OPEC's clout. With the departure in 1992 of Ecuador, following its failure to obtain a higher quota, OPEC's membership stood at twelve. Ecuador's example was followed by Gabon in 1996, and this reduced OPEC's size to eleven members—with all, except Venezuela, being Muslim majority states. In December 1996, when Iraq reentered the world oil market after an absence of over eight years, OPEC made it exempt from its quota system to enable it to repair and rebuild its shattered infrastructure. OPEC's decision in late 1997 to increase its overall output by 10 percent at the behest of Saudi Arabia caused a dramatic drop in price, which fell below $10 a barrel in early 1999. Subsequent cuts in production lifted the price to above $34 in March 2000. Six months later, at the OPEC summit hosted by the current chairman, President Hugo Chavez of Venezuela, in Caracas, to celebrate OPEC's fortieth anniversary, the leaders resolved to promote market stability by developing "remunerative, stable and competitive" pricing policies. The result was an agreement to maintain the price of an oil barrel in the $22–28 range.

The main weakness of OPEC is that it lacks the authority to enforce the quotas it decides for its members every quarter. There is also an inbuilt conflict between OPEC members with (a) large populations—Algeria, Indonesia, Iran, Iraq and Nigeria, and (b) small populations and large reserves—Kuwait, Qatar, Saudi Arabia, and the UAE. Those in category (b) are more interested in extracting as much oil as soon as possible—even if that lowers price—whereas those in category (a) want to restrict output and achieve higher prices in order to improve the living standards of their people. Over the years, buffeted by wild price swings, the two groups have managed to devise a compro-

mise. And to offset low prices of oil, OPEC has made successful deals with such leading non-OPEC producers as Mexico, Norway, Oman, and Russia to cut output in order to improve prices.

Organization of the Islamic Revolution in the Arabian Peninsula: In the course of rioting in late November 1979 during the Ashura [*qv*] processions by Shias [*qv*] in the eastern region of Saudi Arabia [*qv*], the existence of the Shia-dominated Organization of the Islamic Revolution in the Arabian Peninsula (OIRAP) came to light. Buoyed by the emergence of a Shia regime under Ayatollah Ruhollah Khomeini [*qv*] in Iran [*qv*], Saudi Arabian Shias, concentrated along the eastern seaboard, broke the long-enforced ban on the celebration of Ashura and turned the processions into pro-Khomeini demonstrations in important urban centers. The authorities deployed 20,000 National Guard [*qv*] troops to suppress the rioting. But sporadic demonstrations and pitched battles between government forces and Shia militants continued for two months, leading to the death of fifty-seven guards and ninety-nine Shias, and the arrest of about 6,000 people.

Despite the repression suffered by the OIRAP, with its leader, Said Saffran, forced into exile in Iran, it continued to operate secretly. Its adherents made a point of contacting Iranian pilgrims during the *hajj* [*qv*] in order to sustain their views and clandestine organization. Saffran founded a journal in Iran, and continued to broadcast Islamic commentaries against the Saudi royal family. These became vociferous when, following the killing of 402 people, most of them Iranian pilgrims, during the hajj in 1987,

Iran broke off diplomatic relations with Saudi Arabia.

A decade later, when relations between Iran and Saudi Arabia had improved to the extent of Saudi Arabia backing the idea of Iran hosting the triennial summit of the Islamic Conference Organization [qv], the OIRAP became dormant.

Oriental Jews: The term applied to non-Ladino-speaking Jews [qv] from the Arab countries, Iran, India, or Central Asia. In biblical times their ancestors left Palestine [qv] for North Africa or the Middle East [qv]—from where they migrated to Central Asia or the Indian subcontinent. While their religion set them apart from their hosts, they underwent cultural assimilation and adopted the local language as their own. In the late 1960s the 1.5 million Oriental Jews formed about one-ninth of the world's Jewry. They were the dominant group among the Jews in Palestine under the Ottomans. But since the Jewish aliyas [qv] into Palestine between 1882–1939 did not include Oriental Jews (except 45,000 from North Yemen), their proportion in the Jewish community in Palestine declined to about one-fifth of the total on the eve of the Second World War. However, following the 1948–49 Arab-Israeli War [qv], Oriental Jews began to arrive in Israel in large numbers.

Given their higher birth rate, within a generation they formed half of the Jewish population and became a majority during the next decade. But due to the influx of 540,000 Jews from the former Soviet Union from 1990–94, they lost this position to Ashkenazim [qv], a trend that continued with further immigration of the Jews from

that region. Though only the Jews who immigrated from the countries surrounding the Mediterranean followed Sephardic [qv] rituals and practices, those who came from such countries as Yemen, Iraq, and India, with a history of different rituals and practices, often affiliated to the Sephardic chief rabbinate in order to receive public funds for their newly established synagogues [qv].

As for the government, it classifies those Jews born abroad (76 percent of the total population) in its annual *Statistical Abstract of Israel* according to the continent(s) of origin: Europe-America-Oceania (meaning, for all practical purposes, Ashkenazim) and Asia, Africa (taken together, meaning Sephardim). Strictly speaking, the term "Oriental Jew" is geographical whereas the label "Sephardim" is sectarian. However, to describe someone originating in Morocco, Algeria, or Tunisia—part of the Arab West [qv]—as "Oriental" is inexact. The most logical, and ethnically correct, term is "Arab Jew" [qv], which parallels "European Jew" or "American Jew." *See also* Arab Jews and Sephardim.

Orthodox Christians/Church *(Greek: derivative of* orthodoxos, *right opinion):* Official title: Orthodox Catholic Church. Also known as the Orthodox Eastern Church or the Eastern Church. The term applies, literally, to those who follow the right doctrine and not a heretical or heterodox one. As for church denominations, the term applies to the historic churches of Eastern Europe and Southwest Asia that split from the Western Church, based in Rome. They accepted the decrees of the first seven ecumenical councils, held between A.D. 325 and A.D. 787. But the drift between the Western Church led by the Pope in Rome, with Latin as the official language, and the (Orthodox) Eastern Church, led by the Patriarch based in Constantinople (now Istanbul), with Greek as the official language, became unbridgeable with the challenge to papal authority by Patriarch Photius in the ninth century A.D., and irreversible with the mutual excommunication of the Patriarch of Constantinople, Michael Cerularius, and Pope Leo IX in 1054. The Crusades (1095–1272) further embittered feelings between the two sides, and numerous attempts at reconciliation failed.

The Orthodox churches are all noted for their rich liturgical practices and devotional use of icons, but the relationship of various churches with one another is complex. The term Greek Church is applied to the Church of Greece, churches whose liturgy is in Greek, and those affiliated to the patriarchate of Constantinople. There are six other national churches in the (Orthodox) Eastern community: the Churches of Bulgaria, Cyprus, Poland, Rumania, Russia, and Yugoslavia, the most important being the Russian [*qv*].

Orthodox Christians, Armenian: *see* Armenian Orthodox Church.

Orthodox Christians, Greek: *see* Greek Orthodox Church.

Orthodox Christians, Gregorian: *see* Armenian Orthodox Church.

Orthodox Christians, Russian: *see* Russian Orthodox Church.

Orthodox Christians, Syrian: Also known as the Jacobite Church. Unlike other Orthodox churches, the Syrian Orthodox Church rejects the doctrine of the fourth ecumenical council at Chalcedon (A.D. 451), which defined Christ as one person with two natures (human and divine), and accepts that Christ had one nature, as in the monophystic doctrine. The Church was founded in the sixth century by Jacob Baradaeus, assisted by Empress Theodara. Its head is the Patriarch of Antioch and all the East, based in Damascus [*qv*]; its rite is the Antiochene [*qv*]; and its liturgical language is Syriac. The church has a following in Syria, Iraq, and India.

Orthodox Eastern Church: *see* Orthodox Christians/Church.

Orthodox Judaism: Orthodox Jews are those who follow strictly traditional beliefs and practices. They believe among other things that Halacha [*qv*] does not change with time, and that only exceptionally well-qualified authorities can interpret it. They engage in daily worship as well as participate in traditional prayers and ceremonies, study Torah [*qv*], and observe dietary laws and the Sabbath [*qv*]. They separate men and women in the synagogue, where music during the communal service is banned. Orthodox rabbis have successfully challenged the legitimacy of certain non-Orthodox marriages, divorces, and conversions in Israel [*qv*]. In 1998, of the 13.5 million Jews [*qv*] worldwide, one million were Orthodox. Of these, about a half lived in Israel, forming 10 percent of the Jewish population there.

Oslo I Accord: *see* Israeli-Palestine Organization Accord (1993).

Oslo II Accord: *see* Washington Accord (1995).

Oslo Accords: The term includes Oslo Accord I [*qv*] and Oslo Accord II [*qv*].

Oz, Amos (1939–): *Israeli writer* Born Amos Klausner of a scholarly family in

Jerusalem [*qv*], Oz left the city to live in a kibbutz and pursued his further education from there. His first collection of short stories, *Lands of the Jackals* (1965), and his first novel, *Another Place* (1966), are set in kibbutz surroundings. His novella *Unto Death* (1971) is an allegory about a group of crusaders intent on exorcising the Jew among them. In *My Michael* (1972) he uses the central character, Hannah Gonen, as a metaphor for Jerusalem between 1948 and 1967. In *Touch the Water, Touch the Wind* (1973) Oz returns to the kibbutz with the story of two Jews [*qv*] who had survived the Holocaust. His other novels are *Perfect Peace* (1982); *Black Box* (1987), where he argues that ideological conviction is a crutch an individual leans on when his inner world collapses; *To Know a Woman* (1991), about a former Mossad [*qv*] agent who scoured the world deciphering codes and unraveling plots, but failed to understand his wife; and *Fima* (1993), which centers on a Jewish Walter Mitty, a man with big dreams but a shaky grip on reality.

A political activist, Oz was close to Pinchas Lavon [*qv*] and joined his Min HaYesod group. He was injured in the 1956 Suez War [*qv*] and the June 1967 Arab-Israeli War [*qv*]. Following the latter conflict he opposed those who wanted to annex the Occupied Arab Territories [*qv*]. One of the cofounders of the dovish Moked (1973) and Shelli (1977) groups, he was prominent in the Peace Now [*qv*] movement, which emerged in late 1977 after Egyptian President Anwar Sadat's [*qv*] visit to Jerusalem. On the eve of the 1981 general election, he returned to the Labor [*qv*] fold and campaigned for it.

His collection of personal, political and literary essays and articles have appeared as books under the following titles: *In the Powerful Blue Light* (1979), *In the Land of Israel* (1983), *Perfect Peace* (1993), *Israel, Palastine and Peace* (1994), and *Under this Blazing Light* (1996).

His novel *Panther in the Basement* (1998) centers around a 12-year-old jewish boy in Palestine during the last year of the British Mandate, when Oz was nine. *The Same Sea* (2002), a prose poem, dwells on the life and times of Albert, an accoutant, and is the tale of family love and erotic longing.

His books have been translated into many languages.

P

Pahlavi, Muhammad Reza Shah

(1919–80): *Shah-en-shah (Emperor) of Iran, 1941–79* Born in Tehran [*qv*], Pahlavi was educated at a private school in Switzerland and the Tehran Military Academy. Pahlavi succeeded his father, Reza Shah Pahlavi [*qv*], in September 1941, who abdicated in his favor when, angered at his neutrality in the Second World War, British and Soviet troops began to march toward Tehran. Pahlavi allowed Iranian territory to be used by the Allies for supplies to the Soviet Union to bolster its capacity to fight Nazi Germany. At home he placated the clerical establishment, which had been alienated by his father. It was only after the Soviet troops had withdrawn in May 1946 and the Iranian forces had quelled autonomous governments in Kurdistan [*qv*] and Azerbaijan

[*qv*] in December that Pahlavi was able to exercise authority over all of Iran [*qv*].

Following a failed assassination attempt on him in February 1949, Pahlavi imposed martial law and banned the Tudeh Party [*qv*]. However, in his tussle with the nationalist leader, Premier Muhammad Mussadiq [*qv*], Pahlavi yielded to parliament's will to nationalize the British-owned Anglo-Iranian Oil Company (AIOC) in 1951. The ensuing power struggle led to the flight of Pahlavi to Rome on 16 August 1953. But three days later, aided by the U.S. Central Intelligence Agency (CIA) and royalist military officers, Pahlavi staged a comeback.

This inaugurated a period in Iran's history when the United States replaced Britain as the dominant Western power. American companies were preeminent in the Western oil consortium, which was given a contract to run Iran's petroleum industry on behalf of the National Iranian Oil Company (NIOC). In 1955 Pahlavi took his country into the Western-sponsored Baghdad Pact [*qv*], and two years later he subscribed to the Eisenhower Doctrine [*qv*]. At home he established a political police force under military officers, later called Savak (*Sazman-e Amniyat Va Ittilaat-e Keshvar*, Organization of National Security and Intelligence), with strong ties with the CIA, Israel's Mossad [*qv*] and Turkey's National Intelligence Service.

Under pressure from U.S. President John F. Kennedy (r. 1961–63), Pahlavi began a land reform program in 1961. He dissolved parliament and ruled by decree. This led to increased opposition, including from Ayatollah Ruhollah Khomeini [*qv*]. In January 1963 Pahlavi launched a six-point White Revolution [*qv*] and repressed the groups

that called for a boycott of the referendum on it. It won 91 percent approval. His conflict with Khomeini reached a climax in June and led to a nationwide uprising. Pahlavi crushed it, reportedly causing thousands of deaths. Following a general election in September 1963, he eased his grip over the nation slightly. But when, after his release from prison in April 1964, Khomeini resumed his opposition, Pahlavi expelled him from Iran in November.

Pahlavi further strengthened Iran's economic, military, and cultural ties with the West. To persuade the Western oil consortium to increase its output, his government gave further concessions to it. The two ambitious Five-Year Plans between 1963 and 1972 accelerated economic development in agriculture and industry and increased literacy. In October 1971 Pahlavi celebrated 2,500 years of "unbroken" monarchy in Iran (a claim disputed by most experts) at the ancient capital of Persepolis near Shiraz [*qv*].

On the 10th anniversary of the White Revolution in January 1973 Pahlavi announced the nationalization of the Western oil consortium. The petroleum price jump in 1973–74 boosted Iran's export revenue, and fired the grandiose ambitions of Pahlavi. The inflated Five Year Plan of 1973–77, involving *inter alia* high expenditure on Western arms purchases, overheated the economy, causing the rapid migration of rural workers to cities, high inflation and widespread corruption.

With all avenues of secular opposition blocked by Pahlavi's regime, more and more Iranians turned to the mosque and clergy to express their growing discontent. Under pressure from newly elected U.S. President

Jimmy Carter (r. 1977–81), Pahlavi began to moderate his repression of the opposition. This emboldened the dissenters, both secular and religious. Guided by Khomeini, based since 1965 in Najaf [qv], Iraq, religious and secular opposition forces banded together to mount a popular revolutionary movement that was united in its demand for Pahlavi's deposition and influential enough to immobilize the vital oil industry and cause the disintegration of Pahlavi's 413,000-strong military. Pahlavi's last-minute ploy to appoint a dissenter, Shahpur Bakhtiar [qv], as prime minister failed.

On 16 January 1979 Pahlavi left Iran, ostensibly for a holiday in Aswan, Egypt. Pahlavi was allowed to enter the United States clandestinely in October for medical treatment. Iran demanded Pahlavi's extradition, which was refused. In March 1980 Egyptian President Anwar Sadat [qv] invited him to Cairo [qv]. He died there four months later, leaving behind his widow, Farah, and their only son, Reza Cyrus.

Pahlavi, Reza Shah (1878–1944): *Shah-en-shah (Emperor) of Iran, 1925–41* Son of a military officer in a village in northern Mazandaran province, Pahlavi joined the army as a youth. He rose through the ranks, becoming commander of the elite Cossack Brigade with the rank of colonel. At Britain's behest, Pahlavi overthrew the government in February 1921 and forced the monarch, Ahmad Shah Qajar, to appoint Pahlavi's nominee as premier. Pahlavi became war minister, and, later, premier as well. By crushing tribal and other revolts he raised his popular standing. In October 1925, at his instigation, parliament deposed Ahmad Shah Qajar and appointed Pahlavi

as regent. Two months later a freshly elected constituent assembly proclaimed Pahlavi (who had chosen Pahlavi [qv] as his surname) *shah-en-shah* (king of kings) of Iran.

Pahlavi centralized and modernized the state, creating a national civil service and police force. He quickened the pace of economic development, fueled by oil revenues. He unilaterally canceled the economic privileges given to European nations over the past century and increased tariffs on imports. He pressured the Anglo-Persian Oil Company in 1932 to increase its oil royalties and reduced its concessionaire area by 80 percent. To create a national Iranian identity out of many ethnic ones at the popular level, he required all males, by law, to wear Western-style dress and a round peaked cap. He ordered all public places and educational institutions to admit women. He reduced the powers and scope of the Islamic law courts and strengthened the secular, state courts. By manipulating elections he reduced the share of clerics in parliament from 40 percent in the Sixth Majlis [qv] (1926–28) to none in the Eleventh Majlis (1936–38). The building of 14,000 miles of roads and Trans-Iranian Railway by August 1938 boosted industrialization.

Following the rise of Adolf Hitler in Germany in 1933, Pahlavi tried to use Berlin as a counterpoint to the commercial and political dominance of London and Moscow. By the time the Second World War erupted in September 1939, Germany accounted for nearly half of Iran's foreign trade. Pahlavi declared Iran's neutrality in the conflict. The Allies saw the German invasion of the Soviet Union in June 1941 as part of a pincer movement, its other arm being the German thrust into

North Africa. In late August Soviet and British troops invaded Iran at five points. Fearing an imminent march of Soviet troops into Tehran, Pahlavi abdicated on 16 September in favor of his eldest son, Muhammad Reza [*qv*]. He left for the British-ruled island of Mauritius, and then for South Africa.

Pahlavi dynasty: Following a law passed in the spring of 1925, which required all Iranian citizens to acquire a birth certificate and a surname, Reza Khan (later Shah) [*qv*], then Iran's prime minister and commander in chief, chose for his family the name Pahlavi [*qv*], the language of Persians [*qv*] for seven centuries. The Pahlavi rule lasted until January 1979, when Muhammad Reza Shah Pahlavi [*qv*] left the country. He died in exile the following year.

Pahlavi language: Pahlavi evolved in the second century B.C. under the rule of the kings of Parthia, modern northeast Iran [*qv*]. Its alphabet, developed from Aramaic, was written from right to left. It was the principal language of Persians from the third to the tenth century A.D., and the official language of the Sassanians (r. A.D. 226–640). Zoroastrian [*qv*] literature was written in Pahlavi.

Palestine: *(Greek:* Palaistina, *derivative of* Pleshet, *Land of Philistines in Hebrew)* Also known as the Holy Land as it is sacred to Jews [*qv*], Christians [*qv*], and Muslims [*qv*].

Inhabitants and conquerors:

Canaanites and Philistines, before 1250 B.C. and from 1250–1030 B.C.
Israelites, 1030–586 B.C.
Babylonians, 586–38 B.C.
Persians, 538–332 B.C.
Greeks, 332–166 B.C.
Maccebeans (Jews), 166–63 B.C.

(Pagan) Romans, 63 B.C.–A.D. 323
(Christian) Romans, A.D. 323–614
Persians, A.D. 614–28
(Christian) Byzantine Romans, A.D. 628–637
(Muslim) Arabs, A.D. 637 –1072
(Muslim) Turks, 1072–1092
(Muslim) Arabs, 1092–1099
(Christian) Kingdom of Jerusalem, 1100–1187
(Muslim) Arabs, 1187–1517
(Muslim) Turks/Ottomans, 1517–1917
(Christian) British, 1918–1948

History:

In the second century A.D. the Roman emperors called the southern third of their province of Syria, including former Judea [*qv*], Syria Palestina. There has been much variation in the boundaries of Palestine, which has been ruled by Egyptians, Assyrians, Israelites, Babylonians, Persians, Greeks under Alexander the Great and his successors, the Ptolemies and Seleucids, Maccebeans (Jews), Byzantine Romans, Ummayyads, Abbasids, Fatimids, Crusaders, Ayubids, Mamelukes, Ottomans, and British.

Under the Ottomans (r. 1517–1917) there was no single administrative unit called Palestine. What was to emerge as Palestine under British mandate (area 10,435 sq. miles/27,027 sq. km) was divided into three parts under the Ottomans: the southern zone called the *sanjak* (district) of Jerusalem [*qv*], the northern area as part of the *vilayat* (province) of Beirut; and Jerusalem and its suburbs administered directly by Constantinople (now Istanbul). Yet Britain's Balfour Declaration [*qv*] of November 1917 referred to the "establishment in Palestine of a National Home for the Jewish people." The

Ottoman offensive against the Allies in Palestine in 1915 had made London realize the strategic importance of Palestine as a buffer to safeguard Egypt and the Suez Canal [*qv*], Britain's lifeline to its empire in India. Therefore Britain insisted on, and acquired, a mandate—a variant of trusteeship—over Palestine at the meeting of the Supreme Council of the League of Nations in San Remo, Italy, in April 1920. Approved by the League in July 1922, the mandate went into effect in September 1923.

Instead of preparing Palestine for independence—something London had in mind for Iraq—Britain contrived to hold on to it, making full use of the Balfour Declaration, which had been incorporated into the mandate. The discovery of oil in Iraq in 1927 gave further impetus to the British to consolidate their grip over Palestine, which was a gateway to the Iraqi oil fields through the British protectorate of Transjordan [*qv*] (now Jordan).

As a result, the percentage of Jews [*qv*] in the Palestinian population rose from eight in 1918 to eighteen in 1931. The fifth (Jewish) *aliya* [*qv*], from 1932 to May 1939, brought a further 225,000 Jewish immigrants into the country. Among other things this led to an Arab uprising that lasted from 1936–39 and resulted in the death of 3,232 Arabs, 329 Jews and 135 Britons. Responding to this, and anxious to retain Arab goodwill in the region and access to the crucial oil fields in Iran in the increasingly likely event of war with Germany, Britain's White Paper of May 1939 limited Jewish immigration to 75,000 over the next five years, and offered an outline of an independent, binational state in Palestinian by 1949. Earlier, in 1937, the Arabs had rejected the Peel Commission's

recommendation to partition Palestine, creating a Jewish state on the coastal plain and Galilee, and an Arab state to be attached to Transjordan.

Tensions were eased by the Second World War, in which both sides cooperated with Britain, with 43,000 Jews (of both sexes) joining the Allied military and 10,000 of them becoming part of the British Nile Army. After the war the Anglo-American Commission on Palestine recommended in April 1946 that British should continue the mandate. The decision of the Zionist Organization [*qv*] in December to demand an independent Jewish state in Palestine ended whatever hopes London had of solving the problem on its own. It therefore placed the issue before the General Assembly of the United Nations. Its Special Committee on Palestine [*qv*] recommended in August 1947 that Palestine be partitioned—with 45.4 percent of the area going to the Arabs, who made up 70 percent of the population; and 53.5 percent to the Jews, who constituted 30 percent of the population and owned 6 percent of the land. The remaining 1.1 percent, covering Jerusalem and its suburb, was to be placed under international control.

On 29 November the U.N. General Assembly adopted Resolution 181, specifying partition, by thirty-three votes (including the eight-strong Soviet bloc) to thirteen, with twelve abstentions (including Britain). The Arab states challenged the right of the U.N. General Assembly to partition a country against the wishes of the majority of its inhabitants, proposing that the International Court of Justice should rule on the matter. But their proposal was defeated by twenty-one votes to twenty in the General

Assembly. The Jews accepted the partition plan warmly, the Arabs rejected it angrily. Interethnic violence erupted immediately and intensified as Britain's withdrawal date (15 May 1948) approached. By that date some 300,000 Arabs had fled from the areas allocated to the Jews by the U.N. partition plan. After the State of Israel had been proclaimed on 14 May 1948, fighting broke out between the Arab armies and the Zionist forces. *See* Arab-Israeli War I.

Palestine Liberation Army: The Palestine Liberation Army (PLA), the military wing of the Palestine Liberation Organization (PLO) [*qv*], was established in 1964. It was posted in different Arab countries, including Egypt and Syria. Its tank units, stationed in Syria, advanced into north Jordan during the fighting between the PLO and the Jordanian army in September 1970. Lacking air cover from Syria, they retreated when attacked by the Jordanian air force.

After the PLO moved to Beirut [*qv*] in 1972, the PLA consisted of 8,000–10,000 troops, organized into three brigades, two of which were integrated into the Syrian army. In the Lebanese Civil War [*qv*], between October 1975 and January 1976 Syrian President Hafiz Assad [*qv*] dispatched two brigades of the Syrian-officered PLA from Damascus [*qv*] to Lebanon to help the PLO-Lebanese National Movement [*qv*] alliance. In June, under orders from Damascus, these brigades changed sides and backed the right-wing Maronite [*qv*] forces. When Syria redeployed its peacekeeping forces in Lebanon in early 1980, it ceded many of their positions to the PLA. After the June 1982 Israeli invasion [*qv*], the Palestinian forces that left Beirut in early September included 3,500 PLA troops.

Following the break between PLO Chairman Yasser Arafat [*qv*] and Assad in 1983, the PLA in Syria became estranged from the mainstream PLO. In late 1983 the PLA units, backed by the Syrians, encircled Arafat's 5,000 commandos in Tripoli [*qv*], Lebanon, and defeated them. The 8,144 PLO commandos who had been dispersed from Beirut in 1982 to Tunisia, Libya, North Yemen, Jordan, and Iraq were reconstituted as the Palestine National Liberation Army (PNLA), with the host country supervising them. A decade later the strength of the PNLA was put at 11,000. They were stationed in Algeria, Egypt, Iraq, Jordan, Lebanon, Libya, Sudan, and Yemen. Another 4,500 troops, still bearing the old name of Palestine Liberation Army and based in Syria, had nothing to do with the PNLA. Following the Israeli-PLO Accord [*qv*] in September 1993, a minority of the PNLA ranks, having retrained as policemen in Egypt, were recruited into the 10,500-strong police force of the Palestinian Authority (PA) [*qv*]. The estimated strength of Palestinian troops stationed in other Arab countries was 8,000. Later most of them returned to the Palestinian areas controlled by the PA.

Palestine Liberation Organization: An umbrella body, the Palestine Liberation Organization (PLO) was set up in early 1964, to enable Palestinians to play their part in liberating Palestine [*qv*] and determining their own future. The decision to form the PLO was taken at a summit of the Arab League [*qv*], which, by virtue of an annex to its charter, had assumed the right to select an Arab Palestinian to take part in its work. The PLO held its first congress in May–June 1964 in East Jerusalem [*qv*], then under Jordanian control, where it adopted the Palestine National Charter [*qv*], which called for the establishment of a democratic and secular state in the Palestine constituted by the British mandate. Each of the affiliated bodies was represented on the Palestine National Council (PNC) [*qv*], which elected a central council and an executive committee.

The PLO's importance increased in the aftermath of the defeat suffered by the Arab states in the June 1967 Arab-Israeli War [*qv*]. A change in the charter in 1968, which declared armed struggle to be the only way to liberate Palestine, paved the way for the affiliation of radical groups. In 1969 Yasser Arafat [*qv*], leader of Fatah [*qv*], the largest of the parties affiliated to the PLO, became its chairman, replacing Yahya Hamuda, who had taken over from Ahmad Shuqairi [*qv*] after the June 1967 war. Following the Arab-Israeli War of October 1973 [*qv*], the PNC adopted the idea of a Palestinian state in the Occupied Territories [*qv*] as a transient stage for the liberation of all mandate Palestine in June 1974. Later that year the Arab League recognized the PLO as the sole representative of the Palestinian people and granted it membership in the League.

Arafat participated in a debate on the Palestine question at the United Nations General Assembly in mid-November 1974. On 22 November U.N. General Assembly Resolution 3236, describing the PLO as "the representative of the Palestinian people," reaffirmed the Palestinians' right to self-determination and national independence and the right of Palestinian refugees to return to their homes and property. The motion was carried by eighty-nine votes to eight,

with thirty-seven abstentions. The PLO was given observer status at the United Nations by ninety-five votes to seventeen, with nineteen abstentions. Dr. Zehdi Terzi became the PLO's first representative to the United Nations, and he was invited to a U.N. Security Council session on the Palestinian issue in December to participate in the debate. On 22 January 1975 the U.N. Security Council endorsed the General Assembly's stand by adopting a resolution affirming the Palestinians' right to establish an independent state. But the resolution was vetoed by the U.S. administration of President Gerald Ford (1974–77).

By the late 1970s the PLO had won the formal recognition of over 100 countries, far more than Israel. Its annual budget of $500 million consisted of $350 million in grants by oil-rich Arab states and $150 million in indirect Palestine taxes collected by the Arab states, mainly in the Gulf [*qv*], all of which were paid into the Palestine National Fund [*qv*]. It commanded some 23,000 armed guerrillas and 8,000–10,000 troops of the Palestine Liberation Army (PLA). The groups affiliated to the PLO were the Arab Liberation Front, the Democratic Front for the Liberation of Palestine [*qv*], Fatah [*qv*], the Palestine Communist Party [*qv*], the Popular Front for the Liberation of Palestine [*qv*], the Popular Front for the Liberation of Palestine-General Command [*qv*], the Popular Struggle Front, and Saiqa [*qv*]. The PLO's affiliates also included fourteen organizations for students, workers, women, journalists, lawyers, doctors, etc.

Following the Israeli invasion of Lebanon [*qv*] in June 1982, the PLO, including its commandos and PLA troops, were evacuated from Beirut and dispersed to several Arab countries. The PLO headquarters was moved to Tunis. Here its policies became progressively moderate. Yet the Israelis bombed the PLO headquarters on 1 October 1985, killing seventy-one people but missing their main target, Arafat. After the eruption of intifada [qv] in the Gaza Strip [qv] in December 1987, the PLO backed it, and its adherents in the Occupied Territories became part of the United National Leadership of the Uprising [qv].

Following the declaration on 15 November 1988 by the PNC of the independence and establishment of the State of Palestine "on our Palestinian land," on the basis of the U.N. General Assembly's Partition Resolution 181 of November 1947, 70 of the 103 countries that had recognized the PLO accorded it full diplomatic status. In accordance with the resolution adopted by the PNC on the same day, Arafat, named president of the State of Palestine, renounced the use of violence to achieve the PLO's aim, and accepted the idea of Palestinian self-determination in coexistence with Israel.

In December Arafat addressed the U.N. General Assembly, specially convened in Geneva, to reiterate the new PLO position. There was no positive response from Israel, which was on the verge of a rising tide of Jewish immigration from the Soviet Union that was to push the number of immigrants from 13,300 in 1988 to 199,500 in 1990. The PLO's policy then became hardline, with Arafat tilting toward Iraqi President Saddam Hussein [qv] and siding with him in his conflict with the United Nations following his invasion of Kuwait in August 1990. Saddam linked Iraqi's future withdrawal from Kuwait with Israel's evacuation of the Occupied Arab Territories [qv], and this stance had the backing of the Palestinians in the West Bank [qv] and Gaza [qv]. Arafat's support of Saddam resulted in the end of grants for the PLO from the oil-rich Gulf states [qv], a near fatal blow to its finances.

Chastened by the defeat of Iraq in the Second Gulf War [qv] in early 1991, the PLO backed the idea of a Middle East Peace Conference [pv], where Palestinians were to be included in a joint Jordanian-Palestinian delegation. Though this delegation was to exclude any PLO members, the organization was active behind the scenes before and after the conference, which was held in Madrid in October 1991. The subsequent bilateral talks between the Israeli and Jordanian-Palestinian (later functioning separately) delegations made little progress.

Once Israel, now led by a Labor [qv] government, had lifted its ban on contact with the PLO in January 1993, the scene was set for secret talks between the two sides. These took place in Norway. The resulting Oslo Accord [qv], based on mutual recognition of Israel and the PLO (as the representative of the Palestinian people) and providing for limited autonomy for Palestinians in the Gaza Strip and the West Bank town of Jericho [qv], was signed in Washington on 13 September 1993.

Of the ten groups then affiliated to the PLO—the Arab Liberation Front (leader Mahmud Ismail), the Democratic Front for the Liberation of Palestine, the Democratic Palestinian Union (DPU) (leader Yasser Abdu Rabbo), Fatah, the Palestine People's Party (PPP) [qv] (leader Suleiman Najab), the Palestine Liberation Front (leader Muhammad Abul Abbas), the Popular Front for the Liberation of Palestine, the Popular Front for the Liberation of Palestine-General Command, the Popular Struggle Front (PSF) (leader Samir Goshe), and Saiqa—only the DPU, Fatah, PPP, and PSF accepted the deal. Nonetheless, this agreement on principles was transformed into a working document in Cairo [*qv*] in early May 1994. Among other things this gave rise to the Palestinian Authority [*qv*]. Arafat left Tunis in July to administer Gaza and Jericho. The PLO maintained offices in Tunis and Amman [*qv*]. It was the prime mover behind the convening of the joint session of its Central Council, the Palestine National Council, and the Palestinian Authority [*qv*] in Gaza in December 1998 to radically alter the Palestine National Charter. In 2002 the PLO was recognized by ninety-three countries.

Palestine National Charter: Though originally adopted by the Palestine National Council (PNC) [*qv*] at its inaugural session in East Jerusalem [*qv*] in May–June 1964, the Palestine National Charter became significant in July 1968, when the fourth PNC congress in Cairo [*qv*] inserted the statement: "Armed struggle is the only way to liberate Palestine" (Article 9). Of the thirty-three articles in the charter the other important ones were: "Palestine, with the boundaries under the British mandate, is the homeland of Palestinian Arabs [*qv*], and is indivisible' (Articles 1 and 2); 'the Jews [*qv*] who lived in Palestine before the Zionist immigration are considered Palestinian" (Article 6); "the partition of Palestine and the founding of Israel are illegal since they violated the will of Palestinians

and the principle of self-determination included in the United Nations Charter" (Article 19); "the Balfour Declaration [*qv*] and the British mandate for Palestine are null and void" (Article 20); "the Palestinians reject all solutions which are substitutes for total liberation of Palestine" (Article 21); and "Zionism [*qv*], associated with international imperialism, is racist, expansionist and colonial, and Israel is the instrument of the Zionist movement" (Article 22).

Although in November 1988 the PNC abandoned some of the basic principles of the Charter (such as use of the armed struggle to liberate Palestine as constituted under the British mandate), it did not amend the Charter. But on the eve of the signing of an accord between the PLO and Israel in September 1993, PLO Chairman Yasser Arafat [*qv*] stated in a letter to Israeli Premier Yitzhak Rabin [*qv*] that those articles in the Palestine National Charter that denied Israel's right to exist and contradicted the PLO's commitment to renounce terrorism and other acts of violence would henceforth be "inoperative and no longer valid," and added that the PLO would submit to the PNC for formal approval the necessary changes in the Charter. Article 33 of the Charter requires a vote of two-thirds of all PNC members at a special session to effect an amendment. At the joint session of the PLO's 124-member Central Council, the 700-strong Palestine National Council, and the Palestinian Authority's [*qv*] eighty-seven parliamentarians and thirty-four cabinet members in Gaza in December 1998—witnessed by U.S. President Bill Clinton (r. 1993–2001)—the Palestinian representatives passed a resolution radically altering the Palestine National

Charter, with only a few dozen dissenting. The resolution endorsed the letter that Yasser Arafat [qv] had addressed to Clinton in January 1998, revoking those paragraphs of the Charter that clashed with the 1993 Oslo Accord [qv].

Palestine National Council: Official title: National Council of the Palestine Liberation Organization (PLO) [qv]. Founded in May 1964 in East Jerusalem [qv] with 350 delegates representing the various groups affiliated to the Palestine Liberation Organization (PLO) [qv], the Palestine National Council (PNC) was inaugurated by King Hussein [qv] of Jordan [qv]. It adopted the Palestine National Charter [qv] and elected a central council and an executive committee. The fifty-member Central Council, meeting once every three months, acted as an intermediary between the PNC (which was considered a Palestinian parliament in exile) and the executive committee, handling day-to-day affairs as well as deciding broad policy between the sessions of the PNC.

Any Palestinian Arab born in Palestine before 1947 or born of a Palestinian father after that, irrespective of his/her birthplace, was entitled to PNC membership. PNC membership was allocated to affiliated political groups; affiliated mass organizations of workers, students, women, teachers, doctors, etc.; and representatives from the Occupied Territories [qv], and the Palestinian Diaspora in Jordan, Syria, Lebanon, and the Gulf states [qv]. Normally the PNC met once a year. Its acceptance of the resignation of Ahmad Shuqairi [qv] in 1967, followed by its stiffening of the charter in July 1968 in Cairo [qv], which became its headquarters

after the 1967 Arab-Israeli War [qv], paved the way for hardline Palestinian groups to affiliate to the PLO.

With the election of Yasser Arafat [qv] as chairman of the PLO, a new chapter opened in the history of PNC. At its seventh session in April 1972 it rejected King Hussein's plan for a united kingdom of two federated parts: Jordan and a Palestine consisting of the West Bank [qv] and Gaza [qv]. Yet overall it remained a middle-of-the-road body. Of its 292 members at the thirteenth session in March 1977 in Cairo, 172 were moderate and only 69 radical. After the Egyptian-Israeli Peace Treaty [qv] in 1979, thePNC headquarters was moved from Cairoto Damascus [qv].

The expulsion of the PLO from Beirut [qv] in September 1982, followed by the conflict between Arafat and Syrian President Hafiz Assad [qv], had a divisive impact on the PNC. The PNC session in November 1984 in Amman [qv] was boycotted by the radicals, which inter alia made it easier to shift the headquarters from Damascus to Amman. The radicals returned to the eighteenth session of the PNC, now 426 strong, in April 1987 in Algiers only after Arafat had abandoned his earlier agreement with King Hussein on a confederation of Jordan and a future Palestinian state. At the subsequent session in Algiers in November 1988, the radicals, though unhappy at the PNC's acceptance of a Palestinian state in the Occupied Territories [qv] and peaceful coexistence with Israel, accepted the majority decision.

The twentieth session meeting in Algiers in September 1991 elected a new eighteen-member executive committee, with Arafat continuing as chairman. Protesting at the signing of the Israeli-PLO Accord [*qv*] in September 1993, seven of them, including Mahmud Darwish [*qv*], resigned. Of the remaining ten, one each belonged to the Democratic People's Union, Palestine People's Party [*qv*], and Popular Struggle Front, and five were independent, including Archbishop Ilya Khouri. Though on the eve of the signing of an accord with Israel, Arafat promised to submit necessary changes to the charter to the PNC, no such step was taken until April 1996. Then, at its twenty-first session in Gaza in April 1996, the PNC abrogated those articles of its Charter that denied Israel's existence. This was deemed insufficient by Benjamin Netanyahu [*qv*], elected Israeli prime minister in May. Therefore at its twenty-second session in December 1998—bolstered by PLO's Central Council (with 88 of the 124 members attending) and Palestinian Authority's [*qv*] parliamentarians and cabinet ministers in Gaza City [*qv*]—the PNC (with the nominal membership of 700) overwhelmingly passed a resolution endorsing the letter that Yasser Arafat had addressed to U.S. President Bill Clinton (r. 1993—2001) in January, revoking all those paragraphs of the Charter that clashed with the 1993 Oslo I Accord [*qv*].

Palestine National Fund: The Palestine National Fund was set up by the Palestine Liberation Organization (PLO) to meet its financial requirements. Contributions were in the form of grants from Arab and other friendly countries, a general Palestine tax collected by certain Arab states, and an income tax on Palestinians living in the Diaspora [*qv*]. It shared its headquarters with the Palestine National Council [*qv*], first in Cairo [*qv*] and then in Damascus [*qv*] and Amman [*qv*], except for 1987–89, when it functioned from Abu Dhabi [*qv*] before returning to Amman.

Palestine National Liberation Army: *see* Palestine Liberation Army.

Palestine People's Party: *see* Communist Party of Palestine.

Palestine War (1948–49): *see* Arab-Israeli War I (1948–49).

Palestinian Authority: The Palestinian Authority (PA) is the name of the legislative and executive body responsible for exercising all powers and functions devolved by Israel to the autonomous Palestinian areas under the Oslo Accord I [*qv*] in September 1993. The maximum strength of its executive body was fixed at twenty-four. In June 1994 Yasser Arafat [*qv*], its chairman and interior minister, appointed nineteen other members, including Ahmad Krai, who had conducted secret talks with Israel in Norway; Faisal Husseini [*qv*], a nephew of Haajj Muhammad Amin al Husseini [*qv*]; Elias Freij, the Christian [*qv*] mayor of Bethlehem [*qv*]; and Intisar Wazir, widow of the assassinated Khalil Wazir [*qv*]. This arrangement continued until elections were held in the West Bank [*qv*] and Gaza [*qv*] to the eighty-seven-member Palestinian Council (also called the Palestinian Legislative Council, PLC) in January 1996 after Israel had vacated most towns and cities in the West Bank [*qv*] after the signing of the Oslo Accord II [*qv*]. These were boycotted by Hamas [*qv*] Islamic Jihad [*qv*]. Of those elected, fifty-four belonged to Fatah [*qv*], four were Islamists [*qv*] without any party affiliation, one belonged to the Popular Front for the Liberation of Palestine [*qv*], and another to the Palestinian Democratic

Union. Among the remaining deputies, eleven were pro-Fatah independents, and the rest truly independent. Azmi Shuaibi was elected speaker of the PLC. The reconstituted cabinet had twenty-eight ministers chaired by the newly elected President Arafat. According to the law passed by the PLC, its tenure is to expire when Israel has implemented all its obligations under the Oslo Accord II, originally by September 1998. Within a year the PLC passed a draft constitution, which Arafat would sign only in 2002.

With the election of Benjamin Netnyahu [*qv*] as Israel's prime minister in 1996, the Oslo Accords [*qv*] suffered a hemorrhage from, which they did not recover during 1999–2001 when Ehud Barak [*qv*] was the chief executive of Israel. By 1999 complaints about the PA's inefficiency and corruption had risen to the extent that both the European Union and the International Monetary Fund, the chief financial backers of the PA, demanded reform. In January 2000 the PA set up the Higher Council for Development, chaired by Arafat, to ensure transparency of public finances. By then the headquarters of the PA had moved from Gaza City [*qv*] to the West Bank town of Ramallah.

Following the outbreak of the Second Intifada [*qv*], backed by all the Palestinian parties, in September 2000, Israel [*qv*] hit the PA headquarters in Gaza and the West Bank. As violence escalated, the Israeli government under Prime Minister Ariel Sharon (r. 2001–) systematically destroyed the PA's security, administrative, and economic infrastructure , leaving only buildings standing in the PA's Ramallah headquarters, where Arafat was put under house arrest in April 2002.

Thus, within six years of its establish-ment, the PA had reached a peak in 1999— when Israel had finally allowed the establishment of a 20-mile/32-km-long safe corridor for Palestinians between the West Bank and the Gaza Strip, and when the PA had full civilian control over 9 percent of the West Bank and joint control over another 23 percent, and commanded an armed police force of 40,000—to being a threadbare organization.

Palestinian National Authority: This is the term used by some Palestinians for the Palestinian Authority [*qv*].

Palestinian Territories: They consist of East Jerusalem [*qv*], the Gaza Strip [*qv*], and the West Bank [*qv*]. *See* Occupied Territories.

Palmah *(Hebrew: acronym of Plugot Mahatz, Shock Units):* The Palmah, the elite command force of Haganah [*qv*], was formed in May 1941 to accomplish special assignments. It drew its recruits from left-wing *kibbutizm* [*qv*]. Though illegal, it cooperated with British troops and participated in reconnaissance for their Lebanese campaign in June 1941. At the end of the Second World War it was 2000 strong. It cooperated with the right-wing Irgun [*qv*] and the Stern Group [*qv*] in a violent campaign against the British mandate, blowing up railroad tracks, bridges, and radar and other installations. In mid-1946, when the British turned against Haganah and the Palmah, the Haganah leadership ordered the Palmah to focus on illegal Jewish immigration. By the time the United Nations adopted a partition plan in November 1947, the Palmah was 5,000 strong.

During the run-up to the Palestine War (1948–49) [*qv*], the Palmah often cooperated with Irgun and the Stern Group, providing